HISTORY

OF

HOCKING VALLEY, OHIO,

1883

Together with sketches of its cities, villages and townships, educational, religious, civil, military, and political history, portraits of prominent persons, and biographies of representative citizens.

Volume I

A Reprint
by the

HOCKING COUNTY CHAPTER
OHIO GENEALOGY SOCIETY

With additional index by Robert E. and Clara Mae Redd

Milford, Ohio
LITTLE MIAMI PUBLISHING CO.
2000

Originally published and compiled by
Inter-State Publishing Co., Chicago, 1883

Reprinted for the
Hocking County Chapter, OGS
P.O. Box 115
Rockbridge OH 43149-0115

Reprint 2000 by
Little Miami Publishing Co.
P.O. Box 588
Milford, Ohio 45150-0588

© 1991, 2000 Selected Index of Names by Robert E. and Clara Mae Redd
All rights reserved. No part of this added material may be reproduced or transmitted in any form or by any means, electronic or mechanical, including photocopying, recording or by any information storage and retrieval system without written permission from Robert E. Redd.

Printed in the United States of America
Acid-free paper

ISBN 0-966489-7-8
Library of Congress Catalog Card Number 00-108146 (two-volume set)

PUBLISHER'S NOTE: In order to accommodate the size of this publication with the added index, this book has been reprinted in two volumes. Volume 1 includes chapters 1 through 28 of the original publication. Volume 2 includes chapters 29 through the appendix of the original publication and the new index. The table of contents for both volumes is found in volume 1.

John Brown

HISTORY

OF

HOCKING VALLEY,

OHIO,

TOGETHER WITH SKETCHES OF ITS CITIES, VILLAGES AND TOWNSHIPS, EDUCATIONAL, RELIGIOUS, CIVIL, MILITARY, AND POLITICAL HISTORY, PORTRAITS OF PROMINENT PERSONS, AND BIOGRAPHIES OF REPRESENTATIVE CITIZENS.

CHICAGO:
INTER-STATE PUBLISHING CO.
1883.

BLAKELY, MARSH & CO.,
PRINTERS,
155 & 157 DEARBORN ST., CHICAGO.

DONOHUE & HENNEBERRY
BOOKBINDERS,
180 & 182 MONROE ST., CHICAGO.

PREFACE.

IN presenting to the citizens of the Lower Hocking Valley this History, it is with the full knowledge that there may be found within its pages errors, both of omission and commission. It would be strange, indeed, if in recording the many incidents which may have transpired since the Hocking Valley was transformed from the wilderness home of the Indian to the civilization of the white man, that mistakes have not been made and much left unrecorded; yet, notwithstanding this, we feel confident that, by careful research, much has been found, not generally known, worthy of a place in the annals of a local history which, but for this compilation, would have forever remained buried in the dark oblivion of the forgotten past.

To gather these daily incidents of the long ago has been a work of infinite care and attention to detail, and a dependence, in a great measure, upon the memory of early settlers now living, and to the imperfect records of historical events, which in many instances time has effaced, with facts but partially recorded. Of the living pioneers, they have told us of their trials and troubles of by-gone years with all that wonderful simplicity and aptness of illustration for which the "old pioneers" and their first descendants were noted.

'Tis true that their memories at times have sadly faltered, and that they have forgotten much of value and incidents of a thrilling nature, yet enough has been given worthy of a place among the archives of the Lower Hocking Valley's progress to warrant their narration upon the pages of history.

The county, township and city records and the files of old newspapers have been carefully conned, and many facts and figures have been culled by midnight toil. Every available source of information has been explored, and every avenue of investigation exhausted, that only such incidents as were trustworthy might find a place within the pages of this work, making it not only a compendium of acknowledged facts but a useful and valuable book of reference. Intelligent readers may judge of how this labor has been performed and make all due allowance for such errors in names and dates as may be found therein. Perfection in man is not of this world, therefore to say that this work approached that high degree of excellence would savor too much of vanity; but let us say that an honest endeavor has been made to make the HISTORY OF THE LOWER HOCKING VALLEY worthy, in all respects, the careful perusal, if not approval, of the reader.

PREFACE.

One feature of the work is the method and order in which the matter it contains has been compiled and arranged. The biographical sketches of each county are in their respective counties and alphabetically arranged. The portraits of many of the leading citizens of the valley grace the work; and, take it together, while being far from perfect, yet it will be found to be the most complete and correct history of the Hocking Valley that the limits of such a work could contain.

This history appears none too soon. The pioneers have passed away, and the generation that succeeded them, the connecting link between them and the generation of to-day, are fast passing the "dark river," leaving little to tell of a people who dared all and endured all to give the stamp of civilization and Christianity upon our glorious land.

The author is indebted to many for their kindness in assisting him in the collection of the incidents, etc., which go to make up this volume, and most sincerely are our thanks tendered to the "old pioneers" who have so freely and cheerfully responded to requests for the history of the past. To the press of Athens, Nelsonville, Logan, McArthur, Zaleski and Hamden are we indebted for many favors, their files having proved of great value; also to the county officials of the respective counties, to ministers and officers of societies who have cheerfully lent us their aid. To Prof. J. P. Weethee, of Athens County, the author of the scientific chapter; to E. H. Moore and W. W. Knight thanks are due for favors rendered; also to Captain William M. Bowen, author of the war history of Hocking County; Prof. McCray for Logan's school article, and to William Montgomery for valuable assistance. In Vinton County we are indebted to Colonel Homer C. Jones for war history, and to Mrs. Leah, widow of Judge Kaler, Mrs. Rachel Snyder, Robert Sage, Henry Payne and N. C. Darst for much valuable information.

In the hope that this work may meet with a generous welcome and, if found worthy, a cordial approval, it is respectfully submitted.

INTER-STATE PUBLISHING COMPANY.

CONTENTS.

HISTORY OF HOCKING VALLEY.

CHAPTER I.

INTRODUCTORY, BUT STILL HISTORY.
Indians and the White Man's Advent—The Owners of the Territory—The Government Secured It—Ordinance of 1787—The Dunmore War—Locating on Indian Lands—Dunmore's March up the Hocking Valley—The Indian Name and Why...............17-26

CHAPTER II.

EARLY SETTLEMENT AND MATERIAL PROGRESS.
The Ohio Company—The Valley of Hocking—Washington County—Generals Washington and Putnam—Organization—Purchase of Land—Athens and Hocking Counties—First Settlers—Adelphia—Marietta—Indian War—Generals Harmer and St. Clair Defeated—Mad Anthony Victory—First Settlers of College Lands, or Athens County—Making Salt—Pioneer Modes and Pioneer Progress.................................27-48

CHAPTER III.

THE TRIALS AND TRIBULATIONS, CABINS AND COMFORTS OF EARLY DAYS.
Pioneer Life—The Log Cabin—Cooking—Dress—Family Worship—Hospitality—Trade and Barter—Hog Killing—Native Animals—Wolf Hunts—Education—Spelling and Singing Schools—On Their Guard—The Bright Side—A Touch of Pioneer Life—How the Pioneers Advanced Civilization—Women Pioneers........................49-84

CHAPTER IV.

SCIENTIFIC VIEW OF HOCKING VALLEY, PRELIMINARY THOUGHTS.
Topography—Drainage or River System—Geology—Stratigraphical Formation—Archæology—Fauna—Flora—Meteorology—Summary—Conclusion..................85-127

CHAPTER V.

STATISTICS OF THE HOCKING VALLEY, BESIDES RAILROADS AND CANALS, SENATORS AND REPRESENTATIVES.
Lands and Valuation—County Buildings and Valuation—Miles of Railway—Area of Valley—Population and Wheat Growing—Cities and Villages and Population—Boundary of the Mineral Field—Coal Production—Hocking Valley—State Senators of the Hocking Valley and Representatives.........128-145

CHAPTER VI.

ATHENS COUNTY HISTORY—FROM THE WILDERNESS TO ADVANCED CIVILIZATION.
Organic—Act of the Legislature—Organized Feb. 20, 1805—Area—First Session of Court—First Jail and Court-House—Taxation and License—New Court-House, 1818—School Districts and School Moneys—1840 to 1850—Rise and Progress, 1850 to 1860—War and Peace—County Officials—Floods—Devastation and Ruin by the Rushing Waters—Floods of 1847, 1858, and 1873—Destruction of Thirteen Miles of the Hocking Canal—The Swelling Waters of 1875........146-165

CHAPTER VII.

MILITARY HISTORY—WAR OF 1812, MEXICAN WAR, AND THE WAR BETWEEN THE STATES.
Early Patriotism—War with Mexico—The Rebellion—Firing on Fort Sumter—Newspapers Firing the Hearts of the People—Athens County Meets All Demands—Camp Jewett—Mustering In—Camp Denison—Sanitary and Relief—Work—Morgan's Raid—Nelsonville Captured—Ladies Once More to the Front—Grand Encampment—War Ended—President Lincoln's Assassination—The Athens Soldiers by Townships—The Regiments in which they served 166-178

CHAPTER VIII.

STATISTICS OF ATHENS COUNTY—POPULATION, AGRICULTURAL, POLITICAL.
Population by Townships and by Decades—The Value of Real and Personal Property in 1870, 1880, 1881, and 1882—Assessed Valuation in 1846, 1853, and 1859—Record of Marriages and Deaths—Pauperism—Land Sales—Mortgages—Dog and Sheep Statistics—Railroad and Telegraph—Political—Presidential Vote, 1836 to 1880—Governor's Vote, 1836 to 1880—Vote for Secretary of State—The County Vote by Townships....................179-196

CHAPTER IX.

MELANGE—A SERIES OF ARTICLES WORTHY OF ATTENTION.
Perusal—Educational—Normal Institute—Statistical—Agricultural Society—Annual Fairs—Constitution and By-Laws—Pioneer Association—The Death Roll—Officers—Letter of General Thomas Ewing—Future Prospects—New Court-House—The Old Log Court-House of 1807—The Ancient Brick Court-House of 1818—The Pride of Athens County, 1880—Its Cost—Jail—Children's Home—Infirmary—Defalcation........197-224

CHAPTER X.

TOWNSHIP AND CITY OF ATHENS LINKED TOGETHER—ONE AND INSEPARABLE.
Interwoven—Metes and Bounds—1805, and 1851 to 1883—Items—First Post Route—Progressing Slowly—Population and Comparison of Growth—Township Officers, 1806 to 1883—Trustees—Treasurers—Clerks—Justices of the Peace................... 225-232

CONTENTS.

CHAPTER XI.

THE CITY OF ATHENS—THE HOME OF CULTURE, REFINEMENT AND INTELLIGENCE.
What She Was and Is—Advance of Civilization—When Settled and by Whom—Act for the Laying-out of the Town of Athens, 1799—Inception and Growth—Sale of Lots and Purchasers — Incorporation — Growth—Schools—Churches—Cemeteries—Bible Society—Lodges—The Press of Athens—With Biographical Notes.... 233-258

CHAPTER XII.

OHIO UNIVERSITY—ITS INCEPTION, RISE AND PROGRESS.
The Wisdom of Its Conception—The University and Dr. Cutler—Acts of 1802 and 1804—Steps taken for Organization—The Act to Increase Rents—Beginning Active Work—The First Graduate—Pressing Forward—Literary Societies — Beautiful Location — The College Buildings—Biographical Sketches—Presidents of the Faculty—Professors—Preceptors and Principals—Trustees—The Officials.................................259-283

CHAPTER XIII.

INCIDENTS OF TWENTY YEARS—A GROUPING OF FACTS AND A BUSINESS STATEMENT.
Insane Asylum—Light Guards—City Hall—Temperance Movements—From 1829 to 1883—A Challenge — The Whisky Insurrection, 1861—Lynching at Athens—Athens Business Interests—Business Houses and Enterprises—Banks—Gas Light Company—Telegraph—Officers of Athens, 1825 to 1883....... 284-307

CHAPTER XIV.

BIOGRAPHICAL SKETCHES IN THE CITY OF ATHENS AND ATHENS TOWNSHIP.........308-403

CHAPTER XV.

YORK TOWNSHIP—A TOWNSHIP OF INEXHAUSTIBLE MINERAL WEALTH.
Taken from Ames in 1811, Six Miles Square—It is Bounded by—Population and Transportation — Canal and Railroad — Mining its Principal Industry--Some Rich Valley Lands—The Hills Good Sheep Pasture—Development—Official Statistics..............404-411

CHAPTER XVI.

CITY OF NELSONVILLE, THE MINERAL CITY OF THE HOCKING VALLEY.
The Mineral City—Hills of Coal and Iron—Where Located—Some Account of its Early Settlers—First Bridge Over the Hocking River—First Library and Society—Some Old Papers of Value—Settlers in 1827—James Knight's Prophecy—Letter to Dr. Hildreth—The Completion of the Canal—Coal Operators—Manufactures—City Officers—Churches—Public Schools—Lodges and Societies—Business Interests—1866 to 1883......412-436

CHAPTER XVII.

BIOGRAPHICAL SKETCHES OF YORK TOWNSHIP INCLUDING THE CITY OF NELSONVILLE.... .
....437-493

CHAPTER XVIII.

AMES TOWNSHIP—A TOWNSHIP THAT HAD A HISTORY TO RECORD.
The Arrival of the Pale-faces—Who They Were—The Area in 1805—A Few Items—Religious Whisky—Population—Area and Production—Boundary and Valuation—Western Library Association — Township Officers—1802 to 1803—Amesville—Somewhat Historic—When Founded—Growth and Business Interests—Postoffice—Academy—Presbyterian Church—Methodist Church—Biographical..
....494-548

CHAPTER XIX.

ALEXANDER TOWNSHIP--A GIANT IN ITS YOUTH, NOW SHORN OF MOST OF ITS TERRITORY.
As it Was and Now Is—Its Boundary Lines—Topography—Early Settlers—Whisky Transportation--Township Officers—Justices of the Peace – Hubbardsville--- Pleasanton—Woodyard P. O.— Churches, Schools, and Religious and Educational Interests—Biographical....
....549-565

CHAPTER XX.

ROME TOWNSHIP—THE RISE OF ROME AND THE PROGRESS OF THE ROMANS.
Location—Metes and Bounds—Topography — Organization — Population from 1820 to 1880—Schools—Bridges and Mills—Settlers and Progress— Early Historical Facts—The War of 1812—Township Officers—Guysville—Lodges—Stewart Village and Its History—New England, Frost and Big Run—Biographical..566-601

CHAPTER XXI.

LEE TOWNSHIP—SOMETHING OF OLDEN TIMES, AND THE NEGRO'S MECCA.
Organization--Some of the Old Settlers — Population—Elections—Township Officers--Albany, the Negro's Mecca—Postoffice and Postmasters — Mayors of Albany — Atwood Institute, its History—Gifts and Donations--Enterprise Institute—Its Rise and Progress—Schools and Churches—The Wells Library—Lodges and Societies — The Underground Railway Run by a Few Citizens of Albany—Biographical................602-625

CHAPTER XXII.

CANAAN TOWNSHIP—THE LAND OF CANAAN AS SEEN TO DAY.
Location and Description—When Settled--The Hocking River—Population—Rough and Broken—Grazing for Stock Good—Churches and Schools—Township Officers from 1819 to 1883—Cansanville—Its History—A few Closing Remarks—Biographical..........626-649

CHAPTER XXIII.

TROY TOWNSHIP—SOME HISTORY OF COLONIAL TIMES.
Historic — Lord Dunmore's March — His Camp—1774 to 1798—Advance in Population - Dismembered Early Settlers—Township Officers — Coolville—Its Rise and Progress—Its Surroundings—Churches, Schools and Mills—Business Interests—Lodges and Societies—Hockingport -- Its Local History—Torch Condensed--Biographical 650-684

CHAPTER XXIV.

WATERLOO TOWNSHIP -- AGRICULTURAL, MINERAL, AND STOCK.
When Settled--When Organized--Metes and Bounds and Area—Old Settlers--Agriculture and Population — Organization and First Election—Who Elected and Who Voted—All Other Town Officers—Marshfield— Churches—Carbondale — Mineral City—Biographical
....685-700

CHAPTER XXV.

BERN TOWNSHIP — FERTILE SOIL, MINERAL WEALTH, MATERIAL PROGRESS.
Location and Extent of Domain—Metes and

CONTENTS.

Bounds—Some of the Early Settlers—Mineral Deposits—Transportation Only Needed—Churches—Cemeteries—Schools, and Material Prosperity—Biographical...... 701-713

CHAPTER XXVI.

CARTHAGE TOWNSHIP — THE BEAUTY OF ITS LANDSCAPE.
The Act which organized It—Taken from Troy Township in November, 1819—Area—Lost Records—Officeholders—The Pioneers—First Mill—First Postmaster—Population by Decades—Growth Slow but Substantial—Churches and Schools—Biographical...... 714-730

CHAPTER XXVII.

DOVER AND TRIMBLE TOWNSHIPS.
Outline—Early Settlers—Township Officials—Sunday Creek Valley—Mineral Resources—Social Periods—Biographical.......731-789

CHAPTER XXVIII.

LODI TOWNSHIP — AN AGRICULTURAL TOWNSHIP MIXED WITH PETRIFACTIONS AND INDIAN TRADITIONS.
Organization and Bounds — Population — Topography—Petrifactions—First Election, Fourteen Votes—The Pioneers—Schools and Some Few Remarks — Churches, Villages, Business — Township Officers from 1827 to 1883—Biographical 790-812

CHAPTER XXIX.

HISTORY OF HOCKING COUNTY—THE WHITE MAN'S ADVENT AND RED MAN'S EXIT.
Those Who Led the Van of Civilization—The First Pioneers—The County Organization Act — Early Records—Eagle and Salt Creek — County Commissioners' First Meeting—First Grand Jury—Green and Laurel—Townships Organized and Numbered—Items—Falls Gore and Jackson—Marion—Benton—Jail and Court-House — Mineral Talk—Progress—Population, 1840—Taxation—Extracts from Sentinel, 1842—Something of Early Days—Something about a Name—Topography—Metes and Bounds....... 813-834

CHAPTER XXX.

AGRICULTURAL AND MINERAL—LOCAL EVENTS.
Iron Manufacturers—Progress and Flood—Yield of 1859—Local History—Valuation and Taxation—1867 to 1875—Jail—Births and Deaths, 1873—County Infirmary — Its Cost and Officers—Assessment Returns, 1874 and 1876—Agricultural Products and Stocks for 1870, 1875, and 1880—Hocking County Assessment, 1882 — Coal Output—Two Items—Hocking County Agricultural Society—From 1853 to 1882—The Record of a Crime—Murder of the Weldon Family — Patrons of Husbandry—Oil Well—Postal Routes and Tally Ho—Normal Institute—From 1868 to 1882...
....835-851

CHAPTER XXXI.

POLITICAL HISTORY.
Governors of Ohio and Hocking County's Vote—County Officials — Commissioners — Other County Officers—The Vote of Hocking County, 1818 to 1882—Population from 1820 to 1880—Seventh Judicial District—Sub-Districts 1, 2, and 3—Judges from 1818 to 1883—Counties Comprising the Districts and Sub-Divisions—Ten Judicial Districts in the State..852-861

CHAPTER XXXII.

WAR HISTORY OF HOCKING COUNTY—THE GLORIOUS RECORD OF THE GALLANT SONS OF HOCKING.
They Were Born So — Michigan and Ohio Boundary Troubles—Mexican War and Little Hocking—What Ohio Did—The Gallant Seventeenth—A Series of Marches—New Organization—The Slain—The Glorious Thirty-first — Ordered to Travel—The Gallant Dead—The Noble Fifty-eighth—The Sixty-third, Seventy fifth, and the One Hundred and Fifty-first—The End............ 862-883

CHAPTER XXXIII.

FALLS TOWNSHIP — THE PIONEER TOWNSHIP AND ITS STEADY GROWTH.
From 1798 — Something of Its Important Changes of Territory—Railroad, Canal, and River—Timber, Coal, and Iron Ore—Assessed Valuation—Schools—Streams—The Falls of the Great Hockhocking—Under the Surface—Churches — When Located — Cemeteries—Population—Falls-Gore—Railroad and Furnaces—Church—Schools—Societies— Towns — Industries — Business — Land — Water — Boundary—Name 884-893

CHAPTER XXXIV.

THE CITY OF LOGAN—THE PRIDE OF THE VALLEY AND OF THE HOCKHOCKING.
To the Memory of the Mingo Chief, Logan—The Beauty of its Location and Surroundings—From 1825 to 1830—Incorporation of Logan—What She Was—Bridges—the Culver Property—Purchase and Price- Logan Postoffice—Mayors of Logan—Logan Graded School—Business Interests in 1859 and 1883—Professional............................894-902

CHAPTER XXXV.

REFERRING TO RELIGIONS, MORALS, POLITICAL AND BUSINESS INTERESTS.
Presbyterian Church — Methodist Episcopal Church-Catholic Church-Lutheran Churches—People's Bank—First National Bank—The Logan Press—Manufactories—Iron and Steel — Furniture — Woolens — Sash, Doors, and Blinds—Fire Brick—Foundry and Machine Shop- Lodges and Societies..........903-917

CHAPTER XXXVI.

BIOGRAPHICAL SKETCHES OF FALLS TOWNSHIP, INCLUDING FALLS-GORE AND CITY OF LOGAN
....918-1011

CHAPTER XXXVII.

WARD AND GREEN TOWNSHIPS—WARD TOWNSHIP, THE SEAT OF WEALTH, OF COAL AND IRON.
Mineral but not Agricultural—About Ninety Per Cent—Shawnee Ore—Gardner's Trace—Interesting Situation—Dew Farm Organization—Carbon Hill—Orbiston—Murray City—Population and Area—School,etc.—Holocaust—Biographical—Green Township— Organization and Area—Topography—Its Wealth of Waters—Coal and Iron—Craft's Furnace, Saw and Grist Mills—Early Settlement—Haydensville—Churches—Greenland Lodge—Assessed Valuation—Schools—Population—Its Relative Progress--Biographical.....
....1012-1035

CHAPTER XXXVIII.

STARR TOWNSHIP — A TOWNSHIP THAT HAS A HISTORY.
Boundary—Name—Water Courses—Timber—Pioneers—Who They Were— Starr Postoffice — New Cadiz—Haydensville—Schools—Mills—Societies—Political — God's Acre—Religious—Churches — Township Officers—Biographical........................1036-1070

CHAPTER XXXIX.

WASHINGTON AND BENTON TOWNSHIPS — A COMBINATION OF HILLS AND VALLEYS, CAVES AND RAVINES.
Washington — Its Name, Topographically Speaking—Soil and Production—Old Settlers

CONTENTS.

—Population — Schools—Township Officials — Postoffices — Churches — Ilesboro, Ewing Postoffice—New Mt. Pleasant—Point Pleasant — Cemeteries — Biographical—Benton—Metes and Bounds—Area—The Wonders of Queer Creek—Agricultural Resources—Mineral Wealth—Silver and Lead Mines—Description of the Weird Valley — 458 Acres Excess—The Road to H—l—Cedar and Black Jack Falls—Ash Cave-Bloomingville—Business Interests—Township Officers—Population—Biographical 1071-1097

CHAPTER XL.

SALT CREEK AND PERRY TOWNSHIPS—VARIED SCENERY, FERTILE SOIL, A WEALTHY AND PROGRESSIVE PEOPLE.
Salt Creek—What it Comprises—Metes and Bounds—Area, Six Miles by Seven—Population—Pioneers, Schools and Churches—Postoffice and Stores—Township Officers, 1883—Biographical — Perry — Area — Boundary — Scenery — Early Settlers—Mills—Township Officers—South Perry — Laurelville—Buena Vista — Churches — Schools — Population — Valuation—Present Officials — Biographical 1098-1130

CHAPTER XLI.

LAUREL, GOOD HOPE AND MARION TOWNSHIPS—A LAUREL WREATH OF HISTORY BEAUTIFULLY BLENDED.
Laurel — The Laurel Bush — Topography—Boundary—Early Settlement—First Preacher—Churches-School-House—Official Record—Gibisonville — Population — Biographical—Good Hope—Its Bounds—Valleys Productive—Official Record—Rock Bridge Village—Rock Bridge—Churches and Schools—Transportation-Population and Stock—Biographical—Marion— Topography and Boundary—Area—Pioneer Settlers—Population—Valuation — Real and Personal — Churches — Schools—Biographical............1131-1157

CHAPTER XLII.

HISTORY OF VINTON COUNTY — A COUNTY WHICH CAME INTO BEING READY MADE BY TOWNSHIP.
A County Which Had No Pioneer History—Labor — Its Organization, 1850 — Boundary and Area—Early Arrivals—An Interesting Letter—Names of Early Settlers—Political Movements — First Convention — Jail and Contract — Court-House — Mineral Interests —Coal—Iron Ore—Geological Report—Burr-Stone— Agricultural and Stock Statistics—Valuation—Miles of Railroad—County Infirmary—Buildings and Cost—Officia's......
............................1158-1174

CHAPTER XLIII.

THE PRESS AND OTHER ITEMS OF INTEREST—The Vinton County Press — McArthur, Zaleski and Hamden — Agricultural Society of Ante-Bellum Days — Safe Burglary— Contents, $40,000— No Convictions......1175-1184

CHAPTER XLIV.

VINTON COUNTY IN THE WAR OF THE REBELLION.
Introductory--Eighteenth Ohio, Three Years' Service — Second West Virginia Cavalry—Seventy-fifth Ohio Infantry—Ninetieth Ohio Infantry — One Hundred and Fourteenth Ohio Infantry—Twelfth Ohio Cavalry—One Hundred and Ninety-fourth Ohio Infantry..
..................................1185-1207

CHAPTER XLV.

ELK TOWNSHIP, INCLUDING CITY OF MCARTHUR—THE PIONEER ORGANIZATION OF VINTON COUNTY.
The Pioneer Township — The Pioneers of Elk—Personal Recollections of Mrs. C. E. Bothwell—Schools—Church—Population by Decades — McArthur— Location— Incorporation—Village Officers — Fires — Postoffice — McArthur in 1883 — Churches — Societies — Schools—Vinton County Bank—Town Hall —Railroad Statistics—Mills—Biographical..
....1208-1280

CHAPTER XLVI.

MADISON, KNOX AND BROWN TOWNSHIPS, CONTAINING ZALESKI, THE LARGEST CITY IN THE COUNTY.
Madison Township — Original Organization —Surface and Drainage—The Pioneers—Population — Mineral - Schools and Churches—Assessor's Returns, 1883—Zaleski—Its Religious, Educational and Business Interests —Lodges—Manufactories—Knox Township —Identical with Madison—Name and its Origin—Soil and Topography—The First Arrivals—Stock and its Assessment—Only Postoffice—Schools and Churches—Mills—Population—Brown Township—How it Became a Township—Metes and Bounds—The First Settlers—Its Water Supply—What Usually Happens—Religious Denominations—Population—Transportation—New Plymouth—Its Stock Returns for 1883—Agricultural and Mineral— Value as a Stock Township—Biographical......... 1281-1305

CHAPTER XLVII.

SWAN AND JACKSON TOWNSHIPS—WHAT HOCKING LOST WAS VINTON'S GAIN.
Swan Township — Boundary—Early Settlers —First Events—Postoffices—Business— Minera's—Township Officers — Assessment and Stock—Jackson Township—When Changed from Eagle to Jackson—Its Water Courses—Early Settlers—County Honors—Population from 1840 to 1880 — Postoffices — Schools—Stock Returns, 1883—Assessed Valuation—Biographical................ 1306-1332

CHAPTER XLVIII.

EAGLE, HARRISON AND RICHLAND TOWNSHIPS —IN AGRICULTURE, POOR; IN MINERAL DEPOSITS, FAIR.
Eagle—When Organized--Divided by Hocking—First Election, May 9, 1818, and in 1850 Gave Remainder to Vinton—Area and Location— the Old Pioneer—Religion and Education — Stock and Valuation — Harrison Township—A part of Ross Township in 1798 — Topography—Well Watered—A Part of Jackson in 1818—Then Again to Ross—Population—Rapid Gain—Churches—Schools—Stock and Valuation—Richland Township—The Largest Township—Some Good Land—Its Assessed Valuation — Stock Report—North Part Good Farming Land—South Part Minerals, Iron Ore and Coal—A Partial List of Settlers—Churches, Schools and Military—Biographical 1333-1344

CHAPTER XLIX.

WILKESVILLE, VINTON AND CLINTON TOWNSHIPS— A TRIO THAT CONTAINS IMMENSE MINERAL DEPOSITS.
Wilkesville Township—Iron Ore and Coal—Wilkesville Village — Churches—Schools—Hawk Station — Minerton — Valuation of Stocks — Vinton Township — Name—Early Settlement—Schools—Population — Radcliff Station—Mineral Development — Personal Property—Valuation — Clinton Township—Of Athens County, then of Jackson——Once Part of Elk Township—Local History—Postoffice—Lodges—Churches—Dundas—Educational — Population—Valuation— Stock Reports—Biographical 1345-1379

APPENDIX............................1380

CONTENTS.

PORTRAITS.

	Page.		Page.
Alderman, W. N.	437	Mansfield, W. D.	104
Anderson, George S.	335	Mathias, Isaac.	782
Armstrong, William.	1036	McBroom, J. C.	1130
Belt, Raymond.	903	McBroom, Mrs. J. C.	1131
Blackstone, William.	233	McCarthy, T. F	960
Bowlby, W. R	550	McCormick, I. H.	1341
Bowen, Capt. W. M	862	Patterson, John	362
Brawley, Henry B.	284	Poston, A.	412
Brown, John	Frontispiece.	Primrose, I. P.	1256
Buerhaus, Carl H. H	688	Rempel, Col. F. F	813
Carpenter, Abel	1071	Shaw, J. A.	60
Culver, L. A.	27	Shepard, W. P	175
Davis, Levi.	640	Spencer, Smith.	485
Defebaugh, D. K	1098	Stewart, D. B.	259
Friesner, John S	887	Stiers, Wilfred.	1284
Grogan, James R	834	Stiers, Elizabeth.	1285
Grosvenor, C. H.	146	Welch, John F.	515
Hansen, John.	985	White, C. L.	1218
Hart, C. C.	85	Wolf, Andrew	1158
Henry, Charles.	745	Wolf, Joseph.	200
Iles, Jeremiah.	713	Young, W. R.	590
Jones, H. C.	1185		

BIOGRAPHICAL SKETCHES.

	Page.		Page.		Page.
Acker, James N	918	Bason, C	717	Bowen, Wm. M.	925
Acker, Wm. T	918	Bay, T. M.	1371	Bowen, J. C	313
Ackley, John	308	Beam James	797	Bowlby, Wm. L.	928
Addleman, B. T.	309	Bean, Bisco.	555	Bowsher, Nelson.	1101
Akin, G. E		Bean, E. M.	555	Boyd, Daniel.	314
Albin, Samuel	1310	Bean, Edmund	579	Boyd, Wm. G	663
Albin, Wm.	1311	Bean, Harrison	632	Braddock, W. H.	771
Albin, Wm. S.	1110	Bean, Mrs. Lorana	579	Brandeburg, John	580
Alderman, W. N.	437	Beasley, David	556	Brawley, E. H.	519
Allbaugh, Morris.	1292	Beasley, George	516	Brawley, H. B.	517
Allen, B. H	1093	Beasley, J. J	516	Brawley, J. P.	519
Allen, David.	554	Beattie, Alex	439	Brawley, J. W	744
Allen, J. B.	308	Beebe, W. P.	579	Bray, John.	1312
Allen, John, Jr.	1093	Beery, A. W	921	Brehm, G. W.	929
Allen, Josiah	770	Beery, H. P.	1311	Brehm, John	1135
Allender, B. G.	1030	Belford, W. W	1342	Brewer, I. V.	1292
Allison, T. J.	693	Bell, Wm	743	Brewster, Sherman	663
Ames, Bishop E. R.	514	Belt, Raymond.	921	Briggs, James.	1300
Amerine, George.	1094	Bennett, Darius.	1016	Bright, J. G	929
Ambrose, M. H.	919	Bennett, E. H.	1338	Bright, J. L	929
Anderson, Geo. S.	516	Bennett, S. H	440	Bright, S. H.	930
Andrews, M.	437	Benson, J. A	312	Brooke, A. H	931
Angell, R.	796	Berry, James	1134	Brooke, Oliver.	931
Angell, T G	797	Berry, Thomas.	440	Brown, A. G.	315
Ankram, J. A.	1299	Bestow, M. L.	662	Brown, A. M.	1150
Arbaugh, M.	1367	Bethel, A. S.	441	Brown, A. W.	612
Armstrong, C. P.	920	Bethel, L. T.	1046	Brown, C. D.	932
Armstrong, Elmer.	554	Biddison, T.	770	Brown, C. H.	316
Armstrong, E. B	554	Biddison, W.	770	Brown, E. F.	519
Armstrong, F. C.	437	Bingham, H	743	Brown, G. C.	317
Armstrong, Milton.	1110	Bingman, Wm	662	Brown, H. T.	317
Armstrong, Wm.	962	Birge, O. R.	744	Brown, J. D.	318
Armstrong, Wm. H	1044	Bishop, H. H.	1357	Brown, J. E	932
Armstrong, Wm.	1111	Bishop, Harry.	1331	Brown, Gen. John	316
Arnold, Archibald.	1230	Bishop, J.	793	Brown, John.	318
Atkinson, G. E.	1291	Black, Rev. D. P.	1134	Brown, M. B.	933
Atkison, S. L.	1044	Black, John S	612	Brown, Thomas.	1150
Aton, Linza.	797	Black, T. N.	441	Brown, T. J.	933
Austin, J. O.	1045	Blackstone, James.	1076	Bryson, Archibald.	520
Austin, J. S.	1045	Blackstone, W.	811	Buck, A. T.	581
Bailey, Seth.	661	Blackwood, W.	798	Buckingham, Wm. D.	1047
Bailor, Samuel.	1112	Blake, J. R.	442	Buckley, A.	443
Baird, J. W.	631	Blake, S. B.	556	Buerhaus, C. H. H., Jr	934
Baker, Geo. W.	309	Blakeley, G. W.	580	Buerhaus, C. H. H.	934
Baker, S. C.	797	Blazer, George	718	Burge, O. G.	745
Baker, T. E.	920	Blore, John.	1368	Burge, W. W	745
Barker, F. M.	311	Blum, Andrew.	923	Burgess, A. J.	935
Barker, Isaac, Jr.	311	Boden, John.	694	Burgess, H. T.	936
Barnes, James.	1356	Booth, J.	1368	Bumgardner, H. F.	665
Barnes, M. R	1231	Bort, L. S.	923	Bundy, H. S.	1232
Barnes, W.	438	Bothwell, E. P.	1281	Burberry, J.	444
Barnhill, John.	717	Botts, S. M.	1029	Burrell, J. O.	444
Barrowes, G. H.	438	Boudinot, T.	744	Burroughs, Jeremiah.	633
Bartlett, Sylvanus.	1299	Bowen, C. E	924	Burson, J.	799
Bartlett, W. L.	1299	Bowen, David.	1030	Burson, W. N.	799

CONTENTS.

Name	Page	Name	Page	Name	Page
Bushee, J. R.	1113	Cowan, David	800	Dresback, S. S.	455
Butin, J. B.	936	Cowell, Wm. H.	941	Dudleston, H.	1242
Butin, R. J.	1030	Cox, Joseph	1313	Dunlap, C. O.	1243
Butt, P. M.	445	Cozad, A. N.	1343	Earhart, Geo. W.	694
Butt, S. E.	445	Cozad, Henry	1343	Eberst, Nicholas	947
Byron, Mrs. R. S	581	Craig, J. T.	1293	Edgerton, Richard	705
Cable, C. A.	446	Craig, Wm. M.	1049	Edmundson, J. E.	334
Cable, Charles	447	Cram, Daniel	1236	Edwards, E.	1455
Cable, C. W.	448	Cramer, S. F.	1372	Eggleston, S. C.	1301
Cady, T. J.	936	Crane, J. W.	451	Elliott, James	718
Caldwell, J. A.	582	Crawford, Wm. H.	942	Elliott, Moses	719
Caldwell, Joseph	718	Creamer, Joseph	800	Elliott, Richard	706
Calvin, L. W.	1368	Creamer, S. M.	800	Ellis, B. A	522
Camp. J. F.	448	Creesy, J	801	Ellis, Lorenzo	706
Campbell, Geo. K.	665	Cresap, D. J.	942	Ellis, T.	748
Carlton, A. D	666	Crippen, A. S.	586	Endicott, W.	706
Carlton, E. L.	666	Crippen, Eli C	328	England, S. B	1031
Carnes, A. H.	449	Crow, George	1236	England, Wm. N	947
Carpenter, Abel	1144	Crow, M. B	1313	Engle, J, S.	948
Carpenter, E. G	320	Cuckler, J. K.	329	Essex, N. H	1050
Carpenter, F. J.	582	Culver, C. B.	943	Evans, J. D.	719
Carpenter, Harvey	633	Culver, E. S.	943	Evans, L. D	801
Carpenter, Jeremiah	1151	Culver, L. A.	943	Evans, W. E.	456
Carpenter, Oliver	634	Cupp, Charles	1135	Ewing, Alex.	335
Carpenter, Parker	321	Curfman, Wm. H.	521	Ewing, G. K.	1358
Carter, James,	705	Currier, Ebenezer	329	Farabee, William	1293
Case, Oakley	937	Curry, Jennie	1357	Faulkner, James	1314
Cass, S. W.	745	Curtis, E. E.	801	Fants, S.	616
Cather, Quincy	799	Curtis, H. H.	521	Fee, William	1315
Cave, B. E	1113	Dains, E.	747	Ferguson, Vint.	948
Chace, Hosmer	556	Dalton, G. W.	1236	Fetherolf, Nelson	1116
Chappelear, I. E	771	Dana, J. M.	331	Fierce, W. W	1358
Chase, L. C.	614	Dana, J. P.	330	Finch, W. G.	523
Cherry, M. M.	1234	Danford, H. D	772	Findling, C.	456
Clark, Abram.	1234	Danford, S. J	773	Finley, I.	1018
Clark, Robert.	1343	Darby, S. G	1339	Finsterwald, Henry	634
Clegg, Samuel	1016	Darst, N. C	1237	Finsterwald, John	335
Clester, C. P.	746	Davis, E. H	452	Finsterwald, Peter	336
Cline, S. T.	615	Davis, J. A.	452	Finsterwald, Peter	635
Cline, Mrs. Samantha	615	Davis, Jesse	332	Fischer, E	1293
Cline, W. C.	1300	Davis, J. W	944	Fisher, John	558
Clowe, C. W.	938	Davis, Levi	945	Fleming, Daniel	523
Coe, J. J.	557	Davis, M. P	773	Fleming, W. B.	1095
Coe, J. P.	321	Davis, W. B.	1237	Flesher, Draper	636
Coe, Lucius	799	Dawley, Nathan	1017	Fletcher, Edward.	1359
Cohogan, G. W	1030	Dawley, W. N	1017	Fletcher, Hugh	616
Cole, Jefferson	667	Dawson, W. G	1135	Fletcher, Thomas	1359
Coleman, Charles.	583	Day, William	718	Floyd, T. S.	1116
Collins, E. G.	939	Dean, N. W	522	Fogler, Mrs. Eve	1117
Collins, J. L.	940	Dean, Wm. E.	333	Foreman, J. T.	1244
Conaway, James.	1047	Dean, W. T.	557	Fox, G. W.	669
Cone, William	520	Deaver, S. P.	1238	Frame, A. B	336
Connett, L. W	325	Defebaugh, D. K	1115	Frame, A. J.	524
Connett, H	746	Defenbaugh, Calvin	1114	Frame, A. P	669
Constable, R. A.	322	Deffenbaugh, Isaiah	1114	Frame, J. A.	337
Constable, R. E.	323	Deishley, George	946	Frame, John	524
Cook, George.	910	Delay, J. W.	1238	Frasure, G. W.	1151
Cook, J. E.	583	Dennis, E. J	1094	Frasure, Isaiah	1152
Cook, Mrs. L. C	584	Devault, J. L.	1358	Frey, F. W	1050
Cook, Robert.	634	Devoll, Philip	1017	Friday, John	337
Cooley, Mrs. F. E.	667	Devore, G. W.	452	Friday, Leopold	338
Cooley, F. G	450	Dew, James	452	Friend, Jacob.	1118
Cooley, G. L.	450	Dew, Thomas	453	Friend, L. C.	1136
Cooper, T. A.	323	Dewing, John	615	Friesner, J. S	949
Coots, D	746	DeWolf, John.	668	Friesner, Simeon	950
Copeland, Mrs. E.	584	Dickson, J. F.	1240	Friesner, Wm. E.	950
Copeland, John.	585	Dickson, William	557	Friesner, Wm. S.	950
Cornell, Ansley	585	Dille, Geo. A	333	Frost, Abner	802
Cornell, D. W.	586	Dillinger, J. W.	801	Frost, D. G	719
Cornell, J. E	325	Dillon, J	1240	Frost, J. W.	457
Cornell, William	326	Dinsmoor, Wm. A.	668	Frost, Mrs. M. L.	587
Cornwell, D. C.	326	Dixon, W. R	1017	Frost, Samuel	802
Cornwell, John	327	Doan, C. H	453	Fuller, A.	748
Cortney, A. M	941	Doan, Edward	586	Fuller, D. D.	749
Cottrill, William	1235	Dodge, E. D	1241	Fuller, Lemuel	1301
Coulson, J.	747	Dollison, G. W	946	Fuller, L. D.	1301
Coulter, John.	1235	Donaldson, J. H.	946	Fuller, R. N	749
Coultrap, F. S.	540	Dorr, H. K.	334	Fuller, William	1301
Coultrap, H. W	1235	Dorr, Joseph	334	Fulton, D.	749
Courter, Peter	1049	Doughty, J. B.	747	Fulton, J. B	338
Courtney, Alanson	327	Downard, J.	1368	Fulton, L. W.	774
Courtney, A. V M	328	Doyle, Patrick	947	Gabriel, Reason	339
Covert, C.	451	Dreany, J	454	Gallagher, John	951

CONTENTS.

Name	Page	Name	Page	Name	Page
Gardner, Perrin	1360	Hawkins, James	1343	Jennings, C. E. M	354
Gardner, Thomas	525	Haybson, W. J	459	Jennings, Manasseh	673
Geiger, John	1136	Haynes, C. C	1161	Jennings, R. M	354
Gibison, Joel	1136	Haynes, J. S	1101	Jewell, E. W	591
Gilliam, C. F	457	Hays, C. H	671	Johnson, Mrs. A. M	531
Gillilan, Reuben	669	Hays, R. A	1316	Johnson, David	1317
Gilly, James	339	Headley, J. C	750	Johnson, C	1373
Gilly, William	389	Hebbard, P. G	559	Johnson, J. W	591
Gilman, O. W	1244	Hedges, Amos	1118	Johnson, S. H	776
Gilmore, W. B	457	Hedges, Joseph	1118	Johnson, T	463
Ginn, E. H	587	Hedges, S. E	350	Johnson, W	752
Ginn, James	588	Henderson, C. B	350	Jones, D. H	721
Gist, C. D	339	Henkel, Rev. Henry	959	Jones, E. J	354
Glazier, C. W	525	Henry, Charles	797	Jones, George	617
Glazier, E. F	707	Henry, Charles	1388	Jones, H. C	1248
Glazier, J. H	525	Henry, C. M	528	Jones, J. H	776
Glazier, J. W	720	Henry, David	708	Jones, J. W	777
Glazier, Walter	720	Henry, Geo. E	708	Jones, Samuel	1054
Goddard, W. R	707	Henry, James	528	Josten, C	355
Gold, W. D	1245	Henry, John	529	Josten, M	355
Golden, Elmer	340	Henry, Mathew	709	Junipher, A. A	1019
Golden, William	341	Henry, R. B	530	Juniper, A. J	464
Golden Wm. R	341	Henry, Robert	709	Junod, F. L	356
Gompf, Henry	952	Henry, Wm	750	Junod, H. A	356
Goodspeed, C. W	342	Herrold, Joseph	351	Junod, L. F	531
Goodspeed, J. McK	343	Herrold, W. H	352	Kane, Peter	1120
Gordecke, S. M	1018	Hess, James	589	Karns, Cornelius	1319
Gorslene, G. L	344	Hickman, W. C	460	Karns, S. V	1320
Goss, David	952	Hickman, W. G	461	Karshner, Nelson	1102
Goss, Martin	953	Higgins, J. S	352	Karshner, Rufus	1102
Gould, Geo. T	344	Higgins, Judiah	352	Karshner, Samuel	1121
Graham, Elias	617	Hill, Arnold	637	Kastler, Frederick P	532
Graham, F. P	345	Hill, Daniel	527	Kastler, Kilion	532
Gray, Alford	1051	Hill, Loren	527	Keeton, W	1302
Gray, J. T	458	Hill, Solomon	527	Keller, Jacob	963
Green, Jesse	671	Hitchcock, C. B	671	Keller, L. F	964
Green, J. H	526	Hobson. S. N	590	Kelly, John	806
Green Lewis	953	Hoge, Zimri	802	Kelly J. L	806
Green, P. J	1095	Hoey, D. R	1119	Kelly, John L	806
Griffin, John	1077	Hoey, Wm. J	1119	Kempton, J. F	778
Grim, James	346	Hoffhines, Voss	1246	Kempton, S. T	779
Grimm, J	458	Hoisington, N. P	530	Kennedy, William	1102
Grimm, Noah	1152	Hoodlet, J. J	462	Kennedy, W. N	673
Grogan, J. R	953	Hooper, Amsey	353	Kennedy, Wm. P	964
Grosvenor, Hon. C. H	346	Hooper, Clement	559	Kenney, Nathan, Sr	560
Grosvenor, J. M	583	Hooper, G. W	560	Kenney, Nathan, Jr	561
Grosvenor, Mrs. M. C	636	Horton, Paris	1247	Kenney, S. H	561
Groves, Henry	1051	Hoskinson, Z. W	638	Kern, Peter	356
Guard, J. A	1373	Hosom, B. A	1053	Kern, Mrs. Alice	618
Guthrie, J. F	1052	Howard, Wm	803	Kessenger, A	357
Half, Isaac	348	Howdyshell, D. W	1137	Kessler, J. N	964
Ham, Charles J	637	Hudson, W. S	1247	Kessler, Nicholas	965
Hamblin, N. W	954	Hufford, N. D	1153	Keyes, Charles E	674
Hamblin, R. E	349	Hulbert, Geo. B	638	Kidnocker, Robert	1339
Hamilton, David	1153	Hull, H. L	803	Kidwell, P. R	779
Hamilton, W. J	459	Hull, S. T	803	Kincade, John	807
Hammond, James	720	Hull, S. W	804	King, J. H	1249
Hammond. John	721	Huls, O. R	1145	Kitsmiller, Joel	965
Haning, James, Jr	558	Huls, Wm. H	1145	Knight, W. W	464
Haning, John	558	Humphrey, E. C	617	Knipe, Enos	1080
Hansel, John	1078	Humphrey, Milton	671	Knowles, C. L	674
Hansen, John	955	Humphrey, R. F	672	Koerner, T	357
Hansen, R. W	955	Huston, J. E	959	Kolb, F. R	1374
Harden, Ephraim	1079	Hyde, W. S	751	Kontner, S. C	465
Harden, Even	1079	Iler, S. H	1696	Koons, F. M	357
Harned, J. W	1052	Iles, Jeremiah	960	Kreider, P. W	1137
Harper, John	1018	Ingmire, Joseph	1053	Kreider, S. C	965
Harper, R, C	695	Irwin, Thomas	1120	Kreig, Michael	966
Harris, Leander	589	Irwin, W. H	560	Kreppel, H. C	1302
Harris, W. H	349	Jackson, J. H	1019	Krinn, J. G	1137
Harsh, Solomon	956	Jackson, J. W	463	Krinn, John	1138
Hart, Rev. C. C	957	Jackson, O. D	774	Kurtz, Hon. C. L	558
Hartnell, J. E	670	Jackson, Wm	590	Kurtz, W. W	559
Harvey, J	750	James, C. W	962	Kyle, James	807
Hawk, C. E	1361	James, N. W	751	Laird, A	360
Hawk, David	1246	Jarvis, L. R	591	Lamborn, J. M	639
Hawk, F	1361	Jeffers, C B	672	Lane, J. J	465
Hawk, Isaac	1315	Jeffers, George	804	Lantz, D	1250
Hawk, J. F	1246	Jeffers, George W	804	Lantz, G	1250
Hawk, J. H R	1362	Jeffers, L. H	805	Lantz, George	967
Hawk, Lafayette	349	Jeffers, S. J	1369	Lantz, I. M	1251
Hawk O. F	1362	Jeffers, Wm	806	Lash, Abram	561
Hawkin, J. S	1332	Jenkins, J. W	775	Lash, Eli R	360

CONTENTS.

Name	Page	Name	Page	Name	Page
Lash, Isaac	1302	McClure, T. F	1374	Ogg, William	757
Latimer, P. D	1054	McClurg, Alexander	1059	Ogle, Orpheus	1139
Laughlin, Hugh	619	McCollester, Abraham	1058	Oliver, Joseph	620
Lawler, D	1363	McCormick, I. H	1341	Oliver, L	563
Lawrence, Edward	722	McCoy, H. F	754	O'Neal, David W	535
Lawrence, John	722	McCoy, I. N	695	O'Neill, Thomas	1061
Lawrence, Moses	592	McCray, W. W	971	Owen, Horace C	535
Lawrence, N. S	723	McCue, William	1059	Owen, James G	535
Learned, A. J	752	McCuen, Jacob	534	Owens, N. B	641
Learned, M. R	752	McCune, A	1155	Paffenbarger, G	1255
Lee, Elijah	1080	McCune, C. B	710	Paine, B. R	1375
Lee, H. T	466	McCune, J. R	365	Paine, G	1322
Lee, Nelson	1339	McDaniel, George	1303	Paine, J. B	1376
Lefever, B. C	466	McDaniel, Joseph	1303	Painter, A. C	536
Lefever, S. M	780	McDaniel, Zara	1123	Palmer, Augustus	621
Le Goullon, Gustavus	592	McDonald, W. W	972	Palmer, W	781
Lehman, E. D	1031	McDowel, L	454	Parker, J. C	472
Lehman, G. W	1031	McGill, J. P	470	Parker, J. M	472
Lemmon, Rev. R. J	618	McGrath, A. E	1254	Parker, J. M	679
Lewis, Aaron	753	McKee, J. A	755	Parrish, Solomon	1096
Lewis, Abner	675	McKim, Elizabeth	676	Patrick, M	370
Lewis, A. L	1374	McKim, Mrs. M. L	677	Patterson, Amos	595
Lewis, Moses	467	McKitrick, J	755	Patterson, James	536
Lewis, Waterman	675	McLain, Abraham	972	Patterson, John	537
Ley, H. J	467	McLain, J. D	973	Patterson, Joseph	548
Lindsey, William	1121	McLean, C	366	Patterson, R. M	563
Linscott, Seth	532	McManigal, B. C	1060	Patterson, Taylor	539
Linton, Joseph	593	McManigal, R. D	973	Patton, F. B	594
Linton, T. M	467	McManigal, W. J	1020	Payne, F. M	595
Livezey, Samuel	676	McNeil, C	724	Payne, George	1322
Logan, Henry	561	McPherson, J. H	562	Payne, H	1255
Longstreth, J. D	1054	McVey, J. M	1254	Pearce, A	1256
Loomis, J. M	1055	Miller, David	1155	Pelton, L. B	1020
Lottridge, B. B	723	Miller, D. A	974	Perry, Jefferson	595
Lottridge, I. N	1252	Miller, H. McC	470	Persons, Eli P	724
Lottridge, J. D	723	Minear, A. D	619	Pettit, C. H	782
Lottridge, S. H	723	Minear, A. W. S	362	Petty, L	596
Love, J. B	780	Minor, J. K	534	Phelps, Parley	980
Lovell, Lorenzo	710	Mintun, T. L	363	Phillips, E. H	696
Lowden, G. W	724	Mirick, H. D	364	Phillips, Ezra, Jr	539
Lowry, J. M	1253	Mitchell, John	677	Phillips, L. D	1363
Lowry, P	754	Mitchell, Lafayette	678	Phillips, R	371
Lutz, Henry	967	Moler, E. C	620	Pickering, B. W	371
Lutz, Mrs. Minerva	1121	Monahan, S. W	1375	Pickering, F. O	372
Lyons, John	1019	Montgomery, Wm. McA	975	Pickering, J. L	372
Magee, Thomas	1303	Moore, E. H	1392	Pickering, Levi	373
Magoon, Augustus	967	Moore, J. H	1060	Pickering, S	374
Mansfield, George	639	Moore, M. D	976	Pickering, S. W	375
Mansfield, L. E	640	Morgan, Simeon	1321	Pickering, T. M	375
Mansfield, Wm. D	968	Morris, Hon. C	366	Pierce, J	1370
Marshal, T. P	468	Morris, J	756	Pierce, M	725
Marshall, Freeman	562	Morris, J. W	620	Pilcher, C. B	1257
Marshall, George	1122	Morrison, A	368	Pilcher, Rev. J. N	642
Martin, A	754	Morrison, James	593	Pilcher, T. M. D	376
Martin, T. A	1253	Morrison, Joseph	678	Pleukharpe, Peter	1082
Martin, J. M	469	Morrison, Montgomery	679	Pleukharp, Wm. E	980
Martin, J. S	1154	Mosure, A. W	1061	Poling, Noah	1156
Martin, Peter F	360	Motherwell, Robert	976	Pond, Maynard	981
Martindill, J. A	1344	Mourn, J	756	Poston, A	473
Martindill, Moses	1344	Mowrey, H. P	1081	Poston, Elias	642
Mason, G. T	1055	Murphy, A. C	977	Poston, G. W	643
Mason, John	1056	Murphy, L. C	593	Poston, I. G	1033
Mason, Mary	1057	Murray, J	1369	Poston, L. D	474
Mason, T. R	1058	Musselman, John	640	Poston, Samuel	807
Masten, John	619	Myer, Jacob	1139	Poston, William	808
Masters, Robert	1019	Myers, Lloyd	977	Poston, W. S	1033
Matheny, John	533	Nelson, A. W	471	Poston, W. W	474
Matheny, L. G	361	Newman, D. J	978	Potter, J. B	539
Mathews, S. L	562	Newton, A. P	471	Potter, Rev. J. G	757
Mathias, Isaac	969	Nixon, Azariah	978	Potter, W. H	377
Matteson, A	533	Nixon, Silas	1081	Pratt, E	757
Maxwell, L. A	469	Noble, William	1081	Preston, F. L	475
McBroom, J. C	1138	Norton, A	368	Preston, L. P	475
McBroom, M. V	1138	Norton, S. J	1370	Price, A. A	981
McBroom, Robert	1138	Nutter, John	1032	Price, W. H	758
McCarthy, T. F	969	Nutter, J. T	978	Primrose, I. P	476
McCarthy, Wm. D	970	Nutter, T. S	979	Prose, J. R	1323
McCathran, J. A	365	Oberholzer, H. A	534	Pruden, C. C	643
McClannahan, A	1320	O'Bleness, C. B	369	Puden, Judge S. B	377
McClannahan, W. S	1321	O'Bleness, H	369	Pugh, E. B	1258
McClary, M. Andrew	1363	O'Connor, Patrick	594	Pugh, J. C	1258
McClelland, Andrew	619	Ogg, Aaron	711	Pursell, F. S	982
McClelland, Samuel	1122	Ogg, A. J	711	Putz, J. A	1294

CONTENTS.

Name	Page	Name	Page	Name	Page
Raine, John	477	Schlotterback, John	1326	Stevenson, T. M	1304
Rannells, C. S	1294	Schmidt, Conrad	1265	Stewart, D. B	1389
Rannells, D. V	1258	Schwenke, C. W	995	Stewart, D. B., Jr	599
Rannells, J. W	1323	Scott, A. B	384	Stiers, Isaac	997
Rannells, T	1324	Scott, W. F	384	Stiers, J. A	998
Rannells, W. J	1259	Scott, Rev. W. H	384	Stiers, J. B	999
Ratcliff, William	1340	Scott, Winfield	385	Stiers, Wilford	1063
Rathburn, Lewis	540	Secoy, Jasper	565	Stiles, S. D	544
Rauch, J. E	983	Selby, W. W	712	Stimson, Mrs. Emma M.	623
Rauch, Peter	1083	Shafer, G. Van S	479	Stimson, H. S	383
Ream, Isaac	621	Shafler, J	382	Stivison, Samuel	999
Reasoner, Catherine	1304	Shaner, E	750	Stoddard, Grove	1034
Reasoner, P. M	1304	Shaner, Seth	784	Stone, Lemuel	1125
Reber, B. C	990	Shaner, W	784	Stout, Aaron, Sr	727
Reber, M. B	990	Shaw, J. A	1033	Stout, Aaron, Jr	727
Reddick, W. F	1083	Shaw, John	995	Stou, Charles	727
Redfern, E. F	1096	Shaw, J. S	1021	Stout, Cyrenus	728
Reeves, Eliphaz	561	Sheffield, B. B	480	Stout, George	728
Reid, Charles P	435	Sheik, John	1140	Stout, J. M	728
Reid, James	1140	Sheldon, C. R	382	Stout, S. C	728
Reisinger, J. H	1364	Shepard, J. S	481	Stout, W. O	729
Rempel, F. F	983	Shepard, W. P	481	Strahl, J. L	383
Reynolds, Henry	1262	Sheppard, James	482	Strausbaugh, J	1365
Rhodes, J. M	596	Sheppard, Thomas	482	Strausbaugh, M	1365
Rhoads, F. M	991	Sherrard, D. C	1034	Strausbaugh, P	1365
Rhoads, Jacob	991	Sherwood, S. W	1265	Strentz, J. W	998
Rice, Jason	540	Shockey, G. W	1266	Stright, Leander	697
Richardson, A. B	378	Shockey, Jacob	1267	Strong, Frank	1271
Richardson, Thomas	680	Shockey, J. J	1268	Strong, J	1366
Rickey, D. T	564	Shoemaker, Salem	1124	Strous, Allen	1125
Rickey, G. W	1325	Shoop, James B	542	Stump, J. H	1126
Rickey, John	564	Shott, Windell	808	Swaim, J. M	698
Riggs, Samuel	1081	Shrader, A. J	483	Swepston, Thomas	1086
Rineheart, George	1532	Shrader, Mrs. Amy	622	Taylor, J	785
Ring, John	379	Shry, Isaac	1269	Tedrow, Mrs. Mary	599
Risley, D. M	991	Shurtz, Andrew	1327	Tedrow, Noah	599
Roach, A. L	379	Shurtz, G. W	1328	Terrell, I. H	1000
Roads, J. B	992	Sickels, James	622	Thacker, B. W	1342
Robb, J. L	1263	Silvey, W. O	759	Tharp, M. W	785
Robbins, E	1376	Simms, G. B	681	Tharp, T. J	786
Robbins, John	1377	Simms, M. F	1062	Thomas, J. M	1378
Robey, J. J	1033	Sisson, G. W	1269	Thomas, W. A	386
Robinett, Ezekiel	1204	Skelly, Robert	1296	Thompson, J. W	1064
Robinett, Levi	1295	Slater, J	483	Thompson, Samuel	1064
Robinson, Allen	1295	Smith, C. R	760	Tibbles, Francis	729
Robinson, F. C	541	Smith, David	761	Tibbles, John	729
Robinson, J. C	541	Smith, Henry	697	Tinker, C. S	786
Robinson, J. W	782	Smith, H. J	598	Tinker, K	486
Rochester, J. W	992	Smith, John	543	Tobin, J. A	486
Rodeheaver, J. J	993	Smith, Joseph	481	Tompkins, E	386
Romel, J. M	1123	Smith, V	727	Townsend, Hon. C	387
Rose, Charles	994	Smith, W. A	623	Towsley, F. T	388
Rose, C. P	380	Smith, W	761	Towsley, G. W	389
Rose, Cyrus	381	Smith, William	644	Trimmer, Anthony	1272
Rose, J. B	477	Snook, William	1270	Trimmer, S. H	1272
Rossetter, T. K	622	Snowden, G	484	Tritsch, B. K	1001
Roth, F	381	Snyder, H R	996	Tritsch, J. E	1001
Rowell, Wm. M	597	Snyder, Rachel	1270	Troxel, Henry	1146
Runnion, Elijah	725	Sonders, Israel	1086	True, Austin	784
Runnion, M. M	725	Soule, Almond	1364	True, J	787
Runyon, Adam	1062	Southerton, C. W	762	Tucker, Aaron	645
Rush, Peter	758	Southerton, J. P	762	Tucker, Mrs. Caroline	1366
Russell, C. W	477	Spaulding, J	762	Tucker, C. G	600
Russell, David	680	Spaulding, J. M	598	Tucker, Josephus	681
Russell, G. A	782	Speakman, J. J	1340	Tucker, W. S	1126
Russell, James	725	Spencer, Charles	1103	Tullis, John A	434
Russell, John	726	Spencer, Smith	485	Ulmer, Peter	390
Russell, Washington	597	Spicer, J. E	1296	Unkle, David	1140
Russell, William	726	Stalter, Fred	544	Vale, A. P	1370
Salts, A. W	1264	Stalder, Nicholas	645	Vale, J. Q. A	1371
Sams, Nathan	644	Stalder, Samuel	598	Van Atta, R. S	1002
Sanders, H. T	783	Stanley, John	1270	Van Vorhes, Hon. N. H.	390
Sanders, J	758	Stanton, W	1378	Varley, John	392
Sands, J. F	1296	Starkey Wm. W	645	Vickers, Elijah	698
Sands, J. W	381	Starr, N. W	996	Vorhes, Albert	624
Sargent, Isaac	808	St. Clair, Samuel	1156	Vorhes, John	624
Saunders, Amasa	726	Steadman, F. C	383	Vorhes, W. H	486
Saunders, A. N	726	Steel, James S	1124	Vorhes, W. H	699
Scarlott, William	680	Steel, John S	1124	Voris, John	1157
Schaal, Daniel	1085	Steel, M. A	1364	Wadsworth, W. B	1087
Schaeffer, W. T	478	Steel, T. A	1124	Wagner, J. L	1127
Schaff, C. E	478	Stephenson, J. A	763	Walker, A. B	393
Schaff, I. M	479	Steuart, D. G	809	Walker, Daniel	730

CONTENTS.

Name	Page	Name	Page	Name	Page
Walker, G. R	394	Whitcraft, G. W	1141	Wolf, M. D	1067
Walker, J. H	394	White, Alexander	1006	Wolf, S. J	1129
Walker, T. C	682	White, C. L	1274	Wolf, T. B	1130
Walker, William	395	White, Darius	1007	Wolf, William, Jr	1067
Wallace, J. S	487	White, Harlow	1007	Wolfe, Ezra H	712
Wallace, J. W	1379	White, Jacob	1305	Wolfe, Frederick	1097
Wallar, E. H	1329	White, J. F	1008	Wolfe, Joseph H	712
Walsh, Thomas	396	White, J. W	490	Wollett, W. S	492
Warden, T. B	396	White, Lewis	1065	Wood, J. M	401
Warehime, J	787	White, S. C	683	Wood, J P	401
Warren, J. W	1388	White, T. R	788	Wood, R. M	565
Warren, N. O	600	Whitlatch, J. P	1276	Woodard, Ichabod, Sr	1068
Warrener, W. J	545	Whitlatch, William	1276	Woodard, Ichabod	1069
Watkins, Elisha	1021	Wickham, H. H	647	Woodard, L. C	493
Watkins, J. K	809	Wiggins, G. W	1103	Woodard, N. B	1069
Watkins, J. S	1021	Wilder, Jay	547	Woodard, W. N	493
Watson, A	488	Wilkins, C. B	1128	Woodruff, M	402
Waxler, G. W	1273	Wilkins, J. M	1128	Woods, T. D	1141
Weatherby, William	682	Wilkins, John	1129	Woodyard, J. C	402
Weaver, Jacob	1002	Wilkins, J. R	1129	Work, J. W	1008
Weaver, Levi	1127	Will, Daniel	1277	Work, R. R	1009
Webb, Ralph	1003	Williams, A. M	809	Wright, Harvey	601
Webb, Thomas	1004	Williams, B. F	1367	Wright, H. K	1087
Webster, C. D. B	646	Williams, Richason	1065	Wright, O. W	1009
Wedge, F. W	683	Williams, W. M	810	Wright, Robert	1010
Weed, S. T	1305	Willis, S. H	1329	Wright, W. A	1035
Weethee, J. P	764	Willmarth, A. J	769	Wyatt, F. C	648
Weethee, L	769	Wilson, A. J	490	Wyatt, George	713
Weitzell, R. S	1004	Wilson, Mrs. Dorcas	684	Wyatt, J. L	789
Welch, Hon. J	397	Wilson, E	490	Wyatt, John	547
Welch, J. F	488	Wilson, J. G	491	Wyatt, Joshua	648
Welch, J. M	397	Wilson, J	491	Zeigler, David	1142
Wellman, John	1005	Winget, M. C	1297	Zeller, David	1147
Wells, A. H	489	Winn, John T	624	Zeller, Jacob	1147
Wells, R. E	1367	Withers, H. G	810	Zeller, J. N	1011
Wells, W. J	788	Witherspoon, J. S	1330	Zimmerman, Joseph	789
Weltner, John	1147	Wolf, Andrew	1279	Zinn, William	810
Wescoat, N. B	1273	Wolf, Joseph	491	Yaple, W. R	1341
Wheeler, Edmund	546	Wolf, J. D	1066	Young, S	403
Whipple, J. O	400	Wolf, L. H	1035	Young, Wm. R	1130
Whitcraft, D. B	1141	Wolf, L. W	1066		

HISTORY OF HOCKING VALLEY

CHAPTER I.

INTRODUCTORY, BUT STILL HISTORY.

Indians, and the White Man's Advent—The Owners of the Territory—The Government Secured it—Ordinance of 1787—Who was its Author—The Dunmore War—Battle of Point Pleasant—Locating on the Indian Lands—Dunmore's March up the Hocking Valley—The Indian Name and Why.

When the early explorers and missionaries first visited the country afterward described as the "Northwest Territory," they found it under the rule of that famous and powerful tribe of Indians, the "Six Nations." Later, however, their prestige diminished, and during the eighteenth century this region was occupied and owned by several Indian tribes entirely independent of each other. Those in what is now Ohio were the Delawares, the Shawnees, the Wyandots (called the Hurons by the French), the Mingoes (an offshoot of the Iroquois), the Chippewas and the Tawas (more commonly called the Ottawas). The Delawares occupied the valleys of the Muskingum and the Tuscarawas; the Shawnees, the Scioto Valley; the Miamis, the valleys of the two rivers upon which they left their name; the Wyandots occupied the country about the Sandusky River; the Ottawas had their headquarters in the valleys of the Maumee and Sandusky; the Chippewas were confined principally to the south shore of Lake Erie; and the Mingoes were in greatest strength upon the Ohio, below the site of Steubenville. All of the tribes, however, frequented more or less lands outside of their prescribed territory, and at different periods, from the time when the first definite knowledge concerning them was obtained down to the era of white settlement, they occupied different locations. Thus the Delawares, whom Boquet found in 1764 in greatest numbers in the valley of the Tuscarawas, had, thirty years later, the majority of their population in the region of the county which now bears their name; and the Shawnees, who were originally strongest upon the Scioto, at the time of St. Clair's and Wayne's wars had concentrated upon the little Miami. The several tribes commingled to some extent as their animosities toward each other were supplanted by the common fear of the enemy of their race. They gradually grew stronger in sympathy and more compact in union as the settlements of the whites encroached upon their loved domain. Hence the divisions, which had in 1750 been quite plainly marked, became, by the time the Ohio was fringed with the cabins and villages of the pale face, in a large measure, obliterated. In Eastern Ohio, where the Delawares had held almost undisputed sway, there were now to be found also Wyandots, Shawnees, Mingoes, and even Miamis from the western border—from the Wabash, Miami and Mad rivers.

The Delawares, as has been indicated, had their densest population upon the Upper Muskingum and Tuscarawas, and they really were in possession of what is now the eastern half of the State, from the Ohio to Lake Erie. This tribe, which claimed to be the elder branch of the Lenni-Lenape, has by tradition and in history and in fiction been accorded a high rank among the savages of North America. Schoolcraft, Loskiel, Albert Gallatin, Drake, Zeisberger, Heckewelder and many other writers have borne testimony to the superiority of the Delawares, and James Fennimore Cooper, in his attractive romances, has added luster to the fame of the tribe. According to the tradition preserved by them the Delawares, many centuries before they knew the white man, lived in the western part of the continent, and separating themselves from the rest of the Lenni-Lenape migrated slowly eastward. Reaching the Allegheny River they, with the Iroquois, waged war successfully with a race of giants, the Allegewi, and still continuing their migration, settled on the Delaware River, and spread their population eventually to the Hudson, the Susqehanna and the Potomac. Here they lived, menaced and often attacked by the Iroquois, and finally, as some writers claim, they were subjugated by the Iroquois through stratagem. The Atlantic coast became settled by Europeans, and the Delawares being also embittered against the Iroquois, whom they accused of treachery, they turned westward and concentrated upon the Allegheny. Disturbed here again by the white settlers, a portion of the tribe obtained permission from the Wyandots, whom they called their uncles, thus confessing their superiority and reputation of greater antiquity, to occupy the lands along the Muskingum. The forerunners of the nation entered this region in all probability as early as 1745, and in less than a score of years their entire population had become resident in this country. They became here a more flourishing and powerful tribe than they had ever been before. Their warriors numbered not less than 600 in 1764.

OWNERSHIP OF THE NORTHWEST.

Though the actual occupants, and as most will say the rightful owners of this region were these native tribes of Indians, there were other claimants to the soil, who, though for a long time they made little pretense of actual possession, were eventually to dispossess the Indians of their hunting grounds. France, resting her claim upon the discovery and explorations of Robert Cavelier de La Salle and Marquette, upon a sort of nominal occupation of the country by means of forts and missions, and later, upon the provisions of several European treaties (those of Utrecht, Ryswick and Aix-la-Chapelle), was the first nation to formally lay claim to the soil of the territory now included within the boundaries of the State of Ohio, as an integral portion of the valley of the Mississippi and of the Northwest. Ohio was thus a part of New France. After the treaty of Utrecht in 1713, it was a part of the French province of Louisiana, which extended from the gulf to the northern lakes. The English claims were based on the priority of their occupation of the Atlantic coast, in latitude corresponding to the territory claimed; upon an opposite construction of the same treaties above named; and last, but not least, upon the alleged cession of the rights of the Indians. England's charters to all of the original colonies expressly extended their grants from sea to sea. The principal ground of claim by the English was by the treaties of purchase from the Six Nations, who, claiming to be conquerors of the whole country and therefore its possessors, asserted their right to dispose of it. France successfully resisted the claims of England, and maintained control of the territory between the Ohio and the lakes by force of arms until the treaty of Paris was consummated in 1763. By the provisions of this treaty, Great Britain came into the possession of the disputed lands, and retained it until ownership was vested in the United States by the treaty of peace made just twenty years later.

Virginia had asserted her claims to the whole of the territory northwest of the Ohio, and New York had claimed titles to portions of the same. These claims had been for the most part held in abeyance during the period when the general ownership was vested in Great Britain, but were afterward the cause of much embarrassment to the United States. Virginia, however, had not only claimed ownership of the soil, but attempted the exercise of civil authority in the disputed territory as early as 1769. In that year the colonial House of Burgesses passed an act establishing the county of Botetourt, including a large part of what is now West Virginia, and the whole territory northwest of the Ohio, and having, of course, as its western boundary the Mississippi River. It was more in name than in fact, however, that Virginia had jurisdiction over this great county of Botetourt through the act of 1769. In 1778, after the splendid achievements of General George Rogers Clarke,—his subjugation of the British posts in the far West, and conquest of the whole country from the Ohio to the Mississippi,—this territory was organized by the Virginia Legislature as the County of Illinois. John Todd was appointed as County Lieutenant and Civil Commandant of Illinois County, and served until his death (he was killed in the battle of Blue Licks, Aug. 18, 1782). He was succeeded by Timothy de Montburn.

New York was the first of the several States claiming right and title in Western lands to withdraw the same in favor of the United States. Her charter, obtained March 2, 1664, from Charles II., embraced territory which had formerly been granted to Massachusetts and Connecticut. The cession of claim was made by James Duane, Wm. Floyd and Alexander McDougall, on behalf of the State, March 1, 1781. Virginia, with a far more valid claim than New York, was the next State to follow New York's example. Her claim was founded upon certain charters granted to the colony by James I., and bearing date respectively, April 10, 1806, May 23, 1609, and March 12, 1611; upon the conquest of the country by General George Rogers Clarke; and upon the fact that she had also exercised civil authority over the territory. The act was consummated March 17, 1784. Massachusetts ceded her claims, without reservation, the same year that Virginia did hers (1784), though the action was not formally consummated until the 18th of April, 1785. The right of her title had been rested upon her charter, granted less than a quarter of a century from the arrival of the Mayflower, and embracing territory extending from the Atlantic to the Pacific. Connecticut made what has been called "the last tardy and reluctant sacrifice of State pretension to the common good,' 'Sept. 14, 1786.

THE GOVERNMENT OWNED IT.

The United States Government was the only one now claiming authority over the Northwest, and there remained only the task of extinguishing the Indian title before the question of ownership could be finally settled. This was no easy matter, however, as the Six Nations and other tribes were allies of the English, and hostile to the Americans, and they did not relish the idea of giving up their homes without a struggle. The result was a series of hostile movements, and numerous acts of revenge. The Government prosecuted almost a continuous war against them, without bringing about a satisfactory peace, until in 1786, a conciliatory policy was adopted, which proved far more effectual. By a series of purchases and treaties made at various dates, the title of the Indians was peaceably extinguished. It is a fact worthy of note, and one of which we may well be proud, that the title to every foot of Ohio soil was honorably acquired from the Indians.

ORDINANCE OF 1787.

In 1784 a committee, of which Thomas Jefferson was chairman, reported to Congress an ordinance providing for the establishment and maintenance of government in the Northwest Territory. This measure of 1784, although it remained nominally in force until repealed by the ordinance of 1787, was really inoperative—a dead letter. May 20, 1785, an ordinance was passed for the survey of Western lands. A surveyor was chosen from each State, to act under the direction of the Geographer of the United States, in laying off the land into townships of six miles square. The Geographer was instructed to designate the townships by numbers, beginning at the south; and the ranges by numbers, beginning at the east and going westward. It is this simple system of describing land that has been adopted by the Government in the survey of all its lands since that time.

The famous ordinance of 1787, passed July 13, and from its most important provision often termed the "Ordinance of Freedom," was the last gift of the Congress of the old confederation to the country, and it was a fit consummation of their glorious labors. It was the product of what we may call inspired statesmanship, the foundation upon which five great commonwealths were to be built up, the fundamental law, the constitution of the Northwest Territory, and a sacred compact between the old colonies and the yet uncreated States to come into being under its benign influence. "It forever proscribed slavery upon the soil of the great territory that it organized." The Congress of 1787 "builded wiser than it knew," and more grandly. Let us pass the broader significance and vaster value of the ordinance, and look upon it simply as the act of legislation providing for the opening, development and government of the territory; we find it alike admirable and effective. It provided for successive forms of territorial government, and upon it were based all of the territorial enactments and much of the subsequent State legislation. It was so constructed as to give the utmost encouragement to immigration, and it offered the utmost protection to those who became settlers, for "when they came into the wilderness," says Chief Justice Chase, "they found the law already there. It was impressed upon the soil, while as yet it bore up nothing but the forest."

The authorship of the ordinance of 1787 has been variously ascribed to Nathan Dane, a Congressman from Massachusetts, to Rufus King of the same State, and to Thomas Jefferson; and arguments more or less weighty have from time to time been advanced to support their claims or those of their friends. Thomas Jefferson went to France as Minister three years before the passage of the ordinance of 1787, and did not return until eighteen months after. He was, however, identified with the inoperative ordinance of 1784, which introduced the clause prohibiting slavery after the year 1800, which did not pass. Mr. King was undoubtedly the author of the anti-slavery clause in an ordinance which secured some attention in 1785, but he was not even a member of the Congress of 1787. Mr. Dane's claim is combated chiefly on the ground that it was never made while any of the other men who, from their position, were supposed to know about the formation of the ordinance were alive, and on the ground that he had none of those graces of composition which are exhibited in the ordinance Of later years investigation has convinced almost all prominent writers on the subject that Dr. Manasseh Cutler was the real author. The evidence is too lengthy to introduce here, but it has not been refuted, and the supposition accords very well with the well-known facts of history. Dr. Cutler had come before Congress to purchase for a company composed chiefly of Massachusetts men, a large body of public lands. The purchase would have been almost entirely valueless in the opinion of most of the Ohio Company associates if they could not have the land to which they proposed to emigrate covered with the law to which they had been accustomed. The ordinance of freedom was as an act of legislation, the natural predecessor of the sale to the Ohio Company. It was considered by Congress, after the plan had been fully examined, very desirable that the public domain should be advantageously disposed of, and that a colony should be established in the Federal Territory. Such a colony would form a barrier against the British and Indians, it was argued, and this initiative step would be followed speedily by other purchases in which additional settlements would be founded. The South had a greater interest in the West than had New England; and Virginia, especially, from her past protection, future prospect and geographical location, was interested in and eager for the development of the country beyond the Ohio. Virginia, and the South in general, may have justly regarded the planting in the West of a colony of men whose patriotism was well known, a measure calculated to bind together the old and new parts of the nation, and promote union. It is presumable that much was said by Dr. Cutler upon these advantages and that it was their importance in the eyes of Southern members which led them to permit the creation and enactment of such an ordinance.

DUNMORE'S WAR.

Probably but few of the present inhabitants of the Hocking Valley are aware that a fort was established within its limits and an army marched across its borders, led by an English earl, before the Revolutionary War. The building of Fort Gower at the mouth of the Hocking River, in what is now Troy Township, Athens County, and the march of Lord Dunmore's army across the country many years before its first settlement, forms an interesting passage in our remote history.

"Dunmore's War" was the designation applied to a series of bloody hostilities between the whites and Indians during the year 1774. It was the culmination of the bitter warfare that had been waged with varying success between the frontier population of Pennsylvania and Virginia, and the Delawares, Iroquois, Wyandots and other tribes of Indians. One of the most noted of the many massacres of that period was that of Logan's family by the whites, and in retaliation the swift vengeance of the Mingo chief upon the white settlements on the Monongahela, where, in the language of his celebrated speech, he "fully glutted his vengeance."

In August, 1774, Lord Dunmore, then Governor of Virginia, determined to raise a large force and carry the war into the enemy's country. The plan of the campaign was simple. Three regiments were to be raised west of the Blue Ridge, to be commanded by General Andrew Lewis, while two other regiments from the interior were to be commanded by Dunmore himself. The forces were to form a junction at the mouth of the Great Kanawha and proceed, under the command of Lord Dunmore, to attack the Indian towns n Ohio. The force under Lewis, amounting to 1,100 men, rendezvoused at Camp Union, now Lewisburg, Greenbrier Co., W. Va., whence they marched early in September, and reached Point Pleasant on the 6th of October. Three days later Lewis received dispatches from Dunmore informing him that he had changed his plan of operations; that he (Dunmore) would march across the country against the Shawanese towns on the Scioto, situated within the present limits of Pickaway County, and Lewis was ordered to cross the Ohio River at once and join Dunmore before these towns.

This movement was to have been made on the 10th of October. On that day, however, before the march had begun, two men of Lewis's command were fired upon while hunting a mile or so from camp. One was killed and the other came rushing into camp with the alarm that Indians were at hand. General Lewis had barely time to make some hasty dispositions when there began one of the most desperate Indian battles recorded in border warfare—the battle of Point Pleasant. The Indians were in great force, infuriated by past wrong and by the hope of wiping-out their enemy by this day's fight, and were led on by their ablest and most daring chiefs. Pre-eminent among the savage leaders were Logan and "Cornplanter" (or "Cornstalk"), whose voices rang above the din, and whose tremendous feats performed in this day's action have passed into history. The contest lasted all day, and was not yet decided. Toward evening General Lewis ordered a body of men to gain the enemy's flank, on seeing which movement about to be successfully executed the Indians drew off and effected a safe retreat. The force on both sides in this battle was nearly equal—about 1,100. The whites lost half their officers and fifty-two men killed. The loss of the Indians, killed and wounded, was estimated at 233. Soon after the battle Lewis crossed the river and pursued the Indians with great vigor, but did not again come in conflict with them.

Meanwhile Lord Dunmore, in whose movements we are more interested, had, with about 1,200 men, crossed the mountains at Potomac Gap, reviewed his force at Fort Pitt, now Pittsburg, and descended the Ohio River as far as the mouth of the Hocking. Here he landed, formed a camp, and built a fortification which he called Fort Gower. It was from here that he sent word to General Lewis of the change in his plan of campaign, and he remained here until after the battle of Point Pleasant. Leaving a sufficient force at Fort Gower to protect the stores and secure it as a base, Lord Dunmore marched up the Hocking toward the Indian country. There is a tradition that his little army encamped at night successively at Federal Creek, and at Sunday Creek in Athens County. He marched up the Hocking as far as where Logan now stands, and from there westward to a point seven miles from Circleville, where a grand parley was held with the Indians. It was at this council that the famous speech of the Mingo chief was made, beginning, "I appeal to any white man to say if he ever entered Logan's cabin hungry and he gave him not meat," etc. After the execution of a treaty with the Indians, Lord Dunmore returned to Fort Gower by nearly the same route he had pursued in his advance, across the country and down the valley of the Hocking to its mouth. It is probable that his army was disbanded at this point, and returned in small parties to their homes.

ORIGIN OF THE NAME "HOCKING."

"Hockhocking" is a Delaware (Indian) name, and meant in their language, "Bottle River." In the spring of 1765 George Croghan, a sub-commissioner of the British Government, embarked at Pittsburg with some friendly Indians, intending to visit the Wabash and Illinois country, and conclude a treaty with the Indians. Five days from Pittsburg, he notes in his journal that "we passed the mouth of Hochocen, or Bottle River." This translation of the word Hochocen or Hockhocking, is also given by Heckewelder and Johnson, and is undoubtedly correct. The Shawanese called the river Weathak-agh-qua, which meant, in their dialect, the same as Hockhocking; and one of the other tribes called it by a name signifying Bow River. All of these names had reference to the winding, crooked course of the stream. The origin of the name Hockhocking—Bottle River—is thus explained by a writer in an old number of the American Pioneer, who says: "About six or seven miles northwest of Lancaster there is a fall in the Hockhocking of about twenty feet; above the falls, for a short distance, the stream is very narrow and straight, forming a neck, while at the falls it suddenly widens on each side, and swells into the appearance of the body of a bottle. The whole, when seen from above, appears exactly in the shape of a bottle, and from this fact arose the Indian name of Hockhocking." The original name has been corrupted or shortened to "Hocking," and this shortened form has become so universal in its use, that it may now be considered the correct form of the word.

Very truly yours

L. A. Culver

CHAPTER II.

EARLY SETTLEMENT AND MATERIAL PROGRESS.

THE OHIO COMPANY—THE VALLEY OF HOCKING—WASHINGTON COUNTY—GENERALS WASHINGTON AND PUTNAM—ORGANIZATION—PURCHASE OF LAND, 964,285 ACRES—ATHENS AND HOCKING COUNTIES—THE ARRIVALS—NAMES OF THE FIRST SETTLERS—THE CITY OF ADELPHIA—MARIETTA—INDIAN WAR—GENERALS HARMER AND ST. CLAIR DEFEATED—MAD ANTHONY'S VICTORY—FIRST SETTLERS OF THE COLLEGE LANDS, OR IN ATHENS COUNTY—MAKING SALT—PIONEER MODES AND PIONEER PROGRESS.

THE FIRST SETTLEMENT.

The first settlement of the Hocking Valley, or northwest of the Ohio River, was in 1774. Then quite a number settled within the limits of what is now Ohio. There were small villages at Hocking Falls, at the Muskingum, the Scioto, Miami, and along the north banks of the Ohio. The largest appeared to have been Hocking, and there was quite a town on the Mingo bottoms, opposite what is now Wheeling.

In January, 1785, the commissioners to treat with the Indians in possession of the territory, Messrs. George Rogers, Richard Butler and Arthur Lee, were compelled to cease negotiations until the lands west of the Ohio River were dispossessed of the white settlers or pioneers. Ensign John Armstrong was sent by Colonel Harmer to drive these white invaders from Indian soil. Some failed to leave. The Delaware and Wyandot Indians were in possession. This was in March, 1785. It is very probable that these primitive settlements were formed by soldiers from Lord Dunmore's army which, after a short campaign against the Indians in Ohio, was disbanded at the mouth of the Hocking River in the fall of 1774. The fact of the disbandonment of the army, about 1,200 men, at the time and place above named, has been accepted as conclusive, and as no facts to the contrary have ever been presented, nothing seems more plausible than that parties of these soldiers, on discovering the fertility of these valleys, tarried long enough to test their fruitfulness, and afterward sent for their families or friends.

It is fully evident from the foregoing that the whites had fastened themselves upon the country as early as 1774, but there is no evidence at hand to prove that any fixed settlement was founded for the active development of the country until the advent of the Ohio Company. The close of the Revolutionary war, which proclaimed to the world a nation born and liberty triumphant, found the country in an exhausted condition, and the people had little means, either for home comforts or to travel to unknown and far off lands. However, the recuperation of the population from the devastations of a seven-years' war was remarkable for its rapidity, and the desire to explore the then great unknown West became a consuming one. A government of peace, however, had to be founded, laws made, and all the machinery of law, order and the inalienable right of a few people was to be inaugurated that would secure a continuation of that peace which had cost so much, and for a prosperity which was absolutely necessary to the welfare of an impoverished people. This was the labor of years, yet the year 1787 saw the fruition of the work, and a glorious structure was reared which has stood the test of time, the assaults of a foreign foe and a civil strife unparalleled in the history of nations.

Under the ægis of this law the pioneer left his New England home and planted the banner of civilization upon the boundary line of the great Northwest, and from there took up his line of march into the interior, blazing a pathway for others to follow, and, at times, leaving his body as a bloody offering upon the shrine of freedom, and the burning of his cabin a torch to light the footsteps of those who came after. All was not peace in the West when freedom sat enthroned on the Atlantic Coast. The Indians were not willing to give up their hunting grounds without a struggle, and bravely they repelled the pale faces. But destiny had decreed their doom, and the white man was master of the country.

THE CONTROLLING SPIRITS.

A few leading spirits, highly endowed with wisdom, endurance, and a spirit in which, through all the trials and troubles of a pioneer life, remained undaunted, organized for the purpose of settling this country, and took the form of an incorporated body by the name of the "Ohio Company." How they secured this land is a matter of record a few pages further along in this work. The purchase of the land, the contract, the confirmation of the same by Congress, with a copy of the first patent issued by George Washington, completes the entry of that company for the land, and it only became necessary to secure settlers to put themselves into possession of their landed estate. This estate was in part composed of Athens County and a part of Hocking and Vinton counties. The first settlement was at Marietta, on the river, while but a few weeks later Athens seems to have secured both a habitation and a name. Thus it was that Marietta and Washington County became the site of the first white settlement made in the territory of the Northwest, while Athens secured the right to be called the first inland town.

GENERAL PUTNAM'S LETTER.

In the summer of 1783 some 250 officers petitioned Congress for a grant of land in the Western country. General Putnam, who was himself personally interested in the measure, addressed a letter to Washington on the subject, setting forth the plan in detail, and requesting the latter to use his influence with Congress in favor of the grant.

One of the most important suggestions in this letter of General Putnam's was the formation of townships six miles square, and the donation of 3,040 acres of land for the support of churches, schools, and the improvement of the highway. His suggestions were approved, and he thus has the honor of being the father of these beneficent measures. The townships of six miles square were decided upon, and in many of the States, the school sections of 640 acres, set apart in each township for school purposes, is this suggestion of General Putnam practically carried out.

Not long after this a warm friend of General Putnam, General Benjamin Tupper, was appointed by Congress to survey the public lands in the West. This was the first step in the object of securing the grant in which General Putnam and others were successful.

THE INITIATORY STEPS.

In the autumn of 1785 General Tupper started for the Northwest, intending to prosecute the land surveys of that region, but owing to Indian troubles, did not proceed further than the present site of Pittsburg.

After the Indians had been temporarily quieted by treaty, January, 1786, General Tupper made a second journey to the West in the summer of that year and completed, during the season, a survey of most of the territory in this section.

After his *first* visit to the Northwest, during the winter of 1785-'6, General Tupper's mind was filled with the idea of removing to the Ohio country. He soon became thoroughly in earnest, and believing that his friend General Putnam would approve his plans, visited him at his residence in Rutland; and thus were brought together again the two men who originated the idea of the famous Ohio Company. They discussed the subject of Western land and emigration thoroughly, and the result was a call which was published in the newspapers of the State, on the 25th of January, 1786.

It read: " The subscribers take this method to inform all officers and soldiers who have served in the late war, and who are, by a late ordinance of the honorable Congress, to receive certain tracts of land in the Ohio country,--and also all other good citizens who wish to become adventurers in that delightful region,--that from personal inspection, together with other incontestible evidences, they are fully satisfied that the lands in that quarter are of a much better quality than any other known to New England people; that the climate, seasons, products, etc., are, in fact, equal to the most flattering accounts that have ever been published of them; that being determined to become purchasers and to prosecute a settement in this country, and desirous of forming a general association with those who entertain the same ideas, they beg leave to propose the following plan, viz.: That an association by the name of *The Ohio Company* be formed of all such as wish to become purchasers, etc., in that country who reside in the Commonwealth of Massachusetts only, or to extend to the inhabitants of other States as shall be agreed on. In order to bring such a company into existence, the subscribers propose that all persons who wish to promote the scheme should meet in their respective counties at 10 o'clock A. M. on Wednesday, the 15th day of February next, and that each county meeting then assembled choose a delegate or delegates, to meet at the Bunch of Grapes Tavern in Boston on Wednesday, the first day of March next, at 10 o'clock A. M., then and there to consider and determine on a general plan of association for said company; which plan, covenant, or agreement being published, any person (under condition therein to be provided) may, by subscribing his name, become a member of the company.

"RUFUS PUTNAM,"
"BENJAMIN TUPPER."

The result of this call was a meeting of delegates, appointed by several counties of Massachusetts, in Boston on March 1, 1786. These delegates were Winthrop Sargent and John Miles, from Suffolk County; Manasseh Cutler, from Essex; John Brooks and Thomas Cushing, from Middlesex; Benjamin Tupper, from Hampshire; Crocker Sampson, from Plymouth; Rufus Putnam, from Worcester; John Patterson and Jelaliel Woodbridge, from Berkshire; and Abraham Williams, from Barnstable. General Rufus Putnam was chosen Chairman of the meeting, and Major Winthrop Sargent, Secretary. Before the adjournment of this meeting, which was closely followed by a series of others, a committee, consisting of Putnam, Cutler, Brooks, Sargent and Cushing, was appointed to draft a plan of association. At the next meeting, March 3, their draft was presented, a portion of which read as follows: "The design of this association is to raise a fund of continental certificates for the sole purpose and to be appropriated to the entire use of purchasing lands in the Western Territory (belonging to the United States) for the benefit of the company and to promote a settlement in that country." The amount to be raised was not to exceed $1,000,000, exclusive of one year's interest due thereon.

Another part of the plan read: "The one year's interest shall be applied to the purpose of making a settlement in the country, and assisting those who may be otherwise unable to remove themselves thither."

HOW TO BE APPLIED.

The above fund was to "be applied to the purchase of lands in some one of the proposed States northwesterly of the river Ohio as soon as those lands are surveyed and exposed for sale by the Commissioners of Congress, etc." But as this method of obtaining possession of the land was liable to consume too much time, at a subsequent meeting it was unanimously resolved that three directors should be appointed for the company who should make immediate application to Congress for a private purchase of lands. General Samuel H. Parsons, General Rufus Putnam and Rev. Manasseh Cutler were chosen for that purpose.

The consummation of the scheme, however, consumed more time than was anticipated, owing to the slow progress made in raising funds. Steps toward a purchase were not taken until April of the following year, when General Parsons made application to Congress for the purchase of lands on the Muskingum River. A committee from Congress, then sitting at New York, was appointed to confer with him, and he, transcending his instructions, proposed a purchase of the Scioto Valley. The proprietors being dissatisfied with this procedure, appointed in his stead Major Sargent and Dr. Cutler to complete the purchase on the Muskingum. This was done, though the contract was not concluded until the following autumn.

The contract is as follows:

"Contract of the Ohio Company with the Board of Treasury.

"The contract of the Ohio Company with the Honorable Board of Treasury of the United States of America made by the Rev. Mr. Manasseh Cutler and Mayor Winthrop Sargent, as agents for the directors of said company, at New York, Oct. 27, 1787:

"This Indenture, made the 27th day of October, in the year of our Lord one thousand seven hundred and eighty-seven, between *Samuel Osgood*, *Walter Livingston* and *Arthur Lee*, Esquires, (the Board of Treasury for the United States of America), acting by and under the authority of the Honorable, the Congress of the said States of the one part, and *Manasseh Cutler* and *Winthrop Sargent*, both of the Commonwealth of Massachusetts, as agents for the directors of the Ohio Company of Associates, so called, of the other part: Whereas, the Congress of the United States aforesaid, in and by their several resolutions and votes of the twenty-third and twenty-seventh days of July last past, did authorize and empower the Board of Treasury aforesaid to contract with any person or persons for a grant of the tract of land in the said resolutions mentioned, upon such terms and conditions, for such considerations and under such reservations, as in the said resolutions is expressed. And, whereas, by virtue and in consequence of the said resolutions and votes, the said parties of the first part have contracted and agreed with the parties of the second part, agents as aforesaid, for a grant of the tract of land hereinafter mentioned.

"*Now, therefore this indenture witnesseth*, That the said parties of the first part, in order to carry their said agreement, as far as possible, into effect, and for and in consideration of the sum of five hundred thousand dollars well and truly paid into the Treasury of the said United States by the said parties of the second part, before the ensealing and delivery of these presents, the receipt whereof the said Board of Treasury do hereby acknowledge, and do hereby, on the behalf of the said United States, acquit, release, exhonerate and forever discharge the said parties of the second part, and the said Ohio Company of Associates and every of them, their and every of their heirs, executors, administrators and assigns forever, by these presents; and also in consideration of the further sum of five hundred thousand dollars, secured to be paid as hereinafter is mentioned, have, in behalf of the said United States and the Congress thereof, covenanted and agreed, and do hereby covenant and agree, to and with the said parties of the second part, their heirs and assigns, that within one month of the payment of the said last mentioned sum of five hundred thousand dollars, in the manner hereinafter prescribed, a full and ample grant and conveyance shall be executed, in due form of law, under the seal of the said United States, whereby the people of the said United States or the Congress thereof, or such officer or officers as shall be duly authorized for that purpose, shall grant, convey and assure to the said parties of the second part, their heirs and assigns forever (as agents to the directors of, and in trust for the persons composing the said Ohio Company of Associates, according to their several rights and interests under the said association), and to their heirs and assigns forever, as tenants in common, in fee simple, all that certain tract or parcel of land, *Beginning* at the place where the western boundary line of the seventh range of townships, laid out by the authority of Congress, intersects the Ohio, and extending thence along that river southwestwardly, to the place where the western line of the seventeenth range of townships, to be laid out according to the land ordinance of the 20th May, 1785, would intersect the said river, and extending thence northerly on the western boundary line of the said seventeenth range of townships, so far that a line drawn due east to the western boundary line of the said seventh range of townships will, with the other lines of this tract, include one million and a half acres of land, besides the several townships, lots and parcels of land hereinafter mentioned, to be reserved or appropriated to specific purposes; thence running east to the western bounds of the said seventh range of townships, and thence southerly along those bounds to the place of beginning; with the rights, members and appurtenances thereof; which said tract of land shall be surveyed by the Geographer or some other officer of the said United States, to be authorized for that purpose, who shall plainly mark the said east and west line, and shall render one complete map or plat of the said tract to the Board of Treasury of the United States, for the time being, or such other person as Congress may appoint, and another plat or map thereof to the said parties of the second part, their heirs and assigns: *Provided always, and it is hereby expressly stipulated*, That in the said grant, so to be executed as aforesaid, a proper clause or clauses shall or may be inserted for the purpose of reserving in each township, or fractional part of a township, which, upon such surveys as hereinafter are mentioned, shall fall within the bounds of the tract, so to be granted as aforesaid, lot number sixteen, for the purposes mentioned in the said ordinance of the 20th of May, 1785; lot number twenty-nine to be appropriated to the purposes of religion; and lots numbers eight, eleven and twenty-six for the use, and subject to the disposition of the Congress of the United States; and also reserving out of the said tract so to be granted, two complete townships to be given perpetually for the purposes of an university, to be laid off by the parties of the second part, their heirs or assigns, as near the center as may be, so that the same shall be of good land, to be applied to the intended object in such manner as the Legislature of the State wherein the said township shall fall, or may be situated, shall or may think proper to direct. And the said parties of the second part do hereby for themselves, and the directors, and Ohio Company of Associates aforesaid, and every of them, and their and every of their heirs, executors, administrators and assigns, covenant and grant to and with the said parties of the first part, their heirs, executors and administrators (acting, as aforesaid, for and on behalf of the United States, by virtue of the authority so as aforesaid to them delegated and assigned), that within the space of seven years, from and after the outlines of the said tract shall have been so, as aforesaid, run out by the Geographer, or other officer of the United States to be for that purpose appointed, and the plat thereof given as aforesaid (if they are not prevented by incursions or opposition from the savages, or if they are so prevented then as soon as the same can be conveniently thereafter accomplished), the said directors and Ohio Company of Associates, or some of them, their or some of their heirs or assigns shall and will cause the said tract of land to be surveyed, laid out and divided into townships, and fractional parts of townships, and also subdivided into lots, according to the directions and provisions of the land ordinance of the 20th of May, 1785, issued by Congress, and shall and will make, or cause to be made, complete returns of divisions and subdivisions to the Treasury Board of the United States, for the time being, or such other person or persons as Congress shall or may appoint. And, also, shall and will, within one month after the outlines of the said tract shall have been so, as aforesaid, surveyed, well and truly pay, or cause to be paid, into the Treasury of the said United States, the sum of $500,000 in gold or silver, or in securities of the said United States without fraud or further delay. And, inasmuch as it was the true intent and meaning of the said parties to these presents, and of the Congress of the United States, that the said Ohio Company of Associates should immediately cultivate, if they thought proper, a part of the said tract of land, proportionable to the payment which they have so, as aforesaid, already made; and should have full security for the undisturbed enjoyment of the same. *Now, this indenture further witnesseth,* That the said parties of the first part, by virtue of the power and authority to them given by Congress, as aforesaid, have covenanted, promised and agreed, and do hereby covenant, promise and agree, to and with the said parties of the second part, their heirs and assigns, that it shall and may be lawful for the said Ohio Company of Associates, so called, their heirs and assigns, to enter upon, take possession of, cultivate and improve, at their pleasure, all that certain tract or parcel of land, part of the tract hereinbefore described: *Beginning* at the place where the western boundary line of the seventh range of townships intersects the Ohio; thence extending along that river southwesterly to the place where the western boundary line of the fifteenth range of townships, when laid out agreeable to the ordinance aforesaid, would touch the said river; thence running northerly on the western bounds of the said fifteenth range of townships, till a line drawn due east, the western boundary line of the said seventh range of townships, will comprehend, with the other boundary lines of this tract, 750,000 acres of land, besides the several lots and parcels of lands hereinafter mentioned to be reserved or appropriated to particular purposes; thence running east to the western boundary line of the said seventh range of townships, and thence along the said line to the place of beginning; with the rights, members and appurtenances thereof, according to the terms of the said association. Reserving, always, and excepting out of the said tract last mentioned, and the permission to cultivate the same in each township and fractional part of a township which shall fall within the same, according to the land ordinance hereinbefore mentioned, lot number sixteen, for the purposes specified in the said ordinance; lot number twenty-nine for the purposes of religion; lots numbers eight, eleven and twenty-six subject to the disposition of the Congress of the United States, and also reserving and excepting two complete townships for the purposes of an university, to be laid off in the manner hereinbefore mentioned, and to be applied in such manner to that object as the Legislature of the State wherein the said townships shall fall, or be situated, shall or may think proper or direct. And the said parties of the first part do hereby, for and on behalf of the said United States, promise and agree to and with the said parties of the second part, their heirs and assigns, that the said Ohio Company of Associates, their heirs and assigns, shall and may, from time to time, and at all times hereafter, freely and peaceably hold and enjoy the said last-mentioned tract of land, except the said lots and parcels of land and townships so, as aforesaid, excepted: *Provided*, That the covenants and agreements hereinbefore contained on the part of the said parties of the second part are observed, performed and fulfilled. And the said parties of the first part do hereby pledge the faith of the United States to the said parties of the second part, their heirs and assigns, and to the said Ohio Company of Associates, so-called, for the performance of all the grants, promises and agreements hereinbefore contained, which, on the part of the said parties of the first part, or of the said States, are or ought to be kept and performed.

In witness whereof, the parties to these presents have interchangeably set their hands and seals, and the said parties of the first part have caused their seal of office to be hereunto affixed, the day and year first hereinbefore mentioned.

SAMUEL OSGOOD, [L. S.]
MANASSEH CUTLER, [L. S.]
ARTHUR LEE, [L S.]
WINTHROP SARGENT. [L. S.]

There is also given here the act of Congress authorizing the disposition of the land to the Ohio Company, and confirms its sale, and also the first patent to the company signed by Geo. Washington and Thos. Jefferson. There were other patents granted, but not necessary to place here in full.

AN ACT AUTHORIZING THE GRANT AND CONVEYANCE OF CERTAIN LANDS TO THE OHIO COMPANY OF ASSOCIATES.

Be it enacted by the Senate and House of Representatives of the United States of America in Congress assembled, That a certain contract expressed in an indenture executed on the 27th day of October, in the year one thousand seven hundred and eighty-seven, between the then Board of Treasury for the United States of America, of the one part, and Manasseh Cutler and Winthrop Sargent, as agents for the directors of the Ohio Company of Associates, of the other part, so far as the same respects the following described tract of land, that is to say: "Beginning at a station where the western boundary line of the seventh range of townships, laid out by the authority of the United States in Congress assembled, intersects the river Ohio; thence, extending along that river, southwesterly, to a place where the western boundary line of the fifteenth range of townships, when laid out agreeably to the land ordinance passed the twentieth of May, one thousand seven hundred and eighty-five, would touch the said river; thence running northerly on the said western bound of the said fifteenth range of townships, till a line drawn due east to the western boundary line of the said seventh range of townships will comprehend with the other lines of this tract 750,000 acres of land, besides the several lots and parcels of land in the said contract reserved or appropriated to particular purposes; thence, running east, to the western boundary line of the said seventh range of townships, and thence along the said line to the place of beginning," be, and the same is hereby, confirmed: And that the President of the United States be, and he hereby is, authorized and empowered to issue letters patent, in the name and under the seal of the United States, hereby granting and conveying to Rufus Putnam, Manasseh Cutler, Robert Oliver, and Griffin Green, and to their heirs and assigns, in fee simple, the said described tract of land, with the reservation in the said indenture expressed, in trust for the persons composing the said Ohio Company of Associates, according to their several rights and interests, and for their heirs and assigns, as tenants in common.

SEC. 2. *And be it further enacted*, That the President be, and he hereby is, further authorized and empowered, by letters patent as aforesaid, to grant and convey to the said Rufus Putnam, Manasseh Cutler, Robert Oliver and Griffin Green, and to their heirs and assigns, in trust, for the uses above expressed, one other tract of 214,285 acres of land: *Provided*, That Rufus Putnam, Manasseh Cutler, Robert Oliver and Griffin Green, or either of them, shall deliver to the Secretary of the Treasury, within six months, warrants which issued for army bounty rights sufficient for that purpose, according to the provision of a resolve of Congress of the twenty-third day of July, one thousand seven hundred and eighty-seven.

SEC. 3. *And be it further enacted*, That the President be, and he hereby is, further authorized and empowered, by letters patent as aforesaid, to grant and convey to the said Rufus Putnam, Manasseh Cutler, Robert Oliver and Griffin Green, and to their heirs and assigns, in fee simple, in trust for the uses above expressed, a further quantity of one hundred thousand acres of land: *Provided always nevertheless*, That the said grant of one hundred thousand acres shall be made on the express condition of becoming void, for such part thereof as the said company shall not have, within five years from the passing of this act, conveyed in fee simple, as a bounty, and free of expense, in tracts of one hundred acres to each male person, not less than eighteen years of age, being an actual settler at the time of such conveyance.

SEC. 4. *And be it further enacted*, That the said quantities of two hundred and fourteen thousand two hundred and eighty-five acres, and of one hundred thousand acres, shall be located within the limits of the tract of one million five hundred thousand acres of land, described in the indenture aforesaid, and adjoining to the tract of land described in the first section of this act, and in such form as the President, in the letters patent, shall prescribe for that purpose.

Approved, April 21, 1792.

Patent for 750,000 *acres.*

IN THE NAME OF THE UNITED STATES.

To all whom these presents may come.

Know ye, that in pursuance of the act entitled "An Act authorizing the grant and conveyance of certain lands to the Ohio Company of Associates," I do hereby grant and convey to Rufus Putnam, Manasseh Cutler, Robert Oliver and Griffin Green, and to their heirs and assigns forever, the following described tract of land; that is to say, beginning at a station or point where the western boundary line of the seventh range of townships laid out by the authority of the United States in Congress assembled intersects the river Ohio; thence extending along that river southwesterly to a place where the western boundary line of the fifteenth range of townships when laid out agreeably to the land ordinance passed the twentieth day of May, one thousand seven hundred and eighty-five, would touch the said river; thence running northerly on the said western boundary of the said fifteenth range of townships till a line drawn due east to the western boundary line of the said seventh range of townships will comprehend with the other lines of this tract herein specified and described, seven hundred and fifty thousand acres of land beside the several lots and parcels of land in a certain contract executed on the twenty-seventh day of October, one thousand seven hundred and eighty-seven, between the then Board of Treasury for the United States of America of the one part, and Manasseh Cutler and Winthrop Sargent as agents for the directors of the Ohio Company of Associates of the other part, reserved or appropriated to particular purposes; thence running east to the western boundary line of the said seventh range of townships, and thence along the said line to the place of beginning, which said tract contains as computed nine hundred and thirteen thousand eight hundred and eighty-three acres, subject, however, to the reservations expressed, in an indenture, executed on the twenty-seventh day of October, in the year one thousand seven hundred and eighty-seven, between the then Board of Treasury for the United States of America of the one part, and Manasseh Cutler, and Winthrop Sargent, agents for the directors of the Ohio Company of Associates, of the other part:

To have and hold the said described tract of land with the reservations aforesaid in the said indenture so expressed as aforesaid, to the said Rufus Putnam, Manasseh Cutler, Robert Oliver and Griffin Green, and to their heirs and assigns forever, in trust for the persons composing the said Ohio Company of Associates, according to their several rights and interests, and for their heirs and assigns as tenants in common, hereby willing and directing these letters to be made patent.

Given under my hand and the seal of the United States at the city of Philadelphia this tenth day of May, in the year of our Lord one thousand seven hundred and ninety-two, and of Independence the sixteenth.

Go. WASHINGTON.

[L. S.]
By the President :
   TH. JEFFERSON.

WISDOM AND HUMANITY.

The selection of this section of country by the Ohio Company did not seem to some people of that day to have been controlled by either reason or judgment, for the mineral wealth of the region was not known or even thought of. Yet reason guided them, and posterity blesses them for the wisdom of their choice. The lives of the settlers were of the highest consideration to the Ohio Company, and while there might be more inviting fields, from an agricultural point of view, than the hills and valley of the great Hockhocking, there were none that combined so much safety from Indian raids and gave prospects of peace in the future. Then again Virginia had quite a number of settlements on its western border, and these, though some distance away, seemed like near neighbors, and, in case of disaster, a sure refuge. The valley, also, was but the continuation of others which led all the way from Lake Erie to the Ohio River, with but one or two dividing ridges. The valleys of the Cuyahoga and the Muskingum rivers were but extensions of a natural line of communication between the great lakes and the Ohio, which some day would become a great highway of trade, and thus it has proved; and if the Ohio Company did not know of the inexhaustible mineral wealth of this valley or even as a future great highway of traffic and commerce, yet there was wisdom in their choice in what they did know, because humanity guided them and that humanity has received its reward in the productive capacity of the purchase a thousand fold, for Ohio has few, if any, more productive fields than the Hocking Valley. So humanity, the guide of honest and honorable men, has been added to by an abundance of wealth, and posterity blesses the men who preferred what many thought a barren land, rather than to sacrifice to their cupidity, or the merciless tribes of Indians, ever ready to carry out the hellish and cruel work, the men who became purchasers of their estate.

And so to-day these barren hills are turning out large supplies of mineral products, and the rich valleys are teeming with stock and grain, and the then wilderness is now a land fair to look upon, and the home of a joyous, happy and contented people. They meant well, did these humane managers of the Ohio Company, but even they, in all their integrity and wisdom, built wiser than they knew.

THE START.

A meeting of the directors of the company at Brackett's Tavern, in Boston, Nov. 21, 1787, was held to consummate arrangements for forming a settlement, and an advanced expedition was decided upon, with General Putnam as its leader. The trades were represented in the company, for they proposed to build boats to aid in transportation down the Ohio River, the party of mechanics led under the charge of Major Haffield White in December following, while the surveying party and some settlers, under General Putnam and Colonel Ebenezer Sproat, started in January, 1788. They arrived at Sumrill's ferry in February. Having built their boats the party started down the river, April 2, with their baggage.

ON TO ADELPHIA.

The flotilla was composed of one large boat, forty-five feet long and twelve wide, which was roofed over, and had an estimated capacity of fifty tons, a flatboat and three canoes. Laden with the emigrants, their baggage, surveying instruments, weapons, and effects, the little flotilla glided down the Youghiogheny into the Monongahela, and finally out upon the broad bosom of the Ohio, which stream was to bear them to their new home. For several days and nights they pursued their solitary way, urged along only by the current of the beautiful river, whose banks gave no signs of civilized life, nor of welcome to the pioneers. Occasionally a flock of wild turkeys in the underbrush, or a startled deer, drinking at the water's edge, would draw the fire of the riflemen from the boats; and now and then the dusky form of an Indian would be seen darting into the forest. But the emigrants met with no interruption, and on the fifth day reached their destination.

On the 7th day of April, 1788, the company of adventurers landed at Fort Harmer, on the right bank of the Muskingum River, and near its mouth. These were the founders of Marietta, and from the day of their arrival, as above noted, may be said that Ohio dates her existence. The following were their names:

General Rufus Putnam, Superintendent; Colonel Ebenezer Sproat, Colonel R. J. Meigs, Major Anselm Tupper, and Mr. John Matthews, Surveyors; Major Haffield White, Steward and Quartermaster; Captain Jonathan Devol, Captain Josiah Munroe,

Captain Daniel Davis, Peregrine Foster, Captain Jethro Putnam, Captain William Gray, Joseph Wells, Gilbert Devol, Jr., Israel Danton, Jonas Davis, Theophilus Leonard, Joseph Lincoln, William Miller, Earl Sproat, Josiah White, Allen Devol, Henry Maxon, William Maxon, William Moulton, Edmund Moulton, Simeon Martin, Benjamin Shaw, Peletiah White, Josiah Whitridge, John Gardiner, Benjamin Griswold, Elizur Kirkland, Samuel Cushing, Oliver Dodge, Isaac Dodge, Jabez Barlow, Daniel Bushnell, Ebenezer Corry, Phineas Coburn, Allen Putnam, David Wallace, Captain Ezekiel Cooper, Jervis Cutler, Samuel Felshaw, Hezekiah Flint, Hezekiah Flint, Jr., and Amos Porter.

The party at once commenced a settlement, and a town was laid out. The embryo city at the mouth of the Muskingum was named *Adelphia;* the "college bred" members of the little community coming to the front got in their work. They followed this up by calling the largest public square a *Quadranaon*, and the smaller one the *Capitolium*. The wide road, leading up from the river landing to the square, was named *Sacra via*, and the fort, with its inclosure of block-houses, etc., was called *Campus Martius*. At a meeting of the directors held July 2, 1788, which was the first convened west of the mountains, the name of the city was changed to Marietta, in honor Marie Antoinette, Queen of France. Thus by a fortunate change of name, the city of Marietta managed to live and prosper, but it was a narrow escape. Washington County was organized in 1788, and it had something of a territory, comprising, as it did, nearly half of the present commonwealth.

A TERRIBLE AWAKENING.

For a while peace and prosperity had been the lot of the white settlers, and they had been spreading their cabins into the interior, until at last they aroused the red man to a sense of his danger in being dispossessed of his hunting grounds. Then again the frontiersmen, those who in a measure made hunting their occupation, had the impression that an Indian, like a wild beast, was game, and he was generally killed on sight. The Indians were by no means backward in retaliation, and the scalp of a hunter was something they considered a legitimate trophy, and a great one if the hunter was a good fighter. Of course this state of affairs was bound to breed trouble, and when in addition to this the pale faces overran their lands or hunting grounds, they determined upon driving them out of the country. The result was a general rising, in which the shriek of their victims and the light of their burning cabins called upon the Government for immediate action.

THE INDIAN WAR.

Peace overtures having failed and the Indians aggressive to a murderous degree, General Harmer was directed to attack their towns. In September, 1790, with 1,300 men, he marched from Cincinnati through the wilderness to the Indian villages on the Miami, which he burned. On his homeward march he was attacked by a superior force of savages, and, after a desperate battle, was totally defeated. General Harmer was barely able to make good his retreat to Cincinnati. His expedition was a failure and gave the Indians renewed courage and hope.

From this time there were four years of uninterrupted war with the Indians, and sad indeed was the condition of the settlers. Wherever the settlements extended, the whole frontier was lighted by the flames of burning cabins and destruction of improvements. An attack was made on the settlement at Big Bottom, in Washington County, on the Muskingum River, Jan. 2, 1791, characterized by the usual horrible features of stealth and sudden surprise by the savages, of quick massacre and scalping of the victims, and of hasty retreat into the wilderness. In this attack twelve persons were killed and five carried into captivity.

ST. CLAIR'S DEFEAT.

Governor St. Clair was placed in command of a second expedition against the Indians on a larger scale than the first one. He marched against the Indians who were prepared to meet him, and attacked his force with great fury on the morning of the 4th of November, 1791, and totally defeated it. This called for another change of commanders, and General Anthony Wayne was appointed to the command. He arrived at Cincinnati in the spring of 1793, and the work of organizing a third army was commenced. In July, 1794, with a force of about 3,500 men, he marched against the Indians. They had collected their whole force, amounting to about 2,000 men, at the Maumee rapids. Wayne encountered the Indians on the 20th of August. The battle which ensued resulted in the utter defeat of the Indians, and was their downfall in the Northwestern Territory. Wayne followed up his victory, and gathered all its fruits. He burned their villages, destroyed their growing crops, and laid waste their whole country. Forts were erected in the heart of their territory, and they were made to feel, as they had never felt before, the energy and power of the Government. Convinced, at last, of their inability to maintain the contest, or resolved, perhaps, to accept their inevitable doom, they sued for peace. A general council was convened at Greenville (now in Darke County), at which General Wayne represented the United States, and the following tribes were represented by their chiefs, viz.: the Wyandots, Delawares, Shawanese, Ottawas, Chippewas, Pottawatomies, Miamis, Eel-Rivers, Kickapoos, Weeas, Pinkashaws and Kaskaskias. By the treaty here made, Aug. 3, 1795, it was declared that "henceforth all hostilities shall cease; peace is hereby established and shall be perpetual; and a friendly intercourse shall take place between the said United States and Indian tribes." The tomahawk was buried, the Indians gave up their ancient hunting grounds and the graves of their fathers, and the white man's title to the lands of Ohio was never again seriously contested.

THE TWO SURVEYS.

The committee appointed by the Ohio Company to examine the Hocking Valley made the following report Dec. 8, 1795:

"We, the subscribers, being appointed a committee by a resolve of the agents of the Ohio Company of the 9th of Nov. 1790, and for the purpose expressed in said resolve, but being prevented from attending to that business by the Indian war until a treaty took place, since which (in company with Jeffery Matthewson, a surveyor appointed by the superintendent of surveys) having measured and very minutely examined the lands up the Hock-hocking, report that in range XIV., township 10, the following lots or mile squares, viz: Nos. 13, 19, 20, 25, 31 and 32;—range 15, township 12, lots 2, 3, 4, 9, 10, 17, 23, 24, 30, 35 and 36;—range 16, township 13, Nos. 13, 14, 20, 21, 26, 27, 28, 33 and 34, we find are suitable to be laid out into fifth division lots. Having also examined and surveyed the land at the mouth of the Great Hockhocking we find it very suitable for house lots according to map, etc."

Signed, { JNO. DEVOL, ROB'T OLIVER, HAFFIELD WHITE, *Committee.*

The above sections covered most of the river bottom and adjacent upland in Dover and York townships of Athens County, and Green Township of Hocking County.

The two townships, Nos. 8 and 9,—Athens and Alexander,—appropriated by the Ohio Company for the benefit of a university, were located about the same time the above report was made, but by another party. The survey of these lands was made under the personal supervision of General Putnam in 1796 and was, said Ephraim Cutler, "one of the favorite portions of the hunting grounds of the Indians" and upon their surrender to the whites after the disastrous defeat of "Mad Anthony" Wayne, was closed to them forever.

In the early part of 1797 a considerable number of emigrants had arrived at Marietta, eager to obtain lands on the most favorable conditions, and were induced by General Putnam to come to these college lands. Among these were Alvan Bingham, Silas Bingham, Isaac Barker, William Harper, John Wilkins, Robert Linzee, Edmund, William and Barak Dorr, John Chandler and Jonathan Watkins. They made their way down the Ohio and up the Hockhocking in large canoes early in the year 1797. Having ascended as far as the attractive bluff where the town of Athens now stands, they landed and sought their various locations. A few of them fixed on the site of the present town, but most of them scattered up and down the adjacent bottoms. The surrounding country was then covered with dense forests. The bluff and bottoms were heavily timbered with hickory, walnut, ash, poplar, and other trees, indicative of good soil; while the course of the tortuous Hockhocking was marked as far as the view extended by the gigantic sycamores that grew thick set and lofty along its edge.

Hunting parties continued to traverse these hills and valleys, embracing the land watered by Raccoon, Monday, Sunday and the heads of Federal Creek. According to Mr. Cutler the buffalo and the elk were exterminated about the year 1780. A young buffalo, believed to be the last seen in this part of the country, was captured a few miles west of Athens, on a branch of Raccoon, in the spring of 1799, brought to the settlement, and reared by a domestic cow.

The bears continued in considerable abundance until the last great hunt of the Indians in the winter of 1810-'11. That winter was a favorable season for them to effect the object they seemed to have in view, which was to destroy the game, the weather being cold, with several falls of snow. The carcasses of many deer were found in the woods bordering on the settlements in Washington and Athens counties, which appeared to be wantonly destroyed by the savages.

The pioneers soon opened up several clearings about Athens, and the echo of their axes was the first sound of civilized industry heard in all this region. The clearings, however, were irregular and scattered, and no effort was made, as yet, to lay out a town. Early in 1798 a number of emigrants arrived, among whom were Solomon Tuttle, Christopher Stevens, John and Moses Hewitt, Cornelius Moore, Joseph Snowden, John Simonton, Robert Ross, the Brookses and the Hanings. Some of these had families. Some settled in Athens and some in Alexander Township. Mrs. Margaret Snowden, wife of Joseph Snowden, was honored by having "Margaret's Creek" named after her, she being the first white woman who reached this central point in the county.

For the enforcement of laws and preservation of order, Alvan Bingham had been commissioned a Magistrate, and his brother, Silas, a Deputy Sheriff. One of their most difficult duties was to prevent illegal entries and occupations of land by new comers; but this, and their other duties, sometimes delicate and accompanied with danger, they discharged with firmness and general acceptance. Ephraim Cutler, who came in a little later than the Binghams, and settled in Ames Township, was also a Magistrate, and in a certain class of land cases, which required two magistrates and a jury, he and Judge Bingham held court together. In those early times, notwithstanding the primitive state of society, the judges had proper ideas of the sanctity of law and the dignity of a court. It is related that at one of these trials of forcible entry, the leaders of the disorderly class came forward and threatened violence; the magistrates ordered them to leave the room, which they did, but uttering threats to put a stop to such courts. The judges, determined to vindicate their judicial dignity, instantly issued warrants, and ordered the sheriff to arrest the parties immediately, and take them to Marietta. They were arrested accordingly, and it is not easy to conceive of men more frightened; the idea of being taken to Marietta, to be tried by a court that had established a reputation throughout the territory for firmness and strict justice, filled them with terror. Silas Bingham (who, to great shrewdness and dispatch in business, united an unconquerable humor) did nothing to allay their fears, but told them the better way would be to come into court, and, on their knees, ask forgiveness and promise amendment. The ringleader of the offending party replied that "it was too bad to be compelled to kneel down and ask forgiveness of two Buckeye justices;" but he concluded to submit, rather than be taken to Marietta, and the penitential ceremony was accordingly performed. During the first year of the county, the court was held in a private house, obtained for the occasion. In December, 1806, Silas Bingham was allowed $12 for the use of a room occupied by the courts during that year, and an allowance of $6 was made by the county commissioners to "Edmund Dorr and Barak Dorr, for guarding and victualing John Farmer one month." The two Binghams, Judge Alvan and his brother Silas, were natives of Litchfield County, Conn., and had both served in the Revolutionary army. The former was a man of strong common sense, and his judicial mind and well-trained conscience admirably qualified him for the position of judge, which he filled for many years. He is said to have been a person of quiet and dignified manners, stern and uncompromising in his sense of right. Silas was "full of anecdote and humor, social and kind in his feelings, a man of excellent sense, and a terror to evil doers." The promptness with which these men acted in enforcing the laws had the effect to rid the settlement of nearly all disorderly persons. Alvan Bingham was the first Treasurer of Athens County, and Silas was for several years a Constable.

One of the greatest troubles that the pioneers had to contend with was the extreme scarcity of salt, and the high price of that essential article often caused severe privation. At the time of the first settlement of Athens and Ames, it was sold for $6 a bushel, and had to be packed on horseback a great distance. As early as 1788, when the first colony arrived at Marietta, it had been rumored that salt springs existed on a stream, since called Salt Creek, which flows into the Muskingum River, near Duncan's Falls, Muskingum County, and even during the Indian War a party was sent up the river from Marietta to search for them. The exploration was made at great risk, but the springs were not found. White men, held as prisoners by the Indians, had seen them make salt at these springs, and had noted their locality. An accurate description of the country having been gained from these persons, another exploring party of hunters and experienced woodsmen was sent out, a year or two later, to find the springs. This time they were successful, and brought back with them a small supply of the precious article. In 1796 a joint stock company was formed of fifty shareholders, at $1.50 each, making a capital of $75, with the object of buying castings, erecting a furnace, and manufacturing salt. Twenty-four kettles were bought at Pittsburg, and transported by water to Duncan's Falls, and thence, on pack-horses, to the salt springs, seven miles further. A well was dug near the edge of the stream, about fifteen feet deep, to the bed rock, through the crevices of which the salt water oozed and rose, though not very abundantly. The trunk of a hollow sycamore tree was fixed in the well to exclude the fresh water. A furnace was built, of two ranges with twelve kettles each. The water was raised from the well by a sweep and pole. The company was divided into ten sections of five men each, who worked in turns for two weeks at a time, and the works were thus kept in operation day and night, the men standing regular watches. They were thus able to make about 100 pounds of salt in twenty-four hours, using about 1,600 gallons of water. This was the first attempt to manufacture salt in Ohio, and the product was a very inferior and costly article. For several years all of the salt used by the pioneers of the Hocking Valley was brought from these works, and afterward from the Scioto salt licks, in Jackson County, on pack-horses. Yet time changes all things, and the primitive modes of early days gave way to the inventive genius of the people, but the pioneer days were full of incidents in the struggle of life, and the progress of civilization at the hands of the pioneers are here recorded.

CHAPTER III.

THE TRIALS AND TRIBULATIONS, CABINS AND COMFORTS OF EARLY DAYS.

PIONEER LIFE—THE LOG CABIN—COOKING—DRESS, ETC—FAMILY WORSHIP—HOSPITALITY—TRADE AND BARTER—HOG KILLING—NATIVE ANIMALS—WOLF HUNTS—EDUCATION—RATHER LONG-DRAWN-OUT SPELLING AND SINGING SCHOOLS—ON THEIR GUARD—THE BRIGHT SIDE—A TOUCH OF PIONEER LIFE GIVEN—HOW THE PIONEERS ADVANCED CIVILIZATION—WOMEN PIONEERS.

PIONEER LIFE.

The pioneers of Ohio, especially those who settled in the Ohio, Valley and its tributary streams, like the Scioto, Muskingum-Hocking, came generally from the older States which were upon the border, like Pennsylvania and Kentucky, but not a few found their way from the Eastern, or North Atlantic, States. There is little difference in pioneer life even at this day. It is the poor and hard-working element that seek a home in a new country as a general thing, and at this day especially, very few who enjoy the comforts of civilization, of churches, schools, railroads and telegraph, and are able to remain will leave for a residence in the wilds of the West. The exceptions to these are those who may be in fair circumstances, but have large families, who are willing to give up their comforts for the better providing for the future of their children. Thus we find the pioneer generally poor but robust, with an energy which labor increases, and with an endurance that seems to baffle all opposing forces. Poor in purse, but rich in faith, he tackles the wilderness, and it blossoms like the rose.

He has reached his location in the West and he at once commences the erection of his

LOG CABIN,

a description of which may not be uninteresting to the present readers while it will be of profound interest to the generations yet to come, who will be so far removed from pioneer life as to wonder over the primitive styles and habits of long ago. Very few of these old-time structures are now to be seen, but here is their mode of building.

Trees of uniform size were chosen and cut into logs of the desired length, generally twelve to fifteen feet, and hauled to the spot selected for the future dwelling. On an appointed day the few neighbors who were available would assemble and have a "house-raising." Each end of every log was saddled and notched so that they would lie as close down as possible; the next day the proprietor would proceed to "chink and daub" the cabin, to keep out the rain, wind and cold. The house had to be re-daubed every fall, as the rains of the intervening time would wash out a great part of the mortar. The usual height of the house was seven or eight feet. The gables were formed by shortening the logs gradually at each end of the building near the top. The roof was made by laying very straight small logs or stout poles suitable distances apart, generally about two and a half feet, from gable to gable, and on these poles were laid the "clapboards" after the manner of shingling, showing about two and a half feet to the weather. These clapboards were fastened to their place by "weight poles," corresponding in place with the joists just described, and these again were held in their place by "runs" or "knees," which were chunks of wood about eighteen or twenty inches long fitted between them near the ends. Clapboards were made from the nicest oaks in the vicinity, by chopping or sawing them into four-foot blocks and riving these with a frow, which was a simple blade fixed at right angles to its handle. This was driven into the blocks of wood by a mallet. As the frow was wrenched down through the wood, the latter was turned alternately over from side to side, one end being held by a forked piece of timber.

The chimney to the Western pioneer's cabin was made by leaving in the original building a large open place in one wall, or by cutting one after the structure was up, and by building on the outside from the ground up, a stone column, or a column of sticks and mud, the sticks being laid up cob-house fashion. The fireplace thus made was often large enough to receive fire-wood six to eight feet long. Sometimes this wood, especially the "back-log," would be nearly as large as a saw-log. The more rapidly the pioneer could burn up the wood in his vicinity the sooner he had his little farm cleared and ready for cultivation. For a window, a piece about two feet long was cut out of one of the wall logs, and the hole closed sometimes by glass, but generally with greased paper. Even greased deer-hide was sometimes used. A doorway was cut through one of the walls if a saw was to be had; otherwise the door would be left by shortened logs in the original building. The door was made by pinning clapboards to two or three wood bars, and was hung upon wooden hinges. A wooden latch, with catch, then finished the door, and the latch was raised by any one on the outside by pulling a leather string. For security at night this latch-string was drawn in; but for friends and neighbors, and even strangers, the " latch-string was always hanging out," as a welcome. In the interior, over the fire-place would be a shelf, called " the mantel," on which stood the candle-stick or lamp, some cooking and table ware, possibly an old clock, and other articles; in the fire-place would be the crane, sometimes of iron, sometimes of wood; on it the pots were hung for cooking; over the door, in forked cleats, hung the ever trustful rifle and powder horn; in one corner stood the larger bed for the " old folks " and under it the trundle-bed for the children; in another stood the old-fashioned spinning-wheel, with a smaller one by its side; in another the heavy table, the only table, of course, there was in the house; in the remaining corner was a rude cupboard holding the table-ware, which consisted of a few cups and saucers and blue-edged plates, standing singly on their edges against the back, to make the display of table furniture more conspicuous; while around the room were scattered a few splint-bottomed or Windsor chairs and two or three stools.

These simple cabins were inhabited by a kind and true-hearted people. They were strangers to mock modesty, and the traveler, seeking lodgings for the night, or desirous of spending a few days in the community, if willing to accept the rude offering, was always welcome, although how they were disposed of at night the reader might not easily imagine; for, as described, a single room was made to answer for kitchen, dining-room, sitting-room, bed-room and parlor, and many families consisted of six or eight members.

SLEEPING ACCOMMODATIONS.

The bed was very often made by fixing a post in the floor about six feet from one wall and four feet from the adjoining wall, and fastening a stick to this post about two feet above the floor, on each of two sides, so that the other end of each of the two sticks could be fastened in the opposite wall; clapboards were laid across these, and thus the bed was made complete. Guests were given this bed, while the family disposed of themselves in another corner of the room, or in the "loft." When several guests were on hand many ingenious ways were resorted to for the accommodation of the weary traveler.

COOKING.

The pioneer women had very few conveniences which now adorn the kitchens of to-day. The range or stove was then unknown, but the large fire-place was fitted with a crane and a supply of hooks of different lengths, and from one to four pots could be hung over the fire at once. Then the long-handled frying-pan, the bake-pan, the Dutch-oven, and along about 1830 came the tin bake-oven. With these the pioneer women did their hot, laborious work. But they knew how to cook. The bread and the biscuit of those days have not been improved upon.

A better article for baking batter-cakes was the cast-iron spider or Dutch skillet. The best thing for baking bread those days, and possibly even yet in these latter days, was the flat-bottomed bake kettle, of greater depth, with closely fitting cast-iron cover, and commonly known as the "Dutch-oven." With coals over and under it, bread and biscuit would quickly and nicely bake. Turkey and spare-ribs were sometimes roasted before the fire, suspended by a string, a dish being placed underneath to catch the drippings.

Hominy and samp were very much used. The hominy, however, was generally hulled corn—boiled corn from which the hull, or bran, had been taken by hot lye; hence sometimes called "lye hominy." True hominy and samp were made of pounded corn. A popular method of making this, as well as real meal for bread, was to cut out or burn a large hole in the top of a huge stump, in the shape of a mortar, and pounding the corn in this by a maul or beetle suspended on the end of a swing pole, like a well-sweep. This and the well-sweep consisted of a pole twenty to thirty feet long fixed in an upright fork so that it could be worked "teeter" fashion. It was a rapid and simple way of drawing water. When the samp was sufficiently pounded it was taken out, the bran floated off, and the delicious grain boiled like rice.

The chief articles of diet in early day were corn bread, hominy or samp, venison, pork, honey, beans, pumpkin (dried pumpkin for more than half the year), turkey, prairie chicken, squirrel and some other game, with a few additional vegetables a portion of the year. Wheat bread, tea, coffee and fruit were luxuries not to be indulged in except on special occasions, as when visitors were present.

WOMEN'S WORK.

Besides cooking in the manner described, the women had many other arduous duties to perform, one of the chief of which was spinning. The "big wheel" was used for spinning yarn, and the "little wheel" for spinning flax. These stringed instruments furnished the principal music of the family, and were operated by our mothers and grandmothers with great skill, attained without pecuniary expense and with far less practice than is necessary for the girls of our period to acquire a skillful use of their costly and elegant instruments. But those wheels, indispensable a few years ago, are all now superseded by the mighty factories which overspread the country, furnishing cloth of all kinds at an expense ten times less than would be incurred now by the old system.

The loom was not less necessary than the wheel, though they were not needed in so great numbers. Not every house had a loom; one loom had a capacity for the needs of several families. Settlers, having succeeded in spite of the wolves in raising sheep, commenced the manufacture of woolen cloth; wool was carded and made into rolls by hand-cards, and the rolls were spun on the "big wheel." We still occasionally find in the houses of old settlers a wheel of this kind, sometimes used for spinning and twisting stocking yarn. They are turned with the hand, and with such velocity that it will run itself, while the nimble worker, by her backward step, draws out and twists her thread nearly the whole length of the cabin. A common article woven on the loom was linsey, or linsey-woolsey, the chain being linen and the filling woolen. This cloth was used for dresses for the women and girls. Nearly all the clothes worn by the men were also home-made; rarely was a farmer or his son seen in a coat made of any other. If, occasionally, a young man appeared in a suit of "boughten" clothes, he was suspected of having gotten it for a particular occasion, which occurs in the life of nearly every young man.

DRESS AND MANNERS.

The dress, habits, etc., of a people throw so much light upon their conditions and limitations that in order better to show the circumstances surrounding the people of the State, a short exposition of the manner of life at different epochs is here given. The Indians themselves are credited by Charlevoix with being "very laborious"—raising poultry, spinning the wool of the buffalo, and manufacturing garments therefrom. These must have been, however, more than usually favorable representatives of their race.

Dressed deer-skins and blue cloth were worn commonly in the winter for pantaloons. The blue handkerchief and the deer-skin mocassins covered the head and feet generally. In 1800 scarcely a man thought himself clothed unless he had a belt tied round his blanket coat, and on one side was hung the dressed skin of a polecat filled with tobacco, pipe, flint and steel. On the other side was fastened, under the belt, the butcher knife.

Among the Americans home-made wool hats were the common wear. Fur hats were not common, and scarcely a boot was seen. The covering of the feet in winter was chiefly mocassins made of deer-skins and shoe-packs of tanned leather. Some wore shoes, but not common in very early times. In the summer the greater portion of the young people, male and female, and many of the old, went barefoot. The substantial and universal outside wear was the blue linsey hunting shirt. This was an excellent garment. It was made of wide sleeves, open before, with ample size so as to envelop the body almost twice around. Sometimes it had a large cape, which answered well to save the shoulders from the rain. A belt was mostly used to keep the garment close around the person, and, nevertheless, there was nothing tight about it to hamper the body. It was often fringed, and at times the fringe was composed of red and other gay colors. The belt, frequently, was sewed to the hunting shirt. The vest was mostly made of striped linsey. The colors were often made with alum, copperas and madder, boiled with the bark of trees, in such a manner and proportions as the old ladies prescribed. The pantaloons of the masses were generally made of deer-skin and linsey.

Linsey, neat and fine, manufactured at home, composed generally the outside garments of the females as well as the males. The ladies had linsey colored and woven to suit their fancy. A bonnet, composed of calico or some gay goods, was worn on the head when they were in the open air. Jewelry on the pioneer ladies was uncommon; a gold ring was an ornament not often seen.

In 1820 a change of dress began to take place, and before 1830, according to Ford, most of the pioneer costume had disappeared. "The blue linsey hunting shirt, with red or white fringe, had given place to the cloth coat. [Jeans would be more like the fact.] The raccoon cap, with the tail of the animal dangling down behind, had been thrown aside for hats of wool or fur. Boots and shoes had superseded the deer-skin mocassins; and the leather breeches, strapped tight around the ankle, had disappeared before unmentionables of a more modern material. The female sex had made still greater progress in dress. The old sort of cotton or woolen frocks, spun, woven and made with their own fair hands, and striped and cross-barred with blue dye and Turkey red, had given place to gowns of silk and calico. The feet, before in a state of nudity, now charmed in shoes of calf-skin or slippers of kid; and the head, formerly unbonneted, but covered with a cotton handkerchief, now displayed the charms of the female face under many forms of bonnets of straw, silk and Leghorn. The young ladies, instead of walking a mile or two to church on Sunday, carrying their shoes and stockings in their hands until within a hundred yards of the place of worship, as formerly, now come forth arrayed complete in all the pride of dress, mounted on fine horses and attended by their male admirers."

The chronicler of to-day, looking back to the golden days of 1830 to 1840, and comparing them with the present, must be struck with the tendency of an almost monotonous uniformity in dress and manners that comes from the easy inter-communication afforded by steamer, railway, telegraph and newspaper. Home manufacturers have been driven from the household by lower-priced fabrics of distant mills. The Kentucky jeans and the copperas-colored clothing of home manufacture, so familiar a few years ago, have given place to the cassimeres and cloths of noted factories. The ready-made clothing stores, like a touch of nature, made the whole world kin, and may drape the charcoal man in a dress-coat and a stove-pipe hat. The dress goods of England and France give a variety of choice and assortment of colors and shades such as the pioneer woman could hardly have dreamed of. Godey and Demorest and Harper's Bazar are found in our modern farm-houses, and the latest fashions of Paris are not uncommon.

FAMILY WORSHIP.

The ministers in pioneer settlements at that early day seemed more demonstrative in their devotions than at the present time. In those days, too, pulpit oratory was generally more eloquent and effective, while the grammatical dress and other "worldly" accomplishments were not so assiduously cultivated as at present. But in the manner of conducting public worship there has probably not been so much change as in that of family worship, or "family prayers," as it was often called. We had then most emphatically an American edition of that pious old Scotch practice so eloquently described in Burns's "Cotter's Saturday Night:"

> The cheerfu' supper done, wi' serious face
> They round the ingle formed a circle wide;
> The sire turns o'er, wi' patriarchal grace,
> The big ha' Bible, ance his father's pride;
> His bonnet rev'rently is laid aside,
> His lyart haffets wearing thin and bare;
> Those strains that once did sweet in Zion glide;
> He wales a portion with judicious care,
> And "let us worship God," he says with solemn air.
>
> They chant their artless notes in simple guise;
> They tune their hearts,—by far the noblest aim;
> Perhaps "Dundee's" wild warbling measures rise,
> Or plaintive "Martyrs," worthy of the name;
> Or noble "Elgin" beats the heavenward flame,—
> The sweetest far of Scotia's hallowed lays.
> Compared with these, Italian trills are tame;
> The tickled ear no heart-felt raptures raise:
> Nae unison hae they with our Creator's praise.
>
> The priest-like father reads the sacred page,—
> How Abraham was the friend of God on high,
> *   *   *   *   *
> Then kneeling down to heaven's Eternal King
> The saint, the father and the husband prays;
> Hope "springs exulting on triumphant wing,"
> That thus they all shall meet in future days;
> There ever bask in uncreated rays,
> No more to sigh or shed the bitter tear,
> Together hymning their Creator's praise,
> In such society, yet still more dear,
> While circling time moves round in an eternal sphere.

Once or twice a day, in the morning, just before breakfast, or in the evening, just before retiring to rest, the head of the family would call those around him to order, read a chapter in the Bible, announce the hymn and tune by commencing to sing it, when all would join; then he would deliver a most fervent prayer. If a pious guest was present he would be called on to take the lead in all the exercises of the evening; and if in those days a person who prayed in the family or in public did not pray as if it were his very last on earth, his piety was thought to be defective.

The familiar tunes of that day are remembered by the surviving old settlers as being to them more spiritual and inspiring than those of the present day, such as Bourbon, Consolation, China, Canaan, Conquering Soldier, Devotion, Davis, Fiducia, Funeral Thought,

Florida, Golden Hill, Greenfields, Ganges, Kentucky, Lenox, Mear, New Orleans, Northfield, New Salem, Olney, Primrose, Pisgah, Pleyel's Hymn, Rockbridge, Rockingham, Reflection, Supplication, Salvation, St. Thomas, Salem, Windham, Greenville, etc., etc.

HOSPITALITY.

The traveler always found a welcome at the pioneer's cabin. It was never full. Although there might be already a guest for every puncheon, there was still "room for one more," and a wider circle would be made for the new-comer at the log fire. If the stranger was in search of land, he was doubly welcome, and his host would volunteer to show him all the "first-rate claims in this neck of woods," going with him for days, showing the corners and advantages of every "Congress tract" within a dozen miles of his cabin.

To his neighbors the pioneer was equally liberal. If a deer was killed, the choicest bits were sent to his nearest neighbor, a half-dozen miles away, perhaps. When a "shoat" was butchered, the same custom prevailed. If a new comer came in too late for "cropping," the neighbors would supply his table with just the same luxuries they themselves enjoyed, and in as liberal quantity, until a crop could be raised. When a new-comer had located his claim, the neighbors for miles around would assemble at the site of his proposed cabin and aid him in "gittin'" it up. One party with axes would cut down the trees and hew the logs; another with teams would haul the logs to the ground; another party would "raise" the cabin; while several of the old men would "rive the clapboards" for the roof. By night the little forest domicile would be up and ready for a "house-warming," which was the dedicatory occupation of the house, when music and dancing and festivity would be enjoyed at full height. The next day the new arrival would be as well situated as his neighbors.

An instance of primitive hospitable manners will be in place here. A traveling preacher arrived in a distant neighborhood to fill an appointment. The house where services were to be held did not belong to a church member, but no matter for that. Boards were raked up from all quarters with which to make temporary seats, one of the neighbors volunteering to lead off in the work, while the man of the house, with the faithful rifle on his shoulder, sallied forth in quest of meat, for this truly was a "ground-hog" case, the preacher coming and no meat in the house. The host ceased not the chase until he found the meat, in the shape of a deer; returning, he sent a boy out after it, with directions on what "pint" to find it. After services, which had been listened to with rapt attention by all the audience, mine host said to his wife: "Old woman, I reckon this 'ere preacher in pretty hungry and you must git him a bite to eat." "What shall I git him?" asked the wife, who had not seen the deer; "thar's nuthin' in the house to eat." "Why, look thar," returned he; "thar's a deer, thar's plenty of corn in the field; you git some corn and grate it while I skin the deer, and we'll have a good supper for him." It is needless to add that venison and corn bread made a supper fit for any pioneer preacher, and was thankfully eaten.

TRADE.

In pioneer times the transactions of commerce were generally carried on by neighborhood exchanges. Now and then a farmer would load a flat-boat with beeswax, honey, tallow and peltries, with perhaps a few bushels of wheat or corn or a few hundred clapboards, and float down the rivers into the Ohio and thence to New Orleans, where he would exchange his produce for substantials in the shape of groceries and a little ready money, with which he would return by some one of the two or three steamboats then running. Betimes there appeared at the best steamboat landings a number of "middle men" engaged in the "commission and forwarding" business, buying up the farmers' produce and the trophies of the chase and the trap, and sending them to the various distant markets. Their winter's accumulations would be shipped in the spring, and the manufactured goods of the far East or distant South would come back in return; and in all these transactions scarcely any money was seen or used. Goods were sold on a year's time to the farmers, and payment made from the proceeds of the ensuing crops. When the crops were sold and the merchant satisfied, the surplus was paid out in orders on the store to laboring men and to satisfy other creditors. When a day's work was done by a working man, his employer would ask, "Well, what store do you want your order on?" The answer being given, the order was written and always cheerfully accepted.

MONEY.

Money was an article little known and seldom seen among the earlier settlers. Indeed, they had but little use for it, as they could transact all their business about as well without it, on the "barter" system, wherein great ingenuity was sometimes displayed. When it failed in any instance, long credits contributed to the convenience of the citizens. But for taxes and postage neither the barter nor the credit system would answer, and often letters were suffered to remain a long time in the postoffice for the want of the twenty-five cents demanded by the Government. With all this high price on postage, by the way, the letter had not been brought 500 miles in a day or two, as is the case nowadays, but had probably been weeks on the route, and the mail was delivered at the pioneer's postoffice, several miles distant from his residence, only once in a week or two. All the mail would be carried by a lone horseman.

Peltries came nearer being money than anything else, as it came to be custom to estimate the value of everything in peltries. Such an article was worth so many peltries. Even some tax collectors and postmasters were known to take peltries and exchange them for the money required by the Government.

When the settlers first came into the wilderness, some supposed that their hard struggle would be principally over after the first year; but alas! they often looked for "easier times next year" for many years before realizing them, and then they came in so slily as to be almost imperceptible. The sturdy pioneer thus learned to bear hardships, privation and hard living, as good soldiers do. As the facilities for making money were not great, they lived pretty well satisfied in an atmosphere of good, social, friendly feeling. But among the early settlers who came to this State were many who, accustomed to the advantages of an older civilization, to churches, schools and society, became speedily home-sick and dissatisfied. They would remain perhaps one summer, or at most two, then, selling whatever claim with its improvements they had made, would return to the older States, spreading reports of the hardships endured by the settlers here and the disadvantages which they had found, or imagined they had found, in the country. These weaklings were not an unmitigated curse. The slight improvements they had made were sold to men of sterner stuff, who were the sooner able to surround themselves with the necessities of life, while their unfavorable report deterred other weaklings from coming. The men who stayed and were willing to endure privations belonged to a different guild; they were heroes every one—men to whom hardships were things to be overcome, and privations endured for the sake of posterity, and they never shrank from this duty. It is to those hardy pioneers who could endure that the people of to-day owe the wonderful improvements made, and the developments, almost miraculous, that have brought this commonwealth in the past eighty years from a wilderness to the front rank among the States of this great nation.

MILLING.

Not the least of the hardships of the pioneers was the procuring of bread. The first settlers must be supplied at least one year from other sources than their own lands; but the first crops, however abundant, gave only partial relief, there being no mills to grind the grain. Hence the necessity of grinding by hand-power, and many families were poorly provided with means for doing this. Another way was to grate the corn. A grater was made from a piece of tin, sometimes taken from an old, worn-out tin bucket or other vessel. It was thickly perforated, bent into a semicircular form, and nailed, rough side upward, on a board. The corn was taken in the ear, and grated before it got dry and hard. Corn, however, was eaten in various ways. Then followed the horse or band mill as it was called.

Soon after the country became more generally settled, enterprising men were ready to embark in the milling business. Sites along the streams were selected for water-power. A person looking for a mill-site would follow up and down the stream for a desired location, and when found he would go before the authorities and secure a writ of *ad quod damnum*. This would enable the miller to have the adjoining land officially examined, and the amount of damage by making a dam was named. Mills being so great a public necessity, they were permitted to be located upon any person's land where the miller thought the site desirable.

AGRICULTURAL IMPLEMENTS.

The agricultural implements used by the first farmers in this State would in this age of improvement be great curiosities. The plow used was called the "bar-share" plow; the iron point consisted of a bar of iron about two feet long, and a broad share of iron welded to it. At the extreme point was a coulter that passed through a beam six or seven feet long, to which were attached handles of corresponding length. The mold-board was a wooden one split out of winding timber, or hewed into a winding shape, in order to turn the soil over. Sown seed was brushed in by dragging over the ground a sapling with a bushy top. In harvesting the change is most striking. Instead of the reapers and mowers

J. A. Shaw

of to-day, the sickle and cradle were used. The grain was threshed with a flail, or trodden out by horses or oxen.

HOG KILLING.

Hogs were always dressed before they were taken to market. The farmer, if forehanded, would call in his neighbors some bright fall or winter morning to help "kill hogs." Immense kettles of water were heated; a sled or two, covered with loose boards or plank, constituted the platform on which the hog was cleaned, and was placed near an inclined hogshead in which the scalding was done; a quilt was thrown over the top of the latter to retain the heat; from the crotch of some convenient tree a projecting pole was rigged, to hold the animals for disemboweling and thorough cleaning. When everything was arranged, the best shot of the neighborhood loaded his rifle, and the work of killing was commenced. It was considered a disgrace to make a hog "squeal" by bad shooting or by a "shoulder-stick," that is, running the point of the butcher-knife into the shoulder instead of the cavity of the breast. As each hog fell, the "sticker" mounted him and plunged the butcher-knife into his throat; two persons would then catch him by the hind legs, draw him up to the scalding tub, which had just been filled with boiling-hot water with a shovelful of good green-wood ashes thrown in; in this the carcass was plunged and moved around a minute or so until the hair would slip off easily, then placed on the platform where the cleaner would take hold of him and clean him as quickly as possible, with knives and other sharp-edged implements; then two stout men would take him up between them, and a third man to manage the gambrel (which was a stout stick about two feet long, sharpened at both ends, to be inserted between the muscles of the hind legs at or near the hock joint), the animal would be elevated to the pole, where the work of cleaning was finished.

After the slaughter was over and the hogs had had time to cool, such as were intended for domestic use were cut up, the lard "tried" out by the women of the household, and the surplus hogs taken to market, while the weather was cold, if possible. In those days almost every merchant had, at the rear end of his place of business or at same convenient building, a "pork-house," and would buy the pork of his customers and of such others as would sell to him, and cut it for the market. This gave employment to a large number of hands in every village, who would cut and pack pork all winter. The hauling of all this to the river would also give employment to a large number of teams, and the manufacture of pork barrels would keep many coopers employed.

There was one feature in this method of marketing pork that made the country a paradise for the poor man in the winter time. Spare-ribs, tenderloins, pigs' heads and pigs' feet were not considered of any value, and were freely given to all who could use them. If a barrel was taken to any pork-house and salt furnished, the barrel would be filled and salted down with tenderloins and spare-ribs gratuitously. So great in many cases was the quantity of spare-ribs, etc., to be disposed of, that they would be hauled away in wagon-loads and dumped in the woods out of town.

In those early times much wheat was marketed at twenty-five to fifty cents a bushel, oats the same or less, and corn ten cents a bushel. A good young milch-cow could be bought for $5 to $10, and that payable in work.

Those might truly be called "close times," yet the citizens of the country were accommodating, and but very little suffering for the actual necessities of life was ever known to exist.

NATIVE ANIMALS.

The principal wild animals found in the State by the early settler were the deer, wolf, bear, wild-cat, fox, otter, raccoon, generally called "coon," woodchuck, or ground-hog, skunk, mink, weasel, muskrat, opossum, rabbit and squirrel; and the principal feathered game were the quail, prairie chicken and wild turkey. Hawks, turkey buzzards, crows, blackbirds, were also very abundant. Several of these animals furnished meat for the settlers; but their principal meat did not long consist of game; pork and poultry were raised in abundance. The wolf was the most troublesome animal, it being the common enemy of the sheep, and sometimes attacking other domestic animals, and even human beings. But their hideous howlings at night were so constant and terrifying that they almost seemed to do more mischief by that annoyance than by direct attack. They would keep everybody and every animal about the farm-house awake and frightened, and set all the dogs in the neighborhood to barking. As one man described it: "Suppose six boys, having six dogs tied, whipped them all at the same time, and you would hear such music as two wolves would make."

To effect the destruction of these animals the county authorities offered a bounty for their scalps; and, besides, big hunts were common.

WOLF HUNTS.

In early days more mischief was done by wolves than by any other wild animal, and no small part of their mischief consisted in their almost constant barking at night, which always seemed so menacing and frightful to the settlers. Like mosquitoes, the noise they made appeared to be about as dreadful as the real depredations they committed. The most effectual, as well as the most exciting, method of ridding the country of these hateful pests, was that known as the " circular wolf hunt," by which all the men and boys would turn out on an appointed day, in a kind of circle, comprising many square miles of territory, with horses and dogs, and then close up toward the center of their field of operation, gathering not only wolves, but also deer and many smaller "varmint." Five, ten, or more wolves by this means would sometimes be killed in a single day. The men would be organized with as much system as a little army, every one being well posted in the meaning of every signal and the application of every rule. Guns were scarcely ever allowed to be brought on such occasions, as their use would be unavoidably dangerous. The dogs were depended upon for the final slaughter. The dogs, by the way, had all to be held in check by a cord in the hands of their keepers until the final signal was given to let them loose, when away they would all go to the center of battle, and a more exciting scene would follow than can be easily described.

BEE HUNTING.

This wild recreation was a peculiar one, and many sturdy backwoodsmen gloried in excelling in this art. He would carefully watch a bee as it filled itself with the sweet product of some flower or leaf-bud, and notice particularly the direction taken by it as it struck a " bee-line" for its home, which, when found, would be generally high up in the hollow of a tree. The tree would be marked, and in September a party would go and cut down the tree and capture the honey as quickly as they could before it wasted away through the broken walls in which it had been so carefully stored away by the little busy bee. Several gallons would often be thus taken from a single tree, and by a very little work, and pleasant at that, the early settlers could keep themselves in honey the year round. By the time the honey was a year old, or before, it would turn white and granulate, yet be as good and healthful as when fresh. This was by some called "candid honey."

In some districts the resorts of bees would be so plentiful that all the available hollow trees would be occupied and many colonies of bees would be found at work in crevices in the rock and holes in the ground. A considerable quantity of honey has even been taken from such places.

SNAKES.

In pioneer times snakes were numerous, such as the rattlesnake, adder, blood snake and many varieties of large blue and green snakes, milk snake, garter and water snakes, black snakes, etc., etc. If, on meeting one of these, you would retreat, they would chase you very fiercely ; but if you would turn and give them battle, they would immediately crawl away with all possible speed, hide in the grass and weeds, and wait for a "greener" customer. These really harmless snakes served to put people on their guard against the more dangerous and venomous kinds.

It was the practice in some sections of the country to turn out in companies, with spades, mattocks and crow-bars, attack the principal snake dens and slay large numbers of them. In early spring the snakes were somewhat torpid and easily captured. Scores of rattlesnakes were sometimes frightened out of a single den, which, as soon as they showed their heads through the crevices of the rocks, were dispatched, and left to be devoured by the numerous wild hogs of that day. Some of the fattest of these snakes were taken to the house and oil extracted from them, and their glittering skins were saved as specifics for rheumatism.

Another method was to so fix a heavy stick over the door of their dens, with a long grape-vine attached, that one at a distance could plug the entrance to the den when the snakes were all out sunning themselves. Then a large company of citizens, on hand by appointment, could kill scores of the reptiles in a few minutes.

EDUCATION.

Though struggling through the pressure of poverty and privation, the early settlers planted among them the school-house at the earliest practical period. So important an object as the education of their children they did not defer until they could build more comely and convenient houses. They were for a time content with such as corresponded with their rude dwellings, but soon better buildings and accommodations were provided. As may readily be supposed, the accommodations of the earliest schools were not good. Sometimes school was taught in a room of a large or double log cabin, but oftener in a log house built for the purpose. A mud-and-stick chimney in one end of the building, with earthen hearth and a fire-place wide and deep enough to receive a four to six foot back-log, and smaller wood to match, served for warming purposes in winter and a kind of conservatory in summer. For windows, part of a log was cut out in two sides of the building, and may be a few lights of eight by ten glass set in, or the aperture might be covered over with greased paper. Writing desks consisted of heavy oak plank or a hewed slab laid upon wooden pins driven into the wall. The four-legged slab benches were in front of these, and the pupils when not writing would sit with their backs against the front, sharp edge of the writing-desks. The floor was also made out of these slabs or " puncheons," laid upon log sleepers. Everything was rude and plain ; but many of America's greatest men have gone out from just such school-houses to grapple with the world, and make names for themselves and reflect honor upon their country. So with many of the most eloquent and efficient preachers.

Imagine such a house with the children seated around, and the teacher seated on one end of a bench, with no more desk at his hand than any of the pupils have, and you have in view the whole scene. The "schoolmaster" has called "Books ! books!" at the door, and the "scholars" have just run in almost out of breath from vigorous play, have taken their seats, and are for the moment "saying over their lessons" to themselves with all their might, that is, in as loud a whisper as possible. While they are thus engaged, the teacher is perhaps sharpening a few quill pens for the pupils, for no other kind of writing pen had been thought of as yet. In a few minutes he calls up an urchin to say his a b c's; the little boy stands beside the teacher, perhaps partially leaning upon his lap ; the teacher with his pen-knife points to the letter and asks what it is ; the little fellow remains silent, for he does not know what to say ; "A," says the teacher; the boy echoes "A;" the teacher points to the next and asks what it is; the boy is silent again; "B," says the teacher; "B," echoes the little urchin; and so it goes through the exercise, at the conclusion of which the teacher tells the little "Major" to go back to his seat and study his letters, and when he comes to a letter he doesn't know, to come to him and he will tell him. He obediently goes to his seat, looks on his book a little while, and then goes trudging across the puncheon floor again in his bare feet, to the teacher, and points to a letter, probably outside of his lesson, and asks what it is. The teacher kindly tells him that that is not in his lesson, that he need not study that or look at it now; he will come to that some other day, and then he will learn what it is. The simple-minded little fellow then trudges, smilingly, as he catches the eye of some one, back to his seat again. But why he smiled he has no definite idea.

The a-b-ab scholars through with, perhaps the second or third reader class would be called, who would stand in a row in front of the teacher, "toeing the mark," which was actually a chalk or charcoal mark drawn on the floor, and, commencing at one end of the class, one would read the first "verse," the next the second, and so on around, taking the paragraphs in the order as they occur in the book. Whenever a pupil hesitated at a word, the teacher would pronounce it for him. And this was all there was of the reading exercise.

Those studying arithmetic were but little classified, and they were therefore generally called forward singly and interviewed, or the teacher simply visited them at their seats. A lesson containing several "sums" would be given for the next day. Whenever the learner came to a sum he couldn't do, he would go to the teacher with it, who would willingly and patiently, if he had time, do it for him.

In geography, no wall maps were used, no drawing required, and the studying and recitation comprised only the committing to memory, or "getting by heart," as it was called, the names and locality of places. The recitation proceeded like this: Teacher—"Where is Norfolk?" Pupil—"In the southeastern part of Virginia." Teacher—"What bay between Maryland and Virginia?" Pupil—"Chesapeake."

When the hour for writing arrived, the time was announced by the master, and every pupil practicing this art would turn his feet over to the back of his seat, thus throwing them under the writing desk, already described, and proceed to "follow copy," which was invariably set by the teacher, not by rule, but by as nice a stroke of the pen as he could make. The first copies for each pupil would be letters, and the second kind and last consisted of maxims.

About half past ten o'clock the master would announce, "School may go out;" which meant, "Little play time," in the children's parlance, called nowadays recess or intermission. Often the practice was to have the boys and girls go out separately, in which case the teacher would first say, "The girls may go out," and after they had been out about ten minutes the boys were allowed a similar privilege in the same way. Between play-times the request, "Teacher, may I go out?" was often iterated to the annoyance of the teacher and the disturbance of the school.

At about half past eleven o'clock the teacher would announce, "Scholars may now get their spelling lessons," and they would all pitch in with their characteristic loud whisper and "say over" their lessons with that vigor which characterizes the movements of those who have just learned that the dinner hour and "big playtime" is near at hand. A few minutes before twelve the "little spelling class" would recite, then the "big spelling class." The latter would comprise the larger scholars and the major part of the school. The classes would stand in a row, either toeing the mark in the midst of the floor, or straggling along next an unoccupied portion of the wall. One end of the class was the "head," the other the "foot," and when a pupil spelled a word correctly, which had been missed by one or more, he would "go up" and take his station above all that had missed the word; this was called "turning them down." At the conclusion of the recitation the head pupil would go to the foot to have another opportunity of turning them all down. The class would number, and before taking their seats the teacher would say, "School's dismissed," which was the signal for every child rushing for his dinner and having the "big playtime."

The same process of spelling would also be gone through with in the afternoon just before dismissing the school for the day.

The chief text-books in which the "scholars" got their lessons were Webster's or some other elementary spelling-book, and arithmetic, may be Pike's, Dilworth's, Daboll's, Smiley's or Adams's, the old English reader, and Roswell C. Smith's geography and atlas. First, old Murray's, then Kirkham's grammar, were the text-books on this subject. "Book larnin" instead of practical oral instruction, was the only thing supposed to be attained in the primitive log school-house days. But writing was generally taught with fair diligence.

"PAST THE PICTURES."

This phrase had its origin in the practice of pioneer schools which used Webster's Elementary Spelling-book. Toward the back part of that time-honored text-book was a series of seven or eight pictures, illustrating morals, and after these again were a few more spelling exercises of a peculiar kind. When a scholar got over into these he was said to be "past the pictures," and was looked up to as being smarter and more learned than most other people ever hoped to be. Hence the application of this phrase came to be extended to other affairs in life, especially where scholarship was involved.

SPELLING-SCHOOLS.

The chief public evening entertainment for the first thirty or forty years of pioneer existence was the celebrated "spelling-school." Both young people and old looked forward to the next spelling-school with as much anticipation and anxiety as we nowadays look forward to a general Fourth-of-July celebration; and when the time arrived the whole neighborhood, yea, and sometimes several neighborhoods, would flock together to the scene of academical combat, where the excitement was often more intense than had been expected. It was far better, of course, when there was good sleighing; then the young folks would turn out in high glee and be fairly beside themselves. The jollity is scarcely equaled at the present day by anything in vogue.

When the appointed hour arrived, the usual plan of commencing battle was for two of the young people who might agree to play against each other, or who might be selected to do so by the school-teacher of the neighborhood, to "choose sides;" that is, each contestant, or "captain," as he was generally called, would choose the best speller from the assembled crowd. Each one choosing alternately, the ultimate strength of the respective parties would be about equal. When all were chosen who could be made to serve, each side would "number," so as to ascertain whether amid the confusion one captain had more spellers than the other. In case he had, some compromise would be made by the aid of the teacher, the master of ceremonies, and then the plan of conducting the campaign, or counting the misspelled words, would be canvassed for a moment by the captains, sometimes by the aid of the teacher and others. There were many ways of conducting the contest and keeping tally. At one time they would commence spelling at the head, at another time at the foot; at one time they would "spell across," that is, the first on one side would spell the first word, then the first on the other side; next the second in the line on each side, alternately, down to the other end of each line. The question, who should spell the first word was determined by the captains guessing what page the teacher would have before him in a partially opened book at a distance; the captain guessing the nearest would spell the first word pronounced. When a word was missed, it would be re-pronounced, or passed along without re-pronouncing (as some teachers strictly followed the rule never to re-pronounce a word) until it was spelled correctly. If a speller on the opposite side finally spelled the missed word correctly, it was counted a gain of one to that side; if the word was finally corrected by some speller on the same side on which it was originated as a missed word, it was " saved," and no tally mark was made.

Another popular method was to commence at one end of the line of spellers and go directly around, and the missed words caught up quickly and corrected by " word-catchers," appointed by the captains from among their best spellers. These word-catchers would attempt to correct all the words missed on his opponent's side, and, failing to do this, the catcher on the other side would catch him up with a peculiar zest, and then there was fun.

Still another very interesting, though somewhat disorderly, method, was this: Each word-catcher would go to the foot of the adversary's line, and every time he " catched " a word he would go up one, thus "turning them down " in regular spelling-class style. When one catcher in this way turned all down on the opposing side, his own party was victorious by as many as the opposing catcher was behind. This method required no slate or blackboard tally to be kept.

One turn, by either of the foregoing or other methods, would occupy forty minutes to an hour, and by this time an intermission or recess was had, when the buzzing, cackling and hurrahing that ensued for ten or fifteen minutes were beyond description.

Coming to order again, the next style of battle to be illustrated was to " spell down," by which process it was ascertained who were the best spellers and could continue standing as a soldier the longest. But very often good spellers would inadvertently miss a word in an early stage of the contest and would have to sit down humiliated, while a comparatively poor speller would often stand till nearly or quite the last, amid the cheers of the assemblage. Sometimes the two parties first " chosen up " in the evening would re-take their places after recess, so that by the " spelling-down " process there would virtually be another race, in another form; sometimes there would be a new " choosing up " for the " spelling-down " contest; and sometimes the spelling down would be conducted without any party lines being made. It would occasionally happen that two or three very good spellers would retain the floor so long that the exercise would become monotonous, when a few outlandish words like "chevaux-de-frise," "ompompanoosuc" or "baughnaugh-claugh-ber," as they used to spell it sometimes, would create a little ripple of excitement to close with. Sometimes these words would decide the contest, but generally when two or three good spellers kept the floor until the exercise became monotonous, the teacher would declare the race closed and the standing spellers acquitted with a "drawn game."

The audience dismissed, the next thing was to "go home," very often by a round-about way, "a-sleighing with the girls," which of course was with many the most interesting part of the evening's performances.

SINGING-SCHOOL.

Next to the night spelling-school the singing-school was an occasion of much jollity, wherein it was difficult for the average singing-master to preserve order, as many went more for fun than for music. This species of evening entertainment, in its introduction to the West, was later than the spelling-school, and served, as it were, as the second step toward the more modern civilization. Good sleighing weather was of course almost a necessity for the success of these schools, but how many of them have been prevented by mud and rain! Perhaps a greater part of the time from November to April the roads would be muddy and often half frozen, which would have a very dampening and freezing effect upon the souls, as well as the bodies, of the young people who longed for a good time on such occasions.

The old-time method of conducting singing-school was also somewhat different from that of modern times. It was more plodding and heavy, the attention being kept upon the simplest rudiments, as the names of the notes on the staff, and their pitch, and beating time, while comparatively little attention was given to expression and light, gleeful music. The very earliest scale introduced in the West was from the South, and the notes, from their peculiar shape, were denominated "patent" or "buckwheat" notes. There were four, of which the round one was always called *sol*, the square one *la*, the triangular one *fa*, and the "diamond shaped" one *mi*, pronounced *me*; and the diatonic scale, or "gamut" as it was called then, ran thus: *fa, sol, la, fa, sol, la, mi, fa*. The part of a tune nowadays called "treble," or "soprano," was then called "tenor;" the part now called "tenor" was called "treble," and what is now "alto" was then "counter," and when sung according to the oldest rule, was sung by a female an octave higher than marked, and still on the "chest register." The "old" "Missouri Harmony" and Mason's "Sacred Harp" were the principal books used with this style of musical notation.

About 1850 the "round-note" system began to "come round," being introduced by the singing-master. The scale was *do, re, mi, fa, sol, la, si, do*; and for many years thereafter there was much more do-re-mi-ing than is practiced at present day, when a musical instrument is always under the hand. The "Carmina Sacra" was the pioneer round-note book.

GUARDING AGAINST INDIANS.

The fashion of carrying fire-arms was made necessary by the presence of roving bands of Indians, most of whom were ostensibly friendly, but like Indians in all times, treacherous and unreliable. An Indian war was at any time probable, and all the old settlers still retain vivid recollections of Indian massacres, murders, plunder, and frightful rumors of intended raids. While target practice was much indulged in as an amusement, it was also necessary at times to carry their guns with them to their daily field work.

As an illustration of the painstaking which characterized pioneer life, we quote the following remark of an old settler: "The manner in which I used to work in those perilous times was as follows: On all occasions I carried my rifle, tomahawk and butcher-knife, with a loaded pistol in my belt. When I went to plow I laid my gun on the plowed ground, and stuck a stick by it for a mark, so that I could get it quick in case it was wanted. I had two good dogs; I took one into the house leaving the other out. The one outside was expected to give the alarm, which would cause the one inside to bark, by which I would be awakened, having my arms always loaded. I kept my horse in a stable close to the house, having a port-hole so that I could shoot to the stable door. During two years I never went from home with any certainty of returning, not knowing the minute I might receive a ball from an unknown hand."

THE BRIGHT SIDE.

The history of pioneer life generally presents the dark side of the picture; but the toils and privations of the early settlers were not a series of unmitigated sufferings. No; for while the fathers and mothers toiled hard, they were not averse to a little relaxation, and had their seasons of fun and enjoyment. They contrived to do something to break the monotony of their daily life and furnish them a good hearty laugh. Among the more general forms of amusements were the "quilting-bee," "corn-husking," "apple-paring," "log rolling," and "house-raising." Our young readers will doubtless be interested in a description of these forms of amusement, when labor was made to afford fun and enjoyment to all participating. The "quilting-bee," as its name implies, was when the industrious qualities of the busy little insect that "improves each shining hour" were exemplified in the manufacture of quilts for the household. In the afternoon ladies for miles around gathered at an appointed place, and while their tongues would not cease to play the hand was busily engaged in making the quilt, the desire being always manifested to get it out as quickly as possible, for then the fun would begin. In the evening the gentlemen came and the hours would then pass swiftly by in playing games or dancing. "Corn-huskings" were when both sexes united in the work. They usually assembled in a large barn which was arranged for the occasion; and when each gentleman had selected a lady partner the husking began. When a lady found a red ear she was subject to a kiss from her partner; when a gentleman found one he was allowed to kiss his lady partner. After the corn was all husked a good supper was served; then the "old folks" would leave, and the remainder of the evening was spent in the dance and in having a general good time. The recreation afforded to the young people on the annual recurrence of these festive occasions was as highly enjoyed, and quite as innocent, as the amusements of the present boasted age of refinement and culture.

The amusements of the pioneers were peculiar to themselves. Saturday afternoon was a holiday in which no man was expected to work. A load of produce might be taken to "town" for sale or traffic without violence to custom, but no more serious labor could be tolerated. When on Saturday afternoon the town was reached, "fun commenced." Had two neighbors business to transact, here it was done. Horses were "swapped," difficulties settled and free fights indulged in. Blue and red ribbons were not worn in those days, and whisky was as free as water; twelve and a half cents would buy a quart, and thirty-five or forty cents a gallon, and at such prices enormous quantities were consumed. Go to any town in the county and ask the first pioneer you meet, and he would tell you of notable Saturday-afternoon fights, either of which to-day would fill a column of the *Police News*, with elaborate engravings to match.

An old settler quaintly describes some of the happy features of frontier life in this manner:

"We cleared land, rolled logs, burned brush, blazed out paths from one neighbor's cabin to another and from one settlement to another, made and used hand-mills and hominy mortars, hunted deer, turkey, otter and raccoons, caught fish, dug ginseng, hunted bees and the like, and—lived on the fat of the land. We read of a land of ' corn and wine,' and another ' flowing with milk and honey;' but I rather think, in a temporal point of view, taking into account the richness of the soil, timber, stone, wild game and other advantages, that the Hocking Valley country would come up to any of them, if not surpass them.

"Reader, what would you think of going six to eight miles to help roll logs, or raise a cabin? or ten to thirty miles to mill, and wait three or four days and nights for your grist? as many had to do in the first settlement of this country. Such things were of frequent occurrence then, and there was but little grumbling about it. It was a grand sight to see the log heaps and brush piles burning in the night, on a clearing of ten or fifteen acres. A Democratic torchlight procession, or a midnight march of the Sons of Malta with their grand Gyasticutus in the center bearing the grand jewel of the order, would be nowhere in comparison with the log-heaps and brush-piles in a blaze.

"But it may be asked, Had you any social amusements, or manly pastimes, to recreate and enliven the dwellers in the wilderness?

"We had. In the social line we had our meetings and our singing-schools, sugar-boilings and weddings, which were as good as ever came off in any country, new or old; and if our youngsters did not 'trip the light fantastic toe' under a professor of the Terpsichorean art or expert French dancing-master, they had many a good 'hoe-down' on puncheon floors, and were not annoyed by bad whisky. The boys and men of those days had quite as much sport, and made more money and health by their hunting excursions than our city gents nowadays playing chess by telegraph where the players are more than seventy miles apart."

WHAT THE PIONEERS HAVE DONE.

Ohio is a grand State, in many respects second to none in the Union, and in almost everything that goes to make a live, prosperous community, not far behind the best. Beneath her fertile soil is coal enough to supply the State for generations; her harvests are bountiful; she has a medium climate, and many other things, that make her people contented, prosperous and happy; but she owes much to those who opened up these avenues that have led to her present condition and happy surroundings. Unremitting toil and labor have driven off the sickly miasmas that brooded over swampy prairies. Energy and perseverance have peopled every section of her wild lands, and changed them from wastes and deserts to gardens of beauty and profit. Where but a few years ago the barking wolves made the night hideous with their wild shrieks and howls, now is heard only the lowing and bleating of domestic animals. Only a half century ago the wild whoop of the Indian rent the air where now are heard the engine and rumbling trains of cars, bearing away to markets the products of our labor and soil. Then the savage built his rude hut on the spot where now rise the dwellings and school-houses and church spires of civilized life. How great the transformation! This change has been brought about by the incessant toil and aggregated labor of thousands of tired hands and anxious hearts, and the noble aspirations of such men and women as make any country great. What will another half century accomplish? There are few, very few, of these old pioneers yet lingering on the shores of time as connecting links of the past with the present. What must their thoughts be as with their dim eyes they view the scenes that surround them? We often hear people talk about the old-fogy ideas and fogy ways and want of enterprise on the part of the old men who have gone through the experiences of pioneer life. Sometimes, perhaps, such remarks are just, but, considering the experiences, education, and entire life of such men, such remarks are better unsaid. They have had their trials, misfortunes, hardships and adventures, and shall we now, as they are passing far down the western declivity of life, and many of them gone, point to them the finger of derision and laugh and sneer at the simplicity of their ways? Let us rather cheer them up, revere and respect them, for beneath those rough exteriors beat hearts as noble as ever throbbed in the human breast. These veterans have been compelled to live for weeks upon hominy and, if bread at all, it was bread made from corn ground in hand-mills, or pounded up with mortars. Their children have been destitute of shoes during the winter; their families had no clothing except what was carded, spun, wove and made into garments with their own hands; schools they had none; churches they had none; afflicted with sickness incident to all new countries, sometimes the entire family at once; luxuries of life they had none; the auxiliaries, improvements, inventions and labor-saving machinery of to-day they had not; and what they possessed they obtained by the hardest of labor and individual exertions, yet they bore these hardships and privations without murmuring, hoping for better times to come, and often, too, with but little prospect of realization.

As before mentioned, the changes written on every hand are most wonderful. It has been but fourscore years since the white man began to exercise dominion over this region, erst the home of the red man, yet the visitor of to-day, ignorant of the past of the country, could scarcely be made to realize that within these years there has grown up a population of over 3,000,000 people, who in all the accomplishments of life are as far advanced as are the inhabitants of the older States. Schools, churches, colleges, palatial dwellings, beautiful grounds, large, well-cultivated and productive farms, as well as cities, towns, and busy manufactories, have grown up, and occupy the hunting grounds and camping places of the Indians, and in every direction there are evidences of wealth, comfort and luxury. There is but little left of the old landmarks. Advanced civilization and the progressive demands of revolving years have obliterated all traces of Indian occupancy, until they are only remembered in name.

In closing this section it would be well to impress on the minds of the reader the fact that a debt of gratitude is due to those who pioneered this State, which can be but partially repaid. Never grow unmindful of the peril and adventure, fortitude, self-sacrifice and heroic devotion so prominently displayed in their lives. As time sweeps on in its ceaseless flight, may the cherished memory of them lose none of its greenness, but may future generations alike cherish and perpetuate them with just devotion and gratitude.

WOMEN PIONEERS.

Thus far the pioneer has been referred to as of the sterner sex, but were they the only pioneers in these once uncivilized regions ? Was man the only one who suffered privation and want, who worked that a generation, then verging on manhood, might find the way " blazed " to the light of a higher civilization, and that a generation yet unborn might find the fruits of struggle in well-tilled fields, a full granary, and a home blessed with all the art and progress that a new era gave them ? Was it in the culture and refinement of the people of a later day, who had received not only wealth descended from their forefathers, but those benefits which science had discovered hidden in the deep and dark mysteries of nature, and were they to thank men alone for the blessings around them? No! but high on the scroll of fame should the pioneer women of our land have their names emblazoned that generations yet to come, and for all time, may honor and bless the memory of the heroic women who gave themselves to the duties of a pioneer's life, and who proudly and uncomplainingly did the work which came before them, as only women could do it, smoothing their rugged lives with the light of an undying love, and proving in every way the equal of man in carrying forward the work of making a wilderness take upon itself the garb of civilization, and barren plains the wealth of fruitful fields and abundant harvests. Thus have the pioneer women worked and struggled, and the rude cabin to them was a home of love and happiness.

Rude and primitive as that cabin might be, with a floor of mother earth, simple and unadorned, there was found within its walls many a heroine of early days. Not in the palaces of the rich of what is called this enlightened era, was more true life-like happiness found than in those lowly cabins. There was no waiting in those days for a home of splendor before man found his mate, but the heroes and heroines of those days joined hands and hearts, and helped each other down the rugged pathway of life. He went into the field to work, that he might supply the food necessary for life, while she worked on in her own sphere, furnishing her husband's cabin with the smiles of a loving heart, greeting her partner with the evident work of willing hands, keeping her true and womanly talents in full play, not only in preparing the food for the family meal, but in spinning and weaving, cutting and making, not only her own clothing, but the garments of those who were of her household and under her loving care. Much has been written of the "old pioneer" and his struggle in the early years of his life, heavy trials, misfortunes, and, ultimately, his success, but little has been recorded of his noble companion, the light of his cabin, who cheered him in his misfortunes, nursed him in sickness, and in health gave her whole strength to labor for their future welfare and happiness. There was little luxury or ease for the pioneer's wife of those early days, but whatever her destiny might be, it was met with a firm faith and a willingness to do her whole duty, living in the love of her husband and children and trusting in Providence to receive her final reward for the unceasing labor of years, well and nobly performed. Yes, there was something decidedly primitive in the building and furniture of those cabins of old. They were built one and a half stories high, in many cases, that they might have a "loft" to store away things, and sometimes to sleep in. The windows were covered by a light quilt to keep the wind and rain out; the puncheon floor was laid, the stick and mud chimney set up, a table and a chair or two, or stools made of split logs, with auger holes bored to put in the legs ; some shelves made of the same material, holes bored and pins put in to hang up their clothes and other things, and that pioneer heroine was ready to meet her friends and neighbors and the world at-large in a roomy and comfortable house. A house-keeping outfit of that style in these days, would send a young woman into hysterics, make her declare that "she would go right home to her pa," and probably for herself and that young man it would be the best place for her. A calico or gingham dress was good enough to visit in or go to church, but oftener a home-spun dress did duty on the same occasions; then the calico or gingham would last a year or two, and it only took eight yards for a dress. Hoop-skirts had not yet put in an appearance, and pin-backs were of another day and generation. So with a multiplicity of duties the young wife kept on her way. By and by, when a family had grown up around them, cares began to increase; the wife and mother was often compelled to sit up night after night that the husband's and the children's clothes might be mended, their stockings darned, and the preparations for the coming morning's work made ready.

Then it was discovered that woman's work was never done. The household was asleep. The tired husband and father was resting his weary limbs in dreamland, the children were tossing here and there on their beds as restless children always do. Nature itself had gone to rest, and the outer world was wrapped in darkness and gloom, but the nearly exhausted mother sewed on and on, and the midnight candle was still shedding its pale light over the work or the vigils of the loved and loving mother. And this is the record of the thousands of noble women, the female pioneers, whose daily presence, loving hearts, earnest work, and keen judgment made the work of civilization and progress one of success. And the question has often been asked, "What would the men of olden times have done if the women of olden times had not been with them?" And the reply comes back, "Ah! yes, what would they have done?"

These were the kind of women who made civilization a success, and brightened the pathway of material progress with the promise of a glorious future. There are a few yet living of that glorious pioneer band of women who gave their lives to the hard fate of a pioneer's wife. They bore their share of the trials, troubles, and labor of the times. They are deserving the love and veneration of all, and may their pathway to the unknown river be brightened by kind words and loving hearts. Let them glide softly and pleasantly down the river of time, and let no regrets come from them of neglect or coldness. Their young days were days of hardship; let the evening of their life be bereft of care, peaceful and joyous.

Of those who are now sleeping the sleep that knows no waking, they did their duty nobly and well, and while their allotted time on earth has passed they have gone to a better world, a reward to all those whose life's pilgrimage has been worthily performed. And thus the pioneer women pass away. May they be ever blessed while living. One and all, living or dead, deserve a high and honored place in our country's history, and the compiler of the History of the Hocking Valley gives this short tribute to their memory. Not that it is much, but that the lives of those who have done so much to bring this once wild valley to a land of civilization and Christianity, has the veneration of the writer, and of those he has met. And of those who have gone before will he hold a cherished memory until he, too, joins the throng on the golden shore, where time ceases and eternity begins the endless round.

OLD SETTLERS' POEM.

It is almost a hundred years
Since you and I, old pioneers,
   With aspirations free,
A home within this region sought;
But who of us then dreamed or thought
To see the many changes wrought
   That we have lived to see?

From different countries there we came;
Our object and our aim the same—
   A home in this far West.
A cabin here and there was found,
Perhaps a little spot of ground
Inclosed and cleared, while all around
   In nature's garb was dressed.

Here then we saw the groves of green
Where woodman's ax had never been—
   And pleasant valleys, too.
Within these groves so dense and dark
Was heard the squirrel's saucy bark;
The bounding stag was but the mark
   To prove the rifle true.

But all is changed, and cabin's gone,
The clapboard roof with weight-poles on,
   The rough hewn puncheon floor;
The chimney made of stick and clay
Are seen no more— gone to decay;
The men who built them— where are they?
   I need not ask you more.

They're gone, but they're remembered yet,
Those cabin homes we can't forget,
   Although we're growing old;
Fond memory still the spot reveres,
The cabin homes of youthful years
When with compatriot pioneers
   We pleasures had untold.

The dense and tangled woodland, too,
The groves we often wandered through,
   No longer now are there;
The valley with it's sward of green
With flowerets wild no more are seen,
But farms with dusty lanes between
   Are seen where once they were.

Large towns and villages arise,
And steeples point toward the skies
   Where all was desert then;
And nature's scenes have given place
To those of art; the hunter's chase
Has yielded to the exciting race
   Of speculative men.

Ah! what a change the pioneer
In eighty years has witnessed here;
   The country changing still;
How many changes it's passed through,
And we, old friends, are changing too,
There's been a change in me and you,
   And still that change goes on.

And when we think upon the past,
Those friends whose lots with us were cast
   On this once wild frontier,
And pass them all in our review,
As oftentimes in thought we do,
Alas! how very few
   Are there remaining here.

A few more years will come and go
As other years have done, you know;
   And then— ah! yes, what then?
The world will still be moving on;
But we whose cheeks are growing wan
Will not be here! We'll all be gone
   From out the ranks of men.

Our places will be vacant here,
And of the last old pioneer
   The land will be bereft;
The places which we here have filled,
The fields which we have cleared and tilled,
Our barns, though empty or though filled,
   To others will be left.

Let us go back,— in memory go,—
Back to the scenes of long ago,
   When we were blithe and young;
When hope and expectations bright
Were buoyant, and our hearts were light;
And fancy, that delusive sprite,
   Her siren sonnets sung.

'Tis natural that we should think,
While standing on the river brink,
   How wide the stream had grown.

We saw it when 'twas but a rill,
Just bursting from the sunny hill,
And now its surging waters fill
    A channel broad, unknown.

'Tis natural and proper, too,
That we compare the old and new—
    The present and the past—
And speak of those old fogy ways
In which we passed our younger days;
Then of the many new displays
    That crowd upon us fast.

We little knew of railroads then,
Nor dreamed of that near period when
    We'd drive the iron horse;
And 'twould have made the greatest laugh
Had we been told only one-half
The wonders of the telegraph—
    Then in the brain of Morse.

We did not have machinery then
To sow and reap and thresh the grain,
    But all was done by hand;
And those old-fashioned implements
Have long been banished hence,
Or, rusting, lie inside the fence—
    No longer in demand.

Yes, there are grown-up men, I know,
Who never saw a bull-tongue plow,
    A flail, or reaping hook;
And who could not describe, you know,
A swingling board or knife, although
Their grandmas used them long ago
    And lessons on them took.

The young man now would be amused
To see some things his grandsire used,
    Some things he ne'er had seen;
The way in which we cleaned our wheat,
When two strong men with blanket sheet
Would winnow out the chaff and cheat,
And twice or thrice the thing repeat,
    Until the grain was clean.

The single-shovel plow and hoe
To clean out weeds was all the show—
    We knew no better ways;
And now our sons would laugh to scorn
Such poky ways of making corn,
And bless their stars that they were born
    In more enlightened days.

They say the world has wiser grown,
They've got the speaking telephone—
   Talk hundred miles or more.
And preachers now may preach and pray
To congregations miles away;
And thousand other things they say
   We never had before.

And yet I do not know but what
The pioneer enjoyed his lot
   And lived as much at ease
As men in these enlightened days—,
With all the strange new-fangled ways
The world of fashion now displays
   The mind of man to please.

'Tis true we did not live so fast,
But socially our time was passed,
   Although our homes were mean;
Our neighbors then were neighbors true,
And every man his neighbor knew,
Although those neighbors might be few
   And sometimes far between.

Ah! yes! old pioneers, I trow
The world was brighter then than now
   To us gray-headed ones;
Hope pointed us beyond the vale,
And whispered us a fairy tale,
Of coming pleasures ne'er to fail
   Through all the shining suns.

Ambition, too, with smile so soft,
Was pointing us to seats aloft,
   Where fame and honor last.
We had not learned what now we know—
The higher up the mount we go
The storms of life still fiercer blow,
   And colder is the blast.

That though we reach the mountain's top,
Fruition find of every hope,
   Or wear the victor's crown;
Though far above the clouds we tread,
Other clouds there are still o'erhead,
And on the mind there is the dread,
   The dread of coming down.

Ah! yes! old settlers, one and all,
What ever may us yet befall,
   We will not, can't forget

The simple, old-fashioned place,
The ruts in which our fathers ran
Before the age of steam began
    To run the world in debt.

But ere, my friends, we hence embark,
We fain would place some lasting mark
    Upon this mountain shore;
A mark the traveler may see
In coming years, and know that we
Have lived and passed the road that he
    May then be passing o'er.

When death's dark curtain shall be drawn,
And we old pioneers are gone,
    Let truthful history tell
To far posterity the tale
As down the stream of life they sail,
How we with motto " Never Fail "
    Came here, and what befell.

Let history then impartial state
The incidents of every date;
    And that it so may do,
Let pioneers of every age
In this important work engage,
And each of them produce his page—
    His page of history true.

The incidents of early years,
Known only to the pioneers,
    With them will soon be lost,
Unless, before they hither go,
Those incidents are stated so
Posterity the facts may know,
    When they the stream have crossed.

And while we talk upon the past,
Of friends who are dropping off so fast,
    And those already gone,
It may not be, my friends, amiss
For each of us to think of this;
The curtain of forgetfulness
    Will soon be o'er us drawn.

The mind goes back through all the years;
We call to mind the pioneers,
    Those bold and hardy men;
We pass them in the mind's review,
The many dead, the living few,
Those unpretending settlers who
    Were our compatriots then.

> But time would fail to speak of all
> Those changes that our minds recall;
> The world is shifting more,
> And soon its shifting scenes will bear
> The last old pioneer to where
> His lost and loved companions are—
> The bright and golden shore.

The poem closes, more particularly, the career of the old settlers and their work. And it closes in verse a better description of the old pioneer and his work than many pages of prose could have done. Not all has been given which the compiler of this history would have liked to record, and many omissions may be found that should have had a place in the foregoing pages, but what is here given is a record of facts, and will be found to be very full of the passing events of the early settlement of the country. The memory of the old pioneer was not always to be depended upon; dates were seldom remembered, and it was a work of days sometimes to verify a statement and secure the proper date.

C. C. Hart,

CHAPTER IV.

SCIENTIFIC VIEW OF HOCKING VALLEY.

PRELIMINARY THOUGHTS—ITS TOPOGRAPHY—ITS DRAINAGE OR RIVER SYSTEM—ITS GEOLOGY—ITS STRATIGRAPHICAL FORMATION —ITS ARCHÆOLOGY—ITS FAUNA—ITS FLORA—ITS METEOROLOGY —SUMMARY—CONCLUSION.

PRELIMINARY THOUGHTS.

Within an irregular curve, formed by the western water-shed of the Muskingum Valley, and the eastern crest of the Scioto Valley, somewhat parabolic in its contour, lies the Hocking Valley; moderate in its past history, fair in its present, but in its future developments quite unlimited and exceedingly rich.

It is the sixth, in size, of the seven river sections of Ohio. It contains parts of nine counties, and has an area of about 4,000 square miles. Though somewhat limited in its area, yet, in its mineral resources, it is without a peer in Ohio, if in any other part of the world. So many stratigraphical shelves crowded with a variety, profusion and richness of mineral commodities can seldom be found. Nature has seen fit, for some wise and inscrutable purpose, to locate in the Hocking Valley one of her great laboratories, her chemical work-room, where she has abundant materials for future "exposition" of her cabinet of mineralogical wealth. Such a valley demands a scientific record.

The river section, termed "Hocking Valley," contains portions of the following counties: Fairfield, Perry, Hocking, Morgan, Athens, Vinton, Meigs, Gallia and Lawrence. The entire counties are geographically arranged under the Hocking Valley sectional head, except Morgan County, which lies principally in the Muskingum Valley. We have named it among the Hocking Valley Counties for the reason that Sunday Creek, one of the tributaries of Hocking River, drains its western part. The following scientific sketch relates, principally, to that part of the Hocking Valley district which lies along the Hocking River and its tributaries. In our conclusion, however, we shall take in the entire iron and coal fields.

These counties, except Fairfield, lie within the coal measures, and form the southwestern part of the iron ore belt. The surface is quite hilly. The soil is principally native, being formed of the disintegration and wash of its rock structure, or of the decay of vegetable matter. Its limestone ridges make a durable and very fertile soil. The Hocking bottoms contain a very large amount of gravel belonging to the drift period. This will be noticed under its appropriate head.

ITS TOPOGRAPHY.

The topography of Hocking Valley presents a great variety of interesting features. Let us walk about and through its county divisions and gather materials to enable us to construct out of them what would be called in military language an "eye map" —one as perfect as the eye, without instruments, will allow.

The rim of this curvilinear basin has many attractive landscapes. Follow the western divide of the Muskingum Valley, beginning at its southern extremity and traveling northward. Such is the ever changing surface configuration that the eye never tires of seeing. Nature varies your prospect with every change of horizon. The curve which you are following (the curve of the water-shed) changes its course in every yard of advance. Like the hand of a chronometer, or the rise and fall of the mercury in the barometer, the line of your direction is constantly moving to the right or left, toward the heavens, or gradually or abruptly descending. At one time you are climbing a high conical peak from which your view is quite extended and enchanting. Again you descend into a low gap in the divide, where your out-look is circumscribed by surrounding ridges and protracted spurs, shooting forth from the chief divide. At one time you are passing toward the east, heading a long tributary of the Hocking, while, in a few hours, you are driven equally far to the west by a protracted branch of the Muskingum. In this manner you travel, up and down, to the right and left, till, on the evening of the third day, having traveled not less than 130 miles, passing around the heads of the eastern confluents of Hocking, and noted all their hills, spurs, gulches, ravines and tributary valleys describing its northern curve, you arrive at the extreme head fountain of the river some miles to the north of Lancaster.

Your western survey of the Hocking Valley will consume about the same time. During this survey you have an eye view of the western ridges, spurs, slopes, gulches, ravines and valleys, as were seen on the eastern water-shed. The land surfaces in the Hocking Valley present a continued succession of bottom lands, more or less extended, some a mile wide, others presenting but a few rods of level ground ; above these low creek and river bottom lands are a few plains, such as Wolf's Plains, between Salina and Athens, and Tupper's Plains, which are located toward the southeastern part of Athens County. The higher lands consist of side-hill slopes or plains, forming with the horizon every possible angle of inclination, having a face for every point in the heavens.

Other portions of the surface form coves under which were the early creek and river channels, now covered by ancient land slides to the depth of twenty to fifty feet. The crests of the spurs and principal ridges are usually very narrow. Sometimes, however, they are broad, rich, and well adapted to grain and fruit culture.

By cross-sectioning the Hocking Valley through Fairfield and Perry, Hocking and Morgan, and, finally, through Athens counties, the above description of the surfaces of the Hocking Valley will be applicable to all the counties, Fairfield excepted. The surface of the northern two thirds of Fairfield County are quite level and very fertile. The reasons for this exception will appear when we examine its geological features.

In the Hocking Valley, consisting of the river trough, its tributary valleys, its ravines, gulches, plains, river and creek bottoms, coves, side-hill slopes, spurs, and their main ridges, we can find but little waste land. A few acres of swamps and ponds, the remaining parts of old beds of the river and branches, are to be found in the Hocking Valley. It now remains to introduce the agency by which these physical changes, already described, were formed.

ITS DRAINAGE OR RIVER SYSTEM.

The first topographical feature of Hocking, its surface configuration, has been sufficiently examined. Its land formations, whose varieties we have enumerated and described, are a series of effects, the results of adequate causes. The principal agent that has operated through many geological ages to bring about such stupendous results is water. That fluid is an erosive agent, as well as a shipper. It loosens the dissolving elements and transports them into the sea.

Hocking River takes its rise in a large spring some miles northwest of Lancaster, Fairfield County. Flowing from that fountain through Lancaster, having been joined by such tributaries as serve to drain that level part of Hocking Valley, it flows some eight or ten miles to Sugar Grove, where it is joined by an eastern tributary called Rush Creek. By a close inspection of the waters of Rush Creek it will be readily seen that the lesser stream carries the river name (Hocking). It has often been claimed, and very properly, that Rush Creek should have been called Hocking, since it is a third longer, and discharges a larger volume of water. It drains much of Perry County, and the southeastern portion of Fairfield County.

The waters of Hocking and Rush Creek, uniting at Sugar Grove, are the drainage of the level and Waverly division of Hocking Valley. Principally they are the water outlet of a larger territory in proportion to the amount discharged than any other equal section of the river. The reasons are quite obvious: (1) The drainage of flat lands is imperfect; (2) The waters moving sluggishly along their moderately inclined channels are subjected to a greater shrinkage, both by evaporation and by absorption of the soils. For the same reasons water-courses are shortened, as it is invariably the case, with old and well-cultivated lands. Many small branches hat once flowed with water during the four seasons, are now dry during nearly half the year. Rush Creek heads, principally, among the coal measure hills of Perry County, which accounts, in part, for her larger discharge of water. About three miles below Sugar Grove Hocking River receives a tributary from the northwest, the natural drainage of Southwestern Fairfield, and the Northwestern portion of Hocking County. With the exception of Margaret's Creek, Hocking River receives no considerable tributary flowing from the west or northwest from Millville, twelve miles below Lancaster, to Hockingport, at its junction with the Ohio River, a distance of about sixty-five miles, while her eastern branches are large, numerous and long.

As we pass down the river from Millville, Hocking receives no waters except such as drain the river hills, till we arrive at the mouth of Monday Creek, below Nelsonville. Monday Creek is a very important tributary, since its valley is the natural outlet of one of the most magnificent coal and iron districts in Ohio. It was so named by the original survey, the company reaching that creek on that day of the week. Its head waters are in Hocking, Perry and Athens counties. Its confluents are exceedingly numerous, taking their rise principally in Perry County. The most noted branches of Monday Creek are Shawnee Run, the location of the thriving mining and furnace town of Shawnee; Sugar Run, on which New Straitsville is situated; Little Monday Creek; Lost Branch, heading in the same ridge with Sugar Run; Kitchen Run, Sand Run, Dorr's Run, Poplar Run, Snow Fork, with its tributaries, Right Branch, Left Branch, Brush Fork, Case Run, Miligan's Branch, Long Run and Smith's Run. These various branches are noted for their coal and iron interests. No one can examine an accurate and minute map of Monday Creek and its net-work of tributaries, without being convinced that this valley, with its numberless tributaries, was grooved out for a higher purpose than that of drainage. The future of Monday Creek will fully justify the remark.

On the west side of Hocking River are a few small runs flowing into Hocking from the river hills, noted, simply, for their coal works. Three of these are: (1) Lick Run, three miles above Nelsonville, where are located the coal works of the "Lick Run Coal Company," Brettland; (2) Meeker Run; (3) Floodwood, and (4) Brigger Staff.

The Hocking River receives its third large tributary on the eastern side, at Chauncey, six miles above Athens, called Sunday Creek. This branch takes its rise in Perry and Morgan counties. Its head branches are remarkably spread out, east and west, so that its extreme fountains measure a greater distance apart than the length of the stream—wider than long.

The East Branch drains the western portion of Morgan County, joining the Middle Branch in section 6, Trimble Township, Athens County.

The Middle Branch takes its rise in the water-shed, near the town of Moxahala. Along this branch is constructed the Ohio Central R. R. On it are located Rendville and Corning, with their extended coal works. Though by far the smallest of the three Sunday Creek branches, having but a few small tributaries, it is, by far, the most celebrated. Its valley is quite narrow, having but a few patches of bottom lands.

The West Branch has its head waters in the southwestern part of Perry County. It is a large branch of Sunday Creek. Its tributaries are Indian Run, a stream of Perry, Johnson's Run, Windfall and Tucker. The West Branch has at its head waters in Perry some objects of interest—the "Sulphur Springs," visited by invalids; a mill and factory; Buckingham, a coal village. Its head branches are Carter's Fork, Rodgers' Fork, Coal Fork,

West Fork, Hadley's Fork, and Priest's Fork, noted (all these forks) as draining a very remarkable coal development, in one place measuring thirteen feet of excellent coal. From this district was removed a block of coal thirteen feet and over, which was transported to Philadelphia in 1876, and was an interesting specimen in the Centennial. The village of Hartley (Hartleyville) is located on this branch at the mouth of Johnson's Run.

The West Branch is traversed by a branch of the Ohio Central Railroad, which is doing a thriving business in removing coal to the great Northwest. The waters of the three branches form a junction at Sedalia, one mile above the village of Trimble. "Mud Fork" joins the West Branch a few rods above its union with the principal stream at Sedalia. Mud Fork heads in the Snow-Fork ridge. On this branch a shaft was sunk through the "great vein," coal, in which the seam was found to be about twelve feet thick. Strait Run, one of its principal branches, heads with Wolf Run, a tributary of Snow Fork, in a depression or "low gap" of the "divide," between Sunday Creek and Snow Fork. Through this depression a railroad will, probably, soon connect Sunday Creek Valley with that of Monday Creek. Should the two mining districts come under the management of the same company, this union would take place very speedily.

At Trimble, one mile below Sedalia, Sunday Creek receives two other tributaries, McCune's Run from the west, and Congress Run from the east. The junction of these waters and the lay of the valleys (concentering) point to Trimble as a future important mining and iron-making center. With capital in the hands of an enterprising people, Trimble would soon grow into a town of very considerable note. It has an excellent steam flouring mill, a number of stores of various kinds, and shops. Next to Corning, Trimble is the most active, thriving and wide-awake little village in the valley.

Another tributary comes into Sunday Creek from the east, nearly opposite to Jackson and its coal works. It is called Woodbury's Run. This stream, with Congress Run and many small brooks of the East Branch, head with Federal Creek. Jackson, the location of a coal shaft and coal works, is a new village about one mile below the village of Trimble. It takes its name from O. D. Jackson, its proprietor. It will soon become a town of some note.

Trimble and Jackson will, in time, become the upper and lower divisions of one prosperous city.

One mile below Jackson, Sunday Creek receives a western branch, called Green's Run. This branch heads, by two main streams, in the Snow Fork divide. These branches, with their small affluents, cause Green's Run to afford an excellent outlet for the removal of its mineral resources, which are varied and abundant. Near the mouth of Green's Run are two salt wells, where for many years excellent salt was manufactured.

At Millfield, two miles below, Jackson's Run flows in from the east, heading with Woodbury's Run and Federal Creek. Below Millfield, from the east, flow Boon, Stony Camp, and Lick Runs, and with these end all the eastern tributaries of Sunday Creek. On the west, one mile above Chauncey, Sunday Creek receives the waters of Bailey's Run—a stream that gives name to a valuable seam of coal. We have been particular in describing Monday Creek and Sunday Creek and their chief confluents because their mineral resources, especially coal, are so vast, that every creek, branch, branch of branches, brook or rill will be noted among capitalists and miners for some peculiarity of its mineral wealth, either in amount or quality, or in both.

There is a remarkable feature in the head waters of Rush Creek, Monday Creek, and Sunday Creek, to which we desire special attention. Between the mouths of Rush Creek, Monday Creek and Sunday Creek there cannot be less than forty miles, while Rush Creek and Monday Creek have, in part, the same water-shed, while the head waters of Sunday Creek are quite near. The peculiarity is in the sources of Rush Creek. They take their rise among the hills of Perry, on the western slope of the great divide between Monday Creek and Moxahala, and descend from the coal measures of Perry toward the Waverly group of Southeastern Fairfield. The general direction of the flow of these three creeks indicates high lands in the regions of the heavy coal and iron-ore deposits.

The Hocking River has a large western affluent about one mile west of Athens, called Margaret's Creek. This stream is the natural drainage of the western part of Athens County, including principally Athens, Waterloo, Alexander and Lee townships. Near its mouth it receives two branches, Little Factory and Big Factory. Further up the stream comes in another branch, the East Branch; then the middle and west branches. There are many smaller affluents which we have not room, neither is it necessary, to describe. The towns situated on its waters will be noticed in other chapters. The peculiarity of its drainage deserves a brief touch. Margaret's Creek is the water outlet of more surface rainfall than its volume at its mouth would indicate. The philosophy of this fact of science may not be so readily understood. This part of Athens County is peculiar in its surface configuration. It is a high semi-table land, with some hills near Hocking River. Margaret's Creek has grooved this plain to perfect its drainage, though this drainage is as complete as the nature of the territory will allow; still, at the ordinary stage of water, the stream is sluggish, and, therefore, by evaporation and absorption, an unusually large per cent. of its waters never reach the river. Another result is obvious, large rainfalls are at times disastrous. Another inference is, perhaps, correct. Table and flat lands are not generally rich in valuable mineral products, hence the natural process of exposure by rapidly flowing water is not required to expose any deep mineral resources. The Divine Author adapts his means to the ends designed to be accomplished. Drainage is not the entire object of our river systems. Irrigation and exposure of deep and otherwise hidden treasures are evidently had in view by the Author of Nature with all its elementary combinations. He that makes eyeless fishes where no light can ever penetrate would not upheave and plow down the earth's crust without having in view some special object. Hocking Valley is not, by any means, destitute of the foot-prints of the Deity. Hocking Valley is a proof of his handiwork.

About four miles below Athens, Hocking receives another small tributary called Stroud's Run. This stream has nothing worthy of special note. The next branch from the east is Federal Creek, so named from its thirteen branches. This creek heads principally with Sunday Creek and Wolf Creek. The stream is not as large as Sunday Creek, but it has about it many interesting features. Its dividing ridges are rich with limestone formations. They furnish the valley great mineral wealth by the decay of its limestone formations. Federal Creek was early settled by citizens from New England. Its various branches furnished homes for the early pioneers of the county. It was on the Walker Branch that the "Coonskin Library" had its origin. Many of our ablest citizens, those whose names have been heard through the civilized world, claim this valley as their native land. Its minerals, such as iron ore and coal are quite valuable, and will, in coming time, attract public attention. Federal Creek has had many paying oil wells. For some years it furnished a large amount of oil for the general market. The flood waters of Federal Creek are peculiarly rich in lime held in solution. The soil of this creek is the most productive of any other in the county, and quite exhaustless.

Tributaries of Hocking below the mouth of Federal Creek are quite numerous, yet they are small, taking their rise principally in the river hills. They are devoid of sufficient interest to justify any special description. They are short, and flow down steep declivities, making for themselves deep channels in the various rock strata.

We have completed our survey of the river system of Hocking Valley, have carefully noticed its tributaries from its fountain head till its waters are seen mingling with its kindred waters of the noble Ohio. Many questions of interest might be discussed relative to this river system. Of the seven river systems of Ohio, which is the most ancient? for they are, geologically, quite different in their ages and unlike in their growth. Their modes of formation and their movements and their mission are dissimilar. A few thoughts relative to the ages and mission work of the Ohio rivers will enable the reader better to understand the philosophy of the things in the Hocking Valley.

To know that such things exist on and under a given district may be satisfactory to the masses; but, to the mind that desires to look into the reason of things, many questions step forward and demand satisfactory answers. Why do the things exist? Why in such a form? How long have they existed? What made them? Why are they formed? Such queries have correct answers. We are surrounded by an endless variety of objects which, for convenience of explanation, we call "things." They are principally effects. The causes that produced them may often be obscure. It is the object of the science of philosophy to make visible the reasons of things. Cast your eye over a large map of the State. Fix your attention upon one class of objects—rivers, for instance. There are seven river systems. Why differ in so many particulars? In the broadest sense there are but two river systems: (1) The waters flowing into Lake Erie forming one system; (2) Those flowing into the Mississippi forming the other system (the seven being called sections). The causes of these variations lie below the surfaces of each district.

1. The Maumee Valley, embracing eighteen counties, shows glacial action over its entire surface, in its heavy drifts of bluish

clay intermingled with sand, gravel and boulders. Its drainage is peculiar. The St. Joseph River has no tributaries on the south, and the St. Mary is without any on the north. Old drift deposits determine the features of its drainage, whether to the lake or to the Mississippi.

2. The Western Reserve drainage is sluggish, except where the streams head near the lake. Twelve counties lie principally within the lake basin. The rim is about 600 feet, in places, above the surface of Lake Erie. The Cuyahoga and Chagrin rivers are rapid and eroded; deep valleys mark their flow to the lake.

3. The Ohio River section has its peculiarities of drainage. This section numbers four counties. It is drained principally by short affluents of the Ohio, taking their rise in the extremity of the spurs of the river hills. The valleys are, generally, deep erosions.

4. The Muskingum River Valley, having sixteen counties, has its name from its principal river, its system of drainage. It is a valley of erosion, it being noted for its small amount of drift, and, consequently, its large amount of native soil—that which is formed from erosion and disintegration of its own strata. Its drainage extends to the center of the State.

5. The Scioto River section includes fifteen counties. The Scioto River has great length in proportion to its volume of water. Its course is from the north to the south, following one meridian in much of its southern division. Its branches are usually lengthy, its western affluents predominating. The coal-measure hills give rise to its eastern tributaries.

6. The Miami forms another extended river system. It includes fifteen counties, and has an area of 6,440 square miles. This section has the highest and the lowest land in the State; still the surface slopes so gradually, that the country seems somewhat level. The river erosions have been moderate, the waters flowing tardily.

It will be seen, from the sketch above given, that Hocking Valley has its peculiarities of drainage, the closer resemblances being found between it and the Scioto and Muskingum valleys.

Hocking River system of drainage is more active, and, consequently, more perfect than that of any of the other systems, if we except the Ohio River system, which is quite limited.

One other remarkable feature in the Hocking River system is worthy of notice—the direction and flow of the river itself. A single glance at the general course of Hocking River shows us that its flow is in the direction of the greatest dip. It rises in the Waverly group and enters the Ohio River high up in the lower coal measures. Geologically speaking, therefore, its head spring is about 1,200 feet higher than its mouth, and the stream flows up— up the strata, but down the natural slope of the valley. This will be explained under the geological division.

THE GEOLOGY OF HOCKING VALLEY.

Having noticed its surface, structure and drainage, we propose to investigate the causes, which, in the past ages, have superinduced these surface configurations and drainage. The rock formations of the valley are chiefly the coal measures. They are fire-clay, sandstone, limestone, coal and iron stone and shale. In Fairfield County we have the Waverly group, and the glacial drift, which also has its beds down the main valley of Hocking.

The geology of this portion of Hocking Valley, that of Fairfield County, will occupy but little space, since it has no very peculiar features. The northern and western two thirds of the county, are, to the geologist, somewhat monotonous. The fertility of the soil and its large, well-cultivated and well-stocked farms are the objects of attraction in this district. In the southern portion of the county the surface prospects assume a more rugged form; spurs, between which are seen the most lovely valleys, give signs of your proximity to the Alpine district of Ohio.

The drift forms the peculiar geological feature of Fairfield. On the low lands wells reach the blue clay of the drift; and over nearly the entire surface are found gravel and boulders of the drift formation. The immense gravel beds and terraces along the Hocking River come from these immense drift deposits. The boulders, which are profusely scattered over the surface, vary in size from that of a few inches to the one on Baldwin's Run, whose dimensions are eighteen feet by sixteen feet. They are usually granitic, demonstrating their foreign origin. In some cases, however, they are limestone, and are utilized by burning into quick-lime.

Fairfield, though covered in many parts with drift, lies within the Waverly formation, except one lofty hill near East Rushville, showing signs of the coal measures. Fairfield produces no coal. The products of her rich agricultural land are exchanged for fuel.

The Waverly formation, which lies immediately under the coal measures, is seen most distinctly on Rush Creek, in a ravine between East Rushville and West Rushville. The sandstone is fine grained, but too soft for building stone. The Waverly sandstone seen in the cliffs along the Hocking below Lancaster are coarse grained, passing into a conglomerate. Its color is rich yellow and dark brown. At times it is richly variegated. It forms the court-house at Lancaster, and some costly buildings in Columbus.

The Waverly sandstone constitues the only mineral wealth yet found in the Fairfield division of the Hocking Valley. There is an increasing demand for this Waverly sandstone. Quarries are being opened and quite extensively worked. By the proximity of the Hocking Valley R. R. the rock may be readily shipped to the towns farther west. It may, in time, become valuable, and yield a very considerable revenue to the citizens dwelling in this portion of the valley. Still the Fairfield section of Hocking Valley must draw its principal wealth out of its soil. This will always place its industrious citizens among the most wealthy and thriving of the interesting valley.

THE GEOLOGY OF HOCKING COUNTY.

Passing down the Hocking Valley the next county we enter is Hocking. This section of the valley lies principally within the Waverly group. In this county the drift forms terraces along the Hocking River. The rocks of this county are the coarse Waverly sandstone, the conglomerate, and the Logan sandstone. Upon this sandstone as its floor is the Maxville limestone. The south-eastern part of the county comes into the horizon of the lower coal measures. The Waverly rocks have been noticed in their lower formations as seen in Fairfield County. Hocking County is rich in its mineral formations. Its sandstones are excellent for building purposes; its fire-clay has not yet been fully tested. It has lime-stone in considerable quantities, and good. It has beds of excellent ores of iron. Its coal is perhaps the most valuable of its mineral products. This coal field lies on Monday Creek, and its waters flowing into it from the east and west. It contains the great coal seam of Ohio, usually called the " great vein, " or " Nelsonville " coal seam, it having been mined at Nelsonvile and in its vicinity for many years. This coal seam in many localities is a dry, burn-ing coal. It varies in thickness from six feet to thirteen feet. It lies high in the Monday Creek hills, and is mined by drifting. A vertical section passing from the mouth of Monday Creek in Fork Township to a point near New Straitsville, on the divide between

Monday Creek, extending down to the Waverly group and to the highest hill of the aforenamed water-shed would cut the various geological formations in about the following order: A limestone horizon, shales of various degrees of thickness, sandstones, three coal seams, several horizons of iron ore, and about an equal number of horizons of fire-clay, as they usually underlie veins of coal and iron ore. In this section the Bailey's Run coal seam shows an imperfect development, it being located too high in the Monday Creek hills. This will be more fully seen in a section further to the east. The Nelsonville seam shows well, though its location is rather high. One vein of iron ore has been worked to advantage by a number of furnaces. Mining, however, even in this district, is in a crude state, and, consequently, its formations are imperfectly exposed. Many rich beds of iron ore may yet be exposed which have never yet been seen. Prospecting so far has done wonders in discovering and bringing to view its mineral resources. Much remains still to be accomplished in the exposure of its mineral wealth.

THE GEOLOGY OF THE ATHENS COUNTY SECTION OF THE HOCKING VALLEY.

This county takes in the entire valley of Hocking from a point a few miles above Nelsonville to its junction with the Ohio at Hocking port, a distance of nearly forty miles. It lies wholly within the productive coal measures. More or less coal has been developed over the principal portions of the county. For present use we shall have to confine our investigations to the Sunday Creek Valley, including the northen part of Athens County and the southern townships of Perry County. We select this district for various reasons:

1. Of the three eastern tributaries of the Hocking River, Monday Creek, Sunday Creek, and Federal Creek, Sunday Creek is the middle stream. Monday Creek is the stream where the great coal seam is high, and is mined by drifting; and, consequently, there must be a large amount of crop coal, and worthless. On Federal Creek the great vein, if there, is deep and would require very heavy expenses to obtain it by shafting. On Sunday Creek we have the mean between the crop coal and expensive shafting.

2. Along the Sunday Creek Valley is the completed Ohio Central R. R., a road which, from its directions and pecuniary abili-

ties, affords the best shipping facilities that can be found anywhere. Capitalists desiring to invest in coal and mineral property are interested to know what they are purchasing.

In a vertical section 1,100 feet of vertical face, extending below the surface of the valley of the Waverly group, 500 feet; and from the creek to the summit of the most elevated hill, 600 feet, we have the vertical section of 1,100 feet. Beginning at the Waverly and passing upward, we can count the various geological formations. We shall not, at present, enumerate the strata, but simply the different formations:

1. The rock containing brine, from which a vast amount of salt has been manufactured. We then alternate between the limestone shales and sandstone till we reach (2) fire-clay, of which there are many horizons.

3. Above the first fire-clay we have our first coal formation. The entire coal formation of this section measures about twenty-seven feet. Another valuable formation we discover in the face of the section.

4. Iron ore. This appears in various horizons and varies materially in its per cent. of iron.

5. Another valuable geological formation appears—limestone. The limestone formations are numerous and quite pure.

6. Alternating with coal and iron ores, we have heavy shale deposits—still-water formations. There can be seen (7) various layers of sandstone; some of these layers are more than fifty feet thick and excellent for the manufacture of glass. Others are excellent for building stone. There are also beds of flagstone. Flowing in two porous blue (8) sand rocks is petroleum.

9. Illuminating gas flows with the oil and with salt water. All these mineral products are seen in the Sunday Creek Valley, and are found within the 1,100 feet. Let us form them into a list:

Gas, salt water, shale, fire-clay, limestone, sandstone, iron ore and coal. Such are our geological formations.

On Federal Creek and continuing eastward to the rim of the Hocking Valley basin is the Pittsburg coal seam, measuring about eight feet of coal. Above this coal are very heavy horizons of limestone, shales, marls, sandstone and iron ore. On Federal Creek, and on the East Branch of Sunday Creek are oil wells which have produced many thousand barrels of rock oil. The disintegration of the higher limestone formations has made for Federal Creek and other eastern tributaries of Hocking a soil of great productiveness.

Their waters-sheds are full of lime, which being washed down the slopes and into the valleys, produces a black soil, equal to any on the globe. Such is a brief outline of the geological formations of Hocking Valley, between the Waverly and Drift of Fairfield and the buff limestone of the eastern water-sheds. Our space will not allow us to say more about its geological formations. We now come to examine another interesting feature of the Hocking Valley; it may be termed the analysis of its geology.

ITS STRATIGRAPHICAL FEATURES.

In our geological sketch we described each formation as a whole, such as shales, sandstones, limestones, fire clays, marls, iron ores, and coal. We shall now view these formations in their distinct horizons, or layers.

All the formations native to the Hocking Valley are what may be termed sedimentary. The particles of which they are composed were held in solution by the waters of the ocean once covering the entire globe. Hocking Valley cannot date beyond the Waverly. Its age is that of the lower productive coal measures. The valley is, geologically, young. Ages after the Laurentian Mountains of Canada and the Adirondack Mountains lifted their snow heads above the primeval ocean the Allegheny Range quietly slept beneath its turbid brine. In the revolving cycles, the loftiest peaks struggled into atmospheric life; through a series of risings above the sea surface, and fallings beneath it, the mountains stood forth to sink no more. By the upheaval of the Allegheny Mountains and the Cincinnati Arch, the Ohio River trough was formed, the western side of which has, in part, been grooved out into what is now called the Hocking Valley. The valley itself has, therefore, been formed since the deposit of all its eroded strata, and is more recent than the Cincinnati Arch and the Allegheny Mountains. The strata that form the lower coal measures are sedimentary deposits from the ancient ocean. And since coal is of vegetable origin, the forests which produced the coal must have grown above the waters; and afterward, submerged, and made the floor of later deposits. All the other strata, such as shales, fire-clay, limestone, sandstone, iron ore, were submarine deposits.

In our division it is our purpose to notice these distinct sedimentary deposits, which aggregate about 1,100 feet in thickness. The lowest strata in the valley are the Waverly, in Fairfield County, covered by the glacial drift of a more recent date. This floor dates, geologically, far back of the coal measures, since the coal measures rest upon the upper Waverly as its floor; our theme requires us to notice each layer till we reach the eastern water-shed. These strata aggregate about 1,500 feet, in vertical height; by this we mean that the crest of the eastern water-shed of the Hocking Valley is, geologically, 1,500 feet higher than the Waverly floor of Fairfield, and that the mouth of Hocking at Hockingport is, stratigraphically, at least 1,000 feet higher than its fountain source in Fairfield County. When speaking of strata it must not be supposed that each stratum is found in every part of the valley, nor that they are of uniform thickness. Shales vary in thickness from a few inches to fifty feet. As they were still-water deposits, the duration of the stillness and the amount of the clay sediment and clay and sand determine the amount of deposit. Limestone formations are not uniform; nor are the sand rocks, iron ore and coal deposits; they often lie in pockets and lagoons. We shall name such strata only as may be found somewhere in the valley, describing only where they are of special value. As we pass down the valley we shall pass up the strata, as one ascends a flight of stairs, each stratum being a step, or, as the shelves of a mineralogical cabinet, each stratum forming a shelf. Commencing with the Waverly, as the floor of our cabinet, let us note each shelf and its contents as we ascend.

It may be remarked, then, that the first shelf in our coal-measure cabinet has the Maxville limestone; this horizon does not extend over the entire valley, still it is a large deposit in certain localities, and is of considerable value. It is a valuable deposit of the cabinet. The shale stratum is next in order in the ascending stratigraphical shelves. As the shales have not been utilized, only by nature in forming the basis of many of its soils, we shall pass them with a general remark, that they being still-water deposits predominate in our valleys and determine, principally, their extent.

The alternation of mineral rock deposits require sandstone. The sandstone strata are numerous, and vary exceedingly in their texture, Some are too soft for building stone, others hard and shelly; some are conglomerate and coarse grained. The ridges have specimens of glass rock over fifty feet thick. The Hocking Valley abounds in excellent freestone belonging to the lower coal measures. Some of the rocks resemble the best Waverly sandstone. The valley contains extensive beds of excellent flagstone. We therefore place our freestone stratum among our valuable minerals. There are many horizons of fire-clay. These are in places of excellent quality.

They form the floors of our iron ore beds, coal seams, and sometimes underlie limestone formations. The fire-clays are, therefore, of great commercial value. The strata that lies below the coal veins we pass without further notice. Our mining operations will, perhaps, extend only to the lower coal veins, which crop out near Nelsonville, in the Hocking Valley, along Monday Creek, and Lower Snow Fork, at New Straitsville, Shawnee, and is at the depth of about eighty feet in Lower Sunday Creek Valley; at Corning, about forty feet; and at Rendville, but a few feet beneath the surface.

The seams of coal in the Hocking Valley, including its eastern tributaries, number in all six. The first is about twenty-six feet below the "great vein," known as the Nelsonville seam. It measures about three feet. The second vein is the Nelsonville seam. It measures in the Hocking Valley proper about six feet. On Monday Creek it is six to ten feet thick; on the waters of Upper Sunday Creek it measures from seven to ten feet, at one point thirteen feet. In the Lower Sunday Creek Valley, in the shafts, it averages nine feet. This is the only coal which, from Hocking Valley, has reached successfully the general market. Its excellent quality is admitted, and the vastness of the deposit places its value in the front rank of all the mineral deposits of the valley. The third seam of coal is about seventy-five feet above the Nelsonville seam. It averages, in thickness, about four and one-half feet. It is called the Bailey's Run coal, and belongs principally to Sunday Creek and, as it has been the only coal ever used in the Lower Sunday Creek Valley, and lies at the base of its hills, it may be called the Sunday Creek coal. It is not yet known in the general market. It has often been analyzed and coked. For steam generation it is excellent, makes coke, and for domestic uses it is not readily excelled. Should it come into general use for coking it will become of immense value. A fourth seam of coal is found thirty-seven feet above the Bailey's Run coal, too thin, however, for mining except in mining a seam of ore of which it forms the floor. A fifth coal seam, two and one-half feet thick, lies about seventy-five feet above the fourth seam. About 400 feet above the Bailey's Run coal comes in the Pittsburg or Pomeroy coal seam. This seam closes the Hocking Valley coal seams. The amount of coal in Hocking is immense. Centuries will be required to mine and remove and utilize its vast deposits. Alternating with our coal seams and limestone strata are counted thirteen horizons of iron ore. Hocking Valley is located within the iron belt of Ohio. Some of its ores have been in use for iron-making, for at least, one half a century. Its veins of ore are, in certain localities, rich and productive. They vary from six inches to five and one-half feet in thickness. They yield by analysis from twenty-five to sixty per cent. of pure iron.

Mixed with other ores they make an excellent iron.

In Hocking Valley are found twelve horizons of limestone. Four of these spread through half of the valley, the other strata lie along the eastern rim. One deposit is about thirty feet thick, and very pure. Our eastern ridges are formed of heavy limestone layers. The principal strata, which we have enumerated, are found in the higher portion, and in the eastern division of the valley, commencing at the tops (top shelf in our mineral cabinet) of our eastern hills and counting the strata as we descend the rock slopes: (1) The buff limestone; (2) Shales; (3) Sand rock; (4) Limestone; (5) Sandstone; (6) Iron ore; (7) Shale; (8) Pittsburg coal seam; (9) Fire-clay; (10) Rich nodular ore in thirty feet of red marl, nodules yielding fifty-five per cent. of pure iron; (11) Limestone; (12) Sandstone; (13) Iron ore; (14) Ames limestone; (15) Shales; (16) Ferruginous clay stone; (17) Coal, two and one half feet; (18) Ferruginous limestone; (19) Black limestone; (20) Ferruginous limestone; (21) Shales; (22) Black band ore; (23) Coal, one and one half feet; (24) Big vein ore, five and one half feet; (25) Shales under fire-clay; (26) Bailey's Run coal, four and one half feet; (27) Fire-clay; (28) Limestone; (29) Iron ore; (30) Sandstone; (31) Shales; (32) Limestone; (33) Sand rock; (34) Shales; (35) Limestone; (36) Sandstone; (37) Black slate; (38) Nelsonville coal; (39) Fire-clay; (40) Sandstone; (41) Limestone; (42) Shales coal, two and one half feet thick. Here ends the coal seams of the valley.

This inclined plain, which was, by erosion, constructed into the Hocking Valley by the rising of the land, must have had six formative periods when the surface was above the sea and remained above water until the growth of vegetation prepared materials for a vein of coal, when it again subsided, thus rising and falling till the last coal vein was formed, when, after the various strata were deposited, it arose to sink no more. Such appears to be the process by which the Hocking Valley plain was formed. The valley was grooved into this inclined plain by running water. The Ohio River flowed toward the gulf down a series of inclined plains 100 feet below the plains down which its waters now flow. Rain falling on this Hocking plain, the river, as a short river, begins to form by grooving out the strata, and floating the debris, suspended in the running water, till the river had its head waters at Coolville, then as far as Athens, to Chauncey, Nelsonville, Logan, Millville, Sugar Grove, and finally a few miles beyond Lancaster. The tributaries were formed by a similar process, the eroded materials being carried into the main stream. In like manner the branches of the branches, even to the smallest rills, were eroded. This process of erosion is still in progress, and would finally carry all the hills to the ocean, unless a new era should change the order of things. What a vast amount of eroded particles have been taken out of the valley. For the purpose of drainage, irrigation and exposure of the mineral resource, what a work has been, and is being, accomplished in the Hocking Valley. The earth truly is standing out of the water and in the water, and was thus formed; the strata, coal excepted, were formed in or under the water, and the coal elements growing out of the water, but converted into coal under the water.

Thus has the Architect of all the created universe, in his laboratory in the ocean caverns, constructed a rich cabinet of minerals for exposition and future use. After constructing the materials for ages to come, and placing his mineral merchandise upon their appropriate stratigraphical shelves, he raises the entire materials above the deep, and begins the process of opening his grand exposition. We have seen his erosive work. It is our duty to examine the effects that we may discover their intelligent, all-powerful cause. We have now examined the geological make of the Hocking Valley. We have walked up and down its strata, and noted their variety, their position, and searched into the modes of their formation. The age of the valley we have not given, and for the reason of our inability.

ARCHÆOLOGY OF THE HOCKING VALLEY.

What races of men occupied the Hocking Valley before the white man entered it, and its forest began to retire before the march ot civilization? To answer this question intelligently, and with entire satisfaction, requires more data than we are able to command.

When the Europeans first entered the Hocking Valley they found it occupied by the Indians. But who were the Indians? Were they indigenous to the soil, natives, born out of the earth of the valley or were they exotics? Elias Boudinot, LL. D., held that the Indians were of the ten lost tribes of Israel. He made a collection of many of their traditions, manners, and customs, and, from testimony which he deemed sufficient, came to that conclusion.

Be his theory true or false, they were not aborigines of that valley. They came into the valley from some distant country. Their mode of living originated their peculiarities of color and peculiar modes of thought. The Indians were not the Mound-builders, since they do not appear to have any knowledge of the time when the mounds were built, nor by whom they were erected. It is very generally conceded that the mounds are tumuli. Another point is, perhaps, equally true: that they were built over distinguished chiefs, fallen in battle. The mounds occupy grounds, once battle-fields, since they are covered more or less profusely with flint arrow heads. These heads strewn over the ground indicate a battle-field. These mounds are quite numerous in Hocking Valley, on what is called Wolf's Plains, between Salina and Athens, were a number of very large tumuli. Two have been particularly noted. One of these mounds was quite demolished to make room for a school-house, an act of desecration to the tomb of the ancient dead.

One that is now standing is not less than thirty feet high, and quite regular in its form, it being a cone. It was once not less than forty feet high. The materials of which the mounds are composed vary according to the geological formations of the districts where they are erected. On the plains they are formed, principally, of the drift sand and gravel, these materials composing the plains. The materials were carried by many persons, and well packed, or storms of so many centuries as they have seen would have washed them almost to a level with the surrounding plains. The mound of which we are now speaking is in an excellent state of preservation. Though times have been set to have it opened, Providence has defeated all the intentions of the mound desecrators. How long its once living human remains will be allowed to remain in their long and unbroken slumbers is not revealed.

On the farm of Daniel Weethee, in Dover Township, Athens County, two mounds have been opened; the one, about fifty years ago; the other, recently. The one first opened was on the Sunday Creek bottom. It must have been originally twelve or fifteen feet high and about twelve feet in diameter. It was surrounded, when first seen (1798) by a shallow ditch, formed by the removal of the dirt to construct the tumulus. It had on its slope bushes and a large tree. The surrounding lands were thickly sprinkled with flint arrow-heads of all sizes, colors and shapes. Here and there were stone-axes, black and gray. One implement was metallic, and answered, perhaps, for a sword. It has been so many

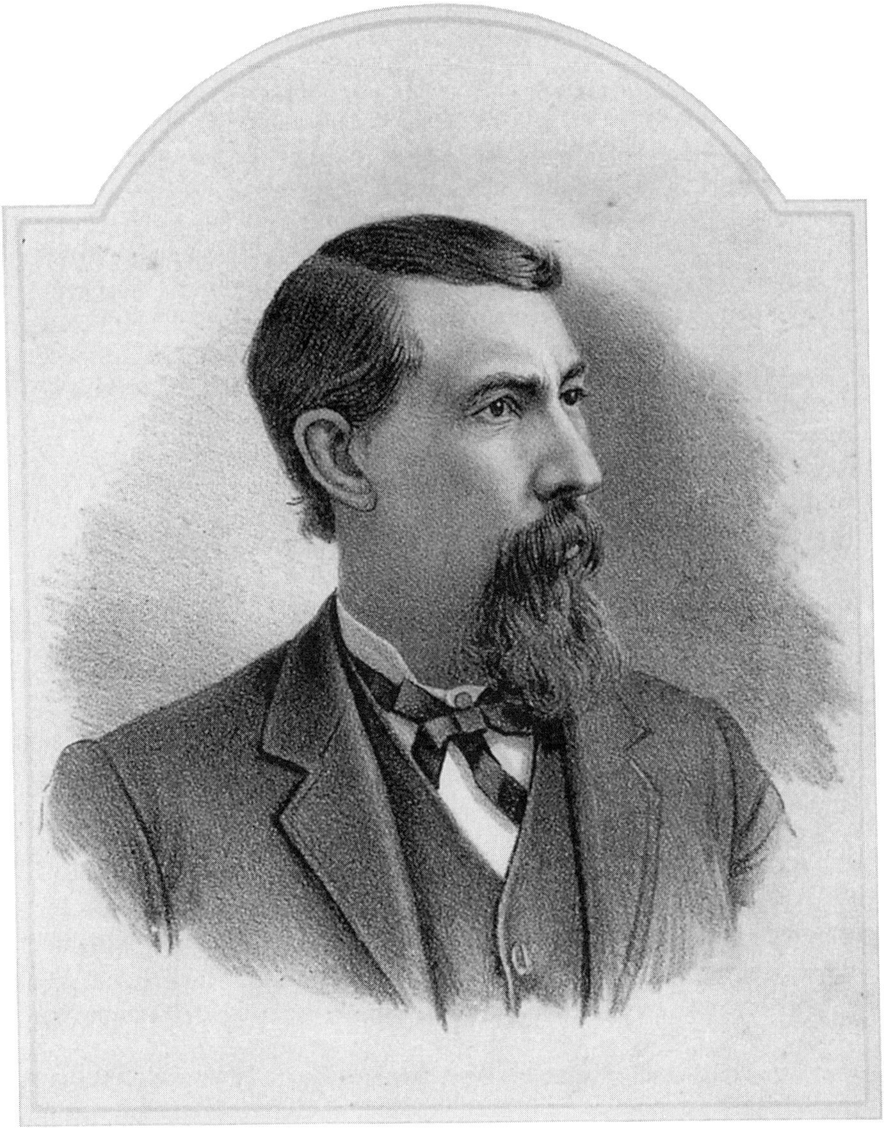

W D Mansfield M.D.

years since I saw it that I cannot describe it intelligently. In the center of the mound's base was a circular heap of dark mold, about two feet in diameter, evidently the dust of the person over whom the mound was erected. In that pile was found a ring, composed of metal, large enough to clasp the human wrist. It was rust-eaten and broken. The mound had been raised around and over the person standing.

This must have been a battle-field, since the implements were those of war. Whether the field, at that time, was cleared, or covered with a dense growth of timber, cannot be clearly ascertained at this late period. We should suppose that the land was then under cultivation, since it would have been difficult to construct such a tumulus in the midst of an unbroken forest of beech, sugar tree, oak and hickory, as it was when Mr. Weethee, the first white man, entered it. If it were a cultivated field, the Mound-builders must have been advanced beyond the purely savage state. They might have been semi-barbarians as their arrow-heads and stone implements indicate. The second mound opened is on a hill. Its size and shape were about the same as those of the one just described. It was constructed of materials that had to be conveyed about one half of a mile, as they could not have been found any nearer.

The contents of this mound were in a much better state of preservation. Near the top were bones of what appeared to be a young child. Three skeletons were found resting on its base. Two o the skeletons were human; the third skeleton resembled that of a dog. This might have been for a fallen chief and his family.

On an adjacent hill, overlooking the 270-acre field first described, is another mound, not opened. It is about the same size as that of the other two. Another mound, of similar size, and unopened, is located on a hill south of the battle-field. Relative to these four mounds and those on Wolf's Plains, if we be allowed to conjecture the occasion of their construction, it would be about as follows: The Sunday Creek Valley and the plains were two great battle-fields, chosen as the ground on which to decide the claims of great rival powers. On the plains was fought the first bloody battle. The defeated army retreated up the Sunday Creek Valley. Being recruited from the north they made a stand. On the North Dover field was fought another engagement, more destructive than the first. Till the dead of those battle-fields can utter their true history, our conjecture will, perhaps, come as near to the facts as our data will allow. The fortifications of the Mound-builders show about the same skill. In a cave, on the same farm on Sunday Creek, is a vessel, worked out of the rock, which was used as a kettle for boiling; whether it was constructed by the Indians or by the Mound-builders we have no means to decide.

The materials out of which their arrow-heads and axes were made came from some other region, since we have no such strata belonging to the valley. They might have obtained their granite from the drift found in the Hocking River terraces, but this drift is foreign. It is true that they might have obtained their black flint from Rush Creek, but whether they found their white and red flints in this locality we are unable to say; perhaps they did.

They had stone implements whose uses we are not able to discern. There is a mound on Minor's Branch of Federal Creek which possesses some peculiar features worthy of special notice. A circular area about twelve feet in diameter is sunk about two and one-half feet below the surface of the earth, around the circumference of which were found lying, heads to feet, six skeletons; in the center of the area rested the seventh and the largest skeleton. Over these the mound was erected. These must have died at the same period, since the seven rest on the same horizontal level and were covered at the same time. This account we have from Dr. Dennis Newton, of Trimble Township, Athens County. It is said that there are 10,000 mounds, and 1,500 circumvallations in Ohio. Of what race were these Mound-builders has not been satisfactorily ascertained. That they were originally from Asia we feel quite sure. From a skull obtained from one of the mounds we are inclined to give them a Mongolian extract. They evidently came to America over Behring's Straits, which they could have crossed on the ice, or in small crafts. It would require centuries to have gone as far south as Central or South America. As they moved toward the south they advanced in their arts. That they came from Northeastern Asia and from that quarter peopled America will appear from this: that the American continent, between the great mountain range (consisting of the Rocky Mountains in North America and the Andes Mountains in South America) and the Pacific Ocean, was first peopled and grew into powerful empires. The memory of the Mound-builders has perished from the earth, and the rude monuments give us a far more imperfect sketch of their being and character than that of the fossils whose tombs are in the earth's strata.

THE FAUNA OF HOCKING VALLEY.

We are requested to describe the Hocking Valley in its three departments, or, kingdoms: Mineral, Animal and Vegetable. We have described its mineral or geological formations; and have dropped a few thoughts relative to its aboriginal inhabitants in their monuments; it now remains to consider its original animal and vegetable kingdoms. What beasts, birds, fishes, and reptiles originally occupied the valley? This department we now propose to investigate.

THE BEASTS OF THE VALLEY.

When the first white man entered within the limits of the Hocking Valley, it was a dark, unbroken wilderness. The silence of its continuous forest was broken by the piercing cry of the eagle, the howling of wild beasts, and the whoop of the savage. The co-mingling of such wild, unusual, and discordant voices produced a sense of loneliness to which the present occupants of the valley are utter strangers. Far from the cheering smiles of quiet civilization he is resolved to take up his abode with these untamed denizens of the valley.

What were they that made his nights so dangerous and gloomy?

A few of its most dangerous occupants deserve special notice. Others will simply be named.

(*a.*) *Puma or Cougar, Felis concolor, leopardus concolor or puma concolor*—one of the largest of the American feliæ, rivaled only by the jaguar. It is called panther (*Felis pardus*) called by the vulgar " painter." It is sometimes called the American lion. It does not often attack man, but has an unusual thirst for blood. One puma has been known to kill fifty sheep in one night, drinking a little blood of each. These monarchs of the forests were not numerous in the Hocking Valley, but their name always carried terror with it. When it was reported that a panther (painter) had been heard or seen in any district, the whole country turned out for a hunt, each man hoping to be the fortunate one to give it the death shot. This animal was the prince of beasts, though sometimes mastered and killed by a single dog.

(*b.*) *Bear*—American black bear (*Ursus Americanus*) were found in abundance, all over the valley. It was rather timid, but had great muscular power. It usually fed on berries; seldom made an attack on man; but, when attacked it was very dangerous. The bear was hunted for the value of his fur and oil. Bear-hunting was a chief pursuit in the early settlement of the valley, and a successful "bear hunter" was enrolled among the honorable. Bear meat was a great relish. Long since has the American black bid adieu to his favorite haunts in the Hocking Valley, and retired to Western lands, from the face of his human foe, there to pursue in secret his own natural calling.

(c.) *The Wolf.*—The gray wolf (*Canis occidentalis*) was the wolf usually found in the Hocking Valley, though now and then a black wolf was caught. The wolves roved in packs, and when hungry disputed with the early settlers the right of possession of the flocks, and at times challenged man to mortal combat. Their barking howl, breaking upon the ear at noon of night, reminds one of those fabled monsters that are said to guard the entrance to the realms of Pluto.

Wolf hunts were very common and quite necessary. They, too, have been driven from the valley, and in a few more years even their name will not be known in the valley.

(d.) *Deer* (*Cervidæ*).—Deer were, in early times, very numerous in the Hocking Valley. They were hunted for their skins and flesh. Many families lived, principally, on venison, and made deer-hunting their chief occupation. The deer have also retired from the valley. Here and there one may be seen, but they are so scarce as to render their hunting quite unsuccessful. The four kinds of animals formed those classes which were, perhaps, the most noted. While these haunted the valley, hunting formed one of the chief occupations. When they disappeared hunting became more of a sporting business. Other wild animals were numerous, some of which were valued for their furs, such as the beaver, foxes, otters, muskrats, minks; others may be enumerated, as the hares, squirrels, mice, rats, weasles, porcupines, badgers. These animals occupied the valley at the time when the white man first entered it. The smaller animals still continue. Foxes have been very numerous and often destructive on the poultry. The opossums were numerous.

BIRDS OF THE VALLEY.

The Eagle Family (*Aquila*)—deserves the first notice as it is the royal family among birds. The eagles were, in the early settlement of the valley, quite numerous, there being many species. The eagle has always been a noted bird. Its extraordinary powers of vision, the height to which it is able to rise, its love for wild scenery, and its longevity constitute it as a bird of poetic associations. "It was associated with Jupiter in the Roman mythology; its figure on the standards of the Roman legions expressed and animated their confidence in victory." It is the emblem of our standard. The American eagle inspires the American soldier in the day of battle. The species of eagles formerly numerous in the Hocking Valley are: (*a*) The white, or bald-head eagle of America; the chosen emblematic eagle of American States, is also an eme, one of the eagle group; (*b*) The forked-tailed eagle was another species quite common in the early settlement of the valley. On almost any clear day of summer its piercing cry would call your attention. Looking toward the sun you would discover the eagle, with expanded wings immovable, and forked tail circling in a spiral path upward till it disappears in the boundless expanse above. That bird has also forsaken the valley. The bald eagle did much damage in the way of carrying-off pigs, lambs and other small animals. Sometimes infants have been stolen.

The Hawk (*Falconidæ*)—is an "ignoble" bird of prey. This family has always had a full representation in the Hocking Valley. The two most noted species are the (1) "hen hawk," so called from its larger size; and (2) the "chicken hawk," one much smaller. A third species may be added, the "blue hawk." The three species are "ignoble" birds of prey. They are far-seeing, and have always been disputants for a large share of the domestic products of the poultry. Our good and wise law-makers placed the family, for a time, under legal restrictions, but, for some reason, wise, perhaps, have signed for them, a reprieve. This large family is pleased with its treatment and fare, and has concluded to continue its residence in the valley.

The Owl (*Strigidæ*).—This family is the nocturnal section of birds of prey. It was once a very large family in the Hocking Valley, and made the nights hideous with its hootings. The owl family has always been one of poor repute, being a family of "evil omen." It has this bad reputation from gloominess of its haunts, such as old, dilapidated buildings, caverns, and the dark solitudes of the woods; and, especially, from its cry, "hollow and lugubrious," but loud and startling, "heard during the hours of darkness, and often by the lonely wanderer. It is evidently from this cry that the name owl is derived, as well as many of its synonyms in other languages, and of the names appropriated in different countries to particular species, in most of which the sound *oo* or *ow* is predominant, with great variety of accompanying consonants. Many of the owls have also another and very different cry, which has gained for one of them the appellation screech owl, and to which, probably, the Latin name *Strix* and some other names are to be referred." Between the settlers and the owl family there has been a continued struggle as to the right of certain kinds of property, the owl being a noted thief and robber, sleeping in the light of day, but wide awake during the hours of darkness—having such a big eye and so peculiarly constructed, that it can see without light. The owl family still remains in the valley, following its old occupation. The eagle, the hawk and the owl were the principal families of prey; what the eagle and the hawk failed to accomplish in the light, the owl finished in the darkness.

Birds of other families abounded in the valley. Enter the dark valley of the primeval forests in the hot and shady months, and the notes of a great variety of "feathered songsters" always salute the listening ear of the lonely traveler. These families prefer the retired wilderness abode to the cultivated lands of civilization. Other families soon formed an intimacy with the new comers of the valley. As the forests removed and the lands were made productive they came in for their share in payment for their "gabble" and musical entertainments. Of these there was a great variety, such as the buzzard, the raven, the crow, the dove, the lark, the quail, the partridge, the black-bird, blue-bird, the humming-bird, the wild turkey, water-fowls, and a great variety of swallows, martins, American mocking-bird (cat-bird), robin, whip-poor-will, yellow-hammer, woodcock, wood-pecker, and many other families; these continue in the valley, and prefer the haunts of civilization. One other family of birds should not be overlooked; since it outnumbered the sum of all others, viz., the wild pigeons. Flocks of pigeons often in their flight darkened the whole heavens. Their roosts were so crowded and large that they broke down forests. This family have now deserted the valley for homes more retired.

FISHES (PISCES) OF HOCKING VALLEY.

The Hocking River and its tributaries, were abundant in their supply of excellent fish. Some have been caught weighing fifty pounds. They were of many varieties, and of nearly all sizes. Those prized most for food were the pike, weighing from one pound to ten pounds; the black perch, sometimes called bass; white bass; the sucker and salmon. The cat fish, sometimes called "mud cat," is now, by far, the most abundant in the Hocking waters. It grows, sometimes, to a very large size, and affords an excellent supply of choice food for the inhabitants of the water courses. During early spring, fishing is made a pleasing and profitable amusement. To fish with a hook and line, standing in the water up to the middle, was one of the early pioneer spring and summer occupations. Should our waters be supplied with foreign varieties of choice fish, the time may come when Hocking River and its affluents will yield the citizens of the valley a satisfactory income. Fish culture, in point of commercial value, will, perhaps, compare favorably with grain products, provided, however, that the culture is properly guarded.

THE REPTILES OF HOCKING VALLEY.

When first discovered, the valley was full of reptiles. (1) Ophidia, or serpents; (2) Sauria, or lizards; (3) Chelonia, or tortoises. The serpents were of many species: (1) The rattle-snake; (2) Copperhead; (3) The black-snake; (4) The striped snake; and (5) The "racer." These were the most common of the serpent family. The rattle-snake and the copperhead were very poisonous. The rattle-snake always gave warning, and was not, therefore, so dangerous as the copper-head, which accomplished its deadly work from an ambush. The racer was not poisonous; still it was dangerous in its mode of attack, coiling about its victim, and, suddenly, and with great power, crushing the object. There were combats between the rattle-snake and the racer which resulted in the total destruction of the former. The serpents of the poisonous species have become scarce, except in a few localities. Lizards in the Hocking Valley are small, and without any special interest. About the same may be said of the tortoises; some few species are used as food.

The insects of the valley were also numerous, some of which are useful. The wild honey-bee belongs to that class. Many species may be placed in the rank of pests. Our space will not allow further notice.

Before closing our notice of the Fauna of the Hocking Valley, it may be well to notice some ancient animals that once occupied the valley but are now either extinct or have long since retired to other regions.

Among these we may reckon the buffalo, and the mastodon. That both of these species once made Hocking Valley their homes, we have sufficient proof. On some of the points of the spurs, on the east of Sunday Creek, in Trimble Township, Athens County, are buffalo beats—spaces covering several square rods of ground. These are trodden very hard. They were localities where, in hot weather, buffaloes congregated to beat flies. The points of ridges were selected by them as watch towers, to give alarm at the approach of an enemy. What proof, it may be asked, is there that the mastodon ever inhabited the Hocking Valley? About fifty-one years since, the Hocking River, during a high flood, on its east bank, on the farm of William Courtney, one mile above Athens, washed out part of the skeleton of a mastodon. It was in the alluvial bank, about thirteen feet below the surface. Its molar teeth and some parts of the jaws remained; still, exposed to the air they began to slack. They were removed to the museum of the Ohio University, where they remained for many years. From the size of those parts obtained the size of the animal was approximately estimated at about eleven feet high and sixteen feet long. It was deposited in the water, or mud of the river. Whether it died there, or washed there from some other part of the valley, cannot be ascertained. It was not found, however, in the glacial drift. That the buffalo and the mastodon once fed upon the banks of the Hocking River, passed up and down its numerous branches, roamed over its ridges, and stood upon its spurs, cannot be a matter of any doubt.

They had left the valley before the white man entered it; how long before is a matter of conjecture. From the condition of skeletons, the mastodon and the Mound-builders might have been face to face.

But, aside from the ancient denizens of the Hocking Valley, let us view the inhabitants of the valley when first seen by the Caucasian. Not a tree has yet fallen before the ax of the white man. Among the waving branches of the heavy timbered bottoms, and on the stately oaks of the hills, are heard the notes and cries of birds of various plumage, new and strange. The Indian whoop, the panther's cry, the hoarse growl of the bear, the howl of the wolf, mingled with thousands of notes of living organism, fall upon his ear, as from the animated beings of a new world. Is he dreaming? or, does he behold the animated beings of a literal country, like the one left behind him?

Are these numberless organisms indigenous to the soil, like the trees that grow out of it? or, are they the offspring of an eastern ancestry, that, in ages long-passed, found their way over a pathless ocean? Have the human family one center, or many? Do animals follow the same law of unity? These points are unsettled in the minds of many learned men. The animals of the new world had their laws of natural combination corresponding with a new human development, each to move in unison as another great whole in the divine government.

THE FLORA OF THE HOCKING VALLEY.

The flora concerns those trees and plants which are indigenous to the district. We shall, under this term, include the botany of the valley, as it was when first settled by Europeans. A few general remarks will be of use to a proper understanding of what shall follow. The Arctic flora of Europe, Asia and America resemble more closely than that of the equatorial regions. The same holds true of their fauna. This affords an argument in favor of the idea of one floral center. Species in the three grand divisions are not alike. Trees of the same name differ in America from those in Europe and Asia. These variations are mostly the result of climate and soil, and not because of different original centers; the families are more alike than their species. The family name is not changed, but the species differ. The American forests, as in Europe and Asia, consist of pines, oaks, birches and willows; but they are not like those that cover the plains and mountains east of the Atlantic. The same is true of other trees, such as poplars, elms, planes, maples, hazels, and other families of trees, and, also, it holds good with roses, brambles, strawberries, bilberries, etc.; it is true also of grasses, common flowers, and weeds. Each zone, therefore, has its peculiar flora. The change in the species is evidently the result of a change in the soil and climate. The oaks and pines on the mountains of Mexico differ from the Arctic oaks and pines of America. Geological formations vary the features. Look at the white oaks, growing on thin hill land, rich north side hills, southern and western exposures, on rich bottom lands, on lands containing much iron, lime or sand, those that are on wet, cold and sour soils. We conclude, therefore, that the flora of a country varies with its geological formation, temperature, light and heat. We speak of a white oak soil, a walnut soil, buckeye soil, beach soil. Each soil is adapted to its peculiar flora. The seeds being in the soils will not germinate unless the laws of germination are met. This is true of all floral seeds. Put a heavy coating of lime on a field and, without sowing, clover springs up from seed already in the earth. These laws of germination understood, we proceed to investigate the flora of the Hocking Valley.

ITS FORESTS.

No one passing for the first time (1883) through the various sections of the Hocking Valley, noting carefully its cultivated fields; its railways, villages, towns and cities; its coal, salt, and iron establishments, can form any fair picture of Hocking Valley and its tributaries one century since. All its bottom lands were then shaded by a very dense, high, and heavy growth of green, healthy trees, composed of immense sycamore, poplars, black and white walnut, black and white ash, buckeye, beech, soft and rock maple, white, black, red and yellow oak, standing so dense when clothed with foliage, as not to allow the sun's rays to penetrate to the earth; turning bright noon-day into twilight. What immense labor to consume those primeval forests. The hills were covered with a dense growth of oak, hickory, ash; here and there pine, poplar, maple and some few other species of forest trees. The ravines, slopes, and plains were covered with a mixture of the bottom and upland growth. These dense forests have given way to the march of civilization. Over a large portion of the valley there is nothing left to teach the rising generation the majestic beauty of nature's original clothing. What is a cornstock beside a venerable oak, or poplar, or ash, or sycamore? What are our steepled houses beside the beauty and the glory of "God's first temple"?

These forests, so wantonly mutilated and destroyed, have been the necessary servants of the citizens of the valley, by supplying them with fuel, bridge, fencing and building materials, and by satisfying various other wants. There has been, however, a great waste of timber; thousands of acres of choice timber were burned The "log rollings" of early times are sufficient testimony of the truth of the assertion. Could that choice timber have been sawed into lumber and protected it would have supplied the wants of many generations, but where then were their portable saw-mills and the men to work them? Steam itself was yet slumbering.

Relative to the flora of the Hocking Valley something should be said relative to its tree families, their location, growth, and particular habits. Many families, each consisting of several members or species of trees, formed the vast wilderness of the Hocking Valley. Sometimes miles were occupied by the members of a single family, such as the oak family; in other localities the family of hickories held almost exclusive possession; in another poplar; beech, another, and so on through the catalogue of families, each family occupying the land that best suited it, forming all over the valley "little squatter" sovereignties. Other localities were covered with family mixtures. Not that they amalgamated, but that they were not exclusive in their habits; they grew up quietly in the same beautiful grove. Such habits do not come by chance; they must spring from philosophical causes. Why such habits among the more noble families of the floral kingdom? Be it true or false, we venture an explanation. Seeds, the parentage of vegetation, were the result of an original creation. Whether they were created in one place and distributed or were formed where they afterward germinated, we do not say. The seeds, through some agency by the waters of the flood, by birds, or by some other means, entered the soils in every quarter of the globe, waiting there for favorable conditions of germination, each variety or family varying in its conditions. They may have been placed there in the original creation. The ground is full of seeds not sown by the hand of man; how long sown there is not known. Seeds retain their vitality many centuries; instances are given which would show that some varieties (grains of wheat about Egyptian mummies) have held their vitality forty centuries. Corn in the tombs of the Incas has vegetated. "After the great fire of London, in 1666, plants not previously common sprang up abundantly on the waste ground; certain plants previously unknown there are sure to appear after a fire in the American forests, in deep trenching of land, or turning up of the soil, by railway or other operations, producing a crop of some kind of plants unknown or rare in the locality." The seeds then that have produced these families may have been in their localities ages before exposed to their various conditions of germination. The seed of the oak might germinate in one place; those of the beech in another; of the poplar in another, each variety of seed germinating in that locality best adapted to its growth. Thus we call one soil a beech soil, another oak, another walnut, because best adapted to that peculiar growth. These tree preferences and habits are well understood, and followed in the purchase of lands.

Each geological formation has its distinct flora. It is not our purpose to discuss fossil botany, but simply to give some account of what might be the origin of the Hocking Valley forests. These forests sprang up among the debris of the lower coal measure, yet they are infants in age compared with the duration of those measures. To the cretaceous formation many of the genera now living are said to belong. "They formed the forests of that period, and the fossil remains show that their appearance was much the same as now. Among the living genera represented were the oak, poplar, plane, willow, beech, sassafras, magnolia, fig, maple, walnut, tulip tree, etc." That the seeds were long in their various localities, and were not therefore brought from the Old World, will appear when we learn that many are natives of America, such as maize (Indian corn) and the potato.

The wild flowers of the Hocking Valley were exceedingly numerous and of many varieties. We have no data by which any botanical description can be given, neither will our limited space permit such a scientific notice. We simply describe it as the first settlers saw it. Wherever the sun was permitted to warm the earth, seeds of unknown plants germinating sprang up in profusion. The deep soils of the river and creek bottoms soon brought them into bloom. One of nature's flower gardens would extend many miles, showing every size, shape and shade of color.

Such a profusion and co-mingling of odors and tints can exist only in the gardens of nature's planting. You might walk seventy miles and still be surrounded with this wild Eden bloom. The rose, the pink, the violet, the tulip and the lilies! Who could count the numbers or tell their varieties? We have floral exhibitions of our times, but they would not favorably compare with one of Nature's exhibitions in the Hocking Valley of those early days. Over hills, up ravines, along the slopes, on the plains, in the valleys, over a space of 2,000 square miles, from April till September, was this beautiful flower garden on exhibition. How true to nature are these lines:

"Full many a flower is born to blush unseen,
And waste its sweetness on the desert air."

METEOROLOGY OF THE HOCKING VALLEY.

Meteorology discusses atmospheric phenomena. We shall confine our remarks to those phenomena that relate to weather and climate. This department of nature has, so far, refused to submit to any regular system of well-defined laws. At least it has been very reticent before the most distinguished savants.

The element that we breathe, and in which we live and move and have our being, is too intimately associated with our health and happiness to allow us not to be familiar with its nature and habits. Let us look into the character of this constant companion. Pure atmosphere is the element of life. Impure air is a death angel. Whatever, then, affects its purity or condition as a breathing element, or as a faithful servant and companion, should be made familiar. The atmosphere is the home of those meteors that so much affect the human family, viz.: Dew, clouds, fog, rain, hail, frost, lightning, and storms of wind, rain, hail and snow. Its temperature and weight are constantly varying. Whatever changes its weight, its temperature, its moisture or its motion or direction has a direct bearing on our health and our enjoyment. We speak, also, of its electricity. In every light, therefore, atmospheric changes affect our happiness more sensibly than any other natural department. All nations are watching its changes, that, if possible, they may discover the laws which govern its greatest meteor storms, how to forecast storms, and, consequently, to avoid their terrible effects. If its tornadoes, or cyclones could be seen twenty-four hours in advance, much of their damages could be avoided. To prevent rains when too abundant, or to cause showers in times of drought, would be a great achievement. We hold that the atmosphere is like water, under the control of specific laws; that these laws will finally be known, and meteorology will be brought under the theorems and problems of all true sciences. This, however, will not be accomplished until the influence of disturbing causes are distinctly ascertained. Then storms will be accurately predicted and their forces ascertained. The 2,000 daily observations taken in all parts of the world is bringing about an important era in the history of meteorology. All that aid in that work are public benefactors.

Every river system has its own meteorological peculiarities. The course of the river and its branches, and the nature of its soils, determine the character of its atmosphere. These, united with temperature and the rapid or tardy flow of the streams—all these combined—make its peculiar atmospheric features, The atmosphere of the Mississippi is subjected to two currents of air, between which there exists a continuous struggle; a cool, dry wind from the north and northwest, and a sultry wind, charged with vapor, from the south and southwest. Were it not for the struggle for the ascendency between these opposing winds the Mississippi Valley would long since have been a desert waste. The reason of this will appear when a third atmospheric current is traced.

A west wind, saturated with vapor, starts from the Pacific, eastward, direct for the Mississippi Valley, in the same latitude. Passing over the Coast Range, with the fall of temperature its capacity to hold moisture decreases. There it parts with a portion of its vapor. It does not recover its full capacity when it meets with its second mountain range (the Nevada), where it makes its second deposit, this range being higher than the coast range. Having passed the third range (the Rocky Mountains) it descends the eastern slope a dry wind. Crossing a vast extent of country with a higher temperature it has no moisture to precipitate, it reaches us a dry west wind. Should there be no north and south winds we should have no rain. Two currents, one cool, the other warm and saturated with vapor, make a general rain fall—what we call "steady rains." Summer showers are produced by the law of condensation, but in another way; a warm, saturated current moving upward meets a cold stratum of air, part of its vapor being condensed is precipitated in the form of rain or hail. The law is the same in each, but they differ in mode and direction; the one is horizontal, the other vertical. With this view before us let us examine the lay and peculiar features of the Hocking Valley. Its course is northwest and southeast, the direction of the two contesting currents of air—the line of advance and retreat of the contending elements. The storm belt is where the contending winds meet. If the wind is southeast the storm is further north; if south, then we have a northwest wind. Our various winds have the following characteristics in Hocking Valley: A south wind, east wind, or southeast wind in the spring, fall and winter bring a storm, because they being warmer and saturated with vapor meet a cold wind which precipitates a portion of its moisture, and will continue to storm till they are driven southward, and the wind, in common language, shifts to the north, northwest. The true expression is, the colder or opposite wind prevails and has driven the warmer wind and, consequently, the storm belt, to the south. The rains in the valley are local, often covering less than a mile square. Severe and protracted droughts are seldom known in the Hocking Valley. The reasons are obvious: The valley has so many hills and ridges that they serve to introduce heated rising currents of moist air; these rising currents carrying their vapor with them it is condensed and falls in rain. Hence it is said that turning up so as to show the under surfaces of the growing leaves is a sign of rain. It shows the existence of upward currents of air, which indicate rain. A west wind is usually a dry wind for reasons already given. East winds, those due east, bring rain only when they are heavily charged with vapor—for meeting a cool, dry west wind, much of its vapor will be absorbed.

The winds of the Hocking Valley are very much broken, owing to so many breaks. Every hill is a wind-break. In the North Fairfield division the winds are more uniform, the country being level. The north and west winds have no obstruction, but in every other section the hills, spurs and ridges " chop " the winds. Among the hills it is difficult to determine the general course of winds, except by the clouds. Within one mile square the wind at different points blows at the same time from every quarter, it meeting with obstructions. Four persons meeting after a heavy blow, might thus speak: A.—We had a severe north wind this morning. B.—No, sir; it was a west wind. C.—You are both mistaken; it was an east wind. D.—You must all have been dreaming, for I was on a hill and know that it came from the south. They were all correct, for (chameleon like) it had a course for each. In this manner the valley in a hot summer's day, when upward currents are forming, is full of eddies or local whirlwinds. The winds of the valley are, therefore, peculiar.

Its climate, for the same reasons, is peculiar also. It has every kind of exposure. On the same farm there are summer gardens and winter gardens, summer fields and winter fields in one locality, owing to the exposures being nearly a month earlier than another. This climatic variety gives Hocking Valley an advantage in fruit culture, since there is scarcely ever a season in which the fruits of all its localities are destroyed.

From its conformation it has its share of fogs and clouds, rains, snows and storms. The valley, at times, has had its tornadoes, yet they have been quite limited, since all the hills combining soon put an end to their devastations. The evaporation of the valley is also very unequal. The whole structure of the valley tends to destroy atmospheric equilibrium. Storms must be the result.

One question deserves further notice : Has the valley civilization changed or modified its meteorological phenomena? What atmospheric changes have resulted from clearing, draining and cultivating the soil, and erecting villages, towns and cities, and establishing manufactories, constructing railways and other improvements?

The writer of this article has kept a weather journal for about fifty years. Much of that time he has been a citizen of the Hocking Valley. He speaks, therefore, from positive knowledge when saying: The seasons are not now what they were one half a century ago. The four seasons have been changed, not that they are opposite in character, but that there has been many atmospheric changes and modifications.

The valley evaporation has been made over and vastly augmented. The letting of the sun's rays, unobstructed by dense forests, falling upon the earth has greatly increased evaporation. Streams that once flowed during the entire summer are dry, only after showers. This vapor, floating in the atmosphere, must change its density and tend to produce local rains.

The cultivated fields are great absorbents, so that the size of the streams, except in heavy rain-falls, is reduced. Much of the land since the removal of its forests lies in its undress. It suffers the extremes of heat and cold, sowing in its bosom the seeds of consumption. This epidemic tendency is communicated to the atmosphere, robbing it of its freshness and vitality. We breathe a cultivated air, impregnated with a thousand malarial impurities.

The improvements of the valley have changed its atmospheric phenomena. Prof. J. P. Espy, the "storm king," used to say: "Give me fuel enough and I can break up any drought." A great upward current thus produced would carry with it a mass of vapor to be condensed and fall in rain. An upward current must be produced to have rain-fall in the summer. It is said that it rains every day in and around London; so many fires in such a small space produce upward rain currents. These disturbing elements are increasing in Hocking Valley, and their results are apparent. Any cause that tends to break up the atmospheric equilibrium introduces a storm element. Man has, therefore, introduced meteorological changes. These disturbing causes will increase as the valley fills up with a working, enterprising population. A coal district is subject to a greater flow of water, and, therefore, affects the atmosphere. Human industry so much changes the meteorological phenomena that it is difficult to predict accurately coming changes of weather. Every person should learn the names and peculiar characteristics of the clouds, winds and all such meteorological phenomena as affect either his health, character or business.

SUMMARY.

The natural history of the Hocking Valley has been briefly outlined. It now remains to aggregate its principal features and sketch its future.

That section of Ohio known as the Hocking Valley was once an irregular block of mineral deposits, about eighty miles long by thirty miles wide, and 1,200 feet deep, resting horizontally on the Waverly group, composed of about six geological formations, viz.: Sandstones, shales, limestones, fire-clay, coal and iron ore; consisting of nearly 100 layers or strata resting upon each other horizontally, as they were deposited from the primeval ocean, and, at that time, under its waters. Its upper surface was smooth, horizontal, and level. That plain was some feet above the highest point of the eastern water-shed, the hills being lowered by ages of erosion. When these strata were finished to the smooth surface of the last and highest stratum, a great geological change took place. The Cincinnati Arch and the Allegheny Mountains arose out of the bosom of the waters, carrying up with them the strata intervening to an elevation above the sea level, and inclining so as to form the longitudinal trough, the bottom of which is now occupied by the waters of the beautiful Ohio. Since that noted upheaval which extended over thousands of miles, there was no further submergence of the Hocking Valley section. The work of the valley formation by erosion then commenced. The Ohio River flowing in a channel 100 feet lower than its present channel, made its tributaries and sub-tributaries erode very rapidly. Hocking River then ran in a channel about 100 feet below its present bed. All its tributaries near their mouths were 100 feet lower than now. This made their flow much more rapid, and the growing process was very active. Every flood carried out of the tributary valleys an immense amount of eroded debris. Thus was the Hocking Valley formed and fashioned into its present size and shape. One other modification of the depth and face of the chief valley deserves notice. A glacial epoch followed with a temperature of Greenland in the Hocking Valley and over the continent. Immense masses of ice were formed, binding up in their glacial fetters millions of tons of sand, gravel and boulders. This was followed by a sinking, so far as to detach icebergs, which, floating south, southeast, by melting, deposited their drift, boulders, clay and gravel. All the Western and Northwestern Ohio was leveled up with this drift. A large amount was deposited along the Hocking Valley, through which the river has cut its modern channel.

Such is a brief sketch of the formation and shaping of the present Hocking Valley. Had it not been for the upheaval there would still have been a sea to occupy its present site; there could have been no erosion; and without erosion, the geological and stratigraphical formation of the valley would never have been known. This great upheaval gave birth to the valley, with all its living organisms. It was evidently elevated above the ocean waters and made and shaped by erosion for some wise purposes. The immense mineral deposits of the Hocking Valley, exposed by the upheaval and erosion, are sufficiently indicative of the intention of its Creator.

The topography of the Hocking Valley is peculiarly varied. It would be a difficult task even to count its ridges, spurs, hills, mounds, gulches, ravines, slopes, valleys and plains; its fountains, rills, rivulets or creeks; and its various bodies of water. Such a pleasing variety never tires the eye. But, to the geologist preparing to benefit mankind by his untiring researches, the Hocking Valley is a theater of unusual interest. Its mineral formations are remarkably rich and exceedingly varied. Of these, its early inhabitants knew but little. There are no remains of any structures in Hocking Valley that indicate any extended use of its sandstones, limestones, shales, fire-clay, coal or iron ores. Flint supplied the place, principally, of iron; cones of earth, that of marble monuments. In the midst of untold mineral wealth, they pursued the chase, and, residing in forests, they subsisted on nature's most simple fare.

Its fauna and flora have changed, and we now behold a valley fast filling up with a population capable of appreciating and utilizing the resources treasured for their use by natures' architect.

CONCLUSION—THE FUTURE OF THE HOCKING VALLEY.

Who knows its future? "Secret things belong to the Lord our God." We forecast only as he furnishes the data and ability. Three terms given, a fourth readily follows. Hocking Valley's future depends upon its mineral resources, the capital to develop and the will; their actual development necessarily follows as the fourth term. In this term is the future of the Hocking Valley. Its future, therefore, can be readily ascertained.

ITS MINERAL RESOURCES.

We shall name no mineral that is not found in the valley, and as herein described. We do not say that each one extends over the entire valley. This would not be true. What we describe is in the valley, and is equal in quantity and quality to our estimates. This is all that any one should require. We would further say that our estimates cover a compact territory of about 600 square miles. We have selected a part of this territory as the basis of our estimates, with which we are quite familiar, Sunday Creek Valley, a mean between the out-crops and deep shafting. What, then, are the mineral resources of the Hocking Valley?

1. *Petroleum.*—The Hocking Valley has its fountains of petroleum. On some of its eastern tributaries, such as Federal Creek and Sunday Creek, thousands of barrels have been obtained. How extensive are its fountains, if properly tested, we cannot say. There is money in it, if diligently worked.

2. *Salt.*—The brine of Hocking Valley comes from the Upper Waverly. It is from 570 feet to 1,000 feet below the surface. It has produced a large amount of salt. Should the brine be drawn up by the power that elevates the coal, and evaporated by the slack of the shaft seam, it could be manufactured with profit. We reckon salt as one of the mineral resources of the valley.

3. *Freestone.*—Building stone is in great abundance. In Fairfield and Hocking counties are the Waverly sandstone. Some of the strata are of excellent quality. In Perry and Athens counties we have the heavy sandstone formations of the coal measures. They are in some localities fifty feet thick, fine grained and sharp, white and pure—a glass-making rock. We have districts where the flag-stone is well developed. The quarries consist of many layers, varying from one inch to six inches thick, sound, and with surfaces as level and smooth as the sawed flag of the Euclid Avenue, Cleveland. A vast amount can be obtained.

4. *Fire-clay.*—This deposit is very abundant in the valley, and much of it is said to be of superior quality. It will, in time, add much to the mineral wealth of Hocking Valley. Three minerals remain, which, from their joint use, should stand as a whole

relatively: iron ore and limestone, and coal employed in their reduction. Profitable iron-making requires that these three minerals should be found in the same localities. This is true of the Hocking Valley.

5. *Limestone.*—Three veins of limestone extend over the most of Hocking Valley, but in the Federal and East Sunday creek hills, that limestone has its heaviest developments. The divide between those two streams is formed principally of limestone of an excellent quality, for quick lime, and for a flux. It may be truly said that the limestone is ample for all its practical uses. Furnaces erected on Federal Creek or on Sunday Creek will have limestone within easy range.

6. *Iron Ore.*—Deposits of iron ore can be found in nearly all sections of the valley, especially in the coal measures. One vein of coal is the floor of an iron ore seam. They occupy different horizons of the same territory. In Sunday Creek Valley we have examined thirteen horizons of iron ore within a vertical space of 400 feet. These veins vary from six inches to five feet. Three veins are, severally, two and a half feet, four feet and five feet thick. One vein, on analysis, yields thirty-three per cent. of pure iron; another, fifty-five per cent., and a third, sixty per cent. These seams extend for miles, and crop out in the opposite slopes of the same hills. Two men of great experience in iron-making, made the following remarks: One from the Cambria Iron Works said: "There is iron ore enough; the per cent. is fair." The one from Mahoning Valley said: "One bushel of the coal should not be taken out of the valley, for it will all be wanted in smelting its ores. Neither of these practical iron masters had seen all the horizons. Such declarations from practical men must have meaning.

7. *Coal.*—We have reserved this mineral to the last, because it is first in value, and well deserves the name of "King of minerals." It is the motive power—the motor of the world's machinery, for its heat generates the steam that moves the world; the treasured sunlight of the carboniferous age; the world's renovator; the fuel for man in his high intellectual life. The value of coal is measured by the power generated in its combustion.

"The power developed in the combustion of a pound of coal is reckoned by engineers as equal to 1,500,000 foot-pounds. The power exerted by a man of ordinary strength during a day of labor is about the same, so that a pound of coal may be regarded as equivalent to a day's labor of a man. Hence, 300 pounds will represent the labor of a man for a year." It has been estimated that 20,000,000 tons of the annual coal product of Great Britain (100,000,000 tons the whole product) is devoted to the development of motive power, and that is equivalent to the labor of 133,000,000 of men.

"These men, in this calculation, are considered as exerting merely brute force,' but they all may be regarded as producers only, and not consumers, the profit on the balance of her coal product (80,000,000 tons) fully covering all expenses, we are safe in estimating the contribution made to the wealth of Great Britain, by her annual coal product, as equivalent (equal) to that of 133,000,000 skilled operatives laboring for her enrichment."—*J. S. Newberry, Chief Geologist of Ohio.*

Making this calculation the basis of our estimates, we will examine the coal treasured up on 600 square miles of the Hocking Valley. Prof. E. B. Andrews estimates the coal of that district, situated on the waters of Monday Creek and Sunday Creek, to average eight feet thick. On 600 square miles, 640 acres to the square mile, would give $600 \times 640 = 384,000$ acres. But a vein of coal of eight feet thick yields about 10,000 tons of coal to the acre, or $384,000 \times 10,000 = 3,840,000,000$ tons. This is thirty-eight and two-fifths times larger than the annual coal product of Great Britain. It would require 133,000,000 men thirty-eight and two-fifths years to produce the same motive power, which would be equal to that of 133,000,000 skilled operatives laboring thirty-eight and two-fifths years for the enrichment of the Hocking Valley. This "Nelsonville" coal vein has its greatest development on Sunday Creek and Monday Creek. Still, more territory is required to make the 600 square miles. Allowing one half of this productive value to exist in its ore veins, the productive value of these two minerals is immense. To these we may add the productive value of the other five and we have an amount truly overwhelming. What a vast amount of labor to utilize the minerals of the Hocking Valley! it would make a Birmingham of every coal valley for centuries. Capitalists begin to see these inevitable results, and are investing their money in these mineral lands. The future, therefore, of the Hocking Valley, as we forecast it, is one of a vast working population, immense labor, and of vast pecuniary resources.

THE FUTURE POPULATION OF THE HOCKING VALLEY,

based upon its coal, its iron ores and its limestone. We assume, what can be readily established, that Hocking Valley has, within itself, all the materials which are necessary to utilize all of its own mineral products, and, consequently, that the entire labor can be more economically done in the valley than anywhere out of it. That being true, we conclude that work, whether by men or machinery, or by both, will be accomplished in the valley. How much work, then, must be done in the Hocking Valley, to utilize its entire mineral deposits, including its petroleum, salt, fire-clay, freestone, limestone, iron ores and stone-coal? We shall base our calculations on the products of three minerals—limestone, iron ore and coal, limestone being necessary as a flux.

If all the coal and limestone (according to the views of a distinguished iron master) will be wanted to reduce the iron ores deposited in that valley where are the heaviest seams of coal and limestone (Sunday Creek Valley), it is safe to say that this will be true of the entire Hocking Valley.

What a vast amount of labor will be required to mine and utilize these three minerals? But the miners and those engaged in placing minerals where they are to be used do not constitute over one fifth of the population.

We know of one district in the Hocking Valley which is about ten miles square, where it would require 2,500 persons, including miners, their families, and necessary help, to mine and remove and utilize each square mile of the minerals in 100 years. Such a population would make a city of the hundred square miles.

We do not propose the above-named districts as a sample for the entire valley, for there are districts in the valley much larger than the one named that are without coal, yet the coal measures of the valley form so much of its surface that we are justified in saying it will have a population far beyond any other district of equal size in the State.

Its Institutions.—There can be no special reasons why its institutions should not occupy a position equally advanced. Mining communities, it is true, have not been celebrated for their love of science or for their elevated morals. We are considering what might be, not what is, or has been. Miners have been degraded in the old, aristocratic countries. Having no means to rise in society, they have formed habits corresponding to their degraded position. Coming to a land of freedom, they, having brought their habits with them, have often become still more debased, giving a bad reputation to the entire business. This state of morals will pass away as the rising generation becomes educated and moral. If miners had no idle hours, there would soon be no drinking, and mining communities would soon occupy an elevated position in society. Hasten that happy day.

CHAPTER V.

STATISTICS OF THE HOCKING VALLEY, BESIDES RAILROADS AND CANALS, SENATORS AND REPRESENTATIVES.

LANDS AND VALUATION—COUNTY BUILDINGS AND VALUATION—MILES OF RAILWAY—AREA OF VALLEY—POPULATION AND WHEAT GROWING—CITIES AND VILLAGES, AND POPULATION—BOUNDARY OF THE MINERAL FIELD—COAL PRODUCTION—HOCKING VALLEY—STATE SENATORS OF THE HOCKING VALLEY AND REPRESENTATIVES—FROM ORGANIZATION TO DATE—RAILROAD HISTORY—MARIETTA & CINCINNATI—COLUMBUS, HOCKING VALLEY & TOLEDO—OHIO CENTRAL—RIVER DIVISION OF THE C., H. V. & T.—THANKS TO CHAS. M. WALKER—MEDICAL SOCIETY.

Condition of lands in the Hocking Valley by counties in 1880:

	Cultivated, No. of acres.	Pasture, No. of acres.	Wood, No. acres	Lying waste, No. acres.	Total No. acres
Athens........	50,801	109,308	62,291	4,473	236,670
Hocking.......	46,119	82,573	58,896	22,509	210,097
Vinton........	39,759	68,531	53,214	17,464	182,448

Total value of lands and buildings in the Hocking Valley, as returned by the State Boards of Equalization in the years 1846, 1853, 1859, 1870 and 1880:

	1846.	1853.	1859.	1870.	1880.
Athens..................	$1,454,592	$2,293,952	$2,813,426	$4,308,282	$4,380,958
Hocking....	910,188	1,707 923	1,992,413	3,125,017	3,152,475
Vinton..................	Not for'd	1,484,842	1,801,030	2,235,663	2,175,563

Total number and value of county buildings existing in the Hocking Valley in 1880:

	No.	Value.
Athens...	4	$63,000
Hocking	3	60,000
Vinton..	4	30,000

Mileage of railway in the Hocking Valley in 1880, by counties:

	1880.
Athens..	90.79
Hocking...	61.59
Vinton..	72.32

AREA OF THE HOCKING VALLEY.

Athens County, 430 square miles; Hocking County, 470 square miles; Vinton County, 400 square miles.

The area of the State is 40,760 square miles. The population of the State, 3,198,062, being the third State in the Union in that regard.

RELATIVE POSITION.

The relative position of the three counties in their assessed wealth as passed upon by the Board of Equalization in 1881, was: Athens County, $5,267,770; Hocking County, $3,661,695; Vinton, $2,436,106.

Table showing population of HOCKING VALLEY from 1810 to 1880 by counties.

	1810	1820	1830	1840	1850	1860	1870	1880
Athens	2,791	3,338	9,787	19,109	18,215	21,364	23,768	28,411
Hocking		2,130	4,008	9,741	14,119	17,057	17,925	21,126
Vinton						9,353	13,631	15,027	17,223

Amount of wheat sown in the HOCKING VALLEY and average grown per acre by counties:

	1871 ACRES	AV.	1873 ACRES	AV.	1875 ACRES	AV.	1877 ACRES	AV.	1880 ACRES	AV.
Athens	15,535	10.48	15,280	9.07	16,458	4.60	14,438	8.45	19,862	11.8
Hocking	14,281	7.31	12,343	8.89	14,124	2.74	9,669	8.26	15,847	10.6
Vinton	7,663	6.14	6,472	7.55	7,419	3.78	5,959	8.19	11,050	9.2

Cities, towns and villages in the HOCKING VALLEY by counties. Population of 1880.

ATHENS COUNTY.		HOCKING COUNTY.		VINTON COUNTY.	
Nelsonville	3,095	Logan	2,666	Hamden	520
Athens	2,457	Bloomingville	165	McArthur	900
Albany	469	Ewing	63	Wilkesville	309
Coolville	323	Falls Gore	445	Dundas	64
Amesville	159	Gibesonville	72	New Mt. Pleasant	44
Buchtel	417	Ilesborough	58		
Chauncey	185	Laurelville	165		
Doanville	136	Mount Pleasant	76		
Floodwood	159	New Cadiz	63		
Hebbardville	92	South Perry	182		
Hockingport	191				
Marshfield	191				
Mineral City	100				
Pleasanton	107				
Trimble	121				
Millfield	105				

BOUNDARIES OF THE COAL FIELD.

The coal basin in Ohio is bounded on the west by a continuous but irregular line running from the Ohio River in Scioto County, to the Pennsylvania line near Sharon, within a line running from that place to Ravenna, Akron, Wooster, Dover, Brownsville, Logan and Hanging Rock. The general course is southwesterly from the northern boundary of Mahoning County to the interior of Licking County, with the exception of two well-defined narrow spurs extending into Geauga and Medina counties. From the southern part of Licking County it passes near the line between Fairfield and Perry counties, with a deep indentation at the Hocking River Valley, extending to the west line of Athens County; thence westward and southwest to include the southeast part of Hocking County, three fourths of Vinton, nearly all of Jackson, and the eastern part of Scioto County.

IRON SMELTING COALS.

Below is the analysis of the best iron-making coals in the State, taken from the records of the State Chemist, Prof. Wormley:

	NELSONVILLE MINES.	STRAITSVILLE MINES.	SUNDAY CREEK MINES.	LOST RUN HOCKING CO. MINES.
Specific Gravity	1.285	1.291	1.287	1.290
Water	6.20	7.90	5.85	6.80
Volatile Matter	31.30	34.63	35.21	36.16
Fixed Carbon	59.80	54.29	53.62	54.99
Ash	2.70	3.18	5.32	2.05
Total	100.00	100.00	100.00	100.00
Sulphur	0.97	0.98	0.51	1.07
Color of Ashes	Gray	Dull White	Fawn.	Light Fawn

Production of coal from the HOCKING VALLEY since 1870 by counties, given in bushels

	1870	1872	1874	1876	1878	1880
Athens	3,278,500	6,419,462	11,218,156	8,057,000	4,169,614	14,727,625
Hocking	1,889,000	2,251,300	1,290,000	1,500,000	5,203,083	4,421,300
Vinton	166,500	1,075,650	1,143,200	894,150	1,217,115	1,547,700

HOCKING CANAL.

This was the first public improvement which opened up the resources of the Hocking Valley. The short lateral canal, or, as it was then called, the "Side Cut," proved of so much value that the Board of Public Works concluded to purchase it for the State and extend it down the Hocking Valley. This information gave intense joy to the people, and in March, 1838, the news was corroborated by an Act passed by the Legislature, authorizing the then Canal Commissioners to purchase the "Side Cut." This was effected Dec. 22, 1838, and the canal purchased for the sum of $61,241.04. The Hocking Valley Canal, which had been projected in 1836, and a portion put under contract, being some sixteen and one-half miles from Lancaster to Bowner's lock in July, 1837, was now rapidly pushed forward, and the work completed as per contract in 1839. A further contract was also let the same year, October, 1837, to build from Bowner's lock to Nelsonville, a further distance of sixteen and one-half miles, the same to be completed within two years. This last, however, was not finished until 1840. In September of this latter year it was opened for business, and the first canal boat, loaded with coal, came out of the Hocking, and the canal was a veritable fact. The boat and its load was a great curiosity to the people along the line and in the upper valley of the Hocking. There were but few of them at that time who knew much about stone coal. Early in 1841 the canal had reached Monday Creek, and later in the same year to Athens. Boats then commenced running the entire length of the canal, from Carroll to Athens, some sixty miles. The canal has thirty-one locks, eight dams, thirty-four culverts, and one aqueduct, with a span of eighty feet.

The total cost of construction was $947,670.25.

At this time the canal from Nelsonville to Athens had been abandoned.

STATE SENATORS FROM THE HOCKING VALLEY.

ATHENS COUNTY.

Washington, Gallia, Muskingum and Athens Counties—1805-'6, Joseph Buell and Hallem Hempsted; 1806-'7, Hallem Hempsted and Leonard Jewett; 1807-'8, Leonard Jewett and John Sharp. Washington and Athens Counties—1808-'9, John Sharp; 1809-'11, Leonard Jewett; 1811-'14, Wm. Woodbridge; 1814-'15,

Wm. Woodbridge (resigned, Wm. R. Putnam, successor); 1815-'17, John Sharp; 1817-'21, Sardina Stone. Washington, Morgan and Athens Counties—1821-'23, Sardina Stone; 1823-'24, Ephraim Cutler. Washington and Athens—1824-'25, Ephraim Cutler; 1825-'27, Ebenezer Currier; 1827-'28, Wm. R. Putnam. Washington, Athens and Hocking—1828-'29, Wm. R. Putnam; 1829-'31, Calvary Morris; 1831-'33, Arius Nye. Washington, Gallia, Meigs, Hocking and Athens—1833-'35, Calvary Morris; 1835-'36, Andrew Donnally. Meigs, Gallia, Lawrence and Athens—1836-'37, Andrew Donnally; 1837-'39, James Rogers; 1839-'41, Simeon Nash. Meigs and Athens—1841-'45, Abraham Van Vorhes; 1845-'47, John Welch; 1847-'49, Horace S. Horton. Jackson, Gallia, Meigs and Athens—1849-'51, Horace S. Horton.

NEW CONSTITUTION.

Hocking, Fairfield and Athens, 9th District—1852-'56, Lot L. Smith; 1856-'58, John T. Brazee; 1858-'62, Newton Schleich; 1862-'64, Alfred McVeigh; 1864-'66, John M. Connell; 1866-'70, Wm. R. Golden; 1870-'74, Michael A. Dougherty; 1874-'78, Robert E. Reese; 1878-'82, B. W. Carlisle.

HOCKING COUNTY.

Pickaway and Hocking Counties—1821-'23, John Barr; 1823-'25, David Shelby; 1825-'27, John Barr; 1827-'28, Joseph Olds; 1828-'36, In Athens District. Fairfield and Hocking—1836-'40, Samuel Spangler. Jackson, Pike, Ross and Hocking—1840-'41, John Hough; 1841-'43, Allan Latham; 1843-'45, John Crouse, Jr. Ross and Hocking—1845-'47, John Maderra; 1847-'49, Wesley Claypool. Fairfield, Perry and Hocking—1849-'50, Henry C. Whitman; 1850-'51, Andrew Faust.

NEW CONSTITUTION.

1852 to 1883, in Ninth District, composed of Athens, Fairfield and Hocking counties; names will be found in Athens list.

VINTON COUNTY.

Lawrence, Gallia, Meigs and Vinton Counties, Eighth District—1852-'54, Alonzo Cushing; 1854-'56, Lewis Anderson; 1856-'58, Chauncey G. Hawley; 1858-'60, Patrick Murdock; 1860-'62, T.

R. Stanley; 1862–'66, Henry S. Neil; 1866–'68, Joseph Bradbury; 1868–'70, Homer C. Jones; 1870–'72, H. C. Jones and T. C. Welch; 1872–'74, Wm. Nash; 1874–'78, J. R. Filson; 1878–'80, Lindsey Kelly; 1880–'82, L. Kelly and W. C. Cline.

REPRESENTATIVES IN STATE LEGISLATURE FROM THE HOCKING VALLEY.

ATHENS COUNTY.

Athens, Washington, Gallia and Muskingum Counties—1805–'6, Elijah Hatch; 1806–'7, Lewis Cass, Levi Barber and Wm. A. Puthoff; 1807–'8, John P. Bureau, James Palmer and John Matthews. Athens and Washington Counties—1808–'9, William Woodbridge and Leonard Jewett; 1809–'10, Wm. R. Putnam and Simeon Pool; 1810–'11, Wm. R. Putnam and Samuel P. Hildreth; 1811–'12, Samuel P. Hildreth and Jehiel Gregory; 1812–'13, Jehiel Gregory and Sardina Stone; 1813–'14, Sardina Stone and Elijah Hatch; 1814–'15, Jehiel Gregory and John Sharp; 1815–'16, Henry Jolly and Robert Linzie; 1816–'17, Sardina Stone and Robert Linzie; 1817–'18, Nathaniel Hamilton and Sylvanus Ames; 1818–'19, Sylvanus Ames and Joseph Barker; 1819–'20, Ephraim Cutler and Elijah Hatch. Athens County—1820–'23, Elijah Hatch; 1823–'24, Ezra Hull; 1824–'25, Edmund Dorr; 1825–'27, Robert Linzie; 1827–'28, Calvary Morris. Athens and Hocking Counties—1828–'29, Calvary Morris; 1829–'30, John Gilmore; 1830–'31, Andrew Crockett; 1831–'33, Ebenezer Currier; 1833–'34, Isaac Lottridge and Andrew Crockett; 1834–'35, Elijah Hatch; 1835–'36, Calvary Morris. Athens and Meigs Counties—1836–'38, David Jones; 1838–'40, Andrew Donnally; 1840–'41, A. Van Vorhes; 1841–'42, J. B. Ackley and Stephen Titus; 1842–'43, J. B. Ackley; 1843–'45, Columbia Downing; 1845–'46, Thomas Irwin; 1846–'47, Horace S. Horton; 1847–'48, Robert G. McLean; 1848–'50, Joseph K. Will, 1850–'52, N. H. Van Vorhes.

NEW CONSTITUTION.

Athens County—1852–'54, N. H. Van Vorhes; 1854–'56, Samuel B. Pruden; 1856–'60, N. H. Van Vorhes; 1860–'62, A. B. Monahan ; 1862–'64, J. W. Bayard ; 1864–'70, Wm. P. Johnson; 1870–'74, N. H. Van Vorhes ; 1874–'78, C. H. Grosvenor ; 1878–'80, Charles Townsend ; 1880–'82, Charles Townsend, elected Secretary of State, C. L. Kurtz, successor; 1882–'84, C. L. Kurtz.

HOCKING COUNTY.

Hocking and Pickaway Counties—1820-'21, John Barr, Samuel Lybrand; 1821-'22, Caleb Atwater, Valentine Keffer; 1822-'24, Samuel Lybrand, Valentine Keffer; 1824-'26, Joseph Olds, Jacob Lindsey; 1826-'27, Jacob Lindsey and Guy W. Doan; 1827-'28, Francis S. Muhlenburg, Valentine Keffer. Hocking and Athens —1828-'29, Calvary Morris; 1829-'30, John Gilmour; 1830-'31, Andrew Crockett; 1831-'33, Ebenezer Currier; 1833-'34, Isaac B. Lottridge, Andrew Crockett; 1834-'35, Elijah Hatch; 1835-'36, Calvary Morris. Hocking and Fairfield Counties—1836-'38, Wm. Medill, John Graybill; 1838-'39, John Brough; 1839-'40, Lewis Hite, James Spencer. Hocking, Ross, Pike, and Jackson Counties— 1840-'41, James T. Worthington, John Stinson, Jos. Kayler; 1841-'42, Le Grand Byington, John James, Daniel Kooshner; 1842-'43, Le Grand Byington, Elihu Johnson, Wm. Nelson; 1843-'44 Wesley Claypool, Joseph Kayler, A. R. Cassidy. Hocking and Ross Counties—1844-'45, Joseph Kayler; 1845-'46, James Gibson; 1846-'47, Joseph Kayler; 1847-'48, J. A. Green. Hocking, Perry, and Fairfield Counties—1848-'49, Isaac Lorimer; 1849-'50, N. P. Colburn. Hocking and Perry Counties—1850-'51, C. W. James.

NEW CONSTITUTION.

Hocking County—1852,-'54, C. W. James; 1854-'56, Reuben Hesten; 1856-'60, George Johnson; 1860-64, Manning Stiers; 1864-'68, Wm. S. Dresbach; 1868-'72, Wm. T. Acker; 1872-'76, Oakley Case; 1876-'78, W. M. Bowen; 1878-'82, S. S. Wolf; 1882-'84, Wm. A. Wright.

VINTON COUNTY. NEW CONSTITUTION.

Vinton and Jackson Counties—1852-'54, D. T. D. Hurd; 1854-'56, Wm. J. Evans; 1856-'58, Ed. F. Bingham; 1858-'60, Robert B. Stephenson, resigned, succeeded by Wm. L. Edmundson; 1860-'62, Alex. Pierce; 1862-'64, John Fee; 1864-'66, E. A. Bratton; 1866-'70, Andrew J. Swaim; 1870-'72, Almond Soule; 1872-'76, Thos. M. Bay; 1876-'80, A. J. Swaim; 1880-'82, Columbus P. Wood.

HOCKING VALLEY RAILROADS.

MARIETTA & CINCINNATI.

The project of building a railroad westward through Southern Ohio to Cincinnati was first discussed about 1840, and finally took shape in the organization, in 1844, of the Belpre & Cincinnati Railroad Company. It was designed to build the road from Cincinnati to Belpre, opposite Parkersburg, Va. (now West Virginia). The company, organized without funds, proceeded to raise the necessary means for prosecuting the work by soliciting subscriptions to its stock from the localities through which the road was to pass, $100,000 being asked of Athens County. The State Legislature, by an act passed March 20, 1851, authorized the Athens County Commissioners to subscribe $100,000 of stock, provided the necessary majority of the legal voters gave their consent. A special election was held August 26 of the same year, resulting favorably to the subscription, and on the 30th day of August the County Commissioners (John Elliott, James Dickey and Zibo Lindley) subscribed for 2,000 shares of $50 each, in the Marietta & Cincinnati Railroad Company. Some years afterward, when the railroad company and the citizens of Athens County were not on the best of terms, an attempt was made to test the legality of the subscription. Some thought the commissioners had transcended their powers in subscribing to the Marietta & Cincinnati, when the people had voted to subscribe to the Belpre & Cincinnati. The question was agitated for some time through the county, meetings being held in several of the townships. All the prominent lawyers were ranged on one side or the other. The county commissioners at one time refused to levy the tax to pay the interest on the bonds, but after some months of discussion they replaced the tax on the duplicate.

ARRIVAL OF THE IRON HORSE.

The company soon began the construction of the road, which was continued in the face of all obstacles until it was completed to Athens in the spring of 1856. There was general rejoicing, not only in the city of Athens, but in the country round about, for they now had communication with the outside world, and a trip to Cincinnati was but a few hours' ride instead of as many days. Tuesday, the 29th day of April, 1856, witnessed the arrival in

Athens of the first railway passenger train over the road, or which had ever reached the city. The citizens turned out *en masse* to give it a welcome with three hearty cheers. Congratulatory speeches were made by several distinguished persons, and the arrival of the "Iron Horse" proved a gala day for the city of Athens.

HOSTILITIES COMMENCED.

Daily passenger trains were at once run between Athens and Chillicothe, connecting at the latter point with trains for Cincinnati. James D. Foster was appointed ticket and freight agent at Athens. Not long after, the road was completed to Marietta. Through bad management, however, the road lost money from the start. It was unfortunate in many things, and the people of Athens and vicinity lost confidence in it. This gradually developed into a decided hostility on the part of many of our prominent citizens, which culminated in tearing up their track, Jan. 1, 1858. It seems that in 1856 the company decided to abandon, temporarily, the tunnel through the hill above Athens, and obtained a lease from some of the citizens for the ground on which to lay a track south of the village, making a kind of *circumbendibus*, as the people said, and again getting upon the old line below town. The lease for this tract expired Dec. 31, 1857, and some days prior to that time the owners of the land gave notice to Mr. Wilson, in writing, to comply with the terms of the lease by vacating the land. This the company failed to do, and on New Year's day, 1858, a number of citizens repaired to the track in question and proceeded to remove some of the rails and ties.

This course was condemned in severe terms by many, particularly by the friends of the road. The Marietta and Chillicothe papers were especially bitter, accusing the Athenians of being blind to their own interests, of being influenced by malicious motives, and even of having committed an offense against the laws of the State. It was, perhaps, a question as to whether the action was politic, or was the best mode of dealing with the company, which of course became only exasperated, and imbued with a decided hostile spirit toward the citizens. The company had never paid any rent for the use of the land; the lease was to expire Jan. 1st, and the company was duly notified in writing several days in advance, by the owners of the land, to remove the track. The company taking no action whatever in the matter, it was clearly the right of the citizens to take quiet possession of their property, and to remove as many of the rails as they pleased.

Soon after this Mrs. Curtis, over whose land the railroad passed, had a portion of the tract removed. The company, however, procured the condemnation of the land by a jury appointed by the Probate Court, and were thus enabled to re-lay their track, and once more run regular trains through to Marietta. The company claimed that in their embarrassed financial circumstances it was impossible for them to complete the expensive tunnel above the town, and that if time was given them they would " make all things right;" but that they would not be enabled to do this if crippled by such opposition as that manifested by the people. The citizens claimed, on the other hand, that they had recognized the straitened condition of the company's resources, and had leased them this temporary right of way merely as an accommodation, it being clearly to their interest to have the road follow the line originally designed; but that the company had neither paid any rent, according to agreement, nor showed any disposition to regard the rights of the owners of the land.

The hostile feeling toward the railroad company was doubtless partly due to the latter's abandoning the original plan of building the road down the Hocking Valley to Belpre, where it could connect with the Northwestern Virginia Road, terminating at Parkersburg, on the other side of the Ohio River. Influenced by the offer of subscriptions from Marietta, Wheeling and Pittsburg to the amount of $1,500,000, the management had turned the road northward toward Marietta instead of toward Belpre, and thus had totally disregarded the interests of the Hocking Valley. The excitement consequent upon the tearing up of the track was of short duration, and after its subsidence Athens and the railroad resumed gradually their former friendly relations.

The original blunder of building the road across the hills to Marietta was rectified at last, after twenty years. The old line had four tunnels between Athens and Marietta, one 1,660 feet long, another 1,400 feet, and two others 300 feet each. Besides, it had a number of high, long and expensive trestles, that made the cost of maintaining the road a constant drain. Worse than all, it had sharp curvatures and heavy grades that made its operations slow and expensive.

In February, 1871, the Baltimore Short-line Company was formed, for the purpose of constructing the short line to Parkersburg. It was composed of parties interested in the B. & O. and the M. & C. roads. The contracts were let in August, 1872, and the last rail was laid Oct. 24, 1874. The line, as built, leaves the old line at Warren's, seven miles east of Athens, and follows the Hocking River for a distance of seven miles, to the valley of Skunk Run, passing through Canaanville, Guysville and within two miles of Coolville. From Skunk Run the road takes an easterly direction, up the valley of that stream, to the summit at Torch; thence striking the valley of Knowles's Run it follows in an easterly and northeasterly direction, coming to the valley of the Ohio River at the mouth of Little Hocking; thence along the Ohio River it passes to Belpre, where it joins the old line.

Athens County has spent considerable money for this railroad, but it has been a good investment. The county took $200,000 of capital stock, but the company pays annually many thousands of dollars to the county as taxes, and the valuation of property in the county has increased by $6,000,000, much of which increase is due to the presence of the road.

COLUMBUS, HOCKING VALLEY & TOLEDO.

The Hocking Valley, as a field for railroad enterprise, early attracted the attention of capitalists and public men, and many projects were started in an early day for building a Hocking Valley railroad to connect with that pioneer of railroads, the Baltimore & Ohio. The State Legislature passed an act as early as March, 1834, authorizing the construction of a railroad from Lancaster to a point on the Ohio River, opposite Parkersburg. Section second of the bill was as follows: "The capital stock of the Hocking Valley Railroad Company shall be $1,000,000, and shall be divided into shares of $50 each. These shares may be subscribed for by any corporation or individuals; and it shall and may be lawful for said corporation to commence the construction of the said railroad, and enjoy all the powers and privileges conferred by this act, as soon as $50,000 shall be subscribed to said stock." The idea of building the Hocking Valley Canal soon after supplanted this project of building a railroad, and nothing was done under the act.

NEW PROJECT.

It was not until 1854, some twenty years after the above charter was granted, that active steps were again taken to secure a railroad through the valley of the Hocking. It again fell through, and active work did not commence until 1856. The former chief engineer of the B. & O. Railroad, B. H. Latrobe, Esq., had examined the route, and was so favorably impressed that he urged the formation of a company and the building of the road. His advice was taken, and a company formed for the prosecution of the enterprise, which was prosecuted with vigor, though active and open opposition was made against it by the Marietta & Cincinnati Railroad Company. The city of Marietta, opposed and personally, undertook to secure legislative action to prevent its construction. This action of its enemies aroused the people of the Hocking Valley, and although the obnoxious legislation passed, it in no way altered the determination of the people of the valley to secure the prosecution of their cherished plans. However, if they could not secure a road to Parkersburg, they could build down the valley, as far as Athens, and let time and circumstances control the extension of the work. Meetings were held, and every effort made to carry forward the work. At the next session of the Legislature, in 1858, the obnoxious act above spoken of as having passed was repealed, and the way for active operation again opened. But the financial crash of 1857 was still severely felt the following year, and although opposition had ceased, the monetary situation prevented further progress. The war then came on, and it was not until the year 1865 that the project was again resurrected. In that year the Mineral Railroad Company was organized, its incorporators being: W. P. Cutler, E. D. Moore, M. M. Green, John Mills and Douglas Putnam. Every effort was made to start the enterprise by arousing the people and showing them the value of the work. The result was, meetings were held along the line, from Columbus to Athens, in the winter and spring of 1866. It was necessary to raise $750,000, and this sum was divided along the route as follows: Columbus, $400,000; Groveport and Winchester, $50,000; Lancaster, $75,000; Logan, $75,000; Athens, $100,000. Athens raised $120,000, and Columbus, $480,000, making, $800,000, which was enough to secure the success of the enterprise, and the people to rejoice. The name of the company was afterward changed, to the Columbus & Hocking Valley Railroad Company. In the spring of 1867, the entire line of seventy-six miles from Columbus to Athens was let to contract, the contractors, Dodge, Wood & Co., receiving for their work $800,000 cash, and the company's bonds for $850,000, or about $21,715, per mile. The ground was broken at Columbus, July, 1867, and on Nov. 7, 1868, twenty-five miles of the road was completed to Lancaster, and the first train of cars arrived at that town at that date, amid the rejoicings of the people. The road reached Nelsonville, June 30, 1869, and Athens in the summer of 1870.

The road is well equipped, and has been a prosperous one from the start. Three passenger trains run each way daily, and thus by affording prompt means of transportation to the coal fields of the Hocking Valley the road has been of untold benefit to both consumers and producers, as well as the welfare of its own exchequer. The Straitsville branch of the Hocking Valley Railroad was constructed at the same time with the main line, which it leaves at Logan; thence running in a circuitous course through the coal beds east of Logan, it returns to the main line at Nelsonville.

The Columbus & Hocking Valley, Columbus & Toledo and Ohio & West Virginia railroads, were consolidated in the summer of 1881, under the present name, Columbus, Hocking Valley & Toledo Railroad. The capital stock of this company was fixed at $20,000,000, divided into shares of $100 each. At the rate paid for the three roads by the syndicate which effected the consolidation, the Hocking Valley stock cost them $4,000,000; Toledo, $1,250,000, and the Ohio & West Virginia, $600,000. The bonded indebtedness of the Toledo road was $2,600,000; Hocking Valley, $2,400,000; Ohio & West Virginia, $1,600,000, a total of $6,600,000, and a total for both bonds and stock of $12,950,000. The new company issued $15,000,000 of bonds, which, with the stock, makes $35,000,000.

OHIO CENTRAL.

The Ohio Central Railroad is a new one, having been built through Athens County within the past two years. It has received no aid from the county and but little from the citizens. It passes through Trimble, Millfield, Jacksonville, Chauncey, Athens, Hebbardsville and Albany, in this county. The road extends from Toledo to Middleport, Ohio, and is being rapidly pushed through Virginia. The line has already proved a valuable auxiliary to the transportation facilities of the valley, and when completed to its terminus on the Ohio and beyond will be still more so. So far as Athens County is concerned its railroad transportation may be said to be completed. Perhaps in the future some few miles of local road may be added, but the prospects are not flattering.

HOCKING COUNTY RAILROADS.

It was as early as 1851 when the railroad fever first showed its symptoms in Hocking and culminated into a violent attack the following year. What caused this first outburst of railroad progression was called the

SCIOTO & HOCKING VALLEY RAILROAD.

On Sept. 2, 1852, the largest railroad meeting ever held in the Hocking Valley came off at Logan. A grand barbecue was given, and the air fairly shook with railroad eloquence. It was a memorable day in the history of Hocking County. The line of route was from Portsmouth, on the Ohio River, running to Jackson, in Jackson County, through McArthurstown, in Vinton County, Logan in Hocking, to Somerset in Perry County, thence to Newark, Licking Co., Ohio, as its terminus. It was computed that 5,000 people were in attendance that day, coming from Jackson, on the south, to Newark, on the north. Perry County turned out the banner delegation, being over a half mile long, accompanied by a band of music. The people of Logan and surrounding country were awakened at sunrise by a Federal salute. Up to that time it was the largest railroad meeting ever held in the State, and few since have exceeded it. It was decided that Perry County should raise $150,000, Hocking County $80,000, and Vinton County $50,000. The road was completed to the town of Jackson in 1853 and the grading completed to Somerset, in Perry County, with the exception of a tunnel at Maxwell and a heavy cut at Union Furnace. Then there was a collapse; the road bed and right of way having been mortgaged, the same was foreclosed and the whole forfeited to the land owners. The most of the stock was held by persons living along the line of the contemplated road. This ended that project and a calm settled over the valley.

THE NEXT MOVE.

A decade had passed, and the white-winged angel of peace, which had soared aloft, again settled upon our distressed country, when another railroad project was being whispered in the ears of the people of Hocking County. This time the connection spoken of was a line to Parkersburg on the Ohio River, to Columbus and Athens, instead of McArthur, the route from Logan. The route is here described, taken from a Northwestern Ohio paper, the Lima *Gazette*. It said :—

"A project for a new railroad that may ultimately be of immense benefit to the people of Lima, Allen County, is now being discussed. It is now, and has been for a year past, proposed (and the route has been surveyed) to construct a road from Columbus, southeast, through Lancaster, Logan and Athens, to Parkersburg, on the Ohio. This the Columbus people and those along the line dream of immense importance, because it opens up the extensive coal and iron deposits of Southeastern Ohio, which are now comparatively cut off, and affords a short cut connecting with the Baltimore & Ohio Road, at Parkersburg. This road will be built, and there necessarily form other combinations in connection with that, of which we propose to speak."

Just what other combinations it had in view, or whether it spoke about them, is immaterial to this history. The route above described is now known as the Columbus, Hocking Valley & Toledo Railroad, which, in this year, 1883, and a few previous ones show a larger net profit per mile than any other road in the State.

The first public meeting to consider the project was on Feb. 16, 1866, and it was reported a success; and the right of way through Hocking and Athens counties was a free gift to the company with but few exceptions. Matters went along, all in good shape, during the summer, and on Dec. 19, 1866, $754,000 had been subscribed and the following Board of Directors elected: Peter Hayden, B. E. Smith, William G. Dishler, W. B. Brooks, William Dennison, Isaac Eberly, George M. Parsons and Theo. Comstock, of Columbus ; D. Tallmadge, of Fairfield County ; J. C. Garrett, of Hocking County ; E. H. Moore and M. M. Greene, of Athens County; and W. P. Cutler, of Washington County.

It was at that time known as the Hocking Valley Mineral Railroad. Logan's contribution was $75,000, and the road was completed through Hocking County to the Athens County line, June 29, 1869, reaching Nelsonville, as previously stated, June 30 of that year. As this was the first railroad to reach Hocking County it was welcomed with loud rejoicing.

OHIO & WEST VIRGINIA RAILROAD.

This was the new name for the "old love," the Scioto & Hocking Valley Railroad, of 1852, with the exception of its terminal point, which was changed from Portsmouth to Gallipolis; the route from Logan through Hocking and Vinton counties was the same.

Work was commenced on this road in the spring of 1879, and the new company followed the old line and grade as far south as Dundas, where it crosses the M. & C. R. R., and then turns from the direction of Portsmouth toward Gallipolis. It was finished the following year so that trains ran from Logan to the Ohio River in December, 1880. The principal owners were residents of Columbus, but they had bonded the road, and Eastern persons held the bonds. The contractors ran the road a short time, then Mr. M. M. Green, of the Hocking Valley Road, was elected its President, which meant that the latter road was in control. This proved true, the road being sold to the Cleveland Syndicate in September, 1881, and re-organized under the name of the River Division of the C., H. V. & T. R. R. By securing this road the Columbus, Hocking Valley & Toledo Railroad secured a line to the Ohio River, their main line terminating at Athens. The road runs through a very rich and inexhaustible mineral region for many miles, which is to a great extent yet undeveloped. It has already a heavy freighting business from the Vinton County ore shipped to the iron furnaces of the Hocking Valley, but this, while considerable, is not a tithe of what the future promises, when the production of coal and iron shall receive from capital that assistance which is required to uncover its hidden wealth and bring it forth for the use of man. Two passenger trains each way run daily.

STRAITSVILLE BRANCH

of the C., H. V. & T. R. R. leaves the main line at Logan, and has some fourteen miles of its length within the limits of Hocking County, but in a circuitous course reaching again the main line at Nelsonville. It touches some of the largest mining country in the valley, and freighting is its principal business.

VINTON COUNTY RAILROADS.

Vinton County has the benefit of a north and south railroad running almost through the center of the county, rather east, perhaps, passing through three townships. This is the River Division of ths C., H. V. & T. Railroad, referred to in the previous pages, commencing at Logan and running to the Ohio River at Gallipolis. It has also a portion of the Marietta & Cincinnati Railroad, which enters the county at the southwest corner of Clinton Township, and, running a general northeasterly course for some twenty miles, passes into Athens County. This gives its central and eastern portion good transportation facilities, the western portion of the county of which the western portion is still void.

The River Division Road was opened for business at McArthur, Aug. 17, 1880, and an account of its freight and passenger traffic at that point will be found in the history of McArthur.

WALKER'S HISTORY OF ATHENS COUNTY.

Charles M. Walker, the oldest son of A. B. Walker, is now editor-in-chief of the Indianapolis *Times*. He was prepared for the legal profession and admitted to the bar, but did not incline to make that his life pursuit. He is somewhat of a politician, and under Lincoln's administration was appointed by Secretary Chase Fifth Auditor of the Treasury, a position which he held for two years. He then entered upon the work of journalism which he has followed since. He was for a number of years connected with the Indianapolis *Journal*. While at Washington he conceived the idea of compiling a history of his native county, and he corresponded with some of the principal citizens concerning the matter. Receiving much encouragement, he proceeded with the work, intending at first to make a book of about 200 pages. The scope of the history enlarged as he progressed, and when completed the History of Athens County appeared as a work of 600 pages. It was well printed and neatly bound. While a few have criticised some features of Walker's History, it is generally conceded to be a well-written and valuable work. A considerable amount of valuable information in this work has been taken from Walker's History by permission, for which our sincere thanks are hereby tendered.

MEDICAL SOCIETY OF THE VALLEY.

This society was organized April 28, 1866, at the court-house in the city of Athens. The following physicians were present:

Drs. A. H. Burrell and A. A. Shepard, of Nelsonville; James Moore, of New England; Hiram G. Witham, of Shade; E. B. Pickett, of Marshfield, James Howe, I. B. Harper, W. P. Johnson, and C. L. Wilson, of Athens; Wm. S. Bell, of Amesville; John Earhart, of Lee, and W. W. Feirce, of Chauncey. A constitution and by-laws were adopted, and the association then proceeded to elect its first officers. These were as follows:

President, Dr. W. P. Johnson; Vice-Presidents, John Earhart

and I. B. Harper; Secretary, C. L. Wilson; Treasurer, Wm. S. Bell. Monthly meetings were decided, and the association started out with twenty-five members. The same officials were re-elected the following year.

1868, for two years—President, E. G. Carpenter; Secretary, C. L Wilson. 1870, for two years—President, C. L. Wilson; Secretary, R. W. Erwin. 1872, for two years—President, I. P. Primrose; Secretary, R. W. Erwin. One year a blank. 1875, for two years—President, I. P. Primrose; Secretary, H. M. Lash. 1877—President, H. C. Rutter; Secretary, H. M. Lash. 1878—President, W. E. W. Shepard; Secretary, Chas. F. Gilliam. 1879—President, Jas. Little; Secretary, Chas. F. Gilliam. 1880—President, H. M. Lash; Secretary, Chas. F. Gilliam. 1881—President, G. W. Pullen; Secretary, E. C. De Steiger. 1882—President, David Little; Secretary, W. N. Alderman. 1883—President, I. P. Primrose; Secretary, K. Tinker; First Vice-President, H. M. Lash; Second Vice-President, G. W. Pullen; Treasurer, S. E. Butt.

The following are the present members of the society, 1883:

Athens County—H. M. Lash, G. L. Gorslene, A. B. Richardson, B. H. Pickering, E. G. Carpenter, Athens; A. H. Shepard, S. E. Butt, C. W. Cable, I. P. Primrose, D. B. Elder, W. E. W. Shepard, W. N. Alderman, C. F. Gilliam, K. Tinker, Nelsonville; W. A. Adair, Huestis, Amesville; H. T. Lee, T. C. Armstrong, Buchtel; James M. Kittrick, Chauncey; H. D. Danford, Trimble; G. W. Blakely, Guysville; H. D. Witham, Shade; B. C. Voris, Albany. Hocking County—David Little, James Little, G. W. Pullen, W. I. Bright, J. H. Dye, E. C. De Steiger, H. G. Campbell, Logan; A. B. Lyons, Sand Run; C. F. Aplin, Carbon Hill; J. C. Wright, Haydenville;——Irwin, South Perry; W. G. Dawson, George Marshall, Gibesonville. Vinton County—J. V. Rannels, Andrew Wolfe, C. O. Dunlap, J. E. Sylvester, McArthur; W. R. Moore, Swan. Perry County—H. C. Allen, W. J. Jones, G. Newton, New Straits

The association is a progressive one, where deep and studious thought, combined with experience, is interchanged in the cause of humanity.

CHAPTER VI.

ATHENS COUNTY HISTORY—FROM THE WILDERNESS TO ADVANCED CIVILIZATION.

ORGANIC—ACT OF THE LEGISLATURE—ORGANIZED FEB. 20, 1805—AREA—FIRST SESSION OF COURT—FOUR TOWNSHIP BOUNDARIES—FIRST JAIL AND COURT-HOUSE—TAXATION AND LICENSE—SOME SHINING LIGHTS—NEW COURT-HOUSE, 1818—SCHOOL DISTRICTS AND SCHOOL MONEYS—1840 TO 1850—RISE AND PROGRESS 1850 TO 1860—WAR AND PEACE—COURT-HOUSE TALK—OLD FATHER TIME—COUNTY OFFICIALS—FLOODS—DEVASTATION AND RUIN BY THE RUSHING WATERS—FLOODS OF 1847, 1858 AND 1873—DAMAGE COMPUTED—DESTRUCTION OF THIRTEEN MILES OF THE HOCKING CANAL—IT IS ABANDONED—THE SWELLING WATERS OF 1875—

ORGANIC.

The county of Washington covered a very extensive territory, so much so that for the convenience of the people who had settled in extreme points of the county, other counties were organized from it. Washington County was organized in 1789, and Athens County was taken from it in 1805. The Athens County of to-day, however, is not the Athens County of 1805, for she, like Washington, has been somewhat curtailed of her former population. The question of organization came up before the third session of the General Assembly, and on Dec. 4, 1804, Governor Tiffin, in reference to the subject of schools and education, referred to the Ohio University and its valuable gift of land, and that these lands might become more valuable if a new county was organized. His message on this point was as follows:

"It is further thought, that it would greatly increase the demand for those lands and town lots, as well as prepare the way for the accommodation and comfort of the youths who may be sent to the university, if a new county were erected and its seat established at Athens. This may conveniently be done without injury to the counties adjacent, and, in my opinion, the convenience of that part of the county imperiously demands it."

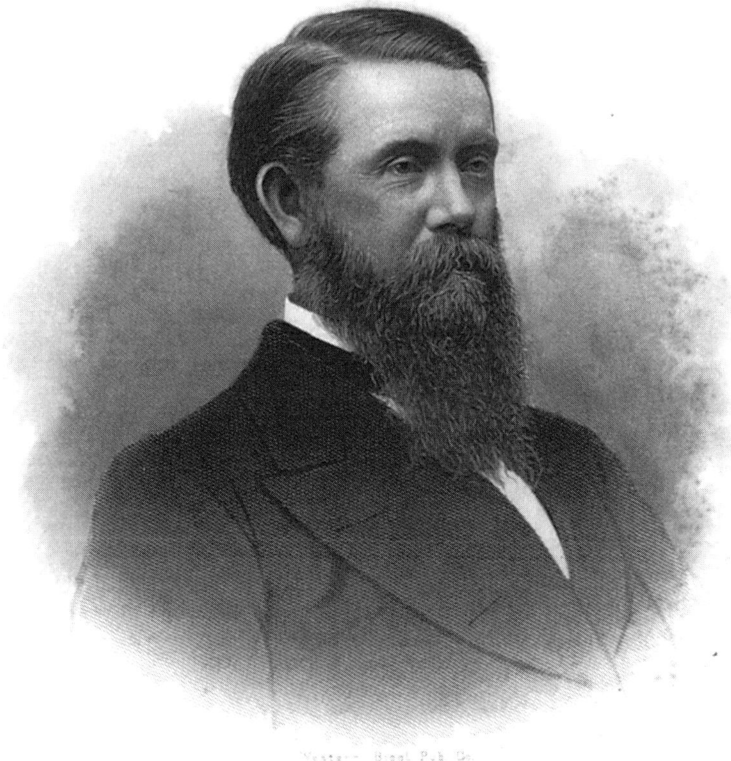

Western Biog'l Pub. Co.

C. H. Grosvenor

These favorable words placed the matter in its proper light before the members of the General Assembly, and before the session closed it was acted upon by them.

Political considerations also hastened this step. The first few years of Ohio's existence as a State were marked by strong political feeling, the advocates of "federalism" being arrayed against those of "democracy."

The act of the Legislature creating the county of Athens, reads as follows.

"*An act establishing the County of Athens.*

"SEC. 1. *Be it enacted*, etc., That so much of the county of Washington as is contained in the following boundaries be, and the same is, hereby erected into a separate county, which shall be known by the name of Athens, viz.: Beginning at the southwest corner of township number ten, range seventeen; thence easterly with the line between Gallia and Washington counties, to the Ohio River; thence up said river to the mouth of Big Hockhocking River; thence up the said Hockhocking River to the east line of township number six, of the twelfth range; thence north on said line to the northeast corner of the eighth township, in the said twelfth range; thence west to the east line of Fairfield County; thence south on said county line and the line of Ross County to the place of beginning.

"SEC. 2. That from and after the first day of March next the said county of Athens shall be vested with all the powers, privileges, and immunities of a separate and distinct county: *Provided always*, That all actions and suits which may be pending on the said first day of March next shall be prosecuted and carried to final judgment and execution, and all taxes, fees, fines and forfeitures which shall then be due shall be collected in the same manner as if this act had never been passed.

"SEC. 3. That the seat of justice of said county is hereby established at the town of Athens, any law to the contrary notwithstanding.

"SEC. 4. This act shall take effect and be in force from and after the first day of March next."

Passed Feb. 20, 1805.

AREA.

The area within the boundary above described, contained 1,053 square miles, or about thirty congressional townships of six miles square. This territory not only included the present county of Athens, but three townships, Ward, Green and Starr, now in Hocking County; seven townships, Brown, Swan, Elk, Madison, Knox, Vinton and Clinton, in Vinton County; five townships now a part of Meigs County, viz.: Columbia, Scipio, Bedford, Orange and Olive; and two townships, Homer and Marion, a part, at this time, of Morgan County; and a strip of land ten miles long and one mile wide, which was afterward made again a part of Washington County. Two years later an act passed the Legislature altering the boundary line between Athens and Gallia counties, and by that act Athens took a strip off of that county ten miles long and one wide. At the same session, about one month later, or Feb. 18, 1807, an act was also passed altering the line between the counties of Washington and Athens, which gave to Athens the portion of Troy Township lying east of the Hocking River, and gave to Washington County a strip fifteen miles long and one mile wide, taken from Athens.

Following up the acts of Legislature, numerous other changes were made, some adding to and others taking territory from Athens. One act making a change was dated Feb. 10, 1814. Then the organization of Jackson County, Jan. 12, 1816, and the creation of Hocking County, Jan. 3, 1818, and a further act dated March 12, 1845, all curtailed the dimensions of Athens County, and added them to the new counties formed. Meigs County, organized Jan. 21, 1819, took off another slice of her territory, and finally by the erection of the county of Vinton, which act was passed March 23, 1850, took the remainder of our outlying possessions in that direction, and the same act detached Ward Township from Athens and gave it to Hocking, thus reducing our boundaries all around to their present limits. The present boundaries of the county include about 430 square miles.

An act of the Legislature was passed Feb. 13, 1804, establishing boards of commissioners, providing that the election for commissioners should be held on the first Mondays of April. The first election in Athens County resulted in the choice of Silas Dean, William Howlett and John Corey, Commissioners.

The first session of the Board of Commissioners took place at

Athens on April 16, 1805, and the records show the following proceedings:—

"Agreeably to an act entitled 'an act establishing boards of commissioners,' passed February the 13th, 1804,

"We, Silas Dean, Wm. Howlett and John Corey, being elected Commissioners for the County of Athens on the 13th day of April, 1805, Silas Dean and John Corey, aggreeably to appointment, met this day in order to proceed to business, and have made choice of John Corey for Clerk, and then proceeded to divide the county into the following townships:

"The township of Ames begins at the northeast corner of the county; thence running west to the northwest corner of said county; thence south to the southwest corner of township No. 12 in the 16th range; thence east to the southeast corner of township No. 7 in the 12th range; thence north to the place of beginning.

"The township of Athens begins at the northwest corner of township No. 12 in the 17th range; thence south to the southwest corner of township No. 12; thence east to the southeast corner of township No. 5, in the 13th range; thence north to northeast corner of the aforesaid township No. 5; thence west to the place of beginning.

"The township of Alexander begins at the northwest corner of township No. 11 in the 17th range; thence south to the southwest corner of township No. 10 in the aforesaid 17th range; thence east to the southeast corner of township No. 3 in the 13th range; thence north to the northeast corner of township No. 4 in the 13th range; thence west to the place of beginning.

"The township of Troy begins at the southwest corner of township No. 4 in the 12th range; thence east on the south line of the county until it intersects with Shade River; thence down Shade River to its junction with the Ohio; thence up the Ohio to the mouth of the Great Hockhocking; thence up the Hockhocking to where the eastern line of the 12th range crosses said river; thence north to the northeast corner of township No. 6, in the 12th range; thence west to the northwest corner of the aforesaid 6th township; thence south to the place of beginning."

After dividing the county into four townships as stated above they next appointed Alvin Bingham, County Treasurer, who produced his bond which was accepted and filed. They also made an order for the erection of a jail, to be built of logs, dimensions to be twenty-four feet long by thirteen feet wide in the clear, with full specifications.

The voting precinct in each township was then made of records, as follows: John Havner's house in Athens; the house of Sylvanus Ames for Ames Township; John Armstrong's house for Alexander Township; and at Ebenezer Buckingham's house for Troy Township. This completed the most important acts of this session, and the board adjourned to the second Monday in June, 1805. The commissioners allowed themselves $1.50 per day, and the session cost the county $19.25.

The next session was principally given over to the question of ferry license, and $2 would get the coveted paper. The license for crossing the Great Hockhocking River, as it was then called, was also $2 and the rates for ferrying was for each foot passenger, 3 cents; for each man and horse, 10 cents; for loaded wagons and team, 50 cents; for every other four-wheeled carriage, or empty wagon and team, $37\frac{1}{2}$ cents; for every loaded cart and team $37\frac{1}{2}$ cents; for every loaded sled, or sleigh, or empty cart and team, 25 cents; for every empty sled or sleigh and team, $12\frac{1}{2}$ cents; for every horse, mare, mule, or ass, and every head of neat cattle, 6 cents; for sheep and hogs, 3 cents.

The rates within the county were the same as the above, but the license was put at $1.

Tavern license was decided to cost as follows: In the town of Athens $8; Ames Township, $4; township of Troy, $5; and that of Alexander $4.50; and for the township of Athens outside of the town limits it was placed at $6.

The levy for a county tax was fixed and a duplicate made for each township, and this assessment amounted to the gross sum of $157.60. The amount of tax in each township was: For Athens and Alexander, $96.40; Ames Township, $39, and Troy Township, $22.20. This closed the second session of the Board of County Commissioners, and it may be said that Athens County was fairly launched upon the world with all the rights and privileges of an independent municipality to paddle her own canoe.

OLD LOG COURT-HOUSE.

The first two years of the county's existence the court-house was a rented room, the property of Silas Bingham and Leonard Jewett, but in 1807 a court-house was erected. It was a substantial log building with the latest improvements, one of which was a brick chimney, instead of one composed of sticks and mud, and the old log court-houses of early days were a very useful auxiliary to the conveniences of a town which had the good fortune to be the county seat. Schools were sometimes held in them, but generally they were churches, amusement halls and court-house, and the place where all public and private assemblies met. In fact, the town got the most of the benefit. This primitive affair remained as a court-house for ten years, and if it could have told the story of its work, or the work and words which transpired within its log walls, history would have repeated some strange episodes of early life. It was in the old log court-house that Hon. Thomas Ewing, then a youth here at college, received the first impressions of the workings of that law of which he subsequently became so marked an embellishment, and so eminent an expounder. Among the distinguished names of those formerly connected with the Athens bar may be mentioned Messrs. Beecher, Irwin, Hunter, Ewing, Brasee, Stanberry and Medill, of Lancaster; Samuel F. Vinton and Simeon Nash, of Gallipolis; Generals Goddard and Convers, of Zanesville; William Woodbridge, Arius Nye and others, of Marietta.

The old log court-house rang with the eloquence of men who became famous in the history of the States, and of others who adorned some of the highest offices in the gift of the country. The societies, schools, etc., that used the house were to furnish the wood for the use of the County Court, and in 1813 the schools secured rooms for their own use. A new court-house was decided upon in 1814, and some contracts made for material. The building was to be of brick and substantially built.

NEW COURT-HOUSE COMPLETED, ETC.

The building was finished in the year 1818, and did duty as such for over sixty years, or, to be exact, sixty-two years. Edmund Dorr furnished the brick, 100,000, at $6 per thousand, payable in county orders.

Notwithstanding the expense of building the new court-house, the county did not go into debt, but managed to pay its running expenses. It continued to grow and prosper. The population increased; the farmers became comfortable if not rich; churches arose in different parts of the county, and schools grew and flourished.

There were ten school districts in the county in 1842, and there was reported the following number of children of school age:—

District No. 1, 44; No. 2, 93; No. 3, 39; No. 4, 58; No. 5, 61; No. 6, 56; No. 7, 83; No. 8, 98; No. 9, 53; No. 10, 56.

The State school money for the same amounted to $299.16.

MEXICO AND CALIFORNIA.

There was nothing to particularly startle the people of Athens County from the even tenor of their ways until 1846, when the declaration of war by Mexico aroused the dormant energies of the citizens, which had become stagnant over a combination of peace and prosperity, which they had enjoyed for a third of a century. The war of 1812 had drawn from Athens County her portion of recruits, and some noble spirits had been sacrificed on the altar of freedom. The war spirit those long years proved not to be dead, but sleeping; and the first bugle blast aroused the people, and acted upon them like an electric shock.

Athens County sent a full company of 100 men under Captain McLean. For two years this war was an all-absorbing theme. But scarcely had the sound of artillery died away amid the chaparrals of Mexico when there was borne upon the wings of the wind, which at first appeared to be a wild, weird and fanciful dream, a report, that upon the Pacific sunlit coast, where the wild waves had dashed in fury when the Storm King was in his wrath, or had laved its pebbly coast with the lullaby of a murmuring sea, that this coast was, veritably, a golden shore. It was not many months before this report was verified, and then came that hegira which has had no equal since the Israelites left Egypt. Athens County had her share of the California fever, and quite a number left the county to make their fortunes in that far off land. Some succeeded; others did not; many returned, but a few made their homes there, while others had crossed the mystic river, time giving place to eternity, as far as their future was concerned. Wealth came to a few, but it is doubtful if the amount of gold brought back, in the aggregate, equaled the amount taken away. If so, Athens County was among the fortunate ones.

1850 TO 1860.

It may be surprising to some to find that Athens County, which rather more than doubled its population between 1830 and 1840, actually lost about 900 during the decade between 1840 and 1850, but this is so, the population in 1840 being 19,109, and in 1850, 18,215. Possibly the Mexican War and the California exodus might have had something to do with it, but these could hardly account for the great loss. The next decade, between 1850 and 1860, showed a respectable gain of a trifle over seventeen per cent. The general prosperity had also been good and the per cent. of material wealth increased fully as much during that decade as at any time during her history.

There were in 1850, 82,168 acres improved, and in 1860, 129,531, making an increase of 47,363 acres improved, or over fifty-seven per cent. increase. In 1860 the value of farms was $4,980,034, against $2,125,967 in 1850, making an increase of $2,754,067, or 133 1-3 per cent. over 1850. One other item will show how the farmers progressed as well as other items, and that is in farm implements. Farm machinery, in 1850, was valued at $92,283, and in 1860 at $156,646, an increase of $64,363, or close to seventy per cent. in ten years. This shows that Athens County, in material wealth, had her full share of the prosperity of the country, and that at the time that the dark and ominous cloud of civil strife first arose upon the horizon, she was riding the wave of progress with exultation, and buoyant with the hope of a magnificent future.

WAR AND PEACE.

When war's dread alarm sounded it found Athens County in the full tide of prosperity, and it also found her ready to do her part in the great struggle for an indestructible union of States. The first bugle blast that called the people to arms had not died away ere her heroic sons had answered the call with a response that told the country that loyal Athens was awake and would, in the language of a once somewhat noted senator of the State: "Welcome all foes of the Union with bloody hands to hospitable graves." Little else was thought or talked of during the conflict, but a prosecution of the war to a successful termination, and for a history of the acts of the gallant sons of Athens County turn to the chapter in this work headed "Military History."

It is not to be supposed that the material prosperity of the people would be greatly enhanced while the constant drain on them for war expenses lasted, but ere the decade which ended January, 1870, had ended, Athens County was once more making commendable progress, both in population and wealth.

RAILROAD FEVER.

It was toward the last of this decade that the railroad fever which had attacked her sporadically in previous years, now assumed a violence which was really to test the enterprise of the people. How successfully the people met the demand upon them can be seen at this time in something over 100 miles of railroad track within her border. Railroads mean progress, and to say that Athens County has nearly doubled her material wealth the past fifteen years is not getting beyond the bounds of truth. Her railroads gave her new life, and even stirred up some of her old fogyish citizens to an exhibition of energy and enterprise that was truly commendable, and the city of Athens, the old borough situated among the "Huckleberry Knobs" of the valley of the Hocking, actually opened wide her dreamy eyes and took an intelligent view, both of the situation and her surroundings, and to her credit, it may be said, she forgot to close them again. So Athens County and her capital city have met the demand of advanced progress, and have kept step with the onward march of the country's prosperity.

COURT-HOUSE TALK.

The general thrift of the people and the awakening of the citizens of the city of Athens to progressive ideas suggested that a city hall, one that would be a credit to the city, would be about the best thing for them to have, and so they erected one of which the city could be proud. The success of this really necessary and desirable work acted upon the citizens very much like a new and highly colored carpet does upon the good house-wife with dilapidated furniture as an accompaniment. The more she looked at the carpet the worse the furniture looked and the more disheartened she became. Just so with the Athenians. They had no sooner withdrawn their gaze of admiration and pride from their new city hall, when, oh, horrors! it fell upon the old rickety court-house. Their pride received a severe shock, and the more they looked the more they felt that the city was everlastingly disgraced, and the citizens, or some of them, would actually go round a block rather than catch a glimpse of the old rat trap, as it was called by many. Of course this could not always be endured, and so it was decided to call upon the citizens of the county to help relieve them of their disgrace, and erect a county court-house that would be worthy the proud city, the seat of culture, refinement, a city hall, an insane asylum. In 1874 the question was put to a vote whether a court-house to cost not over $60,000 should be built. The people said *No*, with an emphasis that was truly staggering to the hopeful Athenians; 2,784 voted no, and 573 yes, which was a majority of 2,211, and about four fifths of the votes in favor were cast by the residents of the ambitious city. This was so disheartening that it took them two years to get up courage enough to again ask that the city's disgrace should be pulled down and a structure reared worthy of Athens County. So in 1876 the question was again asked, and again refused, but the refusal was not in thunder tones, like that of 1874, being but 767 majority against it, and failed to take their breath entirely away. But the people of Athens County soon found that they had one opponent they could not vote down. They could see the pride of the citizens of their capital city humbled, but "Old Father Time" was not to be disposed of in that way, and he soon let the people of the county know that if they did not soon build a new court-house he would rattle the old one down about their ears. This was so unmistakably the case that in June, 1878, the court-house question was carried, but about half the voters stayed at home, knowing that votes enough would be had to carry it, and they, if opposed, might as well accept the alternative of " Old Father Time " and let their vote go by default. Only 1,716 votes were polled, of which 1,213 were in the affirmative, and 503 nays. It was clear that the new court-house was built none too soon, and the citizens of the county certainly can take a just pride in the beautiful and massive edifice known as the Athens County Court-House, one of the most artistic and imposing structures of the kind in the State. The building was completed in August, 1880.

The census of that year, which will be found in another place shows that the county had made excellent forward progress during the decade which had then just ended, and the prosperity then so observant has still a strong and increasing foothold in the county. Her agricultural and mineral productions are still in their infancy, but the future is one so full of promise that hope is in the ascendancy in the breasts of the people. In fact, a book could be written from the standpoint of the present and the probabilities and possibilities of this county, which would read like a fairy tale, or the Arabian Nights, but space is insufficient in this work to even cast a horoscope of her future destiny.

COUNTY OFFICIALS.

Those who attended to the official business of Athens County will be found in the following pages. It is a record of names and dates which will be found invaluable for reference.

COUNTY COMMISSIONERS FROM THE ORGANIZATION OF THE COUNTY.

1805	Silas Dean,	William Howlett,	John Corey—(At special election.)
1805	William Barrows,	William Howlett,	Samuel Moore—(At regular election.)
1806	Alvan Bingham,	William Howlett,	Samuel Moore—(At regular election.)
1807	Alvan Bingham,	Caleb Merritt,	Samuel Moore—(At regular election.)
1808	Alvan Bingham,	Caleb Merritt,	Ebenezer Currier.
1809	Asahel Cooley,	Caleb Merritt,	Ebenezer Currier.
1810	Asahel Cooley,	Zebulon Griffin,	Ebenezer Currier.
1811	Asahel Cooley,	Zebulon Griffin,	Seth Fuller.
1812	Ebenezer Currier,	Zebulon Griffin,	Seth Fuller.
1813	Ebenezer Currier,	Caleb Merritt,	Seth Fuller.
1814	Ebenezer Currier,	Caleb Merritt,	Robert Linzee.
1815	Daniel Stewart,	Levi Stedman,	Robert Linzee.
1816	Caleb Merritt,	Asahel Cooley,	Daniel Stewart.
1817	Caleb Merritt,	Asahel Cooley,	Levi Stedman.
1818	George Walker,	Stambro P. Stancliff,	Levi Stedman.
1819	George Walker,	Stambro P. Stancliff,	James Gillmore.
1820	George Walker,	Stambro P. Stancliff,	James Gillmore.
1821	George Walker,	Edmund Dorr,	James Gillmore.
1822	George Walker,	Edmund Dorr,	James Gillmore.
1823	George Walker,	Edmund Dorr,	James Gillmore.
1824	George Walker,	Edmund Dorr,	James Gillmore.
1825	George Walker,	Daniel Stewart,	James Gillmore.
1826	George Walker,	Daniel Stewart,	Justus Reynolds.
1827	George Walker,	Harry Henshaw,	Justus Reynolds.
1828	George Walker,	Harry Henshaw,	Justus Reynolds.
1829	George Walker,	Harry Henshaw,	Justus Reynolds.
1830	George Walker,	Absalom Boyles,	Justus Reynolds.
1831	Joshua Hoskinson,	Absalom Boyles,	Justus Reynolds.
1832	Joshua Hoskinson,	Absalom Boyles,	Justus Reynolds.
1833	Joshua Hoskinson,	David Jones,	Justus Reynolds.
1834	Joshua Hoskinson,	David Jones,	Justus Reynolds.
1835	Joshua Hoskinson,	David Jones,	Frederic Abbott.
1836	Joshua Hoskinson,	Alfred Hobby,	Frederic Abbott.
1837	Joshua Hoskinson,	Alfred Hobby,	Frederic Abbott.
1838	Joshua Hoskinson,	Alfred Hobby,	William R. Walker.
1839	Joshua Hoskinson,	Elmer Rowell,	William R. Walker.
1840	Joshua Hoskinson,	Elmer Rowell,	Benj. M. Brown.
1841	Joshua Hoskinson,	Elmer Rowell,	Benj. M. Brown.
1842	Joshua Hoskinson,	Arnold Patterson,	Benj. M. Brown.
1843	Silas M. Shepard,	Arnold Patterson,	Benj. M. Brown.
1844	Silas M. Shepard,	Arnold Patterson,	Alfred Hobby.
1845	Silas M. Shepard,	Ziba Lindley,	Alfred Hobby.
1846	Silas M. Shepard,	Ziba Lindley,	Alfred Hobby.
1847	Silas M. Shepard,	Ziba Lindley,	Alfred Hobby.
1848	James Dickey,	Ziba Lindley,	Alfred Hobby.
1849	James Dickey,	Ziba Lindley,	Alfred Hobby.
1850	James Dickey,	Ziba Lindley,	Pearley Brown.
1851	James Dickey,	Ziba Lindley,	John Elliott.
1852	L. D. Poston,	Ziba Lindley,	John Elliott.

1853	L. D. Poston,	Ziba Lindley,	John Elliott.
1854	L. D. Poston,	William Mason,	John Elliott.
1855	John Brown,	William Mason,	Daniel B. Stewart.
1856	John Brown,	William Mason,	Daniel B. Stewart.
1857	John Brown,	Joseph Jewett,	Daniel B. Stewart.
1858	John Brown,	Joseph Jewett,	Daniel B. Stewart.
1859	John T. Winn,	Joseph Jewett,	John E. Vose.
1860	John T. Winn,	John Dew,	John E. Vose.
1861	John Brown,	John Dew,	John E. Vose.
1862	John Brown,	John Dew,	G. M. McDougall.
1863	John Brown,	Hugh Boden,	G. M. McDougall.
1864	John Brown,	W. F. Pilcher,	G. M. McDougall.
1865	John Brown,	W. F. Pilcher,	G. M. McDougall.
1866	John Brown,	W. F. Pilcher,	G. M. McDougall.
1867	John Brown,	W. F. Pilcher,	G. M. McDougall.
1868	Thomas L. Mintern	W. F. Pilcher,	G. M. McDougall.
1869	Thomas L. Mintern	Samuel S. Boyles,	G. M. McDougall.
1870	Thomas L. Mintern	Samuel S. Boyles,	G. M. McDougall.
1871	E. M. Blake,	Samuel S. Boyles,	J. F. Welch.
1872	E. M. Blake,	Samuel S. Boyles,	J. F. Welch.
1873	E. M. Blake,	Samuel S. Boyles,	J. F. Welch.
1874	Alpheus Wilson,	Samuel S. Boyles,	J. F. Welch.
1875	Alpheus Wilson,	E. H. Watkins,	J. F. Welch.
1876	Alpheus Wilson,	E. H. Watkins,	F. Finsterwald.
1877	Elza Armstrong,	E. H. Watkins,	F. Finsterwald.
1878	Elza Armstrong,	E. H. Watkins, A. S. Tidd,	F. Finsterwald.
1879	Elza Armstrong,	W. H. Curfman,	F. Finsterwald.
1880	W. G. Hickman,	W. H. Curfman,	F. Finsterwald.
1881	W. G. Hickman,	W. H. Curfman,	F. Finsterwald.
1882	W. G. Hickman,	W. H. Curfman,	J. W. Murphy.

COUNTY AUDITORS.

The first constitution of Ohio provided for the election by the people of only two county officers—sheriff and coroner; other county officers were, during the first eighteen years of the State's history, appointed by the county commmissioners or by the associate judges of the respective counties. The office of county auditor was created by act of the Legislature, at the session of 1820-'1. Before that time the principal duties of the auditor were performed by the county clerk. Henry Bartlett, so long known in the county as "Esquire Bartlett," was Clerk and *ex-officio* Auditor from 1806 till March, 1821. From this time the successive auditors were:

Joseph B. Miles, appointed by commissioners in 1821, and served nine months.
General John Brown, appointed and served to March, 1827.
Norman Root, elected 1827, served to March, 1839.
Leonidas Jewett, elected 1839, served until 1843.
Abner Morse, elected 1843, served until 1845.
Leonidas Jewett, elected 1845, served until 1847.
E. Hastings Moore, elected 1847, served until 1861.
Simeon W. Pickering, elected 1861, served until 1871.
A. W. S. Minear, from 1871 to 1880.
A. J. Frame, from 1880 to ———.

COUNTY CLERKS.

Henry Bartlett, appointed Dec. 1, 1806; served until Feb 8, 1836.
Joseph M. Dana, appointed Feb. 8, 1836; elected Feb. 22, 1843; served until 1857.
Louis W. Brown, elected 1857.
Edwin M. Phillips, elected 1869.
G. W. Baker, elected 1872.
Silas E. Hedges, elected 1881.

COUNTY RECORDERS.

Dr. Eliphaz Perkins, from 1806, to July, 1819.
Chauncey F. Perkins, from July, 1819, to May, 1826.
A. G. Brown, from May, 1826, to August, 1833.
Robert E. Constable, from August, 1833, to November, 1835.
A. G. Brown, from November, 1835, to October, 1841.
Enos Stimson, from October, 1841, to October, 1844.
John Boswell, from October, 1844, to October, 1847.
A. J. Van Vorhes, from October, 1847, to October, 1850.
W. H. Bartlett, from October, 1850, to December, 1854.
Frank E. Foster, from December, 1854, to November, 1855.
George H. Stewart, from November, 1855, to June, 1861.
Norman Root, from June, 1861, to January, 1862.
Daniel Drake, from January, 1862, to January, 1868.
Josiah B. Allen, from January, 1868.
John W. Andrews, from January, 1880, to January, 1883.
Lafayette Hawk, from January, 1883, to ———.

COUNTY SHERIFFS.

Robert Linzee, from April, 1805, to November, 1807.
Silvanus Ames, from November, 1807, to November, 1809.
Robert Linzee, from November, 1809, to January, 1814.
Thomas Armstrong, from January, 1814, to January, 1818.
Isaac Barker, from January, 1818, to January, 1822.
Jacob Lentner, from January, 1822, to January, 1824.
Calvary Morris, from January, 1824, to January, 1828.
Robert Linzee, from January, 1828, to January, 1830.
John McGill, from January, 1830, to January, 1832.
Amos Miller, from January, 1832, to January, 1836.
Joseph Hewitt, from January, 1836, to January, 1840.
Joseph H. Moore, from January, 1840, to January, 1844.
William Golden, from January, 1844, to January, 1848.
J. L. Currier, from January, 1848, to January, 1852.
J. L. Kessinger, from January, 1852, to January, 1856.
Leonard Brown, from January, 1856, to January, 1858.
H. C. Knowles, from January, 1858, to January, 1862.
Frederic S. Stedman, from January, 1862, to January, 1864.
John M. Johnson, from January, 1864, to January, 1868.

William S. Wilson, from January, 1868, to January, 1872.
A. J. Reynolds, from January, 1872, to March, 1873.
Nehemiah Warren, from March, 1873, to January, 1876.
Parker Carpenter, from January, 1876, to January, 1880.
Tim. B. Warden, from January, 1880.

COUNTY TREASURERS.

Alvan Bingham, from April, 1805, to June, 1806.
William Harper, from June, 1806, to June, 1807.
Ebenezer Currier, from June, 1807, to March, 1808.
Eliphaz Perkins, from March, 1808, to June, 1809.
William Harper, from June, 1809, to June, 1811.
Eliphaz Perkins, from June, 1811, to June, 1815.
Amos Crippen, from June, 1815, to June, 1825.
Isaac Barker, from June, 1825, to January, 1830.
Amos Crippen, from January, 1830, to January, 1832.
Isaac Barker, from January, 1832, to January, 1836.
Isaac N. Norton, from January, 1836, to December, 1836.
Abram Van Vorhes, from December, 1836, to January, 1837.
Isaac Barker, from January, 1837, to January, 1840.
Amos Crippen, from January, 1840, to January, 1842.
Robert McCabe, from January, 1842, to January, 1848.
William Golden, from January, 1848, to January, 1854.
Samuel Pickering, from January, 1854, to January, 1858.
Leonard Brown, from January, 1858, to January, 1860.
Joseph M. Dana, from January, 1860, to January, 1862.
Leonard Brown, from January, 1862, to January, 1864.
A. W. S. Minear, from January, 1864, to January, 1868.
George W. Baker, from January, 1868, to January, 1872.
W. S. Wilson, from January, 1872, to January, 1876.
A. J. Frame, from January, 1876, to January, 1880.
John P. Coe, from January, 1880, to ——.

COUNTY COURT.

The first Court of Common Pleas was held July 8, 1805, Robert F. Slaughter, President Judge; Silvanus Ames and Elijah Hatch, Associate Judges, and Henry Bartlett, Clerk. Since that time the following judges have been elected:

1806—Levin Belt, President Judge; Silvanus Ames, Alexander Stedman and Abel Miller, Associate Judges.

In 1807 Judge Ames became Sheriff and Elijah Hatch became Judge.

1807 to 1812—William Wilson, President Judge, and Alexander Stedman, Abel Miller and Elijah Hatch, Associate Judges.

1813—William Wilson, President Judge, and Jehiel Gregory, Silvanus Ames, and Elijah Hatch, Associate Judges.

1814—William Wilson, President Judge, and Jehiel Gregory, Silvanus Ames, and Ebenezer Currier, Associate Judges.

1815 to 1818—William Wilson, President Judge, and Silvanus Ames, Ebenezer Currier and Elijah Hatch, Associate Judges.

1819—Ezra Osborne, President Judge, and Robert Linzee, Ebenezer Currier, and Silvanus Ames, Associate Judges.

1824—Alvan Bingham, Associate Judge, *vice* Silvanus Ames, deceased.

1825—Amos Crippen, Associate Judge, *vice* Robert Linzee.

1826—Edmund Dorr, Associate Judge, *vice* Ebenezer Currier, and Thomas Irwin, President Judge, *vice* Osborne.

1827—Elijah Hatch, Associate Judge, *vice* Amos Crippen.

1838—George Walker, Associate Judge, *vice* Alvan Bingham.

1833—Ebenezer Currier, Associate Judge, *vice* Edward Dorr.

1834—David Richmond, Associate Judge, *vice* Elijah Hatch.

1840—John E. Hanna, President Judge, *vice* Thomas Irwin.

1840—Samuel B. Pruden, Associate Judge, *vice* Ebenezer Currier.

1841—Isaac Barker, Associate Judge, *vice* D. Richmond.

1845—Robert A. Fulton, Associate Judge, *vice* George Walker.

1847—Arius Nye, President Judge, *vice* John E. Hanna.

1847—Samuel H. Brown Associate Judge, *vice* S. B. Pruden.

1850—Norman Root, Associate Judge, *vice* Samuel H. Brown.

1850—A. G. Brown, President Judge, *vice* Arius Nye.

1852—Simeon Nash, elected first Judge under new constitution, when associate judges were dispensed with.

1862—John Welch, elected.

1865—Erastus A. Guthrie, appointed, *vice* John Welch, elected Supreme Judge.

1866—E. A. Guthrie, elected.

1872—J. Cartwright, appointed.

1872—David Hebbard, appointed.

1873—Joseph P. Bradley, elected.

1873—Samuel S. Knowles, elected.

1882—Hiram L. Sibley, elected.

PROBATE COURT.

(Organized in 1852.)

Jacob C. Frost, elected 1852.

Nelson H. Van Vorhes, elected October, 1855; resigned November, 1855.

Daniel S. Dana, appointed November, 1855.
Calvary Morris, elected October, 1855.
L. Jewett, appointed 1871, elected in October, 1872.
Thomas L. Mintern, elected 1875.
Wm. S. Wilson, elected 1881.

PROSECUTING ATTORNEYS.

E. B. Merwin, from 1806 to 1809.
Benjamin Ruggles, from 1809 to 1810.
Artemas Sawyer, from 1810 to 1812.
Alexander Harper, from 1812 to 1813.
Artemas Sawyer, from 1813 to 1815.
J. Lawrence Lewis, from 1815 to 1816.
Thomas Ewing, from 1816 to 1817.
Joseph Dana, Sr., from 1817 to 1820.
Samuel F. Vinton, from 1820 to 1822.
Thomas Ewing, from 1822 to 1824.
Thomas Irwin, from 1824 to 1826.
Dwight Jarvis, from 1826 to 1830.
Joseph Dana, Jr., from 1830 to 1835.
John Welch, from 1835 to 1839.
Robert E. Constable, from 1839 to 1841
John Welch, from 1841 to 1843.
Tobias A. Plants, from 1843 to 1845.
James D. Johnson, from 1845 to 1847.
Lot L. Smith, from 1847 to 1851.
Samuel S. Knowles, from 1851 to 1855.
George S. Walsh, from 1855 to 1857.
Erastus A. Guthrie, from 1857 to 1861.
Lot L. Smith, from 1861 to 1863.
Rudolph De Steigner, from 1863 to 1870.
Chas. Townsend, from 1870 to 1876.
Leonidas Jewett, from 1876 to 1880.
Emmet Tompkins, from 1880.

The first grand jury drawn in Athens County was in November, 1805, and was composed as follows: John Dixon, John Hewitt, Saml. Moore, Alvin Bingham, Jno. Corey, Peter Boyles, Jeremiah Riggs, Canady Lowry, Wm. Howlett, Robt. Fulton, Josiah Coe and Phillip M. Starr.

THE WATERS AND THE FLOODS.

The Hocking River and its tributaries have frequently risen far beyond their ordinary limits, and carried destruction and ruin in their path. Altogether, property has suffered considerably at different times from high water. One of the most serious floods occurred in 1847, the water rising higher than was known for a generation before, and doing more or less damage throughout the valley. Severe floods were also experienced in 1852.

The next one of importance occurred in the last week of May, 1858. Heavy rains throughout this part of the State caused a general rise in the water-courses. The Hocking was higher than had been known for many years, particularly at Lancaster and Logan. At Athens it was not so high. It did not reach, by twenty inches, the high-water mark of 1847. The destruction of property was considerable. Hundreds of acres of growing grass and grain were entirely or partially ruined. On the uplands, also, the washing of the soil and the consequent injury to grain and grass has been unusually severe. The canal gave way at two or three points, but the breaks were not extensive, and were easily repaired.

Margaret's Creek, running through Alexander and half way through Athens Township, was higher than ever before seen by that notorious personage, "the oldest inhabitant." The bottoms were entire submerged, and the destruction of property necessarily heavy. Several farmers had each as high as eight or ten thousand fence-rails carried away. Along the smaller streams in other portions of the county the destruction of property was similar to that along the Hocking and Margaret's Creek. Several bridges were swept off or greatly injured. The county bridge over Federal Creek, near Big Run, was a total loss.

The damage to the Marietta & Cincinnati Railroad was heavy, but trains were running again in about ten days. East of Athens the greatest obstruction was near Warren's, where some sixty feet of heavy embankment was washed away; and beyond that point were numerous slides. The damage between Athens and Chillicothe was also great.

Scarcely had the waters begun to lower in the streams when, on May 31, the valley was again visited with severe and destructive showers of rain. The smaller streams rose with remarkable rapidity. The west branch of Margaret's Creek, in Alexander Township, in a few hours rose to a point even higher than that reached during the freshet of the previous week, sweeping off fences and causing the sudden destruction of other property. Sunday Creek was higher than had been known for twenty years, and the Hocking was out of its banks.

This storm was followed by another on the evening of the 5th of June. The streams again rose, till, on the 7th, the Hocking lacked but a few inches of being as high as during the first freshet. Monday Creek and other streams rose to a greater height than before, and much damage resulted to bridges, roads, fences and crops. The railroad also suffered further.

And still again in the following June, the 11th, heavy and continuous rains swelled the waters for a fourth time in close succession, the river at this time reaching its highest point since the great flood of 1847. Comparatively little damage was done, however, from the simple fact that there was but little left to destroy. The railroad track was under water for a mile east of Athens, and the approaches to the bridges crossing the river were impassable. The canal was much damaged, there being numerous breaks all along its line. When the floods subsided thousands of acres of land presented the appearance of a desert waste. Mails from Cincinnati were not received over the Marietta & Cincinnati Railroad between May 24 and June 17. This seemed to be a season of general floods, the Hocking Valley not being the only sufferer. The floods were very severe throughout Ohio, Indiana and Illinois.

The severest flood ever known to the inhabitants of the Hocking Valley came in the summer of 1873. The rain commenced falling on Thursday, July 3, and continued, almost without interruption, until Saturday morning following, inundating the whole valley, from Lancaster to the Ohio River. Wheat, corn and grapes were swept to the ground, from Carroll to Hockingport. At Nelsonville fifty families were driven from their homes, the west end of the town being submerged. Among the heavy losses in that vicinity were: The bridge and crops of L. D. Poston, $10,000; bridge and coal works of W. B. Brooks, $5,000; tanyard of J. F. Broadt, $5,000; planing-mill and dry-dock of George Freer, $1,500; crops and lumber of John W. Scott, $3,000; crops of John Herrold, $2,000; and many others. The destructive waters rushed rapidly up the ascent to Main street, impetuously flowing into houses, and mingling in dire confusion their contents. With one exception every bridge in the vicinity of the town was swept away; and the "Robbins' Bridge," though not wholly destroyed, sustained such damages that it had to be virtually rebuilt. At Chauncey five miles north of Athens, the waters entered the second story of the dwellings, and also at Floodwood. At the latter place, about daylight on Saturday morning, the attention of Aaron Lewis, residing near the "Arnold Shaft," was arrested by the shrill screams of a woman. Proceeding in a boat in the direction of the alarm, he found a woman with her two children in the loft of their cabin surrounded by the rapidly encroaching waters; he hurriedly tore through the shingles of the roof and rescued the party, rowing them to his own residence. The works of the Hocking Valley Salt Company were seriously damaged. Their loss in manufactured salt alone exceeded 1,000 barrels. All the smaller bridges in the neighborhood of the works were destroyed. From the residence of Henry Brown, of Chauncey, to the salt works, a distance of half a mile, the entire population were forced to abandon their dwellings during Friday night and Saturday morning. The works at Salina, owned by George T. Gould, lost 3,000 barrels of salt. His loss was estimated at $5,000. Other individual losses in this district were: Those of Henry Brown, $3,000; Infirmary farm, $2,000; A. Courtney, $1,000; Judge and Joseph Jewett, conjointly, $3,500; Joseph Dorr, about $1,000; Hiram Armitage, $1,000; William Courtney, $500.

Coming toward Athens, the destruction was so great as to defy description. Among the heaviest losers here was D. B. Stewart of Athens. Independently of the indirect damages he sustained, his losses included about 100 acres of corn, 80 acres of fine wheat, 1,500 bushels of old corn in crib materially injured; 40 acres of meadow destroyed; 100 cords of wood, and 50,000 feet of lumber swept away, in addition to unestimated damages to mill and fences. Other losers were: Joseph Herrold, between $5,000 and $7,000; E. H. Moore, over $2,000; John Ring, between $1,000 and $1,500; and unestimated: Porter Wilson, Hiram Bingham, Grosvenor and Beaton, R. J. Cable, Jesse Davis, Augustus Norton, Oliver Carpenter, S. H. and Leroy Mansfield, S. S. Boyles, N. O. Warren, Charles Henry, Benjamin Randall, and, indeed, every farmer in the valley, between Athens and the Ohio River.

The damages wrought by the flood to the Hocking Canal and the Hocking Valley Railroad were also of startling magnitude. The canal between Athens and Logan was well-nigh destroyed, the encroachment of the Hocking River completely washing away the tow-path at many points, for stretches, variously, of a half mile and more. So ruinous were the damages to this pioneer public work that it has been discontinued between Nelsonville and Athens. On the Hocking Valley Railroad, bridges, embankments and portions of the road-bed, from a point beyond Lancaster to Athens were wrecked and torn to an extent that required weeks of time and vast expenditures of money to repair. During the height of the flood, as the surging waters swept past Athens and on down the valley, the spectacle was a sublime one, the water bearing upon its swelling surface the fearful havoc it had consummated. Altogether, this general calamity has not been equaled by any similar catastrophe that had previously occurred since the settlement of the country, the extent of the floods of 1832, 1847 and 1858 being materially exceeded by this one of 1873.

In the latter part of July, 1875, the windows of the heavens were opened, and the Hocking Valley once more inundated. Villages were flooded, and crops, bridges and fences carried off. The river was higher than ever before known at Athens, and all the tributaries were swollen beyond their banks. The mails were stopped for several days, and the railroad bridges were swept away, track washed out, etc. At Athens the gas works were flooded, and the citizens were compelled to resort to kerosene lamps and old candle-sticks or to the lights of other days. The damage by this flood was not confined to the valleys, but the hill farms were injured by washing. The losses in the Hocking Valley were probably over   million of dollars.

CHAPTER VII.

MILITARY HISTORY—WAR OF 1812, MEXICAN WAR, AND THE WAR BETWEEN THE STATES.

EARLY PATRIOTISM—WAR WITH MEXICO—THE REBELLION—FIRING ON FORT SUMTER—NEWSPAPERS FIRING THE HEARTS OF THE PEOPLE—ATHENS COUNTY MEETS ALL DEMANDS—CAMP JEWETT—MUSTERING IN—CAMP DENNISON—SANITARY AND RELIEF—WORK—MORGAN'S RAID—NELSONVILLE CAPTURED—LADIES ONCE MORE TO THE FRONT—GRAND ENCAMPMENT—WAR ENDED—GREAT REJOICING—PRESIDENT LINCOLN'S ASSASSINATION—SORROW AND INDIGNATION—THE ATHENS SOLDIERS BY TOWNSHIPS—THE REGIMENTS IN WHICH THEY SERVED.

EARLY PATRIOTISM.

The people of Athens County, in common with the rest of the civilized world, believe that military organization, defense and action are sometimes necessary to patriotism. Some of the early settlers of the county and the ancestors of many more were patriot soldiers during the Revolution, and from them a zeal for the supremacy of the stars and stripes has been inherited, which is so far from cooling with the lapse of time that it seems to grow more fervent in each generation. The first time an appeal was made to the loyalty of Athens County was during the

WAR OF 1812.

A company of volunteers was promptly raised in September, 1812, which was enrolled in the regiment of Colonel Robert Stafford and the brigade of General Ed. Tupper, and which served till March following. It marched northward to Sandusky and Perrysburg, after Hull's surrender, but was not engaged in any actual combat. Jehiel Gregory of Athens, was at first Captain of the company; Nehemiah Gregory, of Athens, was Lieutenant; James Crippen, of Rome Township, was Ensign; and Leonard Jewett, of Athens, was Surgeon of the company. After reaching camp,

Captain Gregory was promoted to Major, Lieutenant Gregory became Captain, and William McKinstry, of Alexander Township, became Lieutenant. Among the privates were Thaddeus Crippen, of Rome; William Stewart, of Rome; Andrew Stewart, of Rome; James Starr, of Rome, and Roswell Poole, of Ames. These volunteers received $8 per month and subsistence for their services. About 1869 the two or three survivors of this band were gladdened by the act of Congress which pensioned all living soldiers of the War of 1812. The last of that company has now gone to "that bourne whence no traveler returns" and their deeds live only in history.

MEXICAN WAR.

The tocsin of war again sounded in 1846, and Athens responded with over 100 volunteers. Most of them went in one company, Captain McLean's, and quite a number of these from York and other townships.

The following is the muster roll of Company E, (Captain McLean's) Second Ohio Regiment in the Mexican War:

First Lieutenant, Michael Earhart; Second Lieutenant, J. K. Blackstone; First Sergeant, E. D. Wall; Second Sergeant, Daniel Nelson; Third Sergeant, John A. Beard; Fourth Sergeant, J. C. Stedman; First Corporal, Thomas Shannon; Second Corporal, Thos. Miller; Third Corporal, A. Steenrod; Fourth Corporal, Charles Barker; Privates, T. Armitage, C. Armitage, J. B. Abbott, Michael Austin, Thomas Arrington, James Andrews, William Bailey, Ezra Bridge, Samuel Brown, Samuel Burns, James Beabout, Martin Bobo, P. A. J. Beard, James Bowen, Samuel Bush, John Crow, F. Chamberlain, A. Carpenter, Richard Carr, Alford Carns, Jonas Clark, Samuel Clark, John Clayton, William Dolen, Isaac Desler, R. De Steigner, G. W. Full, Alexander Francis, James Finsterwald, Homer Gibbs, Columbus Gray, Reason Hull, Harrison Hume, William Hendrixon, L. Holwell, E. D. Hatch, Benjamin Hughs, Jeff Henshaw, H. D. Johnson, Reuben James, Wm. N. R. James, Charles Kemp, Clinton Loudon, A. Liggit, F. Lawrence, Edward Merick, Thomas Macklin, Philip McDaniel, Samuel Older, John Peters, Nathan Pickett, A. Patterson, William Reason, A. M. Smith, Daniel Shepard, Rufus Simmons, Alford Starr, John Thompson and Jerry Thompson.

WAR OF THE REBELLION.

It was in the terrible four years' war of 1861-'65, that the people of Athens County most fully demonstrated their thorough loyalty to the best Government on earth. According to the United States census of 1860, the number of male inhabitants of the county in that year, between the ages of fifteen and fifty, both inclusive, was 5,089. The county furnished to the Government during the war, in all, 2,610 soldiers, or more than fifty per cent. of her men able to bear arms. In other words, of the able-bodied men in the county every other one left his business and his family to aid in suppressing the Rebellion. This is a record of which the county may well be proud—a record which no county in the State of Ohio, and few in all the Northern States, can surpass. The number above given does not include 1,967 men who volunteered and served in repelling the Morgan raid, in 1863, nor 160 "squirrel-hunters," who hurried to the defense of Cincinnati in 1862.

The train of national events which led to the war are too well known to need even a summary of them here. The county was a strong Whig county, and, after the death of that party, its Republican, or "abolition," tendencies were equally strong. Athens was a prominent station on the "underground railway," and many good stories might be told of adventures on that mysterious service.

At the presidential election of 1860, Lincoln, Douglas, Breckenridge and Bell were candidates for the presidency, and the triumphant election of Lincoln was the result. Athens County gave him a majority of 1,200. The South had threatened secession in the event of Lincoln's election, and it now proceeded to execute this threat by the various States passing ordinances of secession, and organizing themselves into a Southern Confederacy. After a number of weeks of negotiation, or attempted negotiation, General Beauregard attacked Fort Sumter, at Charleston, S. C., in obedience to instructions from L. B. Walker, Secretary of War of the Confederate Government at Montgomery, Ala. The startling news of the firing on Fort Sumter produced but one general feeling— that of indignation at the action of the South, and a patriotic determination to support the United States Government in the prompt suppression of the Rebellion. Words can not describe the enthusiasm with which men of all parties in Athens County declared themselves for the Union, the Constitution, and the enforcement of the laws. The spirit of the people was eloquently reflected by the press, which called upon all loyal citizens to stand by their Government, and remember their duties as members of the Republic. We give one or two extracts from the ringing editorial which appeared in the *Messenger* of April 18, 1861:

"The American flag has been violated, American soldiers have been shot down, and a brave commander of a Government fort has been forced to strike his flag and capitulate. Men of Athens County, this news comes home to you. A call will soon be made on Ohio to contribute her portion of men and money to aid the Federal Government in asserting its authority and preserving the honor and dignity of the nation. Will you falter in the hour of your country's peril? Will you stand by and call into question the causes which have produced this state of things? If so the name and memory of Benedict Arnold will be enviable compared with that which future generations will justly apply to you. This is no time for party jealousy or partisan bickering. America expects every man to do his duty, and all must do it, or reap the vengeance of an outraged people. Democrats! Republicans! and no-party men! We call on you to merge the partisan in the patriot, the demagogue into the hero, and rally as the exigencies of the times may indicate, to the support of your country's flag. Let every man be a true American citizen, feeling the responsibilities and patriotism of an American citizen, and those base destroyers of the peace and prosperity of the Union will soon be made to hide their accursed heads in shame before all nations."

Meetings were held by citizens throughout the country, at which patriotic speeches were made, and at which the most zealous determinations to fight for the Union was manifested. A meeting was held at Athens on the 17th, but five days after the firing on Fort Sumter. The stars and stripes were raised over the courthouse, amid the wildest enthusiasm. Republicans and Democrats, with one accord, cheered every Union expression. The townships were urged to hasten the enlistment of volunteers in response to the call of President Lincoln for 75,000 volunteers. April 20 a large and enthusiastic meeting of citizens was held at Chauncey, Dover Township. A pole was raised, and the stars and stripes ran up, amid deafening shouts. The greatest enthusiasm prevailed. A large number volunteered, and steps were also taken to organize a home guard.

At Athens, on the same date, a patriotic meeting was held on the college green. In the center of the concourse were the Ohio State

Guards, of Athens, armed and in full uniform, bearing a beautiful silk banner presented by the ladies of Athens, Feb. 22, 1860, little thinking how soon it would be called to wave amid the smoke of the battle-field. The uniformed recruits were stationed near the college. A beautiful flag, twenty-six by fifteen feet in size, was run up the staff, and as it unfolded to the breeze, it was greeted by three rounds of musketry from the State Guards, and three cheers from the crowd. Patriotic speeches were made; songs were sung by the ladies in attendance. A series of patriotic resolutions were adopted by the students of the Ohio University. A fund started for defraying the expenses of recruits before starting and for the support of their families during their absence reached $2,000 in twenty-four hours.

The following staff officers of the Third Brigade, Seventh Division, Ohio Volunteer Militia, composed of the counties of Athens, Washington, Meigs and Gallia, reported for duty: General R. A. Constable, Brigadier-General, Athens; Major D. Maule, Brigadier-Major, Athens; Amos Layman, Brigadier-Judge-Advocate, Washington; Captain George W. Baker, Brigadier-Quartermaster, Athens; Captain Cyrus Grant, Brigadier-Aid-de-Camp, Meigs; Captain J. L. Vance, Brigadier-Aid-de-Camp, Gallia; Dr. W. P. Johnson, Brigadier-Surgeon; Prof. W. H. Young, Brigadier-Engineer; Rev. J. Pratt, Brigadier-Chaplain. The following call was issued by General Constable:

"The United States Government, through the Governor of Ohio, calls upon the people of the counties of Washington, Athens, Meigs and Gallia for ten companies of infantry, of not less than seventy-five rank and file each. Able-bodied men between the ages of eighteen and forty-five are required. The time of enlistment is three months. Volunteers will be received and enrolled in the cities of Marietta, Athens, Pomeroy, and in Gallipolis."

The volunteers swarmed into Athens in greater numbers than they could be received, and went into camp. Their temporary home at this time received the name of "Camp Jewett," and Camp Jewett was soon a scene of great activity. Fully two hundred men were in a few days quartered here, drilling and organizing for service, under the command of General Constable. Most of the new soldiers were made of the right kind of material, but many fancied that their three months' service would be but a grand pleasure excursion to Washington or to the South, and that they would soon return to their admiring friends "covered all over with glory." They soon found out the reality of war, the hardships of soldier life, etc., and that the war was more than a three months' task. The change from the independence and luxury of Camp Jewett to the rigorous discipline and plain fare of army life, too, was not relished by many; but the majority stoically accepted the situation, and fought the four years' war through.

GOING INTO ACTIVE SERVICE.

The Ohio State Guards, of ninety-six men, was the first company to leave Camp Jewett. It was ordered to Camp Dennison, near Miamiville, where it was mustered into the service of the United States as Company C, Third Regiment. This company, under the command of Captain J. M. Dana, carried the flag of the regiment, and thus occupied the post of honor. It left Athens for Camp Dennison, May 1. The occasion of its departure was one of peculiar interest and solemnity. Many of the volunteers were leaving behind them wives and families, brothers and sisters, and all the fond associations of many years' formation. There was many a moist eye, and many a heart swelled with emotion, but none lacked the courage demanded for the trying scene—the parting of bosom friends from their mates, perhaps forever. Just before their departure each of the volunteers was presented with a New Testament by Revs. Pratt and Porter. A short, patriotic speech was afterward made by Hon. V. B. Horton. Then the shrill whistle of the locomotive screamed, "Good-bye," "God bless you" and "Farewell," were quickly exchanged, and with cheer after cheer they departed. The boys reached Camp Dennison safely, but found poor quarters there even for a soldier. Many of them, without even a blanket, were compelled to lie out all of the first night.

The next company to leave Camp Jewett was Captain E. A. Guthrie's, numbering ninety-nine men, which became Company B, Twenty-second Ohio.

Recruits continued to pour into Camp Jewett, and another company was soon filled. This became Company H, Twenty-second Regiment, and consisted of eighty-nine men. It left Athens for Columbus, May 20, commanded by Captain Nathan Pickett.

Thus in one month's time, Athens County sent forward for the war 300 men. They were fine, able-bodied men, and volunteered with a resolute determination to aid with their whole strength in the suppression of the Rebellion. Captain Pickett's company was raised almost entirely in Dover Township. Two of the commissioned officers, Captain Pickett and Lieutenant Stedman, had seen service in the Mexican War. It is an interesting coincidence that there were seven printers in Captain Dana's company, four of whom were from the office of the Athens *Messenger*. A band of marauders organized in the county and did some desperate deeds. They were lawless characters, who, thinking there was no law, undertook to carry out a programme of thieving and intimidation. They were suppressed.

Among the early appointments to the higher grades of the service was that of W. S. Smith to the position of Assistant Adjutant-General, with the rank of Lieutenant-Colonel, on General Sleich's staff. Colonel Smith was a brother of Lot L. Smith, of Athens, and a graduate of the Ohio University. He was presented, June 5, 1861, just after his appointment as Assistant Adjutant-General, with a beautiful sword by the citizens of Athens, through Hon. S. B. Pruden. On the same occasion a Colt's revolver was presented by C. H. Grosvenor to Captain E. A. Guthrie. Colonel Smith was soon after appointed to the command of the Thirteenth Infantry, and early in 1862 he became a Brigadier-General.

The rapidity with which recruits poured into Camp Wool (the name of "Camp Jewett" was dropped after a few weeks, and the name of "Camp Wool" adopted instead) was fairly astonishing. As if knowing that the war would last for years, and that the Union cause would require all the men that could be spared, the county responded as though animated by one mind. Every township raised a company or half a company of men for three years' service, while those who did not enlist devoted their energies toward raising a good crop, knowing that provisions are the staple necessity of an army. Besides the soldiers of our own vicinity company after company came to Athens from other counties, *en route* to Camp Dennison or some Eastern point. Thus Athens was almost constantly a scene of military activity. By the first of August, 1861, Athens County had raised 1,000 men for the Union army. Eight companies had left, under orders, for Camp Dennison and elsewhere (three of these companies had already seen hard service in West Virginia), while five others were being raised in different parts of the county.

FIRST RETURNS.

The first regiment to return to this part of the State, after the expiration of its term of service, was the Twenty-second Infantry, commanded by Colonel Gilmore. It arrived at Athens, Aug. 4, 1861, and immediately went into quarters at Camp Wool. This regiment had seen the hardest kind of service in marching about from one place to another over the hills and mountains of West Virginia. Four companies, Captain Olmstead's (Company I), Captain Payne's (Company K), Captain Wilhelm's (Company G), and Captain Guthrie's (Company B), were scouting from one place to another nearly all the time after the regiment left Camp Wool until its return. They performed one feat that is worthy of special mention. From Spencer to Glenville, Va., is about forty-two miles. About six miles of this distance was marched in the night. The next morning the four companies started for Glenville, about thirty-six miles distant, where they arrived between eight and nine o'clock in the evening. It rained during the whole day, and the men had to cut away large trees and heaps of rubbish thrown across the road by the rebels in several places. During the day an alarm was given that the advance guard was attacked. Immediately the whole force started off on " double quick," and continued at this rate for a distance of four miles, when they overtook the guard and found the alarm to be false. The Twenty-second remained in camp about two weeks, and were paid off Aug. 21 and 22, and discharged.

One of the brightest pages in the record of Athens County's war history is the remembrance of the sanitary and relief work done by the patriotic citizens—particularly the ladies—all over the county. In October, 1861, an appeal was made for contributions of clothing, etc., for the soldiers. No sooner was it known that these articles were needed, than the citizens immediately took effective measures toward organized relief. A county committee was appointed, known as the " Military Committee," consisting of Joseph Jewett, Rudolph De Steigner, Albert Parsons, H. T. Brown and William P. Kessinger. This committee appointed relief committees in every township, which were urged to act at once, and send in to the county committee such contributions as they could collect. The following are the township relief committees:

Athens.—Judge Barker, Samuel Pickering, Jared Maris and C. W. Goodspeed.

Alexander.—Elmer Armstrong, Hon. James Gibson and William Campbell.

Lee.—John T. Winn, Leonard Brown and Dr. John Earhart.

Lodi.—Joseph Cramer, Dr. Moore and William Jeffries.

Carthage.—James Caldwell, Walter Glazier and Amasa Saunders.
Trimble.—Benjamin Norris, William Russell and Dr. J. Dew.
York.—J. L. Mintern, Charles Ashton and Joseph Brett.
Dover.—Eli F. Brown, Henry Brown and G. T. Gould.
Ames.—N. P. Hoisington, A. W. Glazier and James Bryson.
Bern.—P. W. Lampson, Samuel Wells and George Wyatt.
Troy.—John Frame, E. A. Gibbs and Sherman Brewster.
Rome.—D. B. Stewart, Elmer Rowell and Hiram Gard.
Canaan.—N. O. Warren, Peter Finsterwald and William Burch.
Waterloo.—Hugh Boden, W. H. Allison and P. C. Hewett.

In Athens village the committee appointed some sixteen ladies to solicit contributions. As a result of these prompt steps, large quantities of clothing and other useful articles were sent to our soldiers, which not only aided in making many brave men comfortable, but beyond a doubt saved many a volunteer's life. This work was kept up through the war, and in this way the ladies of the North did effectual service in crushing the Rebellion.

The rebel raid by General John Morgan in the summer of 1863 is well remembered by the citizens of the Hocking Valley, for his forces were for a few days rather "numerous" in this region. He was at that time on a run for life, rather than a raid of destruction; otherwise we should have suffered much more from his presence. The general facts of the raid are well known. His arrival, however, in Athens County, caused considerable consternation among the people, as it did along the line of his march. He had undertaken to cross the Ohio River at Hockingport but the gun-boats were too much for him and he lost about 1,000 of his men at that point, they having surrendered. General Morgan, with about 400, turned toward Gallipolis, crossing the railroad at Vinton, some fifteen miles north of that city, and then turned directly north. About eleven o'clock in the forenoon the people of Nelsonville and vicinity were thrown into confusion by the unwelcome intelligence that the famous General John Morgan and his forces were within a mile of town. In a very short time they came pouring in from all directions, and took complete but quiet possession of the town. Nearly every house was visited and made to serve meals to two or more of the strangers. Never was food given more grudgingly by the usually hospitable people of Nelsonville. The rebels are described by those whom they visited here as being dirty and ragged, of various kinds of dress, and an extremely hard-looking lot of men.

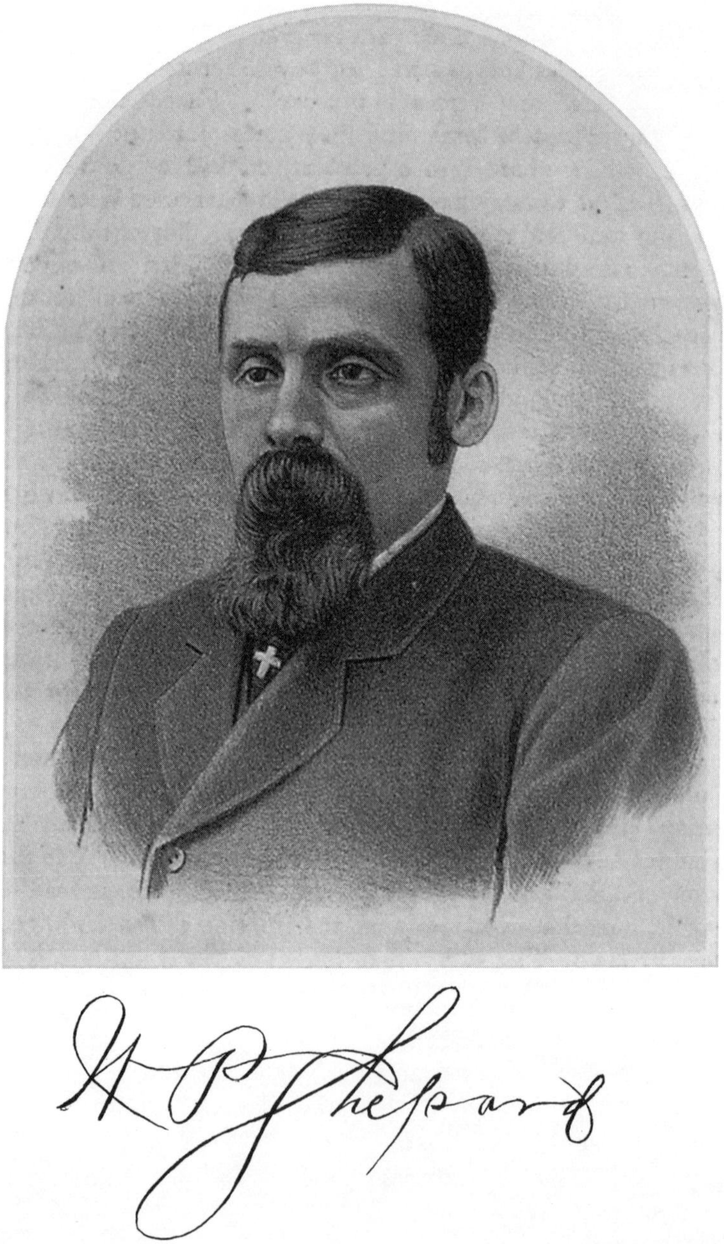
H P Shepard

After they had eaten all they could find in the houses, they entered the stores and helped themselves to new clothes and other things that suited them. They paid for part of them. They then visited all the stables and pastures near town in search of horses, of which they took all that were able to travel. When the news first came of their approach, some rode their horses into the woods to save them, while others were overtaken and had to deliver up. Farmers from the country had their horses unharnessed from their wagons, and were left to get home the best way they could. The plundering was all done in a very quiet manner. Just before leaving they fired the river bridge on which they crossed, and all the canal boats that were in port, about twelve in number, turning families out upon the banks without saving a thing but the clothes on their backs. They kindled a fire in the cabin of one boat where there was a sick woman. Her pleadings were of no avail, and she was obliged to make her escape the best way she could. L. D. Poston's coal-works caught fire from the boats, but were put out after the rebels left without much damage. The plunderers remained in town about two hours, and left between one and two o'clock to spread terror and devastation along their route through the country. Morgan himself was recognized by several persons in Nelsonville. The cavalry in pursuit of Morgan under Major Wolford, entered Nelsonville about five o'clock, but four hours behind him.

Morgan moved northeast through the counties of Morgan, Guernsey, and Harrison, and at noon on Saturday, the 25th, was approaching Wintersville, a place about four miles north of Steubenville. Here he was headed off by militia. Thence he moved north in the direction of the Cleveland & Pittsburg Railroad. He arrived at Salineville, near that road, early on the morning of the 26th, and was met by Major Way with a detachment of the First Michigan Cavalry. After an hour's hard fighting Morgan was completely routed, and the delay occasioned by this engagement enabled General Shackleford, who was only a few miles away, to catch up with Morgan, who surrendered three miles south of New Gibson, Columbiana County.

The part taken by the ladies of Athens County during the week of the Morgan raid was no inconsiderable one. As a proof of their liberality and generous patriotism the following statement is given of the provisions furnished soldiers at Athens for one week: Friday, July 17, dinner on the college green for 65, supper for 300.

Saturday, breakfast for 200, lunch and coffee at the depot, at three o'clock P. M. for upward of 3,000, supper for 80. Sunday, breakfast for 90, dinner for 100, supper for 110. Monday, breakfast at five o'clock A. M. for 150, at six A. M. for 90, dinner at 12 M. for 100, at one P. M. for 90, supper at five P. M. for 90, at six P. M. for 68. Tuesday, breakfast for 90. Wednesday, breakfast for 112. Friday, lunch at the depot for 300. This is, of course, exclusive of those who were provided for at private houses or at the hotels, which were all filled to overflowing. The provisions were supplied for the first two or three days by the citizens of Athens. After that the war committee furnished bacon and coffee. Abundant supplies of bread, biscuit, pies, cake, etc., poured in from the country around, four wagon-loads coming from the patriotic town of Nelsonville alone.

A general order was issued from the Adjutant-General's office Aug. 15, 1863, dividing the State into military districts and directing that there be held in 1863 in each district one officers' muster and encampment, each to continue eight days. The First District included the counties of Athens, Meigs, Washington, Morgan, Hocking, Vinton and Ross, and its officer muster and encampment were directed to be held on the lands of Messrs. Cable and Brooks, at Athens, to be called "Camp Athens." All officers of the militia and volunteers, and also all non-commissioned officers of militia and volunteers of the rank of sergeant, were to attend the camp in their proper district and participate in the drill and instructions throughout the period of its duration; while the various companies of militia, privates as well as officers, were ordered to attend the encampment during the last two days for drill and instruction. The encampment for the First District was appointed for Saturday, Sept. 5, and to last till Saturday, the 12th.

The encampment was held according to appointment, and was a decided success. The weather was fine and favorable for drilling, and a good degree of efficiency was secured for those in attendance. About 6,000 men, including 1,000 militia officers, were in camp. Several companies were completely uniformed. Among these were an artillery company from Washington County, and one from Meigs; and infantry companies from Marietta and Middleport. It was a grand sight on the last two days to see the battalion drill, and it would have been still more imposing, had all been uniformed and armed. The Thirty-sixth Regiment of Ohio Volunteer Militia also met at Camp Athens for drill, Sept. 29, 1863, by order of the regimental officers.

Toward the close of 1863, a "Great Western Sanitary Fair" was held at Cincinnati for the purpose of raising funds, clothing, provisions, etc., to better the condition of our soldiers, and aid in preparing them to endure the winter. A branch organization was perfected in Athens County, with N. H. Van Vorhes as Secretary and Treasurer, and the county was canvassed for contributions, and its offering amounted to about $3,000, over half of which was in cash.

In the spring of 1864 the Governors of Ohio, Indiana, Illinois, Iowa and Wisconsin offered the General Government the services of 85,000 men for 100 days. They thought that the men could be easily raised for this short term of service, and these 100-days men could render efficient service by being placed on guard duty and in garrisons, and enabling the experienced soldiers to go to the front. The Government accepted the tender, and the call for the 100-days men was accordingly made. Ohio's quota was 30, 000, but the militia offered themselves to the number of 38,000. Athens County furnished five companies, which, together with a battalion from Gallia County were organized as the One Hundred and Forty-first Ohio Volunteer Infantry. This regiment was ordered to border duty in West Virginia.

Under the President's call for 500,000 men made in 1863, the quota of Athens County was 250 men, and a general draft was anticipated. But volunteers stepped briskly forward, month after month, induced partly by the liberal bounties, general and private, and when the draft finally came, in the summer of 1864, but eight men were drawn for Athens County. This was just after the county had furnished half a regiment of 100-days men.

The county thus maintained its patriotic record to the end of the war, which came in April, 1865, in the shape of complete victory for the Union arms. Never was there a more jubilant feeling in Athens and vicinity than when the news came of the surrender of Lee. The evening of Friday the 14th saw the town literally ablaze with light, and a brilliant display of fire-works added to the festivities. At the hall the citizens gave vent to their exuberance of feeling in speeches and enthusiastic cheers.

On Saturday morning the joy was unabated, and every one was in the happiest mood when the crushing news came of the assassination of our beloved President—Abraham Lincoln. Twice death had tread the halls of the White House, but never fell a sorrow like this on our people. Business was suspended for want of heart to carry it on, voices were muffled, and the bells tolled the live-long heavy day, in unison with the general sorrow. At night there was a spontaneous meeting of citizens at the M. E. church to testify their sorrow for the nation's loss and to debate over the mournful event. Judge Welch was called to the chair, and A. B. Walker appointed Secretary. An impressive prayer was delivered by Rev. Mr. Prettyman, after which Judge Welch made an appropriate and able address to the audience. A committee of three was then appointed by the Chair, consisting of Hon. C. Morris, Samuel Pickering and E. H. Moore, to prepare resolutions for the action of the meeting. While the committee were out, further remarks were made by Dr. Prettyman, Colonel W. H. Young, Judge Welch and Hon. W. P. Johnson. The committee reported that in view of a more general demonstration soon to be held by the county, they did not deem it necessary to report matters for action at that time. On the 17th a very large and general meeting of the citizens was held at the Atheneum. Dr. W. P. Johnson was appointed to the chair, and A. B. Walker was chosen Secretary. The meeting was addressed briefly by Hon. John Welch, who, at the close of his remarks, offered a series of resolutions appropriate to the heart-rending intelligence of the President's tragic death.

This properly closes the narrative of Athens County's part in the war. The following table shows the number of soldiers furnished by each township:

TOWNSHIPS.	NO. IN U. S. ARMY.	NO. OF 100-DAYS MEN.	TOTAL.
Athens	267	96	363
Alexander	162	58	220
Ames	142	—	142
Bern	108	—	108
Carthage	112	—	112
Canaan	117	10	127
Dover	154	30	184
Lee	117	68	185
Lodi	143	39	182
Rome	156	54	210
Trimble	143	27	170
Troy	181	—	181
Waterloo	162	—	162
York	226	38	264
Total	2,190	420	2,610

The principal regiments in which Athens County was represented were the Third, Eighteenth, Thirty-sixth, Thirty-ninth, Sixty-ninth, Seventy-fifth, Ninety-second and One Hundred and Sixteenth Infantry and the Seventh Cavalry.

CHAPTER VIII.

STATISTICS OF ATHENS COUNTY—POPULATION, AGRICULTURAL, POLITICAL.

POPULATION BY TOWNSHIPS AND BY DECADES—VALUE OF REAL AND PERSONAL PROPERTY IN 1870, 1880, 1881 AND 1882—ASSESSED VALUATION OF IN 1846, 1853, AND 1859—RECORD OF MARRIAGES AND DEATHS—PAUPERISM—LAND SALES—MORTGAGES—DOG AND SHEEP STATISTICS—RAILROAD AND TELEGRAPH—POLITICAL—PRESIDENTIAL VOTE, 1836 TO 1880—GOVERNOR'S VOTE, 1836 TO 1880—VOTE FOR SECRETARY OF STATE—THE COUNTY VOTE BY TOWNSHIPS.

POPULATION BY DECADES.

By the census of 1800, Washington County (then including Athens County) had 5,427 inhabitants.

By the census of 1810, Athens County had

561	males	and	517	females	under	10	years.	
234	"	"	210	" between	10 and 16	"		
241	"	"	260	"	"	16	" 26	"
283	"	"	235	"	"	26	" 45	"
144	"	"	102	"	over	45 years.		
1,463			1,324					

Total population in 1810.................2,787.

POPULATION BY TOWNSHIPS IN 1820.

	MALES.	FEMALES.	TOTAL.
Ames	388	333	721
Athens	582	532	1,114
Alexander	421	433	854
Canaan	193	163	356
Carthage	175	145	320
Dover	330	277	607
Elk	274	271	545
Homer	101	100	201
Lee	185	157	342
Rome	266	231	497
Troy	295	246	541
York	183	158	341
Aggregate	3,393	3,046	6,439

It must be borne in mind that the boundaries of some of the townships underwent changes from time to time till March, 1850, since when there have been no changes.

1830.

Athens Township	1,703
Alexander	882
Ames	857
Bern	223
Canaan	375
Carthage	395
Troy	649
Dover	550
Lee	418
Lodi	276
Elk	822
Vinton	178
Homer	636
Rome	522
Trimble	190
York	871
Waterloo	216
Total	9,763

1840.

TOWNSHIPS.	MALE.	FEMALE.	TOTAL.
Alexander	728	723	1,451
Ames	718	713	1,431
Athens	1,178	1,104	2,282
Bern	196	185	381
Brown	132	125	257
Canaan	421	379	800
Carthage	397	337	734
Dover	679	611	1,290
Elk	647	614	1,261
Homer	451	461	912
Lee	440	408	848
Lodi	394	360	754
Marion	569	510	1,079
Rome	427	425	852
Trimble	385	377	762
Troy	546	510	1,056
Ward	179	157	336
Waterloo	382	359	741
Vinton	108	119	227
York	863	737	1,600
Total white	9,840	9,214	19,054
Colored persons	....	....	55
Aggregate population	....	....	19,109

STATISTICS OF THE COUNTY FOR THE YEAR 1850—POPULATION.

	WHITE MAL'S	WHITE FEM.	TOTAL.	COLORED.	AGGREGATE.
Alexander....	869	859	1,728	7	1,735
Ames........	780	702	1,482	..	1,482
Athens......	1,151	1,179	2,330	30	2,360
Bern.........	432	387	819	..	819
Canaan	589	553	1,142	..	1,142
Carthage......	554	533	1,087	..	1,087
Dover........	628	604	1,232	..	1,232
Lee..........	480	477	957	4	961
Lodi	678	655	1,333	3	1,336
Rome	650	627	1,277	32	1,309
Trimble	482	442	924	..	924
Troy.........	686	735	1,421	..	1,421
Waterloo.....	511	487	998	18	1,016
York.........	745	634	1,379	12	1,391
Total........	9,235	8,874	18,109	106	18,215

CHURCHES.

	NO. OF CHURCHES	VALUE.
Baptist..	2	$ 1,100
Methodist.....................................	12	8,250
Presbyterian...	8	7,000
Roman Catholic................................	1	800
Universalist....................................	1	800
	24	$ 17,950

AGRICULTURAL STATISTICS, 1850.

Acres of land improved in farms...........................	82,168	
Acres of land unimproved.................................	103,109	
Cash value of farms......................................		$ 2,125,967
Value of farming implements and machinery...............		92,283
Number of horses..	3,345	
Number of milch cows....................................	4,302	
Number of working oxen..................................	1,331	
Number of other cattle	6,260	
Number of sheep...	35,945	
Number of swine	15,675	
Value of of live stock.....................................		$314,894
Value of slaughtered animals..............................		75,551
		$ 2,608,695
Bushels of wheat...	72,146	
Bushels of rye..	395	
Bushels of Indian corn	443,546	
Bushels of oats	74,255	
Pounds of tobacco..	58,356	
Pounds of wool...	92,990	

AGRICULTURAL STATISTICS, 1850—CONTINUED.

Bushels of Irish potatoes.................................. 34,447
Bushels of sweet potatoes................................ 2,328
Bushels of buckwheat................................... 7,095
Value of orchard products............................... $ 6,199
Pounds of butter..257,302
Pounds of cheese.. 58,170
Tons of hay... 12,188
Bushels of clover seed................................... 375
Bushels of other grass seeds............................. 229
Pounds of flax.. 7,618
Bushels of flax seed.................................... 348
Pounds of maple sugar.................................. 28,665
Gallons of maple molasses............................... 2,052
Pounds of beeswax and honey............................ 9,983
Value of home-made manufactures .... $ 28,325

POPULATION BY TOWNSHIPS, 1860.

	WHITE MAL'S.	WHITE FEM.	TOTAL.	COLORED.	AGGREGATE.
Alexander....	816	843	1,659	16	1,675
Ames.......	675	657	1,332	3	1,335
Athens......	1,413	1,394	2,807	45	2,852
Bern	482	472	954	68	1,022
Canaan	639	633	1,272	..	1,272
Carthage.....	579	548	1,127	..	1,127
Dover........	722	699	1,421	2	1,423
Lee..........	565	562	1,127	174	1,301
Lodi.........	818	780	1,598	..	1,598
Rome........	787	749	1,536	45	1,581
Trimble.....	574	536	1,110	2	1,112
Troy.........	876	871	1,747	..	1,747
Waterloo....	765	701	1,466	17	1,483
York........	969	853	1,822	14	1,836
Aggregate..					21,364

CHURCHES.

	NO. OF CHURCHES.	VALUE.
Baptist...	1	$ 650
Baptist, Free-Will.....................................	5	4,600
Christian..	3	1,825
Episcopal...	2	700
Methodist...	42	23,565
Presbyterian..	5	10,550
Cumberland Presbyterian..............................	1	1,000
Roman Catholic.......................................	1	800
Union...	1	600
Universalist...	1	600
Total number..	62	$44,890

The valuation of estate, real and personal, in the county for the year 1860, was:—

Real	$6,467,950
Personal	2,600,677
	$9,068,627

AGRICULTURAL STATISTICS, 1860.

Acres of land improved, in farms	129,531	
Acres of land unimproved	123,170	
Cash value of farms		$4,980,034
Value of farming implements and machinery		156,646
Number of horses	5,731	
Number of asses and mules	33	
Number of milch cows	5,658	
Number of working oxen	1,558	
Number of other cattle	11,597	
Number of sheep	36,498	
Number of swine	21,447	
Value of live stock		748,589
Bushels of wheat produced	120,082	
Bushels of rye	721	
Bushels of Indian corn	641,605	
Bushels of oats	66,104	
Pounds of tobacco	275,789	
Pounds of wool	88,968	
Bushels of peas and beans	2,428	
Bushels of Irish potatoes	57,261	
Bushels of sweet potatoes	3,600	
Bushels of barley	476	
Bushels of buckwheat	14,930	
Value of orchard products		$17,799
Pounds of butter	634,872	
Pounds of cheese	89,213	
Tons of hay	19,278	
Bushels of clover seed	104	
Bushels of grass seed	1,098	
Pounds of hops	356	
Tons of hemp	79	
Pounds of flax	2,774	
Bushels of flax seed	118	
Pounds of maple sugar	22,778	
Gallons of maple molasses	2,549	
Gallons of sorghum molasses	28,335	
Pounds of beeswax	554	
Pounds of honey	19,540	
Value of home-made manufactures		15,978
Value of animals slaughtered		122,375

MANUFACTURES, 1860.

	CAPITAL INVESTED.	ANNUAL VAL. OF PRODUCTS
Blacksmithing	$ 1,750	$ 4,452
Boots and shoes	3,700	16,794
Carriages	8,200	4,113
Clothing	7,100	12,150
Coal	49,450	49,700
Flour and meal	70,400	263,938
Furniture	3,950	4,030
Leather	26,815	29,028
Lumber	32,200	46,944
Machinery	3,000	7,100
Marble and stone work	800	3,500
Pottery ware	1,000	800
Printing	3,000	2,400
Provisions—pork and beef	10,000	12,000
Saddlery and harness	2,700	6,141
Salt	96,000	59,050
Tin, copper and sheet iron ware	1,000	2,585
Wagons, carts, etc.	1,400	1,700
Wool carding	1,500	9,860
Total	$331,665	$545,002

STATISTICS OF THE COUNTY FOR THE YEAR 1866.

Products of Athens County in the year 1865–'6.

Number of acres of wheat............13,176,   Number of bushels.....104,893
Number of acres of rye................. 153,   Number of bushels..... 1,450
Number of acres of buckwheat........ 243,   Number of bushels..... 2,450
Number of acres of oats.............. 3,403,   Number of bushels..... 56,445
Number of acres of corn.............15,422,   Number of bushels....546,791
Number of acres of meadow..........15,188,   Tons of hay........... 18,206
Number of acres of potatoes.......... 514,   Number of bushels.... 40,462
Number of acres of tobacco........... 168,   Number of pounds.....136,460
Number of acres of clover........... 755,   Number of tons of hay..   799
Number of acres of sorghum 526,   Number of gall. syrup... 80,253
Number of lbs. of maple sugar.......14,347,   Number of gall. syrup.. 1,391
Number of lbs. of butter............327,480,
Number of lbs. of cheese ....27,705.

Number of sheep in the county.................................. 75,406
Value $221,585
Number of hogs in the county................................... 12,191
Value $60,342
Amount of wool produced, pounds............................... 189,183
Number of dogs in the county................................... 1,082
Number of sheep killed by dogs 304
Number of deeds and leases recorded............................... 713
Number of mortgages recorded...................................... 144
Amount of money secured by mortgage.......................... $124,658
Number of crimes indicted during the year.......................... 42
Number of convictions.. 27
Number of marriages during the same year.......................... 352
Number of divorces... 15
Number of dwellings erected during same year....................... 50
Number of barns... 9
Number of factories... 1
Number of school-houses... 2
Number of civil judgments rendered during same year................ 91
Amount of civil judgments rendered during same year........ $55,026.03

STATISTICS OF THE COUNTY IN 1870.

POPULATION BY TOWNSHIPS.

TOWNSHIPS.	TOTAL.	NATIVE.	FOREIGN.	WHITE.	COLORED.
Alexander	1,511	1,502	9	1,506	5
Ames	1,229	1,220	9	1,195	34
Athens	3,277	3,063	214	3,031	246
Bern	1,014	1,007	7	990	24
Canaan	1,543	1,461	82	1,543	....
Carthage	1,272	1,231	41	1,272	....
Dover	1,697	1,648	49	1,689	8
Lee	1,146	1,133	13	888	258
Lodi	1,551	1,528	23	1,551	....
Rome	1,972	1,897	75	1,861	111
Trimble	1,379	1,365	14	1,373	6
Troy	1,830	1,809	21	1,815	15
Waterloo	1,695	1,587	108	1,663	32
York	2,652	2,465	187	2,618	34
Total	23,768	22,916	852	22,995	773

VALUE OF REAL ESTATE—1870.

Acres of land.................. 305,924
Aggregate number of buildings..466,474
Aggregate value of lands.....$3,790,722
Value in towns of lots and b'ld's $747,428

Total value of real property...$5,004,624

PERSONAL PROPERTY.

Number of horses..6,091
Value of same..$367,158
Number of cattle..17,745
Value of same..$326,670
Number of mules..135
Value of same..$9,215
Number of sheep..45,217
Value of same...$77,269
Number of hogs..17,161
Value of same...$62,763

MARRIAGES AND BIRTHS.

Number of marriages 232
Number of white males born........261 | Number of white females born......217
   "   " colored "   " ......10 | "   " colored "   " 13
Total number of births...501

AGRICULTURAL PRODUCTS—1870.

Total value of farm products..$1,607,698	Bushels of rye.....2,187
Value of orchard products.......91,499	" of Indian corn.......619,447
" " animals slaughtered....387,997	" of oats.....96,012
Bushels of clover seed.......79	" of barley.....110
" " grass seed.......149	" of buckwheat.....586
Pounds of hops.....19	Pounds of tobacco.....207,839
" " flax.....300	" of wool.....201,593
Bushels of flax seed.....14	Bushels of peas and beans.....286
Pounds of maple sugar.....8,118	" of Irish potatoes.....78,721
Gallons of sorghum molasses.....1,027	" of sweet " 1,655
" " maple molasses.....43,820	Gallons of wine.....69
Pounds of beeswax.....486	Pounds of butter.....513,864
Pounds of honey.....17,118	" of cheese.....22,265
Bushels of spring wheat.....468	Gallons of milk sold.....9,029
" of winter wheat.....123,277	Tons of hay.....23,239

STATISTICS OF THE COUNTY IN 1880 AND LATER.

POPULATON BY TOWNSHIPS, 1880.

Alexander.....1,423	Lee.....1,086
Ames.....1,392	Lodi.....1,550
Athens.....4,517	Rome.....2,207
Bern.....1,073	Trimble.....1,367
Canaan.....1,499	Troy.....1,858
Carthage.....1,308	Waterloo.....1,957
Dover.....1,736	York.....5,438

Total.....28,411

POPULATION OF VILLAGES, 1880.

Nelsonville.....3,095	Shade.....175
Athens.....2,457	Chauncey.....185
Carbondale.....500	Amesville.....159
Albany.....469	Floodwood.....159
Buchtel.....417	Pleasant Valley.....150
Lick Run.....400	Torch.....150
Frost.....350	Trimble.....121
Coolville.....323	Pleasanton.....107
Guysville.....250	Millfield.....101
Stewart.....203	Mineral City.....100
Canaanville.....200	Hebbardsville.....92
Jacksonville.....200	New England.....75
Salina.....200	Garden.....50
Hockingport.....191	Lottridge.....50
Marshfield.....191	

AGRICULTURAL STATISTICS, 1880.

Acres of wheat.	19,862
Number of bushels produced.	234,558
Average number of bushels per acre.	11.8
Acres sown for 1881.	19,054
Cost of fertilizers bought for 1881.	13,032
Acres of rye.	179
Number of bushels produced.	1,329
Acres of buckwheat.	170

AGRICULTURAL STATISTICS, 1880—CONTINUED.

Number of bushels produced	1,918
Acres of barley	11
Number of bushels produced	250
Acres of oats	1,667
Number of bushels produced	22,247
Acres of corn	17,301
Number of bushels produced	578,856
Acres of grass other than clover	17,474
Number of tons of hay produced	16,291
Acres of clover	1,022
Number of tons of hay produced	422
Number of bushels of seed	51
Acres of potatoes	1,134
Number of bushels produced	76,234
Acres of sweet potatoes	42
Number of bushels produced	3,079
Acres of tobacco	109
Number of pounds produced	90,146
Acres of sorghum	171
Number of pounds of sugar	65
" " gallons of syrup	13,241
Maple sugar, number of pounds produced	5,315
" syrup " gallons "	2,474
Number of hives of bees	1,294
" pounds of honey produced	17,106
" " butter "	502,696
" " cheese "	14,545
" dozens of eggs "	292,221
Acres of orchards	5,084
Number of bushels of apples produced	186,284
" " peaches "	34,996
" " pears "	658
" " cherries "	4,877
" " plums "	1,749
Acres of vineyard	25
Number of pounds of grapes produced	23,455
" gallons of wine "	502
Pounds of wool shorn	402,832
Sheep killed by dogs	461
Value of same	$1,624
Sheep injured by dogs	191
Estimated damage done	$618
Aggregate of injury done to sheep by dogs	$2,242

STATISTICS, 1881—RAILROADS.

Miles of main lines	54.45
Single track branches	17.42
Sidings, etc	19.92
Total miles	91.79
Value of realty	$ 22,535
" personalty	791,728
Total valuation	$814,216
Taxes for 1881	$16,299.04

LAND SALES, 1881.

Number of sales of agricultural lands..................................	546
" acres in same..	37,440
Average price per acre..	$29.00
Total amount paid for same..	$1,091,409.07
Number of sales of "town acres".....................................	27
" acres in same...	61
Average price per acre..	$132
Total amount paid for same..	$8,060.19
Number of sales of town lots..	270
Total amount paid for same..	$17,624
Mixed sales of land..	6
Sales of lands for one dollar..	37
Total number of sales recorded..	886
Total amount of consideration..	$1,117,093.26

REAL PROPERTY EXEMPT FROM TAXATION.

Common school property, lands................................$	8,350
" " " buildings.................................	54,051
Church property, lands...	3,795
" " buildings...	49,924
Charitable institutions, lands...	9,935
" " buildings...	805,500
Other lands...	20,875
" buildings..	65,600
Cemeteries, etc...	2,865
Aggregate exemptions..	1,020,895

SHEEP KILLED AND INJURED, 1882.

Number of sheep killed by dogs......................................	395
Value " " "...	$1,448
Number " injured ".....................................	259
Damage to " " "...............................	$ 599
Paid for sheep killed...	1,160
" " injured...	506
Total paid...	1,666
Collected from dog tax, including balance.......................	2,710
Transferred to school fund..	823
Balance of "dog tax fund"..	221

BIRTHS, 1881.

White, males...	276
White, females..	294
Colored, males..	13
Colored, females..	6
Total number of births...	581

PAUPERISM, 1881.

Males in infirmary...	47
Females in infirmary...	58
Total in infirmary..	105
Number admitted during year, males..............................	35
Number admitted during year, females............................	41
Whole number admitted during year...............................	76

Paupers otherwise supported by county, males........................... 40
Paupers otherwise supported by county, females........................ 54
Whole number of paupers otherwise supported....................... 94

Total number of all paupers... 275
Cost of keeping infirmary...$ 7,205.71
Cost of keeping other paupers....................................... 3,756.72
Cost of all paupers... 10,962.43
Cost of each pauper per day... .17

DEATHS, 1881.

White, males... 85
White, females.. 102
Colored, females... 5

Total deaths.. 192

MARRIAGES, 1881.

Marriages of white citizens.. 285
Marriages of colored citizens... 7

MORTGAGES.

Mortgages recorded... 350
Amount of same...$ 2,501,883.75
Canceled... 220
Amount of same.. $205,954.42

GRAND DUPLICATE, 1882.

Acres of land.. 313,332

Value of lands... $4,721,849
Value of real estate in cities, towns and villages.................. 855,373
Value of chattel property... 3,018,169

Total value... $8,595,391

5-10 mill tax for payment of State debt.........................$ 3,801.24
1 and 4-10 mill tax for general revenue, State................... 10,643.54
1 mill tax for common school fund............................... 7,602.52
Total State tax, 2 and 9-10 mills................................ 22,047.30
All other than State taxes...................................... 150,091.96
Delinquent taxes, real estate................................... 1,883.99
Delinquent taxes, personal property............................. 1,278.58
Dog tax, one dollar per capita................................... 1,681.00
County tax.. 25,786.17
Poor tax.. 12,033.06
Bridge tax.. 17,190.79
Road tax.. 13,354.63
Township tax.. 9,792.95
Sub-district tax.. 39,222.43
Other special taxes... 18,909.83
City, town and village taxes.................................... 13,801.60

PERSONAL PROPERTY, MONEYS AND CREDITS, 1882.

Number of horses	4,895
Value of horses	$283,103
Number of cattle	12,242
Value of cattle	$192,031
Number of mules	268
Value of mules	$ 17,581
Number of sheep	86,996
Value of sheep	$247,465
Number of hogs	6,752
Value of hogs	$ 22,429
Number of carriages	705
Value of carriages	$ 44,112
Number of watches	658
Value of watches	$ 13,659
Number pianos and organs	415
Value of pianos and organs	$ 26,670
Merchants' stock	$235,337
Manufacturers' stock	85,385
Moneys on hand or in deposit	214,249
Credits, deducting debts	482,057
Stocks, bonds, etc	12,065

EQUALIZED REAL PROPERTY.

Valuation of real property, 1846	$1,655,974
Valuation of real property, 1853	2,676,829
Valuation of real property, 1859	3,225,608
Valuation of real property, 1870	5,064,679
Valuation of real property, 1880	5,267,770

VALUATION AND TAXATION, 1881 AND 1882.

TOWNSHIPS AND CORPORATIONS. ATHENS COUNTY.	1881. VALUATION.	RATE T'X MILLS.	1882. VALUATION.	RATE T'X MILLS.
Athens	$541,185	18.2	$544,843	18.3
Athens Corporation	805,444	28.7	853,333	26.4
Alexander	370,403	17.9	381,630	17.5
Ames	530,990	15.3	522,561	17.6
Bern	333,548	15.4	364,595	18.5
Canaan	494,530	18.6	479,565	17.1
Carthage	568,829	17.7	379,090	19.4
Dover	386,641	18.9	567,827	18.9
Lee	209,827	16.4	220,340	20.3
Albany Corporation	115,720	17.2	129,828	18.0
Albany School District	57,580	15.9	58,705	17.5
Lodi	433,651	18.1	430,230	18.1
Rome	575,621	18.8	579,620	20.8
Troy	370,552	18.6	376,594	18.5
Coolville Corporation	70,956	22.8	69,447	24.0
Coolville School District	30,760	22.0	28,790	22.0
Hockingport School District	35,555	21.0	37,555	21.5
Trimble	402,631	15.2	437,179	20.2
Waterloo	390,964	16.9	400,427	17.5
Marshfield School District	76,795	16.9	75,270	16.5
York	840,614	19.7	1,085,033	17.3
Nelsonville Corporation	546,378	29.3	572,900	30.6

POLITICAL

THE VOTE OF THE COUNTY 1836 TO 1882.

The people of Athens County have always taken an intelligent interest in political matters, and yet they have never indulged in that bitter party strife which has characterized many localities in our country. The attitude of the voters of the county can be most impartially shown by giving, without comments, the vote for the more important officers through a long series of years. We give herewith the vote for President and Governor during the years in which the two great opposing parties have contended:

PRESIDENT, IN 1836.

William Henry Harrison, whig...1098
Martin Van Buren, dem......... 957
Harrison's majority............ 141

GOVERNOR, 1836.

Joseph Vance, whig............. 966
Eli Baldwin, dem............... 736
Vance's majority............... 230

GOVERNOR, 1838.

Joseph Vance, whig............1086
Wilson Shannon, dem............ 732
Vance's majority............... 354

PRESIDENT, 1840.

William Henry Harrison, whig...2094
Martin Van Buren, dem 1322
Harrison's majority............ 772

GOVERNOR, 1842.

Thomas Corwin, whig...........1519
Wilson Shannon, dem...........1278
Corwin's majority............. 241

PRESIDENT, 1844.

Henry Clay, whig..............2050
James K. Polk, dem............1425
Birney, ab.................... 220
Clay's plurality.............. 625

GOVERNOR, 1844.

Mordecai Bartley, whig........1742
David Tod, dem................1267
Leicester King, ab............ 266
Bartley's plurality........... 475

GOVERNOR, 1846.

William Bebb, whig............1189
David Tod, dem................1007
Samuel Lewis, ab.............. 209
Bebb's plurality.............. 182

PRESIDENT, 1848.

Zachary Taylor, whig..........1846
Lewis Cass, dem...............1509
Martin Van Buren, bolter...... 320
Taylor's plurality............ 337

GOVERNOR, 1851.

Samuel F. Vinton..............1294
Reuben Wood, dem..............1162
Samuel Lewis, ab.............. 114
Vinton's plurality............ 132

PRESIDENT, 1852.

Winfield Scott, whig..........1750
Franklin Pierce, dem..........1383
John P. Hale, ab.............. 366
Scott's plurality............. 367

GOVERNOR, 1853.

Nelson Barrere, whig.......... 849
William Medill, dem...........1272
Samuel Lewis, ab.............. 735
Medill's plurality............ 423

The defeat of Scott for the Presidency in 1852 announced the virtual death of the Whig party. Since its formation, in 1854 and 1855, from Whigs and Abolitionists, the Republican party has controlled a strong majority in Athens County.

GOVERNOR, 1855.

Salmon P. Chase, rep..........1634
William Medill, dem........... 974
Allen Trimble, whig........... 98
Chase's plurality............. 660

PRESIDENT, 1856.

John C. Fremont, rep 2299
James Buchanan, dem...........1350
Millard Fillmore, American.... 159
Fremont's plurality 944

CONGRESSMAN, 1856.

V. B. Horton, rep.................2183
William Medill. dem.............1270
Horton's majority.................. 913

GOVERNOR, 1857.

Salmon P. Chase, rep.............1723
H. B. Payne, dem................1319
P. Van Trump, American........ 14
Chase's plurality.................. 404

CONGRESSMAN, 1858.

N. H. Van Vorhes, rep...........2143
C. D. Martin, dem................1303
Van Vorhes' majority............ 840

SUPREME JUDGE, 1858.

William V. Peck, rep............2105
Thomas W. Bartley, dem.........1354
Peck's majority................... 751

GOVERNOR, 1859.

William Dennison, Jr., rep......1843
R. P. Ranney, dem..............1237
Dennison's majority.............. 606

PRESIDENT, 1860.

Abraham Lincoln, rep............2526
Stephen A. Douglas, dem........1491
John Bell, American............. 36
John C. Breckinridge, Union..... 46
Lincoln's plurality............... 1035

CONGRESSMAN, 1860.

V. B. Horton, rep................2580
C. D. Martin, dem...............1386
Horton's majority................1194

GOVERNOR, 1861.

David Tod, rep..................2405
H. J. Jewett, dem............... 642
Tod's majority...................1763

SECRETARY OF STATE, 1862.

Wilson S. Kennon, rep...........1954
W. W. Armstrong, dem..........1194
Kennon's majority................ 760

CONGRESSMAN, 1862.

—— Cutler, rep..................1965
—— Morris, dem.................1185
Cutler's majority................. 780

GOVERNOR, 1863.

John Brough, rep. home vote,....2,788
"   " soldiers' vote.... 609
"   " total vote........3,397
C. L. Vallandingham, dem.
            home vote....1,008
    "   soldiers' vote.. 16
    "   total vote.... 1,024
Brough's majority...............2,373

SECRETARY OF STATE, 1864.

Wm. H. Smith, rep. home vote...2,289
    "   soldiers' vote.. 442
    "   total vote.....2,731
W.W. Armstrong, dem. home vote 1,175
    "   soldiers vote... 27
    "   total vote.....1,202
Smith's majority................1,529

PRESIDENT, 1864.

Abraham Lincoln, rep. home vote 2,474
    "   soldiers' vote.. 566
    "   total vote.....3,040
Geo. B. McClellan, dem. home vote 1,246
    "   soldiers' vote.. 72
    "   total vote.....1,318
Lincoln's majority..............1,722

CONGRESSMAN, 1864.

T. A. Plants, rep. home vote 2,280
    "   soldiers' vote.. 435
    "   total vote.....2,715
James R. Morris, dem. home vote 1,178
    "   soldiers' vote.. 14
    "   total vote.....1,192
Plants's majority...............1,523

GOVERNOR, 1865.

J. D. Cox, rep. home vote........2,541
    "   soldiers' vote.. 50
    "   total vote.....2,591
Geo. W. Morgan, dem. home vote 1,160
    "   soldiers' vote.. 10
    "   total vote.....1,170
Cox's majority..................1,421

SECRETARY OF STATE, 1866.

William H. Smith, rep...........2,647
Benjamin Lafever, dem..........1,210
Smith's majority................1,437

CONGRESSMAN, 1866.

T. A. Plants, rep...............2,640
Martin D. Follett, dem..........1,212
Plants's majority...............1,428

GOVERNOR, 1867.

Rutherford B. Hayes, rep..........2,598
Allen G. Thurman, dem..........1,701
Hayes's majority................ 897

PRESIDENT, 1868.

Ulysses S. Grant, rep............2,908
Horatio Seymour, dem...........1,592
Grant's majority................1,316

SECRETARY OF STATE, 1868.

Isaac R. Sherwood, rep..........2,725
Thomas Hubbard, dem...........1,687
Sherwood's majority.............1,038

CONGRESSMAN, 1868.

E.H. Moore, rep.................2,807
M. D. Follett, dem..............1,590
Moore's majority................1,217

GOVERNOR, 1869.

Rutherford B. Hayes, rep........2,578
Geo. H. Pendleton, dem..........1,644
Hayes's majority................ 932

SECRETARY OF STATE, 1870.

Isaac R. Sherwood, rep..........2,374
William Heisley, dem...........1,417
Sherwood's majority............. 957

CONGRESSMAN, 1870.

William P. Sprague, rep.........2,367
John Cartwright, dem...........1,440
Sprague's majority.............. 927

GOVERNOR, 1871.

Edward F. Noyes, rep............2,505
Gideon W. McCook, dem..........1,540
Noyes's majority................ 965

PRESIDENT, 1872.

Ulysses S. Grant, rep...........3,025
Horace Greeley, dem............1,398
Grant's majority................1,627

SECRETARY OF STATE, 1872.

A. T. Wikoff, rep...............2,798
Aquila Wiley, dem..............1,510
Wikoff's majority...............1,288

CONGRESSMAN, 1872.

W. P. Sprague, rep.............2,644
R. R. Hudson, dem..............1,700
Sprague's majority.............. 944

GOVERNOR, 1873.

E. F. Noyes, rep................2,576
William Allen, dem.............1,455
G. T. Stewart, pro.............. 166
Isaac Collins, lib.............. 34
Noyes's plurality...............1,121

SECRETARY OF STATE, 1874.

A. T. Wikoff, rep...............2,516
William Bell, Jr., dem..........1,684
John R. Buchtel, pro............ 101
Wikoff's plurality.............. 832

CONGRESSMAN, 1874.

N. H. VanVorhes, rep...........2,748
W. H. Oldham, dem.............1,487
Alderman, pro.................. 57
Van Vorhes's plurality..........1,261

GOVERNOR, 1875.

Rutherford B. Hayes, rep........3,192
William Allen, dem.............2,410
Hayes's majority................ 782

SECRETARY OF STATE, 1876.

Milton Barnes, rep..............3,240
William Bell, Jr., dem..........2,152
E. S. Chapman, pro............. 54
Barnes's plurality..............1,088

CONGRESSMAN, 1876.

N. H. Van Vorhes, rep..........3,264
W. W. Poston, dem.............2,044
F. J. Cathers, pro............. 47
Van Vorhes's plurality 1,220

GOVERNOR, 1877.

William H. West, rep...........2,568
Richard M. Bishop, dem........2,051
Henry A. Thompson, pro........ 145
Stephen Johnson, nat........... 15
West's plurality 517

SECRETARY OF STATE, 1878.

Milton Barnes, rep..............2,687
David R. Paige, dem............1,731
Jeremiah N. Robinson, pro...... 327
Andrew Roy, nat................ 447
Barnes's plurality.............. 956

CONGRESSMAN, 1878.

N. H. Van Vorhes, rep..........2,934
A. J. Warner, dem..............1,740
J. M. McElhinney, pro.......... 155
George E. Geddes, nat.......... 362
Van Vorhes's plurality..........1,194

GOVERNOR, 1879.

Charles Foster, rep.............3,361
Thomas Ewing, dem.............2,289
Gideon T. Stewart, pro......... 112
A. Sanders Piatt, nat.......... 73
Foster's plurality..............1,072

SECRETARY OF STATE, 1880.

Charles Townsend, rep............3543
William Lang, dem...............2244
William H. Doan, pro............. 69
Charles A. Lloyd, nat............ 85
Townsend's plurality.............1299

CONGRESSMAN, 1880.

Rufus R. Dawes, rep............ 3580
A. J. Warner, dem..............2260
Wm. Pemrose, pro............... 69
J. W. Martin, nat............... 59
Dawes's plurality...............1320

It will be seen that the Prohibition and National parties both cast their largest vote in this county in 1878. To give an idea of the complexion of the different parts of the county, we give herewith the vote by townships for President in 1876 and 1880, for Governor in 1881, and for Secretary of State and Congressman in 1882:

VOTE FOR PRESIDENT IN 1876, BY TOWNSHIPS.

TOWNSHIPS.	R. B. HAYES, REP.	S. J. TILDEN, DEM.	G. CLAY SMITH, PRO.	PETER COOPER, NAT.	TOTAL VOTE.
Athens......	606	202	14	....	822
Ames........	212	72	1	....	285
Alexander....	191	106	....	....	297
Bern	191	43	1	....	235
Canaan......	120	197	....	....	317
Carthage.....	143	120	....	....	263
Dover........	228	131	....	....	359
Lee.........	201	63	1	....	265
Lodi.........	167	164	5	....	336
Rome........	304	170	5	....	479
Trimble......	180	83	...	....	263
Troy........	251	170	11	...	432
Waterloo....	213	220	....	....	433
York	406	454	....	24	884
Totals.....	3.413	2,195	38	24	5,670

VOTE FOR PRESIDENT IN 1880, BY TOWNSHIPS.

TOWNSHIPS.	JAMES A. GARFIELD, REP.	WINFIELD S. HANCOCK, DEM.	NEAL DOW, PRO.	JAMES B. WEAVER, NAT.	TOTAL VOTE.
Athens......	602	199	20	9	830
Ames...	231	71	....	....	302
Alexander....	208	101	6	....	315
Bern.........	197	38	....	....	235
Canaan......	134	172	6	....	312
Carthage.....	161	103	1	....	265
Dover........	249	120	....	....	369
Lee....	177	56	7	2	242
Lodi.........	178	140	5	....	323
Rome........	324	131	....	......	455
Trimble.....	173	111	2	1	287
Troy........	244	168	11	11	434
Waterloo....	229	162	13	5	409
York........	538	662	....	59	1,259
Total......	3,645	2,234	71	87	6,037

The most remarkable part of the above vote is its number according to the population of the county the same year, which was 28,411, or about one vote to every four and two-thirds persons of the population.

VOTE FOR GOVERNOR IN 1881, BY TOWNSHIPS.

TOWNSHIPS.	CHARLES FOSTER, REP.	JOHN W. BOOKWALTER DEM.	ABRAHAM R. LUDLOW, PRO.	JOHN SEITZ, NAT.	TOTAL VOTE.
Athens	527	228	27	7	789
Ames	214	59	1	..	274
Alexander	159	63	9	....	231
Bern	137	29	5	2	173
Canaan	106	120	2	....	228
Carthage	127	48	10	....	185
Dover	178	83	....	7	268
Lee	131	50	38	1	220
Lodi	132	79	21	....	232
Rome	248	72	2	....	322
Trimble	163	84	....	1	248
Troy	178	111	45	10	344
Waterloo	179	143	7	12	341
York	378	648	50	197	1,273
Total	2,857	1,817	217	237	5,128

VOTE FOR SECRETARY OF STATE, 1882, BY TOWNSHIPS.

TOWNSHIPS.	CHARLES TOWNSEND, REP.	JAMES W. NEWMAN, DEM.	FRED SCHU-MACHER, PRO.	GEORGE L. HAFER, NAT.	TOTAL VOTE
Athens	477	264	24	6	771
Ames	195	159	....	....	254
Alexander	166	72	6	1	245
Bern	117	30	16	....	163
Canaan	111	151	7	....	269
Carthage	138	73	14	....	225
Dover	163	103	3	4	273
Lee	161	61	5	3	230
Lodi	142	73	39	....	254
Rome	244	95	7	....	346
Trimble	135	78	....	6	219
Troy	200	129	23	9	361
Waterloo	191	129	4	20	344
York	484	623	2	188	1,297
Total	2,924	1,940	150	237	5,251

VOTE FOR CONGRESSMAN, 1882, BY TOWNSHIPS.

TOWNSHIPS.	RUFUS R. DAWES, REP.	A. J. WARNER, DEM.	WILLIAM REESE, PRO.	TOTAL VOTE.
Athens	471	295	6	772
Ames	183	71	....	254
Alexander	169	79	1	249
Bern	119	44	....	163
Canaan	96	172	....	268
Carthage	145	75	....	220
Dover	162	106	4	272
Lee	171	60	3	234
Lodi	136	105	....	241
Rome	234	107	....	341
Trimble	141	77	6	224
Troy	191	150	9	350
Waterloo	196	129	19	344
York	487	679	146	1,312
Total	2,901	2,149	194	5,244

CHAPTER IX.

MELANGE—A SERIES OF ARTICLES WORTHY OF ATTENTION—PERUSAL.

EDUCATIONAL—NORMAL INSTITUTE—STATISTICAL—AGRICULTURAL SOCIETY—WHEN INAUGURATED—FAILURE AND RESURRECTION—ANNUAL FAIRS—CONSTITUTION AND BY-LAWS—PIONEER ASSOCIATION—ITS ORGANIZATION—SERIES OF INTERESTING MEETINGS—THE DEATH ROLL—OFFICERS—LETTER OF GENERAL THOMAS EWING—FUTURE PROSPECTS—NEW COURT-HOUSE—THE OLD LOG COURT-HOUSE OF 1807—THE ANCIENT BRICK COURT-HOUSE OF 1818—THE PRIDE OF ATHENS COUNTY, 1880—ITS COST—WHAT THE PEOPLE THOUGHT IN 1874, 1876 AND 1878—ITS SUCCESS AND COMPLETION—JAIL—CHILDRENS' HOME—INFIRMARY—DEFALCATION.

EDUCATIONAL.

The inherited ideas of the pioneers of Athens County, together with the presence for over three quarters of a century of the Ohio University, have ever made the interests of education paramount to most others. The first settlers, being attracted here by the University, were naturally a class of people to benefit by its presence. Common schools and seminaries have from the start received careful attention, and the results have been wonderfully beneficial. The Athens people feel the deep truth of the saying of the eminent Frenchman, Jules Simon, "THE PEOPLE WHICH HAS THE BEST SCHOOLS IS THE FIRST PEOPLE; IF IT IS NOT SO TO-DAY, IT WILL BE SO TO-MORROW."

While this is true, comparatively speaking, it is no less certain that there is yet much room for improvement in educational affairs, a fact to which the people have been awakening during the last few years. It is encouraging to observe a growing tendency to place at the head of the leading schools, and in the important principalships, men and women of ability and culture, and to retain these persons long enough to secure their best services to the community. It is also a favorable sign that the tendency to divide the teaching force somewhat more liberally between the sexes is increasing. It is with reason that two somewhat different elements conspire in the culture of families. Experience demonstrates the wisdom of accepting this suggestion in the organization of schools, where so large a proportion of the intellectual and moral character of the youth of the State is formed.

An occasional tendency to limit too narrowly the salaries of instructors is one of the greatest drawbacks of the present time. The great need of the country is educators, and the fact is beyond dispute that educators can be obtained only through such an organization and management of the school system as shall furnish inducements for educated and enterprising men and women to engage in the business of instruction and to remain in it.

NORMAL INSTITUTES.

One of the most necessary aids to a complete system of education is the Normal Institute. The professional contact of the teachers of a county with each other is quickening, and the influence on the younger and less experienced teachers is always instructive, and tends to awaken ambition and energy.

The first permanent organization of teachers in Athens County was effected Dec. 17, 1853, at the court-house in Athens. S. Howard, President of the University, was chosen Chairman, and J. P. Weethee, President of the Amesville Collegiate Institute, Secretary. The meeting was addressed by Professor J. G. Blair, President Howard, Mr. R. W. Carley, Professor J. F. Given and Superintendent C. Grant, after which it was resolved to organize a teachers' institute. A committee, consisting of Professor Blair, Superintendent Grant and Professor Weethee, reported a brief constitution, which was adopted. Semi-annual meetings were provided for, the first meeting to be held the second Monday in April, 1854. The following persons were chosen to lecture. President Howard and R. W. Carley, at Albany; Professor Blair and Superintendent Grant, at Nelsonville and Chauncey; Professor Given, at Amesville, and President Weethee and Rev. Hand, at Athens. The April meeting was not held, and for some time no further steps were taken for an effectual union of educational interests in Athens County. The organization was kept up continuously, however, and institutes were held occasionally. The first one of which any record is found was held at Coolville on Tuesday, Oct. 7, 1856. George Hanger acted as

President *pro tem*. The session lasted two days, and was of interest to those who attended, although no professional lecturers were present, and the membership not large. The next institute was appointed for Albany, March 31, 1857, but no record of the proceedings, if held, was kept.

Oct. 5, 1857, a very successful institute was held at the Methodist church in Athens, and was entered on the proceedings as being the " tenth semi-annual session." President S. Howard occupied the chair. C. S. Royce, Agent for the Ohio State Phonetic Association, was present and elected a member. He opened the work of the institute by lecturing briefly on elementary sounds. He was followed by Professor McLaughlin in an introduction to the study of arithmetic, and Mr. Royce then addressed the teachers on the subject of phonography. The question of the age at which children should be sent to school was discussed by the institute, and also the usage of tobacco by teachers. An interesting lecture was delivered by Mr. Royce on " Responsibilities of Teachers," and by Mr. Ogden on " Family and School Government."

The next meeting of the association was held in Nelsonville, March 15, 1858, S. Howard being President, and lasted four days The principal lecturers at this institute were Professors Allen, Young and Ogden, Mr. J. C. S. Miller and President Howard. The attendance of both teachers and visitors was large.

The association had adjourned to meet at Albany, where a large institute was held for four days, beginning April 4, 1859. Seventy teachers attended this session, which was presided over by Dr. William Campbell. Mr. Royce, Agent of the Southwestern Normal School, delivered an instructive address on " Moral Culture in Schools." Professor Allen lectured on " English Grammar."

The Normal Institute was again opened in 1860, commencing July 23. The attendance was fair, and one of the principal features was a course of twelve lectures on elocution and literature delivered by Professor I. C. Zachas. This, so far as the records show, was the last one held until 1868. On July 6 of that year, the institute held for two weeks and was largely attended, and proved of unusual interest. The lecturers were Professor Schuyler, on Arithmetic; Professor John R. Scott, Penmanship; Professor Tappan, Geography; Professor Young, the Theory and Practice of Teaching; Professor Gibbons, Grammar; and Professor Kidd on Elocution. The benefits derived from these institutes soon became very apparent, and the standard of qualification took a much higher plane than in former years.

Another of these important institutes was held in the summer of 1870, for one week, with an attendance of twenty-eight males and sixty-five females, which also proved of great interest. This was followed by a session in July, 1873, of one week, with an attendance of sixty-five, and one each in March and August of 1875, holding, also, one week, seventy-five teachers being present. In 1876 a five-days session was organized at which about 100 teachers attended. This was followed by similar sessions in 1878, 1879, 1880 and 1881. The last and largest of all was the two-weeks session of 1882, when 150 teachers and students showed their appreciation of the value of these institutes by their close attendance from the opening to the close, Superintendent R. W. Stevenson, the Hon. T. W. Harvey and Professor Mendenhall conducting the work.

STATISTICAL.

The following educational statistics, taken from the State Commissioner's Report of Common Schools, for the school year ending Aug. 31, 1881, are interesting and instructive. They show in a succinct and clear form the progress that has been made in educational matters in Athens County:

SCHOOL MONEYS—RECEIPTS.

School moneys on hand Sept. 1, 1880	$19,529.81
State tax	13,393.65
Irreducible school fund	1,050.82
Local tax for school and school-house purposes	29,681.64
Amount received on sale of bonds	400.00
Fines, licenses, tuition of non-resident pupils, and other sources	1,639.06
Total receipts	$65,644.98

EXPENDITURES.

Paid primary teachers	$33,224.64
Paid high school teachers	2,790.00
Managing and superintending	1,185.00
Sites and buildings	3,016.45
Interest on bonds	167.96
Fuel and other contingent expenses	6,228.53
Total expenditures	$46,612.58
Balance on hand Sept. 1, 1881	$19,082.40

STATE SCHOOL FUND.

Showing the amount of interest on the several funds constituting the irreducible State debt for the year ending Dec. 31, 1880, due

Joseph Wolf

and payable to counties after Jan. 1, 1881, and paid during the fiscal year ending Nov. 15, 1881.

Section 16, school fund	$784.57
Section 29, ministerial fund	431.46
Total	$1,216.03

SCHOOL POPULATION, ETC., 1881.

White boys between 6 and 21	4,746
" girls " "	4,336
Total white children	9,082
Colored boys between 6 and 21	215
" girls " "	164
Total colored children	379
Whole number	9,461
Population of county, 1880	28,413
Enumeration of persons of school age, 1880	9,237
Per cent. of population	33

SCHOOL DISTRICT, SCHOOL-HOUSES, ETC.

Number of townships	14
" sub-districts	156
" separate districts	6
Sub-divisions included in separate districts	6
School-houses erected in 1881	4
Cost of school-houses erected in 1881	$2,110
Whole number of school-houses	165
Value of school-houses	$112,350

SCHOOL-ROOMS AND TEACHERS.

No. school-rooms, township primary schools	154
" " high "	2
" sep. dist. primary "	27
" " high "	5
Whole number of school-rooms	188
Male teachers in primary schools, township	116
Female " " "	126
Total number	242
Male teachers in primary schools, sep. dist	8
Female " " "	13
Male " high schools, "	2
Female " " "	12
Total number	35
Whole number of different teachers in county	277

AVERAGE WAGES OF TEACHERS.

Males in primary schools, township			$28
Females " "			22
Males " sep. dist.			32
Females " "			30
Males in high schools "			34
Females " "			48

LENGTH OF SCHOOLS.

Number of sub-districts in which schools were taught less than twenty-four weeks within the year 4
Primary schools, in townships, average number of weeks in session 25
Primary schools, in separate districts, average number of weeks in session . 36
High schools in separate districts, average number of weeks in session 36

AVERAGE RATE OF LOCAL TAX IN MILLS.

Townships, 1880–1881	3.2
" 1881–1882	3.5
Separate districts, 1880–1881	3.7
" 1881–1882	4.2

DIFFERENT PUPILS ENROLLLED.

Boys in primary schools, townships	3,157
Girls " "	2,973
Boys in high schools, sep. dist.	84
Girls " "	109
Boys in primary schools "	712
Girls " "	718
Total enrollment	7,753

AVERAGE DAILY ATTENDANCE.

Boys in primary schools, township	1,683
Girls " "	1,556
Total	3,239
Boys in primary schools, sep. dist.	464
Girls " "	424
Boys in high schools "	50
Girls " "	82
Whole average daily attendance	4,259
Per cent. attendance is of enrollment, townships	.72
" " " sep. dist.	.86

DISTRICTS WHOSE ENUMERATION IS OVER 300.

ATHENS.

Enumeration of youth of school age, 1880	759
" " " 1881	645

Total receipts for school purposes..$6,928.63
" expenditures for school purposes within the year 1881............$6,136.51
Local levy for 1881 in mills... 6.5
Number of school-house... 1
Number of school-rooms... 11
Total value of school property, including grounds, school-houses, furniture, apparatus, etc...$ 25,000
Number of teachers necessary to supply the schools....................... 12
Male teachers employed.. 1
Female   "   "   10
Male average monthly wages... $30
Female   "   "   " $33
Superintendent's salary... $1,200
Portion of Superintendent's time employed................................ ½
Pupils enrolled in primary schools... 465
   "   "   "   high   " 33
Average monthly enrollment in primary schools............................ 351
   "   "   "   "   high   " 30
   "   daily attendance   " primary   " 298
   "   "   "   "   high   " 27
Per cent. "   " is of average monthly enrollment in primary
   schools.. 85
Per cent. daily attendance is of average monthly enrollment in high
   school... 90
Number of different pupils enrolled, whose ages were between 16 and
   21... 23
Cost per pupil of the year's expenditure.................................. $12.32

NELSONVILLE.

Enumeration of youth of school age, 1880................................. 1,001
    "   "   "   "   1881................................. 1,028
Total receipts for school purposes.......................................$9,424.30
" expenditures for school purposes...................................... $6,198.50
Local levy for 1881 in mills... $10.00
Number of school-houses... 4
   "   school-rooms.. 12
Total value of school property, including grounds, school-houses, furniture, apparatus etc... $15,500
Number of teachers necessary to supply the schools...................... 7
Male teachers employed... 2
Female   "   "   5
Male average monthly wages... $33
Female   "   "   " $33
Average number of weeks of school... 36
Superintendent's salary... $1,200
Portion of Superintendent's time employed................................ ½
Pupils enrolled in primary schools... 708
   "   "   "   high   " 60
Average monthly enrollment in primary schools............................ 485
   "   "   "   "   high   " 45
   "   daily attendance in primary   " 434
   "   "   "   "   high   " 42
Per cent. daily attendance is of average monthly enrollment in primary
   schools.. 85
Per cent. daily attendance is of average monthly enrollment in high
   schools.. 93
Number of different pupils enrolled, whose ages were between 16 and 21.. 23
Cost per pupil of the year's expenditures................................ $8.07

TOWNSHIPS IN WHICH SCHOOLS WERE HELD LESS THAN TWENTY-FOUR WEEKS.

AMES.

No. of school-rooms in township	14
" " in which schools were held less than twenty-four weeks	1
Average number of weeks schools were sustained in township	25
Rate of local school tax, in mills, 1880-1881	1.3
" " " " 1881-1882	3.0
Average monthly wages, males	$24
" " " females	$23

CARTHAGE.

No. of school-rooms in township	9
" " in which schools were held less than twenty-four weeks	2
Average number of weeks schools were sustained in township	24
Rate of local school-tax in mills, 1880-1881	1.8
" " " " 1881-1882	3.8
Average monthly wages, males	$25
" " " females	$18

ATHENS COUNTY AGRICULTURAL SOCIETY.

The mineral interests of Athens County, while being rapidly developed of late, was not the pioneer business of the settlers. Vast as are the deposits of iron, coal, fire-clay, etc., the agricultural interests of the county are by no means small. The cereals, grasses and stock raised exceed the value of the mineral product as yet, and there are few, if any, counties in the State better adapted to stock-raising than those located in the Hocking Valley. It could be made a vital and important interest in the future growth of these counties.

Agricultural and mechanical associations have, from an early day, been a strong incentive to intelligent farm labor. The rivalry which is excited is one to be commended, and to this spirit it may be said, has the rapid stride been made, which has placed the farm in the front rank of advanced material production and given employment to the inventive genius of man. This is, and always will be, the result of a well-organized and managed agricultural society, and they should be encouraged and fostered. Athens County holds a front rank in agricultural production and stock-raising in the State, but that position could be materially enhanced by enlarging their field of action, and by giving a full week to the exhibition of ALL the products of the county.

WHEN ORGANIZED.

The first agricultural society of Athens County was organized May 19, 1828, under the name of the "Athens County Agricultural Society," and as was stated in the preamble, "was for the purpose of raising a spirit of emulation and improvement in the culture of the soil, and the domestic manufacture of its products." The organization formed a constitution and by-laws which covered the rules and regulations usual to such societies, and appointed committees to solicit subscriptions, etc. The committees were as follows:

Athens.—S. B. Pruden, R. J. Davis, Charles Shipman.

Alexander.—Ziba Lindley, Jr., Asa Stearns, Daniel Dudley.

Ames.—Colonel A. Boyles, Geo. Walker, Jacob Boarman.

Bern.—James Dickey, Wm. T. Brown, Robert Henry.

Canaan.—Parker Carpenter, Martin Mansfield, Harry Henshaw.

Carthage.—Francis Caldwell, B. B. Lottridge, Milton Buckingham.

Dover.—Josiah True, Daniel Herrold, John Pugsley.

Elk.—Thomas Johnson, James Bothwell, Edward Dodge.

Homer.—R. S. Lovell, Selah Hart, Wm. Hyde.

Lee.—Jacob Lentner, Michael Canny, Wm. Brown.

Lodi.—Joseph Thomson, Rufus Cooley, Elam Frost.

Rome.—Elijah Hatch, Daniel Stewart, John Thompson.

Troy.—Charles Devol, Alfred Hobby, Wm. Barrows.

Trimble.—Wm. Bagley, Samuel B. Johnson, James Bosworth.

Vinton.—Daniel H. Horton, Isaac Hawk, Samuel Zinn.

Waterloo.—Joseph Hewitt, Nathan Robinett, Alexander Young.

York.—James Knight, Joseph J. Robbins, Robert Terry.

A meeting was held in July following which showed the work so far advanced as to arrange for a fair. This was accordingly done, and October was designated as the month to hold the first agricultural fair in Athens County, which was also the first held in Southern Ohio. The fair was primitive in many respects, but was considered a success for the times.

At the annual meeting, which took place on the 16th of the following April (1829), an effort was made to enlarge the scope of the society and infuse a new spirit in the enterprise. This was in a measure successful, and the organization received a fresh impulse. The meeting adjourned after electing the following officers for the ensuing year:

President, Ziba Lindley, Jr.; Vice-Presidents, Christopher Wolf, Athens; Samuel McKee, Alexander; Abel Glazier, Ames; James Dickey, Bern; Joshua Hoskinson, Canaan; Fr. Caldwell, Carthage: John B. Johnson, Dover; Justus Reynolds, Elk; H. Alderman, Homer; Jacob Lentner, Lee; J. Thompson, Lodi; Daniel Stewart, Rome; Wm. Barrows, Troy; Wm. Bagley, Trimble; Geo. Utsler, Vinton; Joseph Hewitt, Waterloo; James Knight, York; Treasurer, Thomas Brice; Secretary, A. G. Brown; Directors, Levi Booth, Colonel Absalom Boyles, Robert Linzee, Calvary Morris, S. B. Pruden, Isaac Baker.

There was $75 appropriated at this meeting for premiums at the coming fair. This was not a large sum, but it was considered as about the amount that could be afforded. The largest was to be given for the best stallion, owned and kept by a member of the society, $4. The next largest for the best pair of working oxen and yoke, $3. For the best six merino ewes, $2. Best beef animal, $2.

To the person producing evidence of having killed the greatest number of wolves, two young ones to be counted as one old one, $3.

Best specimen of sewing silk	$1 00
Best five yards fulled cloth, 3-4 wide	1 00
Best ten yards linen	1 50
Best straw or grass bonnet	1 00

This fair was held, as was several others afterward, but the organization was kept up but a few years, when it gradually sank to rest. The General Assembly of the State passed an act Feb. 25, 1832, authorizing the establishment of such societies in the several counties of the State. This was the first general recognition of the farming interest by the State Legislature. Undoubtedly it did some good, but the main trouble was that the country was too young and too thinly settled to make fairs a success in many counties of the State. There was but little further action for a number of years, when the subject was again revived by legislative action.

A NEW DEPARTURE.

An act of the Legislature, passed in 1846, to encourage the formation of agricultural societies, provided that whenever a society might raise $50 as a fund for paying the premiums and other expenses of an exhibition, the State would contibute $50 additional. The subject of forming such a society in this county came up in 1850, and resulted in a call for a meeting to be held Jan. 13, 1851. At that date a number of the citizens of the county met at the court-house, and effected a temporary organization by calling Joseph Post, of Lee Township, to the chair, and appointing George Putnam, of York Township, Secretary. On motion of A. B. Walker it was resolved to proceed to form an agricultural society for Athens County. A committee of five—S. Rice, A. B. Walker, A. Love, Ezra Goodspeed and Hiram Stewart were selected to draft a constitution. They reported the following, which was adopted:

"ARTICLE 1.—The officers of the society shall consist of a president, vice-president, recording secretary, corresponding secretary, treasurer, and five managers, who, together, shall constitute a board of directors for the general management of the affairs of the society; they shall be elected annually by the members of the society, and hold their offices until their successors are appointed.

ARTICLE 2.—Members of this society must be residents of the County of Athens, and pay the sum of $1 annually to the treasurer.

ARTICLE 3.—Competitors for premiums must be members of the society.

ARTICLE 4.—A list of the articles for which premiums are to be awarded by the society must be published in a newspaper or in hand-bills six weeks previous to the day of exhibition.

ARTICLE 5.—All articles offered for premiums must be owned by the persons offering the same, or by members of their families; and products of the soil, or manufactured articles, must be produced or manufactured within the county of Athens.

ARTICLE 6.—Awarding committees of three persons each shall be annually appointed by the directors, for judging the different classes of articles offered in competition, and awarding premiums for the same.

ARTICLE 7.—The awarding committees for the improvements of soils, tillage, crops, manures, implements, stock, articles of domestic industry, and such other articles, productions and improvements as they may deem proper, and calculated to promote the agricultural and manufacturing interests of the county, shall so regulate the premiums and the different grades of the same as that it shall be competent for small as well as large farmers to compete therefor in conformity to the second section of the law of Ohio for the encouragement of agriculture.

ARTICLE 8.—Competitors for premiums on crops shall be required to have the ground and its produce accurately measured by two disinterested persons whose statements shall be verified by affidavit.

ARTICLE 9.—Premiums on grain and grass crops shall not be awarded for less than one acre, and on root crops not less than one fourth of an acre, under the rules in relation to all crops and productions to be agreed on by the directors of the society.

ARTICLE 10.—The annual exhibitions of this society shall be held at such place within the county as may be designated by the directors, on the third Wednesday of October, the premiums on crops, if necessary, to be awarded at a later period.

The members who joined at this first meeting of the society were as follows: Joseph Post, Ziba Lindley, George Putnam, Hiram Stewart, John Ballard, A. Ryors, J. M. Dana, E. B. Talpey, Eleazer Smith, A. J. Wilmarth, E. D. Harper, B. F. Johnson, A. J. Van Vorhes, James D. Johnson, John T. Glazier, E. F. Brown, George Walker, Jr., Alexander Love, N. O. Warren, A. B. Walker, E. Mathews, Chandler Rosceter, H. B. Brawley, Samuel Gillett, N. P. Hoisington, Charles Dickey, James Dickey, John Elliott, John B. Brown, John Welch, Sabinus Rice, James W. Bayard, R. E. Constable, Joseph Herrold, 2d, Joseph Morrison, Ezra Goodspeed, Joseph Goodspeed, Peter W. Boyles, Hugh A. Poston, Alex. Stephenson, John Beabout, J. L. Currier, Daniel Nelson, P. M. Starr, L. Jewett, H. Hay, O. Gillett, N. Root, E. H. Moore, Wm. Golden, W. P. Johnson and Bernard Howson.

The following were chosen as officers: Sabinus Rice, President; Ziba Lindley, Vice-President; George Putnam, Recording Secretary; A. B. Walker, Corresponding Secretary; J. M. Dana, Treasurer; Henry Brawley of Ames, Eleazer Smith of Athens, Hiram Stewart of Rome, Peter W. Boyles of Lodi, and Charles Dickey, of Bern, Managers.

The first fair was held at Athens, Oct. 15, 1851, and, all things considered, was a success. About a hundred premiums were awarded, and the exhibition of stock was satisfactory in most particulars. The productions of the dairy and domestic manufacture were well worthy of commendation. The specimens of grain were remarkably fine, and the quantity raised per acre was also respectable. Forty-five and a half bushels of wheat and 120 of corn to the acre, were reported.

The second annual fair was a decided improvement over the

first. Two hundred premiums were offered and the fair lasted two days—Oct. 14 and 15, 1852, the weather favorable and the attendance good. The first day was devoted exclusively to the exhibition of stock, which was of a much better grade than the first year. At this fair there were entered for exhibition seventy-two horses, sixty-three head of cattle, thirty-two of sheep, and twenty-one hogs. An address was delivered by Hon. John Welch, and short speeches were made by others.

The third fair occupied two days, Oct. 6 and 7, 1853, and the fourth was held on the 5th and 6th days of October, 1854. This was on a larger scale, there being sixteen classes of articles, with a separate committee of judges for each. The admission fee charged was 10 cents. A riding match was held, in which the equestriennes competed for a gold locket, a gold breast-pin and a gold pen. These first fairs, though mere experiments, drew a good number of visitors from all parts of the county, and quite a number from surrounding counties.

The fairs continued to be held annually, and the interest in them increased until the eighth annual fair showed a membership of 500 and the receipts over $1,000. The ninth fair proved the most successful of the series, being held three days under the name of the "Athens County Agricultural and Mechanical Association," and came off Oct. 11, 12 and 13, 1859, with some new features not before given. The attendance was estimated at from 10,000 to 12,000, although Vinton, Hocking, Washington and Ross counties held their fairs at the same time. The membership ran up to about 650. There were 669 entries of articles, and $427 in premiums were awarded. The receipts were $1,500, which placed the society on a sound financial footing. As before, the show of live stock was the best feature, although many were attracted by the trotting races held this year for the first time. Five entries were made. Sorrel gelding "Jake," raised in Athens County, but owned by Dickey & Seamon, of Morgan County, won first money, $20.00. Time, 3:01 and 2:58. Brown mare "Kate" took second money, $10.00. Time, 3:05 and 3:07.

From this time on for some fifteen years annual fairs were held with the exception of 1862. There were little changes to note, with the exception that pleasant weather insured a much more successful fair than wet or bad weather. The sixteenth fair, in 1866, was the best held up to that time, and the only one whose receipts equaled the fair of 1859. The next was the twenty-first, held in 1871, the receipts of which were reported at the same figures as given twelve years previous. From the twenty-first to the twenty-seventh fair, inclusive, the success was but moderate. The twenty-eighth fair showed receipts aggregating $1,700, and that of the twenty-ninth, over $2,000, they being held respectively in 1878 and 1879. The thirtieth annual fair held on Oct. 6, 7 and 8, 1880, was the most successful, for many years, of the series held.

The races this year were also very fine. The gate receipts were over $2,000.

The thirty-first annual fair was held Oct. 5, 6 and 7, 1881. The season had been a very unfavorable one for the farmers, and consequently the number and quality of exhibits showed a considerable falling off. The gate receipts were $1,900, of which $1,250 were paid out in premiums.

The thirty-second annual fair, held Oct. 4, 5 and 6, 1882, was a great success in every respect. The season had been a good one, agriculturally, and the farmers came forward with a goodly number of live stock and farm products. The gross receipts were $2,556.94. The premium list was quite a liberal one, aggregating $1,750.

The society is now in a flourishing condition, and is destined to be a most successful organization for the agricultural and stock interests of Athens County.

ATHENS COUNTY PIONEER ASSOCIATION.

The advantages of organizing pioneer societies to keep alive the memory of early days, to record in permanent shape our early history, and to promote a fraternal feeling among surviving pioneers have been felt and acted upon in most localities. Nearly every county has its organization, and holds reunions at stated periods. Athens County was rather slow to take the necessary steps; but interest was finally awakened, and in pursuance of a call, by a committee previously appointed, a number of citizens of the county met at the court-house in Athens, Dec. 26, 1868. The meeting was called to order by Hon. Calvary Morris, Chairman, with appropriate remarks.

A. B. Walker was chosen Secretary, *pro-tem.*, and the committee appointed for the purpose reported a constitution and by-laws, through Dr. William Blackstone. The following extracts are made:

"The object of this association shall be to gather together and preserve reminiscences, statistics or other information connected with the settlements and history of our town, county and the southern part of Ohio previous to the year 1820.

"Any person may become a member of this association by paying into the treasury thereof the sum of $1 and signing the constitution, provided that he or she has lived in the State of Ohio on or before the 4th of July, 1830.

"The annual meeting for the election of officers shall take place on Saturday succeeding Dec. 25 of each year, and the semi-annual meetings on the fourth Saturday in July, at Athens.

"In case of the death of any member, an attendance upon the funeral, on the part of the members of the association, in a body, shall be observed as far as practicable."

The following persons signed the constitution at this meeting and became members: Isaac Barker, General John Brown, Nathan Kinney, Calvary Morris, Archibald G. Brown, William Blackstone, John Perkins, Francis Beardsley, John N. Dean, Oliver Childs, Jacob Swett, John Brown, Oscar W. Brown, George Putnam, Gilbert M. McDougal, Archibald B. Walker, Daniel B. Stewart, Joseph Tippie, Henry B. Brawley, Peter Stalder, Samuel Pickering, Ephraim C. Brown and William Golden. Also, Matthew A. Patrick, John Ackley and Benjamin T. Randall were elected corresponding members. The members present then proceeded to the election of permanent officers for the ensuing year, which resulted as follows: President, Isaac Barker; Vice-President, General John Brown; Corresponding Secretary, Archibald G. Brown; Recording Secretary, Archibald B. Walker; Treasurer, John Brown; Executive Committee, Calvary Morris, Elmer Rowell, William Blackstone, William Golden and George Putnam. After the transaction of some further business the meeting adjourned.

The next meeting was held April 7, 1869, at the court-house, and several papers of great interest relating to pioneer life and border warfare were read. Brief addresses were also delivered by several of the members.

A very profitable meeting of the association was held Sept. 30, 1869, at New England, in this county. Vice-President General John Brown presided, Judge Barker, then in his ninety-first year, being unable to attend. At this meeting the constitution was amended so as to admit to full membership all females of the families of members who have been in the State the requisite time, without any initiation fee; and the third article was so amended that persons resident of Ohio previous to 1840 (instead of 1830) were eligible to membership. It was also directed that in future the annual meetings be held on the 7th of April (the anniversary of the landing of the first settlers at Marietta), and the semi-annual meetings on the 7th of October, when either or both of said days happen on Sunday, the day following to be substituted instead. T. L. Dewess, Jacob Tedrow, B. F. Johnson, Andrew Dodds and Orange Barrows were added to the list of members, and under the amendment eighteen ladies were received on the list of members. The secretary announced at this meeting the death of several pioneer women of the county, viz.: Mrs. Betsey Parker, Mrs. Apphia Hamilton, Mrs. Maria Dean and Mrs. Lydia Nye. Mrs. Parker was a daughter of Joshua Wyatt, who settled in Ames Township in 1801. Her marriage, May 13, 1803, to William Parker, was the first in that township and the second in the county. She died in Athens, Aug. 8, 1869, in the eighty-fourth year of her age. The following brief sketch of a pioneer was read and entered on the minutes. "Henry Bartlett, a native of Beverly, Mass., came to Marietta in the year 1796, and settled in this county the following year with his young family, living in the town of Athens till his decease, Sept. 9, 1850, in the eightieth year of his age. Mr. Bartlett was on many accounts distinguished among the early pioneers of our county Having enjoyed good opportunities in early life, fitting him for public business, he was appointed by the County Commissioners, Clerk of the board; and of the County Courts in 1805, the year of the organization of the county. He held the position of Clerk of the Court of Common Pleas for more than thirty years, and for a still longer period several other offices, including those of Secretary and Auditor of the Ohio University. His superior penmanship was noticeable among the best writers of the day, and his numerous friends were justly proud of his distinction in that line."

Judge Morris, in a short address, remarked that there were older members present than himself, but that he had lived to see great and important changes in the county, especially in the way of public improvements. In 1828 he rode on the first ten miles of railroad constructed in the United States for the conveyance of passengers, from Baltimore to Ellicott's Mills. The car was made like the body of an omnibus, with seats along the side, and drawn by a single horse, and he thought it a great treat thus to ride on a railroad. In 1842 he witnessed the first public experiment of Professor Morse's telegraph, when the communication extended only from one room of the capitol to another. The Judge then closed with a few remarks upon the rapid growth and extension of improvements generally since that period. The annual meeting, held April 7, 1870, at the court-house, was replete with interest. Judge Barker, then in his ninety second year, presided at the opening, but soon called Judge Morris to the chair. Among the interesting features of this meeting was the presentation to the society, by General John Brown, of a tax duplicate dated June 27, 1807. The following were elected officers: President, General John Brown; Vice-President, Hon. C. Morris; Corresponding Secretary, Hon. A. G. Brown; Recording Secretary, A. B. Walker; Treasurer, John Brown; Executive Committee, H. B. Brawley, William Blackstone, William Golden and G. M. McDougal.

The semi-annual meeting of Oct. 7 following was presided over by Hon. Calvary Morris, the Vice-President, although the President, General John Brown, was present. The principal object of discussion at this meeting was the first public library northwest of the Ohio, the claims of Ames Township (since substantiated beyond dispute) to priority on behalf of the "Western Library Association" having been disputed by Cincinnati. A committee was appointed to investigate the subject and have the question forever settled. General C. H. Grosvenor, Rev. John Stewart, Rev. John Fletcher Stewart, General T. F. Wilder and Charles E. M. Jennings joined the association at this meeting.

The next meeting was the annual one of April 7, 1871, presided over by Vice-President Calvary Morris. The committee appointed to investigate the matter of the first public library in the Northwest made a lengthy report, which was placed on the records, presenting the respective claims of Ames and Cincinnati, and proving that the honor belongs to Ames. A number of interesting and valuable documents were presented to the association. Elmer Armstrong, Leonard Brown, John Ballard, Ziba Hoskison, Dr. S. Howard, Colonel William S. Wilson, Enoch Cabeen, Alfred Morrison and Frederick P. Kassler joined the association. The following officers were chosen: John Perkins, President; H. B. Brawley, Vice-President; A. G. Brown, Corresponding Secretary; A. B. Walker, Recording Secretary; and John Brown, Treasurer. This session was well attended.

A meeting of the association was held at Amestown, July 4, in conjunction with a celebration by the citizens of that vicinity.

General Thomas Ewing was present at this meeting. His father, Hon. Thomas Ewing, had been expected, but could not come on account of failing health. He died soon after. The following is the letter of regret written by him and read by General C. H. Grosvenor:

LANCASTER, *July* 3, 1871.

Gentlemen:

I find it will not be in my power to attend the Amesville pioneer celebration on the 4th. Though my health is tolerable, I cannot endure even a small amount of fatigue; and on consulting my physician, he advises me not to venture. I would be very glad to meet you all, the living friends and associates of my boyhood and early youth, and the descendants of those that are gone; but as I cannot, I send my third son, General Thomas Ewing, Jr., whom I trust you will find a creditable representative of the first pioneers.

I visited Amesville a few weeks since, after an absence of fifty-five years, and found my memory fresh as to places and persons. The streams appeared small, and the valleys narrow, but rich and beautiful as when I last knew them. To me, while I lived in it, and until I left it, it was a happy valley; there was little material wealth in it, but one could see a verification of the assertion of the poet, that a people "though very poor may still be very blest." There can grow up no inordinate wealth here to disturb the quiet tenor of life. While it is abundantly prosperous, its tranquillity is not in danger of being destroyed by those terrible commotions which distract the greater world.

Mr. Walker's History of Athens County marks well the calm and steady progress of this happy valley in population and in mental culture, much of which is due to our early library association; and I am strongly impressed with the opinion that it is entitled to one year's earlier date than his record gives it.

In the spring of 1803 my father removed his family to a small farm seven miles southeast, on the Marietta road. In this I am not mistaken, as I made record of the date on the bark of a beech tree which I have seen often since. I remained on the Amestown farm to go to school, and helped my brother take care of the stock. Judge Walker came in November of that year and occupied the principal cabin, and such of our family as remained, a smaller one on the other side of the little run. I was reading a library book —"The Children of the Abbey"—and had got together a good supply of hickory bark to make me a light, and I rose an hour or two before day and sat on a stool by the fire reading. Henry Bartlett, Esq., who happened to be with us that night, came and sat also and asked to look at my book. I handed it to him, and, as he returned it, it fell open on the fire and scorched and spotted several of the leaves. By the rules of the library there was a fine for every spot; and in counting up the injury in fips and levies, I found myself a bankrupt boy. However, I took the book to the next library meeting, explained the misfortune, and the board very kindly remitted the fines. If the volume (I think it was the second) be still in existence, it must bear the marks of the adventure.

This antedates Mr. Walker's record several months. I think the money was raised and the books bought and on hand before that record was made out, and that it is but an official recognition of a past fact. As to Morse's Geography, I studied it as early as 1800; but it was no doubt a book on hand, afterward turned in by Mr. Cutler and my father as part of their contribution to the library.

I remember a rural scene of the summer of 1800, simple and childish, but illustrative of a fact in history. Mrs. Brown had a handsome little tomato plant of the small round kind, which was then called love-apple. It was not known among us as an article of food until several years after the French inhabitants of St. Domingo had been driven from the island and had taken refuge on our shores, and then its use extended slowly. On the day named, children of the two families were at play in Mrs. Brown's garden, when suddenly the alarm was raised and ran through the little group that Apphia Brown had eaten a love-apple! We sped with the fearful intelligence to the grown up people, who did not partake of our alarm, and it passed off without a catastrophe. It was many years later when I first saw the tomato used on our tables as an esculent.

For many years we had no postoffice nearer than Athens, but my father's little farm on the Marietta road was passed once a week by a mail carried on horseback between Clarksburg, Va., and Chillicothe, one week east, the next week west. I always took care to be on hand when the mail passed. It was carried by a boy of sixteen or seventeen, John Davis, who became my intimate friend, and I fed his horse and mother gave him supper and a bed with me by the fire, as a reward for the news he brought us. I have often sat up till ten o'clock listening for his horn; he was very punctual with his sachel of "news from all nations lumbering at his back."

I am indulging in trifles, but "these little things are great to little men," and I write as I would talk with you, if present. I wish all our assembled friends many happy returns of this glorious day. I am very

Respectfully Yours,
THOMAS EWING.

The semi-annual meeting of October, 1871, was held in Athens, when several reminiscences were presented and the usual routine business transacted.

The annual meeting of April 6, 1872, was held at the courthouse and presided over by John Perkins. John Welch, J. M. Dana, Rev. Justice Reynolds, Dr. Eber G. Carpenter, William Courtney, George Linscott and David Goodspeed were received as members. Hon. John Welch was chosen President; H. B. Brawley, Vice-President; John Brown, Treasurer; A. B. Walker, Corresponding and Recording Secretary; D. B. Stewart, George Putnam, Leonard Brown, Charles H. Grosvenor and T. F. Wildes, Executive Committee. The meeting was well attended.

The semi-annual meeting of Oct. 7, following, was presided over by Hon. John Welch. Joseph Herrold, James G. Owens and William H. H. Mintern were received as members. The most important feature of this meeting was the reading of memorials in regard to a number of pioneers who had recently passed away, among them Mrs. Phœbe Sprague, Mrs. Joseph Post, Mrs. Betsey P. Walker, Mr. Samuel Brown and Dr. Chauncey F. Perkins. The annual meeting in April, 1873, was presided over by Vice-President H. B. Brawley.

The election of officers resulted in the choice of John Ballard as President; H. B. Brawley, as Vice-President; A. B. Walker, Secretary; John Brown, Treasurer; J. H. Glazier, Leonard Brown, D. B. Stewart, C. H. Grosvenor and George Putnam, Executive Committee.

A picnic and meeting of the society was held Sept. 6, following, at Millfield, Dover Township, which was largely attended, and enjoyed by all. John Wyatt, J. P. Weethee, James Henry, A. W. Glazier, John M. Hibbard, J. H. Harris and Ebenezer Pratt were received as members. The deaths of Dr. Solomon Howard, Jacob Tedrow, John Frame, Alexander Caldwell, Isaac Coe, Mrs. Nancy H. Perkins, Mrs. John Haldren and Captain Jasper N. Watkins were announced. A number of interesting communications and donations were received.

The annual meeting, April 7, 1874, presided over by John Ballard, was held at the Presbyterian church in Athens. After an interesting meeting, the following officers were chosen for the ensuing year: President, Hon. N. H. Van Vorhes; Vice-Presid George Putnam; Secretary, A. B. Walker; Treasurer, John Brown; Executive Committee, Leonard Brown, H. B. Brawley, D. B. Stewart, J. H. Glazier and S. W. Pickering.

The annual meeting of April 7, 1875, was held in the M. E. church at Athens, and was presided over by Hon. N. H. Van Vorhes. The following officers were elected for the ensuing year: President, N. H. Van Vorhes; Vice-President, Dr. Wm. Blackstone ; Secretary, A. B. Walker ; Treasurer, Hon. E. H. Moore; Executive Committee, Judge Leonidas Jewett, Dr. E. G. Carpenter, George Putnam and Joseph Herrold. The Secretary reported the death of John N. Dean, June 23, 1874, in the eightieth year of his age; of Nathan Kinney, Aug. 26, 1874, in his ninety-third year; Oliver Childs, Feb. 3, 1875, in his seventy-eighth year; and Nelson McCune, Hon. Jacob C. Frost, Judge L. Jewett, Wm. Mason and Hull Foster were elected members.

The next meeting of interest was held April. 7, 1877, at the new city hall in Athens, Hon. N. H. Van Vorhes presiding. Judge John Welch delivered an instructive address in the afternoon. The following officers were chosen: President, Hon. N. H. Van Vorhes; Vice-President, G. M. McDougal; Secretary, A. B. Walker; Treasurer, E. H. Moore; Executive Committee, H. B. Brawley, M. A. Patrick, D. B. Stewart and Elmer Armstrong.

The annual meeting of April 8, 1878, the tenth since the organization of the society, was held at its room in the court-house, which was tastefully decorated for the occasion with flowers and house-plants, contributed by the ladies. Vice-President Gilbert M. McDougal presided. A large number of contributions of books, papers and reminiscences were received through the Secretary, A. B. Walker. For the ensuing year Gilbert M. McDougal was chosen President; Elmer Armstrong, Vice-President; A. B. Walker, Secretary; E. H. Moore, Treasurer; Executive Committee, Dr. E. G. Carpenter, Hon. John Welch, B. F. Johnson, H. B. Brawley and D. B. Stewart. The deaths of Elmer Rowell, Oct. 26, 1877; John Wyatt, Oct. 31, 1877; and Jacob C. Frost, March 24, 1878, were reported.

The annual meeting for 1879 was held May 7, at the city hall, and was presided over by President Gilbert M. McDougal. The deaths of Dr. William Blackstone, March 18, 1879; Bishop E. R. Ames, April 25, 1879; and George Linscott, April 19, 1879, were announced. A number of contributions were received, and the following officers were elected: President, G. M. McDougal; Vice-President, Samuel Pickering; Secretary, A. B. Walker; Treasurer, Hon. E. H. Moore; Executive Committee, Dr. E. G. Carpenter, Hon. John Welch, B. F. Johnson, D. B. Stewart and H. B. Brawley.

July 4, 1879, an interesting meeting was held at the "grove" near Amesville, the principal features of which were speeches by Hon. Charles Townsend and Judge A. G. Brown. A goodly number of members were received at this time. Their names are as follows: Daniel Fleming, A. W. McLead, Alfred Matteson, George S. Anderson, J. N. Pilcher, George Ed. Henry, S. J. Wells, Jr., Fred Stalder, John Patterson, Solomon Hill, J. H. Blunden, W. M. Henry, Elizabeth Whaley, Lucy Fleming, Rebecca Smith, Annie L. Brown, Mary McLead, Sarah E. Patterson, Sarah E. Matteson, Jane Wells, Lydia A. Blunden and Lavina Henry.

Sept. 1, 1879, a petition praying for the assignment of a room in the court-house for the use of the association, and signed by twenty-five members, was presented to the Board of County Commissioners. This board, then consisting of Messrs. F. Finsterwald, Elza Armstrong and W. H. Curfman, unanimously granted the society the use of the southeast room of the basement.

The next meeting was held April 7, 1880, at the city hall, the room in the court-house not being yet prepared, and was presided over by D. B. Stewart, of Athens. The death of John Perkins, of Athens, one of the oldest merchants in the Hocking Valley, was announced, and a biographical notice prepared by President Scott was read by the Secretary. By a unanimous vote it was decided to hold the annual meetings thereafter on the fourth Wednesday in May. William Nelson, Cephas Carpenter, and William H. H. Mintern presented themselves for membership and were admitted. The election of officers resulted in the choice of the following: President, D. B. Stewart; Vice-President, Eli F. Brown; Secretary, A. B. Walker; Treasurer, Joseph H. Norton; Executive Committee, Dr. E. G. Carpenter, B. F. Johnson, W. H. H. Mintern, Samuel Pickering and Cephas Carpenter.

The annual meeting of 1881 was held May 25, and was the first held at the room in the new court-house. D. B. Stewart presided.

The deaths were reported of Cephas Carpenter, John Ballard, Robert Henry and Judge Leonidas Jewett, members of the association, and of Edwin Corner, Ann C. Grosvenor and Sarah Dains, well-known pioneers, were announced at this meeting. New members were received as follows: Louis C. Butler, Levi Pickering, John Cornwell and A. J. Wilmarth. The association was then photographed, sitting on the steps of the court-house, by Mr. Graham, of Athens. At this meeting Mr. A. B. Walker gave up the office of Secretary, after serving in that capacity for twelve years and over. Mr. L. C. Butler is the present Secretary.

A meeting was held Aug. 13, 1881, to discuss the subject of a "Library Monument," and it was resolved to erect a granite monument at Amesville. A committee was appointed to solicit subscriptions for this purpose.

It has since been decided not to erect any monument of stone; In lieu thereof the society in 1882 authorized the publication of a memorial pamphlet, which was prepared by Judge John Welch, and is now being circulated throughout the county. It has received many favorable notices.

The Pioneer Association of Athens County has been a most useful organization, and contains many noble pioneers yet. May they live long to enjoy the annual reunions of the association.

THE NEW COURT-HOUSE.

Athens County has had during her existence three court-houses, besides renting a room for the first two years of her organization. The first court-house that claimed the name was a log building, with a brick chimney. It was not, as can well be imagined, an expensive building, neither was one of that kind necessary. The county revenue was but $157.60 the first year, and the remaining eleven of its existence were not years of heavy taxation. The twelfth year was the one that inaugurated the second temple of justice and general convenience, which was in 1817 or '18. This last was a more expensive affair, and for the times a fair specimen of the average court-houses throughout the State. The people of the county thought so much of it that had not "Old Father Time" shook his hoary locks at it until it trembled to its very foundation, it would have undoubtedly been there to this day, notwithstanding the refinement of its surroundings and the pride of truly an esthetic people.

The first proposition to build the present court-house was early in 1874, by petition to the County Court to submit the voting of a two-mill tax for four years, for the purpose of building a court-house not to exceed the cost of $60,000. This proposition was submitted to the voters of the county on April 6, 1874, being the day for the spring election. The proposition was lost by a majority of 2,211. The vote by townships is here given:

	FOR.	AGAINST.		FOR.	AGAINST
Athens	383	145	Lodi	8	234
Ames	6	215	Rome	21	222
Alexander	6	200	Troy	44	149
Bern	22	100	Trimble	4	176
Canaan	13	126	Waterloo	23	246
Carthage	1	173	York	10	424
Dover	13	221			
Lee	19	150	Total	573	2,784

This was such an overwhelming defeat that those who favored the project let it rest for a couple of years. The question was again brought before the people for their action at the spring election of 1876 (April 3), but was defeated by a much less majority in an increased vote of 106, the total vote in 1876 being 3,463, against 3,357 in 1874.

The following is the vote again given by townships:

	FOR.	AGAINST.		FOR.	AGAINST.
Athens	469	131	Rome	71	190
Alexander	81	143	Troy	92	143
Ames	54	119	Trimble	51	120
Bern	81	38	Waterloo	58	154
Canaan	120	56	York	104	420
Carthage	6	157			
Dover	94	110	Total	1,348	2,115
Lee	51	122			
Lodi	16	212	Majority against, 767.		

While this was not very satisfactory, it was somewhat encouraging. The opposition had been reduced over 600 votes, while that in its favor had considerably more than doubled. Again, the friends of the enterprise rested for a couple of years, until June 1, 1878, when the proposition was carried by a vote of 1,213 in its favor, to 503 against it, the total vote being only 1,716, or a trifle less than half of the number polled two years before. In fact, the old court-house had given such evidences of decay that the people saw a new building was demanded, and left it to its friends to do the voting. This was as follows:

	YES.	NO.		YES.	NO.
Athens	880	43	Trimble	98	13
Alexander	50	29	Waterloo	79	27
Ames	72	36	York	94	132
Bern	24	3	Lee	26	116
Carthage	20	11	Canaan	63	9
Dover	90	28			
Lodi	35	29	Total	1,213	503
Rome	92	12			
Troy	90	15	Majority, 410.		

Bids were at once advertised for, and Oct. 10, 1878, awards were made as follows: Excavating and grading, D. F. Minihan, $315; stone-work complete, W. W. McCoy, $10,250; steam heating and plumbing, Brown & Robb, $4,230; wrought and cast-iron work, H. O'Blenness, $10,700; galvanized iron, tin and slating, H. O'Blenness; brick-work, concrete and centers, W. W. McCoy, $7,737; painting, glazing and frescoing, W. W. McCoy, $1,635; plastering and stucco work, George H. May and C. W. Mellinish, $1,396; carpenter-work, George Towsley, $5,942. The total of these awards was $44,705. There were over sixty bids. The work was at once begun, and pushed as rapidly as prudent. The cornerstone was laid without formal ceremonies May 22, 1879. In the stone is a copper box containing copies of the Cincinnati *Enquirer*, *Commercial* and *Gazette*, and the Athens *Messenger* and *Journal*; a copy of $500 county court-house bond with coupons attached (on the back of the bond is printed a copy of the act under which the court-house was built); a list of the Presidents of the United States, of the Governors of Ohio, and of the present county and township officers; also the business cards of the several attorneys practicing at the Athens County bar, and cards containing the names of prominent citizens; checks on each of the Athens banks, greenback and State of Ohio dollar bills and specimens of our silver and copper coin.

The court-house as it stands was duly completed in the summer of 1880, and was formally dedicated Sept. 10, with pleasing ceremonies. The building was brilliantly illuminated with gaslight, and the court-room, where the exercises were held, was filled to overflowing with visitors. Entertaining speeches were made during the evening by Hon. A. G. Brown, General Grosvenor, Judge Welch, Homer C. Jones, Esq., of McArthur, and others. Mr. A. B. Walker also read a very elaborate historical sketch appropriate to the occasion. The Second Regiment Band discoursed some of their finest music from the upper balcony.

Athens County now possesses in this, one of the finest county buildings in the State. It is an ornament to the county and town, and is, moreover, built on a scale of substantialness that will conclusively prove its durability and worth.

JAIL.

The first jail of Athens County was built, during the first year of the county's existence, 1805, of logs and was about on a par with the other public buildings of that day. It soon was replaced by a new and better structure, but still not a sufficiently good one to safely confine desperate characters. The number of jail escapes in the history of Athens County is unpleasantly large. The present jail is a great improvement on former ones. It was built in the latter half of the year 1876, by Henry O'Blenness. The contract price was $9,238, but much more than this was required to fit the building for use. The jail is of cut stone, and is adjoining the court-house, in the rear of the sheriff's residence, with which it is connected by a brick office, two stories in height. It is 30 x 47 feet in size and twenty-one feet in height. It contains twelve iron cells, four feet eight inches by six feet eight inches, and seven feet in height.

ATHENS COUNTY CHILDREN'S HOME.

This benevolent institution is a result of the efforts of Mr. John S. Fowler, a Quaker gentleman, living in Washington County. He spent the greater part of the four years prior to 1880 in traveling over the county soliciting private subscriptions for the above institution. In 1880, by an act of the State Legislature, the subscription list, which had been raised to about $12,000, was placed in the hands of the county commissioners. In the same year the commissioners purchased a farm of 125 acres pleasantly situated about one mile east of Athens, lying partly in the river valley and partly on adjoining upland, at a cost of $6,600. In the following year, 1881, the farm and buildings began to be properly improved, and were made ready for occupation in the fall, the farm-house having been thoroughly remodeled and greatly enlarged so as to accommodate sixty inmates, although this number has been overrun most of the time. The subscription list was placed in the hands of the county auditor, who, up to the present time, has received about $9,500. The Home is controlled by a Board of Trustees who are chosen by the commissioners of the county. The first Board, chosen in 1881, consisted of the following men: A.

Norton, John Boden and A. W. S. Minear, Mr. Norton being Secretary. The present Board contains: J. W. Johnson, of Rome Township; Charles Henry, of Athens Township; and A. W. S. Minear, of Athens. The first Superintendent and Matron were: Mr. and Mrs. J. M. Nourse who served until Jan. 1, 1883. They were followed by Mr. and Mrs. W. A. Thomas, who served three months, and were followed by the present Superintendent and Matron, Mr. and Mrs. Elza Armstrong.

There have been received into the Home since it was opened, 117 children. Of this number fifteen have been found good homes in private families, while several have been taken back by their parents or relatives, leaving sixty-four inmates at the present time. A teacher is employed regularly by the Home, and the children are taught in a school-room fitted for that purpose on the farm. The teacher at present is Miss Ella Constable.

INFIRMARY.

This farm, containing 129 acres and located in Dover Township, was purchased in 1857. The farm was put in repair, and an addition made to the building to accommodate 100 persons. The management, both of the farm and the inmates, has been improved. The inmates have numbered as high as 175 in one year. The average for 1882 was eighty-six. The first admission was James Tinkum, May 6, 1857. The farm is now in good order and a productive one. The expenses of the Infirmary for the year 1882, being a fair average, is here given.

EXPENSES, 1882.

For provisions	$ 2,837.50
For apparel	989.10
For improvements	452.87
For building and furniture	121.49
For miscellaneous	296.99
For lights and fuel	364.22
For wages	1,358.29
For conveyances	106.80
For physician and medicines	209.70
For interments	28.00
	$ 6,764.96
Outside relief	6,029.36
Total	$ 12,794.32

This shows an expense, *per capita* of 24 cents per day, which would seem to be about as economically as such an institution *ought* to be managed.

OFFICERS.

The officers of the institution are composed of a Board of Directors, elected by the people, a county superintendent, matron and one general farm hand. The officials for 1883 are as follows:

BOARD OF DIRECTORS.

F. L. Junod, President; T. J. Allison, Secretary; Charles Henry, the three composing the Board; Superintendent, A. Martin; Matron, Mrs. A. Martin; Farm Hand, O. Berge.

DEFALCATION AND FORGERIES.

A. J. Reynolds was elected to the office of Sheriff of Athens County in October, 1871. He continued in office until the night of March 25, 1873, when he left for parts unknown. On examination it was found he was a defaulter to the amount of between $6,000 and $7,000. It was also discovered that he had put out something between $3,000 and $4,000 of forged paper at Athens and McConnelsville. The same summer he was traced to Memphis, Tenn., and there captured by Sheriff Warren, and brought back to the scene of his rascalities. He soon after stood his trial in the Common Pleas Court, found guilty and sentenced to the penitentiary for five years and served his time. His sureties on his official bonds were Joseph Herrold and J. L. Baker, who came forward and paid the amount of the defalcation. The county therefore did not come out a loser, but his sureties did. This was the only defalcation of note which transpired in the county, and the outcome of this was not of a character to make defalcations and forgeries popular among those who served the people in the character of public servants.

CHAPTER X.

TOWNSHIP AND CITY OF ATHENS LINKED TOGETHER, ONE AND INSEPARABLE.

INTERWOVEN—METES AND BOUNDS—1805 AND 1851 TO 1883—ITEMS—BRIMSTONE PUNISHMENT—FIRST POST ROUTE--PROGRESSING SLOWLY—POPULATION AND COMPARISON OF GROWTH—TOWNSHIP OFFICERS, 1806 TO 1883—TRUSTEES—TREASURERS—CLERKS—JUSTICES OF THE PEACE.

INTERWOVEN.

Athens Township is so interwoven with the city of Athens, so blended in their history with each other, that outside of their official acts there is little to record separate. In the exhaustive history of the city here given there is little left of township history to record. Its first settlement in 1798 was at Athens City, and its growth radiated from that point, and this settlement and this growth is fully recorded in the city's history. Its metes and bounds and its official life is here given, which is all that can be said except in a general way.

Athens Township is one of the two selected by Congress as a donation for a university and is six miles square, and is considered about as good a section of land as the Ohio Purchase contained. The valley of the Hocking widens as it nears the Ohio River, and much of Athens Township lies in this valley, and its arable land is rich and fertile. There are other valleys and streams, the latter flowing into the Hocking, and the former with a deep alluvial soil, which yields abundant returns for labor rendered, and these branch valleys are now filled with improved farms, well-built residences, and with an air surrounding them that tells of comfort, thrift and economy.

METES AND BOUNDS.

Athens Township is six miles square with an area in acres of 23,040 on a general average, but perhaps a few hundred acres could be added by measuring both sides of some of the most prominent hills. She has Dover Township on the north; Canaan on the east; her twin township, Alexander, on the south, and Waterloo, on the west.

Athens Township was not always of the present, if it can be so expressed, "regulation" size, but covered a somewhat extensive range of country. At its first organization it was composed of what is now known as Brown and Swan townships, of Vinton County, and Waterloo and Canaan, of Athens County, besides its own present boundary. This gave it thirty miles east and west by six miles north and south. For some reason, perhaps on account of its uneven surface, Southeastern Ohio, as laid off into counties, has been given very queer and irregular shapes, and they seem to have taken it from the forms of the townships, for a good many townships in early days could boast of an area equal to many counties of the present time. The old pioneer may have been educated in many things, but he had little idea of form or compactness, unless it came down to purely home or domestic matters. He could fill a wagon or a canoe until, like an omnibus of modern times, there was always room for more. Even township and range lines were ignored in many cases. Athens County is not so bad as some, but Hocking is thirty miles wide at its widest part, east and west, and Vinton is twenty-four miles north and south, and both out of all conceivable form or shape. However, there is nothing like being used to it, and the people of these counties live and thrive all the same. The few foregoing lines may not be altogether township history, but are facts, and a few facts now and then are not considered barred in historical writings.

ITEMS.

The first preaching done in the township was in 1799.
The survey of the township was completed in 1795.
The first settler came in 1798.
The first school established in Athens Township, says Walker's History, was in 1801, and was taught by John Goldthwaite. The school-house (a log one) was situated on Joseph Higgins's place, about three miles south of Athens. Henry Bartlett taught in this house several quarters, between 1802 and 1806. Michael Higgins, now seventy-four years old, attended Esquire Bartlett's school, and relates that, on one occasion, when the scholars undertook, according to a custom then prevalent, to bar the master out on a certain day, and had made all very fast, Mr. Bartlett procured a roll of

brimstone from the nearest house, climbed to the top of the schoolhouse, and dropped the brimstone down the open chimney into the fire; then placing something over the chimney, he soon smoked the boys into an unconditional surrender.

The first postoffice in the county of Athens was established at Athens in January, 1804, and the first Postmaster was Jehiel Gregory. The office was kept at his house, across the river, east of Athens, where D. B. Stewart's woolen factory is now situated.

The township was organized and given its metes and bounds within the county in the year 1805.

The first mill was built on the river in 1806, known as the Gregory Mill. It stood just east of the city of Athens.

The Miles Bros. erected another mill in 1832 upon the same site.

The Herrold Mill was built in 1816 and 1826. Judge Pruden connected with it the first carding machine and cloth-dressing establishment started in the township.

The first ferry across the Hocking River was that of Arthur Coates, below the South bridge, and the second that of Wm. Harper's which crossed the river just west of Athens. The first was started in 1800 and the latter some later.

The first important bridge built in the township is the one known as the East bridge, in 1834, the West bridge in 1836 and the South bridge in 1839. The first two were erected by Isaac Jackson, the last by Samuel Miller. They were toll bridges.

In 1806 tavern licenses in the township were $4, but those on the road to the salt-works were charged $6.

The first post route through Athens Township was opened in 1802, being the post route from Marietta via Athens, to Chillicothe.

PROGRESSING SLOWLY.

Athens Township, like the county, made but a gradual progress perhaps less so than any other township in the county outside the limits of the town. The growth and prosperity of the township seem to run pretty close together. The wealth showed no more rapid increase than the other.

The population in 1820 was 1,114; 1830, 1,703; 1840, 2,282. Up to this time the gain had been steady, but the next decade it seemed to stand still, even losing nearly all its natural increase. In 1850 the population had reached 2,360, only seventy-eight more than it had ten years previous. In 1860 the gain was better, the number being 2,852, an increase of 492. Neither the actual gain nor the per cent. was quite up to the previous decade, the population of 1870 being 3,277. The population of the town of Athens that year was 1,696, leaving for the township 1,581. The census of 1880 gave the township and city a population of 4,517, the greatest gain in its history, both in town and township. The city increased in number from 1,696 to 2,457, or a net gain of 761, which was considerable more than the city and township had ever before gained in a decade. The township's growth was from 1,851 to 2,060, a net gain of 479, which, up to that decade, was above the average gain of town and township for the previous five decades. The trouble with the valley of the Hocking was, that up to 1871 its only line of travel was the canal and the stage lines. This, of course, prevented its rapid settlement; then its rugged hills were passed by as of little value for a half a century. All this was a drawback. A newer country had been found less rough and broken, easier of access, with the tide of railway building setting toward it as well as immigration, so the old land was passed by and the New West became the Mecca of those who sought a change. But when the iron horse had made his way down the valley and the real wealth of the country became known, with facilities of transportation, and daily intercourse with the outside world a veritable fact, Athens Township felt the inspiration, and township and town took a forward start, that gave it a net gain of about thirty-eight per cent. for the last decade. Since then she has still kept up the new life and progress and prosperity are going hand in hand.

The official records show but little of importance, being simply the natural business which came before them. The names of those who conducted the township business for a period of nearly eighty years, are here added:

TOWNSHIP OFFICERS, ATHENS TOWNSHIP.

The first election for township officers in Athens Township was held at the house of John Havner, on the point of the hill, near where Bing's wagon shop now stands, on the first Monday in April, 1806, when the following persons were elected, viz.:

Jehiel Gregory, John Lowry and William Harper, Trustees; John Hewitt, Robert Linzee, Joel Abbot, Daniel Mulford, Canada Lowry and Uriah Tippee, Supervisors; John Corey, Clerk; Chauncey Perkins, Treasurer; Robert Fulton, Lister; Alvan Bingham and Abel Mann, Overseers of the Poor; Robert Lowry, Philip M. Starr and William Biggerstaff, Constables.

At succeeding elections, the following officers were chosen:

TRUSTEES.

1807	Leonard Jewett,	Jehiel Gregory,	Silas Bingham.
1808	John Havner,	William Harper,	Aaron Young.
1809	Leonard Jewett,	Ebenezer Currier,	John Abbot.
1810	Leonard Jewett,	Jacob Lindley,	John Abbot.
1811	Silas Bingham,	Hopson Beebe,	Joseph B. Miles.
1812	Jehiel Gregory,	Martin Mansfield,	William Harper.
1813	Ebenezer Currier,	Joel Abbot,	Stephen Pilcher.
1814	Robert Linzee,	Wm. Whitesides,	Stephen Pilcher.
1815	Robert Linzee,	Wm. Harper,	Arthur Coates.
1816	Robert Linzee,	Wm. Harper,	Arthur Coates.
1817	Edmund Dorr,	John White,	David Pratt.
1818	Edmund Dorr,	John White,	Abel Mann.
1819	Edmund Dorr,	John White,	Abel Mann.
1820	Edmund Dorr,	John White,	Abel Mann.
1821	Edmund Dorr,	John White,	Abel Mann.
1822	Edmund Dorr,	John White,	Abel Mann.
1823	Edmund Dorr,	John White,	Abel Mann.
1824	Edmund Dorr,	John White,	Silas Bingham.
1825	Edmund Dorr,	John White,	Columbus Bierce.
1826	Edmund Dorr,	John White,	Josiah Coe.
1827	Sol. Goodspeed,	Reuben J. Davis,	Josiah Coe.
1828	Sol. Goodspeed,	Reuben J. Davis,	Josiah Coe.
1829	Sol. Goodspeed,	Reuben J. Davis,	Josiah Coe.
1830	Sol. Goodspeed,	Reuben J. Davis,	Josiah Coe.
1831	Sol. Goodspeed,	Frederic Abbot,	Josiah Coe.
1832	Sol. Goodspeed,	Frederic Abbot,	Samuel Lowry.
1833	John Mintun,	Frederic Abbot,	Samuel Lowry.
1834	John Mintun,	Frederic Abbot,	Daniel Stewart.
1835	Josiah Coe,	Edmund Dorr,	Daniel Stewart.
1836	John Brown,	Solomon Goodspeed,	Samuel B. Pruden.
1837	Justus Reynolds,	John White, Jr.,	Ebenezer Currier.
1838	Justus Reynolds,	John Brown,	Ebenezer Currier.
1839	Edmund Dorr,	John Brown,	Daniel Stewart.
1840	Robert McCabe,	John Brown,	Christopher Sheldon.
1841	Robert McCabe,	John Brown,	Christopher Sheldon.
1842	Amos Crippen,	Norman Root,	Christopher Sheldon.
1843	John R. McCune,	Justus Reynolds,	Christopher Sheldon.
1844	John R. McCune,	Justus Reynolds,	Christopher Sheldon.
1845	John Ballard,	Henry Hay,	Wm. T. Dean.
1846	John Ballard,	Henry Hay,	Wm. T. Dean.
1847	George Connett,	Henry Hay,	Nathan Goodspeed.
1848	George Connett,	Andrew Kessinger,	J. R. McCune.
1849	George Connett,	John Brown,	J. R. McCune.
1850	Leonidas Jewett,	John Brown,	Joseph Morrison.
1851	O. W. Pickering,	John Brown,	Joseph Morrison.
1852	O. W. Pickering,	John Brown,	Joseph Morrison.
1853	O. W. Pickering,	James W. Bayard,	Joseph Morrison.
1854	Peter W. Boyles,	Richard Dobson,	Joseph Morrison.
1855	Peter W. Boyles,	Richard Dobson,	L. R. Jarvis.
1856	Thomas Davis,	Richard Dobson,	Thomas Laughlin.
1857	Thomas Davis,	Charles Goodspeed,	Thomas Laughlin.
1858	Thomas Davis,	Charles Goodspeed,	Richard Dobson.
1859	Thomas Davis,	Charles Goodspeed,	Thomas Laughlin.
1860	Thomas Davis,	Ezra Goodspeed,	Thomas Laughlin.
1861	C. R. Sheldon,	Ezra Goodspeed,	Thomas Laughlin.

230   HISTORY OF HOCKING VALLEY.

1862 C. R. Sheldon,   Ezra Goodspeed,   Alfred Morrison.
1863 C. R. Sheldon,   Jesse Davis,   Jefferson Reynolds.
1864 C. R. Sheldon,   Jesse Davis,   A. J. Reynolds.
1865 Ezra Goodspeed,   B. F. Finney,   A. J. Reynolds.
1866 Ezra Goodspeed,   B. F. Finney,   A. J. Reynolds.
1867 Ezra Goodspeed,   B. F. Finney,   A. J. Reynolds.
1868 Ezra Goodspeed,   Parker Carpenter,   A. J. Reynolds.

TREASURERS AND CLERKS SINCE 1807.

	TREASURERS.	CLERKS.
1807	Chauncey Perkins,	John Corey.
1808	Alexander Stedman,	John Corey.
1809	Alexander Stedman,	John Corey.
1810	Alexander Stedman,	John Corey.
1811	Alexander Stedman,	John Corey.
1812	Alexander Stedman,	John Corey.
1813	Eliphaz Perkins,	Nehemiah Gregory.
1814	William Weir,	Alexander Proudfit.
1815	Charles Shipman,	Alvan Bingaam.
1816	Charles Shipman,	James Gillmore.
1817	Ebenezer Blackstone,	James Gillmore.
1818	John Gillmore	James Gillmore.
1819	John Gillmore,	James Gillmore.
1820	John Gillmore,	James Gillmore.
1821	John Gillmore.	James Gillmore.
1822	John Gillmore,	James Gillmore.
1823	John Gillmore,	James Gillmore.
1824	James Gillmore,	John Gillmore.
1825	James Gillmore,	John Gillmore.
1826	James Gillmore,	John Gillmore.
1827	James Gillmore,	John Gillmore.
1828	James Gillmore,	John Gillmore.
1829	Charles Shipman,	John Gillmore.
1830	Allan V. Medbury,	John Gillmore.
1831	Allan V. Medbury,	David Pratt.
1832	Allan V. Medbury,	David Pratt.
1833	Isaac Barker,	Robert E. Constable.
1834	Isaac Barker,	A. B Walker
1835	A. G. Brown,	A. B. Walker.
1836	A. G. Brown,	N. B. Purington.
1837	Elias Hibbard,	D. W. Cunningham.
1838	Joseph H. Moore,	D. W. Cunningham.
1839	Joseph H. Moore,	D. W. Cunningham.
1840	Joseph H. Moore,	D. W. Cunningham.
1841	Joseph H. Moore,	D. W. Cunningham.
1842	Joseph H. Moore,	D. W. Cunningham.
1843	Joseph H. Moore,	David M. Clayton.
1844	Joseph H. Moore,	David M. Clayton.
1845	E. H. Moore,	David M. Clayton.
1846	Samuel Pickering,	Wm. Loring Brown.
1847	Samuel Pickering,	Wm. H. Bartlett.
1848	Lot L. Smith,	Wm. H. Bartlett.
1849	Joseph L. Kessinger,	Wm. H. Bartlett.
1850	Joseph L. Kessinger,	H. K. Blackstone.
1851	Joseph L. Kessinger,	Daniel S. Dana.
1852	John B. Paul,	Daniel S. Dana,
1853	John B. Paul,	Samuel S. Knowles.
1854	John B. Paul,	Daniel S. Dana.
1855	Wm. P. Kessinger,	Daniel S. Dana.
1856	Wm. P. Kessinger,	George H. Stewart.
1857	Wm. P. Kessinger,	George H. Stewart.

	TREASURERS.	CLERKS.
1858	Wm. P. Kessinger,	George H. Stewart.
1859	Elias Tedrow,	George H. Stewart.
1860	Elias Tedrow,	George H. Stewart.
	Elias Tedrow resigned in December, 1860, and A. D. Brown appointed.	
1861	A. D. Brown,	Norman Root,
1862	A. D. Brown,	Norman Root.
1863	A. D. Brown,	Norman Root.
1864	A. D. Brown,	Norman Root.
1865	A. D. Brown,	Norman Root.
1866	A. D. Brown,	Norman Root.
1867	E. H. Moore,	Norman Root.
1868	E. H. Moore,	C. R. Sheldon.

JUSTICES OF THE PEACE.

1814—John L. Lewis, Abel Miller, Henry Bartlett.
1817—Henry Bartlett, Stephen Pilcher.
1829—Reuben J. Davis, A. G. Brown.
1835—A. G. Brown.
1836—Henry Bartlett.
1838—Abram Van Vorhes.
1842—Henry Bartlett.
1844—Norman Root.
1847—A. G. Brown.
1848—Sumner Bartlett.
1850—H. K. Blackstone, Enoch Cabeen.
1851—Daniel S. Dana.
1852—Norman Root.
1853—Daniel S. Dana, Jacob T. Stanley.
1855—Oscar W. Brown.
1856—Norman Root, Doloro Culley. (Resigned Nov. 10, 1858.)
1858—William Golden, Wm. Loring Brown.
1859—Norman Root.
1861—William Golden, Wm. Loring Brown.
1862—Norman Root.

C. R. Sheldon (Resigned July 18, 1864), May 5, 1864.
Wm. A. Thomas, Oct. 14, 1864.
Wm. L. Brown, Dec. 2, 1864.
Norman Root (Died Sept. 21, 1867), Feb. 15, 1865.
Geo. W. Baker (Resigned Sept. 1, 1868), April 6, 1867.
Oscar W. Brown, Sept. 11, 1867.
Hiram C. Martin (Resigned March 10, 1870), Dec. 4, 1867.
Wm. A. Thomas, Sept. 9, 1868.
Wm. Golden, April 9, 1870.
Sumner Bartlett, Sept. 13, 1870.
R. E. Constable, April 11, 1873.
Wm. Golden, April 11, 1873.
H. L. Baker, Aug. 21, 1874.
R. E. Constable, April 5, 1876.
Wm. Golden, April 5, 1876.
H. L. Baker, Sept. 4, 1877.
Wm. Golden, April 14, 1879.
R. E. Constable, May 6, 1879.
Wm. Golden, April 11, 1882.
Ed. T. Rose, April 11, 1882.
R. E. Constable, May 6, 1882.

OFFICERS SINCE 1869.

1869.—Trustees, Ezra Goodspeed, A. J. Reynolds and Parker Carpenter; Clerk, W. A. Thomas; Treasurer, Thos. H. Sheldon.

1870.—Trustees, Parker Carpenter, A. J. Reynolds and Jacob Lash; Clerk, W. A. Thomas; Treasurer, Thos. H. Sheldon; Justice of the Peace, Wm. Golden.

1871.—Trustees, Jacob Lash, H. L. Baker and Josephus Tucker; Clerk, W. A. Thomas; Treasurer, T. H. Sheldon.

1872.—Trustees, Jacob Lash, H. L. Baker and Parker Carpenter; Clerk, Josiah B. Allen; Treasurer, T. H. Sheldon; Justices of the Peace, W. A. Thomas, Sumner Bartlett.

1873.—Trustees, A. Morrison, Judiah Higgins and H. L. Baker; Clerk, J. B. Allen; Treasurer, T. H. Sheldon; Justices of the Peace, Wm. Golden and R. A. Constable.

1874.—Trustees, A. Morrison, Judiah Higgins and Joseph Dorr; Clerk, J. B. Allen; Treasurer, T. H. Sheldon.

1875.—Trustees, A. Morrison, Judiah Higgins and Joseph Dorr; Clerk, Alex. Ewing; Treasurer, T. H. Sheldon.

1876.—Trustees, Augustus Norton, James H. Irwin and A. Morrison; Clerk, Alex. Ewing; Treasurer, T. H. Sheldon; Justices of the Peace, Wm. Golden and R. A. Constable.

1877.—Trustees, same as above; Clerk, Alex. Ewing; Treasurer, T. H. Sheldon.

1878.—Trustees, A. Norton, C. W. Goodspeed and John Cuckler; Clerk, Alex. Ewing; Treasurer, Judiah Higgins.

1879.—Trustees, C. W. Goodspeed, Josephus Tucker and J. K. Cuckler; Clerk, Alex. Ewing; Treasurer, Judiah Higgins; Justices of the Peace, Wm. Golden and W. H. H. Mintun.

1880.—Trustees, C. W. Goodspeed, J. K. Cuckler and Joseph Dorr; Clerk, Alex. Ewing; Treasurer, D. H. Moore, Jr.

1881.—Trustees, same as above; Clerk, Alex. Ewing; Treasurer, D. H. Moore.

1882.—Trustees, C. W. Goodspeed, Joseph Dorr and Parker Carpenter; Clerk, Alex. Ewing; Treasurer, D. H. Moore; Justices of the Peace, Wm. Golden, R. A. Constable and Ed. T. Rose.

1883.—Trustees, C. W. Goodspeed, P. Carpenter and A. H. Simms; Clerk, Alex. Ewing; Treasurer, D. H. Moore.

Dr. Blackstone

CHAPTER XI.

THE CITY OF ATHENS—THE HOME OF CULTURE, REFINEMENT AND INTELLIGENCE.

WHAT SHE WAS AND IS—ADVANCE OF CIVILIZATION—FOOTSTEPS OF THE OLD PIONEER—WHEN SETTLED AND BY WHOM—ACT FOR THE LAYING OUT THE TOWN OF ATHENS, 1799—INCEPTION AND GROWTH—CONDENSED HISTORY—COMPARISON NOT NEEDED—SALE OF LOTS AND PURCHASERS—INCORPORATION—GROWTH—SCHOOLS —CHURCHES—CEMETERIES—BIBLE SOCIETY—LODGES—THE PRESS OF ATHENS—WITH BIOGRAPHICAL NOTES.

WHAT SHE WAS AND IS.

The City of Athens is situated in the beautiful valley of what in olden times was called the "Great Hockhocking." Placed upon its hundred hills in this magnificent valley, it was a pioneer settlement in Southeastern Ohio, and the second in the territory now known as the State of Ohio. Standing upon a high bluff, the scenery is one of beauty, and the Athenians can not only be proud of its surroundings, and its early or pioneer existence, but also because it has arisen from the wilderness a veritable rose blooming, and fragrant with beautiful life, a seat of learning, and the record of a noble generation of men, who have made a glorious name in the annals of State history. Her pioneers were men of education, men who stood in the front rank of culture, and intelligence in the Puritan States, and whose children and children's children have proven themselves worthy sons of noble sires. Such were the founders of the proud and beautiful city of Athens. Cultured, refined and hospitable, it was no wonder that she drew to her other noble men of those early days, and that she has since become famous throughout the State for the true nobility of her people, the beauty of her surroundings, her culture and refinement, and the unostentatious generosity of her sons and daughters.

THE ADVANCE OF CIVILIZATION.

The hunter first trod the site of the city of Athens, and within her limits the buffalo, the bear, the deer and wild turkey, gave up their lives, but they soon left for more quiet fields, and, like the red men, gave way before the steady march of civilization, the ring of the woodman's ax and, last, but not least, before the unerring rifle of the pale-face. Scarcely can there be found within the broad limits of our magnificent commonwealth a more beautiful site for a city than this of Athens. Lying upon the banks of the murky Hocking, with an extended view of the valley, which is everywhere recognized not only for its beauty, but for the richness of its deep alluvial soil, the great fertility of which after nearly a century of cultivation has not failed or allowed its resources to diminish; surrounded by valleys and hills, and looking out upon a broad expanse of well-cultivated fields, guided by intelligent labor, she invites to her those natures who wish to rise to a higher plane, those who wish to retire from the vortex of business strife to give their minds and talents to those researches which develop man's best nature and brings forth his greatest intellectual force and endeavor. So the Athens of to-day is the seat of culture, education and refinement, and her future is but brightened by the noble record of her past.

FOOTSTEPS OF THE PIONEER.

Following the footsteps of the hunter the old pioneer was not long in finding this favored spot, and still less time in deciding that it would be his present and future home. In 1797 the first permanent white settler located in this county, and in 1798 the first one built his cabin on the site of the city of Athens. Of course the country was a wilderness, an unbroken forest; and it was the woodman's ax, while clearing the land, that marked the era of civilization, and of progress which time has not diminished. It was early in the year 1798 that Athens was first inhabited and the first Indian corn waved its grim foliage to the breeze, the proof of man's labor and the date when progress should henceforth rule the country and become the light which was to shed its rays upon a people prosperous, peaceful and happy. Quite a number settled in and around the site of the city, and there were, perhaps, a score of families within the radius of a few miles before the new year of 1799 entered upon its diurnal course. Of course not all of these settled upon the immediate site of the city of Athens. Walker's History gives the number of only six families who resided within the present city limits, but this was an error of nearly one half, or in other words, there were twelve to fifteen families located here. That Gillespe killed the buffalo is probably true; that deer and wild turkeys were killed on the site is also true; but when this land was surveyed and platted for a town or city, it was known to the settlers who came here as under the auspices of the Ohio Company. The college grounds were located in 1796, the survey having been commenced the previous year, or in 1795. Two settlements started almost together—Amesville and Athens—and around these two points the pioneers located first; and as immigrants continued to arrive they spread over a greater extent of country. A company came in 1799, more than half of whom settled at Athens or immediately around the present site of the city —none on the hills, but all in the valley.

"At this time, December, 1800, there were not more than five or six cabins on the town plat. Mr. Earhart lived on the brow of the hill where Bing's carriage shop is situated. Othniel Tuttle had a cabin on the southwest corner of the old graveyard. Dr. Perkins bought this cabin, moved it down the road and added it to his own near where Dr. E. G. Carpenter now lives. Solomon Tuttle lived on the corner of the Atkinson lot opposite the Currier homestead. Christian Stevens had a cabin just back of the college green, and a man by the name of Brakefield lived twenty or thirty rods east of the southeast corner of the green. Alvan Bingham, known by older citizens as "Old Judge Bingham," lived half a mile northeast of where our Auditor, A. W. S. Minear, now resides. During the next four or five years, though increasing but slowly it received the addition of numbers of valuable citizens.

"The first school-house on the town plat was a small brick building, which stood on the site now occupied by the city hall. It was built in 1806. David Pratt taught here several years. Some of those who succeeded him in giving shape to the growing thought of the present and preceding generations are Mrs. Sarah Foster, Miss Sallie Jewett, Rev. James McAboy, Prof. Andrews, Rev. Joseph Marvin, Dr. Charles Townsend, Samuel Marsh, Rev. J. M. Stevenson, Miss Haft and others."

The act of laying off the town of Athens was passed and approved by General Arthur St. Clair, Dec. 18, 1799, a little less than two years from the time the first cabin was erected. This act reads as follows:

WHEREAS, In the county of Washington, within this territory, the townships Nos. 8 and 9, in the 14th range have been appropriated and set apart for the purpose of endowing a university; and *whereas*, the application of the same to the purpose aforesaid has been entrusted to the Legislature of this Territory; therefore, to enable the said Legislature the better to determine the situation whereon to establish the said university:

Be it resolved by the Legislative Council and House of Representatives in General Assembly, That Rufus Putnam, Benjamin Ives Gilman and Jonathan Stone, Esquires, be requested to lay off, in the most suitable place within the townships aforesaid, a town plat which shall contain a square for the college, also lots suitable for house lots and gardens, for a president, professors, tutors, etc., bordering on or encircled by spacious commons, and such a number of town lots adjoining the said commons and out-lots as they shall think will be for the advantage of the university, who are to make a return of the said town plat and lots, describing their situation within the said townships, to the Legislature at their next session, and shall receive such compensation for their services as the Legislature shall and may direct and allow.

EDWARD TIFFIN,
Speaker of the House of Representatives.
H. VANDERBURGH,
President of the Council.

On receiving a copy of this act of the Territorial Assembly, the gentlemen named therein took steps to carry out its provision, and did so, being ready to report at the next session of the Territorial legislation. That body, on receiving the report, passed the following act entitled,

An act confirming the establishment of the town of Athens in the County of Washington.

WHEREAS, By a resolution of the Legislature of this Territory, of the 18th day of December, 1799, Rufus Putnam, Benjamin Ives Gilman and Jonathan Stone, Esquires, were requested to lay off a town in the most convenient place within the townships numbered 8 and 9, in the 14th range of townships as set apart by the agents and directors of the Ohio Company, for the uses and purposes of a university, which should be so laid off as to contain a square for colleges, and lots suitable for house-lots and gardens for a resident, professors and tutors, with out-lots and commons. And, *whereas*, the said Putnam, Gilman and Stone, in conformity to the said resolution, have laid off the said town within the ninth, tenth and fifteenth, sixteenth and twenty-second sections of the aforesaid ninth township, and have returned a plat of the same; therefore, to establish and confirm the same:

SECTION 1. *Be it enacted by the Legislative Council and House of Representatives in General Assembly*, And it is hereby enacted by the authority of the same, that the return and report of the said Putnam, Gilman and Stone be accepted and approved, and that the said town shall be confirmed and established by the name of the town of *Athens; Provided*, That the trustees of the university therein to be established shall have power to alter the plan of said town, by extending the house lots into the commons or out-lots which adjoin the town, or by altering the streets, when, on actual survey, they may find it necessary or convenient; *Provided also*, That such alterations be made and a plat of the town, out-lots on commons, with a designation of the uses of the commons, be recorded in the office of the recorder of the proper county, prior to the offering to lease any of said lots.

SEC. 2. *And be it further enacted;* That the house-lots numbers 55 and 56 in the said town of Athens, or some other two lots therein, equally as well situated, to be designated and set apart by the trustees of said university when appointed, shall be reserved for the accommodation of public buildings that may be necessary to be erected for the use of said town and the county in which it may be situated; which two lots, when agreed upon by said trustees, shall be particularly noted on the plat of said town and vested in the county to and for the uses designed thereby.

EDWARD TIFFIN,
Speaker House of Representatives.

Approved, Dec. 6, 1800.
ARTHUR ST. CLAIR,
Governor.

ROBERT OLIVER,
President of the Council.

When the last act of the Territorial Legislature was passed, Athens could well boast of from fifteen to twenty families, and instead of Cincinnati being a town on paper at that time, or credited with 750 inhabitants, it had more thousands than hundreds above given, the cause being that it was the western and southern outpost of the Northwest Territory at that time. Athens County, while being probably settled first, was only because it was nearer the eastern border; but while some stopped here, others followed the river, and Cincinnati did not lag far behind. It was from that point that Mad Anthony Wayne made the first successful campaign against the Indians, after Generals Harmar and St. Clair both had met with overwhelming defeat and disaster. General Harmar was defeated in September, 1790; St. Clair in November, 1791, and General Anthony Wayne commenced the formation of his army, at Cincinnati, in April, 1793, but did not move against the Indians until the following year, 1794. His celebrated battle was fought Aug. 20 of that year, and peace was declared in 1795. So an army of 3,500 men left Cincinnati in July, 1794. This would show that Walker had made a very great mistake in putting the population of Cincinnati in the year 1800 at 750 when in fact the census of that year gave the county of Hamilton 14,692, and the city of Cincinnati held most of it. Ten years later Athens County had a population of 2,791.

It has been thought best to correct this statement here, as the history above mentioned is much quoted, and its errors of figures resulted probably from a want of correct statistics at hand. In making the above correction, however, in regard to the population of Cincinnati, it is done only for the purpose of conforming to known history and to the census of that year.

INCEPTION AND GROWTH.

The following early history of Athens is condensed from an address by Mr. A. B. Walker, delivered in June, 1875, on the occasion of the opening of the new city hall. It contains facts which can not be gathered from any other source, and will be found of particular interest in this connection. The portions taken are mainly such as pertain alone to the town of Athens.

At the public opening of the new city hall in Athens, June 8, 1875, Mr. A. B. Walker, an aged and respected citizen of the place, delivered the following address, a familiar historic narrative sketch of the town of Athens:

"The occasion which we celebrate is peculiarly fitted to direct our minds and lead our thoughts to reminiscences bearing upon the history and growth of our town. The first opening of a new city hall is an event of sufficient moment to arouse the municipal consciousness and reanimate the local patriotism which must belong to all who have common interests and common surroundings.

" Each achievement, like the present, is a milestone that marks our progress ; every such occasion places us on a height where we can glance back on the path already traversed.

" Since the shades of the native forest fell on this spot a momentous·and salutary change has taken place in the physical, intellectual and social condition of this people.

" The material resources requisite to produce a public hall at a cost of perhaps $30,000, and the felt need of a place of public entertainment convenient of access, are matters of the highest commendation, and such as may well lead to an inquiry into the sources of our corporate life. Let us therefore examine in brief some of the causes that have operated in producing Athens.

" On the evening of the 6th of April, A. D. 1788, while a heavy mist hung over the river, a little flotilla of one large boat, one flat-boat and three canoes dropped quietly down the beautiful Ohio, and lodged on a point at the mouth of the Muskingum. It was a winged seed, which contained the germ of the subsequent civilization of this broad State.

" Of the four natural divisions of Ohio,—the lake country, the Miami country, the Scioto country and the Muskingum country, the Ohio Company wisely (as time has proved) decided in favor of the Muskingum country, which gave to our section of the State priority of occupation. The letters patent granted by Congress gave them about 1,000,000 acres, lying within the limits of Washington County. Indeed, at that time, the ambitious boundaries of Washington County reached out to the headwaters of the Big Miami, and encircled the present sites of Portsmouth, Cleveland and Columbus.

" The auspicious location of our town is more than evinced when we consider it in its wider geographical connections. The Scioto and the Muskingum form a parallelogram which, lying north and south, or nearly so, is bisected diagonally by the Hockhocking River, having its source near Columbus, on the Scioto, ninety miles above the mouth of the latter, and emptying into the Ohio only a few miles below the mouth of the Muskingum. Now the Hockhocking, with its tributaries, contains the great mining field of Ohio, and Athens County enjoys the happy distinction of occupying the preferred portion of this charming valley, while the town of Athens is the central point in the valley, as it is the middle point between Parkersburg and Marietta on the east, and Chillicothe on the west.

"Every access by the river and that general fertility and picturesqueness which invited first the occupation of water-courses, may have fixed this bluff and the adjacent bottoms as an eligible site for a settlement. The haste to found the college would prompt to a selection of the most accessible place, which at the same time should be sufficiently interior. Thus it appears that the college and town were mutually parent and child to each other; for while the growing village was intended to become a source of revenue and nourishment to its infant charge, the university, on the other hand, became a leading and efficient cause in hastening the inception of a corporate town, in giving it a local habitation so desirable, and a name linking it with the choicest associations of literature and learning in the distant past.

"The county of Athens was first settled in 1797, but was not regularly erected into a separate county by legislative enactment until the year 1805—eight years after its first settlement. It is singular however, in being the second county in Ohio, as the town of Athens is the second town in the State. Upon the latter fact we may be pardoned in indulging a natural pride, since antiquity is no slight element in the historic estimate of a place."

The town of Athens was incorporated by the following act:

"'*An act to incorporate the town of Athens, and for other purposes.*

"'*Jan.* 28, 1811.—Sec. 2. That the trustees of the Ohio University are hereby authorized and directed to lease to the commissioners of the county of Athens for the time being, in-lots numbers 35 and 37, on which the court-house and jail now stand, and also in-lot number 18 reserved for the purpose o building a school-house and meeting-house, on a nominal rent for ninety-nine years, renewable forever; also, to lease on the terms aforesaid, the ground reserved for a burying ground.

"'This act to be in force from and after the passage thereof.'

"About the year 1820 a company for that purpose bored a well for salt water on Sunday Creek, to a considerable depth, but abandoned the undertaking. Ten or twelve years after other parties resumed the boring and soon struck a vein of good salt water. This was the first successful salt-well bored in the Hocking Valley. The manufacture of salt in this valley soon became a prosperous business, imparting of its advantages to all the surrounding interests of the county. To provide for its export with other surplus productions, two channels of traffic were opened, which, though now in disuse, bore quite a prominent part in the early commercial history of our town.

"Athens, with its surplus pork, flour, wheat and other agricultural productions, and now engaged in the very considerable manufacture of salt, must not only make use of the Hockhocking River, as it offered the advantages of descending navigation during the spring and autumnal freshets, for the passage of large flat-boats loaded and intended for the Southern markets, but to facilitate the transit of salt to the interior and central part of the State a canal down the Hocking Valley to Athens, for the double purpose of transporting both the salt and the coal to the interior of the State, was justly deemed indispensable to all the interests of the valley. For the timely construction of the Hocking canal, we are largely indebted to our late townsman, Hon. Calvary Morris. It was through his indefatigable endeavors that the canal was chartered and pushed vigorously to completion in the face of the most stubborn opposition of the commissioner and a majority of both Houses of the Legislature. A public dinner was tendered to Judge Morris on his return, as a token of the high estimation in which his services were held. The canal opening up the valley to the north was an outlet toward the middle portion of the State and the Western markets generally.

"The middle section of this town's history presents fewer salient points to the eye, but we may say in general that the several causes that operated in giving the place early notoriety, were still active in controlling its subsequent advancement. Athens, in its type, is a pioneer town, and is well built for one of its class. Its central position in the thickly settled Southern part of Ohio; the growth of a thrifty, agricultural and stock-raising county of which it is the natural focus and constituted seat of justice; the seminal principles of a rugged virtue and industry unconsciously engrafted upon it by its founders; the intellectual and moral atmosphere diffused by its schools, courts, churches and university; its handsome situation and picturesque surroundings; all these have ever made Athens an attractive place of residence.

"Few towns have retained such a hold upon their people as is evinced by the large number of old inhabitants in proportion to the population. This circumstance coming into notice has given rise to the proverb that 'No one can permanently remove from Athens who has once tasted the waters of the Hockhocking.'

"Situated in one of the two college townships, Athens may well regard herself as a natural custodian of the college allotment or endowment lands; rejoicing in its elevation; guarding with jealous interest against any encroachments tending to abridge its power, and doing as much as may be to aid its future advancement.

"It is gratifying to be able to say concerning the town that its old age, which entitles it to some degree of veneration, appears to bring with it no indications of decrepitude. For all purposes of internal improvement and energetic action in securing advantages of a public nature from without, Athenian enterprise has suffered no abatement. The exterior dress of the town is proof enough of this. Its recently improved streets, both in grades and pavements; its multiplied shade-trees; its gaslights; its beautiful new cemetery, and more particularly its asylum for the insane, are all features that at once strike the eye of a stranger, producing a decidedly favorable impression; and last, but not least, we make mention of our railroads and telegraphic communications of the most important character; all not only combine to reflect the highest credit upon the action and enterprise which secured them, but are also encouraging as harbingers of an era that may one day, in the early development of this valley, make Athens one of the noticeable and important railroad centers of Ohio."

COMPARISON NOT NEEDED.

Athens needs no comparison with other points, nor is she envious of their growth and prosperity. Comparisons are said to be odious, and this is so in this case, for it *is* entirely unnecessary. Athens is not, cannot be, and would not be a commerical emporium if she could. If so, she would not be Athens; and the fact that she is ATHENS, is her pride and boast. Anything else would be her destruction. She represents a seat of learning the oldest in the State, and she herself is really an enlarged edition of the famed college. She is the home of all that goes to make an intellectual paradise on earth. Refined, cultured, generous and hospitable, situated in one of the most beautiful valleys in the State, nature and art have combined to make her, what comparison would but lower. The first tavern, built of logs, was kept by Wm. McNichol, nearly opposite to where the old Abbott House stood. Wm. Dorr built a store. Dr. Perkins's cabin was on what is now State Street, and that of Dr. Leonard Jewett was on College street. The town seemed to take on new life after it was incorporated, and attracted considerable attention at that time from the outside world. Game was abundant all through the country, and Athens became somewhat of a trading point, dealing in the furs brought in and also in wild meats, for it furnished most that the inhabitants used at that time. Hogs and cattle were scarce, and few would kill them for meat.

Athens was not experiencing any very rapid progress, but it was steady. The first circuit preachers appear to have been Rev. Jno. Meek and Rev. James Quinn, who were appointed to the Hocking Circuit in 1804. The Rev. Joseph Williams was on the circuit the following year. The trustees in charge of the town passed an ordinance for the sale of lots to take place Nov. 5, 1804. It was their desire that Athens should become the county-seat of the new county which was shortly to be organized, and was organized the following year, 1805. The town was at once surveyed, laid off and platted, in readiness for the above sale, and rules prescribed for the purchase and payment of lots. The sale came off on the above date, and in Walker's History is the following account of the sale.

THE FIRST SALE.

NO. OF LOT.	PURCHASER.	PRICE.	PURCHASER'S RESIDENCE.
1	John Havner	$132.00	Athens.
4	Wm. Mc Nichol	46.00	Salt Works.
7	Silas Bingham	40.50	Athens.
10	Jarrett Jones	27.00	Middletown.
13	Silas Bingham	62.00	Athens.
16	Silvanus Ames	51.00	Ames.
19	Moses Hewitt	61.00	Middletown.
23	Wm. McNichol	25.00	Salt Works.
26	Eliphaz Perkins	30.00	Athens.
28	"	101.00	"
29	Rufus Putnam	59.00	Marietta.
32	John Simonton	27.00	Middletown.
36	John Johnson	20.00	Wheeling.
40	Rufus Putnam	20.00	Marietta.
43	"	30.00	"
46	Henry Bartlett	17.00	Middletown.
49	Canaday Lowry	14.00	"
52	Daniel Mulford	13.00	"
55	Jehiel Gregory	42.00	"
59	Timothy N. Wilkins	22.00	"
63	John Wilkins	10.00	"
65	Rufus Putnam	30.00	Marietta.
68	Wm. McNichol	23.00	Salt Works.
71	"	30.00	"
73	"	101.00	"
74	Wm. Dorr	65.00	Middletown.
77	Wm. McNichol	42.00	Salt Works.

This was thought to have been a very fair sale, and the prices were satisfactory to the trustees. The town took a start after this sale, and Athens's future seemed to be assured. Steady growth in town and country for a little over two years resulted in another sale of lots, which came off Nov. 25, 1806, and while not realizing so high an average, was considered a profitable one, from the fact that the lots were not so eligibly situated as those of the first sale. The prices and names of purchasers will be found below:

SECOND SALE OF LOTS.

NO. OF LOT.	PURCHASER.	PRICE.	NO. OF LOT.	PURCHASER.	PRICE.
1	Joel Abbot	$72.00	36	Moses Hewitt	18.00
2	"	40.50	48	"	6.00
3	Ebenezer Currier	36.50	21	Silas Bingham	15.00
4	Wm. Skinner	15.00	22	"	22.00
5	Silvanus Ames	15.00	23	Rufus Putnam	10.00
6	Leonard Jewett	15.00	25	"	16.00
8	"	15.00	34	"	26.00
9	"	13.00	27	Saml. Luckey	14.00
10	John Walker	12.50	30	James Buell	15.00
12	"	26.00	32	"	11.00
11	Wm. Skinner	7.50	31	Benajah Seaman	20.00
29	"	16.00	43	"	12.00
33	"	35.00	38	David Boyles	17.00
14	Silvanus Ames	35.00	39	Timothy Wilkins	14.00
16	"	15.00	41	"	17.00
15	Wm. Dorr	18.00	40	Dudley Woodbridge	11.00
17	Ebenezer Currier	52.00	42	"	10.00
19	Moses Hewitt	35.00	44	Jehiel Gregory	6.00
20	"	40.00	47	"	6.00
24	"	11.00	45	Henry Bartlett	6.00

INCORPORATION AND GROWTH.

An act for the incorporation of the town of Athens was passed by the Legislature Jan. 28, 1811, and the act covered what was known as the town plat, as recorded in the recorder's office of the county of Washington. It was given the name of the "Town of Athens," with all the rights and privileges accorded corporate bodies, and provided for annual township elections. At that time Athens had, probably, a population of about 200 inhabitants, and her growth from that time up to the opening of the Civil War was slow, reaching in the neighborhood of from 1,250 to 1,300 in population. The decade between 1860 and 1870 was a marked era of dullness, and Athens made but little progress, either in population or material progress. The year 1870, however, found her recovering from the prostration of preceding years and she commenced that decade with a population of 1,696. Undoubtedly this recovery from her former listless activity resulted from the fact that in 1867 she had secured to her site the Southern Lunatic Asylum. The struggle to secure this aroused all the dormant energies of her people, and, although the good effects of this important element to her growth was not at first felt, yet by the opening of the decade between 1870 and 1880, its great benefit began to leave its mark on the daily progress of her business life. The prize was won and the citizens showed of what stuff they were made by promptly purchasing, adjoining the city, 150 acres of land, known as the Coates farm, commanding a most beautiful view of the valley of Hocking, and lying upon an elevation, which gives of itself and the magnificent buildings which adorn its crest, as pleasant a scene as man's eye need rest upon. The blue of heaven, the lofty hills lying in the background, and God's earth surrounding it with a carpet of green, make it one of the most attractive of sights; and if insanity cannot be cured, it has in this instance a home where Nature in her most glorious garb, blended with art, has done her best for the comfort and happiness of the afflicted ones. From 1870 to 1880 the city of Athens made somewhat more rapid strides toward metropolitan greatness, her population increasing during that decade nearly fifty per cent., the census giving her 2,457. The improvements made were also of a more substantial nature, and few cities of the State of her size can boast of finer brick blocks, a growth more stable, handsomer residences, or more beautiful lawns and pleasant surroundings than the city of Athens.

SCHOOLS.

The Union system of schools was adopted in Athens in the year 1850. At a meeting of citizens held Jan. 12 of that year, at which S. Miller acted as Chairman and F. F. Baker as Secretary, the following Board of Directors was chosen: L. Jewett and O. W. Pickering, three years; E. H. Moore and William Walker, two years; E. P. Talpey and William Golden, one year. This board chose L. Jewett as President and E. H. Moore as Secretary. Salaries of teachers in those days were surprisingly low. We find from the records that in 1853 C. Grant received $450 for his services one year; Miss Rice, $5.50 per week; Miss Gould, $5.00 per week; D. S. Dana, $8.30 per week; Misses Sanderson and Beaton, $4.00 per week, each.

Several different buildings were used for the schools before the present fine building was erected. Among the many eligible sites offered for school purposes, the board finally decided to accept the Frost lot, consisting of in-lots 132, 130, 150 and 151. Sept. 17, 1853, $8,000 were voted for a school building, to be raised in four annual levies of $2,000 each, and afterward $4,000 more were voted. Various sums have since been appropriated for the improvement of grounds, and other purposes, $2,000 having been spent in the last ten years. The property is now valued at about $30,000. The building was first used in 1858.

The first Superintendent of the Athens schools was Cyrus Grant, chosen Dec. 23, 1853. He served till Oct. 15, 1855, a period of one year and ten months, at $450 per year. He was succeeded by John H. Pratt, who served five months, until March 22, 1856. J. K. Mower was then chosen Superintendent, holding the position two years and eight months. He was followed by J. H. Pratt, for three months. The next to hold the office was J. H. Doan, for two years and five months, resigning Aug. 9, 1861. M. M. Travers then served one year, and after him for one year and a half the Superintendent was W. H. Scott, now President of Ohio University. C. A. Barker was chosen Feb. 6, 1864, and served two years and five months. July 16, 1866, the present Superintendent, J. M. Goodspeed, was elected. His salary was at first $600, but has been variously increased, and is now $1,200.

The present corps of instructors includes J. M. Goodspeed, Superintendent; Miss Kate Boyd, High School; Miss Emma Dana, Mrs. Stalder, Ella White, Clara Weiher, Lizzie Cochran, Ollie Wilson, Sallie Kessinger, Fronie Foster and Ella Pickering. The present Board of Directors are Judiah Higgins, President; J. M. Wood, H. M. Lash, E. B. Clarke, E. J. Jones and A. B. Frame. Superintendent Goodspeed is Clerk of the Board. The course of study comprises five years in the Primary School, four years in the Grammar School and three years in the High School. The High School course is an English course, none of the languages being prescribed as studies. Students may, however, elect to pursue Latin for two years. The roll of graduates comprises 109.

CHURCHES OF ATHENS.

Presbyterian.—The First Presbyterian Society of Athens was organized in the autumn of 1809, by the Rev. Jacob Lindley. The original members of the organization were but nine in number, viz.:

Joshua Wyatt and wife, Josiah Coe, Arthur Coates, Dr. Eliphaz Perkins, Alvan Bingham, Mrs: Sally Foster and the Rev. Jacob Lindley and wife.

Public service was held for a time in the little brick school-house which stood just east of the present site of the Presbyterian church, and afterward in the court-house until the year 1828, when the present brick church was built. In 1815 the church numbered forty-seven members, and a revival that year added forty-three. In the year 1820 there were fifty-six added to the church, and the whole number of church members at that time was 177.

Articles of association were drawn, written in the hand of Joseph B. Miles, and adopted by the society in the early days of its existence.

Though among the earliest religious societies organized in the State, this church was not incorporated till 1828. The act, passed Feb. 7 of that year, names as the incorporators: Columbus Bierce, Isaac Taylor, Joseph B. Miles, Charles Shipman, Francis Beardsley, Samuel Miller, Eben Foster, John Perkins, Hull Foster, John Gillmore, and Cephas Carpenter, and Messrs. Miles, Bierce, Taylor, Beardsley and Carpenter were constituted Trustees of the church, to act as such till the first annual meeting. The Rev. Jacob Lindley acted as Moderator of the session and Pastor, until about 1828, since when eighteen ministers have served the church either as stated supply or as Pastors. The entire list in the order of time is as follows:

Rev. Jacob Lindley, contemporary; Rev. Samuel Davies Hoge, contemporary; Rev. Robert G. Wilson, Rev. John Spaulding (now of New York City), Rev. William Burton, Rev. Timothy Stearns, Rev. N. B. Purington, Rev. Wm. H. McGuffey, Rev. Wells Andrews, Rev. Aaron Williams, Rev. Moses A. Hoge, Rev. Addison Ballard, Rev. Alfred Ryors, Rev. S. Dieffendorf, Rev. John H. Pratt, Rev. James F. Holcomb, Rev. Ernst W. Schwefel, Rev. J. M. Nourse, and Rev. Isaac W. Montfort.

Rev. John H. Pratt began his labors here in 1854, laboring one year as " stated supply," after which he received a call as Pastor. During the period of his pastorate (fourteen years), 200 members were added to the church. The deaths and removals of members during the same period were, however, numerous—the latter especially so—so that the present active membership is only about 170.

Some years since, the church was rebuilt and a lecture-room added. The old-fashioned lofty pulpit has given place to a modern platform. In those days the pulpit being in the front end of the church, the congregation faced about on taking their seats.

The church is prospering, and a Sunday-school is connected which is doing effective service in its sphere.

The Methodist Episcopal Church—Is the pioneer religious organization of Athens, and indeed of the whole Hocking Valley. The Methodists have had a society here from the year 1800, when a Rev. Mr. Quinn made a missionary tour up the Hocking Valley and preached in Athens, and during the early as well as later years of their church history here, have numbered among their preachers some very able, earnest and useful men. In 1805 Rev. Jacob Young preached on this circuit; Rev. George C. Light preached here about the same time. In 1806 Peter Cartwright, who afterward became celebrated in the church, visited Athens and Alexander townships, preaching and forming societies. About 1815 Rev. Thos. Morris (afterward Bishop Morris) was on this circuit and preached statedly at Athens. Among the early Methodist preachers here were Rev. Cornelius Springer, Rev. Daniel Limerick, Rev. Curtis Goddard, Rev. Abraham Lippett, Rev. John Ferree, Rev. Abraham Baker, Rev. Henry S. Fernandez, Rev. Absalom Fox, Rev. Asa Stroud and Rev. Robert O. Spencer, some of them being on the Muskingum and some on the Athens circuit.

For the first few years the Methodists held their meetings at different houses, but in 1812 or 1813 they built a brick church, now owned by Henry Wright. In 1825 they erected a brick parsonage adjoining. The church building, having been used as such nearly thirty years, fell into decay and was then used for some years as a foundry; it has now disappeared. The parsonage forms a part of Mr. Wright's present house. The present Methodist church was built in 1837 and thoroughly remodeled in 1861. Other important improvements have been made at short intervals up to the present time, one of the most important being the addition of a fine lecture-room in the rear of the main building in 1875. The present parsonage, situated on College street, was built in 1876. It is to be regretted that the records of this old and useful church society have not been better preserved. The Pastors since the war have been: Rev. Ansel Brooks, appointed in 1865; Rev. J. M. Jamison, 1867; Rev. J. H. Creighton, 1869; Rev. E. H. Heagler,

1870; Rev. W. T. Harvey, 1873; Rev. O. J. Nave, 1875; Rev. J. W. Peters, 1876; Rev. J. M. Weir, 1877; Rev. M. V. B. Evans, 1879; Rev. S. D. Hutsinpillar, 1881. The church is now in a state of gratifying prosperity. A Sabbath-school is kept up by the church society throughout the year. It is well attended and is very prosperous. The superintendency has changed hands several times in the last few years, Mr. D. L. Sleeper holding the position at present.

Catholic Church.—The St. Paul's Catholic Church of Athens was organized about the year 1846. No regular service was held for a while, but irregular meetings were held in the court-house.

The first regular service was conducted by Father John Albrick, of Pomeroy, who came over once a month. Father Albrick was succeeded by Father McGee, a Dominican from Somerset, Ohio. Father Gells, from Pomeroy, succeeded him, and he in time was succeeded by Father Tenerie, from Vinton County. During all these changes the church was growing stronger, both in number and influence, and if not rapid was sure. It was during Father Tenerie's administration that the timber for a church building was gotten out. This was in the year 1861. During the service of Fathers Madzell and Curtzen the church was completed and ready for occupancy in 1863. Since then services have been held by the Reverend Fathers in the order named, viz.: Fathers O'Reily, Slavens, Campbell, Hartnedy, T. J. Lane and John Madden. The church is attached to the diocese of Columbus, Ohio, and has at this time a membership of 300. It is progressive and prospering.

Colored Churches.—The colored citizens of Athens have two church organizations of the denominations of Methodist and Baptist. They also have two church buildings, one a brick church belonging to the Methodist congregation and the other a frame, that of the Baptist. The churches are fairly supported and in a fair condition, though some money is yet due upon their buildings.

CEMETERIES.

For considerably more than half a century, says Walker's History, after Athens was settled, the dead were buried in the old graveyard northwest of town, which was set apart for that use by the trustees of the university in 1806. The place never was ornamented to any extent, and for many years only a few forest trees have given it their grateful shade. Here, a little apart from their surviving friends, rest the fathers of the village.

> "The breezy call of incense-breathing morn,
> The swallow twittering from the straw-built shed,
> The cock's shrill clarion or the echoing horn
> No more shall rouse them from their lowly bed."

In January, 1864, the citizens of Athens, feeling the need of a more beautiful burying ground, organized the Athens Cemetery Association, with a capital stock of $4,000, divided into shares of $100, which was incorporated under a general law of the State. An eligible site was selected west of the town, and a purchase made of twelve acres, which has since been tastefully laid off into winding walks and drives, and handsomely ornamented with shrubbery. Some appropriate and costly monuments already adorn the new cemetery, which is a place of pleasant resort for the residents of Athens, and is a credit to the town. The organization is officered as follows: Calvary Morris, President, H. J. Topky, Secretary; A. B. Walker, Treasurer, and Calvary Morris, J. W. Harris, J. H. Pratt, W. P. Johnson and Jesse Van Law, Trustees.

ATHENS COUNTY BIBLE SOCIETY.

This society was founded in Athens County in 1822, as an auxiliary of the American Bible Society. Since its organization it has donated to the parent society in cash nearly $2,000 and expended in the purchase of books for home use about $7,000. It has circulated, in sixty-one years, upward of 16,000 copies of the Holy Bible in home and foreign fields. The present officers are: D. B. Stewart, President; Cyrus Rose, Secretary, and James D. Brown, Treasurer.

SOCIETIES.

Paramuthia Lodge, No. 25, F. & A. M., was chartered Oct. 2, 1814, and is one of the oldest lodges in the State of Ohio. The records have been unfortunately destroyed by fire. The Past Masters since 1867 have been: C. L. Wilson, 1867; J. M. Goodspeed, 1869; H. M. Lash, 1875; J. M. Goodspeed, 1878; H. C. Will, 1879; J. H. Walker, 1880; J. L. Pickering, 1882. The present officers are: Peter Kern, W. M.; E. P. Cooke, S. W.; J. P. Dana, J. W.; Judiah Higgins, Treas.; George R. Walker, Sec.; H. B. Stewart, S. D.; G. G. Lewis, J. D.; Joel Moe, Tyler. The next election of officers occurs Dec. 11, 1883. The stated communications are held the second and fourth Tuesdays of each month.

Athens Chapter, No. 39, *R. A. M.*, was chartered Jan. 20, 1849, since which time the office of High Priest has been held successively by Leonidas Jewett, 1849–'52; S. P. Pruden, 1853–'5; J. M. Dana, 1856–'8; L. W. Brown, 1859–'61; J. M. Dana, 1862–'74; J. M. Goodspeed, 1875–'83. The present officers are: J. M. Goodspeed, H. P.; H. M. Lash, K.; L. M. Jewett, S.; J. P. Dana, C. H.; H. B. Stewart, P. S.; E. R. Lash, R. A. C.; E. P. Cooke, G. M. 3 V.; J. L. Pickering, G. M. 2 V.; B. W. Pickering, G. M. 1 V.; Wm. H. Brown, Treas.; C. Mc Lean, Sec.; Joel Moe, Guard. The next election of officers occurs Dec. 14, 1883. The stated communications are held on the second Friday of each month.

Sereno Lodge, No. 479, *I. O. O. F.*, was organized June 29, 1871, by A. Pearson, D. G. M. The seven charter members were: J. O. Jones, W. G. Cooley, J. H. Earhart, G. W. Ullom, J. H. Thurston, J. W. Harris and W. H. Mintun. The first officers were: J. O. Jones, N. G.; W. G. Cooley, V. G.; G. H. Earhart, Rec. Sec.; G. W. Ullom, Per. Sec.; J. W. Harris, Treas. The present officers are: W. C. Leesger, N. G.; W. J. Hastings, V. G.; Mr. Myers, Rec. Sec.; D. C. Conwell, Per. Sec.; G. W. Ullom, Treas,; C. B. O'Bleness, P. G. The lodge meets every Friday evening, and is in excellent condition, financially and otherwise.

Athenian Lodge, No. 104, *K. of P.*, was instituted Jan. 15, 1877, by Leroy S. Dungan, of London, O., and T. Q. Collins, of Toledo, O., with eighteen charter members, as follows: C. B. O'Bleness, P. C.; E. R. Lash, C. C.; H. B. Stewart, V. C.; F. O. Pickering, P.; E. H. James, K. of R. and S.; A. L. Gabriel, M. of F.; T. M. Pickering, M. of Ex.; John Graham, M. at A.; L. W. Connett, J. L. Swett, C. P. Rose, E. Z. Stedman, E. R. Gabriel, W. F. Jourdan, A. Laird, S. M. Shepard, H. C. Gabriel and F. F. Custar. The present membership is forty-five. It meets every Monday night. The present officers are: C. P. Rose, P. C.; L. W. Connett, C. C.; George Ford, V. C.; A. Laird, P.; E. R. Lash, K. of R. and S.; John P. Coe, M. of Ex.; F. O. Pickering, M. of F.; C. B. O'Bleness, M. at A.

Athens Council, No. 15, was chartered Oct. 15, 1850. The records having been destroyed by fire, a new charter was granted June 3, 1853, since which time the office of Thrice Illustrious Master has been filled as follows: S. B. Pruden, 1853; W. H. Young, 1859; J. M. Dana, 1864; L. W. Brown; J. M. Goodspeed, 1873; J. A. Slattery, 1875; G. W. Baker, 1878; A. Selig, 1882; J. L. Pickering, 1883. The present officers are as follows: J. L. Pickering, T. I. M.; A. J. Frame, D. M.; J. M. Goodspeed, P. C. W.; L. M. Jewett, Treas.; C. McLean, Rec.; E. R. Lash, C. of G.; Dean Stickney, C. of C.; Peter Kern, Steward; Joel Moe, Steward. The next election of officers occurs Dec. 19, 1883. The stated communications are held third Wednesday of each month.

Athens Commandery, No. 15, was chartered Oct. 16, 1857, since which time the office of Eminent Commander has been filled by Samuel Pruden, 1857–'64; Norman Root, 1865; Wm. H. Young, 1866; C. L. Wilson, 1867–'8; J. Q. Mitchel, 1869–'72; Joseph Jewett, 1873; N. H. Van Vorhes, 1874; J. M. Goodspeed, 1875–'6; C. H. Grosvenor, 1877–'8; J. M. Goodspeed, 1879–'83. The present officers are : J. M. Goodspeed, E. C.; E. R. Lash, Gen.; H. B. Stewart, Capt. Gen.; J. P. Dana, Prelate; J. L. Pickering, S. W.; Dean Stickney, J. W.; A. J. Frame, Treas.; C. McLean, Rec.; C. W. Harris, St. B.; W. P. Shepard, Swd. B.; Peter Kern, Warder; Joel Moe, Sent. The next election of officers occurs Nov. 28, 1883. The stated communications are appointed to be held the fourth Wednesday of each month.

Grand Army of the Republic.—This order was established June 24, 1881, by David Lanning, of J. C. McCoy Post, of Columbus, Ohio. It is called the Columbus Golden Post, No. 89, being named after Columbus Golden, who was the first man who fell in the civil war from Athens County. The post belongs to the Department of Ohio, and was organized with twenty-five charter members, R. A. Constable, elected Post Commander and J. L. Pickering, Adjutant. The post has had a successful life so far and its future is one of promise. Its present officers are R. A. Constable, Post Commander and F. T. Towsley, Adjutant. Its membership now numbers 212, and its treasury holds a surplus of $800.

R. A. Constable was the delegate to the National Council in 1882, and the delegate to the National Encampment in 1883 was C. H. Grosvenor, the only one from Ohio. A portion only of the members of the post (thirty) are uniformed besides the officers. The Columbus Golden Post stands high among its brethren in the State, and has strong influence in the State and National Council.

NEWSPAPERS.

Athens Mirror and Literary Register.—This was the pioneer newspaper of the Hocking Valley, as well as of Athens County. It was started in 1825 by A. G. Brown, as editor and proprietor. He was assisted pecuniarily in this enterprise by several citizens of Athens. The press was bought second-hand at Marietta, and with the press came Isaac Maxon as foreman, and John Brough, afterward Governor of Ohio, as apprentice. He lived with Judge Brown for several years, working on the paper, and between the two there grew a warm friendship. The press above alluded to was a Stanburg press, "double pull," and the ink was distributed by leather-covered balls, the only method at that time known. The first isssue of the *Mirror* appeared the first week in April, 1825. The paper was political and literary in its character, printed once a week, of sixteen pages, about 9 x 5 inches to each number. It continued through five years. In February, 1829, the publisher announced that "all who wish to see the fifth volume of the MIRROR published, are desired to send in their names before the first day of May next," and earnestly solicits increased patronage.

Among the contributors to the *Mirror* was Rev. Samuel D. Hoge, a son of Rev. Moses Hoge, President of Hampden-Sidney College, of Virginia, and a brother of Rev. James Hoge, of Columbus. The circulation of the *Mirror* was usually about 400 to 500. It was succeeded in 1830 by

The Western Spectator, which was edited and published by Isaac Maxon, formerly foreman under Mr. Brown. Under his management it continued about six years. It was a good local newspaper. In 1836 it was bought by Abraham Van Vorhes, who changed the name to the

Athens Messenger and Hocking Valley Gazette.—Under this name Mr. Van Vorhes edited and published the paper for several years, enlarging it, printing it on new press and type, and otherwise greatly improving it. In 1844 he sold out to his sons, N. H. and A. J. Van Vorhes. From Jan. 18, 1850, to July 14, 1851, S. N. Miller was a member of the firm. July 8, 1853, N. H. Van Vorhes was obliged to resign his duties temporarily, on account of failing health, and his brother conducted the paper until Oct. 19, 1856, when the office was sold to G. S. Walsh. Mr. Walsh conducted it but a year, when N. H. Van

Vorhes again took the paper. He continued as editor till 1861, when he entered the Union army, having sold the *Messenger* to T. F. Wildes, afterward editor of the *Journal*. He retained the *Messenger* but a short time, selling out to Jesse and S. C. Van Law, the latter of whom withdrew in September, 1863, leaving Jesse Van Law sole editor and proprietor. He was the "war editor," and under his control the paper maintained the reputation made for it by Mr. Van Vorhes. The news from the scenes of conflict during the war were fuller in the *Messenger* than in almost any other paper of its size in the State. Mr. Van Law sold to J. W. Stinchcomb in November, 1865, and on Oct. 25, 1866, J. R. S. Bond became the proprietor and editor. He sold to the present editor, C. E. M. Jennings, March 5, 1868. Since taking possession of the paper, Mr. Jennings has twice brought out the *Messenger* in a new dress. The size of the paper has been changed several times during its long life. It is now eight pages in size, and contains six columns to the page. It is published every Thursday. The *Messenger* has always been uniformly Republican in principles, since the organization of that party, and before 1855 equally consistent in its support of Whig doctrines. It continues to be one of the most influential papers in Southeastern Ohio.

The Athens Herald.—The Athens *Herald* is yet in its infancy, its first issue being of date Sept. 25, 1882, but it is a lusty, vigorous child of the art typographical. It was started by a stock company, of which J. M. Wood, J. P. Wood and L. C. Butler were the principal stockholders, Mr. L. C. Butler assuming the editorship, and the name given being as above. Politically it is Republican or represents the principles of the party so designated at this time, and is in size a quarto of eight pages, six columns to the page. Mr. Butler retired from the editorship May 9, 1883, and at this time the paper does not have its editor's name at the head of its columns. Mr. Malcolm Jenning became city editor Oct. 23, 1882, and is still upon the editorial staff of the paper. The publication of the *Herald* has proved a marked success from its first issue, and the *Herald* Publishing Company is at this time in a prosperous condition.

The Athens Journal.—The Athens *Journal*, since its founding, has been one of the leading newspapers in the county. Although for a period in its history it was independent in politics, it has always been a guide to public opinion on the leading topics of the day, and has done not a little to affect the political phases of the county and elsewhere, so far as it has reached. Its history is considerably varied, having made two radical changes in its political doctrine, and been in the hands of several different, but always able, editors. It was founded by Hiram C. Martin, a citizen of Athens, who was proprietor and editor. The first issue appeared on Wednesday, Dec. 15, 1869, but it did not appear regularly until Thursday, Jan. 6, 1870, the number issued on this date being marked No. 1, of Vol. 1. It was Republican in politics, but rather than to political agitation its tendency was in the direction of a critical and literary journal, having among its contributors such public-spirited and educated gentlemen as David H. Moore, W. H. Scott, then Professor of Greek in the Ohio University, W. F. Boyd, of Cincinnati, Rev. A. C. Hirst, then Professor of Latin in the Ohio University, Rev. Jesse Van Law, John R. Scott, Earl Cranston, John E. Sanders and John Ackley under the *nom de plume* of "Daddy Hague." The paper continued under this management until 1871 when, Mr. Martin's health failing, he sold out to a joint stock company and retired from the paper but retained an interest in it by becoming a stockholder. Of this new company, called the *Journal* Printing Co., Mr. Henry T. Brown, of Athens, was the President and Dr. Thomas W. Sparrow, Secretary and Treasurer. Dr. Sparrow assumed the business control. Although for several months after this change no name appeared as editor, it is well known that the editorial work was done chiefly by General Thomas F. Wildes, then a resident of Athens. At the beginning of the year 1872, according to previous announcement, the editorial responsibility was undertaken by W. H. Scott, while Hiram C. Martin became business manager and local editor In October following the management was transferred to Oscar W. Brown, who also supervised the editorial department.

In December, 1873, the *Journal* Company sold out to D. Montague and James A. Miller, whose names appear as joint proprietors and editors, but who failed to fulfill the contract of purchase, and it fell back into the hands of the company in January, 1875.

At the beginning of this management the name was changed from the Athens County *Journal* to its original name, the Athens *Journal*, and it was also changed in politics to an independent paper. In the issue of Jan. 14, 1875, Montague and Miller presented their valedictory, making known to the public their sale of the paper to Colonel R. W. Jones, who was to take possession at once. At this time it was the intention of Mr. Jones to make it a partisan paper, and change the name to the *Democratic Standard*. Although public announcement to that effect had been made, since it was found that the *Journal* Company were still the real owners, it was only leased to Mr. Jones, and continued as an independent paper, as the owners, being all Republicans, refused to allow it to become Democratic.

At the time of the completion of this change the following card appeared in the columns of the *Journal*; "The *Journal* Company have made arrangements with Colonel R. W. Jones to continue the publication of the *Journal* as an *independent* paper. Under the new management the patrons of the paper, and the public, may be assured that its interest as a public journal will be increased, and its usefulness and circulation extended.

" Colonel Jones has had large experience as an editor and publisher, and is thoroughly conversant with every department of the newspaper business.

" The prompt encouragement of the friends of the *Journal* by way of subscriptions, job-work and advertising is earnestly solicited, and will, we are confident, assure the complete success of the present arrangement.

Signed,
F. L. JUNOD,
H. T. BROWN,
H. C. MARTIN,
T. W. SPARROW,
PETER HIXSON,
GEO. PUTNAM,
and LEONARD BROWN,
Journal Company."

Soon after this, the paper was enlarged to nine columns, the size it has since preserved.

Mr. Jones won friends and confidence in the paper by his sarcastic wit and masterly ability. Limited as he was by the requirements of its owners, that the paper should be independent, his strength as a political advocate was not known until after April, 1876, when it passed entirely under his control.

He made the paper strictly Democratic in doctrine, expressing through it, without fear, his views on all subjects. During his editorial control, which lasted until near the time of his death, in 1881, the paper was characterized by vigor and independence, the editor's motto being, " Give me the liberty of the press and I will tear down corruption from its towering height, and bury it beneath the ruin of the abuses it was meant to shelter."

Since the death of Mr. Jones the paper has remained in the hands of his family, and has continued the same in appearance and political doctrine. The editorial control has been assumed by his daughter, Jennie Jones, who has proven her ability to maintain the usefulness and strength of the paper as an influential public organ.

PERSONAL SKETCH FROM THE FUNERAL DISCOURSE.

Robert Wilmeth Jones was born in Belmont County, O., June 17, 1826. On his father's side he was of Welsh extraction, and on the maternal side a lineal descendant of that brave sailor, Rear-Admiral Carter, who, with Admiral Russell, commanded the English and Dutch fleets in the battle of La Hogue, and who, being mortally wounded in the engagement, gave his last command in the memorable words, "Fight the ship while she can swim." Colonel Jones was the third child of Wilmeth Jones and Sarah, his wife, *nee* Carter, and one of seven children. At the age of fourteen years he began to learn the mysteries of "the art preservative of all arts," serving seven years as apprentice and foreman with John Irons, of Uniontown, Pa., in the office of the *Genius of Liberty*, which paper he edited for about two years of that time. On the 2d of March, 1847, he was united in marriage with Anna M. Sturgis, of Uniontown, who survives him after a wedded life of thirty-four years. To them were born six children, two of whom only are now living.

In 1847 Colonel Jones began the publication of the *Cumberland Presbyterian*, the organ of the church whose name it bore, at Uniontown, and continued it at Brownsville and afterward at Waynesburg, Pa., with a short interval, till 1865. He began the publication of the *Messenger*, a political paper, at the latter place in 1861, but in 1865 abandoned all newspaper work for more active business pursuits, which he continued at Philadelphia and other points with varying success till he came to Athens, and assumed editorial and business control of the *Journal*. He took an active part for many years in all business and political questions, often occupying responsible positions in the counsels of his party, and at one time holding a military commission as aid to Governor Pollock, of Pennsylvania. He was of a social and genial disposition, with a host of friends, and best beloved by those who knew him best. As a journalist he was a pleasing writer, wielding a facile and often trenchant pen; clear, sparkling and direct in style; accurate in facts and convincing in deductions and argument. To all these qualities he united a high sense of justice, great industry and fine business capacity. He amassed a handsome fortune, but financial losses came to him with railway and other investments. During the days of his greatest prosperity his friends shared in all his good fortune. In the season of adversity he bore with philosophical equanimity his reverses, and took up anew all the labors of life, with a serene determination to extract the largest measure of comfort for self and family from his surroundings; and with temper unsoured and disposition as genial and sunshiny as ever, he worked on till death, with no unkind hand, without lingering or great conscious suffering, and in the midst of his activity and labors, called him to rest.

The *Journal* has been continued by his daughter, Jennie Jones, who undertook to carry out all the plans of her father. She was born at Brownsville, Pa., and was educated at Philadelphia, graduating from the High School there in the spring of 1872. When her father began his connection with the *Journal*, she went into the office as his bookkeeper and took charge of the mailing department, holding that connection until his death, when she became the sole editor and publisher, and has so continued to the present time.

D. B. Stewart

CHAPTER XII.

OHIO UNIVERSITY—ITS INCEPTION, RISE AND PROGRESS.

THE WISDOM OF ITS CONCEPTION—THE UNIVERSITY AND DR. CUTLER—ACTS OF 1802 AND 1804—GIVEN IN FULL—STEPS TAKEN FOR ORGANIZATION—THE ACT TO INCREASE RENTS—BEGINNING ACTIVE WORK—THE FIRST GRADUATE—PRESSING FORWARD—LITERARY SOCIETIES—BEAUTIFUL LOCATION—THE COLLEGE BUILDINGS—BIOGRAPHICAL SKETCHES—PRESIDENTS OF THE FACULTY—PROFESSORS—PRECEPTORS AND PRINCIPALS—TRUSTEES.—THE OFFICIALS.

THE WISDOM OF ITS CONCEPTION.

Almost simultaneously with the final erection of this new Empire of America, provision was made by the governing power of the nation for the establishment of an institution of learning in the great West, the exact location to be fixed at a future time. Too high a tribute to the far-reaching wisdom of those men who conceived and worked out the destiny of this project can hardly be paid. It was an idea worthy of the conjecture of an old and established country; but these men were only members of a then feeble nation, of unknown resources and an uncertain future, just recovering from a terrible conflict for life. This move to plant a seat of learning far in the West, beyond the bounds of civilization, that should in time rival the English universities of Cambridge and Oxford, indicated a prophetic faith in the development of the new country almost unprecedented. Now, civilization has reached and gone far beyond the spot chosen, and if the University has failed to come up to the cherished hopes of its founders, that it should deserve and retain the homage of all the Western country as its pride and shining light, and be its mother of intelligence and learning, it is not the fault of those who gave it life, for they did well their part and there all the honor lies. If the Rev. Manasseh Cutler and General Rufus Putnam could now come and review the blunders of some of those in whose hands they had placed the care of their ward, and see the careless disregard shown to the University by many who have grown up within her very shadow, they would surely say, "There's something grimly wrong in this."

But if this institution has failed to fulfill early anticipation, its career has by no means been void of usefulness. Its location on the site of Athens presented attractions greater than those of any other portion of all the Northwest Territory. For healthfulness and beauty of situation, for the lay of its ground and its commanding scenery, it can hardly be surpassed. The Hocking Valley, beside the compliment to its beauty by securing the location of the university, is better for its possession and especially Athens, the child of the college, which, like a natural child, has grown up from earliest infancy beneath her brow.

THE UNIVERSITY AND DR. CUTLER.

One of the first great steps taken by the revolutionary heroes after the close of the war, was to make arrangements for settling the country north of the Ohio River, called the Ohio country. In the growth and adoption of the plan for such a settlement, which culminated in the ordinance of 1787, the idea of providing for a university was always present. This ordinance was passed in July, 1787, while the Constitutional Convention was in session at Philadelphia, thus preceding the first permanent encroachment of civilization upon the vast wilderness west of the Alleghanies by ten years. It was, in fact, intended as an integral part of the foundation then laid for the political and social fabric which has since been reared in the Northwest. In authorizing the Board of Treasury to contract this sale of lands to the Ohio Company, Congress agreed that two complete townships should be given perpetually to the uses of a university, to be laid off by the purchasers as near as possible to the center of the purchase, but that it should be good land and applied to the intended object by the Legislature of the State. This was the first university ever thus endowed by Congress with land for its support, but the policy then begun was continued and now Indiana, Illinois, Michigan, Alabama, Missouri, Mississippi and other States have similarly endowed universities. This great principle which has done so much toward shaping the intellectual features of our country may be said to have resulted from the propriety of such a measure as impressed upon Congress by Dr. Manasseh Cutler in securing the endowment for the Ohio University. To this man, Dr. Cutler, perhaps more than to any other, is due the founding of this pioneer institution. He was a member of the Ohio Company, and being a man of culture and ability, was able to appreciate the value of higher education as a source of individual happiness, its value as an element of political liberty, and doubtless was the first to conceive and set forth the idea of establishing the University. At the first organization of the company he had urged the advantage of employing a competent instructor for the proposed settlement, and was himself authorized to secure a proper person. He afterward conceived the idea of the University and impressed it so strongly upon the members of Congress as to secure the above result. He urged that the location of the college lands should be as nearly as practicable in the center of the first million and a half of acres that the company should pay for; for, he said, to fix it in the center of the proposed purchase might too long defer the establishment.

Dr. Cutler found a ready supporter of his plans and a valuable helper in another member of the Ohio Company, General Rufus Putnam. He, in charge of the first colony, came to Ohio, helped to view the country, located the college lands and the site of the college, and was an interested and efficient worker for the University scheme to the end of his life. The college townships were not located and surveyed till 1795, when townships 8 and 9 in the 14th range were selected. These are the townships of Athens and Alexander. For some years after that, the dense forests that covered the whole region were but slightly invaded by settlers, and it was not until the town of Athens had been laid out and "confirmed and established" by the Territorial Legislature, that any action was taken by that body toward carrying into effect the compact for the establishment of the University. On Dec. 18, 1799, the Territorial Legislature appointed Rufus Putnam, Benjamin Ives Gilman and Jonathan Stone " to lay off in the most suitable place within the townships, a town plat which should contain a square for the college; also, lots suitable for house lots and gardens for a president, professors, tutors, etc., bordering on or encircled by spacious commons, and such a number of town lots adjoining the said commons and out-lots as they shall think will be for the advantage of the University." This work having been done, a resolution was adopted by the Legislature, Dec. 6, 1800, approving and accepting it. In that year, also, Dr. Cutler sent to General Putnam his draft of an incorporating act for the University. In a letter which accompanied the draft, he said: "As the American Congress made the grant which is the foundation of the University, no name appeared to be more natural than *American University*. The sound is natural, easy and agreeable, and no name can be more respectable. There i a Columbian College and a Washington College, etc., already in the country, but no American College. I hope the name will not be altered."

It is evident from this passage that the founders of the University entertained large expectations of its future. The same fact is no less manifest from Dr. Cutler's comments on the eighth section of his draft. Speaking of a limitation of the income by the Legislature, he said: "$40,000 and $50,000 can not be too high, as it must be applied to one of the most useful and important purposes to society and to Government. The sums sound large, but no one can say to what amount the income of the endowments of this University may arrive in time. The income of Oxford and Cambridge in England is much greater."

ACTS OF 1802 AND 1804.

The act referred to above was passed by the Territorial Legislature in 1802. It was an able instrument and largely copied in the act of 1804, but it does not appear that any effective action was ever taken under this law. It provided that the institution should be known as the "American Western University," and that the Hon. Rufus Putnam, Joseph Gilman, Return J. Meigs, Jr., Paul Fearing, Rev. Daniel Story, Griffin Greene, Robert Oliver, Ebenezer Sproat, Dudley Woodbridge and Isaac Pierce, together with the president, yet to be selected, should constitute a body politic by the name of "The President and Trustees of the American Western University."

The next legislative act on this subject was a joint resolution passed by the first Legislature of the State, Jan. 27, 1804, which read as follows:

"*Resolved*, That Samuel Carpenter, James Wells, and Henry Abrams be appointed commissioners to appraise the land included within the two college townships, in the county of Washington, at its real value in its original and unimproved state; to divide and value said land into four different qualities or rates and make return of the quantity contained in each division, as near as may be, and the value thereof to the next General Assembly on oath. And that the said commissioners also value the land in its present situation, mentioning the number of houses and quantity of cleared land contained within the two townships.

"*Resolved*, That the trustees appointed by the act entitled an act establishing a university in the town of Athens, be, and they are, hereby required to report to the next General Assembly of this State, what measures they have taken to carry the said act into operation."

On the 18th of February, 1804, the Legislature passed another act establishing a university at Athens, which differed in some respects from the one of 1802. This is the fundamental act under which the institution was actually founded and remains to-day, the origin of the present University. The following is an exact copy of the law:

Act of State Legislature establishing a University in the town of Athens.

WHEREAS, Institutions for the liberal education of youth are essential to the progress of arts and sciences, important to morality, virtue and religion, friendly to the peace, order and prosperity of society, and honorable to the government that encourages and patronizes them: Therefore,

SEC. 1. That there shall be a University instituted and established in the town of Athens, in the ninth township of the fourteenth range of townships, within the limits of the tract of land purchased by the Ohio Company of Associates, by the name and style of the "Ohio University," for the instruction of youth in all the various branches of liberal arts and sciences, for the promotion of good education, virtue, religion and morality, and for conferring all the degrees and literary honors granted in similar institutions.

SEC. 2. That there shall be and forever remain in the said University a body politic and corporate, by the name and style of "The President and Trustees of the Ohio University;" which body politic and corporate shall consist of the Governor of the State (for the time being), the president, and not more than fifteen nor less than ten trustees, to be appointed as hereinafter is provided.

SEC. 3. That Elijah Backus, Rufus Putnam, Dudley Woodbridge, Benjamin Tappan, Bazaleel Wells, Nathaniel Massie, Daniel Symmes, Daniel Story, Samuel Carpenter, the Rev. James Kilbourn, Griffin Greene, Sr., and Joseph Darlington, Esquires, together with the Governor as aforesaid, and the president of the said University (for the time being), to be chosen as hereinafter directed, be, and the same are hereby created, a body politic and corporate, by the name of "The President and Trustees of the Ohio University;" and that they and their successors, and such others as shall be duly elected members of the said corporation, shall be and remain a body politic and corporate in law, by that name forever.

SEC. 4. That the said trustees shall have power and authority to elect a president, who shall preside in the University, and also to appoint a secretary, treasurer, professors, tutors, instructors, and all such officers and servants in the University as they shall deem necessary for the carrying into effect the designs of the institution, and shall have authority, from time to time, to determine and establish the name, numbers and duties of all the officers and servants to be employed in the University, except wherein provision is otherwise made by this act, and may empower the president or some other member of the corporation, to administer such oaths as they shall appoint and determine, for the well ordering and good government of the University: *Provided nevertheless*, That no corporation business shall be transacted at any meeting, unless seven of the trustees at least shall be present.

SEC. 5. That the said corporation shall have power and authority, from time to time, to make and ordain reasonable rules, orders and by-laws for the government of the corporation, not incompatible with the constitution, laws and ordinances of the United States or this State, and the same to repeal as occasion may require, and also to determine the salaries, emoluments and tenures of their several officers.

SEC. 6. That the said corporation shall have power and authority to suspend or remove the president or any member of the said corporation, who shall, by his misconduct, render himself unworthy of the office, station or place he sustains, or who, from age or other infirmity, is rendered incapable to perform the duties of his office ; and the said corporation shall have power and authority to suspend or remove from the University any professor, instructor or resident student, or servant, whenever the corporation shall deem it expedient for the interest and honor of the University.

SEC. 7. That whenever the president or any member of the corporation shall be removed, by death, resignation or otherwise, during the recess of the Legislature, the corporation shall hold a meeting (due notice of the design of which meeting shall be given to the several members) for the supplying such vacancy; and the person elected shall continue in office until the end of the next session of the Legislature, and no longer, by virtue of such appointment; and in order to choose a president or member of the corporation, there shall be, at least, two thirds of the whole number of said trustees present, and the said election shall be by ballot.

SEC. 8. That when any member of the corporation shall be removed by death, resignation or otherwise, such vacancy shall be supplied at the next meeting of the Legislature of the State.

SEC. 9. That the president and such professors, tutors and instructors as the corporation shall appoint for that purpose shall be styled, "The Faculty of the University," and shall have power and authority, from time to time, to ordain, regulate and establish the mode and course of education and instruction to be pursued in the University, and also to make, publish and execute such code of rules, regulations and by-laws as they shall deem necessary for the well ordering and good government of the University, and to repeal or amend any part thereof; which rules, regulations and by-laws shall continue in force until altered or disapproved of by the corporation; and it shall be the duty of the faculty to lay before the corporation, from time to time, accurate statements of all their proceedings; and the faculty shall direct and cause to be holden in the said University, quarterly, in every year, a public examination, at which time the faculty shall attend, when each class of the students shall be examined relative to the proficiency they shall have made in the particular arts and sciences, or branches of education in which they shall have been instructed.

SEC. 10. That the said corporation may have and keep one common seal, which they may change or renew at pleasure; and that all deeds or instruments of writing, signed and delivered by the treasurer, and sealed with the corporation seal, by order of the president and trustees, shall, when made in their corporate name, be considered in law as the deed and act of the corporation; and the said corporation shall be capable of suing and being sued, pleading and being impleaded, in any action, real, personal or mixed, and the same to prosecute and defend to final judgment and execution, by the name of "The President and Trustees of the Ohio University:" *Provided*, That when any suit shall be commenced against the said corporation, the process shall be by summons, and the service made by the officer leaving an attested copy of such process with the treasurer of the said corporation, at least twenty days before the return day of such process; and the said corporation shall be capable of having, holding and taking, in fee simple, or any less estate, by gift, grant, devise or otherwise, any lands or other estate, real or personal.

SEC. 11. That the two townships numbered 8 and 9 in the 14th range of townships, within the grant of land made by Congress to the Ohio Company of Associates, be, and they are, hereby vested in the corporation, by this act created, in trust, for the sole use, benefit and support of the said University, forever.

SEC. 12. That one or more of the aforesaid trustees (to be appointed by the board for this purpose), shall, within six months from the passage of this act, proceed (by the oath of three disinterested and judicious freeholders) to lay off the lands in said townships (those included in the town of Athens excepted), or such part thereof as they may deem expedient, into tracts not less than eighty nor more than 240 acres, and to estimate and value the same as in their original and unimproved state (for which service such compensation shall be allowed as the trustees shall think reasonable, to be paid out of the funds of the University) and having thus laid off and estimated said lands, the trustees, after giving four weeks' notice in the newspaper printed at Marietta, shall proceed to make out leases of the said tracts to such of the present occupants as shall apply for the same, within three months after such notice given, and to all persons that shall apply hereafter, for the term of ninety years, renewable forever, on a yearly rent of six per centum on the amount of the valuation so made by the said freeholders; and the land so leased shall be subject to re-valuation at the expiration of thirty-five years, and to another re-valuation at the expiration of sixty years, from the commencement of the term of each lease; which re-valuation shall be conducted and made on the principles of the first, and the lessee shall pay a yearly rent of six per centum on the amount of the re-valuation so to be made, and forever thereafter on a yearly rent equal to and not exceeding six per centum of the amount of a valuation to be made as aforesaid, at the expiration of the term of ninety years aforesaid (which valuation the trustees and their successors are hereby authorized and directed to make).

Provided, however, That such last-mentioned rent shall be subject to the following regulations, to-wit: At the expiration of the aforesaid period of ninety years, three referees shall be appointed, the first by the corporation of the University, the second by the lessees, under the provisions of this section of this act, and the third by the two referees thus chosen (or in case either or both of the parties shall neglect to choose such referee or referees, or said referees shall neglect to choose an umpire, the General Assembly, at its next session, shall appoint such number of referees, not exceeding three, as the case may require), which referees shall meet within a reasonable time, to be agreed on between them, at the town of Athens, and then and there determine on and declare the medium price per bushel of the article of wheat; which determination shall be grounded on a calculation of the average price of said article at the town of Marietta, for the five preceding years; which declaration shall be made in writing, and entered of record on the books of the corporation; and at the commencement of each and every succeeding period of twenty years thereafter, the amount of rent for such period shall be fixed on and determined by referees, to be chosen upon the principles hereinbefore directed, from a comparison of the aforesaid recorded price of wheat with its average price at Marietta, for the five years which shall have been then last past; in which leases shall be reserved a right of distress and re-entry for non-payment of rent, at any time after it shall have been due two months: *Provided, always,* That the said corporation shall have power to demand a further yearly rent on the said lands and tenements, not exceeding the amount of the tax imposed upon property of like description by the State, which rents shall be paid at such time and place, to such person, and collected in such a manner as the corporation shall direct.

SEC. 13. That the trustees shall lay off the aforesaid town of Athens, conformably to a plan made out by Rufus Putnam and others, in pursuance of a resolution of the Territorial Legislature of the eighteenth December, one thousand seven hundred and ninety-nine, with such variations, however, as they may find it expedient to make; and the same being thus laid off and a plat of the same with a designation of the uses of the several parts recorded in the office of the recorder of the proper county, and six weeks' previous notice given, in at least two of the newspapers of this State, may proceed to sell, from time to time, at public auction, such of the houses and out-lots as they may think proper, for which lots, on payment being made or satisfactory security given, according to the conditions of such sale, they shall execute to the purchasers respectively, leases for the term of ninety years, renewable forever on an annual rent, equal to, and not exceeding, six per centum of the amount of the purchase money, which lots, with the improvements which may be made on the same, shall be subject to such further yearly rent as may be equal to the tax imposed, from time to time, on property of like value and description, by the State; and they are likewise authorized to deliver a reasonable compensation for the improvements which have been made on lands within the town of Athens, to be paid out of the funds of the University.

SEC. 14. That the clear annual rents, issues and profits, of all the estate, real and personal, of which the said corporation shall be seized or possessed, in their corporate capacity, shall be appropriated to the endowments of the said University, in such manner as shall most effectually promote the end of the institution: *Provided nevertheless,* That any donation which shall hereafter be made and received for particular purposes, relative to the design of this institution, shall be applied in conformity to the intention of the donor or donors.

SEC. 15. That the treasurer of the said corporation shall, before he enters upon the duties of his office, give bonds to the said corporation, in such sum and with such sureties as they shall approve, conditioned for the faithful discharge of the duties of the said office, and for the rendering a just and true account of his doings therein, when required; and also, for the delivering over to his successor in office all moneys, securities and other property that shall belong to the president and trustees of the said University, together with all the books and papers in which his proceedings, as treasurer, shall be entered and kept, that shall be in his hands at the expiration of his office; and all money that shall be recovered by virtue of any suit at law upon such bond shall be paid over to the president and trustees aforesaid, and be subject to the appropriations above directed in this act.

SEC. 16. That the said corporation shall have full power, from time to time, to contract for, and cause to be erected, such building or buildings as they shall deem necessary for the accommodation of the president, professors, tutors, pupils, and servants of said University; as also, to procure the necessary books and apparatus, for the use of said University, and shall cause payment therefor to be made out of the funds of the University, and shall reserve such lot or lots in said town of Athens as they may deem necessary for the purposes aforesaid, and for the erection of buildings for the use of the town and county.

SEC. 17. That the lands in the two townships, appropriated and vested as aforesaid, with the buildings which are or may be erected thereon, shall forever be exempted from all State taxes.

SEC. 18. That until a president of the said University shall be elected, and shall have entered upon the duties of his office, and also, in all cases of a vacancy or the absence of the president, the said trustees shall appoint one of their members to preside in their meetings, and all the doings and acts of the trustees, while acting under such circumstances, shall be considered in law as the doings and acts of the corporation, as fully and completely as when the president of the University shall be in office and preside.

SEC.' 19. That it shall be the duty of the Governor to fix the time for holding the first meeting of the said corporation, which shall be in the town of Athens, of which he shall give notice in writing, to each member, at least twenty days previous to such meeting, and all subsequent meetings of the said corporation shall be in the said town of Athens.

SEC. 20. That all acts and parts of acts, containing anything within the purview of this act, shall be and they are hereby repealed.

STEPS TAKEN TOWARD AN ORGANIZATION.

From the records of the first meeting of trustees the following is taken:

"At a meeting of the trustees of the Ohio University, convened at the house of Dr. Eliphaz Perkins, in the town of Athens, on the first Monday of June, 1804, the day ordered by His Excellency Edward Tiffin, Esq., Governor of the State of Ohio, for the first meeting. The following trustees present, viz.: His Excellency Edward Tiffin, Elijah Backus, Rufus Putnam, Dudley Woodbridge, Daniel Story, Samuel Carpenter and James Kilbourne."

The board elected Governor Tiffin, President, Dudley Woodbridge, Secretary, Eliphaz Perkins, Treasurer, and adjourned till next day, June 5. This first session of the board lasted three days, and was principally spent in arranging for the appraisal and leasing of the college lands. Rufus Putnam and Samuel Carpenter were appointed to lay off and appraise such lands in the two townships as were claimed and occupied. Since the surveying of these townships in 1795, numbers of new settlers had come in and occupied the lands. Some of these were rough and determined characters, and were bent on maintaining possession. To adjust these cases, settle disputed titles, etc., required patience, tact, and wisdom. The persons had either to be mollified and induced to come to terms, or be ejected from the lands. The first business of the board was to adjust the claims of conflicting persons, secure titles and protect the corporation in its rights. These matters, together with the surveying and laying out of lots, classifying lands, etc., employed the trustees during this session.

It is worthy of remark that the meeting of these men, under the circumstances, afforded a high proof of their character—of their appreciation of the value of education, and their honest devotion to the welfare of the new country. They had traveled fifty, seventy-five or a hundred miles by blind paths or Indian trails through the dense and wild forest to this embryo village, for the purpose of establishing an institution of learning. By the following November the sale of house and out-lots of the town of Athens amounted to $2,223.50; average of house-lots, $43.33 1-2; of out-lots, $39. In the south township (Alexander), seventy-five tracts, or 11,000 acres, were applied for. In the north township (Athens), seventy-five applications for leases, covering 8,760 acres, had been made.

Notwithstanding this favorable outset toward a disposition of the college lands the State Legislature at their following session passed an amendatory law which was probably designed to hasten the disposition of the lands. However this law may have fulfilled its intended design, it has certainly been the means of much concern to the future welfare of the University. The following is a copy of the act:

An act to amend an act, entitled " An act establishing a University in the town of Athens."

SECTION 1. That James Denny, Emanuel Carpenter, Jr., Isaac Dawson, Pelatiah White and Ezekiel Deming, residents of this State, are appointed appraisers of the two college townships, numbered 8 and 9, in the 14th range of townships within the grant of land made to the Ohio Company of Associates, and the said appraisers, or any three of them, on oath or affirmation, are hereby required to appraise the townships aforesaid, within nine months, at the present real value as in its original and uncultivated state, and make report thereof to the Board of Trustees of the said University; and the said trustees shall lease the same to any persons who have or may apply, agreeable to law, for the term of ninety-nine years, renewable forever, with a fixed annual rent of six per centum on the appraised valuation: *Provided*, That no lands shall be leased at a less valuation than at the rate of one dollar and seventy-five cents per acre.

SEC. 2. That the commissioners aforesaid shall meet on the first day of April next, at the town of Athens, who shall then proceed to discharge the duties imposed on them by this act, and the act to which this act is an amendment, and the same to have performed within the time mentioned in this act.

SEC. 3. That the trustees of the corporation of the said University lands are hereby authorized and empowered to remove, by due course of law, all persons living on said lands, in case such persons refuse or neglect to take leases within six months after the valuation of the lands aforesaid.

SEC. 4. That the secretary of this State shall cause notice to be given as soon as convenience will permit, to each of the commissioners aforesaid, of their appointment under this act, and the commissioners respectively, on receiving the notice aforesaid, shall within a reasonable time thereafter, forward to the Governor of this State their determination to accept, or not to accept, the appointment under this act made.

SEC. 5. That so much of the aforesaid act, passed the eighteenth day of February, one thousand eight hundred and four, as is contrary to this act, be, and the same is, hereby repealed.

This act shall be in force from and after the passage thereof.
Passed Feb. 21, 1805.

It will be seen that this law conflicts, to a certain extent, with the original act, and partially repeals the founding act of 1804, but the extent of the real confliction is the question which has given rise to extensive and important litigations between the lessees of the college lands and the authorities of the University. Prior to 1875 the authorities of the University had made no attempt to put into force that part of section 12 of the act of 1804, reading, "*Provided, always*, That the said corporation [meaning the president and trustees of the University] shall have power to demand a further yearly rent on the said lands and tenements, not exceeding the amount of the tax imposed upon property of like description by the State," etc. Although numerous laws had been passed from time to time touching indirectly upon this subject, the next move directly, and that which was the immediate cause of the litigations referred to, was the passage of the following act in 1875:

An act to require trustees of institutions of learning to collect certain rents.

Sec. 1. *Be it enacted by the General Assembly of the State of Ohio*, That the trustees of any institution of learning, holding leasehold lands and having authority, under the laws of the State, to demand a yearly rent on such lands, and the tenements erected thereon, not exceeding the amount of the tax imposed on property of like description by the State, said rent being in addition to a yearly rent at six per centum on the appraised valuation of said lands and tenements, are hereby required to demand and collect said rents for the support of said institution.

Sec. 2. This act shall take effect from and after the first day of July, eighteen hundred and seventy-five.

March 30, 1875.

This was followed by a resolution of the trustees of the University in June, 1876, instructing the treasurer to collect additional rents in accordance with the above act, the date of such additional rents to begin on the first day of July, 1875. The lease-holders, believing that that part of the law of 1804, to which the act of 1875 might in this case apply, had been repealed by the act of 1805, refused to comply with the demand for the additional rent and at once entered suit against the president and trustees of the University. The case has passed through the Court of Common Pleas and the Supreme Court of Ohio, in both of which decision was given in favor of the University, and is now awaiting decision in the Supreme Court of the United States.

During the fourteen years following 1805, nearly as many laws were passed by the State Legislature relative to the University, many of them amendments to former acts, and a number of them on the subject of land rents. One passed in 1809 provided that the renters might pay in produce; and one in 1826 authorized the trustees of the University to dispose of certain lands by conveyance in *fee simple*.

BEGINNING ACTIVE WORK.

But to return more directly to the early work of the commissioners. The year 1806 was consumed in settling titles, appraising the lands, and accumulating a small fund with which to begin the actual educational work. The second meeting of the Board of Trustees was called for Nov. 20, 1805, but no quorum was present and they adjourned. The third meeting was held April 2, 1806, when the committee for selling town lots reported, and other business was transacted relative to titles and leases. At this session it was

"*Resolved*, That Jacob Lindley, Rufus Putnam and William Skinner be a committee to contract with some person or persons for building a house in the town of Athens for the purpose of an academy, on the credit of the rents that will hereafter become due."

At the meeting of the trustees Dec. 25, 1806, pursuant to the above resolution, a plan for a building was reported and the committee was empowered to contract for a building. This was the old academy which stood east of the present buildings, partly outside of the present enclosure. It was a two-story brick building, twenty-four feet by thirty, containing one room on each floor. For ten years this was the only building of the University. After the college classes were organized, the lower room was occupied by the preparatory department, while the upper one accommodated the higher classes. After the completion of the building, at a meeting held March 2, 1808, Rev. Jacob Lindley, Eliphaz Perkins and Rufus Putnam were appointed a committee to report a plan for opening and conducting the academy and providing for a preceptor, which they did at the same meeting. A few days later Mr. Lindley was chosen Preceptor and entered on his duties in the spring of 1808.

Thus, in a scantily inhabited wilderness, the University began its active career which has now extended over three quarters of a century. The attendance at first was necessarily small and the curriculum incomplete, but then, as since, the institution was characterized by proficiency of its instruction and the thoroughness of work done by students. For the first few years Dr. Lindley was the only instructor, he alone constituting the Faculty of the Ohio University. In 1812 Mr. Artemus Sawyer, a graduate of Harvard University and an excellent scholar, was appointed assistant instructor. Prior to this time it had not assumed pretentions beyond those of a grammar school; but the instructor had done good work and the school was now well qualified to adopt a more thorough course of study. In the year 1815

THE FIRST GRADUATE

received from the University the degree of Bachelor of Arts. The man who had not only this honor of being the first to go forth with the blessings of the Ohio University, but the first to receive a collegiate degree in the State of Ohio, was the Hon. Thomas Ewing, Sr., whose after career is well known throughout this country. He had entered the institution three years previously and pursued his studies with great energy, spending his later vacations in surveying and helping to lay out county roads to raise money for his college expenses.

In 1815 the success of the University was thought to be so far assured, and the necessity for increased facilities was so apparent, that the trustees resolved to erect a new college building. June 4, 1816, a committee, consisting of Jacob Lindley, Eliphaz Perkins, and J. Lawrence Lewis, appointed in September previous, reported to the board that, after due advertisement and consultation with an architect, they had contracted with William T. Dean for 370,000 bricks at $4.50 a thousand; with Christopher and Daniel Herrold for 27,964 feet of lumber, to be delivered and piled up during the summer, at $1.12 per hundred feet; with Messrs. Bingham & White for stone; with Pilcher & Francis for laying the foundation of the rough stone, and making the window and door sills; and with Wm. and James Wier for digging the cellar—which last was already completed. The corner-stone of the building, now known as the center college, was laid in the summer of that year. The work was pushed forward as rapidly as the condition of the treasury would permit, and the building was completed in 1817. In order to raise funds for this expense, the trustees had, in June, 1814, petitioned the State Legislature to grant a lottery, the proceeds of which was to be given to the college. The Legislature granted the request, and prescribed the method, but for some reason the scheme was never carried out.

In 1819 Mr. Sawyer having some time before ceased his connection with the institution, Professor Joseph Dana, a man of rare scholarly attainments, was secured as a teacher of languages. He was especially fitted for this chair by his knowledge of the classics, and remained in connection with the University a number of years.

PRESSING FORWARD.

The pecuniary embarrassments of the University were so far overcome by 1822 that its complete organization was effected in that year, and the faculty was constituted as follows: Rev. James Irvine, President and Professor of Mathematics; Joseph Dana, Professor of Languages; Rev. Jacob Lindley, Professor of Rhetoric and Moral Philosophy; Rev. Samuel D. Hoge, Professor of Natural Sciences, and Henry D. Ward, Academical Preceptor.

From this period dates the complete working system of the University. Its history from this on to the present time has been almost uniform in the routine duties of ordinary college work. The usual four years' course was adopted, the curriculum embracing higher studies in mathematics, natural sciences, philosophy, and the classics.

The classes graduating each year have ranged from fourteen down. The attendance gradually increased up to the time of Rev. Wm. H. McGuffey's administration (1839-'43), when it reached nearly 250 students. This, and a short time following the close of the war of the Rebellion, are the two most flourishing periods in the University's history. For the decade from 1855 to 1865 the average annual attendance was 150, and for the college year of 1865-'6 the attendance was 243. This sudden rush of students resulted, doubtless, from the fact that the great number of young men throughout the country, who had just been released from the service, were without employment, and being generally supplied with ready money, as well as many of them being entitled to free tuition by a law passed in 1864, saw no better way to spend a year or two than in attendance at the University. Since 1870 the average annual attendance has been about 110.

The two

LITERARY SOCIETIES

were established in 1836 and in 1839 by special acts of the State Legislature. The first, entitled "An act to incorporate the 'Athenian Literary Society of Ohio University,' in the town of Athens," was passed Dec. 19, 1836, and the other, entitled "An act to incorporate the 'Philomathean Society of the Ohio University' in the town of Athens," March 9, 1839. By these laws, the above societies were each created a body corporate and politic by the names given above, capable of suing and being sued as such, and invested with the usual privileges granted to other corporated bodies, the only provision made being that the annual income of either shall not exceed the sum of $1,000. The first was created with perpetual succession, and the second with succession for thirty years. These societies have each a hall in one of the University buildings, own the property with which it is furnished, and are each governed by separate constitutions and by-laws which provide for a regular succession of officers. Since these are the only societies of the kind connected with the institution, each has had in its membership since organization about half the students of the University. The public exercises of these societies consist of an annual literary contest between the two. There are also four Greek letter fraternities in the University, the Delta Tau Delta, Beta Theta Pi, Phi Delta Theta, and a ladies' society, Kappa Alpha Theta.

Ladies were admitted to equal privileges with the gentlemen in the University in 1868, the first lady graduate being Miss Margaret Boyd, in the class of 1873.

THE BEAUTIFUL LOCATION

of the University can not fail to excite the admiration of all lovers of natural scenery. The winding valley of the Hocking and the wooded hills beyond, together with the asylum building across the wide bottom on the opposite hill, with its lakes and improved grounds in front, all make a series of landscape views seldom surpassed in quiet and varied beauty. The immediate site of the University buildings is unusually charming even for this region of rural beauty. The campus is an enclosed square of ten acres, higher than the adjacent portions of the surrounding town and sloping gently from the center. The buildings, grouped nearly in the center of this extended lawn, are partially hidden from a front view by the growth of forest trees, except the tower of the main building, which lifts its head high above and overlooks all. The entire grounds are carpeted with a fine growth of grass, are laid out with improved walks, and the north half covered with tall forest trees evenly distributed, and skirted along the lower edge by a row of magnificent elms.

THE COLLEGE BUILDINGS

are four in number. The main building was erected in 1817, and is the oldest college edifice, as the University itself is the oldest institution of learning, northwest of the Ohio River. This venerable structure, made dear to many by a thousand strong and tender associations, and to many more by the names of eminent men who have studied or taught within its walls, has recently been remodeled, and, while retaining the same general proportions, is, to all intents, a new building. It is admirably planned and well finished. With its slate roof and massive cornice, its lengthened windows and handsome colors, its convenient arrangement and pleasant appointments, it will compare favorably, in appearance and in adaptation to its purpose, with most college buildings in the West.

The two wing buildings, erected in 1836, contain the dormitories, and will accommodate about sixty students. The west wing contains also the preparatory recitation-room, three music-rooms, and one large room which is at present used as a chapel. On the completion of the new chapel, however, the last-named room will be devoted to other purposes.

The new building stands on an eminence at the western side of the campus. In design it is unique and elegant; the material is brick with cut-stone trimmings. Its dimensions are forty feet in width by seventy-six feet in length, and two stories in height. It has two fronts, one on the west toward Court street, which is the principal street of the town, and one on the east toward the main building. The first floor contains the chapel or assembly-hall, two corridors and stairways, and a waiting-room. The second floor contains two society-halls, with a committee-room attached to each.

The University comprises only a literary department, which offers two courses, the classical and philosophical. The quality of work done is equal to the best institutions in the West. The usual degrees are given. The University library, in connection with those of the two literary societies, is one of the best in the State. Connected with it is a large reading-room, supplied with standard newspapers and periodicals, which is open daily to the students. The long roll of graduates from this institution contains many who have achieved more than a local fame, and nearly all have in their several walks of life reflected credit upon their *alma mater*.

With the recent improvements and additions in buildings, apparatus and library, for which liberal appropriations were made by the State, and the recent re-organization and enlargement of the faculty, it is generally believed that the University is about to enter upon a new, prosperous and more useful career than it has ever before known.

Following are brief sketches of the first preceptor and the subsequent presidents of the Ohio University:

JACOB LINDLEY.

Mr. Lindley, the Preceptor, was born in Pennsylvania, June 13, 1774, graduated at Princeton in 1798, and was appointed a

Trustee of the Ohio University in 1805. From 1808 to 1822 he was President of the Board, and Preceptor of the Academy; from 1822 to 1824, Professor of Rhetoric and Moral Philosophy; from 1824 to 1826, Professor of Mathematics. His connection with the Board of Trustees continued till 1838, when it was dissolved by reason of his removal to the State of Mississippi. He died in 1857.

REV. JAMES IRVINE, A. M.,

the first President of the Ohio University, was born in Washington County, New York. Immediately after his graduation at Union College, he was elected Professor of Mathematics in the University, in 1831; and in the following year became the President. Owing to ill-health, he was the next spring allowed leave of absence and never returned to his post.

REV. ROBERT G. WILSON, D. D.,

a native of North Carolina, was born Dec. 30, 1768. He graduated at Dickinson College, Carlisle, Pa., and, after studying theology, was ordained to preach May 22, 1794. He spent the first ten or eleven years, of his ministry in Abbeville District, S. C.; removed thence, in 1805, to Chillicothe, O., where he was for nineteen years Pastor of the Presbyterian church. In 1824 he was elected President of the Ohio University, and during the next fourteen years administered its affairs with ability and success. In 1838, at the age of seventy, he resigned his position. He died April 17, 1851.

REV. WILLIAM HOLMES MCGUFFEY, D. D., LL. D.

was born in Washington County, Penn., Sept. 23, 1800. When he was but a child his parents removed to Trumbull County, Ohio. He prepared himself and entered Washington College, Pennsylvania. In March, 1826, he was elected Professor of Ancient Languages in Miami University, Ohio, and in 1832 he was transferred to the chair of Mental Philosophy. In 1836 he was chosen President of Cincinnati College and in 1839, President of the Ohio University, which position he retained until 1843, when he returned to Cincinnati. In 1845 he was chosen Professor of Mental Philosophy in the University of Virginia, where he continued until his death, May 4, 1873.

REV. ALFRED RYORS, D. D.

Rev. Alfred Ryors, D. D., was born in Philadelphia, June 28, 1812. Being left an orphan at a very early age, he was received into the family and select school of Rev. Robert Steel, D. D., at Abington, Pa. He graduated at Jefferson College, Pa., in 1835, and in May, 1836, he was elected Professor of Mathematics in the Ohio University where he remained till 1844. In that year he was called to the same chair in Indiana State University. In 1848 he was elected President of the Ohio University, and filled the office for four years.

REV. SOLOMON HOWARD, D. D., LL. D.,

was born in Cincinnati, Nov. 11, 1811. At twenty-two he graduated at Augusta College, Kentucky. He was elected to a professorship in St. Charles College, Mo. He entered the Ohio Conference of the M. E. church in 1835; was elected Principal of the Preparatory Department of the Ohio Wesleyan University in 1843, and Principal of Springfield High School in 1845. On leaving this position he became President of Springfield Female College; and in 1852 was elected President of the Ohio University. He retained this office till 1872, when, on account of ill-health, he resigned. He died at San Jose, Cal., June 9, 1873.

WM. H. SCOTT

was born at Chauncey, Ohio, Sept. 14, 1840. He entered the Ohio University as a student in 1859, graduating in 1862. Was Superintendent of the public schools of Athens from 1862 to 1864, and Principal of the Preparatory Department of the Ohio University from 1864 to 1865. He joined the Ohio Conference of the M. E. church in September, 1864; was Pastor of Main Street Church, Chillicothe, Ohio, from 1865 to 1867, and of Town Street Church, Columbus, Ohio, from 1867 to 1869. He was elected Professor of Greek in the Ohio University in 1869; served in that position three years. He was acting President of the University for 1872-'3 and elected President of the same in 1873, still retaining that position.

PRESIDENTS OF THE FACULTY.

Rev. James Irvine, A. M., 1822-1824; Rev. Robert G. Wilson, D. D., 1824-1839; Rev. William H. McGuffey, D. D., LL. D., 1839-

1843; Rev. Alfred Ryors, D. D., 1848-1852; Rev. Solomon Howard, D. D., LL. D., 1852-1872; Rev. William H. Scott, A. M., (acting) 1872-1873; Rev. William H. Scott, A. M., 1873.

PROFESSORS OF ANCIENT LANGUAGES.

Joseph Dana, A. M., 1818-1819; Rev. John B. Whittlesey, A. M., 1819-1821; Joseph Dana, A. M., 1822-1835; Daniel Read, A. M., 1836-1838; Daniel Read, A. M., Latin and Political Economy, 1838-1843; Rev. Elisha Ballentine, A. M., Greek, 1838-1840; Rev. John M. Stephenson, A.M., Greek, 1840-1842; James Irwin Kuhn, A. M., Greek, 1842-1844; Rev. Aaron Williams, D. D., 1844-1853; Rev. Addison Ballard, A. M., Latin, 1848-1852; Rev. E. E. E. Bragdon, A. M., 1853-1854; Rev. Clinton W. Sears, A. M., 1854-1855; Rev. John M. Leavitt, A. M., 1855-1857; Rev. Robert Allyn, A. M., 1857-1859; William H. Young, A. M., 1859-1869; Rev. William H. Scott, A. M., Greek, 1869-1872; Rev. Augustine C. Hirst, A. M., Latin, 1869-1870; Rev. John L. Hatfield, A. M., Latin, 1870-1882; Charles W. Super, A. M., Ph. D., Greek, 1879; David J. Evans, A. M., Latin, 1882.

PROFESSORS OF MATHEMATICS.

Rev. James Irvine, A. M., President, 1821-1824; Rev. Jacob Lindley, A. M., 1824-1826; William Wall, A. M., 1827-1836; Rev. Alfred Ryors, A. M., 1836-1844; Rev. Lorenzo Dow McCabe, A. M., 1844-1845; Rev. William J. Hoge, A. M., Rhetoric, 1848-1851; Rev. Addison Ballard, A. M., 1852-1854; Rev. John M. Leavitt, A. M., 1854-1855; William H. Young, A. M., 1855-1859; Eli T. Tappan, A. M., 1859-1860; Rev. Richard A. Arthur, A. M., 1861-1864; Eli T. Tappan, A. M., 1864-1868; William H. G. Adney, A. M., 1869-1872; Rev. Daniel M. Blair, A. M., *pro tempore*, 1872-1873; Russell S. Devol, A. M., 1873.

PROFESSORS OF MORAL AND MENTAL SCIENCE.

Rev. Jacob Lindley, A. M., 1822-1824; Rev. Robert G. Wilson, D. D., President, 1824-1839; Rev. William H. McGuffey, D. D., LL. D., President, 1839-1843; Rev. Alfred Ryors, A. M., President, 1848-1852; Rev. Solomon Howard, D. D., LL.D., President, 1857-1872; Rev. William H. Scott, A. M., President, 1873.

PROFESSORS OF NATURAL SCIENCE.

Rev. Samuel D. Hoge, A, M., 1826, died 1826; Thomas M. Drake, M. D., 1827-1834; Rev. Frederick Merrick, A. M., 1838-1842; William W. Mather, A. M., 1842-1850; Rev. Joseph S. Tomlinson, D. D., 1851-1852; Rev. James G. Blair, M. D., D. D., 1852-1864; Rev. Alexander S. Gibbons, A. M., M. D., 1864-1872; William H. G. Adney, A. M., 1872-1873; J. McC. Martin, A. M., 1873-1882; Carl Leo Mees, M. D., 1882.

PROFESSORS OF HISTORY AND ENGLISH LITERATURE.

Rev. Randolph Stone, A. M., 1838-1839; Rev. Wells Andrews, A. M., 1840-1842; Cynthia U. Weld, 1882.

PRECEPTORS AND PRINCIPALS OF THE PREPARATORY DEPARTMENT.

Rev. Jacob Lindley, Preceptor, 1809-1822; Henry D. Ward, A. M., Preceptor, 1822-1824; A. G. Brown, A. M., Preceptor, 1824-1825; Daniel Read, A. B., Preceptor, 1825-1836; Rev. Wells Andrews, A. M., Preceptor, 1837-1840; Rev. Amos Miller, A. M., Principal, 1844-1845; Rev. Aaron Williams, A. M., Principal, 1845-1847; Rev. O. M. Spencer, A. M., Principal, 1851-1852; Rev. James F. Given, A. M., Principal, 1852-1854; W. H. Young, A. B., Principal, 1854-1855; Francis Brown, A. B., Principal, 1855-1859; Hugh Boyd, A. B., Tutor in Mathematics, 1859-1860; Edward H. Guthrie, A. M., Tutor in Language, Principal, 1859-1863; Rev. William H. Scott, A. B., Principal, 1863-1865; William H. G. Adney, A. M., Principal, 1865-1868; Rev. John M. Davis, A. B., Principal, 1872-1874; Rev. John A. White, A. B., Principal, 1874-1877; George B. Coler, Principal, 1881-1882; L. W. Sheppard, Principal, 1882.

Trustees.—Elijah Backus, Marietta, 1804-1806; General Rufus Putnam, Marietta, 1804, died 1824; Hon. Dudley Woodbridge, Marietta, 1804, died 1823; Hon. Benjamin Tappan, Steubenville, 1804-1808; Bezaleel Wells, Steubenville, 1804-1808; General Nathaniel Massie, Chillicothe, 1804--1808; Hon. Daniel Symmes, Cincinnati, 1804-1808; Rev. Daniel Story, Marietta, 1804, died 1804; Samuel Carpenter, Lancaster, 1804, died 1821; Rev. James Kilbourne, Worthington, 1804-1820; Griffith Green, Marietta, 1804-1808; Joseph Darlington, West Union, 1804-1815; Hon. William Creighton, Jr., Chillicothe, 1805-1808; General Joseph Buell, Marietta, 1805, died 1812; Benjamin Tupper, Zanesville, 1805, died 1814; Rev. Jacob Lindley, Waterford, 1805–1838; Michael Baldwin, Chillicothe, 1805–1809; Rev. Stephen Lindsley, Marietta, 1806–1826; William Skinner, Marietta, 1806, died 1840; Dr. Eliphaz Perkins, Athens, 1806–1819; Hon. Sylvanus Ames, Athens, 1808, died 1823; Hon. Jehiel Gregory, Athens, 1808–1812; Hon. Abel Miller, Athens, 1808–1825; Dr. Leonard Jewett, Athens, 1808–1813; Moses Hewett, Athens, 1808, died 1814; Rev. Robert G. Wilson, Chillicothe, 1809–1819, Hon. Jesup N. Couch, Chillicothe, 1809, died 1821; Major J. P. R. Bureau, Gallipolis, 1809–1812; Hon. Elijah Hatch, Athens County, 1809, died 1849; Henry Abrams, Lancaster, 1809–1814; Dr. Samuel P. Hildreth, Marietta, 1812–1819; Seth Adams, Zanesville, 1812–1838; Hon. William Wilson, Newark, 1813–1819; John Lawrence Lewis, Washington County, 1815–1819, Joseph Wood, Washington County, 1815–1838; Rev. James Culbertson, Zanesville, 1815, died 1847; Hon. Charles R. Sherman, Lancaster, 1815–1833; Hon. Edwin Putnam, Putnam, 1820–1839; Hon. Ephraim Cutler, Marietta, 1820–1849; Hon. Thomas Scott, Chillicothe, 1820–1838; Hon. Robert Linzee, Athens, 1820–1839; Hon. Alexander Harper, Zanesville, 1821–1839; Hon. Return J. Meigs, Marietta, 1822, died 1825; Hon. Levi Barber, Marietta, 1822, died 1833; William Rufus Putnam, Marietta, 1823–1843; Rev. James Hoge, D.D., Columbus, 1823–1852; Hon. Thomas Ewing, Lancaster, 1824–1832; Rev. David Young, Zanesville, 1825–1849; Rev. Dudley Woodbridge, Jr., Marietta, 1825–1833; Hon. Calvary Morris, Athens, 1825–1848; Hon. Lewis Summers, Virginia, 1829, died 1843; Hon. John L. Frye, Virginia, 1829–1839; General James T. Worthington, Chillicothe, 1830–1846; Rev. James McAboy, 1831, died 1833; Rev. Amos Miller, Athens County, 1832; Dr. A. V. Medbury, Athens County, 1834–1839; William B. Hubbard, Columbus, 1834, died 1865; General Samuel F. MacCracken, Lancaster, 1834, died 1857; Hon. Nathaniel C. Reed, Cincinnati, 1840–1845; Hon. John Brough, Columbus, 1840–1843; Hon. William Medill, Lancaster, 1840–1847; Hon. A. G. Brown, Athens, 1841; Rev. James M. Brown, Virginia, 1842–1859; Hon. John H. Keith, Chillicothe, 1844, died 1875; Hon. V. B. Horton, Pomeroy, 1844; Joseph Olds, Circleville, 1844–1846; Rev. William Aiken, McConnelsville, 1846–1866; Rev. William Cox, Lancaster, 1846–1856; William H. Trimble, Hillsboro, 1846–1849; Benjamin F. Hickman, Somerset, 1847–1849; Hon. Samuel F. Vinton, Gallipolis, 1848–1859; Hon. John Welch, Athens, 1848;

Hon. Wm. P. Cutler, Chillicothe, 1849-1853; Hon. Leonidas Jewett, Athens, 1849-1881; Joseph M. Dana, Athens, 1851, died, 1881; Hon. Samuel B. Pruden, Athens County, 1851, died 1862; Dr. M. Z. Kreider, Lancaster, 1851, died 1855; Hon. Robert Wright, Logan, 1852; Horace Wilson, Columbus, 1853; Hon. John E. Hanna, McConnelsville, 1854; Rev. Wm. T. Hand, Marietta, 1854, died 1860; Hon. John McLean, LL. D., Cincinnati, 1856, died 1861; Hon. George M. Woodbridge, Marietta, 1857; Hon. Calvary Morris, Athens, 1859, died 1871; Rev. J. M. Trimble, D. D., Columbus, 1860-1876; Rev. B. N. Spahr, Columbus, 1861-1877; Rev. J. M. Leavitt, New York, 1861-1864; Hon. E. H. Moore, Athens, 1861; Wm. Waddle, M. D., Chillicothe, 1864; Hon. H. S. Bundy, Jackson, 1864; Hon. W. P. Johnson, M. D., Philadelphia, 1866; Hon. Bellamy Storer, Cincinnati, 1866, died 1875; Hon. R. De Steiguer, Athens, 1871; Hon. Thomas Ewing, Lancaster, 1875; Hon. G. W. Boyce, Cincinnati, 1875; Hon. W. W. Johnson, Ironton, 1876; Hon. John Hancock, Dayton, 1877; Hon. James W. Bannon, Portsmouth, 1881; Hon. Perry Wiles, Zanesville, 1882.

Presidents.—Governor Edward Tiffin, *ex-officio*, 1804-1806; General Joseph Buel, 1806-1808; Rev. Jacob Lindley, A. M., 1808-1822; Rev. James Irvine, A. M., *ex-officio*, 1822-1824; Rev. Robert G. Wilson, D. D., *ex-officio*, 1824-1839; Rev. Wm. H. McGuffey, D. D., LL. D., *ex-officio*, 1839-1843; Hon. Calvary Morris, 1845-1847; Rev. Alfred Ryors, D. D., *ex-officio*, 1848-1852; Rev. Solomon Howard, D. D., LL. D., *ex-officio*, 1852-1872; Rev. William H. Scott, A. M., *ex-officio*, 1873.

Secretaries.—Hon. Dudley Woodbridge, 1804-1808; Henry Bartlett, 1808-1841; A. G. Brown, 1841-1853; Horace Wilson, 1853-1857; J. M. Dana, 1857-1881; R. De Steiguer, 1881.

Treasurers.—Eliphaz Perkins, M. D., 1804-1807; Leonard Jewett, M. D., 1807-1808; Joseph B. Miles, 1808-1814; Hon. Ebenezer Currier, 1814-1824; General John Brown, 1824-1875; Hon. E. H. Moore, 1875.

Auditors.—Henry Bartlett, 1813-1850; Wm. H. Bartlett, 1850, died 1855; Hon. Calvary Morris, 1855, died 1871; J. M. Dana, 1871-1881; L. M. Jewett, 1881.

CHAPTER XIII.

INCIDENTS OF TWENTY YEARS—A GROUPING OF FACTS AND A BUSINESS STATEMENT.

INSANE ASYLUM—ITS GENERAL HISTORY—A BARBECUE—LIGHT GUARDS—CITY HALL—TEMPERANCE MOVEMENTS—FROM 1829 TO 1883—A CHALLENGE—THE WHISKY INSURRECTION, 1861—LYNCHING AT ATHENS—JUDGE LYNCH DECIDES TO HANG A MURDERER, AND IT IS DONE—ATHENS'S BUSINESS INTERESTS—SOME GENERAL REMARKS—BUSINESS HOUSES AND ENTERPRISES—BANKS—GAS LIGHT COMPANY—TELEGRAPH—OFFICERS OF ATHENS, 1825-1883.

ATHENS ASYLUM FOR THE INSANE.

Through the efforts of Dr. W. P. Johnson, Representative from Athens County, and other citizens, the State Legislature passed an act which was approved April 13, 1867, providing for the erection of an additional lunatic asylum. It directed the appointment by the Governor of three trustees, to select and purchase, or receive by gift or donation, a lot of land, not less than fifty nor more than 100 acres, suitably located for the erection of an asylum to contain 400 patients. W. E. Davis, of Cincinnati, D. E. Gardner, of Toledo, and Dr. C. McDermont, of Dayton, were appointed Trustees; a vacancy occurring in this committee, through the death of Dr. McDermont, E. H. Moore, of Athens, was appointed in his place. There were various competing points, and for some time the contest was sharp and close; but Athens finally secured the asylum. To carry the point, the citizens purchased and made a gift to the State of 150 acres of land, lying south of the town, known as the Coates farm. It is a magnificent site, overlooking the Hocking Valley, and presenting a fine view of the city on the opposite hill. The location was fixed by the trustees in August, 1867, and contracts let for the various parts of the work. About 18,500,000 bricks were used in its construction, all of which were made on the ground.

H. B. Bowley

The corner-stone of the asylum was laid on Thursday, Nov. 5, 1868. The day was delightful, and the people came pouring into Athens until the streets were thronged with those who had come to witness the event. The ceremonies were conducted by the Masonic order, not less than 1,000 members of the order, from various parts of the State, being present to participate in the exercises. The people of Athens had made every preparation for the reception, and a cordial and generous welcome was given to all. The procession formed at two o'clock, on Washington street, in the following order, and marched to the asylum grounds: 1st, Athens Brass Band; 2d, Choirs of the Methodist, Episcopal, and Presbyterian churches; 3d, Masons; 4th, Judges, mayor, members of town council, magistrates, county officers, etc.; 5th, Citizens on foot; 6th, Citizens in carriages; 7th, Citizens on horseback. This procession was imposing in the extreme. General D. W. H. Day acted as Grand Marshal.

Having arrived at the asylum grounds, the exercises of laying the corner-stone were performed by Howard Mathews, the Grand Master of the order in Ohio, assisted by the grand officers carrying the emblems of corn, wine and oil. Both vocal and instrumental music by the Athens Brass Band and the united choirs of the Methodist, Episcopal and Presbyterian churches added much to the pleasure of the occasion, while deep interest was manifested in the ceremonies as conducted by the Grand Lodge. The Grand Treasurer made the following deposits in the corner-stone: Holy Bible; Constitution of Ohio and of all the States of the Union; names of members of the Fifty-eighth General Assembly of Ohio; names of State officers of Ohio; proceedings of the Grand Lodge of Ohio for 1867; laws of Ohio, 1867; programme of this day's proceedings; roll of members of Paramuthia Lodge, No. 25; one copy of daily Cincinnati *Commercial;* one copy of daily Cincinnati *Gazette;* one copy of daily Cincinnati *Chronicle;* one copy of weekly *Enquirer;* one copy of Athens *Messenger;* specimens of coins of the United States; a list of grand officers of Ohio Masons. After the ceremonies at the asylum, the procession moved to Athenæum Hall, where Past Grand Master Thrall delivered the oration. It was a beautiful and scholarly production, and was listened to with great attention.

The asylum was completed and furnished for the reception of patients Jan. 1, 1874. The building was 853 feet in length in a straight line, and it is 4,072 feet around it. It is divided into an administration building, with two wings for patients at the sides, and a series of buildings extending from it in the rear, for domestic and other purposes. The administration building is four stories in height, and comprises a front and rear divisions. The first includes, on the first floor, an entrance hall sixteen feet wide by fifty-five long, on each side of which are the offices of the superintendent, assistant physicians and steward, a general reception room for visitors, and the large stairways to the stories above. The second story of this division contains the apartments of the superintendent. The third and fourth stories comprise similar rooms for the other officers of the institution. In the rear division of the administration building, a central hall twelve feet wide leads from the front to the rear, on either side of which are the passages to the patients' wards.

In the basement of this division are placed the kitchens, sculleries and other domestic rooms for the general household, and beneath these are cellars. On the first floor are the dining-room and kitchen of the officers, reception-rooms for friends of patients, and general store-rooms. On the second floor the central hall leads to the amusement room, 66 x 42 feet, and twenty-eight feet in height, occupying both second and third stories. Above this room, in the fourth story, is a room of similar size, sixteen feet high, designed for religious services. Besides these rooms, there are on each side of these stories two rooms for reading, sewing and other purposes, and on every floor bath-rooms.

On either side of the administration building in the wings are the wards for patients. Each wing is of three stories high, except at the end, where a fourth story is placed over a part of the third section. Each wing is divided into three sections, connected together, but receding in succession. Thus ten wards are made on each side, providing for the classification to that extent of each sex. Each ward contains a central corridor, fifteen feet wide, with the rooms opening into it on each side. In the center of the front part of each ward is the parlor, a handsome room 24 x 16, with bay window. A dining-room and associate dormitories, bath-rooms, lavatory and water-closets are attached to every ward. An iron stairway leads in every section from basement to attic, and communicates with each floor therein. The single bed-rooms are about 9 x 11 feet, and vary in height from twelve to fifteen feet. The associate dormitories vary in size from 10 x 20 to 20 x 20 feet.

Under the wings is a basement connecting with the kitchens and basement of the administration building, in which is a railway for the conveyance of food to the dumb-waiters of the dining-rooms of each ward, and the chambers for the steam coils and pipes connecting them to heat the wards above. In the rear of the administration building are the laundry and boiler-house. The connecting building contains a long corridor continuous with the central hall of the main edifice, having on one side eight rooms for domestic or other purposes. In the basement is a similar corridor, and also a passage for steam pipes, etc. Below this is the air duct for supplying air to steam coils of main building. The laundry building has two stories and a basement, in the center of which is situated the water-tower, sixty-eight feet high, containing four large iron tanks, capable of holding 8,000 gallons of water. Still further in the rear is the boiler-house, in which are located the six boilers for heating purposes, the entire building being heated by steam. The asylum contains 544 rooms at present. The original cost of the building was about a half million dollars, but the present needs of the county call for an addition that will probably cost $100,000.

The visitor to the asylum cannot fail to be favorably impressed at the humane methods used in the treatment of the unfortunates and at the absence of prison-like surroundings. But few patients require seclusion, and these only at times. This, too, is the only form of mechanical restraint in use. Patients are encouraged, and in many cases required to take out-door exercise. In the last report of the able and efficient Superintendent, Dr. A. B. Richardson, it is stated that the daily average for some months of those who were given out-door walks, equaled half the number of patients in the asylum; and, as a rule, on every suitable day, scarcely a dozen males fail to get some form of out-door exercise.

The reports show that at least one fourth of the whole number of patients, or an average of over 150, have been allowed the privilege of the grounds unattended. This exhibition of confidence in the integrity of the patients is found to operate well. It does much to remove the feeling of imprisonment which is often so depressing in its influence. The instances of misplaced confidence have been infrequent. During the past year, out of a total of over 250 persons who were accorded special privileges, but sixteen attempted to escape, and in not one of these cases did any bad results follow.

Regular weekly religious services are held in the chapel, and opportunities are afforded the patients for social enjoyment Thursday evening of each week in the amusement hall. The health of the patients is remarkably good, the death-rate being from two to three per month, out of a total number of 631 patients on the average at the asylum.

OFFICERS, 1880.

H. M. Horton, Pomeroy, President; John E. Hanna, McConnelsville, S. W. Pickering, Athens, George W. Boerstler, M. D., Lancaster, Theo. F. Davis, Marietta, Trustees; A. B. Richardson, M. D., Superintendent; E. P. Cook, M. D., Asst. Physician; B. W. Pickering, M. D., Asst. Physician; Robt. E. Hamblin, Steward; S. C. Adams, Store-Keeper; Mrs. J. D. Richardson, Matron.

UNION SOLDIERS' BARBECUE.

One of the greatest days Athens ever saw was the 30th of August, 1866, when a grand barbecue was held, by the ex-soldiers and citizens of Athens County. The barbecue had its origin in a desire to cement more firmly the relations existing between the citizens and survivors of the gallant band who for so long a time breasted the storm of battle for love of country. The day was propitious, and the town of Athens, the streets having been cleaned, never appeared in a neater dress. The streets were thoroughly policed from end to end. A train of ten cars came from the West and two loaded trains from the East, bringing over 3,000 persons. But from every wagon-road came, not here and there a wagon, but a grand unorganized series of processions which had been formed spontaneously on the main thoroughfares from all the smaller roads and paths, and finally culminated in the grand throng, which filled every nook and corner of the town. Some 15,000 people came into Athens that day.

The decorations were a leading feature. They were planned by the ladies with great taste and skill, and they with their own hands did most of the labor. Banners and streamers spanned the streets at all the principal corners, while an ingenious and beautiful arch from the court-house yard to the block opposite was the admiration of all. A rope was the main support of the arch, while smaller ropes beautifully decorated with evergreens formed the principal ornamentations. The likenesses of Generals Grant and Sherman and the mottoes "The Nation Honors her Defenders," and " Welcome, Brave Men," occupied a place in the center. Nearly every place in town was decorated, some of them on a magnificent scale.

The dinner was served on the college green, and was a great success. Vast as was the hungry throng, there was enough for all to eat. A good idea of the amount of edibles required can be obtained by perusing a few figures showing the amount of the contributions from one or two places. Athens Township gave 138 pounds of bread, 26 pounds of butter, 280 pounds of mutton, 60 pounds of cheese, 26 chickens, 50 dozen pickles, 21 large cakes, 7 dozen tarts, 28 dozen small cakes, 167 pies and $600 in cash. About $200 of this sum was invested in bread. Lodi Township brought 300 pounds of bread, 400 pounds of beef, 60 pounds of mutton, 20 chickens, 55 pounds of butter, 60 pounds of cheese, 25 pies and 50 small cakes. Alexander Township gave 44 pies, 17 chickens, 9½ dozen small cakes, 15 large cakes, 250 pounds of mutton, 71 pounds bread, 20 dozen pickles, 6 pounds of butter, 1 turkey, 1 peck pop-corn, 1 cheese and $10 in cash. Rome, Ames, Lee, Dover and other townships all furnished their quota of provisions.

Eloquent and interesting speeches were made by Governor Dennison, W. H. Gibson, Hon. T. A. Plants, Colonel W. B. Stokes (of Tennessee), Colonel T. B. Pond, and Hon. Mr. Bundy (of Jackson). The barbecue was pronounced a grand success, and reflected credit on all concerned.

ATHENIAN LIGHT GUARDS.

This military organization, the only one worthy of mention in Athens since the war, was formed in the spring of 1878, with L. P. Harper, Captain; John P. Dana, First Lieutenant, and H. B. Stewart, Second Lieutenant. Three months after the organization, Captain Harper was elected Colonel and John P. Dana was elected Captain; H. B. Stewart, First Lieutenant, and W. F. Scott, Second Lieutenant. In 1879 Captain Dana was appointed Quartermaster of the Eighteenth Regiment, O. N. G., and H. B. Stewart was elected Captain; W. F. Scott, First Lieutenant, and Chas. W. Potter, Second Lieutenant. In 1881 Stewart and Potter resigned when W. F. Scott was elected Captain; C. W. Harris, First Lieutenant, and H. T. Hoyt, Second Lieutenant. The first year of the company's existence it was a detached company. The second year it was made Company C, of the Eighteenth Regiment, O. N. G., and remained so until the following year when the Eighteenth and Second Regiments were consolidated and continued under the name of the Second Regiment, of which the A. L. G. still formed Company C. The company averaged about forty-five members, were well uniformed, and armed by the State with breech-loading rifles. The company's band, also organized from Athens, was in 1879 detailed as a regimental band, at which time it was enlarged to about twenty-five pieces, being an unusually fine military band, of which A. B. Lowry was leader. The company went into camp each year of its existence at Marietta in 1878 and 1879; at Cambridge in 1880, and at Barnesville in 1881. It was a well-drilled company, being above the average in proficiency. Among the evidences of the appreciation in which it was held by the public was the presentation of a fine silk banner in 1878 by the ladies of Athens.

CITY HALL.

The construction of the fine town hall of Athens was begun in the summer of 1874, Henry O'Bleness being the contracting architect. The following extracts from the plans are given: "Frontage on Washington street, fifty-four feet; depth, 104 feet; height, two stories; first story thirteen feet in the clear, second story, twenty-five feet. A corridor thirteen feet in width extends through the building, on each side of which corridor are three apartments suitable for offices, with large closets attached." The postoffice is located in two of the east rooms. Two broad flights of stairs ascend from the front entrance to the second story, and one staircase ascends from the rear of the building to the rear of the stage. These latter stairs are designed for private use. The entire height of the structure to the top of the cupola, in which latter is a fine town clock, with four faces, is 102 feet. The hall on the second floor, designed for public occasions, is fifty-one feet wide, seventy feet in length, and twenty-five feet in height. The stage is 16 x 26 feet, with a private apartment 12 x 14 on each side. The seating capacity of the hall is from 500 to 600.

The corner-stone was laid Monday, Aug. 24, 1874, with imposing ceremonies by the Masonic order, witnessed by a large concourse of people both from home and abroad.

The following articles were deposited within the stone: One copy each of the Cincinnati *Commercial*, *Gazette*, *Times* and *Enquirer;* the Athens *Messenger* and *Journal*, the Nelsonville *Miner;* the *Prohibition Era*, *Western Christian Advocate*, *Masonic Review* and Wooster *Republican*; specimens of the several denominations of fractional currency; a one dollar note on the State Bank of

Ohio, Athens Branch; a two dollar U. S. note and silver half dollar of 1874 ; roll of officers of the Athens Masonic bodies and of the Grand Lodge of Ohio, and municipal officers of Athens.

This hall was completed in the spring of 1875, and opened formally June 8.

TEMPERANCE MOVEMENT.

The warfare between King Alcohol and the friends of temperance has been waged constantly for forty years with varying success. A detailed history of the temperance work will not be attempted here, but it is deemed fitting to notice some of the principal agitations.

The first temperance movement of record is found in a sermon preached on that subject by the Rev. Robert G. Wilson, Jan. 22, 1829. This sermon was published in full in the Athens *Mirror* of that date.

A society was formed, of which Dr. Wilson was President, the Rev. John Spaulding, Vice-President, and Prof. Joseph Dana Secretary, and a pledge was kept at the *Mirror* office for signatures The movement was pushed with great earnestness and success by the good men who inaugurated it, and doubtless there was sufficient need of reform. Some of the seed sown fell on good ground in Ames Township, and blossomed forth into the following unique advertisement, which appeared in the *Mirror* of April 25, 1829 :

"A CHALLENGE.

"ATTENTION GROG DRINKERS ! !

"SAMUEL L. MOHLER, of Ames Township, having been for sixteen years in the constant habit of *drinking*, and getting drunk on an average as often as once a month, has resolved to refrain entirely from the practice in future; and as a test of his sincerity, he offers to pledge the new wood work to a good wagon against any property of equal value that he will refrain from drinking ardent spirits longer than any other man who has been in the habit an equal or half the length of time ; provided both live to make the trial. Any person disposed to take him up can give notice to that effect.

"April 10, 1829."

Whether this interesting challenge was ever accepted or not is not known.

The Washingtonian movement, which started in the East about the year 1848, became very popular throughout Athens County. In July, 1848, there were seven of this order organized and at work in this county, as follows: Philos Adelphos Division, No. 129, located at Athens; McArthurstown Division, No. 210, at McArthur, now Vinton County; Amesville Division, No. 277, at Amesville; Hebbardsville Division, No. 296, at Hebbardsville; Nelsonville Division, No. 445, at Nelsonville; Albany Division, No. 487, at Albany; and Savannah Division, No. 485, at Savannah.

"THE CRUSADE."

The famous temperance "crusade" produced much excitement in Athens. The initial step here was a meeting held in the Presbyterian church Feb. 6, 1874, when a "Woman's Temperance League" was organized. Mrs. Angie C. Brown was elected President, Mrs. James L. Ballard and Mrs. Lewis Steenrod, Vice-Presidents, and Mrs. Angele C. Davis, Secretary. Daily prayer-meetings were held for some time. A number of pledges were prepared and circulated. The first was a pledge for the members, declaring lasting warfare on all kinds of liquor dealing. A pledge of total abstinence was signed by many citizens, binding for one year, and another binding for life. Still another pledge for the citizens was one promising aid and sympathy to the women in their work. The "property-holders' pledge" promised that the signers would not lease any property for use in connection with the liquor traffic. The physicians' and druggists' pledges promised not to prescribe or sell liquor for medicine except when absolutely necessary. Most of these pledges were liberally signed.

Tuesday, Feb. 10, a meeting was held in the Methodist church, when a call was made for volunteers to go upon the street and personally appeal to the druggists and saloonkeepers. Two thirds of the ladies present volunteered for this duty, and the rest of the ladies with a number of gentlemen remained in the church to pray. The crusaders went forth to visit the places where liquors were sold in the town, and, by singing and praying, endeavored to induce the proprietors to give up their business. All such places were visited, but the object in view was attained only with a few. Various promises were secured, but when the excitement subsided the town was but little better off in this respect than before. Nelsonville and other places in the county had a similar experience.

MURPHY MOVEMENT.

The well known "Murphy movement" of 1877 reached Athens May 9, of that year. A series of meetings was held, beginning with that date, which almost carried Athens by storm. In ten days 1,000 signatures to the pledge were received. The meetings were attended by immense crowds. These meetings were held in the city hall, except a mass meeting on the college green, held on Saturday, May 19. Much good was doubtless effected by these meetings, but still the enthusiasm was comparatively short lived. Meetings were for a time held almost constantly all over the county, and several thousand persons were pledged to total abstinence.

WHISKY INSURRECTION.

On the last day of the session of the Legislature, in the spring of 1861, a law was passed by an almost, if not quite, unanimous vote, prohibiting the sale of intoxicating liquors within two miles of any encampment of soldiers, and authorizing the officers of the military, as well as civil officers, under certain circumstances, to destroy the liquor. This law was soon enforced in Athens. On the night of Wednesday, May 22, some of the recruits in Camp Jewett found the means of leaving the camp, and after visiting the grog shops of the town, were prepared to play the soldier on their own account. Mistaking gate posts for rebel officers, and the pickets for secession armies, they charged upon the foe, and when victory perched upon their banners there were fewer front fences in Athens than before. Of course a stir was created in town, and no less a one in camp. It was soon ascertained where the liquor had been obtained, and a squad of soldiers, with muskets and bayonets, were detailed to "execute the law." And they did execute the law with summary promptness. From shanty to saloon, and from doggery to hotel, the squad marched, and in their trail flowed, if not blood, streams of very bad whisky.

This summary execution of a wise law was repeated in a milder manner, Aug. 4, 1861. The Eighteenth Infantry was at that time rendezvousing at Camp Wool, at Athens, for reorganization, under the supervision of Major C. H. Grosvenor. Certain "liquor shanty" proprietors on the outskirts of town were on several occasions ordered not to sell liquor to the soldiers, but this prohibition was persistently disregarded. Accordingly, early on the morning of the date above mentioned, Major Grosvenor appeared on the streets with a squad of soldiers, and accompanied by "Cart" Davis with his horse and dray, proceeded to gather up the whisky from the different places where it was kept for sale. Several loads of whisky were thus captured, and placed under lock and key.

LYNCHING IN ATHENS!

The greatest event in the criminal history of Athens County was the crime and punishment of Christopher C. Davis, a mulatto, in the fall of 1881. Davis was a farm-hand who had been working in the vicinity of Albany. He had done some work for and was acquainted with a widow, Mrs. Lucinda Luckey by name, a most estimable lady of about fifty-two years of age. Between eight and nine o'clock on Saturday evening, Oct. 29, 1881, Davis went to Mrs. Luckey's house, which was in an isolated situation, and made indecent proposals to her, which were indignantly repelled. She succeeded in inducing him to quit the house, but he returned again at midnight and broke into the house with an ax. Without a word he assaulted the poor woman, who stood near the doorway, wild with terror, striking her in the face and choking her to the floor. It is supposed that he then forcibly outraged her person. After accomplishing this hellish purpose he took the ax to complete his deadly work, and struck her with it about the head several times, fracturing the frontal and parietal bones of the skull, and cutting frightful gashes, portions of the scalp and the integuments of the head being torn completely off. Mrs. Luckey lay unconscious for several hours, but in the early morning managed to make her way to a neighbor's house, and tell her terrible story. She finally recovered.

Davis was arrested and taken before the Justice at Albany, who bound him over to court in the sum of $300. He was taken to Athens and imprisoned there. But when the enormity of the crime charged against him became known, there were mutterings and threats of vengeance both loud and deep, which induced Sheriff Warden to remove him to Chillicothe for safe keeping. After a time, when the excitement had apparently subsided, he was brought back to the Athens jail.

Between one and two o'clock on the morning of Monday, Nov. 21, 1881, a band of about thirty armed men from the vicinity of Albany and other parts of the county made their appearance in Athens for the purpose of hanging Davis. They were thoroughly organized, and used great care in their operations. They stationed guards at the residence of Marshal Scott, at the Brown House, where it was supposed Deputy Sheriff Sands roomed, at the churches and city hall, so that no alarm could be given by the ringing of bells. They then proceeded to the residence of the sheriff, overpowered him, got into the jail, and finding Davis, placed a rope around his neck, and the crowd proceeded to the South Bridge. Davis at first maintained his innocence, but finally confessed. He was given three minutes to pray, and then, the rope being fastened, was cast off the bridge. Watching him till life was extinct, the crowd then quietly dispersed. The testimony before the grand jury did not show who were the leaders in this summary execution, and no one has ever been brought to justice for complicity in it. In fact, public sympathy was so strong that little effort was made to investigate the facts.

ATHENS BUSINESS INTERESTS.

In the business interests of Athens can be seen better than in any other way her actual growth and true progress. For years her growth was slow, her business languishing. This was while she had no outlet to the busy world, but was surrounded by her everlasting hills, which looked down serenely upon the gem which rested so quietly upon the bosom of the valley below. The first impulse or movement which gave life to her sluggish nature, for it was becoming such from long inactivity, was the completion of the Hocking Valley Canal. It was the end of water route, and as such she received much business. She was the shipping point for quite an extensive scope of country, which gave her quite a name as a business point. It did not much, as the census shows, increase the population, but her mercantile class received a wonderful increase to their business, and one they welcomed most heartily. On the completion of the Marietta & Cincinnati Railway, the Hocking Valley and the Ohio Central, she had been placed in a commanding position, and her trade has advanced most rapidly. The isolated town among the hills is assuming a commercial look, and it will not be long before her business interests will be, like her University and Asylum, something that people can point to with pride.

IN 1819.

The record of the above year of Athens's business interests shows that she had five general stores, three taverns, and the Ohio University, one of the most celebrated seminaries in the State, and the Hocking River. There was also stated that there were five practicing physicians in the county. From that date the town grew, and further arrivals and a more extended business gathered within her limits, but the next record found was after a lapse of nearly a half a century.

1866.

It was not until 1866 that another statement was found of the business interests of Athens, and the contrast between that and 1819 is certainly great; while taking the half century that had passed into consideration, the city had nothing whatever to be proud of. A far greater contrast will be found between 1866 and 1883. One other point in this last growth of seventeen years: It has not only grown in the number and variety of its business houses, but the old firms have in many instances trebled and quadrupled their sales. One house in Athens now does a larger business than all in 1819, and has a fair margin over. There can be ten business houses of 1883 selected that would, in amount of their sales, exceed the combined mercantile interests of 1866. It is this business growth which has exceeded the increase of population. The statistics of 1866 are given below:

There were 218 dwelling houses, 2 tanneries, 2 grist-mills in operation besides one out of repair, 2 spinning and weaving factories, 2 carding machines, 2 wagon and buggy shops, 4 blacksmith shops, 13 carpenters, 2 coopers, 2 tinshops, 2 hardware stores, 2 drug stores, 2 book and stationery stores, 1 tobacconist, 2 butchers, 4 fresh meat sellers, 2 bakeries, 1 general land agency, 1 planing mill, 3 coal merchants, 2 salt works, 1 company sinking shaft for coal, 3 hotels, 2 barber shops, 1 express company, 1 telegraph office, 5 plasterers, 1 clothing store, 5 dry-goods stores, 2 boot and shoe stores, 2 silversmiths, 5 groceries, 1 huckster shop, 4 saloons, 2 millinery shops, 2 saddle and harness shops, 2 tailor shops, 2 draymen, 2 warehouses, 1 foundry and machine shop, 3 livery stables, 1 stage-coach line, 7 lawyers, 7 doctors, 1 bank, 2 churches (Methodist and Presbyterian), jail and county buildings, 4 passenger and 4 freight trains arriving and departing daily, 1 printing office, 1 fancy sign-painter, 2 house-painters, 2 dentists, 1 university with large and commodious buildings, a large and one of the finest union school-houses in Ohio, and "an old court-house."

There have been some changes in Athens since that time, and

decidedly for the better. The last item of the above was undoubtedly a sore spot to the chronicler, "An old court-house." He seemed to have an utter contempt for the "old affair," and yet it rang with as much eloquence, and the law had as many great expounders as ever will the new. There are no doubt brainy men at the bar of Athens to-day, but somehow their reputation is not national and they but fill a State and local field. So we will drop a parting tear to the "old court-house," to Tom Ewing and his compeers, before the old love is thrown off for the new.

BUSINESS DIRECTORY.

Adams' Express Company, Frank Falloon, agent; B. F. Addleman, photograph artist; Robert Arscott, brickmaker; Athens Gas Light Company, J. M. Welch, President, W. H. Harris, Secretary; Athens Water Wheel and Machine Co., D. B. Stewart, President, H. R. Mathias, Secretary; G. W. Baker, general insurance agent; Bank of Athens, James D. Brown, Cashier; First National Bank, A. Norton, President, D. H. Moore, Jr., Cashier; W. D. Bartlett, hardware; Bayard, Ullum & Co., hardware; E.C. Berry, restaurant; E. T. Bingman, musical instruments and sewing machines; Thomas Bradford, barber shop; W. H. Brown & Co., wholesale groceries; T. W. Woodyard, proprietor Brown House; Brown & Koons, attorneys at law; W. R. Calkins & Bro., hardware; Wm. Caven, blacksmith; R. E. Constable, attorney at law; John Cornell, proprietor Cornell House; Jesse Cornell, restaurant; D. C. Cornwell, jewelry and silverware; Cushman Crippen, blacksmith; Dana & Kaler, dry goods and clothing; De Steiguer & Jewett, attorneys at law; G. A. Dille, dentist; H. K. Dorr, drugs and medicines, two stores; David Dyson, boots and shoes; David Edgar, brick-maker; J. E. Edmundson, dentist; Falloon & O'Bleness, furniture manufacturers and dealers in lumber and building materials; James Farrell, meat market; F. Fensel, brick-maker and saloon keeper; Frank E. Foster, groceries; W. B. Foster, livery stable; A. B. Frame, physician and surgeon; J. A. Frame, physician and surgeon; James B. Fulton, groceries; Elmer Golden, groceries; G. L. Gorslene, physician and surgeon; Frank Gibbs, barber shop; F. P. Graham, photograph artist; James Grim, livery stable; Grosvenor & Jones, attorneys at law; Henry Hagy, saloon; Isaac Half, furniture; Frederick Heisner, tobacco and cigars; C. B. Henderson, drugs and medicines; the *Athens Herald*, published by the Herald Company, edited by L. C. Butler; Henry Herrold, flouring mill; T. J. Herrold & Co., groceries; Judiah Higgins, harness and saddles: C. C. Holmes, bakery and confectionery; The *Athens Journal*, published and edited by Jennie Jones; P. Kern & Son, boots and shoes; James King, blacksmith; F. M. Koons, grocer and dealer in lumber and building material; Kurtz & Minear, books, jewelry, stationery and wall paper; Justin Laird & Co., carriage manufacturers, and dealers in carriages, wagons, farming implements, harness, whips, etc.; E. R. Lash, drugs and medicines; H. M. Lash, physician and surgeon; A. Love, Bakery; W. F. Mann, saloon; J. Maxey, gunsmith; C. McLean, jewelry; W. F. Scott, agent M. & C. R. R. and Express Co.; Gus. Mensler, meat market; The *Athens Messenger*, published and edited by C. E. M. Jennings; Mintun & Fuller, groceries; M. P. Murphy, cigars, tobacco and sample room; Henry Nelson, dry goods and clothing; Pickering & Walsh, groceries; S. Pickering, cigar manufactory; T. M. D. Pilcher, furniture; W. H. Potter, restaurant; John Ring, meat market; A. L. Roach & Son, groceries; F. S. & H. M. Roach, Jr., groceries; Harvey M. Roach, groceries; R. W. Roach, groceries; F. Roth, tannery; Cyrus Rose, harness and saddles; Ryan & Bell, groceries; Jacob Shaffler, merchant tailor; Chas. P. Shutt, carriage manufactory, dealer in carriages, wagons, etc; Singer Sewing Machine Co., sewing machines and fixtures; Albert Sloan, tobacco, cigars and jewelry; O. B. Sloan, dry goods; Sam. Sommers, dry goods; W. H. Statey, boots and shoes; D. B. Stewart, flouring mill; H. S. Stinson, physician and surgeon; Emmett Tompkins, attorney at law; Townsend & Sleeper, attorneys at law; E. L. Walker, boots and shoes; G. R. Walker, books and stationery; J. H. Walker, undertaker; C. H. Warden & Bros., produce shippers; Granville C. Brown, proprietor Warren House; J. E. Weidman, cigar manufactory; C. S. Welch, attorney at law; Welch & Welch, attorneys at law; Western Union Telegraph Co., Mrs. Ella Guerin, operator; James West, barber shop; John West, barber shop; Mrs. M. C. White, milliner; J. O. Whipple, groceries; Wilson & Morse, marble works; C. H. Winger, confectioneries, cigars and tobacco; Wood & Wood, attorneys at law; D. Zenner & Co., dry goods and clothing; one new courthouse; one new city hall and postoffice; Ohio University with additional building; an insane asylum; one fine public school building.

BANKS.

The first bank in Athens, and the first in the Hocking Valley, except at Lancaster, was the Athens branch of the State Bank of Ohio, established in 1848. For the purpose of forming this bank, a number of citizens met at the court-house May 17 of that year, over which meeting Ezra Stewart presided. Articles of association were adopted and signed by the forty-nine stock-holders. The capital stock was $100,000, divided into 1,000 shares of $100 each. This was the minimum amount which the law of 1845 allowed to be used as the capital of a branch of the State Bank. The following nine gentlemen were chosen as the Directors of the bank: John Ballard, John Welch, Ezra Stewart, A. B. Walker, Joseph M. Dana, Leonidas Jewett, Douglas Putnam, Samuel Pickering, and Joseph K. Will. John Welch, of Athens, was elected President; Charles H. Cornwell, previously Teller of a bank at Chillicothe, was chosen Cashier, at a salary of $800; and Enos Stimson, Jr., of Athens, was named as Teller, at a salary of $500. The cashier's bond was fixed at $20,000, and the teller's at $10,000. The bank was located in a brick building erected by Pickering & Carley, opposite the court-house, and began business in the latter part of July, 1848. John Ballard was chosen President for 1849, and held the office as long as the bank existed as a branch of the State Bank. Mr. Cornwell resigned in December, 1850, and John R. Crawford was chosen Cashier in his place. He remained six years, and was succeeded by L. H. Stewart in 1857. Mr. Stewart's health failing him, he was obliged to leave in 1863, after which time A. G. Brown was the Cashier. The year 1863, in which was passed the law providing for National banks, brought a revolution in banking, and the State banks gave way to the banks of the present day.

The First National Bank of Athens was the natural successor of the Athens Branch of the State Bank, and was organized Dec. 29, 1863, with a capital stock of $50,000, divided into 500 shares, the first owners of which were as follows: Noah L. Wilson, of Chillicothe, 62; John Welch, of Athens, 19; John Ballard, of Athens, 110; Eliakim H. Moore, of Athens, 40; Archibald G. Brown, of Athens, 100; Douglas Putnam, of Marietta, 50; Charles B. Hall, of Marietta, 54; David C. Skinner, of Marietta, 50; Milbury M. Greene, of Athens, 15. The Directors first chosen were, N. L. Wilson, John Welch, John Ballard, E. H. Moore, J. C. Skinner, Douglas Putnam, and A. G. Brown. E. H. Moore was elected

President, a position he retained until January, 1879, when A. Norton became President. A. G. Brown was Cashier until 1868, when he was succeeded by Thomas H. Sheldon. Mr. Sheldon resigned in 1882, and since Jan. 1, 1883, the position has been held by David H. Moore. David Kessinger was Teller from 1868 to 1876, in September of which year D. H. Moore was elected Teller. On Mr. Moore's being promoted to Cashier, John J. Welch became the Teller. The present Board of Directors consists of A. Norton, J. M. Welch, E. H. Moore, A. G. Brown, Emmett Tompkins, J. M. Goodspeed, and E. W. Nye. The charter of the bank was renewed Feb. 24, 1883. The capital stock was some time since increased to $75,000. Since the establishment of the bank, it has declared over $80,000 in dividends.

The Bank of Athens.—Messrs. John Brown and James D. Brown started in the banking business in Albany in 1867, under the firm name of John Brown & Son. In October of the following year they removed, with their business, to Athens, where their bank has since been known as the "Bank of Athens." The elder Mr. Brown died in October, 1875, since which time the business has been conducted by Mr. J. D. Brown. Mr. R. H. Stewart was with the bank as Teller for about ten years, leaving in July, 1882. Charles W. Harris, the present Teller, entered the bank in January, 1876. W. B. Golden entered the bank in August, 1882. The bank of Athens has until this year (1883) occupied one of the oldest buildings of the village, having been built in 1812. This has been taken down, and at the present writing Mr. Brown is erecting a new building 38 x 46 feet, with an L 18 x 19 on the same corner. The banking-room will be 18 x 26; private office 10 x 11.

ATHENS GAS-LIGHT COMPANY.

This company was organized as a joint stock company in 1872, its object being the manufacture of gas for lighting the city. The original capital was $30,000. The facilities were all completed for operation in the fall of 1873, since which time gas has been used for lighting the streets, also the public and private buildings of the city. The original directors of the company were: John Ballard, G. T. Gould, C. H. Grosvenor, D. B. Stewart and L. W. Brown, John Ballard being President and L. W. Brown, Secretary. The present Directors are: J. M. Welch, D. B. Stewart, A. W. Ullum, Emmett Tompkins and W. D. Bartlett. J. M. Welch is

President and W. H. Harris, Secretary. This company has also built up a large trade in lime and cement in which, at present, they are the leading dealers in the city.

TELEGRAPH LINES.

The first telegraph line which passed through Athens City was that of the New Orleans & Ohio Telegraph Company. The first message received at Athens was on Oct. 6, 1848, and the line is still a public institution for private profit. The Pomeroy & Athens line was the next which opened for business, in January, 1859.

OFFICERS OF THE TOWN OF ATHENS.

The records of the town, from the date of incorporation, 1811, to that of 1825, inclusive, were lost. The latter year, however, it was known that James Gilman was President of the Council, and Joseph B. Miles, Recorder.

The election for town officers, March 6, 1826, gave a total poll of forty-three votes, and the following persons were elected members of the Town Council, viz.: Thomas Brice, by thirty-four votes; Columbus Bierce, by thirty-four votes; Ebenezer Currier, by thirty-one votes; John Brown, Jr., by thirty-three votes, and Joseph B. Miles, by twenty-three votes. The following town officers were elected: Samuel Knowles, Marshal; Eben Foster, Supervisor; A. G. Brown, Treasurer; Calvary Morris, Collector; John Gillmore, Assessor. The council elected Ebenezer Currier, President, and Joseph B. Miles, Recorder.

March 5, 1827.—Charles Shipman, Columbus Bierce, John Brown, Jr., Thomas Brice and Isaac Taylor were elected Councilmen; William W. Bierce, Marshal; John Gillmore, Assessor; James J. Fuller, Collector; A. G. Brown, Treasurer; Eben Foster, Supervisor. The council elected Columbus Bierce, President, and John Brown, Jr., Recorder for the ensuing year.

March 10, 1828.—An election was held, pursuant to an act of the Legislature, passed Jan. 24, 1828, entitled "an act to incorporate the town of Athens, in the county of Athens." Nine councilmen were chosen, whose term of office was afterward decided by lot, as follows, viz.: Joseph Dana, Thomas Brice and Jeremiah Olney, to serve three years; Isaac Barker, John Gillmore and Amos Crippen, to serve two years; and Ebenezer Currier, Eliphaz Perkins and Norman Root, to serve one year. The council elected of their own number, Joseph Dana, Mayor, and Norman Root, Recorder; and they appointed from the citizens, A. G. Brown, Treasurer; John McGill, Marshal; John Porter, Surveyor of wood and lumber, and William Golden, Clerk of the market.

March 9, 1829.—Joseph Dana was elected Mayor; Ebenezer Currier, Calvary Morris and Norman Root, Councilmen; and John McGill, Marshal. Norman Root was chosen Recorder for the ensuing year; A. G. Brown, Treasurer, and John Porter, Surveyor of wood and lumber. The mode of electing the mayor and marshal had been changed by an act of the Legislature, passed Feb. 28, 1829, which made these officers elective by the people, instead of by the Town Council.

March 8, 1830.—John Gillmore, Amos Crippen and Isaac Barker were elected to the Town Council, for three years, and John Perkins for one year; Joseph Dana was elected Mayor, and John Sampson, Marshal. Norman Root was appointed Recorder, John Porter, Surveyor of wood and lumber, and Dr. A. V. Medbury, Treasurer.

March 14, 1831.—Joseph Dana, Thomas Brice and John Perkins were elected Councilmen; Joseph Dana was elected Mayor, and John Sampson, Marshal. The Council appointed Norman Root, Recorder; Dr. A. V. Medbury, Treasurer, and Wm. D. Bartlett, Surveyor of wood and lumber for ensuing year.

March 12, 1832.—Hull Foster, Wm. D. Bartlett and Francis Beardsley were elected Councilmen; John Gillmore, Mayor, and Thomas Francis, Marshal. The Council appointed Thomas Brice, Recorder, and Dr. Medbury, Treasurer.

March 11, 1833.—Samuel Miller, Oliver Childs and Isaac N. Norton were elected Councilmen; Samuel Miller, Mayor, and John Sampson, Marshal. Joseph Dana was appointed Recorder, and Dr. Medbury, Treasurer.

March 10, 1834.—Thomas Francis, A. B. Walker and Charles Cunningham were elected Councilmen; Samuel Miller, Mayor, and John Sampson, Marshal. A. B. Walker was appointed Recorder, for the ensuing year, and Dr. Medbury, Treasurer.

March 9, 1835.—Norman Root, James J. Fuller and Francis Beardsley were elected Councilmen; Samuel Miller, Mayor, and John Sampson, Marshal. Edgar P. Jewett was appointed Treasurer, and A. B. Walker, Recorder, for the ensuing year.

March 14, 1836.—I. N. Norton, John Welch and Leonidas Jewett were elected Councilmen; I. N. Norton, Mayor, and Cyrus

Gibson, Marshal. John Welch was appointed Recorder, and P. S. Baker, Treasurer.

March 13, 1837.—Henry Bartlett, John N. Dean, Cephas Carpenter and Thomas Francis were elected Councilmen; Henry Bartlett, Mayor, and Samuel Miller, Marshal. Norman Root, appointed Recorder, and P. S. Baker, Treasurer.

Record of 1838 missing.

March 11, 1839. — John Brown, Jr., H. R. Gillmore and Cephas Carpenter were elected Councilmen for three years, and Norman Root, Robert McCabe and Francis Beardsley, for two years. John Brown, elected Mayor, and Dr. C. Bierce, Marshal. Norman Root appointed Recorder, and P. S. Baker, Treasurer.

March 9, 1840.—P. S. Baker, John N. Dean and Cephas Carpenter, were elected Councilmen; John Brown, Mayor, and I. K. Norton, Marshal. Norman Root appointed Recorder, and A. B. Walker, Treasurer.

March 8, 1841.—James J. Fuller, E. Cockerill and Enos Stimson, were elected Councilmen; John Brown, Mayor, and Benjamin Brown, Marshal. Enos Stimson appointed Recorder, and A. B. Walker, Treasurer.

March 14, 1842.—Leonidas Jewett, Norman Root and J. L. Currier were elected Councilmen; Norman Root, Mayor, and John Sampson, Marshal. Enos Stimson appointed Recorder, and A. B. Walker, Treasurer.

March 13, 1843.—John Brown, Ezra Stewart and Francis Beardsley were elected Councilmen; John Brown, Mayor, and Jacob C. McCabe, Marshal.

March 11, 1844.—John Ballard, Cephas Carpenter, Sumner Bartlett and Dr. Wm. Blackstone were elected Councilmen; John Brown, Mayor, and William Smith, Marshal. Leonidas Jewett appointed Recorder, and Benjamin Brown, Treasurer.

Record of 1845, missing.

March 9, 1846.—Ezra Stewart, Francis Beardsley and John Brown elected Councilmen for three years; Sumner Bartlett, Wm. R. Smith and J. W. Bayard for two years; John Brown, Mayor, and Abel Stedman, Marshal. J. W. Bayard appointed Recorder, and O. W. Brown, Treasurer.

March 8, 1847.—John Ballard, Dr. Wm. Blackstone and Cephas Carpenter were elected Councilmen; John Brown, Mayor, and Abel Stedman, Marshal. J. W. Bayard appointed Recorder, and O. W. Brown, Treasurer.

March 13, 1848.—Samuel Miller, Wm. R. Smith and Joseph Jewett were elected Councilmen; Samuel Miller, Mayor, and Wm. H. Abbott, Marshal. Joseph Jewett appointed Recorder, and O. W. Brown, Treasurer.

March, 12, 1849.—John Brown, Andrew Kessinger and Wm. Walker were elected councilmen; John Brown, Mayor, and Abel Stedman, Marshal. Joseph Jewett appointed Recorder, and O. W. Brown, Treasurer.

March, 11, 1850.—Joseph M. Dana, Lot L. Smith and Samuel Pickering were elected Councilmen; Samuel Miller, Mayor, and Abel Stedman, Marshal. Joseph Jewett appointed Recorder, and Leonidas Jewett, Treasurer.

March, 10, 1851.—John Brown, Joseph M. Dana, Andrew Kessinger, E. P. Talpey and Wm. Walker, Councilmen; Samuel Miller, Mayor; Joseph Jewett, Recorder, and Leonidas Jewett, Treasurer.

March 10, 1852.—Wm. Walker, Norman Root, John B. Paul, Samuel Miller, J. M. Dana, Councilmen; John Brown, Mayor; Joseph Jewett, Recorder, and L. Jewett, Treasurer.

April 14, 1853.—John Brown, Samuel Miller, John B. Paul, Joseph Jewett, Wm. Walker, Councilmen; Norman Root, Mayor; J. M. Dana, Recorder, and L. Jewett, Treasurer.

April 15, 1854.—John Brown, Wm. Walker, H. K. Blackstone, D. M. Clayton, Henry T. Hoyt, Councilmen; Norman Root, Mayor; J. M. Dana, Recorder; and L. Jewett, Treasurer.

April, 1855.—Henry T. Hoyt, Jesse Davis, J. Lawrence Currier, J. C. Frost, N. H. Van Vorhes, Councilmen; Norman Root, Mayor; J. M. Dana, Recorder; L. Jewett, Treasurer.

April, 1856.—H. K. Blackstone, Wm. P. Kessinger, Oliver W. Pickering, L. Jewett, E. H. Moore, Councilmen; Norman Root, Mayor; J. M. Dana, Recorder; L. Jewett, Treasurer.

April, 1857.—Lot L. Smith, H. K. Blackstone, Wm. P. Kessinger, Geo. W. Baker, O. W. Pickering, Councilmen; Norman Root, Mayor; J. M. Dana, Recorder; H. K. Blackstone, Treasurer.

April, 1858.—Henry T. Hoyt, N. H. Van Vorhes, Lot L. Smith, Hiram R. Crippen, Thomas Davis, Councilmen; N. Root, Mayor; J. M. Dana, Recorder; H. T. Hoyt, Treasurer.

April, 1859.—H. T. Hoyt, L. L. Smith, Charles H. Grosvenor, Thomas Davis, Hiram R. Crippen, Councilmen; N. Root, Mayor; J. M. Dana, Recorder; H. T. Hoyt, Treasurer.

April, 1860.—L. Jewett, W. P. Johnson, H. T. Hoyt, Wm. Golden, Rufus P. Crippen, Councilmen; N. Root, Mayor; F. H. Stedman, Recorder; H. T. Hoyt, Treasurer.

April, 1861.—L. Jewett, W. P. Johnson, H. T. Hoyt, Wm. Golden, H. S. Stimson, Councilmen; N. Root, Mayor; F. H. Stedman, Recorder; H. T. Hoyt, Treasurer.

April, 1862.—H. T. Hoyt, Wm. Golden, E. H. Moore, Josephus Tucker, E. C. Crippen, Councilmen; N. Root, Mayor; F. H. Stedman, Recorder; H. T. Hoyt, Treasurer.

April, 1863.—H. T. Hoyt, E. C. Crippen, Josephus Tucker, Charles P. Ballard, Jesse Davis, Councilmen; N. Root, Mayor; F. H. Stedman, Recorder; H. T. Hoyt, Treasurer.

April, 1864.—Abner Cooley, A. D. Brown, H. K. Blackstone, Josephus Tucker, R. P. Crippen, Councilmen; Joseph M. Dana, Mayor; Simeon W. Pickering, Recorder; A. D. Brown, Treasurer.

April, 1865.—Jesse Van Law, N. H. Van Vorhes, H. K. Blackstone, Elmer Golden, A. D. Brown, Councilmen; J. M. Dana, Mayor; S. W. Pickering, Recorder; A. D. Brown, Treasurer.

April, 1866.—A. D. Brown, H. K. Blackstone, J. W. Harris, N. H. Van Vorhes, Jesse Van Law, Councilmen; J. M. Dana, Mayor; S. W. Pickering, Recorder; A. M. Brown, Treasurer.

April, 1867.—H. K. Blackstone, N. H. Van Vorhes, Jesse Van Law, J. H. Falloon and Wm. P. Johnson, Councilmen; George W. Baker, Mayor; Frederick L. Ballard, Recorder; H. H. Van Vorhes, Treasurer.

April, 1868.—N. H. Van Vorhes, H. K. Blackstone, C. L. Wilson, H. S. Stimson and Alexander Cochran, Councilmen; J. M. Dana, Mayor; F. L. Ballard, Recorder; N. H. Van Vorhes, Treasurer.

1869.—Hiram C. Martin, Mayor; F. L. Ballard, Recorder; N. H. Van Vorhes, Treasurer; H. K. Blackstone, H. S. Stimson, Josephus Tucker, N. H. Van Vorhes, C. L. Wilson and F. L. Ballard, Councilmen.

1870.—Wm. Golden, Mayor; S. W. Pickering, Eli C. Crippen, H. S. Stimson, John Ring, W. W. Kurtz and W. W. Love, Council; C. H. Grosvenor, Solicitor; C. R. Sheldon, Clerk; James D. Brown, Treasurer; Robert White, Street Commissioner and Marshal.

1871.—The same as 1870, except Elza Jones, Marshal, in place of R. White, resigned.

20

1872.—Wm. Golden, Mayor; L. W. Brown, George T. Gould, Jacob Grones, W. W. Kurtz, W. W. Love and J. Ring, Council; C. H. Grosvenor, Solicitor; C. R. Sheldon, Clerk; James D. Brown, Treasurer; Robert White, Street Commissioner; M. B. Port, Marshal.

1873.—Members of Council, Louis W. Brown, George T. Gould, J. Grones, R. P. Crippen, Judiah Higgins and Nehemiah Warren; other officers the same as in 1872.

1874.—Wm. Golden, Mayor; James D. Brown, Treasurer; C. R. Sheldon, Clerk; L. M. Jewett, Solicitor; Robert White, Street Commissioner; J. Cart. Davis, Marshal. Council, J. Higgins, N. Warren, J. Grones, E. H. Moore, N. H. Van Vorhes and Winfield Scott, and George W. Baker, from Nov. 5, to fill vacancy of N. H. Van Vorhes, resigned.

1875.—Council, S. W. Pickering, J. Higgins, Winfield Scott, E. M. Moore, H. K. Blackstone and J. Grones; other officers the same as in 1874.

1876.—Mayor, Wm. Golden; Solicitor, Emmett Tompkins; Clerk, C. R. Sheldon; Treasurer, J. D. Brown; Marshal, M. B. Port; Street Commissioner, Peter Finsterwald; Council, Messrs. Leonard Brown, H. S. Stimson, E. H. Moore, W. H. Brown, J. Higgins and S. W. Pickering.

1877.—Council, E. B. Clarke, H. M. Lash, T. B. Warden, H. S. Stimson, E. H. Moore and Leonard Brown; other officers held over from 1876.

1878.—Mayor, Emmett Tompkins; Solicitor, Evan J. Jones; Clerk, C. R. Sheldon; Treasurer, J. D. Brown; Marshal, M. B. Port; Street Commissioner, Peter Finsterwald; Council, Peter Kern, Winfield Scott, George W. Ullum, E. B. Clarke, H. M. Lash and T. B. Warden.

1879.—Council, E. B. Clark, F. O. Pickering, T. H. Sheldon, P. Kern, G. W. Ullum and Winfield Scott; other officers held over from 1878. Dec. 31, J. P. Wood appointed Mayor to fill vacancy of Emmett Tompkins, resigned.

1880.—J. P. Wood, Mayor; C. R. Sheldon, Clerk; C. McClain, Treasurer; Walter Howe, Marshal; Peter Finsterwald, Street Commissioner; R. H. Stewart, John Graham, W. H. Brown, T. H. Sheldon, F. O. Pickering, E. B. Clarke, Councilmen.

1881.—J. H. Calkins, Harry M. Roach, T. H. Sheldon, W. H.

Brown, John Graham, R. H. Stewart, Councilmen; W. M. Scott, Marshal; other officers held over.

1882.—Mayor, J. P. Wood; Marshal, W. M. Scott; C. R. Sheldon, Clerk; C. McClain, Treasurer; Peter Finsterwald, Street Commissioner; D. L. Sleeper, Solicitor; Council, W. H. Brown, Conrad Josten, Peter Kern, J. H. Calkins, T. H. Sheldon and H. M. Roach.

April 3, 1883.—Mayor, J. P. Wood; Solicitor, D. L. Sleeper; Clerk, C. R. Sheldon; Treasurer, C. McLean; Marshal, Peter Finsterwald; Street Commissioner, F. O. Pickering; Members of Council, Jesse H. Cornell, James D. Brown, H. M. Roach, W. H. Brown, C. Josten and P. Kern.

CHAPTER XIV.

BIOGRAPHICAL SKETCHES IN THE CITY OF ATHENS AND ATHENS TOWNSHIP.

John Ackley, civil engineer and ex-County Surveyor of Athens County, was born in Washington County, Pa., May 31, 1825, He is the second of the five sons of Jehu and Elizabeth (Eaton) Ackley, who came to Ohio in 1836 and settled in Lodi Township, Athens County. His mother died when he was eleven years old. He lived with his father till he was twenty years old, working on a farm and attending the common schools. In 1846 he entered the Ohio University at Athens, taking an irregular course, studying and teaching till 1849, when he was elected Surveyor of Athens County, holding the position six years, and since then at intervals till January, 1883, although the most of his time has been spent in surveying and civil engineering. He has also been engaged in farming in the vicinity of Athens since 1868. Dec. 31, 1849, he married Jerusha Haning, of Lodi Township. They have five children—Lavinia, wife of W. F. Lewis, of Waxahachie, Ellis Co., Tex.; Ida; Hattie, wife of H. A. Brown, of Scioto County, Ohio; Eber G., and Eliakim H. Mr. Ackley is Master of Grange No. 422, Athens, and County Deputy.

Josiah Benton Allen, late Recording Clerk in the office of the Secretary of State at Columbus, Ohio, was born near Cadiz, Harrison Co., Ohio, July 14, 1842. He is the son of David and Mary (Wilkin) Allen. He lived with his parents until he was seventeen, receiving his education in the common schools and the De Camp Institute at Pagetown, Ohio. July 4, 1861, he enlisted in Company C, Thirtieth Ohio Volunteer Infantry as a private. In April, 1862, he was promoted to First Orderly Sergeant. He participated in a number of battles and skirmishes, the most important being Giles Court-House, Carnifax Ferry, Second Bull Run, Centerville, South Mountain, Antietam, Haines's Bluff, Jackson, Champion Hill, Black River and Vicksburg. At the last, May 22, 1863, while storming Fort Gregg, he being in command of his company at the time, all but fourteen of his men were killed, he himself losing his left arm. After submitting to two amputations of the same arm, and being unfitted for service thereby, he was discharged for disability in 1864. He returned to Athens and attended the Ohio University until the close of the college year in 1866, then went to Missouri and that fall was engaged in the insurance business. During the winter he taught school in the village of Maysville, of that State; returned to Athens in April, 1867, and the following fall was, without opposition, elected Recorder of Athens County on the Republican ticket. He held that office by being re-elected, for twelve years. From January to June, 1880, he held the stewardship of the Athens Asylum for the Insane. Losing that position through a change in the administration, he was appointed Recording Clerk in the office of the Secretary of State at Columbus, in December, 1880, remaining there until January, 1883. April 14, 1871, he was married to Miss Sue E. Racer, of Marietta, Ohio. He is a member of J. C. McCoy Post, No. 1, G. A. R., and holds a membership in the council of administration of that order, of the State of Ohio.

Benjamin Thomas Addleman, photographer, Athens, Ohio, was born near Richmond, Wayne Co., Ohio, Jan. 28, 1827. At the age of nineteen he went to Richmond and worked as an apprentice eighteen months to learn the gunsmith's trade. He then worked as a journeyman until 1849, when he opened a gunsmith shop in Richmond, remaining there until 1852, when he went to California and mined successfully in Canyon Creek until 1859. He then returned to Ohio and purchased a farm in Preble County near New Paris, and farmed nearly two years, when, selling his farm, he returned to Richmond and dealt in iron with his brother, J. P. Addleman, until 1861. He then purchased another farm in Wayne County and pursued farming until 1864, when he again returned to Richmond and engaged in photography until 1869. He removed to Hagerstown, Ohio, and engaged in photography until 1873 when he came to Athens and established his present gallery. In April, 1860, he married Miss Margaret Tenney, of Montgomery County, Ohio. They have six children—Charles L., bookkeeper for the Singer Sewing Machine Company of Athens; Adell; Clara Belle, wife of Clement H. Hooper, of Athens County; Lula, William A. and Frank.

George Washington Baker, general insurance agent, Athens, was born near Athens, O., May 2, 1829, where he was reared, receiving only a common-school education. His father, Nicholas Baker, was one of the pioneers of Athens County, and came with his parents from Massachusetts in 1814. His mother, Clara

(White) Baker, was born in Washington County, O. The subject of this sketch came to Athens when twenty years of age and was employed as a clerk in the drug store of John Perkins for two years. He then went to California where he worked in the gold mines in Placer and Butte counties about two years, returning home in February, 1854, making his adventure a success. In March of the same year he became associated with his former employer, John Perkins, in the drug business, under the firm name of Perkins & Baker, they doing business until 1859. He then engaged in the clothing and merchant tailoring business with F. L. Ballard under the firm name of Baker & Ballard, they discontinuing in 1861. In July of that year he entered the Union army as Captain of Company C, Thirty-ninth Regiment, Ohio Volunteer Infantry, and served as such until November, 1862, when he was commissioned Commissary of Subsistence by President Lincoln, and served under General Sherman until the fall of Vicksburg in July, 1863, when, broken down in health, he was sent home on a leave of absence. In the following November he was ordered to report to General Stephen A. Hulburt at Memphis, Tenn., and was by him ordered on duty at La Grange, Tenn., where he remained until March, 1864, when he served as Commissary of General A. J. Smith's command during the Red River expedition, until May, 1864. Having returned with that command to Memphis his health again became impaired and he was ordered by the General War Department to report to General Pope at Milwaukee, Wis., and by him to report to General Sibley at St. Paul, Minn., who ordered him on duty as Commissary of the Post at Fort Snelling, where he remained until Nov. 22, 1864, when he was ordered to report to General A. J. Smith at Nashville, Tenn., and remained with that command during the battle of Nashville, and the pursuit of the enemy to Eastport, Miss. Soon after the command was ordered to New Orleans where it was organized into the Sixteenth Army Corps, and our subject was commissioned Chief Commissary with the rank of Lieutenant-Colonel, and was with that corps at the siege and capture of Mobile and Montgomery, Ala., until April, 1865. At Montgomery he served as Chief Commissary of that department until December, 1865, when he was ordered to report at St. Louis, Mo., and from there home to Athens to await further orders; was mustered out of the service there Jan. 16, 1866. During that summer he went to West Virginia, and engaged in the oil business until the spring of 1867, when he returned to Athens and was elected Mayor and Justice of the Peace, and served as such until September, 1869, when he was elected Treasurer of Athens County and held that office by re-election for two terms. In 1872 he was elected Clerk of the Courts of Athens County and filled that position for nine consecutive years. For six months in 1881 he owned a half interest in the *Athens County Republican,* when he sold and then established his present business. May 2, 1854, he married Amanda Mahon, of Blairsville, Pa. They have four children—Edward H., attorney at law, Cincinnati, O.; Anna B., Clara A., and Rollins M., at home. He is a prominent Mason and member of the lodge, chapter and commandery of Athens. Himself, wife and three of his children are members of the Methodist Episcopal church.

Francis M. Barker, farmer, of Athens Township, eldest son of Joseph and Ruth (Griffith) Barker, was born in Athens Township, Athens Co., Ohio, April 23, 1836. At the age of twenty-one years he began working for himself. In 1858 he began farming for himself on his father's and other farms. Nov. 4, 1861, he enlisted in Company D, Seventy-Fifth Ohio Volunteer Infantry, for three years, as a private, and was appointed Corporal of his company. He was with his company on duty until March 26, 1862. While at Huttonville, W. Va., he was accidentally wounded, and returned home on furlough, and remained until June following, when he returned to his command at Middletown, Va. From there he was sent to Baltimore, Md., to the hospital, and there discharged for disability, Aug. 9, 1862. He then returned to his home in Athens County. In 1863 he purchased eighty acres joining his father's farm, and lived there until 1865. He then sold his farm and purchased the one on which he now resides. Nov. 11, 1858, he married Amanda, daughter of Derick and Eliza (Saring) Byrd, of York Township. They have five children—Charles, Thaddeus W., Bertha B. (wife of Clarence Winget, of Lee Township), Rutha E. and Michael L. He is a Master Mason, and a member of Constitution Lodge, No. 426, Marshfield, Ohio; is Senior Warden of the lodge. He is also a member of Columbus Golden Post, No. 89, G. A. R., Athens, Ohio. His wife is a member of the Protestant Methodist church.

Judge Isaac Barker, Jr., came to Athens when a young man, in 1798, where he lived continuously until the time of his death, March 30, 1873, at the age of ninety-four years. It is not, though, by virtue of his long residence here or the fact that he was a pioneer, that we give him a place in this chapter, but because he was a man of ability and accomplishments, a public man of model character and habits. Judge Barker was born at Long Plains, near New Bedford, Mass., Feb. 17, 1779, the son of Isaac and Rhoda (Cooke) Barker. Isaac Barker, Sr., was a lineal descendant of Robert Barker, a Welshman, who emigrated to Plymouth Colony prior to 1630, and afterward became a colonial official. In 1789 he came with his father's family to Ohio, where they settled on a farm near the present site of Belpre, a mile above the garrison soon afterward built and known in pioneer history as "Farmer's Castle." At the outbreak of the Indian war of 1790-'94, the savages commenced warfare on the settlement, killing and harrassing the field laborers and capturing prisoners, compelling a part of each family to stand on guard while the remainder worked and slept, destroying their stock and scanty crops until the entire settlement was compelled to take refuge in the garrison, where they suffered from disease and privation for two or three years, and were only relieved by the final treaty of peace concluded by General Wayne. Here in Belpre our subject spent the nine years of his pioneer life, having as companions the Putnams, Devols, Smiths, Danas, Rouses, Stones, Cookes, Bents, Brownings and many other families of more or less prominence in pioneer annals. In 1798 the family removed to Athens, then a village of half a dozen cabins, and settled on a farm. Judge Barker's education was acquired principally by private study. His first business on his own account after coming to Athens was that of hotel keeping. His hotel was on the site of the old Brown House, just in front of the college. After remaining here three years he removed to his long residence on the corner of College and State streets in 1818. During his residence in Athens, Judge Barker served ten years as Associate Judge of Common Pleas Court, and held the offices of County Sheriff, County Treasurer, and Collector of rents for the University, each a number of years.

James Ashton Benson, Superintendent of the Hamley Run coal mines, was born in the city of Buffalo, N. Y., Jan. 7, 1837. When he was five years of age his parents, Michael and Harriet (Ashton) Benson, removed to Sheboygan, Wis. He was educated in the public schools of Sheboygan and at the Lawrence University, at Appleton, Wis. When becoming of age he followed teaching school in Manitowoc and Sheboygan counties until 1862, when he came to Ohio and located at Nelsonville, Athens County, where he was employed to take charge of a store for his uncle, Charles Ashton. In 1865 his uncle died, and he and A. B. Walker were appointed administrators of the estate, requiring a year or more to settle it up. In February, 1865, he removed to Athens and engaged in the mercantile business until September, 1868, when he removed his business to Nelsonville. In 1873 he gave up merchandising and was employed as weigh-master at the coal mine of W. B. Brooks until 1878. He then went to Shawnee, O., where he carried on the mercantile business until 1882, when he returned to Athens and took charge of the Hamley Run coal mines as Superintendent for H. C. Wells & Co., of Columbus, O. While residing in Nelsonville, in 1873, he was elected City Clerk and during 1873 and 1874 served as a member of the Board of Education of that city. May 29, 1865, he was married to Aggie, daughter of Cornelius Steinrod, of Nelsonville. They have three children—George Edwin, Hattie and Abbie. Mr. Benson is a member of Paramuthia Lodge, No. 25, A. F. & A. M., of Athens.

James Crawford Bower was born Jan. 30, 1835, near Pittsburg, Pa., where he was reared and received a common-school education. He was the third of seven sons of Alexander and Martha (Couch) Bower, with whom he lived till fifteen years of age when he was apprenticed to learn the blacksmith's trade, serving three years and seven months. After working as a journeyman about a year, he, in March, 1855, came to Athens County, Ohio, and established himself in a shop at Pleasanton, where he remained till 1862, being at the same time engaged in farming. In 1862 he was commissioned a recruiting officer with the rank of First Lieutenant, and recruited Company I, Ninety-second Ohio Infantry, going into the service with them as First Lieutenant. He served about nine months when he resigned on account of sickness. In April, 1864, he went to Montana; worked at his trade there till October, 1866, and then returned to Athens County, locating in Albany, where he opened a shop. In 1877 he moved on to a farm in the vicinity of Albany and carried on the farm in connection with blacksmithing. In 1880 he came to Athens, where he is now engaged in the dairy business. Aug. 15, 1855, he married Louisa Cooley, of Pleasanton. They have five children—Loduska, Emma, William, Charles, and Hattie. Mr. Bower has been Coroner of Athens County since the fall of 1878. He is a Master, Royal Arch, Council and Knight Templar Mason, and a member of lodge, chapter, council and commandery at Athens. He has served as Junior Warden of his lodge. He is also a member of Athenian Lodge, No. 497, K. of P., and Columbus Golden Post, No. 89, G. A. R.

Daniel Boyd, deceased, was born in the county of Donegal, in the Northern part of Ireland, in September, 1794. His ancestors came from Scotland. His opportunities for obtaining an education were limited, but by improving his spare hours while learning the weaver's trade, he acquired a good education. He had a natural love of books, and was a constant reader, and in after life whatever luxuries his circumstances might compel him to forego, newspapers and periodicals were always to be found in his home. In boyhood he had become familiar with the wrongs and hardships of the Irish people. His father, Robert Boyd, possessed a small leasehold estate, which he intended to divide among his four sons. But Daniel, having read of the rich land and free air of the western world set his heart on seeking a new home free from exacting tithes and odious rents. Succeeding in obtaining sufficient money with which to pay his passage he came to America, landing at Philadelphia in 1819. He walked over the mountains to Steubenville, Ohio, where he found employment as a teacher and afterward as a weaver. In 1827 he removed to Keene, Coshocton County, where he engaged in the mercantile business, near which place he had located his parents and younger brothers and sisters who followed him to America in 1822. His business proving a failure he became deeply involved in debt. In 1838 he removed to Athens County, Ohio, and settled on a farm in Carthage Township, where he died in 1867, and where for nearly thirty years he was highly respected as a man of the strictest integrity, warm sympathy, and generous impulses. Here, after many years of hard labor, he succeeded in paying off his indebtedness with its heavily accrued interest. He was a member of the Methodist Episcopal church, and gave liberally of his means for its support, and at his house the "itinerant" was always a welcome guest. He took a deep interest in educational institutions, especially the common schools of the vicinity. In 1825 he was married to Jane Elliott, a sister of Rev. Charles Elliott, widely known in the Methodist Episcopal denomination as a minister, editor and author. They were blessed with nine children—John Elliott, a physician, who died at Columbia in 1855; Mary Ann, who died in 1867; Jane, a prominent teacher of Athens County; Kate, Principal of the Athens High School; Hugh, a graduate of Ohio University in class of 1859, afterward a member of the Ohio Conference of the Methodist Episcopal church, and since 1871 Professor of the Greek and Latin Languages in Cornell College, Iowa; Lucy, formerly a teacher in the Nelsonville school, but now teaching in the Orphan's Home of Xenia; William Fletcher, a graduate of the Ohio University in the class of 1866, now attorney at law at Cincinnati; Fanny Blair, wife of Charles Lawrence, Esq., of Carthage Township; and Margaret, who taught for several years in the Cincinnati Wesleyan College and is now Principal of the High School at Martinsville, Ind. She is the first lady graduate of the Ohio University. After the death of their father, in 1867, the family sold the farm and removed to Athens where they procured a pleasant home and where those remaining at home still live, and with them their mother, happily and contented at the age of eighty years.

Hon. Archibald Green Brown, born at Waterford, Washington Co., Ohio, April 16, 1798, is of Puritan stock. His father was Captain Benjamin Brown of Revolutionary fame, who came from Massachusetts in 1776, and settled in Washington County, Ohio. Our subject was educated in the Ohio University at Athens, graduating in the close of 1822, and is now the oldest living graduate of that institution. In the latter part of 1822 he went to Columbus, Ohio, where he taught in an academy until the following year, when he returned to Athens and taught in the preparatory department of his *alma mater* from September of that year until the spring of 1825. In the summer of 1825 he established the Athens *Mirror*, the first paper published in Athens County, the publication of which he continued until 1830. In July, 1825, he was appointed, by the Court of Common Pleas, Recorder of Athens County, which he subsequently held, by election, for a period of thirteen years. Prior to 1826 he was elected Justice of the Peace of Athens, and held that office continuously until about 1850. In 1834, while filling the office of Justice of the Peace and County Recorder, he taught a private school in Athens, and, having in the meantime privately studied law, was admitted to the bar at Athens, during the same year. In April, 1850, he was elected member of the Constitutional Convention that framed the present Constitution of Ohio, and in July of the same year was appointed Presiding Judge of the Eighth Judicial Circuit, to fill a vacancy, and held that office until February, 1852. Since then he has devoted his life to his profession and has built up an enviable reputation as a real-estate lawyer. In 1841 he became a Trustee of the Ohio

University, and still fills that position. Jan. 8, 1824, he married Priscilla K. Crippen, by whom he had five children—Henry T., attorney at law, Athens; Louis W., late of Athens, who was for some fifteen years Clerk of the Court of Athens County, and who died Sept. 29, 1873, at the age of forty-two; the others died in infancy. He has been a member of the First Presbyterian Church of Athens since 1819 and a Ruling Elder since 1833.

Charles Henry Brown, born Nov. 26, 1846, in Athens, Ohio, is the youngest of three children of Charles Pitt and Angeline Elizabeth (Crippen) Brown, and grandson of the late General W. Brown, an old pioneer of Athens County. He was educated in the Athens High School and the Ohio University, it being his intention to graduate from the latter, in the class of 1865. He was suspended for a minor offense, and afterward reinstated, but considering the suspension unjust he withdrew from the class, and spent the next two years in teaching. April 7, 1867, he married Ann Eliza, daughter of Harvey and Abbie (Calvert) Carpenter, of Canaan Township, who died Oct. 23, 1867. After his marriage he settled on a farm in Canaan Township, which he still owns and carries on in connection with his other business. In 1874 he was employed by the Adams Express Company and worked for them in different capacities for five years. In 1879 he received his present situation as bill clerk for the M. & C. R. R. In 1877 he married Ada Earhart, from whom he was divorced in 1880. Feb. 7, 1881, he married Ada J., daughter of Hiram Hill, of Marietta, Ohio.

General John Brown was a resident of Athens County from 1799 to the time of his death, March 28, 1876. He was born in Rowe, Mass., Dec. 1, 1785, descended from a good family, a number of his ancestral relatives holding high positions, both military and civil. He came with his father's family to the Northwest Territory in 1799, settling in Ames Township. He took advantage of the superior school advantages at that time in Ames Township, supplementing his education by private study. He married, in 1811, Miss Sophia Walker, daughter of Dr. Ezra Walker, and removed to Athens in 1817, where he resided continuously to the time of his death. For the first year he kept a hotel on the lot afterward owned by Judge Barker, and then purchased the lot and built the house long known as the Brown House, in front of the college campus. Here he kept hotel continuously until 1865, a period of forty-seven years. In 1808 he was elected Captain in the militia, was subsequently made Colonel, and in 1817 was elected Brigadier-General. He was County Auditor from 1822 to 1827, and was Treasurer of the Ohio University from 1824 until June, 1874, more than half a century. He was Mayor of Athens for several years and held the office of Coroner two terms. He was a man universally respected and for many years kindly regarded as one of the most worthy fathers of the village, "who has come down to us from a former generation." He had a kind heart, good judgment, and perfect honor.

Granville Currier Brown, of the firm of G. C. Brown & Co., proprietors of the "Warren House," Athens, was born in Athens, May 16, 1853, where he was reared and educated in the public schools. He is the son of Oscar W. and Adaline S. (Currier) Brown. At the age of seventeen he began to clerk in the store of W. W. Love & Co., at Athens, remaining with them three years. He was then variously employed for one year, and in 1874 began to clerk in the Brown Hotel, for Major Elmer Golden, remaining with him in that and the Warren House until November, 1882, when he became associated with W. H. Brown, under the firm name of G. C. Brown & Co., proprietors of the Warren House, Athens, he having the full charge of the house. He is a Master Mason, and member of Paramuthia Lodge, No. 25, Athens.

Henry Thomas Brown, attorney, Athens, was born in Athens, Nov. 11, 1825. He is the oldest of two sons of Hon. Archibald Green Brown, a pioneer lawyer, and a native of Ohio. His mother, Priscilla King Crippen, was a native of New York. He was educated in Ohio University, at Athens. He chose his father's profession, and at the age of nineteen began the study of law in his office. He was admitted to the bar by the Supreme Court at Pomeroy, Ohio, in 1846, and at once began to practice at Athens. In 1852 he became associated with his father, under the firm name of A. G. & H. T. Brown. In 1860 L. A. Koons became associated with them, changing the firm name to Brown & Koons. In 1864 Mr. Brown entered the Union Army as First Lieutenant and Quartermaster of the One Hundred and Forty-First Regiment, Ohio National Guards, and served five months. Dec. 16, 1847, he married Charlotte M. Fuller, of Athens, by whom he has five children—Charlotte E., wife of Henry D. Mirick, of Athens; Herbert H., of Parsons, Kan.; Mabel King and Bertha B., living at home; and Harold, of Nebraska. They lost one son, Carlos Louis, who died at Athens, June 30, 1878, at the age of twenty-two. He s an Odd Fellow, and a member of Sereno Lodge, No. 479, and of Athens Encampment, No. 175, and has held all the positions in both bodies. He is a member of the First Presbyterian Church of Athens.

James Dickey Brown, a banker of Athens, son of John and Susan (Green) Brown, was born at Albany, Athens Co., Ohio, Aug. 27, 1845. He was educated in the High School of his native town. In the spring of 1865, at the age of nineteen, he became associated with his father in the mercantile business at Albany, under the firm name of John Brown & Son. They discontinued the mercantile business in the fall of 1867, and engaged in private banking at Albany, under the same firm name. In the fall of 1868 they removed to Athens, and established the Bank of Athens, carrying on private banking together there, until the death of the senior member of the firm, Oct. 18, 1875. Since then our subject has carried on the business alone. In 1865 he enlisted in Company H, One Hundred and Forty-First Ohio Volunteer Infantry, as a private, and served on guard duty 100 days, at Barboursville, W. Va. May 23, 1867, he married Lizzie, daughter of Elmer Armstrong, Esq., of Athens County. They have two children, John and Jennie Jaynes. Mr. Brown and wife are members of the First Presbyterian Church, of Athens, of which church he has been a Ruling Elder since April, 1875. Our subject is a Mason, a member of Paramuthia Lodge, No. 25, A. F. & A. M., of Athens.

John Brown.—The founder of the Brown family in America was William Brown, who came to this country from England in 1660, and settled in Hatfield, Mass. Sixty years later, in 1720, the family removed to Leicester, Mass., where, at an advanced age, William Brown died. Captain John Brown, son of William, came with the family to Leicester, and was there elected to the Massachusetts Legislature and served with ability for twenty successive years. He was twice married and the father of nineteen children. His eldest son was John Brown, a Revolutionary soldier, who was twice wounded at the historic battle of Bunker Hill. He came to Ohio in 1797, settling in Washington County. His eldest son, Samuel Brown, father of our subject, was also a Revolutionary soldier. He came to Ohio with his parents in 1797, landing at Marietta, and settled in Athens County, Dover Township. His wife was Lydia Thayre, of Taunton, Mass. They were the parents of seven children, five of whom were born before and two after they came to Ohio. Their names, in the order of their birth, were—Samuel

B., William T., Phœbe, Lydia, Betsey, Harriet and John. John Brown was born in Ames Township, Athens, (then Washington) Co., Ohio, Dec. 23, 1801. While he was still a child his parents removed to a farm within nine miles of Marietta. In 1836 he married Susan Green, of Washington County, who was a faithful wife to him and a devoted mother to his children till her death, Aug. 19, 1859. In 1838 he removed to Trimble Township, and two years later to Albany. In 1868 he took up his residence in Athens, where he remained till his death, Oct. 18, 1875. Throughout his career he sustained a marked character. In whatever community he lived, wherever his influence extended, he was recognized as a man of sagacity and strength. Without high official station and without undue self-assertion, he was, by inherent superiority, a public man. The only public office he ever held was that of County Commissioner, to which he was three times elected without his consent and against his wishes, and he was probably the ablest, or at least one of the ablest, that ever filled that position in Athens County. In any suitable notice of the man a prominent place must be given to his intellectual character; and first, when the circumstances of his life are considered, one cannot but be struck by his mental force and individuality. His educational advantages were limited. At ten years of age he went one or two terms to a district school, and at nineteen went about half a year to the High School in Marietta. At the former he learned little, if anything, beyond reading and spelling, but on this foundation, slender as it was, he never ceased to build. When thirteen years old he began the study of arithmetic at home, and having, with his mother's assistance, mastered the fundamental rules, he pressed on alone. During the six or seven months he spent at Marietta he devoted eighteen hours a day to study and recitation. Not being satisfied with the work required in school, he took up besides both chemistry and physics, and pursued them in private with his usual exactness and thoroughness. Soon after leaving school he became a teacher, and for twelve or fourteen years taught in winter and worked on his farm in summer. To the general public he was best known as a business man. In practical matters he displayed clear perceptions, sound judgment and great caution, and he managed his affairs with such care and discretion that he succeeded in building up no inconsiderable fortune. He was a man of exact and general information, and made himself familiar with geology, botany, chemistry, astronomy, physics, and was also well read in medicine.

Like Terence he could say, "I count nothing pertaining to man foreign to me." His moral character was as sharply defined as his intellectual character. His life was pure, temperate and honest. The most distinctive features of his moral character were courage and justice. His courage had nothing of bravado; he took a courageous position as a matter of course. In an early day to be an Abolitionist was to suffer ostracism. Yet he was one of the few to openly and strongly avow himself a friend of the slave. Abolitionism was no mere sentiment with him; he studied the subject till he was more than a match for his ablest opponents. He was a man of much kindness and even tenderness of feeling. Toward cases of distress he was among the most benevolent. At the time of his death he was President of the Bank of Athens, his son James D. being Cashier. He always merited as he received the confidence and patronage of the public, and in his death Athens lost one of her best and most influential citizens.

Eber Green Carpenter, M. D., is a native of New Hampshire, the son of Dr. Eber and Judith Green Carpenter. He was born in Alstead, Cheshire County, August, 1808, and was reared and educated in his native town. His father and brother being physicians, he studied medicine under them and graduated as M. D. from the Berkshire Medical College, an adjunct of Williams College, in 1831. He then practiced at Lempster, N. H., until 1833 when he came to Ohio and located at Chester, the county seat of Meigs County. On account of impaired health during 1836 he made a visit to his native State, and on returning to Ohio, permanently located at Athens, where he practiced continuously until March, 1879, when he had the misfortune to fracture the neck of his thigh bone, the result of a fall, which not uniting rendered him a cripple. Not being able to endure the fatigue of practicing, he was obliged to abandon it. October, 1833, he married Miss Mary Kellogg Stanley, a daughter of the late Timothy Stanley, of Marietta, Ohio. They have had five children—Mary P., wife of R. De Steiger, of Athens; George H., deceased, a physician who was accidently killed in Missouri in 1861; Helen M., wife of J. L. Hatfield, recently a Professor in the Ohio University at Athens, but now of Missouri; Emma, unmarried; and Julia, wife of Dr. R. W. Erwin, of Bay City, Mich. Dr. and Mrs. Carpenter are members of the First Presbyterian Church of Athens. He was made a Master Mason at Alstead, N. H., in 1832.

Parker Carpenter, son of Frederick and Mary W. (Johnson) Carpenter, was born in Rome Township, Athens Co., Ohio, Nov. 4, 1831. When he was four years of age his parents came to Athens Township, where he was reared and has spent the most of his life, engaged in farming. From 1863 to 1868 he combined tanning with his farm labor. In 1869 he was elected Assessor of Athens Township, serving a year. In 1872 he was nominated Sheriff of Athens County on the Republican ticket, but was defeated. In 1874 he was again nominated by the same party and elected, and in 1876 was re-elected to the same office, serving continuously four years. From 1872 to 1874 he served as Deputy Sheriff under Sheriff N. Warren. In 1882 he was elected Trustee of Athens Township, still holding that office. Oct. 12, 1853, he married Elizabeth C. Knowles, of Alexander Township, who died June 18, 1874. Feb. 26, 1876, he married Jane D. Cook, of Alexander Township. They have three children—Frederick, R. F., and Hattie May. Mr. Carpenter is a member of Sereno Lodge, No. 479, I. O. O. F., Athens.

John Porterfield Coe, Treasurer of Athens County, was born in Ohio County, W.Va., Oct. 5, 1842. His father, Silas Coe, was a native of Pennsylvania, and his mother, Emily (Porterfield) Coe, of Ohio. In his seventh year he came with his parents to Athens County, they settling on a farm near Athens, where he lived with them until his nineteenth year. He was given only a common-school education. On leaving home, in 1861, he enlisted in the Union army as a private in Company C, Thirty-sixth Regiment, Ohio Volunteer Infantry, and served during the war. In 1863 he was promoted to Corporal, to Sergeant in 1864, and to First or Orderly Sergeant in May, 1865, but had acted as Orderly Sergeant from May, 1864. During his time of service he was only twice on the sick list, once by camp fever and again by an injured ankle, caused by a spent ball. He participated in all the battles in which his regiment took part, the most important being South Mountain, Antietam, Chickamauga, Mission Ridge, and the battles in the Shenandoah Valley, during Sherman's campaign. He was mustered out of the service in August, 1865, when he returned home to Athens County. In March, 1866, he went to Vinton County, where he engaged in farming and dealing in stock. In the fall of 1867 he returned to Athens County, and again engaged in farming and dealing in stock, making sheep a specialty. In the fall of 1879 he was the Republican nominee for Treasurer of Athens County.

and was elected by a handsome majority, and was elected his own successor without opposition in the fall of 1881. In 1870 he was elected Clerk of Lee Township, which he held for nine consecutive years, until his election as County Treasurer in 1879. Oct. 25, 1866, he married Lucy, daughter of Edward Blake, late County Commissioner of Athens County, by whom he has five children— Flora Alice, William Wallace, Perry Glenn, Frank Edward, and Mary Elsa. He is a member of Athenian Lodge, No. 104, K. of P., of which he is Treasurer. Himself and wife are members of the First Alexander Cumberland Presbyterian Church of Alexander Township.

Colonel Robert Albert Constable, attorney at law, Athens, is the only son of the late Robert E. Constable, a prominent lawyer of Athens, a native of Maryland, who came to Athens in 1826, and died at that place Jan. 19, 1883. His mother was Elizabeth H. (Barker) Constable, a native of Athens. He was born at Athens in March, 1830, where he was reared and educated in the private school and at the Ohio University. At the age of seventeen, in 1847, he began the study of law in his father's office and was admitted to the bar by the Supreme Court at Delaware, O., in June, 1851. However he did not enter upon the practice of law at once, but engaged in the mercantile business until 1854, when he became associated with his father and formed the law firm of Constable & Constable. They remained together until 1878 when, on account of failing health, his father retired from the firm. At the breaking out of the war in 1861, being a Brigadier-General of militia, his brigade being composed of Washington, Athens, Meigs and Gallia counties, he, with Captain J. M. Dana, went to Columbus and offered his services to Governor Dennison, by whom he was authorized to recruit 2,000 men for the United States service, which he did and sent forward. In 1861 he helped to raise the Seventy-fifth Regiment, Ohio Volunteer Infantry, and was commissioned Lieutenant-Colonel. Soon after, the Colonel, N. C. McLane, being promoted to Brigadier-General, he was promoted to Colonel. At the battle of McDowell, Va., in April, 1862, while sick with typhoid fever, he was taken prisoner by the Confederates, and was incarcerated at Libby Prison and Salisbury four months, and at Belle Island one day, when he was exchanged under the first cartel for the exchange of prisoners. He then returned home on a leave of absence and remained until October of that year, when he rejoined his regiment at Fairfax Court-House, Va. In 1863 he, not endorsing President

Lincoln's emancipation, like many others, resigned his commission, returned to Athens and resumed the practice of law. June 10, 1851, he married Martha S., daughter of Professor Joseph Dana, of Athens, by whom he has four children—Elizabeth A., wife of W. R. Flinn, of North Adams, Mich.; Ethel Dana, Anna and Henry Lee, at home. He is a member of Columbus Golden Post, No. 89, G. A. R., of which he is Commander, and also is a member of the National Council of Administration of the same order.

Robert E. Constable was born at Chestertown, Kent Co., Md., Nov. 29, 1809. He began his education in Maryland, and became very thoroughly grounded in the languages before he came to Athens, in July, 1826. Here he entered the Ohio University, and remained as a student until about half through the senior year, when he was married to Elizabeth H. Barker, daughter of Judge Isaac Barker, May 5, 1829. Soon after that time he was elected Recorder of Athens County. He studied law during his term of office and was admitted to the bar in the spring of 1835, at Jackson, O. He entered upon the practice of law in Athens County and was elected soon afterward Prosecuting Attorney. This position he resigned, in order to be able to practice as criminal lawyer and counselor. He was a leading and successful lawyer in this part of the State until his health failed him, when he was obliged to retire from practice. He was very active in all his undertakings. As a lawyer he was markedly successful in addressing a jury, and his ability was most specially adapted to the conducting of criminal cases. He was an orator of merit, and was chosen at different times as chief speaker on important occasions, being a devoted member of the old Whig party. In his most active days he was as a politician justly considered as entitled to the respect and confidence of the people. In the later years of his life he was so afflicted that it was impossible for him to be active in the scenes of public and social life. In the year 1827 Mr. Constable became a Christian and joined the Methodist Episcopal church; but in later years he became a member of the Episcopalian society, organized at Athens. He had been reared as an Episcopalian originally. He died at Athens, Jan. 19, 1883, leaving one son, R. A. Constable.

Thomas Andrew Cooper, carpenter and joiner, was born near Chestnut Flat, Walker Co., Ga., Sept. 16, 1838, the eldest of twelve children of Andrew and Nancy (White) Cooper. He received a limited education in the common schools of that country, and worked on the farm with his father until he was nineteen years old.

He continued farming for himself until March, 1862, when circumstances forced him into the service of the Confederate States, and he was assigned as a private to the Army of Virginia under Jackson, and participated in the battles of Bristow Station, second Bull Run, Fredericksburg, Chancellorsville, Spottsylvania Court-house, Monocacy, Md., Lynchburg, Va., and in the several engagements in the Shenandoah Valley during the campaign of 1864. In September, 1864, he came to Parkersburg, W. Va., and engaged to work at gardening for T. T. Davidson, near that place, until January, 1865, when he was employed by the New York Oil Company as carpenter, in Wood County, W. Va., until March of the same year. He then came to Marietta, O., and entered the employ of the Marietta & Cincinnati Railroad Company as bridge carpenter under S. M. Wright, foreman. In February, 1868, he entered the employ of Gould & Smith, contractors, on the Columbus & Hocking Valley Railroad, as bridge carpenter, and worked for them until November, 1868. He then formed a partnership with T. T. Davidson, near Parkersburg, W. Va., for the purpose of market gardening, the firm name being Davidson & Cooper. In September of same year they dissolved partnership, and Mr. Cooper came to Athens, O., and again entered the employ of Gould & Smith and worked for them until the Hocking Valley Road was completed. In July, 1870, he was employed by Gould & Wright as bridge carpenter in the construction of the Hope Furnace branch of the M. & C. R. R., and also the Straitsville branch of the Columbus & Hocking Valley Railroad. In November, 1870, he was employed by the Salina Salt and Coal Company, until July, 1871; then by the Columbus & Hocking Valley Railroad Company until May, 1872; then by Joseph Herrold until January, 1873; then by S. M. Wright at Hamley Run Coal Works till January, 1874; then by G. T. Gould at Salina until January, 1877; and by the Hocking Valley Coal and Salt Company at Chauncey, Ohio, until January, 1878. During the years of 1878, 1879 and 1880 he was variously engaged at the trade in Athens, and in the spring was employed by the C. & H. V. Railroad Company at Columbus, where he worked until April, 1882. He was then employed by William Gladfelter, of Springfield, O., contractor and builder, and worked for him until Oct. 9, 1882, when he returned to Athens. Aug. 9, 1857, he was married to Miss Sarah Elizabeth, daughter of Sexton and Martha Ann (Williams) Humphres. They have five living children—Annie; Lizzie, wife of W. H. McGill, Columbus, O.; Carrie May, Alfred Mintun and Leola Rosalie. Mr. Cooper is a Master Mason and member of Paramuthia Lodge, No. 25. He has filled the office of Senior Deacon two years, 1880 and 1881.

Lewis William Connett, proprietor of the Stewart Flouring Mills, Athens, was born in Dover Township, Athens County, Aug. 23, 1851, a son of George and Lydia (Dorr) Connett. He was educated in the schools of his native county and at the Ohio University. His mother died when he was fourteen and he then began to work for himself. When nineteen years of age he went to Chauncey and clerked for J. C. McCracken a year. He then went to Greenfield, Ind., and engaged in the mercantile business there till 1874. In 1875 he came to Athens and was employed till 1877 as bookkeeper in the Grange store. He then engaged in the grocery business till 1881, when he rented the Stewart Flouring Mill. He was married May 4, 1881, to Mary, daughter of Henry Brown, of Athens. They have one child—Lewis Henry. Mr. Connett is a member of the Methodist and his wife of the First Presbyterian Church, of Athens. He is a member of Lodge No. 104, K. of P., of which he is Chancellor Commander.

John Everett Cornell, proprietor of the Cornell House, Athens, Ohio, was born at Chester, Meigs Co., Ohio, July 5, 1847. He lived with his parents, Frank and Amelia (Branch) Cornell, until his sixteenth year, when he was employed as a clerk in the wholesale hardware house of R. W. Booth & Co., Cincinnati, Ohio, one year, and then as cashier in Hunt's dining rooms of the same city for nearly two years. He then went to Guysville, Ohio, where he clerked in the store of his father and uncle until 1868, when he removed with his father to New Vienna, Ohio, where he clerked for him until 1869. At that time he was employed as bookkeeper in the office of the C., H. & D. R. R. Company at Cincinnati until 1870. He then came to Athens County and engaged in farming in the vicinity of Athens until 1871, when he went to Washington C.-H., Fayette Co., Ohio, and kept a confectionery store and restaurant until August, 1872, when he returned to Athens and opened the Cornell House with his father, as F. Cornell & Son. In 1881 his father retired from the firm and he became sole proprietor. March 29, 1870, he was married to Miss Lizzie West, of Martinsville, Ohio. They have two children—Blanch and Adine.

William Cornell, farmer, is the second son of Eli and Elizabeth (Dilley) Cornell, and was born near Elizabethtown, Wood Co., W. Va., Aug. 17, 1836. When a small boy his parents came to Athens County, O., and purchased a farm near Salina, where he was reared, and was educated in the common schools. He began business for himself, mining coal at Salina, O., and was thus engaged for six years. In 1859 and 1860 he and his brother Rufus were engaged in farming. April, 1861, they enlisted in Company A, Twenty-second Ohio Volunteer Infantry, as privates, for three months. At the expiration of his term of enlistment he was mustered out at Athens, O., and returned home, his brother Rufus enlisting in the First West Virgina Cavalry for three years. After remaining at home for a few months, he enlisted in Company I, Sixty-third Ohio Volunteer Infantry, at Chillicothe, for three years, or during the war, as a private. At the organization of his regiment, he was elected First Lieutenant of his company, and served as such until July, 1863, when he was promoted to Captain of Company D, same regiment, and commanded the company until their term of service expired, Dec. 21, 1864. He was engaged in the battles of New Madrid, Island No. 10, Fort Pillow, Farmington, Parker's Cross Roads, Iuka, and Corinth, Miss. He was with Sherman to the sea, and was in the battles of Dallas, Kennesaw Mountain, Siege of Atlanta, and all the battles to Savannah, where his regiment was discharged. He has served as Trustee of his township for four years. He is a Master Mason and member of Paramuthia Lodge, No. 25, F. & A. M., Athens, O. He has been twice married. May, 1860, he married Sarah, daughter of Thomas and Barbara (Young) Wilson, of Athens Township. January, 1861, his wife died. Nov. 11, 1866, he was married to Annie C., daughter of Isaac and Christie Ann (Harper) Matheny. They have five children—Angie B., Cora D., Manley G., Russel R., Stella M., all living at home. Their daughter, Ella W., died April 9, 1882, in her eleventh year. Himself and wife are members of the Methodist Episcopal church. His brother Rufus, of the West Virginia Cavalry, was killed while reconnoitering in front of the enemy near Antietam, Md., Sept. 4, 1862.

David Colman Cornwell, jeweler, of Athens, was born near Athens, Oct. 15, 1844. He lived with his parents, John and Ann (Cowell), Cornwell, until manhood, and learned the jeweler's trade in his father's shop in Athens. After becoming of age he engaged in farming near Athens two years, when he went to Nelsonville and worked at his trade nearly two years, which, not agreeing with his health, he abandoned and again pursued farming for two years. In 1871 he established his present business at Athens. He has been twice married. He married his first wife, Mary A. Tedrow, of Athens, March 21, 1865. She died June 15, 1868, leaving two children—Mary Luella and Eber H. May 21, 1873, he married Sarah J., daughter of James Thomas, of Londonderry, Ross Co., Ohio. They have four children — David B., Alma E., Sadie T. and Clifford. Mr. and Mrs. Cornwell are members of the Methodist Episcopal church. He is a member of Sereno Lodge, No. 479, I. O. O. F., of which he is Secretary. Politically he is an avowed Prohibitionist. During the late Rebellion, in 1865, he enlisted in Company B, One Hundred and Forty-first, O. N. G., for 100 days, and served on guard duty at Barboursville, Ky.

John Cornwell was born in Hallowell, Prince Edward Co., Upper Canada, May 17, 1812. He is of English ancestry. His father, David Cornwell, and his mother, Phœbe Gilbert Goldsmith, emigrated from England and settled in Canada in early times. When five years of age our subject came, with his parents, to Ohio, settling near Gallipolis, where he lived with them until he was seventeen. After living in Meigs County two years, he, in 1831, came to Athens, where, after attending the Ohio University one year, he settled, and engaged in the jewelry business till 1852, when he went to California and mined for gold, and was variously employed until 1856. He then returned to Athens and resumed the jeweler's business, remaining here till 1871, when he removed to McArthur, Vinton County. April 20, 1837, he married Ann Cowell, who was born in Berkshire, England, Sept. 20, 1815. When four years of age she immigrated to America with her mother and relatives, her father being dead. They had nine children, five sons and four daughters. He resided at McArthur until the death of his wife, Feb. 20, 1878, when he began to live with his children. He is now living with his son, David C. Cornwell, at Athens. He experienced religion in 1830 and joined the Presbyterian church, from which he withdrew in 1834 and joined the Methodist church. In 1851 he was ordained a Deacon. He has been a member of the church at Athens since 1868.

Alanson Courtney, farmer, was born near Newport, Washington Co., Ohio, Aug. 26, 1797. He is the oldest son of Neal and Mary (McLane) Courtney. He lived with his parents until manhood, receiving a common-school education. At the age of twenty-one years he purchased a farm in Dover Township, Athens Co., Ohio, and has farmed it up to the present time. May, 1818, he married Nancy, daughter of Samuel and Mary Camby, of Athens County. They had nine children, seven now living—Mary, wife of Joseph Eten, of Chauncey, Ohio; Caroline, wife of Peter Hixson, Ames Township; Louisa, wife of Robert Carpenter, of Monroe County, Ohio; Allen V. M., Rufus, Henrietta and Zimrode. His son, Alonzo Courtney, enlisted in Company A, Sixty-third Ohio Infantry, Oct. 20, 1861, as First Sergeant, and was with his regiment in all the battles from New Madrid, Mo., to Atlanta, Ga., and re-enlisted as a veteran in the same regiment, Dec. 22, 1863, as a private. He was taken prisoner near Atlanta, Ga., July 22, 1864, and was confined in Andersonville Prison for a time, and from there to Florence, where he died Feb. 5, 1865, at the age of twenty-four years. His son William died May 21, 1875, at the age of forty-eight years. His wife died Aug. 31, 1851. March 24, 1856, he married Mrs. Mary Pyle, widow of Jesse Pyle, of Belmont County, Ohio. They had no children. She died May 10, 1861.

Allen V. M. Courtney, farmer, of Dover Township, second son of Alanson and Nancy (Camby) Courtney, was born in Dover Township, Athens Co., Ohio, Oct. 22, 1828, and has lived with his father up to the present time. He was educated in the common schools. In May, 1863, he enlisted in the Fourty-fourth Regiment, Ohio Home Guards, Company A; remained with the regiment until Nov. 10, 1863, when he enlisted in Company H, Eighteenth Ohio Infantry, as a private, and served a short time, when he was transferred to Company A, same regiment. In July, 1864, he was appointed Military Postmaster's Clerk at Chattanooga, Tenn., and filled that position until Aug. 4, 1865. He then reported to his regiment at Augusta, Ga., where he was mustered out, receiving his discharge at Camp Chase, Ohio, Oct. 9, 1865. He then returned home and has continued farming up to this time. He is a Master Mason and member of Paramuthia Lodge, No. 25, F. & A. M., Athens, Ohio, and is also a member of the chapter. He is a member of the Methodist church.

Eli Cushman Crippen, an old resident of Athens, was born Dec. 28, 1814, in that city, where he was reared and has lived all his life. His parents were Amos and Amelia (Steadman) Crippen. His father was a man of some prominence, being at one time Associate Judge of the Court of Common Pleas of Athens County, and having served as Treasurer of the same county for eight years. He was also Postmaster of Athens a number of years. He was by trade a blacksmith, Eli learning the trade of him when a boy. After attaining his majority our subject became associated with his father in the business, under the firm name of Amos Crippen & Son. The firm existed until the death of the senior member, in February, 1856. Since then our subject has carried on the business alone. In 1865 he was appointed Postmaster of Athens by President Lincoln, and served as such three years, when, not meeting with approbation during President Johnson's administration, he was removed from office. Dec. 2, 1841, he married Kate C. Whipple, daughter of Jeremiah Whipple, residing near Athens. Mr. and Mrs. Crippen have three children living—Henry C., mail agent on the M. & C. R. R.; Carrie, wife of Rev. Silas Pruden, of Brownsville, Cal., and Celia A., wife of Rev. David Morgan, of St. Paul, Minn. They have lost two children—Willie C., who died in infancy, and Frank M., who died Feb. 4, 1875, at the age of seventeen. Mr. Crippen is a member of the Universalist church at Rutland, Meigs Co., Ohio; his wife, of the First Presbyterian Church at Athens.

John K. Cuckler, son of W. H. and Elizabeth Cuckler, was born in Belmont County, Ohio, Dec. 15, 1840. When he was eleven years of age his parents came to Athens County and located in Athens Township. During the late war he enlisted in Company B, One Hundred and Forty-first Ohio Infantry, and served four months. He was married Oct. 20, 1870, to Jennie Bartley, of Pike County, Ohio. They have three children—Minnie L., William B., and Maggie J. Mr. Cuckler has a fine farm of 150 acres and a good residence and farm buildings. He has one of the best orchards in this township. He has been Township Trustee four years. He is a member of the Methodist church.

Judge Ebenezer Currier came to Athens in 1806, where he was a leading citizen until his death, March 2, 1851. He was prominently connected with every laudable public enterprise during his time; was possessed of ample means, and was a most reliable man, especially in his time, when most of those about him were in poor circumstances. By his generosity and the interest he took in aiding the pioneer settlers to secure permanent homes he soon became known as the poor man's friend, to whom all looked with confidence when substantial aid was needed. We give an example of the way this man helped to promote the early development of the country: He would furnish poor men the money to pay for land, and although securing himself with a mortgage, would accept, in some cases, 50 cents on the dollar or let the debts run forty years, or as he did some, until after his death, without foreclosing the mortgage. To such men as this too much credit can hardly be given for the success of new countries, and we feel justified in saying that no man deserves more credit for the success of Athens County than Judge Currier. He was born at Hempstead, Rockingham Co., N. H., Dec. 15, 1772. His early education was received at the public schools, afterward completed at Exeter, Mass., where he was a schoolmate of General Lewis Cass. He came to Marietta in 1804, and to Athens in 1806. His permanent business was that of a merchant, doing a large wholesale and retail business. Besides this he owned and superintended a farm and carried on a private banking business. He filled, during his lifetime, a number of minor offices, among them Justice of the Peace, County Treasurer and County Commissioner. He was for many years Treasurer of the Ohio University, taking great interest in the success of that institution. He was four times elected to the State Legislature, serving both as Senator and Member of the Lower House, and was Associate Judge of the Court of Common Pleas for about twenty-one years. He was a great reader, devoting much of his time to the study of the science of government and to American politics. He took an active interest in both local and national politics, being the recognized leader of his party in his own county. He was married in 1807 to Miss Olive Crippen, who, with her mother, came from the East to Ohio in its earliest settlement. She survived her husband seventeen years

John Perkins Dana, merchant, Athens, was born at Athens, Aug. 27, 1846, and is the son of Captain Joseph M. and Catharine F. (Perkins) Dana. His mother died when he was two years old. He lived with his father until manhood, and was educated at the Ohio University, at Athens, graduating in the class of 1867. When becoming of age, in 1867, he was employed as traveling salesman by the wholesale house of J. N. Harris & Co., of Cincinnati, and, with the exception of one year that he traveled for D. M. Ferry & Co., Detroit, Mich., was employed by them until June, 1876. That year he visited the Centennial, at Philadelphia. In the fall of 1877 he was employed as clerk in the First National Bank, of Athens, where he remained until 1878, when he received the appointment of Deputy Revenue Collector, of the Fifteenth Revenue District, of Ohio, and served until 1880. In 1863, while a student at the university, he became a member of Company B, One Hundred and Forty-first Regiment, Ohio Volunteer Infantry, and served 100 days on picket duty at Barboursville, Va. At the expiration of his time of service he served as First Lieutenant of a company in the Eighteenth Regiment, Ohio National Guards, and afterward as Captain of Company C, Second Regiment, Ohio National Guards, acting as Quartermaster until it was disbanded in 1881. He is a Master, Royal Arch, and Knight Templar Mason and member of the lodge, chapter, and commandery at Athens. He is a charter member of Columbus Golden Post, No. 89, G. A. R., and is one of the staff of the command of the State, as District Inspector, with the rank of Lieutenant-Colonel.

Captain Joseph M. Dana, a descendant of an old Huguenot family, of which Richard Dana, who settled at Cambridge, Mass., about twenty years after the landing of the Mayflower, was the first representative in this country, was the son of Professor Joseph Dana, who long occupied the Chair of Languages in the Ohio University, and Anna C. Dana. He was born in Athens, Ohio, March 22, 1822, and this continued his place of residence during a life extending to nearly sixty years. Captain Dana was as favorably as he was widely known in this county and throughout this portion of the State. The warm, generous and social qualities which he early developed and which notably characterized his whole life, enlisted and preserved the friendly regard of all who had personal business relations with him. Beginning active business at the early age of sixteen as Deputy in the office of his father, the then Clerk of the Court of Common Pleas, entire charge of the affairs of the office soon devolved upon him. Feb. 22, 1843, he was appointed his father's successor and retained the office, with great popularity, for a period of fifteen successive years, during which time he married Miss Catherine F. Perkins, daughter of one of the pioneers of the State, John Perkins, Esq., of Athens, Ohio, in September, 1845, who died in the faith of Christ, Jan. 28, 1848, regretted by all who knew her, leaving one child, John Perkins Dana. On the first day of May, 1851, he again married, Miss Ann E. Colwell, daughter of Judge A. R. Colwell, of Urbana, Ohio, by whom he had five children. Two died in infancy and three are still living—Mrs. Kate D. Cramer, Emma K. Dana and Joseph H. Dana. During his term in the clerk's office he studied law and was admitted to the bar in 1852. He formed his first partnership with Hon. Horace Wilson, now of Columbus, Ohio. In 1859 he was elected Treasurer of the county, during which incumbency and thereafter he continued to practice law until the breaking out of the Rebellion, when he promptly entered the military service of the United States, tendering the services of the Ohio State Guard, a local company of which he had been for several years in command, which was accepted, and had the honor of being the first company from the county sending more soldiers to the war according to the population, than any in the State. Captain Dana's company was assigned to the Thirteenth Regiment, Ohio Infantry, and afterward, prior to leaving the State, was transferred to and became Company C, Third Regiment, Ohio Infantry. At the end of eight months, his health proving inadequate to the physical demands of active military service, he resigned his commission and resumed his law practice. In 1866 he entered into a law partnership with General C. H. Grosvenor, which continued fourteen or fifteen years. Among the positions in civil life which he honorably and creditably filled were those of Director of the Athens branch of the State Bank of Ohio; member of the Board of Education for twenty years or more, and Treasurer of the same for a long term of years; Mayor for many consecutive terms; member of the Board of Trustees of the Ohio University, being Secretary and Auditor of that time-honored institution many years, resigning finally on account of infirm health, which rendered him unable to attend to the responsibility of its position. One of his most prominent and distinguished traits was his sterling and uncompromising integrity and honesty, which marked his every dealing in professional and business life, equally in small as in large affairs. As a Mason he was zealous and prominent, presiding many times in the different bodies. Was High Priest of Athens R. A. Chapter fifteen years, and Treasurer of all the bodies many years. He was a charter member of Athens Commandery of Knights Templar, No. 15, and for many years represented the different orders in the Grand Bodies, and took a very active part in their proceedings, usually being assigned to positions upon the most important committees. Captain Dana was a member of the Methodist Episcopal church, and was a zealous Republican. Of friends he had legions; of enemies none. He died at Athens, O., July 10, 1881.

Jesse Davis was born in Cadiz, Harrison Co., Ohio, Jan. 30, 1828. When ten years of age he came with his brother Thomas to Athens, where he has since resided. His mother died when he was five, and his father when he was twelve years of age. He was thus early thrown on his own resources. He received a common-school education, and when twelve years of age was apprenticed to learn the wool-carding business; but, not liking the business, at the end of his three years, began to learn the shoemaker's trade, which he afterward worked at ten years. Since then he has been in the grocery and mercantile business. July 3, 1850, he married Elizabeth Warren, of Canaan Township. They have eight children—Ambrose, George W., Fred, Lancaster, Lou, Jesse, Ida and Bee. Mrs. Davis is a member of the Methodist church of Athens. Mr. Davis is a member of Paramuthia Lodge, No. 25, Athens. He has served as Trustee of Athens Township four years, and as a member of the City Council two years.

William Eben Dean, stone-mason, was born in Athens, Aug. 2, 1840, where he has lived all his life, excepting when serving in the Union army. In April, 1861, he enlisted in Company C, Third Ohio Infantry, and served three months, when he again enlisted in Company D, Fourth W. Va. Infantry, and served until the spring of 1863, when he re-enlisted in the same company and regiment as a veteran and served until the close of the war, being discharged at Wheeling, Va., in March, 1865. He then returned to Athens, and was soon after appointed Postal Clerk in the House of Representatives at Washington, D. C., under Colonel Given, the Postmaster of that body, and served as such until the close of the session in 1867, when he returned to Athens, and has pursued the vocation of a stone-mason ever since. May 2, 1868, he was married to Miss Martha Gabriel, daughter of William Gabriel, of Athens. They have two children—Frank C. and Minnie F. Mr Dean is a member of Columbus Golden Post, No. 89, G. A. R.

George Albert Dille, a dentist of Athens, was born near the village of Ontario, Ohio, May 3, 1849. He is the son of John R. and Nancy (Rogers) Dille, with whom he lived until he was twenty, and was given a good education. In his nineteenth year he began teaching school and taught for two years, when, in 1870, he began the study of dentistry in the office of Dr. F. D. Coleman, at La Salle, Ill., and studied under his tutorship eighteen months. He then went to Mansfield, Ohio, and studied eighteen months under Dr. L. W. Nevins, forming a co-partnership with him in dentistry at the end of that time, under the firm name of Nevins & Dille. The co-partnership was dissolved Nov. 1, 1875, Mr. Dille going to Lima, Ohio, where he practiced until June, 1879, when he came to Athens and established his present practice. Oct. 14, 1875, he married Lou C., daughter of Esau W. Numbers, of Iberia, Ohio. They have three children—John Mar, Iva Pauline and Anna Helen. Mr. Dille and wife are members of the First Presbyterian Church at Athens, of which he is a Ruling Elder, and also Superintendent of the Sabbath-school.

Hadley King Dorr, druggist of Athens, is a son of Joseph and Dorcas (Mathena) Dorr. He was born near Athens, Sept. 10, 1852; there lived with his parents until he was seventeen, and was educated in the common school and Ohio University. On leaving home, which he did in 1870, he became associated with his brother, Dr. Eber G. Dorr, in the drug business at Athens, under the firm name of E. G. Dorr & Co. In 1873 the firm name was changed to H. K. Dorr & Co., his brother, though still associated with him, opening a drug store at Columbus, Ohio. In 1876 his brother retired from the firm. Since that time he has continued the business alone, at Athens. Mr. Dorr is a Mason and a member of Paramuthia Lodge, No. 25, and an Odd Fellow, and member of Sereno Lodge, No. 479, of Athens.

Joseph Dorr, a resident of Athens, was born in the vicinity of Athens, June 1, 1816. He was reared a farmer and has pursued that avocation all his life in Athens Township, excepting one year, during which he lived in Dover Township. He worked as a farm-hand until 1844, when he purchased a farm on Sugar Creek, three miles north of Athens, on which he lived until 1854, when he sold it and purchased a farm on Wolf's Plains, three miles west of Athens. There he lived until 1871; since that year he has had it farmed by tenants and he himself has resided in Athens. March 1, 1844, he married Dorcas, daughter of John Mathena, of Athens. They have four children—Dr. Eber G., of Texas; Lucy C., now wife of David C. Casto, of West Virginia; Hadley K., druggist of Athens, and Laura Frances. Mr. Dorr is a member of the Methodist Episcopal church of Wolf's Plains.

Joseph Eli Edmundson, dentist at Athens, was born July 25, 1840, in Pittsburg, Pa., where he was reared, and educated in the common schools until he was fifteen. He then attended the Iron City College of Pittsburg, for three years, and Duff's College, of the same city, one year. He then taught bookkeeping and penmanship in Ohio about one year, and then began the study of medicine and dentistry in private. In 1861 he entered the dental office of Dr. Jacob Greenawalt, of Pittsburg, and was under his tutor-

Geo S Anderson

ship some four years, in the meantime acting as an assistant in the surgical hospital at Pittsburg. In 1865 he located on Smithfield street, Pittsburg, having formed a partnership in dentistry with Dr. Hoffman, under the firm name of Edmundson & Hoffman. Six months later he retired from the firm and traveled through Ohio and Pennsylvania until the spring of 1866, when he located at Plymouth, Ohio. In the spring of 1870 he removed to Athens and established his present dental practice. March 7, 1867, he married Margaret Black, of Pittsburg, six children being born to them— Mary E., William T., James L., Charles G., Clyde M. and Edith. Mr. Edmundson and wife are members of the Methodist Episcopal church at Athens. Our subject is an Odd Fellow, and a member of Sereno Lodge, No. 479, of Athens.

Alexander Ewing, assistant in the Auditor's office at Athens, was born in Lancaster County, Pa., Aug. 23, 1824. When he was two years old his parents, Thomas and Mary (Gallaway) Ewing, removed to the region of Mount Pleasant, Ohio, where he was reared, receiving a common-school education. At the age of fifteen he began the woolen manufacturing trade in McKei's woolen mills near Mount Pleasant, where he worked until 1848. From 1849 until 1857 he was engaged in the livery business at Warrenton, Ohio. In 1858 he was elected County Recorder of Jefferson County, and re-elected in 1861. From 1865 to 1868 he acted as insurance agent and traveling salesman. He came to Athens in April, 1868, and rented the Herrold Woolen Mills, manufacturing woolen goods until 1872. He entered the County Auditor's office at Athens as an assistant, December, 1872, and has remained there ever since. In March, 1849, he was married to Mary A. Moore, of Mount Pleasant, Ohio, three children being born to them — George Y., now station agent at McArthur's Junction; Jane, still at home, and John A., now telegraph operator at Big Springs, Texas. Mr. Ewing is an Odd Fellow, a member of Goodwill Lodge, No. 143, Steubenville, Ohio, also a charter member of Athens Encampment, No. 175, of Athens.

John Finsterwald, a farmer of Athens Township, was born in Ames Township, Athens County, Jan. 1, 1820. His parents, John and Catherine (Stalder) Finsterwald, came from Switzerland in 1819, and settled in Ames Township, where he was born. His father died when he was fifteen years of age and he lived with his mother until manhood. In April, 1842, he was married to Mary Ann, daughter of Jonathan Hill, of Ames Township. He farmed as a renter until 1844, when he was employed by Judge B. Pruden to work in his salt works near Athens, nine years. He then purchased a farm in the vicinity of Athens and followed farming until 1858, when he was employed in the Ballard Salt Works until 1867. He then went to McCuneville, in Perry County, and worked in the McCune Salt Works until 1870, when he returned to his farm, where he still resides. He has been Road Supervisor of Athens Township seven years. He has eight children —Catherine, wife of Pearson Duffy, of Perry County; Lucy, wife of Spence Hill, of the same county; Eliza, Ada, Peter, Marshall, of Athens; Henry, of Ludlow Grove, Ohio; Charles, of Athens Township, and John, an attendant of Athens Asylum for the Insane.

Peter Finsterwald, Marshal of Athens, was born in Ames Township, Athens Co., Ohio, Feb. 23, 1843. He was reared a farmer and lived with his parents, John and Mary (Hill) Finsterwald, until he was nineteen years of age, when, in 1862, he enlisted in Company A, Ninety-second Ohio Infantry, as a private. He participated in the battles of Mission Ridge, Chickamauga, Dalton, Kennesaw Mountain, Resaca, Peach Tree Creek, Atlanta, Savannah, Charleston and Bentonville. He was discharged as a Sergeant at the expiration of his term of service at Washington, D. C., June 20, 1865. He then returned home and worked on the farm with his father until 1867, when he rented a farm where he lived till 1871. He then came to Athens and followed teaming until the spring of 1875, when he was elected Street Commissioner, and has held the office by re-election ever since. In 1882 he received the appointment of Marshal of Athens. He has been twice married. His first wife was Emma M. Bing, of Athens, whom he married in August, 1867, and who died in 1873, leaving four children—Frederick, Elsie, Carlos and William. In October, 1876, he was married to Mary O. Crippen, of Rome Township, Athens County. They have two children—Artemus and Gertrude. Mr. Finsterwald is a member of the Knights of Pythias and of Columbus Golden Post, No. 89, G. A. R.

Adolphus Benjamin Frame, M. D., was born in Coolville, Athens Co., Ohio, Jan. 4, 1840. He is the son of John and Mary (Nesmith) Frame. He remained at home until September, 1859, at which time he entered Marietta College, attending there until the fall of 1862, when he entered the Union Army as Second Lieutenant of Company I, One Hundred and Sixteenth Ohio Volunteer

Infantry, being commissioned by Governor David Todd, Aug. 16, 1862. He was promoted to First Lieutenant, Jan. 31, 1863, and to Captain, Dec. 27, 1864. He served with his regiment in the Shenandoah Valley, under Generals Melroy, Seigle, Hunter, Crook and Sheridan, until December, 1864, when it was transferred to the Army of the James. March 1, 1865, he was honorably discharged, by order of the War Department, and on the following day was commissioned Adjutant of the One Hundred and Eighty-sixth Ohio Volunteer Infantry. He served with this regiment in the Army of the Cumberland from March, 1865, until September of the same year, when the regiment was mustered out, at the close of the war. Immediately after quitting the service, he began the study of medicine with Dr. A. B. Monahan, at Jackson, Ohio. He graduated from the medical college at Cincinnati, in March, 1868, after taking two full courses of lectures. He then practiced at Coolville, Ohio, until May, 1872, when he came to Athens. Dec. 24, 1868, he married Miss Mary Elizabeth Morris, daughter of Charles Morris, of Athens. They have one child— Mary Lydia. Jan. 5, 1874, Mr. Frame was appointed United States Pension Examining Surgeon, by the Government. March 7, 1877, he was appointed a Trustee of the Athens Asylum for the Insane, by Governor Thomas L Young. He is a member of the Paramuthia Lodge, No. 25, A. F. & A. M., at Athens, and also one of the charter members of the Columbus Golden Post, No. 89, G. A. R., he being Surgeon of the post and Deputy of Ohio.

John Adrian Frame, M. D., was born at Coolville, Athens County, Feb. 26, 1850, and is a son of John and Mary (Nesmith) Frame. He lived with his parents until manhood at his birthplace, and was educated in the High School of that place. In October, 1879, he began the study of medicine in the office of Dr. G. W. Harman, at Coolville, and was under his preceptorship for three years. He graduated as M. D. from the Ohio Medical College at Cincinnati—after taking two courses—in 1872. He then began his practice in Coolville, where he remained until 1875, when he went to Jacksonville, Ohio, and practiced nine months. He then came to Athens and established himself in his present practice. June 3, 1874, he married Miss Elizabeth Morrison, daughter of Alfred Morrison, of Athens County. They have one child— Adrienne.

John Friday, of the firm of D. Zenner & Co., merchants of Athens, was born near Nuremberg, Bavaria, June 11, 1834. He was educated in the schools of Nuremberg up to the year 1849, when, at the age of fourteen, he emigrated to America. He was employed as clerk in stores at Cincinnati, Ohio, and Rushville, Ind., until 1853. He then engaged in the mercantile business at Salem, Ohio, Rochester, Ind., and Wellsville, Ohio, until 1858, when he removed to Steubenville, Ohio. Here he engaged in the mercantile business until 1867, when he came to Athens and became associated with D. Zenner, under the firm name of D. Zenner & Co. In October, 1868, he married Miss Rebecca Zenner, daughter of D. Zenner, of Athens. He is a demitted Mason, a member of Good Will Lodge, No. 143, and Nimrod Encampment, No. 3, I. O. O. F., at Steubenville, Ohio.

Leopold Friday, of the firm of D. Zenner & Co., of Athens, was born near Nuremberg, Bavaria, July 13, 1842. At the age of fifteen he was apprenticed to learn the mercantile business at Bayreuth, serving three years. He then clerked for his father until he reached his majority. In 1864 he emigrated to America. He was employed as stockman in a wholesale house at Cincinnati for about six months, at very low wages; then went to Nashville, Tenn., and clerked one year. He then went to Memphis and thence to St. Louis; not finding employment, went to Dakota Territory, where he worked at manual labor, enduring all the hardships and privations of a frontier life for three years. He returned to Ohio in 1869 and was employed for some six months as a farm hand by D. Zenner, living near Athens, when by the advice of his relatives and friends he entered, as a clerk, the store of D. Zenner & Co., his brother being the company. By hard work and attention to business he became a member of the firm in 1875. June 14, 1876, he was married to Julia, daughter of D. Zenner. He is a Master, Royal Arch and Council Mason, and a member of the lodge, chapter and council at Logan, Ohio. He is a member of Sereno Lodge, No. 479, and Athenian Encampment, No. 175, I. O. O. F., at Athens, and has passed all the chairs in both subordinate lodges and encampments. He is also a member of Hockhocking Lodge, No. 1,880, K. of P., of Logan.

James B. Fulton, grocer, Athens, was born in Athens Township, Nov. 10, 1855, where he was reared and educated. He is the youngest of three sons of Robert and Elizabeth (Robinson) Fulton. He began business for himself in 1878, by dealing in wool. During 1880 he was employed as clerk in the grocery store of J. O. Whipple, Athens. In 1882 he opened the store where he is now doing a good business. Nov. 8, 1882, he married Etta Wilson, of Vinton County, O. They are members of the Methodist Episcopal church. Mr. Fulton is a member of Sereno Lodge, No. 479, I. O. O. F., Athens.

Reason Gabriel, born Sept. 28, 1815, in Alexander Township, Athens Co., Ohio, is the third of four sons of Abram and Polly (Higgins) Gabriel. Dec. 31, 1835, he married Elizabeth, daughter of Tederman Allen, of Philadelphia, Pa. He purchased a farm in Waterloo Township where he lived three years; then sold it and bought one in Athens Township, which he still owns. In 1855 he moved into Athens, where he still resides, his farm being carried on by tenants. Mrs. Gabriel died Oct. 25, 1862. They had seven children—Sarah A., now Mrs. Asa Love, of Athens; Abram, of Athens; Mary M., now Mrs. C. S. Rose, of Columbus; Orpha, now Mrs. John Wyland, of Columbus; Elizabeth, now Mrs. Henry Kilburn, of Columbus; Charles, of Columbus, and one who died in infancy. Jan. 10, 1875, Mr. Gabriel married Elizabeth, daughter of John and Serena (Andrew) Clutter, of Washington, Pa. Mrs. Gabriel is a member of the First Presbyterian Church, Athens.

James Gilly, son of William and Frances Gilly, was born Nov. 22, 1845, on the farm where he now resides. His youth was spent in working on the farm and attending the common schools of the neighborhood. He was married when twenty years of age to Sarah Johnson, of this township. They have two children— Luella and Tabitha. Mr. and Mrs. Gilly are members of the Methodist Episcopal church. Mr. Gilly has a good farm of 118 acres, all well improved.

William Gilly, son of William and Sarah Gilly, was born in Pennsylvania, Dec. 15, 1816. When he was twelve years of age his parents came to Ohio, settling in Alexander Township, Athens County. He was married when twenty years of age to Frances Hill, of Athens County. Their children are—Calvin, Frank, Henry, William, Becky, Frances, James and Elizabeth. Mr. Gilly has a fine farm of 740 acres, which he has acquired by his frugality and industry.

C. Dent Gist was born Muskingum County, O., Jan. 13, 1844. He is the second son of Charles W. and Melinda (Wilson) Gist, his father a native of Frederick County, Md., and his mother of Muskingum County. Our subject was reared on a farm and received his early education in the common schools, and completed it at New Plymouth Academy, Vinton County. He enlisted as a private in Company F, One Hundred and Fourteenth Ohio Infantry, Aug. 22, 1862, and during his service was promoted to Commissary Sergeant. He participated in many of the hard-fought battles of the Rebellion, and bravely performed the duties of a soldier until the close of the war, and was mustered out at Houston, Texas, July 17, 1865. He then returned home and became engaged in the mercantile business, which he has since pursued. He was married Nov. 30, 1871, to Susie Allen, daughter of David and Mary J. Allen, who were among the pioneers of Athens. By this union are three children—Dollie, born Sept. 1, 1872; Gracie, born March 28, 1875; John D., born Oct. 7, 1878. Mr. Gist is a member of the G. A. R., Columbus Golden Post, No. 89, which is located at Athens, Ohio.

Major Elmer Golden, grocer, was born in Alexander Township, Athens Co., Ohio, April 12, 1835, the son of William and Jane (Crossen) Golden. He was reared in Athens County. At the age of twelve years he began to clerk in the store of Oliver Pickering, and afterward clerked in different stores in Athens until 1855, when he became associated with D. Zenner in the mercantile business, the firm name being Zenner & Golden. In July, 1862, he received a recruiting commission as Captain, and in ten days' time recruited 143 men; out of that number Company A, Ninety-second Ohio Infantry, was organized, of which he was elected Captain. The excess of men were transferred to other companies. He served as Captain until March, 1863, when he was promoted to Major of his regiment. He was discharged Dec. 8, 1863, for disability, and returned to Athens. He participated in the battles of Chickamauga, Mission Ridge and others of less importance. In 1865 he retired from the firm of Zenner & Golden and was employed as salesman in the wholesale dry goods house of Thompson & Keen, of Cincinnati. In 1866 he engaged in the hardware business at Jackson, Ohio. In 1868 he removed with his stock of hardware to Garnett, Kan., where he remained until March, 1874, when, discontinuing the business, he returned to Athens and became proprietor of the Brown Hotel. In May, 1878, he took charge of the Warren House, which he kept until November, 1882. March 1, 1882, he engaged in his present grocery business. Dec. 6, 1856, he was married to Miss Mary B. Cooley, of Athens, who died March 13, 1862, leaving two children—Will B., a clerk in the Bank of Athens, and Bessie P., wife of Dr. Charles A. Cable, of Logan. He was again married, Sept. 20, 1866, to Miss Hattie A. Butin, of Logan, Ohio. Major Golden is a Freemason, demitted from the lodge at Jackson, Ohio. He is a member of Columbus Golden Post, No. 89, G. A. R., of Athens, of which he is Junior Vice-Commander.

William Golden, Esq., Justice of the Peace of Athens, was born near Lewistown, Pa., Oct. 5, 1799. He is the son of Barnabas and Mary (Campbell) Golden. His mother died when he was an infant and he was left in the care of an uncle in Mifflin County, Pa., with whom he lived, receiving a common-school education, until he was fourteen; at that age he began to maintain himself by various employments. In his seventeenth year he went to Allenville, Mifflin County, and was apprenticed to learn the trade of plasterer, serving three years, when, in 1818, he came to Ohio and worked at his trade in Wooster, Wayne County, until 1820. During the winter, when he could not work at his trade, he taught school. He then went to Perry County, living there until 1823, when he came to Athens, working there as a plasterer till 1829, when he purchased a farm in Alexander Township, five miles south of Athens, where he farmed until 1843. Being at that time elected Sheriff of Athens County, he removed to Athens. He held this office two terms of two years each. In 1847 he was elected Treasurer of Athens County, and held this position, by re-election, for six years. While living in Alexander Township he served as Justice of the Peace for six years. He is now Justice of the Peace of Athens Township, and has held that position since 1864. He also served as Mayor of Athens eight years. Nov. 28, 1822, he married Miss Jane Crossen, of Perry County, O. She died at Athens, April 17, 1876. They had nine children, only three of whom are now living—John C., of Texas; Sarah A., wife of Lewis Steinrod, of Nelsonville, and Major Elmer Golden, of Athens. His children all lived to maturity excepting one that died in infancy. His son, Columbus Golden, in honor of whom the Grand Army of the Republic of Athens named their post, died from wounds received at Sugar Creek, Ark., in 1862. He was the first resident of Athens County who fell in that war. Mr. Golden is the oldest Freemason in Athens County. He has taken the Master, Royal Arch, Council and Knight Templar degrees, and is a member of the lodge, chapter, council and commandery at Athens. He has also held high positions in these bodies for many years.

Hon. William Reed Golden's career was among the men of to-day. As a lawyer and a politician his abilities have been seldom excelled, if ever, in this portion of the State. He was born at Athens, April 11, 1827, where he died Feb. 17, 1880, aged nearly fifty-three years. He passed his boyhood on his father's farm in Alexander Township, where he attended the district school. He afterward, for three years following 1846, attended the Ohio University. He then studied law in Athens with Hon. Lot L. Smith, and after two terms in the National Law School at Ballston, N. Y., graduated from it and was admitted to the bar in 1851. He at once began the practice of law in Athens, meeting with good success from the start. He was married in May, 1852, to Miss Kate K. Foster, to whom was born six children, five of them surviving the father. He was twice elected to the Ohio State Senate, in 1865 and 1868, serving four years, representing the district composed of Athens, Hocking and Fairfield counties. In this body he was an able and important member. In the dark days of the Republic, although from a natural defect unable to take up arms, he was, in sympathy, true to his country. His career as a politician was that of an honorable, patriotic and shrewd gentleman. For many years he was the leading spirit in his, the Democratic, party in this part of the State, and whether on the stump or in the committee room was a formidable adversary to his party opponents. As a lawyer he was polite to those about him, and exceptionally shrewd in the conduct of a case. He was not only shrewd, but well informed on the substantial principles of the science of law, being able to conduct his business in a prompt and masterly way. His natural ability was, however, generally supposed to be far in advance of his real attainments. Being of a careless disposition, he let his impulsive nature take its course, unrestrained by a desire for self-improvement or by moral precept. But for all this, he never forgot the instincts of honor to his fellowmen and to the laws of his country. He was of a genial and cordial disposition, steadfast to his friends and honorable toward all. His faults were the weaknesses of human nature, in which he injured none so much as himself. He made no pretension to be other than what he was—equally as honorable and outspoken in this as in his public and professional business. He was highly respected and honored as an able and genial companion by his associates at the bar.

Charles William Goodspeed, a farmer of Athens Township, where he was born Sept. 17, 1829, is a son of David and Clarissa (Baker) Goodspeed. After becoming of age he lived on the homestead with his parents until his marriage with Nancy Coats, daughter of Arthur Coats, of Athens, June 27, 1858, when he settled on a farm he had purchased in Athens Township, on which he lived twelve years. In 1870 he returned to the homestead, which he now owns. His farm, in all, embraces 500 acres. With farming he does an extensive teaming business by contract. He is now a Trustee of Athens Township and has served as such several years. He has served nine years as Assessor and one year as Land Appraiser. He has three children—George Elza and Mary Elma (twins), and Mattie Florence, all still at home. He is a Master, Royal Arch, Council and Knight Templar Mason, and member of the lodge, chapter, council and commandery at Athens.

Joseph McKendree Goodspeed, Superintendent of the Union Public Schools of Athens, was born near Athens, June 20, 1834. He is the only son of Ezra and Matilda (Rose) Goodspeed, with whom he lived until manhood, and was given a classical education. He graduated from the Ohio University in the class of 1859. He had, however, taught school several terms before his graduation, and afterward, during 1859 and 1860, he taught the school in Middleport, Meigs County. In September, 1860, he accepted the position of Principal of the Carrollton College at Carrollton, Ky. At the breaking out of the war, in 1861, he resigned his position and, returning to Ohio, was commissioned a Second Lieutenant and recruited Company E, Seventy-fifth Infantry, Ohio Volunteers. Upon the organization of the company he was elected First Lieutenant and so commissioned, serving as such until November, 1862, when he resigned his commission on account of failing health. While serving he participated in the engagements at McDowell, Strasburgh, Slaughter Mountain, Freeman's Ford and Second Bull Run. In May, 1864, he went out with the One Hundred and Forty-first Regiment, O. N. G., as Adjutant. He served 100 days, and then served with his regiment on guard duty at Barboursville, W. Va., until the expiration of his term of service. In the fall of 1864 he was employed in the commission house of R. H. Stewart at Cincinnati, and while there, Jan. 14, 1865, he was married to Mary C. Clark, daughter of Rev. J. W. Clark, of that city. He then returned to Athens County and farmed his father's farm until September, 1866, when he was elected Superintendent of the Union Public Schools of Athens, by the Athens Board of Education, and has filled that position seventeen years. April 1, 1874, his wife died at Athens, aged twenty-eight years, leaving him two children—Gertrude and Eliza, the latter dying in October, 1877.

Mr. Goodspeed is a prominent Mason and has taken the degrees up to thirty-second of the Scottish rite. From 1869 to 1875 he was Worshipful Master of Paramuthia Lodge, No. 25, of Athens; High Priest of Athens Chapter, No. 39, from 1874 to the present time; Eminent Commander of Athens Commandery from 1874 to 1876, also from 1877 to the present time (1883). During 1880 and 1881 he was Most Illustrious Master of the Grand Council of Ohio, and during the same years was Senior Grand Warden of the Grand Lodge of Ohio. In 1882 he was elected Deputy Grand Master of the Grand Lodge of Ohio and now holds that position. Mr. Goodspeed is a Director of the First National Bank of Athens, and President of both the Citizens Building and Loan Association and the Home Building Association, of Athens.

Granville Lucius Gorslene, M. D., of Athens, was born at Athens, July 16, 1837. He is the son of James M. and Maria (Quimby) Gorslene. He was educated by taking an irregular course at the Manual Labor School, at Albany, now the Atwood Institute. At the age of twenty he began the study of medicine under the tutorship of Dr. C. L. Wilson, at Albany, with whom he studied and practiced four years. He then practiced and studied at Hamden, Vinton County. He graduated as M. D. from the Starling Medical College, at Columbus, Ohio, Feb. 28, 1865. He continued his practice at Hamden until 1873, when he came to Athens and became associated with Dr. H. M. Lash, under the firm name of Lash & Gorslene. Two years later he withdrew from the firm and practiced alone until 1876, when he removed to Austin, Texas, and practiced there one year, when, on account of impaired health, he returned to Ohio and practiced at Hamden until 1879, when he again came to Athens and established his present practice. In April, 1882, he was appointed one of the Board of Examiners at Athens by the Pension Commissioner. May 29, 1862, he married Miss Mary Charlotte Strahl, daughter of John and Hannah (Snitt) Strahl. They have two children—James M., a student of the Ohio University, and Clara Lula. He is a member of the First Presbyterian Church of Athens and has served as Ruling Elder since 1874. He is a Master, Royal Arch and Council Mason, and a member of the lodge at Hamden and of the chapter and council at Athens.

George T. Gould, of Athens, was born at Kennebunk Port, a coast town in the State of Maine, Nov. 24, 1825. His father, Thomas F. Gould, of Scotch ancestry, was a sea captain and finally lost at sea. His mother, Lyntha Miller, was of English descent. George T. Gould was educated in the public schools at Lewiston, Maine, where the family moved when he was yet a child. He came to Ohio in November, 1852, brought hither by the construction of the Marietta & Cincinnati Railroad, on which he was a contractor. After the completion of this road, he, in connection with M. M. Green, of Columbus, engaged in business at Salina, where they invested a large amount of capital and carried on various businesses, including salt-making, coal-mining, pork-packing, and dealing in grain, wool and general merchandise. After a residence at Salina of twelve or fourteen years he removed to Lancaster when the Columbus & Hocking Valley Railroad was being built, and on which he had a contract for the construction from Lancaster to Athens. A number of years previous to the close of business at Salina, Mr. Green had withdrawn and Mr. Gould was alone. In 1878 he went to South America, where he was, for a time, superintendent of the mines of the Telimbia Mining Company, of which he was a member. For a few years following this he was in California superintending mines, a part of the time having as many as four different mines under his control. For the last few years he has been engaged in various pursuits. Few men have had so wide an experience in business pursuits as Mr. Gould. To mention in detail all of his business relations would, in his own language, "make a book of itself." In this short sketch we have only noticed those pursuits in which he was more permanently established. More than as many more in which he has been to a great or less extent engaged, might be mentioned. In his business pursuits he has traveled through more than two thirds of the States and Territories of the Union, and through a greater part of both Upper and Lower Canada and parts of South America. He was married Oct. 24, 1855, to Miss Minerva Brown, daughter of the late John B. Brown, of Ames Township. They have six children, five daughters and one son, all living.

Finley Perry Graham, photographer at Athens, was born near McKeesport, Pa., Nov. 28, 1842. He lived with his parents, George and Mary Jane (Maines) Graham, until he was nineteen, when he joined the Union army, enlisting in Company F, Thirty-sixth Ohio Volunteer Infantry, serving three years. He participated in a number of battles and skirmishes, the most important being South Mountain, Antietam (being wounded at the battle), Hoover's Gap and Kernstown. At the battle of Kernstown he was taken prisoner and imprisoned at Winchester, Lynchburg, Danville and Libby Prison, making in all seven months of imprisonment; at the end of this time he was exchanged at Annapolis. He was then granted a furlough, his health being impaired by his prison life, when he returned to Ohio to gain strength. He rejoined his regiment at Winchester, Va., and served until his discharge at the expiration of his term of service, June, 1865. He then returned to his father, at Plymouth, Washington Co., Ohio. The following August he went to Chesterfield, Ohio, and began learning the art of photographing, with his uncle, William S. Waugh, remaining with him four months, when he returned to Plymouth, where he did photographing until 1872. He afterward carried on the same business at Lexington and Logan until 1874, when he came to Athens and established his present gallery. Nov. 8, 1866, he married Hattie T. Selby, of Athens County, Ohio. They have four children—George H., Clarence Arthur, Mabel L. and Lulu Selby. They lost one by death—Ida A., who died at Logan, Aug. 5, 1873, at the age of nine months. Mr. Graham and wife are members of the Methodist Episcopal church at Athens. Our subject is a member of Columbus Golden Post, No. 89, G. A. R.

James Grim was born April 4, 1835, near New Lisbon, Ohio. When fifteen years of age he went to Salem and learned the molder's trade, serving an apprenticeship with Samuel Taylor. In 1853 he went to Cleveland and worked in the foundry of Merchant & Ingersoll a year. In 1856 he came to Athens and was employed as molder in the foundry of W. W. Love until 1866, being absent only 100 days, while serving in Company B, One Hundred and Forty-first Regiment, O. N. G. In 1867 he engaged in the hucksterng business with John Davis, under the name of Davis & Grim. In 1868 Mr. Davis withdrew and Mr. Grim continued the business till 1872. From 1872 to 1877 he was in the grocery business, but sold out and was variously employed till August, 1880, when he became established in the livery business. In September, 1862, he married Eliza J. Pierce, of Athens. They have seven children— Emma F., Robert T., Charles A., James C., Eliza J., Myrtle A., and Holly H., all living at home.

Hon. Charles H. Grosvenor, attorney at law and a member of the law firm of Grosvenor & Jones, at Athens, and Grosvenor & Vorhes, at Pomeroy, was born at Pomfret, Conn., Sept. 20, 1833. At the age of five he came with his parents, Peter and Ann

(Chase) Grosvenor, into Athens County, where they settled in 1838. He is of English ancestry, being a descendant of John Grosvenor, who died at Roxbury, Mass., in 1690, from whom, it is believed, have descended all who bear his name in America. His grandfather, Thomas Grosvenor, served on the personal staff of General Washington during the Revolutionary War, with the rank of Colonel. He was afterward Judge of the Circuit Court of Connecticut. His father served in the war of 1812, and was promoted to the rank of Major of Militia. Our subject received his rudimentary education in the district schools of Athens County, and, being thrown upon his own resources at an early age, he was obliged to teach school, tend store and work on a farm in order to obtain means to further pursue his studies. In his private study he was assisted by his mother, an amiable and intelligent lady, to whom the marked characteristics that distinguish Mr. Grosvenor as a lawyer and advocate are largely due. He studied law under the tutorship of Hon. Lot L. Smith, and was admitted to the bar by the District Court at Athens in 1857, and at once began the practice of his profession. In 1858 he formed a law partnership with Hon. S. S. Knowles. During the war he enlisted in the Eighteenth Ohio Infantry, and was soon promoted to Major of his regiment. In June, 1863, he was promoted to Lieutenant-Colonel, and in April, 1865, to Colonel, with the brevet title of Brigadier-General, he having commanded a brigade at the battle of Nashville, and having been recommended by General Steedman, on account of gallant action on the field. The recommendation was endorsed by General George H. Thomas as follows:

"Respectfully forwarded and earnestly recommended. Lieutenant-Colonel Grosvenor has served under my command since November, 1862, and has on all occasions performed his duties with intelligence and zeal."

At the close of the war he returned to Athens and resumed the practice of law, becoming associated with J. M. Dana, Esq., under the firm name of Grosvenor & Dana, this co-partnership lasting nearly fourteen years. Besides being a prominent lawyer, with an extensive practice in the Supreme Court of Ohio, and all the lower courts in this section of the State, he has the reputation of being an eloquent orator, a successful campaign speaker and a formidable opponent. During the hotly contested Maine campaign of 1879 his assistance was earnestly requested by Hon. James G. Blaine and other distinguished Republicans of that State. Accepting the invitation, he made his first speech at Portland, Aug. 13. He made in all thirty speeches, his stay covering a period of several weeks, he fully vindicating his reputation as an eloquent and popular speaker. In 1872 he was elected one of the Republican Presidential Electors, and was chosen to carry the returns from Ohio to Washington. In 1880 he was elected Presidential Elector at large on the Republican ticket, and took an active part in that campaign, making speeches in five States. Dec. 2 of that year the Republican Presidential Electors and other distinguished citizens of Ohio visited President-elect Garfield to tender him their congratulations on the successful issue of the campaign just closed, and Mr. Grosvenor was chosen spokesman. In 1873 he was elected a member of the House of Representatives, from Athens County, and while a member of that body formed one of several important committees. He was re-elected in 1875, and at its organization was chosen Speaker of the House. Mr. Grosvenor is now a member of the law firms of Grosvenor & Jones, Athens, and Grosvenor & Vorhees, Pomeroy; the latter firm has existed since 1868. Dec. 1, 1858, he married Samantha Stewart, of Athens County. She died April 2, 1866, leaving one daughter. He was again married, May 21, 1867, to Louise H. Currier, also a native of Athens County. They have two daughters.

Isaac Half, upholsterer and dealer in furniture and carpetings, of Athens, was born in Hagueneaw, Alsace, July 17, 1842. He was educated in the schools of his native city and Strasbourg, where he went at the age of thirteen, and attended the Industrial School four years. He then, 1860, emigrated to the United States, landing in New York City, July 4. He was first employed in the upholstery house of M. Steinhous, where he remained until the fall of 1861, when he came to Athens and was employed as a clerk in the store of I. Selig & Co. He was employed by the same at Athens, Albany and Logan until 1864, when he, with L. Selig, purchased the stock of I. Selig & Co., and established themselves in the mercantile business at Athens, under the firm name of L. Selig & Co. In 1868 M. and A. Selig became associated with them, changing the firm name to M. Selig & Co. The firm dissolving in December, 1882, Mr. Half, the following February, established himself in his present business. He has been a member of the Board of Education of Athens for seven years. He is a Master, Royal Arch and Council Mason and also an Odd Fellow. He is, by birth and education, a Hebrew, and has always adhered to that faith. February, 1865, he married Eva Selig, of Philadelphia, seven children being born to them—Filx, Gertrude, Rodolph, Morris, Samuel, Sophia and Leopold.

Robert Emmett Hamblin, Steward and Financial Manager of the Athens Asylum for the Insane, born in Logan, Hocking Co., Ohio, Aug. 14, 1852, is the son of Emmett and Celestia (Cook) Hamblin. He received his literary education in the schools of Logan and took a commercial course in the Zanesville Business College in 1872. At the age of nineteen he began to teach school, and taught until July, 1874, when he received the appointment of Steward of the Athens Asylum for the Insane. In May, 1878, on account of a change of administration, he was superseded by another. In May, 1880, without being solicited, he was again appointed Steward of the asylum and still holds the position. He is a Master, Royal Arch and Knight Templar Mason and member of the lodge, chapter and commandery at Athens.

William Hunter Harris, Superintendent and Secretary of the Athens Gas Light Company, was born at Clarksville, W. Va., Sept. 8, 1845, where he lived with his parents, James W. and Permelia (Burton) Harris, until he was eighteen years of age. He attended schools in Clarksville until his sixteenth year, when he was employed as a clerk in the store of B. F. Shuttleworth for two years. He then came to Athens with his parents and, with his father, engaged in the marble business until 1873, when he became Superintendent and Secretary of the Athens Gas Light Company and has since held that position. Oct. 27, 1869, he married Miss Bettie, daughter of the late George Putnam, of Athens. They had two children—May Putnam and Bessie. Mr. and Mrs. Harris are members of the First Presbyterian Church of Athens. He is a member of Paramuthia Lodge, No. 25, A. F. &. A. M.

Lafayette Hawk, Recorder of Athens, was born at Wilksville, Vinton Co., Ohio, Aug. 24, 1843, where he was reared, and lived with his parents until his seventeenth year. He was educated in the common schools. When first leaving home he enlisted in Company C, Thirty-sixth Regiment, Ohio Volunteer Infantry; he served as a private about two years, when he was promoted to Corporal, and three months after, in July, 1863, to Duty Sergeant. July 18, 1864, he was detailed as Sergeant-Major of his regiment. In September of that year he was taken prisoner while in an engagement at Kernstown, in the Shenandoah Valley, and was imprisoned at Danville, Va., until Oct. 10, when he, with others, made his escape and returned to the Union lines at Gauley Bridge, Va., being out twenty-eight days. He was returned to his regiment at Cumberland, Md., in January, 1865; he was soon after promoted to Orderly or First Sergeant. May 16, 1865, he was commissioned Second Lieutenant of Company A, of the same regiment; in July, 1865, he was mustered out of the service at Columbus, Ohio, when he returned home to Vinton County. During 1866 he farmed his father's homestead, and in 1867 he came to Marshfield, Athens County, and engaged in merchandising until 1871, when he engaged in shipping produce at the same place until 1872. He was then employed as a traveling salesman by wholesale houses in Chillicothe and Portsmouth, Ohio, which he followed, with the exception of three years, until August, 1881. For a short time he was employed as a clerk at Guysville, Athens County. In the fall of 1882 he was elected by the Republican party, Recorder of Athens County, and has just entered upon the duties of that office. Oct. 18, 1866, he married Jennie, daughter of James Mayhugh, of Marshfield, Athens County. They have two children living—Eva and Nellie; they lost one—Nettie—who died June 1, 1879, at the age of twelve years. Mr. Hawk is a Master Mason and member of Constitution Lodge, No. 426, Marshfield, and of Columbus Golden Post, G. A. R., No. 89, Athens.

Silas Elson Hedges, Clerk of the Court of Common Pleas of Athens County, is the son of William F. and Sarah (McElhiney) Hedges, and was born in Homer Township, Morgan Co., Ohio, Sept. 26, 1847. He was educated in the common school, besides attending one term at Mount Auburn, Ohio. In 1868 he took a commercial course at Small's Business College, at Zanesville, Ohio. He was associated with his father, who was a merchant, as clerk and partner until the death of his father in 1880. After this event he did not engage in any particular occupation until the fall of 1881 when he was elected Clerk of the Court of Common Pleas of Athens County by the Republican party. Sept. 18, 1871, he married Miss Sarah J., daughter of Jackson Franklin, of Morgan County, Ohio. They have three children—William F., Flora H. and Fred A.

Charles Booth Henderson, druggist, Athens, was born Feb. 23, 1856, at Parkersburg, W. Va., a son of Richard H. and Anna W. (Shanklin) Henderson. His parents removed to Wheeling and from there to Belpre, Ohio, and when he was twelve years of age, to Marietta, Ohio. He was educated in the schools of Belpre and

Marietta. When nineteen years of age he returned to Belpre and entered the drug store of C. H. Johnson, with whom he learned the business, clerking for him three years, till 1878. During 1879 he was employed as bookkeeper for J. W. Moore, of Harmar, Ohio, six months, returning to Athens in December, 1879, when he was employed as clerk by F. E. Waterman a year. In January, 1881, he, in company with P. Carpenter, purchased the drug store of Mr. Waterman and carried on the business under the firm name of Carpenter & Henderson. In January, 1882, he withdrew from the firm, and in February established his present business. Mr. Henderson is a Master, Royal Arch and Knight Templar Mason, and a member of lodge, chapter and commandery at Athens.

Joseph Herrold, a farmer and mill owner of Athens Township, was born in Ames Township, Athens County (then Washington County), Feb. 2, 1809. He is the son of Christopher and Martha (Cable) Herrold, who came to Washington County in 1798. His father dying when our subject was only thirteen years of age he began to support himself at that age by working as a farm hand at $8 per month. In 1833 he worked, under a contractor, on the Ohio Canal for $24 per month. In the latter part of that year he returned to Athens County and worked for Captain Bingham for $20 per month, and while with him, in 1834, built a flat-boat and ran it to Cairo for him. In 1836 he began to work as a bridge-builder and continued so until 1849. Many of the bridges built by him are still standing. In 1840 he purchased the mills now known as Herrold's Mill, on Hocking River, which he rebuilt in 1858 with a run of five pairs of burrs. In 1850 he went to California for his health, accompanied by C. H. Armitage, Isaac Deshler and Isaiah Baker. While in California they established a mercantile house in a mining district, and he was to receive a percentage of their profits for the first eighteen months. He then cruised on the Pacific and Atlantic coasts and returned home during the latter part of 1850. In 1854 he built the Woolen Mills at Athens, which he ran up to 1873. In 1858 he purchased 400 acres of coal lands at the mouth of Monday Creek, in York Township, and opened up the Herrold coal mines, employing many miners and shipping his coal to various places on the Hocking Valley Canal up to 1873. In 1860 he purchased the Ballard Salt Works, Athens County, which he enlarged and worked till 1880. In 1857 he again went to California, having been appointed administrator of the estate of C. H. Armitage, who was murdered at Virgin Bay, on the Pacific

Coast, when on a return trip to Athens; and while there, prospected on the North Fork of the American River and returned to Athens in 1858. He has been twice married. His first wife was Elizabeth Barker, whom he married in 1830, who died in January, 1849, from the effects of injuries received by a falling bridge near Pomeroy. They had eleven children, five of whom are still living. He married his second wife, Mrs. Orpha Baker, in December, 1849. In 1871 he built his present residence near Athens, it being one of the finest in Athens County. He is a Master, Royal Arch and Knight Templar Mason and member of the lodge, chapter and commandery at Athens. He has been a member of the Methodist Episcopal church since 1837 and an exhorter for many years.

William Henry Herrold, proprietor of Herrold's Mills, is the son of Joseph and Elizabeth (Barker) Herrold, and was born near Athens, April 8, 1833, where he was reared, and received a common-school education. When seventeen years of age he commenced to assist his father in his extensive coal mining, milling and salt manufacturing business. He worked for his father till 1876, when he became associated with him in the milling business. In 1880 his father gave him two thirds of the mill as his share of the estate, and sold him the remaining third. Mr. Herrold is a practical business man, having received a business education in boyhood, and entered upon a business career before reaching manhood. He was married June 16, 1862, to Orpha Reynolds, of Athens. They have one daughter—Rosa.

Joseph S. Higgins, farmer, stock dealer and market gardener, Athens Township, second son of Michael and Mary (McClintick) Higgins, was born in Athens Township, June 30, 1828, and lived with his parents until he was twenty-two years of age; then continued in business with his father until 1862, when he purchased the farm on which he now resides, and was engaged in farming until July 28, 1863; he then enlisted in the Independent Battery of Ohio Volunteer Artillery for sixty days; was appointed Corporal and served as such with his battery through the Morgan invasion of the State. At the expiration of his term of enlistment he was discharged at Camp Denison, Ohio, in November, 1863, and returned home, and has been actively engaged in farming, gardening and stock-dealing to the present time. He has served as Assessor of his township several years. He has been a member of the Board of Agriculture of Athens County for twenty years, serving as Vice-President eight years, and President two years. He is a Master Mason and member of Paramuthia Lodge, No. 25, F. & A. M., Athens, Ohio. Sept. 2, 1851, he married Hannah W., daughter of John M. and Amity L. (Lyons) Hibbard, of Athens Township; they have had ten children, nine living—Charlotte E., wife of William H. Wood, of Smithfield, Jefferson County, Ohio; Joseph W., married and living near his father; Cyrus M., Daniel N., John M., Charles H., Mary E., Hannah E., Nettie A. A., all at home. They lost their second child, Sarah E., who died Feb. 22, 1874, at the age of twenty years. Mrs. Mary (McClintick) Higgins, his mother, now resides with him, on the farm she settled on in the year 1817.

Judiah Higgins, harness-maker, was born near Cadiz, Ohio, May 7, 1837. When he was two years old his parents, Edward and Nancy (Collins) Higgins, removed to Athens Township, Athens County. When fifteen he came to Athens and was apprenticed to J. W. Bayard to learn the harness-making trade and served three years. He worked as a journeyman until 1867, when he established his present shop at Athens. In 1873 he was elected a member of the Council at Athens and re-elected in 1875. In 1873 he was also elected Township Trustee of Athens Township and held the office by re-election for three years. In 1878 he was elected Treasurer of Athens Township and re-elected in 1879. In 1880 he was elected a member of the Board of Education of Athens and still holds that office. In 1858 he was married to Miss Jane Umbowers, of Athens. They have two children—William Edwards and Katy K. Mr. Higgins is a member of the Masonic and Odd Fellows fraternities at Athens.

Amsey Hooper, manufacturer of the Gem bed-springs, Athens, was born in Alexander Township, Athens Co., Ohio, Feb. 11, 1856. He is the fourth of five sons of Clement and Rhoda (Axtel) Hooper, with whom he lived till twenty-one years of age. March 8, 1877, he married Maggie Angel, of Lodi Township, and went to farming, following that occupation till 1881, when he came to Athens and was employed as a clerk in the grocery of John Graham for eighteen months; then clerked for J. B. Fulton till Jan. 1, 1883. He is now engaged in the manufacture of the Gem bed-springs, for which there is at present a market in Athens and adjoining counties, with the demand constantly increasing. Mr. and Mrs. Hooper have one child—Ola.

Charles E. M. Jennings was born March 9, 1837, at Catawissa, Columbia Co., Pa., and was brought by his parents the same year to Ohio. They located in Fairfield County, where he lived with them on a farm till the fifteenth year of his age. In 1852 he went into the office of the Lancaster *Gazette* to learn the trade of a printer. In 1857 he went to Logan, and assumed the editorial control of the *Hocking Valley Republican*. During the war of the Rebellion he was Chief Clerk to the Provost Marshal General of Ohio, serving with Colonel Edward A. Parrott of the First Ohio Infantry and Colonel Joseph H. Potter of the regular army. For some time after the war he was the Columbus correspondent of the Cincinnati *Gazette*, relinquishing the position in 1868, when he purchased the Athens *Messenger*, of which he has since been editor and proprietor. The *Messenger* is the old established Republican paper of the county and now, under the editorialship of Mr. Jennings, continues to be one of the most influential papers of Southeastern Ohio. He is an able and easy writer, fearless of all contemporaries, and dauntless in advocating the principles of truth and justice.

Robert Malcolm Jennings was born in Cairo, Ill., Oct. 17, 1861. His father, Robert M. Jennings, was a son of Junia Jennings, of Marietta and was well known along the Ohio River, he having been prominent in steamboat circles for many years. The mother of the subject of this sketch was a grand-daughter of Elijah Hayward, who held the office of Commissioner of the Land Office during Jackson's administration, and who subsequently held various offices in Ohio. Mr. Jennings received a grammar-school education and learned the printer's trade at the *Messenger* office in Athens. In October of 1882, shortly after the establishment of the Athens *Herald*, he became a member of the company publishing that paper and has since been connected with it as Associate Editor.

Evan J. Jones, of the law firm of Grosvenor & Jones, Athens, was born near Centerville, Gallia Co., Ohio, Oct. 3, 1849. His mother dying when he was about eight years old, he remained in his father's family until his sixteenth year, when he went to Ewington and attended the Ewington Academy one year, he defraying the expenses by teaching district school at Portland and Madison Furnace, Jackson Co., Ohio. In the spring of 1869 he went to Lebanon, Ohio, and attended the National Normal School for four months, when he came to Athens and entered the Ohio University and graduated in the class of 1873, in the mean time having in 1872 and 1873 taught at Burlington, Ohio. Immediately after his graduation he accepted the Principalship of the Grammar School at Norwalk, Ohio, where he taught one year, at the same time privately studying law. In December, 1874, he was admitted to the bar by the Supreme Court, at Columbus, and in August, 1875, became associated with Hon. Charles Townsend, forming the law firm of Townsend & Jones, at Athens. In 1878 he became associated with Hon. Charles H. Grosvenor and formed the present law firm of Grosvenor & Jones. In 1878 he was elected City Solicitor of Athens, and by subsequent election held the position for four years. In the fall of 1881 he was appointed to fill a vacancy in the School Board of Athens and was elected to the same position in 1882. Dec. 17, 1879, he married Miss Lucy Johnson, of Pennsylvania. They have one child—Helen. Mr. Jones is a member of Sereno Lodge, No. 479, I. O. O. F., of Athens, and of the Delta Tau Delta Society, a fraternity of Ohio University. He is a member of the Baptist church at Norwalk, Ohio.

Conrad Josten, of the firm of Laird, Josten & Co., manufacturers of wagons and carriages, and dealers in agricultural implements at Athens, was born in Wheeling, Va., July 1, 1850. When eight years of age he came to Athens County with his parents, Mathias and Elizabeth (Bricker) Josten, settling in Lodi Township, where he lived with them until he was sixteen years old, when he went to Gallipolis and learned the blacksmith trade with Louis Munzt, being with him four years. He then worked at blacksmithing at various places until 1878, when he became associated with Armstrong Laird at Athens, the firm being Laird & Josten, and engaged in manufacturing carriages and general repairing. In 1882 his father became associated with them, changing the firm to Laird, Josten & Co. In 1882 he was elected a member of the Council of Athens. May 3, 1880, he married Miss Maggie Shay, of Athens. They have one child—James M. Mr. Josten is a member of St. Paul's Catholic Church at Athens.

Mathias Josten, of the firm of Laird, Josten & Co., was born in Prussia, Oct. 1, 1820. At the age of sixteen he was apprenticed to learn the trade of calico printer, at Mettlock. He afterward worked in print factories in Austria, Bavaria and Prussia until 1846, excepting two years he served in the Prussian army. In 1846 he came to America and settled in Pottsville, Pa., where he was variously employed until 1849, when he removed to Wheeling, W. Va.; thence to Athens County, Ohio, in 1857, where he settled on a farm in Lodi Township, and pursued farming for twenty-five years. In 1882 he sold his farm and came to Athens and became associated with A. Laird, and his son, Conrad Josten, in manufacturing wagons and carriages, and dealing in farming implements. Feb. 17, 1848, he married Elizabeth Bricker, of Armstrong, Pa. They have four children—Conrad, Peter, Mary and Lizzie. Mr. and Mrs. Josten are members of St. Paul's Catholic Church of Athens.

Frederick Lewis Junod was born in Canaan Township, Athens Co., Ohio, Jan. 30, 1832. When he was an infant his parents, Frederick Lewis and Ursula (Stalder) Junod, removed to Ames Township, where he was reared. His father died June, 1852, and he remained on the homestead farm with his mother till 1867, when he bought the farm in Dover Township, where he now resides. Mr. Junod was Trustee and Justice of the Peace in Ames Township several years. He has been a member of the Board of Education in Ames and Dover townships the most of the time since 1854, and has also been a Trustee in Dover Township. In 1880 he was elected one of the Directors of the Athens County Infirmary. Nov. 30, 1852, he married Lydia Ann Stephenson. They have ten children, seven sons and three daughters. Mr. and Mrs. Junod are members of the Sugar Creek Methodist Episcopal church.

Herbert Augustus Junod, son of Frederick L. and Lydia (Stephenson) Junod, was born in Ames Township, Athens Co., Ohio, Sept. 17, 1854. When he was thirteen years old his parents removed to Dover Township. He was educated in the district schools of the county, and at the Ohio University, Athens, after which he taught school two years. He then was a salesman for the Singer Manufacturing Company a year, and then was employed by F. M. Koons, lumber dealer, two years. In 1883 he accepted the situation as salesman for O. D. Jackson, proprietor of the coal mines at Jacksonville, Athens County. He is a member of the Methodist Episcopal church at Sugar Creek, and of Sereno Lodge, No.479, I. O. O. F., Athens.

Peter Kern, dealer in and manufacturer of boots and shoes, was born near Chambersburg, Pa., Oct. 10, 1837. When two and one-half years old his parents removed to Ohio and settled at Logan, Hocking County, where his father died when he was about four years old. He lived with his mother at Logan until he was nineteen. At the age of sixteen he began to learn the trade of a shoe maker, serving three years. He then worked as a journeyman at Logan and Pella, Iowa, until 1863, when he came to Athens and engaged in manufacturing and in dealing in boots and shoes. He was associated with several parties at different times, under various firm names, up to 1879, when he became sole proprietor and carried on business alone until August, 1882, when his son, Harry E., became associated with him, under the firm name of Peter Kern & Son. In April, 1879, he was elected a member of the Council of Athens for a term of two years, and re-elected in April, 1882. Oct. 18, 1860, he was married to Annie M. Reynolds, of Athens County. They have two children—Lizzie and Harry Ellsworth. He is a member of the Masonic fraternity, and has taken the degrees as high as Knight Templar.

Andrew Kessenger, deceased, was a native of Virginia, born in Rockingham County in 1800. He came to Ohio with his mother in 1812, and lived in Muskingum and Fairfield counties till 1842, when he came to Athens County, and engaged in merchandising and milling at Athens, until his death in 1853. He was an enterprising business man and one of the substantial citizens of the county. He was a member of the Methodist Episcopal church from his boyhood.

Theodore Koerner, born in Milwaukee, Wis., Feb. 25, 1845, is a son of Frederick Hugo and Amelia Margaret (Rampmire) Koerner. In August, 1862, he enlisted as a drummer in Company K, Twenty-sixth Wisconsin Infantry, and served till the close of the war. He participated in the battles of Chancellorsville, Gettysburg, Mission Ridge, Atlanta, and was with Sherman from Atlanta to the sea. He was discharged June 29, 1865. After his return to Milwaukee he was apprenticed to learn the trade of an iron-molder, serving over two years. In 1868 he started out as a journeyman and worked in towns in Iowa, Nebraska, Missouri, New York and West Virginia. In 1875 he came to Athens, and is now employed in the foundry of the Athens Water-wheel and Machine Company. Aug. 22, 1872, he married Mary Priscena Baker. They have three children—Anna Lee, Julia Belle and Louisa. Mr. Koerner is a member of Paramuthia Lodge, No. 25, A. F. & A. M.; Sereno Lodge, No. 479, I. O. O. F., of which he is Past Grand, and of Columbus Golden Post, No. 89, G. A. R.

Francis Marion Koons, grocer and dealer in lumber and building hardware at Athens, was born in Dover Township, Athens Co., Ohio, Nov. 9, 1848. His parents were George S. and

Chloe A. (Wemmer) Koons. His father died when he was an infant, and he remained with his mother until he was fourteen, when he began to maintain himself. Up to that time he had received a limited education. After becoming of age he attended two terms at a select school in Dover Township. In 1864, at the age of sixteen, he went to Mount Pleasant, Mich., and was employed on farms or in lumber camps until 1867, when he returned to Athens County, remaining there until the winter of 1868–'9. He then returned to Michigan and worked in the pineries until 1870, when he again returned to Athens County. In 1871 he began to sell goods by peddling in Athens and adjoining counties, at first carrying a pack and afterward running a wagon. He followed this business for two years. In the fall of 1873 he purchased a farm in Dover Township, where he pursued farming until 1878, and during that period taught four terms of school. Selling his farm in 1879, he purchased a tract of timber land in the vicinity of Chauncey, Athens County, where he manufactured lumber until 1880, when he removed to Athens and opened a lumber yard. January, 1882, he added to his lumber business that of groceries and building hardware. In 1880, before removing to Athens, he was elected Land Appraiser of Dover Township, and also Census Enumerator of the same township. Nov. 12, 1873, he married Martha J. Orme, of Dover Township. They have five children—Stella Irene, Leopold Wordworth, Inez Leona, Eva Maud and George Wilmarth. Mr. Koons is a Master, Royal Arch and Knight Templar Mason, and a member of the lodge, chapter and commandery at Athens.

Honorable Charles Lindly Kurtz, member of the Ohio State Legislature and senior member of the firm of Kurtz & Minear, booksellers, stationers and jewelers, Athens, is the son of W. W. Kurtz, the present Postmaster of Athens, and Isabella, *nee* McEllroy, Kurtz. He was born in Albany, Athens County, May 4, 1854. In 1865 he came with his parents to Athens where he received a common-school education. At the age of fourteen he was employed as a clerk in the book store of J. & T. W. Van Law. Some time after his father and C. D. Norris became the Messrs. Van Law's successors, and our subject had the management of the business until 1881, when he became associated with A. W. S. Minear, and they became the successors of his father and Mr. Norris, and now continue the business under the firm name of Kurtz & Minear. In 1880 he was elected by the Republican party of Athens County for member of the Sixty-fourth General Assembly of the State of Ohio, to fill a vacancy caused by the election of Major Charles Townsend as Secretary of State. He was re-elected in 1881, and is the present Representative of Athens County. Sept. 11, 1878, he married Annie, daughter of Edgar P. Jewett, Esq., of Athens County. They have two daughters, Ione and Eleanor. Mr. Kurtz is a member of the First Presbyterian Church of Athens.

William Wyland Kurtz, Postmaster of Athens, is the son of George A. and Mary (Divender) Kurtz. He was born near New Vienna, Clinton Co., Ohio, March 16, 1823. When he was an infant his parents removed to Allegheny City, Pa., where he was reared and given a common school education. He lived with his parents until manhood, and when a youth learned the carpenter trade. In 1851 he came to Athens County and settled near Albany where he pursued farming and working at his trade until the fall of 1865. During three years of that time he was Postmaster of Albany, and also served as Clerk of Lee Township about six years, and Township Trustee three years. He came to Athens in 1865, and engaged in dealing in drugs, books and stationery with a silent partner, under the firm name of W. W. Kurtz & Co., until 1868, when he became associated with C. D. Norris as booksellers, jewelers and stationers, under the firm name of Kurtz & Norris. In 1870 he received the appointment of Postmaster of Athens. His son, Charles L., was the manager of the business until 1881, when the same son and A. W. S. Minear became the successors of Kurtz & Norris. Since that time he has devoted his time wholly to the Athens postoffice. During 1864 he was commissioned Captain of Company H, One Hundred and Forty-first Regiment, Ohio National Guards, and served at Barboursville, W. Va., nearly four months. Since living in Athens he has served on the City Council three years. June 8, 1848, he married Isabella, daughter of William McEllroy, then editor of the daily *Pittsburgher*, of Pittsburg, Pa., by whom he has seven living children—William M., of Columbus, Ohio; Mary Ellen, wife of John W. Doud, Superintendent of the schools of Toledo, Ohio; George A., Hon. Charles L. and Oscar H., all of Athens; Edward B., of Columbus, and Jennie A., attending the Ohio University. They lost one, Benjamin F., a twin brother to Jennie, who died at Athens, Feb. 7, 1882, at the age of eighteen. Himself and wife are members of the Free Baptist church, of Albany, Athens County.

Armstrong Laird, senior member of the firm Laird, Josten & Company, manufacturers of wagons and carriages, and dealers in farm implements, Athens, was born near Athens, May 16, 1852, son of John and Susannah (Hooks) Laird. He attended school until sixteen years of age, and then commenced to learn the carriage-maker's trade of J. G. Cornwell, serving an apprenticeship of three years, after which he worked on a farm a year. Nov. 30, 1872, he married Rebecca M. Sams, of Canaan Township, Athens County, and came to Athens and rented a small shop where he made and repaired carriages and wagons. In the fall of 1874 he formed a partnership with John Graham, under the firm name of Laird & Graham, increasing his stock. In the spring of 1877 they sold out and established themselves in the grocery business under the firm name of Graham & Laird, but the following fall Mr. Laird withdrew his interest and engaged again in the manufacturing of wagons, etc., with Conrad Josten, under the name of Laird & Josten. In 1882 Mr. Josten's father, M. Josten, was admitted to the firm, the name changing to Laird, Josten & Co. Mr. and Mrs. Laird have two children—H. A. and Mattie A. Three children died in infancy. Mr. Laird is a member of Athenian Lodge, No. 104, K. of P., Athens. He has filled all the chairs, being at the present time Prelate.

Eli Reynolds Lash, a druggist at Athens, was born in Alexander Township, Athens County, Nov. 20, 1848. He is the son of Jacob and Susan (Morrison) Lash, with whom he lived until he became of age. He then left home, in 1869, and entered the Ohio University at Athens, attending two years. In 1871 he was employed as a druggist's clerk by Dr. E. G. Dorr, with whom he remained until 1873, when he purchased the drug store of John Perkins and established himself in the drug business at Athens. In November, 1875, he married Alice, daughter of James M. Johns, of Athens. They have two children—Rey and Florence. Mr. Lash is a Master, Royal Arch, Council, and Knight Templar Mason. He is also an Odd Fellow and a Knight of Pythias; has held important positions in all these bodies, and represented his lodge in the Grand Lodge, K. of P., of Ohio, in 1879.

Peter Fisher Martin, farmer, is the eldest of two sons of William and Mary Ann (Bodine) Martin, and was born in Bloomsbury, Hunterdon Co., N. J., Sept. 28, 1832. After arriving at manhood he was employed by his father at home on the farm, until they removed to Ohio. In 1851 he came to Ohio with his parents, and settled in Athens Township, Athens County, and pursued farming there until 1856. In the fall of 1856 he moved to Henry County, Ill., and was there employed in improving a new farm for five years. In the fall of 1861 he returned to Athens County, purchased the Willis farm, and lived there two years. He then worked on the Jewett farm one year. In the spring he moved on the Zenner farm where he lived seventeen years. In the spring of 1880 he purchased the Leonidas Jewett farm, on which he now resides. March 11, 1851, he married Mary Ann, daughter of John and Margaret (Hacket) Hoppock, of New Jersey. They have had five children, three now living—Isabel, wife of Gaston Coe, of Dover Township; John H., married, living in Dover Township; Walter H., at home. William W. was drowned in the Hocking Canal at the age of nine years; George W. died in infancy. In February, 1865, he obtained a divorce from his wife. April 20, 1865, he married Charetta H., daughter of David and Margaret (Sidders) Shafer, of Athens County. They have one son—Curtis James. Himself and wife are members of the Methodist Episcopal church.

Loring Glazier Matheny, farmer, Athens Township, oldest son of Isaac and Chistia Ann (Harper) Matheny, was born June 1, 1840, in Tyler, Dover Township, Athens County. He lived with his parents until manhood. He was educated in the common schools, the Albany Manual Laboring Institute, and attended the Ohio University at Athens three terms. He began teaching school at the age of eighteen. Oct. 20, 1861, he enlisted in Company A, Sixty-third Ohio Infantry, as a private, and was mustered into the service at Chillicothe, Ohio. He was appointed First Sergeant of his company, Feb. 20, 1862, and served as such until June 27, 1863, when he was commissioned Second Lieutenant of Company B, same regiment. He participated with his command in the battles of New Madrid, Island No. 10, Fort Pillow, Farmington, Tenn., Iuka, Corinth and Parker's Cross Roads, Tenn. He was with Sherman from Chattanooga to the sea, and participated in all the battles in which his regiment was engaged. He was mustered out of the service and discharged near Savannah, Ga., Dec. 21, 1864. He then returned to his home in Athens County, Ohio. During the year 1865 he was in the employ of the Hocking Valley Oil Company. May, 1866, he removed to Johnson County, Mo., and there engaged in school teaching until the fall of 1868, when he returned to Athens County and taught until the spring of 1870. He then engaged in farming until March, 1877, when he removed to Scotland County, Mo., and there engaged in farming. March, 1879, he returned to Athens County, and has followed farming to the present time. Nov. 17, 1869, he was married to Hannah M., daughter of William and Mary Ann (Bodine) Martin, of Athens Township. They have six children—Edward L., Gertrude M., Charles M., Luella, William M., and Mary E. Mr. and Mrs. Matheny and two oldest children are members of the Methodist Episcopal church, and he is Steward of the church and local preacher. He is a member of Columbus Golden Post, No. 89, G. A. R., of Athens.

Alexander Watts Shaw Minear, of the firm of Kurtz & Minear, booksellers, stationers and jewelers, Athens, was born in Harrison County, W. Va., Dec. 6, 1835. He came to Ohio with his parents, Jonathan and Nancy (Parrill) Minear, when he was in his fifth year, they settling near Coolville, in the southern part of Athens County, where he lived with them until his twentieth year, when he went to California and was employed as a clerk in a store for nearly two years. He then went to the gold diggings at the junction of the North and South Yuba rivers and mined until the spring of 1859, when he returned home. After his return, the same year, he purchased a half interest in the Coolville flouring-mill. Selling the same in 1860, he became associated with his brother, E. R. Minear, in the mercantile business at Guysville, Athens County. The war breaking out soon after, he sold his interest in the store to his brother and entered the Union army as First Lieutenant of Company C, Eighteenth Regiment, Ohio Volunteer Infantry, he having assisted in raising the company. At the battle of Stone River he was shot through the body, the ball penetrating his left lung. The wound was received while making a charge through a cedar thicket. It being considered fatal, his wife left her home to visit him, and although it was the order of the War Department not to let any one pass through the lines on account of a scarcity of provisions, she, by secreting herself among a load of pork-barrels covered with a large tarpaulin, succeeded in passing through the line. She remained until his convalescence, in March, 1863, when he returned home with her. Being entirely disabled for service he resigned his commission in the following April, and in the fall of that year he was elected Treasurer of Athens County, and re-elected in the fall of 1865. At the expiration of the term, having held the office for two consecutive terms, he was ineligible for re-election. In 1868 he became associated

John Patterson

with Drs. Johnson and Wilson in the drug business, under the firm name of A. W. S. Minear & Company. They discontinuing the business in 1870, he was not especially engaged in any business until the fall of 1871, when he was elected County Auditor, which he held by re-election for nine consecutive years, up to November, 1880. In the spring of 1881 he became associated with C. L. Kurtz in his present business, as Kurtz & Minear. April 20, 1860, he married Fannie, daughter of N. O. Warren, of Athens County. They have two daughters—Minnie and Rosa. He is a Master and Royal Arch Mason, and a member of the lodge and chapter at Athens.

Thomas Leazenby Mintun, ex-Probate Judge of Athens County, was born in Hampshire County, Va., June 11, 1809. When he was about six months old his parents, John and Sarah (Leazenby) Mintun, removed to Parkersburg, where his mother died about three months later. In 1812 he came with his father, who married again that year, to Athens County, O., and settled near Wolf's Plains, where he lived until he was seventeen. Having no opportunities to go to school, he received but a meager education. On leaving home, which he did in 1826, he came to Athens and became apprenticed to learn the trade of carpenter and joiner, which trade he followed until 1855. In 1837 he removed to Nelsonville, where he lived until 1876. In 1850 he was elected Justice of the Peace of York Township, and filled that office at Nelsonville, by re-election, until 1863. In 1863 he was appointed Postmaster at Nelsonville, and served as such until 1867. In the spring of 1867 he was again elected Justice of the Peace of York Township, and served until 1876. In the fall of 1867 he was elected one of the County Commissioners of Athens County for two terms of three years each. He also served as Mayor of Nelsonville several terms. In October, 1875, he was elected Probate Judge of Athens County, and served as such for two terms of three years each. In 1876 he removed to Athens, where he still resides. Jan. 14, 1830, he married Miss Nancy E. Herrold, of Athens. They have six children living—Thomas, now living in Illinois; William H., now in Cincinnati, O.; Charles H., now residing in Athens; Sarah, now wife of J. F. Welch, of Nelsonville; Lucinda E., now wife of Dr. D. G. Gillian, of Columbus, O.; and Emma, now wife of G. B. Rain, of Nelsonville. Mr. Mintun is a member of the Methodist Episcopal church. In 1842 he was licensed to preach the gospel, and was ordained as Deacon by Bishop Janes.

Henry Dustin Mirick, son of Augustus and Caroline Dustin (Prichard) Mirick, was born March 3, 1836, in Worcester, Mass. His father was by trade a printer, and during his life was a prominent journalist and publisher in Massachusetts. At the time of his death, Feb. 1, 1864, he was doing a general book and job printing business in Greenfield, Mass. His mother is a descendant of the Dustins and Prichards, families of prominence, of whom mention is made in the early histories of Massachusetts. Henry D. Mirick received a good common-school and some academical education, and learned the printer's trade of his father, being in business with him from March, 1857, till August, 1862, when he went to Cincinnati and was in the wholesale boot and shoe store of Prichard, Alter & Co. until June, 1867. He then went to Des Moines, Ia., where he was in the boot and shoe business about two years. In April, 1869, he sold out and was an agent for the Cranberry Iron property at Cranberry Forge, N. C., till the following November, when he was offered a position in the land office of the Union Pacific Railroad Company, at Humboldt, Kas. In April, 1870, he was appointed general freight and ticket agent of the Missouri, Kansas & Texas Railroad (which had assumed control of the Union Pacific), with headquarters at Junction City, Kas. July 1, 1870, owing to the increase of business, this double office was divided, Mr. Mirick retaining the position of general freight agent, with headquarters at Sedalia, Mo. In March, 1873, he was appointed assistant to the general manager of the road. He left this position in December, 1875, to take the one of assignee of the Land Grant Railway & Trust Company, headquarters still at Sedalia, filling this position till January, 1878. In addition to this and other business he was Auditor of the Hannibal & St. Joseph Railroad from February, 1876, to January, 1877, and was afterward extensively engaged in Southern Kansas and Northern Texas. From 1878 to 1879 he was Secretary and Treasurer of the Dennison & Pacific Railroad Company. In 1880 he became connected with the Osage Coal-Mining Company at Parsons, Kas., being its Vice-President and Treasurer, and at the same time became Vice-President of the First National Bank, of Parsons. In 1881 he came to Athens with the intention of making this his permanent home. Oct. 14, 1874, Mr. Mirick married Harriet S., daughter of John Brown, of Athens. She died at Sedalia, Mo., Dec. 23, 1875, leaving an infant son, and her remains were brought to Athens for burial. July 22, 1879, Mr. Mirick married Charlotte E., daughter of Henry T. Brown, of Athens. They have one child—Carlos Brown.

John A. Mc Cathran, manufacturer of carriages and buggies, Athens Township, second son of John and Mary (Stevens) McCathran, was born in Guernsey County, Ohio, April 3, 1840. He lived with his parents until manhood, receiving a common-school education. When about eight years old his parents removed to Pennsylvania, and remained there near seven years. He then went to Virginia, near Holiday's Cove, and remained nearly two years, when he went to Steubenville, Ohio, where he learned the trade of cabinet-maker. He remained at Steubenville some eighteen months, and then went to Cambridge, Ohio, where he resided two years. He then went to Bishopville, Morgan Co., Ohio, and remained there three years, when he came to Athens County. May 2, 1864, he enlisted in Company G, One-hundred and Forty-first Regiment National Guards, at Athens, Ohio, as First Sergeant of his company for 100 days, and served for four months; was mustered out and discharged at Gallipolis, Ohio, Sept. 1, 1864, and returned to Athens, Ohio. He then entered the employ of T. M. D. Pilcher in his furniture factory and worked for him about eighteen months, when he went to Hebbardsville and purchased property and began manufacturing carriages. In 1870 he sold his Hebbardsville property and purchased property near Athens and continued the manufacture of carriages there until 1876, when he sold out and purchased property near Wolf's Plains. In February, 1882, he removed to Nelsonville, Ohio, and remained four months, returning to the Plains, where he now resides. March 27, 1864, he married Fannie F., daughter of John and Elizabeth (Fierce), Stage, of Athens Township. They have two children—Nettie R., and Lizzie L. Their oldest daughter, Eva M., died July 30, 1865. Himself and wife are members of the Free Methodist church.

John Russell McCune was born in Lycoming County, Pa., June 24, 1795, a son of James and Martha (Russell) McCune, who emigrated to America from Ireland in 1790. When six years of age his friends removed to Fayette County, Pa. After arriving of age he worked the homestead farm till 1824, when, Nov. 24, he married Maria King, of Somerset County, Pa., and purchased a farm, where he lived till 1838, when he sold out and came to Athens County, Ohio, and settled on a farm two miles south of Athens. In 1861 he moved into Athens and lived four years, returning to the farm in 1865. In 1879 he retired from farm life and moved into Athens to spend the remainder of his days. Mrs. McCune died Jan. 5, 1882. He has six children—Harriet, now Mrs. W. P. Wilkin, of Missouri; Maria, now Mrs. J. N. Patterson; Ellen, now Mrs. W. A. Thomas; Ann, now Mrs. W. W. McVey; John King, and Samuel. The latter son is supposed to be living somewhere in the West. In 1851 he went to California and remained till 1857, when he went to Oregon, a volunteer in the war against the Indians. After serving about eighteen months he was taken prisoner by the Indians, by whom he was kept in bondage three years, and then exchanged to another tribe and kept by them three years. He made his escape in 1863 and reached Fort Hall, where he first heard of the Rebellion. From there he went to Salt Lake City and engaged in teaching school and acting as Indian interpreter, since which he has never been heard from. Mr. McCune has been a member of the Methodist Episcopal church over fifty years. In 1883 he visited Fayette County, Pa., where he spent his boyhood and early manhood, and married his wife, and was cordially received by relatives and friends.

Cinney McLean, jeweler, was born in Washington, Fayette Co., Ohio, Aug. 17, 1846, a son of Samuel and Eliza (Robinson) McLean, with whom he lived at his birthplace until maturity. At the age of nineteen he began to learn the jeweler's trade, serving four years. Sept. 15, 1868, he came to Athens and established his present business. In 1880 he was elected Treasurer of Athens City, and re-elected in 1882, the term of office being two years. Feb. 29, 1880, he was married to Miss Annie, a daughter of William Edwards, of Athens. They have two children—Ben and Willie. Mr. McLean is a Master, Royal Arch, Council, and Knight Templar Mason, and a member of the lodge, chapter, council and commandery at Athens.

Hon. Calvary Morris was born near Charleston, W. Va., in 1798, and spent his youth in the Kanawha Valley, laboring on a farm, and battling with the hardships of pioneer life. In 1818 he married the eldest daughter of Dr. Leonard Jewett, of Athens, and in the spring of 1819 located permanently in that town. "Finding myself," said Mr. Morris, "a stranger in a strange land, and obliged to make provision for the support of my family, my first step was to rent five acres of ground, upon which to raise a crop of corn. While cultivating that ground, during the summer of 1819, the Rev. Jacob Lindley (then acting president of the

Ohio University) came to me and said that a school teacher was much needed in our town, and proposed that I undertake it. I informed him that I was not at all qualified—that reading, writing, spelling, and a limited knowledge of arithmetic was the extent of my education. He said that the wants of the community required that arithmetic, geography, and English grammar be taught in the school, and 'now,' said he, 'I will tell you what to do. I have the books and you have brains; take my books, go to studying, and recite to me every day for three weeks, and by that time I will have a school made up for you; you will then find no difficulty in keeping ahead of your scholars so as to give satisfaction in teaching, and no one will ever suspect your present lack of qualifications.' I consented, went to work, and at the end of three weeks went into the school. I taught and studied during the day, and cultivated my corn-field part of the time by moonlight, and if there was ever any complaint of my lack of qualifications as a teacher, it never came to my knowledge."

In 1823 Mr. Morris was elected Sheriff of Athens County, and re-elected by an almost unanimous vote in 1825. In 1827, at the close of his term as Sheriff, he was elected to the lower branch of the State Legislature, and re-elected in 1828. In 1829 he was elected to the State Senate, and re-elected in 1833. In 1835, when the project of the Hocking canal was being warmly agitated, Mr. Morris was elected again to the popular branch of the Assembly from Athens and Hocking counties, as the avowed friend of that measure, and in the belief that he was the best man to engineer it through. To his adroit management and indefatigable efforts the measure was mainly indebted for success, as he had to overcome the almost unanimous opposition of both branches of the Legislature and the whole Board of Canal Commissioners. He had the pleasure of seeing the bill triumphantly passed a few days before the close of the session, and on his return home his constituents tendered him a public dinner.

In 1836 Mr. Morris was elected to Congress, and re-elected in 1838 and '40. In 1843 he retired from public life and engaged, to some extent, in wool growing and in the introduction of fine-wooled sheep into the county, in which business he rendered great service to the farming community. In 1847 he removed to Cincinnati and engaged in mercantile pursuits, which finally proving unfortunate. he returned to Athens in 1854, and in 1855 was elected Probate Judge of the county.

Few men of the county have filled a larger part in its official history than Judge Morris, and, during his varied services, he discharged every trust with honor and fidelity. In his latter days, secure in the confidence and respect of all his neighbors, he had the rare and happy fortune of being able to review his whole career without shame and without remorse.

Judge Morris was a brother of the Reverend Bishop Morris of the Methodist Episcopal church; William D. Morris, of Illinois, and Levi Morris, of Louisiana, were the other brothers. He died at Athens, Oct. 13, 1871.

Alfred Morrison, son of Joseph and Susan Morrison, was born in Jefferson County, Ohio, Aug. 21, 1820. He was the sixth of a family of seven children, and when only four years old his father died. His mother then took her children to Belmont County and lived there eleven years. They then came to Athens County and settled on the same farm where Mr. Morrison now lives. Nov. 15, 1842, he married Minerva Benson, of Monroe County, Ohio. They have seven children—Joseph, Emma J., Susan, Elizabeth, E. B., Lydia A. and George. Mr. Morrison has a fine farm of 220 acres, with a good residence and farm buildings. Politically he is a Democrat. He has been School Director many years, and takes an active interest in the welfare and education of the young. He is a member of the Masonic fraternity, Lodge No. 25, Athens.

Augustus Norton, President of the First National Bank of Athens, is the only son of Joseph H. and Rosannah (Johnson) Norton. He was born at Athens, Dec. 19, 1837, where he was reared and educated in the Ohio University. In early boyhood he began clerking in his father's store, and upon becoming of age became associated with his father in the mercantile business, under the firm name of J. H. Norton & Son, and so continued until the breaking out of the war. In June, 1861, he enlisted in the Union service as a member of Company F, First Ohio Volunteer Cavalry. At the organization of his company he was elected First Lieutenant, and was commissioned by Governor F. H. Pierpoint. He served as such until July 25, 1862, when he resigned and returned to Athens. In the following August he raised Company I, Seventh Ohio Volunteer Cavalry, and was commissioned Captain of that company by Governor David Tod, Sept. 2, 1862. The Seventh Regiment was composed of three battalions, his company being one of the Second. Dec. 28, 1862, he was commissioned Major of his regiment and placed in command of that battalion, and served until Jan. 30, 1864, when he was discharged for disability, caused by an injured ankle. He participated in many battles and skirmishes, the most important being those of Winchester, Port Republic, Mount Sterling, Strawberry Plains and Cumberland Gap. After resigning he returned to Athens, and in the following spring resumed business with his father, whose interest he purchased in 1868. In 1870 he discontinued the mercantile business on account of impaired health and purchased a farm in the vicinity of Athens, where he still lives, and with other business pursues farming. In 1879 he became connected with the First National Bank of Athens, and at the same time was elected its President. He has served as Trustee of Athens Township two terms. At the organization of Athens County Children's Home, in 1881, he was commissioned by the county commissioners as one of its Trustees. March 26, 1866, he married Miss Sarah W., daughter of George Putnam, Esq., of Athens. They have five children—Frankie J., S. Alberta, Joseph Augustus, Alice and Willie. They have lost two—George Putnam, who was drowned in the Hocking River, June 5, 1879, at the age of twelve; and Wyatt Parker, dying in infancy. Himself and wife are members of the First Presbyterian Church of Athens.

Cornelius Battelle O'Bleness, carpenter and joiner, was born at Newport, O., Sept. 23, 1853. [For genealogy see biography of his brother, Henry O'Bleness.] He left home in his twentieth year and came to Athens and became apprenticed to his brother, Henry O'Bleness, to learn the carpenter's trade, serving three years. He then, in 1876, went to Sidney, O., and worked one year, when he returned to Athens, where he has since resided. Sept. 20, 1878, he married Miss Belle Johns, of Athens. They have one child— Frank Bernard. Mr. O'Bleness is a member of the Masonic, Odd Fellows and Knights of Pythias fraternities of Athens. He was the first Past Chancellor of Athenian Lodge, No. 104, K. of P., of Athens, and has represented his lodge in the Grand Lodge of the State of Ohio.

Henry O'Bleness, architect, contractor and builder, is a descendant of a sturdy Hollander who came from over the sea long before the Revolution, bringing with him his wife whose maiden name was Mary Devoe. They settled in the city of New York, and in time possessed considerable property, owning a large portion of Manhattan Island. To them was born Henry (their third son), in

New York City, March 15, 1771. He was married in the city of New York, May 15, 1796, to Rachel (Rickman) Davenport, a widow. He emigrated to Ohio in 1817, and settled in Washington County, near Marietta. To them was born John Vark, at Kingsbridge, near New York City, Aug. 21, 1809, who came with his parents to Ohio in 1817. He was married in Lawrence Township, Washington Co., O., Oct. 29, 1829, to Susan Hoff, and settled at Newport, near Marietta, where the subject of this sketch was born to them, June 16, 1842. He lived with his parents until he was nineteen and learned his father's trade, that of carpenter and joiner. He enlisted in 1861 in Company F, Eighty-fifth Ohio Infantry, to serve three months. After being discharged at the expiration of his term of service he went to Marietta and worked at the carpenter's trade until May 2, 1864, when he enlisted in Company G, One Hundred and Forty-eighth Ohio National Guards, to serve 100 days, going out as a Sergeant. When discharged from service he again returned to Marietta and resumed the carpenter's trade. In the spring of 1865 he returned to Newport and engaged in contracting and building, also in dealing in lumber until the spring of 1869, when he came to Athens and became associated with W. W. McCoy, as McCoy & O'Bleness, and took the contract to construct the wood work of Athens Asylum for the Insane, he having the full charge of the business. Mr. McCoy remained with him for three years. Mr. O'Bleness completed the contract, requiring a period of five years, after which he determined to remain at Athens and has either superintended or built by contract the city hall, court-house, university building and many of the business houses and private residences of Athens. March 7, 1871, he was married to Josephine M. Shearer, of Belpre, Washington Co., Ohio. They have four children—Henry Clifford, Charles Garnett, Ralph Alphonso and Mary Lulu. Mr. and Mrs. O'Bleness are members of the Methodist Episcopal church. He is a Master and Royal Arch Mason and member of the lodge and chapter at Athens.

Matthew Patrick, son of Jacob and Sarah (Spicer) Patrick, was born Jan. 28, 1811, in Sullivan Township, Madison Co., N. Y., where he was reared and received a common-school education. When sixteen years of age he went to Lyons, N. Y., and clerked in his brother's store five years. In 1832 he came to Ohio to sell fanning-mills for his brother-in-law, Zalmon Rice, traveling for him three years. In 1835 he went into the mercantile business at Lithopolis, Ohio, and in 1837 removed his stock of goods to Athens, and was one of the leading merchants here several years. In 1856 he bought a farm in the vicinity of Athens where he lived till 1866, when he again moved to Athens. Mr. Patrick was married May 1, 1839, to Lydia S., daughter of John Walker, of Athens. One son was born to them—John J., who died Sept. 7, 1861, aged twenty-one years. Mrs. Patrick died Feb. 1, 1879. Aug. 10, 1880, Mr. Patrick married Mrs. Martha A. Davis, widow of John Davis, who died at Athens, Dec. 30, 1871. Mrs. Patrick has had two children—Ella, who died Feb. 9, 1873, aged nineteen, and Mary Hattie. Mr. and Mrs. Patrick are members of the Methodist church, of which he has been Steward and Trustee for forty years.

Richard Phillips, a native of Hunterdon County, N. J., born Jan. 11, 1807, was a son of Thomas and Mary (Angell) Phillips, natives of England. He lived on a farm till seventeen years of age and then went to learn the boot and shoe maker's trade, an occupation he followed many years. In December, 1831, he married Leah Bishop. They had ten children—John B., Mary, Thomas, Wilson, Kate, Elizabeth, David, W. H. L., Jane and Belle. In May, 1842, Mr. Phillips started for Athens County, with his family and household goods. He was on the road a month, arriving in Athens, June 4. He settled in Lodi Township on the farm now owned by Thomas Angell. Here, with the assistance of his sons, he cleared 160 acres of timbered land. In 1856 he sold the farm and removed to Canaan Township. He lived there till 1870 and then bought his present home, where he has fifty acres of good land and is surrounded with all the comforts of life. His wife died in October, 1868, and June 6, 1870, he married Jane Robinson, a native of England. Mr. Phillips is a member of the Methodist Episcopal church, and has been a Steward and Class-Leader. He started in life poor, and by his own exertions has acquired the property he now has.

Belford Wood Pickering, M. D., assistant physician in the Athens Asylum for the Insane, a son of Samuel and Catherine (Wood) Pickering, was born at Athens, July 26, 1853. He was educated in the Union schools of Athens and the Ohio University. In the fall of 1873 he began the study of medicine in the office of Dr. A. B. Frame, and was under his preceptorship three years. He graduated from the Medical College of Ohio at Cincinnati, in the spring of 1875, after taking two courses of lectures. In 1878 he began to practice at Stewart, O., and in the fall of 1880 he was appointed assistant physician of the Athens Asylum for the Insane. April 23, 1879, he married Miss Susie D. Foster, of Washington County, O. They have one child—Julia D. Dr. Pickering is a Master, Royal Arch, and Knight Templar Mason, and member of the lodge, chapter and commandery at Athens.

Francis O. Pickering, born near St. Clairsville, Belmont Co., O., Dec. 26, 1837, is the eldest of eight sons of Levi and Susannah (Spiller) Pickering. He was given a common-school education, living with his parents till he was of age, and coming with them to Athens Township in 1854. In 1858 he went to Wheeling, Va., and purchased a stock of notions and stationery, which he sold by running a peddler's wagon through Athens, Meigs, Washington and Morgan counties. He followed that business till August, 1862, when he enlisted in Company I, One Hundred and Sixteenth Ohio Infantry, and served till the close of the war. He enlisted as a private and after serving as such a year was promoted to Commissary Sergeant. The most important battles in which he participated were Moorefield, Winchester, Fisher's Hill, Cedar Creek, Lynchburg, siege and capture of Petersburg, and Richmond; was present at the surrender of Lee's army at Appomattox Court-House. He was discharged in June, 1865, and returned to Athens, where he has followed farming together with dealing extensively in coal. He has been twice married. His first wife was Hannah E. Tedrow, whom he married March 9, 1860. She died in December, 1861, leaving one son—William F., who was drowned in the Hocking River, in July, 1867, aged six years. June 7, 1866, he married Mary Jane, daughter of Robert C. Clark, of Athens Township. They have had six children, only five now living—Francis C., Warrington Addison, Thomas O., Charles G., and Sarah May. Clarence Edward died March 26, 1873, aged six years. Mr. Pickering was a member of the City Council from 1880 to 1881. He is a member of Columbus Golden Post, No. 89, G. A. R., of which he has been Vice-Commander.

Joseph L. Pickering, postal clerk on the Columbus & Athens route on the C., H. V. & T. Railroad, is a son of Samuel and Catherine (Wood) Pickering, and was born in Athens, Aug. 11, 1846, where he was reared, and educated in the Ohio University. When fifteen, in 1862, he enlisted in Company H, Eighty-seventh Ohio Infantry, to serve three months, but served five, as a Corporal. His company was under a siege of four days at Harper's Ferry, when they were taken prisoners in September, 1862, and released on parole. He was discharged with his regiment at Delaware, O., in October, 1862, but still under parole, and was not exchanged until the following February. In July, 1863, when Morgan made his raid through the border counties of Ohio, he, with other citizen soldiers, shouldered his musket and joined in the pursuit, and while on duty near Cheshire, Gallia County, was slightly wounded. In May, 1864, he enlisted in Company B, Fourteenth Ohio National Guards, to serve 100 days, and with his regiment was on detached duty as guard in the Fort at Barboursville, W. Va., and was discharged Sept. 3, 1864. Soon after, being a member of the Athens Light Artillery, he was called out for duty at Camp Dennison, O., and served three months. He then attended Ohio University until the spring of 1866, when he went to Maryville, Mo., and engaged in the insurance business until November, and during the winter of 1866–'67 he taught school at Xenia, returning home in the following spring. In the spring of 1868 he was employed as an engineer in the coal regions in the vicinity of White Oak, W. Va., where he remained until January, 1869. He then returned to Athens and was variously employed until 1872, when, with his father and brother, he engaged in the grocery business at Athens, under the firm name of S. Pickering & Sons. They remained in the business until 1876. While in the grocery business, in 1875, he was appointed express agent for the Adams Express Company and held this position until March, 1882, when he was appointed Postal Clerk on the C., H. V. & T. Railroad, between Athens and Columbus. He is a Master, Royal Arch, Council and Knight Templar Mason.

Levi Pickering, Assessor of Athens Township, was born in St. Clairsville, Belmont Co., Ohio, March 24, 1815. He was the second of five sons of Levi and Susannah (Crozier) Pickering. He remained on the homestead farm till 1840 when he came to Athens, and was employed a year by Pickering & Corley (his brother Samuel being a member of the firm) to superintend the construction of a section of the Hocking Valley canal. He then returned to Belmont County and purchased a farm, living there till 1853, when he sold out and came again to Athens County, buying a farm in the vicinity of Athens, where he still resides. In 1854 he was elected Assessor of Athens Township and has held the office by re-election ever since, with the exception of four years. During the war he was appointed by Captain Barber, Provost Marshal, Special Agent of the Fifteenth Provost District of Ohio. In

1837 he married Susannah Spiller, of Belmont County. They have had fourteen children, twelve of whom, seven sons and five daughters, are still living. Mr. and Mrs. Pickering are members of the Methodist church, of which he has been a Class-Leader and Steward for twenty-five years. He is an ancient Odd Fellow, holding a card but a member of no lodge.

Samuel Pickering, manufacturer of cigars and dealer in wool at Athens, was born near St. Clairsville, Ohio, June 24, 1811. He lived with his parents, Levi and Susannah (Crozier) Pickering, until his nineteenth year, and was given a good common-school education. On leaving home he taught school two years, when, in 1832, he engaged in the mercantile business at St. Clairsville, until the fall of 1836. He then removed his business to Concord, Ohio, where he remained until 1838 when he came to Athens, still continuing the mercantile business until 1854. Upon being elected Treasurer of Athens County he gave up his business. In connection with his merchandising he also, in 1838, became associated with R. W. Corley as Corley & Pickering, and built two locks on the Hocking Valley canal, requiring three years to complete the contract. During the winters of 1847 and 1848 he engaged extensively in packing pork at Beardstown, Ill. He was also a dealer in stock in connection with his mercantile business, driving horses, cattle and sheep to the Eastern markets. In 1856 he was re-elected Treasurer of Athens County, holding the office for two terms, until 1859. He then engaged in farming and bred and dealt in sheep for several years, and during the late war bought horses for the Government. In 1872 he engaged in the grocery business, his sons, Joseph L. and Ernest C., being associated with him, under the firm name of S. Pickering & Sons. They also constructed a section of the Baltimore & Ohio Shortline R. R. under contract. They discontinued the grocery business in 1876. In 1882 he began to manufacture cigars at Athens. He has served several years in the City Council of Athens, and at the organization of the First National Bank he was chosen one of its Directors and served three years. He was the first President of the Athens Loan & Building Association. In May, 1842, he was married to Catherine G. Wood, of Athens. They have four living children—William B., of Carthage, Tenn.; Joseph L., a postal clerk on the C., H. V. & T. Railroad; Ernest C., express messenger on the Ohio & Virginia R. R.; and Belford W., a physician in the Athens Asylum for the Insane. They have lost two children—Frank Belmont, who died Oct. 8, 1853, at the age of three years, and Levi C., who was killed at the battle of Perryville, Ky., Oct. 8, 1862. Mr. Pickering is a Master, Royal Arch and Knight Templar Mason.

Simon Woodrow Pickering, son of Levi and Susannah (Crozier) Pickering, was born in St. Clairsville, Belmont Co., O., Feb. 4, 1819. He received his education in the common schools of his native town and at the Franklin Institute, Harrison Co., O. He lived at home until he arrived at manhood, clerking, when a boy, at intervals, in his father's store. After becoming of age he clerked for his father till 1845, when he became associated with him as a partner, under the firm name of L. Pickering & Son. In 1851 he withdrew his interest and came to Athens and formed a partnership with his brother, Samuel Pickering, and R. W. Corley, the firm name being Pickering, Corley & Co. In 1856 W. L. Brown succeeded Messrs. Corley and Samuel Pickering, changing the firm to Pickering & Brown. In 1858 he withdrew from the mercantile business and became connected with the Big Sand Furnace Company in Vinton County. In 1860 he was elected Auditor of Athens County, and held that office by re-election till 1871. From that time till 1881 he was connected with the Columbus & Hocking Valley Railroad Company, being one of the Directors. During the same time, from 1875, he was engaged in the milling business at Zanesville, O., a member of the firm of Pickering, Grant & Co., proprietors of the Casel Flouring Mills. In 1881 he retired from business, except dealing in real estate and being a stockholder in the Nelsonville Coal & Coke Company. He has served several terms in the City Council of Athens, and also as a member of the School Board. Since 1880 he has been a Trustee of the Athens Asylum for the Insane. June 20, 1843, Mr. Pickering married Miss Elizabeth Collins, of St. Clairsville, O. They have three children—Charles C., in business at Columbus, O.; Ella, wife of H. C. Will, of Columbus, and Woodrow S., Assistant Paymaster of the Hocking Valley & Toledo Railroad Company. Mr. Pickering is a Master and Royal Arch Mason, a member of lodge and chapter at Athens.

Theodore Marcus Pickering, born April 7, 1844, near St. Clairsville, Belmont Co., Ohio, is the second of eight sons of Levi and Susannah (Spiller) Pickering. In September, 1864, he enlisted in Company D, One Hundred and Seventy-fourth Ohio Infantry, and served till the close of the war. A month after going out he was promoted to Corporal. He participated in the battles of Murfreesboro, Overall's Creek and Kingston; was discharged at Columbus, O., July 5, 1865, and returned to Athens County, and attended the Ohio University nearly four years. Aug. 20, 1870, he married Sarah J. Talbott, of Ashley, O., who died June 29, 1875, leaving one child—Pearl. After his marriage he settled on a farm in Athens Township, where he lived till 1875, when he came to Athens and engaged in the coal business with his brother, Francis O., at the same time carrying on his farm. From 1878 to 1880 he carried on the coal business alone, and since that time has been dealing largely in produce in Athens. March 15, 1877, he married Charlotte White, of Athens. They have one child—Mary Nellie. Mr. and Mrs. Pickering are members of the Methodist Episcopal church at Athens. He is a member of Athenian Lodge, No. 104, K. of P., of which he is Past Chancellor, and of Columbus Golden Post, No. 89, G. A. R.

Thomas Murray Drake Pilcher, manufacturer of sashes, blinds and furniture, and dealer in furniture, at Athens, was born in the vicinity of Athens, April 22, 1832. His parents, John and Laura (Warren) Pilcher, both died before he had reached the age of sixteen. At that age he came to Athens and was apprenticed to W. B. Bartlett, to learn the trade of cabinet-maker, serving three years. He then engaged in furniture-making at Athens, remaining in the business one year, when, in December, 1851, he went to California, where he mined and worked at the carpenter's trade at Jacksonville until September, 1854. He then returned to Athens and soon after went to Logan, Hocking County, engaging in the clothing business for about six months, when he sold out and again went to Jacksonville, Cal., working at the carpenter's trade until 1856, when he returned to Athens, and the same year became associated with W. B. Bartlett in the furniture business, under the firm name of Bartlett & Pilcher. Our subject retired from the firm in 1857, and went to Logan, engaging in the furniture business there until Nov. 8, 1861, when he received a recruiting commission as Second Lieutenant, and assisted in recruiting Company H, Seventy-fifth Ohio Volunteer Infantry. Upon the organization of the company he was selected for Captain, and so commissioned by Governor Tod. He served until May, 1862, when he resigned on account of ill health. He returned to Logan and was soon after employed by Joseph Herrold as superintendent of his coal mine at the mouth of Monday Creek, in Athens County. In 1866, he became associated with Mr. Herrold in a planing-mill at Athens, under the firm name of Herrold & Pilcher. In 1867 Mr. E. H. Moore became Mr. Herrold's successor, the firm name being changed to T. M. D. Pilcher & Co. They built an extensive factory, which was burned down in March, 1879. The following April Mr. Pilcher built his present commodious factory at Athens, and has continued in the manufacturing business ever since. May 20, 1856, he married Martha B. Herrold, daughter of Joseph Herrold, of Athens. They have three children—Charles A., now an employe in his father's factory; Thomas Milroy, now a student in Ohio University; and Hastings Moore. Mr. Pilcher and wife are members of the Methodist Episcopal church at Athens. Our subject has served as Class-Leader, Trustee and Steward many years. He is a member of Sereno Lodge, No. 479, I. O. O. F.; and of Columbus Golden Post, No. 89, G. A. R., at Athens.

William Hull Potter, grocer, Athens, was born at Providence, R. I., Feb. 9, 1818, where he was reared and educated in the private schools. At the age of sixteen he went to Edwardsville, Ill., and clerked in the store of S. Kidmore & Hall for a short time, when he returned to Providence and entered his father's store as a clerk, and was so employed until his father's death in 1839, when he became his successor. He discontinued the business in 1843, and in 1844 he removed to Pittsburg, Pa., and engaged in manufacturing cigars until 1845. He enlisted in Company K, First Regiment Pennsylvania Volunteers, called the De Quense Greys, Colonel Wyncoop, and served during the Mexican war. He participated in the besiegement and capture of Vera Cruz, Cerro Gordo, Huamanta and the investment of the city of Mexico. After being mustered out of the service at Pittsburg, Aug. 22, 1847, he resumed manufacturing cigars. The following year he came to Athens and engaged in the same business until 1852, when he discontinued it, and since then has been in the grocery business. June 24, 1839, he married Eliza, daughter of Jeremiah Whipple, of Providence, R. I., who died at Athens, Feb. 5, 1855. They had six children, two of whom are living—Lizzie, wife of C. D. Norris, Superintendent of the Ohio & West Virginia Railroad, at Cincinnati; and Charles W., insurance agent of Athens. He is an ancient Odd Fellow, and one of the charter members of Sereno Lodge, at Athens.

Judge Samuel B. Pruden spent forty-eight years of his manhood a resident of Athens County. His wealth, all acquired by honorable industry, his great business ability and his public enterprise justly place him in position of eminence in this work. He was the son of Silas and Rebecca Pruden, born near Morristown, N. J., Jan. 17, 1798. Of his early education there, little is definitely known, but he never graduated from any institution of learning, having acquired his education principally by private study and reading. The family came to Athens County, O., in 1815, where they became well known, one of the daughters becoming the wife of Governor Brough. Samuel B. Pruden was married to Miss Mary Cranston, of Athens, in 1821. On entering business he was careful and industrious, and successful from the first. Among other business interests his attention was principally given to the milling and wool-carding business in the Bingham Mills, west of Athens, for ten years following 1826. In 1836 he transferred his business to his own permanent establishments about two miles south of Athens, on the bank of the Hocking River, the location being since known as Harmony. Here he erected an oil-mill, a grist and saw mill and in 1840 bored wells and began the manufacture of salt. A coal bank was opened for the use of the salt furnaces and for years the product of salt here and at Mr. Pruden's works at Chauncey was many thousand bushels annually. His business at Harmony gradually extended until a village grew up around him, occupied mostly by people in his own employ. He was elected by the State Legislature a Trustee of the Ohio University in 1851. As was his habit in his own business, he was punctual and judicious in the discharge of this trust, taking a deep interest in the welfare of the institution to the end of his life. Though not a man of collegiate education, yet by much reading, his literary, and especially his scientific, attainments were highly creditable. He was elected to the Ohio Legislature to represent Athens County during its second session under the new constitution in the winter of 1854-'5, and served one term as Associate Judge on the Common Pleas bench. He also held a number of minor offices, among them that of County Surveyor for a number of years. In the Masonic fraternity he passed through the successive degrees until he became Commander of Athens Encampment of Knights Templar. He was ever gentlemanly in his bearing, and in every position honorable in the highest sense of the term. He died Dec. 10, 1863.

Alonzo Blair Richardson, M. D., Superintendent of the Athens Asylum for the Insane, was born near Portsmouth, Scioto Co., Ohio, Sept. 11, 1852, a son of Edward W. and Mary (Blair) Richardson. He was educated in the public schools of his neighborhood, and the Ohio University, at Athens. At the age of sixteen he began to teach school and taught while pursuing his literary and professional studies, and while pursuing his medical studies, in 1873, taught as Principal of the public schools at Ravenswood, W. Va. In the fall of 1872, immediately after leaving the University, he began the study of medicine under Dr. D. B. Cotton, at Portsmouth. He graduated as M. D. from the Bellevue Hospital Medical College of New York, in the spring of 1876, after taking two courses of lectures. He afterward also graduated from the Medical College of Ohio at Cincinnati. In March, 1877, he received the appointment of assistant physician in the Athens Asylum for the Insane and filled that position until May, 1878. He then went to Portsmouth and practiced until March, 1881, when he was appointed Superintendent of the Athens Asylum for the Insane. Oct. 25, 1876, he was married to Miss Julia D., daughter of J. W. Harris, of Chillicothe, Ohio. They have three children—William Waddle, Mary Bertha and Edith. Dr. and Mrs. Richardson are members of the Methodist Episcopal church at Athens.

John Ring, born in Somersetshire, England, June 30, 1814, was a son of John and Bridget (Long) Ring. His parents removed to Devonshire when he was still an infant, where they both died before he was seven years old. He then lived with his grandfather, William Ring, till he was fifteen years old when he went to Taunton, Somersetshire, and was apprenticed to learn the butcher's trade, serving four years, after which he remained with his master as an employe about ten years. From 1842 to 1856 he pursued farming and butchering at Creech St. Michael, near Taunton. He then came to America, settling in Athens, Ohio, where he was employed by Abraham Newton two years. In 1858 he bought Mr. Newton's interest and established his present business. May 24, 1842, he married Amelia Watson, of Taunton. They have two children—William and Ellen (Mrs. Ezra Phillips, of Amesville). Mr. and Mrs. Ring are by education Episcopalians, but Mrs. Ring is now a member of the First Presbyterian Church, Athens. Mr. Ring has served twice in the Athens City Council.

Alonzo Lawrence Roach, grocer of Athens, was born near Lowell, Ohio, Aug. 22, 1828. His parents were John and Anna (Roach) Roach. His father dying when he was but two years old, he remained with his mother until he was seventeen, when he was employed as cabin-boy on a steamboat on the Muskingum River.

He passed through all the grades of steamer-life, from cabin-boy to second mate. In 1859 he quit steamboating and attended school, and was variously employed until October, 1853, when he came to Athens, where he worked at the carriage trade until February, 1859; then engaged in the hardware, stoves and tinware business at Athens. He followed this business until 1869, and during that time was in partnership, at different periods with H. J. Topky, Oliver Childs and James Ballard. In January, 1869, he established himself in his present business, his sons, Frank S. and Harry M., being associated with him, they keeping two groceries in Athens. He married Maria Louisa, daughter of Oliver Childs, of Athens, Oct. 5, 1853, three children being born to them—Frank Spencer, Emma Louisa and Harry Milton. Feb. 1, 1858, he married his second wife, Mrs. Clarissa Eleanor Post, daughter of David Goodspeed, of Athens County, and widow of the late John Post, Esq., who left two daughters—Lizzie Noble, who died at Athens, March 20, 1865, at the age of five years, and Cora Anna.

Charles Perry Rose, born July 4, 1840, in Canaanville, Athens Co., Ohio, is the youngest of the five sons of Mathias and Lydia M. (Dewey) Rose. When an infant his parents removed to Coolville, and when he was nine years of age they went to Barlow Township, Washington County. When fifteen years of age he came to Athens and went into his brother Cyrus's shop, with the intention of learning the saddler's trade, but was obliged to abandon it on account of weak eyes. He then attended the High School a year, defraying his expenses by serving as janitor. He afterward attended the Ohio University a year, receiving the free tuition due one from each county in the State. He then returned to Washington County, and remained till the breaking out of the Rebellion, when, in August, 1861, he enlisted in Company F, First West Virginia Cavalry, re-enlisting in November, 1864, and serving till the close of the war, being mustered out July 9, 1865. He was in the battles of Winchester, second Bull Run, Culpeper, Hagerstown, Monterey and numerous others. After his return home he attended the Atwood Institute, at Albany, four months. He then came to Athens where he was variously employed until 1873, and since then has been foreman of the stables at the Athens Asylum for the Insane. June 14, 1867, he married Matilda Duncan, of Athens Township, who died Nov. 6, 1882. He has three children—Jessie L., Alice Irene and Mattie May. Mr. Rose is a Master Mason, a member of Paramuthia Lodge, No. 25, Athens; is Past Chancellor of Athenian Lodge, No. 104, K. of P., and a member of Columbus Golden Post, No. 89, G. A. R., Athens.

Cyrus Rose, saddler and harness-maker, was born near Watertown, N. Y., Feb. 4, 1831. His parents came to Ohio when he was four years of age, living at Athens, Chillicothe and Coolville. When he was fifteen he went to Marietta and learned the saddle and harness-maker's trade with Charles Cambers & Co., serving an apprenticeship of four years, after which he attended the Harmar Academy a year and the Wesleyan University at Delaware two years. He then worked at his trade in Harmar a year, and in 1853 he came to Athens and worked for E. P. Jewett a year. In 1854 he established his present shop, where he is doing a good business. He was married Sept. 20, 1853, to Cornelia S., daughter of Major Reed, Esq., of Reedsville, Meigs County. They have six children—Edward T., Justice of the Peace, Athens; Alice L., graduate of the Athens Union School, class of 1877; Charles Otis, Belle, Frank C. and Fannie. Mr. and Mrs. Rose are both members of the Methodist church. He is a local preacher; was ordained Deacon by Bishop Thomas A. Morris, Sept. 30, 1866.

Frederick Roth, proprietor of Athens Tannery, was born in Mecklenburg Schwerin, Germany, Oct. 23, 1838. When sixteen years of age he came with his father to America, going first to Harmony, near Springfield, Ohio, where they worked in a tannery about three years. In the meantime his mother and the remainder of the family had followed them to America. They then went to Jeffersonville and established a small tan yard, working together about twelve years. In 1870 Frederick withdrew his interest in the business and went to farming near Jeffersonville. In 1875 he sold his farm and came to Athens, where he is now extensively engaged in the tanning business. June 16, 1869, he married Margaret Coons, of Fayette County, Ohio. Mr. Roth is by birth and education a Lutheran, and though a member of no church adheres to the faith of the Lutheran church.

James W. Sands, Deputy Sheriff of Athens County, was born Oct. 22, 1854, in Ogle County, Ill., son of William H. B. and Nancy A. (Sanderson) Sands. When he was eight years old his parents removed to Zaleski, Vinton Co., Ohio. He received his education in the schools of his native town, New Plymouth, Ohio, and the Ohio University, graduating from the latter in the class of 1879. He was employed in the freight and telegraph offices of the M. & C. R. R., at Zaleski and Roxabell, a short time, and in the fall of 1879 came to Athens and commenced the study of law, under the preceptorship of Hon. C. H. Grosvenor. In January, 1880, he was appointed Deputy Sheriff, by Sheriff Tim. B. Warden, and is now serving in that capacity, still pursuing the study of law. He is a Master, Royal Arch, and Knight Templar Mason, and a member of the lodge, chapter and commandery at Athens.

Jacob Shafler, merchant tailor, Athens, born in Munich, Germany, Feb. 23, 1847, is a son of Nicholas and Madlaine (Moore) Shafler. He was educated in the business college of his native city and learned the trade of a tailor. In 1879 he came to America, first stopping in New York City about three months. He then came to Athens and worked for Enneking & Bunnemire four months, after which he went to Portsmouth, Ohio, and from there to Rushville, Ind., returning to Athens Oct. 1, 1880, when he established his present business. Sept. 1, 1881, Mr. Shafler married Miss Lionne Bodine, of Rushville, Ind. He is a member of the Paramuthia Lodge, No. 25, A. F. & A. M.; Portsmouth Lodge, No. 416, I. O. O. F., and Athenian Lodge, No. 104, K. of P. Jan. 1, 1883, he was elected a member of the Board of Directors of the People's Building and Loan Company, of Athens.

Christopher Remington Sheldon, City Clerk of Athens, was born at Pawtuxet, R. I., July 15, 1823, the son of Christopher and Amelia (Holmes) Sheldon, with whom he came to Athens County, Ohio, in 1835. Previous to that time he had attended the schools of his native town, and after arriving at Athens he attended school two terms. In 1837 (then being fourteen years old) he went to Coshocton, Ohio, and clerked two and a half years when he returned to his father and pursued farming on the homestead farm until 1852. He then removed to Athens where he worked at the carpenter's trade until 1861, after which he was in the grocery business until 1880. In April, 1861, he was elected a Trustee of Athens Township, and being re-elected served four years. In 1866 he was appointed Clerk of Athens Township, to fill a vacancy, and in the subsequent spring was elected to the same office. Since 1870 he has been City Clerk of Athens. He has been twice married. His first wife was Miss Melvina Rice, of Athens, whom he married Nov. 30, 1846, and who died in September, 1850, leaving him two sons—Thomas H., of Colorado, who has been Teller and Cashier of the First National Bank seventeen years, and Charles A., now a farmer of Athens Township. He married his second wife, Miss Ann E. Childs, of Athens, Oct. 12, 1851. They have three children—George F., of West Liberty, Iowa; Christopher C., Cashier for Selig & Co., of Athens, and Ida C., wife of H. E. Dickason, Cashier of the First National Bank, of Jackson, Ohio.

Frank C. Steadman, junior member of the firm of W. H. Brown & Co., wholesale grocers, Athens, was born in this city March 13, 1853, where he was reared and educated. He is a son of Frederick and Louisa (Golden) Steadman. When sixteen years of age he commenced to clerk for W. H. Brown, and in 1873 became associated with his employer, under the firm name of Brown & Steadman. In 1876 he withdrew his interest and went to Philadelphia and carried on a hotel for the National Surgical Institute till 1880, when he returned to Athens and again became associated with W. H. Brown in the wholesale grocery business, under the firm name of W. H. Brown & Co. Aug. 1, 1880, he married Etta Crouse, of Philadelphia. Mr. Steadman is a member of Paramuthia Lodge, No. 25, A. F. & A. M., Athens.

Hoit Spencer Stimson, M. D. son of Dr. Stephen and Abigail (Shaw) Stimson, was born March 18, 1823, in Jericho, Chittenden Co., Va. When he was nine years of age his parents came to Ohio, living a year at Mt. Vernon and then going to Homer, Licking County. He received his education at the High School in Homer, and a seminary in Delaware, Ohio. His father being a physician he early had a desire to study the same profession, and spent considerable time in his father's office. When seventeen years of age he began the actual study of the profession, remaining under the preceptorship of his father till twenty years of age. In 1843 he went to Nelsonville and was associated with his brother, Dr. B. C. Stimson, three years. He then went to Guysville and practiced three years, and in 1849 came to Athens, where he has built up a large practice. Nov. 20, 1846, he married Amanda, daughter of Abraham and Lydia (Lawrence) Cornish. Dr. Stimson has served as a member of the City Council of Athens seven years.

John Leign Strahl, proprietor of South Planing Mill, Athens, was born in Athens County, Ohio, April 12, 1854, a son of John and Hannah Jane (Smith) Strahl. When he was two years of age his parents removed to Vinton County and lived three years; then removed to Albany, Athens County, where he grew to manhood. When nineteen years of age he engaged in the cabinet and undertaking business, following it till 1876. In 1875 he added a planing mill to his other business. In 1880 he moved his mill to Athens. Nov. 20, 1880, he married Phœbe Aurilla Rigg, of Albany. They have one child—Fred. Mr. and Mrs. Strahl are members of the Baptist church at Albany.

Alexander Bothwell Scott, deceased, was born at Putnam, Ohio, in October, 1808, of Scotch-Irish parents, they both emigrating from Ireland when very young. When he was quite young his parents removed from Putnam to Harmar, thence to Belpre, Ohio, and later to McConnelsville, where he lived until 1858, and was variously employed. At one time he ran a general store, and during that time carried on the mercantile business one year (1840) at Chauncey. In 1842 he took charge of the flouring mill of Doster & Cassel at McConnelsville, and was so employed for thirteen years. He was again variously employed until the spring of 1858 when he took charge of the Herrold Mills, of Athens, removing his family to that city in the spring of 1859. He remained in that position until the spring of 1864 when he took charge of Stewart's Mill near Athens. He died Jan. 3, 1866, at his home in Athens, having been in failing health for two years. Dec. 29, 1839, he was married to Miss Susan Rutledge, of McConnelsville. They had four children—William H., President of Ohio University; John R. Winfield, freight and ticket agent for the Washington & Baltimore R. R., at Athens; Anna M., who died in infancy, and Wilbur F., express agent at Athens. Mr. Scott was a member of the M. E. church the greater part of his life. He was well informed, being a great reader, and above the average in intelligence. He was devoted to his family and took great pains to educate his sons, placing in their hands the best literature.

Wilbur Fisk Scott was born at McConnelsville, Morgan Co., Ohio, Dec. 25, 1850, the youngest son of Alexander B. and Susan (Rutledge) Scott. Soon after his birth his parents came to Athens, where his father died when he was fifteen years old. He received a common-school education and was variously employed until his twentieth year, when he entered the M. & C. R. R. office as clerk under his brother, W. Scott. He was married March 3, 1881, to Sadie, daughter of George E. and Eliza (Carpenter) Whipple, of Athens. They have one child—Nellie. Mr. Scott is a member of Paramuthia Lodge, No. 25, A. F. & A. M., Athens.

Rev. William Henry Scott, Professor of Mental, Moral and Political Science and President of Ohio University, Athens, was born in Chauncey, Ohio, Sept. 14, 1840. When about one year old his parents, Alexander B. and Susan (Rutledge) Scott, removed to McConnelsville, Ohio, where he attended school until he was sixteen. At that age he began to teach school and taught two years, in the meantime preparing himself, by private study, to enter college. In the spring of 1859 he entered Ohio University, from which he graduated in the class of 1862. The last two years of his attendance at the University he taught in the Preparatory Department. Immediately after graduating he was elected Superintendent of the Union Schools of Athens and filled that position until February, 1864, when he was appointed by the Executive Committee of the Board of Trustees of the Ohio University temporary Principal of the Preparatory Department, to fill the vacancy caused by the death of Prof. E. H. Guthrie. In the following June he was chosen as permanent Principal by the Board of Trustees. In June, 1865, he resigned that position to enter upon the ministry, having previously, in October, 1864, been ordained by Bishop Ames, and connected himself with the Ohio Conference of the Methodist Episcopal Church. His first charge was the Main Street M. E. Church, of Chillicothe, Ohio, where he officiated until the fall of 1867, when he was sent by his conference to the Towns Street Church, Columbus, Ohio. In the summer of 1869 he was elected Professor of Greek by the Board of Trustees of Ohio University. He filled that chair until the summer of 1872 when he was appointed by the Executive Committee of the Board of Trustees, Acting President, vice Dr. Solomon Howard, resigned. At the next meeting of the Board of Trustees he was elected President and still holds that position. Aug. 9, 1863, he was married to Miss Sarah A. Felton, of Athens. They have six children— Charles Felton and Emma, students at the Ohio University; Bertha, Herbert, Ernest and Dudley.

Winfield Scott, freight and ticket agent of the Cincinnati, Washington & Baltimore R. R., at Athens, was born at McConnelsville, O., Feb. 3, 1846. When twelve years of age he removed to Athens with his parents, Alexander and Susan (Rutledge) Scott, living there until he was seventeen. He was educated in the schools of his native town and Athens. He left home in January, 1863, enlisting in Company A, Thirty-ninth Ohio Volunteer Infantry, as a private, serving until August, 1865. He was with his company in the engagement at Atlanta, Ga., and also in Sherman's "march from Atlanta to the sea." After his discharge at the expiration of his term, he returned to Athens and became associated with his father in the milling business, remaining in the business until 1868, when he obtained the appointment of freight and ticket agent for the Cincinnati, Washington & Baltimore R. R. Company, and he has held this position ever since. Nov. 15, 1870, he was married to Miss Anna F., daughter of George E. Whipple, of Athens, six children being born to them—Guy, Anna, Winfield, Jr., Paul, Grace and Homer. Himself and wife are members of the Methodist Episcopal church. He is an Odd Fellow, a member of Sereno Lodge, No. 479, and Encampment, No. 175, at Athens; also a member of Columbus Golden Post, No. 89, G. A. R., at Athens.

William Austin Thomas, Superintendent of the Athens County Children's Home, was born near Chillicothe, O., Sept. 9, 1835, the youngest of seven sons of James and Tamzon (Wilkins) Thomas. His mother died when he was five years old. He received his rudimentary education in the common schools, completing it at the Ohio Wesleyan University, Delaware, and Ohio University, Athens. In August, 1861, he enlisted in the Regimental Band of the Sixty-ninth Ohio Infantry, and served nearly a year, when, by an order from the War Department, all regimental bands were disbanded. He then returned to Ohio and taught in Ross County till December, 1862, when he came to Athens and engaged in the grocery business two years. Feb. 25, 1864, he married Ella A., daughter of John R. and Maria (King) McCune, of Athens. In May, 1864, he enlisted to serve 100 days, in Company C, One Hundred and Forty-first Regiment Ohio National Guards. At the organization of the regiment, his company having an excess of men, he was transferred to Company G, and promoted to Orderly Sergeant, but served as Post-Adjutant at Guyandotte most of his time of service. At the expiration of his time he returned to Athens and the same year was elected Justice of the Peace, holding the office six years. During this time he studied law with Knowles & Martin, and was admitted to the bar at Marietta in 1867. He soon after went to Hamilton, Butler County, and with his brother B. F. formed the law firm of B. F. & W. A. Thomas, but did not remain there long. Returning to Athens, he dealt in musical instruments and taught vocal and instrumental music till January, 1883, when he accepted the Superintendency of the Athens County Children's Home. Mr. and Mrs. Thomas have one child—Mabel. They and their daughter are members of the Methodist church, Mr. Thomas having been a local preacher since 1870. He is a member of Sereno Lodge, No. 479, I. O. O. F., Athens.

Emmett Tompkins, Prosecuting Attorney of Athens County, was born in McConnelsville, Morgan Co., Ohio, Sept. 1, 1853.

His parents were Hon. Cydnor B. and Mary A. (Fouts) Tompkins; both died before his eleventh year. In his twelfth year he came to Athens County and was reared by his guardian, W. B. Vorhest, with whom he lived until manhood. He was educated in the Ohio University at Athens. After leaving the University he began the study of law with Hon. C. H. Grosvenor. He was admitted to the bar by the District Court of Vinton County, Sept. 7, 1875. He then established himself in the law practice at Athens. In the spring of 1876 he was elected City Solicitor of Athens and served the term of two years. In 1878 he was elected Mayor of Athens, which office he resigned in 1879 to accept the office of Prosecuting Attorney, to which he was elected that year. He was elected his own successor in 1881 and is still the incumbent of that office. Sept. 21, 1875, he married Martha L., daughter of John M. Welch and granddaughter of Hon. John Welch, late Judge of the Supreme Court of Ohio. They have one child—Cydnor Welch. Politically, he is a Republican. He is a Master Mason and member of Paramuthia Lodge, No. 25, Athens, and of the Phi Delta Theta, a college fraternity.

Hon. Chas. Townsend, ex-Secretary of State and attorney at law, Athens, Ohio, was born Dec. 22, 1834, at Harrisville, Belmont Co., Ohio, but was reared on a farm in the vicinity of Athens. In his seventeenth year he entered the Ohio University from which he graduated in the class of 1861. He defrayed the expenses of his education by teaching, receiving no assistance. He had substantially completed his college course in 1857, but graduated at the term before mentioned. At the breaking out of the late war he was Principal of the Decamp Institute, Meigs County, Ohio, but relinquished his position, and, without appointment or commission, recruited 120 men for the Union service, who were enlisted in Company C, Thirtieth Ohio Infantry, and mustered in at Camp Chase, Ohio, in July, 1861. On the organization of the company he was elected Captain and received his commission from the Governor of Ohio. He was immediately assigned to duty with his company under General Rosecrans in West Virginia, and next under General Pope, with whom he served until after the second battle of Bull Run. He then served under General Geo. B. McClellan until the battle of Antietam, when his regiment was transferred to the Army of the Tennessee, where he served in Sherman's corps until the siege of Vicksburg and the battles around and about that city. He served with his regiment in the same corps in Georgia, having been promoted to Major. He was tendered a Colonel's commission to take charge of another regiment, but preferred to remain with his own. He was through the Atlanta campaign, and while storming a battery at Nickajack was seriously injured by the explosion of a shell from which he was so disabled that he was obliged to leave the service and return home just as the war was about to close. In 1866 he graduated from the Law Department of the University at Cincinnati, Ohio, and immediately entered upon the practice of law at Athens. In October, 1869, he was elected Prosecuting Attorney of Athens County and re-elected in 1871 and 1873. In 1876 he was elected a Representative in the Ohio Legislature and re-elected in 1878. In 1880 he was elected Secretary of State of Ohio, his term of office expiring January, 1883. In October, 1859, he was married to Miss Margaret J. Allen. They have three children—Helen M., Charles H. and Mary. Mr. Townsend is a Master, Royal Arch and Knight Templar Mason.

Franklin Tichenor Towsley, eldest son of Darius and Mary E. (Clogston) Towsley, was born Aug. 5, 1843, in Marietta, O. He worked with his father at the trade of carpenter and bridge-builder from his eleventh year till after the breaking out of the late war. March 26, 1862, he enlisted in Battery K, First Ohio Light Artillery. During his three years' service he participated in many prominent battles and forced marches, among which are the battles of McDowell, Franklin, Shenandoah Valley, Chattanooga, Lookout Mountain. Sept. 1, 1864, he was appointed by General Thomas Postmaster at Stevenson, Ala. On one occasion the mail agents refused to take the mail to Huntsville, a distance of seventy miles, on account of the danger, the road having been in the possession of the rebels for some time. He telegraphed to General Thomas at Nashville, offering his services, which were accepted, and with a locomotive, tender, and one box car, and no guards, he made a successful run down and back. March 11, 1865, he was discharged at Nashville, Tenn., and returned to Marietta, O., and again took up his former occupation. The latter part of that year he, with three other mechanics, loaded a flat-boat with the materials for building a dwelling in Memphis, and after a pleasant voyage arrived in that city during the great riot between the ex-slaves and rebels. He was an eye-witness to the murder of several negroes, and twice refused to fall into the ranks of the rebel mob. For more than a week the city was illuminated with the burning of the Government barracks occupied by the negroes. After his return to Marietta he was employed as carpenter on several of the river boats. He has, since then, built or helped to build a number of river steamers now plying the Ohio, Cumberland and Kanawha rivers. In March, 1873, while making a trip on the Arkansas River, the boat struck a snag at midnight, and sank in thirteen feet of water and immediately caught fire, burning to the water's edge. Of fifty-one souls on board seventeen were lost. F. T. Towsley was highly complimented by all the river newspapers from Pittsburg to New Orleans for his heroic conduct in saving the lives of the passengers and crew. Having lost all his clothes and tools he returned to Marietta and worked at his trade until November, when he came to Athens and assisted in finishing the asylum for the insane. Since then he has assisted in building many of the finest buildings in the State. June 24, 1881, Columbus Golden Post, G. A. R., was mustered in at Athens, and he was appointed Sergeant-Major, holding the position till 1883, when he was appointed Adjutant. Feb. 9, 1882, he was appointed mustering officer of the Thirteenth District, composing the counties of Athens and Morgan, and since then he has mustered in T. R. Stanley Post, Zaleski; Stewart Johnson Post, McConnelsville; Wesley Weller Post, Deavertown; Thomas Dew Post, Buchtel. Previous to this he had assisted in mustering in Hill Post, at New Straitsville. In February, 1883, he was appointed mustering officer of the Ninth District, comprising Athens and Hocking counties, and has re organized Phil. Kearney Post, Nelsonville; Chilcotte Post, South Bloomingville; and mustered in the Thomas F. Wildes Post, Coolville, and Luther Devoe Post, Carbon Hill. He was a delegate from Athens to the Departmental Encampment at Youngstown. Jan. 1, 1883, he married Jennie F. Ulmer, and is now living on the McGill property recently purchased by his father-in-law.

George Weaver Towsley, contractor and builder, of Athens, a son of Darius and Mary E. (Clogston) Towsley, was born at Marietta, Ohio, June 23, 1850. He was educated in the schools of Marietta. His patriotism developed itself at an early age, as when only eleven years of age, in 1861, he went out with the Eighty-seventh Ohio Volunteer Infantry, as drummer boy and served six months. While out he was taken prisoner at Harper's Ferry, when General Miles surrendered that post to the Confederates, and was released on parol. In 1862, with his drum, he aided in producing martial music that inspired young patriots to enlist in the One Hundred and Twenty-fifth Ohio Volunteer Infantry, he himself enlisting as Drum-Major. His father objecting, he reluctantly yielded to parental authority and remained at home. However, in 1864, after earnest entreaties, he was permitted to enlist in the One Hundred and Forty-sixth Ohio National Guards, as a drummer boy, for 100 days, and was on duty in front of Petersburg during his whole time of service. After his discharge he returned home and began to work at the carpenter and joiner's trade under his father, remaining with him until 1870. He then came to Athens and worked for Henry O'Bleness as journeyman and foreman until 1877, when he began to contract for himself. April 15, 1874, he was married to Mary M., daughter of W. M. Vorhess, of Athens. They have two children—Mabel and Jessie. Mr. Towsley is a member of Paramuthia Lodge, No. 25, A. F. & A. M., at Athens. He is a member of Columbus Golden Post, No. 89, G. A. R., of Athens.

Peter Ulmer, carpenter and joiner, was born in Nockamixon Township, Bucks Co., Penn., Aug. 17, 1824. His mother dying while he was an infant, he was adopted by Jacob Bougher, with whom he lived in Bucks and Allegheny counties until 1844, when he came with him to Ohio and settled in Lodi Township, Athens County, remaining with him until attaining his majority in 1845. In boyhood he worked in the cooper shop of a son of his foster father and learned that trade. In 1846 he built a shop in Lodi Township and carried on coopering there until the fall of 1860, when he removed to Harmony, Athens Co., and worked for S. B. Pruden until 1868. In the latter year he came to Athens and opened a shop and worked at the cooper's trade during the winter months, and at the carpenter and joiner's trade during the remainder of the year until 1878, when he abandoned the cooper's trade. April 12, 1847, he married Miss Mary Jane Saddler, of Lodi Township. They have four children—Jacob, Josephine, Jennie and Effieanettie.

Hon. Nelson H. Van Vorhes.—Among the eminent dead of the Hocking Valley, Nelson H. Van Vorhes stands in the front rank, doubtless the foremost in public life. From the time he was a young man up to the date of his death, Dec. 4, 1882, he has been held in high esteem, regarded as worthy of filling almost any position of trust. Not only has he been worthy of the public honors conferred upon him, but by the faithful and honorable discharge of every trust he has deserved the perfect confidence of his fellowmen and his life has been well honored with public positions. At the age of twenty-one he assumed the editorial control of a newspaper; at twenty-six was a member of the Ohio Legislature, having been nominated without opposition, and elected by a majority exceeding that of his ticket. At thirty-four he was Speaker of the House and the choice of his party for a seat in the National Congress, and though failing of election at this time, he was, later in life, twice elected to that body. He was born in Washington County, Pa., Jan. 23, 1822, whence he removed with his father's family to Athens County at ten years of age. His father, Abraham Van Vorhes, was a man of unusual strength of mind and character, and, like his son, had been honored with public positions, among them a seat in the State Legislature. He first settled on the present site of Hebbardsville, which town he founded. After four years' residence here he became the proprietor and editor of the *Western Spectator*, published at Athens, and removed to that place. At this time young Nelson entered the newspaper office as an apprentice, having had but little schooling and that only such as was then afforded by the district schools. While in this position his father became a member of the House of Representatives, and he was left in control of the paper. In 1844 he and his brother, A. J. Van Vorhes, purchased the paper, the Athens *Messenger and Hocking Valley Gazette* as it was then called, and he became the leading editor and manager. A few years later S. N. Miller bought one third of the paper when the firm name became N. H. Van Vorhes & Co. Mr. Miller withdrew in a short time, as did also Mr. Van Vorhes a few years later, but only temporarily on account of failing health. He returned to the paper again in 1856 and continued its editor and proprietor until 1861, when he sold out and entered the Union army. He was one of the first to respond to the call for troops, entering the first company organized at Athens, as a private. He was in active duty nearly two years when his failing health compelled him to resign. During this time he was successively promoted through a number of subordinate offices to that of Colonel, which he held at the time of his resignation. In 1865 he formed a partnership with W. D. Bartlett in the hardware business, the business and the partnership continuing up to within a few months of his death. His entrance into public life was in 1850 when he was elected by the Whigs to represent Athens and Meigs counties in the State Legislature. He continued to represent Athens County until 1854. In 1853 he was nominated by his party for Secretary of the State, but was defeated with the rest of the ticket. The following year he was elected Probate Judge, but before the expiration of his term he resigned, to enter the House of Representatives, having been again elected in 1855. During this term he served for the first time as Speaker. In 1857 he was again elected a Member of the House. The following year he was a candidate for Congress from his district but, although running ahead of his ticket, was not elected. In 1869 he was again chosen to the Ohio House of Representatives, and still again in 1871, when he was a second time made Speaker. In 1874 he was elected to Congress and in 1876 was re-elected. Much against his own inclination he was made a candidate for a third election in 1878 but, the district having recently been made strongly Democratic, he failed of election, General Warner, of Marietta, being the successful candidate. During all his public career he was never even suspected of complicity in anything the least dishonorable. He retired from public life with clean hands, as much a public favorite as ever. Throughout life he was feeble in health, having a delicate constitution, but by his upright and mild nature and his cordial fidelity to all, he secured and retained the confidence and friendship of all with whom he became associated. Mr. Van Vorhes was married to Elizabeth B. Foster, Oct. 23, 1845. He was the father of three children—Charles, who died in 1851; Louis A. and Nellie H. who, with their mother, still survive him.

John Varley, section boss of the C., H. V. & T. R. R., was born in Galway County, Ireland, Nov. 9, 1821, and is the eldest of five sons of Martin and Bridget (Gilmore) Varley. When twenty years of age he came to America, landing at New York City, April, 16, 1841. He first went to Morrison County, N. J., where he was employed as foreman stone cutter, but not liking the climate he went to Portland, Me., and was foreman on the Maine Central R. R. two years. He then went to Hartford, Conn., and worked in the same capacity on the Hartford & Waterbury Railroad eighteen months. From this time till 1856 he was at Bridgeport, Port Chester, White Plains, Haverstraw, Philadelphia, Baltimore, Pittsburg and Parkersburg. In 1856 he came to Ohio, and during that year was employed as foreman of the stone cutting on the M. & C. R. R. In 1857 he purchased a farm near Fleming, where he lived till 1864, being during that time employed as foreman of the hands that dug the four-mile tunnel on the M. & C. R. R. From 1865 to 1868 he was section boss on the same road.

During 1868 he had charge of the track of the Junction Road from Cincinnati Junction to Cambridge City. From 1868 to 1872 he was employed by the contractors as foreman on the Cincinnati & Hocking Valley Railroad, and since 1872 has been section boss of the same road. Aug. 4, 1853, he married Ann Costello, of New York City. They have had six children, five now living—Thomas, train dispatcher of the C. & H. V. R. R., at Columbus; Martin, telegraph operator at Athens; Katie, John and William. Sarah died at Nelsonville, March 2, 1870, aged fifteen years. Mr. and Mrs. Varley are members of St. Paul's Catholic Church, Athens, of which he is Trustee.

Archibald B. Walker, son of Dr. Ezra Walker, was born in Poultney, Rutland Co., Vt., Oct. 15, 1800, and came to Ames Township with his father's family when ten years old. In this excellent neighborhood he enjoyed the advantage of good common schools in the winters, and was occupied most of the year in assisting to open and cultivate a small farm, thus forming well established habits of industry, and acquiring a relish for early pioneer life. In 1825 he married Lucy W., daughter of Judge Silvanus Ames, and in 1826 they removed to the town of Athens, where they have since resided continuously over half a century, and reared a family of two sons and four daughters. On coming to Athens, Mr. Walker spent a few years in the clerk's office as Assistant Clerk which proved of great advantage to him in all his subsequent life. This was followed by an extensive business, for those years, with his brother-in-law, Mr. James J. Fuller, including pork-packing and buying and selling produce. To this was added, about the year 1839, the manufacture of salt at the furnace opposite Chauncey, afterward owned by Judge Pruden; and soon after they bored the wells and erected the furnaces at Salina, since owned by M. M. Greene & Co. For a period of twenty years the firm name of Fuller & Walker was well and favorably known in the valley and in the central and southern parts of the State. The partnership was dissolved in 1853. Since that time Mr. Walker has not engaged in active business on his own account. During his long residence in the county he has always been prompt to embrace and ardent in the support of every useful local enterprise. At home and abroad, in personal intercourse and through the press, he has ever been ready and efficient in advocating the development of the county, and presenting her claims. He was one of the original Friends, and for several years a Director of the

Marietta & Cincinnati Railroad, and an early and strenuous advocate for the construction of the Hocking Valley Railroad, which has been subsequently built under the energetic control of younger men, and which he is gratified to have been spared to see completed, and witness its wonderful success. Those who are familiar with the history of Athens County and the Hocking Valley are unanimous in according to Mr. Walker a large measure of credit for the faithfulness with which he has worked for the welfare of the valley in all things. He is universally respected as an upright citizen and a true Christian. Mr. Walker has had, as is stated above, two sons and four daughters. Of the sons, the eldest is Charles M., editor of the Indianapolis *Times*, who is mentioned more fully in connection with " Walker's History of Athens County." The second son is Ezra M., a merchant of Athens at the present time. He is unmarried, and resides with his father. The eldest daughter, Laura, is now Mrs. James Ballard, residing in Athens. Miss Augusta resides at home. Alice is now Mrs. Frederick L. Ballard, of Philadelphia; and Helen, the youngest, also resides at home.

George Ralph Walker, dealer in books, stationery, pictures and picture frames, and musical instruments, was born in Athens, Dec. 29, 1850. His parents were William and Matilda (Claxton) Walker, with whom he lived until manhood. He was educated at the Ohio University, graduating in the class of 1872. He then began the study of medicine, and after studying some eighteen months was obliged to abandon it on account of too close application impairing his eye-sight. In October, 1873, he established himself in his present business at Athens. Dec. 9, 1874, he was married to Miss Ida M. Mingus, daughter of Gideon Mingus, of Bowling Green, Ky., by whom he has one child—Lelia M. Mr. and Mrs. Walker are both members of the Methodist Episcopal church at Athens. He is a member of Paramuthia Lodge, No. 25, A. F. & A. M., of which he is Secretary. He is also an Odd Fellow and member of the subordinate lodge and encampment at Athens, and is Past Grand and Past Patriarch.

John Henry Walker, undertaker, was born in Athens, Feb. 6, 1836, a son of William and Matilda (Claxton) Walker. He was reared and educated at Athens and lived with his parents until his sixteenth year, when he went to Coolville to serve an apprenticeship of three years with Isaac A. Dinsmore, to learn the carpenter's trade. He then worked at the trade until the spring of 1859, when, in connection with carpentering, he took charge of his father's farm in the vicinity of Athens, until 1862. In September of that year he enlisted in Company I, Seventh I. V. Cavalry, under Captain A. Norton, going out as a Corporal. Feb. 28, 1863, he was promoted to Sergeant, but acted as First or Orderly Sergeant from September, 1863, to April, 1864. He participated in the battles of Dutton Hill, West Farm, Monticello, Mount Sterling, Blue Spring, Raytown, and many others. He was discharged at Nashville, July 8, 1865, and returned to Athens and worked at the carpenter's trade until 1867, when he was employed in the Pilcher Furniture Factory at Athens, in which he worked eight years. In 1875 he established his present business. March 7, 1860, he married Amelia Crippen Higgins, of Athens County. They have six living children—Adie M., Nettie M., Edward H., Frederick B., Bertha C. and Nellie H. They have lost one, William H., who died June 30, 1879, at the age of eighteen years. Mr. and Mrs. Walker are members of the First Presbyterian Church of Athens. He is a Master and Royal Arch Mason, and member of the lodge and chapter at Athens. He is a Past Master of his lodge. He is an Odd Fellow and member of Sereno Lodge, No. 479, of which he is a Past Grand. He is a charter member of Columbus Golden Post, No. 89, G. A. R., and has filled the position of Officer of the Day since its organization.

William Walker, deceased, was born in Yorkshire, England, Dec. 30, 1808. In 1819, when eleven years old, he came with his parents to the United States, settling at Athens. His father being a horse-shoer by trade, William learned that part of the blacksmith's trade with him. When nineteen years of age, with only $6 in his pocket, he went on foot to Cincinnati and completed his trade, and returned to Athens when he was twenty-one. He then established himself in the blacksmithing business and followed it until 1856, when he removed to a farm one mile south of Athens, where with farming he also carried on blacksmithing until 1857, when he had the misfortune to lose his right arm in a threshing machine. He then pursued farming until 1866, when, retiring from business, he returned to Athens where he lived until his death, Dec. 3, 1877. He was noted for his skill in blacksmithing, especially in making edged tools. Sept. 8, 1831, he married Matilda Claxton, daughter of Thomas and Mary J. (Blatch) Claxton. She was born in the Northern part of London, England, June 24, 1810. When an infant her parents emigrated to the United States, settling at Baltimore. At the breaking out of the war of 1812 they came to Ohio and settled at Chillicothe, and lived there until 1820, when they came to Logan where she lived with them until her marriage. Mr. and Mrs. Walker had six children, only three now living. Mr. Walker became a member of the Methodist Episcopal church when he was nineteen years of age, and was a consistent member of that church until his death, and for many years officiated as Class-Leader. His wife, who still survives him, is also a member of that church.

Thomas Walsh, a farmer and resident of Athens and lately a merchant of that city, was born in County Longford, Ireland, in May, 1844. When he was four years of age his parents, James and Catherine (O'Riley) Walsh, came to the United States. They settled in Athens Township, Athens Co., Ohio, where he was reared a farmer and given a good common-school education. His father dying when he was fourteen years of age, he continued to live with his mother and had charge of the farm for her until becoming of age. He remained on the homestead farm until 1875, when he came to Athens and engaged in merchant tailoring until 1879. He is now engaged in overseeing his farm in Canaan Township, but resides in Athens. Sept. 5, 1878, he was married to Uphema McGravy, of Logan, by whom he has two children—Katy Estella and Jessie Genevieve. Himself and wife are members of St. Paul's Catholic Church, of Athens.

Timothy Burr Warden, Sheriff of Athens County, was born at Mt. Vernon, Knox Co., O., Aug. 25, 1848. He is the son of Henry P. Warden, who was for some fifteen years freight agent for the Sandusky, Mansfield & Newark Railroad, via the Baltimore & Ohio, at Sandusky. He lived with his parents at his birthplace until his fifteenth year, when he removed with them to Sandusky. At the age of twenty, in 1868, he came to Amesville, Athens County and became associated with his brother, C. H. Warden, in the mercantile business, under the firm name of C. H. Warden & Brother. In 1871 they removed to Athens where they engaged in shipping produce, and are doing an extensive business. In 1879 Mr. Warden was elected Sheriff of Athens County on the Republican ticket. The election was warmly contested, there being four candidates in the field, he receiving a majority of 267 votes. He was re-elected in 1881 by a majority of nearly 1,500 votes. During his term of office in 1881, the lynching of the notorious Charles C. Davis by a furious mob took place at Athens, a history of which can be found elsewhere in this volume. Sept. 15, 1871, he married Miss Augusta, daughter of Dr. Lorenzo Fulton, of Amesville, by whom he has four children—Harry F., Ella W., Mary E. and Winnie A. He is a Master, Royal Arch and Knight Templar Mason, and member of lodge, chapter and commandery at Athens. He is also an Odd Fellow and member of Sereno Lodge, No. 479, Athens.

Hon. John Welch, ex-Judge of the Supreme Court of Ohio, belongs pre-eminently in the honorable rank of self-made men. He shared the hardships of pioneer life, struggled against ill health, and wrenched success out of the hard hand of poverty. He was born in Harrison County, Ohio, Oct. 28, 1805. The region was then, to a great extent, a wilderness, and John's father was one of the earliest pioneers who undertook the task of subduing it, and converting it into a cultivated and productive land. He was a poor man with a large family, consisting of seven sons and four daughters. The child of such a household who would have prosperity, manifestly must work it out for himself. It certainly would not be thrust upon him, no matter how ardent the parental love, or how strong the parental wish to have things better than they are, for those who come after. John Welch was one to work out results for himself. He had early set his heart on success, and his purpose never faltered, no matter how discouraging the obstacles that presented themselves. He worked with his father upon the family farm until he was eighteen years of age, and during that time he acquired such education as was to be gained by attending the country district school during the winter months. These opportunities were not very great for scholastic attainments. Meager as were the facilities offered in the common schools of that day, and the short period of three months out of each year for attendance, does not mean much compared with the school privileges of the present day. Such opportunities were made the most of in this case. When he was eighteen years of age he was "given his time" by his father, and then he began in serious earnest to obtain the education he had early determined to procure. He taught school, that he might earn money, and the money earned was spent in the prosecution of liberal studies, under the best auspices within his reach. He had entered Franklin College, Ohio, and for five years, by this system of alternate teaching and attendance upon school, he maintained himself in that institution, and in September, 1828, graduated from that college with honors. He had decided upon the law as his future profession, and in January, 1829, commenced his legal studies under Hon. Joseph Dana, of Athens, Ohio. Excessive study and sedentary habits impaired his health long before his course of study had been completed, and for a time it seemed as if his cherished purpose of becoming a lawyer must be abandoned. His physician assured him that the surest means of restoring his broken health was to resume the active and laborious habits of his boyhood. In compliance with this assurance, he accordingly engaged in attending a saw and grist mill. This engagement offered a double advantage: It not only promised to restore his lost health, but would also, in a very desirable manner, reinforce the finances of the young student, who was in great need of such reinforcement. The mill work did not come altogether as an interruption either of his legal studies, as it is said that the studious mill hand would " set the saw and then read Blackstone while it was running through the log." Be this as it may, he continued his legal studies in connection with his mill work; and so, while he was gaining new health and renewing his store of money, he was also drawing nearer to the object of his endeavors. He continued thus to work and study, until 1833, and in the meantime he had taken a wife, marrying Martha Starr, daughter of Captain James Starr, formerly of Connecticut, but at this time a resident of Ohio. The marriage took place soon after he engaged in the milling business, and on the 3d of June, 1833, when he gave up that business, his family consisted of a wife and two children. With this family he removed to the town of Athens, where he established his residence and where he has ever since continued to reside. In the month of November of the same year he was admitted to the bar, and at once began the practice of his profession. His practice grew rapidly, and he was soon established as a prosperous lawyer, with important and laborious work always on his hands. He brought to the practice of his profession the same ability, diligence, energy and fidelity that had marked his preparatory career, and they are qualities which win ready recognition and yield material results. In his case they were recognized, and yielded results outside the immediate circle of his profession. In 1845 he was elected a member of the State Senate of Ohio, and served a term of two years in that body. In 1850 he was elected to Congress as the successor of Hon. Samuel F. Vinton. During his term the Congressional District from which he was elected was changed, and, in consequence of this fact, he failed of re-election in 1852. During his sitting in the National Legislature he made two important speeches, one on the Tariff, the other on the Public Land Question. Both were able, thorough, and marked by the clear sagacity and the straightforward honesty that characterized the man. The speech on the Public-Land Question attained the honor of a publication in full in the columns of the *National Intelligencer*, of Washington. In the year 1852 he served as a delegate in the Baltimore Convention which nominated General Winfield Scott for President of the United States, and in 1856 he was a member of the Electoral College which cast the vote of Ohio for John C. Fremont. In 1862 he was called from the bar to the bench, having been, in February of that year elected Judge of the Court of Common Pleas. He sat upon the bench of the Common Pleas Court until February, 1865, when he was appointed Judge of the Supreme Court, vice Hon. Rufus P. Ranney, resigned. He remained upon the Supreme bench until 1878, having been re-elected to the position three times. Since his retirement from the bench, Judge Welch has continued to practice law up to the present time. He now spends the most of his time in his library and garden, but continues to take an active part in politics and the affairs of life. He has been an industrious reader all his life, and has a very extended knowledge of literary and scientific subjects. He attends a reading club in Athens, occasionally delivers a lecture in the University Chapel on "Mathematics," on "Religion, and Morality," on "Mob Law," etc. He lately wrote a "History and Memorial" of the Amestown Library, the first library established in the Northwest Territory. He has now in the hands of the printers for publication a work to be entitled "Mathematical curiosities," consisting mainly of new and original rules, puzzles and surprises, and including an interest table on an entirely new plan. Soon after his first election as Judge of the Supreme Court, his *alma mater*, Franklin College, conferred upon him the honorary degree of LL. D. As a writer, Judge Welch has an easy and elegant style, and his productions, by their clearness and originality, are always full of interest. His opinions while on the Supreme bench take rank among the first authorities on legal questions.

Johnson Morton Welch, of the law firm of Welch & Welch, Athens, was born in Rome Township, Athens Co., Ohio, April 20, 1832. He is the son of Hon. John and Martha L. (Starr) Welch. When he was fifteen months old his parents removed to Athens, where he was reared and educated at the Ohio University, graduating at the age of twenty, in the class of 1852. Immediately after graduating he made a sea voyage for the benefit of his health. In 1856 he entered his father's office to study law, and was admitted to the bar at Athens in 1858, and at once became associated with his father, under the firm name of Welch & Son. In 1861 he entered the Union army as Captain of Company C, Eighteenth Regiment, Ohio Volunteer Infantry. He was promoted to Major of his regiment in 1863 and was soon after appointed a member of General James S. Negley's staff, in command of Second Division of the Fourteenth Army Corps of the Army of the Cumberland. He took command of his regiment immediately after the battle of Chickamauga and commanded it until the spring of 1864, when he was made Provost-Marshal of the city of Chickamauga and served as such until the expiration of his term of service in October of that year. He was mustered out Nov. 9, 1864. when he returned to Athens and resumed his law practice. In February, 1878, he became associated with his father and formed the present law firm of Welch & Welch. In 1881 he was chosen President by the stockholders of the Athens Gas-Light Company, and in 1882 became Vice-President of the First National Bank of Athens, both of which positions he still holds. He has been twice married. His first wife was Miss Adaline Carpenter, daughter of Harvey Carpenter, of Athens County, whom he married Sept. 14, 1853, and who died at Athens, July 25, 1866. They had five children— Martha, afterward wife of Emmet Tompkins, attorney at Athens; Jessie, wife of Dr. E. C. De Steiguer, of Logan, Ohio; Charles, now of Abiline, Kan.; John, Teller of the First National Bank of Athens, and George, a student of Ohio University. June 15, 1873, he married his second wife, Miss Ella Cadwallader, daughter of the late Alfred Cadwallader, of Zanesville, Ohio. They have four sons—Edward Guy, Dudley W., Thomas C. and Philip.

Jeremiah Ouey Whipple, grocer, was born in Athens, Ohio, April 16, 1849, where he was reared and educated in the Union Public Schools. His parents are George E. and Eliza (Carpenter) Whipple. At the age of fifteen he was employed as a clerk in the store of his uncle, W. H. Potter, and remained with him three years. In 1868 he went to Parkersburg, W. Va., and was, for a short time, employed in the same capacity by the Oak Oil Company. He was then employed in the grocery store of H. H. Welch, at Cincinnati, until 1871, when he returned to Athens, and was employed in the dry-goods house of M. Selig & Co. until 1873. He then clerked in the hardware store of H. J. Topky until the latter part of 1876, and in 1877 he went to Columbus, Ohio, and engaged in the grocery business until 1879, when he returned to Athens and established his present grocery. May 12, 1873, he married Miss Mary Ellen, daughter of John Vernoy, of Columbus, Ohio. They have three children—Abbie, George E. and Dana. He is a member of Sereno Lodge, No. 479, I. O. O. F., of Athens.

James Perry Wood, attorney at law and Mayor of Athens, is the son of James Perry and Rebecca (Mauk) Wood. He is the youngest of nine children and was born at Rio Grande, Gallia Co., Ohio, April 21, 1854. In 1864 his mother, then a widow, removed with her family to Cheshire, Gallia County. In 1870 he became a member of the family of his uncle, Joseph Mauk. He was educated at Cheshire Academy and Hillsdale College, Michigan. In 1874 he commenced teaching in Atwood Institute at Albany, Athens County, and was made Principal of that school in the fall of 1876, which position he resigned in 1877 in order to take charge of the graded schools at Detroit, Ohio. While teaching he studied law privately, and in April, 1878, was admitted to the bar by the District Court at Pomeroy, Ohio. The following August he formed a law partnership with Charles Townsend, under the firm name of Townsend & Wood. In July, 1880, he withdrew from the firm, and associated himself with his brother, J. M. Wood, in the law practice, forming the present law firm of Wood & Wood. In January, 1880, he was appointed Mayor of Athens in the place of Emmett Tompkins who resigned. The following April he was elected to that office, and in April, 1882, was re-elected. Nov. 14, 1876, he married Florence Ellen Vorhes, daughter of John and Ellen Vorhes, of Albany, Athens Co., Ohio. They have one child—John Vorhes, born Jan. 14, 1880.

Joseph Mauk Wood, senior member of the law firm of Wood & Wood of Athens, is the second son of James Perry and Rebecca (Mauk) Wood. He was born on a farm near Rio Grande, Gallia Co., O., July 28, 1850. On the death of his father, Aug. 15, 1863, he was the oldest child at home. He remained on the farm two years, when his mother removed with her family to Cheshire in the same county. He attended the academy at that place for about two years, when he went to live with his brother-in-law, Rev. I. Z. Haning, at Albany, Athens Co., O., where he completed his education in the Atwood Institute. March 22, 1871, he was married at Albany to Miss Emily Bingham Pullins, daughter of Samuel and

Margaret Pullins. They have four children—Augustus Palmer, Mary Ellen, James Perry, and one unnamed. In the fall of 1871 he was elected Principal of Atwood Institute, at Albany, and held that position four years, when he resigned in order to accept the Superintendency of the public schools at Clifton, West Va., where he remained two years. In the spring of 1876 he began the study of law, in private, and was admitted to the bar at Athens in the fall of 1878. He then became associated with A. H. and H. T. Brown in the law practice, at Athens, under the firm name of Brown & Wood. In July, 1880, he withdrew from that firm and became associated with his brother, J. P. Wood, and formed the present law firm of Wood & Wood. He is a member of the Free Baptist church.

Merrill Woodruff, son of Samuel and Phœbe (Sharp) Woodruff, was born in Alexander Township, Athens Co., O., April 4, 1841, where he was reared and educated. He followed farming till 1863, when he enlisted in Company K, Second Ohio Heavy Artillery, and served till the close of the war. He enlisted as private and was promoted to Duty Sergeant, Drill Master and Forage Master. He was discharged at Munfordville, Ky., May 18, 1865, and returned to Athens County, resuming farming. In 1873 he began to deal in stock, and in December, 1881, came to Athens, where he is extensively engaged, both selling at home and shipping abroad. Dec. 23, 1862, he married Lucinda J., daughter of A. C. Murphy, of Alexander Township. They have had eight children—seven now living—Albert, Columbia, Cora B., Mary E., Mattie, Charles and Joseph. Nellie died at the age of seven months. Mr. and Mrs. Woodruff have been members of the Methodist Episcopal church at Pleasanton for fourteen years. He is a member of Columbus Golden Post, No. 89, G. A. R., of Athens.

Jeremiah Chase Woodyard, son of Jeremiah and Hannah (Chase) Woodyard, was born in Alexander Township, Athens Co., O., Oct. 21, 1832. He attended and taught school till 1861, when he enlisted in Company H, Twenty-second Ohio Infantry, to serve three months. He served four months and then re-enlisted in Company H, Seventy-third Ohio Infantry, and served three years and three months, being mustered out at Columbus, in January, 1865. The last eight months he was detailed Mail Messenger by General Sherman. He participated in the battles of Culpeper Court-House, second Bull Run (where he was captured and imprisoned at Belle Isle eighteen days), Chancellorsville, Gettysburg, and many others. After his discharge he returned to Athens County and began to deal in live-stock and wool at Albany. In May, 1882, he came to Athens where he carries on the same line of trade. Oct. 15, 1867, he married Ella M., daughter of John Brown, late of Athens. They have one son—John B. Mr. and Mrs. Woodyard are both members of the Free-Will Baptist church of Albany, of which he is a Deacon. He is a Master, Royal Arch, and Knight Templar Mason, and a member of the lodge, chapter and commandery at Athens.

Sylvester Young, carpenter and joiner, was born in Canaan Township, Athens Co., Ohio, Sept. 20, 1826. His parents were Ephraim and Driscilla (Bean) Young, with whom he lived until attaining his majority. His father being a carpenter and joiner, he learned his trade with him. He came to Athens in April, 1864, and permanently settled. Sept. 7, 1862, he enlisted in Company I, Seventh Ohio Cavalry, as a private, to serve three years. In the following March he was promoted to Corporal. With his company he participated in the battles of Sherman's campaigns from Buzzard's Roost to the close of the seige of Atlanta. He met with many narrow escapes but was never absent from his company on account of wounds or sickness, excepting being laid up in camp a short time on account of an injury received by his horse falling. He was discharged at Nashville, Tenn., July 4, 1865, when he returned to Athens and resumed his trade. Aug. 10, 1848, he married Mary Jane Kincade, of Canaan Township, Athens County, who died at Athens, Feb. 26, 1856, leaving two children—Mary Alice, wife of Dr. John Armatage, of Portland, Ohio, and William Le Roy of Rainier, Oregon. He was married again, April 22, 1858, to Ann H. Matheny, of Athens. They have two children—Charles Henry and John Clifford. Mr. Young is a member of Sereno Lodge, No. 479, and Encampment, No. 175, I. O. O. F., of Athens. He has passed all the chairs in both bodies and is now the Treasurer of his encampment.

CHAPTER XV.

YORK TOWNSHIP—A TOWNSHIP OF INEXHAUSTIBLE MINERAL WEALTH.

TAKEN FROM AMES IN 1811, SIX MILES SQUARE—IT IS BOUNDED BY—POPULATION AND TRANSPORTATION—CANAL AND RAILROAD—MINING ITS PRINCIPAL INDUSTRY—SOME RICH VALLEY LANDS—THE HILLS GOOD SHEEP PASTURES—DEVELOPMENT—OFFICIAL STATISTICS.

A PART OF AMES TILL 1811.

The territory which composes York Township was a portion of Ames until 1811. When Dover Township was organized it included all the territory to the west line of the county. This remained Dover Township until June, 1818, when the present York Township was organized with 23,040 acres of land, or a congressional township six miles square. It is bounded on the east by Dover Township, south by Waterloo Township, and west and north by Hocking County. Topographically speaking, it is mostly hills with about one fourth valleys, very rough and broken, but the hills while not all of grazing value are mostly so, while the small valleys, running from twenty acres to perhaps a 100 each, are fair agricultural lands. Those that lie immediately upon streams of living water are rich and fertile; the others, small ones which seem to be simply indentures of the surface, are not so productive, the erodings of the hill covering the original soil too deep for cultivation, and this covering being of little agricultural value. It is, in fact, one of the richest mining regions in this or any other State, and its resources in both coal and iron are simply inexhaustible. Fruit could be bountifully raised, for these side hills could be made very valuable with but little labor in making them into orchards. It is also a good stock township, especially for sheep. Its great industry, however, is mining.

TRANSPORTATION AND POPULATION.

Its transportation facilities are good because it became a necessity. The Hocking Valley Railroad, called the C., H. V. & T. Railway, passes through the township from the northwest to the southeast, bearing, however, to the north of the center of the township, but following the river, which also traverses the township from northwest to southeast. In addition to this the Monday Creek Branch of this railroad is started from Nelsonville and passes through Bessemer and other points, giving freighting facilities to the several mining towns located in this rich mineral country. The Hocking Valley Canal, although now in but little use, also passes through the township and was at one time the only medium of transportation. It will be thus seen that her mining interest will not suffer for want of transportation. This interest has given the township a wonderful growth, both rapid and permanent, and while other townships in the county have felt the hands of decay or stagnation upon them, York has gone forward with rapid strides, not only in population but in wealth.

While in 1820 York Township could boast of a population of 341 only, in 1850 it had risen to 1,399. Here was the doubling of the original number for three successive decades. In 1860 it was 2,563, and in 1870, 2,652, which showed a slow advance caused by the civil war, but the last decade it more than doubled its population, having in 1880 no less than 5,438. Since the census was taken the growth has been equally marked, and it will without doubt again double itself the present decade, and in 1890 it will show a population of from 10,000 to 12,000. As has been remarked above, the leading industry of the township, and the one which has given it such rapid growth, is mining. The easy access to the upper coal beds which crop out of the hills and the valuable quality of the coal has always designated this locality as particularly attractive to enterprising men. Besides the coal deposits, the iron ore in the hills has attracted the attention of iron men, and a number of iron furnaces have been built within the last few years.

NEW TOWNS.

There are a number of villages in the township besides the towns of Nelsonville and Buchtel, but they are so dependent upon the operations of the miners and of such a temporary nature as to hardly deserve the name of village. It has therefore followed that wherever the capitalists have designated a convenient place to open a mine, they have at once constructed a number of cheap dwellings for the use of their employes. It enables the miner to more closely attend to his work, and being erected in close proximity to the mine, is of a great convenience to those who labor at or in the mines. They generally remain in the possession of the operator, but in some cases a few of the more thrifty laborers have preferred owning their houses to paying rent, and have bought of their employers, paying in labor. All such operators have a store, out of which they pay for labor. Merchandise, and generally a postoffice, is kept in the store. Such in York Township are Floodwood, New and Old; Lick Run, Laurel Hill and Doanville. The most important of these is Floodwood, situated on the river about three miles below Nelsonville. It has sprung up within the last three years and, should the anticipations of the proprietors be fulfilled, will soon be a seat of considerable industry. Two large iron furnaces have been built, a large store building and about 600 wooden dwellings. But as yet the furnaces are cold and the houses without inhabitants. Just across the river is the older village designated as Old Floodwood. It has about fifty houses. Laurel Hill and Lick Run are owned by different companies, but are near enough together to be accommodated with one postoffice. They are situated near the river, in the northwestern corner of the township, and contain about 150 houses.

DEVELOPMENT.

The township has shown much progress outside of its mining interests, and has developed much interest in schools, churches and societies. It has also a fair amount of stock within its borders. It is a well-watered township, and peculiarly adapted to sheep-raising. Beside the valley of the Hocking, which is rich and fertile, and the Hocking River, there is Monday Creek, a fine stream of pure water, and several branches, and Minker Run on the south side of the Hocking River. Springs, besides, are abundant.

OFFICIAL STATISTICS.

The organization of the township required township elections, and the first was held in 1819, and the voting precinct was at the house of Ebenezer Blackstone, and there the voting was done. The following is a list of the township officers from 1844.

TOWNSHIP OFFICERS.

1844.—Trustees, Joshua Sheffield, T. M. Boyles and James H. Devore; Clerk, Robert Miller; Treasurer, Cornelius Steenrod; Justice of the Peace, Wm. E. Brown.

1845.—Trustees, Joshua Sheffield, T. M. Boyles and W. W. Poston; Clerk, Noah Wilder; Treasurer, C. Steenrod; Justice of the Peace, Noah Wilder.

1846.—Trustees, Joshua Sheffield, T. M. Boyles and W. W. Poston; Clerk, Noah Wilder; Treasurer, C. Steenrod; Justice of the Peace, Christian Harmon.

1847.—Trustees, Joshua Sheffield, T. M. Boyles and W. W. Poston; Clerk, Noah Wilder; Treasurer, C. Steenrod; Justice of the Peace, Christian Harmon.

1848.—Trustees, Joshua Sheffield, T. M. Boyles and W. W. Poston; Clerk, Noah Wilder; Treasurer, C. Steenrod; Justice ot he Peace, B. F. Harper.

1849.—Trustees, Alvin Baker, L. D. Poston and Pierson Vore; Clerk, Thomas L. Mintun; Treasurer, C. Steenrod; Justice of the Peace, Noah Wilder.

1850.—Trustees, Alvin Baker, L. D. Poston and John Dew; Clerk, John Cheshire; Treasurer, C. Steenrod; Justice of the Peace, Thomas L. Mintun.

1851.—Trustees, Thomas Dew, Joseph Brett and A. H. Cowen; Clerk, J. B. Harper; Treasurer, J. E. Price; Justice of the Peace, Alvin Baker.

1852.—Trustees, J. G. Myers, Joseph Brett and A. H. Cowen; Clerk, C. Steenrod; Treasurer, J. E. Price; Justice of the Peace, Alvin Baker.

1853.—Trustees, Joshua Sheffield, Joseph Brett and A. H. Cowen; Clerk, John Cheshire; Treasurer, J. E. Price; Justice of the Peace, Joseph Brett.

1854.—Trustees, Joshua Sheffield, Aaron Lewis, and J. G. Myers; Clerk, Lewis Steenrod; Treasurer, C. Steenrod; Justices of the Peace, Joshua Sheffield and Thomas L. Mintun.

1855.—Trustees, Joshua Sheffield, John Hull and Thomas L. Mintun; Clerk, L. Steenrod; Treasurer, C. Steenrod; Justices of the Peace, Joshua Sheffield, and Thomas L. Mintun.

1856.—Trustees, Joshua Sheffield, John Hull and Aaron Lewis, Clerk, L. Steenrod; Treasurer, C. Steenrod; Justices of the Peace, Joshua Sheffield and Thomas L. Mintun.

1857.—Trustees, Joshua Sheffield, John Hull and Aaron Lewis; Clerk, L. Steenrod; Treasurer, C. Steenrod; Justices of the Peace, Joshua Sheffield and Thomas L. Mintun.

1858.—Trustees, Joshua Sheffield, M. D. Socie and Ashford Poston; Clerk, L. Steenrod; Treasurer, C. Steenrod; Justices of the Peace, Joshua Sheffield and Thomas L. Mintun.

1859.—Trustees, Joshua Sheffield, John G. Myers and John Hull; Clerk, Ashford Poston; Treasurer, C. Steenrod; Justices of the Peace, Joshua Sheffield and Thomas L. Mintun.

1860.—Trustees, Joshua Sheffield, G. L. Cooley, and Moses Lewis; Clerk, Ashford Poston; Treasurer, C. Steenrod; Justices of the Peace, Joshua Sheffield and Thomas L Mintun.

1861.—Trustees, Joshua Sheffield, G. L. Cooley and Moses Lewis; Clerk, Ashford Poston; Treasurer, C. Steenrod; Justices of the Peace, Robert R. Patterson.

1862.—Trustees, Richard Matheny, G. L. Cooley and Wm. Allbright; Clerk, Samuel N. Poston; Treasurer, C. Steenrod; Justice of the Peace, Joseph Brett.

1863.—Trustees, Richard Matheny, G. L. Cooley and J. G. Meyers; Clerk, Samuel N. Poston; Treasurer, C. Steenrod; Justices of the Peace, Ashford Poston and Robert Patterson.

1864.—Trustees, Richard Matheny, Ashford Poston and J. G. Meyers; Clerk, John Harrison; Treasurer, John W. Scott; Justices of the Peace, Ashford Poston and Robert Patterson.

1865.—Trustees, Richard Matheny, Ashford Poston and J. G. Meyers; Clerk, John Harrison; Treasurer, John W. Scott; Justices of the Peace, Ashford Poston and Robert Patterson.

1866.—Trustees, Richard Matheny, Ashford Poston and J. G. Meyers; Clerk, John Harrison; Treasurer, John W. Scott; Justices of the Peace, Ashford Poston and Robert Patterson.

1867.—Trustees, Aaron Lewis, P. H. Moore and J. G. Meyers; Clerk, John Harrison; Treasurer, John W. Scott; Justice of the Peace, Thomas L. Mintun.

1868.—Trustees, Moses Lewis, R. R. Patterson and J. G. Meyers; Clerk, John Harrison; Treasurer, John W. Scott; Justice of the Peace, Thomas L. Mintun.

1869.—Trustees, Wm. Comstock, S. N. Poston and John Beckler; Clerk, John Harrison; Treasurer, John W. Scott; Justice of the Peace, W. C. Hickman.

1870.—Trustees, P. H. Moore, C. Steenrod and J. S. Butt; Clerk, John Harrison; Treasurer, J. S. Scott; Justice of the Peace, Thomas L. Mintun.

1871.—Trustees, J. G. Meyers, John Thompson and Harrison Atwood; Clerk, L. S. Aisles; Treasurer, J. S. Scott.

1872.—Trustees, John G. Meyers, Chas. A. Cable and John Beckler; Clerk, W. C. Hickman; Treasurer, J. S. Scott.

1873.—Trustees, J. G. Meyers, Chas. A. Cable and John Beckler; Clerk, W. C. Hickman; Treasurer, J. S. Scott; Justices of the Peace, Thomas L. Mintun and Moses Lewis.

1874.—Trustees, J. G. Meyers, John Beckler and Wm. W. Poston; Clerk, W. C. Hickman; Treasurer, J. S. Scott.

1875.—Trustees, Wm. W. Poston, R. R. Patterson and A. H. Wells; Clerk, W. C. Hickman; Treasurer, John C. Parker; Justices of the Peace, Wesley C. Hickman and R. R. Patterson.

1876.—Trustees, J. G. Meyers, Wm. W. Poston and A. H. Wells; Clerk, W. C. Hickman; Treasurer, J. C. Parker; Justice of the Peace, Moses Lewis.

1877.—Trustees, A. H. Wells, Mason Andrews and Chas. A. Cable; Clerk, John F. Camp; Treasurer, J. C. Parker.

1878.—Trustees, Chas. A. Cable, Thomas P. Scott and Mason Andrews; Clerk, John F. Camp; Treasurer, J. C. Parker; Justices of the Peace, David Putnam and R. R. Patterson.

1879.—Trustees, W. G. Hickman, James Dew and J. G. Meyers; Clerk, J. R. Hickman; Treasurer, J. C. Parker.

1880.—Trustees, W. G. Hickman, James Six and A. H. Wells; Clerk, J. R. Hickman; Treasurer, J. C. Parker; Justice of the Peace, John Grimm.

1881.—Trustees, A. H. Comes, James Six and A. H. Wells; Clerk, J. R. Hickman; Treasurer, J. C. Parker; Justices of the Peace, J. A. Stick and W. C. Hickman.

1882.—Trustees, James Six, W. J. Hayburn and A. H. Wells; Clerk, J. R. Hickman; Treasurer, J. C. Parker; Justice of the Peace, John F. Camp.

BUCHTEL VILLAGE.

The village of Buchtel is situated in the northern part of York Township, part of it being across the line in Hocking County. It is situated near Snow Fork, a branch of Monday Creek, and on the Monday Creek branch of the C., H. V. & T. Railway. The village was laid out by John R. Buchtel, of Akron, Ohio, in the spring of 1876, having a short time before, as representative of the Akron Iron Company, purchased upward of 2,000 acres of mineral land in Athens and Hocking counties. The same year the furnace at this place was built, which, in all its departments, immediately offered employment to over 600 men. The village grew rapidly, and in the course of a few months nearly 200 houses had sprung up, most of which were built by the Akron Iron Co. This company still owns 178 of the houses, at least one half of which are occupied by two or more families. The inhabitants are almost all laborers and clerks in the employ of the company. It has, at present, two physicians, H. T. Lee and F. C. Armstrong, with about 1,500 inhabitants. Two churches are in course of erection, a Roman Catholic and a Methodist Episcopal. The store at this place, erected by the company in 1881, is decidedly the most extensive mercantile establishment in the Hocking Valley. Since the early history of the village a store had existed which was controlled by the company, but managed by Mr. O. D. Jackson, who was an independent partner in the store. The present store is a massive brick structure, 60 x 130 feet in dimensions, two stories high, with a cellar under the entire building. It handles nearly everything known to the mercantile business and comprises four departments, each of which occupies a large store-room, the average stock carried being worth $70,000. The store building and fixtures cost over $30,000. On the second floor, besides a large store-room, is an opera hall with a seating capacity of 500, a hall occupied by the Odd-Fellows lodge, and a doctor's office. The furnace at Buchtel is one of the largest in the valley, and this, together with the coal mining at this place, makes it an important mining center. The postoffice was established in the fall of 1877 by Mr. O. D. Jackson, he being the first Postmaster, serving until April, 1882, when Mr. W. J. Hamilton was appointed, Mr. Jackson having gone out of business at this place and left the village.

SOCIETIES.

Buchtel Lodge, No. 712, *I. O. O. F.*, was instituted July 6, 1882. The charter members were: Thos. N. Black, N. G., Wm. Palmer, V. G.; W. N. Black, R. S.; L. A. Whitmore, P. S.; J. J. Lane, George Sowers, Wm. Snyder, Wesley Duffee, Thomas Clark, George Littlejohn, W. B. Gilmore, Nicholas Brown, E. A. Petty, Samuel Campbell, Theodore Hedge and Henry Gaver. The membership, at present, is about seventy-four. The present officers are: J. J. Lane, N. G.; Henry Gaver, V. G.; D. W. Conner, R. S.; and H. W. Veon, P. S.

Keystone Assembly, No. 1,516, *K. of L.*, located at Buchtel, was established April 15, 1880, with twenty charter members. The original officers were: John McMahon, M. W.; Robert Bradley, W. F.; Ebenezer Moses, R. S. The present officers are: S. D. Hannah, M. W.; Jacob Kautz, W. F.; Charles Covert, R. S. The present membership of this assembly is about seventy-nine. Another assembly of the same order, the

Humboldt Assembly, a German society, holds its meetings in the hall owned by the above.

York Lodge, No. 75, K. of P., located at Buchtel, was transferred from Nelsonville in the fall of 1882. It then had sixty members, and has since grown to sixty-seven. The leading officers are: W. D. Marshall, B. C.; E. W. Woody, C. C., and A. L. Horton, V. C.

The Tom Dew Post, G. A. R., located at Buchtel, was established Jan. 4, 1883, with twenty charter members. The officers are as follows: J. J. Lane, Commander; Joseph Robison, Vice-Commander; Thomas McMaster, Junior Vice-Commander; W. R. Gilmore, Quartermaster; Geo. Snowden, Adjutant; Ferd Conner, Officer of the Day; John Clark, Officer of the Guard, and W. D McLain, Chaplain.

CHAPTER XVI.

CITY OF NELSONVILLE, THE MINERAL CITY OF THE HOCKING VALLEY.

THE MINERAL CITY—RATHER ELONGATED—HILLS OF COAL AND IRON—WHERE LOCATED—SOME ACCOUNT OF ITS EARLY SETTLERS—FIRST BRIDGE OVER THE HOCKING RIVER—FIRST LIBRARY AND SOCIETY—SOME OLD PAPERS OF VALUE—SETTLERS IN 1827—JAS. KNIGHT'S PROPHECY—LETTER TO DR. HILDRETH—THE COMPLETION OF THE CANAL—COAL OPERATORS—HEAVY WORK—MANUFACTURES — CITY OFFICERS — CHURCHES — PUBLIC SCHOOLS — LODGES AND SOCIETIES—BUSINESS INTERESTS—1866—1883.

THE MINERAL CITY OF THE VALLEY.

Nelsonville is not only the largest city in the Hocking Valley, but is also the most important point in mining interests in Southeastern and Southern Ohio. It is located on the Hocking River, in the midst of one of its most fertile portions, and extends back to the hills, which rear their majestic proportions, giving from their bold outlines a pleasing view in contrast to the valley in which the town lies, and which has extended itself for nearly a mile in length—still growing and still elongating, with but little prospect of stopping until another mile or so of the valley is wrapped in its loving embrace. It is so rich in its mineral surrounding, so inexhaustible in its coal supply, and so fertile is the valley upon whose bosom it lies, that Nelsonville is destined to retain the prestige she now holds of being the largest and most important city in the rich and beautiful valley of the Hocking River. She has not so commanding a site as Athens, neither can she show so wide a plain, gentle elevations and handsome drives as Logan, but the wonderful wealth of those massive hills which surround her gives a very beautiful look to the eye of the man of business and practical knowledge when he gazes upon them, which, with but a flimsy covering of a few feet of earth, hold within their embrace a world of wealth. So Nelsonville, confined in the narrow valley, will gradually extend herself up and down for

A. Poston

miles, while her breadth will scarcely, at any point, exceed a quarter of a mile. And under her black and unprepossessing look she carries a warm heart, and he who wishes to make a home here is received with open arms, and the race for a competency or wealth is opened to him, free, to exercise his own best talent and judgment to win the prize. Nelsonville is situated in the northern part of York Township, a small portion of the incorporated land lying over the border in Hocking County. It lies on the left bank of the Hocking River, on the line of the C., H. V. & T. Railway, and the Hocking Canal. The Monday Creek branch of the C., H. V. & T. Railway leaves the main line at this point, connecting it with New Straitsville and other mining towns in Perry and Hocking counties.

EARLY DAYS.

Prior to 1814 two families, named Johnson and Hurlbert, had settled in the wilderness of the Hocking Valley, building their log cabins within sight of each other, very near to the present site of Nelsonville. This was the only interruption to an unbroken wilderness between the then scanty settlement of Athens and the early settlements near Logan. In 1814 Mr. Daniel Nelson, an intelligent and prosperous citizen of Shrewsbury, Mass., purchased a large tract of land from an agent of the Ohio Company, and came with his family to settle and improve it. He reached the site of Nelsonville in August, 1814, and, as soon as possible, erected a double log-cabin for a dwelling, on the ground where now stands the dwelling of Mr. John Burberry, just west of W. B. Brooks's store.

The following is from the Centennial address of W. C. Hickman at Nelsonville, July 4, 1876. "In June, 1818, York Township was organized, and on the 16th of the same month Daniel Nelson laid out the village of Nelsonville, which was properly named in honor of the founder, who well deserved that and greater acknowledgment, for his public-spirted energy of character, and for his foresight and generosity to the then weak, struggling village. Let me say here, that no selfish act nor an instance of close exacting dealing is shown, by such items of history as we can now gather, to have been perpetrated by Daniel Nelson toward the village he founded, or toward those who had cast their lot in it. He has long since passed to his final account; but these words can truthfully be said of him, and it is his due that they be thus publicly expressed. His death occurred on the 20th of May, 1835. The original plat comprised fifty-seven lots, numbering from one to fifty-seven. Two streets were named—Columbus and Mulberry. In the month of October, 3d day, 1825, Mr. Nelson laid out twenty additional town lots, numbering from fifty-eight to seventy-seven, both inclusive. At that time the town had not developed to any great extent; but those who lived here had faith in its future, and were getting ready for its growth. When Captain John Hull came there were but eight houses here. The oldest of these, a cabin, belonging to ——Johnson, stood south of Steenrod & Poston's mill, between the present bed of the canal and the railroad.

EARLY SETTLERS.

Mr. Nelson was a man of great energy, and was soon making more permanent improvements than were common to new settlements, and drawing about him men of an enterprising disposition. In 1816 Mr. Josiah Coe located near and built a flouring mill on the river bank, the same one now owned by Mr. Chas. Robbins. Soon after, in about 1820, Mr. Thomas Thompson came and kept a hotel on the south side of the public square, only a few rods from the present Dew House. He was succeeded in the hotel business by Mr. Claudius L. Fisk, who built a brick tavern on the site of Mr. Chas. A. Cable's residence. Mr. James Knight, an energetic and enterprising Englishman, came in 1822 and inaugurated the mercantile business, bringing a small stock of goods with him on his first arrival. His store was a small frame building, standing on the lot now occupied by his son, Wallace W. Knight, the building now being attached to and forming a part of the store of Mr. A. H. Carnes. Thus gradually but slowly the infant settlement grew. Although but a few people had gathered in, a town was laid out by Mr. Nelson in 1823, he at that time deeding to the village the public square and the lot on which now stands the public school building, the latter to be used for a church and school lot. Between 1816 and 1820 Mr. George Courtauld, a wealthy Englishman, purchased land and settled on what is now a part of Longstreth's Addition, about one mile from the original village of Nelsonville. He brought with him among others a family of grown children, some of whom were married, all of whom began earnestly to prosecute the plan of establishing a village. Considerable land was cleared, a store was kept by Mr. Courtauld, and through his efforts a postoffice was established in 1821, which he kept in his store. This community prospered and bid fair to fulfill the anticipations of its proprietor, until, when on a business trip to the East, Mr. Courtauld suddenly died and the remainder of the company soon gave up the enterprise and returned to England. Coal was known to exist in the hills about Nelsonville even at this date, but it was not mined and did nothing toward developing the village until several years later. Inhabitants were attracted by the beauty and convenience of location, and the fertility of the soil. The principal industry was clearing and cultivating the land and transporting the products to market. An avenue for this purpose was supplied by the Hocking River, on which plied the flatboats of active tradesmen, transporting goods to and from the greater markets. The growth of the village in its early days was due, however, in a great measure to the efforts of Mr. Nelson and a few others; through their efforts roads were opened connecting the village with other settlements in this part of the State, a bridge was built across the river, said to be the first to span the Hocking and many other efforts were put forth to secure prosperity and growth.

After the death of Mr. Courtauld in 1823, Mr. Nelson was appointed to succeed him as Postmaster, and he removed the office to his own village Jan. 1, 1824, the name of the office being changed to Nelsonville.

FIRST BRIDGE OVER THE HOCKHOCKING.

The next move of importance was the building of a bridge across the Hocking River. This was started in 1827. May 21 of that year an advertisement was put up on trees and other places, saying a committee of four persons would receive proposals to build a bridge across the Hocking River, and that plans, etc., would be found in the hands of Mr. James Knight. The plans and specifications of this, the first bridge ever built across the Hocking River, is now in the hands of W. W. Knight, his son, and are well worthy of examination. A subscription paper was taken around for contributions. The largest donation was $20, and the smallest 50 cents. The subscription paper read, that those wishing to pay their subscriptions in labor could do so, and they would be allowed the munificent sum of 50 cents per day, and they board themselves. Corn would be received at 25 cents per bushel, wheat at 50 cents per bushel, whisky at 25 cents per gallon, and pork at

$2 per 100 pounds. There was one man from Columbus who subscribed $5, one from Marietta $5, four from Lancaster, in all $16, being two of $5 each and two of $3, and the township of York $10 from the road fund. There were some four bids, but Mr. Nelson secured the job by agreeing to take the subscription paper at par and do his own collecting. The subscription amounted to $442.50, and Mr. Nelson got $400 out of it, and made to the commissioners the following statement: Bridge, per contract, $410; extra work, $85; total $495; subscription list, $440.50; bad, $40.50; net, $400; out of pocket, $95. The bridge was completed and accepted by the commissioners Oct. 23, 1828, and on May 5, 1829, that bridge started down the Hocking River on a voyage of discovery, and, so far as the people of Nelsonville know to the contrary, is still prosecuting its search. It was to stand one year, and resulted in a lawsuit and loss to the contractor. Some years later, in 1832, another bridge was erected.

FIRST LIBRARY.

In 1827 there was also a movement for the establishment of a village or town library, and a report of this was made Sept. 7, 1828, when it was shown they had forty-seven volumes of miscellaneous works in their possession.

Mr. Knight has in his possession, in the original, an several of them, headed, "An Essay on the Deity of Jesus Christ," by Thos. Scott, Rector of Aston Sanford, and dated Nov. 5, 1774. Part of these writings are in short-hand, and some of the passages are strikingly original. Some of the reverend gentlemen of Athens County might find food for thought in perusing this manuscript, or at least get some idea of what was the belief or the doctrine held over 100 years ago.

EARLY SETTLERS.

The first settlers of Nelsonville have been given, but the following named persons were residing in the village Jan. 1, 1827, as their names were found on the subscription paper in January and February of that year, to the Hocking Bridge: Jas. Knight, C. L. Fisk, Wm. Biggerstaff, Wm. Harper, Robert Thompson, Amorn Entsminger, Jas. Pickett, Jos. Brett, Saul Pickett, Jonathan White, Daniel Nelson, Jas. Tenants, Wm. Long, John Rochester, M. B. Lovewell, Samuel K. Harrington, Jacob Feirce, Jacob

Skeiver, Calvin Thompson, Richard Mills, Thos. Thompson, Geo. Mills, Wm. Gleason, John McKeye, Abijah Weaver, Martin L. Sheppard, Thos. Campbell, F. Billinghurst, John Hume, E. Stewart, David Robert, Thos. Brien, John Brown, B. Brice, Chas. Shipman, Robt. Callis, Isaac Barker, Hocking H. Huhler, Wm. Stewart, G. Kincannon, Harry Henshaw, Harvey Weill, Geo. Walker, Christian Eby, Justus Reynold, Leroy Allen, Norman Root, John Beach, Jos. B. Miles, A. Cormac, David Johnson, Calvary Morris, Solomon Finney, Dwight Jarvis, John Wight, A. Brown, John Noble, G. Browning, E. Hibbard, John Wright, Henry Bartlett, Thos. Irvin, Ebenezer Currier, R. E. Constable, Jno. Dana, Cephas Carpenter, J. J. Fuller, Emery Newton, E. Burnett, Thos. Harris, Chas. O'Neil, S. F. McCracken, S. B. Pruden, C. F. Perkins, Samuel Entsminger, Benjamin Johnson, Jacob Claypool, David Skiver, John Graham, John S. Putman, Elias Spencer, Nicholas Bates, George French, Elijah Watkins, Samuel Lewis, John Counch, Daniel Jacob, Thos. Watkins, Jas. Coe, Jos. S. Rollins, John Entsminger, David Dunham, Solomon Tuttle, Rufus P. Danir, Peter M. Dodd, John Conrad, John Weavin, Daniel Boomer, Moses Lewis, Edmund Terry, John Samson, Jacob Benjamin, Henry Hansen, Edmund Weavin, Thos. Snider, Solomon Roberts, John Roberts, John Chamberlin, John Dodd, Michael Weavin, John Perkins, Amos Crippin, Wilmarth Allen, Seth Morge.

ORIGINAL PAPERS OF VALUE.

The first society organized in Nelsonville was in the fall of 1823, and was called the "York Township Amicable Library Society." No person living outside of York Township was allowed to become a member. It flourished for several years, held debates on various subjects, and was really the foundation of what was called the "Nelsonville Library," which assumed the name in 1827. The original papers of this library are in the hands of W. W. Knight, left him by his father, Mr. James Knight. Mr. Knight has many other papers of interest left him by his father, but there is one of singular importance and prophesy, a copy of a letter written to Dr. Hildreth, of Marietta, Ohio, by Mr. Knight, which shows him to have been one of the shrewdest men of his time, and had he lived (he died Aug. 26, 1836) would have held a prominent, if not the foremost, one, in the history of the town and county. He at that day, 1833-'34, had already divined the future of Nelsonville and the Hocking Valley, and he prophesied truly when he said, "These hills were not placed here without design, nor without their uses; man has not yet found out their value." He was indeed a prophet, a man of clear sense, a mind given to analysis and tracing effects from causes. In the light of the facts which have been developed the past few years, and the future which may now be considered known of this great valley, Mr. Knight's prophesy has come true, and only his observing eye and clear mind were able at that time to grasp the future of the valley of the great Hockhocking. Here is the letter, and it is well worthy a place in the historic pages of Ohio history:

COPY OF A LETTER SENT TO DR. HILDRETH, OF MARIETTA, OHIO, JAN. 17, 1834.

This letter was dated Jan. 14, 1834, but filed on the 17th as sent at that time.

NELSONVILLE, OHIO, *Jan.* 14, 1834.

"DR. S. P. HILDRETH, *Dear Sir:*—Yours of the 25th of December came safely to hand. I have to thank you for your very complimentary communication. I assure you nothing would give me more pleasure than to give you a reply in full to all your queries, did I feel myself sufficiently qualified to answer them in such a scientific manner as would be understood. The only answer I could possibly give you at this time is in general terms, as the time (1st of February) which you wish to have all the queries answered is so near at hand, and the season of the year so unpropitious for actual observation or research, as to render it impossible with me to do half justice to so interesting an enquiry. I thought it best to give a general answer without delay, and at the same time to say that as soon as the season of the year will allow you to leave home with any degree of comfort, to just take your horse and ride out here and pass a few days with me. In the interval I will make minutes where will be found the most interesting spots for our attention to be directed. I shall take great pleasure in spending a few days in this way—it is what I have long wished to do in company with some person of science. I believe here will be more found that relates to the mineral kingdoms worthy of particular notice than is generally known, or than you can form any correct idea of.

"In the first place we have the coal strata, and those which are most particularly known to us are such as have presented themselves by the washings of runs and hollows in the hills. Veins are to be found from one to ten feet thick, in this vicinity, above the level of the bottom land. I believe I could show you at least 100 that have presented themselves. I opened a bank the other day, on the side of a hill (at a lick), which was certainly from twenty to twenty-five feet higher in the strata than one which I knew only about one quarter of a mile distant. The one I opened was only two feet to two feet, three inches in thickness. The one referred to a quarter of a mile distant has a strata of from five to six feet. The quality of our coal is better than I ever had on my fire in England. I learn also that in sinking the salt well on Sunday Creek, that the first strata of coal was a few feet below the surface, and that another was passed through eleven feet thick, 100 feet below the first. My personal observation has not been sufficiently particular to state for a fact on what level the thickest stratas are to be found, but I believe it is to be in general just above the bottom lands level.

"We have limestone, also, on most of our hills, in some places in considerable quantity, and I have observed it, also, in several gulleys that are far below the usual line of level of the hill-tops.

"IRON ORE, I believe in quantity inexhaustible will be found here. My impression is, that in the hills there are large quantities, from the pieces that have presented themselves in plowing, etc. In many other places not far distant I know it exists in large quantities and easily attainable.

"The large sandstone rocks are generally found near the top of the hills, and frequently below them is a kind of shelly soapstone, often impregnated strongly with alum; then layers of freestone, say ten inches to a foot in thickness, which will, in time, be uncommonly valuable. In some instances large flat stones of two inches thick, suitable for paving, are found. It is under these the coal generally presents itelf—though not in all cases. I am fully persuaded that there is slate in this vicinity, of a hardness sufficient to cover a house.

"I know a place, also, where thin fine stone, say from one-third to one-half inch in thickness, can be found that could be dressed for the same purpose—it would be worked profitably were it in England.

"Alum, salt-peter and copperas are known to exist in many places. These I will endeavor to get full information of by the time you visit us. I believe I could introduce you to a spring that possesses all the virtues of the Saratoga.

"Here is also a fire-clay, when dry perfectly white, and apparently free from any impure admixture. It does not appear to possess the virtue of marl. I think fine earthenware could be made of it.

"In short, Nature has been so bountiful in this part of the country that we know not yet how to appreciate the value. A week's research of a few scientific men would discover more than *all* that is yet known. I have always been of the opinion, and daily experience tends to confirm it, that this will be in a very few years the richest section of the State of Ohio. These hills were not placed here without design, nor without their uses. Man has not yet found out their value. We merely stir a little of their surface with no enterprise to go farther, but the time is not far distant when all our lands will be explored, and these hills which have so long been considered as of no value, and not worth paying taxes for, will be the most carefully sought. Excuse this hasty and unconnected communication.

"I am very respectfully yours,
"JAMES KNIGHT."

Mr. Knight had been in correspondence with Mr. Hildreth over two years previous to this date, back in 1832, and had been strenuous in his efforts to get a few scientific men and geologists to thoroughly examine the country around. He had divined its wealth and he wished for a full exploration to test his belief. Whether Prof. Hildreth came and examined the country or not, as this letter seems to carry out the idea that he promised to do, we know not, but it was not long after this that the country began to attract attention in regard to its coal deposits and its iron ores and fire-clay, etc. This brought forward the canal project to ship this coal, and this, having been started and every prospect of its being completed in a few years, brought capitalists who largely invested in the coal lands.

CANAL COMPLETED.

On the completion of the canal in 1840 an efficient means of transportation was offered and Nelsonville was soon transformed into an active and growing mining town. While mining and shipping coal was a new business it was engaged in by almost every one who owned land or was able to lease mines, but on a small scale, as the modern facilities for extensive mining were not known, or if known could not be afforded. Of course the completion of the canal was the placing of Nelsonville upon a secure foundation.

The mining operations began to increase largely and rapidly, and it was not many years before it passed into the hands of capitalists who could combine and carry out larger business interests.

The first coal put to use in Nelsonville was taken from the river bed, but the use was very limited, being confined almost entirely to the blacksmith shops. Two wagon loads of this river coal were hauled to Columbus in April, 1830, the first being a six-horse load, fifty-eight bushels, sold by James Knight to Gill and Greer, of Columbus, at four cents a bushel, delivered. But little coal was taken to market until the canal was finished, when it began to be mined and shipped in small quantities, although a bank had been opened on the north side of Johnson's Hill to supply the local demand, which is believed to be the first mine opened in the valley.

COAL OPERATORS.

Soon after the location of the Hocking Valley Canal Eastern capitalists and others of our own State made extensive purchases of land along the line of the canal from Lick Run to Chauncey. Among the most extensive purchasers were Thomas Ewing and Samuel F. Vinton, who shortly afterward associated with themselves Nicholas Biddle and Elihu Chauncey, of Philadelphia, under the name of Ewing, Vinton & Co. The firm made an opening for coal about the time of the completion of the canal to Nelsonville. Their mine was located in the hillside on the Nelsonville seam of coal, at the Dorr Run canal basin, on what is now the west end of the incorporated village of Nelsonville.

Shortly after the mine of Biddle, Ewing & Vinton was opened another opening by Fuller & Walker (James Fuller and A. B. Walker, of Athens,) was made a little further up the river. Then C. Fay, John Crothers, C. Steenrod, Launcelot Scott, J. F. Somers and L. Steenrod were found among the pioneer miners of the valley. Their mines were situated on both sides of the Hocking River, at Nelsonville, and the coal was hauled in wagons from the mouth of the mines to the canal, dumped on the wharf and loaded on the boats with wheelbarrows.

Steenrod & Scott operated in what is known as the old Steenrod works, just below the village. They were in partnership, but soon after dissolved, Steenrod keeping the old works and Scott opening new mines in what is now known as Robbin's Hill. These mines were successfully worked by Mr. Scott for a number of years when, on his death, the business passed into the hands of Mr. L. D. Poston, a son-in-law, who followed it up on a more extended scale. Among the more prominent early operators were also Mr. Mathew Vanwormer, of Boston, who conducted a mine just back of the village, and Dr. Robert Fulton, who operated across the river in what was afterward known as Brooks's mines. The completion of the C. & H. V. Railway gave another great impetus to the coal trade in the valley, and consequently added much to the business and growth of Nelsonville. Since the village has been until recently dependent upon the operations in coal, and its growth virtually governed by such operations, it is deemed proper to trace, in a brief way, a history of the business of some of the leading enterprises as identical with the growth of the village. *Mr. W. B. Brooks*, though a resident of Columbus, has done much to assist the growth of Nelsonville and secure the development of its natural wealth. He came to Nelsonville in 1859 and, with Mathew Vanwormer, under the style of Vanwormer & Brooks, purchased 300 acres of land all across the river from the town. They opened mines and conducted the coal trade on a large scale until June, 1860, when Vanwormer withdrew and the business passed under the control of W. B. Brooks.

These mines were supplied with an ice-breaking machine and continued shipping the year round. From the first the coal was transferred from the mine to the canal in cars, and there loaded into their own boats, for shipment. In 1869 Mr. Brooks purchased another tract of 600 acres immediately back of and north of Nelsonville, known as section 19. Mines were opened on this land; the two works were run together until within a few years back, when the old mine became nearly exhausted. In the new mines were placed all the latest facilities for rapid and successful mining, including mining machines, an improved set of screens, and a system of pumps for relieving the mine of water. The mining machines and pumps are run by compressed air power, the pumps being automatic in their actions. Mr. Brooks, as one of the leading citizens, has been liberal in the support of worthy enterprises. He has been also largely in the mercantile business since he came to Nelsonville to inaugurate his mining enterprises, and erected the large brick store on the corner of the square, now occupied by the firm, in 1872. Mr. Brooks has recently taken his son into partnership, under the firm name of W. B. Brooks & Son, they are doing a large business, and now put out some 200,000 tons of coal annually. Their largest day's work was the loading and shipping of 105 cars.

L. D. Poston began operating in coal soon after the completion of the canal in 1840. His first business was in connection with Mr. Launcelot Scott, who, as already stated, operated in Robbin's Hill. When on the death of Mr. Scott the business fell into the hands of Mr. Poston, he greatly improved and enlarged the facilities, soon becoming one of the foremost operators in the valley. At this time the coal was wagoned from the mines to the wharf. The business steadily increased and the works became gradually more extensive by the application of new methods until the late war of the Rebellion, when the business sprang to double its former proportions. A short time previous to the war Mr. Poston had purchased the lands in which he had operated, having had them leased up to this time. When the C. & H. V. Railway was built the business was again enlarged, large quantities being shipped both by railroad and canal.

In 1872 he bought a tract of 250 acres of land lying just east of the town and opened the mines. Having made all the preparations for extensive mining the property was leased to his sons, C. L. and Wm. W. Poston, and a son-in-law, E. P. Pendleton, for twenty years, himself retiring entirely from the business in 1875. The business was continued under the firm name of Poston & Pendleton. In 1880 Wm. W. Poston and Pendleton sold their interest to McClintick and Smith, of Chillicothe, Ohio, who are the present partners of C. L. Poston, under the firm name of C. L. Poston & Co. This firm recently purchased 400 acres of mineral land in the Monday Creek Valley, and are mining about 100,000 tons of coal a year, having constantly in its employ about 165 men. They own a large store on the public square, doing a business of about $50,000 a year.

Thaddeus Longstreth.—This gentleman began operating in coal at Nelsonville in the summer of 1867. He came from Warren County, Ohio, and bought an interest in the coal works of W. G. Power & Co., who were working mines leased of Rhodes & Phillips. In 1869 Mr. Longstreth bought out his partners and about the same time bought the land on which the works were situated. Since that time he has been operating alone, the business constantly increasing. In December, 1878, he purchased a large tract of coal land in Hocking County and opened extensive works on it. He employs, at Nelsonville, about 200 men and ships about

120,000 tons of coal a year. In 1871 he laid out the eastern part of Nelsonville, known as Longstreth's addition, which consists of 178 lots laid out on improved and well-laying ground. This addition is already mostly taken up by dwellings, and will probably be, in a few years, a valuable portion of the city. The store owned by Mr. Longstreth is a large and substantial brick building situated in the *addition*. It was built in 1874, is 30 x 90 feet in dimensions, with a cellar under the whole of it. Mr. Longstreth, by supporting public enterprises, and by the extent of his individual business interests, has done much for the welfare and growth of Nelsonville. These are the largest and oldest of coal interests, but there are several other operators well deserving of mention, both in the extent of their mining operation and their energy and enterprise. Among these are Johnson Bros. & Co., Juniper Brothers, Nelsonville Mining Company, L. Steenrod and W. A. Shoemaker & Co. There are between 1,000 and 1,200 miners at work in these several mines, and very many of them are owners of their own dwellings. The price now paid for mining is 80 cents per ton.

NOT ALL MINING.

Nelsonville has, beside her mining and manufacturing interests, a number of elegant and substantial public buildings, among them the Methodist Episcopal church, which is an exceptionally fine and substantial structure; the Opera House, a substantial structure situated on the public square, and a number of very fine store buildings. She has at present a population of about four thousand inhabitants.

The town was incorporated by act of the Legislature in 1838. The first election for town officers was held April 27, 1839, when Charles Cable was elected Mayor; A. J. Bond, Recorder; John Coe, S. M. Shepard, John Hull, W. W. Poston and James Rusk, Trustees. Luther Burt was appointed Marshal of the village, and Robert Miller, Treasurer. James Rusk declining to serve as Trustee, Thomas L. Mintun was appointed in his place. Since then the following persons have filled the town offices; up to 1870 only the Mayors are named: Charles Cable, elected in 1838; Wm. Burlingame, 1840; Ebenezer Fenimore, 1841; Solomon Roberts, 1842; James Deaver, 1843; R. G. McLean, 1845, 1846-'47, no record; Lewis Steenrod, 1848 (Mr. Steenrod resigning, A. J. Guitteau was appointed for his unexpired term); B. A. Lincoln, 1850; Thomas L. Mintun, 1852; L. Hutchins, 1853; H. H. Myers,

1854; A. M. Burgess, 1855; C. T. Hyde, 1856; J. E. Price, 1858; A. H. Burrell, 1859; J. E. Howe, 1861; M. A. Stewart, 1862; James Eddington, 1864; H. H. Myers, 1865; Jacob C. Frost, 1866; R. R. Patterson, 1867; John F. Welch, 1868.

1870.—Mayor, John F. Welch; Clerk, W. C. Hickman; Treasurer, John C. Parker; Council, Wm. Comstock, James Eddington, S. C. Koutner and C. Steenrod.

1871.—Mayor, S. W. Butt; Clerk, J. A. Benson; Council, Geo. Somers, A. N. Bull, S. Spencer, James Verity and Frank Jones.

1872.—Mayor, Thomas L. Mintun; Clerk, A. D. Miller; Council, A. N. Bull, S. Spencer, A. Poston, James Verity and J. F. Welch.

1873.—Mayor, Thomas L. Mintun; Clerk, L. L. Scott; Council, J. F. Welch, S. N. Poston, Thomas Berry, Geo. Somers and S. C. Koutner.

1874.—Mayor, Wm. Gilliam; Clerk, James Verity; Council, W. W. Poston, J. W. Scott, J. M. Martin, Geo. Somers and S. C. Koutner.

1875.—Mayor, A. J. Schrader; Clerk, James Verity; Council, John T. Gray, B. C. Lefevre, S. C. Koutner, J. M. Martin, J. W. Scott and W. W. Poston.

1876.—Mayor, R. R. Ellis; Clerk, J. D. Jackson; Council, C. A. Cable, J. T. Gray, J. F. Welch, B. C. Lefevre, S. C. Koutner and W. W. Poston.

1877.—Mayor, R. R. Ellis; Clerk, L. C. Steenrod; Council, J. F. Brodt, John T. Gray, S. F. Robinet, C. A. Cable, J. F. Welch and W. W. Poston.

1878.—Mayor, John F. Camp (R. R. Patterson filling out unexpired term); Clerk, L. C. Steenrod; Council, C. A. Cable, W. B. Devore, T. R. Blake, J. F. Brodt, John T. Gray and S. F. Robinet.

1879—Mayor, Asher Buckley; Clerk, L. C. Steenrod; Council, Wm. Comstock, Geo. F. Gardner, Branson Poston, C. A. Cable, W. B. Devore and T. R. Blake.

1880.—Mayor, Asher Buckley; Clerk, Wm. Fisner; Council, Frank Cooley, Calvin Haines, T. P. Marshall, John T. Gray, Branson Poston and G. F. Gardner.

1881.—Mayor, Asher Buckley; Clerk, Wm. Fisner; Council, Branson Poston, I. P. Primrose, T. R. Blake, T. P. Marshall, John F. Gray and Frank Cooley.

1882.—Mayor, James A. Tobin; Clerk, J. W. Bates; Council, E. H. Davis, W. P. Shepard, Jacob Stoneburner, I. P. Primrose, T. R. Blake and Branson Poston.

1883.—Mayor, James A. Tobin; Clerk, Eben Wilson; Council, T. R. Blake, E. H. Davis, Jacob Stoneburner, I. P. Primrose, John Hill and W. P. Shepard.

THE POSTOFFICE.

The office was established Aug. 7, 1821, by Mr. George Courtauld, who was appointed Postmaster, and who kept the office in his store, in what is now Longstreth's Addition. The office was called Englishtown while kept at this place until Jan. 1, 1824, when it was removed to Nelsonville and the name changed. Mr. Daniel Nelson was at this time appointed Postmaster, holding the position until 1832, although the business of the office was done by Mr. James Knight, who acted as Mr. Nelson's clerk, and in 1832 became his successor. Since then the Postmasters have been as follows: James Knight, 1832 to 1836; John Lillabridge, 1836 to 1839; Henry Parkson, 1839 to 1840; L. D. Poston, 1840 to 1848; John H. Tucker, 1848 to 1850; Charles Cable, 1850 to 1852; Alfred Condon, 1852 to 1855; C. A. Cable, 1855 to 1857; M. A. Stuart, 1857 (two quarters); Joseph Brett, 1857 to 1862; T. L. Mintun, 1862 to 1866; John F. Welch, 1866 to 1871; Elliott Gardner, Dec. 9, 1871, to 1878; J. W. Frost, 1878 to present time. It was made a money-order office Aug. 1, 1870, the first order being issued on that day to John Mankoph, payable to the *Times Chronicle* Co., Cincinnati, O., for the amount of $2.00. Up to the present date, March 29, 1883, 1,635 orders have been issued. It was changed from a fourth to a third class office Jan. 1, 1882. The sale of stamps for the year 1882 amounted to $2,826.96.

CHURCHES.

The Methodist Episcopal.—This society was first organized about 1836. Prior to this time the only church society which existed here was the United Brethren, who held meetings in the school-house or in a dwelling, as opportunity was afforded. This society was of short duration, being to a great extent absorbed by the Methodist society when it was formed. For a time this society used for its meetings dwellings and new buildings until they erected a building in 1838. It was a frame building 40 x 60 feet in dimensions, situated where the present church building now stands. The first regular preacher was Ezekiel Gavet. Until 1868 the appointment belonged to a circuit, when it became a station belonging to the Ohio Conference. The successive pastors after it became a station have been Revs. Richard Doughty, I. Sminger, Samuel Bright, Jr., George W. Burns, Z. Fagan, H. B. Westervelt and J. H. Gardner, the present Pastor. The old church was replaced by a new one in 1877, which is a very fine structure, costing about $20,000. Besides an auditorium it has a large Sabbath-school room.

The Presbyterian Church at Nelsonville was founded by Rev. Thomas J. Downie, Nov. 1, 1868, he being engaged to locate as Pastor the same year. The church at this time, and for a number of years after, held its meetings in the hall of the Odd Fellows society. On the first organization of the society the following officers were elected:

Elders, Jacob C. Frost, John G. Myers, Samuel N. Poston, Charles A. Cable. Deacons, W. H. Burrill, John T. Gray, J. H. E. Howe, J. F. Brodt. Trustees, John W. Scott, William Comstock, John C. Barrow, William J. Power, J. F. Brodt.

Mr. Downie remained Pastor up to the time of his death, March 31, 1869. For a time, the church being without a pastor, Thomas L. Mintun occasionally filled the pulpit until Rev. W. L. S. Clark, of Western Missouri, visited the society in November of the same year, and he was engaged to officiate as Pastor unti March, 1870. The church was again without a pastor until Aug. 1 of the same year, when James Stickle, of Cincinnati, O., was chosen Pastor, remaining one year, when he resigned on account of poor health, and the Rev. Julius Straus succeeded him, who remained until Oct. 7, 1874, when he, too, resigned. Jan. 1, 1875, Rev. Silas Cooke, of Canonsburg, Pa., became Pastor, he and also Mr. Straus having been regularly installed pastors. Mr. Cooke resigned in December, 1877, and was succeeded by the Rev. A. B. Rice, of Beverly, O., March 13, 1878, and filled the pulpit until April 13, 1881. Rev. A. A. Jameson, of Fairmount, W. Va., was then engaged as a supply for one year, resigning July 23, 1882, being followed by the Rev. James H. Hawk, of Franklin, O., who is the present Pastor. In the fall of 1873 the First Presbyterian Church of Nelsonville, was begun, and made ready for occupation in 1876. It was dedicated April 2, 1876, the dedicatory sermon being preached by Rev. A. B. Boyd, of Lancaster, O. It is a fine brick building worth about $12,000. It is 40 x 60 feet in dimensions, has a Sabbath-school room, and is furnished with steam heating apparatus.

The Church of Christ.—This church was established in Nelsonville in 1857 by Rev. L. M. Harvey. The organization took place in the residence of W. P. Roberts, and for some time after the meetings were held in private houses and school-houses. In 1859 a small house was built by the society on the hill-side now called Madison street. This building was sold for a private residence in 1873, and a new church, the present one, was built on Fort street. The church property also includes a parsonage on the same lot with the church. The church building is not large but it is elegantly finished on the inside, and well located. It cost about $6,000. The Pastors during the church's history have been, Revs. L. M. Harvey, Nathan Moody, John Moody, A. P. Frost, W. B. Thompson, A. B. Wade, A. W. Dean, M. A. Harvey and A. P. Frost, whose second pastorate began Nov. 19, 1882. Prominent among the evangelists who have labored with this church are: B. F. Franklin, T. D. Garvin, T. J. Clark, Elisha White, S. H. Bingman, Daniel Sweeney, R. G. White and Ira J. Chase, the latter having conducted three successful meetings during the last twelve years. The church is out of debt and in a very prosperous condition, claiming among its membership some of the most cultivated and influential residents of the city.

PUBLIC SCHOOLS.

One of the early and most prominent features of the village was its strong desire for educational advantages. To this end Daniel Nelson donated the school lot upon which the present plain but substantial three-story brick school-house now stands. The school interest has grown with its growth, and there is probably no better graded school in Southeastern Ohio than that of Nelsonville, under, at this time, the superintendency of Prof. F. S. Coultrap. The growth of Nelsonville compelled the erection of the brick building above mentioned in 1856, but there was very little record kept until since the late civil war. A portion of that also is missing. In the year 1865 the School Board was composed of B. F. Harper, A. Poston and C. Steenrod, the latter acting as clerk. In 1866 it was C. Steenrod, A. Poston and C. A. Cable, the latter also assuming the duty of clerk. This continued to be the number of the members of the board for a few years, when it changed to six members, with an addition of a treasurer and secretary. The brick school-house of three stories has been for several years too small for the growth of the town, and there are now three other buildings used. In the meantime while the population of school age was rapidly increasing and increased expenses occurring for more room and a greater number of efficient teachers, the startling fact became apparent that the source of taxation and supply for school purposes was rapidly diminishing. So long as the property was in the hands of small operators, each being assessed, the valuation of real and personal estate was rather advancing than receding, but consolidation and large holdings were returned for taxation at so much less than their true or honest value that the real estate and personal property of Nelsonville decreased on the assessor's books no less than $246,378 within six years, to wit: Assessed valuation of real and personal property for the year 1875, $821,390; 1880, $575,012; total loss, $246,378; and in 1881 that assessment was still further reduced, net, $85,028. As above remarked, expenses and children of school age increased, and thus it was cutting both ways. Eight teachers only were employed in 1875, and fifteen were found necessary in 1881. In 1875 there were 708 pupils in attendance, and in 1880, 1,001, while the annual levy, in amount was exactly the same in 1880 as in 1875, notwithstanding the large increase.

SOMETHING HAD TO BE DONE.

A meeting was called in May, 1881, to take into consideration the proposal to vote a three-mill tax, or 30 cents on the $100 valuation for school purposes, in excess of the State fund, and in that call the Board of Education submitted to the people a carefully prepared circular compiled by Prof. Coultrap of the facts above given, and from which this paragraph has been taken, in substance. The same circular gave a comparison of teachers' salaries in Nelsonville and Logan not very flattering to the citizens of the former town.

The statement made seemed to have a beneficial effect, for it aroused the people to the fact that a long-cherished institution was not receiving that care and nourishment to sustain it with vigorous life, and which in early years had been the pride of the city.

There are now seventeen teachers employed in the public schools of Nelsonville, name and position as follows: F. S. Coultrap, Superintendent; Alice C. Pierce, Principal; Lucy A. Bell, Assistant; Meda Riddill, Helen T. Musser, Sarah Washburn, Mattie Warren, Ida B. Maxwell, Kate Gabriel, Callie Carnes, Retta Eckles, Elta Riddill, Emily Saumenig, Mary Weihr, Mrs. S. S. Keyser, Lizzie M. Howe and Lillie M. Butterworth, teachers.

There are 1,084 children of school age, and an average enrollment of 780. The State school fund the past school year amounted in all to $1,666.00, and there is a school fund tax levy of ten mills.

BOARD OF TRUSTEES AND OFFICERS, 1883.

T. P. Marshall, President; Dr. I. P. Primrose, Josiah Wilson, W. G. Hickman, W. W. Poston, Geo. W. Devore; J. C. Parker, Treasurer; F. S. Coultrap, Secretary.

LODGES AND SOCIETIES.

Philodorean Lodge, No. 157, *A. F. & A. M.*—This lodge was instituted May 20, 1848, and its charter is of date Sept. 28, 1848. The following were its charter members: Lincoln D. Chamberlain, W. P. Johnson, Jas. E. Price, Noah Wilder, Thos. Miller, R. G. McLean, Obediah J. Eckley and Jas. Pugsley. The officers who received their appointment by this charter were, Wm. P. Johnson, 1st Master; Jas. E. Price, 1st Senior Warden; Obediah J. Eckley, 1st Junior Warden. At the time the charter was given them M. Z. Kreeder was M. W. G. M. of the State, and his signature was affixed to the charter.

It has been for many years supposed that Lincoln D. Chamberlain was the first Past Master, but this is a mistake, W. P. Johnson held that position. Mr. Chamberlain's name is the first written of the charter members. These facts are taken from the original charter, and of course are correct. The Past Masters would then be the same as published, leaving out the first name. They were given us as follows: W. P. Johnson, 1849; J. E. Price, 1850; Thomas Shannon, 1851; J. E. Price, 1853; B. A. Lincoln, 1854; Thomas Shannon, 1856; William Gilliam, 1857; Thomas Shannon, 1859; Jos. H. Butterworth, 1864; S. S. McDivitt, 1865; Thomas Older, 1866; W. P. Roberts, 1867; S. S. McDivitt, 1868; J. F. Camp, 1869; H. S. Preston, 1872; J. F. Camp, 1874; H. S. Preston, 1875; John T. Gray, 1876.

Officers, 1883: John T. Gray, W. M.; Chas. H. Decker, S. W.; Wm. Hayburn, J. W.; J. F. Brodt, Treasurer; E. S. Jennings, Secretary; Calvin Haynes, S. D.; P. P. Andrews, J. D.; B. F.

Martin, Tyler; Alexander Beattie and Thomas Johnson. Stewards.

Unity Lodge, No. 568, *I. O. O. F.*, located at Nelsonville, Ohio, was instituted June the 5th, 1874. The charter members and first officers installed were as follows: Joseph Barnecut, N. G.; W. G. Hickman, V. G.; T. B. Prichard, R. S.; M. W. Davis, P. S.; James M. Riddle, Treasurer; S. F. Robinet, Samuel C. Breakey, J. S. Speelman, J. J. Hoodlet, Henry A. Harris, John S. Wilson, Calvin Millinger, G. W. Mitchell, Joseph Smith, Wm. Barnes, Thomas C. Wilson, Joseph P. Dean, J. M. Parker, Frederic Wend and Paul Cummins. The Past Grands are: J. J. Hoodlet, 1876; Wm. Barnes, 1876; S. C. Breakey, 1877; Joseph P. Dean, 1878; S. F. Robinet, 1878; W. C. Sidman, 1879; James Six, 1879; James M. Riddle, 1880; John S. Wright, 1880; Calvin Millinger, 1881; George V. Shaffer, 1881; Nathan Coy, 1882; Charles Ellwanger, 1882. The present membership is about 104. The present officers are: Wm. E. Evans, N. G.; W. F. Brandon, V. G.; Wm. J. Daniels, R. P.; W. H. Barnes, P. S., and S. F. Robinet, Treasurer.

The Phil Kearney Post, No. 38, was chartered July 16, 1880, with the following charter members: Chas. E. Cutler, Wm. M. Phillips, James Hartly, C. K. Lansley, Jacob Hammond, Thomas R. Blake, Wm. Rankin, Wm. Justice, I. P. Primrose, Albert Woody, Wm. A. Worley, Hiram Rosser, John F. Welch. The following roster of officers was duly elected, and installed by Chief Mustering Officer P. W. Stanhope: Chas. E. Cutler, Post Commander; Hiram Rosser, S. V. C.; T. R. Blake, J. V. C.; Wm. A. Worley, Post Adj.; C. K. Lansley, Q. M.; Albert Woody, Chaplain; I. P. Primrose, Surgeon; Wm. Rankin, O. of the day; Wm. Justice, O. of the Guard; James Hartley, 1st G., and Wm. Phillips, 2d G. The following year was a prosperous one for the post. Roster for 1883: John O. Burrell, P. C.; Alonzo Newton, J. V.; Lemuel Cline, Surgeon; I. P. Primrose, Chaplain; Jas. A. Wilson, P. A.; Albert Woody, Q. M.; O. of the D., Frank Morgan; John Figgins, O. of the Guard. At this date, March 24, 1883, the post seems to be imbued with new life, and is on the road to prosperity, with all dues paid and some money in hands of Quartermaster.

Hockhocking Lodge, No. 339, *I. O. O. F.*—This lodge has had its records lost or mislaid and but little could be had of its previous history.

Thursday, July 8, 1858, Hockhocking Lodge, No. 339, I. O. O. F., was permanently organized here. The charter members were:

Messrs. C. A. Cable, E. W. Poston, E. C. Washburn, J. W. Fulton and John Burberry. That this lodge has been prosperous we have abundant evidence. Precisely eleven years afterward (in July, 1869), Nelsonville Encampment, No. 121, was instituted. The charter members were: S. N. Poston, Wm. Comstock, Smith Spencer, I. P. Primrose, E. W. Newton and others. At this time, May, 1883, Joseph Barnicut is N. G., and T. P. Marshall, Secretary. A further history was promised us, but has failed to come to hand.

BUSINESS INTERESTS.

Nelsonville grew slowly until an impetus was given by the opening of railroad transportation. While the canal had been a great help, it was not as capable of moving the mineral wealth when mined as capital was ready to dig out this wealth, and on the 1st of February, 1866, the year following the close of the war, it had but the following houses: 137 dwelling houses, 2 churches, 1 school-house, 4 schools, 5 dry-goods stores, 10 groceries, 1 drug store, 1 saddler shop, 2 shoe shops, 1 cabinet shop, 3 carpenter shops, 2 barber shops, 3 blacksmith shops, 1 wagon-shop, 1 millinery store, 2 dressmakers, 2 mills, 1 hotel, 2 boarding houses, 2 bark yards, 3 doctors, 1 dry-dock, 2 lodges (I. O. O. F. and A. F. & A. M.), 1 tannery, 1 silversmith, a canal and several of the finest coal banks in the country.

This amount of business with a population of between 800 and 900 was Nelsonville in the spring of 1866.

In 1870 Nelsonville had a population of 1,080, and in 1880 of 3,095, or a gain of nearly 200 per cent. The completion of the railroads gave an impetus that is yet pressing her forward, and in 1890 she may show another gain of 200 per cent, or a population of 10,000. Her business interest now is composed of 13 general stores, 8 exclusive grocery stores, 4 drug stores, 2 boot and shoe stores, 1 clothing store, 2 jewelry stores, 1 furniture and stove store, 2 sewing-machine agencies, 3 hardware stores, 1 furniture store, 4 restaurants, 2 confectionery stores, 2 bakeries, 17 saloons, 2 livery stables, 1 flour and feed store, 4 meat markets, 3 barber shops, 3 millinery stores, 1 cigar manufactory, 1 tanyard, 2 tailors, 2 painters, 7 carpenters, 2 planing mills, 1 lumber yard, 2 dealers in plaster and cement, 1 foundry and machine shop, 2 flouring mills, 1 saw-mill, 1 bank, churches, schools and lodges, newspaper and job offices, etc.

The *Times* was started in September, 1872, and the *Mirror*, now *Gazette*, in September, 1873, by Geo. Cook.

PROFESSIONS.

Lawyers—James A. Tobin, Asher Buckley, W. C. Hickman, A. J. Schrader. Fire Insurance Agents—Asher Buckley, W. C. Hickman, Wilson Kessinger. Physicians—Aaron Shepard, I. P. Primrose, W. N. Alderman, W. E. W. & S. M. Shepard, K. Tinker, C. F. Gilliam & S. E. Butt, J. W. Johnson, A. J. Shrader.

It is possible that some few items of business interest have been overlooked, but the showing for 1883 is sufficiently wonderful to satisfy the most extravagant wishes or views of the people. Add to the above the mining interest and the railroad and there is something to excite extravagant hopes, also, for the future. It only needs capital and brawn to double the present output of the mines, and transportation will be found for it all.

Iron furnaces are what is wanted, and rolling mills, in fact machinery of all kinds. Coal and iron at hand, and where, with such means of shipment, can the workers of iron find a cheaper place for manufactures or a better market than what can be easily reached by rail and water?

MERCHANTS AND MINERS' BANK.

This is the only bank in Nelsonville; was organized in 1873, opening business Sept. 9, on an individual liability. At the first election of officers, Charles Robbins was elected President, John W. Scott, Vice-President, and Charles A. Cable, Cashier. The original stockholders were Charles Robbins, John G. Myers, John W. Scott, Charles A. Cable, W. B. Brooks, of Columbus, and E. H. Moore, of Athens. The entire stock is now owned by Charles Robbins, Charles A. Cable, E. H. Moore and Eugene J. Cable. Mr. Robbins is the President, and Mr. C. A. Cable, Cashier.

NEWSPAPERS OF NELSONVILLE.

Times.—The first paper started in Nelsonville was called the Nelsonville *Times*. It was a six-column weekly paper, but only lived a short time. In the following year (1873) the

Nelsonville Miner was published by George Cook. He made a lively and progressive paper of it, and always took the laborer's part. The coal operators got down on him for his independent spirit, and he closed out in December, 1875, to J. A. Straight, after publishing as good a paper as was ever seen in Nelsonville.

Mr. Straight kept up the wide-awake spirit of the paper. This was followed by the *Mirror*, and it was succeeded by the *News*.

The Nelsonville News.—The Nelsonville *News* may be said to be the successor of the Nelsonville *Mirror*, although the latter was of short life. The *News* was established by John A. Tullis in 1879. On his coming to Nelsonville in 1878 he purchased the press and office supplies from the proprietor of the *Mirror*, but used the press only for job work. The first number of the *News* was issued Jan. 16, 1879. It was a seven-column paper, 24 x 36 inches, and so continued up to the 26th of the following June, when it was changed to an eight-column paper. Mr. Tullis has been its sole editor and proprietor from the start. The career of this paper has been as prosperous as could be expected under the circumstances. It has been steadily growing in strength, and is now on a firm basis, being not only self-supporting but producing a reasonable profit to its proprietor. It is neutral in politics, the editor's motto being: "An independent journal, devoted to the interest of its patrons." It is issued every Thursday, the subscription price being $1.50.

John A. Tullis, editor of the Nelsonville *News*, was born Nov. 11, 1836, near Donnelsville, Clarke Co., O. His father was a farmer in moderate circumstances, keeping his son on the farm with him. In 1844 the family removed to Champaign County, O., still remaining on a farm. His father being unable to send him to college, young Tullis obtained what education he could at the public schools. He afterward attended a seminary in Clarke County, but was not able to continue until completing the course. When he became a man, his health being delicate, he decided to go into a life of business. He consequently engaged in and followed for a number of years, as long as his health permitted, wholesale produce shipping to New York and Philadelphia markets. The last four years he was in this business he was located at St. Paris, O., where he was also engaged in the printing business. When he retired from business there, he came to Nelsonville and established his paper, on which he has worked faithfully ever since. Great credit is due to his perseverance and good management, as he is the first man who succeeded in permanently establishing a newspaper in Nelsonville, although numerous attempts had been made. He has well maintained the reputation of his profession, by endeavoring to infuse new and animated life in his fellow-citizens. He has advocated public and private improvements, and it is not at all improbable that some of this seed has fallen in good soil, since at no time in the town's history has the progress of improvement been so great as at the present time.

He was married to Miss Susan E. Deaton, of Addison, Champaign County, March 31, 1859. Of this union there are three children, all daughters and all living—Addie A. was born Feb. 5, 1860; Anna V., April 23, 1875, and Mabel, April 5, 1878.

Athens County Republican.—The *Athens County Republican*, published at Nelsonville, O., was founded by James A. Miller and Charles Logan, at Athens, O., in May, 1881. The first issue appeared June 1, 1881, the name of the paper at that time, and for several months after, being the Athens *Republican*. Miller & Logan were the proprietors and editors up to Jan. 11, 1882, when the paper appeared with the name of James A. Miller as sole editor, Mr. Logan continuing to be part owner. As the name indicates, the paper is Republican in politics, its public statement being, "To be devoted to the promotion and interests of the Republican party." In February, 1882, Mr. Miller became the sole proprietor. By the next issue the paper had again changed hands, the names of G. W. Baker, J. M. Wood and J. P. Wood appearing as proprietors, and that of G. W. Baker as editor and manager. The last number issued at Athens is dated Aug. 30, 1882, it having been sold to Charles P. Reid, its present owner, and taken at once to Nelsonville. Originally the *Republican* was a six-column four-page paper. It was subsequently enlarged, Aug. 3, 1881, to seven columns, and May 10, 1882, to eight columns, its present size. It was purchased by Charles P. Reid, who took possession Sept. 1, 1882, removing it to Nelsonville, where he issued the first number the following Thursday. Mr. Reid's name has appeared from that time to the present as sole editor and proprietor. It is issued regularly every Thursday, the subscription price being $1.50.

Charles P. Reid, editor of the *Athens County Republican*, was born Aug. 18, 1858, at Piqua, Miami Co., O. He received a good school education, finishing at Wapakoneta, O., in April, 1875, at which time he apprenticed himself to O. J. Powell, publisher of the Wapakoneta *Republican*. He removed with Mr. Powell to Chicago Junction, Huron Co., O., in the winter of 1875-'6, but returned to Wapakoneta in about one month, and immediately accepted a situation as foreman with Davis & Mc-

Murray, publishers of the *Auglaize County Democrat*. In November, 1879, he became associated with Trego & Binkley, publishers of the Sidney (O.) *Journal*, and later went to Piqua and took the foremanship and local chair on the Piqua *Journal*. In July, 1880, he accepted a situation with Colonel R. W. Jones, publisher of the Athens *Journal*. He remained but seven weeks, when he returned to his old situation as foreman of the *Auglaize County Democrat*, and in December, 1880, when Mr. Davis, the publisher, was taken with hemorrhage of the lungs, he assumed editorial control of the *Democrat*, being then only twenty-three years old. He continued in that capacity until after Mr. Davis's death, June 19, 1881, when the office was sold by Mrs. C. P. Davis, and he returned to the position of foreman, and so continued until he purchased the *Athens County Republican*, Aug. 26, 1882, from Baker & Woods. He was married to Miss Carrie E. Davis, daughter of C. P. Davis, Jan. 10, 1882. Immediately after taking charge of the *Republican*, Sept. 1, 1882, he removed to Nelsonville, issuing the paper the following week, as usual, without missing a number.

MANUFACTORIES.

The manufacturing interests of Nelsonville are as follows:

Nelsonville Foundry and Machine Co.'s works, established April, 1880. They are owned by a joint stock company, the President being John R. Buchtel, of Akron, O. Among the products are steam-pipes and steam-fittings, and mining cars are a specialty.

Two *Flouring Mills*, a water mill, owned by Charles Robbins, and a steam mill, owned by C. Steenrod & Co.

Two *Planing Mills*, owned by M. Craig & Sons, and the Nelsonville Planing Mill Company, Asher Poston, President.

This closes the history of the largest city in the valley of the Hocking, and its future destiny is very bright and promising. Energy, enterprise and morality will give her a prestige that no city in the valley can rival. May this be her lot.

W. N. Alderman M.D.

CHAPTER XVII.

BIOGRAPHICAL SKETCHES OF YORK TOWNSHIP, INCLUDING THE CITY OF NELSONVILLE.

William Nelson Alderman, M. D., was born in Oxford, Morgan Co., Ohio, Nov. 27, 1853, a son of Nelson J. and Susannah (Weimer) Alderman. He received a common-school education, remaining at home till eighteen years of age. On leaving home in 1871, he became associated with his brother, S. J. Alderman, in the mercantile business, in Bishopville, Ohio, under the firm name of S. J. Alderman & Bro. In 1874 he retired from the firm and began the study of medicine with Dr. George E. Carpenter, of Athens; was under his preceptorship one year and then went to Oxford and studied with Dr. H. D. Dantford, remaining with him until his graduation from the Medical College of Ohio, at Cincinnati, Feb. 28, 1877. He practiced with his preceptor till the following September, when he went to New York and took a course of lectures in the Bellevue Hospital Medical College, graduating in February, 1878. In July, 1878, he located in Nelsonville, and in the spring of 1879, became associated with Dr. I. P. Primrose. Feb. 25, 1880, he married Sarah A., daughter of Dr. Primrose. They have one daughter—Addie P. Dr. Alderman is a member of Philodorean Lodge, No. 157, A. F. & A. M., Nelsonville.

Mason Andrews was born in Ames Township, Athens County, May 27, 1844, a son of David and Christiana (Mowery) Andrews. He was reared on a farm and educated in the common school, living with his mother until he grew to manhood. He was married Dec. 29, 1863, to Miss Eve Howard, only daughter of Loyd and Elizabeth (Weimer) Howard. They are the parents of five children—Loyd R., Emma V., William M., Ira E. and Hulda E. In 1874 Mr. Andrews purchased his present farm containing 114 acres of good land, under a high state of cultivation. He and his wife are members of the M. E. church. He is a member of the I. O. O. F., Hockhocking Lodge, No. 339.

Frank C. Armstrong, M. D., physician and surgeon, was born in the city of Columbus, Ohio, Feb. 2, 1859, a son of Thomas and Jane

(Chadwick) Armstrong. His youth was spent in attending school. He began the study of medicine with Dr. S. W. Fowler, of Delaware, Ohio, and graduated at the Ohio Wesleyan Seminary in the summer of 1880, and at the Columbus Medical College in the winter of 1881 and 1882. He first commenced to practice with his preceptor in Delaware, and, in the fall of 1882, located in Buchtel, where he has met with good success. He is a member of the K. of P., York Lodge, No. 75.

William Barnes was born in Wirt County, W. Va., June 15, 1842, a son of Nathan and Mary (Cornell) Barnes. When he was an infant his parents came to Ohio, and settled at Chauncey, Athens County, where he was reared and educated. In April, 1861, he enlisted in Company H, Twenty-second Ohio Infantry, for three months, but served four months, and the following August re-enlisted in Company A, same regiment, for three years. In January, 1862, his regiment was consolidated with the Sixty-third Ohio Infantry, his company retaining the same letter. In January, 1864, he re-enlisted in the same company and regiment as a veteran to serve till the close of the war. July 22, 1864, he was taken prisoner at Decatur, Ga., and confined at Andersonville eight months. He was then taken to a parol camp, at Vicksburg, and kept a month, and then, April 22, 1865, was released on parol and taken with 2,200 released prisoners on board the transport steamboat Sultana, *en route* for Camp Chase, Columbus, Ohio, then a camp of distribution. When a few miles above the city of Memphis, on the morning of April 27, the boiler exploded, completely destroying the vessel and killing 1,600 men. Mr. Barnes was rescued at Memphis by clinging to a bale of hay. He and 400 or 500 of his comrades lay three days at Memphis awaiting transportation and recovering from the effects of the disaster. May 1, 1865, he was taken on board the mail boat Belle Memphis and arrived at Cairo the following morning, and May 4 arrived at Camp Chase, where he was discharged May 18, the war closing. He returned to Athens, remaining there till 1871, when he came to Nelsonville, and a greater part of the time since then has been in the employ of W. B. Brooks. April 5, 1877, he married Mary A. Shannon, of Nelsonville. They have one child—Mary F. Mr. Barnes is an Odd Fellow, a member of Unity Lodge, No. 568, and of Nelsonville Encampment, No. 121.

George Henry Barrows, proprietor of Barrows's saloon and billiard hall, of Nelsonville, was born in Albany, Maine, July 14, 1833, in which place he lived with his parents, Harvey and Hannah (Beckley) Barrows, until he was eighteen years of age. His school opportunities were very limited. On leaving home he went to Yarmouth, Maine, where he was employed in a saw-mill nearly a year, when he went to Abington, Mass., and drove an express wagon for L. A. Ford for the same length of time. In 1853 he began to learn the shoemaker's trade at Abington, at which he worked till Nov. 14, 1854, when he went to New Bedford, Mass., and embarked on the whaling vessel, Benjamin Cummings, on which he cruised on the Pacific and Atlantic oceans until June, 1859, a period of nearly five years. During 1860 he worked as a section hand on the Grand Trunk Railroad until July when he worked on the farm and in the saw-mill of Peter C. Fickett at West Paris. In 1861 he was employed in the same town in a chair factory until the fall of 1862, when he enlisted in the war of the Rebellion, in Company F, Twenty-third Regiment of the Ohio Infantry, and at the end of nine months was discharged with his regiment. While out, he was on duty in guarding Washington City, D. C. After his discharge he again worked on the Grand Trunk Railroad as section foreman until the spring of 1864, when he went to Bath, Maine, and was employed in a saw-mill there until December, 1865. In March, 1866, he came to Ohio and was engaged as foreman of the switch yard at Piqua for the C., C. & I. C. R. R. Company until March, 1867, after which he was employed in the same yard as fireman on a switch engine until the summer of 1869. He then went to Fairfield County and was employed by Dodge, Case & Co., contractors on the C. & H. V. Railroad as foreman of the track layers until November. He was then engaged as engine dispatcher by the C. & H. V. R. R. Company at Nelsonville, after which he was employed at Athens in the same capacity until June, 1871, when he was placed in charge of a switch engine at Nelsonville until September, 1872, after which he engaged in his present business. Dec. 25, 1870, he was married to Miss Martha Smith, of Nelsonville. They have seven children, viz.: Harvey A., Peter, George A., John, Charles, Alonzo and James M.

Alexander Beattie, Marshal of Nelsonville, was born in Ayr, Scotland, Aug. 15, 1851. When two years of age he came with his parents, Alex. and Sarah (Robinson) Beattie, to the United States, settling in Johnstown, Pa. He lived with them there, and in McKeysport, Pa., and Pomeroy, Ohio, and Sharon, Pa., until manhood, and was educated in the schools of those places. In 1872 he came to Nelsonville and was employed in the coal mines of W.

B. Brooks & Son until 1879, when he was appointed one of the policemen of Nelsonville and served as such until April, 1882, when he was elected Marshal. Sept. 23, 1874, he was married to Miss Christiana A. Laird, of Sharon, Pa. They have two children—Estella May and Eva L. Mr. Beattie is a Master Mason and member of Philodorean Lodge, No. 157, of Nelsonville, of which he has filled the station of Junior Warden.

John W. Bennett, farmer and stock-raiser, was born in Baltimore, Md., Aug. 17, 1849, a son of James and Priscilla C. (Luken) Bennett. In 1859 his parents came to Ohio and located in York Township, Athens County, near Nelsonville, where he resided till manhood. He was married April 20, 1871, to Mary L. Thornton, daughter of Madison and Sarah C. (Hicks) Thornton. They have had six children, only four now living—Loring R., Frank N., Charles W. and John M. Mr. Bennett's father was born in Baltimore County, Md., March 24, 1801. When eighteen years of age he was employed in the Patterson Rolling Mills near Baltimore, and remained there thirty-seven years. Sept. 23, 1844, he married Priscilla C. Luken, a native of Hartford County, Md., but reared in Baltimore County. They were the parents of seven children, six now living. They came to Athens County in 1859, and located near Nelsonville, where Mr. Bennett died Nov. 18, 1865. Mr. and Mrs. Bennett were members of the Christian church, he having been Deacon over thirty-five years.

Thomas Berry, Superintendent C. & H. Coal and Iron Company, is a native of Allegheny County, Pa., born April 3, 1837, and reared near the city of Pittsburg. His youth was spent in mining coal which he has since followed, coming to Nelsonville Sept. 23, 1858. He was married Nov. 27, 1859, to Miss Hannah Charlton, a native of England, but reared in Ohio. During the late civil war he enlisted in Company K, One Hundred and Sixteenth Ohio Infantry, Aug. 21, 1862. He participated in many hard-fought battles, among them, Winchester, Va., in June, 1863; Piedmont, in June, 1864; Cedar Creek, Lynchburg, and Petersburg. He was captured Feb. 16, 1863, but was soon after paroled. After the close of the war he returned to Ohio and settled in Nelsonville where he has since made his home. He secured his present position as Superintendent, July 1, 1874. Mr. and Mrs. Berry are the parents of five children, only four living—Charles M., born Sept. 23, 1860; Josephine Elizabeth, born Nov. 7, 1862; Inez Estella, born July 15, 1867; Thaddeus Huxly, born July 24, 1875, died

Nov. 18, 1879; Ethel May, born Dec. 27, 1882. Mr. Berry is a member of the A. F. & A. M., Philodorean Lodge, No. 157.

Albert Slater Bethel, merchant and farmer, Nelsonville, was born in Guernsey County, Ohio, near Cambridge, June 19, 1846. When about nine years of age he came with his parents, Lemuel T. and Rebecca (Slater) Bethel, to Athens County, settling in Trimble Township, where he lived with them until his twenty-second year, and received a common-school education. Being reared a farmer he followed that avocation until 1874, when, selling his farm, he was employed in the store of John W. Scott, a coal operator at Lick Run, Athens County, and was in his employ until 1878, when he came to Nelsonville and engaged in the mercantile business with his brother, J. C. Bethel, under the firm name of Bethel Brothers. In April, 1882, his brother retired from the firm. In connection with his mercantile business he also carried on farming to some extent. He has been twice married. His first wife was Miss Hannah Ann Anderson, of Athens County, whom he married Nov. 22, 1866, and who died in Trimble Township, Aug. 17, 1870, leaving him two children—George Lemuel and William J. June 6, 1876, he married Miss Sarah Luetta Anderson, of Ames Township, Athens County. They have three children—Charles Sherman, Lucy May and Webster Garfield. Mr. Bethel is a Master, Royal Arch, Council and Knight Templar Mason, and member of Philodorean Lodge, No. 157, Nelsonville, and the chapter and council at Logan, and Commandery No. 15, at Athens.

Thomas N. Black was born in Lanarkshire, Scotland, Oct. 12, 1829. In 1847 he came to the United States and located in Allegheny County, Pa., where he followed coal-mining until 1860, when he came to Ohio, and located in Zanesville. In June, 1877, he came to Buchtel, where he has since resided. He is Superintendent of the coal and iron mines of the Akron Iron Company. He was first married, April 18, 1854, to Margaret McKinnel, a native of Edinboro, Scotland; three children were born to them —William N., Elizabeth and Isabella. His wife died May 14, 1865. He was again married, Oct. 24, 1866, to Louisa Romine, a native of Muskingum County, Ohio. They have six children— Louisa, Mary, Annie, Jennie, Margaret and Flora. Mr. Black is a member of the A. F. & A. M. and I. O. O. F. fraternities. He has been an Odd Fellow over thirty years, and is now a member of the Buchtel Lodge, No. 712.

James Rider Blake, a coal-miner in the Johnson Brothers & Patterson's coal mines, at Nelsonville, was born in Devonshire, England, April 3, 1823, where he lived until he was twenty years of age. He lived with his parents, Nathaniel and Joannah (Rider) Blake, until his ninth year when he was put out to a farmer, with whom he lived until April 25, 1843, when he enlisted in the Plymouth Division of the Royal Marines, and, after being drilled in the infantry and ship gun drill, embarked on board Her Majesty's ship Vanguard, in February, 1845. In the following May, on account of receiving an injury, he was placed in the Hasslar Hospital, at Gosport, England, where he remained four months, when he was transferred to the Marine Barracks at Portsmouth, where he remained a short time, after which he embarked on board Her Majesty's ship Superb, on which he served two months, when he was sent to the Stone House Barracks, and from there on board Her Majesty's ship Nimrod, on which he served four years and cruised around the Peak of Teneriff to Island of Ascension, thence to Sierra Leone, thence to Cape Mount, Cape Miserata, thence to the Cape of Good Hope. He cruised off the southeast coast of Africa, visiting all the ports, and thence through the channel of Mozambique to the Islands of Mozambique and Madagascar. He then cruised back to the Cape of Good Hope, the Island of St. Helena, thence to the East Indies and then back to England, making a cruise of nearly four years. He afterward embarked on Her Majesty's ship Bella Ropher. After serving as a marine eight years and six months he, in September, 1851, bought his discharge, and until the following January served as convict keeper at Dartmoor Prison. Feb. 18, 1852, he started to the United States, landing at New York City, March 29. He first went to Pittsburg, Pa., where he mined coal four months, and from there he went to Tuscarawas Valley, where he worked in the mines of G. W. McIlvain until 1853. He afterward followed mining in Illinois, Missouri and West Virginia until August, 1857, when he came to Nelsonville and permanently settled. Feb. 8, 1855, he married Rebecca Prout, of Suffolk County, England. They have six children—Mary E., wife of Albert Michem; Sarah Jane, Nathaniel R., Susannah, Addie (deceased), Hester M. and Cora B. Oct. 20, 1861, he enlisted in Company G, Eighteenth Ohio Volunteer Infantry, as a private, to serve three years, and during his service participated in many battles, the most important being Athens, La Vergne, Stone River, Chattanooga, Chickamauga, Davis Cross Roads, Lookout Mountain and Mission Ridge. From Oct. 17, 1863, to Feb. 14, 1864, he was detailed to take charge of the watch on the transport Paint Rock on the Tennessee River. He was discharged Nov. 10, 1864, being mustered out as First or Orderly Sergeant, having served as such for one year, and part of the last year being in command of his company, his superior officers being detailed to different posts of duty. After his return home he was immediately afflicted with blindness, the result of overwork and exposure while in the service, and had to be lead for three years. He finally recovered the partial sight of one eye through the skill of Dr. E. Williams, of Cincinnati. He has been elected twice and held the office of Councilman of Nelsonville, and is now an incumbent of that office. He is a member of Phil Kearney Post, No. 38, G. A. R., and has served as Junior Vice-Commander.

Asher Buckley, attorney at law, Nelsonville, was born in Canaan Township, Athens County, July 6, 1828, where he lived with his parents, Aratus and Margaret (Long) Buckley, until his fourteenth year, when he went to Clarksburgh, Harrison Co., Va., and learned the trade of saddle and harness making with Edward Link, working with him six years. In 1848 he returned to Athens County and engaged in the saddle and harness business at Guysville until 1853, when he removed his business to Coolville. While carrying on his business at Coolville he studied law under the preceptorship of the Hon. Charles Townsend, of Athens, and was admitted to the bar by the District Court at Athens, Sept. 1, 1876. In the spring of 1875 he came to Nelsonville and began the practice of law. While living in Coolville he was Mayor of that village four years. In the spring of 1878 he was elected Mayor of Nelsonville for a term of two years, and re-elected in the spring of 1880, holding the position for four years. In August, 1862, he enlisted in Company I, One Hundred and Sixteenth Regiment, Ohio Infantry, to serve three years, and was discharged at the close of war, at Camp Dennison, July 2, 1865. He participated in the battles of the Shenandoah Valley, under Generals Sheridan, Hunter and Sigle, and at the siege and capture of Petersburg. April 25, 1852, while at Clarksburgh, Va., he married Miss Margaret Southworth. They have three living children— Harry C., a farmer, of Jackson County, W. Va.; Leverett K., of Youngstown, Ohio, and Gertrude, still at home. Mr. Buckley is a member of Philodorean Lodge, No. 157; Hockhocking Lodge, No. 339, and Nelsonville Encampment, No. 121.

John Burberry, shipping clerk for C. L. Poston & Company, coal operators of Nelsonville, was born in Sussex County, England, Dec. 1, 1816, where he lived with his parents, John and Rebecca (Peskitt) Burberry, until his sixteenth year, receiving his education in the common school, when he immigrated with them to the United States, they arriving at Nelsonville, July 31, 1832. In 1833 he went to Lancaster, Ohio, where he learned the tailor's trade with George H. Smith, serving an apprenticeship of four years, after which he did journey work for a short time. About the year 1837 he began business for himself at Lancaster, continuing till the spring of 1841, when he removed to Bremen, Ohio, remaining there till 1844, and while there he served as Constable and Assessor for two years, holding both offices at the same time. Leaving Bremen he returned to Lancaster, where he continued the tailoring business till 1849, after which he was engaged in the store of L. D. Poston, of Nelsonville, for the following eight years. In 1857 he became associated with Mr. Poston as a coal operator, and after several years he was employed as a general manager of Mr. Poston's coal business, staying with him till 1875. Since then he has been employed by Mr. Poston's successor, C. L. Poston & Company, in various branches of their extensive business. May 14, 1874, he was married to Miss Mary, daughter of William and Mary Ann (Hampshire) Thayer. She was a native of Sussex County, England, and came with her parents to this country at the same time and on the same ship as our subject. Mr. and Mrs. Burberry are members of the M. E. church, of Nelsonville, of which he is Steward and Trustee.

John Oscar Burrell, carpenter and stair-builder, of Nelsonville, was born in Newport, Maine, Oct. 12, 1837. When he was an infant his parents, Almond H. and Almira P. (Wilson) Burrell, came to Ohio and located in Alexander Township, Athens County. When he was twelve years of age they moved to Nelsonville. When eighteen years of age, in 1856, he went to Marietta and began to work in the Marietta *Republican* office under A. W. McCormick, to learn the printer's trade. He worked about one year, when, not liking the trade, he left the office and for a short time was employed on a steamboat on the Ohio River as a "Texas Tender." In the fall of 1858 he returned to Nelsonville, and in the spring of 1859 began to work at the carpenter's trade. In June, 1862, he enlisted in Company H, Eighty-fifth Ohio Infantry, to serve three months. At the expiration of that term he re-enlisted in Company A, One

Hundred and Twenty-eighth Ohio Infantry, for three years, serving as Quartermaster-Sergeant. His company participated in the capture of Cumberland Gap and siege of Knoxville. After his discharge he returned to Nelsonville and resumed work at the carpenter's trade, which he still follows. April 19, 1865, he was married to Maria P. Wilson, of Wolf's Plain, Athens Co., Ohio, who died Jan. 25, 1883, leaving one child—Amos Guy. Mr. Burrell is a member of the Methodist Episcopal church of Nelsonville. He is a member of Phil Kearney Post, No. 38, G. A. R., of which he is Commander.

Peter Matthew Butt, proprietor of the Home saloon, Nelsonville, was born in New Philadelphia, Ohio, Feb. 24, 1837. When fourteen years of age he began to maintain himself, and came to Nelsonville and began to work in and about the coal mines. In the spring of 1861 he went to California and engaged in gold mining in Placer County, until the fall of 1863, when he returned to Nelsonville and again engaged in coal mining until the fall of 1866, when he became established in his present business. He has served one term in the City Council of Nelsonville. He has been twice married; his first wife was Miss Irene Butt, a cousin, of Nelsonville, whom he married in December, 1855, and who died at Nelsonville, in November, 1858, leaving one child—Samuel Edgar, a physician of Nelsonville. Oct. 2, 1864, he married Miss Maria Lytle, of Logan, Ohio. They have five living children—Frank, Kate, Fred, Eugene and George, all living at home. They have lost two children—Emma M., who died Aug. 8, 1880; Mertie Blanch, who died Dec. 20, 1880.

Samuel Edgar Butt, M. D., Nelsonville, was born in that city April 12, 1857, and was educated in the common and High School. He is the son of Peter M. and Irene (Butt) Butt. His mother dying before he was two years old, he was taken by his grandmother and lived with her until he was seven years old, when his father married again and took him to live with him. When about seventeen he was employed as a surveyor, filling that position two years, when he took up the study of medicine under Dr. W. E. W. Sheppard, of Nelsonville, studying with him three years and graduating from the Medical College of Ohio at Cincinnati, in March, 1880. He then became associated with Dr. C. F. Gilliam at Nelsonville in the practice of medicine, they mutually dissolving in 1882. He was City Physician of Nelsonville during 1880-'81. Oct. 26, 1881, he married Miss Addie Koutner, daughter of S. C.

Koutner, of Nelsonville. She was formerly a teacher for some time in the Nelsonville public schools. They have one child—Solomon Edgar.

Charles Augustus Cable, Cashier of the Merchants and Miners' Bank of Nelsonville, and a member of the firm of C. A. Cable & Co., hardware, stoves, tinware and furniture dealers, was born in Nelsonville, April 6, 1834, where he was reared. He was educated in the public schools of Nelsonville and a select school at Athens. He is the son of Charles and Julia G. (Nye) Cable, with whom he lived until manhood. At the age of fifteen, while making his home with his parents, he engaged in the grocery and provision business at Nelsonville for about two years, when, in 1851, he became associated with his father in the general merchandising business. His father dying one year after, he carried on the business with his mother until 1856. He then carried on the business alone until 1858, when he discontinued it. From that time until 1861 he was employed as traveling salesman for the wholesale grocery house of Mead & Co., of New York City, and as clerk by Charles Ashton and Charles Robbins, at Nelsonville. Sept. 27, 1861, he enlisted in Company G, Eighteenth Ohio Infantry. On the organization of the company he was elected First Lieutenant. His regiment served in the Army of the Cumberland. From January to May, 1863, he was Acting Adjutant of his regiment, and as Quartermaster from May to June, 1863, when he was promoted to Captain and took charge of his company until after the battle of Chickamauga, when he became Acting Assistant Adjutant-General on the staff of Colonel T. R. Stanley, commanding an engineers' brigade at Chattanooga, Tenn. In the spring of 1864 Colonel Stanley was relieved from the command of the engineer brigade and assigned to the command of the post of Chattanooga, Tenn., our subject still holding the position of Acting Assistant Adjutant-General under him until Oct. 20, 1864, when, at the expiration of his term of service, he returned home with his regiment and was mustered out. He participated in a number of battles, the most important being Athens, Ala.; La Vergne, Tenn.; Stone River, Davis Cross Roads, Ga.; Chickamauga, Brown Ferry and Mission Ridge. In March, 1865, he engaged in the grocery and provision business at Nelsonville, following it one year when he estalished the hardware store, adding furniture to it in the spring of 1870. In that year his brother, Eugene J., became associated with him under the present firm name. In the fall of 1873 he was one of the stockholders that organized the Merchants and Miners' Bank of Nelsonville, and was appointed its Cashier. During 1854-'55 he was Postmaster of Nelsonville, appointed under President Pierce. He was City Clerk of Nelsonville in 1855-'56, and has served as member of the City Council and Board of Education of Nelsonville and Trustee of York Township, several years each. In 1875-'76 he was one of the Trustees of the Athens Asylum for the Insane, at Athens. April 23, 1857, he married Miss Sarah A. Scott, daughter of Launcelot Scott, of Nelsonville. They have four children—Charles W., a physician of Logan, Ohio; Don Carlos, Teller in Merchants and Miners' Bank; and Eugene W. and Edith G., attending school. Mr. and Mrs. Cable are members of the First Presbyterian Church of Nelsonville, of which he is a Ruling Elder and a Trustee. He is a member of the Hockhocking Lodge, No. 339, I. O. O. F., and is now Past Grand. He is a member of Phil Kearney Post, No. 38, G. A. R., Nelsonville.

Charles Cable (deceased), one of Nelsonville's old pioneers, was born at Jefferson, New York, Jan. 31, 1809. He came to Ohio about 1816 with his father, who settled at Athens. At the age of twelve he was apprenticed to learn the tanner's trade, and with the exception of one year he worked at his trade at Athens till 1833 when he went to Nelsonville, where he engaged in tanning till his death, which occurred April 2, 1852. During 1848 and 1849, in connection with his other business, he kept a hotel known as the Cable House, and at the time of his death was engaged in the general mercantile business and had dealt extensively in real estate. In 1838, when Nelsonville was first incorporated, he was elected its first Mayor. He has filled the positions of member of the Council and Township Trustee, besides various others during his life. Jan. 1, 1833, he was married to Julia G. Nye, of Dover Township, Athens County, by whom he had two sons—Charles A. and Eugene J. In the spring of 1851 his son, Charles A., then seventeen years of age, became associated with him in the general mercantile business and continued with him till his death. From 1849 to the end of 1851 he was Postmaster of Nelsonville. His wife survived him nearly twelve years, she dying Jan. 12, 1862. She had belonged to the Christian church since girlhood, always taking an active part in church affairs. Mr. Cable, although not a member, always took an active part in promoting the growth of the church work. He was a man of great endurance and strength until 1846, when his health became broken down by over work.

Charles Walter Cable, M. D., Nelsonville, was born July 25, 1859. He is the oldest of four children of Charles A. and Sarah A. (Scott) Cable, with whom he lived until manhood and received a High School education in his native city. At the age of seventeen he began the study of medicine under Dr. Richard Gundry, Superintendent of the Columbus Hospital for the Insane at Columbus, and was under his preceptorship eighteen months, when he went to Athens and studied under Dr. A. B. Frame eighteen months. He graduated from the Medical College of Ohio, at Cincinnati, March 2, 1880. He then continued his studies until the following winter when he went to New York City and attended a course of lectures at the Bellevue Hospital Medical College, from which he graduated March 10, 1881. He then began the practice of medicine at Nelsonville. Oct. 12, 1881, he married Bessie, daughter of Elmor and Mary (Cooley) Golden, of Athens. They are both members of the First Presbyterian Church of Nelsonville.

John French Camp, real estate agent, Nelsonville, and Justice of the Peace of York Township, was born in Alexander Township, Athens Co., Ohio, March 11, 1829. He is the youngest of two sons of Edward and Charlotte (Taylor) Camp. His father dying when he was two years of age, he lived with his mother until he was twelve, when he began to maintain himself by working as a farmer's boy. At the age of sixteen he apprenticed himself to J. C. Frost, of Athens, to learn the tailor's trade, and remained with him two years, receiving his board and $40 per year for his services as an apprentice. He then, feeling the importance of having an education, entered the Preparatory Department of the Ohio University at Athens and attended two years, defraying the expenses of his board and tuition by working during the hours he was not in school and during vacations. In 1851 he engaged in teaching in the public schools and taught in Athens and Hocking counties until 1861, and in the meantime was Superintendent of the schools of Nelsonville for several terms. Oct. 2, 1861, he enlisted in Company G, Eighteenth Ohio Infantry, as a private. In the following November he was promoted to First, or Orderly Sergeant, and served as such until April 1, 1864, when he was commissioned Second Lieutenant of Company C, same regiment, and served in that capacity until he was mustered out at the expiration of his term of enlistment in 1864. He was in fourteen battles. The most important were Stone River, Chickamauga and Davis Cross Roads. After his discharge he returned to Athens County and taught until 1877. He located at Nelsonville in 1866 where he has since resided. He has been elected to and filled the office of Mayor of Nelsonville two terms, and has also served as Clerk of York Township two terms. In 1882 he was elected Justice of the Peace of York Township. In 1882 he became associated with Alexander W. Nelson in the real estate business, under the firm name of Camp & Nelson. April 25, 1851, he was married to Miss Mary Lutitia, daughter of Rev. John W. Brown, of Nelsonville. They have four children—Florence Iota, Julius French, William Preston and Angie Charlotta. They have lost one, Eva Sophia, who died July 22, 1864, at the age of nine years. Mr. Camp is a demitted Master Mason and also a demitted Odd Fellow, and has filled all the stations in both orders.

Alfred Harrison Carnes, senior member of the firm of Carnes & Shepard, merchants of Nelsonville, was born near Leesburgh, Loudoun Co., Va., Aug. 10, 1824. When he was seven years old he came with his parents, James and Mary (Scatteday) Carnes, to Ohio, settling near McConnelsville, Morgan County, and from there came to Athens County when he was thirteen. His parents both died the year before he was fifteen and he was thrown on his own resources. The first year after their death he lived with William Jolliffe in what is now Ward Township, Hocking County, working for him and attending school one year. He then went to Eggleston salt works on Sunday Creek, Athens County, and was engaged as fireman and engineer for two years, when, in 1842, he came to Nelsonville and located. He worked in the coal mines until the spring of 1856, when, by the request of a friend, Matthew Van Wormer, he entered his store as a clerk, remaining with him until the fall of 1860, when W. B. Brooks became Mr. Van Wormer's successor. He worked for Mr. Brooks until the fall of 1871, when he purchased the business house and stock of Lewis Steenrod and engaged in the mercantile business, W. P. Shepard being associated with him under the firm name of Carnes & Shepard. He has been a Trustee of York Township one year; a member of the Council three years, and of the School Board of Nelsonville. He has been twice married; his first wife was Miss Sarah A. Crothers, of Nelsonville, whom he married in the spring of 1850, and who died Oct. 21, 1858, leaving five children, three of whom are living—Sarah L., wife of W. P. Shepard; Nancy V., wife of Robert J. Hickman, and Mary Z., wife of Thomas Johnson; Charles A. died Sept. 5, 1873, at the age of eighteen, and Emily

Effie, wife of Winfield Scott, died Dec. 6, 1882, at the age of thirty years. May 23, 1860, Mr. Carnes married Miss Emily M. Bridge, of Nelsonville. They have two children—Ina May and Clara Amanda. Mr. and Mrs. Carnes are members of the Methodist Episcopal church of Nelsonville.

Frank Gideon Cooley, only living son of Gideon L. and Harriet (Hull) Cooley, was born Feb. 23, 1852, at Nelsonville, Ohio, where he was reared and educated in the Union School of that place. When nineteen years old he began to clerk in his father's store, and on attaining his majority he became a partner of the present mercantile firm of G. L. Cooley & Son, of Nelsonville. He was married Dec. 15, 1872, to Miss S. J. Riddle of Nelsonville. They are the parents of the following children—Hattie Olive, Sylvia Winnie, Lew Pierce and James Garfield. Mr. Cooley is a Master Mason and member of Philodorean Lodge, No. 157, at Nelsonville.

Gideon Leonard Cooley, of the firm of Cooley & Son, merchants, of Nelsonville, Ohio, was born at Springfield, Mass., March 1, 1816. He is the son of Jesse and Polly (Leonard) Cooley. His father dying before he was eight years old, he went to Allegany County, N. Y., near Angelica, where he lived with strangers until he was eighteen, when he returned to his birthplace in Massachusetts and remained a year. He then went to Troy, Bradford Co., Penn., where he lived over two years, employed on a farm. In the spring of 1839 he came to Ohio, and located at Nelsonville. He followed farming two years, and then worked in the coal mines thirty years. He then, in 1872, engaged in the mercantile business, and in the following year his son Frank became associated with him, the firm name being Cooley & Son. He has served three terms in the City Council of Nelsonville, and in the spring of 1861 was elected one of the Trustees of York Township, and served three years. July 3, 1840, he married Miss Harriet Hull, of Nelsonville. They have had four children, only one of whom, Frank, is living. John died June 30, 1844, aged two and a half years. Hattie, wife of W. W. Poston, died Nov. 18, 1870, aged twenty-five years; and Charles L. died April 21, 1880, aged thirty-three. Mr. and Mrs. Cooley are members of the Presbyterian church, of Nelsonville.

Fletcher Stanton Coultrap entered the Ohio University of Athens in his eighteenth year (in 1869), and graduated in June, 1875. The following September he took charge of the Union schools of Wheelersburg, Ohio, and remained there two years. In September, 1877, he came to Nelsonville and accepted his present position as Superintendent of the Nelsonville Public Schools. He has been very successful, and is universally respected and esteemed, and, as an evidence of their appreciation, at the closing exercises of the schools in 1880, Rev. A. B. Brice, in behalf of the board, presented him with an elaborate silver water pitcher and cup, on which was engraved: "Presented to Prof. F. S. Coultrap, by the Board of Education of the Nelsonville Union Schools, May 31, 1880."

Charles Covert was born in Boone County, W. Va., Jan. 17, 1849, a son of John and Sarah Covert, his father a native of Butler County, Pa., and his mother of Boone County, W. Va. Our subject spent his youth in attending school, his father being a school teacher. In 1861, although a small boy, he took an active part in the Confederate service. His father and grandfather were both in that army, and were both taken prisoners, and held at Camp Chase. His grandfather died while a prisoner of war. After the war Mr. Covert went to farming, following that occupation until 1871, when he went to Kentucky and remained a year. He then came to Ohio and located in Lawrence County, and engaged in mining until 1878, when he came to Athens County and settled in Buchtel. He was married Oct. 8, 1874, to Miss Caroline Thompson, a native of Lawrence County. They have had four children, only three of whom are living—Albert S., John A. and Frank A. Mr. Covert is a member of the K. of L., Keystone Assembly, No. 1,516; K. of P., York Lodge, No. 75, and I. O. O. F., Buchtel Lodge, No. 712.

James Wilson Crane, of the firm of Vorhes & Crane, brickmakers, contractors and builders, Nelsonville, was born in the vicinity of Zanesville, Ohio, Aug. 13, 1830, where he lived with his parents, James and Mercy (Wartenbe) Crane, until he was eighteen years of age. In 1848 he came to Nelsonville, and was employed as a coal-miner in the mine of VanWormer & Brooks, until 1864. Jan. 1, 1865, he was employed by W. B. Brooks as mine boss, remaining in his employ until February,1879. That year he became associated with W. H. Vorhes in brickmaking, contracting and building, under the firm name of Vorhes & Crane. He has been three times married. His first wife was Mary M. Crothers, of Nelsonville, whom he married Oct. 28, 1852. She died Jan. 20, 1864, leaving four children—Florence M., wife of Alfred Powell, of Muskingum County, Ohio; Lucinda E., wife of Vincent Green, of Hocking County ; Vesta M., wife of Charles W. Sanders, of Hocking County, and Mercy C., unmarried. He married his second wife, Margaret E. Carnes, of Nelsonville, March 26, 1865. She died April 3, 1875, leaving five children—Sylva M., Eliza M., Charles W., James A., and William A. He married his third wife, Mrs. Margaret Davis, of Lancaster, Dec. 20, 1876. Mr. Crane is a Master and Royal Arch Mason, and has served as Senior and Junior Deacon and Senior and Junior Warden of his lodge. He is also an Odd Fellow, and is a Past Grand.

Edward Homer Davis, proprietor of Davis's livery stables at Nelsonville, was born in York Township, Athens Co., O., April 15, 1859. His parents were Joseph A. and Alvira (Judd) Davis. His father dying when he was a child, he lived with his mother on the homestead until her death, when he was fourteen. At that age he began to work for himself. In 1876 he traded his interest in his father's estate for the livery business, in which he is now engaged at Nelsonville. In the spring of 1882 he was elected a member of the Council of Nelsonville, and is now an incumbent of that office.

Joseph A. Davis (deceased) was born in Athens County, Ohio, near the mouth of Monday Creek, Dec. 1, 1825. His parents were Rufus P. and Clarrissa (Allen) Davis. He was married to Alvira Judd, Oct. 24, 1850. They had seven children, five of whom are living—John F., Lizzie Armitage, Charles J., Edward H. and Clinton L. Seth P. died in childhood and Susan A. in infancy, Mr. Davis spent his whole life on the farm on which he was born, heiring part of the land and purchasing the balance, where he pursued farming up to his death, July 16, 1866.

G. W. Devore is a native of York Township, Hocking Co., Ohio, born Nov. 28, 1843, a son of Henry and Nancy (McKee) Devore. He was reared on a farm and received his education in the common schools and at the Ohio University. He spent several of his vacations in teaching school. In 1868 he entered the employ of the Nelsonville Coal Company, and April 2, 1870, was employed by T. Longstreth. He has been promoted from time to time, and at present is Superintendent of the store and offices of this district of the Columbus & Hocking Coal and Iron Company. He was married, Oct. 14, 1869, to Carrie McGill. They have three children—Carrie C., Belford L. and George E. Mr. and Mrs. Devore are members of the Methodist church.

James Dew, proprietor of the Dew House, Nelsonville, was born at Zanesville, Ohio, Sept. 6, 1839. In 1840 his parents, John and Sarah (Zane) Dew, came to Athens County, and settled in York Township on a farm, where he was reared. His father was a pioneer of Athens County, and came with his brother, Thomas Dew, when eight years old from Cumberland, Md., in 1819. His mother was a descendant of the Zane family, founders of the city of Zanesville, Ohio. Our subject lived with his parents until manhood, and was given a common-school education. In his boyhood he was placed in charge of his father's farm, and did not begin to do any thing for himself until his father's death, in 1863. Receiving his share of his father's estate, he made no investments until 1878, when he built the Dew House, a brick structure in Nelsonville, which he rented until May, 1882, when, with his son Dudley, he took charge of it as James Dew & Son. In January, 1881, he purchased a farm of 530 acres in the vicinity of Frankford, Clinton Co., Ind., where he is also engaged in farming and stock-raising. In 1881 he was Trustee of York Township. In 1859 he married Miss Margaret Charlton, of Nelsonville. They have three children—Dudley, Capitola and Stanley. They have lost one son—Orlaf.

Thomas Dew was born in July, 1815. He lived near Nelsonville, and was a farmer and stock-dealer. He enlisted in the late war and was a Captain of the Eighteenth Ohio Regiment, which position he held until his health failed, when he was obliged to resign and come home. He died at his home at Bessemer, Sept. 30, 1868, from disease contracted in the army. He left a family and a host of friends to mourn his loss. He was married to Miss Nancy Zane, daughter of Silas and Annie (Bland) Zane. Mr. Zane was the founder of Zanesville, Ohio, and was a very wealthy and influential man at that time. Mrs. Dew was born May 4, 1821, and is the only one of the family now living. Mr. and Mrs. Dew were the parents of eight children, three of which are living—Thomas E., Silas, and Mark; James, Joel, Isah, John and Orlaf are deceased.

Charles Henry Doan, junior member of the firm of Lama & Doan, coal operators and merchants of Nelsonville, was born at Harveysburgh, Ohio, Jan. 7, 1852. When about four years old his parents, Nathan and Anna E. (Downing) Doan, moved to Richmond, Ind., where our subject remained till he was sixteen years of age. He was educated in the public schools and in Holingworth's Commercial College at Richmond. In 1868 he was employed in a planing mill for a year, and afterward worked about two years in a boot and shoe store. In 1870 he began operating in coal at Richmond till November of the following year, when he came to Nelsonville and accepted the position of general manager of the New York & Ohio Coal Company's stores at Nelsonville, which position he held till 1874. He was then engaged as bookkeeper till the following year in the store of Whitman & Bates. In March, 1875, he was employed as bookkeeper for the Nelsonville Mining Company, staying there till it was discontinued, in January, 1879. In 1881 he with J. E. Lama became the proprietors of the same mine in which they are now operating under the firm name of Lama & Doan. Previous to his becoming associated with Mr. Lama, he, in 1880, engaged in general merchandising at Nelsonville, which he carried on till December, 1881. June 23, 1873, he was married to Miss Jennie Austin, of Richmond, by whom he has two children—Robert A. and Frank C. Mr. Doan is an Odd Fellow, being Past Grand of Hockhocking Lodge, No. 339, and is also Past Chief of Nelsonville Encampment, No. 121.

Levi McDowel, photographer, Nelsonville, was born in Muskingum County, O., March 24, 1848. He lived on his father's farm until he was twenty-one, when he engaged in the cattle and stock trade. In 1873 he went to Columbus, O., and learned the photographer's trade, remaining at this point until 1874, when he went to Adamsville, Muskingum Co., O., and some six months later went to Plainfield, O., remaining there two years; then he located in Logan, O., and one year later came to Nelsonville and established his present business, where he has one of the best galleries in the Hocking Valley. He was married to Miss Laura Risley May 26, 1881. She was born in Logan, O., a daughter of James A. and S. A. (Prince) Risley, natives of Virginia and Maryland. Mr. and Mrs. Levi McDowel are members of the Methodist Episcopal church.

John Dreany, merchant, of Nelsonville, was born Feb. 22, 1832, in County Armagh, in the north of Ireland, where he lived till he was twenty-one years old. He then emigrated to the United States, landing at New York in June, 1852. He first went to Pittsburg and engaged himself as a miner in the Sawmill Run coal mines until 1854, when he went to Virginia and worked as a miner till 1856. The same year he came to Nelsonville, where he was again engaged as a miner for one year, after which he became a coal operator and carried on the business until November, 1859. He then began boating on the Hocking Valley & Ohio Canal, and in July, 1863, during the Morgan raid, his boat was burned and his best horses taken by Morgan's men. In 1870 he gave up boating and engaged in the mercantile business, which he still follows. March 27, 1865, he married Elizabeth Cawthorn, who died June 4, 1874, when he, Aug. 1, 1877, married Anna Matheny, who died Oct. 13 of the same year. In February of the following year he was again married, this time to Lavina Dashler, of Athens County. Mr. Dreany is a Master Mason of Philodorean Lodge, No. 157, of Nelsonville, and also an Odd Fellow, and belongs to Hockhocking Lodge, No. 339.

Samuel Smith Dresback, of the firm of Dresback & Hall, grocers and coal operators, Nelsonville, was born at Bloomingville, Hocking Co., O., Dec. 22, 1843, where he was reared a farmer and received a good common-school education. He lived with his parents, David and Jane (Smith) Dresback, until manhood. His father dying at about the time our subject became of age, he remained on the farm with his mother six years, and during that time taught school during the winter months. In 1870 he was employed by the Lick Run Coal Company as a bookkeeper, and was in their employ two and one-half years. In 1873 he was employed as assistant bookkeeper and weighmaster by T. Longstreth. In the spring of 1878 he engaged in the grocery business at Nelsonville. In October, 1882, George E. Hall became associated with him, under the firm name of Dresback & Hall, in the grocery business, and added that of operating in coal, their mines being in the vicinity of Nelsonville. Nov. 27, 1879, he was married to Jane Snyder, of Nelsonville. Himself and wife are members of the First Presbyterian Church. He has served both as Deacon and Ruling Elder for several years.

Ellis Edwards was born in Flintshire, North Wales, in 1854. When he was eighteen years of age he went to Durham County, England, and worked in the coal mines thirteen years. While there, in 1858, he married Isabelle Caldwell, of Bouden Close, England. In 1865 he came to America and first located in Dunmore, Luzerne Co., Pa., where he worked in the coal mines a year. He then went to Wilkesbarre, Pa., and worked for Parish & Thomas a year. In 1867 he came to Ohio and worked in the railroad shops in Lancaster a year, and in 1868 came to Nelsonville and worked for Phillips & Powers four years. He then worked for W. B. Brooks most of the time till 1882 and since then has been employed by Johnson Bros. & Patterson. In 1864 his wife died very suddenly of heart disease, leaving four children—Joseph, Mary

Elizabeth (recently a graduate of Nelsonville High School), Isabella and Cora. In 1868 Mr. Edwards married Mrs. Emily McLaughlin of Nelsonville. They have one child—Stella L. Mr. Edwards is a member of the First Presbyterian Church, Nelsonville. He has served as Deacon several years and is now a Ruling Elder. He is a member of Hockhocking Lodge, No. 339, I. O. O. F.

William Edward Evans, President of the Hocking Valley division of the Miners' Association of the State of Ohio, was born at Grayson, Ky., July 1, 1847, where he was reared and lived with his parents, David and Frances (Evans) Evans, until manhood. At the age of eighteen he began to work in the coal mines at Mandy Furnace, Ky., remaining there until he was of age, when he came to Ohio and was employed in the coal mines at Sheridan, Lawrence County. He afterward returned to Kentucky and worked in the mines at Coalton until 1874 when he came to Nelsonville and has been employed in the various mines at that place ever since. July 1, 1881, he was elected President of the Hocking Valley division of the Miners' Association of Ohio. Sept. 8, 1870, he married Elizabeth Rust, of Ironton, Lawrence Co., Ohio. They have six children—Charles Edward, William Henry, Frank, Harry, Stella and an infant. Mr. Evans is a member of Franklin Assembly, No. 453, Knights of Labor, being at present Treasurer. He is also an Odd Fellow and member of Unity Lodge, No. 568, of which he is Noble Grand, and of Nelsonville Encampment, No. 121.

Christopher Findling was born in Germany, Sept. 12, 1849. When he was six years of age he came with his father's family to the United States and settled in Pomeroy, Meigs County, O., where he was reared and received a limited education. During his youth he worked in the coal mines, and when he was seventeen years of age he went to work in the woolen mills at Middleton, where he remained two years. At the end of that time he came to Athens County and was employed in the coal mines at Nelsonville. In 1879 he came to Bessemer, where he has since resided, and has been engaged in the grocery business. He was married March 4, 1872, to Miss Corithine Rinestetter, a native of Hocking County. They had two children—Charley (died in 1877) and Lizzie. His wife died in 1875. He was married Nov. 4, 1880, to Miss Missouri Stuart of Athens County. They have had one child—Bertha, who died Sept. 2, 1881. Mr. Findling is a member of K. of P., York Lodge, No. 75.

Jacob William Frost, Postmaster of Nelsonville, was born in Athens, Ohio, Nov. 9, 1847, where he was reared and received a common-school education. He is the son of Jacob C. and Mary (McCabe) Frost, with whom he lived until manhood. His father being a tailor, he learned that trade in his boyhood. In the fall of 1863 he came to Nelsonville and engaged in tailoring until 1870, when, on account of his health, he was obliged to change his business, and was employed as a clerk in the stores of Nelsonville until 1878, when he received the appointment of Postmaster. He is a Master, Royal Arch, Council and Knight Templar Mason and member of the lodge at Nelsonville, and chapter and council at Logan, and commandery at Athens. He has served several terms as Senior Deacon of his Lodge.

Charles Frederick Gilliam, M. D., Nelsonville, Ohio, was born in Logan, Ohio, Nov. 9, 1853. He is the son of William and Mary E. (Bryan) Gilliam. He began to support himself at the early age of thirteen by working in the nail factory of Clifton, W. Va. In his nineteenth year he was employed as a clerk at Middleport, and afterward at Nelsonville. When about twenty he began to clerk for his brother, Dr. D. T. Gilliam & James Dew, druggists at Nelsonville. He afterward succeeded Mr. Dew and was in business with his brother, under the firm name of Gilliam & Brother, until 1877, and during that time he studied medicine under his brother. Having a certificate to practice from the County Medical Society, Athens County, for several years, he was only required to take one course of lectures before graduating. He graduated from the Columbus Medical College in March, 1878, and established himself in his present practice at Nelsonville. From July, 1878, to September, 1881, he served as Township Physician of York Township. March 12, 1879, he married Miss Mattie Frost, daughter of J. C. Frost, of Nelsonville. They have one child—Charles Frederick, Jr.

William B. Gilmore was born in Pickaway County, Ohio, Sept. 10, 1835. His youth was spent in attending school. At the age of eighteen years he engaged in running an engine for a saw-mill. About a year and a half later he went to the Vinton County furnaces and ran the engine for four years. At the breaking out of the Rebellion he enlisted in Company K, Eighth Ohio Cavalry. He participated in many hard-fought battles and remained in active duty until the close of the war, receiving an honorable discharge Aug. 7, 1865. He returned to Vinton County, and was in the employ of the Hamden Express Company for a year and a half. In the spring of 1867 he went to Stewart County, Tenn., where he engaged with the Lagrange Iron Company as engineer for four years. In August, 1871, he returned to Ohio, and for five years was employed by the Union Furnace Company, of Hocking Valley. In 1877 he came to Buchtel, where he has since been in the employ of the Akron Iron Company as engineer. He was married April 9, 1860, to Miss Caroline Cramer, a native of Vinton County, Ohio. They had two children—Addie and Annie. His wife died March 14, 1871. He was married Dec. 21, 1872, to Miss Diantha Tucker, a native of Hocking County, Ohio. Mr. Gilmore is a member of the I. O. O. F., Hocking Valley Lodge, No. 262, and of Tom Dew Post, No. 288, G. A. R.

J. T. Gray was born in Prince George County, Md., Nov. 23, 1825, a son of Elias and Delilah Gray. Mr. Gray received a common education in the public schools, and moved to Nelsonville in 1867, where he has since made his home. June 27, 1849, he was married to Eliza Specht, daughter of Peter Specht. They have two living children—Alice and Emma, both married. Jonas died at the age of twenty years and one month. Mr. Gray enlisted first in the Ninety-second, and afterward in the One Hundred and Fifty-fifth Ohio Regiment, under General Ben Butler. He has been a Mason for a number of years, and is at present Master of the Nelsonville Lodge, No. 157. He was also a member of the I. O. O. F. for a brief period. He has served as Village Counsel three terms of two years each. Mr. Gray is by trade a tanner.

John Grimm is a native of Baden, Germany, born March 9, 1833. His father, Philip Grimm, was Secretary of State for twenty-seven years in his native country, and his three elder brothers were men of military rank. One was Major in the German army, and the other two were Captains in the regular service. Our subject came to the United States in 1848, landing in New York. He learned the blacksmith's trade in Brooklyn, serving three years as an apprentice and one year as journeyman in the same shop. He then visited nearly all the principal cities of the United States, and in 1854 came to Ohio, and located in Cincinnati. Oct. 17, 1857, he married Miss Rachel Wollbrand, a native of Sleswick, Holstein, Germany. He resided in Cincinnati until November, 1859, when he removed to Meigs County, Ohio, and remained until the breaking out of the late civil war. In 1861 he enlisted in the Seventh Ohio Battery Light Artillery, as a soldier of the ranks, but was soon promoted to Artificer of the blacksmith's department. June 6 he met with a serious accident by the fall of a horse, having his left leg and five ribs broken, and was confined to the hospital until October 23 following, when he was honorably discharged by a special order of General Sherman, but the following May he returned to his old regiment as a veteran, and received his former position, where he served until the close of the war. He was mustered out Aug. 27, 1865, and returned to his home in Meigs County, and there pursued his trade until 1876, when he came to Athens County and lived at Stewart for one and a half years. He then came to Buchtel, where he has since resided, and has been foreman of the blacksmith shops for the Akron Iron Company. He was elected Justice of the Peace in 1880, and re-elected in 1881. Mr. and Mrs. Grimm are the parents of nine children, only seven of whom are living—Charles, Mary E., Florinda, Sophia, James, Augustus and Gustus (twins); John and Rachel, deceased. Mr. and Mrs. Grimm are members of the Methodist Episcopal church. He is a member of the A. F. & A. M., Lodge No. 457, and of K. of L., Keystone Lodge, No. 1,516.

W. J. Hamilton, Postmaster, Buchtel, a son of Samuel and Mary (O'Neal) Hamilton, was born in McKeesport, Allegheny County, Pa., June 17, 1848, where he was reared and educated. When he was old enough to work he engaged on the public works of the mines. He afterward clerked for his uncle, John O'Neal, at Pine Run, where he remained for seven years, after which he engaged in weighing coal for the same company two years. He then engaged as carpenter for the P. V. & C. R. R. Co., where he remained for about two years, and in the summer of 1877 came to Ohio and located at Buchtel, Athens County, where he has since resided. The first six months he was engaged in the mines, after which he was weighmaster until April 1, 1882, when he received his appointment as Postmaster. He was married Jan. 16, 1875, to Lizzie Cawean, a native of West Elizabeth, Allegheny Co., Pa. They have two children—Cora B. and Norrinne. He is a member of I. O. O. F., Buchtel Lodge, No. 712, being a charter member, and the encampment at West Elizabeth, No. 212; also a member of the K. of P., York Lodge, No. 75.

W. J. Haybson was born in Hamden, Vinton Co., O., Sept., 30, 1844, a son of Richard and Rachel (Gregory) Haybson, where he was reared and received his education in the common school. His youth was spent in working on a farm and attending school until he was sixteen years of age when he went to learn the blacksmith's trade with Wm. Newton in his native county, where he remained one and a half years. He then went to work for the M. & C. R. R. for two years, after which he went into the railroad shops at Zaleski, Ohio, where he served eight years. In the spring of 1877, he came to Athens County and located in Buchtel and engaged with the Akron Iron Company, where he has since been employed. He was married Oct. 6, 1868, to Ellen Robb, a native of Clarion County, Pa. They have three children—Irenos J., Franklin and Ira S. Mr. Haybson is a member of the K. of P., Buchtel Lodge, No. 78. He is also a member of the Blue Lodge, Nelsonville, No. 157; Logan Chapter, No. 75, and Hockhocking Council, No. 39, A. F. & A. M., and Knights of Labor, Keystone Assembly, 1,516. He holds the office of Township Trustee of York Township, elected in 1882.

Wesley Clark Hickman was born near Chesterville, Knox Co., Ohio, Dec. 30, 1832, a son of Robert F. and Harriet (Nichols) Hickman, his father a native of Chester County, Pa., and his mother of Leesburg, Va. When he was four years of age his parents removed to Mt. Vernon, Ohio, remaining there till the fall of 1842, when they went to Somerset, Perry County. In 1843 he went into his father's printing office to learn the trade, working part of the time and attending school the rest of the time for six years. Early in 1849 he left home and worked as a jour printer in Indiana, Ohio and Michigan for three or four years, spending part of the time, however, in attending school in Somerset, to Rev. A. J. Weddell. In the latter part of 1852 he began the study of law, and was admitted to the bar in 1854. In the spring of 1855 he was married to Catherine M., daughter of James and Amelia (Kelley) Porter, of Fultonham, Ohio, who died in 1856, leaving two children, a son and a daughter. The son, James Robert, still lives; the daughter died at the age of four and a half months. After the death of his wife he served two years as Deputy Clerk of Probate Court of Perry County, his father being Probate Judge. He then assumed the control of the Somerset *Review*, but it proved unsuccessful, and through that and other unsuccessful business ventures he found himself involved in debt. He closed his office and went to Cincinnati and entered an office as compositor, and from the fall of 1859 till April, 1861, worked at the case, principally in the office of the Daily *Times*. He then enlisted in Company I, Fifth Ohio Infantry, for three months. The company organized under the name of Franklin Guards, and was composed almost wholly of "typos." In June, 1861, the regiment reorganized as a three years' regiment, and Mr. Hickman re-enlisted. He served in the ranks as a non-commissioned officer till August, 1863, when, on account of failing health, he was transferred to the Veteran Reserve Corps. Objecting to the transfer which was made against his will, he only remained with the "reserves" till Sept. 27, 1863, when he rejoined his regiment at Washington, D. C., and accompanied his old command to Tennessee. He remained with his regiment till Dec. 23, when an order for his arrest was forwarded to his regiment and he was returned to Washington and the charge of "desertion" preferred against him by the Captain of the Seventh Company, Second Battalion, V. R. C., Emil Sturmfels. After being kept in the guard house a few days he was put on trial as a "deserter" before a general court martial, Colonel Guile, of Philadelphia, presiding, but before the result of the trial was announced the Adjutant General graciously removed the charge and remanded him to duty. During his military service he was in the campaigns of West Virginia in 1861, and in the Shenandoah Valley in 1862, participating in the engagements at Winchester, Port Republic, Cedar Mountain and others, and did duty as scout a short time. He was in the service thirty-eight months, being with the Fifth Ohio two years, in the hospital seven months (as patient part of the time and about four months as clerk at Harper's Ferry General Hospital), and about six months in the Veteran Reserve Corps. In June, 1864, he returned to Perry County, and resumed the practice of law. In June, 1866, he was appointed Clerk of Courts of Perry County, but at the election was beaten by his Democratic competitor by a majority of 145. In October, 1867, he came to Nelsonville. He served one term as Justice of the Peace of York Township, from 1869–'72, but refused re-election at the end of the term. In 1875 he was again elected and still holds the office. In September, 1865, he married Kate, daughter of Hixson and Ann (Pruner) Hunt. They have had six children born to them, only three now living—Paul H., Katie and John M. Fletcher died at the age of five months, Annie H. at the age of two years, and Sam aged one year.

Willis Gaylord Hickman, County Commissioner of Athens County, and druggist of Nelsonville, was born in Mount Vernon, Ohio, Oct. 16, 1839. He is the son of Robert F. and Harriet (Nichols) Hickman. His mother died at Somerset when he was three years of age, and he lived with his father until he was seventeen, and ~~was~~ given a common-school education. He worked at the printer's trade until he was eighteen, but not liking that trade began to learn the blacksmith's trade, and worked at it for four years, when, in March, 1862, he enlisted in Company E, of the First Battalion of the Eighteenth U. S. Infantry, and served three years, being discharged at Lookout Mountain, Tenn., March 27, 1865. He participated in the battles of Corinth, Perrysville, Stone River, Hoover's Gap, Tullahoma, Chickamauga, Mission Ridge, Dalton, Resaca, Burnt Hickory, Kenesaw Mountain, Smyrna Church, Peach Tree Creek, Chattahoochee, the siege and capture of Atlanta and Jonesboro. After being discharged he returned to New Lexington, Ohio, where his father had removed while he was in the service, and from there he went to Lebanon, Ohio, and attended the Southwestern Normal School for nearly two years. He then returned to New Lexington, and was deputy clerk under his father in the probate office at that place one year, when in May, 1868, he came to Nelsonville and engaged in the drug business, being associated with his brother, W. C. Hickman, under the firm name of Hickman Brothers. In 1873 Joseph Smith became his brother's successor, and changed the firm to Hickman & Smith. In July, 1876, Mr. Smith retired from the firm, and since then Mr. Hickman has carried on the business alone. In the spring of 1878 he was elected Treasurer of the village of Nelsonville for a term of two years, and re-elected in the spring of 1882. He served as Township Trustee of York Township during 1878-'79, and on the School Board of Nelsonville from 1881 to 1883. In 1880 he was elected one of the Commissioners of Athens County for a term of three years. Nov. 2, 1871, he married Miss Lorana L. Wolf, of Hocking County, Ohio, who died at Nelsonville, May 31, 1878, leaving two children — Robert D. and Perley W. He married Miss Dora Wolf, of Nelsonville, Aug. 8, 1880. They have one child—Emma E. Mr. Hickman is a member of Philodorean Lodge, No. 157, A. F. & A. M.; of Hockhocking Lodge, No. 339, I. O. O. F., and of Nelsonville Encampment, No. 121. He is Past Grand of the subordinate lodge, and Past Worthy Patriarch of the encampment. He is also a member of Phil Kearney Post, G. A. R.

Jacob James Hoodlet, blacksmith, of Nelsonville, was born near Somerset, Ohio, April 7, 1835. He lived with his parents, Peter and Catherine (Klise) Hoodlet, in Perry and Hocking counties until manhood. At fourteen years of age he began to learn the blacksmith's trade with James Edington, at Old Straitsville, Perry County, with whom he worked some three years, after which he worked for his brother, John Hoodlet, at Gore, Hocking County, until 1857. He then returned to Old Straitsville and began business for himself, remaining in that place till 1862, when he came to Nelsonville and established the shop in which he still continues to work. He was married Aug. 6, 1856, to Miss Elizabeth Johannah Johnson, of Hocking County, who has borne him twelve children, nine of whom survive, viz.: Henry P., John W., Mary A., Charles L., Isaac P., Ella L., Maria J., Kate L. and Nancy M. He and wife are members of the Methodist Episcopal church of Nelsonville, of which he is Steward. Mr. Hoodlet served as Councilman of Nelsonville in 1867. He is an Odd Fellow, being a member of Unity Lodge, No. 568, of Nelsonville. In 1864 he enlisted in Company D, One Hundred and Forty-fourth Regiment, O. N. G., and served on guard duty at Barboursville, Va., four months.

John Wesley Jackson, of the firm of Wilson & Jackson, proprietors of the Central Meat Market at Nelsonville, was born in Manchester Township, Morgan County, April 30, 1829. At an early age he came with his parents, Robert and Rebecca (Hollister) Jackson, to York Township, Athens County, where he lived until he was fifteen years old, after which he went with them to Ward Township, Hocking County, where his father died in 1845. Soon after he returned with his mother to York Township. He was reared as a farmer, and educated in the district schools. At twenty-two years of age he rented the homestead of his mother, and began to farm for himself. After a short time he and his brother-in-law bought the interest of the other heirs, and he became owner of the portion on which he lived for twenty-eight years. In 1879 he rented his farm, removed to Nelsonville and formed his present partnership with Clark Wilson. He was married April 14, 1864, to Miss Kate S. White, of Athens. They have two children living, viz.: Robert Hiram and Harry Hays. Lizzie Lillian died at Nelsonville, April 30, 1880, at the age of fifteen years. Mr. Jackson was elected Township Assessor of York Township in 1878, and served one year. He and wife are members of the Methodist Episcopal church of Nelsonville, of which he is Trustee and Steward.

Thomas Johnson, of the firm of Johnson Brothers & Patterson, consisting of Thomas, Edward and Charles Johnson, Joseph Slater and David Patterson, coal miners and dealers, of Nelsonville, was born near Birmingham, England, Dec. 6, 1853. When he was about eight years of age he came to the United States with his parents, Thomas and Ann (Slater) Johnson, first settling at Niles, Ohio. He lived with them there, at Sharon, Pa., and Akron, Ohio, until 1873, when he, with his brother Charles, came to Nelsonville. He was given only a common-school education and was brought up a miner. He followed that avocation at Nelsonville until 1879 when he and his brothers, Charles and Edward, and half brother, Joseph Slater, leased the Salt Well Hollow coal mines at Nelsonville and began to mine and ship coal. In August, 1881, David Patterson, of Columbus, Ohio, became associated with them and formed the present firm of Johnson Brothers & Patterson. Oct. 4, 1881, he married Mary Zephyr, daughter of A. H. Carnes, of Nelsonville. They have one child—Thomas Alfred. Mr. Johnson is a Master Mason and member Philodorean Lodge, No. 157.

Andrew Jackson Juniper was born in York Township, Athens County, on Nov. 2, 1853, and at the age of four years accompanied his parents, Thomas and Charlotte (Taylor) Juniper, to Wisconsin. They returned from there to Athens County in 1861, where he was educated in the schools of Nelsonville. At the age of twenty he began to work as a coal miner for W. B. Brooks, and continued to do so for five years. In 1878 he was employed by John W. Scott as Superintendent of the Lick River coal mines for one year, after which he was engaged as a clerk in the store of the Floodwood Coal Company about one year. In 1860 he came to Nelsonville and engaged in merchandising, and in 1881 he also began operating in coal. In December of the latter year his brother, Abner Juniper, became associated with him under the firm name of Juniper Brothers. They employ some seventy-five miners annually and are permanently located in Nelsonville. Dec. 17, 1871, he was married to Miss Anna More, of Nelsonville, and they are the parents of two children, viz.: Ida and Edward.

Wallace Washington Knight, an old resident of Nelsonville, was born Nov. 13, 1825, on the spot where he now resides. He is a son of James and Sarah (Redmond) Knight, who emigrated from England and settled in Nelsonville in July, 1821. His father died Aug. 26, 1836, and his mother, Aug. 6, 1867. Our subject received his education in the district school. At the age of fifteen he began to learn the tanner's trade, working at it six or seven years, but not liking that trade he was variously employed until 1868, when he retired from active business. Oct. 11, 1857, he married Miss Josephine Everts, of Athens County, daughter of Eli and Oril (Howe) Everts. She was born in Canada, and came to Athens County with her parents when she was quite young. They have two children—James S., a clerk with C. A. Cable & Co., and Wallace Wade, attending school.

Solomon Charles Kontner, proprietor of meat market, Nelsonville, Ohio, was born at Deavertown, Morgan Co., Ohio, Nov. 29, 1832. When about six years of age he came with his parents, Solomon and Mary (Bagley) Kontner, to Nelsonville, where he was reared. His father dying when he was sixteen years old he began to maintain himself. He was employed as a driver on the Hocking Valley & Ohio Canal during the summer season, until 1857; has served in all the positions, from driver to captain. Since 1857 he has been engaged in his present business at Nelsonville, with the exception of three years, when he was operating in mining coal. He has served as Marshal of Nelsonville nine years, and Councilman five years. March 15, 1855, he married Mary A. Lazarus, of Deavertown. They have five children—Ida, Addie (wife of Dr. S. E. Butt), Charles S., Cora and Verna. Mr. Kontner is an Odd Fellow and member of the Hockhocking Lodge, No. 339, and Nelsonville Encampment, No. 121.

Joseph J. Lane, mechanic, Buchtel, was born in Washington County, Pa., June 7, 1839, a son of Joseph and Margaret (McKeever) Lane. His youth was spent in assisting his father in a cabinet shop, and attending school. When sixteen years of age he went to Ripley, Brown Co., Ohio, and served an apprenticeship of four years at the machinist's trade. At the breaking out of the late civil war, he was the first man in Washington County, Pa., to offer his services in defense of his country, enlisting on the 12th day of April, 1861, in the three months' service. He served in the Eastern army until his term of enlistment expired, after which he re-enlisted in the Ringgold Cavalry, an independent battalion, where he served until the close of the war. He participated in many hard-fought battles; among some of the most prominent were: Winchester, Cedar Creek, Gettysburg and Knoxville. He enlisted as a soldier of the ranks, but received promotion through all the non-commissioned offices, and in February, 1864, received the commission of Second Lieutenant. He was honorably discharged Dec. 12, 1865, thus serving his country faithfully for a period of nearly five years. After being mustered out he returned to his native county. In 1867 he came to Ohio and settled in New Lexington, and went to work at carpentering, remaining there until 1880, when he came to Buchtel, where he has since resided. He was married Nov. 4, 1862, to Miss Martha Wilkins, a native of Washington County, Pa. They have had five children, only four of whom are living—Maggie, Lulu A., Samuel S. and Nora. Mr. Lane is a member of Buchtel Lodge, I. O. O. F., No. 712, and of the Tom Dew Post, No. 288, G. A. R., Buchtel.

H. T. Lee, M. D., was born in Muskingum County, Ohio, Jan. 26, 1856, a son of James H. and Rachel (Baldwin)Lee. He received his early education in the common schools, and completed it at the Atwood Institute, Albany, Athens Co., Ohio. After leaving school he engaged in teaching for about four years. He began the study of medicine in April, 1878, under the preceptorship of Dr. A. C. Allen, of Straitsville, Ohio. He took his first course of lectures in the winter of 1879–'80, at the Ohio Medical College, after which he returned to Straitsville, and remained with his preceptor until the next winter, when he took his second course of lectures, and graduated in 1882, at the same college, after which he located in Buchtel, where by strict attention to his profession he has built up a large practice, and met with remarkable success. He is a member of the K. of P., Buchtel Lodge, No. 78. He is also a member of the I. O. O. F., Buchtel Lodge, No. 712.

Barnet Columbus Lefever, Superintendent of the Nelsonville Planing Mill Company, was born at Butler, Butler Co., Pa., May 27, 1830. In his sixth year he came with his parents, Isaac and Elizabeth (Step)Lefever, to Ohio and lived in Trimble Township till he attained the age of manhood. At the age of twenty he began to learn the carpenter's trade with James M. Bishop, of Morgan County, with whom he worked about two years. He next worked as a journeyman at different places in Athens, Hocking and Morgan counties for three years, and in 1855 he located in Albany, Athens County, where he lived one year, when he removed to a farm in York Township, where he pursued farming with his trade till 1871. In that year he came to Nelsonville and engaged as a contractor and builder and undertaker, in which he is still engaged. In January, 1882, at the organization of the Nelsonville Planing Mill Company, he became a stockholder and was elected Superintendent, and still holds that position. In 1875 he was elected one of the Athens County Infirmary Directors for a term of three years; has also served as Councilman of Nelsonville two terms; as member of the School Board one term, and on the School Board of York Township about ten years. He was married Jan. 19, 1855, to Miss Rebecca Miranda, daughter of Robert and Rebecca Jackson, of York Township, Athens County. They have had six children, but Edmund Burns is the only one living at present. Three died in infancy. Thomas Orlando died in 1872, at the age of sixteen, and Charles Welch in 1874, aged over three years. Mr. Lefever is a Master Mason and member of Philodorean Lodge, No. 157; an Odd Fellow, a member of Hockhocking Lodge, No. 339, of which he is Past Grand.

Moses Lewis, deceased, was born in Athens County, Ohio, April 19, 1816, a son of Samuel Lewis, who was a son of Daniel Lewis, and came to Athens County among the early settlers. He was reared on a farm and educated in the common schools. He was married May 9, 1843, to Miss Sarah Harrington, a daughter of Samuel K. Harrington, a native of New York. Soon after our subject's marriage he moved on the farm, where his widow now resides. They were the parents of fifteen children, eight of which are still living. He and his wife were members of the Methodist Episcopal church. Mr. Lewis held the office of Justice of the Peace for about eight years besides many other local offices of trust and responsibility. He departed this life May 29, 1882. Mrs. Lewis has a large farm of 336 acres of well-cultivated land.

Henry J. Ley was born in Alsace, Germany, Nov. 14, 1855, where he was reared and educated. He came to the United States in 1873, and located in Akron, Summit Co., Ohio. In 1876 he came to Bessemer and worked at the stone-mason's trade about three months, when he went to work in the iron mines. He was married June 2, 1881, to Miss Josephine Gross, a native of Lawrence County, Ohio. They have one child—Henry P. Mr. Ley is a member of the K. of L., Keystone Assembly, No. 1,516, and of the K. of P., York Lodge, No. 75.

Thomas Manning Linton, a miner in the coal mines of Nelsonville, was born near Frederick City, Frederick Co., Md., Aug. 12, 1838, where he lived until he was ten years of age. In the fall of 1848 he came with his parents to Ohio, settling near Maxville, where they lived until 1850, when they came to Hocking County and located on Monday Creek. In 1858 he came to Nelsonville and engaged in mining, which he followed until April 21, 1861, when he enlisted in Company B, Twenty-second Ohio Infantry, for three months. He served until Aug. 19, 1861. Oct. 2, 1861, he enlisted in Company G, Eighteenth Ohio Infantry, for three years. He was discharged at Camp Chase, Columbus, Ohio, Nov. 9, 1864. He participated in the battles of Athens, Ala., LaVergne, Tenn., Stone River, Tenn., Elk River, Chattanooga, Davis Cross Roads, Chickamauga, Rossville, Brown's Ferry, Missionary Ridge and Pulaski. In January, 1863, he was promoted to Duty Sergeant, and served as such until his discharge. After his discharge he returned to Nelsonville and resumed mining, and has been connected with that business ever since. Jan. 13, 1868, he married Emma Tedrow, of Nelsonville. They have four children—Eugene M., Emma May, Flora and Purley. Mr. and Mrs. Linton are members of the Methodist Episcopal church. He is a member of Philodorean Lodge, No. 157, A. F. & A. M., and of Hockhocking Lodge, No. 339, I. O. O. F.

Thomas Porter Marshall, of the Maple Hill Coal Company, Nelsonville, was born May 30, 1827, in Philadelphia, Pa., a son of William and Rebecca (Beaty) Marshall. When he was two years of age his parents removed to Darlington, Pa., where he was reared and educated. When he was twenty years of age he went to work for J. C. Hartman to learn the trade of a millwright, serving an apprenticeship of three and a half years, and in 1850 became associated with his employer in business. In 1854 they went to Iowa and worked in Marshall and Hardin counties till 1861. In August, 1861, he enlisted in Company H, Thirteenth Iowa Infantry, and was elected Captain of his company. He was afterward promoted to Major of the regiment. He participated in the battles of Shiloh, siege of Corinth, second battle of Corinth, siege and capture of Vicksburg, and was in the Atlanta campaign. After the fall of Atlanta, while at home on furlough, he was assigned to General Thomas's command, Army of the Cumberland, stationed at Nashville, Tenn., and placed in command of a regiment of the provisional division of the Army of the Tennessee, and while there participated in the two days' battle before Nashville. He remained in command of the regiment till its disbandment in April, 1865, when he returned to his own regiment at Goldsboro, and after the surrender of Johnston went to Washington, and was discharged April 9, 1865, after a service of nearly four years. He returned to his old home in Beaver Co., Pa., his family having moved there in his absence. He was engaged in the oil business two years, and in 1867 began operating in and mining coal. In October, 1873, he came to Nelsonville and was appointed Superintendent of the Laurel Hill Coal Company, of Columbus, remaining with them till Feb. 28, 1882. March 6, 1882, he was employed as Superintendent of the Maple Hill mines. April 1, 1883, a new organization was formed, and called the Maple Hill Coal Company. Mr. Marshall became a member of the company, still retaining the position of Superintendent. In 1857-'58, he was Justice of the Peace of Greencastle Township, Marshall Co., Iowa, and was Coroner of that county in 1859. In 1880-'81 he was Councilman of Nelsonville, and since 1881 has been a member of the Board of Education, being at present President of the Board. Nov. 10, 1852, he married Rachel Dawson, of Columbiana Co., O., who died Sept. 6, 1873, leaving three children—William Dawson, Almira H. and Etta Florella. In December, 1875, Mr. Marshall married Rachel Snyder, of Zaleski, O. They have two children—Ralph Everett and Ethel Ida. Mr. Marshall belongs to the Masonic fraternity, and is a member of Philodorean Lodge, No. 157, of Nelsonville, and Liverpool Chapter, No. 100, of East Liverpool; an Odd Fellow and a member of Hockhocking Lodge, No. 339, and Nelsonville Encampment, No. 121, and also of York Lodge, No. 15, K. of P.

James Monroe Martin, watchman in the coal mines of W. B. Brooks, was born in Lancaster, Fairfield Co., Ohio, April 7, 1818. where he lived for thirty years. When eighteen years of age, in 1836, he became apprenticed to George Ring, of Lancaster, to learn the woolen manufacturer's trade, which he followed till 1878, carrying it on at Nelsonville from 1848 until 1878, being associated with J J. Robbins. From 1878 till 1881 he was not in any active business, but since then has been employed in his present position. He has held the office of Councilman of Nelsonville one term. March 25, 1841, he was married to Mary Moutice, of Lancaster, who died April 21, 1864, at Nelsonville, leaving two children—Joseph C. and William Scott, both of Nelsonville. June 25, 1865, he was married to Mrs. Susan A. Bates, of Nelsonville, who died Sept. 20, 1879. Mr. Martin is an Odd Fellow and member of Hockhocking Lodge, No. 339, of which he is Past Grand.

Lindley Alonzo Maxwell, station agent of the C., H. V. & T. R. R. at Nelsonville, was born near Malaga, Monroe Co., O., March 31, 1854, a son of John L. and Phœbe J. (Carlton) Maxwell. He attended school till fifteen years of age and then clerked in a store at Lancaster a year, after which he went into the office of the C., H.

V. & T. R. R., at Lancaster, and learned telegraphy. He was employed in the office as extra operator about six months, and then as night operator eight months. From Lancaster he went to Columbus, Ohio, and was employed as extra operator there and afterward in other places till Nov. 9, 1873, when he received the appointment of day operator at Nelsonville, and Aug. 4, 1881, he was promoted to station agent. Sept. 11, 1878, he married Sarah I. Smith, of Nelsonville. They have two children—Charles L. and Lula J. Mr. Maxwell is a member of York Lodge, No. 75, K. of P., of which he is now Past Chancellor.

John Perry McGill, junior member of the mercantile firm of Parker & McGill, Nelsonville, was born in Canaan Township, Athens Co., O., May 3, 1837, where he lived with his parents, John and Susan (Mansfield) McGill, until he was eight years old, when they moved to Waterloo Township. In 1847 they removed to Hamley Run, in Dover Township, and when he was eighteen to York Township, and in 1857, to Starr Township, Hocking County, where he lived four years. He remained with his father's family, his father being a cripple, until he was twenty-seven years of age. Sept. 5, 1864, he enlisted in Company D, One Hundred and Seventy-fourth Ohio Infantry, and served until the close of the war. He then returned to Athens County, and in the fall of that year engaged in saw-milling and farming at Mineral City, carrying on that business until the following year. He then went on the M. & C. R. R., working in different capacities until 1869, when he took charge of the telegraph wires on the Columbus & Hocking Valley Road, having charge of the lines from Athens to Columbus. His father died Dec. 24, 1869, at Mineral City. In March, 1883, he became associated with J. M. Parker in the general mercantile business at Nelsonville. Aug. 17, 1865, he was married to Elvira Burlingame, of Albany, Athens County. They have one daughter—Flora. Himself and wife are members of the Methodist Episcopal church. He is an Odd Fellow and member of Hockhocking Lodge, No. 339, of Nelsonville.

Hosea McC. Miller was born in Preston County, W. Va., Feb. 19, 1846. He was reared on a farm and received his education in the common schools, living with his parents until he grew to manhood. After he reached his majority he learned the blacksmith's trade with his father, working with him three years. He then went to Grafton, W. Va., and worked in the Baltimore & Ohio Railroad shops two years. In 1873 he came to Hocking County, O., and worked at the Union Furnaces until May 9, 1877, when he came to Buchtel, where he has since been in the employ of the Akron Iron Company. He was married Sept. 22, 1868, to Mary M. Rodeheaver, a native of Preston County, W. Va. They have two children— Frank G. and Clarence W. Mr. Miller is a member of the K. of P., York Lodge, No. 75. His wife is a member of the Methodist Episcopal church.

Alexander Warden Nelson, real estate agent, was born in Nelsonville, Sept. 4, 1825. He is the second of three sons of Daniel and Sarah (Smith) Nelson. His father was the original owner of the site of Nelsonville and an extensive land owner. He laid out the plot of Nelsonville in 1818. Our subject was reared and has spent his whole life at Nelsonville. His father dying when he was ten years of age he was thrown upon his own resources. In his boyhood he began to work on the Hocking Valley & Ohio Canal by driving a cart-horse, and after its completion followed canaling, from driver to captain, until 1861. In that year he assisted in recruiting soldiers for the Union army, he being a staunch Union man. In the latter part of that year he enlisted in Company G, Eighteenth Ohio Infantry, and served only eighteen months when he was discharged at Huntsville, Ala., for disability caused by diseased eyes, having at that time nearly lost his eyesight. He then returned home, and although still afflicted, assisted in raising recruits. He has been under treatment for years but has not fully recovered his sight. He for a time tried to work in the coal mines, but was obliged to abandon it. He was then variously employed until 1875, when he engaged in the real estate business and lately became associated with J. F. Camp, under the firm name of Camp & Nelson. July 18, 1850, he was married to Miss Alpha Steinrod, of Muskingum County, O. They have eight children—Josephine, wife of Albert Riggs; Ella, Douglas Ward, Orilla, Daniel, Alpha, Amos and Angie. They have lost one—Louisa, who died at the age of seventeen years. Mr. Nelson is a member of Phil Kearney Post, No. 38, G. A. R., of Nelsonville.

Alonzo Pugsley Newton, Street Commissioner of Nelsonville, was born at Nelsonville, Oct. 10, 1835. He is the son of Gershom and Clarissa (Fisk) Newton, with whom he lived until he was eight years old, when he was taken by his uncle, Aaron Lewis, living with him until he was twenty-one. He then engaged in boating on the Hocking Valley & Ohio Canal until 1861, when, Oct. 9, he enlisted in Company G, Eighteenth Ohio Infantry, and served three years. He was in the battles of Athens, Ala., Pulaski, Tenn., and Stone River. He was discharged at Camp Chase, Ohio, Nov. 4, 1864. He then returned to Nelsonville and was employed in the coal mines until 1879, when he was elected Street Commissioner of Nelsonville, and has held that position by re-election ever since. Jan. 29, 1865, he married Miss Rebecca Anders, of Nelsonville. They have four children—Ella, Berta, Minnie and Fred. Mr. Newton is a member of Phil Kearney Post, No. 38, G. A. R., of which he is Senior Commander.

James Milton Parker, senior member of the firm of Parker & McGill, merchants, Nelsonville, was born near Logan, Hocking Co., Ohio, May 26, 1843, where he was reared and lived with his parents, Albert and Malinda, *nee* Bancroft, Parker, until manhood, and was given a common-school education. After becoming of age he was variously employed until 1871, when he was employed as a clerk in the store of W. B. Brooks, of Nelsonville, until 1882, when he became associated with John P. McGill in the mercantile business, under the firm name of Parker & McGill. Sept. 12, 1865, he was married to Miss Lydia Woodard, daughter of Nathan B. and Sarah (Nelson) Woodard. Her grandmother was a descendant of Daniel Nelson, the founder of Nelsonville. They have had two children; one died in infancy, and the other, Luetta, died at Nelsonville, Feb. 26, 1871. Mr. and Mrs. Parker are members of the Methodist Episcopal church, of Nelsonville, of which he has been Steward eleven years, Class-Leader two years, and Sabbath-school Superintendent eight years.

John Calvin Parker, salesman for Charles Robbins, Nelsonville, was born near Deavertown, Ohio, April 4, 1839, a son of Albert and Malinda (Bancroft) Parker. He was reared in Logan, Hocking County, where he received his elementary education, completing it in the Union School, Lexington, Ohio. He began teaching when twenty years of age, and taught five winters in Starr Township, Hocking County. In June, 1864, he came to Nelsonville and opened a photograph gallery, but the next June sold out and became associated with M. W. Benson in the mercantile business. In November, 1867, he retired from the firm and entered the employ of Charles Robbins. Since 1873 he has been dealing in real estate, and since his boyhood he has dealt in horses, being one of the best judges of that animal in the county. He was elected Township Clerk in 1868, serving a year; has served as Township Treasurer ten years; a member of the Board of Education of

Nelsonville seven years, and Treasurer of the village School Board nine years. May 30, 1860, he married Sarah A. Woodard, a descendant of Daniel Nelson, the founder of Nelsonville. They have one child—Orilla M., wife of Fred. W. Bull, of Buchtel. Mr. and Mrs. Parker are members of the Methodist church. He is a member of Philodorean Lodge, No. 157, A. F. & A. M., and of Hockhocking Lodge, No. 339, I. O. O. F.

Ashford Poston was born near Hanging Rock, Hampshire Co., Va., Nov. 7, 1814, the eldest of three sons of Richard and Elizabeth (Thompson) Poston. He was reared on his father's farm, and received but a limited education in the ordinary subscription schools of that day. The year he was twenty-one he came to Ohio with his parents, locating in the vicinity of Zanesville, where he began to work for himself, and was variously employed till 1837, when he became established in the grocery business with his cousin, E. S. Poston, in Nelsonville, the firm name being E. S. & A. Poston. Four years later they added general merchandise to their stock of groceries. He was also engaged in driving horses and cattle to the Philadelphia and Baltimore markets until 1844, when he retired from the mercantile and stock business, and engaged in boating on the Hocking Valley & Ohio Canal, and in buying and selling produce. In 1856 he retired from active business, but in 1863 became interested in mining and shipping coal, and was thus engaged until 1881. In connection with mining, in 1873 he was in the hardware and furniture business with S. N. Poston, the firm name being A. & S. N. Poston. In 1876 he purchased a dry-goods house, but in 1880 rented his coal mine and retired from all active business. Since 1858 he has been an extensive dealer in real estate. Although not actively engaged in business he is a member of the Nelsonville Planing Mill Company, of which he is President, Treasurer and Director. During the many years of his residence in Nelsonville he has served in most of the offices of its municipal and township organization. He has been twice married. His first wife was Margaret Parkinson, of Athens County, whom he married in 1838, and who died in 1842, leaving two children—Mary E. (now Mrs. Abraham Williams), and William B. Dec. 2, 1857, he married Miss M. C. Butt. They have three children—Maggie L., wife of William H. Hatch; Dennie A., widow of Cassius Dew, and Emma May. They have lost two children—Allie Monema, died March 3, 1869, aged ten years, and Annie, died in infancy.

Lorenzo Dow Poston was born in Hampshire County, Va., March 22, 1812, and moved to Athens County in 1830 and engaged in buying and selling cattle until about 1835, when he moved to Nelsonville and went into the mercantile business. He owned a large tract of land in and near Nelsonville, and in 1852 went into the mining business, in which he was very successful. Nov. 26, 1835, he was married to Martha Wilson, who only lived about two years. Sept. 26, 1838, he married Lucinda Parkinson. They had five children, two of which are living—William W., and Lucinda, wife of E. P. Pendleton. In 1852 he was married to Miss Hannah Scott. They had three children—Winfield, Irvin and Clarence E. Mr. Poston died Dec. 16, 1875. He was a man of fine business talent, and his death was mourned by all that knew him. He was a member of the Methodist Episcopal church for many years before his death, and had been Class-Leader several years. When a young man he used to work by the month at any kind of work he could obtain, but when he died he was one of the wealthiest men in the county. He obtained it all by his own good management and hard work. Mrs. Hannah Poston, wife of the deceased, was born Sept. 15, 1830, in England, and came to America with her parents when she was about three and one-half years old. They settled on the Ohio River and lived there until she was about ten years old, when they moved to Nelsonville.

Webster Wesley Poston, of the firm of Steenrod & Poston, proprietors of Eagle Flouring Mills, of Nelsonville, and also a member of the Nelsonville Planing Mill Company, and of the Nelsonville Foundry and Machine Company, was born in Nelsonville, June 29, 1844, where he was reared and educated. He lived with his parents, Wesley W. and Mary E. (Dew) Poston, until manhood. At the age of fourteen he entered the store of his father and was variously employed until the death of his father, Feb. 2, 1875. After his death he, with his brother, James D., settled up the estate. He then engaged in business with Amos Steenrod, and purchased the Eagle Flouring Mills. In 1881 he became a stockholder in the Nelsonville Foundry and Machine Company, of which he is Treasurer, and in 1882 became a member of the Nelsonville Planing Mill Company, of which he is one of the Directors. He is also largely interested in coal lands now being worked by leasers. He has been twice married. His first wife was Miss Hattie O., daughter of G. L. Cooley, of Nelsonville, whom he married Nov. 26, 1865, and who died in October, 1869, leaving two children—

Frank W. and Ella Vell, the latter dying in the fall of 1876, at the age of six years. He married his second wife, Miss Belle G. Cresap, of Logan, Ohio, April 22, 1873. They have three children—Webster C., Charles E. and Mabel Lefever.

Fred Lorenzo Preston, of the firm of L. P. Preston & Son, was born at Delaware, Ohio, Jan. 10, 1854, and is the eldest of four sons of Lorenzo P. and Laura L. (Dix) Preston. When he was an infant his parents removed to Columbus, where they lived until he was thirteen, when they came to Nelsonville. He was educated in the schools of Columbus and Nelsonville until he was seventeen, attending the High School of Columbus through part of the junior year, when he returned home to Nelsonville, and was employed as a clerk for W. B. Brooks. He afterward became bookkeeper and was with him about ten years. In August, 1881, he became associated with his father in the mercantile business at Nelsonville, under the firm name of L. P. Preston & Son. March 31, 1879, he married Ella, daughter of John Herrold, of Athens County. They have one child—Perry.

Lorenzo Perry Preston, senior member of the firm of Preston & Son, merchants, Nelsonville, was born in Montpelier, Vt., Feb. 3, 1817, where he was reared a farmer, and lived with his parents, Samuel and Lydia (Short) Preston, until manhood, and was given a good English education. When seventeen years of age he began to teach in country schools, and taught in various places in Vermont, at the same time pursuing his studies. After becoming of age, in the spring of 1838, he came to Ohio, and located at Columbus, where he was employed as clerk in the store of Stone, Carr & Co. for one year, when he become associated with Charles Kelton in the mercantile business, under the firm name of L. P. Preston & Co. In 1844 he formed a co-partnership with his brother, S. D. Preston, in the mercantile business at Columbus, under the firm name of S. D. & L. P. Preston, remaining in business together till the fall of 1854. Mr. Preston was then employed as a clerk in the store of his brother, W. B. Preston, until 1858, when he was employed as postoffice clerk at Columbus by Samuel Medary for six months. He was elected associate clerk of the Ohio Legislature, serving the winter of 1858 and '59. In the spring of 1859 he was employed by Fitch, Bortle & Co., to take charge of a store in connection with the furnace at Logan, and was in their employ until January, 1860. In the spring of 1860 he received the appointment of census-taker in the townships of Franklin, Jackson, Hamilton and Pleasant, in Franklin County, Ohio, and after completing that work went to Cambridge, Guernsey County, and was employed in the store of R. E. Champion & Co., until the spring of 1863, when he returned to Columbus and engaged in the grocery business, continuing until 1865. In 1866 he was employed by W. B. Brooks, as buyer and manager of his store at Nelsonville, with whom he remained until 1877. He then went to Mechanicsburg, Ohio, and engaged in the mercantile business until the spring of 1882 when he removed with his business to Nelsonville, when his son, Fred L. Preston, became associated with him, forming the present mercantile firm of L. P. Preston & Son. He has been twice married. His first wife was Miss Elsie Clark, of Montpelier, Vt., whom he married June 20, 1844, and who died in Columbus, November, 1851, leaving one child, Kate, who died in April, 1856, at the age of seven years. March 3, 1853, he married Miss Laura Dix, of East Montpelier, Vt. They had four children—Fred L., Samuel Decatur, Gilbert Dix and Leonard Shubael.

Isaac Porter Primrose, M. D., Nelsonville, Ohio, was born in Uniontown, Muskingum Co., Ohio, Oct. 18, 1831, the eldest of six children of Reuben H. and Hester Ann (Cannon) Primrose. He was reared in Muskingum and Perry counties, receiving his education in the common schools and the High School of Somerset. In 1857 he began the study of medicine with Dr. Nicodemus Hafford, of Old Straitsville, Perry County, studying and practicing the profession till August, 1861, when he enlisted in Company A, Thirty-first Ohio Infantry. On the organization of his company he was elected Second Lieutenant, and in February, 1862, was promoted to First Lieutenant. In November, 1862, he resigned on account of his eyes and a catarrhal trouble and returned to Old Straitsville. In February, 1863, he came to Nelsonville and assisted in raising Company A, Thirty-sixth Ohio National Guard, and was appointed its Captain, but on the organization of the regiment he was chosen Colonel. His regiment retained its organization till the close of the war, but was never called into active service. In the winter of 1864–'65 he attended Starling Medical College, Columbus, Ohio, from which he graduated Feb. 26, 1865. He has been a member of the City Council of Nelsonville three years, of the School Board two years, and President of the Athens County Medical Society five years. He is a Master Mason and member of Philodorean Lodge, No. 157; also a member of Phil Kearney Post, No. 38, G.

A. R. In April, 1852, he married Jane Harbaugh, of Old Straitsville. They have five children—Hester A., now Mrs. S. W. Jones, of Kingston, Ohio; Sarah A., now Mrs. W. N. Alderman; Binnie L., now Mrs. F. J. Hill; Loving and Blanch H. They have lost two children—Kittie Greenwood, died in July, 1862, aged six months, and Adie C., died July 11, 1879, aged twenty years. Dr. and Mrs. Primrose are members of the Methodist Episcopal church. June 16, 1883, the Doctor received the nomination of the Republican party for Representative to the State Legislature.

John Raine was born in Stanhope, county of Durham, England, Dec. 22, 1813, a son of George and Elizabeth (Brown) Raine. When he was thirteen years of age he went to work in the lead mines with his father, but soon after his father died. His mother died in 1835. He remained in the lead mines till 1838 and then went into the coal mines, remaining there till 1844, when he embarked for the United States, landing in New York, May 24. He came to Nelsonville and was first employed in the coal mines of J. F. Sommers, remaining with him three years. He was then employed by the late L. D. Poston eighteen years. Since 1865 he has worked for W. B. Brooks & Son, and though seventy years of age, still retains much of his youthful vigor, and enjoys life better when at work than when idle. April 9, 1844, on the eve of his departure for America, he married Miss Eliza Taylor, who is still living, having shared all the changing vicissitudes of a Western home with her husband. They have no children. They are members of the Methodist church, of Nelsonville, Mr. Raine having been Trustee, Steward and Treasurer.

James B. Rose was born in Pickaway County, Ohio, Dec 25, 1856. He was reared on a farm, and received his education in the common schools of his native county. He remained with his parents until he reached his majority, after which he engaged as a fireman on a locomotive for the C. & H. V. R. R. He afterward went to Straitsville, Ohio, where he was employed by a mining company as clerk in their store. In the fall of 1880 he came to Buchtel, and entered the employ of the Akron Iron Company, as salesman in their mercantile establishment, having charge of the dry-goods department. He is a member of the A. F. & A. M., Lodge No. 84, Straitsville, Ohio.

Curtis William Russell, blacksmith, Nelsonville, was born in Middleport, Meigs Co., Ohio, Oct. 3, 1849, where he lived until twenty years of age. He is the son of Benjamin Franklin and Jane

(McNeil) Russell. He was given a common-school education. At the age of sixteen, in the fall of 1864, he became apprenticed to John Rightnyse, at Rutland Corners, to learn the blacksmith's trade, serving three years. He then came to Nelsonville, and has since been employed in the blacksmith shop of W. B. Brooks & Son, coal operators. June 29, 1873, he was married to Caroline Woltz, of Hocking County. They have two children—Lena May and Jennie Maud. They lost one—Luella J., who died Oct. 1, 1874, at the age of eighteen months. Mr. and Mrs. Russell are members of the Christian church of Nelsonville, of which he is now a Deacon. He is an Odd Fellow, and a member of Unity Lodge, No. 568, and Mineral Encampment, No. 121, at Nelsonville, and served as Warden in the subordinate lodge.

William T. Schaeffer was born in Dayton, Ohio, June 6, 1850. His youth was spent in attending school, living with his parents until manhood. He received his early education in the schools of Dayton; afterward he attended the Miami Commercial College, taking a thorough course, after which he engaged as bookkeeper for his father, Thomas Schaeffer, broker and banker at Dayton, for about three years. In 1876 he came to Nelsonville, and engaged with T. Longstreth as clerk, and May 23, 1882, he was promoted to the position of manager of the store, which position he still occupies. He was married May 23, 1872, to Miss Addie J. Balser, a native of Piqua, Ohio, born Aug. 31, 1851. They have had four children, two now living—Oliver T., born Aug. 5, 1873, and Mary C., born July 30, 1878. Maud, born Feb. 28, 1875, died March 6, 1875; Elsie May, born April 9, 1880, died July 27, 1880.

Charles Ellsworth Schaff, son of Isaac and Angelina N. (Cleaves) Schaff, was born Feb. 4, 1853, in Kirkersville, Licking Co., Ohio. When one year old his parents moved to Grafton, W. Va., where they lived some time, and then moved to Newburgh, W. Va. When our subject was twelve years of age, they returned to Ohio, and settled at Uhrichsville, in Tuscarawas County, and in 1871 they went to Columbus, Ohio. Mr. Ellsworth was educated in the schools of Newburgh, W. Va., and graduated from the High School of that place in 1869. In that year he was employed as brakesman on the P., C. & St. L. R. R., and in 1872 became a fireman on the C. & H. V. R. R. until 1874. In that year he became baggage-master and express messenger on the same road, which position he held till August, 1876, when he became conductor, and in 1882 assumed his present position as yard master at Nelsonville for the

Columbus & Hocking Valley Railroad. He was married Dec. 31, 1878, to Miss Leila Belle, daughter of George White, Jr., of Columbus. They have been blessed with one child, Howard E. Mr. Ellsworth is a Master, Royal Arch and Knight Templar Mason, of Magnolia Lodge, No. 20, of Columbus; Logan Chapter, No. 75, at Logan, and Athens Commandery, No. 15, at Athens. He is a member of Court Forest, No. 12, United Order of Foresters at Columbus, of which he is Past Chief Ranger.

Isaac M. Schaff was born near Newark, Licking Co., Ohio, July 18, 1834, a son of John and Charlotte (Hartzill) Schaff. He was reared a farmer, following that avocation till twenty-two years of age. In 1856 he was employed in the machine shops of the old S. & I. Railway, now the Pan Handle Road, at Newark, and the following year went on the B. & O. R. R. as brakeman, and four months later was promoted to conductor, running from Wheeling, Va., to Harper's Ferry. He retained that position from August, 1857, till September, 1865. After the war, in 1865, he returned to Ohio and was employed by the Pan Handle Road as freight conductor, remaining with them till 1872. He ran the second train that went into Pittsburg on that road. Since November, 1872, he has been conductor on the C., H. V. & T. R. R. He has never had any accident on his train and can look back over a period of a quarter of a century spent as conductor with the satisfaction that no one has been injured through any fault of his. He has never been discharged or suspended for misdemeanors, but his changes have been of his own making. Aug. 29, 1854, he married Angeline Cleaves, of Winchester, Ohio. They have nine children—Charles E., yard master of the C., H. V. & T. R. R.; Flora, wife of T. C. Galvin, conductor on the C., H. V. & T. R. R.; Ella, wife of C. H. Myers; D. F., bookkeeper for Croft's Iron Company, Greendale, Ohio; D. M., baggage clerk at Nelsonville, for the C., H. V. & T. R. R.; Hattie, Franklin, Mary and Harry.

George Van Sickle Shafer, merchant, of Nelsonville, is the son of David and Margaret (Sidders) Shafer, and was born near Wilford, N. J., Feb. 19, 1839. When eleven years of age he came with his parents to Ohio, settling in Athens Township, Athens County, where he lived with them until manhood. At the age of thirteen he was afflicted with inflammatory rheumatism, caused by bathing in the early spring, and was for seven years almost a helpless cripple. He was restored to health by being placed under the treatment of Dr. W. P. Johnson, then of Athens, and while being treated by him through his kindness he was enabled to attend the Ohio University, thereby receiving a good business education. At the age of twenty-two he had so recovered that he was employed as a clerk in the store of Isaac Silves, of Athens, six months, when he was employed in the same capacity by D. Zenner & Co., of the same place, with whom he remained three years. In 1865 he went to Salina, Athens County, and engaged in keeping a saloon until 1867, when, having lost all he had saved while clerking, by the assistance of friends he engaged in the grocery business at the same place. In 1878 he removed to Nelsonville, where he is now carrying on a general mercantile business, and besides his residence and business house in Nelsonville he also owns a small farm in the vicinity of Salina. In December, 1869, he was married to Mary M. Shoemaker, of Meigs County, Ohio. They have six children—Edward, Eva May, Luella, Harvey H., Dow Frost, and Clinton Davis. Himself and wife are members of the Christian church of Nelsonville, of which he is a Deacon. He is an Odd Fellow and belongs to the lodge and encampment at Nelsonville.

Burton B. Sheffield, Floodwood, was born on Block Island, R. I., Feb. 7, 1829, and came to Athens County with his parents in the fall of 1836, and settled on Floodwood Creek, in York Township. He was brought up on the old homestead and educated in the Ohio University at Athens, graduating from that institution June 17, 1858, and delivering the valedictory address. While attending college Mr. Sheffield taught at intervals to obtain means with which to defray his college expenses, and thus educated himself. Prior to entering college he worked in the coal mine at Salina for two years. The autumn after graduating he took charge of the Collegiate Institute at New Vienna, Ohio; but on account of his eyes was obliged to abandon all literary pursuits. Mr. Sheffield engaged for several years in the saw-mill business, but is at present engaged in general merchandising, also operating extensively in coal at Floodwood. His bank produces some of the best coal in the Hocking Valley. He owns 700 acres of valuable land, mostly mineral, though part of it is well adapted to farming and stock-raising. He resides on river lot 613, Floodwood, on the same spot that his father settled in 1836. In June, 1861, he married Seviah, daughter of Hosea Guernsey. She was born at Woodstock, Canada, June 10, 1843. They have had six children—Genevra, Homer, Clara, Burton B., Stella S. and Frances May. Joshua Sheffield, father of the above, was also born on Block Island, and came to this county in 1836, where he died in 1861, at the age of fifty-seven years. He married Nancy Briggs. They had seven children, six living—Burton B., Nathaniel B., Benjamin F., Joshua, Almira (now Mrs. Hosea Guernsey of Kansas), and Hannah A. Nathaniel married Alvira Guernsey (now deceased). Mr. Sheffield's grandmother, Mrs. Huldah Briggs, died in 1880, at the age of ninety-nine years.

Jerome S. Shepard, druggist, Nelsonville, was born near McConnelsville, Ohio, Feb. 16, 1849, a son of Aaron H. and Elizabeth J. (Powell) Shepard. When six or seven years old he came with his parents to Nelsonville, where he was educated in the High School. In 1863, when only fourteen years of age, he enlisted in Company K, One Hundred and Sixteenth Ohio Infantry, under Captain John Hull, to serve as a musician, but by order of the War Department disallowing men to be mustered in as musicians, he returned home, after being out with the regiment some four months. He enlisted again in 1864, in Company G, Eighteenth Ohio Infantry, and was sworn in, but the mustering officer at Marietta rejected him on account of his youth. He then returned to Nelsonville and went to work in the mines. In the spring of 1871 he went to Kansas and stopped with an uncle near Columbus, Cherokee County, until the following fall, when he returned to Nelsonville, and in the spring of 1872 became established in the drug business. Nov. 10, 1878, he married H. Addie Lewis, daughter of Moses Lewis, of Nelsonville. They have three children—William Perley, Jerome Blaine and Laura Bernice, twins. Mr. Shepard is a member of the Christian and his wife of the Methodist Episcopal church. He is a member of Philodorean Lodge, No. 157, A. F. & A. M., of Nelsonville.

William P. Shepard, junior member of the firm of Carnes & Shepard, merchants, Nelsonville, was born near McConnelsville, Morgan Co., Ohio, May 8, 1847, a son of Aaron and Elizabeth (Powell) Shepard. When he was seven years of age his parents came to Nelsonville where he was reared, receiving his education in the public schools. In 1862 he enlisted in Company G, Eighteenth Ohio Infantry, and served till the close of the war, being mustered out at Columbus, Ohio, Oct. 25, 1865. Although a mere youth he followed the regiment in all its numerous engagements. At Nashville the regiment went into battle with 200 men and had seventy-five men killed. After his discharge he returned to Nelsonville, and in 1868 took a course at Duff's Commercial College,

Pittsburg. In the fall of 1871 he formed his present partnership with A. H. Carnes in the mercantile business. In April, 1882, he was elected a member of the City Council of Nelsonville, still retaining that position. He belongs to the Masonic fraternity; is a member of Philodorean Lodge, No. 157, Nelsonville, and has been Secretary four years and Junior Warden one year of Logan Chapter, No. 75, and of Athens Commandery, No. 15, being Sword-bearer in the latter. He is also a member of Phil Kearney Post, No. 38, G. A. R. March 21, 1869, Mr. Shepard married Sarah L., daughter of A. H. Carnes. They have four children—Charles J., Grace G., Frank S. and Florence E.

James Sheppard was born near Halifax, Yorkshire Co., England, in 1817. He came to this country in 1841. He located at West Point, N.Y., and was engaged as a master workman in making the pipes for, and laying the foundation of, the Croton River waterworks. He worked on them two years, until they were completed. He was married in 1841 to Miss Margaret Taylor, who was also born in England, near Manchester, in 1819; she came to this country in 1839, and settled near Poughkeepsie, N. Y. They removed to Nelsonville, Athens County, in 1850, and bought property and started an iron foundry. He carried on an able and successful business until his death, in 1862. He left a wife and two children—Thomas and Ellen.

Thomas Sheppard, Superintendent of the coal works, Buchtel Coal and Iron Company, Floodwood, was born near West Point, N. Y., April 14, 1842, a son of James and Margaret (Taylor) Sheppard. He came to Nelsonville with his parents in 1850 and was here reared and educated. When he was fourteen years of age he began to work in his father's foundry, remaining there two years, and then worked for L. D. Poston two years. In October, 1861, he enlisted in Company G, Eighteenth Ohio Infantry, for three years. Six months after enlistment he was promoted to Duty Sergeant and served as Ensign during his term of service. He participated in the battles of Stone River, Davis Cross Roads, Chickamauga and Mission Ridge. He was mustered out of service in the fall of 1864, and returned to Nelsonville and entered the employ of W. B. Brooks, remaining with him till 1873, when he was given the charge of the New York & Ohio Coal Works, in the vicinity of Nelsonville. In 1875 he was employed by Poston & Pendleton as overseer of their mines, and remained with them till 1881, when, in August, he accepted his present position. Jan.

1, 1866, he married Maria, daughter of C. R. Smith, of Chauncey, Ohio. They have four children—Margaret Ellen, James Taylor, Gertrude Esther and Charles Grosvenor. Mr. Sheppard is a member of Hockhocking Lodge, No. 339, I. O. O. F., and of Phil Kearney Post, No. 38, G. A. R.

Andrew Jackson Shrader, M. D., Nelsonville, was born near Plymouth, Washington Co., Ohio, March 7, 1821, where he was reared. He was educated in the school of Amos Miller, in Athens County. He is the son of Philip and Catherine (Montgomery) Shrader, with whom he lived until manhood. He began the study of medicine under Dr. Gilbert, in 1846, finishing his study with Dr. Jacob Myers, of Plymouth, in 1851. He took one course of lectures at Cleveland Medical College, in 1850–'51. He began his practice at Lancaster, Ohio, in 1851, where he remained thirteen years. In 1864 he removed to Logan, where with his medical practice he also practiced law, until the spring of 1868, when he came to Nelsonville, where he has since practiced both medicine and law. In 1874 he was elected Mayor of Nelsonville, serving two years. Nov. 28, 1841, he was married to Sarah Blair, of Belpre, Washington Co., Ohio. They have five children—Jane, wife of Isaac N. Coakley, of Knoxville, Ill.; Catherine wife of J. B. Doughty, of Chauncey, Ohio; Susan, wife of Robert Beattie, of Nelsonville; Eliud, of Hocking County, Ohio, and Sarah, wife of Chas. S. Newton, of Hocking County.

Joseph Slater, a silent partner of the firm of Johnson Brothers & Patterson, coal operators, of Nelsonville, was born in Staffordshire, near Birmingham, England, Jan. 10, 1851. His father, Joseph Slater, dying some three months before his birth, he was reared by his grandfather until he was eighteen years of age. His mother, Mrs. Ann Slater, afterward married Thomas Johnson, and is the mother of Thomas, Charles and Edward Johnson, his half-brothers, with whom he is now associated. He never had any educational advantages, but educated himself so as to be able to do business. At the age of eighteen, in June, 1869, he emigrated to the United States, arriving in New York in July. He then went to Dennison, Summit County, Ohio, where he was employed as a coal-miner until January, 1870. He afterward worked in the Potomac coal mine in Maryland, and in the blast furnaces of the North Chicago Rolling Mills, of Chicago, Ill., until the great fire of 1871, when he came to Nelsonville and was employed in the coal mines of W. B. Brooks & Son. In 1873 he went to England on a visit, returning in 1874, when he was again employed in the same coal mines until September, 1879, when he leased coal land and began to operate in coal-mining. In June, 1880, his half-brothers, Charles, Thomas and Edward Johnson, became associated with him as Johnson Brothers, and in July, 1881, David Patterson, of Columbus, became associated with them under the firm name of Johnson Brothers & Patterson, when they began a more extensive business. Nov. 17, 1875, he was married to Miss Barbara A. Coulter, of Nelsonville, by whom he has three children—Clarence C., Edward Earl and Gertrude Nellie. His wife is a member of the Methodist Episcopal church. He is a Master Mason and member of Philodorean Lodge, No. 157, of Nelsonville.

Joseph Smith, grocer, Nelsonville, was born in Bradford, Yorkshire, England, Sept. 7, 1848, a son of Peter and Mary (Blackburn) Smith. When he was six months old his parents came to the United States, landing in New York, where they remained about a year, and then came to Nelsonville, where he was reared and educated. When he was nine years of age he went to work with his father in the coal mine of M. M. Butt and J. Smith. He afterward worked in the mines and attended school alternately till sixteen years of age. He then was employed by W. B. Brooks till 1873, and from that time till 1882 engaged in different kinds of business with varied success. In the latter year he became established in his present business. In January, 1881, he was appointed Constable of York Township. Nov. 18, 1869, he married Mary Coulter, of Logan, Hocking County. They have five children— Jessie A., William A., Florence A., Joseph L. and Mary H. Mr. Smith is a member of York Lodge, No. 75, K. of P., of which he is Past Chancellor. In 1875 he represented his lodge in the Grand Lodge of Ohio, at Cleveland. He is also an Odd Fellow, a member of Unity Lodge, No. 568, and of Nelsonville Encampment, No. 121, of which he is Past Worthy Patriarch.

George Snowden was born in County Durham, England, May 25, 1839. His father was killed when our subject was an infant by the explosion of a mine. In 1849 his mother came to the United States and located in Meigs County, Ohio, where he lived until 1856, when he went to Peoria County, Ill., and remained until the breaking out of the late civil war. April 16, 1861, he enlisted in the three months' service, but there being a mistake in the mustering papers he only served seven weeks, when he returned to Meigs County, Ohio, and soon after joined Captain William R.

Smith Spencer

Brown's corps, Company E, Fourth Virginia Regiment, and was detailed by General Garfield as a scout, serving in that capacity until the fall of 1862, when he was detailed to drill the officers of the Thirteenth Virginia Regiment, and there received a commission as Second Lieutenant. He afterward acted as spy in the Rebel General Jenkins's camp for a time, after which he took command of the scouts until Sept. 19, 1863, when he was severely injured by the falling of a horse, which disabled him from active duty for a time. July 16, 1864, he entered General McCausland's camp in rebel uniform and gathered some valuable information, but received a severe wound from which he has never recovered. After the close of the war he went to Illinois, and accepted the position as superintendent of two large mines, which he held for seven years. In 1876 he returned to Athens County, where he has since resided. He was married Oct. 12, 1865, to Miss Ellen Thompson, of Middleport, Ohio. They have seven children—Annie L., John G. and Mary C. (twins), Ellen M., Ladie J., William T. and Sadie B. Mr. Snowden is a member of Tom Dew Post, No. 1,516, G. A. R., and the Odd Fellows Lodge, No. 242, Pomeroy.

Smith Spencer was born in Burnley, Lancashire, England, March 22, 1825, a son of Henry and Maria (Smith) Spencer. He received but a meager education in his native town, his father dying when he was an infant. When a very small boy he began to work in the cotton factory. He worked in the different departments of a cotton-cloth manufactory till 1852, when he came to the United States, arriving in New York, June 9 of that year. He located in Tamaqua, Pa., where he worked in a blacksmith's shop a year. In June, 1854, he came to Nelsonville and worked for Joseph H. Thompson till 1856. From that time till 1873 he worked for the late L. D. Poston. He then became a member of the Nelsonville Coal Mining Company. Two years later, in 1875, he went to Monday Creek Furnace, working there about a year. He then worked in the Bessemer mines, and the mines of W. B. Brooks & Son, till December, 1880, when he retired from active business, and is now living quietly in Nelsonville, enjoying the fruits of a well-spent business life. March 22, 1845, he married Susannah Clagg, daughter of Joseph and Jane (Etching) Clagg, of Calne, England. They have seven children—Henry, a druggist of Straitsville, Ohio; Jane, wife of James Winchett, of Athens County; Maria, wife of Clarence Swackhammer, of Nelsonville; Joshua, John, Ella, wife of William Bates, of Nelsonville, and

Ama, at home. Mr. Spencer is a member of Hockhocking Lodge, No. 339, and Nelsonville Encampment, No. 121, I. O. O. F., and is Past Grand and Past Worthy Chief.

Kossuth Tinker, M. D., of Nelsonville, was born in Trimble, Athens Co., Ohio, Feb. 6, 1855. He is the son of Solomon H. and Angeline (Campbell) Tinker, with whom he lived until manhood, and was given a common-school education. In 1874 he began the study of medicine under Drs. Shepard & Dew, at Nelsonville, studying with them three years. He graduated from the Medical College of Ohio, at Cincinnati, Feb. 28, 1877. He then located in Albany, Athens County, and began the practice of medicine, remaining there until February, 1880, when he came to Nelsonville and established himself in his present practice by becoming associated with Dr. W. E. W. Shepard, Tinker remaining with him until December, 1882. Oct. 12, 1882, he married Anna Golden Steadman, of Athens. He is a member of Philodorean Lodge, No. 157, A. F. & A. M., of Nelsonville.

James Alpheus Tobin, attorney at law, and Mayor of Nelsonville, was born at Bremen, Fairfield Co., Ohio. When about four years old he removed with his parents, Elijah and Julia (Williams) Tobin, to Lancaster, Ohio. He lived with them until he was sixteen, educating himself principally by private study. He was thrown on his own resources at sixteen, and maintained himself by working on a farm, and afterward as a stone-cutter. In 1875 he began to teach school, and while teaching to study law under the preceptorship of Hite & Dolson, of Lancaster. He was admitted to the bar by the Supreme Court at Columbus, June 30, 1880. He then came to Nelsonville and established himself in his present practice. He served as Township Clerk of Hocking Township, Fairfield County, from 1878 to 1880, resigning when he came to Nelsonville. In the spring of 1882 he was elected Mayor of Nelsonville for a term of two years. Feb. 1, 1881, he married Miss Ella S. Graybill, of Lancaster. They have one child—Leland.

William Harrison Vorhes, of the firm of Vorhes & Crane, contractors, builders and brickmakers, of Nelsonville, was born in Somerset, Perry Co., Ohio, June 24, 1840. He removed with his parents, Isaiah and Nancy (Hughes) Vorhes, to Hocking County in 1850, where he lived until he was twenty-three years of age. His father being a contractor and brickmaker, he was brought up to that business. In 1864 he began for himself by working for Samuel

Boardman, as a sawyer in his mill near Logan, and was so employed until 1866, when he removed to Nelsonville, where he engaged in mining coal in the mine of W. B. Brooks until 1872. In 1872 he engaged in manufacturing brick at Nelsonville, and also as a contractor for mason work and plastering. In 1876 Elliott Gardner became associated with him, under the firm name of Vorhes & Gardner. In 1878 J. W. Crane succeeded Mr. Gardner, changing the firm to Vorhes & Crane. Mr. Vorhes, either alone or in company with others, has built the walls of a majority of the substantial residences, public and business buildings, machine shops and foundries of Nelsonville and vicinity; among them the Opera House building, Dew Hotel, Methodist Episcopal church, Akron Iron Furnace. April 16, 1864, he was married to Miss Frances Stacy, of Hocking County. They have five children—Wesley, Flora, Vernon Harrison, Charles and Nancy. Mr. Vorhes is a Mason, and an Odd Fellow, and a member of the lodges at Nelsonville.

John Shaw Wallace, machinist, in the employ of W. B. Brooks & Son, coal operators of Nelsonville, was born at Coatbridge, Lanarkshire, Scotland, May 16, 1852, where he was reared, and was educated in Gartsherrie Academy, at Coatbridge. He is the son of William and Jane (Shaw) Wallace. His mother dying when he was seven years old, he was taken by his grandparents, with whom he lived until manhood; when he was thirteen he began to act as an engineer on a small boat, on the Forth & Clyde Canal. He was thus employed four years, when, in 1869, he became a fireman on the North British R. R., and eighteen months later was promoted to locomotive engineer. In May, 1873, he came to the United States, and located at Laurel Hill, Athens Co., Ohio; was variously employed about the mines of the Laurel Hill Coal Company for two years, when, in the summer of 1875, he came to Nelsonville, and was appointed locomotive engineer in the coal mines of T. Longstreth. In 1877 he was given the position of mining machinist for the same company. In the summer of 1880 he returned to Nelsonville and was employed as mine machinist of W. B. Brooks & Son. In 1875 he invented a valve indicator for steam engines, which is now extensively in use. In 1881 he invented an automatic water elevator, which he had patented in August, 1882. In the latter part of 1882 W. B. Brooks, Jr., became associated with him and formed the Wallace Automatic Water Elevator Company of Nelsonville, and they are fast introducing their elevators and bringing them into use in pumping water from mines. Jan. 7, 1872, he was married to Miss Barbara Macauly, of Coatbridge, Scotland. They have five children—William, Jeanetta, Alvin, Sylvia and John. They have lost one, Alexander, who died in 1877, aged nearly three years. Mr. Wallace is a member of the Odd Fellows lodge, at Haydenville, Ohio, and of the Knights of Pythias lodge at Nelsonville, of which he is Past Chancellor commander.

Albert Watson, born in Morgan County, Ohio, March, 1855, is a son of William and Henrietta (Anderson) Watson. When he was eight years of age he came with his father's family to Athens County, where he has since resided. He was reared on a farm and received his education in the common schools. When he was sixteen years of age he commenced to learn telegraphy, and worked for the C. & H. V. R. R. until the fall of 1879, when he came to Buchtel and was employed as salesman in the store of the Akron Iron Company, where he has since been engaged. By attending faithfully to his duties he has been promoted, and is now purchasing agent for the largest mercantile establishment in the Hocking Valley. He was married Dec. 16, 1882, to Miss Alice Mankopf, a native of Athens County.

John Forbes Welch, son of Robert and Nancy (Perry) Welch, was born in Dresden, Muskingum Co., Ohio, Sept. 30, 1837. His mother died when he was nine years of age, and he was then thrown on his own resources. He made his home with a married sister till thirteen years of age, and in April, 1850, came to Nelsonville, walking from Windsor, Ashtabula County. He arrived here in the night, a tired boy and an entire stranger in the city. He soon found employment, and by his earnings supported himself and attended school during the winter months, thus acquiring a good education. At the age of fifteen he began to learn the carpenter's trade with J. C. Barron, remaining with him three years. He then, with Joseph Bates, purchased a canal boat on the Hocking Valley & Ohio Canal, and followed boating till 1857, when, as a result of the financial panic, they lost all they had made and found themselves in debt. He began anew, resuming his trade, and in 1858 paid his indebtedness of $180. In July, 1861, he enlisted in Company C, Thirty-ninth Ohio Infantry, and was elected First Lieutenant of his company. In 1862 he resigned his position and was commissioned First Lieutenant of Company K, One Hundred and Sixteenth Ohio Infantry. In 1864 he was promoted to Captain of Company B, same regiment, and served till the close of the war, being mustered out at Camp Dennison, Ohio,

June, 1865. He was in the battles of New Madrid, Pittsburg Landing, Winchester, all the battles of the Shenandoah Valley, the siege and fall of Richmond, and was present at the surrender of Lee at Appomattox Court-House. In 1866 he formed a partnership with J. A. Mintun in the grocery and provision business. In 1868 he retired from the firm, and in the spring of that year became associated with B. C. Lefever in contracting and building. In 1870 he abandoned the carpenter's trade, and with Captain C. A. Cable, William Comstock and Edward Pendleton formed the Hocking Valley Stave and Lumber Company, of which he was Superintendent. In 1873 the company dissolved, and Mr. Welch speculated in real estate till 1874, when he and A. Poston, W. W. Poston and C arles Robbins formed the Nelsonville Mining Company, of which he is President and Superintendent. In 1880 he with C. P. L. Butle, S. W. Pickering, W. H. Jennings, R. L. Doty, Robert Sheldon and George Hardy formed the Nelsonville Coal and Coke Company. He served as Superintendent till August, 1882, and is now one of the Directors. In the spring of 1882 he became a member and director of the Nelsonville Planing Mill Company. From 1866 till 1871 he was Postmaster of Nelsonville. He has been Marshal, Councilman, Mayor and a member of the School Board of Nelsonville, several terms each. In 1871 he was elected one of the Commissioners of Athens County, serving two terms of three years each. Sept. 11, 1859, he married Sarah A., daughter of Judge Thos. L. Mintun. They have five children— Allie M., wife of L. D. Lampman; Ellen L., Charles E., Lelia A. and Harry R. One son, John W., died Oct. 1, 1871, aged three years. Mr. and Mrs. Welch are members of the Presbyterian church. He is a member of Philodorean Lodge, No. 157, A. F. & A. M.; Hockhocking Lodge, No. 339, I. O. O. F., and Phil Kearney Post, No. 38, G. A. R.

Albert H. Wells, farmer and stock-raiser, was born in Athens County, Ohio, March 18, 1847, the youngest son of Samuel J. Wells. He lived with his parents till manhood, attending and afterward teaching school in Athens County. In 1868 he went to Missouri and remained a year, returning again to Athens County, Sept. 25, 1869. He married Electa, daughter of Thomas M. Boyles. They have one son—Samuel J. Mr. Wells is a member of Nelsonville Lodge, No. 157, A. F. & A. M. He has held the office of Township Treasurer seven terms.

Jesse W. White, farmer and stockraiser, was born in York Township, Athens County, Oct. 29, 1843, a son of Joseph and Margaret (Allen) White. He was reared on a farm and educated in the common schools. He enlisted Aug. 3, 1862, in Company A, Ninety-second Ohio Infantry, and participated in many hard-fought battles. Among the more prominent were: Hoover's Gap, Chickamauga, Chattanooga, Mission Ridge, the Atlanta campaign, and with Sherman on his march to the sea, serving until the close of the war, when he was discharged, June 22, 1865, and returned to his native county. He was married March 15, 1866, to Miss Angeline S. A. Wilt, a native of Hocking County. They have had eight children, seven now living—Ida V., Mintor L., Emma M., Earl R., Clarence R., Rolley A., and Warren H. Mr. White has a farm of 285 acres of improved land under a high state of cultivation.

Amos Joseph Wilson, junior partner of the firm of Wilson Brothers, was born at Wolf's Plains, Athens County, Sept. 10, 1852. He is the youngest of the six sons of Eben and Jane C. (Matheny) Wilson, with whom he lived till he was eighteen years of age, receiving his education in the district school of his native place. On leaving home, he was employed in the Brook's coal mines at Nelsonville for two years, after which he worked at the carpenter's trade for three years. From 1875 until 1881 he was again engaged in coal-mining, after which he became associated with his brothers in the mercantile business at Nelsonville. On April 4, 1875, he married Miss Sadie, daughter of Philemon and Mary (White) Crawford, of Pennsylvania. Their children are—Blanche Nell and Mabel Coe. He is a Knight of Pythias, of York Lodge, No. 75, of Nelsonville.

Eben Wilson, son of Eben and Jane C. (Matheny) Wilson, was born at Wolf's Plains, Athens County, June 17, 1849. When twelve years of age, he went to Athens and began to learn the trade of printing in the office of the *Messenger* with Thomas Wilds, and continued with his successor, Jesse Van Law. He then worked in the *Journal* office for a time, and on Sept. 20, 1869, he came to Nelsonville, and was employed in the coal mines till 1873. In the fall of 1874 he went in partnership with his brother Josiah in the boot and shoe business, which they carried on till the spring of 1878, when they engaged in general merchandising. He was married to Miss Allie Austin, of Richmond, May 5, 1881. Mr. Wilson is a Knight of Pythias, of York Lodge, No. 75, of Nelsonville, of which he is Past Chancellor. He has represented his lodge for two years in the Grand Lodge of Ohio.

Jehiel Gregory Wilson, operator in coal, Nelsonville, was born at Wolf's Plains, Athens Co., Ohio, May 13, 1834, where he was reared. He is the eldest of six sons of Eben and Jane C. (Matheny) Wilson, with whom he lived until he was twenty years of age, and was educated in the common school, also attending the Ohio University at Athens two years. After leaving the University, in 1856, he taught school in Athens County one year. May 10, 1857, he married Miss Jennie M. Brown, of Athens County, daughter of Ephraim Brown, of Sunday Creek, and went to Zaleski, Ohio, and engaged in dealing in lumber for a year. In 1858 he went to Flora, Clay Co., Ill., and engaged in farming until 1862, when he was employed as a carpenter on the Ohio & Mississippi Railroad until 1866, when he returned to Athens County and engaged in the manufacture of wagons and carriages for twelve years. In 1878 he located at Nelsonville, where he kept a hotel one year, when he engaged in his present business. He has five children— Ota, Lincoln, Charles, George and Leon. Himself and wife are members of the Methodist Episcopal church, of Nelsonville. He has been a Class-Leader for six years and Sunday-school Superintendent ten years.

Josiah Wilson, of the mercantile firm of Wilson Brothers, of Nelsonville, was born at Wolf's Plains, Athens Co., Ohio, Sept. 20, 1843, where he was reared and educated in the district school. He is the son of Eben and Jane C. (Matheny) Wilson, with whom he lived until he was twenty years of age, when he went to Hocking County and was employed in the Floodwood coal mines eleven years. In 1874 he came to Nelsonville and opened a boot and shoe store, and soon after his brother Eben became associated with him under the firm name of Wilson Brothers, and in 1882 Amos J., a younger brother, became a partner in the firm. Oct. 19, 1865, he was married to Miss Emma Burrell, of Nelsonville. They are the parents of two children—Harry L. and Clarence Almond. He and wife are members of the Methodist Episcopal church, of Nelsonville. He has been a member of that body for twenty-one years, and has been a Class-Leader about six years. He is a Knight of Pythias, a member of York Lodge, No. 75, of Nelsonville. In 1878 he was elected a member of the School Board of Nelsonville, and re-elected in 1882.

Joseph Wolf was born in Porter County, Ind., Jan. 1, 1836, a son of William and Mary (Matheny) Wolf. His grandfather, Christopher Wolf, came to Athens County in 1797 and settled on what has long been known as Wolf's Plains, near the city of Athens. He was prominently identified with the early settlement of Athens County. Our subject was brought by his parents to Athens County when an infant, and lived here till six years of age. His parents then removed to Hocking County where he was reared and educated. Upon reaching his majority he bought the farm where he now resides, in York Township. He is one of the most successful farmers of the township, his farm showing that a man of superior judgment and skillful management is at its head. In connection with farming he has been extensively engaged in the manufacture of lumber, and for five years was superintendent of the coal mines at Old Floodwood. Mr. Wolf is a practical business man, and through his own industry has accumulated his large property. He has 600 acres of fine land, valuable both for agriculture and mineral resources. His home is beautifully located in the heart of the Hocking Valley coal regions. His residence, situated in the valley, surrounded by natural shade and ornamental trees, his commodious stables and farm buildings, indicate the thrifty farmer. Nov. 15, 1857, Mr. Wolf married Sarah N., daughter of James Rodgers, who was prominently identified with the early settlement of Hocking Valley. Twelve children have been born to them, eleven still living—Frank L., Eugene O., Charles J., Sylvester E., Lizzie B., James W., Dora M., Homer V., Minnie F., Nellie B., Mertie A. Cora A. died in infancy. Mr. Wolf is giving his children the advantage of a good practical education. He is a public spirited man and subscribes liberally to all laudable enterprises that benefit and interest his township. He and his wife have been members of the Methodist church twenty-eight years and take an interest in all that pertains to their church. Mr. Wolf is a member of Philodorean Lodge, No. 157, A. F. & A. M., and Hockhocking Lodge, No. 339, I. O. O. F.

William S. Wollett, son of Peter and Ann Eliza (Davis) Wollett, was born March 2, 1846, in York Township. His parents came from Bedford County, Pa., in 1832, and located in Athens Township, Athens Co., Ohio. In 1844 they came to York Township, where William S. was reared and educated. He enlisted Aug. 2, 1862, in Company A, Ninety-second Ohio Infantry. He remained in West Virginia till the spring of 1863 and then joined the Army of the Cumberland and participated in many hard-fought battles, among them Chattanooga, Mission Ridge, Lookout Mountain, Atlanta, and was with Sherman to the sea. He was mustered out June 22, 1865, and returned to Athens County. He soon after took a trip through the Western States, returning in May, 1867, when he purchased the farm where he has since resided. He has 167 acres of good land and one of the finest orchards in the township. He was married April 18, 1868, to Lucinda J. Haines, of Athens County. They are the parents of one child which died March 6, 1869. Mr. and Mrs. Wollett are members of the Christian church. He is a member of Philodorean Lodge, No. 157, A. F. & A. M., and Hockhocking Lodge, No. 399, I. O. O. F.

Lewis Clinton Woodard, a clerk with Parker & McGill, of Nelsonville, was born in Starr Township, Hocking County, April 27, 1851. He is the fourth of five sons of Ichabod and Eleanor (Nelson) Woodard, his mother being a daughter of Daniel Nelson, the founder of Nelsonville. He first attended the district school of the township, after which he went to Union High School at Logan, completing his education at the Ohio University at Athens. He began to teach in 1871, and taught in several schools in Hocking County, until 1881, when he came to Nelsonville and engaged in butchering, continuing in that business till the spring of 1883. He then accepted his present position. He was married April 26, 1881, to Miss Jennie Gilliam, of Nelsonville, and both are members of the Methodist Episcopal church of that place.

W. N. Woodard was born in Starr Township, Sept. 29, 1841. He is a son of Ichabod and Eleanor Woodard. He is a grandson of Daniel Nelson, the founder of Nelsonville, and one of the early settlers and old pioneers of this county, who died about 1835 or 1836. Ichabod Woodard died on his farm in Starr Township, March 16, 1868. Mr. Woodard received a common education in the public schools of his township. He enlisted July 25, 1862, at the age of twenty-one years, in Company E, Ninetieth Ohio Infantry, and was in several battles of importance, under General Sherman. March 25, 1875, he was married to Violet Smith, a daughter of John and Sarah Smith, of Moundsville, W. Va. They are the parents of four children, three of which are living—Estella V., Lulu and Clyde B. John C. died when he was about six weeks old.

CHAPTER XVIII.

AMES TOWNSHIP — A TOWNSHIP THAT HAD A HISTORY TO RECORD.

THE ARRIVAL OF THE PALEFACES—WHO THEY WERE—THE AREA IN 1805—SQUIRREL AND CROW SCALPS—A FEW ITEMS—RELIGIOUS WHISKY—POPULATION—AREA AND PRODUCTION—BOUNDARY AND VALUATION — WESTERN LIBRARY ASSOCIATION—ITS HISTORY — TOWNSHIP OFFICERS—1802 TO 1883—AMESVILLE — SOMEWHAT HISTORIC—WHEN FOUNDED—GROWTH AND BUSINESS INTERESTS— POSTOFFICE — ACADEMY — PRESBYTERIAN CHURCH — METHODIST CHURCH—BIOGRAPHICAL.

OLD SETTLERS.

The first visit to Ames Township was in the spring of 1797, by Lieutenant Geo. Ewing and Judge Ephraim Cutler; and their second visit in the fall of the same year, Captain Brown accompanying them. In the following spring Lieutenant Ewing located the first farm or residence in the township, which was on the 1st of March, 1798, followed by Judge Cutler and Captain Benjamin Brown. These were the first three, but Ewing located first, and that farm is now known as the Tom Gardner farm. Judge Cutler settled on his place in 1799 and Wm. P. Cutler owns the homestead. Captain Brown settled at the same time, and his farm is now the Daniel Fleming farm. Just how many came the next few years is hard to tell, but when Ames Township was organized in 1802, the following were citizens of the township but widely located: Samuel Brown, Nathan Woodberry, Sylvanus Ames, Christopher Herrold, Jonathan Swett, Daniel Weethee, Josiah True, Daniel Converse, Ambrose Evarts, Benjamin L. Brown, Joseph Pugsley, Alvin Bingham, Benjamin Brown, John Brown, Joshua Wyatt, Jacob Boyles, Edmund Dorr, Wm. Brown, Silas Dean, Azel Johnson, George Wolf, Noah Linscott, Edmund Neal, Solomon Tuttle, Oheniel Tuttle. Jonathan Swett, Jr., Stephen Swett, David Boyles, Ezra Green, Jason Rice, John Brown, Jr., Isaac Stephens. In 1804 the following were residents: Hosea Neal, Samuel McCune, John McCune, Wm. Green, Nehemiah Davis, Nehemiah Davis,

Jr., Moses Kay, Abel Glazier, Moses Everett, Thomas M. Hamilton, Upton Farmer, Frederic Fought. There were others who were residents of the township as then formed, but they were too widely scattered to be named.

Ames Township then comprised not only its present limits as well as the whole north tier of townships in the county, but it had within its limits the present townships of Ward, Green and Starr, now in Hocking County; Marion and Homer townships, in Morgan County. The following townships were taken from Ames in this county, viz.: York, Trimble, Dover and Bern. Its boundary was then described as follows: "Beginning at the northeast corner of the county, thence running west to the northwest corner of said county; thence south to the southwest corner of said township 12, range 16; thence east to the southeast corner of township 7, range 12; thence north to the place of beginning." This was a territory but a trifle less in extent than the present area of the whole county of Athens, but was rapidly lessened on the organization of Hocking County, Jan. 3, 1818, and Morgan County, March 1, 1818, which was then followed by the reorganization of township, when, in about 1851, after Vinton County had been organized, Athens County had been reduced to her present size. The first meeting of the Township Board of Trustees was June 1, 1802, at the house of Sylvanus Ames; in 1803 the next annual meeting, on March 7, was at the house of John Swett, and from this time up to the year 1812 the meetings were held at the house of Christopher Herrold.

Quite an influx of settlers came in the following years, and in 1805 to 1809 these old-time settlers made their home in the township, to-wit: Reuben Hurlbut, Reuben I. Davis, Samuel Beaumont, Joseph Fuller, Samuel Lewis, John Mansfield, Joseph Ballard, Robert Palmer, Zebulon Griffin, Silas Dean, Jonathan Watkense, Jacob Haysenton, David Rathbern, Luther Danielson, William Beckerstaff, Abner Connett, John Wright, Henry Johnson, Joseph Linscott, Amos Linscott, Samuel Mansfield, Jr., Jeremiah Cass, William H. Hasse and Uriah Tippy.

In 1807 the trustees decided to give a premium on squirrel and crow scalps, shot between the first day of February and the first day of July, to be three cents for squirrels and six cents for crows if shot within, as was worded, "two miles of a plantation." These had become a pest to the growing corn, and it was proposed to lessen their number.

SOME ITEMS.

The first road-tax was levied in 1805, and it was the same amount as the county tax. They could pay the cash, or they had the privilege of working it out on the road at 75 cents per day and board themselves.

The first white child born in Ames Township, or in Athens County, was Margaret Strong, daughter of a Judge Strong, and the birth of this child is given as 1797. There is evidently a slight mistake of date here. Ames Township was not settled, so far as known, until 1798, although Cutler and Ewing visited it in 1797. The date is probably 1799, for up to January of that year there were only three or four families in the township. Two weeks later Judge Gustavus A. Evarts, a son of Ambrose Evarts, was born, and he was the first white male child born in the township or county. At his birth there were but seven families, and Mr. Evarts's was one of them, then in the township. The name of Judge Strong was not among the early settlers. It is therefore impossible to vouch for the absolute truthfulness of the above statement, but it is probable that it is true and the date 1799.

The first physician known to have practiced in the township was a Dr. John Baker, whose first case was in the Ewing family, in 1801.

The first horse-mill was owned by Christopher Herrold. This was in 1800 or 1801. Up to that time, or the two previous years, hand-mills had been used, except when they took a trip of from fifteen to twenty miles to get their corn ground. Henry Barrows put up the first water-mill on Federal Creek about 1801.

The first school was taught in the township in 1802, by Mr. Charles Cutler, and the children of all the early settlers attended. It was here the Hon. Thomas Ewing, so prominent both in State and nation as a lawyer and statesman, first received the rudiments of education.

The first marriage was that of Betsy Wyatt and William Parker, May 13, 1802.

Judge Cutler, one of the most prominent men of that early day, and who, though living there but a few years, left the impress of his strong mind upon the infant settlement, removed from the township, in 1806, to Washington County, as also did Lieutenant George Ewing, the father of Thomas, who made Perry County, Ind., his home in 1818.

RELIGIOUS WHISKY.

The pioneers did not at all times have preaching among them, but many of them at that day, like Deacon Wyatt, could give the settlers some sound advice and religious teaching. The Revs. Austin Thomas and Dickson were among the first resident preachers, but the circuit riders made their visits at times for many years before the settlers could afford stated preaching. Walker's History gives this novel incident connected with early preaching among the pioneer settlements:

"An incident connected with early preaching among the pioneer settlements may be mentioned. A neighborhood in the lower settlement in Ames Township, in which 'Squire John Brown lived, secured the services of Elder Asa Stearns, a Free-Will Baptist, to preach for them once a month during the year, to be paid with *three barrels of whisky*. Mr. Stearns had an arrangement with Ebenezer Currier, at Athens, to take the whisky and allow him therefor $24 to be credited to him toward the farm he had bought of Judge Currier. The contract was faithfully carried out on all hands, Elder Stearns visiting his little congregation every third Saturday of each month during the year, at the end of which he received his salary in whisky and made the transfer of it as agreed to Judge Currier."

So that in this case it was in the use and not the abuse of whisky which did a power of good in that community for twelve months. So whisky with its manifold sins had one credit mark on the right side of the ledger.

Sylvanus Ames was another of the old pioneers whose rugged sense and energy of character made a marked influence in the community. He was naturally a leader among men, and yet he scarcely knew it, and neither did his neighbors, in that sense, yet Sylvanus Ames was ever to the front of progress, and his neighbors followed. Judge Ames served in nearly every official capacity in the history of his town and county, and when a member of the Legislature he soon became noted for his strong sense and his ability to command a hearing and a following, and his house was for many years the headquarters for the leaders of Southern Ohio, for the planning of their political movements. He died in his prime, being only in the fifty-third year of his age. His death occurred Sept. 23, 1823.

POPULATION.

The township, like the county, gradually progressed, and the population of the latter was given as 2,787 in 1810. Ames Township must then have had a population of between 700 and 800. Before the census of 1820 came around, she had been shorn of her territory lying in Hocking and Morgan counties. The census gave her 388 males and 333 females, or a total of 721 inhabitants. The next ten years, or in 1830, she gained only 136, but this was again owing to loss of territory in a measure. Still it was not a decade of progress in either population or wealth. The stagnation which has thus shown to have ruled for several years was changed and the growth between 1830 and 1840 proved that the people had thrown off their sloth and were again on the highroad to prosperity. The gradual increase of the population of Ames Township from 1820 to 1880 inclusive is here given, and as the ratio of wealth has rather more than kept even with that of population the material progress of the township can be pretty accurately seen by decades. The figures are as follows:

CENSUS RETURNS.

Population of Ames Township, 1820, 721; 1830, 857; 1840, 1,431; 1850, 1,482; 1860, 1,335; 1870, 1,229; 1880, 1,392. These figures show no rapid progress, and for a couple of decades a loss. This is, however, but the result of late years in the purely agricultural townships of the counties, where the development of the mineral resources of the county has assumed greater proportions. There is coal in Ames Township, but it is not mined to any great extent.

PRODUCTION AND AREA.

It was not until 1850 that the boundary lines of Athens County were finally established, and therefore many of the township lines were changed from time to time by the establishment of new independent municipalities. Undoubtedly for the convenience of the people a congressional township, in size, is the best, or six miles square of territory. This at last became the size of Ames Township, or an area of 23,040 acres of land. It is in the valley of Federal Creek and its branches, rich and fertile, and the hills good grass and pasture lands. There is plenty of water, being beside Federal Creek, McDougal Creek, and other streams and springs innumerable. This gives it value for stock-raising purposes, and the people have taken advantage of this feature, for it is the largest stock-raising township in the county. The only returns at hand were the assessment returns of 1867, when Ames Township had 14,129 sheep, nearly double any other township in the county, the next highest being Alexander, with 7,808. It was second in horses, having 552, Lodi having 564, yet the assessed valuation of the former exceeded the latter. This was also the case with cattle. Lodi led with 1,917, assessed at only $28,691; Rome, 1,527, assessed at $23,732, while Ames, with 1,513, was assessed at $37,176, nearly $4,000 more than any other township in the county. This would seem to prove that the farmers of Ames were raising a better class of stock than any of its sisters.

BOUNDARY.

Through the years of trials and tribulations and the curtailment of her territory, Ames at last emerged out of the wreck a township on the north border of the county, and second from the eastern border of the county, reserving to herself the location and grounds of her first settlement, which through the prominence and ability of her early pioneers had become historic. Ames Township is bounded on the north by Morgan County, east by Bern Township, south by Canaan, and west by Dover Township.

The assessed valuation in 1881 was a total of $530,990, and in 1882 was $522,561, the difference being a trifle less on assessment in some items. It is the fifth township in the county in wealth, while it is the tenth in population.

WESTERN LIBRARY ASSOCIATION.

The Pioneer Association of Athens County published, about the close of 1882, a carefully prepared and neatly printed "Memorial and History of the 'Western Library Association.'" From this memorial we condense the following brief account:

The Western Library Association, or as it was sometimes called in later years, in half-derision, the "Coonskin Library," originated in 1801, in what is now Ames Township, Athens County, and the founders were an offshoot from Marietta, where the first settlement in Ohio was made. In the chapter on Ames Township an account is given of the early settlement made by George Ewing, Judge Ephraim Cutler, Captain Benjamin Brown, Sylvanus Ames, Deacon Joshua Wyatt and others. The hardships of pioneer work, some of which are portrayed in the chapter on "Pioneer Life," are well known to all our readers. One would think that under such circumstances there could be but little time or energy left for the greater work of providing for the wants of their higher nature. Not so with these hardy pioneers. They seemed to realize that they were founding an empire, that they were engaged in laying one of the foundation-stones, on which the great States of the Northwest Territory were to be erected ; that they were making history, to be read with profit by posterity ; that a little taper light to be kindled by them in this obscure pioneer settlement would in time unite with other lights, and illumine the great Northwest. They apparently acted under an inspiration like that of the poet, who describes the night ride of Paul Revere, rallying his neighbors to the battle of Concord.

> "And yet through the gloom and the light,
> The fate of a nation was riding that night;
> And the spark struck out by that steed in his flight,
> Kindled the land into flame with its heat."

In 1803 the inhabitants of Ames assembled in public meeting, to consider the subject of roads, which, having been disposed of, the intellectual wants of the settlement became a topic of discussion. They were entirely isolated and remote from established schools and libraries, and felt keenly the necessity of providing some means for their own and their children's mental development. The establishment of a library was suggested, and all agreed that this was the readiest way to meet the case, provided funds could be raised and the books obtained. The scarcity of money seemed an almost insuperable obstacle. The little transactions of the colony were carried on almost wholly by barter and exchange in kind. In this great scarcity of money the purchase of books for a library seemed like an impossibility; but the subject was canvassed by the meeting, and it was resolved to attempt it. Before the end of the year, by dint of economy, and using every ingenious device to procure necessary funds, a sum of money was raised. Some of the settlers were good hunters, and there being a ready cash market for furs and skins, which were bought by the agents of John Jacob Astor and others, these easily paid their subscriptions. Samuel Brown was just ready to make a business trip to New England. He was furnished with letters to Rev. Thaddeus M. Harris and Rev. Dr. Cutler, who accompanied Mr. Brown to Boston, and selected a valuable collection of fifty-one books. These books cost

$73.50, and comprised the following: Robertson's North America; Harris's Encyclopedia, four volumes; Morse's Geography, two volumes; Adams's Truth of Religion; Goldsmith's Works, four volumes; Evelina, two volumes; Children of the Abbey, two volumes; Blair's Lectures; Clark's Discourses; Ramsey's American Revolution, two volumes; Goldsmith's Animated Nature, four volumes; Playfair's History of Jacobinism, two volumes; George Barnwell; Camilla, three volumes; Beggar Girl, three volumes, and some others. Later purchases included Shakespeare, Don Quixote, Lock's Essays, Scottish Chiefs, Josephus, Smith's Wealth of Nations, Spectator, Plutarch's Lives, Arabian Nights, Life of Washington, etc.

This was the first public library formed in the Northwest Territory, though not, as some have supposed, the first incorporated. The "Dayton Library Society" was incorporated Feb. 21, 1805; a library "at Granville, in the County of Fairfield," Jan. 26, 1807; one at Newton, Hamilton Co., Feb. 10, 1808. The Western Library Association was incorporated by an act passed Feb. 19, 1810.

On the 2d day of February, 1804, at the house of Christopher Herrold, articles of association were regularly entered into for the government of the Library Association. The amount of a share was fixed at $2.50, and the owner was required to pay in for the use of the library 25 cents additional every year on each share. The names of the subscribers to the Articles of Association, with the number of shares taken by each, were as follows: Ephraim Cutler, 4 shares; Jason Rice, 2; Sylvanus Ames, 2; Benjamin L. Brown, 1; Martin Boyles, 1; Ezra Green, 1; George Ewing, 1; John Brown, Jr., 1; Josiah True, 1; George Ewing, Jr., 1; Daniel Weethee, 2; Timothy Wilkins, 2; Benjamin Brown, 1; Samuel Brown, 2d, 1; Samuel Brown, Sr., 1; Simon Converse, 1; Christopher Herrold, 1; Edmund Dorr, 1; George Wolf, 1; Nathan Woodbury, 1; Joshua Wyatt, 1; George Walker, 1; Elijah Hatch, 1; Zebulon Griffin, 1; Jehiel Gregory, 1; George Castle, 1; Samuel Brown, 1. Among the subscribers in later years appear the names of Ezra Walker, Othniel Nye, Sally Rice, Lucy Ames, John M. Hibbard, Seth Child, Ebenezer Champlin, Amos Linscott, Elisha Lattimer, Nehemiah Gregory, Thomas Ewing, Jason Rice, Cyrus Tuttle, Perley Brown, Robert Fulton, R. S. Lovell, Michael Tippie, and James Pugsley.

The library has long since ceased to exist as such, and has been succeeded by other more modern sources of information. The books had accumulated to several hundred volumes—a considerable library for the place and period. Many years later it was divided, and part taken to Dover Township (where some of the original stockholders lived), where it formed the nucleus of another library, which was incorporated by act of the Legislature passed Dec. 21, 1830. The portion retained in Ames Township, was sold by the shareholders in the year 1860 or 1861 to Messrs. J. H. Glazier, A. W. Glazier and E. H. Brawley, and they afterward sold it to Hon. W. P. Cutler, of Washington County. In conclusion we quote from the memorial before mentioned:

"The simple history of this unpretending Library Association is sufficient to challenge the admiration and homage of every true American. It was one of the springs which have made up the great ocean of our State and national prosperity. It is to be hoped that an effort may be made to redeem these old historic books, such of them as can be found, and place them in proper form in some secure public place. The worm-eaten and dilapidated volumes are intrinsically of little value, but they are priceless as mementoes of the past."

OFFICIALS OF AMES TOWNSHIP.

1802.—Trustees, Samuel Brown, Nathan Woodbury and George Ewing; Clerk, Daniel Weethee; Overseers of the Poor, Samuel Brown, Josiah True; Fence Viewers, Joseph Pugsley, Nathan Woodbury and Jno. Sweet; House Appraiser, Christopher Herrold; Lister, Daniel Converse; Constables, Daniel Converse and Sylvanus Ames; Supervisors, Samuel Brown and Benjamin L. Brown.

1803.—Trustees, Benjamin Brown, Sylvanus Ames and Daniel Weethee; Clerk, George Ewing; Overseers Poor, Nathan Woodbury and Joshua Wyatt; Fence Viewers, Jno. Brown, Benjamin L. Brown and Samuel Brown; House Appraisers, Jacob Boyles and Edmund Dorr; Lister, Josiah True; Constables, William Brown and Josiah True; Supervisors, Jno. Brown, William Brown and Josiah True. First Grand Jurors from this township were: Silas Dean and Nathan Woodbury; and Petit Jurors, Azel Johnson, George Wolf and John Brown. The same year Ephraim Cutler and Samuel Brown were elected Justices of the Peace. The first Justice of the Peace was Alvin Bingham in 1802.

1804.—Trustees, David Boyles, Azel Johnson and Nathan Woodbury; Clerk, Benjamin L. Brown; Overseers Poor, David Boyles and Daniel Weethee; Fence Viewers, Benjamin Brown,

Joshua Wyatt and Christopher Herrold; House Appraisers, Silas Dean and Ezra Green; Lister, Ezra Green; Constables, Hosea Neal and William Green; Supervisors, Samuel McCune, Jason Rice, Edmund Dorr and Edmund Neal; Treasurer, Sylvanus Ames—first Township Treasurer.

1805.—Trustees, Benjamin Brown, Daniel Weethee and Josiah True; Clerk, Harris Parsons; Treasurer, Sylvanus Ames; Overseers Poor, Ephraim Cutler and Nathan Woodbury; Fence Viewers, Moses Everett and Isaac Stephens; House Appraisers, Ephraim Cutler and Josiah True; Lister, Josiah True; Supervisors, Joshua Wyatt, Abel Glazier, Moses Kay, Hosea Neal and Daniel Weethee.

1806.—Trustees, Ephraim Cutler, John Brown and Daniel Weethee; Clerk, George Walker; Treasurer, Ephraim Cutler; Overseers Poor, Edmund Neal and Jacob Boyles; Fence Viewers, George Wolf and Joshua Wyatt; House Appraisers, Christopher Herrold and Martin Boyles; Lister, Martin Boyles; Constables, Josiah True and Thomas M. Hamilton; Supervisors, Upton Farmer, Nathan Woodberry, William Brown, Isaac Stevens, John McCune, Ezra Green and Frederic Fought.

1807.—Trustees, Abel Glazier, Benjamin Davis and Liberty Griffin; Clerk, Benjamin Davis; Treasurer, Seth Fuller; Overseers Poor, Abram Pugsley and Samuel Beaumont; Fence Viewers, Nathan Woodberry and George Wolf; House Appraisers, Josiah True and Martin Boyles; Lister, Martin Boyles; Supervisors, William Brown, George Walker, Joseph Pugsley, John Brown, Joseph Fuller, Joseph Ballard, John Mansfield and Thomas M. Hamilton.

1808.—Trustees, Robert Palmer, Reuben Davis and George Walker; Clerk, Martin Boyles; Treasurer, Zebulon Griffin; Overseers Poor, Seth Fuller and John Brown; Fence Viewers, Benjamin Davis and Samuel McCune; House Appraisers, Nathan Woodberry and John Brown, Jr.; Lister, John Brown, Jr.; Constables, Martin Boyles and Reuben I. Davis; Supervisors, Christopher Herrold, Horace Parsons, Samuel Lewis, Reuben Hurlbut, Joshua Wyatt, Silas Dean, Zebulon Griffin and Abel Glazier.

1809.—Trustees, Seth Fuller, Josiah True and George Wolf; Clerk, George Walker; Treasurer, Zebulon Griffin; Overseers Poor, Robert Palmer and James Fuller; Fence Viewers, Abram Pugsley and Ezra Green. House Appraiser, Jason Rice; Lister, Zebulon Griffin; Constables, John McCune and Zebulon Griffin; Supervisors, Othniel Tuttle, Thomas M. Hamilton, William Brown, Samuel McCune, Ezra Green, Samuel Beaumont, Azel Johnson, Reuben Hurlbut and Samuel Mansfield, Jr.

1810.–Trustees, Seth Fuller, Josiah True and George Wolf; Clerk, George Walker; Treasurer, Zebulon Griffin; Overseers Poor, Joshua Wyatt and Robert Palmer; Fence Viewers, Zebulon Griffin and George Walker; House Appraisers, Christopher Herrold and Zebulon Griffin ; Lister, Zebulon Griffin; Constables, Nehemiah Davis, Jr., Zebulon Griffin and James Pugsley; Supervisors, George Ewing, Jr., George Walker, Joshua Wyatt, John Brown, Martin Boyles, Luther Danielson, Daniel Weethee, Solomon Tuttle, Reuben Hurlbut, Joseph Fuller and William Beckerstaff.

1811.—Trustees, Sylvanus Ames, George Ewing and Daniel Weethee; Clerk, George Walker; Treasurer, Seth Fuller; Overseers Poor, Joshua Wyatt and Nathan Woodbury; Fence Viewers, Uriah Tippy and Abel Glazier; House Appraisers, Samuel Brown and Ezra Walker; Lister, Ezra Walker; Constables, William Henry Hass, James Pugsley and Jeremiah Cass; Supervisors, John Wright, Henry Johnson, Abner Connett, Joseph Fuller, Josiah True, Azel Johnson, Reuben I. Davis; District No. 1, Jason Rice; District No. 2, Samuel Brown; District No. 3, Samuel McCune; District No. 4, Martin Boyles; District No. 5, Ezra Green.

1812.—Trustees, Joshua Wyatt, Seth Fuller and John Brown, Jr.; Clerk, George Walker; Treasurer, John Brown; Overseers Poor, Joseph Linscott and Amos Linscott; Fence Viewers, Ezra Green and Samuel McCune; House Appraisers, William Brown and John Boyles ; Lister, John Boyles ; Constables, Jeremiah Cass and John Boyles ; Supervisors, District No. 1, Jason Rice; District No. 2, Abel Glazier ; District No. 3, John McCune; District No. 4, Joab Hoisington; District No. 5, Ezra Green; District No. 6, David Rathburn; District No. 7, Elisha Alderman, Jr.

TRUSTEES SINCE 1813.

1813–1815, Ezra Green, Seth Fuller and John Brown, Jr.; 1816, Jason Rice, Russell S. Lovell and Daniel Phillips; 1817, Sylvanus Ames, Russell S. Lovell and Jason Rice; 1818, Jacob Boarman, Russell S. Lovell, Ezra Green; 1819, Jacob Boarman, John Brown, Ezra Green; 1820, Seth Fuller, James Cable, James Mitchell; 1821, Seth Fuller, James Cable and Ezra Walker; 1822–'23, John Wyatt, Charles Cutler, Alanson Hibbard; 1824, John

Wyatt, Jacob Boarman, David Trowbridge; 1825, John Columbia, John Boyles, John M. Hibbard; 1826, Charles Cutler, Elisha McEvers, Morris Bryson; 1827-'28, Sabinus Rice, L. G. Brown, Morris Bryson; 1829, Absalom Boyles, Jacob Boarman, John B. Brown; 1830, James Brawley, Jacob Boarman, Gulliver Dean; 1831, Daniel Cable, George Black, Gulliver Dean; 1832, Silvanus Howe, George Black, Jonathan Buzzard; 1833, John Carter, Sabinus Rice, Jonathan Buzzard; 1834, John Carter, Absalom Boyles, Silvanus Howe; 1835, L. G. Brown, John B. Miller, Silvanus Howe; 1836, L. G. Brown, Lewis Rathburn, Daniel S. McDougal; 1837, R. G. Carter, Lewis Rathburn, Daniel S. McDougal; 1838, R. G. Carter, Charles Cutler, Daniel S. McDougal; 1839, Daniel Rose, William Robinson, Daniel S. McDougal; 1840 -'45, John T. Glazier, John Carter, James G. Owen; 1846-'49, John T. Glazier, D. S. McDougal, Solomon Koons; 1850, George Linscott, D. S. McDougal, Solomon Koons; 1851-'52, James Patterson, D. S. McDougal, Solomon Koons; 1853, James Patterson, G. M. McDougal, Solomon Koons; 1854-'55, James Patterson, G. M. McDougal, George Linscott; 1856-'57, Almon Henry, G. M. McDougal, George Linscott; 1858, John E. Vore, G. M. McDougal, George Linscott; 1859-'60, John E. Vore, F. L. Junod, George Linscott; 1861, Moses Curtis, Solomon Koons, E. P. Henry; 1862, F. L. Junod, C. J. Brown, G. W. Wright; 1863, F. L. Junod, C. J. Brown, C. H. Wyatt; 1864-'65, N. P. Hoisington, C. J. Brown, Daniel Fleming; 1866, N. P. Hoisington, Almon Henry, Daniel Fleming; 1867, N. P. Hoisington, Edmund Wheeler, O. N. Owen; 1868, N. P. Hoisington, Daniel Fleming, Ezra Wolfe; 1869, N. P. Hoisington, Daniel Fleming, Ezra Wolfe; 1870, N. P. Hoisington, Daniel Fleming, Ezra Wolfe; 1871, N. P. Hoisington, Daniel Fleming, W. G. Finch; 1872, Fred Stalder, Daniel Fleming, W. G. Finch; 1873, Fred Stalder, Daniel Fleming, Silas Sayres; 1874, Fred Stalder, Daniel Fleming, Silas Sayres; 1875, Fred Stalder, Daniel Fleming, Silas Sayres; 1876, Fred Stalder, W. H. Curfman, Silas Sayres; 1877, Fred Stalder, W. H. Curfman, Silas Sayres; 1878, Harvey Linscott, Daniel Fleming, C. A. Hines; 1879, Harvey Linscott, Daniel Fleming, J. H. Phillips; 1880, C. A. Hines, Daniel Fleming, J. H. Phillips; 1881, J. P. Bradley, Daniel Fleming, Harvey Linscott; 1882, J. P. Bradley, Daniel Fleming, Harvey Linscott; 1883, J. P. Bradley, Daniel Fleming, Harvey Linscott.

TOWNSHIP CLERKS SINCE 1809.

1809–'18, George Walker; 1819–'22, Benjamin Davis; 1823–'24 Sabinus Rice; 1825–'26, David Trowbridge; 1827–'28, George Walker, Jr.; 1829–'30, Wm. R. Walker; 1831, Hiram Cable; 1832–'44, R. A. Fulton; 1845 to 1879, J. H. Glazier; L. H. Glazier, 1880 to present time.

JUSTICES OF THE PEACE SINCE 1802.

1802, Alvin Bingham; 1803, Ephraim Cutler, Samuel Brown; 1805, John Brown; 1806, Daniel Weethee; 1807, George Walker; 1808, John Brown, Jonathan Watkins; 1810, George Walker, Benjamin Davis; 1811, Thos. M. Hamilton; 1813, George Walker—served till 1830; 1819, Martin Boyles—served till about 1828; 1828, John Brown; 1831, Wm. R. Walker, John B. Brown; 1834, Sabinus Rice, Charles Carter; 1837, R. A. Fulton; 1840, H. B. Brawley, R. A. Fulton; 1843, R. A. Fulton, H. B. Brawley; 1845, James Bryson, Lewis Rathburn; 1846, Henry Clark, Lewis Rathburn; 1847, Henry Clark, James Bryson; 1849, J. M. Mitchell, Wm. Mason; 1850, Henry Clark, James Bryson; 1852, J. M. Mitchell, J. G. Owen; 1853, James Bryson; 1855, R. A. Fulton, Jas. G. Owen; 1857, Gilbert M. McDougal; 1858, Robert A. Fulton, James G. Owen; 1860, Gilbert M. McDougal; 1861, Robert A. Fulton, William Mason; 1862, James G. Owen; 1863, F. L. Junod, R. R. Ellis; 1864, Lewis Carpenter; 1865, Frederick P. Kasler, James M. Mitchell; 1866, N. P. Hoisington; 1868, Lorenzo Fulton, David L. Rathburn; 1869, N. P. Hoisington; 1871, A. W. Glazier, W. G. Finch; 1872, N. P. Hoisington; 1874, A. W. Glazier, W. G. Finch; 1875, N. P. Hoisington; 1876, W. G. Finch, O. N. Owen; 1878, Fred Stalder; 1880, W. G. Finch, O. N. Owen; 1881, Fred Stalder; 1883, A. W. Durfee, W. J. Warrener.

AMESVILLE.

Situated on a rising eminence in the beautiful valley of Federal Creek, with quite an extended view, comprising that also of McDougal Creek, with the bold outlines of the surrounding hills, there are very few rural scenes that will surpass that of Amesville and her surroundings. Away from the busy world, surrounded by a farming neighborhood, rich in this world's goods, and in manly honor and honesty, Amesville rests in her quiet retreat, willing to take passing events as it finds them, content with her rich soil, pure air, and the material prosperity that comes from the daily avocations of life, faithfully and earnestly performed. Settled in the beginning of the century, it was this valley of Federal Creek, nestling among the hills with its varied scenery, bracing atmosphere and a look of quiet repose, that first caught the eye of Cutler, of Ewing and of Ames—men whose names have since become historic, and the impress of whose wonderful characters has been stamped indelibly upon the people. The pleasant valley is still there, and from the few log cabins of primeval days has arisen a quiet village that basks in the sunshine of peace, prosperity, health and happiness. Such is Amesville in the year 1883.

WHEN FOUNDED.

The village was laid out in the year 1837. James Pattison is now the oldest living resident, as he was the first. Rev. John Hunt came next, then Samuel McDaniel, Mr. Gregg and John Hardy and Hiram Cable. John Pattison, brother of James, came in 1839. The first year of its existence it could boast of one general store, one carding machine, one blacksmith and wagon shop, one tailor shop.

It is stated that the second school-house built in the county of Athens was erected upon the present village site of Amesville in 1804, and a man by the name of Moses Everett was the teacher. The next was erected on the farm of Sylvanus Ames, in 1811, and used also for church purposes. Dr. Ezra Walker and his daughter Sophia both taught in this last school-house. The oldest building now in the village is a part of the residence of W. H. Curfman's. It has a handsome and substantial school building which was erected as early as 1852, which has been painted and repaired not long since, and has stood the test of time with great credit to the honesty and faithfulness of its builders. Its cost, at the time of its erection, was $2,000. One fact is referred to by the citizens with pride, and that is the fact that no liquor saloon has ever been opened in Amesville. The village had a population, in 1880, of 159, and it has now about 175. Some improvements are now going on, and, though Amesville will never become a large town, it will probably hold its own, advancing as the surrounding country increases in population and wealth.

ITS BUSINESS INTEREST.

The following represents the business interests of the village, May 1, 1883: John Pattison, general store; W. H. Curfman, general store; A. C. Painter, general store; F. H. Gibson, drug store; A. C. Young, saddle and harness store; W. Gilligan & Bro., wagon and carriage shop; S. Balderson, blacksmith shop; J. W. Warren, shoe store; J. B. Buckingham, shoe store; J. B. Shoop, planing mill; J. B. Shoop, cabinet shop; V. Lots, butcher shop; Taylor Pattison, house and sign painter; Jas. Crawford, carpenter; Dr. W. A. Adair, Dr. J. Huestis, physicians. There is only one brick store in the village, that of John Pattison. This is a fine building, two stories high, 27 x 75 feet, and is a decided ornament to the town. The Presbyterian church and school building are both creditable affairs, and the village has many fine residences. In this last regard the citizens have displayed good taste, both in their building and their pleasant surroundings.

POSTOFFICE.

The postoffice is kept at the brick store and John Pattison is the Postmaster, a position he has held for the past ten years. This office was established in 1821, and the following have been the persons in charge: Loring B. Glazier, 1821-'29; Robert Henry, 1829-'34; Hiram Cable, 1834-'37; N. Dean, 1837-'41; Loring B. Glazier, 1841-'42; Hiram Cable, 1842-'46; Everet V. Phillips, 1846-'49; Lorenzo Fulton, 1849-'61; A. W. Glazier, 1861-'62; Lorenzo Fulton, 1862-'70; C. L. Warden, 1870-'73; John Pattison, 1873, present Postmaster.

AMESVILLE ACADEMY.

It has been and is the pride and boast of Amesville that it has within its limits one of the best educational institutes in the county. The building itself has been referred to on a previous page: The school took its inception from a meeting of the citizens of Amesville in November, 1852, the moving spirits of which were George Wyatt, Robert Henry, J. T. Glazier, James Pattison and A. S. Dickey. These gentlemen were appointed a committee to decide upon the best plan of securing the desires of the citizens. They reported on the 25th of the above month their views and acts upon the important question, which were probably adopted, for it was but a short time before the building was begun and finished, which gave to Athens County, as well as Amesville, one of the most efficient educational institutions in the State, so far as the branches of studies taught are considered. Its Superintendents have been. J.

P. Weethee, from 1854 to 1856; P. B. Davis, from 1856 to 1857; A. C. Kelly, from 1857 to 1858; Mr. McGonagle, from 1858 to 1860; E. P. Henry, from 1860 to 1861; J. H. Doan, from 1861 to 1862; J. M. Goodspeed, from 1862 to 1864; Miss L. M. Dowling, from 1864 to 1866.

Rev. H. C. Cheadle, principal, and Miss M. G. Keyes, assistant, from 1866.

CHURCHES.

The Presbyterian Church, of Amesville, was organized March 26, 1829, by the Rev. John Spalding, of Athens. The original members were Bildad Curtis and wife, Thankful; Elder John Jackson, Hannah McDougal, Abigail, wife of Wm. R. Walker, and John Walker.

Bildad Curtis and John Walker were appointed Elders. The fellowship of the church was given by Joseph B. Miles and Charles Shipman, Elders of the Athens church, and David Shields, of the Canaan church. Rev. Charles R. Fisk was the first Pastor.

The church at the above date was situated about one-half mile from the present site of Amesville and was called the Mudsock church. Nabby L. Ames joined the church on the 14th of May following, and the first baptized were Clark, Julia, Henrietta and Abraham Dodd, May 2, 1830. These were children of Andrew Dodd.

Chauncy and Patty Ward joined the church in 1830, and Chauncy Ward was made Elder.

The Rev. James McAboy succeeded the Rev. Charles R. Fisk, in May, 1832, and was installed as Pastor Dec. 1, 1832, and resigned his charge in May following. He dedicated the church which had been erected in 1832.

There had been no clerk up to 1832, the moderator keeping the minutes, who was the pastor, but on Feb. 19, 1832, Bildad Curtis was chosen as such, and remained clerk until August, 1836.

On the resignation of Rev. Jas. McAboy the church remained without a regular pastor until the spring of 1834, when the Rev. Ebenezer Hebbard was called, March the 18th, and took charge of the church the following May. He continued his pastorate until his death, which occurred Sept. 9, 1835.

May 1, 1836, the Rev. John Hunt served as Pastor for one year, but continued his charge for several years, being succeeded in 1844 by the Rev. Luke De Witt.

E. Ward was appointed Clerk August, 1836, to succeed Bildad Curtis. In 1841 Wm. R. Walker was elected and continued clerk of the Sessions until his death, which took place June 17, 1855. The church records were either not kept or a large portion were lost from 1844 to 1850. In 1836 Wm. R. Walker, Jno. B. Brown and John Jackson were elected Ruling Elders. The records show that John Wyatt succeeded Walker as Elder in 1843, the others remaining. The next Pastor found in charge of the church was the Rev. Roswell Tenney, who took charge August, 1849, and was still Pastor in 1855, and probably remained until 1858, as on April 12, 1858, the Rev. Chas. Merwin was installed.

In 1853 the Elders were: John B. Brown, Jas. Pattison and John Wyatt, and they were such in 1858.

After the death of Wm. R. Walker, in 1855, there seems to have been no record kept, and when Dr. Merwin assumed the pastorate he was also installed as Clerk of the Sessions, but no record was ever found and the opinion was formed that he had entirely neglected this important duty. The next date had advanced to Dec. 9, 1865. There was a membership of seventy-seven in 1846, and the last record previous to the war was 167 members.

The church, which had been irregularly attended and supported during the civil strife, was re-organized at Amesville, and again started to exercise a power and influence for good which had sadly lapsed the few preceding years.

In November, 1865, the Rev. H. C. Cheadle was called to the pastorate, and the Trustees in charge were James Pattison, C. H. Wyatt and A. W. Glazier. A handsome church was erected at a cost of $4,000, and was dedicated Dec. 8, 1867. Dr. Cheadle continued his labors until April 1, 1872, when he retired. It was not until July, 1873, that another minister was secured, but on the twentieth of that month the Rev. L. N. Woodruff was installed and continued until Sept. 30, 1882, since which time the pastorate has been vacant. The present membership is ninety. W. A. Adair is Clerk. The church is in good condition and it is not expected to be without a pastor much longer.

The First Methodist Society formed in Ames Township was formed by Rev. Curtis Goddard in 1824, at the house of Gulliver and Mary Dean (his wife). The society was composed of the following persons: Mr. and Mrs. Dean, Mr. and Mrs. Hart and their four daughters were the original class of eight persons. In 1825, under the ministry of Rev. James Laws, there were twelve or fifteen persons added to the society, among whom were Mr. Kelion Kaslar and wife, Mr. Rathburn and wife, Mrs. Samuel McCune, Mr. John Bigford and wife, Mr. Hyde, Class-Leader. The only one now living of that society is Mary B. O. Neal, in her seventy-second year. Among the early pastors were: John Feree, Henry S. Fernandes, Orvil Shelton, Robert O. Spencer, Martin Kellog, George G. West, Samuel Harvey, Benjamin Ellis, Joseph S. Brown, Levi S. Munsell, James McCutchen. As the society increased in numbers it was removed to a log school-house near where Edwin Lehon preached occasionally (since a Southern Methodist Bishop). The circuit or charge embraced the territory of what is now Stewart charge, Amesville charge, part of Rosseau and part of Chester Hill. In 1844–'5 a church was built in Amesville, a frame 30 x 50 feet, a king-post roof apparently as solid to-day as when built thirty years ago, and cost $1,300. Colonel Absalom Boyles, Gulliver and Leonard Dean were the building committee. Colonel Boyles framed the building and had a general oversight of the work; Gulliver and Leonard Dean furnished the stone and did the stone-work; Henry B. Brawley furnished the hewed timber, William Johnson the oak flooring, Harvey Goble the plastering lath, other members contributing in like manner as was needed. Abraham Curtlich and Charles H. Lawton were among the first Pastors after the church was built in 1846–'7. Rev. Lawton organized the first Sabbath-school, Henry B. Brawley, Superintendent; John T. Glazier, Secretary; Gulliver Dean, James Henry and Isaac Hedge, Managers. The Sunday-school has been kept up ever since. The Superintendents since its organization were, in addition to Mr. Brawley: John T. Glazier, R. R. Ellis, G. M. Ross, John L. Brown, William Moore, George E. Henry, John Walsh, L. L. Munsell, John P. Brawley, E. H. Brawley and James Gillian, the present very efficient Superintendent. Miss Kate Brawley was for many years the loving and beloved teacher of the primary class, and endeared herself to the little ones by her thoughtful care and kindness.

PASTORS FROM 1847 to 1883.

The pastors who have served the church since 1847 are named here in the order they officiated: Rev. Levi Cunningham, afterward Presiding Elder; Rev. Uriah Redferren (he died on the circuit, 1850), Revs. W. R. Litinger and Amos Wilson; 1851, Revs. W. R. Litinger and David Mann; 1852, Revs. Cherrington and

Catlin; 1853, Revs. Cherrington and Gregg; 1854, Revs. Street and Anderson; 1855, Revs. Hopkins and Anderson; 1856, Revs. Hopkins and Kelley; 1857, Revs. Kelley and Nichols; 1858, Revs. Ryland and Rankin; 1859, Revs. Ryland and D. Ricketts; 1860, Revs. Thurston and Pardon Cook; 1861, Revs. Thurston and D. Ricketts; 1862, Lewis Brothers, who resigned and entered the service of the Union army; 1863, Revs. Wolf and Spencer; 1864, Revs. Wolf and Porter; 1865, Rev. M. D. Vaughan; 1866, Rev. L. W. Mensell; 1867, Rev. Lounis; 1868, Revs. Durant and David Morgan, the latter is now living at St. Paul, Minnesota,—and the following in the order named: Revs. Cash, Arbuckle, Morris, Fry, S. B. Ricketts, J. G. Jones, for two years; Rev. T. S. Armstrong, an outspoken defender of the Christian faith, who was a prisoner for a year in Libby Prison, having been taken prisoner while a soldier in the Federal army. The Rev. R. A. Le Maston is the present Pastor.

Under the ministry of the Revs. J. Hopkins and A. C. Kelley, there was an active revival, and among those who then joined and became an active member was John L. Brown, now deceased, who afterward was Superintendent of the Sabbath-school, and a young man of talent and promise.

The pastorship of Rev. S. B. Ricketts was noted for a gracious revival which added between twenty-five and thirty to the membership of the church, and in 1880 the church was again revived and strengthened by additional members, under the active spiritual work of the Rev. J. G. Jones.

PRESIDING ELDERS.

The following named persons have been Presiding Elders from 1848 to 1865, inclusive: Uriah Heath, deceased; E. M. Boring, from 1853 to 1856; J. W. Clark, to 1859, deceased; B. N. Spahs, to 1863; and J. T. Frewgar, to 1865. Since then S. M. Merrill (now Bishop Merrill) presided several years; also Eskridge Dixon, James Kendall, Henry Gartner and S. M. Frampton, the present Elder. The present Stewards are: William Jackson, J. B. Rhodes, F. L. Junod, R. R. Marquis, Daniel Hixon, Edmund Wheeler and J. P. Brawley. The latter is also Class-Leader. The church is prospering and one of power and influence.

LODGES.

Amesville Lodge, No. 278, *A. F. & A. M.*, held its first meeting at Amesville, in their present lodge-room, Feb. 18, 1856, the following officers being in charge: Watson Harris, W. M. *pro tem.;* J. G. Woolman, S. W.; A. S. Dickey, J. W.; Job S. King, Treas.; J. P. Harris, Sec.; John Patterson, S. D.; G. W. Pewthers, J. D.

The only business before this meeting was the reading of three petitions for initiation, which were properly referred, signed by Hiram Black, William H. Curfman and Francis Ginn. At the meeting of the lodge, Sept. 20, 1856, the following exhibit of work for the seven months of its existence was reported: Number of initiations, fifteen; number passed, fourteen; number raised, twelve.

With this, their Grand Lodge report, they met the G. L. at Zanesville, Ohio, Oct. 22, 1856, and asked that body to grant them a charter, which was done, the charter being signed by the following officers of the Grand Lodge: W. B. Dodds, M. W. Grand Master; B. F. Smith, R. W. Deputy Grand Master; M. D. Brock, R. W. S. G. W.; Barton S. Kyle, R. W. J. G. W.; John D. Caldwell, R. W. Grand Secretary.

The following names appear upon the charter as charter-members of the new lodge: John Patterson, A. S. Dickey, O. W. Pickering, William Golden, L. Fulton, J. P. Harris, Abner Cooley, D. L. Dana, J. F. Woolman, George W. Baker, J. L. Kessinger.

Thus equiped with a charter the lodge began its Masonic life, which has continued harmoniously for twenty seven years. One of the first business undertakings of the lodge was to contract a debt of over $400 for building and furnishing a lodge-room. It was built by a stock company, mostly Masons. Although largely in debt, and the members of the lodge not being wealthy, they began at once to practice that greatest of virtues, charity. Very seldom has a worthy applicant been turned away from this lodge empty handed. This charitable practice has wrought itself so thoroughly into the character of the lodge that they remain contented with a very plain lodge-room to point with pride to their long list of charitable bestowments.

The workings of the lodge ran along smoothly, without interruption, receiving into its membership many honorable and intelligent men, until the spring of 1861, when many of her members offered themselves to their country, engaging in the great struggle for the nation's life. No member of this lodge sympathized with the Southern Confederacy. At the close of the war regular meetings, which had been suspended, were resumed, and have been kept up to the present time.

When labor was resumed some confusion was to be encountered in the affairs of the lodge. Debts had accumulated, the lodge-room had run down, and many of the members had died or moved away. Those who were left equal to the emergency began the work of restoring the lodge; the lodge-room was repaired and refurnished, the lodge placed under new management, and the debt, which had never ceased to grow from the beginning, began gradually to decrease. The entire debt was at length paid, and the lodge is now on a good basis in every respect.

In July, 1871, a number of the members who lived near Guysville, Athens County, asked for and were granted permission to establish a lodge at that place. In the establishment of this, Amesville Lodge not only lost some of her best members, but also a large portion of her best territory, which fell into the jurisdiction of the new lodge.

In August of the same year the old lodge was again asked to divide her members and territory for the establishment of a new lodge at Bishopville, Morgan County. Although crippling her severely in membership and territory, she gave consent, and Bishopville Lodge was formed. Since the establishment of these two new lodges, owing to reduced territory, the membership of Amesville Lodge has not grown so rapidly as before. None of the interests of the order, however, have been forgotten or neglected, the members are fully alive to their obligations, and each is doing his duty, while perfect harmony prevails.

The entire membership of the lodge since its organization, excepting charter members, is 125; of this number seven have died while members of the lodge, fifty-one have been demitted, and thirteen have been expelled, leaving a membership of fifty-four at the present time.

BIOGRAPHICAL.

Edward R. Ames, D. D., a native of Ames Township, Athens Co., Ohio, born May 20, 1806, was a son of Judge Sylvanus Ames. His early education was plain and practical. A natural taste for reading was fostered by a local library to which he had free access, and when twenty years of age he entered the Ohio University at Athens. There he remained many years, supporting himself mainly by teaching. In 1828 the Ohio Conference of the Methodist Episcopal Church met at Chillicothe, and he attended

John F. Welch

its meetings. Bishop Roberts, the presiding officer, was so impressed with the young man's appearance that he invited him to accompany him to the Illinois Conference at Madison, Ill. He there made the acquaintance of several prominent Methodist clergymen, and opened a school at Lebanon, Ill., which was the germ of McKendree College. In August, 1830, he entered the itinerant ministry, and was licensed to preach by the Rev. Peter Cartwright. He was sent to the Shoal Creek Circuit, which covered an almost unlimited territory, and when the Indiana Conference was organized, in 1832, he went with the new conference, and was ordained a Deacon by Bishop Soule. In 1834 he was ordained an Elder by Bishop Roberts, and was employed in several fields of labor, including two years spent in St. Louis, Mo., till 1840. He was that year appointed a delegate to the General Conference in Baltimore, and was by that body elected Corresponding Secretary of the Missionary Society for the South and West. He was the first Chaplain ever elected by an Indian Council, having served the Choctaw General Council in that capacity in 1842. In 1848 he was elected President of the Asbury University, Indiana, but declined the honor. In the General Conference in 1852 he was elected Bishop, together with Bishops Scott and Simpson; and he was the first Methodist Bishop who ever visited the Pacific Coast. When the question of the separation of the Methodists came up in 1844, he opposed the division, and afterward did all he could to foster a fraternal spirit. When the ecclesiastical property of the Methodist Episcopal Church South was confiscated for the time being, he was commissioned by President Lincoln and Secretary Stanton to take charge of it. This was a most delicate duty, and in its performance he visited New Orleans and other Southern cities, organizing so cieties and appointing white and colored preachers. During the twenty-seven years in which Bishop Ames was in the episcopacy, his whole public life was marked by a strict adherence to the rules and discipline of Methodism, and even when the most difficult points came up for settlement he displayed a far-seeing judgment and quickness of apprehension, which enabled him to grapple successfully with them. Although grave and dignified in manner, there was a magnetism about him which attracted, and his preaching was always thoroughly enjoyed. He could scarcely be styled an orator, and yet his quiet reasoning, apt aphorisms, pertinent illustrations and earnestness, impressed more than mere declamation. He died at Baltimore, Md., April 25, 1879. He had been twice married, and left a son and two daughters.—*Appleton's Annual*, 1879.

George S. Anderson was born in Belmont County, Ohio, Nov. 11, 1811, where he lived till he was sixteen years of age. In 1827 he went with his father to Guernsey County. When he was eighteen years of age his father died, and, being the eldest son, the care of his widowed mother and the management of the farm devolved on him, which duty he performed faithfully until his mother's death. He was married June 6, 1833, to Sarah Smith, a daughter of English parents. They had twelve children, all of whom lived to be men and women, and ten still survive. His wife died Sept. 17, 1870. He was again married July 3, 1871, to Amanda Beal, a native of Ohio. They have three children. He is a member of the Universalist church, and his wife a member of the Methodist Episcopal church. Mr. Anderson has held many local offices of trust, having held the office of Township Trustee for thirteen years, and the office of Justice of the Peace for nine years. He came to Ames Township, Athens County, in 1873.

George Beasley, farmer and stock-raiser, was born Oct. 15, 1811, the eldest son of John and Elizabeth Beasley, who came from Virginia and located in Bern Township, in 1823, where our subject was reared on a farm and received his education in the subscription schools, living with his parents until he was nineteen years of age. He was married April 15, 1830, to Mary A. Gardner, a daughter of Thomas Gardner, a pioneer of Ames Township. By this union there were twelve children, eight of whom still survive—Rosanna, Elizabeth, David, John J., Adeline, Sarah E., Calley M. and Charles M. His farm contains 204 acres of improved land under a high state of cultivation. In his chosen avocation, that of a farmer, he has been very successful.

John J. Beasley, farmer and stock-dealer, born in Ames Township, Athens Co., Ohio, April 5, 1847, is the third son of George and Mary (Gardner) Beasley. He was reared on a farm and received his education in the schools at Amesville. At the breaking out of the late civil war, though only a boy, he went out in defense of his country, enlisting in Company G, Fifty-third Ohio Infantry, in which capacity he participated in many hard-fought battles, served until the close of the war, and received an honorable discharge Aug. 13, 1865. After the close of the war he returned to his native village, and the subsequent year he was sick and unable to attend to active business. After he recovered he engaged in the mercantile business for several years, after which he engaged in the live-stock business, which he has since followed with marked success, and has for several years been identified with the leading stock dealers of Southern Ohio. He was married Aug. 15, 1871, to Mazeppa Hill, a daughter of Solomon Hill, a pioneer of Athens County. They have one child—Austin. Mr. Beasley is the owner of a fine farm containing 235 acres of good land under a high state of cultivation, admirably adapted to the purpose for which it is used—that of raising stock. His residence is in the village of Amesville.

Henry B. Brawley, deceased, was born in Brownsville, Pa., Dec. 19, 1806. When he was ten years of age his widowed mother came with her four sons to Ohio and settled in what is now Ames Township, Athens County. Their struggle for a livelihood was a hard one, but it was firmly maintained, and all the sons were reared to manhood. Mr. Brawley was married Oct. 31, 1833, to Elizabeth McCune, daughter of Samuel and Mary McCune. She was born near the present site of Amesville, Feb. 17, 1812. She died June 22, 1863, leaving four children, two sons and two daughters. She had been a member of the Methodist church since fourteen years of age, and was known and honored by all the Amesville circuit for her hospitality and kindness. Mr. Brawley began life without pecuniary help. He first rented land just north of Amesville, but a few years later bought the farm, where he resided till his death. By industry, care and frugality he gradually accumulated a valuable estate. In business transactions and in the discharge of numerous trusts that were committed to him he was perfectly upright and faithful, being as conscientious in the performance of public as he was in private affairs. Considering his early opportunities, he attained an unusual degree of intelligence and culture. Fond of books and diligent in the improvement of his time, his reading was extensive and varied. He had an excellent general acquaintance with history and historical personages. He sought information on public questions with as much interest as if they were private and personal. His favorite kind of reading, especially the latter years of his life, was poetry, and nearly all the standard poets were to be found in his house. With some of them he was very familiar and was fond of making quotations from the large number of passages with which his mind was stored. He was hospitable at home, genial and pleasant in every circle. The children of other persons were in several instances committed to his care.

He received them into his home and dealt with them as with his own, and they became attached to him as to a father. He was a man of careful judgment and settled convictions. One of the most beautiful things in his life was his tender, but manly, devotion to the memory of his wife, whose death preceded his by sixteen years. He was a member of the Methodist church forty years. In 1845 he was appointed Steward, a position he held till his death. He was frequently honored by being a representative to the annual conferences, and the punctuality, precision and efficiency with which he discharged the duties of his post is seldom equaled among church officials. He was not a mere business man of the church; though quiet and undemonstrative, he cherished a deep religious life, and his influence was felt in every part of his circuit of which he was for many years the most conspicuous and widely known member. He died June 5, 1879, but long will he live in the memory of those who knew him. Of his four children, three are still living—Edward H., M. E. and John P. His youngest daughter, M. Kate, died April 19, 1881. She was a most devoted Christian, and when the Methodist church called for women to labor in behalf of foreign missions, she gave herself, heart and soul, to the work. She was chosen a District Secretary, and for more than eight years gave her time and labor to the cause. Being of a timid and nervous disposition, the position was a very trying one, as she was often called upon to appear as a public speaker, and she never succeeded in overcoming her embarrassment. The amount of writing she did, considering her feeble health and the demands of domestic duties, deserves especial notice. Her correspondence was necessarily extensive; her preparations for her public efforts required considerable time, and she sometimes wrote for the press, her articles being generally for children and appearing in the *Western Christian Advocate*, *Ladies' Repository*, and the *Nursery*. From the numerous testimonials of her excellence and worth we subjoin the following, passed at the annual session of the Cincinnati Branch of the Woman's Foreign Missionary Society, held in Hillsboro a few days before her death:

"WHEREAS, Our beloved friend and co-worker, sister M. Kate Brawley, the efficient Secretary of Marietta District, has in the providence of an All-wise Father been called from doing to suffering his will,

"*Resolved*, That we hereby tender our sincere regrets at her absence at this our annual feast, and extend our warmest sympathy with the hope that, if consistent with his holy will, a restoration to health may permit her to again enter the work she loved so well.

"MARY WARNER,
"MARY E. SOSMANS,
"Committee.

"*Hillsboro*, April 14, 1881."

Edward H. Brawley, farmer and stock-raiser, born in Ames Township, Athens Co., Ohio, Jan. 2, 1835, is the oldest son of the late Henry B. and Elizabeth (McCune) Brawley. His youth was spent in assisting his father in the management of the farm and attending the common schools, where his early education was obtained. After he grew to manhood, being ambitious, he attended the Ohio University at Athens for a time. He now has a fine farm of 140 acres. In connection with his farming pursuits he has been engaged in dealing in wool, and has met with good success and won the confidence and esteem of the community. He was united in marriage April 7, 1862, to Miss Jenny McCollom, who was born in Ohio but at the time of her marriage was a resident of Indiana. They have had six children, three of whom are living—Robert G., Mary Gertrude and Bertha Florence. Mr. Brawley has held many local offices of trust. In 1870 he was appointed Assistant United States Marshal for this district. He is a member of the A. F. & A. M., Amesville Lodge, No. 278. He and his wife are members of the Methodist Episcopal church.

John P. Brawley, farmer and stock-raiser, was born in Ames Township, Sept. 8, 1848, the youngest son of the late Henry B. and Elizabeth (McCune) Brawley. His youth was spent in assisting his father on the farm and attending the common schools, residing with his parents until he grew to manhood. He was married Sept. 8, 1875, to Miss Allie E. Wedge, of Coolville, Athens Co., Ohio. They have three children—Jessie, Lizzie and Mamie. Mr. Brawley has a fine farm of 221 acres of good land, a part of the old home farm. He and his wife are active members of the Methodist Episcopal church.

Eli F. Brown was born in Ames Township, April 1, 1814, a son of John and Polly Brown. His youth was spent in assisting his father on the farm and attending the subscription schools. When he reached the age of twenty-one years he went to Lancaster, where he spent three years with an auctioneer, and subsequently for forty-one years he was engaged as a public auctioneer in his native county. Mr. Brown has during his life been actively engaged in business of almost every description, and he has gained a wide reputation as an energetic and enterprising citizen. He was first married Aug. 27, 1834, to Amy Eddic, a native of Providence, R. I. By this union there were three children, only two of whom still live. He lost his wife April 3, 1867. He was again married March 12, 1868, to Nancy A. L. Dean, daughter of Gulliver and Mary (Cutler) Dean, and a granddaughter of the late Judge Ephraim Cutler, who was prominently identified with the early settlement of Ames Township. They have two daughters and two sons—Mary E., Julia A., Abel G., and Walter G. Mr. Brown now lives on the old homestead of Judge Cutler, afterward of Gulliver Dean. It had never been owned by any but the family. He has been elected to many local offices of trust and responsibility. He is a member of the A. F. & A. M., Amesville Lodge, No. 278. He and his wife are members of the Methodist Episcopal church.

Archibald Bryson, born in Bedford County, Penn., Aug. 27, 1813, is the son of David and Elizabeth (Kearns) Bryson. He has from a child been identified with this township, his parents coming here in 1816. His father entered a tract of unimproved land, where he reared his children and lived till his death, in September, 1854, aged seventy-seven years and ten days. His wife died in 1864, aged eighty-one years. Mr. Bryson, the subject of our sketch, lived with his parents till manhood. He was married Oct. 11, 1835, to Henrietta Davis, daughter of John and Matilda (Atwood) Davis. He purchased the place where he now lives in 1835. At that time there was a small log house and a log stable on it, and but a small portion cleared. He now has 120 acres of the best land in Athens County. Mr. and Mrs. Bryson are the parents of twelve children, only seven now living—David W., John D., Fannie F., Elizabeth J., Morris O., George W. and Eliza D. Mrs. Bryson is a member of the Methodist Episcopal church.

William Cone, farmer, born in Ames Township, Sept. 11, 1822, is the oldest son of Albert B. and Sarah Cone, who were among the early settlers of Athens County. His young days were spent on a farm, and at the age of twenty he began learning the trade of a blacksmith, at which he worked for several years. In 1856 he purchased the farm on which he now resides, and has since devoted his time to farming and stock-raising. He was first married Dec. 25, 1846, to Miss Mary Ketler. They were the parents of two children—Augustus W. and Mary E. Mrs. Cone died Jan. 17,

1854. Mr. Cone was again married Aug. 29, 1856, to Ruth McCune. To them were born two children—Julien and Charles. His wife died Oct. 15, 1871, and he was married April 15, 1873, to Mrs. A. P. Lamb, of Marietta. They have one child—Frank W. Mr. Cone is a self-made man and has accumulated his property by his own exertions.

William H. Curfman, merchant, was born in Frederick County, Md., March 28, 1832. When he was five years of age he came with his parents, George and Cordelia (Hemsworth) Curfman, to Ohio and located in Morgan County. Here he was reared and educated until he was sixteen years of age, when he went to learn the carpenter's trade, which he followed three years. He then came to Amesville and engaged as clerk with George Walker, Jr., in the mercantile business. He served in that capacity for three and one-half years, when he purchased an interest in the business, which they carried on successfully until his partner, Mr. Walker, died, and our subject being unable to control such an extensive business, sold out and engaged as clerk with Patterson Bros. in the same place, and remained with them two years. He then went to Salina, Athens Co., Ohio, where he continued in the same occupation for a period of seven years. He then returned to Amesville and formed a partnership with John Patterson and carried on a successful mercantile business until 1879. At this time they met with a severe loss by fire, amounting to about $10,000. He immediately purchased a stock of goods which he placed in the store he has since occupied. During Mr. Curfman's many years in the mercantile business, he has by fair dealing won the respect and confidence of his many patrons. He has never aspired to publicity, but in 1878 his friends urged him to accept their proffered suffrage for the office of County Commissioner. He was elected by a large majority, and has since held the important position with honor to himself and credit to his constituents. Mr. Curfman was married Nov. 30, 1854, to Julia A., daughter of L. B. and Jane (Henry) Glazier. By this union there were four children—O. A., Louie, Mattie and Maud. Mr. and Mrs. Curfman are consistent members of the Presbyterian church, he being an Elder of the organization. He is a member of the A. F. & A. M., Amesville Lodge, No. 278.

Henry H. Curtis, farmer and stock-dealer, born in Ames Township, Athens Co., Ohio, is the oldest son of Moses and Sophia (Henry) Curtis. He was born June 15, 1837, reared on a farm, and received his education in the common school. Shortly after he reached his majority his father died, leaving the management of a large estate to our subject. He was first married Sept. 9, 1860, to Jane Sundland, of Maryland. By this union were two children, one still living—Edwin C. Antie C. died Jan. 15, 1865. Mrs. Curtis died Sept. 23, 1869. He was again married Oct. 4, 1870, to Miss Sarah E. Sundland, a sister of his first wife. They have one child—Effie B. Mr. Curtis is the owner of 380 acres of good land which is admirably adapted to the purposes for which it is used. His residence is beautifully located in the suburbs of the village of Amesville.

Nathan W. Dean, farmer and stock-raiser, is the oldest son of Nathan and Fanny (Lane) Dean, and a grandson of Nathan Dean, who was prominently identified with the early settlers of Ames Township. Our subject was born in Bristol County, Mass., Nov. 1, 1818, and when about six months old came with his parents to Ames Township, Athens Co., Ohio. They made the journey in a wagon, and our subject was suspended from the bows of the wagon cover in a clothes-basket. His father having the contract of carrying the mail from Amesville to Marietta, when our subject was twelve years of age he assisted him in these duties. At the age of seventeen years his father died, leaving his mother and sisters and the management of the farm to the care of our subject. He has since followed assiduously the avocation of farming. He was married in 1846 to Miss Catherine McDannald, a native of Pennsylvania. They had two sons, only one of whom still survives—Nathan Edgar. Henry L. died Nov. 9, 1873, at the age of twenty-two years. He still lives on the old homestead, which contains 224 acres of good land under a high state of cultivation. His son, Nathan E., resides with him. He was married Oct. 11, 1876, to Roena E. Owens. They have two children—Mertie Lee and Linnie May. He is engaged in farming and stock-raising with his father, but in connection with his farming pursuits has for the last ten years been engaged as a public auctioneer.

B. A. Ellis was born in Perry County, Ohio, in 1846, and when about two years of age came with his parents, R. R. and F. S. Ellis, to Athens County and settled in Amesville, where his youth was spent in attending school and clerking in a store until he was sixteen years old. In response to his country's call, though yet but a boy, he enlisted in the One Hundred and Twenty-ninth Ohio Infantry for six months but served nine months before being mustered out of the service. Again in 1864, he enlisted in the One Hundred and Sixty-fifth Regiment, where he served for four months, and in 1865 re-enlisted in the One Hundred and Eighty-fourth Regiment, where he served until the close of the Rebellion. He participated in many severe skirmishes but in no regular engagement. After the close of the war he returned to Amesville and attended school for two years, working on a farm a portion of the time, after which he engaged in painting, which occupation he followed for four years. He was married March 16, 1871, to Lois S., a daughter of Moses and Sophia (Henry) Curtis, who were prominently identified in the early settlement of Ames Township. By this union were two sons and one daughter—Frank and Fred (twins), and Edna May. After his marriage Mr. Ellis engaged in farming, which avocation he followed until the spring of 1880, when he accepted a position as clerk in the establishment of John Patterson, where he has won many friends and gained the confidence of his employer. He and his wife are members of the Presbyterian church, and he has ever been an ardent worker in the temperance cause.

Walter G. Finch was born in Washington County, Ohio, Sept. 15, 1823. He was reared on a farm and received his education in the common schools. He was left an orphan at the age of eight years and thrown on his own responsibility. He found a home with Gulliver Dean, of Ames Township, with whom he lived until he reached his majority. He was married Nov. 1, 1849, to Miss Juliette Smith, a native of New York City. They have seven children—Charles, Sarah, Alice, Nina, Edward, Juliette and William. Mr. Finch purchased his present farm in 1855, where he lived for three years, when he sold out and six years later again purchased it. He has 200 acres of good improved land. He has held the office of Justice of the Peace since 1871. He is a member of the A. F. & A. M., Amesville Lodge, No. 278.

Daniel Fleming, farmer and stock-dealer, born in Athens County, Ohio, in 1822, is a son of John and Christina Fleming. John Fleming was born in Germany in 1777, and at the age of fifteen years came to the United States and located in New York, and at an early age engaged in the coal business, in which he met with marked success. In 1819 he came to Athens County, Ohio, and purchased an interest in the Ohio Land Company's grant. He having considerable means contributed liberally by his influence and from his personal means to improve the country, which was then a wilderness. After remaining about six years he returned to New York, but still retained his interest in the Ohio lands. He was married March 11, 1806, to Christina Smith, a native of New York City. By this union there were eleven children, six of which lived to be men and women, and three still living—Martin, Jane and Daniel. John Fleming died in New York City in 1841, and his wife died in Ames Township in 1863, at the advanced age of seventy-nine years. Our subject was reared in New York City, his youth being spent in attending school. At the age of twenty-two years he returned to the place of his birth, where he has since resided, and since his arrival in this county he has followed assiduously the avocation of farming and stock raising and dealing, and by good management he has met with remarkable success. He was married May 16, 1846, to Lucy P. Gardner, daughter of Thomas and Margaret (Smith) Gardner, who was born in 1824. Thirteen children were born to them, eight of which still survive—Joseph, William, John, Theodore, Lincoln, Lucy, Julia and Edith.

A. J. Frame, Auditor of Athens County, Ohio, the eldest of nine sons and ten children of John and Mary (Nesmith) Frame, was born at Coolville, Athens County, Aug. 21, 1834, where he was reared and educated in the public school and the Coolville Seminary, attending the latter four years. In 1856 he became associated with his father in the mercantile business and so continued until 1865, when his father retired from business. His brother, A. P. Frame, then became associated with him, he himself retiring from the business in 1874. In 1875 he was elected Treasurer of Athens County, and re-elected in 1877, holding the office four years. In 1880 he was elected Auditor of Athens County, and re-elected in 1882. Besides being a county officer he has held the office of Treasurer of Troy Township for many years. Politically he is a Republican. July 14, 1856, he was married to Harriet Smith, of Racine, Meigs Co., Ohio, who died May 31, 1882. They have three children—R. A. and J. F., both telegraph operators on the Marietta & Cincinnati Railroad, and E. C., attending school. Mr. Frame is a member of the Athens Commandery, No. 15, Knights Templars.

John Frame, deceased, a pioneer of Troy Township, Athens County, was born in Crawford County, Pa., Sept. 20, 1807. Although born and reared on a farm he as an apprentice learned the tailor's trade, serving six years. In 1832 he emigrated to Ohio and settled at Coolville, Athens County, where he followed his trade until 1840, when he engaged in general merchandising, and also dealt in wool, grain and produce. In November, 1833, he was married to Mary Nesmith, of Dover Township. They were blessed with a large family, nine sons and one daughter, all of whom are living excepting one son. He retired from active business in 1865. He held the offices of Township Treasurer and School Director for many years. Politically he was a Democrat, a thorough and uncompromising Union man, but after the late war up to his death took no part in politics. He died Aug. 27, 1873, a truly representative man, who had endeared himself to his neighbors and associates by his many genial and amiable qualities. He was a member of the Congregational church, as is also his wife, who still survives him.

Thomas Gardner, farmer and stock-raiser, Ames Township, was born in New York City, Feb. 1, 1814, and in the fall of the same year his parents came to Ames Township, Athens Co., Ohio, and settled on the farm where he has since lived, formerly known as the Thomas Ewing homestead. He remained with his parents until he grew to manhood. He was married Jan. 28, 1852, to Phebe Beasley, daughter of the late John Beasley, a native of Virginia. He has followed assiduously the avocation of a farmer, in which he has been highly successful, and now ranks among the larger land-owners of Athens County, having 511 acres of land under a high state of cultivation, on which he is engaged in raising stock and grain, making a specialty of cattle and sheep of the higher grades.

C. W. Glazier, merchant, Amesville, is the youngest son of Abel and Sallie (Brown) Glazier, who were among the early settlers of Athens County. He was born in Ames Township, Sept. 7, 1821, reared on a farm and educated in the common schools. His father died when he was sixteen years of age, when he was thrown on his own responsibility. He followed the avocation of farming until 1862, when he became engaged in the railroad business, which he followed for several years. He was first married in 1842 to Eliza Cook, a native of New York. By this union there was one daughter—Frances. His wife died in September, 1869. He was again married in 1872 to Mrs. Sarah E. Walker, of this county. Mr. Glazier has for several years been successfully engaged in the mercantile business at Amesville, and bears an unsullied reputation among his fellow townsmen.

John Henry Glazier, farmer, section 8, Ames Township, was born in this township Dec. 13, 1820, and is the son of Loring B. and Jane (Henry) Glazier, grandson of Abel Glazier, and great-grandson of Captain Benjamin Brown, who was prominently identified for many years among the early settlers of Athens County. Our subject was reared on a farm and educated in the schools of Amesville. He lived with his parents until their death and then succeeded them on the old homestead. He was married Jan. 1, 1851, to Sarah Ann, daughter of Mathew and Mary Henry, who settled in Athens County in the year 1839. By this union were five children, four of whom still live—Alice (deceased), Edna, Loring H., Emma D and Louis B. Mr. Glazier has always stood in the foremost rank to aid every laudable enterprise which would be of interest and benefit to the community. In the year of 1845 he was elected to the office of Township Clerk. This position was not at that time a very remunerative one, as he only received $5 per year; yet by his strict attention to the duties thereof he gained the confidence of the people and was by them re-elected each year until 1880. He has also held many offices in the agricultural society, an enterprise in which he takes great pride. He is physically a man of great personal strength and courage, and intellectually possesses great common sense and unusual native mental vigor. In his chosen avocation, that of a farmer, he has been highly successful and uses his accumulated wealth to the best advantage in surrounding himself and family with all the comforts of life, and giving to his children a thorough and practical education. Besides caring well for those of his own household he is not unmindful of the wants of others, and his unostentatious generosity contributes to relieve the necessities of many. Upright in his dealings with his fellowmen, charitable to the weaknesses of others, generous to the deserving poor, conscientious in the discharge of every duty, he receives, as he deserves, the considerate respect of his fellow-citizens, and has always the respectful obedience and affectionate regard of those of his own household. He has a fine farm containing 400 acres of good land under a high state of cultivation on which is a large and commodious residence surrounded by beautiful shade trees and shrubbery.

John Henry Green was born on the farm where he now lives in Ames Township, Athens Co., Ohio, March 18, 1842. His father, Steven W. Green, was born on the same farm March 2, 1814. His grandfather, Ezra Green, was born in Worcester County, Mass., Oct. 8, 1776, and married Sally Proctor, Oct. 2, 1805, and soon after came to Ohio and settled on the above-mentioned farm, where he lived till after the death of his wife, Nov. 25, 1819. He then went to Washington County, where he married Mrs. Dodge and passed the remainder of his days. His death occurred Sept. 21, 1822. Steven W. Green went with his father to Washington County and resided until after his death. He was married Sept. 1, 1836, to Miss Lucy Green, a native of Washington County. After his marriage he returned to the old homestead in Ames Township, Athens County, where he followed the avocation of farming until his death. They were the parents of eleven children, five of whom are living. Mr. Green died March 26, 1864. Mrs. Green still resides with our subject. She is a member of the Presbyterian church. Our subject was reared on a farm and educated in the common schools, and has always lived on the old homestead. He was married Nov. 24, 1870, to Miss Mattie Hatfield, a native of Wabash County, Ind. They have two children—Frank C. and Charles W. Mr. and Mrs. Green are members of the Presbyterian church.

Daniel Hill, farmer and stock-raiser, was born in Canaan Township, Aug. 15, 1829, son of John and Nancy (Arnold) Hill. He was reared on a farm and educated in the common schools. At the age of twenty-three he purchased the farm on which he has since resided. It contains 320 acres of improved land. In connection with his farming he has been extensively engaged in shipping stock to Eastern markets. He was married June 11, 1858, to Miss Flora Lewis, a native of Noble County. They have had six children, four still living—William E., Annie M., Oliver E. and Linnie. Charles and an infant are deceased. Mr. and Mrs. Hill are both members of the United Brethren church.

Loren Hill, farmer and stock-raiser, was born in Ames Township, Jan. 21, 1837, the second son of Amos and Mary Ann (Miner) Hill. He lived with his parents on the farm during his minority, receiving a common-school education. April 28, 1875, he married Lucinda, daughter of Nelson and Lucy McCune. They have four children—Herbert H., Luella M., Carny C., and an infant. After his marriage Mr. Hill bought a farm and lived on it till 1879. He then returned to the old homestead, where he has since resided, taking charge of the farm. Mrs. Hill is a member of the Presbyterian church.

Solomon Hill was born in Spencer, Mass., Aug. 15, 1814, and when three years of age came with his parents to Athens County and settled on a farm about two miles from where the village of Amesville now stands. The days of his youth were spent in assisting his father on the farm and attending the subscription schools. He resided with his parents until their death, and then succeeded them on the old homestead, which was purchased by his father in 1825. He has added to it until he has now 260 acres of good land. He has been extensively engaged in raising stock and sheep of the higher grades. He was married March 13, 1844, to Miss Ellen P. Mitchell. They are the parents of four children, all daughters—Alice A., Margaret J., Emma L. and Florence A.

Charles Mathew Henry, farmer and sheep-raiser, was born in Ames Township, Athens County, Ohio, Nov. 6, 1842, the youngest son of Mathew and Mary (Park) Henry. He was married Sept. 16, 1867, to Elizabeth C. Goble, daughter of Thomas L. and Mary J. (Law) Goble. Her father was born in Athens County and her mother in Guernsey County, Ohio. By this union there are two children—Herbert, born Jan. 11, 1869, and Lizzie Alma, born March 27, 1873. He has a fine residence in Amesville, built, on the foundation of the old home where he was born, in 1877. His farm is a part of his father's original purchase, containing 210 acres of improved land. He has taken great interest in the raising of fine sheep and has been to great expense in the importation of blooded stock, having a large flock of thoroughbred sheep. Mr. Henry is a member of the Presbyterian church and his wife of the Methodist Episcopal. He is a member of the A. F. & A. M., Amesville Lodge, No. 278.

James Henry, farmer, section 3, Ames Township, born in Washington County, Ohio, in 1807, is a son of John Henry, who emigrated to the United States, from Ireland, settling in Pennsylvania for a short time, and in 1781 came to Ohio and settled in Washington County, and in 1817 came to Athens County, where he purchased of the Ohio Purchase Company 640 acres of land, and here our subject was reared and educated. Mr. Henry was first married Oct. 29, 1835, to Sophronia Goodspeed, a native of Massachusetts, but her parents were among the pioneers of Athens County. By this union there were three daughters—Sarah E., Mary J. and Flora E. His wife died Nov. 11, 1871. He was again married June 2, 1875, to Mrs. Sarah C. Rolston, who was a sister of his first wife. Mrs. Henry has one daughter by her former marriage—Miss Fannie Rolston, a young lady of rare intellect and refinement. Mr. Henry has held many offices of trust, and by his honorable and upright dealing has made many warm and true friends. He has a fine residence situated about one mile from Amesville, and his farm contains 175 acres of improved land. He has by industry accumulated a large property. He and his wife are members of the Methodist Episcopal church.

John Henry, the second child of Robert and Mary Henry, was born in Derry County, Ireland, in March, 1763. His mother's maiden name was Woodburn. He came to America in 1788, landing at Philadelphia, near where he remained about three years, working most of the time on a farm in Chester County. At this time he concluded to return to Ireland, and hoping to add something to his scanty means he decided to invest his earnings in flax-seed. With this merchandise he sailed for Ireland to join his family, but on the coast of that island, in sight of his home, the vessel was wrecked and his flax-seed went to the bottom of the ocean. By this accident he lost nearly all of the fortune he possessed. After remaining there about two years he again sailed for Philadelphia, bringing with him his wife and youngest son, leaving his eldest son, John, with his father. John remained in Ireland until he grew to manhood, when he came to Nova Scotia and there engaged in farming. As no communication between him and the rest of the family has taken place for many years it is not known what became of him. Mr. Henry, after arriving in America the second time, settled in Chester County, Pa., and remained there until 1801, when he came to Washington County, Ohio. Here he rented a farm in Newport Township and remained on it about five years, when he bought a farm on the Ohio River, five miles below Harmar, to which he at once removed and spent a number of years in improving. He had, when a young man, learned the trade of a wheelwright, and after he came to Ohio was able to turn this knowledge to profitable account, there being a good demand for flax-wheels among the early settlers, where almost every family used one for the manufacture of its own cloth, and by industry he could make two wheels a week, which were worth $4 each. The high water in the Ohio River in 1815 decided him to sell this farm, and in the spring of 1817 he removed to Athens County, having already bought section 33 in Bern Township. Here he lived until the time of his death, which occurred Feb. 27, 1854, a few days before he was ninety-one years old. During his long life he was a continuous example of industry and economy. He was twice married. His first wife was Miss Rachel Henry, whom he married in Ireland in 1787. She died in 1809. In 1811 he married Miss Margaret Mc-Nutt, who survived him about three years. His children by the first wife were five sons and four daughters, and by the last, four sons and six daughters, in all nineteen children; one daughter died in infancy, but the remaining eighteen Mr. Henry lived to see grow to manhood and womanhood. Mr. Henry is the progenitor of many children, grandchildren and great-grandchildren. At the time of his death he had nearly sixty grandchildren and ten great-grandchildren living, the latter number having since been raised to nearly ninety. These do not include the children and grandchildren of John Henry, Jr., who lived in Nova Scotia. The descendants of Mr. Henry are pretty generally farmers, there being only a few exceptions. They are industrious and in good circumstances, and as a class are good and useful citizens.

R. B. Henry, farmer and stock-raiser, was born in Ames Township, Athens Co., Ohio, May 15, 1840, the fourth son of Mathew and Mary (Park) Henry, who came to Athens from Washington County in 1839 and located in Bern Township, and the subsequent year moved to Ames Township and settled on the farm near the village of Amesville, where our subject was reared and educated. He was married Oct 17, 1865, to Eliza, daughter of Moses and Sophia (Henry) Curtis, who were prominently identified with the pioneers of Athens County. She is a lady of refinement and culture. This union was blessed with four children, two of whom are living— Edward Payson was born July 31, 1866, and died May 16, 1876, after a severe illness of typhoid pneumonia; Alice Glazier, born Sept. 4, 1870, died Oct. 26, 1878, when eight years of age; Vesta Curtis, born June 5, 1877, and Jesse Louis, born Nov. 29, 1880. Mr. Henry has a fine farm, a part of the old homestead, containing 182 acres of improved land adjoining the village of Amesville, on which he makes a specialty of raising sheep of the higher grades. His residence in the village was erected in 1876 and has all the conveniences of a modern house. He and his wife are members of the Presbyterian church.

Nathaniel P. Hoisington, farmer and stockraiser, was born in Ames Township, Nov. 19, 1819, the youngest son of Joab and Annie B. (Green) Hoisington. His father was a native of Vermont and came to Athens County in 1804, and his mother a native of Massachusetts and came here in 1802. Our subject was reared on a farm and received his early education in the common schools, living with his parents until he reached his majority. He then took charge of the old homestead until the death of his parents. He was married Dec. 3, 1843, to Miss Elizabeth Weis, daughter of Jacob and Rosanna (Stalder) Weis, who came from Newburn, Switzerland, about the year 1818. They have had a family of eight children, seven still living—Dudley W., Rose, Mary, John B., Lou M., William P. and Kittie. Jacob L. is deceased. Mr. Hoisington purchased his present farm in 1857. It contains 230 acres of excellent land and is one of the best farms in Athens County. He has held several offices of trust in the township. He and his wife are members of the Presbyterian church at Amesville.

Mrs. Ann M. Johnson is the daughter of James Cook. Her grandfathers, Thomas Cook and James Reaves, were both soldiers in the Revolutionary War. She was born in Fairfax County, W. Va., March 6, 1812. She was united in marriage Feb. 14, 1835, to William T. Johnson, born in the same county, April 14, 1808. In 1838 they came to Ohio and settled on a farm in Washington County, where they lived until 1843, when they came to Athens County and settled on a farm in Ames Township, belonging to William Cutler. Although Mr. Johnson was a hard-working man he was unable to provide his family with anything more than the necessaries of life, and Feb. 19, 1847, he died, leaving his widow and five small children in almost destitute circumstances. Being a woman of remarkable energy, she supported her family by her daily labors, and for several years walked a distance of two miles, did a hard day's work and returned home. In this way she educated her children so that as they grew up they were all able to teach school. When the late civil war broke out, her only son, William Thomas Johnson, then little more than a boy, went out in the defense of his country. He enlisted in July, 1861, in Company B, Thirty-sixth Ohio Infantry, and was engaged in some of the hardest fought battles of the Rebellion. He served his country faithfully for four years, never flinching from his duty, and at the close of the war received an honorable discharge and returned to his native home, and two months subsequent, Oct. 14, 1865, died, leaving his widowed mother and four sisters and a large number of his old comrades to mourn his loss. Mrs. Johnson is an ardent worker in the cause of Christianity, having united with the Methodist Episcopal church in 1842.

L. F. Junod was born in Ames Township, Athens Co., Ohio, Sept. 1, 1853. He was reared on a farm and received his early education in the common schools, finishing at the Ohio University at Athens, living with his parents until he grew to manhood. He was married March 7, 1878, to Alice Southerton, of Athens County. They have one child—Ida Mabel. Mr. Junod and his wife are members of the Methodist Episcopal church. He has a fine farm of 275 acres of improved land.

Kilion Kasler, deceased, was born in Norwich, Vt., Aug. 27, 1788, and married Mandana Pembers, who was born in Poultney, Vt., Feb. 27, 1793, and in 1818 they came to Ohio, having only 12½ cents when they arrived here; but by industrious and economical habits they were able to accumulate a large property. They were the parents of seven children, six of whom still live. They were active members of the Methodist Episcopal church for many years, and both lived to an advanced age. Their youngest son, Andrew J. Kasler, was born in Ames Township, Athens Co., Ohio, April 3, 1831. He was reared on a farm and received his education in the common schools. He lived with his parents until the death of his father, when he succeeded him to the homestead and cared for his aged mother until her death. He was married Oct. 4, 1855, to Mary A. Rathburn, of Ames Township. They hav had five children, only four of whom are living—Marvin M. (deceased), Lillie D., Lewis W., Asa A., Sally A. Mr. K. has a fine farm of 150 acres of good land under a high state of cultivation.

Frederick P. Kasler was born in Clinton County, N. Y., Aug. 29, 1817, and when one year old came with his father's family to Ohio, and settled in Ames Township, Athens County. He was the second son of Kilion and Mandana Kasler. His youth was spent in assisting his father in clearing and opening up their frontier home, and attending school. He was married April 10, 1843, to Jane L. Minor, a daughter of Nathan L. and Hannah L. Minor, who were prominently identified with the early settlers of Ames Township. Seven children were born to them, six now living—Kilion, Royal P., Ellen, Alice, Warren V., Georgiana, and Charles (deceased). Mr. Kasler has always followed assiduously the avocation of a farmer, having moved on his present farm in 1843. He has accumulated a good property, and by his honest and upright dealings, has won the confidence and esteem of the entire community. He has held many local offices of trust. His wife died Feb. 20, 1871. His farm contains 153 acres of improved land on which, in the year 1881, he erected one of the best farm houses in the township.

Seth Linscott, farmer and stock-raiser, was born in Ames Township, Athens Co., Ohio, Aug. 2, 1836, a son of George and Sarah (Davis) Linscott, and a grandson of Israel Linscott, who was one of the early settlers of Ames Township. He was reared on a farm, and received his education in the common schools, residing with his parents until he was twenty-two years of age. He was married Jan. 10, 1858, to Miss Elizabeth Morris, of Athens County. They have had twelve children, of whom ten are living—George I., Perley J., Harvey L. D., Sarah C., Daniel S., Charles O., Nora M., Adeline D., Alonzo V. and Emmit. Mr. Linscott has always followed the avocation of farming, and by his own industry and exertion has accumulated a large property. His farm contains 200 acres of improved land, under a high state of cultivation. He and his wife are active members of the Church of the Disciples.

John Matheny, farmer, was born in Athens Township, March 20, 1841, the son of John and Rebecca Matheny. He was reared on a farm, and has during his whole life followed that occupation. On reaching his majority he purchased a farm in Athens Township on which he resided about eight years. In 1867 he came with his family to Ames Township and purchased his present home, which is a fine farm containing 122 acres of improved land. He was married April 17, 1862, to Miss Mary E. Boyles. They are the parents of three children—George G., Minerva E., and Electa F. Mr. Matheny has been very successful through life and uses his accumulated wealth in surrounding himself and family with the comforts of life. Mrs. Matheny is a member of the Methodist Episcopal church.

A. Matteson, Ames Township, Ohio, farmer and stock-raiser, was born in Bennington County, Vt., Sept. 14, 1843, a son of Leland and Livia Matteson. Our subject was reared on a farm and received his early education in the common schools and finished at the Mt. Auburn Seminary. He was married in 1869 to Miss Sarah Wilmarth, a daughter of Ambrose, who was the only surviving son of Rufus Wilmarth, who emigrated to Washington County in 1815, settling near Plymouth, where he passed his remaining days. Ambrose Wilmarth purchased the farm now occupied by A. Matteson in 1840. He was married in the fall of 1833 to Miss Sarah E. Larue. By this union was one child, a daughter. His wife died in 1862, and he was again married in 1866 to Miss Laura Pugsley, of Hocking County. In 1867 Mr. Wilmarth moved to Clinton County and remained until 1870, when he returned to Athens County, purchasing the property where he still resides, near Salina. Mr. Matteson since his marriage has resided on his present farm, where he has been engaged in raising fine stock, in which avocation he has been highly successful and gained a wide reputation. They are the parents of four children, of whom three are still living—Orson S., Livia G. and Sarah E. His farm contains 160 acres of fine land under a high state of cultivation, admirably adapted for the purpose for which it is now being used.

Jacob McCuen, was born on the 25th day of May, 1801, a son of John and Mary (Boyles) McCuen, who were from Bedford County, Penn., and came to Ames Township, Athens Co., Ohio, in 1796, where they lived the remainder of their days. Our subject spent his youth in assisting in clearing and improving the farm, and received a limited education in the subscription schools. After he grew to manhood, in connection with his farming pursuits, he worked at carpentering for many years. Much of his leisure time was spent in hunting wild game, which was abundant at that early day, and as a marksman Mr. McCuen had no superior. He was united in marriage, Jan. 18, 1823, to Lyda Owens, a native of Washington County. By this union are five children—Nancy, Vesta, Adaline, Charles O. and Theodore A.

Joseph K. Minor, farmer and stock-dealer, was born in Columbus, Ohio, Jan. 28, 1827, the son of Nathan and Hannah Minor. During his infancy his parents came to Athens County and settled in Homer Township, which is now in Morgan County. His father died when he was five years old, and he soon after went to live with Nathan Hill, with whom he remained until he reached his majority, and during this time was able to save $100. He has always followed farming, and in 1863 became connected with J. B. Brown, in the stock business, in which he continued for nineteen years, meeting with considerable success. He now owns a fine farm of 158 acres of good land. He was married Jan. 13, 1848, to Eliza A. Mitchell, a native of Ames Township. They have had six children, five still living—Edith J., Helen S., Albert G., Oliver D. and Lawrence L. Charles K. is deceased.

H. A. Oberholzer was born in Bern, Switzerland, Nov. 8, 1812, and came to the United States with his parents in 1819, locating in Athens County. Here our subject was reared, and for the greater part of his life resided. When about eighteen years of age he went to work on the Ohio Canal, and followed this occupation for about four years. He then returned to Ames Township, and has since been engaged in farming. In 1833 he entered eighty acres of Government land and afterward bought forty acres, which constitute his present farm. He was married Dec. 2, 1841, to Miss Nancy, daughter of Albert B. and Sarah Cone. They have had four children, three of whom are living—Mary S., William A. and Louis W. Frederick H. is deceased. Mr. Oberholzer has held several offices of trust in his township. He and his wife are members of the Methodist Episcopal church.

David W. O'Neal was born in Ames Township, Athens Co., Ohio, April 12, 1843, a son of Samuel and Mary (Bryson) O'Neal, who were among the pioneers of Athens County. He was reared on a farm and received his education in the common schools. When he was fourteen years of age his father died, leaving our subject to manage the farm of about thirty acres cleared land, with an incumbrance of $700, and care for his mother and sisters. By strict attention to his work he had the debt paid off before he was twenty years of age. He was married Sept. 14, 1862, to Susan M. Johnson, of Ames Township. They are the parents of seven children, five of whom are still living—Elsworth D., John T., Charles V., Samuel R., Osro Ben Eddie. Mary and one infant are deceased. Mr. O'Neal has an improved farm of 170 acres of good land. He and his wife are active members of the Methodist Episcopal church.

Horace C. Owen was born in Ames Township, March 31, 1861, son of James P. and Minerva J. (Carter) Owen. His education was received in the common school and completed at Bartlett's Academy and at the Northwestern Ohio Normal School. He was engaged for a time with the C., C., C. & I. R. R., as car tracer, and in other capacities. He is now engaged in the mercantile business at Bishopville, where he receives, as he deserves, a large portion of the public patronage. He was married April 11, 1883, to Mattie G., daughter of Wm. H. Glazier, a lady of culture and much refinement. Mrs. Owen is an active member of the Presbyterian church.

James G. Owen was born in Washington County, June 25, 1805, a son of James Owen, who came to Ohio in 1788. His wife is said to be the first white woman in the Northwestern Territory, and as near as can be learned, the Ohio Purchase Company donated her 100 acres of land on that account. After the Indian war they settled in Adams Township, Washington County, where Mrs. Owen died in 1800, after which Mr. Owen married the mother of our subject, Miss Zuby Brown, a daughter of John Brown, a native of Massachusetts, and a soldier in the Revolutionary War, who, at the battle of Bunker Hill, received two severe wounds. Ten years after the death of his first wife, Mr. Owen died, leaving a widow with three small children—James G. being an infant. His youth was spent at the home of his Grandfather Brown. He was first married Nov. 27, 1823, to Polly B. Palmer. They were the parents of eight children, seven of whom are still living. His wife died in March, 1861. He was again married Aug. 24, 1862, to Mrs. Ann Thompson, who was a sister of his first wife. He came to Athens County in 1827, where he has since resided. Mr. Owen has accumulated a large property by his own industry, having nothing to start with, and in his old age he has a competence. Although eighty years of age, he retains the physical and mental vigor of his youth to a remarkable degree.

A. C. Painter, merchant, Amesville, a native of Westmoreland County, Pa., was born Nov. 12, 1834, and when eight years of age came with his parents, Isaac and Eliza Painter, to Ohio, settling on a farm in Washington County. When he was thirteen years of age the family, consisting of the mother and eleven children, were bereaved by the loss of a generous and affectionate husband and a kind and indulgent father. At the age of nineteen he went to learn the shoemaker's trade, which avocation he followed assiduously for a period of eleven years, after which he entered the store of John Patterson, as clerk, and continued in this capacity for a term of nineteen years. By his genial and courteous manner he won the confidence of his employer and the esteem of the general public; and, by his prudence and economy, he was enabled to enter the mercantile business for himself in the fall of 1882, in the village of Amesville, where he receives a generous share of the public patronage. He was married Feb. 11, 1864, to Lauretta F., daughter of the late Dr. J. W. Moore, who was for many years a prominent physician at Amesville. She is a lady of intelligence and refinement. This union has been blessed by two sons—William and Fred.

James Patterson is the oldest son of Jordan Patterson, who was born in North Carolina in 1792, and in 1807 came to Ohio and located in Jefferson County, where he lived until 1836. He was united in marriage, Oct. 27, 1814, to Mary Lipsey, born in 1798, daughter of Amasa Lipsey, who in the year 1801 assisted in surveying what is now Jefferson County, to which place, the subsequent year, he moved his family, it being then the frontier, inhabited only by Indians and native denizens of the forest. He settled on a farm, passing there the remainder of his days. Mr. Patterson came to Athens County in 1836 and located on a farm in Bern Township, where he resided until his death, Feb. 2, 1864, at the age of seventy-two years, having lived with his wife happily and contentedly for a period of over fifty years. They were the parents of eleven children, six of whom still live. He followed, since his early youth, the avocation of a farmer, and by an honest and upright life won the respect and esteem of all who knew him. He gave his children every advantage obtainable in that early day to gain a good English education, and when he passed away he caused his wife to mourn the loss of a generous and affectionate husband, and his children a kind and indulgent father. He and his wife were consistent members of the Society of Friends from their early youth. Mrs. Patterson still lives with her son James in Amesville, having reached the advanced age of eighty-five years. Her physical powers are but little impaired and she retains to a remarkable extent the mental vigor of her youth. Our subject was born in Jefferson County, May 27, 1816. His youth was passed in assisting his father on the farm and attending the subscription schools. At the age of seventeen he was apprenticed to a blacksmith where he spent three years in learning the trade. In 1836 he came with his parents to Athens County and located in Bern Township, where he erected a small shop and followed for one year blacksmithing. He then came to Ames Township and located near where the village of Amesville now is. During that time he built the first dwelling in the place, into which he moved his family, consequently he became the first resident of the now old village. Soon afterward he moved his shop and followed his chosen avocation assiduously for a period of over forty years. In connection with his regular business he carried on extensively the manufacturing of wagons and carriages. Mr. Patterson was united in marriage in June, 1838, to Martha, daughter of John and Margaret Henry. By this union there were four children, two of whom still live—Mary M. is the wife of J. L. Dunbar and Lucy A. is the wife of Dr. A. Adair. Mr. Patterson was, during the oil excitement, engaged with a large New York company in leasing land, and employed a large number of men in prospecting. During the period of about three years he leased over 6,000 acres of land. He and his wife are both active members of the Presbyterian church, he having officiated as Deacon for over thirty years. They are also members of the old pioneer society. He was, politically, formerly of the Whig party, and since the formation of the Republican party has ever been in the first ranks.

John Patterson, merchant, Amesville, is the son of Jordan and Mary (Lipsey) Patterson, who were among the old settlers of Athens

County. Our subject was born in Jefferson County, Ohio, Aug. 21, 1824. When twelve years of age he came with his parents to Athens County and settled on a farm in Bern Township. Mr. Patterson lived on a farm until he reached the age of fifteen years. He received his education in the common-schools. About the year of 1839 he came to Amesville where he was engaged in assisting his brother James in a blacksmith shop and attending school for about six years, after which he purchased a stock of goods and engaged in the mercantile business in the village of Amesville, which he carried on for one year, when he sold out and entered the store of Brown & Dickey as clerk, remaining with them one year. In the fall of 1848 he again engaged in business for himself, and has for a period of thirty-five years been prominently identified among the leading merchants of Athens County. In the spring of 1879 he met with a serious loss by fire which consumed his store and entire stock of goods amounting to $10,000. He immediately built a large brick building and filled it with a complete stock and has now one of the finest stores in Athens County, where he does a very extensive business, amounting to about $25,000 a year, and by his strict attention to business has accumulated a large property and has, by his honorable and upright dealings with his patrons, won the confidence and respect of all who know him. He has held the office of Town Treasurer more than thirty successive years. He was appointed Postmaster soon after Grant was first elected President, which office he still retains. Mr. Patterson was first married, Jan. 2, 1851, to Emma J. Glazier a daughter of L. B. Glazier. By this union there are two daughters—Ella F., and Bell I., who is the wife of S. G. Adair. Mrs. Patterson died Sept. 16, 1862. He was again married, June 1, 1865, to Sarah E. Glazier, a sister of his first wife. They have one daughter—Emma. He and his wife are active members of the Presbyterian church. John Patterson was initiated in the first-degree of Masonry in Mount Olive Lodge at Chester Hill, Ohio, July 7, 1855. He was passed to the degree of F. C. July 27, and raised to the sublime degree of M. M. Aug. 22 of the same year. At the first meeting of the Amesville Lodge, U. D. which was held Feb. 18, 1856, Mr. Patterson was appointed S. D. At the next election of officers, Dec. 8, 1856, he was elected S. D., which office he held two years. In 1858 he was elected S. W., in which office he was retained for two years. In 1860 he was elected W. M., to which he was re-elected the two following years. In 1863 he was elected Treasurer, which office he filled until 1865. At this time he was elected J. W. In 1866 he was again elected W. M. which he held until 1878, with the exception of two years. In 1878 he was elected Tyler, and in 1881 he was elected W. M., which office he still holds.

Taylor Patterson, painter, Amesville, was born in Athens County, Dec. 19, 1848, a son of M. D. and Angeline (Sedgwick) Patterson. The father of our sketch was born in South Carolina, Nov. 11, 1821, and came to Athens County in 1841 and followed the avocation of farming and carpentering until the breaking out of the Rebellion. When his country needed brave and true men he answered the appeal by going out in the defense of the old flag and gave his life in defending his country. He was married Dec. 19, 1838, to Angeline, daughter of William and Elizabeth Sedgwick, who came to Athens County from Maryland in the year 1826. By this union were two children—Lucy J. and Taylor Patterson, the subject of this sketch, who was reared and educated in Ames Township. Since he reached his majority he has followed the avocation of painting in his native village of Amesville. Mr. Patterson is a man of an ambitious disposition and for several years has been at work in his leisure hours on an invention, a steam-propelling wagon, which without doubt in the near future will be of great benefit to the public at large.

Ezra Phillips, Jr., farmer and stock-dealer, born in Ames Township, Athens Co., Ohio, April 3, 1835, is the oldest son of Ezra and Mary Ann (McDougal) Phillips, who have been prominently identified with the interests of Ames Township since its early settlement. He was reared on a farm and received his education in the common schools, living with his parents until he grew to manhood. He has always followed the avocation of farming and stock dealing in which he has been remarkably successful. He was married March 7, 1872, to Miss Ellen Ring, a daughter of John Ring, who came from Somersetshire, England, in 1857, and located in Athens. They have had three children, two of whom are living—Ezra and William. John is deceased. Mr. Phillips has a fine farm of 447 acres under a high state of cultivation.

J. B. Potter was born in Wheeling, W. Va., Sept. 7, 1836, and when three years of age went with his parents to Perry County, Ohio, where he was reared. His father being a blacksmith he was early put to work in the shop, which avocation in connection with farming he followed until 1865. During the late war he engaged extensively in buying horses for the Government, meeting with good success. He was married Aug. 15, 1858, to Miss M. J. Gift, a native of Morgan County, but at the time of her marriage a resident of Perry County. They had seven children, five of whom are living—Bertha J., Perley A., Ida B., Blanche A. and Willie. Mr. Potter came to Athens County in October, 1872, and purchased his present farm, which contains 270 acres of improved land. In 1880 he met with a serious loss by fire, having his residence and contents entirely consumed. Mrs. Potter is a member of the Methodist church.

Lewis Rathburn was born in Delaware County, N. Y., Sept. 22, 1808, and came with his parents, David and Elsie (Lewis) Rathburn, to Ames Township, Athens Co., Ohio, in 1809. He was reared on a farm, and received his education in the subscription chool, living with his parents until he reached his majority. He was first married in 1829 to Sally Kearns, of Washington County, Ohio, and by this union were six children, five of whom are still living. He purchased his present home about 1830, where he has resided for over fifty years. His wife died May 17, 1880, and he was again married in August, 1881, to Mrs. Mercy Dille, a daughter of Israel Linscott, who was among the pioneers of Ames Township.

Jason Rice was born in Waterford, Ohio, in 1801, and came with his parents, Jason and Sarah (Hibbard) Rice, to Ames Township, Athens County, in 1804, where he has since resided. When twenty years of age his father gave him one year of his time as his share of the estate. He was married Nov. 12, 1826, to Caroline Duffee, a native of Rhode Island, who came to Ohio in 1817. By this union there were seven children, four of whom lived to be men and women, and two still living—Melona A. and Elizabeth C. After his marriage he resided on the old homestead for one year, after which he purchased a farm on Sunday Creek containing eighty-four acres of unimproved land, where he resided for eight years. He then sold out and purchased his present home, which contains about 200 acres of improved land under a high state of cultivation, where he has resided for a period of over forty-seven years. Mr. Rice is among the foremost in contributing liberally to all enterprises that will be of interest and benefit to the community. Although eighty-two years of age, with the exception of his hearing being somewhat impaired, he retains his physical and mental vigor to a remarkable degree.

Francis C. Robinson, farmer and stock-raiser, born in Ames Township, Athens Co., Ohio, Oct. 2, 1832, is the eldest son o John C. and Eliza A. Robinson, who were prominently identified with the early settlement of Ames Township. He was reared on a farm and educated in the common schools, remaining with his parents until he was twenty-three years of age. He was married Nov. 17, 1855, to Miss Mary J. Johnson, a daughter of Joseph and Dorcas Johnson, also pioneers of Athens. They have ten children—Eliza T., Delila J., Thomas G., Calvin C., Margaret L., William D., John Q., Polly E., Joseph F. and Mary E. Mr. Robinson owns a large farm on which he is nicely situated. He and his wife are members of the Disciple church.

John C. Robinson was born in Wood County, W. Va., March 22, 1803. When he was two years of age he came with his mother's family to Ohio and settled in Warren Township, Washington County, where they lived until he was thirteen years of age, when they removed to Ames Township, Athens County, where with the exception of a few years he has since lived. His father died when he was an infant, leaving his mother with a family of five small children in limited circumstances. The first year after they came to this county they located temporarily on an improved farm, after which they moved into the woods on school land, where the small boys cleared the land and supported their widowed mother. In 1818 they returned to Washington County, where they resided for two years. They then came again to Athens County and purchased a farm in what is now Bern Township. In 1826 Mr. Robinson, taking great interest in all the leading questions that were of benefit and interest to the community, with one or two others, started a petition to separate Bern and Ames townships. He was married Sept. 17, 1826, to Elizabeth Ann Gardner, a daughter of Thomas Gardner. She was born in the city of New York in the year 1809. To them were born seven children, only five still living—Margaret and Polly (deceased), Frances C., Sarah E., James L., Delilah J., Lewis L. He moved on his present farm in 1836. It contains eighty-six acres of good land, under a high state of culture. Mr. Robinson never aspired to publicity, and could never be persuaded to accept the support of his friends to county or local offices. He has been a member of the Baptist church for about sixty years. His wife was a member of the same church. She died April 15, 1876. Mr. Robinson is eighty years of age, and by a long life of honest and upright dealings he has won a large circle of warm and true friends, and the confidence and esteem of the entire community.

Captain James B. Shoop, a resident of Amesville, Athens Co., Ohio, since the year 1866, was born Feb. 2, 1842, in the old town of Marietta, Ohio. From thence, about the year 1850, his parents moved to McConnelsville, Morgan Co., Ohio, at which place and the neighboring village of Malta he continued to reside until his settlement at Amesville as above stated. His father, though a skillful and industrious cabinet-maker, having a large family to support by his daily labor, was able to afford his son but a limited common-school education. He was early assigned work at the bench with his father, thus contributing his help to the family's support until his enlistment in the Union army in 1861. The war record of Captain Shoop is one of which he and his friends may be justly proud. When the Rebellion arose as a mighty hurricane and smote the Government with a force that made its strong pillars to shake, young Shoop was astir to support the cause of freedom and union. When, as yet, many with more favored opportunities were going to and fro, in doubt and indecision, a company, hastily recruited at his native city, Marietta, under President Lincoln's first call for troops, passed through McConnelsville, hurrying to defend the beleaguered capital city. This company Shoop joined, went to Zanesville and quartered the first night in the old market house. The next morning he was rejected at roll call, by the intervention of his older brother, Hewett, who, taking his place in the company, sent him reluctantly and disappointed to his home. Immediately on his return, however, he enlisted, one of the first in the county, in the company then forming, and was soon mustered into the three months' service, as a private in Company H, Ohio Volunteer Infantry, forming at Camp Anderson, near Lancaster, Ohio. In this campaign he served for nearly four months, discharging his duties in such a soldierly manner that assured his later and greater success. Soon after being mustered out President Lincoln issued his proclamation for volunteers for three years, or during the war. Shoop entered the service in Company B, Ohio Volunteer Infantry, forming at Camp Goddard, near Zanesville. Enlisting as a soldier of the ranks, always prompt in the discharge of his duties, never asking, he nevertheless promptly earned and received promotion, passing through all the grades of non-commissioned officers. He was first commissioned as First Lieutenant in August, 1863, and was assigned the command of Company B, and in 1864 he was awarded a Captain's commission, in which rank he closed his military career. The Captain won all these honors without home influence, solely by his soldierly virtues in sight of all his comrades. He participated in many of the hardest fought battles of the war. In the bloody charge on Fort Wagner, on Morris Island, S. C., he received a severe wound in his side, from which he is still a sufferer. Always preferring to share the hardships and perils of his comrades he went into the charge on Wagner, although on the sick list and excused from duty. He had many assurances and testimonials of the universal respect and esteem in which he was held by his command, one of the proudest of which was an elegant sword, sash and belt, presented to him by his old Company B, on Christmas, 1863, at Hilton Head Island, S. C. At the close of the war he was honorably discharged and he returned to his home in Morgan County, where on the 18th of July, 1865, he was united in the holy bonds of matrimony to Lizzie Koons, of McConnelsville. By this union there were six children, of whom five still survive—Daisy (deceased), Fred, Hugh, Nellie, James and Edith. In 1866 Captain Shoop located in business in Amesville, where he has followed assiduously the avocation of a cabinet-maker, during which time he has met with several severe losses by fire. First in 1870 his home and contents were totally destroyed, and in 1873 a building in which he had furniture stored caught fire, by which our subject met with a loss of $300. In 1875 he was again visited by the fire fiend, when his shop, tools, and entire stock were wholly destroyed. But being a man of great energy he again started in business and has built up a fine trade. He is among the foremost to contribute to every laudable enterprise which will be of interest and benefit to the community, lending his influence and donating from his own personal means to all worthy objects of charity. He was first made a Free and Accepted Mason in March, 1868, an organization in which he takes great pride, having held nearly all the offices to be conferred, and is among the first to promote the usefulness of the order. He is a Republican in politics and takes great interest in all political questions of the day. He and his wife are active and consistent members of the Amesville Presbyterian church.

John Smith, farmer, was born in Ames Township in 1825, and is the son of Nicholas Smith, who was one of the pioneers of Athens County. Our subject remained with his parents until he reached his majority, and then purchased the farm on which he now resides, which contains 700 acres of well improved land. He was married in

1847 to Miss Rosanna Weis, daughter of Jacob Weis. They have had seven children, four of whom are living—Mary E., Peter W., John L., Hiram B.; Jacob W., Lydia A. and Betsy are deceased.

Fred Stalder was born in Ames Township, Athens County, July 17, 1842, a son of Frederick Stalder, a native of Switzerland, who came to the United States and settled on the farm in Ames Township, Athens Co., Ohio, where our subject now resides, in 1819. He was reared on a farm and received his early education in the common schools, completing it at Bryant's Commercial College, at Chillicothe, Ohio. At the breaking out of the late Rebellion he enlisted in Company B, Thirty-sixth Ohio Infantry, in the summer of 1861, where he participated in many hard-fought battles, of which were Shiloh, siege of Corinth, Vicksburg, Jackson, Mission Ridge, New Hope Church, Atlanta and many others. At the last named he received a severe wound which disabled him from active duty for two months, and from which he has never recovered. He enlisted as a soldier of the ranks but earned and received promotion, passing through all the grades of the non-commissioned offices, and in the summer of 1863 receiving his commission as Second Lieutenant, and in a short time was promoted to First Lieutenant, which office he held until his term of enlistment expired. He received an honorable discharge Dec. 24, 1864, after which he returned to his native home and engaged in farming, which avocation he has since followed. He was united in marriage Nov. 8, 1872, to Lydia Ashman, a native of Cincinnati. They have one child—Harry G. He has held many local offices, and in 1878 he was elected to the office of Justice of the Peace, and re-elected in 1881. He is a member of the Columbus Golden Post, No. 89, G. A. R.

Samuel D. Stiles, a native of Pennsylvania, was born Nov. 26, 1835, the son of Enos and Mary Stiles. When he was five years old he came to Ohio with his parents and located in Alexander Township, Athens County, and three years after moved to Portsmouth, Ohio. His parents died when he was fourteen years of age and he was thrown upon his own resources. He became engaged in the fruit business which he followed for six years, meeting with good success. During the late civil war he was engaged as a teamster in the Quartermaster's department. He was married July 10, 1865, to Miss Susan E. Frisby. They have had nine children, six of whom are living—Martha A., Nathan C., Joseph E., Clarence W., Cary C. and Franklin W. Mr. Stiles has labored under many disadvantages through life yet has been enabled to raise a large family of children, and has given each of them a good education. Mr. and Mrs. Stiles are members of the Methodist Episcopal church.

Judge George Walker was born in Boston, Mass., in 1774. His father, John Walker, came from an old family in Leicestershire, England, was a graduate of the University of Edinburgh, and was a barrister at law. He removed to America in 1753, was married in Boston, and settled in Hartford, Conn. George received a good business education, engaging first in mercantile business at Cooperstown, N. Y. Through the dishonesty of his partner, he met with heavy losses and came to the territory of the Northwest in 1804. Here he purchased and settled on a farm near the present town of Amesville, where he remained all his life. When he came onto it the farm was a forest and he was without any practical knowledge of clearing or farming, but by patient endeavor he conquered all obstacles, coming out not only with means to support and educate his own family, but he took a great interest in, and contributed much to, the public welfare. He was one of the founders and principle supporters of the Western Library Association, the library being for a number of years kept at his house. He was also a leading supporter of the schools and all laudable enterprises. Soon after his arrival in the township he was made a Justice of the Peace, an office which he held continuously for about twenty-four years. He was County Commissioner for sixteen years, and was elected by the State Legislature an Associate Judge on the Common Pleas bench, holding this position fourteen years. His son, George Walker, Jr., was for many years a business man in Amesville. Of his seven daughters the eldest was married to Colonel Charles Cutler, the second to Edgar Jewett, two of the others married physicians, one a banker, one a merchant, and one was the wife of Rev. Alford Ryors, formerly of the Ohio University.

Rev. Wm. John Warrener, the eldest son of John Metham and Martha Warrener, was born at Bayswater, London, England, Aug. 3, 1845. He attended the common schools till he was ten years of age, when, on account of a weak physical constitution and failing health, he had to leave and go to work with his father, who was a house carpenter. During the next three years about one-half of the time was occupied at work and the other in attending school, after which he followed the occupation of a farmer until he left England in 1869. Desiring to become something more than a

35

mere mechanic, he at the age of seventeen attended the Government School of Art at South Kensington, where he studied geometry, perspective and free-hand drawing, and architecture. These studies were pursued in the evening from seven till nine, after his day's work of ten hours was done, for a period of two years, after which he made many designs of buildings, etc., which were afterward executed. When nineteen years of age he became converted and united with the General Baptist church. One year thereafter he organized the Canterbury-road Baptist Sunday-school at Kilbourne, London, and began to speak in public on religious and temperance topics. Having been asked by his aunt to come to America, he left the home of his boyhood Aug. 11, 1869, and landed in New York City on the 24th and reached Ames Township on the 26th of the same month. On the 23d of September, 1871, he was, in Baltimore, Md., married by the Rev. J. T. Murray to Rachel A. Kelly, of London, England, born Nov. 4, 1843. She is a lady of much refinement and cultivation. Mr. Warrener was naturalized in 1874, and has since taken an active part in public affairs. He is widely known as an able speaker and writer on political, social and religious subjects. In 1876, after much careful investigation and thought, he united with the Christian church, and on Aug. 14 of that year was ordained as minister of the gospel, and received as a member of the Ohio Eastern Christian Conference. In this, his favorite work, he has made rapid progress, and has represented it in its quadrennial session of the American Christian Convention in 1878 and 1882. His education was acquired in greater part by study after his day's toil of manual labor was done. Mr. and Mrs. Warrener are the parents of five children—John M., Sydney K., Harrison P., Emily W. and Annie A.

Edmund Wheeler, farmer and stock-raiser, was born in Athens County, Ohio, March 4, 1827, the oldest son of Ezra and Rachel Wheeler. His youth was spent on a farm and his education was received in the common schools. His father died when he was sixteen years of age, and he went to live with George Walker, Jr. At the breaking out of the Mexican war he enlisted. On arriving at Baton Rouge he was taken seriously ill, and was unable to attend to active duty. He received an honorable discharge and returned home to Ames Township, where he has since resided. He was first married Feb. 5, 1847, to Nancy McCuen, a daughter of Jacob and Lyda McCuen, of Ames Township. They had one child, a daughter, Adaline, the wife of L. F. Beasley, of Ames Township. Mr. Wheeler lost his wife Feb. 5, 1852. He was again married June

23, 1858, to Georgiana L. Walker. He has a fine farm containing 150 acres of improved land adjoining the village of Amesville. He and his wife are active members of the Methodist Episcopal church.

Jay Wilder, Ames Township, lumber manufacturer, was born in Oakland, Ohio, Feb. 22, 1852, where he lived until he was twelve years of age, when he went to Morgan County and remained until 1870. He then came to Athens County, where he engaged in the lumber business. In 1873 he went to Virginia and remained until 1878, returning to Ames Township, Athens County, and engaging in the same business, which he has since followed. He was married Feb. 22, 1872, to Alpha Bailleau, of Bern Township. They have two children—Lillian and Pearley E. He is a member of the A. F. & A. M., Amesville Lodge, No. 278. Mrs. Wilder is a member of the Presbyterian church of Amesville.

John Wyatt, deceased, was the eldest son of Deacon Joshua and Elizabeth Wyatt, and was born in Westmoreland County, Pa., Aug. 26, 1793. With his father's family he came to the then Territory of Ohio, in the spring of 1800, and after stopping one year at Marietta moved, in 1801, to the unsettled, uncleared and uninviting locality now Ames Township, then in Washington, now in Athens, County, O., where he spent the greater part of his long and active life. While at Marietta he attended school, taught by Mr. David Putnam, and afterward, in addition to the limited educational advantages furnished by the new settlement, he was for a limited period a student of the Ohio University, at Athens. About 1818 he was united in marriage with Emily Carpenter, a daughter of Captain Parker Carpenter. Ten children were born to them, seven sons and three daughters, all but two of whom grew to man and womanhood. Mr. Wyatt was a man of great energy and industry, and it may be well said of him he never ate the bread of idleness. Moving soon after his marriage upon a part of the same tract upon which his father lived, he soon cleared up his farm and caused the waste places and wilderness to blossom as the rose. His industry and frugality were not unrewarded, for he was not only enabled to furnish to each member of his numerous family a good farm as soon as they became of age, and render them material assistance all through his life, but had a large competency left for benevolent purposes and subsequent distribution. He was also a man of distinguished piety, and having united with the Presbyterian church at the early age of nineteen, first at Athens and subsequently at Amesville, he continued an active, earnest, steadfast and devoted member to the day of his death. But not willing that his work should end at his death, the church at Amesville, toward the erection of which building he had so generously contributed, and the cause so liberally sustained all through his long life, was made the recipient of the munificent sum of $1,000, the annual interest of which is to be toward sustaining the gospel as long as the church shall exist. "Verily the good men do shall live after them." Mr. Wyatt was ever foremost in espousing the cause of the needy, destitute and oppressed, it mattered not in what form presented. No one went from his door hungry. This same hatred of oppression made him affiliate politically with the Abolition party when Abolitionism was far from being popular. The pursued slave ever found a safe haven in the house of John Wyatt. Another characteristic was his fondness for children and his desire to point them to the Savior. This was beautifully exemplified but a few minutes before he breathed his last, by a little three-year-old granddaughter bidding him good-bye before retiring, when he took up and repeated with her the simple and familiar prayer of, "Now I lay me down to sleep," etc. But the life of Mr. Wyatt was not without its trials and difficulties. Six of his ten children passed the Jordan of death before him. His wife was summoned by death in 1865, and that loathsome disease, cancer, was for several years slowly but surely eating away his life. Death was a welcome messenger, coming Oct. 31, 1877. After the death of his wife he lived with his daughter, Mrs. Howe, at Belpre, Ohio, where he died. In accordance with a long-cherished desire his remains were taken to Amesville for interment, and deposited by the side of his wife and children.

Joseph Patterson, proprietor of the Isham House, Jackson, Ohio, was born in Jefferson County, Ohio, in 1818, a son of Jordan and Mary Patterson. When he was nineteen years of age his parents moved to Athens County and located on a farm. When twenty-one years of age he started in life for himself, and soon after married Grace Beck, who died fifteen months later, leaving one child—Mary. Two years later he married Martha Van Pelt, who died in 1864, leaving six children. Mr. Patterson then married Mary E. Pattent, by whom he has one child. In the early part of his life Mr. Patterson was in the mercantile business in Athens County, but since 1873 has been engaged in the hotel business. In 1874 he removed to Jackson, and succeeded I. T. Monahan as proprietor of the Isham House. The conveniences of the house are good; the guests are at all times treated with due courtesy, and the house deserves the patronage of the public. Mr. Patterson is a genial landlord, and at all times exerts himself to make comfortable the many guests who visit his house.

CHAPTER XIX.

ALEXANDER TOWNSHIP—A GIANT IN ITS YOUTH, NOW SHORN OF MOST OF ITS TERRITORY.

AS IT WAS AND NOW IS—ITS BOUNDARY LINES—TOPOGRAPHY—EARLY SETTLERS—WHISKY TRANSPORTATION—TOWNSHIP OFFICERS—JUSTICES OF THE PEACE—HEBBARDSVILLE—PLEASANTON—WOODYARD P. O.—CHURCHES, SCHOOLS, AND RELIGIOUS AND EDUCATIONAL INTERESTS.

AS IT WAS AND NOW IS.

When Athens County took upon itself the robes of official life, and secured a local habitation and a name among her sister counties of the State, Alexander Township was one of the four into which the county was divided. It originally included the territory which now forms eleven townships, viz.: Bedford, Scipio and Columbia, of Meigs County; Vinton, Clinton, Elk, Madison and Knox, of Vinton County; and Lee, Lodi and Alexander, of Athens County. In territorial extent it was equal to Ames, and twice as large as Athens. The township was located and surveyed in 1795. This township with Athens, were the "college townships," and these naturally being in close connection, Alexander was for a long time known as "South Town." The township is a congressional township in size, and is located in the south tier of sections and second from the west line of the county. It is bounded on the north by Athens, on the east by Lodi Township, on the south by Meigs County, and on the West by Lee Township. Its general appearance is hilly and uneven, yet within its borders are to be found many excellent farms, and the entire township is well adapted to stock-raising and wool-growing, in which pursuits its citizens are principally engaged.

EARLY SETTLERS.

Among the early settlers of Alexander Township, were: Robert Ross, William Gabriel, Amos Thompson, Enos Thompson, Edward Martin, Isaac Stanly, John, Jonathan, Joseph, Thomas and Isaac Brooks, Matthew Haning, Thomas and John Armstrong, Jared,

Israel and Martin Bobo, Caleb Merritt, Joel Lowther, Michael Bowers, William Stroud, Esquire Bowman, Abner Smith, Charles and Isaiah Shepherd, Thomas Sharp, Richard and William Reaves. These all came as early as 1805. There was little difference in he settlement of this township from the others. They had their trials and hardships to contend with. Game was abundant, and the marksmanship of the old settlers proverbial. They wasted very little powder and lead, and when the bead was drawn and the sharp crack of the rifle heard, it was pretty certain death had claimed a victim. Two of the early settlers, who were noted hunters, Jeremiah Clements and Israel Bobo, killed sixty-five bears in one season, on the site and its surroundings, where the town of Hebbardsville now stands. These same old pioneers were very fond of whisky, and to procure the desired article took a load of bear skins to the Ohio River and traded them for a barrel of the same, and to get it home they made a sort of a drag of two poles to be drawn by the horses, and in this way conveyed it through the woods to their home. This was the first barrel of whisky ever brought into Alexander, but in after years the use of it became very common and fashionable, but at the present time the people are more temperate, and there are no saloons in the township.

OFFICIAL.

The early records of the township were destroyed by fire in the house of John McKee, in about 1828, but as nearly as can be ascertained the first Trustees were Caleb Merritt, John Brooks, and Thomas Sharp. The first Justice of the Peace was Caleb Merritt. The following is a list of the township trustees and justices since 1829.

TRUSTEES.

1829, Ziba Lindley, Sr., Sam'l McKee, N. Misner; 1830, Ziba Lindley, Sr., Sam'l McKee, E. N. Nichols; 1831, Ziba Lindley, Jr., Sam'l McKee, E. N. Nichols; 1832, Samuel Earhart, Asa Stearns, B. Parks, Jr.; 1833, Samuel Earhart, J. V. Brown, B. Parks, Jr.; 1834, Ziba Lindley, Jr., J. M. Mahon, B. Parks, Jr.; 1835, Ziba Lindley, Jr., John Brooks, Samuel Earhart; 1836, Daniel Dudley, Ami Conde, Archelaus T. Clark; 1837, Samuel Earhart, John Brooks, Jr., Archelaus Stanley; 1838, Wm. B. Reynolds, John Brooks, Jr., Franklin Burnham; 1839, Wm. B. Reynolds, John Brooks, Jr., Franklin Burnham; 1840, John

Wm R Bowlby

Rickey, Peter Morse, John W. Drake; 1841, Franklin Burnham, John Grey, A. Love; 1842, Franklin Burnham, J. H. Brooks, A. Love; 1843, J. W. Drake, Ziba Lindley, Jr., A. Love; 1844, J. W. Drake, Ziba Lindley, Jr., A. Burtnett; 1845, J. W. Drake, Moses Patterson, A. Burtnett; 1846, George Bean, Daniel Teters, A. Burtnett; 1847, George Bean, John H. Brooks, Abram McVey; 1848, Archelaus Stanley, John H. Brooks, Abram McVey; 1849, James S. Hawk, A. G. Henderson, William Wood; 1850, John Rickey, Joseph W. Blackwood, John W. Drake; 1851, John Rickey, George Bean, William Wood; 1852, John Rickey, Franklin Burnham, William Wood; 1853, Daniel Teters, Peter Long, William Wood; 1854, Missing; 1855, Alexander Love, James H. Martin, Abram Coe; 1856, Alexander Love, James H. Martin, William Campbell; 1857, Moses Patterson, William Wood, William Campbell; 1858, Moses Patterson, Isaac Stanley, George W. Sams; 1859, E. N. Blake, John Rickey, George W. Sams; 1860, E. N. Nichols, John Rickey, George W. Sams; 1861, E. N. Blake, John Rickey, George W. Sams; 1862, E. N. Blake, John Rickey, George W. Sams; 1863, E. N. Blake, Isaiah Bean, Isaac Brooks, Jr.; 1864, E. N. Blake, Isaiah Bean, Isaac Stanley, Jr.; 1865, B. Rickey, Isaiah Bean, Peter Long; 1866, B. Rickey, Isaiah Bean, Homer Chase; 1867, S. B. Blake, Isaiah Bean, P. G. Hibbard; 1868, Samuel Blake, Isaiah Bean, William Bean; 1869, I. Bean, S. B. Blake, P. G. Hibbard; 1870, S. B. Blake, S. L. Matthews, John Rickey; 1871, S. B. Blake, John Rickey, J. J. Coe; 1872, S. B. Blake, John Rickey, J. J. Coe; 1873, S. B. Blake, John Rickey, J. J. Coe; 1874, W. B. Smith, J. N. Scott, Henry Logan; 1875, W. B. Smith, J. F. Biddle, Henry Logan; 1876, W. B. Smith, J. F. Biddle, Henry Logan; 1877, W. B. Smith, J. F. Biddle, S. B. Blake; 1878, Daniel Drake, H. B. Rickey, E. Reaves; 1879, P. G. Hibbard, H. B. Rickey, E. Reaves; 1880, J. F. Biddle, H. B. Rickey, S. B. Blake; 1881, Robert Buchanan, Daniel Drake, S. B. Blake; 1882, Robert Buchanan, Daniel Drake, G. W. Hooper; 1883, Daniel Drake, G. W. Hooper, W. H. Irwin.

JUSTICES OF THE PEACE.

1829, Ami Conde, J. M. Gorsline; 1831, Samuel McKee; 1832, J. M. Gorsline, Alfred Dunlap, Samuel Earhart; 1834, Josiah Wilson; 1835, William Golden; 1837, Josiah Wilson; 1838, William Golden; 1849, Franklin Burnham; 1850, John Camp, Joseph W. Blackwood; 1852, Franklin Burnham; 1853, John Camp, Joseph

W. Blackwood; 1854, Joseph McPherson, George Adair; 1855, Daniel Drake; 1857, Joseph McPherson, A. S. Coe; 1858, Daniel Drake; 1860, James Strite, L. Oliver; 1861, L. C. Crouch, Wm. B. Dickerson, A. S. Coe, A. C. Murphy, S. H. Kinney; 1863, Leven Oliver; 1864, Wm. Watson, Amos C. Murphy; 1866, Leven Oliver; 1867, Wm. Watson, Amos C. Murphy; 1868, Peter Vorhes; 1869, L. Oliver, A. C. Murphy, Peter Vorhes; 1870, L. Oliver, S. L. Matthews, Peter Vorhes; 1871, L. Oliver, S. L. Matthews, C. Hooper; 1872, R. S. Dent, S. L. Matthews, C. Hooper; 1873, R. S. Dent, S. L. Matthews, C. Hooper; 1874, R. S. Dent, S. L. Matthews, C. Hooper; 1875, R. S. Dent, S. L. Matthews, C. Hooper; 1876, R. S. Dent, S. L. Matthews, C. Hooper; 1877, R. S. Dent, S. L. Matthews, Henry Logan; 1878, R. S. Dent, S. L. Matthews, Henry Logan; 1879, R. S. Dent, S. L. Matthews, Henry Logan; 1880, R. S. Dent, S. L. Matthews, Henry Logan; 1881, W. R. Northrop, S. L. Matthews, Henry Logan; 1882, W. R. Northrop, S. L. Matthews, Henry Logan; 1883, W. R. Northrop, S. L. Matthews, B. F. Shamel.

HEBBARDSVILLE.

This quiet little town is located in the northwestern part of the township. It has never reached a very large size and now only contains about 100 inhabitants. Its business interests consist of a store and hotel both kept by B. Bean; one blacksmith, shop, by Jonas Lewis; a shoe shop, by J. J. Coe, who is also Postmaster at the present time; one wagon shop, by W. R. Northrop. There is a Methodist Episcopal church located here and the Cumberland Presbyterian near by. It also has one school. Near the Cumberland Presbyterian church is located the principal cemetery of the township, which is pleasantly laid out and tastefully arranged. The people may well look with pride upon this beautiful City of the Dead which they have provided as the last resting place of those who pass on to the "other shore."

PLEASANTON

is situated in the eastern part of the township, on the road from Athens to Pomeroy, and at the present time contains nearly 100 inhabitants. The first house was built in 1817 by Simon Pierce, and other settlers located from time to time and a postoffice was established in 1851, with the very appropriate name of Pleasanton.

The town has a high and commanding view of the surrounding country. In this place is located another of the Methodist Episcopal churches which is called McKendree's Church, and was built in 1869. Pleasanton has one general store kept by Henry Logan, Esq., while Dr. Bean attends to the wants of the sick and afflicted in this community. In the extreme southern part of the township is another postoffice, established in 1880, and called Woodyard's postoffice, with Mr. Woodyard as Postmaster.

Alexander Township has nine churches, three Baptist, three Methodist Episcopal, two Methodist Protestant and one Cumberland Presbyterian, all in a flourishing condition. The citizens of this township are generally of a peace-loving, church-going disposition, and take great interest in religious, as well as educational, matters. The pleasant church and school buildings which are so numerous speak well for the people who support them, and are monuments to their intelligence and enterprise.

The First Cumberland Presbyterian Church, of Alexander Township, Athens Co., Ohio, was organized Oct. 10, 1832, at a camp-meeting held on the farm owned by Mr. Ziba Lindley, which was conducted by Revs. John Morgan and Jacob Lindley. At the time of organization six Elders were chosen as follows: Jacob McVey, Ziba Lindley, Jr., A. Van Vorhes, Elijah Goodspeed, Samuel Earhart and Josiah Wilson.

The following is a list of the original members: Dennis Drake, Abel Bower, Jemima Bower, Anna McVey, Louis P. McLead, Mary McLead, Purnell Drake, Almus Lindley, Permelia Lindley, Thomas Armstrong, Sarah Gray, Abram McVey, Lucinda McVey, Eliza Blakeway, Octava A. Farlin, Mary Farlin, Festus McVey, Richard M. Drake, Melinda R. Drake, Susan Gabriel, McCraven Bean, John Clutter, Nathan Kinney, Abigail Wilson, Abram McKee, Elias Gabriel, Wm. Gabriel, Cyrena Clutter, Jane Van Vorhes, Lydia Kinney, Abigail West, Laurence King, Mary A. King, Julia Brown, Dennis Drake, Jr., Olive Drake, Eliza Day, Chloe Goodspeed, Phebe Brown, Andrew Gabriel, William Brown, William Bean, William Hanbury, James McKee, John B. King, Joseph Post, Sarah Post, Eliza Tippie, Elisha Hibbard, Sela Hibbard, Daniel McLead, Elias Day, Cornelius Moore, Elizabeth Moore and Andrew Gabriel.

The first regular pastor was Rev. Samuel Aston. Since that time about twenty ministers have served the church stately for longer or shorter periods, and about thirty have preached transiently. Twenty-three elders have served the church from first to last.

The present Elders are: Charles Jolley, Harvey Clutter, Daniel Drake, William Johnson, Peter Vorhes and Richard M. Drake.

The present Pastor is Rev. T. A. Welsh, who has served the congregation at different times for forty years.

The present membership is 130. Since the organization of the church more than 1,000 persons have been members of the same.

BIOGRAPHICAL.

David Allen, born in Fayette County, Pa., June 12, 1816, is a son of Josiah and Susan Allen, also natives of Pennsylvania. In 1818 his parents removed to Harrison County, Ohio, where his father died in 1842, aged eighty-three years. May 10, 1839, he married Mary Jane, daughter of John and Margaret (Porter) Wilkins, a native of Washington County, Pa. In 1847 Mr. Allen came to Athens County and located in Athens Township, living there sixteen years. He then came to Alexander Township and, in 1876, bought the farm where he now resides. He has 220 acres of land well cultivated, and a good residence. Mr. and Mrs. Allen have seven children—Margaret J., J. B., Clarinda Susan, John H., George D., William A. and Lillie A. Politically, he is a Democrat.

Elmer Armstrong, born in Athens County, Jan. 17, 1812, is a son of Thomas and Alice (Crawford) Armstrong. His father came to this county from Greene County, Pa., in 1799, and settled on the farm where his son now lives. Jan. 7, 1844, Mr. Armstrong married Permelia Booth, of Medina County, Ohio. They have four children—Elizabeth, Olive A., Elza B. and Addie A. During the war Mr. Armstrong was a strong Union man. He gave $1,000 to the One Hundred and Sixteenth and the Ninety-second Ohio regiments. He went out as Sutler of the former, and June 15, 1863, was taken prisoner and had all his goods taken by the rebels. He was taken to Castle Thunder, Libby Prison, and confined four months. Having considerable money concealed on his person and being allowed to go out without a guard, he was able to be of great assistance to his fellow prisoners. He is still living on the old homestead farm, engaged in farming and stock-raising, making a specialty of the latter.

Elza B. Armstrong was born in Alexander Township, Dec. 25, 1849, the son of Elmer Armstrong. His education was received at the Atwood Seminary, Albany, and at the Ohio University.

His early life was spent in assisting his father on the farm, and he is now in partnership with him under the firm name of Elmer Armstrong & Son. They have a fine farm of 600 acres and are making a specialty of fine stock, Clydesdale and thorough-bred trotting horses; also thorough-bred short-horn Jersey and Holstein cattle of the finest families bred constantly for sale. They have a large deer park and fish pond, and a number of Scotch coolie dogs. They have one of the best stock farms in the county. It is also rich in metal and has valuable coal beds and potter's clay of a fine variety. Mr. Armstrong was married Sept. 5, 1876, to Mary E., daughter of P. G. Hebbard. They have two sons—Elmer and Charles Crawford.

Bisco Bean, born in Hardy County, Va., Jan. 7, 1819, is a son of John G. and Dyanna Bean, who came to Athens County when Bisco was twelve years of age, and settled in Canaan Township. He was reared a farmer and educated in the common schools. He was married June, 17, 1840, to Orena Catlin. They have four children—Cyrus, J. F., Louisiana and Alonzo. In 1858 Mr. Bean came to Alexander Township, locating near Pleasanton. Mrs. Bean died in 1870, and Mr. Bean afterward married M. E. Cayton, daughter of William and Malinda Cayton, of Ross County. He then went to Ross County where he lived two and a half years, then returned to Pleasanton and remained nearly four years. In 1881 he bought his hotel and store in Hebbardsville, and is now engaged in the general mercantile business, having a good assortment of dry goods, groceries, boots and shoes, notions, etc.

E. M. Bean, M.D., born in Hardy County, Va., April 28, 1820, is a son of Thomas and Sarah (Hill) Bean. He received his education at Savannah Seminary, and commenced the study of medicine with Drs. Hill and Rice; was with them two years, then went to Dr. George Bean, remaining with him four years. He afterward attended the Physio-Medical College, at Cincinnati, where he graduated, receiving the degree of M. D. in 1871. In 1839 he came to Athens County, locating first in Rome Township. After his graduation he came to Pleasanton, Alexander Township, where he has since resided. He has a very extensive practice, frequently being called from a distance of seventy-five miles, and having letters from and sending medicine to patients in most of the States. A number of the prominent physicians now located in different States received their instruction from Dr. Bean. His library is one of the best in the county, both in a professional and literary point of view. Dr. Bean was married in December, 1845, to Adaline Culver, daughter of James Culver, of Athens County. They have three children—Emma Jane, Curnce Ann and Ida May. Dr. Bean and family are members of the Methodist church,

David Beasley, son of George Beasley, a pioneer of Athens County, was born March 12, 1838. During his early life he resided at home, attending the farm of his father. Nov. 12, 1861, he enlisted in Company G, Fifty-third Ohio Infantry; was wounded in the battle of Pittsburg Landing and discharged on account of disability. Regaining his health, he re-enlisted in the same regiment, Feb. 13, 1864. He was captured while on a foraging expedition and remained a prisoner forty-two days. He was discharged June 19, 1865, at Camp Chase, Ohio. After his return home he settled in Bern Township; then lived in Dover Township two years, in Ames Township two years, and on a farm in Alexander Township nine years. He then went to Hebbardsville and engaged in merchandising and keeping a hotel two and a half years, when he traded his property there for the place he now owns in Pleasanton. Nov. 8, 1857, he married Nancy, daughter of Aaron Evans, of Ames Township. They have three children—L. D., Florence and G. E. Their eldest daughter, Rachel Malvina, died at the age of three and a half years. Politically, Mr. Beasley is a Republican. He is a member of the Methodist Episcopal church.

Samuel B. Blake, born March 2, 1817, in Alexander Township, was a son of S. L. Blake, a native of Connecticut, who came to this township in 1816, and resided here till his death, March 15, 1859. He resided at home till twenty-six years of age, receiving his education in the common schools. He was married March 25, 1845, to Polly C., a daughter of John Camp, and a native of Connecticut. They have six children—William H., Henry C., Hattie, Mary, John and Charles. Mr. Blake has a farm of 157 acres where he has lived since 1848. He has a large two-story frame house and good farm buildings. Politically he is a Republican. He has held the office of Township Trustee for fifteen years. Mr. and Mrs. Blake are members of the Free-Will Baptist church.

Hosmer Chace was born on his father's farm in Alexander Township, Athens County, Oct. 2, 1833. Here among the beautiful hills of his nativity he spent his boyhood days, received his education and grew to manhood. July 1, 1862, Mr. Chace enlisted in the war for the Union and was mustered in as Sergeant of Company I, Seventh Ohio Cavalry, and was subsequently promoted to Lieutenant. Mr. Chace was married to Miss Nancy Reeves, of Meigs County, Ohio, and to them six children were born—Elsworth, Ellwood, Annie, Celia, Ella, and Mary Alice. Mr. Chace married for his second wife Sarah Ellen Robison, Oct. 23, 1877, who was a native of Alexander Township, Athens County. Three children were born of this union—Bertha, Ada and Ida; the two latter were twins. Seven of the nine children survive, all living with their father on the beautiful homestead where they were all born.

J. J. Coe, born in Knox County, Ohio, Nov. 11, 1829, is a son of John K. and Isabella Coe, natives of Washington County, Pa. He was the fourth of a family of seven children, and when five years of age his parents came to Athens County, locating at Chauncey, where they lived five years and then removed to Meigs County. When twenty years of age Mr. Coe came to Hebbardsville and worked at the shoemaker's trade a year with J. G. Wilson. He then went to work for himself, and by his fair dealing has gained a good custom, both in shoe and harness making. He has been Postmaster of Hebbardsville twenty years, and has been Township Trustee three terms. In May, 1856, he married S. W., daughter of John Calvert, of Meigs County. They have nine children—Anna, Lizzie, Estella, Edith, John, Mary, Maggie, Daisy and Earl. Mr. Coe is a member of the Cumberland Presbyterian church. He is a member of the Masonic fraternity, Lodge No. 156, Albany.

W. T. Dean, an enterprising farmer of Alexander Township, was born Jan. 14, 1850. His father, W. T. Dean, died when he was sixteen months old, and his mother, Mary J. (Beard) Dean, when he was six years old. He was reared by D. M. Clayton, of Athens, and received his education in the schools of that place. During the late war he enlisted, but was rejected on account of his age. When seventeen years of age he commenced to learn the trade of a stone mason and followed that occupation several years. He now has a fine farm of 103 acres and one of the best residences in the township. He was married Feb. 21, 1872, to Mrs. Kate (Walters) Coates, of this county. She had two daughters—Bell K. and Emma M. Coates. Mr. Dean is a member of the Masonic fraternity, Lodge No. 25, Athens.

William Dickson, born in Belmont County, Ohio, May 29, 1819, is a son of Henry Dickson, a native of Maryland. When he was a child his parents moved to Guernsey County, and when he was fifteen years old came to Athens County. March 16, 1843, he married Maria Lentner, a native of Delaware, and a daughter of Jacob Lentner. They have eight children—J. M., Joanna, Albert Hanford, J. W., Nancy, Mary L., Lizzie M. and Elisha B. In 1854 he bought the farm where he now resides. He has 310 acres of good land which is under a good state of cultivation. Politically, he is a Republican.

John Fisher, born in Columbiana County, Ohio, July 15, 1839, is the eighth of eleven children of Michael and Eliza (Dawson) Fisher. In October, 1862, he enlisted in Company F, Seventy-sixth Ohio Infantry. He participated in some of the hardest fought battles of the Rebellion, among them the siege of Vicksburg, Lookout Mountain, Mission Ridge, Ringgold, Resaca, and was with Sherman to the sea. After the war he settled in Meigs County Ohio, and lived there till 1881, when he bought the place where he now resides. He has one of the best farms in the township, having 310 acres all well improved, with a good two-story dwelling and commodious farm buildings. He was married Dec. 15, 1869, to Olive A., daughter of Elmer Armstrong, a prominent pioneer of Athens County. They have one child—Mabel B., born July 15, 1873.

Rev. James Haning, Jr., Lodi Township, Athens County, was born in Meigs County, Ohio, April 12, 1819, and is the son of James Haning, Sr., who came to Athens County in 1796, and was a soldier in the war of 1812. Our subject's parents moved to Alexander Township where they remained about seven years; then moved to Lodi where he was reared a farmer, receiving his education in the common schools. He was married when nineteen years of age to Miss Hannah Dudley, of Athens County. This union was blessed with one child—Emily. Mrs. Haning died July 18, 1842. Mr. Haning was again married March 4, 1843, to Miss Eliza Dudley, a sister of his first wife. They are the parents of four children—Hannah, Eliza J., Sarah and Mary. Mr. H. has a fine farm containing 242 acres of land under a high state of cultivation on which is one of the best coal beds in the county. He is a zealous worker in the cause of Christianity, and his lectures on sacred ordinances are very fine.

John Haning, born in Alexander Township, Athens Co., Ohio, Aug. 30, 1815, is a son of James Haning, a native of Washington County, Pa. When he was two years of age his parents moved to Scipio Township, Meigs Co., Ohio, where they lived six years. They then returned to Alexander Township and lived seven years, when his father bought 320 acres of wild land in Lodi Township, where he has since resided. He owns 184 acres, all under a good state of cultivation, with residence and barn built in modern style. He was married in September, 1837, to Delia Reeves, of Meigs County. They have four children—Margaret, John R., Joseph M. and Charles W. Mr. Haning is a member of the Free-Will Baptist church, and has been one of its most liberal supporters, it being through his instrumentality that the church in Lodi was built.

P. G. Hebbard, born in Dover Township, Athens County, Ohio, Aug. 10, 1830, is the second of four sons of Alanson and Becca (Grow) Hebbard, his father an early pioneer of Athens County, coming here from Vermont in 1819, and his mother a daughter of Judge Peter Grow, of Meigs County, Ohio. He was reared on a farm and educated at home under his father's instruction. He afterward taught seven years. April 20, 1854, he married Jane E. Davis, of York Township. They have seven children, six still living—Mary E.; Emma J., Charles A., Becca B., P. G., Jr., and Nettie. Mr. Hebbard has a fine farm of 163 acres, but makes a specialty of stock dealing, at which he has been very successful. His youngest daughter is a musical prodigy, and when two and a half years old could play accurate accompaniments on the piano to the most difficult pieces, and now, though but six years of age, is a musical wonder.

Clement Hooper, son of Stephen and Ellen Hooper, was born in Wheeling, Va., April 23, 1824. When he was quite young his parents removed to Belmont County, Ohio, where they lived till 1835, and then came to Athens County, settling on the land now owned by their son. July 9, 1845, Mr. Hooper married Rhoda Axtell, of Alexander Township, formerly of Mercer County, Pa. They had a family of twelve children—Elizabeth Ann, Stephen F., G. W., Jerusha A., Mary Jane, E. A., Amasa, R. S., Ida B., Victoria Blanche, Ellen and an infant. Mrs. Hooper died Oct. 22, 1881. May 11, 1882, Mr. Hooper married Thula Coughenour, of Gallia County, Ohio, a daughter of David Coughenour. Mr. Hooper has a large, fine farm well improved. He has one of the best residences in the township. He has been engaged in dealing in stock more or less for a number of years. Politically he is a Republican. He has been Justice of the Peace six years. He is a member of the Free-Will Baptist church.

G. W. Hooper, son of Clement Hooper, was born in Athens County, Oct. 22, 1849. His early life was spent on a farm and in attending school. He was married Aug. 3, 1873, to Susannah Sisson, daughter of William Sisson, of Columbia Township, Meigs County. They have five children—Albert, John W., Elden W., Lulu B. and Ralph. Mr. Hooper settled on the farm where he now lives in 1874. He has eighty-seven acres of well-improved land, and is engaged in general farming and stock-raising. He has held the office of Constable seven years, and is at present Township Trustee. He is a member of the Methodist Episcopal church.

W. H. Irwin, a native of Alexander Township, was born Sept. 18, 1840, a son of John Irwin. He was married Feb. 13, 1866, to Isabelle Sisson, a native of Meigs County. They have six children —William W., John C., O. L., Emma V., George B. and Cora M. Mr. Irwin has a farm of 150 acres, under a good state of cultivation, with a good house and farm buildings. Politically he is a Republican. In early life Mr. Irwin assisted his father on the farm, receiving his education in the common schools. He commenced life for himself with comparatively little but strong hands and an honest heart, and by hard work and good management has acquired a home where he is surrounded with all the comforts of life. He is one of Alexander Township's most worthy citizens, a man always alive to the interests of the township, and ready to do all in his power for its improvement and advancement. He is truly a public-spirited man, one of whom his fellow-citizens may well be proud.

Nathan Kenney, Sr., deceased, was born in Randolph County, Vt., in 1790. His early life was spent in Vermont, and when a young man he came to Athens County, locating about a mile east of Athens. He afterward moved northwest of Athens, and after a residence there of about ten years moved to the southern part of the county, settling on 300 acres of wild land, where he lived till 1863. Being too old to have the care and management of the farm he retired and moved to Athens, where he died Aug. 25, 1874. He was married Nov. 1, 1812, to Clarissa Abbott, of Cape Cod. They had a family of twelve children—Lydia, Lordrick, Marianne, Maria, Jofanna, Samuel, Nathan, Nahum, Josephus, Clarissa, Emeline and Eliza. Mr. Kenney was a member of the Cumberland Presbyterian church.

Nathan Kenney, Jr., son of Nathan and Clarissa Kenney, was born in Athens Township, Oct. 1, 1827. His early life was spent in assisting his father on the farm and attending the district schools. He resided on the homestead farm till 1858, when he went to Taylor County, Iowa, and settled on Government land, remaining there five years. He then returned to Athens County and lived on the old homestead till 1877, when he moved to his present farm, where he has 138 acres, all well improved. He is engaged in farming and stock-raising. Mr. Kenney was married Oct. 30, 1851, to Samantha Teeters, daughter of Daniel and Mary Ann Teeters. They have a family of seven children—Georgiana, Sidney Howard, Charles Lewis, Frank Albert, Edward T., Mary C. and Laura N. Mrs. Kenney died March 12, 1883. Mr. Kenney is a member of the Methodist Protestant church. Politically he is a Democrat.

S. H. Kenney, son of Nathan Kenney, was born in Athens County, Ohio, March 1, 1825. In 1850 he came to Alexander Township, where he has permanently located, being one of its prominent citizens. He owns a farm of 160 acres in Alexander Township. He has served in all the offices of the township. Politically he was a Jackson Democrat until 1880, when he became a staunch Prohibitionist. He was married Jan. 8, 1850, to Minerva, daughter of Daniel Drake, of Athens County, Ohio. They have reared a family of nine children, whose names are—Augusta B., Lafayette H., Winfield W., Wayne B., Webster D., Luelma M., Murdock D., Missouri R., Sierra Nevada, all of them residing in Athens County.

Abram Lash, postoffice Athens, was born Aug. 5, 1817, son of William Lash, a native of Pennsylvania. Our subject's early life was spent on a farm, and he received his education in the common schools. He was married Jan. 30, 1840, to Eleanor Beal, of this county. They were the parents of three children—John, William and Elizabeth. He was married the second time, Feb. 17, 1850, to Isabella McKinstry, of this county. To them were born six children—Josiah, Leander, Martha, Jeremiah, Mary and George. Mr. Lash resides on a fine farm of 460 acres, eighty acres of which his father first settled, Mr. Lash having purchased the rest. He has been a member of the Baptist church forty years.

Henry Logan, merchant, a native of Alexander Township, was born Nov. 21, 1832, the son of John Logan, who was of Irish descent. He was reared a farmer and received his education in the common schools. Arriving at the age of manhood, he engaged in the mercantile business, which he has since followed. He has served as Township Clerk six years, Trustee three years, and Justice of the Peace six years. He was appointed Postmaster in 1862, and has served since that time. June 9, 1853, he married Caroline Bean, daughter of Dr. George Bean, of this township. They have seven children—Rettie, Reppie, W. G., Ella, Flora, Earle and Frank; all have been given the advantages of a good education and are well fitted to perform the duties of life. Mr. Logan is a zealous member of the Methodist Episcopal church. He keeps a large assortment of goods, and by fair and honorable dealings has secured the confidence and trust of all who know him.

Freeman Marshall, son of William and Susan Marshall, was born in Carroll County, Ohio, Oct. 2, 1823. His early life was spent on the farm and in attending the common schools. In June, 1845, he married Ellen M. Twaddle, of Jefferson County, Ohio. They have nine children—Mahan, David, Ethan, William, Sylvester, Howard, Izetta, Ida and Ira. Mr. Marshall purchased the farm where he now resides, in 1854. He has 300 acres of well-improved land, with a good residence and commodious farm buildings. He is an influential man of his township and has served as School Director for many years.

S. L. Mathews, born in Guernsey County, Ohio, Aug. 6, 1825, is a son of Newman Mathews, a native of Massachusetts, but an early settler of Guernsey County. He was married at the age of thirty-eight, to Henrietta Matheny. They have two children—Carrie Alta and Charles Grant. Mr. Mathews bought the farm where he now resides, in 1865. He has 100 acres of good land, with commodious buildings, and is engaged in farming and stock-raising. During the late war he enlisted in the One Hundred and Forty-first Ohio Infantry. He has been Justice twelve years. Mr. and Mrs. Mathews are members of the Methodist Episcopal church.

John H. McPherson, born in Belmont County, Jan. 18, 1828, son of Joseph McPherson, of Scotch ancestry. At six years of age he moved with his parents to Morgan County, Ohio, where he was reared and received a common-school education, together with Methodistical religious culture, and upon the temperance question, prohibition. It would be unjust to not here mention that his mother, whose maiden name was Elizabeth Hart, of English descent upon her mother's side, and German on her father's, was an example of the finer virtues of feminine character and especially that of self-government. The subject of this narrative commenced teaching school at twenty years of age. He married Maria J., daughter of Rezin and Nancy Calvert, the former of German-English, and latter of Irish ancestry, and both of religious aspirations. John H. and Maria J. McPherson's children consist of two boys and eight girls—Rezin M., Flavius M., Mary M., Susanah M., Elizabeth M., Florence M., Nancy M., Eliza M., Adah M. and Emma M., all living and healthy. Mr. McPherson enlisted in Company I, Seventh Ohio Volunteer Cavalry, Sept. 12, 1862; was disabled in a charge on the enemy near Mount Sterling, Ky., Feb. 27, 1863, by rupture and injury to diaphragm, the result of being thrown upon pommel of saddle, after which he served the Government as clerk until June 7, 1865, when he was discharged by reason of Surgeon's certificate of disability. Politically he is a Prohibitionist Republican. His residence is at Pleasanton, Athens County, Ohio. His present occupation *Legal Studie.*

L. Oliver, born Jan. 22, 1825, in Harrison County, Ohio, is a son of Jesse Oliver, a native of Virginia. When he was four years of age his parents removed to Guernsey County, where his early life was spent on a farm and in attending the common schools. He was married Oct. 16, 1851, to Elizabeth Adair, a native of Guernsey County, and a daughter of George Adair. They have seven children—Adandra, Joanna, Horton, Clara, Elizabeth, Ernest and William. Mr. Oliver has a good farm of forty acres, where he has lived since 1854. He has held the office of Justice for twelve years. Politically he is a Republican. He is a member of the Presbyterian church.

R. M. Patterson, born in Athens County, Ohio, Jan. 1, 1850, is the youngest son of William and Elizabeth Patterson. He was reared on a farm and has always followed that occupation, owning at present 270 acres of land under a good state of cultivation. He makes a specialty of Spanish merino sheep, having a large flock and spending considerable time and money on them. He was married Sept. 5, 1872, to Lizzie Cuckler, of Athens, Ohio. They have six daughters—Birdie E., Alice G., Cina E., Nellie L., Mary F. and Lena E. Politically Mr. Patterson is a Republican. He has been Township Clerk three successive years. He is a member of the Cumberland Presbyterian church. Mr. Patterson's father, William Patterson, deceased, was born in Washington County, Pa., Jan. 24, 1808. When twenty-two years of age he married

Elizabeth Cooper, and in 1832 they came to Athens County, settling on wild land. They reared a family of eight children—Levina, Martha, Maria, Eunice, Elizabeth, John C., Mary C. and R. M. Mr. Patterson was for eight years agent for the American Tract Society. He died Jan. 8, 1872.

Eliphaz Reeves.—As far back as 1801, at the age of three years, David Reeves, father of Eliphaz, came with his parents to Athens County and settled on the farm where the Wines school-house now stands. The Reeveses were among the early pioneers of this section of Ohio, coming here from Pennsylvania, where David Reeves was born, near Pittsburg, in 1798. Mr. Reeves is still living, past eighty-five years of age, and is probably the oldest man living in Athens County, who came here as early as 1801. His wife was Matilda Woodyard, and they were married in 1825. Eliphaz Reeves was born near the Woodyard church, Alexander Township, Nov. 27, 1832. He was reared, engaged in business and continued to live in the same neighborhood, spending his time in farming and trading, and is now, 1883, merchant and Postmaster at Wood yard. April 2, 1874, he was united in matrimony with Marticia C. Shumwa, of Meigs County, Ohio. Lulu May, their only child was born July 7, 1876. Mr. and Mrs. Reeves are members of the Woodyard Methodist Episcopal church, in which he is Class-Leader. During the war Mr. R. served as Orderly Sergeant in the Ohio State militia, and has at various times held the township offices.

Daniel T. Rickey.—On a farm in Greene County, Penn., June 6, 1830, Mr. Rickey was born and reared to the age of maturity. His father was Abraham C. Rickey, and his mother Pheba Throckmorton, both natives of the Keystone State. In 1855, at the age of twenty-five, Daniel Rickey left his native State, and came direct to Athens County, where he has since lived. He enlisted under Colonel Jones in the late war, but was soon after discharged for physical disability. June 10, 1856, Mr. Rickey was married to Harriet Williams, a daughter of A. M. Williams, of Lodi Township. Their children are—Milan A., born March 15, 1857; Clara, born Sept. 26, 1858; Blanche, born Aug. 13, 1865; Imogene, born Sept. 16, 1867, and Annetta C., born Aug. 1, 1872. He and wife are members of the Cumberland Presbyterian church of Albany.

John Rickey, born in Jefferson County, Ohio, Oct. 12, 1801, is a son of John and Nancy Rickey. His parents were among the first settlers of Jefferson County. They moved to Belmont County about 1815. His father was a soldier of the war of 1812, and died from a cold contracted while in the service. John was reared on a farm, receiving but a limited education. He was married Sept. 15, 1825, to Michal Jones, a native of Virginia. In 1830 he moved to Morgan County, where he lived six years. In 1836 he came to Athens County, settling in Alexander Township. In 1875 he bought the farm where he now lives. He is a member of the Free-Will Baptist church, and one of its strongest supporters. Mrs. Rickey died in July, 1874, after rearing a family of eight children —R. J., Jane, James, Narcissa, Elza A., Matilda, John and Henry. In March, 1875, Mr. Rickey married Hetty Jane Robneth, a sister of his former wife.

Jasper Secoy, born in Carthage Township, Athens Co., Ohio, Nov. 28, 1839, is a son of David Secoy, a native of New York, and an early settler of Carthage Township. In the spring of 1861 he came to Alexander Township, and the following August enlisted in Company I, One Hundred and Sixteenth Ohio Infantry, serving till 1865. He was in the battles of the Shenandoah Valley, Fisher's Hill, etc., following the regiment on all its numerous marches and campaigns. After his return home, March 26, 1865, he married Sarah, daughter of Samuel Woodruff. They have five children— Hattie, Samuel, Franklin, George and Mildred. In 1878 Mr. Secoy bought the farm where he now resides, consisting of fifty acres of good land. Mr. and Mrs. Secoy are members of the Methodist Episcopal church. Politically he is a Republican.

R. M. Wood, section 7, Alexander Township, was born in this township Aug. 21, 1827, a son of William and Margaret (Brooks) Wood. He was reared on a farm, receiving but a limited education in the common schools. In February, 1848, he married Amanda Drake, of this township. They have eight children— Emma, William, Fremont, Cassie, Eulelia, Estella, Carrie and Jennie. In 1867 Mr. Wood removed to Meigs County, where he lived two years. In 1869 he bought the farm where he now resides. He has ninety-six acres of land well cultivated with good improvements. During the war Mr. Wood was taken prisoner by Morgan's men, and lost two fine horses.

CHAPTER XX.

ROME TOWNSHIP—THE RISE OF ROME AND PROGRESS OF THE ROMANS.

LOCATION—METES AND BOUNDS—TOPOGRAPHY—ORGANIZATION—POPULATION FROM 1820 TO 1880—SCHOOLS—BRIDGES AND MILLS—SETTLERS AND PROGRESS—EARLY HISTORICAL FACTS—THE WAR OF 1812—TOWNSHIP OFFICERS—GUYSVILLE—LODGES—STEWART VILLAGE AND ITS HISTORY—NEW ENGLAND, FROST AND BIG RUN—BIOGRAPHICAL.

ABOUT THE YEAR 1811.

Rome Township lies on the eastern border of the county, and is bounded on the north by Bern Township, on the east by Washington County, on the south by Carthage, and on the west by Canaan Townships. Its eastern border encroaches upon Washington County, about one mile east by two miles north and south, which adds about two sections of land over a congressional township. This would give it about thirty-eight sections, or 23,320 acres of land.

TOPOGRAPHICALLY

speaking, it is hilly and broken, but the valley of the Hocking is rich in agricultural wealth, for its soil is deep and fertile. The river crosses the township from east to west, meandering in its course, and forms a portion of the eastern line of the township, the stream turning and running almost due south in its course for about three miles and then in a southeasterly direction. Federal Creek flows into the Hocking River within its boundary, and some good agricultural and grazing lands are found on its border. It is known as a township of timbered land, and it is still rich in timber resources. The mineral development has not yet proven very great, but coal is known to exist, and has been mined to a small or limited extent. It is, however, an agricultural township, and for cereal and stock raising has few superiors in the county. Its territory may also be said to have been among the earliest settled, for it became a township in 1811, being on April 4 of that year

ORGANIZED

The organization read as follows.

"*Thursday, April* 4, 1811.—*Ordered* by the commissioners, That so much of the township of Troy as is contained in the original surveyed townships, numbered 5 and 6, in the 11th range, and 6 in the 12th range, be erected into a new township by the name of *Rome*. . . . .

"*Ordered* by the commissioners, That their clerk notify the inhabitants of the township of Rome to meet at the house of Amos Crippen, in said township, on Saturday the 20th instant, for the purpose of electing township officers."

But no election was held under this order, and on the 4th of June ensuing, the commissioners

"*Ordered*, That the boundaries of the township of Rome be as follows, to wit: Beginning at the southwest corner of township number 6 in the 12th range, thence east on the township line until it intersects the river Hockhocking, thence up said river until it intersects the range line between the 11th and 12th ranges, thence on said range line (being the line between the counties of Athens and Washington) to the south boundary of Ames Township, thence west on said township line to the township of Athens, thence south to the place of beginning, and that the remainder of the township of Rome be and is hereby attached to the township of Troy. [This refers to the previous order of April 4.]

"*Ordered* by the commissioners, That their clerk notify, by advertisement, the inhabitants of the township of Rome to meet at the house of Daniel Stewart, on Saturday, the 15th instant, for the purpose of electing township officers."

The township was taken from the territory of Troy Township as above bounded, and it continued thus until Feb. 10, 1814, when the Legislature passed an act giving to Athens County and to Rome Township the two sections of land lying on the west side of the Hocking River. These sections were 31 and 32 of congressional township No. 6, of range No. 11, making a turn in the county line.

It is one of the most thriving among the agricultural townships of the county, and its people are progressive, economical, and combine energy with intelligent labor.

POPULATION.

Just what the population of the township was in 1811 is not known, but it probably did not exceed 200. In the census of 1820 it was 497; in 1830, 522; in 1840, 852; in 1850, 1,309; in 1860, 1,581; in 1870, 1,972; in 1880, 2,207.

While there is nothing remarkable in this increase, the figures show one very desirable fact, and that is, that it has never gone back, but grown steadily and surely with increasing years. It may be said to have sustained the general average of the county and State during the different decades with but one exception, that between 1820 and 1830.

Daniel and Archelaus Stewart, who settled in the township in 1802, were the first to move for the organization of a church society, and a Methodist church was organized at a very early day, probably a few years before its organization into a township, and Rev. Jacob Young, then on the Marietta circuit, came to the residence of Mr. Daniel Stewart, held service and organized a society. The original members were William Pilcher and wife, Job Rutler and wife, Eliphalet Case and wife, and Elijah Rowell and wife. From this small but happy beginning three Methodist congregations have grown up, and three substantial and neatly furnished church buildings have been erected.

The first service held in the township was by the Rev. Cyrus Paulk, Jr., who preached as early as 1803 at the cabins of the settlers. He was a Baptist, and continued his ministration for several years.

SCHOOLS.

Among the settlers of those early days there was nothing that received their more earnest attention than that of the education of their children. To read, write and cipher and to be a good speller was what they deemed a necessity, and added that of grammar and geography when they could. A good common-school education was generally the summit of their ambition, and it was only when a boy became ambitious for a higher course, refused the plow and stuck to his books, that money was raised by the sacrifice of a horse or other stock to give him the desired schooling. In fact, having become worthless on the farm, for if he was sent in the field to work, he was generally found under a tree or in the crook of the fence, perfectly oblivious to all surroundings and deep in the mysteries of his favorite study, the old man at last got weary and gave it up and the book worm was soon in his glory, for he was going to the academy and then to college.

The first school-house erected in Rome Township was in 1804, and was built by subscription—that is, the neighbors joined in the work, each doing their part. The house above mentioned was built of logs, about sixteen feet square, and was located on the east bank of Federal Creek, near its mouth. The first teacher was Abram Richards, and a daughter of Ebenezer Barrows, Mrs. Polly Driggs, was the next. Of course it was not long before other school-houses were erected and schools taught.

In 1841 the Rev. Amos Miller started a private school on his farm and called it "Miller's Academy." It flourished for more than twenty years, a large two-story building being erected to furnish accommodations. It was about one mile from Savannah or Guysville. It suspended during the civil war and was never resurrected.

There is at present an academy located at Savannah, the management of which has been quite successful. It was founded in 1867, by a number of public-spirited citizens, and its first Trustees were: Fred Finister, Peter Boyles, Vincent Caldwell, Harvey Peirce, and Harvey Caldwell. Its first teacher in charge was Prof. George W. Bryce, and the fact that 140 scholars enrolled themselves the first year shows that the citizens were imbued with the right spirit.

BRIDGES AND MILLS.

In 1808 the first bridge in the township was built over Federal Creek, near its mouth, by Elijah Hatch, and in 1818 a second one was built at the same place. In 1842 a fine bridge was erected by Peter Beebe, Isaac Jackson being the architect; it was at first a toll bridge, but is now free. About the year 1851 or 1852 a bridge was built over Federal Creek, near the mouth of Big Run, but was soon swept away; another has since been erected on the same site. The bridge at Savannah was built about 1858, the funds being supplied partly by the county and partly by subscription. Another has been built over the Hocking, about two miles below Savannah, the funds being raised in the same manner.

The first grist and saw mill in the township was built in 1802 by George, Henry and James Barrows, on Federal Creek, about a mile from its mouth. The mill is a log building with only one run of stones, which were made of the "Laurel Hill granite," and run by a large undershot wheel. Before this the nearest mill where wheat could be ground was Devol's, on the Muskingum, at least forty miles distant. Many families, however, possessed that great desideratum of pioneer life, the primitive hand-mill and the "hominy block." There were also a few horse-mills in the county, but they were only used for grinding or, as it was called, "cracking" corn. In 1818 Reuben Farnsworth built the first mill on the Hocking River within the township limits. This was one of the most solid and substantial mill structures ever erected in the county. Farnsworth failed, and the mill passed into the hands of Peter Beebe, who afterward sold it to Thomas Welch. It was sold by Mr. Welch to Cook, Crippen & Co., and subsequently passed into the hands of a son of Mr. Cook, who is the present owner.

In 1820 the Savannah mill (grist and saw mill) was built by Ezra Stewart and his brother Charles, sons of Esquire Daniel Stewart. It has three run of stones and does a great amount of custom work. It is situated on the Hocking River, in the village of Guysville, about three miles from the west line of Rome Township. About 1834 Alexander Stewart and George Warren built the Stewart Mill (a saw-mill), near Savannah; but it was soon destroyed by fire, and a large three-story grist and saw mill was erected on the site by Daniel B. Stewart. In 1844 Mr. Stewart connected a woolen factory with the establishment, which is now owned by a daughter of Mr. Stewart, Mrs. Charles Byron. In runs 470 spindles, has four looms, four carding machines, two spinning jacks and a full set of fulling and dressing machinery. The grist and saw mill are still in active operation. Two miles above Savannah are the Kincade Mills, built in 1842 by John and Allen Kincade, and rebuilt by John Kincade on an enlarged plan and in a more substantial manner in 1868, and was again rebuilt in 1880 by D B. Stewart. About 1854 Heman Frost, son of Abram Frost, one of the pioneers of Carthage Township, built a grist and saw mill three miles below Cook & Crippen's mill; it was subsequently replaced by a saw mill, which was swept off by high water in the spring of 1867, but rebuilt by Allen Kincade.

SETTLERS AND PROGRESS.

What was called in those days the "Upper Settlement" in this ownship was first settled in 1808, when Joshua Selby, John Thompson, Robert Calvert, and Jonathan Simmons came from Virginia, and Richard, George, and James Simmons, from Pennsylvania. They were all good citizens. In 1810 or 1811 Christopher Herrold, one of the pioneers of Ames Township, settled in Rome. He was a Pennsylvania German and a man of enterprise and thrift. He afterward removed to Dover.

A strong evidence of the enterprising spirit of the early settlers is afforded by the fact that in 1811 a sea-going vessel was built in Rome Township, a mile below the mouth of Federal Creek, on the south bank of the Hocking. She was launched and taken to New Orleans in the spring of 1812. The vessel was built by Captain Caleb Barstow, from Providence, Rhode Island, and was called The Enterprise.

Between 1800 and 1810 the township received a number of good settlers. John Johnson and father, on the Hockhocking, opposite Federal Creek; Job Ruter, with his sons Martin and Calvin, on the river about two miles above Federal Creek; and about the same time came Nathan Connor, Rev. Moses Osborn, the Calverts, the Thompsons, the Selbys, and the Mitchells, all of whom settled on the river. Most of these came from Virginia. Also prominent among the early settlers were Abraham Sharp, for whom Sharp's Run and Sharp's Fork of Federal Creek were named; Francis Munn, a revolutionary soldier; Archibald Dorough, Thos. Richardson, Dr. Seth Driggs, Jeremiah Conant, Wm. Pilcher, Aaron Orme, Thos. Swan, Aaron Butts, Eli Catlin, Daniel Anderson (a Lieutenant in the Revolutionary army), David Chapman, Rev. Enos Thompson (Methodist) and the Hewitts.

EARLY HISTORICAL FACTS.

Esquire Elmer Rowell, a pioneer and a valuable and prominent citizen of Rome Township during its early days, who died a few years back, leaves the following reminiscence of pioneer days: "When I first settled here the nearest postoffice was at Athens, sixteen or seventeen miles distant, and I have frequently gone that distance for a single expected letter; now there are four postoffices in the township. Then we went thirty miles to obtain our necessary dry goods, groceries, hardware, etc.; now there are seven or eight good country stores in the township. While musing on the times and people of fifty-five years ago, the whole scene for thirty miles up and down the valley seems photographed on my memory—the men and women, their costumes, the log cabins and the cleared patches. The men all dressed in homespun during summer, and during winter a great part of the clothing consisted of buckskin; the females, both matron and lass, dressed for every day in homespun, except in later years, when one now and then began to appear in a 'factory dress,' and all had for Sunday and holidays the more costly and gayer calico and cambric dresses. Those were the days of warm friendships and close attachments. Common hardships and labors begot a fellow feeling. If there was a cabin to raise, every man for miles around turned out with alacrity to help raise it and put on the last clapboard. If there was any job too heavy for one man to do, all assisted. When a hunter or any one else was belated, be he a stranger or acquaintance, he found a home and a welcome in any log cabin he might chance to find."

THE WAR OF 1812.

Rome Township having been or was the home of several of the Revolutionary patriots and soldiers of 1776, when the war of 1812 was declared they found her sons willing patriots to enter the field and defend the soil of their country from the footsteps of an invader. Athens County being called upon for a company of infantry, to be composed of fifty men or volunteers, the militia regiment of the county, then commanded by Colonel Edmund Dorr, was summoned to meet at Athens and volunteers called for. The men stepped promptly to the front, and of this number Rome Township was the residence of nine who enlisted. Their names were Jas. Crippen, Peter Beebe, Thaddeus Crippen, Ebenezer Hatch, Chas. Stewart, Wm. Starr, Andrew Stewart, John Wickham and Daniel Muncie. The company was then raised to sixty men and Rome added one more volunteer, George Driggs, or one sixth of the number. In 1813, when the Governor of Ohio called for forty days' mounted riflemen, George Barrows, Montgomery Perry and a young man named Swann went from Rome.

William T. Hatch, son of Elijah Hatch, was the first male child born in the township, and his sister Harriet, the late Mrs. Hill, is said to have been the first female. Mrs. Elijah Hatch, mother of Judge Hatch, was the first person who died in the township. A portion of the facts here given were taken from Walker's very interesting history of Athens County. The growth of the township and its increase in population has been spoken of in previous pages, and to this might be added the fact that its material progress has been a marked feature in its history, and prosperity seems to have taken a firm hold upon the township.

TOWNSHIP OFFICERS.

1811.—Trustees, Job Ruter, Elijah Hatch and James Crippen; Clerk, Caleb Barstow.

1812.—Trustees, Daniel Stewart, George Barrows and John Thompson; Clerk, Amos Crippen.

1813.—Trustees, Elijah Rowell, James Crippen and John Thompson; Clerk, Elijah Hatch.

1814.—Trustees, Daniel Stewart, James Crippen and Joshua Selby; Clerk, Elijah Hatch.

1815.—Trustees, Daniel Stewart, James Crippen and William Barrows; Clerk, Elijah Hatch.

1816.—Trustees, Daniel Stewart, Elijah Hatch and Joshua Selby; Clerk, William Stewart.

1817.—Trustees, James Crippen, John Thompson and Henry Barrows; Clerk, Wm. Stewart,

1818.—Trustees, James Crippen, Archelaus Stewart and Henry Barrows; Clerk, Wm. Stewart.

1819.—Trustees, James Crippen, Archelaus Stewart and Henry Barrows; Clerk, Wm. Stewart.

1820.—Trustees, James Crippen, Archelaus Stewart and Daniel Stewart; Clerk, Wm. Stewart.

1821.—Trustees, James Crippen, John Thompson and Daniel Stewart; Clerk, John Green.

1822.—Trustees, Elijah Hatch, Joshua Selby and Daniel Stewart; Clerk, Daniel Stewart.

1823.—Trustees, James Crippen, Elmer Rowell and Archelaus Stewart; Clerk, Elijah Hatch.

1824.—Trustees, Wm. S. Doan, Joshua Selby and Henry Barrows; Clerk, Elijah Hatch.

1825.—Trustees, Daniel Stewart, Elijah Dalbey and Peter Beebe; Clerk, Elijah Hatch.

1826.—Trustees, Daniel Stewart, Elijah Dalbey and James Crippen; Clerk, John Thompson.

1827.—Trustees, Daniel Stewart, Josephus Butts and Joshua Selby; Clerk, Samuel Thompson.

1828.—Trustees, John Thompson, Josephus Butts and Joshua Selby; Clerk, Samuel Thompson.

1829.—Trustees, John Johnson, Josephus Butts and Joshua Selby; Clerk, Edmund Cook.

1830.—Trustees, John Thompson, Josephus Butts and Daniel D. Cross; Clerk, Guy Barrows.

1831.—Trustees, John Johnson, Josephus Butts and Joseph Mitchell; Clerk, Guy Barrows.

1832.—Trustees, Wm. S. Doan, James E. Hatch and Joseph Mitchell; Clerk, John Welch.

1833.—Trustees, Levi Stewart, James E. Hatch and Joseph Mitchell; Clerk, Elijah Hatch.

1834.—Trustees, Levi Stewart, James E. Hatch and Joseph Mitchell; Clerk, Wilson Selby.

1835.—Trustees, Alexander Stewart, James E. Hatch and Peter Beebe; Clerk, Thos. Newcomb.

1836.—Trustees, Joseph Mitchell, James E. Hatch and Samuel Hill; Clerk, Blanford Cook.

1837.—Trustees, Joseph Mitchell, S. T. Richardson and George Warren; Clerk, Blanford Cook.

1838.—Trustees, James E. Hatch, Joshua Calvert and George Warren; Clerk, Elmer Rowell.

1839.—Trustees, Peter Beebe, Wilson Shelby and William P. Doan; Clerk, Elmer Rowell.

1840.—Trustees, Peter Beebe, Joseph Mitchell and Levi Stewart; Clerk, Wilson Selby.

1841.—Trustees, Peter Beebe, Joseph Mitchell and Levi Stewart; Clerk, Wilson Selby.

1842.—Trustees, Daniel B. Stewart, William Mitchell and Nelson Cook; Clerk, Wilson Selby.

1843.—Trustees, Wm. P. Doan, Wm. Crippen and B. F. Johnson; Clerk, E. B. Parrill.

1844.—Trustees, Peter Grosvenor, Wm. R. Winner and Joseph Mitchell; Clerk, Wilson Selby.

1845.—Trustees, Peter Grosvenor, Levi Stewart and Joseph Mitchell; Clerk, Wilson Selby.

1846.—Trustees, D. B. Stewart, Wm. Simmons and B. F. Johnson; Clerk, Joshua Calvert.

1847.—Trustees, D. B. Stewart, Wm. Simmons and Abraham Parrill; Clerk, Joshua Calvert.

1848.—Trustees, Elmer Rowell, Artemus S. Crippen and Levi Stewart; Clerk, B. F. Johnson.

1849.—Trustees, Elmer Rowell, Peter Grosvenor and Levi Stewart; Clerk, Sydney S. Beebe.

1850.—Trustees, Nelson Cook, Peter Grosvenor and Connell Roberts; Clerk, B. F. Johnson.

1851.—Trustees, Nelson Cook, Peter Grosvenor and T. F. Jones; Clerk, B. F. Johnson.

1852.—Trustees, Levi Stewart, Peter Grosvenor and Wm. R. Winner; Clerk, Joshua Calvert.

1853.—Trustees, Elmer Rowell, D. B. Stewart and Wilson Selby; Clerk, B. F. Johnson.

1854.—Trustees, Elmer Rowell, D. B. Stewart and Wilson Selby; Clerk, B. F. Johnson.

1855.—Trustees, Elmer Rowell, D. B. Stewart and Wilson Selby; Clerk, B. F. Johnson.

1856.—Trustees, T. R. Rider, Perry Barrows and Harvey Pierce; Clerk, Charles H. Grosvenor.

1857.—Trustees, T. R. Rider, Voltaire Barrows and Harvey Pierce; Clerk, Chas. H. Grosvenor.

1858.—Trustees, Josephus Tucker, Perry Barrows and Elmer Rowell; Clerk, Robert Bean.

1859.—Trustees, James Rice, Herman Frost and Artemus Buckley; Clerk, Blanford Cook.

1860.—Trustees, James Rice, Josephus Tucker and W. L. Petty; Clerk, Blanford Cook.

1861.—Trustees, James Rice, Josephus Tucker and W.L. Petty; Clerk, Blanford Cook.

1862.—Trustees, A. S. Crippen, Artemus Buckley and G. S. Simpson; Clerk, Blanford Cook.

1863.—Trustees, A. S. Crippen, P. W. Boyles and James Cross; Clerk, James Moore.

1864.—Trustees, Blanford Cook, P. W. Boyles and James Cross; Clerk, Harvey Pierce.

1865.—Trustees, Blanford Cook, P. W. Boyles and J. W. Johnson; Clerk, Harvey Pierce.

1866.—Trustees, Blanford Cook, Joseph Patterson and Harvey Pierce; Clerk, Charles Dean.

1867.—Trustees, Blanford Cook, Amos Patterson and Robert Bean; Clerk, George M. Ross.

1868.—Trustees, Blanford Cook, Amos Patterson and Robert Bean; Clerk, George M. Ross.

1869.—Trustees, Amos Patterson, Harvey Pierce and J. W. Johnson; Clerk, D. W. Cornell; Treasurer, B. F. Johnson; Justices of the Peace, R. A. Fulton and Elam Frost.

1870.—Trustees, Amos Patterson, J. W. Johnson and V. A. Caldwell; Clerk, D. W. Cornell; Treasurer, B. F. Johnson.

1871.—Trustees, Amos Patterson, J. W. Johnson and V. A. Caldwell; Clerk, D. W. Cornell; Treasurer, B. F. Johnson; Justices of the Peace, J. S. Devol and S. S. Beebe.

1872.—Trustees, Amos Patterson, J. W. Johnson and V. A. Caldwell; Clerk, D. W. Cornell; Treasurer, D. M. Burchfield.

1873.—Trustees, Amos Patterson, E. Vickers and J. W. Johnson; Clerk, John L. Cross; Treasurer, D. M. Burchfield.

1874.—Trustees, Amos Patterson, J. W. Johnson and Jefferson Perry; Clerk, J. L. Cross; Treasurer, D. W. Cornell.

1875.—Trustees, Jefferson Perry, Edwin Glazier and Clark Dodds; Clerk, J. E. Cook; Treasurer, D. W. Cornell; Justices of the Peace, R. M. Wilson and Edwin Glazier.

1876.—Trustees, Jefferson Perry, Clark Dodds and J. A. Caldwell; Clerk, J. E. Cook; Treasurer, D. W. Cornell; Justice of the Peace, Silas E. Hedges.

1877.—Trustees, Noah Tedrow, Frank Patton and Elijah H. Bean; Clerk, J. E. Cook; Treasurer, D. W. Cornell; Justice of the Peace, S. S. Beebe.

1878.—Trustees, B. S. Plumley, Riley Crippen and Jefferson Perry; Clerk, J. E. Cook; Treasurer, D. W. Cornell; Justice of the Peace, James Malcolm.

1879.—Trustees, B. S. Plumley, Riley Crippen and Amos Patterson; Clerk, S. B. Pickering (resigned), L. M. Fowler; Treasurer, D. W. Cornell; Justice of the Peace, Silas E. Hedges.

1880.—Trustees, Riley Crippen, Amos Patterson and Eli Brooks; Clerk, L. M. Fowler; Treasurer, D. W. Cornell; Justice of the Peace, S. S. Beebe.

1881.—Trustees, Amos Patterson, J. W. Murphey and J. W. Johnson; Clerk, L. M. Fowler (serving part of the year, and S. N. Hobson appointed to fill out the term); Treasurer, H. J. Smith; Justice of the Peace, William King.

1882.—Trustees, J. W. Murphey, J. W. Johnson and Eli Brooks; Clerk, S. N. Hobson; Treasurer, H. J. Smith; Justice of the Peace, P. F. Bush.

1883.—Trustees, Hiram Burden, Henry Finsterwald and Eli Brooks; Clerk, S. N. Hobson; Treasurer, Harvey J. Smith; Assessor, William Skinner; Justices of the Peace, S. S. Beebe and Henry Crippen.

GUYSVILLE.

The village of Guysville is situated near the southwestern corner of Rome Township, on the bank of the Hocking River, and on the new line of the Marietta & Cincinnati Railroad. It was laid out in 1836 by Chauncey Carpenter, who at that time owned the mill at that place. The postoffice was established about three years later through the efforts of Mr. Guy Barrows, who was appointed the first Postmaster, and for whom it was named, although the village has always been known by the name of Savannah. Among the first settlers were a Mr. Conner, a blacksmith; Laban Heth, a shoemaker; Barton Ferris and Amos Calvert. The village has a population, at present, of about 250 inhabitants. It has a flouring mill, owned by J. W. Murphey; a tannery, owned by Gustavus LeGoullon; a hotel, owned by D. W. Cornell; a Methodist Episcopal church with a membership of about fifty, and two physicians, G. W. Blakely and G. B. Parker. The merchants are D. W. Cornell and Brown & Lawrence, general merchandise; John Picket and L. C. Murphey, drugs; and John D. Sand's furniture and undertaking store. It has also a millinery store, two harness shops and two blacksmith shops. There being a good bridge across the river at this point to connect it with the surrounding country on the opposite side of the river, and that being particularly a stock-raising section, this village has lately become the most important live-stock shipping point in the county. The most active parties in this business are Samuel Stalder and J. W. Murphey (partners), Henry Stalder, Jefferson Perry and William Rhodehaver. The postoffice is at present kept in the store of Brown & Lawrence, Mr. H. H. Brown, of that firm, being the Postmaster.

Savannah Lodge, A. F. & A. M., was established June 28, 1872, with the following charter membership: A. B. Dickey, Master; B. W. Calvert, Sen. Warden; J. E. Cook, Jun. Warden; D. M. Burchfield, Secretary; J. A. Hawley, Hiram Burden, William Johnson, Vincent Caldwell, Charles Byron, J. W. Johnson, E. D. Merwin and J. A. Caldwell. The present officers are: G. W. Blakely, Master; S. N. Hobson, Sen. Warden; D. W. Cornell, Jun. Warden; C. L. Bean, Secretary.

STEWART.

The village of Stewart is situated on the Hocking River and the Marietta & Cincinnati Railroad, about two miles below Guysville.

It was laid out by Mr. D. B. Stewart, on a part of the Stewart homestead, in 1875, about the time of the completion of the railroad to that point. Mr. Stewart built the first five houses, and furnished lots and dressed lumber for a number of others, waiting on the occupants for pay. A mill and church had marked the site for many years, and a postoffice had been in the locality since 1830, but was not located at this particular place until 1873. Previous to the establishment of the village the postoffice had been called Federalton. The village has its church; a flouring mill, owned by Mrs. Ruth Byron; a planing mill, owned by D. B. Stewart; one physician, Dr. W. E. Webb; and two stores, kept by H. G. Smith and S. N. Hobson, Mr. Hobson being the present Postmaster. Stewart has a population of about 200.

NEW ENGLAND.

The village of New England, situated near the western boundary of Rome Township, on the old line of the Marietta & Cincinnati Railroad, sprang up soon after it was known that the railroad would pass through that point, about 1853, and was laid out by Jacob Tedrow, E. H. Moore and A. G. Brown, of Athens, being his partners in the ownership. The postoffice was established immediately after trains began running on the railroad in 1859. The first residence was built by Thaddeus Rider, and the first store by Chapman & Rider. The store stood on the lot now used for the Methodist Episcopal parsonage, Mr. Rider's dwelling standing just south of it on an adjoining lot. Then followed, in succession L. R. Jarvis, who built a store; Hiram Gard, who kept a store in the depot building, and Joseph and Amos Patterson, who built the store and residence now occupied by J. M. Rhodes. The village has two churches, Methodist Episcopal and Presbyterian, the former having a membership of about fifty-four, and the latter a membership of over ninety. The merchants are L. R. Jarvis, J. M. Rhodes and Harvey Patterson. Mr. Rhodes is also the present Postmaster and keeps the office in his store. Since the abandonment of the railroad through this village the population has greatly decreased, being now not more than 150.

FROST.

Frost Village is in the southeastern part of Rome Township, on the Marietta & Cincinnati Railroad, and has been built since the completion of the railroad. The merchants are C. D. Smith, F. M. Payne and Washington Russell. The population is about 100.

BIG RUN.

Big Run was a station on the old line of the Marietta & Cincinnati Railroad, and is situated in the northeastern part of the township. The postoffice remains, and one store, owned by H. Gordon & Son.

BIOGRAPHICAL.

Edmond Bean was born in Hardy County, Va., Aug. 5, 1805, and came to Athens County in 1833. He has a good farm of 120 acres on section 25, Rome Township, and is engaged in both farming and stock-raising. His land borders on the Hocking River, and is well adapted for general farming. He was married in 1833 to Mahala Bean, a native of Hardy County, Va., born Jan. 10, 1814. They have no children. Both Mr. and Mrs. Bean are members of the Methodist Episcopal church. Mrs. Bean's sister, Mrs. Clara E. Holmes, and her daughter, Fannie E. Holmes, are members of Mr. Bean's family. Mr. Holmes was drowned in the Hocking River, Jan. 22, 1862. He and Mr. Bean and two other men were crossing the river in a small boat to go to church when the boat capsized. Mr. Holmes was seemingly more anxious to save the others than himself, and by his self-denying efforts lost his own life. Mrs. Holmes and her daughter have since that time made their home with Mr. and Mrs. Bean.

Mrs. Lorana Bean was born in Athens County, Ohio, Aug. 30, 1829. June 7, 1849, she married Robert Bean, a native of Hardy County, Va., born July 12, 1825. Five children were born to them —Samantha, born Aug. 17, 1851; Matilda Jane, July 20, 1859; Louis Franklin, Jan. 25, 1863; Rosa Alice, July 29, 1868; Ervine Hebert, born May 15, 1871. Samantha married Daniel M. Cole, Oct. 4, 1867. Matilda J. married M. Baker, Nov. 3, 1877; she has one child—Robert E., born Feb. 5, 1879. Mr. Bean died Oct. 26, 1876. Mrs. Bean has 104 acres of well-improved land on section 25. She is a member of the Methodist Episcopal church.

W. P. Beebe, proprietor of the Beebe House, was born in Rome Township, Dec. 5, 1819. His father, Peter Beebe, was a native of Washington County, N. Y., born Oct. 15, 1792. His mother, Melissa (Cook) Beebe, was born in Connecticut in 1801, and died

March 6, 1821. His father then married Betsy Vaughn, who died leaving four children—Louisa, Harriet, Villa and Mary. Mr. Beebe then married Ann Eliza Kincade. They had five children— Elmira, Melissa, Helen, Henry and Henrietta. Mr. Beebe died May 10, 1849. W. P. Beebe was married Aug. 9, 1853, to Louisa Davis, a native of Rome Township, born Feb. 7, 1837. They have nine children—Edwin, born Oct. 22, 1854; Peter, born April 22, 1856; Owen, July 20, 1858; Emerson, Dec. 14, 1860; Hanley, March 27, 1863; Fannie, April 30, 1866; Augusta, Aug. 27, 1868; Bessie, Dec. 27, 1872; Millie, Sept. 13, 1876. Mr. Beebe now owns the farm of 175 acres once owned by his father and grandfather. He also owns the hotel and other town property in Stewart.

G. W. Blakeley, M. D., son of Harvey and Susan Blakeley, was born in Athens County, Ohio, Aug. 12, 1851. His father was born in Pennsylvania, June 19, 1803, and came to Ohio in 1844, and is now living on a farm near Athens. His mother was born in New York in 1807, and died in December, 1854. G. W. was the youngest of eleven children. He was educated in this county, and read medicine with Dr. H. M. Lash at Athens, graduating from Columbus Medical College in 1878. He located in Guysville, where he now has a large practice. He was married Sept. 15, 1880, to Ollie M. Pruden, a native of Athens County, born Jan. 18, 1862. Dr. Blakeley is a member of the Methodist Episcopal church. He belongs to Savannah Lodge, No. 466, A. F. & A. M., and has been W. M. four years.

John Brandeburg was born in Jefferson County, Ohio, Feb. 20, 1845, and when two years of age removed with his parents to Washington County. Nov. 21, 1863, he enlisted in Company K, One Hundred and Twenty-fifth Ohio Infantry; was in the battles of Mission Ridge, Dandridge, Buzzard's Roost and Resaca. He was wounded at Resaca, Saturday, May 14, 1864, and lay on the field until nine o'clock Sunday morning. He was then taken to the hospital where he remained nine months. He rejoined his regiment in February, 1865, at Blue Springs, E. Tenn., and was then in the battles of Franklin and Nashville. He was discharged June 5, 1865, and returned home and has since been engaged in farming. He now owns thirty-eight acres of good land on section 32, Rome Township. Dec. 25, 1872, Mr. Brandeburg married Nancy Jewell, a native of Athens County, born Sept. 22, 1851. They have four children—Elmer Ellsworth, born April 24, 1874; Effie

Jane, Oct. 25, 1875; Nettie Leota, Oct. 24, 1877; William Eugene, Dec. 25, 1882. Politically Mr. Brandeburg is a Republican.

Abraham T. Buck was born in New York, June 9, 1810, and came to Ohio at the age of six. He has always made Athens County his home. He has a farm of 160 acres of fine land on section 15, Carthage Township, Athens County. He has held the office of School Director in Carthage Township several terms. Mr. Buck came to Guysville in 1880, where he still resides. In 1833 he married Miss L. Davis, a native of Ohio, born in 1818. They have had nine children—Alden, who was wounded in the battle of Gettysburg, and died in the hospital; Rachel M., now Mrs. John Weatherly; Alonzo, Wesley, George, James, Charles, Dow, and John A., who died when quite small. Mr. Buck and wife are members of the Methodist Episcopal church.

Mrs. Ruth S. (Stewart) Byron was born in what is now the tov of Stewart, Rome Township, Athens Co., Ohio, Jan. 14, 1842. He father, D. B. Stewart, born in the same township, Nov. 26, 1812, has always lived in this county. He has carried on farming, milling, woolen manufacturing, etc., all his life. The mother of our subject, Mrs. Sarah (Carter) Stewart, was born in Morgan County, Ohio, Feb. 11, 1820. She was married April 7, 1836, and died Oct. 16, 1874. She was the mother of nine children, six of whom are living—Ruth, Hannah, Matilda, Juliette, Frank C. and D. B., Jr. Her husband, C. Byron (deceased), was born in Yorkshire, England, April 14, 1832, and was brought to America in 1833. During the gold excitement he went to California, and remained there until 1859, making one visit home in 1856, of six months' duration. In 1859 he returned to Stewart, and went into business with his father, buying and selling wool and making cloth in the factory at Stewart. April 9, 1861, he enlisted as private in the Third Ohio Infantry. On the 27th of the same month he was married. He served his country three years and eight months. He was first commissioned Lieutenant, and afterward, in 1863, Captain of his company. He was selected by Colonel Streight to command 100 picked men in making a raid upon Rome, Ga., for the purpose of destroying a Confederate armory. While on this raid he was taken prisoner and confined in Libby Prison one year and eight months. November, 1864, he escaped, and was thirty-one days in reaching the Union lines. In crossing the Savannah River, one mile wide, and full of ice, he was obliged to wade, which permanently impaired his health. Five months after reaching home he was mustered out at

Columbus, Ohio. In the spring he bought the Stewart woolen mills, and was engaged in the manufacturing business at the time of his death, which occurred Dec. 25, 1878. There were present at the funeral nearly 100 members of the Freemason lodges at Guysville, Athens, Amesville and Coolville.

James A. Caldwell was born in Carthage Township, Athens Co., Ohio, March 9, 1820. His education was received in the district schools. He has always been a farmer, and now owns 300 acres of fine, well-improved land. He held the offices of Justice of the Peace, Township Clerk, School Trustee and Township Assessor in Carthage Township, and in 1860 was Land Appraiser. He came to Rome Township in the spring of 1862. He was married Dec. 29, 1843, to Harriet Branch, of Meigs County. They have one child— Margaret Ann. She was married in 1860 to E. D. Erwin, who died in 1880, leaving two sons—James and E. C. Mrs. Erwin and her sons now live with Mr. Caldwell. Mrs. Caldwell and her daughter are members of the Presbyterian church. Mr. Caldwell is a member of Guysville Lodge, No. 466, A. F. & A. M. Mr. Erwin was also a member of that order. Mr. Caldwell's father, Alexander Caldwell, was born in Ireland in 1797, and came to America in 1808. He was married in 1824, to Margaret Fesler, of North Carolina. They had five children—James, Polly, Fesler, Belinda and Margaret. Polly and Belinda are deceased. Fesler and Margaret are living in Macon County, Mo. Mr. Caldwell died in 1875.

F. J. Carpenter, farmer, was born in Athens Township, Athens Co., Ohio, Dec. 10, 1844, on the farm recently bought and called the Children's Home. He lived there until the spring of 1856, when he came to Rome Township, where he has since resided, engaged in farming. His father died in September, 1848; his mother, Mary Wyatt (Johnson) Carpenter, was born in Rome Township, Athens County, and is still living. She has been the mother of six children three now living—Parker, born in 1831; Louisa, now Mrs. John Bailey, born in 1842, living in Bates County, Mo., and the subject of this sketch. Our subject was married Jan. 11, 1866, to Augusta Rowell, a native of Rome Township, born in 1842. They had two children—Mattie, born Oct. 1, 1866, and Maie, born July 28, 1868. Mrs. Carpenter died Sept. 18, 1875, and Oct. 10, 1877, Mr. Carpenter married Dell Schraden. She was born in Rome Township, Athens County, March 16, 1855. They have one child—Bertie, born Sept. 18, 1879. Mr. Carpenter has a farm of 200 acres, located in

Rome Township. He is a member of the order of Freemasons, Coolville Lodge, No. 337. In August, 1862, he enlisted in Company A, One Hundred and Twenty-ninth Ohio Volunteer Infantry, serving ten months, when he was mustered out at Cleveland, Ohio, and returning home re-enlisted in Company I, One Hundred and Eighty-sixth Volunteer Infantry; served eleven months, and was mustered out at Columbus, Ohio. He participated in the siege of Knoxville, Tenn., and various skirmishes. John Johnson, the grandfather of Mr. Carpenter, was born in Bucks County, Pa., in 1779, and died in 1865. His wife, Sallie (Wyatt) Johnson, was born in Beverly, Mass., Dec. 28, 1777, and died Dec. 30, 1859. They were the parents of seven children, Mr. Carpenter's mother being the second child, born in Rome Township, Athens County, July 10, 1809. April 11, 1829, she married Frederick Carpenter. He was born in Hartford County, Conn., in April, 1802, and died Oct. 11, 1848. Mrs. Carpenter and her husband were members of the Methodist Episcopal church. When Mrs. Carpenter's father settled in this county services were held only once in four weeks, it being in the early days of the church.

Charles Coleman, farmer, was born in Muskingum County, Ohio, Dec. 29, 1828. He left there and came, in 1840, to Athens County, where he has since resided. He owns ninety acres of land where he lives, on fraction 32, Rome Township, Athens Co., Ohio. He has been considerably engaged in constructing railroads, working on the Baltimore Short Line, the D. & S. E. Narrow Gauge R. R., the Scioto Valley R. R., also the Chesapeake & Ohio R. R. He has also farmed to some extent. He was married in 1850, to Margaret M. Boyles. She was born in Athens County in 1831, and is the mother of four children—Francis M., Sarah, William and Charles E. Mrs. Coleman is a member of the Methodist Episcopal church. The father of our subject was Charles Coleman, born in Maryland in 1786 and died in Athens County in 1852. His mother, Elizabeth (Fuller) Coleman, was of German descent; she died in Morgan County, Ohio, in 1834. They have had six children, four of whom are living—Rachel (now Mrs. Josephus Day), John, Mary Ann (now Mrs. William Abbott, of Carter County, Ky.), Elizabeth (now Mrs. Luther Withum, who lives in Meigs County, Ohio).

John E. Cook was born in Rome Township, Athens Co., Ohio, April 9, 1836. He was married July 4, 1859, to Susan J. Ginn, a native of Morgan County, Ohio, born in September, 1837. They had two children—John N. and Jennie. His wife died June 17,

1865. Dec. 17, 1866, he married Phœbe J. Kelly, a native of Athens County, born April 6, 1838. They have one child—Charles S. Aug. 27, 1862, Mr. Cook enlisted in Company C, Third Ohio Infantry, and served three years; was in the battles of Perryville and Stone River. At the latter place he was captured and was in Libby Prison a week. He was then paroled and came home, and two months later was exchanged and returned to his regiment. He was then on the famous raid to Rome, Ga., with Colonel Streight, and at Rome was captured and sent to Belle Isle. From there he was paroled but never exchanged, and after being at home three months returned to the field and was on detached duty a year. He was attached temporarily to the Thirty-third Ohio, and during the time was in the battles of Marietta, Altoona, Kennesaw, Old Shanty, Atlanta, Jonesboro, Fort McAlister, Averysboro and Bentonville. From there he went to Richmond, thence to Washington, where he was mustered out June 5, 1865. He was also with Sherman on his raid, and was captured at Rockingham, S. C., and sentenced to be hanged, but two girls, Emma and Lucretia Smith, planned his escape. Mr. Cook is a member of Savannah Lodge, No. 466, A. F. & A. M.; the Grand Army the Republic, and the Ex-Prisoners of the War Association.

Mrs. L. C. Cook was born in Rome Township, Athens Co., Ohio, Nov. 19, 1815. April 17, 1834, she married B. Cook, a native of New York, born in September, 1810. He came to Ohio in 1815, and died July 23, 1879. Mrs. Cook has two sons—Harley A., born Feb. 13, 1842, and Wyatt J., born Oct. 9, 1847. Harley A. is engaged in the mercantile business and is also carrying on the farm. He has been Postmaster since 1879. He was married Aug. 30, 1866, to Christina J. Done, a native of Rome Township, born in 1842. They have four children—Frank T., born Sept. 27, 1868; Josephine, Oct. 14, 1869; Alberta, July 13, 1873; Ora F., Feb. 1, 1880. Wyatt J. has a saw and grist mill, situated two miles east of Stewart, on the Hocking River. He has six children, Rosamond W., G. R., Roland B., Elbert C., Orland L. and Leroy W. Mrs. Cook and her children are members of the Universalist church. She owns a farm of 270 acres.

Mrs. Esther Copeland, daughter of James and Jane Milligan, was married March 19, 1828, to William Copeland, a native of Westmoreland County, Penn., born June 25, 1798. He died Aug. 15, 1875. They had a family of eleven children, seven now living—Josiah, Samuel, Thomas, Clark, Aikin, David and Carr.

Six sons were in the late war, and three were in the battle of Pittsburg Landing. Their eldest son, Robert C., was killed by being caught in the machinery of a saw-mill at Taylor's Station. David S. was married March 29, 1877, to Emma Biggins, a native of Washington County, born in 1856. They have two children— Ervilla, born Dec. 21, 1877, and Fred, born April 22, 1879. Mrs. Copeland's father was a native of New York. He was a soldier in the war of 1812, under General Harrison. He died in 1815. Her mother was a native of Ireland. She died in Ohio in 1862.

John Copeland, farmer and stock-raiser, was born in Guernsey County, Ohio, May 28, 1839. He came with his parents to Athens County when a year old, and settled on a farm where he has lived ever since. His father, John Copeland, was born in Pennsylvania, July 2, 1795, and died in Athens County, Ohio, Dec. 20, 1855. His mother, Jane (Dick) Copeland, was born in Pennsylvania, May 5, 1800, and died in Athens County, Nov. 29, 1881. They have had nine children—William, Ellen, Jane, Jonathan, Susannah, Samuel, Mary, John and Ann. John, the subject of this sketch, is next to the youngest child. He was married April 26, 1864, to Sarah Jane Marquis. She was born in Noble County, Ohio, in 1848. They have five children—David A., Eliza A., Clara V., William A. and Addie J. Mr. Copeland owns 180 acres of good land in Rome Township. He is a member of the New School Presbyterian church. He enlisted in Company H, Eighteenth Ohio Infantry, Oct. 7, 1861, and served three years; was mustered out at Louisville, Ky., Oct. 27, 1863. He was in the battle of Stone River, Tenn., and a great many skirmishes.

Ansley Cornell, Guysville, was born in Albany, New York, Aug 7, 1829, and came to Meigs County, Ohio, in the spring of 1832. He lived there until 1875, when he came to Guysville, where he has since resided. He was engaged in the hotel business one year, but has since then been occupied as saddler and harness-maker. April 11, 1856, he married Harriet E. Ellis, a native of Lawrence County, Ohio, born April 5, 1837. They have had three children, two of whom are living—Ida M., born March 19, 1857, now Mrs. Louis Finsterwald, married March 14, 1878, and Ira E., born Dec. 11, 1860. The father of our subject, Dr. John Cornell, was born in New York, and came to Ohio in 1832, where he died in 1873. His wife, Christiana, was born in Pennsylvania, and died in 1876. All their ten children are living, the youngest now forty years old. Mrs. Cornell's father, Hiram Ellis, was born in New York in 1799, and died May 18, 1876. Her mother, Harriet (Gillett) Ellis, was born in Connecticut in 1800, and died Jan. 18, 1856. Mr. and Mrs. Ellis were the parents of thirteen children, Mrs. Cornell being next to the youngest.

D. W. Cornell was born in Chester, Meigs Co., Ohio, Jan. 20, 1842. In 1858 he entered the Ohio Institute at Athens and graduated in 1863. In 1866 he became established in the mercantile business in Guysville. He held the office of Township Clerk three years, and Township Treasurer ten years. He is a member of Savannah Lodge, No. 466, A. F. & A. M. Oct. 10, 1869, he married Amy Calvert, a native of Rome Township, born Feb. 8, 1840. Mr. Cornell's parents, Dr. John and Christine (Spraker) Cornell, were natives of New York, his father born in December, 1798, and his mother in 1802. They were married in 1820, and came to Ohio in 1832. They had a family of ten children, all of whom are living and married but one. Dr. Cornell practiced his profession in Meigs County till about ten years prior to his death. He died Sept. 19, 1873.

A. S. Crippen was born March 4, 1810, in Rome Township, Athens Co., Ohio, and has always made this his home. When a young man he followed flat-boating on the Ohio and Mississippi rivers, and has visited Memphis when there were but two stores there. For forty years he ran the Crippen grist and saw mill on the Hocking River, two miles east of Stewart, but gave up milling in 1871 and now lives a more retired life on his farm, where he has 238½ acres of fine land. He was married in 1836 to Theodocia Frost, a native of Rome Township, born in 1814. She died in June, 1875, leaving three children—Adaline, born Dec. 25, 1836; Mary, born in January, 1841, and Charles, born March 16, 1843. Their eldest daughter, Adaline, married Laughlin Devine, a native of Pennsylvania, born Oct. 21, 1828. They have one son—Owen Crippen, born Oct. 9, 1881. Mary married Peter Finsterwald. Mr. Crippen has never belonged to a church or a society of any kind. Mrs. Crippen's mother, Keziah Frost, was a native of New York, born in 1796, and came to Ohio with her parents in 1800. Her father, Elijah Hatch, was a Representative of the Northwestern Territory, now Washington, Athens and a part of Vinton counties, thirteen terms.

Edward Doan, born in Rome Township, Nov. 14, 1837, is a son of William P. and Julia (Frost) Doan. His father was born in Washington County, Ohio, and died in 1847. His mother was born in Athens County in February, 1815, and is now the wife of Rev. P. F. Jones. There was a family of four children—Franklin, Edward, Charles and Christiana. Mr. Doan enlisted, June 20, 1861, in Company C, Third Ohio Infantry, and served three years. He was in the battles of Rich Mountain, Perryville, Stone River and many skirmishes. He was with Colonel Streight on his raid through Georgia, and was captured at Rome and sent to Belle Isle. He was discharged in 1864. Dec. 21, 1865, he married Mary E. Potter, a native of Washington County, Ohio, born July 12, 1843. Nine children have been born to them—Oliver M., born Oct. 12, 1866, died Sept. 22, 1879; Julia, born Aug. 2, 1868; Edward C., born Sept. 11, 1870; Louisa, born July 18, 1872; Hattie, born Jan. 17, 1874; Franklin, born June 24, 1876; Annie, born Dec. 19, 1877; Osa, born Aug. 12, 1880, and Clara, born Sept. 8, 1882. Mrs. Doan's father, Edward Potter, was born in Maine, Aug. 11, 1812, and died near Lynchburg, Va., in 1847. Her mother, Louisa (Beebe) Potter, was born in Rome Township, March 20, 1823. They had a family of three children—Mary E., born July 12, 1843; Maria L., born April 27, 1845, and Horace C., born Dec. 5, 1846.

Mrs. Melvina L. (Washburn) Frost was born in Coolville, Athens County, Feb. 10, 1827. March 29, 1851, she married C. C. Frost, of Rome Township, born June 23, 1827. They had one child—Leura B., born Sept. 9, 1856, now Mrs. John Lemmon, of Baltimore, Md. Mr. Frost enlisted in Company I, One Hundred and Sixteenth Ohio Infantry, and died June 29, 1864, of a wound received in the battle near Staunton, Va. July 16, 1866, Mrs. Frost married Harvey G. Frost, a native of Athens County, born June 4, 1819. He died May 3, 1881. He enlisted in Company K, Thirty-ninth Ohio Infantry, and served one year; was discharged on account of disability. Mrs. Frost has twenty-four acres of good land and considerable village property in Frost. She is a member of the Congregational church. Her father was born in Massachusetts, Dec. 18, 1794, and died May 17, 1874. Her mother, Leura (Cleveland) Washburn, was a native of New York, and died July 9, 1839. Her parents had a family of ten children. Her father married a second wife, Anna Parsons, of Athens County. She died July 9, 1859, leaving five children.

Edward H. Ginn was born in Morgan County, Ohio, Nov. 16, 1831, and came to Athens County in 1836. In 1856 he went to Illinois and lived in Mercer and Rock Island counties about eight years, returning to Ohio in 1863. In 1876 Mr. Ginn fell from a trestle thirty-five feet high, on the M. & C. Railroad, and broke his left arm in two places and five of his ribs. For the past eighteen months he has been running a stationary engine, pumping water for the M. & C. Railroad, at Stewart. He was married April 25, 1853, to Robena Welch, a native of Pennsylvania, born Dec. 31, 1836. Eleven children have been born to them, nine now living—Elizabeth, now Mrs. L. A. Patterson, born in 1856; William A., born in 1858; Daniel F., born in 1860; Edward E., born in 1863; Charles S., born in 1866; George P., born in 1867; John S., born in 1870; Frederick J., born in 1871, and Lewis, born in 1880. Mr. and Mrs. Ginn are members of the Methodist church. Politically he is a Republican.

James Ginn was born in Morgan County, Ohio, Oct. 3, 1828. In 1836 he came with his parents to Athens County and settled in Ames Township. In 1840 they moved to the farm where he now lives, in Rome Township, where his father died in 1842. He was married Sept. 11, 1851, to Cynthia Hill, a native of Athens County, born June 1, 1826. They have three children—Ida, Ella and Hattie. Mr. Ginn and his family are members of the Methodist church. He has a fine farm of 105 acres on section 35, Rome Township. His father was a native of Ireland, born March 2, 1805, and came to America in 1810, landing in South Carolina. In 1812 he came to Ohio, locating in Morgan County. His mother, Mary (Benton) Ginn, was born in Guernsey County, Ohio, in 1805, and now lives in Clyde, Ohio. They had a family of eight children, five of whom are living—James, Edward, Francis, Sarah and Rosa. Mrs. Ginn's parents, Nathan and Lucy (Bennett) Hill, were natives of Massachusetts, her father born in 1779, and her mother in 1782. Mr. Hill died in March, 1864, and Mrs. Hill, Sept. 11, 1867. They had a family of eight children—Sallie, Amasa, Lucius, Solomon, Lucy, Polly, Nancy and Cynthia. Lucius died in February, 1882.

J. M. Grosvenor was born in Windham County, Conn., Oct. 22, 1832, and came to Athens County, Ohio, in 1839, locating in Rome Township, where he has since resided. He now owns 150 acres of good well-improved land. He enlisted in November, 1861, in Company H, Eighteenth Ohio Infantry, and served till October, 1865. He enlisted as private and was promoted to Second Lieutenant, then First Lieutenant, then to Regimental Quartermaster of the old regiment, and afterward was First Lieutenant and Quartermaster of the new Eighteenth. He served under General Mitchell in Kentucky; was with General Rosecrans at the battles of Stone River and Chickamauga; afterward was under General Grant; then at Mission Ridge and Nashville, Tenn., in the Fourteenth Army Corps, under General Thomas; then through Alabama, and with General Steadman to Augusta, Ga., and from there to Columbus, Ohio, where he was mustered out. Mr. Grosvenor is a member of Columbus Golden Post, No. 89, G. A. R. He was married in 1854 to Sarah Jane McColloch, a native of Marshall County, Va., born in 1833. They have three children—Frank, Peter and Fannie.

Leander Harris was born in Morgan County, Ohio, Feb. 22, 1841, and when nine years of age came to Bern Township, Athens County. June 22, 1861, he enlisted in Company D, Fourth Virginia Infantry, and served three years. The first eighteen months he was in a number of skirmishes in West Virginia; afterward was in the battles of Jackson, siege of Vicksburg, Resaca, Mission Ridge and Dallas. He was discharged July 8, 1864, two days before the battle of Kennesaw Mountain. He was married April 9, 1865, to Sarah A. Hodcroft, a native of Athens County, born Dec. 15, 1845. They have had eight children, only six now living —Arza E., born March 31, 1866; Vesta V., born Jan. 24, 1868; Addie M., born Feb. 13, 1870, died June 1, 1871; Ruth E., born March 16, 1872; Fannie E., born Feb. 28, 1874; Augusta, born July 25, 1876; Flora B., born March 13, 1879, died June 13, 1880; Georgianna, born Sept. 21, 1882. Mr. and Mrs. Harris are members of the Methodist Episcopal church. Mr. Harris is a member of Savannah Lodge, No. 466, A. F. & A. M. Mr. Harris came to Stewart in April, 1876, and now has a pleasant home and good trade.

James Hess, carpenter and farmer, was born in Warren County, N. J., Jan. 3, 1839. His father, Abraham Hess, was born in Pennsylvania in 1808, and died in Athens County, October, 1877. His mother, Elizabeth (Smith) Hess, was born in New Jersey about 1811, and died in Athens County in 1856. They were the parents of eight children—William, Jane, James, Sarah E., Peter, Martin, Isaac and Lewis. James came with his parents to this county in 1848, and has since resided here, most of the time following farming. For the last five or six years he has followed the carpenter's trade. He married, Nov. 3, 1861, Angeline Weethee, born in Athens County, Dec. 16, 1844. They have one child—Margaret Ann, born June 11, 1864. Mr. Hess lives in fraction 25, Rome Township, where he has a pleasant home.

Samuel N. Hobson, Postmaster, was born in Jefferson County, Ohio, April 5, 1833. He removed with his parents to Washington County in 1851, remaining there until 1865, when he moved to Beverly. He removed to Morgan County in 1870, and in 1877 came to Athens, where he has since resided. He has been engaged in the mercantile business many years, and has for ten years been acting Postmaster in Athens, Morgan and Jefferson counties. He has been a notary public five years, and has been elected County Surveyor. He was married Nov. 20, 1853, to Anna M. Heald, a native of Columbiana County, Ohio, born April 18, 1836. They have three children—Marianna, now Mrs. J. A. Lovell, of Morgan County, born in August, 1855; Addie, now Mrs. O. M. Lovell, born in 1857; R. Estella, born March 9, 1876. Mr. Hobson joined the Freemasons April 4, 1863, Bentley Lodge, No. 293, Washington County, Ohio. He is a member of the Methodist Episcopal church, of Stewart. During the late war he enlisted in Company G, One Hundred and Forty-eighth Regiment, O. N. G.; was under General Sigel at Harper's Ferry, Va., and under General Grant at City Point, Va. He was mustered out at Marietta, Ohio, returning home to Washington County. Since that time he has been engaged in the mercantile business now in conjunction with the postoffice at Stewart.

William Jackson was born in Canaan Township, Athens Co., Ohio, Feb. 15, 1816. He has lived in Ames and Rome townships ever since he was seven years of age. He learned the cooper's trade when he was eighteen years old and worked at it until 1838. He came to New England in 1860, and is still a resident of that place. He was married to Anna Tedrow, Jan. 3, 1839. She was born in Pennsylvania, May 22, 1811. Mr. and Mrs. Jackson are members of the Methodist Episcopal church. His father, John Jackson, was born in Pennsylvania in 1790, and died Nov. 27, 1867. His mother, Mary Calvert, was born in Virginia, and died in 1839, in Ames Township, Athens Co., Ohio. They had a family of seven children—Sallie, William, Matilda, Robert, David, Deborah, and Jane. Mrs. Jackson's father, Reuben Tedrow, was born in Pennsylvania in 1759, and died in 1839. Her mother, Jane Leech, was born in Pennsylvania in 1768. She died in 1854. They had thirteen children—John, Phebe, Thomas, Jacob, Sarah, Rebecca, Reuben, Jane, Joseph, David, William, George and Anna. Mr. and Mrs. Jackson have no children of their own but have an adopted daughter, Ella M., born May 7, 1862. She is also a mem-

W R Young

ber of the Methodist church. Mr. Jackson owns about thirty-two acres of land adjoining New England, and considerable town property.

L. R. *Jarvis*, a native of Belchertown, Mass., born Sept. 29, 1817, left there in 1843 and came to Athens Township, where he worked at his trade of gun-smithing, and in 1850 moved to the town of Athens, and followed the same trade for three years. In 1853 he was employed to superintend the building of the M. & C. R. R. In October, 1857, he came to New England, remaining here the greater part of the time, being absent from the State in 1859 and 1860. He has been employed as conductor on the T. H., A. & St. L. R. R. He is now engaged in the general mercantile business and farming. He has 73$\frac{1}{3}$ acres in Canaan Township, also several town lots in New England. Oct. 6, 1838, Mr. Jarvis married Susan Thomas, who was born in Lenox, Berkshire Co., Mass., in 1816. They have had five children, two of whom are living— George P., born Oct. 29, 1842, in Berkshire County, Mass., and Leonora D. M. (now Mrs. H. J. Smith), born May 15, 1850, at Athens, Ohio.

E. W. *Jewell*, born in Philadelphia, Penn., Feb. 10, 1822, was a son of Samuel and Mary (Winner) Jewell, his father a native of New Jersey, and his mother of Bucks County, Penn. He came with his parents to Athens County, Ohio, in 1842, and located in Rome Township. He was married in the spring of 1845 to Rebecca Simmons, a native of Rome Township, born July 4, 1825. They have nine children—W. G., born April 7, 1847; Jonathan S., born Oct. 13, 1848; Nancy J., born Sept. 22, 1851; Mary E., born May 11, 1852; Angenetta, born Nov. 22, 1854; Marcellus, born Nov. 18, 1856; Caroline, born Jan. 22, 1858; Franklin, born May 2, 1862; Perley, born Jan. 2, 1865. Mr. Jewell and his two eldest sons enlisted in the Eighteenth Ohio Infantry, he in Company C, W. G. in Company I, and Jonathan in Company H. They were in the Army of the Cumberland under Generals Thomas and Rosecrans; were in the battles of Stone River, Duck River, Hoover's Gap, Davis Cross Roads, Chickamauga, and Nashville. Mr. Jewell owns 120 acres of land in fraction 4, Rome Township. He and his son W. G. are members of Columbus Golden Post, No. 89, G. A. R. He is neutral in his political views.

J. W. *Johnson*, born in Rome Township, Athens Co., Ohio, Sept. 27, 1818, was the fifth of seven children of John and Sarah (Wyatt) Johnson, natives of Pennsylvania and Massachusetts. His mother was born Dec. 23, 1777, and died Dec. 30, 1859. His father also died in this county. Mr. Johnson has a fine farm of 1,100 acres of the best land in the Hocking Valley. He was married March 7, 1841, to Catherine Beebe, a native of Rome Township, born in September, 1824. They have had six children, five now living—Eliza, now Mrs. H. P. Mineer; Mary, now Mrs. F. B. Patton; William, Charles and John. Mr. Johnson is a member of Lodge No. 466, A. F. & A. M.

Moses Lawrence was born in New Hampshire, Jan. 2, 1820, and when sixteen years of age came to Ohio, locating first in Carthage Township, Athens County. He afterward removed to Lodi Township and bought a farm of 236 acres, where he lived thirty years. In 1880 he came to Guysville, Rome Township. June 12, 1843, he married Laura T. Skeels, a native of New York, born May 3, 1821. They have five children—Harriet R., now Mrs. H. Stalden, born Oct. 25, 1847; George R., born Nov. 28, 1851; Caroline M., now Mrs. H. Brown, born June 15, 1854; John E., born Feb. 2, 1858; Arthur E., born Dec. 7, 1867. Mr. Lawrence's parents, Moses and Sarah (Johnston) Lawrence, were natives of Massachusetts, his father born July 14, 1775, and his mother, Feb. 16, 1776. His mother died July 19, 1844, and his father, Sept. 8, 1844, in Athens County. Mrs. Lawrence's father, Sylvanus Skeels, was born in Vermont, Aug. 16, 1789, and died in Troy Township in 1866. Her mother, Calista (Benjamin) Skeels, was born Feb. 14, 1798, and died Dec. 10, 1876. Mrs. Lawrence is the fourth of a family of seven children, six now living.

Gustavus LeGoullon was born in Beaver County, Pa., Oct. 12, 1842. In 1862 he enlisted in Company I, One Hundred and Fifty-fifth Pennsylvania Infantry; was in the battles of Antietam, Fredericksburg, Chancellorsville, Gettysburg, battle of the Wilderness, Laurel Hill, North Anna River, Cold Harbor and Petersburg. June 28, 1864, he was wounded in the left foot and was in the hospitals at New York and Pittsburg, Pa., ten months. He was mustered out at Pittsburg and returned to Beaver County. June 28, 1868, he married Dora Massey, a native of Loudoun County, Va., born Nov. 2, 1847. They have seven children—Florence, born Dec. 10, 1869; Francis, Sept. 28, 1871; George, Aug. 7, 1873; Harold, May 4, 1875; Blanche, Dec. 1, 1876; Anna, Dec. 20, 1879; Earl G., May 30, 1882. Mr. Le Goullon came to Guysville, Athens Co., Ohio, in April, 1880, and built a tannery. He pays the highest prices for hides and makes first-class leather. He has the only tannery between Parkersburg and Athens and furnishes all the leather that is needed by the shoemakers in this vicinity.

Joseph Linton, son of James and Mary (Montgomery) Linton, natives of Ireland, was born in County Derry, Ireland, in 1827, and came to America in 1849, landing in Boston. He went to Philadelphia and remained a few weeks, then went to Rochester, N. Y., and from there to Pittsburg, where he lived six months. He then came to Ohio and bought a farm of forty acres in Washington County. He now owns 320 acres of fine, well-improved land on section 32, Rome Township, Athens County. He was married May 29, 1849, in Scotland, to Nancy Chestnut, a native of Antrim, Ireland, born Nov. 15, 1822. They have seven children— William J., born Aug. 1, 1855; Hannah L., March 11, 1856; Mary E., April 6, 1858; Nancy, Jan. 6, 1860; Perlina C., April 8, 1862; Joseph C., July 25, 1864; and Daniel, July 20, 1867. Mr. Linton was reared in the faith of the Presbyterian church. Politically he is a Republican. He has held the office of School Director. His mother died in 1829 and his father in 1833. Joseph was the youngest of three sons. Mrs. Linton's parents, William and Nancy (Coyles) Chestnut, were natives of the north of Ireland and died there, her father in 1843 and her mother in 1830. Mrs. Linton is the seventh of eight children.

James Morrison was born in Washington County, Pa., Oct. 11, 1840. He was a resident of Guernsey County, Ohio, a few years, and has lived in Athens County about twenty-five years. March 17, 1869, he married Julia Dewese, a native of Athens County, born March 22, 1847. She died June 2, 1873, leaving one son— Seth Clarence, born April 7, 1871. Jan. 2, 1878, Mr. Morrison married Mrs. Jane Johnson, widow of Calvin Johnson. They have three children—Jessie May, Lon T. and William. Mrs. Morrison also has four children by her first marriage—Cynthia, Nancy, Maggie and Callie. Mr. Morrison enlisted in the late war in Company H, One Hundred and Eighty-sixth Ohio Infantry, and served till the close of the war. He owns 130 acres of good land on section 36, Rome Township, and is engaged in general farming and stock-raising.

L. C. Murphy, druggist, was born in Pleasanton, Athens Co., Ohio, June 22, 1858. His parents, A. C. and Martha (Baker) Murphy, were natives of Belmont and Athens counties, Ohio. They had a family of twelve children, eight of whom are now living—Finley J., Lucinda J., O. B., Wm. S., L. C., Eber R.,

Lewis and Flora E. L. C. was educated in this county and taught school several terms till 1881. Nov. 7 of that year he became established in the drug business in Guysville and now has a good trade. He was married Dec. 31, 1877, to Emma Sams, a native of Pleasanton, born in 1858. They have two children—Maud M., born in 1878, and Arthur G., in 1881. Mr. and Mrs. Murphy are members of the Methodist Episcopal church.

Patrick O'Connor, son of Martin and Bridget O'Connor, was born in Ireland, March 18, 1827. He came to America with his parents in 1852, landing in New York, May 3. Three years later his parents returned to Ireland, where his father died in 1860 and his mother in 1865. Mr. O'Connor lived a few weeks in Maryland and then went to Clarksburg, W. Va., and lived five years. He then lived four years in Missouri, two years in Kentucky, and two years in Indiana. From the latter State he came to Athens County and has since resided here, engaged in the grocery business. He was married Jan. 19, 1863, to Mary Patton, a native of Ireland, born May 13, 1845. They have six children—Mary E., born Feb. 2, 1864; Agnes, Aug. 8, 1866; Margaret, Oct. 22, 1870; Kate, March 11, 1872; Sarah, Sept. 13, 1874, and Nora, Aug. 8, 1877. Mr. O'Connor and his family are members of the Catholic church. Mrs. O'Connor's parents, Thomas and Ellen (Gallagher) Patton, were natives of Ireland, and came to America, her father in 1845 and her mother in 1852. Mrs. O'Connor is the third of their eight children.

Francis B. Patton was born Oct. 20, 1838, in Athens County, Ohio. He enlisted in the late war in Company A, Ninety-second Ohio Infantry, and served two years and ten months; was in the battles of Hoover's Gap, Chickamauga, Chattanooga, and with Sherman to the sea. He came home via Washington and was mustered out at Columbus, Ohio. He was married Sept. 11, 1877, to Mary Johnson, a native of Rome Township, born June 28, 1846. Mr. Patton and his brother, Preston I., own 186 acres of good land on fraction 3, Rome Township. Mr. Patton is a member of Coolville Lodge, No. 337, A. F. & A. M., and Columbus Golden Post, No. 89, G. A. R., Athens. His parents, Joseph and Permelia Patton, are both natives of Ohio, his father born April 24, 1815, and his mother April 24, 1818. They have five children—Francis B., Preston I., Martha, Oscar and Mary. Mrs. Patton's parents, J. W. and Catherine (Beebe) Johnson, are both natives of Athens County. They have five children—Eliza, Mary, William, Charles and John, all residents of this county.

Amos Patterson was born in Jefferson County, Ohio, Dec. 25, 1828. His father, Jordan Patterson, was born in North Carolina in 1796, and went to Jefferson County, Ohio, about 1805, and in 1838, came to Athens County, where he died in 1867. His mother was Mary (Lipsy) Patterson, born in Jefferson County, Ohio, in 1797, and is still living in Amesville, Athens Co., Ohio, at the age of eighty-six years. Mr. and Mrs. Patterson have had ten children, six living—James, Joseph, Amasa, John, Amos and Sarah. Amos was married Nov. 7, 1852, to Eunice Vampelt, born in Highland County, Ohio. They have four children living—A. D., H. W., L. A. and Linnie. Mr. and Mrs. Patterson are members of the Presbyterian church. Mr. Patterson is a member of the order of Freemasons, Amesville Lodge. He resides in New England, Rome Township, and owns 200 acres of good land.

F. M. Payne, merchant, Frost, Ohio, was born in Washington County, Ohio, Jan. 24, 1843. He was reared and educated in this State. He went to Illinois and remained a year, but returned to Ohio. He came to Frost in 1881, where he now has a large stock of groceries, boots and shoes, notions, etc. He was married Nov. 28, 1865, to Adda L. Smith, a native of Plymouth, Ohio, born in April, 1842. They have two children—Fred, born April 23, 1867, and Estella, born Dec. 2, 1872. Mr. Payne is a member of Lodge No. 527, I. O. O. F. His father, Gabriel Payne, was born in Clinton, N. J., Oct. 18, 1818, and came to Ohio when fourteen years of age. His mother, Mahala (Gossett) Payne, was born in Washington County, Ohio, July 4, 1817. They have two children—J. D., born April 12, 1838, and F. M.

Jefferson Perry was born in Rome Township, on the farm where he still lives, April 16, 1840. Aug. 9, 1862, he enlisted in Company I, Ninety-second Ohio Infantry, and served till the close of the war. He was in West Virginia four or five months, and then went to Carthage, Tenn.; was afterward at Chattanooga, siege of Atlanta, followed Hood to Alabama, then again to Atlanta, Savannah, Fayetteville and Raleigh. He returned home via Richmond and Washington, and was mustered out at Columbus, Ohio. Dec. 29, 1869, he married Rebecca J. Townsend, a native of Meigs County, Ohio, born March 10, 1845. They have two children—Emma E., born Jan. 10, 1872, and Frank O., born Nov. 2, 1877. Mr. Perry is a member of Columbus Golden Post, No. 89, G. A. R., at Athens. His father, John M. Perry, was born in Berkshire County, Mass., June 28, 1805, and died Oct. 25, 1872. He married Filma Wells, a native of Massachusetts, born Oct. 15, 1807. She died Jan. 11, 1832, leaving three children—Huldah P., P. W. and Oliver H. Mr. Perry then married Polly Simmons, a native of Ohio. She died Oct. 3, 1846, leaving four children—Matilda, Jackson, Jefferson and William. March 29, 1847, Mr. Perry married Rebecca Townsend, widow of John S. Townsend. She was born in Alexander Township, Athens County, Dec. 13, 1804. She had four children—Sophia C., born March 6, 1822; William, July 24, 1824; Willard A., July 24, 1827, and John C., Sept. 9, 1840.

Waterman L. Petty was born in Rome Township, Athens Co., Ohio, Nov. 14, 1841. His father, Willis Petty, was born in Prince William County, Va., in 1804, and came to Ohio in 1831. He died in Rome Township in 1876. His mother, Abigail (Johnson) Petty, was born in New Hampshire in 1812, and came to Ohio in 1834. She is still a resident of this county. There was a family of nine children—Willard, Teresa, Sallie Ann, Samantha, Waterman, Loran, Lawrence, Lydia and Edward. Mr. Petty enlisted in Company A, Ninety-second Ohio Infantry, and served three years; was in the battles of Hoover's Gap and Chickamauga. He was captured at Chickamauga, Sept. 20, 1863; was in Libby Prison six weeks, Danville five months, and Andersonville twelve months, and was only released at the final surrender of the rebels. He was mustered out June 25, 1865. At the time of his capture his weight was 145 pounds, and when released was only ninety-four pounds. Oct 12, 1868, Mr. Petty married Lizzie McDaniel, a native of Grafton, Va., born Nov. 7, 1841. They have three children—Emma Maud, born Nov. 5, 1871; Myrtle, born March 8, 1874, and Ulysses, born Nov. 3, 1876.

J. M. Rhodes, general merchant, New England, was born in Noble County, Ohio, Oct. 16, 1841. He was reared on a farm, remaining with his father until twenty years of age. He enlisted in the Twenty-fifth Regiment, Ohio Volunteer Infantry, June 20, 1861, and was mustered out June 18, 1866, lacking only two days of serving five years. He was in the battles of Chancellorsville, second Bull Run, Gettysburg and many others. He was wounded at Gettysburg in the left foot; was absent from his regiment three months. He rejoined his regiment at Folly Island in time to cast his first vote for President, casting it for Abraham Lincoln. He was kept on duty at Columbia, S. C.; was discharged at Columbus, Ohio. He then returned to Noble County, Ohio, and engaged in the grocery business, remaining in that business nine months.

March 14, 1867, he married Hattie Curtis. She was born in Geauga County, Ohio, March 5, 1844. They have had five children, three of whom are living—Jessie M., born April 8, 1868; William S., born July 26, 1877, and Russell R., born Aug. 3, 1880. After Mr. Rhodes was married he went to Bailey's Run, Athens County, and farmed three years; from there to Chauncey and entered the store of the Hocking Valley Coal and Salt Company. He remained there until April, 1874. In January, 1875, he came to New England and since then has been engaged in the general mercantile business. He has been Postmaster ever since he came here. He and his wife and daughter Jessie are members of the Methodist Episcopal church. He is a member of the Freemasons, Savannah Lodge, No. 466. He was also railroad agent at New England as long as there was any business done on the road at that place.

William W. Rowell, born in Athens County, Ohio, Sept. 20, 1834, was a son of Elmer Rowell, a native of Vermont, born in 1794 and died in 1875. His mother was born in New York in 1802 and died in 1872. William is the youngest of two sons, his brother being Ohiolus. He has a good farm of 150 acres in township 6, range 17. Dec. 20, 1855, he married Corisanda Barrows, a native of Athens County, born May 25, 1837. They have eight children—Theodore, Alva M., Anderson, Aldie E., Joshua H., Everett, Orange S., and Iola. Theodore married Esther Jarvis, and Aldie E. married Alza E. Tibbells; the others are still at home. During the late war Mr. Rowell enlisted in Company E, One Hundred and Forty-fourth Ohio National Guards and served about four months. He is a member of Hocking Grange, No. 904.

Washington Russell was born in Meigs County, Ohio, Aug. 31, 1843, and came to Athens County in 1845. In 1859 he moved to Washington County and lived till 1879, when he returned to Athens County and located in Frost. He now has a first-class general store, keeping a good stock of boots and shoes, dry goods and notions. He enlisted in the late war in August, 1862, in Company A, Ninety-second Ohio Infantry, and served till June, 1865; participated in the battles of Chickamauga and Mission Ridge; was through the Atlanta campaign and with Sherman to the sea. He was married in September, 1869, to Mary J. Mills, a native of Athens County, born in May, 1847. They have three children—William L., Jessie E. and Charles E. Mr. Russell is a member of Coolville Lodge, No. 337, A. F. & A. M.

Harvey J. Smith established his present place of business in Stewart in 1880. He has a good stock of watches, clocks, jewelry, and general merchandise. He was born May 3, 1849, in Plymouth, Washington Co., Ohio, where he was educated and lived till 1873, when he went to Colton, Ohio. He remained there till 1879, engaged in the mercantile business. He was married Oct. 1, 1873, to Leonora Jarvis, a native of Athens, born in 1852. They have two children—Leonard H., born in June, 1875, and Daisy V., born in November, 1879. Mr. Smith is now serving his second term as Township Treasurer. His father, Harvey Smith, was a native of New York, and came to Ohio about sixty years ago. He died in 1877. His mother, Eliza (Dixon) Smith, was born in Pennsylvania about 1809. She is now living in Athens. There was a family of nine children, six now living— Columbus C., L. D., Adaliza, Lucina, C. D. and Harvey J.

John M. Spaulding was born in Vermont, Oct. 7, 1818, and came to Athens County, Ohio, in 1843. He was married Aug. 12, 1852, to Nancy M. Fulton, a native of Amesville, Ohio, born April 10, 1825. Six children have been born to them, only three now living—Addie M., born Nov. 21, 1857; Louie A., Dec. 30, 1859, and Eli A., Feb. 10, 1863. Both daughters are teaching school. The son is a farmer and inventor. March 6, 1883, he obtained a patent for his Duplex Hand Seed Planter, a machine for planting and depositing the fertilizer at the same time. When only ten years of age he made a wooden sewing-machine about five or six inches square. It was entirely of wood except the needle, which was a common sewing needle turned upside down, and sewed nicely, making a chain stitch. Mr. and Mrs. Spaulding and their daughters are members of the Presbyterian church. Mrs. Spaulding's brother, Robert A. Fulton, was born in Hartford, Conn., Feb. 13, 1808. He was Lieutenant-Colonel of the Fifty-third Ohio Infantry. While on a march one dark stormy night, his horse fell down an embankment, and Mr. Fulton received a wound from his sword which finally caused his death, July 23, 1874. His regiment presented him with a fine sword which cost $500.

Samuel Stalder was born in Athens County, Ohio, Aug. 30, 1842. He has always been a farmer, and for the past eighteen years has dealt extensively in live stock. He owns a good farm of eighty acres on sections 25 and 26, his residence being on section 25. He was married March 22, 1866, to Samantha Hammond, a native of Athens County, born in 1845. They have had two children, only one now living—Nettie A., born March 12, 1867. Herbert was born Oct. 11, 1870, and died Nov. 16, 1875. Mr. Stalder is a member of Savannah Lodge, No. 466, A. F. & A. M. His parents, Nicholas and Barbara Stalder, were natives of Switzerland, and came to America when they were children. They were married about 1838, and had a family of twelve children, only six now living—Henry, Samuel, Philena, Helena, Ida and Augusta.

D. B. Stewart, Jr., miller, was born in Stewart, Rome Township, Athens Co., Ohio, Oct. 2, 1859. He lived here nine years, then moved with his parents to Athens, remaining there about twelve years, when he went to Colorado, in 1880, where he remained until July, 1882. He then returned to Athens and thence came to Stewart, where he is now engaged in running the flouring mill known as Byron's mill, and is doing a good business. His father, D. B. Stewart, now living in Athens, was the founder of the town of Stewart. His mother, Sarah (Carter) Stewart, died in Athens eight or nine years ago. Our subject is the only son now living. He has five sisters—Matilda, now Mrs. D. M. Birchfield; Ruth S., who married C. Byron, deceased; Julia, now Mrs. J. M. Case, and Frank, now Mrs. S. B. Pickering. Our subject bids fair to be, as was his father, one of Stewart's best business men.

Mrs. Mary (Kooser) Tedrow was born in Somerset County, Penn., Sept. 3, 1800. Sept. 5, 1820, she married Jacob Tedrow, also a native of Somerset County, born June 7, 1792. They came to Ohio in 1836 and settled near where Mrs. Tedrow now resides. They had a family of eleven children, nine now living—Drusilla, born Sept. 30, 1822, now the widow of George Wyatt; Harriet, born Feb. 2, 1826, now the widow of J. McHorten; Noah, born Feb. 1, 1828; Rebecca, born Dec. 2, 1829, now Mrs. James Robertson; Jane, born Dec. 3, 1832, now Mrs. Samuel Copeland; Oliver, born Sept. 16, 1836; Mary Ann, born Feb. 2, 1838; Effie, born Feb. 1, 1841, now the widow of Henry Norris, and Charles, born July 3, 1844. Mrs. Tedrow has 166 acres of fine land on section 35, Rome Township. She and her daughter Mary are members of the Presbyterian church at New England. Mr. Tedrow died July 1, 1873.

Noah Tedrow, born in Somerset County, Penn., Feb. 1, 1828, is the second child of Jacob and Mary (Kooser) Tedrow. He came to Ohio with his parents in 1837, and, with the exception of six months spent in Muskingum County, has since that time resided in Athens County. He was married Oct. 7, 1855, to Nancy Yazer, a native of Greene County, Penn., born Feb. 2, 1830. They have three children—Sarah, born Dec. 19, 1857, now Mrs. G. W. Parker; Mary, born March 16, 1862, and George, born Dec. 5, 1868. Mr. Tedrow has 700 acres of fine land in Rome Township, his residence being on section 35. He makes a specialty of stock-raising. Mr. and Mrs. Tedrow and their daughters are members of the Presbyterian church.

C. G. Tucker was born in Athens County, Ohio, Dec. 1, 1847. He was married April 19, 1879, to Margaret A. Jackson, a native of Athens County, born in 1851. They have two children—Jessie M., born Jan. 25, 1880, and Charles Guy, born Dec. 2, 1882. Mr. Tucker has been Constable of Rome Township twelve or fifteen years, and Township Assessor seven years. He has sixty-five acres of land where he resides, on fraction 24, and an interest in other land in this county, and also owns land in Iowa. He is now dealing in sewing-machines, and is special collector for Southern Ohio. Mrs. Tucker is a member of the Methodist church. Mr. Tucker's father, Nathan Tucker, was born in Maryland in 1814, and is now living on fraction 33, Rome Township. His mother, Barbara A. Tucker, was born in Somerset County, Penn., in 1805. She first married Joseph Tedrow. He died in 1833, leaving six children—Henry, Silas, Aaron, Joseph, Freeman and Susan. Aaron died in 1865. Freeman is a resident of Ohio; the others are living in Iowa. Mr. and Mrs. Nathan Tucker are members of the Methodist church.

Nehemiah O. Warren was born Sept. 22, 1799, in Connecticut, and when twenty-one years of age went to Hudson, N. Y., where he was engaged in the live-stock business about five years. He then came to Athens County, Ohio, and located in Canaan Township, remaining there till 1871, engaged in various kinds of business. He established his first dry-goods store in 1840, in Guysville, and afterward started a store in Stewart. In 1871 he came to Rome Township, and now lives on a fine farm of 450 acres. In 1879 he discontinued his commercial career, and is now settling up his business with a view to living a more retired life. Mr. Warren claims to have bought and sold more horses than any other man in the county, and has probably borrowed more money and paid more interest than any other man. He at one time owned over 1,600 acres of land. He was married April 19, 1818, to Hannah Deway, a native of Connecticut, born June 27, 1800. They had a family of nine children, five now living—Jane, born

Feb. 2, 1819; Hannah, March 12, 1821; Levinda, April 16, 1831; Elizabeth, Sept. 14, 1833; Joseph W., July 30, 1838. Mrs. Warren died Jan. 31, 1866. Mr. Warren has been four times married. He was married the last time to Mary Frost, May 31, 1874. He is a member of the Methodist Episcopal church.

Harvey Wright, carpenter and contractor, was born in Ames Township, Athens Co., Ohio, May 10, 1836. At the age of twelve he went to Washington County, Ohio, and remained eight years. At the expiration of that time he came to New England and lived two years, then went to Sugar Creek, Athens County, where he lived four years. In 1862 he again moved to New England, where he has since remained, building railroad bridges and working at the carpenter's trade. He married, Dec. 6, 1861, Susan Smith, who was born in Columbiana County, Ohio, Dec. 6, 1835. They are the parents of three children—Minnie M., born Nov. 6, 1864; Perley S., Jan. 4, 1868; William H., March 5, 1872. Mr. and Mrs. Wright are members of the Presbyterian church. Henry Wright, the father of Harvey, was born in New York in 1803, and died in 1867. His mother, Louisa (Otis) Wright, was born in New York in 1804, and is still living in Athens County, Ohio. Mr. and Mrs. Henry Wright had a family of fifteen children, seven living—John N., Simeon M., Henry H., Harvey, Sophia, Electa and James O. Thomas Smith, Mrs. Harvey Wright's father, was born in Pennsylvania, in October, 1809, and died in 1879. Her mother, Sarah (Draper) Smith, was born in Pennsylvania in 1809, and is still living. Mr. and Mrs. Smith have had seven children, six living—Julia A., Thomas D., Susan D., Celisa, Mary C. and Louisa B.

CHAPTER XXI.

LEE TOWNSHIP—SOMETHING OF OLDEN TIMES, AND THE NEGRO'S MECCA.

ORGANIZATION—SOME OF THE OLD SETTLERS—POPULATION—ELECTIONS—TOWNSHIP OFFICERS—ALBANY, THE NEGRO'S MECCA—POSTOFFICE AND POSTMASTERS—MAYORS OF ALBANY—ATWOOD INSTITUTE, ITS HISTORY—GIFTS AND DONATIONS—ENTERPRISE INSTITUTES—ITS RISE AND PROGRESS—SCHOOLS AND CHURCHES—THE WELLS LIBRARY—LODGES AND SOCIETIES—THE UNDERGROUND RAILWAY RUN BY A FEW CITIZENS OF ALBANY—BIOGRAPHICAL.

ORGANIZATION.

Lee Township was organized November, 1819, and her territory was taken from Alexander Township. It is the southwest township of the county, and in size the smallest, having but twenty-four sections of land, or two-thirds of a congressional township, being six miles north and south and four miles east and west, or 15,360 acres. It is bounded on the north by Waterloo Township, on the east by Alexander Township, south by Meigs County, and west by Vinton County. The land is generally rolling, and in some parts quite hilly, but nearly all portions suited for farming purposes, well suited for cultivation. The hills in some places are rather steep, but the soil is good and grasses grow luxuriantly. In fact there is very little waste land. The soil is not deep, neither is it very strong, but it is fertile enough to raise fair average crops. There are not many living streams of water, but then there are numerous springs, and water is reached by wells at from ten to forty feet. This spring water is pure and splendid for stock, and the farmers are giving largely of their attention to stock-raising, and to the best breeds. In this respect the farmers of Lee Township can boast, for her stock is the equal of any in the county.

SOME OF THE SETTLERS.

Among the earliest settlers of the township were: Captain John Martin, of Revolutionary fame; Phillip Smith, Henry Cassel, Ziba McVey, Daniel Knowlton, George Canney, Jno. Holdred, William Brown, William Graham, Jacob Lentner, James McGonnegal, Francis Thomas, Samuel Luckey, Hiram Howlett and John Doughty. These settlers were characteristic of the times, earnest, progressive, honest and well educated, and they brought with them a strong determination to see that in respect to educational facilities their children should not suffer by settling in the wilderness of the West. Schools were therefore among the first provided for, and their efforts in this direction met with success. Their action in this regard is worthy of all commendation, and the erection of churches, school-houses and support of libraries, attests their devotion to these important elements of moral progress, and the culture and refinement everywhere exhibited at their homes.

POPULATION, ETC.

This township, like one or two others, has shown a slight decline the past ten years in its population. In fact, its largest population was in 1860. The loss during the decade between 1860 and 1870 might be laid at the door of the late civil war, but there is no such excuse during the last, and it can possibly be attributed to too large a colored population. The population by decades from 1820 is here given: That year it was 342; in 1830, it was 418; in 1840, it was 848; in 1850, it was 961; in 1860, it was 1,301; in 1870, it was 1,146; in 1880, 1,086. This showing gives the township but 125 more in 1880 than it had in 1850, a period of thirty years.

The organization being in November of 1819, the first election for township officers did not take place until the following April, 1820, and these officers and subsequent ones are recorded here.

TOWNSHIP OFFICERS.

1820.—Trustees, Jacob Lentner, James McGonnegal and Ephraim Martin; Justice of the Peace, Isaac Baker.

1821.—Trustees, Francis Thomas, James McGonnegal and Elisha Chapman.

1822.—Trustees, Ephraim Martin, James McGonnegal and Daniel Rowell; Justice of the Peace, Abner C. Martin.

1823.—Trustees, Joseph Wallace, Francis Thomas and Wm. Brown; Justice of the Peace, Isaac Baker.

1824.—Trustees, Ephraim Martin, Francis Thomas and James McGonnegal; Justice of the Peace, Joseph Wallace.

1825.—Trustees, same as above; Justices of the Peace, McCowen Bean, Michael Canney and James McGee.

1826 and 1827.—Trustees, same as above.

1828.—Trustees, Samuel Martin, Francis Thomas and James McGonnegal; Justice of the Peace, Jacob Lentner.

1829.—Trustees, James McGee, George Reeves and McCowen Bean.

1830.—Trustees, same as above.

1831.—Trustees, Wm. Graham, Wm. Thompson and McCowen Bean; Justices of the Peace, McCowen Bean and Abner C. Martin.

1832.—Trustees, Joseph Martin, Wm. Thompson and John Havener; Justice of the Peace, Jacob Lentner.

1833.—Trustees, Wm. Graham, James McGonnegal and Joseph Martin.

1834.—Trustees, same as above; Justice of the Peace, Abner C. Martin.

1835.—Trustees, same as above; Justice of the Peace, Jacob Lentner.

1836.—Trustees, Joseph Post, Wm. Thompson and Nimrod Dailey.

1837.—Trustees, Wm. Graham, Michael Canney and Nimrod Dailey; Justice of the Peace, Abner C. Martin.

1838.—Trustees, same as above; Justice of the Peace, John Dickson.

1839.—Trustees, same as above; Justice of the Peace, Lucius Beckley.

1840.—Trustees, same as above; Justice of the Peace, Abraham Enlow.

1841.—Trustees, John T. Winn, Joseph Post and Jacob Lentner; Justice of the Peace, A. Warner.

1842.—Trustees, same as above; Justice of the Peace, John T. Winn.

1843.—Trustees, Wm. Graham, Wm. Henderson and Jacob Lentner; Justices of the Peace, George Means and Francis E. Clark.

1844.—Trustees, same as above; Justice of the Peace, Edmund Morse.

1845.—Trustees, F. E. Clark, A. G. Henderson and James Greathouse; Justices of the Peace, A. G. Henderson and Peter Morse.

1846.—Trustees, same as above; Justice of the Peace, Francis E. Clark.

1847.—Trustees, F. E. Clark, Travis Wilson and James Greathouse; Justice of the Peace, George Holdren.

1848.—Trustees, F. E. Clark, John Brown and George Holdren.

1849.—Trustees, Andrew Means, John Dewing and George Holdren; Justices of the Peace, D. M. Ross and F. E. Clark.

1850.—Trustees, F. E. Clark, D. M. Ross and A. W. Brown; Justice of the Peace, Joseph Post.

1851.—Trustees, F. E. Clark, Leonard Brown and D. M. Ross.

1852.—Trustees, James Holmes, B. Goodrich and John T. Winn; Justices of the Peace, James Clements and F. E. Clark.

1853.—Trustees, James Holmes, A. Enlow and John T. Winn; Justice of the Peace, Joseph Post.

1854.—Trustees, same as before; Justice of the Peace, George Johnson.

1855.—Trustees, James Holmes, Samuel Shuster and John T. Winn; Justices of the Peace, James Clements, John Brown and Jacob McVey.

1856.—Trustees, James Holmes, Jacob McVey and John T. Winn; Justice of the Peace, Harvey L. Graham.

1857.—Trustees, James Holmes, James Clements and John T. Winn.

1858.—Trustees, James Holmes, James Clements and Benjamin Rickey; Justices of the Peace, James Clements and Jacob McVey.

1859.—Trustees, James Holmes, James Clements and A. W. Brown; Justice of the Peace, Harvey L. Graham.

1860.—Trustees, James Holmes, W. W. Kurtz and A. W. Brown; Justice of the Peace, Peter Morse.

1861.—Trustees, James Holmes, A. Wilson and A. W. Brown; Justice of the Peace, E. R. Cooper.

1862.—Trustees, James Holmes, A. Jennings and A. W. Brown; Justice of the Peace, James M. Gorslene.

1863.—Trustees, same as above.

1864.—Trustees, James Holmes, A. Wilson and A. W. Brown; Justice of the Peace, E. R. Cooper.

1865.—Trustees, James Holmes, Wm. C. Lindley and Robert Dickson; Justice of the Peace, James M. Gorslene.

1866.—Trustees, Lemuel Cline, Jacob McVey and Robert Dickson.

1867.—Trustees, same as above; Justices of the Peace, John Q. Mitchell and Isaac Friedlein.

1868.—Trustees, Albert Vorhes, Jacob McVey and Robert Dickson; Justice of the Peace, Abraham Enlow.

1869.—Trustees, Jacob McVey, W. W. Blake and A. C. Daily; Clerk, A. Palmer; Treasurer, John Dewing.

1870.—Trustees, W. W. Blake, John Molher and L. Cline; Clerk, A. Palmer; Treasurer, John Dewing.

1871.—Trustees, L. Cline, John H. Molher and Alpheus Wilson; Clerk, John P. Coe; Treasurer, S. R. Hibbard.

1872.—Trustees, J. H. Molher, W. C. Lindley and Thomas Daily; Clerk, John P. Coe; Treasurer, A. Palmer.

1873.—Trustees, W. C. Lindley, J. H. Molher and Thomas Daily; Clerk, John P. Coe; Treasurer, A. Palmer.

1874.—Trustees, W. C. Lindley, J. H. Molher and Abraham Crossen; Clerk, John P. Coe; Treasurer, A. Palmer.

1875.—Trustees, Abraham Crossen, Elias Graham and Hugh Fletcher; Clerk, John P. Coe; Treasurer, A. Palmer.

1876.—Trustees, A. Crossen, John Snyder and A. H. Holmes; Clerk, John P. Coe; Treasurer, A. Palmer.

1877.—Trustees, Jacob McVey, Elias Graham and Amos Knowlton; Clerk, John P. Coe; Treasurer, A. Palmer.

1878.—Trustees, Elias Graham, Jacob McVey and Amos Knowlton; Clerk, John P. Coe; Treasurer, A. Palmer.

1879.—Trustees, Jacob McVey, Elias Graham and James Sickles; Clerk, John P. Coe; Treasurer, A. Palmer.

1880.—Trustees, Elias Graham, James Sickles and J. N. Patterson; Clerk, W. Cline; Treasurer, A. C. Daily; Justices of the Peace, D. J. Canny and S. P. Armstrong.

1881.—Trustees, Elias Graham, J. N. Patterson and S. V. Knowlton; Clerk, W. W. Cline; Treasurer, A. C. Daily.

1882.—Trustees, Elias Graham, W. C. Lindley and James Sickles; Clerk, W. W. Cline; Treasurer, A. C. Daily.

1883.—Trustees, Jacob McVey, Wm. C. Lindley and M. J. Dixon; Clerk, John Ritchie; Treasurer, S. T. Cline; Justice, D. J. Canny.

ALBANY.

The village of Albany is situated in the eastern part of the township, on the line of the Ohio Central Railroad. It was laid out into lots by Wm. Graham in 1832 or 1833, the first house in the village being built by Lucius R. Beckley on the ground now owned by

Cline & Daily and known as the old Brown store. In 1840 John Brown purchased this property and commenced selling goods. Albany has now a population of about 700 inhabitants, with the usual complement of business men and mechanics. The leading business establishments at present are J. H. Vorhes & Bro., Cline & Daily and W. A. Smith, dealers in general merchandise; J. C. P. Moore, dealer in hardware, and T. D. Moore, dealer in tinware and harness. Albany is a neat village, surrounded by a beautiful farming country. It having been, until recently, an inland town, its business has been necessarily limited. The buildings are almost all of wood and generally of the style of farm buildings. It has two institutions of learning besides the public schools, five church societies, a public library, one Masonic lodge, two hotels kept by G. W. Hill and R. M. Figley, and two physicians, J. H. Winn and B. C. Vorhes. Albany was incorporated in 1844. At the first election for town officers John V. Brown was chosen Mayor and J. M. Gorslene, Clerk. For a number of years afterward there was no election, but since 1855 the elections have been regular. The Mayors have been as follows: John V. Brown, 1844 to 1855; Albert Vorhes, 1855 to 1857; A. Palmer, 1857 to 1858; Almus Lindley, 1858 to 1859; W. B. Dicksen, 1859 to 1860; S. M. Preshaw, 1860 to 1861; John Brown, 1861 to 1862; James M. Gorslene, 1862 to 1872; J. C. Woodyard, 1872 to 1874; George Bean, 1874 to 1876; J. M. Wood, 1876 to 1877; J. C. P. Moore, 1877 to 1882; A. C. Daily, 1882 to present time.

The Postoffice at Albany (Lee P. O.) was first established in 1829, on the old Athens and Chillicothe mail road, about two and one-half miles northwest of the present village of Albany. It remained here until 1836, when it was removed to the village by James Wilson. The Postmasters, with their times of service, have been as follows: Jacob Lentner, 1829 to 1836; James Wilson, 1836 to 1837; Lucius R. Beckley, 1837 to 1840; J. McCully, 1840 to 1841; Jonathan Winn, 1841 to 1846; John V. Brown, 1846 to 1847; John Earhart, 1847 to 1849; Peter Morse, 1849 to 1853; James M. Gorslene, 1853 to 1861; Peter Morse, 1861 to 1865; W. W. Kurtz, 1865 to 1866; Augustus Palmer, 1866 to present time. It was made a money-order office Aug. 1, 1870, the first order being issued to P. C. Hewitt, payable to Jacob Wycoff, Mt. Ayr, Iowa, for the amount of $20. The office has issued 4,778 orders up to the present time. The sale of stamps for the year 1882 was about $720.

ATWOOD INSTITUTE.

This Institute, located at Albany, was originally called the Albany Manual Labor University. A brief sketch of its origin is as follows: In 1847 Mr. William S. Lewis removed with his family from Oberlin, Ohio, and settled at Albany. Soon after their arrival his daughter, Miss Lamira Lewis, opened a school for children in a part of their residence, the house now occupied by Mrs. Mitchell. In 1848 Mr. Lewis bought a lot and built upon it a house especially for school purposes. The school here soon became very prosperous, and in order to make room for the students a second story was added to the building. Students were admitted to this school regardless of color, caste or sex. Mr. Lewis having assumed control of this school continued it in his own building until 1851, when others gave their influence and a joint-stock company was formed, made up of shares of $25 each. The first meeting of the executive board of this company was held Sept. 25, 1851, when the following officers were elected: John T. Winn, Chairman; John S. Lewis, Secretary, and George Hanger, Treasurer. It was this organization that gave to the school the name of the Albany Manual Labor University. The first plan adopted by the management was to require those borrowing money from the institution to give so many hours a week of manual employment to students of the University, the amount being regulated by the amount of money borrowed and the rate of interest paid. In 1852 Dr. J. A. Bingham, now a resident of Medina County, Ohio, a soldier of the war of 1812, and a man of great energy, was induced to act as traveling agent to secure funds for the University. A little later Rev. J. Cable was elected to solicit funds, and the success of both soon enabled the association to buy 300 acres of land which was converted to the use of the institution. The present building, now known as the Atwood Institute, was erected in 1857. It is a frame building, 40 x 100 feet in dimensions, and three stories high. From 1857 until 1862 the school was conducted by two men named McLanthin and Cable. Under them the school averaged about eighty students. In 1862 Prof. T. D. Garvin and James Dodd took charge of the school. They being members of the Christian church a sectarian element was introduced into the school, and the manual-labor feature was discontinued. Under this management the school had, at times, over 100 students. In 1866 the school fell into the hands of the Free-

Will Baptist church, by whom it is controlled at present. This change was, in effect, a revolution in the school's history. From this time colored students were denied admission, the school was placed on a firm footing by a donation from Mr. Nehemiah Atwood of $3,500, and its name was changed to the Atwood Institute. Others of the Free-Will Baptist denomination contributed liberally, and the school was transferred to the Athens Quarterly Meeting, under whose control it still remains. Lyman C. Chase, A. M., a graduate of Hillsdale College, Mich., was the first Principal under its present management. For three years, from 1866 to 1869, Mr. Chase, assisted by Rev. J. M. Rayser and Rev. M. W. Spencer, A. B., conducted a very prosperous school, the attendance ranging from seventy to over one hundred students. After Mr. Chase's resignation, in 1869, the school changed hands several times within the next ten years. For a number of years J. M. and J. P. Wood, now attorneys at Athens, Ohio, conducted the school in a successful manner. In 1880 the Board of Trustees called again L. C. Chase to the Principalship, and Mrs. Hattie Chase, Preceptress of the school, they having an attendance of fifty-three students the last term. Mr. Chase's health failing he retires from the school at the end of the present year, and through his aid the board has secured Mr. C. H. French, of Boston, Mass., as Principal, with Misses Maria Ward and Nellie B. Porter, assistants. Prominent among the donors, besides Mr. Atwood, in the early history of the Institute are: General John Brown, who gave $1,000; John T. Winn, who gave $500; Webber Wilson and H. L. Graham.

The Enterprise Institute was first established in 1864. When the Atwood Institute came under the control of the denominational churches, colored students were denied admission and some of the more influential colored citizens conceived the idea of founding a school especially for colored pupils. Donations were solicited from wealthy men in this and other States, and among the liberal aids received were a gift of $3,000 worth of real estate from Thomas Carleton, of Syracuse, Ill., and an appropriation from the Freedmen's Bureau of $2,000. Many other liberal donations were received but these are the most important. Young colored people of both sexes were admitted, and for a time the school was very prosperous, receiving patronage from different parts of this State, and from adjoining ones. Mr. T. J. Ferguson, an able and well-educated colored gentleman, has been the principle teacher up to the present time. The school building is a two-story brick, the lower floor only being used for the school at present, the upper being used by the colored Baptist church for a place of worship. It is pleasantly situated on the outskirts of the village of Albany.

The Village School for white children is a well-conducted school, occupying two rooms and having two teachers. The building is a good one, two stories high, situated on a high piece of ground in the center of the village. There is also in Albany a common school for colored children.

CHURCHES.

The Free-Will Baptist Church, of Albany, is the oldest church society in the village. It was founded about 1854 by Ira Z. Haning. Mr. Haning was followed in the pastorate by O. E. Baker, who conducted, in 1857, the most successful revival meeting in the history of the church, securing the addition of sixty persons to its membership. Mr. Baker was followed successively by Revs. S. E. Root, J. M. Kayser, M. W. Spencer, J. W. Martin, David Powell, A. Streamer and D. Powell again, the present Pastor. The society owns a good church building which was erected in 1857.

The Methodist Episcopal Church society, of Albany, was founded in the winter of 1876 by Rev. Elias Nichols. The society is a prosperous one, numbering at present about fifty-five members. Mr. Nichols was followed by Revs. James Ricketts, Mr. Murphy, B. F. Jackson, Edward Howe and Mr. Kendall. Mr. Jacob Spring is the present Class-Leader. The society has, up to the present time, rented the first floor of the Masonic Hall for a place of holding meetings.

The Cumberland Presbyterian Church was founded at Albany, Aug. 25, 1880. A. Lindley, A. L. Patterson, A. Vorhes, S. P. Armstrong and Hugh Fletcher were elected Trustees. Rev. R. J. P. Lemon was made the Pastor and remains such to the present time. The society finished a new church building in September, 1881, at a cost of $1,850.

The Colored Churches at Albany are a Baptist and Methodist Episcopal, and are well attended by the colored brethren.

The Wells Library is an institution of which the citizens of Albany are justly proud. It was founded by Mr. Henry Wells, who, dying in 1860, bequeathed $250 for the immediate purchase of books for a public library, and $1,000 to be a perpetual fund, the interest to be used for the purchase of new books and keeping in repair the old ones. The money was securely invested in 1861, by Mr. E. H. Moore, of Athens, whom Mr. Wells made his trustee for this purpose. The proceeds averaging until recently about $70 a year, have been carefully expended for books until the library has been swelled to 1,124 volumes of well-selected miscellaneous works, besides a useful collection of public documents and books of reference. The expense of the library is kept up by a light tax laid upon the property of the incorporate village. For some time the library was kept in a room gratuitiously furnished by the Freemasons of Albany, but in March, 1868, Mrs. Mary Weethee, mother of the founder of the library, bequeathed a frame building to be used as a library room, provided the town should keep it in repair and pay the taxes. By the rules of the library, any family, living within the corporation may, for $1 a year, draw out two volumes at a time for not more than four weeks, and the library is open two hours every Thursday for members. The library is a settled and highly valued institution, and is a splendid example of a wise and useful disposition of property.

Albany Lodge, No. 156, A. F. & A. M., was founded under the old dispensation, Feb. 15, 1848, at Hebbardsville, Ohio, where it remained until 1855, under the name of the Hebbardsville Lodge. The charter was obtained Sept. 27, 1848. The first officers were: Ziba Lindley, Jr., W. M.; Wm. Russell, S. W.; J. B. Gray, J. W.; Josiah Wilson, Treas.; Harvey Pratt, Sec.; John Arnold, S. D.; A. Lindley, J. D., and John W. Drake, T. The following is a list of the Past Masters:

Ziba Lindley, Jr., 1848–'49; J. B. Gray, 1850; John Arnold, 1851; J. B. Gray, 1852; John Arnold, 1853; A. B. Dickey, 1854; (1855–'56, no record); J. B. Gray, 1857; C. L. Wilson, 1858 to 1861; Joseph Jewett, 1862; A. D. Jaynes, 1863; C. L. Wilson, 1864; J. Q. Mitchell, 1865; James McClure, 1866–'7; J. Q. Mitchell, 1868; James McClure, 1869; J. L. Carpenter, 1870 to 1872; J. Q. Mitchell, 1873; Isaac Stanley, 1874–'75; J. L. Carpenter, 1876; R. S. Dent, 1877 to 1881; A. L. Rutherford, 1882. The lodge is in a prosperous condition and owns a good hall building.

Before leaving the village of Albany something should be said of it as a station in the old "underground railway" system. In the days of great excitement over the slave question, while the fugitive slave law was being enforced, and slaves were being transported secretly to Canada, no community of persons in this portion of the State took a more active part in protecting the transfer than did the city of Albany in this humane but unlawful work.

THE ALBANY ECHO.

The Albany *Echo* is published at Albany (Lee postoffice), Athens County, by D. A. R. McKinstry, editor and proprietor. It is a six-column weekly, published every Thursday. In politics it is independent. It was first published "semi-occasionally" on the co-operative plan, by D. A. R. McKinstry, of the Lee Insurance Company, as an advertising sheet. The *Echo* was established as a weekly journal in January, 1877, by a joint stock company of which the late Dr. Alex. Richardson was President, J. H. Vorhes, Secretary, and A. C. Dailey, Treasurer. At the end of the first year, Mr. McKinstry and J. S. Black bought up these shares and became proprietors as well as editors. In October this partnership was dissolved by mutual consent, J. S. Black retiring. The paper has been well received from the first, maintaining a good circulation, and having a fair advertising patronage.

BIOGRAPHICAL.

John S. Black was born at Greenock, Scotland, June 5, 1826, and when quite young came to America alone. He landed in New York and remained there two years; then went to Canada West and lived four years; then spent a year in Pontiac, Mich., and from there went to Sheboygan, Wis. He learned the carriage-maker's trade, and worked at it a year in Wisconsin. In 1855 he came to Athens County, and located in Albany, where he has since been engaged in manufacturing carriages. In 1877, in company with D. A. R. McKinsley and J. P. Wood, he started the *Echo*. In 1878 Mr. Wood sold his interest, and two years later Mr. Black sold out. Mr. McKinstry is now managing the paper. He has been a member of the Board of Education for the past nine years. He has been Clerk of the corporation four years, and is at present a member of the Town Council. July 14, 1858, he married Rhoda E. Bissell, a native of Meigs County, born May 25, 1828. They have two children—Agnes S., born Dec. 17, 1859, and Elizabeth A., born Dec. 26, 1864.

A. W. Brown, born in Ames Township, Aug. 21, 1814, was a son of William and Polly L. Brown, natives of Massachusetts, his father born Feb. 22, 1779, and his mother Sept. 14, 1782. His father died Feb. 18, 1859, and his mother Feb. 7, 1849. They had a family of nine children, five now living—Elizabeth, now Mrs. B. S. Williams; Lydia A., a resident of Woodbury, N. J.; A. W.; Leonard, now living in Woodbury, N. J., and Daniel T., of Fort Madison, Iowa. Mr. Brown was married April 19, 1838, to Almira Van Vorhes, a native of Washington County, Penn., born May 3, 1818. They had four children, only one now living—Edwin A., born Oct. 5, 1839. He was married in 1871 to Phœbe Brownlee, a native of Athens County, born Dec. 25, 1843. They have three children—Harry L., born in May, 1873; Nellie, in June, 1876, and Minnie M., in October, 1879. Edwin A. enlisted June 24, 1861, and served nearly four years; was in the battles of Lewisburg (where he was wounded), second Bull Run and Antietam. He was transferred to the Army of the Cumberland, and was in the battles of Mission Ridge, and Chickamauga. Edwin A. is living on the home farm with his father. They have fifty acres of land on section 8, Lee Township, within the corporation of Albany. Mr. Brown's son, William V., was born Feb. 12, 1842. He learned the printer's trade and was foreman in the Athens *Messenger* office. He enlisted in Company D, Fourth Virginia Infantry, and died of small-pox at Vicksburg, Miss., March 9, 1863. Another son, D. N., born March 23, 1844, enlisted in 1863, and served one year in Virginia. After his return home he studied medicine, and graduated from the Cincinnati Medical College in 1869. He married, Oct. 11, 1870, Laura Graham. He died Feb. 10, 1873, leaving one child—Myra, born Feb. 7, 1872. A daughter, Emma J., born May 20, 1847, married Dr. W. A. Adair, Oct. 22, 1871, and died March 16, 1873. Mr. and Mrs. Brown and their daughter-in-law are members of the Cumberland Presbyterian church. Mrs. Brown's father, Abraham Van Vorhes, was born in Washington County, Penn., in December, 1793, and came to Ohio in 1831. He was the first editor of the *Hocking Valley Gazette*, now the Athens *Messenger*. He was appointed by President Taylor Register of the first land office in Minnesota, and the last years of his life were spent in that State. In 1840 he was elected to the Lower House of the Ohio Legislature, and afterward was sent to the Senate four terms. He was County Surveyor of Athens County six years and County Treasurer one year. He was appointed Territorial Auditor by Governor Ramsey, and in 1860 was a Commissioner to locate the capitol and university lands appropriated by Congress. He was Postmaster at Stillwater several years. Major Van Vorhes's wife was Mary W.

Vorhes, a native of Washington County, Md. They had a family of eight children, five of whom are living—Almira, Jane, Elizabeth, Maria and Henry C. The son is now living in Stillwater, Minn.

Lyman C. Chase, A. M., Principal of Atwood Institute, was born Oct. 2, 1839, at Rutland, Meigs Co., Ohio. He was a son of Charles Chase, the latter being a son of Abel Chase, who emigrated from Bangor, Me., in 1807; his mother, before marriage was Miss Mary Holt, daughter of Rev. Aaron Holt, a Baptist minister, who emigrated from New Haven, Conn., in 1802, each being among the first settlers in that part of Ohio. Lyman resided at Rutland and attended the district school at Side Hill till the spring of his fifteenth year. Early in the spring of this year he went to Prestonsburg, Ky., to visit his brother, Dr. O. G. Chase, who at the time was a practicing physician in that town, and while there he engaged to teach his first school. Mr. Chase at this time rather hesitatingly assumed the control of the village school as he was only fifteen years old and some of the pupils, of whom there were about sixty, were several years older than himself. He, however, in early summer assumed the responsibilities of the school, entering upon his work with a determination to succeed. He finished his term and returned to Ohio in the fall. He attended the district school at home through the winter of 1856-'7, and the following summer taught in the same district. After this he attended school for a year and a half at Albany University, now known as Atwood Institute, and after several years of teaching and going to school, in February, 1860, being then twenty years old, he entered Hillsdale College. Dependent upon his own efforts in securing an education, he graduated with honors in 1866. In the month of June of that year he returned to his home in Rutland, and soon after, through the solicitations of Rev. I. Z. Haning, of Albany, he consented to take charge of Atwood Institute. This was a change in the plans of Mr. Chase somewhat, as he had contemplated the taking of a Theological course. However, Jan. 3, 1869, he was set apart to the work of the Christian ministry, according to the usages of the Free-Will Baptist denomination, and in June following he tendered his resignation as Principal of Atwood Institute. For some years subsequent to this he was engaged in the ministry. He held pastorates at Conneaut, Ohio, Cromwell, Iowa, and preached several years in Illinois. In the fall of '81 he resumed the Principalship of Atwood Institute, and on the 9th of March, 1882, he was married to Miss Hattie Lawson who, for two years, had formerly been a student of Mr. Chase's in the Institute. This marriage took place in the church in which Mr. Chase was ordained to the gospel ministry about fourteen years before. At this writing Mr. Chase is still an occupant of Atwood Institute, is pastor of a church, but will shortly retire, for a time, from the duties of the institution, as health demands a change.

S. T. Cline, born in Athens County, Ohio, Aug. 10, 1841, is a son of John and Elizabeth (Townsend) Cline, natives of Virginia, his father born March, 1818, and his mother Aug. 9, 1821. His parents had a family of seven children—S. T., Ruth and Rachel (twins), George, James, Arclisse and John E. When he was quite small his parents moved to Meigs County, and he lived there till 1879. He then came to Albany and bought a stock of drugs, boots and shoes, and has since added dry goods and groceries. He married, April 14, 1862, Lydia M. Gillogly, a native of Meigs County, born April 5, 1844. They have two children—Anna E., born Jan. 6, 1865, and John H., born May 31, 1872. Mr. and Mrs. Cline are members of the Methodist church. Mr. Cline is a member of Lodge No. 156, A. F. & A. M.

Mrs. Samantha Cline, born in Lee Township, May 11, 1830, is a daughter of Nimrod and Mary (Cottrill) Dailey. Her father was born in Virginia in 1800, and her mother in 1803. They have five children—Emily, Nancy, Samantha, Thomas and Andrew. Mrs. Cline was married Feb. 15, 1849, to Lemuel Cline, a native of Virginia, born July 10, 1827. They had a family of six children—Mary R., born Dec. 5, 1849; Sarah J., born Dec. 27, 1852; Nancy E., born Oct. 13, 1854; William W., born Aug. 24, 1856; Nimrod D., born March 11, 1859; Flora, born Jan. 10, 1863, and Howard, born April 12, 1869. Mr. Cline died in 1872. Mrs. Cline has a fine farm of 164 acres on section 19, Lee Township. She is a member of the Methodist church.

John Dewing was born in Norfolk, Mass., Jan. 18, 1813. His father, Elijah Dewing, was born in Dover, Mass., July 11, 1761, and served at West Point during the Revolutionary war. He was at West Point about the time Benedict Arnold was trying to surrender the fort to the British. He died in 1843, at Medway, Mass., aged eighty-three years. His wife, Betsey (Reed) Dewing, was born in Needham, Mass., in 1769, and died the same day as her husband, and they were buried in the same grave. Mr. Dewing came to Athens County in 1841, and located at Hebbardsville. In the latter part of 1844 he came to Albany, where he has since resided. He learned the trade of a cutler in Worcester, Mass., in 1830, in the first cutler's shop in America, and afterward learned to make spectacles, and was engaged in that business several years after coming here. Of late years he has been buying and collecting notes and doing a general brokerage business. He has sixty acres of land on section 11, Lee Township, and considerable town property. In 1849 he went to California via the isthmus, and remained eighteen months. He has been Township Assessor six years. He is a member of Albany Lodge, No. 156, A. F. & A. M. Jan. 13, 1836, he married Mindwell R. Cleveland, a native of Harwinton, Conn., born Sept. 17, 1817. They have one daughter—Mary M., now Mrs. James H. Holmes. She has one child—Angie G., born Aug. 4, 1881. Mr. Dewing has the record of his father's ancestors from 1644 to the present time. Andrew Dewing, one of the first settlers of Needham, was a member of the ancient artillery of Boston in 1644.

S. Fauts, contractor and bridge builder, was born in Morgan County, Ohio, Aug. 15, 1824, and lived there till twenty-two years of age. From 1846 to 1852 he was engaged in manufacturing windmills in Ohio and Illinois. From 1853 to 1861 he was engaged in general contracting and building. May 15, 1862, he enlisted in Company H, Eighty-seventh Ohio Infantry, and served five months. He was taken prisoner at Harper's Ferry, Va., in September, 1862. In 1863 he came to Albany, and took charge of the wood work in the colored school building, and has since that time been engaged in contracting and bridge building. He has a pleasant home in Albany, where his family are surrounded with the comforts of life. He was married July 4, 1847, to Catharine Neff, a native of Pickaway County, Ohio, born May 2, 1830. They have three children—Cydnor T., Charles W. and Mary A. Mr. and Mrs. Fauts are members of the Methodist church. He belongs to Columbus Golden Post, No. 89, G. A. R., Athens.

Hugh Fletcher was born in County Donegal, Ireland, May 13, 1809, and came to America in 1824. He landed in New Jersey and went direct to Greene County, Penn. In 1836 he came to Athens County, Ohio, and located in Alexander Township. In 1838 he went back to Europe but returned again to America in 1840 and settled in Lee Township. In 1843 he went to Wisconsin, and in the fall of 1846 went again to Europe. In 1851 he came again to Lee Township. He bought a farm in Waterloo Township and lived there till 1857, when he came to Albany, where he has since resided. He was married Jan. 17, 1855, to Margaret Entsler, a native of Vinton County, Ohio. They have two children—Charles E., born April 1, 1856, and Mary E., born March 14, 1866. Mr. and Mrs. Fletcher are members of the Cumberland Presbyterian church.

Elias Graham, born in Albany, May 8, 1825, was a son of William and Nancy (Cassel) Graham. His father was born July 2, 1783, and died May 31, 1854. His mother was born Feb. 14, 1788, and died March 26, 1851. They had a family of twelve children —Henry (the second male child born in Lee Township), Elizabeth, Sophia, Ivy, William, James, Samuel, Hannah, Elias, Martha, Wilson and Nancy. Elias was married April 24, 1838, to Diantha Martin, a native of this township. Four children were born to them, only three now living—Rebecca J., Martha and William T. Mr. Graham has 190 acres of good land and is engaged in farming and stock-raising, making a specialty of the latter. He is a member of Lee Grange. His father built the first hotel in Athens in 1800.

E. C. Humphrey, carpenter, was born in Washington County, Ohio, May 3, 1823, and in 1846 came to Lee Township, Athens County. He was married in September, 1846, to Sarah Rigg, a native of Pennsylvania, born May 29, 1826. They have had four children, only two now living—William E. and Joseph E. Their eldest son, John A., enlisted in the late war, and at the battle of Winchester, July 24, 1864, he was shot through the thigh, and as the Union forces left the field to the rebels, he fell into their hands and is supposed to have died as he has never since been heard from. Mr. Humphrey enlisted Feb. 1, 1862, in Company C, Seventy-fourth Ohio Infantry, and was discharged Nov. 5, 1862, on account of disability. March 1, 1864, he raised a company to take a wagon train to Cumberland Gap. On their arrival at Camp Nelson, Ky., it was formed into a pack-mule train, and he was appointed its Captain. During the John Morgan raid in Ohio he enlisted in the State Militia and served till after Morgan's capture. Mr. and Mrs. Humphrey are both members of the Free-Will Baptist church.

George Jones was born in Belmont County, Ohio, Jan. 19, 1821, When ten years old he went to Morgan County, and in 1846 came to Athens County, where he has since resided. He has eighty-eight acres of good land on section 33, Lee Township. He was married June, 1846, to Hannah Jackson, a native of Delaware

County, Ohio, born in 1814. They have six children—James H., Jesse (now in Washington Territory), George W., Eliza J., Sarah and Libbie. Mr. and Mrs. Jones and three of their children are members of the Christian church.

Mrs. Alice Kerr was born in Pennsylvania June 13, 1807. She was married Jan. 19, 1836, to David Kerr, a native of Pennsylvania, born Dec. 17, 1804. They moved to Virginia in 1837, and in 1842 came to Ohio and settled on section 2, Lee Township, where Mr. Kerr died Dec. 9, 1880, and where Mrs. Kerr now resides. Mrs. Kerr has six children—Salome, born Nov. 5, 1836; H. Huston, Jan. 16, 1838; Mary L., Oct. 31, 1839; Margaret, March 16, 1841; Rebecca, Dec. 8, 1842, and Phœbe A., Dec. 16, 1844. Mr. and Mrs. Kerr were both members of the Cumberland Presbyterian church. The children are all members of the Free-Will Baptist church. Mrs. Kerr's daughter, Mary L., commenced to teach school when sixteen years of age and taught sixteen years, in Ohio, Illinois and Nebraska. For the past three years she has been managing the home farm.

Rev. R. J. Lemmon, pastor of the Cumberland Presbyterian church, was born in Dubois County, Ind., Feb. 12, 1832. Nov. 6, 1856, he married Miss Jane Turner, a native of Bloomfield, Ind., born Feb. 8, 1833. They have five children—Jessie, now first assistant in the graded schools of Taylorville, Ill.; D. Donnell, R. Bell, Annie D., and Fannie Grace. After his marriage Mr. Lemmon took charge of the church in Bloomfield. In 1860 he went to Dale, Ind., and in connection with his pastoral work was employed to raise money to build an academy. At the breaking out of the late war the project was abandoned, and in 1863 he was called to the pastorate of the church in Taylorville, Ill. His health failing he resigned in 1866 and was appointed agent to obtain funds to endow Lincoln University, Lincoln, Ill. In 1869 he assumed the charge of the church at Albion, Ill. He afterward went to Newbury, Ind., and remained two years, when his health again being delicate, he was sent by the Board of Missions of the church to California, and remained there two years and a half. He was then called to the general financial management of the Waynesburg College, Waynesburg, Pa. In 1880 he came to Athens County, and in August of that year organized the church at Albany, and was instrumental in building the church in addition to his other pastoral labors. Mr. Lemmon has been a very prominent man in his church and has been an earnest worker in its behalf.

Hugh Laughlin was born in Jefferson County, Ohio, May 5, 1825. He was married in September, 1864, to Margaret Beveridge, a native of Athens County, born in 1821. They have had six children, only three now living—Mary, now Mrs. John Bowman; Nancy and Albert. Mr. Laughlin has fourteen acres of good land on section 12, Lee Township, and is engaged in farming and stock-raising, making a specialty of raising cattle. He was at one time a member of the Methodist church, but for the past eighteen years has not been connected with any denomination.

John Masten was born in Ritchie County, W. Va., Oct. 4, 1845. He came to Lee Township in 1864 and has since resided here engaged in farming. He now has sixty acres of good land on section 12. In October, 1873, he obtained a patent for his Climax churn, which has taken the premium at several county fairs, and also at the Ohio State Fair in 1878. Mr. Masten's address is Lee, Athens Co., Ohio, and he will be pleased to correspond with any one wishing a good churn. He was married April 21, 1866, to Catherine Llewellen, a native of Lee Township. They have eight children—Charles, Nora, Ora, Perley, Lucy, John, Rawliegh and Leander.

Andrew McClelland was born in Jefferson County, Ohio, Aug. 23, 1813, and when eight years of age went to Pennsylvania. When sixteen years of age he commenced to learn the shoemaker's trade and served an apprenticeship of four years. He was married Nov. 9, 1834, to Nancy Pratt, a native of Pennsylvania. They have had nine children, only seven now living—Mary, Sarah, Harriet, Eliza, Catherine, Rebecca M. and Salina. In 1847 Mr. McClellan came to Ohio and lived seven years in Hebbardsville, and in 1854 came to Albany. He enlisted Dec. 18, 1861, in the Seventy-ninth Ohio Infantry, afterward consolidated with the Seventy-fifth Ohio, and served three years; was in the battles at McDowell, second Bull Run, Chancellorsville and Gettysburg. He is a member of Albany Lodge, No. 156, A. F. & A. M.

A. D. Minear was born in Lee Township, Dec. 10, 1838. He enlisted in the late war in Company A, Ninety-second Ohio Infantry, and served three years. He participated in the battles at Chickamauga and Mission Ridge; was shot through the hips at the latter place and lay in the hospital three months, then received a furlough of a month, and returned to his regiment at Ringgold, Ga. From there went to Atlanta, Savannah, the Carolinas, Richmond and Washington, where he was mustered out; thence to Columbus, Ohio, for discharge. He returned to Lee Township and has since been engaged in farming and stock-raising. He has a fine farm of 345 acres, his residence being on section 16. He was married Dec. 10, 1865, to Sarah J. Cooper, a native of Ohio, born in 1847. She died Sept. 21, 1879, leaving two children—Aldo Z., born Jan. 3, 1868, and Holland M., born March 2, 1874. Mr. Minear is a member of the Methodist church. He is prominently associated with the Patrons of Husbandry.

E. C. Moler was born in Perry County, Ohio, June 7, 1847, and when six years old went to Vinton County. He came to Athens County in the spring of 1868 and settled in Lee Township, where he now has a fine farm of sixty acres on fraction 36, and seven acres in the limits of Albany. He is engaged in buying and selling stock in connection with farming. He was married in September, 1868, to Celestia A. Means, a native of Athens County, born Feb. 4, 1849. They have five children—Herbert, Cora, James, Jennie and Minnie.

J. W. Morris, carpenter, was born in Kent County, Md., Dec. 27, 1841. Oct. 11, 1869, he left Maryland and went to Cincinnati, and from there to Meigs County, but in 1870 came to Athens County and located in Albany. He was married in 1874 to E. M. Martin, a native of Meigs County, born in February, 1852. They have one child—C. R., born July 26, 1880. Mr. Morris's father, William Morris, was born in Maryland in 1811, and was killed by lightning in 1864. His mother, S. A. (Kankey) Morris, was born in 1808, and died in 1869. There was a family of seven children —C. K., J. H., W. T., E. S., G. W., J. W. and Anna Jane.

Joseph Oliver, farmer, was born in Guernsey County, Ohio, May 19, 1828. In 1859 he came to Athens County and lived in Alexander Township eighteen months, and then came to Lee Township. He has nine acres of good land in the corporation of Albany. For fifteen years he drove a hack from Albany to Marshfield, and a part of the time to Pomeroy. Three years of the time he was United States mail carrier, and was also employed during this time by the Adams Express Company. He was married Feb. 3, 1853, to Rebecca B., daughter of William and Margaret Figley, a native of Harrison County, Ohio, born Aug. 30, 1827. They have had seven children, five now living—Mary, J. D., Lizzie J., John M. and Addie M. Mr. and Mrs. Oliver and their daughter Mary are members of the Free-Will Baptist church. Mr. Oliver's father, Jesse Oliver, was born in Virginia in 1799, and is now living in Noble County, Ohio. His mother, Rebecca Oliver, was born in Harrison County, Ohio, March 25, 1805, and died March 15, 1882. There was a family of nine children, seven of whom are living—Leven, L. B., Joseph, William, Maria, Martha and Mary. Mrs. Oliver's father was born in Harrison County, Ohio, in 1800, and died in January, 1881. Her mother died when Mrs. Oliver was only three years old, leaving three children—Margaret A., Rebecca B. and Martha J.

Augustus Palmer, Postmaster, was born in Washington County, Ohio, Jan. 26, 1827. He learned the saddler's trade in 1846, in Plymouth and then came to Albany and opened a shop. Five years later he sold out and went into the mercantile business with Charles Lindley, but after two years sold out to Brown & Jaynes. In 1866 he was appointed Postmaster of Lee, and has served in that capacity longer than any other man in Athens County. He was married in 1858 to Samarie, daughter of Jabez and Margaret (Simpson) Hubbell. She was born in Meigs County, Dec. 28, 1831. They have no children. Mr. Palmer's father, J. F. Palmer, was born in Vermont, Aug. 31, 1787, and died in Washington County, Ohio, in 1843. His mother, Lydia (Brown) Palmer, was born Nov. 1, 1789, and died in 1856. They had three children—Harriet, born Dec. 17, 1822, and died in Missouri in 1874; John, born Feb. 12, 1825, and Augustus.

Isaac Ream was born in Fairfield County, Ohio, July 2, 1812. In 1840 he came to Athens County and made four miles of the Hocking Canal. He was then overseer at Judge Pruden's salt works ten years. In 1854 he followed boating on the canal. The next six years he kept a dairy, having sixty cows. In 1870 he went to Vinton County and worked for a stock importer four years. He then bought a farm in Vinton County and remained there till 1882. In April of that year he bought a farm of eighty acres in Alexander Township, Athens County, where he now resides. He was married in 1839, to Elizabeth Williamson, of Fairfield County, Ohio, a native of Virginia, born in 1815. They have two children —Ellen, now Mrs. D. M. Cooper, born April 3, 1853, and Sarah, now Mrs. Charles Martin, born Sept. 3, 1859. Mr. Ream enlisted in 1862, in Company E, Seventy-sixth Ohio Infantry, and served three years. He participated in the battle of the Wilderness, both battles at Bull Run, Gettysburg, and was eight months in front of Charleston, S. C. His regiment was mounted and sent to Florida. He was discharged at Hilton Head, Fla., and returned to Athens

County. He participated in twenty-six hard-fought battles besides skirmishes, and was never wounded.

T. K. Rossetter was born in New Hartford, Conn., Sept. 14, 1822. When sixteen years old he came to Ohio and settled on Shade Creek, Alexander Township, Athens County, where he lived twenty-two years. He then came to Albany, Lee Township, and now has a farm of 170 acres on section 4. He was married in 1847 to Matilda J. Wheeler, a native of Athens County, born in 1827. They have four children—Chandler M., Mary M., Hattie A. and Lou T. Mr. Rossetter is a member of Albany Lodge, No. 156, A. F. & A. M.

Mrs. Amy Shrader, daughter of Samuel and Almira (Tracy) McCune, was born in Athens County, Jan. 26, 1826. Her father is a native of Canaan Township, this county, and was born Aug. 9, 1798. Her mother is a native of New York, born June 7, 1808. They have twelve children, all married—Amy, Henry, Jane, George, Susan, Levi, Charles, William, Eliza, Sarah, Lucy and Samuel R. The subject of this sketch was married in February, 1845, to David Shrader, a native of Washington County, Ohio, born July 21, 1825. Six children were born to them, only four now living—Henry, born June 23, 1850; Jennie, born April 14, 1859; Maggie E., born March 15, 1861; D. M. born Sept. 5, 1863. Maggie E. has been teaching school since fourteen years of age in Athens and Vinton counties. Mrs. Shrader has been a member of the United Brethren church thirty-four years.

James Sickels was born in Waterloo Township, Athens Co., Ohio, May 5, 1835. In 1854 he was employed by the M. & C. R. R. contractors in getting out timber for the road; worked 200 days for one man. In 1855 he went to Illinois and remained fourteen months. He then returned to Ohio, and in Chillicothe met his father who had started for Kansas, and wanted James to accompany him. When they reached St. Louis they found that the Missouri River was frozen over, so turned their course downward and went to Louisiana. From there they went to Natchez and Vicksburg, Miss. When they arrived at Paducah, Ky., on their way home, the Ohio River was frozen over and they had to abandon the boat, the captain returning the money for the remainder of the trip. Mr. Sickels then went to Tennessee, from there to St. Louis, Peoria and Galesburg, Ill., and returned to Ohio in April, 1858. Since 1868 he has been engaged in the lumber business, furnishing large quantities of lumber and timber to the railroad as well as to the general public. He was married Oct. 29, 1858, to Sarah Ann Hawk, a native of New Jersey, born in 1836. They have nine children—Albert L., J. E., William L., George E., Julietta, Anna E., Jane, Mary and James H. Mr. and Mrs. Sickels are members of the Protestant Methodist church.

William A. Smith was born in Beaver County, Penn., Feb. 7, 1844. He worked on the farm with his father and attended school till twenty years of age. He then taught every winter for ten years, and in the spring of 1874 attended the commercial college at Pittsburg. In the fall of 1874 he came to Ohio, and Nov. 1 located in Wilkesville, Vinton County. He was employed as clerk in the mercantile house of John Wilson, afterward changed to J. & H. S. Wilson, four years. In 1879 he opened a store of his own in Wilkesville, and in 1882 moved his stock of goods to Albany, where he is now doing a good business. He was married March 2, 1876, to Susan E. Riggs, a native of Washington County, Ohio, born March 16, 1846. They have two children—Ira Dwight, born Aug. 20, 1878, and Norma A., born Sept. 24, 1881. Mr. Smith was reared in the United Presbyterian church, and Mrs. Smith in the Methodist church, but since coming to Albany have joined the Cumberland Presbyterian church. Mr. Smith's father, Jacob Smith, was born in Allegheny County, Penn., in 1818 and his mother, Sophia (Alexander) Smith, in Lawrence County, Penn., in 1818. They are now living in Beaver County, his father being Postmaster at Rome. They had three children, only two now living—William A. and Calvin A. Mrs. Smith's parents, Hezekiah and Elizabeth (Moreland) Riggs, were natives of Pleasant County, W. Va., and Washington County, Ohio. They have had nine children, only five living—James W., Mary R., Susan E., Ellen and Perlina E.

Mrs. Emma M. Stimson was born in Washington County, Ohio, Feb. 22, 1852, and when four years of age came to Lee Township, where she was reared and educated. She taught twenty-seven terms of school in Athens and Vinton counties. She was married Oct. 24, 1877, to Dr. Stephen H. Stimson, a native of Alexandria, Licking Co., Ohio, born in 1849. He was a son of Dr. B. C. Stimson, of Alexandria. Dr. Stimson was killed Oct. 15, 1879, by falling from a pile of lumber in Athens, where he had gone to rejoice with thousands of others over the election of Oct. 14. Dr. Stimson was a skillful physician, a sympathetic, pleasant counselor at the sick-bed, and his services have been sadly missed. He was young and his prospects were bright for a brilliant future. His friends were legion, and many were the sad hearts that followed him to his last resting place. Mrs. Stimson has two sons—Chauncey M., born Nov. 4, 1878, and Stephen H., born Jan. 15, 1880.

Albert Vorhes, a native of Washington County, Penn., born Nov. 29, 1818, was a son of Peter and Elizabeth (Burnett) Vorhes, natives of New Jersey, his father born in January, 1791, and his mother Sept. 2, 1792. His father died Sept. 13, 1854, and his mother Nov. 8, 1862. They had a family of seven children—John, Sarah, Albert, Maria, William, Peter and Andrew. Andrew died Dec. 4, 1875. Mr. Vorhes lived on a farm till 1853, when he located in Albany, and established the mercantile house now in charge of his sons. He retired from active business in 1876, and the firm since that time has been J. H. Vorhes & Bros. He has a farm of 120 acres where he now resides, enjoying the benefits of an active early life. He was married in 1846 to Jane Morse, a native of Lawrence County, Ohio, born March 16, 1825. She died Feb. 2, 1866, leaving seven children. Mr. Vorhes afterward married Ollie Gorslene, a native of Athens County. He is a member of the Presbyterian and his wife of the Baptist church. He belongs to Albany Lodge, No. 56, A. F. & A. M. The firm of J. H. Vorhes & Bros. do an annual business of $75,000. In 1871 and '72 they handled over 200,000 pounds of wool.

John Vorhes was born in Greene County, Penn., Aug. 7, 1815. When twenty-one years of age he came to Athens County and settled in Alexander Township, and five years later came to Lee Township and lived on a farm on section 11 till 1849. He moved into Albany in November of that year, and opened a dry-goods store. In 1864 he sold out to Isaac Stanley, and since then has been operating largely in real estate. He has been Town Councilman and Treasurer several terms. In August, 1841, he married E. M. McGrath, a native of Watertown, N. Y., born in 1823. They have had eight children, only five now living—A. W., Elizabeth, Albert, B. C., and F. Ellen. Mr. Vorhes has 1,000 acres of fine land, 200 acres being near Albany.

John T. Winn was born in Canada West, Oct. 7, 1812. In 1816 he moved to Meigs County, Ohio, and in September, 1834, came to Athens County, and has since lived in Lee Township. He owns 300 acres in this township and 130 acres in Knox Township, Vinton County. He was married June 2, 1840, to Mary A. Graham, a native of Meigs County, born March 12, 1820. They had four children—A. J., born June 10, 1841, now living in Knox County, Ill.; Mary E., born Nov. 12, 1842, now Mrs. A. M. Aplin; Nancy M., born March 2, 1846, now living in San Bernardino, Cal.; John H., born May 7, 1850. Mrs. Winn died March 20, 1851. Oct. 20, 1852, Mr. Winn married Phœbe B. Ripley, a native of Morgan County, born Aug. 19, 1825. They have three children—Wm. S., Lucy A. and Benjamin F. Mrs. Winn is a member of the Methodist church. Mr. Winn is a member of Lodge No. 156, A. F. & A. M. In 1872 he was admitted to the bar of Athens County. He has served as County Commissioner one term and Justice of the Peace three years. In 1860 he went to the Rocky Mountains, forty miles west of Denver, returning to Athens County after a year's absence.

CHAPTER XXII.

CANAAN TOWNSHIP—THE LAND OF CANAAN AS SEEN TO DAY.

LOCATION AND DESCRIPTION—NORTH AND SOUTH CANAAN—WHEN SETTLED—THE HOCKING RIVER—POPULATION—ROUGH AND BROKEN—LAND ON THE HILL POOR—GRAZING FOR STOCK GOOD—CHURCHES AND SCHOOLS—TOWNSHIP OFFICERS FROM 1819 TO 1883—CANAANVILLE—ITS HISTORY—A FEW CLOSING REMARKS—BIOGRAPHICAL.

A CENTRAL TOWNSHIP.

This township lies east of and adjoining Athens Township. The Hocking River passes through the middle of it, the township from west to east dividing it into two almost equal parts, which are locally designated as North Canaan and South Canaan. It is difficult to separate the first settlement of Canaan Township from that of Athens, of which Canaan was originally a part. It will have been noticed that the pioneer settlements clung pretty closely to the water courses. In the absence of roads or any other means of communication, the navigable streams always decided the movements of emigrants. The Hocking was, from all accounts, a considerably deeper stream and carried much more water eighty-five years ago than now, and was easily navigable for heavily laden barges. It thus became valuable as a means of communication and supplies, and the regions accessible to it were the first to be settled in the county. Accordingly many of the first settlers of Athens Township located within the present limits of Canaan, whose rich bottom lands proved very attractive.

POPULATION AND ORGANIZATION.

The township was organized in 1819. The name Canaan was suggested by Judge Walker, of Ames Township, one of the County Commissioners at this time.

The population of the township in 1820 was 356; in 1830 it was 375; in 1840 it was 800; in 1850 it was 1,142; in 1860 it was 1,272; in 1870 it was 1,543, and in 1880 the census gave 1,499.

Back from the river bottoms the land is rough over almost all of this township. Along the bottoms and over parts of the upland the soil is very fertile, but a great deal of the hilly part of the township is too steep or too poor for cultivation, and is devoted to grazing. Some coal is mined in the township, but the hill beds are thin, and it is mined only for local use. At present there are four banks open in different parts of the township.

AGRICULTURALLY DISPOSED.

The industry of the inhabitants of this township is almost exclusively farming. There is but one store in the township, and but one postoffice. The only manufactory in the township is the flouring mill at Canaanville. It was first built in 1824, by Ephraim Young and Henry Barrows, but has been since rebuilt by C. D. B. Webster in 1872.

In the township there are thirteen school districts and five churches—two Methodist Episcopal, two United Brethren, and one Baptist.

ELECTION AND OFFICERS.

The first election for Township Trustees was held at the house of Edward Pilcher, April 5, 1819. John C. Carico and Stephen Pilcher were Judges, and Joshua Hoskinson and John McGill, Clerks of the Election. The township officers up to the present time are as follows:

1819.—Trustees, Parker Carpenter, Stephen Pilcher and George Bean; Justices of the Peace, Stephen Pilcher and Martin Mansfield.

1820.—Trustees, Martin Mansfield, Stephen Pilcher and George Bean; Justice of the Peace, Wm. Stewart.

1821.—Trustees, Martin Mansfield, Martin Boyles and George Bean.

1822.—Trustees, Parker Carpenter, Martin Boyles and Elijah Pilcher; Justice of the Peace, Martin Mansfield.

1823.—Trustees, Martin Mansfield, A. J. Hoskinson and Samuel Warren; Justice of the Peace, Stephen Pilcher.

1824.—Trustees, Martin Mansfield, A. J. Hoskinson and Phillip M. Starr.

1825.—Trustees, Joshua Hoskinson, Stephen Pilcher and John Boyles; Justice of the Peace, Wm. Thompson.

1826.—Trustees, John C. Carico, George Boyles and Wm. Hallert.

1827.—Trustees, Stephen Pilcher, Parker Carpenter and John Boyles; Justice of the Peace, Stephen Pilcher.

1828.—No election—old Trustees acted; Justice of the Peace, Wm. Thompson.

1829.—Trustees, Stephen Pilcher, Parker Carpenter and Joshua Hoskinson.

1830.—Trustees, Martin Mansfield, Martin Boyles and Elijah Pilcher; Justice of the Peace, Joshua Hoskinson.

1831.—Trustees, Martin Mansfield, Martin Boyles and Stephen Pilcher; Justice of the Peace, Martin Mansfield.

1832.—Trustees, Wm. Burch. George Bean and Stephen Pilcher.

1833.—Trustees, Wm. Burch, George Bean and Stephen Pilcher; Justice of the Peace, John McGill.

1834.—Trustees, Wm. Burch, Martin Mansfield and Robert Bean; Justice of the Peace, George Bean.

1835.—Trustees, Elijah Pilcher, Joshua Hoskinson and Robert Bean; Justice of the Peace, John McGill.

1836.—Trustees, Martin Mansfield, Joshua Hoskinson and Frederic Wood.

1837.—Trustees, Amos Miller, John G. Bean and Parker Carpenter; Justice of the Peace, George Bean.

1838.—Trustees, Martin Mansfield, Jacob Tedrow and Parker Carpenter; Justice of the Peace, Joshua Hoskinson.

1839.—Trustees, Elijah Pilcher, John Boyles and John G. Bean.

1840.—Trustees, Elijah Pilcher, John Boyles and John G. Bean; Justice of the Peace, George Bean.

1841.—Trustees, E. C. Wright, Richard Poston and David Jordan; Justice of the Peace, George N. Reade.

1842.—Trustees, D. M. Pruden, Richard Poston and David Jordan.

1843.—Trustees, D. M. Pruden, Isaac Long and David Jordan; Justice of the Peace, Robert Bean.

1844.—Trustees, D. M. Pruden, G. N. Reade and David Jordan; Justice of the Peace, G. N. Reade.

1845.—Trustees, D. M. Pruden, G. N. Reade and David Jordan.

1846.—Trustees, Clayton Starr, G. N. Reade and Harrison Halbert.

1847.—Trustees, Clayton Starr, G. N. Reade and D. M. Pruden; Justice of the Peace, D. M. Pruden.

1848.—Trustees, Wm. Henry, N. O. Warren and John Druggan; Justice of the Peace, A. Buckley.

1849.—Trustees, David Jordan, N. O. Warren and John Druggan.

1850.—Trustees, Richard Poston, Peter Sams and Peter Stalder; Justices of the Peace, Nathan S. Pilcher and Aaron Hull.

1851.—Trustees, A. Buckley, George Mansfield and Peter Stalder; Justice of the Peace, Richard Poston.

1852.—Trustees, Peter Davis, Nathan S. Pilcher and David Jordan.

1853.—Trustees, Peter Davis, Nathan S. Pilcher and David Jordan; Justices of the Peace, Nathan S. Pilcher and Aaron Hull.

1854.—Trustees, Peter Davis, Peter Stalder and Peter Finsterwald; Justices of the Peace, Elijah Tucker and Thomas Grosvenor.

1855.—Trustees, Peter Davis, Peter Stalder and Peter Finch.

1856.—Trustees, David Jordan, Peter Stalder and Peter Finch; Justices of the Peace, Joseph Border, Charles C. Pruden and Peter Davis.

1857.—Trustees, David Jordan, Peter Stalder and Peter Finsterwald.

1858.—Trustees, Nicholas Stalder, James Sams and Peter Davis.

1859.—Trustees, Nicholas Stalder, Joseph Border and Thomas Grosvenor; Justices of the Peace, David Love and J. W. Baird.

1860.—Trustees, Nicholas Stalder, Henry Finsterwald and E. D. Sheridan.

1861.—Trustees, Nicholas Stalder, Henry Finsterwald and E. D. Sheridan; Justices of the Peace, David Love and J. W. Baird.

1862.—Trustees, L. D. Bean, Henry Finsterwald and S. L. Mohler.

1863.—Trustees, Curtis Bean, Henry Finsterwald and William Burch; Justices of the Peace, David Love and J. W. Baird.

1864.—Trustees, S. McLeade, Henry Finsterwald and William Burch.

1865.—Trustees, C. B. Cunningham, J. W. Baird and Joshua Wyatt; Justices of the Peace, David Love and J. W. Baird.

1866.—Trustees, Curtis Bean, N. Warren and J. W. Baird.

1867.—Trustees, Curtis Bean, N. Warren and Peter Finsterwald.

1868.—Trustees, Curtis Bean, F. C. Wyatt and Peter Finsterwald; Justice of the Peace, T. W. Stewart and Arnold Hill.

1869.—Trustees, Curtis Bean, F. C. Wyatt and Peter Finsterwald; Clerk, J. W. Hoskinson; Treasurer, L. D. Bean.

1870.—Trustees, Curtis Bean, F. C. Wyatt and Peter Finsterwald; Clerk, J. W. Hoskinson; Treasurer, L. D. Bean.

1871.—Trustees, Curtis Bean, F. C. Wyatt and Peter Finsterwald; Clerk, J. W. Hoskinson; Treasurer, L. D. Bean; Justices of the Peace, T. W. Stewart and Arnold Hill.

1872.—Trustees, N. Stalder, J. O. Hill and William Stewart; Clerk, W. D. Mansfield; Treasurer, C. D. B. Webster.

1873.—Trustees, J. O. Hill, William Stewart and Elias Poston; Clerk, W. D. Mansfield; Treasurer, C. D. B. Webster.

1874.—Trustees, J. O. Hill, Elias Poston and D. D. Dowler; Clerk, E. B. Hoskinson; Treasurer, C. D. B. Webster; Justices of the Peace, T. W. Stewart and A. Tucker.

1875.—Trustees, Elias Poston, D. D. Dowler and Z. W. Hoskinson; Clerk, E. B. Hoskinson; Treasurer, C. D. B. Webster.

1876.—Trustees, Z. W. Hoskinson, T. W. Stewart and Robert Dunlap; Clerk, E. B. Hoskinson; Treasurer, C. D. B. Webster.

1877.—Trustees, Z. W. Hoskinson, Robert Dunlap and J. M. Lamborn; Clerk, E. B. Hoskinson; Treasurer, C. D. B. Webster; Justices of the Peace, D. D. Dowler and J. M. Maxwell.

1878.—Trustees, J. M. Lamborn, William Marshall and J. McClanahan; Clerk, E. B. Hoskinson; Treasurer, C. D. B. Webster.

1879.—Trustees, J. M. Lamborn, J. McClanahan and William Marshall; Clerk, J. W. Baird; Treasurer, C. D. B. Webster.

1880.—Trustees, Henry Finsterwald, J. McClanahan and William Marshall; Clerk, D. Flesher; Treasurer, C. D. B. Webster.

1881.—Trustees, J. B. Phillips, Peter Finsterwald and Frank Finsterwald; Clerk, D. Flesher; Treasurer, F. M. Webster; Justice of the Peace, J. O. Hill.

1882.—Trustees, Peter Finsterwald, J. B. Phillips and C. I. Ham; Clerk, D. Flesher; Treasurer, F. M. Webster.

1883.—Trustees, C. I. Ham, J. O. Maxwell and Robert Patterson; Clerk, D. Flesher; Treasurer, F. M. Webster.

CANAANVILLE.

The only village in Canaan Township, Canaanville, is situated on the Marietta & Cincinnati Railroad, about the center of the township. It never was laid out in lots, and has only a population of about fifty-five inhabitants. It has one store, kept by J. W. Baird, who also keeps the postoffice; one flouring mill, owned by the

Webster Brothers, and one blacksmith shop, kept by Draper Flesher. Considerable lumber and timber is shipped from the station at this point. A village was laid out in this township about a quarter of a mile east of Canaanville in 1855, on the land of Nathan Pilcher, but it never was settled upon to any extent. The name of this imaginary village is *Detroit*. The postoffice was established and originally kept near its present location, on the old Athens and Marietta mail route. The first Postmaster was Stephen Pilcher, who held the office from 1834 until 1839. He was followed by N. O. Warren, who was Postmaster from 1839 until 1866, when J. W. Baird, the present Postmaster, was appointed. The village has also a hotel kept by N. B. Owens.

A FEW REMARKS.

The township has not improved much the past decade, and its population proved to have been a trifle less in 1880 than in 1870. The southern portion of the township is watered by Willow Run, and through that portion of the township the land is fertile. The northern section of the township is more broken and the valley smaller after leaving the Hocking River. The Valley of McDougal's Creek lies in the northeastern part and is extremely rich, and the hills excellent pasturage grounds. Stock and sheep raising especially is an important element of wealth to the farmers. It is bounded on the north by Ames Township, on the east by Rome, south by Lodi, and west by Athens townships. The Hocking Valley Railroad, following the river bank, also runs through the township from west to east and has one station, Warren depot, about midway or central in the township, which gives the farmers splendid shipping facilities, the most distant point being but a trifle over three miles from the station. The fact that Canaan Township has retrograded the past ten years instead of growing, when the nature of the township is known, the nearness of railroad facilities, schools, churches and the county seat, is something hard to understand, but there seems to be a disposition to congregate in the mining townships. While the present outlook is not flattering, it is not altogether without promise.

BIOGRAPHICAL.

J. W. Baird, merchant, was born in Sullivan County, New York, June 6, 1827, and is the son of C. C. and Sarah (Barlow) Baird, who came to Athens County in 1836 and located in Rome Township where N. O. Warren now resides. Our subject was educated in the common schools and completed it at Miller's Academy. At the age of fifteen he became engaged as a clerk in a store, in which he remained until he was married, Dec. 31, 1847, to Miss Lorinda Warren, a daughter of the venerable N. O. Warren, of Rome Township. Mr. and Mrs. Baird have seven children—Waldo, Lydia, Charles, Lot L., Augustus, Grace and Wade. At the time of his marriage Mr. Baird became engaged in farming, in which he continued until 1860. He then became a partner of C. D. B. Webster in the mercantile business at Canaanville, which partnership existed until 1878. He then purchased Mr. Webster's interest and still continues in the business, where he receives, as he deserves, a liberal share of the public patronage. Although he never craved office, yet the people had such perfect confidence in him that they have given him nearly all the offices of trust in the township. He has held the office of Justice of the Peace for nine years, and at the same time held the office of Township Clerk and Assessor. He has been Postmaster at this point for about twenty years. He took the census of the township in 1880. He owns 160 acres of land and has been generally successful in all his undertakings.

Harrison Bean, farmer, Canaan Township, was born in Hardy County, W. Va., July 31, 1829, and is the son of John G. and Dianna Bean, who came to Athens County about 1830 and settled in Canaan Township, on a farm located at the mouth of Willow Creek, where our subject now resides. He was reared on his father's farm and educated in the common schools. Mr. Bean was married in November, 1855, to Margaret W., daughter of Martin and Abigail Mansfield, residents of Athens County. This union was blessed by the birth of ten children, nine of whom are living —Martin L., Parker (deceased), Emeline E., Rosa Lee, Fred H., Arlow W., Cyrus B., Annette, Elsie E. and Mary F. Mr. Bean has a fine farm containing 150 acres of improved land, on which are substantial buildings. He has followed his chosen avocation very successfully and been enabled by his industry to surround himself and family with the necessary comforts of life. When a young man he made sixteen trips to Cincinnati, Ohio, in flat-boats, this being their only way of carrying the products of the farm to market. His father, who has reached the advanced age of ninety-four, retains his strength and faculties remarkably. He resides near Springfield, Ill.

Jeremiah Burroughs, farmer, was born in Canada West, May 10, 1813, and is the son of James and Marian Burroughs, who were among the early settlers of Athens County. They were born in New York State, and went from there to Canada, and when General Harrison went in there he was very much wanted by the British, as a soldier, but he remained loyal to the country of his birth, and was enabled to escape with the United States army with his family to the United States, coming across the lake, and located in Huron County, Ohio, where he remained a short time and then came to Belpre, Washington County, where he remained about two years and then came to Athens County and located first in Rome Township; remained a little over two years and then came to Canaan Township and settled near where the store of J. W. Baird now stands. Here he passed the remainder of his life. Our subject was married in 1844 to Elizabeth Bean, daughter of Thomas Bean. Mr. Burroughs has a fine farm containing about fifty-eight acres of improved land. He has, by his industry, been enabled to accumulate a property sufficient to keep him comfortably during his remaining days. He is physically a strong man and retains his faculties to a remarkable degree for a man of his years. His first vote was cast for William Henry Harrison, and he always voted with the Whig party as long as it remained in existence, and since the formation of the Republican party he has ever been a staunch adherent to its principles.

Harvey Carpenter, farmer and stock-raiser, Canaan Township, was born in Windham County, Conn., Aug. 11, 1802, and is the son of Parker and Mary Carpenter, who were prominently identified among the early settlers of Athens County, coming here in the year 1817 and locating in Canaan Township. Our subject, at the time of coming here, was fourteen years of age, and has been able to note the rapid development of the country about his adopted home. He remained with his parents until he reached his majority, receiving his education in the common schools. At this time he purchased a farm near that of his father's, and began life for himself. He was married about 1820 to Abbie Arnold, a daughter of Thomas Arnold, who was also a pioneer. By this union were five children, two of whom still survive—Oliver and Mary; John, Adeline and Ann Eliza are deceased. Mr. Carpenter was bereft of his wife Dec. 18, 1880. He has followed assiduously his chosen avocation, that of a farmer, and by his industry has been able to accumulate a property sufficient to surround himself during his remaining days with all the comforts of life.

Oliver Carpenter, the oldest son of Harvey and Abbie (Arnold) Carpenter, was born in Canaan Township, April 20, 1827. He was reared on his father's farm and was educated in the common schools. He was married in 1849 to Laura Bartlett, a daughter of William D. and Julia (Bingham) Bartlett, of Athens. By this union are six children—Addie M., William D. B., John H., Edward D., Percy H. and Elizabeth S. Mr. Carpenter has been engaged in farming a greater portion of his life and has resided with his father quite a portion of the time. In 1862 he was employed by the United States Government as an inspector of horses, being stationed at St. Louis, and in 1863-'4 was engaged as recruiting officer for Canaan Township; and by his efforts they avoided the draft by keeping their quota filled.

Robert Cook, farmer, Canaan Township, was born in Manchester, England, and is the son of William and Mary Cook, who were of Irish descent. His mother died when he was only one year old, and at the age of seven he came to America with his father, who settled in Washington County, Pa., where our subject lived on a farm until he was eighteen years of age. At this time he learned the tailor's trade which he followed for ten years. He was married Sept. 2, 1850, to Mary B., daughter of Jonathan and Mary Minear, natives of Virginia. They have five children—Mary N., Elizabeth V., William E., Emma M. and Robert S. After their marriage they resided in Pennsylvania for about seven years, then coming to Athens County and locating in Troy Township, where they still own property. In 1877 they came to Canaan Township and located on the farm where they now reside. He has a fine farm containing $148\frac{3}{4}$ acres of improved land on which he has erected a very pleasant residence. Mr. Cook has by his industry been able to accumulate a handsome property which he uses in surrounding himself and family with all the necessary comforts of life. Mrs. Cook is a member of the Congregational church.

Henry Finsterwald, farmer and stock-raiser, Canaan Township, Athens County, was born in Fairfield County, Ohio, Jan. 23, 1827, and is the son of John and Catharine Finsterwald, who came to Athens among the early pioneers, coming from Switzerland in the year 1819 to America, crossing the ocean in a sailing vessel, and landing in New York before steamships and railroads were known. They came from New York to Pittsburg, Penn., in teams, where they purchased a flat-boat and came down the Ohio River to Marietta, where the women and children remained until the men could go out and build a house for them in the woods, as it was at that time. They came to Canaan Township and built a large log house near the place now owned and occupied by Elijah Woods. They then returned to Marietta for their families and moved them into the new house, arriving in November, the whole colony of about seventy persons occupying this one house the first winter. The following spring they each bought and settled on their future homes, our subject's parents settling in Ames Township, where they lived for a few years. They then went to Fairfield County, where his father died when our subject was six years of age. At this time his mother and family returned to Ames Township. Mr. Finsterwald remained with his mother until he was sixteen years of age, and then came to Canaan and became engaged in coal-mining, which he followed for about twenty-eight years. He was married April 20, 1855, to Miss Lucy Hill, daughter of Jonathan and Nancy (Arnold) Hill, who was among the early settlers of Athens County. By this union there are seven children—Franklin, Alice, Mary, Henry, Samuel, Carrie D. and Pharis. In 1872 Mr. Finsterwald purchased his present home, a farm containing 226 acres of well-improved land, well adapted to raising stock and grain. Mr. Finsterwald has followed his present vocation assiduously, and by his industry has been able to accumulate a handsome property which he uses in surrounding himself and family with the necessary comforts of life and carries with him the respect of his fellow citizens.

Peter Finsterwald, farmer, was born in Canaan Township, Jan. 15, 1823, the son of John and Catharine (Stalder) Finsterwald, who came from Switzerland to America in 1819. He was reared on a farm until eighteen years of age. He then went to Harmony and went to work in a salt manufacturing establishment, in which business he remained for about twenty-five years, and for the past eight years has been engaged in farming. He was married in 1844 to Barbara A. Davis, a resident of Athens County. They had one child —Jessie. Mrs. Finsterwald only lived one year after their marriage. In 1846 he chose for himself a second wife in Miss Isabel Liggett, and this union was blest by the birth of four children, one of whom still survives—Amanda. His wife died Feb. 5, 1866. He was again married Feb. 9, 1867, to Amanda Liggett, a sister of the preceding wife, and they were the parents of three children, two still living—Lorinda and Frederick. This wife died April 12, 1873, and he was married to his present wife, who was Mrs. Dorcas Sams,

April 11, 1874. He is the owner of 217 acres of improved land, and as a farmer he has proved a success. He has held several different township offices, and is at present one of its Trustees. Mr. and Mrs. Finsterwald are members of the Methodist Episcopal church, an organization in which they take great interest. He is a member of the A. F. & A. M., Paramuthia Lodge, No. 25, located at Athens.

Draper Flesher, blacksmith, Canaan Township, was born Sept. 16, 1850, in Lewis County, W. Va., and is the son of John and Minerva (Camden) Flesher. He received his early education in the subscription schools, and at the age of fifteen he entered the employ of a blacksmith as an apprentice, in which he served for four years, coming to Athens in October, 1869, with his employer and settling in Canaan Township. In the fall of 1871 he commenced business for himself in the shop where he now successfully prosecutes his trade. He was married Jan. 18, 1871, to Miss Catharina Reining, daughter of George and Christina Reining, residents of Athens County. By this union there are four children— Mary L., Henry M., Lawrence G. and Lena E. Mr. Flesher is a member of the Athenian Lodge, No. 104, K. of P., located at Athens. In 1880 he was elected to the office of Township Clerk, and was re-elected in 1881, and again in 1882, which office he still holds and fills with credit to himself and honor to his constituents, and carries with him the confidence of his fellow townsmen.

Mrs. Mary C. Grosvenor is the daughter of the late John and Emily (Carpenter) Wyatt, and was born in Ames Township, March 19, 1828, and received her early education in the common schools, completing it at the academy in Chester, Meigs County, Ohio. She was married Nov. 1, 1847, to Thomas Grosvenor. By this union there were seven children, only six of whom are living— Henrietta, Ann E., William P. (deceased), Mary A., Hattie, John H. and Sarah E. Mr. Grosvenor died April 14, 1862. At the breaking out of the late civil war he was among the foremost to answer the appeal, enlisting in November, 1861, in the Eighteenth Ohio Volunteer Infantry, and lost his life on the date above mentioned. Mrs. Grosvenor is the owner of a nice farm containing seventy-five acres of well-improved land, on which is a very pleasant residence in which she is surrounded with the comforts of life. She has been a member of the Presbyterian church for several years and takes an interest in the good work, and has taken an active part in the missionary cause, being the President of the society at New England.

Charles J. Ham, farmer and stock-raiser, Canaan Township, was born in Kennebec County, Maine, July 29, 1831, and is the youngest son of Thomas and Mary (Smith) Ham. He received his education in the common schools, completing it at the academy at Monmouth, Maine. On reaching his majority he came to Ohio. locating in Athens County, and immediately became connected with the old M. & C. R. R., as a contractor, following this avocation for a period of sixteen years, and was also a greater part of the time superintendent of bridges, and by strict attention to the duties thereof he gained the confidence and esteem of the managers of the company. In 1870 he went to Springfield, Ill., and engaged in the construction of bridges for the S. E. & S. E. R. R., which position he occupied for a period of four years, after which he returned to his adopted home, in Ohio, and re-entered his former position with the M. & C. R. R., where he remained for about four years, when he severed his connection with the company and purchased the homestead of the late William Henry, where he has since resided. His farm contains 390 acres of improved land, which is well adapted to the purposes for which it is used, raising grain and live-stock, and on which are commodious and substantial buildings. He was married in October, 1858, to Jane Henry, daughter of William and Eunice Henry, and a granddaughter of the late John Henry, who was one of the pioneers of Ames Township. There are two children, a son and daughter—Charles W. and Emma D. By his industry and strict attention he has been able to accumulate a large property, which he uses to the best advantage in surrounding himself and family with all the comforts of life. He is a man of generous disposition, and is ever ready to aid in forwarding any laudable enterprise which will be of interest and benefit to the public, and by his honesty and integrity he carries with him the justly deserved respect and esteem of the entire community.

Arnold Hill, farmer, was born in Zanesville, Ohio, Nov. 9, 1824, the son of Jonathan and Nancy (Arnold) Hill, who were among the early settlers of the county, coming here from Massachusetts in 1817 and locating in Ames Township. He was the builder of one of the first bridges across Federal Creek. He came to Canaan Township about 1826, and located [on what is now known as the N. O. Warren farm, where he remained until a short time before his death, which occurred in Ames Township, Feb. 26, 1862. Our subject was reared on the farm and remained with his parents until he was twenty-two years of age. He was married Aug. 25, 1855, to Mary Pruden, daughter of Samuel Pruden, a pioneer of the county. By this union there were ten children; nine still live— Charles C., Romma, Samuel B., Silas, Hattie, Eva, Nathan, Mida and Ella. He is the owner of 430 acres of land, 300 of which is improved and on which is a valuable deposit of coal, which he has operated quite successfully. He has held several different offices at the hands of the people and has in discharge of these duties given satisfaction to his constituents. He always takes a lively interest in educational matters and has been School Director for twenty-seven years.

Ziba W. Hoskinson, farmer, Canaan Township, section 8, was born in Canaan Township, Athens County, April 18, 1818, and is the second son of Joshua Hoskinson, who came from Maryland to Athens County in 1810, and grandson of Elisha Hoskinson, who was one of the first settlers of Canaan Township. Our subject was reared on his father's farm. He lived with his parents until their death, and still remains on the old homestead on which his parents first settled in 1826, which contains about 200 acres of good land, located at the mouth of Willow Creek. He was married May 19, 1842, to Mary Bean, daughter of John Bean, who was one of the pioneers of Rome Township. By this union there are four children—Elza B., Elmira, Clarissa, Hoyt. Mr. and Mrs. Hoskinson are active and consistent members of the Free-Will Baptist church, he being Clerk of the church. His father was the first Township Clerk, and our subject officiated in the same capacity for a period of ten years. In 'his chosen avocation, that of a farmer, he has been very successful, and uses his accumulated wealth in surrounding himself and family with all the comforts of life.

Geo. B. Hulbert, farmer, was born in Canaan Township, March 3, 1838, and is the son of Harrison and Nancy (Bean) Hulbert, who were among the pioneers of the county, as Mr. Hulbert was born here as early as 1804. Our subject was reared on the farm of his father and remained with him until he was about twenty-five years of age. He was at this time married to Annie Mansfield, daughter of Martin Mansfield, a resident of Lodi Township. They have four children—Elzina, Caroline, Elsie and an infant. When about thirty years of age he purchased the farm on which he now resides, containing 160 acres of improved land, on which he has erected a fine residence. The comforts with which he and his family are surrounded were gained by strict attention to his pursuits, and the good will of his fellow-men has been won by his integrity and man-like bearing.

John Milton Lamborn, farmer and stock-raiser, Canaan Township, Athens County, was born in Washington County, Pa., March 2, 1826, and is the son of Joel and Jane (Chapman) Lamborn who were natives of Pennsylvania. Our subject received his early education in the common and select schools. At the age of eighteen he became engaged as a clerk in the grocery business in Louisville, Ky., in which he remained for about three years. He then returned to his native State and taught school about three years. He then became engaged in the dry-goods business for himself in which he continued for about three years with a fair degree of success. He then sold out and became engaged in farming, in which he continued until 1868, in his native State, having purchased a farm in 1864. During the years of 1862-'3 he dealt largely in stock. In 1868 he came to Ohio where he spent a short time in looking for a place to locate, and in March, 1860, came to Canaan Township and located on the farm where he now resides. He was married in September, 1849, to Matilda Morrill, a native of Pennsylvania, daughter of George and Hester Morrill. By this union there were six children, five of whom are still living—Rosalia Florence (deceased), Virginia C., Olive C., Byron L., Lizzie M. and Milton M. Mr. Lamborn has a fine farm containing 150 acres of improved land well adapted to raising stock and grain, on which is a very pleasant residence and substantial farm buildings. He has held the office of Township Trustee for several years and performed the duties thereof with credit to himself and honor to his constituents. Mr. and Mrs. Lamborn are members of the Christian church. He is politically a conservative Democrat, always striving to use his influence for the right.

Geo. Mansfield, farmer, was born in Canaan Township, Oct. 19, 1813, and is the oldest son of Peter and Susan Mansfield, who were among the earliest settlers of the county, coming here from Pennsylvania in 1797, locating at the mouth of Willow Creek. Here our subject was reared and remained until he was nearly twenty-eight years of age. He was united in marriage, Jan. 19, 1841, to Catherine S., a daughter of William T. Dean, who was a pioneer, coming here from Massachusetts in 1815. By this union were seven children, five of whom still survive—William Dean, Mary A., Susan M. (deceased), Lewis, Nancy J., Catherine E. (deceased), and Harriet A. He was bereft of his wife Jan. 19, 1873. He has a fine farm containing 300 acres of improved land, and in following his chosen avocation he has been quite successful. He is an active member of the United Brethren church, as was also his wife until her death, in which they have always taken great interest. His children have all taken unto themselves companions for life.

L. E. Mansfield, farmer and stock-raiser, Canaan Township, Athens County, is the youngest child of Martin and Margaret Mansfield. Martin Mansfield was a native of Sussex County, N. J., and when a child went to Huntingdon County, Pa., where he lived until he was sixteen years of age, when, in the year 1795, he came to Athens County, Ohio, and in 1797 purchased a farm and built a cabin on the same place where our subject's residence now stands. Margaret Denham was born in Delaware, and came to Athens County in 1795. They were married in Ames Township. They were the parents of twelve children, eleven of whom lived to be men and women. They started in life without means, and with nothing to aid them but strong hands and willing hearts; but after passing through the hardships and privations of a frontier life, they were enabled by careful management to accumulate a large property. They gave to their children all the advantages possible at that early day to gain a good and practical education, which fitted them for good and useful men and women in society. After living an honorable and useful life, and winning the confidence and esteem of all who knew him, he died Aug. 7, 1860, at the advanced age of eighty-one, having been an active and consistent member of the Methodist Episcopal church for fifty-three years. His wife survived him three years, her death occurring Aug. 28, 1863, she having been a member of the same church for fifty-six years. Our subject was born on the 9th of April, 1833. His youth was spent in assisting on the farm and attending school, receiving his education at the Ohio University at Athens. He has always resided on the homestead on which his father first settled, where he makes a specialty of raising live stock. He has a fine brick residence, where he enjoys all the comforts of life. Mr. Mansfield is an ardent worker for the cause of temperance, never having used either liquor or tobacco.

John Musselman, miller, Canaan Township, was born in Ross County, Ohio, March 12, 1830, and is the son of Michael and Rebecca Musselman, and grandson of Henry Musselman, who settled in Ross County in 1799, and was one of the pioneers, and

Levi Davis

built and operated one of the first flouring mills in that county, which avocation was followed by his son, and also by our subject. Mr. M. was educated in the common schools, attending for one term the Academy at Chillicothe, Ohio. He came to Athens County, March 1, 1865, and located in Canaan Township. He has been engaged ever since he came to the place in the flouring mill, which he still successfully operates, and has won the confidence of the entire community by his strict attention to his pursuits and fair dealing with his fellow men. He was married Dec. 30, 1852, to Angeline Hanson, daughter of James and Elizabeth Hanson. By this union are five children—Edward, Charles, Minnie May, Chauncey W. and Zoa. He was bereft of his wife Jan. 11, 1861. He was again married in October, 1869, to Martha W. Gibson, a native of Ross County. She died July 4, 1874, leaving one daughter—Ina Maud. Mr. M. is a member of the A. F. & A. M., Paramuthia Lodge, No. 25, located at Athens. Politically, he is a Republican.

Nelson B. Owens, Canaan Township, was born in Ames Township, May 3, 1833. He is the oldest son of Gardner and Abigail (Nichols) Owens, who were among the pioneers of Ames Township. Our subject was reared on a farm, and his education was obtained in the common schools. At the age of twenty-two he purchased a farm adjoining the old homestead, and began life for himself. He was married June 14, 1855, to Annie Carpenter, the youngest daughter of Samuel and Annie Carpenter, of Morgan County. By this union are two children—Roena E. and John G. At his mother's death, Mr. Owen returned to his old home and resided with his father for a short time. In 1861 he went to Morgan County and engaged in the mercantile business, which he followed for about eight years. In 1869 he went to Rome Township, where he remained a short time, then returned to his native town and engaged in carrying the United States mail between there and New England postoffice, in Rome Township, in which service he remained for three years. In May, 1873, he became engaged in the hotel business at Amesville, in which he continued for about seven years. In 1880 he engaged himself in stock trading and operating a flouring mill. He came to Canaanville in August, 1882, where he now resides on what is known as the old " Jocky " Warren farm. He is a man of obliging disposition, and has won for himself many warm friends.

Rev. J. N. Pilcher was born in Canaan Township, Feb. 15, 1833, and is the son of George F. and Elizabeth (Saunders) Pilcher, who came to Athens County from Hampshire County, Va., in 1804, and settled in Canaan Township, near the residence now occupied by their son. They were among the early pioneers of the county, and were instrumental in the development of the county, which was at that time one vast wilderness, with but few to aid them and to bear with them the hardships attendant upon the early settlement of the county. Our subject was reared on his father's farm and was educated in the common schools, attending for one term Miller's Seminary, and completing it at the Ohio University, at Athens. In 1858 he connected himself with the Ohio Conference of the Methodist Episcopal Church, and remained in this work for a period of thirteen years, being first located on the Plymouth circuit, in Washington County; afterward at Chester, Meigs County, Mt. Pleasant, in the counties of Hocking and Vinton, Hamden, Vinton County, Piketon, which was at that time the county seat of Pike County, Jackson C. H., Jackson County, Pleasanton charge in Athens County. During the tenth year of this work he was in charge of the Ladies Seminary at Worthington, Ohio, and the following year was passed in California, after which he returned to his native State and was located at Westerville, Franklin County, and the last year at Plain City, Union County. At this time his health became impaired and his voice failing him he was obliged to abandon his chosen work, in which he always took so much interest. In 1871, hoping to regain his health he visited the Pacific Coast, where he remained for seven months. He then returned to Canaan Township and now resides on the old farm where he passed the days of his youth. He was married in July, 1861, to Florence M., daughter of Rev. Ezekiel and Phœbe Sibley, who were at that time residents of Nelsonville, Athens Co. Their seven children are: Herbert Holmes, George Sibley, Francis Nelson, Henry Merrill, Alice Florence, Charles Summerfield and Benjamin Luther. Mr. Pilcher and his wife are very sincere, earnest workers in the cause to which they gave their lives when young, the Christian religion, through which they strive to make the pathway of others bright and their burdens easy to bear, and in so doing gain for themselves in their remaining days true peace and happiness.

Elias Poston, farmer, was born in Hampshire County, W. Va., Sept. 13, 1832, and is the son of John and Elizabeth Poston, who came to Athens County in 1836 and settled in Ames Township, where they resided about two years, and then came to Canaan Township and located on the farm on which they resided until their death. Our subject was reared on the farm and received a common-school education. He lived with his parents the most of the time until he was twenty-six years of age. At this time he purchased the farm on which he now resides. He was married Feb. 1, 1867, to Fostina Young, a daughter of Ephraim and Drusilla Young, residents of Canaan Township. By this union were four children, three of whom are living—Dow L., Charles H., and John. Mrs. Poston died Oct. 29, 1875, thirty-nine years of age. Mr. Poston has a fine farm of 161 acres of well-improved land on which he has built a neat and comfortable home and surrounded it with shade trees and shrubbery. He has followed his chosen avocation very successfully, and has been able, by his industry, to accumulate a property sufficient to give himself and family every comfort, and is respected by all his fellow-townsmen.

Geo. W. Poston, farmer and stock-raiser, was born in Canaan Township, Feb. 27, 1846, son of Ashford and Mary Poston, natives of Virginia, who came to Athens County about 1837 and located on the place on which they resided until shortly before Mr. Poston's death. Our subject was reared on the farm and educated in the common and high schools, and remained with his parents until he reached his majority. He then went to Virginia and engaged in the lumber business, in which he continued for eight years, and taught school the two following years. In 1875 he purchased the old homestead where he has since resided. Mr. Poston is principally engaged in buying and selling stock, in which he is quite successful. He also takes an active interest in educational matters. He was married June 9, 1878, to Luella Blaine, daughter of Zarah Blaine, a resident of Mason County, W. Va. Mrs. Poston is a member of the Missionary Baptist church.

Charles C. Pruden, salt manufacturer, Canaan Township, Athens County, was born in Athens, Aug. 17, 1827, and is the son of Samuel B. and Mary (Cranston) Pruden. When a young man he was engaged in assisting his father in his business. He received his education in the common schools, and has in his possession the teacher's quarterly report of the first school which was held in the place, with his name thereon as a student. He was married Sept. 24, 1860, to Miss Lucy A. Howard, daughter of Cyrus and Lucy Howard, residents of Hamilton County, Ohio. They have had two children—Olive M. and Ulysses Grant (deceased). Mr. Pruden has in his possession several articles of interest, among which is his grandfather's clock, an old family Bible, which is over 100 years old, and other articles of antiquity. Mr. and Mrs. Pruden reside in the large brick residence built by his father in 1840, and are surrounded with the comforts of life. He has his father's library, which contains many books of interest, in which he takes a great pride. They have the respect and esteem of the community in which they live.

Nathan Sams, deceased, was born in Belmont County, Ohio, Aug. 6, 1833, and was the son of Peter and Elizabeth (Jenkinson) Sams, who came to Athens County about 1845, and located in Canaan Township, on the place now owned by Hector Angel, where they lived for several years, and then moved to the place adjoining that of their son, where they remained till their death. Our subject was reared on his father's farm, and remained with his parents until he reached his majority. He was married June 19, 1856, to Henrietta Bishop, daughter of Daniel and Susan Bishop, natives of Pennsylvania, who came to this county in 1845. By this union there were five children, only two of whom are living—Elizabeth E., George Wesley (deceased), Charles Andrew (deceased), Daniel Albert and William Hastings (deceased). Mr. Sams died Feb. 7, 1877, bearing the respect of all. Mrs. Sams now resides on the old homestead, together with her only remaining son. The farm contains 100 acres of well-improved land. Mrs. Sams has been for several years a member of the Methodist Episcopal church, as was also her husband till his death.

Wm. Smith, farmer and stock-raiser, Canaan Township, Athens County, was born in Columbiana County, Ohio, Sept. 25, 1834, and is the son of Michael and Rebecca Smith, who came to this county in 1852, and located in Canaan Township, on the farm where they resided until their death. Our subject was reared on the farm and received his early education in the common schools. He was married April 16, 1857, to Ruth Smith, daughter of Nicholas Smith, a resident of Athens County. By this union there were six children, only five of whom are still living—Elenora, James, May, Ezra and Aida. After his marriage he went to Missouri and lived eleven years; then returned to the old homestead where he now resides. He has a fine farm of 280 acres of well-improved land, on which is a very pleasant residence and substantial farm buildings. He has followed his chosen avocation, that of a farmer, very successfully, and by his industry has been enabled to accumulate such a property as to be able to surround himself and family with the comforts of life.

Nicholas Stalder, farmer and stock-raiser, was born in Switzerland, Feb. 9, 1812, and is the son of Jacob and Annie Stalder, who came to America in 1819, and settled in Canaan Township, Athens County, near the farm now owned and occupied by Elijah Woods. They were among the early settlers of the county. He was reared on his father's farm and was educated in the common schools, as educational advantages were at that time limited. Our subject was married in 1840, to Barbara Ninegar, who also came to America at a little later period than Mr. Stalder. By this union were twelve children, six of whom still live—Henry, Samuel, Philena, Helen, Ida and Augusta. Mr. Stalder was bereft of his wife and companion in 1880. They were both active and consistent members of the United Brethren church. He has a fine farm containing 205 acres of well-improved land, on which he has built a neat and comfortable residence. Mr. S. has by his industry and economy been able to accumulate such a property as to enable him to surround himself and family with the neccessary comforts of life, and bears the respect of his fellow citizens.

William W. Starkey, farmer, was born in West Virginia, Jan. 24, 1837, and came to Ohio in 1855. He lived in Rome Township, Athens County, till 1881, when he bought 137½ acres of fine land in Canaan Township. He was married April 1, 1858, to Charity Durand, a native of New York, born in 1865. They have three children—John, Charles and Mary. Mr. Starkey's father, Joseph Starkey, was born in Virginia and came to Ohio in 1855, and is still living in Canaan Township. His mother, Cassy (Masters) Starkey, died in Virginia in 1853, leaving three children—Edward, Chloe and William. His father afterward married Susan Baker, of Ohio. She died leaving one child—George. Mr. Starkey then married Martha Cocondouer, of Virginia. They have no children.

Aaron Tucker, farmer, was born in Hardy County, W. Va., Nov. 11, 1826, and came with his mother, Martha Tucker, to Athens County in 1829 and located in Canaan Township, on the farm immediately east of the railroad station at Canaanville. At the age of nine years he went to live with Edmund Bean, of Rome Township, with whom he remained four years, and the three following years he lived with John Salter, of Rome Township. At the age of sixteen he went to Nelsonville, York Township, and made his home with C. S. Kimmey until he was nineteen years old. He was married Dec. 31, 1845, to Sarah L. Camby, daughter of Thomas and Annie (Mansfield) Camby. They have one child, a daughter—Edith. Mrs. Tucker's grandfather was Fife Major in the Revolutionary war, his son Simon H. served in the same capacity in the war of 1812, and his son William held the same position in the late civil war. Mr. Tucker was elected by the people to the office of Justice of the Peace in 1874 and again in 1880, and has always discharged the duties thereof to the entire satisfaction of the people. Mr. Tucker's mother resides with him and has reached the advanced age of eighty-two, but still retains her strength and faculties to a remarkable extent. Mr. Tucker and his wife have been consistent Christians and members of the church the greater portion of their lives, and he is at the present time Ministerial Trustee for the township, a position he has held for the past ten years.

C. D. B. Webster, deceased, merchant and mill-owner, Canaan Township, was born May 23, 1825, in Portland, Me. The days of his youth were passed on his father's farm, and his education was such as could be derived from the common schools. He was married Jan. 8, 1853, to Miss Joanna Morrell, at Bridgeton, Me., and by this union are two children, both of whom still survive—Frank C. and Fred M. He came to Athens County in 1853, and located at Athens, and was engaged in the survey and construction of the M. & C. R. R. (now the C., W. & B. R. R.). At the completion of the road he came to Canaan Township and engaged in the mercantile business, in which he continued with remarkable success till within two years of his death. He was prominently identified with the business interests of the place, and in 1865 he purchased the flouring mill situated on the Hocking River, which is still retained by his family. He was a man of excellent judgment and shrewd business tact, which enabled him to accumulate a large property, which he used in surrounding himself and family with the comforts of life. He was ever mindful of the wants of others, and did much by his counsel to assist his fellowmen, and with his ever ready means to relieve the wants of the worthy poor and needy. He was bereft of his first wife March 22, 1863, and was again married Nov. 29, 1864, to Almira Musselman, a resident of Ross County, Ohio, this union being blessed by the birth of three children—Charles W., Henry M. and Dana B. Mrs. W. still resides in the pleasant home so thoughtfully provided by her husband. By his death, which occurred Feb. 5, 1881, his wife was bereft of an honored and affectionate husband, and his children of a kind and indulgent father, and the entire community of a generous and noble citizen. He was a member of Paramuthia Lodge, No. 25, A. F. & A. M. His two eldest sons, Frank C. and Fred M., succeed their father in his business, and it is their desire to carry out the plans laid out by him. They are young men of industry and integrity, and to a degree maintain the confidence of the people which their father had borne. Frank C. is, in connection with his other business, station agent and operator for the C., W. & B. R. R. at Canaanville. He was married, Oct. 21, 1881, to Libbie Smith, daughter of Ezra and Rebecca Smith, of Amestown. They have one daughter, Mertie Morrell. Fred M. gives his whole attention to the management of their business, and is also Township Treasurer, which office he fills with entire satisfaction to the people who placed him there.

Hadley H. Wickham, farmer and stock-raiser, Canaan Township, was born in Rome Township, Athens County, April 9, 1842, and is the oldest son of Warren W. and Harriet (James) Wickham, and grandson of John Wickham, who was a soldier in the war of 1812, and a great-grandson of Joseph Wickham, who was forced to enter the British army during the Revolutionary War, but at the first opportunity left it and joined the American army. Our subject was reared on his father's farm, and received his early education in the common schools. At the breaking out of the late civil war he was among the first to answer the appeal "to arms," enlisting, Aug. 3, 1862, in Company A, Ninety-second Ohio Infantry. He went to Kanawha, thence by steamer to Tennessee, after which he participated in many hard-fought battles, viz.: Chickamauga, Lookout Mountain, Missionary Ridge, and Rocky Face, Ga. In the first-named battle he received a wound which disabled him for several weeks, and was again severely wounded Feb. 25, 1864, at Rocky Face, in the left arm, which disabled him from active duty for about three months. May 24 of the same year he returned to his regiment, and passed through the Atlanta campaign to Atlanta, Ga., thence with General Sherman to Savannah, Ga. He was engaged in the last battle with Johnston, in North Carolina, on the 19th of March, 1865, and was mustered out of the service June 11, 1865. After receiving an honorable discharge he returned to Athens County and attended school for a time, and then engaged in teaching school and farming until 1870. He then became engaged in the mercantile business at Mineral City, which he continued till 1878, when he purchased his present home, a fine farm containing 250 acres of well-improved land. He was married Sept. 16, 1869, to K. E. Broadnell, a native of Cincinnati, Ohio. Mr. Wickham is a member of the A. F. & A. M., Amesville Lodge, No. 278; also of the G. A. R., Columbus Golden Post, No. 89, of Athens. He is a member of the Universalist church, and is always ready to lend his aid to any laudable enterprise which will be of benefit to the public. He carries with him the respect of the entire community, and is numbered among its leading men. Politically Mr. Wickham is a staunch Republican, and takes a great interest in all the political issues of the day.

Frederick C. Wyatt, farmer and stock-raiser, was born in Ames Township, Aug. 14, 1823, and is the son of John and Emily (Carpenter) Wyatt. His father came from Pennsylvania when he was eleven years of age, about 1803, when there were very few inhabitants to aid in the development of the county, and bear the hardships incident to an early settler's life. Our subject was reared on his father's farm, and remained with his parents till he reached his majority. He then came to Canaan Township and located on the farm where he now resides. He received his early education in the common schools. He was married in September, 1848, to Polly Smith, a daughter of Nicholas Smith, a resident of Athens County. By this union there were twelve children, nine of whom are living—John, Nicholas (deceased), Frederick, Joshua (deceased), William H., Charles, Alice, Barnard, Drusilla, Ruth A., Herbert E. and Beatrice B. (deceased). Mr. Wyatt has a fine farm containing 146 acres of improved land. He has erected a very pleasant residence and substantial farm buildings. He has been enabled, through his industry, to accumulate a handsome property, which he uses in surrounding himself and family with the comforts of life. He has held the office of Township Trustee for several years. Near the close of the late civil war he enlisted for the one-hundred-days' service in Company A, One Hundred and Forty-first Ohio Volunteer Infantry, and went into West Virginia. At the close of his term of enlistment, and after receiving an honorable discharge, he returned to his home.

Joshua Wyatt, deceased, was born in Ames Township, Sept. 26, 1825, and was the son of John and Emily (Carpenter) Wyatt. Our subject was reared on his father's farm, and remained with his parents until he was twenty-two years of age. His father then gave him the farm, on which he resided until his death, and he began life for himself. He was married Nov. 2, 1848, to Hannah M. Phillips, daughter of Ezra Phillips. She was born Jan. 16, 1829. By this union there were three children, only one of whom still survives—Emily (deceased), Ezra (deceased), and Lucy A. Mr. Wyatt, at the breaking out of the late Rebellion, enlisted in the One Hundred and Forty-first Ohio Volunteer Infantry for the one-hundred-days' service. He died June 2, 1870, and his wife was bereft of an honored and affectionate husband and his children a kind and indulgent parent. Mrs. Wyatt resides on the homestead. She has a fine farm containing 102 acres of well-improved land, on which she has a very pleasant residence which her husband provided during his life. He was a man of excellent character, and always gladly used his accumulated means in providing the comforts of life for his family, in which he always took a great interest.

CHAPTER XXIII.

TROY TOWNSHIP—SOME HISTORY OF COLONIAL TIMES.

HISTORIC—LORD DUNMORE'S MARCH—HIS CAMP—1774 TO 1798—ADVANCE IN POPULATION—DISMEMBERED—EARLY SETTLERS—TOWNSHIP OFFICERS—COOLVILLE—ITS RISE AND PROGRESS—ITS SURROUNDINGS—CHURCHES, SCHOOLS AND MILLS—BUSINESS INTERESTS—LODGES AND SOCIETIES—HOCKINGPORT—ITS LOCAL HISTORY—TORCH CONDENSED—BIOGRAPHICAL.

SOMEWHAT HISTORIC.

It was in the latter part of the eighteenth century that Troy Township was first settled. It was, like the most of Athens County, the property of the Ohio Company. There is no doubt that it was one of the favorite spots of the Indian, for from its position at the mouth of one river and on the banks of another, the beautiful Ohio, it was undoubtedly a well-frequented region. For a hundred years, at least many scores, before the pale faces made it their home, the light bark canoe floated upon the waters of the Hockhocking, gliding swiftly and silently down its rippling waters to the deeper and more quiet bosom of the majestic Ohio.

It was in the year 1798 that a company of emigrants, numbering forty persons, left their New England homes and westward found their way until they reached Belpre, and the following year, 1799, arrived and settled in Troy Township, or a part of what now constitutes its boundary. Among those who constituted some of the members of the party were Eleazier Washburn, the Noahs, Cyrus and Xerxes Paulk, Horace Parsons and Ephraim Frost. Xerxes Paulk and Horace Parsons were Baptist preachers, and the latter was pastor of the first Baptist church in the township for some thirty years.

LORD DUNMORE'S CAMP.

While the first settlements of a permanent nature were made in 1798 and 1799, the tread of armed men had been heard within its boundaries nearly a quarter of a century before. Lord Dunmore, who made his campaign against the Indians in 1774, traversed this township on his line of march. He had also built a fort at the mouth of the Hocking River in the same year, and when the permanent settlers of 1798–'99 came, many relics were found proving that he had camped at least one night, if not more, within the limits of Troy Township. The camping ground had the appearance of an old field, and numerous articles, such as hatchets, bullets, gun-barrels and an old sword, etc., were plowed up within this space, grown up then with underbrush. Several of these mementoes of early history were preserved for a long time, the sword finding a resting place in the College Museum at Athens.

ORIGINALLY AND AT PRESENT.

Troy, as its boundaries were originally defined by the County Commissioners at their first meeting, comprised the territory which now constitutes the townships of Orange and Olive in Meigs County, and Rome, Carthage and Troy in Athens County. At that time the Hocking River was the dividing line between Athens and Washington counties, but by an act of the Legislature passed Feb. 18, 1807, the portion of township No. 5, range 11 (now Troy), lying east of the river was detached from Washington and added to Athens County. The formation of Carthage Township in 1810, and of Rome in 1811, and the erection of Meigs County in 1819, taking off two townships, reduced Troy to its present limits. The population of the township in 1820 was 541; in 1830 it was 459; in 1840 it was 1,056; in 1850 it was 1,421; in 1860 it was 1,747; in 1870 it was 1,830, and in 1880 the census gave 1,858. The first election of township officers was held in 1805 at the house of Ebenezer Buckingham. Stephen Buckingham was township lister for that year. These men were the founders of the Buckingham family, which became celebrated for wealth and social influence.

Troy has increased but a trifle in many years. She has been shorn of the best of her estate in an agricultural point of view, by the division of her territory. From 1820 to 1860 she continued to hold her own with other townships, but since that time has not been even benefited by the natural increase, having really gained but 112 in population in twenty years. This is not a showing that will suggest pride either in the present or probable future of the township.

Rome Township being stricken off from Troy in 1811 took with it many of the prominent early settlers, as Asahel Cooley, Levi

Stedman, Daniel Stewart, and others. Kingman Dutton, father of Samuel Dutton, settled at the mouth of the Hocking with his family in 1806. At that time there were only two roads in the township: one passed through the center, running from Belpre to Chillicothe, the ferry of which was kept about two and a half miles above the present site of Coolville by Xerxes Paulk; and another from Belpre down the Ohio to the mouth of the Hocking, thence by the ridge (through Carthage Township) to Athens. About 1815 a road was laid out from the mouth of the Hocking up the eastern bank of the river to Federal Creek, where it intersected the Federal Creek road from the Ames settlement. At this early period the great majority of the emigrants to Athens County used to come down the Ohio to the mouth of the Hocking, and then ascend that river in pirogues or canoes. Kingman Dutton kept a number of these craft, and he and his son carried on the business of conveying emigrants and their goods up the Hocking. Abram Brookhart settled in Troy in 1811, and was Township Trustee for several years; Jonas Smith, who came in 1810, was Township Trustee for several terms; Silas Blizzard and Martin Griffin came in 1810. The township records prior to 1837 are lost.

TOWNSHIP OFFICERS.

1837.—Trustees, M. L. Bestow, Jesse Derry and Samuel Dutton; Clerk, Isaac A. Dinsmore, Treasurer, R. B. Blair; Justice of the Peace, John Pratt.

1838.—Trustees, M. L. Bestow, Jesse Derry and Samuel Dutton; Clerk, Isaac A. Dinsmore; Treasurer, R. B. Blair; Justice of the Peace, John Pratt.

1839.—Trustees, Nicholas Baker, Jedediah Fuller and Ferdinand Paulk; Clerk, C. F. Devol; Treasurer, R. B. Blair; Justice of the Peace, Roswell Washburn.

1840.—Trustees, Nicholas Baker, Jedediah Fuller and William Kincade; Clerk, Eps Storey; Treasurer, John Frame; Justice of the Peace, Roswell Washburn.

1841.—Trustees, Nicholas Baker, Samuel Dutton and Heman Cooley; Clerk, Eps Storey; Treasurer, A. C. Wedge; Justice of the Peace, Sylvester A. Gibbs.

1842.—Trustees, Joseph Tucker, Samuel Dutton and William W. Barrows; Clerk, R. H. Lord; Treasurer, John Frame; Justice of the Peace, Roswell Washburn.

1843.—Trustees, Josephus Tucker, Nicholas Baker and John Brookhart; Clerk, R. H. Lord; Treasurer, John Frame; Justice of the Peace, Sylvester A. Gibbs.

1844.—Trustees, Josephus Tucker, Nicholas Baker and John Brookhart; Clerk, R. H. Lord; Treasurer, John Frame; Justice of the Peace, Sylvester A. Gibbs.

1845.—Trustees, Samuel Dutton, Nicholas Baker and M. L. Bestow; Clerk, R. H. Lord; Treasurer, John Frame; Justice of the Peace, Roswell Washburn.

1846.—Trustees, Josephus Tucker, Nicholas Baker and Ferdinand Paulk; Clerk, R. H. Lord; Treasurer, John Frame; Justice of the Peace, Sylvester A. Gibbs.

1847.—Trustees, Josephus Tucker, Nicholas Baker and Samuel Humphrey; Clerk, R. H. Lord; Treasurer, John Frame; Justice of the Peace, William F. Pilcher.

1848.—Trustees, J. M. Maxwell, R. M. Wilson and R. K. Bridges; Clerk, R. H. Lord; Treasurer, John Frame; Justice of the Peace, William F. Pilcher.

1849.—Trustees, Heman Cooley, Samuel Dutton and Thomas Richardson; Clerk, R. H. Lord; Treasurer, John Frame; Justice of the Peace, William F. Pilcher.

1850.—Trustees, R. M. Wilson, Samuel Humphrey and J. M. Maxwell; Clerk, R. H. Lord; Treasurer, John Frame; Justices of the Peace, Sylvester A. Gibbs and William F. Pilcher.

1851.—Trustees, Stephen Warren, Josephus Tucker and J. M. Maxwell; Clerk, R. H. Lord; Treasurer, John Frame; Justices of the Peace, Sylvester A. Gibbs and Wm. F. Pilcher.

1852.—Trustees, M. L. Bestow, Josephus Tucker and Samuel Humphrey; Clerk, R. H. Lord; Treasurer, John Frame; Justices of the Peace, Sylvester A. Gibbs and Wm. F. Pilcher.

1853.—Trustees, M. L. Bestow, Josephus Tucker and Samuel Humphrey; Clerk, R. H. Lord; Treasurer, John Frame; Justice of the Peace, Jonathan Pussey.

1854.—Trustees, Samuel Dutton, Josephus Tucker and C. Creesy; Clerk, R. H. Lord; Treasurer, John Frame; Justice of the Peace, Wm. F. Pilcher.

1855.—Trustees, Thomas Richardson, Josephus Tucker and C. Creesy; Clerk, M. L. Bestow; Treasurer, C. W. Waterman; Justice of the Peace, Sylvester A. Gibbs.

1856.—Trustees, S. A. Gibbs, Josephus Tucker and C. Creesy; Clerk, M. L. Bestow; Treasurer, Jefferson Cole; Justice of the Peace, Sylvester A. Gibbs.

1857.—Trustees, M. L. Bestow, Josephus Tucker and Thomas Richardson; Clerk, John Mitchell; Treasurer, A. J. Frame; Justice of the Peace, Wm. F. Pilcher.

1858.—Trustees, M. L. Bestow, Josephus Tucker and Thomas Richardson; Clerk, John Mitchell; Treasurer, A. J. Frame; Justice of the Peace, Sylvester A. Gibbs.

1859.—Trustees, M. L. Bestow, Josephus Tucker and Thomas Richardson; Clerk, John Mitchell; Treasurer, A. J. Frame; Justice of the Peace, Wm. F. Pilcher.

1860.—Trustees, M. L. Bestow, Samuel Humphrey and James T. Morrison; Clerk, John Mitchell; Treasurer, A. J. Frame; Justice of the Peace, Wm. F. Pilcher.

1861.—Trustees, Thomas Richardson, Samuel Humphrey and James T. Morrison; Clerk, John Mitchell; Treasurer, A. J. Frame; Justice of the Peace, D. P. Scott.

1862.—Trustees, R. K. Bridges, Shephard Humphrey and James T. Morrison; Clerk, John Mitchell; Treasurer, A. J. Frame; Justice of the Peace, Wm. F. Pilcher.

1863.—Trustees, M. L. Bestow, Shephard Humphrey and Thomas Richardson; Clerk, John Mitchell; Treasurer, A. J. Frame; Justice of the Peace, Wm. F. Pilcher.

1864.—Trustees, John Frame, E. H. Williams and Thomas Richardson; Clerk, John Mitchell; Treasurer, A. J. Frame; Justice of the Peace, D. P. Scott.

1865.—Trustees, John Frame, E. H. Williams and F. W. Tipton; Clerk, John Mitchell; Treasurer, A. J. Frame; Justices of the Peace, Wm. F. Pilcher and Wm. G. Boyd.

1866.—Trustees, Thomas Smith, E. H. Williams and Thomas Richardson; Clerk, John Mitchell; Treasurer, A. J. Frame; Justice of the Peace, Wm. F. Pilcher and Wm. G. Boyd.

1867.—Trustees, R. F. Parrish, James B. Dutton and Thomas Richardson; Clerk, John Mitchell; Treasurer, A. J. Frame; Justices of the Peace, Wm. F. Pilcher and Wm. G. Boyd.

1868.—Trustees, R. F. Parrish, James B. Dutton and Thomas Richardson; Clerk, John Mitchell; Treasurer, A. J. Frame; Justices of the Peace, Wm. F. Pilcher and E. W. Johnson.

1869.—Trustees, C. W. Waterman, R. F. Parrish and Warren Patten; Clerk, John Mitchell; Treasurer, A. J. Frame; Justices of the Peace, Wm. F. Pilcher and E. W. Johnson.

1870.—Trustees, R. F. Parrish, R. K. Bridges and C. W. Waterman; Clerk, John Mitchell; Treasurer, A. J. Frame; Justices of the Peace, Wm. F. Pilcher and E. W. Johnson.

1871.—Trustees, R. O. Knowles, C. W. Waterman and R. K. Bridges; Clerk, John Mitchell; Treasurer, A. J. Frame; Justices of the Peace, E. W. Johnson and Wm. F. Pilcher.

1872.—Trustees, R. K. Bridges, Titus Shotwell and Warren Patten; Clerk, John Mitchell; Treasurer, A. J. Frame; Justices of the Peace, E. W. Johnson and Wm. F. Pilcher.

1873.—Trustees, Thomas Jones, C. E. Dinsmore and Andrew McAin; Clerk, John Mitchell; Treasurer, A. J. Frame; Justices of the Peace, Wm. F. Pilcher and E. W. Johnson.

1874.—Trustees, R. K. Bridges, T. Shotwell and C. W. Waterman; Clerk, John Mitchell; Treasurer, A. J. Frame; Justices of the Peace, Wm. F. Pilcher and M. R. Franklin.

1875.—Trustees, G. K. Campbell, C. W. Waterman and Titus Shotwell; Clerk, John Mitchell; Treasurer, J. Cole; Justices of the Peace, Wm. F. Pilcher and M. R. Franklin.

1876.—Trustees, C. W. Waterman, Titus Shotwell and G. K. Campbell; Clerk, John Mitchell; Treasurer, J. Cole; Justices of the Peace, Wm. F. Pilcher and M. R. Franklin.

1877.—Trustees, R. K. Bridges, Ezra Barrows and Seth Russell; Clerk, John Mitchell; Treasurer, J. Cole; Justices of the Peace, A. McVicker and F. W. Tipton.

1878.—Trustees, Seth Russell, A. D. Carleton and M. D. Humphrey; Clerk, John Mitchell; Treasurer, J. Cole; Justices of the Peace, F. W. Tipton and Wm. A. Dinsmore.

1879.—Trustees, Seth Russell, A. D. Carleton and M. D. Humphrey; Clerk, John Mitchell; Treasurer, J. Cole; Justices of the Peace, F. W. Tipton and Wm. A. Dinsmore.

1880.—Trustees, E. H. Parker, F. S. Monahan and D. C. Richardson; Clerk, John Mitchell; Treasurer, J. Cole; Justices of the Peace, W. R. Baker, E. W. Johnson and Wm. A. Dinsmore.

1881.—Trustees, E. H. Parker, F. S. Monahan and D. C. Richardson; Clerk, John Mitchell; Treasurer, J. Cole; Justices of the Peace, W. R. Baker, E. W. Johnson and Wm. A. Dinsmore.

1882.—Trustees, E. H. Parker, D. C. Richardson and John Palmer; Clerk, John Mitchell; Treasurer, J. Cole; Justices of the Peace, E. W. Johnson, Wm. A. Dinsmore and Samuel Fitch.

1883.—Trustees, G. K. Palmer, John Palmer and George Simms; Clerk, John Mitchell; Assessor, George Fox; Treasurer, J. Cole.

COOLVILLE

is in one of the oldest settled portions of Athens County, not quite so rough and broken as is many other portions, but fair to look upon and fertile in production. Coolville was not laid out until 1818, and there are very few towns in the county that were laid out sooner, Athens and Nelsonville being perhaps the only ones. It is very pleasantly situated upon rising ground, on the banks of the Hocking River, in the midst of a splendid fruit country, but has no railroad communication nearer than two miles. So far this has neither been a detriment to its progress, nor has it been the cause of any very rapid growth.

Some four years before the date above given, or in the year 1814, Simeon W. Cooley and his brother Heman settled upon the land upon which the village is located, and in 1818 Simeon W. laid out, or caused to be laid out, the village of Coolville. The village became, in those early days, quite a center of trade, and beside the Cooleys there were John Frame, Jedediah Fuller (who made an addition to the village), John Pratt, Waterman Lewis, Reuben Blair, Harley and Loran Lewis, Eleazer and Roswell Washburn, J. A. Dinsmore, Jabez Hoyt, Alfred Hobbie, M. L. Bestow, Nathan Hatch, Jacob S. Miller, Henry Lord, J. Press and Curtis Sherman. These settlers were nearly all from New England, and the town has much of the appearance and management of some of the old towns of Massachusetts. It still holds its local trade and has steadily progressed in proportion to the increased growth of the township. Its population is now 365.

BUSINESS INTERESTS.

A. P. Frame, general store; J. A. Palmer & Co., general store; J. Cole & Co., general store; Davis & White, furniture; Taylor & Son, drugs; W. C. Higley, drugs; H. C. Cooley, groceries; Mrs. and Allie White, millinery; Roberts & Fuller, millinery; Misses Pewthers, millinery; Albert Wedge, shoe store; Joseph Cary, shoe store; Wm. Lyons, shoe store; Seth Bailey, hotel; L. L. Lomann, blacksmith; John Knowles, wagon-shop and blacksmith; R. R. Wilson, blacksmith; George King, tannery; J. M. Tidd, saddlery and harness.

The postoffice of Coolville was established in 1822. The Postmasters up to the present time have been as follows: Jacob S. Miller, from 1822 to '24; Alfred Hobby, from 1824 to '40;

R. B. Blair, from 1840 to '41; Eps Story, from 1841 to '42; James M. Miller, from 1842 to '43; John Pratt, from 1843 to '57; James K. Davis, from 1857 to '62; Wm. F. Pilcher, from 1862 to '76; Fannie Pilcher, from 1876 to '81; A. S. Tidd, since 1881. It was made a money-order office in the year 1879, the first order being issued to Mrs. Helen A. Davis, for $3.50, and payable to M. H. Mallory & Co., of New York. Up to date over 2,000 orders have been issued. The annual sales of stamps are between $600 and $700.

COOLVILLE SEMINARY.

The people were anxious to establish a higher grade of instruction than that furnished by the common schools of the day, and this wish culminated in the establishment in 1846 of the Coolville Seminary, which flourished for some twenty years, finally closing its existence in 1865. The school was established by the united efforts of A. S. Tidd, Daniel Boyd, Andrew Dudder, Sherman Pelf and A. C. Wedge, under the auspices of the M. E. church. It afforded an excellent opportunity for the young men of the day to fit themselves for college, and was much patronized by those who intended to enter a professional life. The building since 1866 has been leased to the town for school purposes. Two teachers are employed there, and the village has one other school employing one teacher.

MILLS.

The Cooleys were also the pioneers in the milling business in Troy Township, and the brothers Simeon and Heman erected the first flouring mill with a saw-mill attachment in the township. This mill, or mills, was put up in 1817. It stood until 1882, having been owned in succession by quite a number of persons, and was then torn down and upon its site is erected as fine a mill as can be found in Athens County, and to the extent of its capacity the equal of any. The owners are Jas. T. Morrison, Jas. A. Palmer, Jos. Harknell, John Mitchell and Alexander Fish.

The building is a massive one, being 36 x 48 in size and 75 feet high in the main building. It has an addition for an engine-room 20 x 30 feet in dimension. The machinery is all of the latest milling patents and has a capacity of 100 barrels of flour every 24 hours. It has five run of burrs, cost $25,000, and has both water and steam power.

CHURCHES AND SOCIETIES.

The Methodist Episcopal Church is one of the oldest religious organizations in the county, dating from 1820. It was in that day in the Marietta circuit, afterward joined to Athens, and is now one of the five which form the present circuit—Coolville, Bethel, Hockingport, Torch and Little Hocking. The present church building is a fine structure, costing $2,000, erected a few years since. The first church was built in 1830, the second in 1855, and was followed by the one above mentioned. It has met with no reverses of moment the past sixty years, having had regular services and now numbers a membership of fifty. Its present Pastor is the Rev. J. H. McKusky. A flourishing Sunday-school with an enrollment of 130 scholars is connected with the church, under the superintendency of Geo. K. Campbell. The Trustees are Geo. K. Campbell, Jas. A. Palmer, A. C. Wedge, F. W. Wedge and A. S. Tidd.

Congregational Church.—This church was established in 1841, but was, up to the year 1859, tributary to the church at Hockingport, at that time the larger and more influential society. The members erected their first church building at Coolville in 1848, which was destroyed by fire in 1854. The Universalists at that time were building a church, but feeling some doubt of their ability to finish, sold it to the Congregationalists and the latter completed it, making a plain but substantial frame church, neatly finished, with a seating capacity of about 200. The Pastors were first, the Rev. L. C. Ford, then in the order named, Revs. C. D. Curtis, F. Bartlett, W. Bay, J. H. Jenkins, A. Brown, C. Mowery and the present Pastor, Rev. T. C. Walker. The church is in a flourishing condition, out of debt, and a membership of seventy.

The Camp-Meeting Association of the Marietta District, Methodist Episcopal church, holds its annual meetings about one mile from Coolville, on the road running from the village to the depot. The grounds consist of twenty acres, finely situated on a high piece of ground, with improvements in fences and buildings already to the amount of $3,500. It contains an auditorium, boarding-house, preacher's tent, and a number of private cottages. The Association was organized in September, 1880, electing D. B. Stewart, of Athens, Shephard Humphrey, G. K. Campbell and J. A. Palmer, of Coolville, L. R. Curtiss, of Little Hocking, and Calvin Lesure, of Belpre, Trustees. This site for holding the meetings was chosen for its beauty and convenience of location, a good supply of pure water, and the favorable condition of surrounding society. The ground has been leased for sixteen years, and is under the control of the trustees. The officers of the Association are: D. B. Stewart, President; —— Frampton, Vice-President; J. A. Palmer, Secretary; and A. S. Tidd, Treasurer. Annual meetings are held, beginning the third Wednesday in August, lasting three weeks.

Coolville Lodge, No. 337, A. F. & A. M., was established Oct., 16, 1861, with the following charter members: W. W. Hurley, W. M. Bancroft, M. L. Bestow, William Mason, Andrew Fisher, Alpheus Hayden, John A. Lytle, D. P. Scott, J. M. Harris, S. Dewey and H. Z. Adams. At the first election the officers were: Master, W. W. Hurley; Senior Warden, Wm. M. Bancroft; Junior Warden, M. L. Bestow; Secretary, D. P. Scott. The present officers are; Master, G. W. Harmon; Senior Warden, F. S. Monahan; Junior Warden, J. A. Palmer; Secretary, E. L. Carleton. The membership at present is about eighty-four.

Coolville Lodge, I. O. O. F., was organized July 12, 1872. The charter members were: W. J. Griffith, Noble Grand; Edgar Humphrey, Vice Grand; W. W. Bay, Secretary; and E. W. Johnson, George Simms, W. C. Bay and A. O. Frame. The membership now reaches seventy, the present officers being: John Bailey, Noble Grand; Orin Oakley, Vice Grand; J. E. Hartwell, Secretary; G. K. Campbell, Permanent Secretary.

The Troy Grange, located at Coolville, was organized and chartered in May, 1873, the membership at that time numbering sixteen. The original officers were: C. B. Jeffers, Master, and Edward Dudder, Overseer. The membership now is about twenty-five, the officers being: E. H. Parker, Master, and D. H. Frost, Overseer. Both this and the two preceding societies have separate and nicely furnished halls.

HOCKINGPORT.

Hockingport is located at the mouth of the Hocking River, on the Ohio River, and is one of the oldest settlements in the county. Charles Devol, E. H. Williams, Samuel Dutton, Sylvester A. Gibbs, Benjamin Huntington, Benjamin Brookhart, David Davis, George Williams and Alonzo Williams were among the first settlers. It was formerly, before the coming of the Marietta & Cincinnati Railroad, the most important point in the county besides Athens. It was the shipping point for the whole lower half of the Hocking Valley, and was well known to business men. It is now comparatively a quiet place. The population is now about 150.

There are two church organizations, the Methodist Episcopal and the Baptist, both of them very old. There is also a Congregational society, but it holds no services at present.

The present business of the town is represented by S. C. White, general store; J. Huntington, grocery; George Simms, hotel and postoffice; Heman Bumgardner, saw-mill; W. G. Boyd, coopering; William Goen, coopering; John Dickerson, coopering; Miss Clara Dutton, millinery; E. G. Franklin, cigar factory.

A fine iron bridge was built across the Hocking at this point in 1882, which was never crossed by passengers. It was the finest bridge in the county, the abutments being forty-four feet high, and the bridge itself being 173 feet long. It was supposed to be well put up, but in February, 1883, before it was completed, the stone foundations gave way, unexpectedly, and the bridge sank into the river. It cost $10,781. At the present writing it is being raised, and it will be replaced this year (1883).

The Southern Ohio Normal School is located at Hockingport, the building and grounds being owned by the Principal, Professor Charles E. Keyes. The school was formerly known as the *Hockingport Seminary*, but the building having been recently enlarged and improved, and the authorities believing it to be about to enter upon a new career, changed the name to its present one. It has a good library and literary society, and gives instruction in both the common and higher branches, being designed to prepare students for college. Instruction is also given in instrumental and vocal music.

The Hockingport Baptist Church was organized in 1875 by Rev. B. M. Stout, assisted by Revs. G. R. Gear, J. W. Riddle and R. W. Malcolm. Its first officers were: Rev. B. M. Stout, Pastor; J. W. White, Clerk; William Goens and W. B. Spencer, Deacons; J. W. White, William Goens and W. B. Spencer, Trustees; Mrs. Virginia Spencer, Treasurer. The church edifice was built in 1875. It is 30 x 60 feet in size and cost about $1,200. Rev. J. W. Riley succeeded Rev. Mr. Stout as Pastor, and remained two years. At present there is no regular pastor. The membership of the church is seventeen. The present officers are: William Goens, Deacon; J. W. White, Clerk, and Lizzie White, Treasurer. The Union Sunday-school has a membership of forty, under the superintendency of J. W. White.

The Hockingport Congregational Church was organized by Rev. Lucien Ford, of the Home Missionary Society. Mr. Ford held the first services at the house of Douglass Putnam, with an audience of seventy-five or 100 persons. He preached to this society for some time. The organization of the society at Coolville reduced the membership here somewhat. The church, which cost $2,000, is now used by Prof. Keyes for his normal school.

The Methodist Episcopal Society here is very old—one of the oldest in this part of the State. It now belongs to the circuit comprising Hockingport, Coolville, Torch, Bethel and Little Hocking.

TORCH.

The settlement of Torch is located in the eastern part of Troy Township, and has a population of about seventy-five. It has two stores, kept by William Walden and A. H. Knowles, a blacksmith and wagon shop, and a steam flouring mill, owned by a Mr. Bell. The village has sprung into existence since the railroad was built, and consequently does not boast of the antiquity of Coolville and Hockingport. The postoffice has been established about twenty-five years.

BIOGRAPHICAL.

Seth Bailey, born Sept. 9, 1806, on what was then known as Vienna Island, is a son of Seth and Polly (James) Bailey, natives of Massachusetts and Connecticut. In 1790 his parents came to Ohio and located in Washington County, where they both died. His grandfather, Seth Bailey, was a native of England. He was one of the early settlers of Ohio, coming here in 1780. His Grandfather James once owned the islands above Parkersburg, now known as the Bailey and James Islands. Mr. Bailey received such education as those early times afforded, frequently having to take a load of wood five and a half miles to market, return home and walk two miles to school. Until recently Mr. Bailey has lived on a farm. He still owns a fine farm of eighty acres, adjoining the village, and also owns the property known as the Bailey House. In 1833 he married Sarah McLure, of Washington County, Ohio. Mrs. Bailey died in 1835 leaving one daughter—Mary, now Mrs. Martin Athey, of Nebraska. In 1840 Mr. Bailey married Mary Ann, daughter of John and Nancy (Patterson) Scott, who was born in 1814. They have seven children—Nancy and teachers in Kansas; Lydia is the wife of David Sinclair, of Pennsylvania; Seth Austin; Julia, widow of J. B. Douglass, is a teacher in Coolville; Alice and Elizabeth (deceased). Mr. and Mr. Bailey are members of the Methodist church. Politically Mr. Bailey is a Republican.

Marcus L. Bestow, postoffice Coolville, tanner and currier, a son of Job and Luranah (Curtis) Bestow, was born in Massachusetts in 1805. He learned the trade of a tanner at Pittsfield, Mass., and from there came to Meigs County, Ohio, in 1826, where he lived some four years. From there he came to Coolville, where he has resided since with the exception of some four years. April 5, 1829, he married Fanny D., daughter of Peter and Sally (Haskell) Derry, who was born in Oneida County, N. Y., June 7, 1806. This union has been blessed with five children, three living—Luranah M. (Mrs. A. S. Tidd, died in 1850), Fanny M. (wife of J. M. Tidd), Marcus P., Mary E. (Mrs. Hine, deceased), and M. Augusta. Each of the deceased left two children. Mr. Bestow and wife are members of the Congregational church. Mr. Bestow is also a member of the F. & A. M. fraternity. He is one of the oldest Masons in the United States, having become one in 1826, in Chester Lodge, Meigs County, Ohio. Politically he was an old-line Whig, but now votes the Republican ticket. The son, Marcus P., enlisted in the war for the Union and served four years. He was appointed Adjutant on General T. J. Wood's staff, of the regular army, with the rank of Colonel; he is now a successful attorney in the city of New York.

William Bingman, the subject of this sketch, was born March 31, 1831, in Belmont County, Ohio. His boyhood days were spent in farming with his father until he was about nineteen years of age. His education was limited to some extent, there not being schools of any note there at that date. He moved from Belmont County to Morgan, where he was married, Dec. 28, 1845, to Susan Coler, a daughter of George E. and Catherine Coler, both deceased. Mr. Bingman is a son of Stephen Bingman, who was born Feb. 28, 1799. His mother was born Nov. 29, 1802. His father died April 5, 1872, and his mother, June 30, 1863. Mr. and Mrs. Bingman are the parents of thirteen children, only seven now living—Stephen T., Wilsey A., William E., Abraham, Strod P., Mary J. (now Mrs. Russell) Lillie B. (now Mrs. Nist) and Susan E. Mr. Bingman was both a farmer and merchant, owning two stores at the time of his death. He was a man whom everyone looked to both for advice and information. He died Dec. 4, 1882, mourned by all who knew him, and his place as a social citizen and neighbor can never be filled. The Ireland Literary Society, which met in his neighborhood, tendered the bereaved family resolutions of their deepest sympathy, and a copy of the same was printed in the county paper. At his death the county lost a leading business man, and his family a kind and affectionate husband and parent.

William George Boyd, cooper, Hockingport, is a son of John and Mary (Murdick) Boyd, natives of Wilmington, Del., where they died. W. G., the oldest of eight children, was born March 14, 1814. He was educated in Wilmington, Del., and learned the trade of a cooper of his father. He lived in Pennsylvania about fourteen years, and then moved to Longbottom, Ohio, where he lived three years. In 1861 he came to Hockingport. In 1849 he married Mary Ann, daughter of John and Ann (Boyd) Rowan, natives of Delaware. She was born in Delaware, June 27, 1818. They have lost one child by death. Mrs. Boyd is a member of the Congregational church. Mr. Boyd was an Odd Fellow when he came to Hockingport. Politically he is a Republican. He has been Justice of the Peace three years, and Supervisor of the township.

Sherman Brewster, a son of Levi and Lydia Brewster, was born Dec. 19, 1822. He is a descendant of William Brewster, who came over with the Mayflower and landed at Jamestown, Va. His boyhood days were spent in college in Smyrna, where he completed his course of study at the age of thirteen, coming out with high colors. He immediately came to Washington County, where he went to teaching. Being so young, it was difficult for him to govern a school, although his knowledge of discipline and teaching was superior, and his mother, being a teacher in former days, governed the school for him. He afterward made teaching his life-work. Sept. 27, 1851, he was married to Miss Nancy Mc Laughlin, who was born Sept. 27, 1831, a daughter of Davis and Mary N. McLaughlin, who are residents of this county. They had a family of eight children, only five now living—Alice, infant twins and Emma (deceased), Edward, Ella, Henry and Cyrus. Mr. Brewster was a well-respected citizen, and had taught about eighteen terms of school in and about Torch. He died June 3, 1863. He was a man of superior talent and was respected by all with whom he was associated, both in and out of the school-room. We give below some lines written by him on the death of his daughter Emma:

"Died in Troy Township, Athens Co., Ohio, March 5, 1862, of measles, Emma, second daughter of Sherman and Nancy Brewster, aged four years, five months and twenty-six days.

"A lovely child has gone to sleep,
 No sounds disturb her sweet repose,
She can not hear poor Alice weep;
 Nor calm her parents' deeper woes.

"The baby's cry and Edward's call
 No more demand her watchful care;
Between them now there is a wall
 That none can pass who enter there.

"Though far beyond the reach of praise
 We think of all her goodness now;
We think how happy were her days,
 When health and joy were on her brow.

"Our wishes were her only guide,
 No angry words her tongue did speak,
But full of love her life did glide,
 Until a home she went to seek.

"How could a child so young and fair
 Leave all her dearest friends and kind
And pass the vale of dark despair
 Without one wishful look behind?

"Who drew the bow? Who aimed the dart?
 Who raised on high the chastening rod?
Who gave the blow that smote the heart
 And sent our child to dwell with God?

"'Tis vain to say we will not grieve
 Because our child has gone to rest;
We feel the stroke we did receive,
 Though she may be forever blest.

"Oh, Emma! child of human birth,
 Though placed in regions far above,
Wilt thou forget thy home on earth
 And all thy parents' care and love?

"It would be joy to know but this,
 That thou, while here, so good and mild,
When in a land of heavenly bliss
 Wilt never cease to be our child.

"And when we all shall meet again
 Without a sigh, a pain, or care;
Where purest joys forever reign,
 Then, then thou wilt be happy there,

> "Alone with the light of day
> That path the best of men have trod;
> The gate is a straight and narrow way,
> That leadeth to the throne of God.
>
> "Farewell, dear child! we give thee up,
> And prostrate fall before his throne;
> But as we drink the bitter cup,
> We wish O, God! *Thy will be done.*"

H. F. Bumgardner, manufacturer and dealer in all kinds of lumber, Hockingport, is a son of Andrew and Esther (Cooley) Bumgardner, natives of Virginia and Athens County, Ohio, his father of German and his mother of New England descent. H. F. was born April 20, 1837. He was educated in Ohio, and followed farming till 1875 when he engaged in the mercantile business in this village. Being burned out in 1878 he then bought the saw-mill which he at present runs. In 1861 he married Henrietta, daughter of Milton and Mary (McPherson) Humphrey, natives of Athens County, Ohio, and Indiana. She was born June 26, 1839. Mr. and Mrs. Bumgardner are the parents of nine children, seven living—Mary Esther, born Dec. 16, 1862, wife of J. L. Hansen, of Parkersburg, Va.; Lucy H., born Dec. 10, 1864; Rose F., born June 2, 1867; Frank H., Oct. 23, 1872; Eugene, Feb. 4, 1875; Elton, Jan. 31, 1876; Clara Edna, born July 21, 1879. Mr. Bumgardner and wife are members of the Methodist Episcopal church. Mr. Bumgardner is a member of the A. F. & A. M. fraternity. Politically he is a Republican.

Geo. K. Campbell, postoffice Coolville, farmer, son of Edward and Margaret (Kauffman) Campbell, natives of the North of Ireland and Maryland respectively. His father came to the United States about 1820. He died in 1863, at the age of fifty-eight, in Athens County, Ohio. George K. Campbell was born in Belmont County, Ohio, Dec. 12, 1834. He received a common-school education and has followed farming through life; he now owns 160 acres of good land on sections 30, 31 and 32. In 1859 he married Lois, daughter of Heman and Abigail (Cowdrey) Cooley, who was born June 15, 1830. Mr. and Mrs. Campbell are members of the Methodist Episcopal church. Mr. Campbell is a member of the I. O. O. F. He votes the Republican ticket. He enlisted in 1862, in Company B, One Hundred and Sixteenth Regiment, and served three years; was in the battles of Winchester and the Shenandoah Valley of 1863, and the battles about Nashville; also in one of the last battles of the war—Kinston, N. C. He was mustered out at Columbus, Ohio,

July 7, 1865, having been through most of the severe service of the Union army. In August, 1864, he was commissioned Captain and transferred to the One Hundred and Seventy-fourth Ohio, and took command of Company E, in that regiment, in which position he remained until the close of the war. Mr. Campbell has always taken a very active part in school matters and has taught for many years. He is considered one of the ablest and best teachers in the county.

A. D. Carlton was born Oct. 3, 1841, in Athens County, Ohio, a son of John and Annie (Dinsmore) Carlton. His father was one of the first settlers of the county, and was a very prominent man. When he was about ten years old his parents moved to Coolville, where he attended school until seventeen years of age when he returned to the farm. He then went West and remained until 1862, when he enlisted as a private in Company I, One Hundred and Sixteenth Ohio Infantry. He was in the battle of Winchester, where he was taken prisoner and spent fourteen days on Belle Island, Va. He was then paroled and walked home from Annapolis, Md., starting Aug. 6, and arriving Aug. 26 at Coolville. He was afterward in the battles of Cedar Creek, Fort Gregg and several others of less importance. Oct. 10, 1866, he was married to Phœbe Ewers, daughter of Jonathan and Rosana Ewers. They are the parents of six children—Martha L., George E., Anna M., Harry, Ethel and Phœbe J. Mr. Carlton is one of the enterprising farmers of Athens County. He is a member of the Masonic Lodge, No. 337. He owns 110 acres of fine farming land located about one mile northeast of Coolville. He has held the office of Township Trustee two years.

Edwin L. Carlton, M. D., P. O. Coolville, son of John and Ann Matilda (Dinsmore) Carlton, natives of New Hampshire, who came to Ohio at an early day and settled in Athens County, was born Nov. 16, 1838, and was reared on a farm. He was educated in Coolville, and in the Ohio Wesleyan University at Delaware, taking his medical course and graduating at the Starling Medical College, Columbus, Ohio. In 1865 he began the practice of medicine in Vinton County, but soon returned to Coolville, where he has since built up a very successful practice. In March, 1865, he married Martha Ann, daughter of E. H. and Elinda (Frost) Stone. This union has been blessed with seven children— Emma R., born Dec. 30, 1865; Mary E., born Jan. 10, 1867; John S., born Aug. 30, 1868; Clara J., born July 6, 1871; Edwin Carl, born Sept. 5, 1873 (deceased); Grace, born June 1, 1875; Kate Ruth, born May 20, 1879. Mrs. Carlton is a member of the Methodist Episcopal church. Dr. Carlton is a member of the A. F. & A. M. fraternity. He votes the Prohibition ticket, and is one of the most respected citizens of Coolville. In 1861 he enlisted in Company K, Thirty-ninth Ohio, Captain Rood. He was with Colonel Groesbeck some time, and was promoted to the Eighth Corps for spilling a lot of whisky, and was afterward detailed to the hospital, where he served the balance of his time; he was discharged in 1864.

Jefferson Cole, merchant, P. O. Coolville, son of Nathan and Lavina (Bryan) Cole, natives of New York and Virginia respectively. They came to Ohio about 1800, when this State was settled principally by Indians and wild animals, locating in Washington County, where they lived some years. Then came to Athens County, where they died, aged eighty-six and eighty-one respectively. Jefferson was born in Ohio, Oct. 30, 1826; in early life he followed farming. In 1848 he began a mercantile life, and in 1853 went into business for himself; he has been prosperous and has a fine trade in dry goods, groceries, and everything pertaining to a well-stocked store. During the war Mr. Cole was in the Quartermaster's Department, and after the war resumed his present business. In 1855 he married Phœbe W., daughter of Reuben Davis. By this union there are three children, two living—Eva L., born June 12, 1857 (deceased); Elmer, born March 25, 1863; Minnie, born May 17, 1877. Mrs. Cole is a member of the Presbyterian church. Mr. Cole votes the Republican ticket and has held the office of Assessor two years. Has been Corporation Treasurer, and he is now Township Treasurer, which office he has held several years. He is one of the well-to-do and much respected citizens of the county.

Mrs. Fanny E. Cooley was born in Carthage Township, Athens Co., Ohio, Aug. 22, 1828. She was married in 1847 to Leonard Jewett Cooley. He was born Jan. 15, 1821, a son of Heman and Abigail (Cowdry) Cooley. He was educated in Ohio and learned the trade of a carpenter, but soon after bought a farm and followed that vocation till the breaking out of the civil war. In 1862 he enlisted in Company B, One Hundred and Sixteenth Ohio Infantry, and died in the hospital at Annapolis, Nov. 9, 1864. Four children were born to Mr. and Mrs. Cooley—Sarah Jane, born April 6, 1850, was married Feb. 28, 1871, to James

Runnion, and resides in Minnesota; Frances Abigail, born May 4, 1853; Moses Elliott, born May 2, 1855, was married Aug. 19, 1879; Heman, born Sept. 10, 1858, was married Oct. 30, 1882, and resides in Minnesota. Mrs. Cooley is a member of the Methodist Episcopal church.

John De Wolf, farmer, is a son of Clement and Nancy (Kasson) De Wolf, natives of Connecticut. His parents moved to Pennsylvania and lived some years; then moved to Ohio in 1817. He was a teacher and made that his life-long labor. John was born in Pennsylvania, April 4, 1813. He was educated in Ohio; now owns 100 acres of land on section 33, where he lives. In 1839 he married Harriet, daughter of Jonas and Jerusha (Waterman) Smith, natives of New York; they moved to Pennsylvania, and in 1810 moved to Ohio. They followed farming some time and boating for many years on the Ohio. They died in Ohio. Mrs. De Wolf was born Oct. 6, 1809. This union has been blessed with three children, two living—Amanda, born July 11, 1842, wife of Matthew Humphrey, of Troy; John, born Sept. 14, 1852, married and lives with his parents; one child died in infancy. Mr. De Wolf, politically, is a Republican.

William A. Dinsmoor, son of Isaac and Hannah (Little) Dinsmoor, was born Oct. 3, 1814, in New Hampshire. His parents were natives of New Hampshire and came to Ohio in May, 1834, and located in Lodi Township, Athens County, where they both died. Mr. Dinsmoor's paternal ancestors were originally from Scotland, but settled in Ireland, and at an early day came to America. In 1834 he went to Western New York, and in 1836 came to Athens County, where he has since lived engaged in farming. Nov. 4, 1838, he married L. L., daughter of William and Laura (Cleveland) Tubbs, and a native of Athens County, born Oct. 17, 1821. They have had seven children, six now living— John C., born Jan. 14, 1840, is deceased; Mary Ann, born July 24, 1841, is the wife of W. L. Saffreed, of West Virginia; Samuel P., born March 8, 1843, is living in Jersey County, Ill.; Elizabeth C., born July 6, 1846, is the wife of D. W. Gardner; Theresa J., born May 8, 1851, is a school teacher; Franklin P., born Feb. 21, 1853, is living in Stewart; Rosa L., born June 23, 1857, is the wife of Wm. Pruden, of West Virginia. Mr. Dinsmoor is a member of the Christian Union, and his wife of the Methodist Episcopal church. He belongs to the Masonic fraternity. Politically he is a Democrat, and has held several of the township offices.

A. P. Frame, postoffice Coolville, general merchant, a native of Athens County, Ohio, born in 1837, is a son of John and Mary (Nesmith) Frame, natives of Pennsylvania and Maine respectively. They came to Ohio at an early day, where John died in 1873. A. P. received a common-school education, and has followed the mercantile business. In 1863 he married Eletha, daughter of Thomas and Osee (Slack) Smith. They came to Ohio many years ago and died here. By this union there are four children—Richelieu L., born in 1864; Mary A., born in 1867; Osee I., born in 1869, and Ralph, born in 1876. Mr. and Mrs. Frame are members of the Congregational church. Mr. Frame is a member of the A. F. & A. M. fraternity. He votes the Democratic ticket. He has been very successful in business and carries a stock of everything usually found in a country store.

G. W. Fox was born June 19, 1850, in Doddridge County, W. Va., the son of S. H. and Charlotte (Pinnell) Fox. His grandmother is yet living at the age of 101 years; can see to read without spectacles; walked two and a half miles with Mr. Fox last fall without a cane; never took a dose of medicine in her life; only has a few gray hairs in her head; is the mother of eleven children, and her teeth, except one, are as sound as a dollar. Mr. Fox spent the early part of his life on the farm with his father. When fourteen years old he enlisted in Company C, Sixth West Virginia Infantry, and served about ten months. Dec. 23, 1873, he was married to Miss Emma Mickle, daughter of Andrew and Fannie M. Mickle. They are the parents of four children, but one living —Perry D., who was born Dec. 23, 1878. Mr. Fox came to this county in 1872, settling at Torch, but afterward bought the farm known as the Chambers property, where he now lives. He has fifty-five acres of good land. Although his educational advantages were limited, he obtained a good education, and has been one of the most successful teachers of Athens County, having taught twenty-five terms. He is the present Assessor of Troy Township. He is a member of the I. O. O. F., Coolville Lodge, No. 527.

Reuben Gillilan, farmer, Coolville, is a son of Reuben and Lucy (Frost) Gillilan, natives of Vermont and Ohio respectively. He was born in Orange Township, Meigs Co., Ohio, Jan. 23, 1841. He has followed farming most of his life, and now owns 166 acres of land where he lives. In October, 1861, he enlisted in Company I, Thirty-third Regiment, Ohio Volunteer Infantry, Captain William McKain, and served three years. He was in the battles of Perryville, Ky., Stone River, Chickamauga, Lookout Mountain, Ringgold, Ga., Resaca and Atlanta, besides numerous skirmishes. He was wounded, and was discharged. In 1866 he married Sarah J., daughter of Abraham and Phebe (Smith) Webster, natives of Ohio. There have been by this marriage six children—Lewis R., born May 22, 1867; Seldon E., born March 23, 1869; Winfred, born Aug. 16, 1871; Phebe Alverna, born Dec. 11, 1875; Bertha Eveline, born March 1, 1879; Berton Everet, born Oct. 10, 1881. Mrs. Gillilan is a member of the Methodist Episcopal church. Politically Mr. Gillilan is a Democrat.

Jesse Green, farmer, postoffice Coolville, son of Benjamin and Martha (La Rew) Green, natives of Indian Creek, Va., is the sixth of eleven children. He was born in Virginia, and came to Ohio in 1859. His father died in 1862. After coming to Ohio Mr. Green bought a farm of thirty-five acres, where he now lives. In 1853 he married Martha A., daughter of Shelton and Rachel (Heflin) Smith, natives of Virginia. By this union there are six children, four living—Elijah M., born Nov. 7, 1854, lives in Union County, Ohio; Roxa L., born Nov. 17, 1856, wife of William Cooper, living in Virginia; Ella J., born March 24, 1862, wife of Carson Lewis, living in Troy Township; Ida M., born July 18, 1865, wife of Luther Tiffany, of Meigs County, Ohio. Mr. and Mrs. Green are members of the United Brethren church. Politically he is a Republican. In 1862 he enlisted in Company I, One Hundred and Sixteenth Regiment Ohio Volunteers, and served three years. He was in several of the severe battles of the war—Winchester, Piedmont, Lynchburg, Richmond and several others; was at Richmond when General Lee surrendered, and was discharged at Richmond.

J. E. Hartnell, postoffice Coolville, miller, was born March 25, 1851. He is a partner in the new and fine flour-mill built here in 1882. He is a son of Richard and Sarah (Harris) Hartnell, natives of Western England. Sarah died when J. E. was one year old. He was educated in England and learned the trade of a miller, which he has since followed. He came to America in the spring of 1872, locating in Gallipolis, Ohio; remained there six months, then went to Charleston, W. Va., and from there to his present home. In 1871 he married Mary Jane, daughter of William and Hannah Hunt, natives of England, where they still live. Mrs. Hartnell was born Dec. 12, 1845, in England. By this union there are three children—Walter Bailey, born June 13, 1872;

Ida Jane, born Dec. 12, 1873; Minnie Belle, born Oct. 17, 1880. Mrs. Hartnell is a member of the Episcopal church, and Mr. Hartnell of the Methodist Episcopal church. He is a member of the I. O. O. F. lodge.

C. H. Hays, one of the old residents and survivors of Southern Ohio, moving to this State from the East at the time of Martin Van Buren's election, and coming to Athens County in 1861, was born in Connecticut in 1791. When the second struggle for independence seemed to be staring the American people in the face he, like all other brave-hearted Americans, shouldered his gun and marched in the van. He served in the war of 1812 under General Jackson, and now draws a pension on account of disability caused by exposure and servitude in that war. He is now ninety-two years of age, and is very feeble. Perhaps before this work comes before the public, he will have passed from time to eternity, but let it be remembered by all who may chance to look on this page that he is one among the *very* few who are yet living that helped to win our independence and make the nation what she is.

C. B. Hitchcock, Coolville, music teacher, vocal and instrumental, is a son of Quartus and Ardelia (Bond) Hitchcock, natives of Massachusetts, who moved to Ohio in 1846, and located in Belpre, remaining there some twenty-seven years; then moved to Chester, Meigs County, where they still live. C. B. was born in Hawley, March 16, 1825. He was educated in that State, and took a musical academic course under Mason & Webb. He has made music his life-long business, teaching in some eight States, and has been very successful as a teacher. Where many have failed he has always met with success. In 1864 he married in Vermont, Fannie A., daughter of Joseph and Polly (Bowker) Snow, natives of Sandgate, Bennington Co., Vt. Mr. Snow died in Vermont, and Mrs. Snow is now with her daughter in Ohio. Mrs. Hitchcock was born Nov. 4, 1842. To Mr. and Mrs. Hitchcock have been born three children—Annie M., born May 7, 1866; Herbert R., born Sept. 3, 1869, and Louie B., born Jan. 27, 1876. Mr. Hitchcock and family are members of the Congregational church. He votes the Republican ticket.

Milton Humphrey, son of Jacob and Mary (Spacht) Humphrey, was born in Troy Township, Aug. 31, 1809. His grandfather came to the United States from England in 1776, landing in Philadelphia, where he shouted "Glory to God" for being permitted to see a land where he could worship God according to the dictates of his own conscience. He was arrested by the police who thought him crazy, but was soon released. He lived in Pennsylvania a year or two and in 1798 came to Ohio and located on Wolf Creek, but afterward moved to Waterman Hill, Troy Township, where he died in 1829. Jacob was the second son of a family of five children. He was married in 1804, and had a family of thirteen children, eleven growing to maturity. His son John was the first child born in the township. Milton is now the oldest native resident of the township. He at one time owned a section of land, but has given a portion of it to his children, having reserved 240 acres for himself. He was married in 1835 to Mary, daughter of Samuel and Elizabeth (Forgy) McPherson, who was born Sept. 22, 1816. Ten children have been born to them—Joseph, born March 24, 1837, is a resident of Hardin County; Henrietta, born June 26, 1839, is the wife of Heman Bumgardner; Martha, born Jan. 7, 1842, wife of John Gabert; Pratt, born Oct. 30, 1844, resides in Carthage Township; Marshall, born Feb. 25, 1846, resides on the homestead; George, born May 7, 1848, a resident of Troy; Mary Eliza, born Sept. 29, 1850, is the wife of Edward Doderer, of Meigs County; Lucy Ellen, born Dec. 26, 1854, is the wife of William Price, of Meigs County; Selden, born Jan. 13, 1857, lives in Troy Township, and Albert, born Dec. 12, 1858, lives in Hockingport. Politically Mr. Humphrey is a Republican.

R. F. Humphrey, farmer, P. O. Coolville, son of Isaac and Harriet (Sawyer) Humphrey, was born Nov. 5, 1820. He was educated in Ohio. He now owns a farm of 162 acres, on fraction section 19. In January, 1851, he married Elizabeth L., daughter of Job and Lydia (Weatherby) Coggeshall, natives of Rhode Island and New Jersey. She was born in Washington County, Ohio, June 18, 1824. By this union there has been six children—Isaac Edward, born Nov. 2, 1851, left home and went to the Western mining region thirteen years ago, and for the last five years nothing has been heard from him; A. O. Wesley, born April 2, 1854, married, and living in Champaign County, Ohio; Nelson, born May 16, 1856; Harvey J., born Oct. 12, 1860; Lydia, born April 14, 1863; Estella Blanche, born Aug. 27, 1867. Mr. Humphrey belongs to the United Brethren church, Scioto Conference; Mrs. H. belongs to the Methodist Episcopal church. Politically Mr. Humphrey is a Republican.

Cornelius B. Jeffers, farmer, son of Asa P. and Eliza (Jakeway) Jeffers, natives of Pennsylvania, was born in Carthage Township, Aug. 27, 1831. His parents came to Ohio about 1815. His mother died in August, 1869. His grandfather came first to Ohio in 1804, but returned to Pennsylvania and lived some years, then came again to Ohio, where he died at the age of ninety years. Cornelius B. had the privileges of a common-school education. He has settled down to farming, and now occupies ninety acres of fine land on section 31, and has 125 acres in Decatur County, Iowa. In 1857 he married Margaret, daughter of Truman and Elizabeth (Duke) Perfect, natives of Kentucky and Pennsylvania respectively, who came to Ohio in 1805, where they died. By this union there were two children, both deceased. Mrs. Jeffers died June 2, 1860. Dec. 29, 1864, Mr. Jeffers married Margaret, daughter of James and Sarah (Morrow) McCain, natives of Pennsylvania, who came to Ohio in 1847, where they died in 1857 and 1858. Mrs. Jeffers was born Feb. 28, 1830. By this union there is one child—Charles, born June 16, 1866 (deceased). Mr. and Mrs. Jeffers are members of the Presbyterian church. Mr. Jeffers is a member of the grange. Politically he is a Democrat.

Manasseh Jennings, farmer, Coolville, is a son of Jeremiah and Amy (Carns) Jennings, natives of New Jersey, who moved to Jefferson County, Ohio, at an early day. They had a family of nine children, Manasseh being the seventh child. He was born in Jefferson County, Ohio, Dec. 9, 1811. He was educated in Ohio and has followed farming for a livelihood. In 1839 he married Phebe, daughter of John and Betsey Palmer, natives of Pennsylvania and New Jersey respectively. Mrs. Jennings was born Oct. 15, 1815. Eight children have been born to them, seven living—Malinda Almira, born Jan. 9, 1841, wife of Wm. Shafer, of Nebraska; Mary Elizabeth, born Dec. 22, 1843, wife of Stephen W. Hull; John R., born Sept. 16, 1844, and was killed at the battle of Chickamauga; Anna Maria, born Oct. 2, 1846, wife of Austin Secoy; Sarah Alma, born Nov. 4, 1848; Margaret Jane, born Jan. 24, 1850, wife of Timothy A. Price, of Meigs County, Ohio; Rachel Emeline, born March 23, 1852, and Hannah Lucinda, born Oct. 16, 1856. Mr. and Mrs. Jennings are members of the Presbyterian church. Mr. Jennings votes the Republican ticket. He owns forty acres of fine land on section 34.

W. N. Kennedy was born Feb. 1, 1834, in Wheeling, Va., and is a son of Susana Kennedy. His father was born in Scotland, and came to this country about 1815, settling at Pittsburg, where he worked at his trade—that of a silk weaver—many years. Mr. Kennedy spent his early life in a weaving factory. When about twenty years old he went into the grocery business, and two or three years later went to steamboating. In February, 1865, he enlisted in the war of the Rebellion, serving until its close. He was then engaged in a rolling mill for four or five years, and from there came to the farm where he now lives. May 8, 1874, he was married to Mrs. Mary J. Branyan, a widow with one child—Frank E. They have no children. Mr. Kennedy owns fifty acres of farming land, and is at present engaged in general farming and stock-raising.

Charles E. Keyes, Principal of the Southern Ohio Normal School, P. O. Hockingport, is a son of Edwin and Sibyl (Sargent) Keyes, natives of Ohio and Massachusetts, respectively. His parents were married in Ohio, and settled in Hockingport in 1858. From thence, in 1860, moved to Tupper's Plains, where his father built a seminary, of which he was the Principal. In 1862 he enlisted in Company B, One Hundred and Sixteenth Ohio Infantry, and was elected Captain. He enlisted most of the company himself, they being largely students. In 1864 he was wounded at the battle of Lynchburg, Va., and died in the hospital there a month later. His wife died May 16, 1879. Charles E. was born in Laurel Furnace, Ky., Aug. 31, 1855. He was educated at Tupper's Plains Seminary and at Marietta College, Ohio, and since then has been engaged in teaching. For three years he was Superintendent of Belpre graded schools. Since coming to Hockingport he has built a large and commodious school building for the establishment of the Southern Ohio Normal School. Aug. 24, 1882, he married Mary, daughter of Charles and Mary (Curtis) Cook, natives of Parkersburg, Va., and Little Hocking, Washington Co., Ohio. Mrs. Keyes was born in Belpre, Nov. 30, 1855. Mr. and Mrs. Keyes are members of the Congregational church. Mr. Keyes is a member of the I. O. O. F. Politically he is a Republican.

C. L. Knowles, a son of William and Sally (Woodward) Knowles, was born Sept. 26, 1833. His father died in 1870, at the age of eighty-one years, and his mother in 1871, aged seventy-one years. Mr. Knowles was reared on his father's farm, and received a moderate education in the old-fashioned log school-houses. In May, 1861, he enlisted in the Thirty-ninth Ohio Infantry, under Captain Rhodes, for three years, and when his time had expired re-enlisted and served till the close of the war, when he was mustered out at Louisville, Ky., July 9, 1865. He was in the battles of Atlanta, New Madrid, second battle of Corinth, Savannah, Bentonville, S. C., and several others of less importance. April 22, 1868, he was married to Miss

S. M. Cole, daughter of John and Mary Cole. Her father is yet living in Washington County, Ohio. Mr. Knowles takes pride in having fine stock. He owns a good farm of about 300 acres, and stands in the front rank with the farmers of Athens County.

Abner Lewis, farmer and blacksmith, P. O. Frost. His parents were Jonathan and Nancy (Randolph) Lewis. They came to Ohio in 1812, and located in Belmont County, then moved to Morgan and then to Athens County, where they died after living to the ripe old age of eighty-three years. Abner was born in Belmont County, Ohio, May 2, 1821. He was educated in Ohio, and has followed farming and blacksmithing. He now owns forty acres of land on section 11, and also works at his trade. During the war he worked one and a half years as Government blacksmith under General Rosecrans. In 1842 he married Joanna, daughter of Benjamin and Hannah (Deweese) Grimes. By this union there were five children—Hannah, born April 17, 1843, wife of Benjamin Dailey; Nancy M., born Jan. 14, 1845, wife of John Lewis; George G., born July 2, 1847, married Minerva Goodwin; Amanson, born Nov. 13, 1850, married Elizabeth Black, living in Warren County, Ohio; Joanna T., born March 24, 1853, wife of Jacob Kerschenschlager, of Chillicothe, Ohio. Mrs. Lewis died April 30, 1856. Mr. Lewis married in 1856, Mary Ann, daughter of Shepley and Nancy (Nice) Martin. By this union there were five children, only one living—Mary, born Aug. 4, 1861, wife of James Robinson, of Madison County, Ill. Mrs. Lewis died July 22, 1867, and Mr. Lewis married Mary Ann, daughter of Henry and Elizabeth (Hull) Hartley. She was the widow of Benjamin Hart, who died in the army. She had three children—John, born July 25, 1857; Eliza Jane, born April 26, 1860, wife of Charles Thompson; Benjamin Franklin, born Nov. 10, 1862. Mr. and Mrs. Lewis have five children—Elizabeth, born Nov. 30, 1868; Edna, born Jan. 14, 1870; Sarah, born March 26, 1873: Henry, born May 11, 1875; Eda, born Oct. 8, 1877. Mr. and Mrs. Lewis are members of the Baptist church. Politically he is a Republican.

Waterman Lewis, postoffice Coolville, farmer, is a son of Henry and Lovina (Slater) Lewis, natives of Rhode Island and Massachusetts respectively, who moved from Berkshire County, Mass., in 1813, to Belpre, Ohio, and in 1832 moved to Illinois and bought Government land near Quincy, where they died. Waterman was born in Berkshire County, Mass., Feb. 11, 1804, and came to Ohio with his parents. He was educated in Ohio and Parkersburg, Va.

He taught school some years, but the most of his life has been spent in farming. He came to Coolville in 1829 and went to work in a store for Charles Devol. A short time after, he and his employer bought out a distillery which they carried on, in connection with the store, about eleven years. In the meantime they bought cattle, taking them to pasture lands the other side of the mountains, and from there driving them each year to Philadelphia and Baltimore, and sometimes sending a boat-load to New Orleans. After a few years Mr. L. bought his present farm adjoining the village of Coolville, where he has since lived. In March, 1833, he married Matilda, daughter of Caleb and Matilda (Buckingham) Cooley, natives of the East, and among the first settlers of Troy Township. She was born Oct. 15, 1813, and died Jan. 31, 1882. She was the mother of eight children, three living—Lovina, born Aug. 11, 1835, now the widow of Charles Nesmith (she has two children—Henry and Carrie); Carson, born Jan. 6, 1851; Martha, born Dec. 27, 1854. Mr. Lewis is a member of the Congregational church. He votes the Republican ticket, and has held most of the township offices, faithfully discharging his duty. Two of his daughters, after the age of womanhood, were drowned in the Hocking River only a few rods from his door. He is one of the oldest and most respected citizens of the valley.

Samuel Livezey was born July 18, 1802, in Pennsylvania, a son of John and Ann Livezey, who were also natives of that State. His father died Sept. 9, 1834, and his mother, Feb. 24, 1854, aged eighty-six years. When Mr. Livezey was young, he went to Philadelphia and learned the tailor's trade, which he followed for about fifteen years, when he returned home and lived with his parents fifteen years, and then moved, in 1840, to Morgan County, Ohio, where he pursued farming until 1866, when he came to Troy Township, Athens County, where his widow now lives. Sept. 22, 1841, he was married to Rebecca Kind, daughter of James and Rebecca Kind, natives of Pennsylvania. They had a family of nine children, seven now living—John C., Lewis K., Samuel, Ann (now Mrs. McVeigh), Martha (now Mrs. Chambers), Emma and Sarah. Ames and Thomas S. are deceased. Mr. and Mrs. Livezey both have a birthright to the Quaker or Friends church.

Elizabeth McKim, wife of A. J. McKim, deceased. He was a native of Pennsylvania. His father was Andrew and his mother Mary (Edgar) McKim, also natives of Pennsylvania, who moved to Ohio many years ago, where both died. A. J. followed the mercantile business for a livelihood, and was a very successful business man. In 1844 he married Elizabeth, daughter of Peter and Susan (Ridenour) Hoffman, natives of Maryland, but moving to Athens County, Ohio, in 1840. They had seven children. Mrs. McKim was born in Cumberland, Md., Dec. 21, 1819. Eight children were born to Mr. and Mrs. McKim, two living—Charles, born June 26, 1851, and Frank E., born June 22, 1861. Mr. A. J. McKim died in 1877. Mrs. McKim has a fine property. She is a member of the Congregational church, and a much respected lady.

Mrs. Mary L. McKim, born in Athens County, Ohio, April 14, 1819, is the daughter of William and Elizabeth (Boyd) Whiteside, natives of Mercer County, Pa., who came to Ohio in 1812. She was married to Nicholas Edgar McKim April 9, 1835. He was a native of Butler County, Pa., born Dec. 17, 1811, and a son of Andrew and Mary (Edgar) McKim. He came to Ohio in 1823, but afterward returned to Pittsburg and learned the cabinet-maker's trade, finally locating in Hockingport, where he died in 1878. Mr. and Mrs. McKim had seven children, only four now living—Andrew Jackson, born Feb. 19, 1838, is now a Presbyterian clergyman in the city of Mexico; Mary Elizabeth, born Feb. 5, 1840, is the wife of Benj. Hoodman; Olive Frances, born April 3, 1848, is a teacher and living at home; Thomas, born June 22, 1850, is a Methodist clergyman, located at Strawberry Point, Iowa. One son, now deceased, was a physician, and another a lawyer.

John Mitchell, hotel keeper, Coolville, born Feb. 3, 1815, in Allegheny County, Pa., is a son of William and Esther (McNeal) Mitchell, natives of Pennsylvania, who came to Ohio about 1820, locating in Jefferson County, and in 1837 moved to Harrison County, where his father died in 1845. He was educated in the Ohio common schools, and began life as a teacher, which he followed some fifteen years. He then went to farming and afterward was in the mercantile business until the breaking out of the Rebellion, locating in Coolville in 1855. In 1837 he married Hannah, daughter of John M. and Sarah (Turner) Morrison, natives of Pennsylvania, who came to Ohio about 1818, and died in this State. Mrs. Mitchell was born in June, 1819. By this union there have been three children—William N., born in 1840; John N., in 1842; James T., in 1847; all married and in business in Parkersburg. Mrs. Mitchell died July 12, 1881. Mr. Mitchell and wife were members of the United Presbyterian church. Mr. Mitchell is a member of the A. F. & A. M. fraternity, and votes the Republican ticket. He has held the office of Clerk since 1857, has been Assessor a year, and Justice of the Peace a short time, and has been for many years a notary public.

Lafayette Mitchell, farmer, P. O. Coolville, is a son of William and Margaret (Spence) Mitchell, natives of Pennsylvania and Ohio respectively. His father came to Ohio about 1820, where he died in 1865. His wife died in 1840, and he married, in 1844, Clarissa Webster, who now lives in Meigs County. Lafayette was born in Athens County, Nov. 15, 1830. He was educated in Ohio, and has taught school most of his life winters, and summers has worked on farms. June 20, 1852, he married Hannah Maria, daughter of Edward and Hannah Maria (Sweet) Lawrence, natives of New Hampshire, who came to Ohio about 1840, and now live in Athens County. Mrs. Mitchell was born Oct. 11, 1835. By this union there have been six children, five living—Ann Maria, born April 26, 1854, wife of Andrew J. Athey, of Clay County, Neb.; Mary Florence, born July 21, 1859; Arthur Edwards, born Sept. 1, 1862; William Elmer, born July 19, 1868; Walter Lawrence, born Aug. 5, 1872 (deceased); Nettie Evern, born Feb. 15, 1880. Mr. and Mrs. Mitchell are members of the Methodist Episcopal church. Mr. M. is a member of the A. F. & A. M. fraternity. Politically he is a Democrat.

Joseph Morrison, farmer, P. O. Coolville, is a son of John and Sarah (Turner) Morrison, natives of Pennsylvania. They came to Jefferson County, Ohio, and from there to Troy Township, where they died in 1875 and 1876. Joseph was born in Pennsylvania, Oct. 11, 1815. He has followed boating and farming all his life, and now owns 425 acres of land on fraction section 23, mostly well improved. In 1843 he married Fidelia L., daughter of Jacob and Anna (Paulk) Barrows. She was born Aug. 19, 1822. To them were born ten children, nine living—John M., born Sept. 30, 1844, married and living on the homestead; Sarah, deceased; James T., born Sept. 30, 1848, living in Troy Township; Martha Jane, born April 8, 1851, wife of Dean Ewers, of Coolville; Henry B., born Feb. 14, 1853; Samantha M., born July 20, 1855, wife of Alonzo Palmer, of Troy Township; Alexander M., born July 8, 1857; Mary A., born Dec. 8, 1860; Douglas, born July 14, 1862, and Delmer F., born March 28, 1865. Politically Mr. Morrison is a Democrat.

Montgomery Morrison, farmer, Coolville, is a son of John M. and Sarah (Turner) Morrison, natives of Pennsylvania. They came to Jefferson County, Ohio, about 1815. Montgomery was born in Jefferson County, where he was educated. He has followed farming most of his life, always living on one. He now owns 220 acres of land on section 11, all under improvement, and an undivided half of 220 acres in Athens Township, also cultivated. In 1848 he married Samantha, daughter of Seneca and Lucy (Parsons) Brown, natives of New York and Ohio, now living in Lodi Township. Mrs. Morrison was born within a half a mile of where she now lives. By this union there were three children, all deceased. Mr. and Mrs. Morrison are members of the Baptist church. Politically Mr. Morrison is a Democrat.

John M. Parker, farmer, postoffice Hockingport, is a son of Thomas and Ann (Bracy) Parker, natives of Pennsylvania. His parents came to Ohio in 1836. John was the second of their eight children. They lived in Meigs County, where Mrs. Parker died. Mr. P. died in Hockingport, at the house of his son. John M. was born in Beaver County, Penn., Aug. 13, 1824. He came to Ohio when young and was educated here; he followed farming for a time and then learned the trade of a blacksmith, which he followed for several years. In 1861 he enlisted in Company D, Seventy-fifth Ohio Volunteers, and served three years and forty-five days; was discharged at Jacksonville, Fla., in 1865; was on detached service as blacksmith most of the time. On returning home he engaged as a farmer, which occupation he has since followed, now owning forty acres of land. In January, 1851, he married Ethelinda, daughter of Craig and Susan (Paulk) Dutton, natives of Virginia and Massachusetts, respectively. They came to Ohio at an early day, Mr. Paulk locating here in 1798. Mr. Dutton was a farmer and died in 1866. Mrs. Dutton is living in Mr. Parker's family at the advanced age of eighty-nine years. Mrs. Parker was born Dec. 18, 1826. Mr. and Mrs. Parker are the parents of six children, four living—Charles C., born Oct. 22, 1851; Mary Eunice, born Oct. 3, 1857; Edwin K., born Feb. 29, 1860; Myrta, born Feb. 22, 1866. Thomas Scott and Addison Wilmer are deceased. Mrs. Parker is a member of the Methodist Episcopal church. Mr. Parker is a member of the I. O. O. F. He votes the Republican ticket, and has held several of the township offices. He takes considerable interest in the cause of education, having several times been a member of the School Board.

Thomas Richardson, farmer, postoffice Frost, the first child of a family of five children, of Abraham and Vashti (Paulk) Richardson. His mother was the widow of Mr. Frost when she married Mr. Richardson, and was one of the first settlers in Troy Township, coming here about the year 1800, when Troy Township was very wild and unsettled. Thomas was born on the farm where he now lives and has always made it his home, March 21, 1811. His is a record few other men can show of having lived seventy-two years on one farm, and that the one their parents settled and died on. The homestead has 400 acres, about 275 acres under good improvements. Mr. Richardson was married to Miranda, daughter of William and Saloma (Barrows) Frost. Her father is deceased, and her mother is perhaps the oldest person living hereabouts. This union was blessed with ten children, six now living—D. C., born Feb. 28, 1838, living in Troy Township; Lewis, born Aug. 17, 1839; Olive was a twin, born April 12, 1841, wife of Charles Beebe, living in Arkansas; Samaria, born April 22, 1843, wife of Samuel Splee, of Belpre; Martha, born April 20, 1845; Harvey T., born Aug. 16, 1847, living on the homestead. The others are deceased. Mrs. Richardson died Feb. 10, 1854. Mr. Richardson married in 1857, Emily, daughter of Xerxes and Miranda (Barrows). Paulk. By this union there were two children, both deceased. Mr. Richardson votes the Republican ticket.

David Russell is a well-known farmer near Coolville, Ohio, and with the exception of C. H. Hays, whose sketch is found elsewhere, is the only survivor of the war of 1812 in Southern Ohio. In 1811 he enlisted in the war under General Harrison and went to New Orleans, where he began his campaign. He was promoted to the rank of First Lieutenant, served as such till the close of the war, when he was mustered out and came home. He was born April 25, 1795, in Pennsylvania. Although he is now eighty-seven years old, his mind is remarkably clear and his power of delivery is more than ordinary.

William Scarlott was born July 14, 1815, a son of John and Catherine (Woodfield) Scarlott. His father was born in 1781, and died in 1844. Mr. Scarlott's boyhood days were spent on the farm with his father, going to school in the winter until he was about twenty years old, when he turned his attention entirely to farming. In 1851 he moved to the place where he now lives, engaged in farming and stock-raising. He has a good farm of 115 acres. Jan. 24, 1850, he was married to Miss Anne Noble, daughter of James

Noble. They have four children—James N., who is now watch on the Helper at Torch, O.; John W., who is on the farm with his father; Mary E., wife of David Marlow, of Virginia, and William E., who is now helping run a saw-mill. Mr. Scarlott is a strong advocate of the temperance cause and is emphatically a Prohibitionist. He is a member of the Methodist Episcopal church.

G. B. Simms, hotel-keeper, farmer and Postmaster, Hockingport, is a son of Oliver and Mary (Simpson) Simms, natives of Virginia, and Corinth, Penobscot Co., Maine. They moved to Meigs County, Ohio, in 1817, where they lived till 1852, when they moved to Athens County, where Mr. Simms died in 1863. G. B. was born in Meigs County, Ohio, Jan. 21, 1838. He was educated in this State and remained on the farm till twenty-six years of age. In 1861 he enlisted in Company K, Thirty-ninth Ohio, and served four years. He was discharged at Camp Denison, in July, 1865; he was train-master and several times shouldered his musket and did duty as a soldier also. After the war he went to the Western Territories—Kansas, Nebraska, Dakota, Nevada, Colorado and New Mexico—spending some two years, then returned to Hockingport, where he has since resided. In 1875 he married Sarah E., daughter of Joshua and Mary (Morrison) Safreed, natives of Chester County, Pa., and Jefferson County, Ohio, now living in Hockingport. Mrs. Simms was born in Jefferson County, Ohio, June 25, 1837. They have one child—Delmer Frank, born Feb. 26, 1878. Mr. Simms is a member of the I. O. O. F. fraternity and votes the Republican ticket. He has held several of the township offices; was appointed Postmaster in 1874 and still holds the office.

Josephus Tucker was born Oct. 24, 1821, in Athens County, and is a son of David and Susan (Austin) Tucker, who emigrated from Virginia. His father died in December, 1846, and his mother in March, 1879. He spent his early days in hard work on the farm and in attending the public school in winter. When seventeen years old he began working by the month. He has worked hard, and has managed well, and at present owns 125 acres of good farming land, and has it well stocked. March 23, 1848, he married Eliza A. Fulton, daughter of Samuel Fulton. They have had eight children, only five now living—Joanna (now Mrs. Goodrich), Zalinda (now Mrs. Mansfield), Mary (now Mrs. Persons), Hala, George W., Elijah, Samuel D. and Charles H. Mr. Tucker has held the office of Township Trustee for four years. He and his wife are members of the Methodist Episcopal church.

Theodore C. Walker, postoffice Coolville, adopted son of James B. Walker, of Wheaton, Ill., was born in Michigan, July 29, 1839, and was educated at Oberlin, Ohio. He enlisted in 1861, in Battery I, First Regiment, Ohio Light Artillery, and served three years and four months, being in many of the severe battles of the war: second Bull Run, Chancellorsville, Cross Keys, McDowell, Fredericksburg, Lookout Mountain, Resaca, and all the principal battles to Atlanta. He refused promotion and went through the war as he enlisted—a fighting private. He was mustered out at Camp Denison, Dec. 9, 1864. He went from there to Michigan, and engaged in teaching music and elocution in Grand Traverse College. After this he was elected County Clerk and Register of Deeds of Benzie County, Mich., with only one vote against him. Then he moved to Manistee County, and was Deputy Clerk for six years. After this he had charge of one of the newspaper offices, and was engaged in the abstract and real-estate business. From there he moved to Sandusky, Ohio, where he engaged in a manufacturing business. He was store-keeper and Private Secretary of the Ohio Reform School for a time, and then went to Virginia, where he began preaching, being ordained at Marietta. He now has charge of the Congregational church at Coolville. In September, 1868, he married Mary P., daughter of M. C. and Mary D. (Dunlap) Metcalf. By this union there were four children—Arthur H., born July 12, 1870; Samuel Willis, born 1876; Dean A., born February, 1878; Mary E., born Jan. 27, 1881. Mrs. Walker died March 9, 1881. Mr. Walker married, June 23, 1882, Emma L., daughter of John J. and Lovina (Ulm) Catt, who was born in Mason, Warren Co., Ohio, May 10, 1855. She is a member of the Disciple church. Mr. Walker votes an independent ticket.

William Weatherby, postoffice Coolville, farmer, a son of Isaac and Elizabeth (Kennedy) Weatherby, was born in Washington County, Ohio, Nov. 27, 1819, and was educated in Athens County. He has followed farming and boating all his life. He now owns sixty acres on section 19, where he lives. In 1838 he married Elizabeth, daughter of John and Nancy (Armitage) Cole, natives of Pennsylvania. By this union there were four children, three living—Salina, born March 24, 1839; John Wesley, born Aug. 17, 1840; George Armitage, born July 24, 1845 (deceased); and Emily Jane, born Aug. 18, 1849, wife of Augustus Coe, of Nelsonville. Mrs. Weatherby died June 17, 1850. Mr. Weatherby married, Jan. 29, 1852, Lorania, daughter of James and Deborah

(Cole) Weethee. They had a family of fourteen children—George, William, Mary, Clarissa, Charles, Lucinda, Sally, Sylvester, James, Daniel, Lorania, Ann, Caroline and Wallace. Mrs. Weatherby was born Dec. 28, 1831. Five children have been born to Mr. and Mrs. Weatherby, two now living—Walter Fremont, born July 28, 1856; Emma, born Nov. 23, 1858. Those deceased are—Arminta Maria, Elza Elwood and Eva Viola. Politically Mr. Weatherby is a Republican.

F. W. Wedge, farmer, born in Washington County, Ohio, Sept. 26, 1821, is a son of Ira and Elizabeth (Leach) Wedge, natives of Connecticut, who came to Washington County, Ohio, about 1820. His father died in Washington County and his mother in Coolville, March 17; 1882. He was educated in Ohio, and followed farming till he was about twenty-one years of age; then learned the trade of a carpenter, which he followed several years, building saw-mills, etc. He afterward again began farming, and now owns a farm of 100 acres on sections 30 and 31. He was married in November, 1845, to Emily A., daughter of Heman and Abigail (Cowdrey) Cooley. By this union there were five children, three living —Caroline Ellen, born Aug. 21, 1846, wife of A. C. Young, of Amesville, this county; Allie E., born Oct. 29, 1849, wife of J. P. Brawley, of Ames Township; Emma A., born Oct. 1, 1856, is the widow of Charles L. Pewthers. Simeon, Waldo and Ambrose are deceased. Mr. and Mrs. Wedge are members of the Methodist Episcopal church. Mr. Wedge votes the Prohibition ticket. Mrs. Wedge's father and brother built the first flour-mill ever erected at Coolville in 1816, and did the flouring for many miles around. It was torn down about one year ago, and a large new one now occupies the old site.

S. C. White, merchant, P. O. Hockingport, son of Joseph and Sarah (Hall) White, was born in Wood County, W. Va., March 26, 1823. He was educated in Virginia. His early life was spent as a boatman on the Ohio, where he owned several craft. Since coming to Hockingport he has been engaged in the mercantile business, and now has a well-filled store of dry goods, groceries, boots and shoes, hats, caps, hardware, etc. In 1874 he married Mary Isabel, daughter of Joshua and Mary (Morrison) Safreed. She was born Aug. 12, 1841. They have two children—Sarah, born June 10, 1875, and Arthur, born Feb. 3, 1879. Mr. White is a member of the I. O. O. F. fraternity. He votes the Republican ticket.

Mrs. Dorcas Wilson, is the widow of Nathan S. Wilson, who died July 27, 1881. She was born in Harrison County, Ohio, Nov. 3, 1834, and is a daughter of John and Dorcas (Busbee) Ford, natives of Maryland. June 11, 1856, she was married to Alexander, son of John and Hannah (Lyell) Winters, of Pennsylvania. There was one child by this marriage—Aurelius Stanley, born Dec. 24, 1857. Mr. Winters died May 20, 1864, and Mrs. Winters, April 1, 1877, married Charles Green, son of Ebenezer Green. Mr. Green died Aug. 18, 1879, and Mrs. Green married, Feb. 10, 1881, Nathan Spencer Wilson, a native of Washington County, Ohio. He died July 27, 1881. Mrs. Wilson is a member of the Methodist Episcopal church. She owns a farm of fifty-five acres on section 33.

CHAPTER XXIV.

WATERLOO TOWNSHIP—AGRICULTURAL, MINERAL AND STOCK.

WHEN SETTLED—WHEN ORGANIZED—METES AND BOUNDS AND AREA—OLD SETTLERS—AGRICULTURE AND POPULATION—ORGANIZATION AND FIRST ELECTION—WHO ELECTED AND WHO VOTED—ALL OTHER TOWN OFFICERS—MARSHFIELD—CHURCHES—CARBONDALE—MINERAL CITY—BIOGRAPHICAL.

WHEN IT WAS ORGANIZED.

While the territory which composes the township of Waterloo was not organized into a separate township until March, 1826, it was one of early portions settled by the pioneers of those days. Its first settlement dates back just one score of years before it received its memorable name, a name which holds a prominent place in English history, and which a few of her sons, although transplanted to American soil, still remember with a glowing pride. Thus when her people asked for a separate local government, this name was chosen, and her people in the battle of life have shown the heroic courage of those who fought and won upon its memorable but blood-stained field.

METES AND BOUNDS AND AREA.

The township is one of the three which lies upon the western line of the county, and is a congressional township in size, being six miles square, and containing 23,040 acres of land. It is bounded on the north by York Township, east by Athens Township, south by Lee Township and Vinton County, and west by Vinton and Hocking counties, and is the central township on the border. Originally, and for the first quarter of a century of its existence, or nearly so, it was a part of Athens Township, and many of its citizens were prominent in the history of Athens County in early times.

OLD SETTLERS.

The township was first permanently settled in the year 1806, and Moses Hewitt was the first to stake his claim and raise his cabin within its limits. His family was soon joined by others, and these came in the order named: Abram Fee, who settled on what was afterward called the Foster place; Ezekiel Robinett, Sr., and Colonel Wm. Lowry. Mr. Lowry's father first settled near Athens in 1797, when William was eighteen years of age. The nearest mill at that time was a floating one at Vienna, eight miles from the mouth of the Kanawha River. The old settlers did not always go that distance, but pounded their corn, if a hand or a horse mill could not be found. Game was abundant and the trusty rifle furnished the meat.

AGRICULTURAL AND POPULATION.

Waterloo Township cannot be said to be the best agricultural township in the county, yet it has stretches of excellent land where grains and grasses grow most fruitful and luxuriantly. The topography of the township is hilly, and in many places rough and broken. It is, however, a good stock-raising township, for the hills and ravines make excellent pastures. The hills and broken surface are far from being waste ground, for under their surface lie beds of splendid coal, and although not as yet mined to any great extent, is still there awaiting the pleasure of capital and the brawny arms of the miner. It has exhibited its share of the steady growth of the county since its organization. Its first census was taken in 1830, and its population, 216; in 1840, 741; in 1850, 1,016; in 1860, 1,483; in 1870; 1,695; in 1880, 1,957.

The progressive spirit of her people is shown in well-cultivated fields, cozy residences, improved stock, and a general spirit of thrift which is seen on every hand. Waterloo received quite an influx of settlers, among whom were the families of Robert Cotton, Lewis Davis, James Mayhugh, Hugh Boden, Daniel McCoy, Samuel Allison, William Johnson and Joseph Johnson. They proved a valuable addition, and came from the counties of Morgan and Muskingum.

The first mill was erected in 1801, on Margaret Creek, by John Hewitt.

The first grist and saw mill in the township was built by Joseph Brookson, and when worn out, some years after, a sawmill was rebuilt upon the same spot by Nelson Hewitt.

ORGANIZATION AND ELECTIONS.

The organization of the township in March, 1826, required the election for township officers, and for that purpose an election was ordered to take place April 3, 1826, and the voting precinct was at the house of Joseph Hewitt. The Judges of the Election were: Abram Fee, Joseph Bullard and Silas Bingham, and Andrew Glass and Pardon C. Hewitt were appointed Clerks. From Walker's History the following names of the voters were taken:

William Lowry, James Lowry, Joseph Hewitt, P. C. Hewitt, Ezekiel Robinett, Lemuel Robinett, Nathan Robinett, William Young, William Young, Jr., Silas Bingham, Andrew Glass, Joseph C. Martin, Horace Martin, Abram Fee, Joseph Bullard, John Bullard, Samuel Lowry, Jr., Abram Gabriel, Elias Gabriel and Elias Young.

The election results were as follows: William Lowry and Joseph Hewitt were elected Justices of the Peace; Alexander Young, Elias Gabriel and Silas Bingham, Trustees; Andrew Glass, Clerk; Horace Martin, Treasurer; William Young and Ezekiel Robinett, Overseers of the Poor; Joseph Lowry and Samuel Lowry, Fence-Viewers; William Young, Nathan Robinett, and John Bullard, Supervisors; William Lowry and Joseph Hewitt, Constables. At this time William Lowry and Joseph Hewitt were the only two Whigs in the township, yet they were both elected Magistrates, showing that party feeling did not enter greatly into the election.

The following list gives the principal officers of the township for the succeeding years, the elections being held annually:

TOWNSHIP OFFICERS.

1827.—Trustees, William Lowry, Elias Gabriel and Silas Benjamin; Clerk, Andrew Glass; Treasurer, Horace Martin.

1828.—Trustees, William Lowry, Abram Gabriel and Hezekiah Robinett; Clerk, Elias Gabriel; Treasurer, Lemuel Robinett.

1829.—Trustees, William Lowry, Abram Gabriel and Hezekiah Robinett; Clerk, Elias Gabriel; Treasurer, Isaac Pearce.

1830.—Trustees, William Lowry, Abram Gabriel and Hezekiah Robinett; Clerk, William Young; Treasurer, Alexander Young.

1831.—Trustees, William Lowry, Daniel Lowry and Jeremiah Thompson; Clerk, Samuel Lowry; Treasurer, Wilson Phillips.

1832.—Trustees, William Lowry, Daniel Lowry and Jeremiah Thompson; Clerk, William Handberry; Treasurer, Wilson Phillips.

1833.—Trustees, William Lowry, Daniel Lowry and Jeremiah Thompson; Clerk, William Handberry; Treasurer, Joseph Brooks.

1834.—Trustees, William Lowry, Daniel Lowry and Jeremiah Thompson; Clerk, William Handberry; Treasurer, Joseph Brooks.

1835.—Trustees, William Lowry, William Handberry and Samuel Lowry; Clerk, Elijah Lowry; Treasurer, Joseph Brooks.

1836.—Trustees, John Mintun, William Handberry and George Hewitt; Clerk, David G. Benjamin; Treasurer, Daniel Lowry.

1837.—Trustees, John Mintun, William Handberry and William Lowry; Clerk, David G. Benjamin; Treasurer, Elias Gabriel.

1838.—Trustees, Hugh Laughlin, William Mills and Elias Gabriel; Clerk, William Johnstone; Treasurer wanting.

1839.—Trustees, Hugh Laughlin, William Mills and Elias Gabriel; Clerk, R. H. Cotton; Treasurer, Alexander Young.

1840.—Trustees, William Handberry, William Herron and Elias Gabriel; Clerk, R. H. Cotton; Treasurer, Alexander Young.

1841.—Trustees, William Handberry, Pardon C. Hewitt and Elias Gabriel; Clerk, William Young; Treasurer, Alexander Young.

1842.—Trustees, William Handberry, Pardon C. Hewitt and Elias Gabriel; Clerk, James Holmes; Treasurer, Elijah Lowry.

1843.—Trustees, William Handberry, Simon Elliott and Elias Gabriel; Clerk, James Holmes; Treasurer, Alexander Young.

1844.—Trustees, William Handberry, Daniel McCoy and Elias Gabriel; Clerk, James Holmes; Treasurer, Alexander Young.

1845.—Trustees, John Mintun, Simon Elliott and Pardon C. Hewitt; Clerk, W. C. Allen; Treasurer, Alexander Young.

1846.—Trustees, John Mintun, William Lowry and Pardon C. Hewitt; Clerk, W. C. Allen; Treasurer, Alexander Young.

1847.—Trustees, John Mintun, Hugh Boden and Robert McNeal; Clerk, James Holmes; Treasurer, Alexander Young.

1848.—Trustees, John Mintun, Hugh Boden and John Means; Clerk, W. C. Allen; Treasurer, William Herron.

1849.—Trustees, Andrew Herron, Robert McNeal and John Means; Clerk, W. C. Allen; Treasurer, William Herron.

1850.—Trustees, Hugh Boden, Robert H. Cotton and John Means; Clerk, W. C. Allen; Treasurer, William Herron.

1851.—Trustees, Hugh Boden, Robert H. Cotton and Robert Spear; Clerk, David W. Mintun; Treasurer, William Herron.

1852.—Trustees, Hugh Boden, Robert H. Cotton and Joseph McNeal; Clerk, David W. Mintun; Treasurer, William Herron.

Carl H. Burrhaus

1853.—Trustees, Hugh Boden, John Means and Joseph McNeal; Clerk, William C. Allen; Treasurer, William Herron.

1854.—Trustees, John Mintun, Samuel Spencer and P. B. Wilson; Clerk, George Dixon; Treasurer, William Herron.

1855.—Trustees, William Lowry, Robert Spear and P. B. Wilson; Clerk, George Dixon; Treasurer, William Herron.

1856.—Trustees, William Lowry, Charles Burr and Jonathan Mintun; Clerk, Asa Thomas; Treasurer, William Herron.

1857.—Trustees, William Lowry, Charles Burr and P. B. Wilson; Clerk, George Dixon; Treasurer, William Herron.

1858.—Trustees, William Lowry, Charles Burr and P. B. Wilson; Clerk, Bingham Goodrich; Treasurer, Hugh Boden.

1859.—Trustees, Robert H. Cotton, William Swaim and Samuel Cagg; Clerk, Bingham Goodrich; Treasurer, Hugh Boden.

1860.—Trustees, Robert H. Cotton, William Swaim and Samuel Cagg; Clerk, S. C. Teeters; Treasurer, Hugh Boden.

1861.—Trustees, Moses Gabriel, William Swaim and Samuel Cagg; Clerk, A. G. Patterson; Treasurer, Hugh Boden.

1862.—Trustees, Moses Gabriel, William Swaim and Samuel Cagg; Clerk, John Nichols; Treasurer, Hugh Boden.

1863.—Trustees, Moses Gabriel, William Swaim and Peter Beckter; Clerk, John Nichols; Treasurer, Thomas Withers.

1864.—Trustees, James Boden, William Swaim and Richard Dowler; Clerk, A. G. Robinett; Treasurer, Thomas Withers.

1865.—Trustees, James Bell, James Mayhugh and Moses Kennard; Clerk, Marcus L. Griswold; Treasurer, Nelson Squires.

1866.—Trustees, James Bell, Daniel McCoy and Joseph McNeal; Clerk, H. C. Wilson; Treasurer, A. G. Patterson.

1867.—Trustees, T. J. Allison, Abraham Martin and Joseph McNeal; Clerk, Lafayette Hawk; Treasurer, A. G. Patterson.

1868.—Trustees, Samuel Cagg, E. H. Phillips and Richard Inns; Clerk, J. B. Miller; Treasurer, A. G. Patterson; Assessor, C. M. Carman; Constables, H. C. Wilson and Joshua King; Justice of the Peace, L. P. Armstrong.

1869.—Trustees, W. C. Foster, P. B. Wilson and Richard Inns; Clerk, M. L. Griswold; Treasurer, F. A. McVay; Assessor, C. M. Carman; Constables; H. C. Wilson, and G. H. Harper; Justice of the Peace, Robert McNeal.

1870.—Trustees, Richard Inns, Samuel Cagg and E. H. Phillips; Clerk, M. L. Griswold; Treasurer, F. A. McVay; Assessor, J. T. Dickerson; Constables, L. M. Holmes and S. T. Allen.

1871.—Trustees, S. D. King, A. Condon and E. H. Phillips; Clerk, Levi Hunter; Treasurer, William Herron; Assessor, J. T. Dickerson; Constables, Elihu Cox and John Maxwell.

1872.—Trustees, J. A. Armstrong, P. B. Wilson and C. M. Carman; Clerk, M. L. Griswold; Treasurer, James Love; Assessor, J. D. Dickerson; Constables, Elihu Cox and S. R. Lowry.

1873.—Trustees, P. B. Wilson, L. D. King and E. H. Phillips; Clerk, M. L. Griswold; Treasurer, James Love; Assessor, J. T. Dickerson; Constables, S. R. Lowry and D. Mayhugh; Justice of the Peace, Daniel Hester.

1874.—Trustees, E. H. Phillips, T. J. Allison and R. McNeal: Clerk, M. L. Griswold; Treasurer, James Love.

1875.—Trustees, E. H. Phillips, Robert McNeal and T. J. Allison; Clerk, M. L. Griswold; Treasurer, James Love; Assessor, J. T. Dickerson; Constables, C. V. Lewellyn and J. D. Cox; Justice of the Peace, John Boden.

1876.—Trustees, E. H. Phillips, T. J. Allison and Robert McNeal; Clerk, H. H. Williams; Treasurer, James Love; Assessor, C. M. Carman; Constables, E. W. Gilbert and S. R. Lowry.

1877.—Trustees, E. H. Phillips, A. Condon and John Young; Clerk, M. L. Griswold; Treasurer, James Love; Constables, S. R. Lowry and E. W. Gilbert.

1878.—Trustees, R. C. Harper, Samuel Cagg and John Young Clerk, C. V. Lewellyn; Treasurer, John Boden; Assessor, Robert McNeal; Constables, S. R. Lowry and John Shaffer; Justice of the Peace, John Boden.

1879.—Trustees, John Young, E. Jones and E. H. Phillips; Clerk, L. V. Pickens; Treasurer, John Boden; Assessor, J. M. Swaim; Constables, John Shaffer and G. S. Clendenning; Justice of the Peace, Daniel Hester.

1880.—Trustees, P. B. Wilson, E. T. Davis, and John Young; Clerk, M. L. Griswold; Treasurer, John Boden; Assessor, S. R. Lowry; Constables, G. W. Ely and H. W. Sayles.

1881.—Trustees, P. B. Wilson, P. Jones, and A. Condon; Clerk, M. L. Griswold; Treasurer, Leander Stright; Assessor, S. R. Lowry; Constables, G. W. Ely and J. N. McNeal.

1882.—Trustees, E. Vickers, A. Condon and C. C. Pierce; Clerk, W. G. Galligher; Treasurer, John Boden; Assessor, John Young; Constables, Samuel Might and William McCoy; Justice of the Peace, Daniel Hester.

1883.—Trustees, P. B. Wilson, C. C. Pierce and P. Jones; Clerk, H. Fuller; Assessor, S. K. Lowry; Treasurer, L. Stright; Constables, J. M. Stewart and John Kennard.

MARSHFIELD.

The village of Marshfield is in the central portion of the township, on the C., W. & B. Railroad, and about seven miles from Athens. It has a population of about 250. The following are the business firms of the village:

William McPherson, general store; Joseph Kaler, general store; W. G. Gallagher & Co., drugs and groceries; L. Stright & Son, tannery.

The postoffice was established in 1859, since which time the following have officiated as Postmasters: Hugh Boden, 1859 till 1865; A. G. Patterson, 1865 to 1866; David Mayhugh, 1866 till 1867; James Mayhugh, 1867; F. A. McVay, 1867 to 1870. M. L. Griswold was appointed in 1870, and is the present incumbent.

CHURCHES.

There are three churches, the Methodist Episcopal, Protestant Methodist, and the Christian, all holding regular services.

Christian Church.—In 1870 a few earnest spirits united in the work of organizing a church, and their names were: T. J. Allison, J. M. Swaim, Daniel Conkey, Marcus Griswold, H. W. Hewitt and a few others whose names were not remembered. They erected a neat and substantial place of worship, in connection with the A. F. & A. M., whose lodge-room is over the church. Their present able and efficient Pastor is the Rev. George Van Pelt. The church was dedicated Oct. 18, 1870. The dedication sermon was preached by the Rev. S. H. Bingman, as Pastor. The membership at the organization numbered forty, and the present membership is 125. Since its organization there has been connected with the church 300 members.

The Methodist Protestant Church was erected in the year 1860, and dedicated in November of that year by its Pastor, Rev. William Bawden. The membership at organization in 1860 was seventy; and the present membership fifty-two. The Pastor at this time is the Rev. D. G. Shirer, and the church is at this time growing stronger.

The Methodist Episcopal Church, was organized in 1869, by quite a number belonging to that denomination, who had heretofore acted without that unity so desirable in church progress. The first members were: Prof. Miller and wife, Norman McLeod, wife and daughter, Alexander Shalis and wife, Joseph McPherson and wife, William McPherson and wife, and Byron McVay and wife. Soon after the organization steps were taken to erect a place of worship, which was completed the same year. Their first Pastor was the Rev. —— Dickson, who did much to encourage its progress. The present Pastor is Rev. C. D. Nichols. There are at this time twenty-eight members.

Constitution Lodge, No. 426, A. F. & A. M., was chartered Oct. 20, 1869, the first meeting under dispensation having been held Feb. 22, 1869. The charter members were: William Golden, F. A. McVay, James Love, H. M. Cotton, R. C. Harper, William McPherson, David Mayhugh and E. B. Pickett. Of this number two are dead—F. A. McVay and E. B. Pickett. The lodge owns a nice hall, and is in a prosperous condition. Ninety-five have joined the lodge since organization. The present officers are: J. Boden, W. M.; F. M. Barker, S. W.; W. C. Holmes, J. W.; J. M. Swaim, Treas.; I. N. McCoy, Sec.; Elmer Gabriel, S. D.; W. G. Galligher, J. D., and J. M. Stewart, Tyler.

CARBONDALE

is a flourishing mining village, with a population numbering between 250 and 300. The coal works were opened in 1867, and soon after a branch railroad was laid and completed before the end of the year. The coal vein is four feet in thickness. Mining in the neighborhood is in its infancy. These works are said to have been the first opened in Southeastern Ohio. They are operated by McClintock & Smith. There are two general stores, one owned by P. J. Beckler and the other by the mining company, who employ from 150 to 175 men. They have no church building, but have one school. The postoffice was established in 1880, and Mr. Charles Smith is still Postmaster.

MINERAL CITY

is a protege of the Marietta & Cincinnati Railroad Company, having been laid out by them. It has about 150 inhabitants, two stores with general stocks, Mr. E. Vickers owning one, and the other owned by Vorhes, Earhart & Co. There is also a drug store owned by Dr. Coleman, who is also a practicing physician. They have one flourishing public school and a postoffice, of which E. Vickers is the Postmaster. The future of the town does not come under the head of Great Expectations, but as it is a great convenience the citizens and farmers around are satisfied.

BIOGRAPHICAL.

T. J. Allison, farmer and stock-raiser, was born in Athens County, Ohio, Dec. 24, 1839, and is the son of William H. and Dorcas (Gabriel) Allison. Mr. Allison was a native of Maryland, coming to Ohio when young, and settled in Jefferson County. In 1837 he moved to Morgan County and shortly after to Athens, where he remained for about three years, and then came to Waterloo Township, where he resided until 1864, with the exception of three years, during which time he was engaged as a stone mason in Athens. While a resident of this township he was engaged in farming and sheep-raising, in which he was very successful. In 1864 he went to Chillicothe, Ross Co., Ohio, where he became engaged in wool-buying, in which he was generally very successful, but at one time was a heavy loser by the "Boston fire," as he had a large amount of wool there. His loss amounted to about $60,000, from which he partially recovered before his death, which occurred in August, 1880. Our subject was reared on the farm and remained with his parents until he reached his majority. He was married Oct. 2, 1859, to Miss Elizabeth A. Huron, a daughter of William Huron, a resident of this township. They were the parents of eleven children, ten still living—Arthur M., Mary L., Nettie M., William L., Ida A., Dorcas L., William H., Nora Z., Abbie G. and Sadie. Mr. Allison's farm contains 270 acres of well-improved land, on which he has erected a pleasant residence. During the wool season he deals largely in the commodity. He has held at three different times the office of Township Trustee, and his administration has ever been satisfactory to the people. He is a member of Constitution Lodge, No. 426, A. F. & A. M., in which he has held the office of Treasurer at three different times. Mr. and Mrs. Allison are active and consistent members of the Christian church, he being one of the Elders, and also Sabbath-school Superintendent, an organization in which he takes a great interest. Politically he is a staunch Republican. He is one of the Directors of the County Infirmary, in which capacity he has served for three terms.

John Boden, station agent, M. & C. R. R., Marshfield, was born in Morgan County, Ohio, March 21, 1837, and is the son of Hugh and Ellen (Elliot) Boden, who came to Athens County in 1840 and located on a farm about one mile from Marshfield, where they remained until 1856. Mr. Boden was at this time appointed station agent for the M. & C. R. R. at this point, being the first agent after the completion of the road. He held several offices of trust—County Commissioner, Township Treasurer and Justice of the Peace for several years each. He was a member of the A. F. & A. M., Paramuthia Lodge, No. 25. He and his wife were both members of the Protestant Methodist church. Our subject was reared on the farm and remained with his parents until he was twenty-seven years of age. In 1864 he came to Marshfield and became engaged in the mercantile business, in which he continued for four years meeting with fair success, and on his father leaving he was appointed to his position as station agent. He was married Sept. 28, 1858, to Miss Malvina Gabriel, daughter of Elias Gabriel, one of the early pioneers of the township. By this union there were five children, four of whom still survive—Orland G., Elza E. (deceased), Mary E., George and Lafayette O. As he deserves, the people have confidence in him and have given him several offices of trust. He has been Township Treasurer four years and Justice of the Peace eight years. In 1881, on the opening of the Children's Home of this county, he was appointed one of its Trustees. His performance of these duties have given credit to himself and honor to his constituents. He is a member of Constitution Lodge, No. 426, A. F. & A. M.; Athens Chapter, No. 39, and Commandery No. 15. He is at present Master of his lodge, which office he has held for six years. Mr. Boden is unassuming in his manners, gentlemanly and courteous in his connection with others, and is highly respected by all. Mrs. Boden is a member of the Protestant Methodist church.

George W. Earhart, of Vorhes, Earhart & Co., merchants, Mineral P. O., was born in Lee Township, Athens County, June 24, 1856, and is the son of Dr. John and Ruth (McVey) Earhart. He received his early education in the common schools and completed it in the academy at Albany and in Holbrook's Normal Institute at Lebanon, Ohio. In 1879 he entered the store of Vorhes Bros, at Albany, as a clerk, and continued with them for two years. The following year he was engaged with S. K. Hibbard in the same capacity. He purchased an interest in the store of W. H. Vorhes at Mineral, in which he still continues. He and his partner are young men of sterling qualities, and by their strict attention to the business receive, as they deserve, the confidence of the community about them and a liberal patronage. Mr. Earhart was married Sept. 27, 1880, to Miss Mary Hibbard, daughter of Henry Hibbard, a resident of Athens Township. They have one child—John Douglas.

Robert C. Harper, farmer, local preacher and Elder in the Methodist Episcopal church, was born in Athens Township, Sept. 16, 1823. He was reared on a farm, and his early education was acquired by a limited attendance in the common schools. His religious life began when he was seven years old. He united with the Methodist Episcopal church at the age of sixteen under the labors of Samuel Mattox, and has ever aimed to follow his teachings. He always took an active part in church matters, and has for the last thirty-five years been a preacher of the gospel. During this time he has taken over 1,100 persons into the church, and has preached over 1,300 funeral sermons. One year he preached seven over an average of one per day for the entire year. He is the owner of a fine farm containing 150 acres of improved land, on which are substantial buildings. He was married June 20, 1844, to Miss Catherine Six, daughter of George Six, a resident of Waterloo Township. Seven children were born to them, three still living —Leo (deceased), Vinton (deceased), Isador F., Serepta F. (deceased), Henderson (deceased), Mary E. and William W. He married his present wife April 4, 1867. She was Maria Caldwell, daughter of James and Maria Caldwell, residents of Pickaway County, Ohio. They have two children—Robert C. and Amanda M. Mr. Harper is a member of the A. F. & A. M., being a charter member of Constitution Lodge, No. 426, located at Marshfield.

I. N. McCoy, school-teacher, was born in Waterloo Township, Nov. 10, 1847, and is the son of Daniel and Eve (Enlow) McCoy, natives of Washington County, Pa., who came to Athens County in 1836, and located in this township, where they remained until their death. They were both active members of the Methodist Episcopal church and were ever mindful of the wants of others and friends of the deserving poor. Mr. McCoy was politically a staunch Republican. Our subject was reared on his father's farm, and received his early education in the common schools and completed it at the Ohio University at Athens. As a teacher he has been very successful, always gaining the confidence of the pupils and the respect of their parents. He married Carrie, the youngest daughter of John Clutter, of Athens Township. This union was blessed by the birth of two children—Myrtie A. and Don Hadley. By the death of his wife, Oct. 22, 1879, Mr. McCoy was bereft of an affectionate companion, and the children of a loving mother. During the late civil war, when only seventeen years of age, he enlisted, Feb. 26, 1864, in Company C, Thirty-sixth Ohio Volunteer Infantry, and went from Marietta, Ohio, where they were mustered in, to Chattanooga, Tenn., and there joined the army of General Thomas, and about May 1 was transferred to West Virginia, and was on the famous Lynchburg raid, participating in the battle of Lynchburg; was mustered out at Wheeling, W. Va., July 27, 1865, and returned to his native home. He is a member of the A. F. & A. M., Constitution Lodge, No. 426, being the first to apply for membership after it received its charter. He, at the present time, holds the office of Secretary.

E. H. Phillips, farmer and stock-raiser, son of E. V. and Tacy (Hopkins) Phillips, was born in Ames Township, Aug. 27, 1824. His father came to Athens County in 1808, and located in Ames Township, where he remained till his death, Aug. 21, 1859. His mother now resides in New England, Rome Township, and has reached the advanced age of seventy-six years. Our subject remained with his parents until he was twenty-two years of age. He learned the shoemaker's trade of his father, and worked with him in the shop and on the farm most of the time during his minority. At the age of twenty-two he began business for himself in the shop at home. A year later he purchased the property now known as Dunbar's Hotel, and in connection with his trade carried on the hotel business for three or four years. He then went to Rome Township and purchased a farm near New England. After living here about twelve years he sold out and went to Alexander Township and purchased the Patterson farm, and resided there about two years. He then moved to Waterloo Township, on to the farm where he now resides. His farm contains 355 acres of well-improved land. Mr. Phillips is an excellent farmer, and has been enabled to accumulate a handsome property. He has held the office of Township Trustee for nine years, to the satisfaction of his constituents. Politically he is a Democrat, and was one of the first of his party to be elected to office in the township after the war. He is a man of liberal ideas, and is ever willing to lend his aid to forward any laudable enterprise. He was married April 10, 1850, to Miss Allinda Breyfogle, a daughter of George Breyfogle, a resident of Canaan Township. By this union there were nine children—Augusta M., Franklin P., George E., Alice A., John E. (deceased), Lizzie T., Lucy M., Lena A. and William T.

Henry Smith, carpenter, Marshfield, was born in Washington County, Pa., Nov. 16, 1800, the son of William and Catherine Smith. His parents came to Ohio in 1812, and located in what is now Morgan County, it being at that time unorganized and in its natural state—a dense wilderness. Here they remained until their death. Our subject was reared on the farm and at the age of nineteen became apprenticed to a carpenter, and spent two years in learning the trade. After this he went to work on his own account, and has followed his trade the greater part of his life. He was married in 1818 to Miss Mary Collins. They had five children—Louisa, Jackson M., Leander, William (deceased), and John. His wife died in 1863, and he was again married March 1, 1865, to Mrs. Catherine Pierce, widow of Andrew M. C. Pierce. She had a family of eight children, three of whom are now living—Sarah V. (deceased), William S., Georgiana M. C., Susan J. (deceased), Manfred (deceased), M. Olivia, Sarah P. (deceased), Andrew M. (deceased). Mr. Smith came to Athens County in 1847 and located in Bern Township, where he resided till 1866, when he moved to Amesville and was engaged in the grocery business, in which he continued until 1881. He then came to Marshfield, and is now keeping the Swaim Hotel. Mrs. Smith is a member of the Presbyterian church.

Leander Stright, tanner and currier, Marshfield, born in Mercer County, Pa., June 6, 1835, is the son of Young R. and Rachel (Scott) Stright. His parents came to Ohio in 1853 and located in Vinton County, where they resided two or three years, then came to Lee Township, Athens County, and remained five years. From this place they went to Harrison County, Iowa, where their father died. The mother now resides in Henry County, Mo., and has reached the advanced age of seventy-four years. When sixteen years of age, Mr. Stright became apprenticed to a tanner and currier and served four years. Mr. Stright came to Ohio in 1855, and purchased a tannery at Hebbardsville, where he resided until 1860, then moved to Albany and carried on the same business for three years. In 1863 he came to Marshfield and purchased the property he now owns. During the late civil war he enlisted, May 25, 1862, in Company H, Eighty-seventh Ohio Volunteer Infantry, forming at Camp Chase, Columbus, where they were mustered into the service. He went with his regiment to Baltimore, Md., and from there to Harper's Ferry. His company was sent from here to Knowland Ferry, to intercept General Lee. After being out on a skirmish for several days, returned to Harper's Ferry, where they were all captured by the rebels, but were fortunately paroled the following day and returned to their friends at Frederick City, Md., and thence via Philadelphia to Delaware, O., where they were mustered out. He now carries on the business of a tanner and currier at Marshfield, where he does a thriving business. He was married Oct. 1, 1855, to Miss Catherine J. Fox. They have had seven children, five of whom are still living—Elizabeth A. (deceased), Mary E., Hiram B., Janet A., Florence J., Cora (deceased), and Mabel Lee. Mr. Stright has always taken an active interest in the matter of education and music, and is ever among the foremost to forward any enterprise that will be of benefit to the community. He is a member of Constitution Lodge, No. 426, A. F. & A. M. Mr. and Mrs. Stright are consistent members of the Presbyterian church.

J. M. Swaim, farmer, son of William and Susan (Culberson) Swaim, was born May 5, 1831, in Athens County, in what is now Vinton County. He was reared on the farm and remained with his parents until thirty years of age, and was afforded only a common-school education. He was married Oct. 9, 1851, to Miss Mary Grimm, a daughter of Thomas Grimm, a resident of this county. They are the parents of seven children—Thomas A., William E., Diantha E., Susan A., James F., John M. and Fay M. He has a fine farm containing 200 acres of improved land, well adapted to the raising of stock and grain, on which he has erected a pleasant and commodious residence. He has by his industry been enabled to accumulate a property sufficient to surround himself and family with the comforts of life. In 1879 he was elected to the office of Township Assessor, which he filled with credit. He is a member of the A. F. & A. M., Constitution Lodge, No. 426, in which he has held several offices. Mr. and Mrs. Swaim are members of the Christian church, he having united when he was nineteen years of age.

Elijah Vickers, merchant, Mineral City, was born in Belmont County, Ohio, April 30, 1828, and is the son of Thomas and Hannah (Harmar) Vickers, who came from Pennsylvania to Ohio and located in Belmont County at an early day. In 1840 they moved to Washington County, where they resided until Mrs. Vicker's death. Mr. Vickers then sold out, and after remaining with his children for a short time went to Iowa, where he now resides, having reached the advanced age of ninety-two years. The subject of this sketch was reared and remained with his parents on the farm until he reached his majority, receiving his education in the common schools. He was married, Oct. 30, 1849, to Miss Letitia McGirr, daughter of Alexander McGirr, a resident of Washington County, Ohio. By this union there were four children, only two of whom are now living—Sylvester (deceased), Alexander (deceased), Arthur and Ethel L. His eldest son was killed by lightning while at work in the field near the house, when the storm seemed as yet to be in the distance, the sky overhead being perfectly clear. After his marriage Mr. Vickers continued farming in Washington County until 1860, when he went to Marietta and lived for one year. In 1861 he came to Athens County and located at Big Run Station, on the old line of the M. & C. R. R., where he became engaged in the mercantile business, in which he continued until 1872. He then went to Guysville and carried on the same business until 1876. He at this time moved to the farm now owned by H. H. Wickham, in Canaan Township, where he remained for one year; then went back to Guysville and remained till 1878, when he came to Mineral City. On coming here he again entered upon a mercantile life, in which he still continues, receiving, as he deserves, a liberal share of the public patronage. He was bereft of his wife Sept. 19, 1876, after a lingering illness of about nine months. He was again married Nov. 27, 1879, to Margaret A. Alexander, a resident of Muskingum County, Ohio. She is a lady of pleasant manners and refinement. His aim through life has ever been to be temperate in everything, and a consistent Christian.

W. H. Vorhes, of Vorhes, Earhart & Co., merchants, Mineral P. O., was born in Lee Township, Athens County, Aug. 13, 1852, and is the son of Albert and Elizabeth (Morse) Vorhes. He remained with his parents until he reached his majority, and received his early education in the common schools, completing it in the academy at Albany. During his minority he was engaged in assisting his father in the store at Albany. On reaching his majority he purchased an interest with his brother in their father's business, in which he continued three years, meeting with good success. He then sold out his interest and was engaged in farming and dealing in stock one year. The following year he clerked in the store at Albany, and the next year went to Kansas, where he purchased a ranch and was engaged in sheep-raising until the following January. He returned to Ohio, May 1, 1880, and built the store which he now occupies, and filled it with a line of general merchandise. He was married May 10, 1874, to Miss Ollie Whaley, daughter of John Whaley, a resident of Lee Township. They have one son—Arthur B.

CHAPTER XXV.

BERN TOWNSHIP—FERTILE SOIL, MINERAL WEALTH, MATERIAL PROGRESS.

LOCATION AND EXTENT OF DOMAIN—METES AND BOUNDS—FROM THE RECORDS—LIST OF TOWNSHIP OFFICIALS—SOME OF THE EARLY SETTLERS—MINERAL DEPOSITS—TRANSPORTATION ONLY NEEDED—CHURCHES—CEMETERIES—SCHOOLS AND MATERIAL PROSPERITY—BIOGRAPHICAL.

ITS LOCATION AND EXTENT OF DOMAIN.

This townshp lies in the extreme northeast corner of Athens County, is six miles from north to south, and five miles from east to west, and contains only thirty sections of land, or 19,200 acres, the eastern tier of sections having been set off to Washington County in 1807. The general nature of the county is hilly and broken, yet a large portion of its land cannot be surpassed for fertility. It is well watered by Federal Creek and Sharp's Fork, both of which traverse it from north to south, and there are several smaller creeks which flow into them. Besides these there are innumerable springs all over the township.

The township has been exclusively settled by farmers and stockraisers, there being no town or village within its borders, and as yet it has no postoffice—probably accounted for by its ample accommodations through postoffices in its borders.

METES AND BOUNDS.

It is bounded on the north by Morgan County, on the east by Washington County, on the south by Rome Township, and on the west by Ames. It was originally included in Ames Township and was not separately organized till 1828, consequently much of its early history will be found in connection with that township.

FROM THE RECORDS.

Bern was set off from Ames Township by the county commissioners March 3, 1828, and the electors were directed to meet at the house of John Henry on the first Monday of April to elect township officers. The following is a list of its officers from its organization to the present date inclusive:

TRUSTEES.

1828-'30, John Henry, James Dickey, John Wickham; 1831-'3, John Henry, David James, Jeffrey Buchanan; 1834, Dyar Selby, Sen., John Wickham, J. Dickey; 1835, W. J. Brown, John Wickham, J. Dickey; 1836, W. J. Brown, David James, J. Dickey; 1837, Matthew Henry, David James, J. Dickey; 1838, Matthew Henry, David James, Wm. J. Brown; 1839, Matthew Henry, James Dickey, Wm. J. Brown; 1840, J. E. Vore, James Dickey, John Work; 1841, David James, Thornton Swart, John Work; 1842, David James, James Dickey, Dyar Selby, Jr.; 1843, Joseph McCune, James Dickey, Dyar Selby, Jr.; 1844, Joseph McCune, James Dickey, Reuben Hague; 1845, David James, James Dickey, Reuben Hague; 1846, Jesse Carr, Dyar Selby, John Work; 1847, David Colvin, Robert Henry, Wm. Rardin; 1848, David Colvin, Levi Ellis, Wm. Rardin; 1849, David Colvin, Edward Ginn, Calvin Tracy; 1850, James Henry, Edward Ginn, J. E. Vore; 1851, Lewis Dille, Reuben Hague, Calvin Tracy; 1852, Lewis Dille, Edward Ginn, Calvin Tracy; 1853, Andrew Ogg, P. W. Lampson, J. E. Vore; 1854, Andrew Ogg, J. S. King, J. E. Vore; 1855, H. C. Selby, J. S. King, John Whaley; 1856, H. C. Selby, P. W. Lampson, David Gilchrist; 1857, David James, Edward Ginn, David Gilchrist; 1858, Levi Rardin, J. M. Smith, George Wyatt; 1859, Clark Dodds, W. Endicott, George Wyatt; 1860, Dyar Selby, W. Endicott, H. T. McCune; 1861, H. C. Selby, W. Endicott, W. W. Wickham; 1862, Dyar Selby, Thomas Dickson, W. W. Wickham; 1863, E. Hanson, Thomas Dickson, W. W. Wickham; 1864, O. Gifford, Thomas Dickson, W. Endicott; 1865, Levi Rardin, Thomas Dickson, W. Endicott; 1866, H. C. Selby, Thomas Dickson, W. Endicott; 1867, H. C. Selby, L. Driggs, Elijah Hanson; 1868, S. J. Wells, Elijah White, Elijah Hanson; 1869, Elijah Hanson, D. W. Lambert, George E. Henry; 1870, Elijah Hanson, W. M. Marquis, D. W. Lambert; 1871, W. Endicott, D. W. Lambert, Wm. M. Marquis; 1872, W. Endicott, H. T. McCune, Wm. M. Marquis; 1873, Charles Henry, G. H. Moore, G. W. Armstrong; 1874-'5, Henry Broadwell, George H. Moore, G. W. Armstrong; 1876, Henry Broadwell, Wm. M. Marquis, G. W.

Armstrong; 1877, A. C. Smith, Wm. M. Marquis, Abner Lambert; 1878, A. C. Smith, John Marquis, Abner Lambert; 1879, A. C. Smith, Abner Lambert, H. Broadwell; 1880, A. C. Smith, Charles Henry, Elijah Hanson; 1881, Charles Henry, C. B. McCune, Elijah Hanson; 1882, C. B. McCune, J. R. Wickham, Daniel Parkins, Jr.; 1883, J. R. Wickham, Isaac Armstrong, J. A. Marquis.

JUSTICES OF THE PEACE.

1828, Thaddeus Crippen, Wm. T. Brown; 1831, Matthew Henry, Wm. T. Brown; 1834, Levi Ellis, Robert Henry; 1836, David Dille; 1837, Robert Henry; 1839, Dyan Selby; 1840, Robert Work; 1841, Calvin Tracy; 1843, John Brawley, P. W. Lampson; 1844, Dyar Selby, Jr.; 1846, John Brawley; 1847–'50, Dyar Selby, Jr.; 1852, Philip W. Lampson; 1853, Thomas Bruce; 1854, Elijah Hanson; 1855, P. W. Lampson; 1857, Elijah Hanson; 1858, P. W. Lampson; 1859, Robert Henry (refused to qualify), Seaborn Carr; 1860, Aaron Smith; 1862, Seaborn Carr; 1863, Watson Harris; 1864, W. W. Wickham; 1866, Watson Harris; 1867, Edwin T. Glazier; 1868, Hiram C. Selby; 1870, Geo. E. Henry; 1871, H. C. Selby; 1873, Geo. E. Henry; 1874, B. C. Pickering; 1876, Geo. E. Henry; 1877, B. C. Pickering; 1879, Geo. E. Henry; 1880, H. C. Selby; 1882, Geo. E. Henry; 1883, Elijah Hanson.

D. L. Dille has been Township Clerk and Richard Edgerton Treasurer for the past fifteen years.

EARLY SETTLERS.

Among the early settlers of Bern Township were: John Henry, a native of Ireland, who came here in 1817; John Wickham, a native of Vermont; David and Daniel James, and Philip W. Lampson settled here in 1820; James Dickey, of Pennsylvania, and of Irish descent, in 1821. These with a few others, perhaps, formed the nucleus of what is now a prosperous and enterprising community, and by hard labor, undergoing trials which the present generation know nothing of, developed what was then a dense wilderness, turning it from its natural state into luxuriant fields of grain and grass, dotted over with pleasant residences and substantial farm buildings.

MINERAL DEPOSITS.

There are valuable deposits of coal and iron in the township, and when properly developed will become a source of great wealth.

A railroad by which the coal could be cheaply transported to the different markets is all that is needed to make Bern Township one of the busy coal fields of the Hocking Valley. Such a road is in anticipation, and has been surveyed, running through the township from north to south along the valley of Federal Creek and Sharp's Fork of the same. There also exists an excellent quality of salt water, and in such quantities as would justify its being worked.

CHURCHES.

Methodist Protestant Valley Church was organized in 1856 with seven charter members, to-wit: John Whaley, Lucy Whaley, David Whaley, Sarah Whaley, Watson Harris, Nancy Harris and Sarah Vanzant. At its organization the Rev. Henry Lawson became its first Pastor. The house in which they worship was built the same year of their organization, and the church has been blessed with much good and a large membership, it numbering at one time eighty-six members. Its present membership is twenty-one, and the pastorate is under the charge of Rev. Luman.

The Methodist Episcopal Church was organized in 1856 at the Valley Church, and its original members, twenty in number, among whom were: Rev. Oren Gifford, Olive Gifford, Ruby Gifford, Peter Ingle and wife, David Gilchrist and wife. Its first Pastor was Elder Clark and its present Pastor the Rev. D. W. Windsor. It has now a membership of about forty, which includes some of the best citizens of the township.

United Brethren—Mt. Hermon.—This church was organized in 1857. There was formerly an organization of this denomination, but there are only three members left who formed the first members of Mt. Hermon church—William Rardin, Rebecca Hanson and Elizabeth Work. The church was built in 1858 and has now a membership of about forty, with Rev. William Burnsworth as its Pastor.

Westland Church was organized in 1877 with Rev. E. Robinson for its first Pastor and about twenty members, among which were: J. Brille and wife, E. White and wife, Robert Brille, Sarah Vanzant, M. Watson and Sarah Funk. Its present membership is about twenty-five, and its Pastor, Rev. Wm. Burnsworth.

Mt. Carmel Church was organized by Rev. Phillips, its first Pastor, in 1881, with ten members, as follows: Lewis Dille and wife, Albert Brooks and wife, F. W. Taylor and wife, Wm. Wanless and wife, Joseph Harris and Clyde Harris. Its present Pastor is Rev. Wm. Burnsworth.

The Universalists organized a church in 1860, and among the first members were: John Wickham and wife, T. Crippen and wife, Warner Wickham and wife, Mrs. Oldcraft and Mrs. Ogg. Its first pastor was Rev. F. Jones, and the pulpit is now occasionally supplied by Rev. McMasters, of Marietta.

SCHOOLS.

There are nine school-houses in this township and the report for winter of 1882–1883 shows a full average attendance and fair progress in all of them. The example set by the citizens of Athens has become infectious and educational progress has kept step with advanced civilization. This has made the people intelligent and progressive, and material prosperity has been the result. If Athens County has shown a great many educated and talented men who have made history, it can be traced to the fact that one of the pillars upon which was reared a temple of progressive people was built upon an educational foundation.

BIOGRAPHICAL.

James Carter, Homer Township, Morgan County, was born in Bedford County, Penn., July 25, 1812, a son of George Carter, who came to Athens County, Ohio, in 1815 and located in Ames Township, where our subject was reared and educated, living with his parents until he grew to manhood. He was married in 1836 to Elizabeth McDonnald. By this union there were nine children, only three of whom are living—Melissa, George and Elizabeth. He and his wife are members of the Church of the Disciples. He is an ardent worker in the temperance cause.

Richard Edgerton, was born in Belmont County, Ohio, April 7, 1827, and came with his father's family to Athens County and settled in Marion Township, now Morgan County, in 1835, where he was reared and educated, residing with his parents until he was twenty-one years of age. He was married April 20, 1848, to Tama Vernon, a native of Belmont County. Eight children were born to them, only six now living—William (deceased), Jeptha H., Mary Z., Sarah P., John C., Ruth A., Edward R. (deceased), James A. Mr. Edgerton has always been engaged in farming, but in connection with his farming pursuits, from 1868 to

1876, he engaged in the mercantile business at Plantsville. His farm contains 400 acres of good land where he makes a specialty of raising high grades of live stock. He has been elected by the people to many local offices of trust and responsibility. He and his wife are members of the society of Friends.

Richard Elliott was born in Highlandshire, Scotland, in 1831, and came with his father's family to the United States in 1837, and settled on a farm in Bern Township, where he was reared and educated. He was married Sept. 18, 1857, to Miss Margaret J. Barton, a native of Athens County. They have eight children— John B., Alphia, Mary J., Charles, George, Eva, William and Lewis. He purchased his present farm in 1859, where he has since resided. It contains 150 acres of good land under a high state of cultivation.

Lorenzo Ellis was born in Morgan County, Ohio, July 15, 1819; the oldest son of Levi Ellis, who came to Ohio from Vermont about the year 1815, and in 1843 came to Bern Township, Athens County. He afterward moved to Chesterfield, where he passed the remainder of his days. His wife, Lucy Gibson, was also a native of Vermont. They were the parents of seven children, six of whom are still living. They were active and consistent members of the Baptist church for many years. Our subject was reared on a farm and received his education in the subscription schools. He was married March 17, 1851, to Miss Mahalia Dorithy, a native of Morgan County, Ohio. They have two daughters—Emma J. and Lucy A. Mr. Ellis purchased his present farm in 1865, containing 245 acres of improved land. He and his wife are members of the Christian church.

Washington Endicott was born in Belmont County, Ohio, a son of Charles Endicott, of Pennsylvania, and of English descent. He was born March 26, 1821. His father died when he was thirteen years of age, and he went to live with an elder brother until he was seventeen, after which he worked by the month until he was twenty-two. He was married Nov. 17, 1842, to Susana Hanson, a native of North Carolina. To them were born nine children, only seven now living—Isaac N., Mary M., Hannah I., Charles E., Samuel M., Washington J. and Eliza M. John W. and Elijah H. are deceased. After his marriage he rented land and followed the avocation of farming, and by strict attention to his farming pursuits he has been highly successful, and gave his children a good and practical education, and fitted them for useful citizens. In

1855 he came to Bern Township, Athens County, where he has since resided. He has a fine farm with all the modern improvements. He has been elected by the people to nearly all the local offices of trust and responsibility.

Edwin F. Glazier was born in Bern Township, Athens County, June 30, 1842, where he was reared on a farm and educated in the common schools. At the breaking out of the late civil war he enlisted in Company B, Fifty-third Ohio Volunteer Infantry, and participated in many hard-fought battles. In 1863 his term of enlistment expired, and he re-enlisted and served until the close of the war, and was mustered out of the service; returned to the home of his birth and for a time attended school, after which he engaged in farming, which he has since followed. In connection with his farming pursuits in 1875 he purchased the store at Big Run, Ohio, and engaged in the mercantile business for about four years, when he sold out and returned to his farm. He was married Oct. 19, 1870, to Hannah N. Greenwalt, of Washington County. They have three children—Arla M., Effa B. and William E. F.

W. R. Goddard was born in Washington County, Ohio, March 24, 1849. He was reared on a farm, and received his early education in the common schools, and spent three years at the Marietta College, after which he engaged in teaching school about three years. In the latter year he was elected to the office of County Treasurer of Washington County. He was first married, May 8, 1878, to Annie Black, of Washington County. They had two children—Blanche and Charles. His wife died Feb. 23, 1881. He was again married, Sept. 14, 1882, to Fanny E. Henry, a daughter of Charles and Fanny (Dean) Henry, of Bern Township, Athens County, Ohio. He has a fine farm of 232 acres of good land on Federal Creek. His wife is a member of the Presbyterian church at Amesville. He is a member of the I. O. O. F., Palmer Lodge, No. 351.

Charles Henry was born in Bern Township, Athens County, Ohio, April 18, 1821, son of John and Margaret Henry, who settled on the farm where our subject now lives, in 1817. He received his education in the schools at Amesville. He has always lived on the old homestead and cared for his parents in their old age. He was married Sept. 18, 1848, to Fanny M., daughter of Nathan and Fanny Dean, of Ames Township, Athens County. They have had five children—Charles E., Nathan Wm., Fanny E., Carlos D., Augusta M. (deceased). He has given his children upon their reaching their majority each a good farm. The homestead contains 360 acres of land, and is one of the finest in the county. He has a fine residence and large and commodious barns and stables. He has a large and beautiful fish pond, well-stocked with the choice varieties of fish. Mr. Henry has always led a quiet life, never aspiring to publicity, but in 1881 he was persuaded by his friends to accept their proffered suffrage, and was elected by a large majority to the office of Director of the Athens County Infirmary, which he has filled with honor to himself and credit to his constituents.

David Henry was born in Bern Township, Athens County, Jan. 19, 1827, son of John and Margaret Henry, where he was reared on a farm and educated in the common schools. He was united in marriage April 11, 1850, to Miss Margaret A. Owen, of Ames Township, Athens County. They are the parents of eight children, seven only now living—Florina, Marcela, Ray, Jennie, Mary, Nora, George B. and Bradford. He has a fine farm containing 160 acres of land under a high state of cultivation.

George E. Henry, the youngest son of Robert and Lavina (Glazier) Henry, was born in Bern Township, on the same farm and in the house where he has since resided, Aug. 15, 1841. Received his early education in the common schools of his native township, finishing in the Ohio University, at Athens. His youth was spent in assisting his father on the farm and attending school. After leaving school he engaged in teaching until the breaking out of the late civil war, when he enlisted, June 24, 1863, in Battery K, Second Ohio Volunteer Heavy Artillery, and was appointed Quartermaster-Sergeant, but served on detached duty as clerk in the office of Provost Marshal and Provost-Marshal Generals at Knoxville, Tenn., until March, 1865, when he was appointed Hospital Steward at Knoxville, and served in that capacity until Aug. 12, 1865, when he was mustered out of the service, after which he returned to his home in Bern Township and took charge of the farm where he has since resided. After serving in various township offices he was elected to the office of Justice of the Peace, serving since 1870. He was united in marriage, Sept. 18, 1872, to Sarah C. Demming, daughter of Daniel and Louisa (Curtis) Demming, born in Washington County, July 15, 1850. They have one son—Heber Homer, born July 13, 1877. Mrs. Henry is a member of the Presbyterian church at Amesville. He is a member of the A. F. & A. M., Amesville Lodge, No. 278. He is also a member of Columbus Golden Post, No. 89, G. A. R.

Captain Robert Henry, deceased, was born of Irish parents in Chester County, Penn., Dec. 14, 1797, and came with his father's family to Newport, Washington Co., Ohio, in 1801, and five years later removed to Warren, four miles below Harmer, and in the spring of 1817 came to Athens County, and located in what is now Bern Township, where he assisted his father in clearing his land and opening up their frontier home. Having more than an ordinary education he engaged in the winter in teaching school, working on his farm in the summer. He was united in marriage to Lavina Glazier, Nov. 30, 1826, by Judge George Walker. He immediately moved on his farm, where he continued to reside until his death, a period of over fifty-four years. During his life he held several local offices of trust and responsibility. He was naturally of a retiring disposition, which prompted him to refuse places of this kind unless tendered him under circumstances that left no doubt in his mind that it was the earnest wish of his friends that he should accept their proffered suffrage. In 1826 he was commissioned by Governor Jeremiah Morrow Captain of the Second Light Infantry Company, First Brigade, Third Division, Militia of Ohio, which office he held until 1830, when he resigned his commission. In the fall of 1829 he received the appointment as Postmaster at Amesville, being the second Postmaster in that township. In 1834 he was elected Justice of the Peace, which office he held for several years. Mr. Henry and his wife were ardent workers in the cause of Christianity, and united with the Presbyterian church at Amesville, at the time of its organization in 1832. He was very affable, courteous and gentlemanly in his intercourse with mankind, and received, as he deserved, the confidence and respect of all who knew him. His wife died Oct. 31, 1857, and he, Jan. 5, 1881, leaving four sons and two daughters and a large number of relatives and friends to mourn his loss.

Mathew Henry, deceased, was born in Ireland in October, 1792, a son of John and Rachel Henry, and when he was about six months of age he came with his parents to the United States, and located in Chester County, Penn., where he lived until 1801, when they removed to Ohio and settled in Newport, Washington County. Five years later they moved to Warren, where they resided until August, 1817, when they came to Athens County, settling in what is now Bern Township, where he spent the remainder of his days. He was married Aug. 16, 1817, to Lavinia Proctor, who was born in Danvers, Essex Co., Mass., April 12, 1793, and came with her parents to the then Northwestern Territory in the same year and located in Washington County, where she was reared and educated. After their marriage they settled on a part of the tract of land previously purchased by his father, where he set to work clearing his land and improving his home. He followed the avocation of a farmer until his death, and was highly successful. Although he never aspired to publicity he accepted the proffered suffrage of his friends and was elected to many local offices of trust and responsibility, having served as Township Trustee for several years, and Justice of the Peace several years. Mr. Henry and his wife were active members of the Presbyterian church, having joined at the time of the organization in 1832. They were the parents of eight children, five still living. Mr. Henry died March 17, 1865, at the advanced age of seventy-three years, having retained the mental and physical vigor of his youth to a remarkable degree. Nov. 23, 1882, his wife followed, at the age of eighty-seven years.

Lorenzo Lovell was born in Morgan County, Ohio, July 13, 1840, a son of Thomas R. and a grandson of Thomas S. Lovell, who was prominently identified with the pioneers of the county. Our subject was reared on a farm and received his education in the common schools. In 1861 he went to California and engaged in the lumber business in which he met with good success, and returned to Athens County in 1864. He was married Feb. 7, 1867, to Hannah T. Hopkins, of Morgan County. They have three children—Thomas S., Hannah S., George O. After his return from California he engaged in farming, and raising and dealing in livestock. His farm contains 263 acres of good land under a high state of cultivation.

Charles B. McCune, farmer and stock-raiser, was born in Bern Township, Oct. 14, 1843, the fourth son of Samuel McCune. He was reared on a farm and educated in the common schools, living with his parents until the breaking out of the late civil war, when he enlisted, in September, 1862, in Company I, Seventh Ohio Cavalry. He participated in many hard fought battles; among some of the more prominent were the siege of Atlanta and Nashville. Just after they raised the siege of Atlanta he was taken prisoner. While out gathering feed for the horses the enemy made a charge and took several, and while going toward the enemy's lines our subject started for the woods and hid behind the trees and thus escaped, walking six miles without shoes, hat or coat. He was the only one who escaped. Three others afterward died in Andersonville Prison. He served for three years and at no time was he unable to attend to his duty, although once sent to the hospital but returned to his regiment without orders. He was discharged July 4, 1865, and returned to his native home, where he engaged in the avocation of farming, which he has since followed. He was married Nov. 29, 1871, to Nannie Marquis, a daughter of William M. Marquis, a native of Noble County. They have two children—Bernice G. and Effie I. He first purchased his present farm in 1871 containing fifty acres, and by strict attention to his pursuits he has added to it from time to time until he has a fine farm of 110 acres of good land under a high state of cultivation, where in 1880 he erected a fine residence.

Aaron Ogg was born in Athens County, Ohio, Oct. 5, 1826. He was reared on a farm and educated in the common schools. He was married Sept. 17, 1851, to Theodosia Wickham. Ten children were born to them—William W., Izola, Clarinda, Lucy, Elmer E., Arthur, Lydia, Lindley, Leonard and Charles. Mr. Ogg followed the avocation of farming until the breaking out of the late civil war, when he was among the first to answer to the call for men, and enlisted in August, 1861, in Company B, Fifty-third Ohio Volunteer Infantry. He engaged in the battle of Pittsburg Landing, when he was taken seriously ill and was unable for active duty, and received an honorable discharge in November, 1862, and returned to his home in Athens County and again engaged in farming. He now has a farm of seventy-five acres of good land. He is a member of the Columbus Golden Post, G. A. R., and also a member of A. F. & A. M., Amesville Lodge, No. 278.

Andrew J. Ogg, farmer and stock-raiser, was born in Athens County, Oct. 11, 1827, a son of Andrew and Lucy (Wright) Ogg, who came to Athens County among the first settlers. Our subject was reared on a farm. When he was about sixteen years of age he began work for himself, working out by the month for John Brown and George Walker for a period of ten years. About 1847 he purchased forty acres of land in Bern Township. He was married March 22, 1855, to Elizabeth Rathburn. Four sons and one daughter were born to them—David L., Sally A., Andrew L., William N. and Silas F. Mr. Ogg is a self-made man, having accumulated a large property by his own exertion and industry.

He has a farm of 400 acres of good land, where he makes a specialty of growing live stock. About 1857 he moved to Morgan County where he resided for about sixteen years, after which he returned to his native county where he has since resided. He is a member of A. F. & A. M., Amesville Lodge, No. 278.

Warren W. Selby was born in Washington County, Ohio, Dec. 7, 1822, a son of D. Selby. When our subject was about twelve years of age he came with his parents to Bern Township, Athens County, and settled on the farm where he has since lived. He received his education in the common schools. He was married Jan. 1, 1850, to Emily Garratson, a native of Jefferson County, but a resident of Morgan County. Six children were born to them—Ida E., Susan, J. W., F. M., A. D. and Metta A. Mr. Selby's home contains 300 acres of improved land with a fine brick residence erected in 1867, which with its surroundings has no superior in the township. He has one of the finest orchards in the county.

Ezra H. Wolfe was born in Ames Township, Athens Co., Ohio, Dec. 15, 1833, a son of George P. and Eliza (Walker) Wolfe. He was reared on a farm, and received his education in the common schools, residing with his parents until he was twenty-three years of age, when he went to Lee County, Ill., and remained two years. He was married Feb. 26, 1860, to Miss Polly Swett, a daughter of Johnson and Polly Swett, who were among the pioneers of this county. By this union there are five children—Addie A., Lolie B., A. O., Lizzie L. and Frank C. After his marriage he remained on the old homestead for about three years, when he purchased a farm of sixty-six acres, which he added to from time to time until it contained 100 acres of improved land, where he resided seven years. In 1871 he purchased the farm where he now lives, in Homer Township, Morgan County. It contains 150 acres of good land, under a high state of cultivation. Mr. Wolfe takes great interest in all the political questions of the day, and casts his suffrage with the Republican party.

Joseph H. Wolfe, Homer Township, Morgan County, was born in Porter County, Ind., Jan. 22, 1835, a son of Frederick and Margret Wolfe, who were natives of Ames Township, Athens County. When he was two years of age he came to Athens County with his parents, where he was reared on a farm and received his early education in the common schools, completing it in the Normal School at Albany, Lee Township, Athens Co., Ohio. After leaving

Jeremiah Iles

school he engaged in farming in the summer and teaching school in winter for about six years. He was married Nov. 1, 1855, to Nancy A. Sayers, a daughter of Stacy Sayers, who came to Athens County from Marshall, W. Va., in 1835. They have five children —Stacy F., Lona H., Nina R., Margie C. and Ettie J. Mr. Wolfe is the owner of 320 acres of improved land. He has been elected to nearly all the local offices in the township. Mrs. Wolfe is a member of the Church of the Disciples. He is a member of A. F. & A. M., Bishopville Lodge.

George Wyatt, deceased, was born in Ames Township, Athens Co., Ohio, Aug. 21, 1821, the oldest child of John and Emily (Carpenter) Wyatt, and a grandson of Joshua Wyatt, who was prominently identified with the first settlers of Ames Township. He was reared on a farm and received his education in the schools at Amesville, and by strict attention to his study he obtained more than an ordinary education. He was married Dec. 20, 1842, to Miss Drusilla Tedrow, a daughter of Jacob and Mary Tedrow, who were among the pioneers of Rome Township. They had ten children, only eight now living—Emily (deceased), Julia A., Chauncey P., Mary J., George E., Nettie L. (deceased), Charles S., Genevieve A., Leonna D., Byron W. Mr. Wyatt came on the farm where his family now lives immediately after his marriage. He and his wife have been members of the Presbyterian church since 1842. Mr. Wyatt was foremost in lending his influence and donating from his own liberal means to every laudable enterprise that would be of interest and benefit to the county in which he resided. Besides caring well for those of his own household, he was not unmindful of the wants of others, and was the means of relieving the wants of many. He died April 9, 1873.

CHAPTER XXVI.

CARTHAGE TOWNSHIP—THE BEAUTY OF ITS LANDSCAPE.

The Act Which Organized it—Taken From Troy Township in November, 1819—Area—Facts and Fiction Combined—Lost Records—Office Holders—The Pioneers—A Panther's Familiarity—First Mill—First Postmaster—Population by Decades—Growth Slow, but Substantial—Churches and Schools—Biographical.

THE ACT THAT MADE IT.

Carthage Township was not organized until 1819, the territory being taken from Troy, and in the records of the County Commissioners the following resolution appears:

"Nov. 10, 1819—*Resolved*, That all that part of the township of Troy included in township 5, range 12, and the east half of township 4, range 13, be a separate township by the name of *Carthage*."

The township is six miles square and has 23,040 acres of beautiful and fruitful land. It is bounded on the north by Rome Township, on the east by Troy Township, on the south by Meigs County, and on the west by Lodi Township, and lies in the south tier of sections, and second from the eastern boundary line of the county. It is watered by the east branch of Shade Creek and several others of less magnitude. The surface is somewhat hilly, but of a less rough and rugged nature than some of her sister townships. The soil is of such a nature as to yield to the husbandman excellent crops of grain, and its green hilltops afford the best of grazing, which is one of the essentials to successful stock-raising. Thus it is found that land and water, hill and valley, are so united in this township as to combine all the essentials which go to make farming a success. It is therefore not surprising that Carthage Township, with its rich virgin soil, should entice the early settler to locate here and secure the rich lands which produce such abundant returns for the labor expended. The emigrant

"Sought fresh fountains in a foreign soil,
The pleasures less'ning the attending toil."

When we take the beauty of its surroundings and the fertility of its soil, there is little more to wish for to the farmer or stock-raiser of Carthage Township, and he would indeed be hard to please if, in choosing an agricultural life, the lands of this township did not fill the full meed of his desire. Upon the organization of the township the inhabitants were directed to meet on a specified day and elect township officers. The records of the township prior to 1855 have been lost, consequently no list of its early office-holders can be given, but among the first Trustees of the township were Stephen Buckingham, Joseph Guthrie, Francis Caldwell, Alex. Caldwell, Moses Elliott and B. B. Lottridge. The first Justice of the Peace in the township was Milton Buckingham, and Joseph Guthrie and Francis Caldwell were among the earliest, also, who held that office.

FIRST SETTLERS.

The first known white settler of Carthage Township was Ashabel Cooley, Sr., who came from near Springfield, Mass., and after traversing the dense wilderness between Muskingum and the Hocking, settled in this township in the year 1799, and with the aid of his grown-up sons soon prepared a home. He was a man possessed of great native mental vigor, shrewd business tact, and by his industry and integrity did much toward the advancement of civilization, and for many years held offices of trust in both township and county. In 1800 came Abram Frost who, with his large family, settled in this township, and in 1801 were joined by Ebenezer Buckingham, Sr., and his brother Stephen. In 1805 came Bernardus B. Lottridge, a native of New York. At the time of his coming there was not more than a dozen inhabitants in the township, and the forests were full of their native denizens. A large panther walked into the cabin of Mr. Lottridge one evening and stood before the fire, whereupon Mr. Lottridge seized a large butcher knife and would have attacked him had it not been for the entreaties of his wife; her screams frightened the animal and it soon darted through the door and beat a hasty retreat. These early settlers were soon followed by Alex. Caldwell, William Jeffers, Moses, John and James Elliott, James Baker and many others, and the township became generally settled at an early day, all its parts having some attraction for the pioneer.

FIRST MILL.

The first grist-mill in the township was built by Joseph Guthrie, in 1820, on his farm near the southeast corner of section 6. The power was derived from a small stream which took its name from him and is still known by the name of Guthrie's Creek. Since that time there has been several saw and grist-mills erected in the township, but they have all gone out of existence. There are none in the township at the present time worthy of mention. The business of Carthage is solely agricultural and there is not a village within its limits. It has one postoffice, established in 1851, called Lottridge postoffice from its being located in the Lottridge neighborhood. The first Postmaster was Edward Lawrence, who retained the position for many years.

POPULATION.

As before stated, the township was not organized until 1819, and in 1820 the population was 320. During the following ten years it only increased seventy-five in its population, in 1830 being 395.

The next decade it nearly doubled, as the census report of 1840 showed a population of 734. In 1850 it was 1,087; in 1860, 1,127; while in 1870 it was 1,272, and in 1880 it had reached 1,308. It will be seen by these figures that the growth of the population in Carthage Township has been slow, even below what should have been its natural growth, but it has an enterprising, thrifty class of people which gives stability to the community in which they are located. There has been nothing of importance to disturb the serenity of the people of this township for many years. With this steady means of population the area of cultivated lands has become more extended, and with it those great additions to the progress of civilization and Christianity, schools and churches.

CHURCHES.

Carthage Township has five churches, as follows: Two Methodist, one Presbyterian, one United Brethren and one Christian.

The Methodists were the pioneers of this township, their society being organized as early as 1812. One of their churches is located in the extreme western part of the township, on section 35, and the other on fraction 2, near the residence of John Lawrence. The Christian church was the next to organize and is located in the southern part of the township on section 19. The organization was effected in about 1835, and the United Brethren in about 1840.

The Presbyterian Church was organized in 1850 and they have a very neat church located on section 23. The churches in this township are all in a flourishing condition and only need energetic work to extend their usefulness and the greater exercise of their influence for good. With their surroundings they have a splendid field for labor, and should be fully used to extend their power and for the good of the churches and for the glory of God.

SCHOOLS.

The schools of Carthage Township number nine and are all in a condition of progressiveness. In fact, if there is any one thing that has shown the sound judgment of the people of this township it has been their determined and persevering effort in the cause of education.

BIOGRAPHICAL.

John Barnhill, born in Jefferson County, Ohio, June 26, 1828, is a son of Robert Barnhill, a native of Ireland, who came to America when quite young. When he was seven years old his parents removed to Coshocton County, where he lived till twenty-one years of age. He then came to Athens County and lived a short time, and then went to Wayne County, Ill., returning after three years to Carthage. He was married Feb. 17, 1859, to Margaret Swiss, of Carthage Township. They have eight children— Elizabeth C., John W., Burgett, Louisa J., Rosilla, Sarah E., Samuel and Catharine F. Mr. Barnhill received but a limited education in his youth, but by careful observation and study he has acquired a good practical education. He is giving his children the best advantages that the county affords, that they may be fitted to fill any station in life.

C. Bason, born in Coshocton County, Ohio, Dec. 10, 1834, is a son of Joseph Bason, a native of Pennsylvania, born in 1805, now residing with his son. When he was four years of age his parents moved to Washington County, where he was reared and educated. In 1855 he came to Carthage Township, and in 1869 bought the farm where he now resides. He has 200 acres of well-improved land, with a fine residence and farm buildings. He was married

March 15, 1860, to Elizabeth J. Alger. Four children were born to them—Joseph, J. M., Esther A. and Sarah Ellen. Mrs. Bason died May 27, 1867. Politically Mr. Bason is a Republican.

George Blazer, son of David and Mary (Davis) Blazer, was born in Washington County, Pa., April 16, 1801. When twenty-one years of age he went to Columbiana County, Ohio, and engaged in coal-mining and in salt works eight years. In October, 1836, he came to Athens County, and settled on what is now known as the old Burson farm. He was for many years engaged in buying and selling land, so has changed his residence a number of times, though the most of the time he has lived in Lodi Township. Since 1878 he has made his home with his son-in-law, William Day. Aug. 12, 1825, he married Susan Moore. They reared a family of eleven children—Cyrus, David, Hiram, James, Mordecai, William, Charles, Harriet, Mary, Sarah A. and Joanna. Six sons and two sons-in-law were in the Union army during the war of the Rebellion.

Joseph Caldwell, deceased, was a native of Pennsylvania, and settled in Carthage Township in an early day, where he improved a good farm. He married Mary Fish, a native of Meigs County, Ohio. They had one child—Mary, who married A. W. Nickeson, of Meigs County, Dec. 8, 1880, and is now living on the old homestead. They have a fine farm of 240 acres all under a good state of cultivation. Mr. Caldwell died June 16, 1862, aged forty-three years, five months and nine days.

William Day, born in Lodi Township, Athens Co., Ohio, April 26, 1838, is a son of James and Lucy H. (Pearson) Day, his father a native of New Jersey, and his mother of New Hampshire. He is the oldest of a family of three sons and one daughter. He was married May 13, 1858, to Sarah A. Blazer, and settled on section 1, Lodi Township, where he lived four years. He then bought the farm on section 25, Carthage Township, where he still resides. He has 215 acres of good land and is engaged in general farming, making a specialty of raising sheep and cattle. Aug. 27, 1864, he enlisted in Company E, One Hundred and Seventy-fourth Ohio Infantry, and was discharged June 28, 1865. He is a member of the A. F. & A. M. fraternity, at Coolville.

James Elliott, son of Moses Elliott, was born Jan. 22, 1826, in Carthage Township. He resided on the farm where he was born till 1879 when he bought the farm where he now lives. He has 300 acres of well-improved land, with good buildings. Mr. Elliott has served as Township Clerk fourteen years and Township Treasurer twelve years. Jan. 22, 1875, he was appointed Postmaster at Lottridge. He was married April 12, 1855, to Catherine, daughter of Peter and Jane Hammond. They have three children—Ann Jane, born May 10, 1857; Charles Lincoln, July 9, 1860, and Robert Grant, Aug. 29, 1864.

J. D. Evans, son of Hans and Elizabeth Evans, was born Sept. 22, 1837, in Morgan County, Ohio. When he was quite small his parents came to Lodi Township and settled on what is now the Windell Shott farm. When he was eight years of age they moved to Bedford Township, Meigs County, where our subject was reared and educated, spending the greater portion of his early life in farming and milling. May 1, 1864, he enlisted in Company C, One Hundred and Forty-first Ohio Infantry. His term of enlistment was short but was distinguished by memorable events in the Shenandoah Valley, on the James River, around Petersburg and Richmond, in the intrenchments before Washington and other important service. In the fall of 1870 he came to Athens County and settled on the farm where he now resides. He has ninety acres of good land well improved. He was married March 13, 1862, to Augusta, daughter of S. T. Hull, of Lodi. They have four children—Samuel E., Martha J., Hiram and Grove. Politically Mr. Evans is a Republican.

Moses Elliott, deceased, was born in County Donegal, Ireland, Feb. 1, 1784, a son of John and Fanny (Blain) Elliott. He came to America in 1819, landing at New York, after being fifteen weeks at sea. He first settled in Washington County, Pa., where he lived four years. Dec. 5, 1825, he came to Athens County, stopping first at Hockingport, and Dec. 8 came to Carthage. He was married in 1815 to Jane, daughter of James Cuscaden. They reared a family of seven children—John, Mary, Susannah, Eliza Jane, James, Frances Ann and Sarah. The two eldest were born in Ireland, the next three in Washington County, Pa., and the two youngest in Athens County. Mr. Elliot was Justice of the Peace twelve years and Township Clerk and Trustee several years. In religious faith he was a Methodist. Politically he was a Republican. He died Dec. 19, 1854.

D. G. Frost, born in Lodi Township, Athens Co., Ohio, March 7, 1831, is a son of Abner and Rachel (Sullivan) Frost. In 1835 or '6 his parents moved to Meigs County, and years after his father went to Wisconsin, where he died, in 1852. D. G. was educated in the common schools, and when twenty years of age went to learn the cabinet-maker's and carpenter's trades, working at the two combined a number of years. July 1, 1855, he married Ruth Ann, daughter of Aaron Stout, a pioneer of Carthage Township. Aug. 12, 1862, he enlisted in Company B, One Hundred and Sixteenth Ohio Infantry. The regiment was in the battles of Moorfield, Winchester, New Market, Piedmont, Lynchburg, Fisher's Hill, Hatches Run, and numerous others. He was discharged June 24, 1865, and returned home. In the spring of 1867 he bought the farm where he now resides. He has 100 acres of good land, which he has improved in a fine manner. Mr. and Mrs. Frost have four children—Clarence, Elwood, Albert and Allen. Politically Mr. Frost is a Republican. He has held most of the township offices. He is a member of the Christian church.

J. W. Glazier, son of Walter Glazier, was born Jan. 14, 1844, in Athens County, Ohio. Aug. 18, 1862, he enlisted in Company I, One Hundred and Sixteenth Ohio Infantry; was in the principal battles of the Shenandoah Valley and around Petersburg and Richmond; was slightly wounded twice, and was taken prisoner and taken to Belle Isle. Was paroled and exchanged, and came home for a short furlough, then rejoined the regiment at Martinsburg, and was with them till the close of the war, being present at the surrender of Lee's army; was discharged at Richmond, mustered out at Camp Denison, and returned home. May 6, 1868, he married Mary M., daughter of Seneca and Irena Hatch, of Rome Township. They have two children—Frank W. and Fannie Fern. In 1871 Mr. Glazier moved on his present farm, where he has ninety-seven acres of good land. He is engaged in farming and stock-raising, making a specialty of Alderny cattle. Politically Mr. Glazier is a Republican.

Walter Glazier, son of Abel and Sally Glazier, was born July 6, 1807, in Ames Township, Athens Co., Ohio. In June, 1831, he married Elizabeth Bolander, of Ross County, Ohio. Seven children were born to them—R. B., Mahala, Laura, Lavinia, James, Mary Jane and Elizabeth. Dec. 21, 1850, Mr. Glazier married Mrs. Laura P. Glazier, daughter of Elijah Hatch, of Athens County. They have three children—Sybil V., E. P. and Addie Rosella. Mr. Glazier came to Carthage Township in 1837, and now owns a farm of 262 acres of fine land.

James Hammond, son of Peter and Jane Hammond, was born Dec. 19, 1826. He received but a limited education, his assistance being required on the farm. He lived at home till thirty years of age. April 6, 1864, he married Susan, daughter of H. H.

and Susan Parsons. They have no children, but have adopted James W. Kincaid and Abertha Bursons into their home. They are members of the Presbyterian church, and are among the influential citizens of Carthage Township. Mr. Hammond has a farm of 300 acres, well improved, with a good dwelling and commodious barn.

John Hammond, born in Jefferson County, Ohio, Oct. 15, 1822, is a son of Peter and Jane (Long) Hammond, natives of Pennsylvania, his father of English and German, and his mother of Irish and German descent. He was the third of a family of nine children—William, Eliza, John, Oliver, James, Mary, Katherine, Margaret and Seth. His early life was spent on a farm, his education being received in the common schools and by studying at home. In 1842 he came to Carthage and built a tan house, following that business six years very successfully. He then bought 100 acres of wild land on section 24, which he cleared and improved, living there till 1865, when he bought the farm where he now lives. He has 242 acres which is well adapted for the raising of stock, in which Mr. Hammond is extensively engaged. He has a fine two-story residence, built in modern style and well furnished. Aug. 28, 1844, he was married to Belinda Caldwell, who died leaving three children—Samantha, Mary and Edward. Oct. 30, 1867, he married Catharine Caldwell. They have three children—Henry, Bettie J. and James Arthur. Mr. Hammond has held the office of Justice of the Peace six years.

D. H. Jones, son of H. B. and Susan Jones, was born July 30, 1844, the second of a family of eight children, also one of four of the family that served their time out during the war. He enlisted June 9, 1861, in the war of the Rebellion, in Company C, Third Ohio Infantry; was mustered in the service at Camp Denison, then sent to Virginia under the command of McClellan; was at the battle of Rich Mountain and through the campaign of Virginia until December, 1861, then transferred to the Western army under General Mitchell's command. In May, 1862, he had his jaw broken in a skirmish near Governor Clay's farm in Alabama. He was also in a skirmish in 1862 at Bridgeport; in the battle of Perryville in 1862, receiving a slight wound, and in the battle of Stone River was wounded in the right side, from the effect of which he has never recovered. He, with the rest of the regiment, was detailed mounted infantry in Streight's raid through Georgia; during the time was in some severe skirmishes; was taken prisoner with the rest of the command and taken to Belle Isle, paroled and returned to Camp Chase, Ohio; from there engaged in the Morgan raid through Ohio, then returned to the army, but did only guard duty on account of commanding officers being prisoners. He was discharged June 20, 1864, and returned home. Feb. 18, 1865, he married Mary St. Clair, who died leaving one son, John H. March 25, 1868, he married Lurena Rogers, daughter of John Rogers, a soldier in the war of 1812. They have three children—Geneva B., William C, and Myrtle A. Mr. Jones owns one of the best farms in the township. He has 100 acres with a two-story residence built in 1882, and a good barn and farm buildings.

Edward Lawrence, son of Moses and Sarah Lawrence, was born in Grafton County, N. H., April 16, 1810. He was the sixth of a family of ten children, three of whom are now living. He was married Jan. 19, 1832, to Maria Sweet, a native of New Hampshire, and five years later he came to Athens County, locating on the farm, where he still resides. It was only partly cleared, but he has improved it, till now he has one of the best farms in the township. He was the first Postmaster of this township, holding the position twenty-four years. He has been Township Trustee two years and Treasurer two years. Mr. and Mrs. Lawrence have four children—Hannah, Nathan, Elza and Charles. One son, Arthur, enlisted in Company K, Thirty-ninth Ohio Infantry; was wounded at Atlanta, Ga., July 22, 1864, and died Aug. 27, 1864. Mr. Lawrence has been a member of the Methodist church thirty years. Politically he is a Republican.

John Lawrence, born May 2, 1808, in Grafton County, N. H., was a son of Moses and Sarah (Johnson) Lawrence. His early life was spent on a farm, and he received but a common-school education. In 1837 he started for Athens County, coming with teams; was forty-two days on the road. He settled in Carthage Township on the place where he now lives. It was then a wild, heavy timbered piece of land, but now, through the industry of Mr. Lawrence, it is a fine, well-cultivated farm of 200 acres, with first-class improvements. March 20, 1831, Mr. Lawrence married Keziah J. Sweet, of Belknap County, N. H. They have five children—Anna, Charles, Mahala, Horace and Mary. A son, Wesley, enlisted in Company E, One Hundred and Seventy-fourth Ohio Infantry, at Newton, N. C. He was wounded, from the effects of which he died March 14, 1865. Mr. Lawrence has been a member of the Methodist Episcopal church sixty years.

N. S. Lawrence, son of Edward and Maria (Sweet) Lawrence, was born in Carthage Township, Jan. 6, 1844. In May, 1864, he enlisted in Company K, One Hundred and Fortieth Ohio Infantry, and was discharged Sept. 3, 1864. Oct. 8, 1867, he married Martha, daughter of Francis and Catharine (Flick) Griffin, of Troy Township. In November, 1867, he moved to the farm where he now resides. He has 186 acres of land under a high state of cultivation. In 1877 he built a fine two-story residence. Mr. and Mrs. Lawrence are members of the Methodist Episcopal church. Politically he is a Prohibitionist.

Bernardus B. Lottridge, son of Thomas and Elizabeth Lottridge, was born in Rensselaer County, N. Y., in 1780. When nineteen years of age he married Abigail Bull, and removed to Niagara, where he lived four years. In 1803 he came to Athens County, being among the first settlers, and located on wild land. He improved, with the help of his two sons, 525 acres of heavily timbered land, and at the time of his death was one of the well-to-do citizens of the county. Mr. and Mrs. Lottridge's children were—Isaac, John, Caroline, Simon, Emma, Maria, Thomas, Sarah, George, Joseph, Amanda, Catharine and Marcus. Mr. Lottridge was a member of the Methodist church forty years.

J. D. Lottridge, section 3, Carthage Township, was born Jan. 2, 1818, the son of B. B. Lottridge, one of the pioneers of this county. Our subject was reared on a farm, and received his education in the common schools. In August, 1838, he married Margaret McCleon. Five children were born to them—Geraldine, Ellozine, Caroline (deceased), Josephine V. and William. Mrs. Lottridge died March 8, 1880. May 10, 1881, he married Mrs. Rebecca J. Robertson. She is the mother of one child—Nettie R. Mr. Lottridge has a fine farm of 170 acres, all well improved.

Simon H. Lottridge, the oldest native of Carthage, now living in the township, was born Feb. 3, 1807, son of B. B. and Abigail (Bull) Lottridge. He was married in March, 1829, to Elizabeth, daughter of Ben Coddington, an early settler of Troy Township. After his marriage he removed to Marietta, Ohio, and remained about a year; then removed to McArthur, which was then in Athens and now Vinton County, where he lived seven years engaged in the wool-carding business. In February, 1838, he returned to the old homestead, where he has since resided. He has a fine farm of 260 acres, all well improved. He has held the office of Justice two terms, Assessor two years, and Township Trustee several years.

Politically he is a Republican. Mr. and Mrs. Lottridge have had eight children, six now living—Catharine, Lydia, Almira and Alvira (twins), Sarah and May. Abigail and Mary Jane are deceased. Mr. Lottridge is a member of the Methodist Episcopal church.

G. W. Lowden, born in Meigs County, Ohio, Feb. 5, 1841, is a son of John and Margaret Lowden, natives of England, who settled in Meigs County in 1833. He enlisted in the war of the Rebellion in the Second West Virginia Cavalry, and served three years and four months; was in the battles of Pottsville, Lewisburg, Lynchburg, Winchester, Cedar Creek and numerous others; was discharged at Wheeling, W. Va. He married Sarah Lax, of Meigs County, and a daughter of George and Elizabeth Lax. They have five children—Thomas S., Lizzie, John, George and Earl E. One daughter, Annie, died in March, 1882, aged eight years. Mr. Lowden owns a farm of eighty acres under a good state of cultivation. Politically he is a Republican. He is a member of the I. O. O. F.

C. McNeil, deceased, was born in Meigs County, Ohio, April 29, 1827, the son of Archie McNeil, a native of New York. He was reared a farmer, and received his education in the common schools. He was married Nov. 14, 1850, to Lydia A. Gleason, of Vinton County. He came to Carthage Township in 1855. Feb. 14, 1865, he enlisted in Company F, One Hundred and Eighty-ninth Ohio Infantry. He died April 15, 1865, leaving a wife and two children—Hiram H. and Perry P. Mr. McNeil was a member of the United Brethren church; a kind husband and father, and a good neighbor, he was respected by all who knew him. Mrs. McNeil still resides on the old farm with her son Perry P., who is a teacher.

Eli P. Persons, born Dec. 24, 1827, in Carthage Township, Athens County, Ohio, is a son of Sylvester and Lydia Persons, natives of Connecticut and Virginia respectively. His father died when he was twenty years old, and the next four years he worked by the month at farming. He was married Oct. 24, 1851, to Susan Bail, a native of Pennsylvania. Aug. 25, 1862, he enlisted in Company K, Seventy-third Ohio Infantry, but by the exposures of army life he lost his eyesight, and in November he was granted a furlough, but not recovering was discharged in February, 1863. Mr. and Mrs. Persons have five children—Sylvester, Almira J., Samuel, Elizabeth and Horace. Politically Mr. Persons is a Republican.

M. Pierce, born Sept. 29, 1823, in Meigs County, Ohio, is a son of Isaac and Fanny (Stout) Pierce. When three years of age he lost his father. When sixteen years of age he commenced to learn the tanner's and shoemaker's trades, at which he worked about six years. In 1845 he purchased the farm where he now resides, which he has brought under a good state of cultivation. He is now engaged in general farming and stock-raising. In September, 1845, he married Mercy Daily, daughter of Benjamin Daily, a pioneer of Athens County. They had a family of five children— Mary Jane, Florinda, Isaac, Louis Eldora and Emma Serilla. Mrs. Pierce died Jan. 6, 1875. Jan. 9, 1876, Mr. Pierce married Mrs. Mary (Day) Swarts. She has five children—Merzer, John, Israel, James and Mary Elizabeth. Mr. and Mrs. Pierce are members of the Christian church. He has been an Elder in the church several years.

Elijah Runnion, born in Lewis County, W. Va., March 25, 1811, is a son of Samuel and Ann (Batty) Runnion. When eleven years of age his parents moved to Kanawha County, W. Va., and soon after to Jackson County, where he was reared and educated, remaining there till 1849. In the latter year he came to Ohio, settling first in Meigs County, and moved to Athens County in 1861, where he still resides. He was married Aug. 29, 1833, to Harriet B. Smith, a native of Virginia, and a daughter of John and Susan Smith. They have six children—Rebecca, Mary, Catherine, James, Milo and Alexander. Mr. Runnion has been a member of the Methodist church sixty years. Politically he is a Republican.

M. M. Runnion, Carthage, was born March 14, 1847, a native of Virginia. He was reared on a farm and received his education in the common schools. At the age of sixteen he enlisted in Company F, Sixtieth Ohio Infantry. He was in several battles, and was discharged in August, 1865. Sept. 12, 1877, he married Ann Jane Elliott. They have two children—Lonna T. and Robert J. Mr. and Mrs. Runnion are members of the Methodist Episcopal church. In politics Mr. Runnion is a Republican.

James Russel, son of David Russel, was born in Coshocton County, Ohio, July 7, 1828, and came with his parents to Athens County in 1837. He lived at home till he arrived at manhood, receiving a limited education in the common schools. He was married Nov. 22, 1863, to Perezinda Price, a native of Athens County, and a daughter of James M. Price. They have seven children—Lincoln,

Sheridan, Adson, Clinton, Emma, Ada, Alma. Mr. Russel bought the farm where he now lives in 1858. He has 133 acres. Politically he is a Republican.

John Russell, son of David Russell, of Troy Township, was born in Coshocton County, Ohio, Dec. 26, 1819. He came to Athens County with his parents in 1838, and lived in Troy Township till he was of age. He was married May 27, 1847, to Nancy Morrison, of Jefferson County, Ohio, daughter of John Morrison. They have seven children—Winfield, Hannah, Timothy, Eber, Grant, Lot and Mahlon. Mr. Russell has a fine farm of 218 acres, with a good two-story house and comfortable farm buildings. Politically he is a Republican.

William Russell, a native of Coshocton County, Ohio, born May 19, 1824, is a son of David Russell. His parents came to Athens County when he was thirteen years old and settled in Troy Township, where his father still resides. Dec. 1, 1853, he married Mary Elliott, a daughter of William Elliott, a native of Ireland. They have four children—Almira, Selden C., David E. and William. Mr. Russell bought the farm where he now resides in 1854. He has 180 acres of good land with a good residence and farm buildings, where he has all the comforts of a home. He is a genial, whole-souled man and has the respect and confidence of all who know him.

Amasa Saunders, a native of Delaware County, N. Y., and a son of Jonathan and Mary (Buck) Saunders, was born March 20, 1809. He was the second of a family of eight children. When he was nine years of age his parents came to Athens County, locating in Carthage Township, which at that time had but few voters. His early life was spent in helping to clear the heavily timbered land, and he received but a limited education in the subscription schools. April 16, 1834, he married Louise Alden. They have but one child, a son—A. N. Saunders, a prominent man of this township. Mr. Saunders has been a member of the Methodist Episcopal church fifty-two years, and is one of its liberal supporters. He has one of the best farms in the township, and has acquired it by his industry and good management.

A. N. Saunders, proprietor of Slade Valley stock farm, is a son of Amasa Saunders. He was born in Carthage Township, July 20, 1835, and was reared and educated in his native township. Nov. 29, 1860, he married Harriet A., daughter of Moses and Roxanna Flanders. They have three children—Arthur B., Eva

M. and Ida R. Mr. Saunders moved to his present farm in 1866. He has one of the best farms in the township, consisting of 690 acres, and makes a specialty of high grade and registered Spanish merino sheep. He spends both time and money for their improvement and is rewarded by being the owner of the best flock in Athens County, having taken the first premium wherever he has exhibited them. Politically he is a Republican. He is a member of the Methodist church.

V. Smith, son of Frederick and Elizabeth Smith, was born Nov. 16, 1813, in Germany. He learned the weaver's trade in his native country and worked at it till 1843, when, wages being low, he determined to come to America. He landed in New York after a voyage of thirty-two days, and came to Athens County, settling in Lodi Township, where he now has a good farm of 150 acres. He has a store of general merchandise, having a good stock of dry goods, boots and shoes, etc., where he has a good trade. He was married in Germany to Miss P. Richport. They have eleven children—Anthony, Peter, John, Fred, George, Jacob, Phœbe, Sophia, Elizabeth, Mary and Michael. Politically, Mr. Smith is a Democrat. He is a member of the Catholic church.

Aaron Stout, Sr., was born near Trenton, N. J., June 2, 1768. He came to Ohio in 1806, settling in Meigs County. In 1814 he came to Athens County and settled on section 19, Carthage Township. He married Sarah Praull, and to them were born nine children—Letitia, George, Abner, Fanny, Mary, Ruth, Charles, Aaron, and John.

Aaron Stout, Jr., was born in Meigs County, Ohio, July 6, 1810. When four years of age he came to Carthage Township, where he was reared and educated. He was married March 23, 1833, to Martha McIntyre, a native of Pennsylvania, born May 11, 1808. They had a family of six children—Lizzie, Ruth Ann, Sophia, Harrison, J. M. and Sarah Jane. Mr. Stout was a member of the Christian church. He died May 5, 1866.

Charles Stout, son of George and Eliza Stout, was born on the farm where he now resides April 24, 1827. November, 1854, he was married to Ellen Gregory, of Carthage Township. Mrs. Stout died Nov. 11, 1868, leaving one child—Addie. Nov. 20, 1870, Mr. Stout married Louise Wiley, daughter of James Wiley, of Meigs County. They have one daughter—Mary Belle, born Oct. 19, 1876. Mr. Stout has 402 acres of well-improved land with a fine dwelling, well furnished, and surrounded by shade and ornamental trees. Politically he is a Republican.

Cyrenus Stout, son of George and Eliza Stout, was born in Meigs County, Ohio, and came to Carthage Township, Athens County, when four years of age, where he was reared and educated. Nov. 18, 1841, he married Mary Childs, daughter of Seth and Dinah Frost Childs. They had three children—Leander, Elmedia and George W. In 1841 Mr. Stout settled on the farm where he now resides. He has 640 acres of good land which he has brought from a wild state to its present highly cultivated condition. He has a good residence, well furnished, where his family have all the comforts of a good home. Mr. Stout's present wife was Sarah M., daughter of Moses Elliott. They were married Nov. 3, 1859, and have three children—Horace, John and Jerome. Politically Mr. Stout is a Republican. He has held the offices of Township Trustee and Treasurer, and Assessor.

George Stout, deceased, son of Aaron Stout, Sr., was born near Trenton, N. J., March 17, 1792. When fourteen years of age he came with his parents to Ohio. He was married in 1820 to Eliza Buzzard, a daughter of Peter Buzzard. In 1825 he came to Athens County and settled on section 19, Carthage Township, which at that time was wild timbered land, but he went bravely to work and brought it under a good state of cultivation. Mr. and Mrs. Stout had a family of three children—Cyrenus, Charles and Fannie (Mrs. Hecox). Mr. Stout was a member of the Christian church for over thirty years. He died April 21, 1875, aged eighty-three years. Mrs. Stout died Aug. 17, 1869.

J. M. Stout, son of Aaron and Martha Stout, was born in Carthage Township, Sept. 19, 1842, where he was reared and educated. Aug. 12, 1862, he enlisted in Company B, One Hundred and Sixteenth Ohio Infantry, and was in all the regiment's engagements except the fight round Petersburg, when he was detailed at headquarters. He enlisted as private, and was discharged as Duty Sergeant June 23, 1865. July 4, 1867, he married Lulinda Hecox, daughter of Truman Hecox, of Meigs County. They have five children—Adella Moselle, Emerson, Elmont, Mrytie Jeanette and Elmy. Mr. Stout has a good farm of 182 acres, and is engaged in general farming and stock-raising. He is a member of the Christian church. Politically, he is a Republican. He has never been an aspirant for office, though frequently urged by his friends to accept one.

Selden C. Stout was born in Carthage Township, July 7, 1833. He received a good education in the common schools and at Coolville Seminary. When twenty-six years of age he married Mary Jane, daughter of J. Davies, of Meigs County. He first settled on section 25, where he lived seven years. He then bought a farm on section 32 where he still resides. He has 460 acres of good land, well improved, and is engaged in general farming and stock-raising. In August, 1864, he enlisted in Company E, One Hundred and Seventy-fourth Ohio Infantry, and was discharged at the close of the war. Mr. and Mrs. Stout have four children—Anna S., Ida Rosilla, Elmer C. and Dora Aurilla. Mr. Stout's father, Charles Stout, came to Carthage Township in 1814 and lived here till his death, July 2, 1856. He married Roxy Childs, and to them were born three children—Selden C., Marinda and Samantha.

W. O. Stout was born in Meigs County, Ohio, Dec. 15, 1851, a son of Aaron and Mary (Hoffman) Stout. His education was received in the common district schools and at Tupper's Plains Seminary. When twenty years of age he embarked in the mercantile business at Osage, and five years later came to Carthage. In 1879 he moved to his brother-in-law's farm, which contains 260 acres of land under a good state of cultivation, with good buildings, and is engaged in general farming and stock-raising. Oct. 1, 1873, he married Mary A., daughter of John Lawrence. They have two children—Nora May and Charles Leslie. Politically, Mr. Stout is a Republican, and is at present Clerk of Carthage Township. He is a member of the Methodist church.

Francis Tibbles, son of John and Jane Tibbles, was born in Carthage Township, Athens Co., Ohio, Jan. 26, 1826. His youth was spent in assisting his father to improve the farm, receiving but a limited education in the subscription schools. He now owns a fine farm of 200 acres, all well improved. May 21, 1856, he married E. J. Elliot, a native of Ireland, and a daughter of William Elliot, who settled in Athens County in 1842. They have three children—Elza G., Sarah Frances and William E. One son, Albert, died in 1861; another, Addison B., died April 2, 1883, and a daughter, Nellie, died in 1882. Politically, Mr. Tibbles is a Democrat. He is a member of the Masonic fraternity.

John Tibbles, deceased, was born in Pennsylvania, Sept. 16, 1796, a son of Thomas and Elizabeth (Hayes) Tibbles. He was reared in his native State, and in 1817 came to Athens County, Ohio, and settled on the farm now owned by his son Francis. It was wild, heavily timbered land, the nearest house being four miles east of it. He improved a farm of 130 acres, and, being a brick-maker by trade, made the brick of which his residence is built. He was married in 1818 to Jane Caldwell, a native of Ireland, who came to America when five years of age. They had a family of six children—James, Alexander, Francis, Elizabeth, John, Joseph. Joseph and Alexander were members of the Seventy-fifth Ohio Infantry and died in the service in 1862 and 1863. Mr. Tibbles died Jan. 4, 1866, and his wife, April 19, 1878.

Daniel Walker, born in Indiana County, Pa., Oct. 11, 1800, was a son of Adam and Hester (Chance) Walker. His father died in 1813, of yellow fever. When fifteen years of age he came to Jefferson County, Ohio, and resided about five years. May 1, 1820, he was hired to drive a four-horse team to Orange Township, Meigs County. Jan. 28, 1825, he married Mary Ryther, a native of Ohio, who died Aug. 28, 1876, leaving two children—Sarah Ann and R. Becky. In the fall of 1826 Mr. Walker bought a farm on section 25, where he lived five years and then traded it for 100 acres in the southwestern part of the section where he still resides. June 10, 1880, he married Mrs. Ruth (Wingate) Frost, a native of Pennsylvania. She has two children—Olive and Angeline. Mr. Walker has an adopted son—Charles Albert Sarson. Politically he is a Democrat. He has held the office of Township Trustee a number of years. In religious faith he is a Methodist.

CHAPTER XXVII.

DOVER AND TRIMBLE TOWNSHIPS.

OUTLINE—EARLY SETTLERS—TOWNSHIP OFFICIALS—SUNDAY CREEK VALLEY—MINERAL RESOURCES—SOCIAL PERIODS—BIOGRAPHICAL.

Every locality, however contracted, or, in the estimation of the masses, without anything worthy of note, has its historical materials that deserve to be collected, and accurately written and faithfully preserved. Such is strictly true of the territory whose history we propose to sketch.

But few pages of this history are occupied with the Dover and Trimble divisions, and Sunday Creek Valley plays a very subordinate part in the county affairs, while worthy of a far more extended notice.

OUTLINE VIEW OF THE WHOLE DISTRICT.

There is a high elevation, like a natural mound, in southern Trimble, which throws within your horizon the whole territory, including the valleys of Sugar Creek, Hocking and Lower Sunday Creek, with its eastern and western tributaries. The scenery from this elevated position is exceedingly varied and beautiful. Nature, in this landscape, has evidently scouted at every feature of dull monotony. She has scattered profusely her hills and dales. The eastern and western ridges with their numerous spurs have formed a very interesting kaleidoscope. The eye never tires with views so constantly changing. South Dover, including some five or six sections situated on both sides of Hocking, constitutes the river division. Wolf's Plains, together with Chauncey and Salina with their surroundings, are flat, being covered with gravel beds of the drift period. These river sections are rich in soil, and valuable. The plains are noted for their immense tumuli, covering the remains of great warriors that fell in battle. Along this part of Hocking were located the rude mills that supplied the early inhabitants with flour and corn meal. The salt works of Chauncey and Salina were very productive for many years, being a source of considerable revenue to their proprietors, and giving employment to many hands. Through South Dover down the Hocking Valley are now two completed railroads, the Hocking Valley and the Ohio Central. These railways will, in time, make this district quite valuable. Should Chauncey and Salina be occupied by a new class of enterprising capitalists who shall turn their attention to coal and iron, these towns would soon enter upon their resurrection life. Within this district is located the County Infirmary. It has a farm of about 130 acres. It is a valuable tract, situated principally on the river bottom, and aids the county materially to sustain her poor. This institution is a creditable specimen of county infirmaries.

IN SOUTH DOVER

are situated two villages—Chauncey and Salina. Chauncey is situated on a level plot of ground forming a tongue of land between the mouth of Sunday Creek and Hocking. It has been a town of considerable trade, especially during those years of the active manufacture of salt. Its location is favorable for the building up of a large town. There is ample building room for 20,000 inhabitants. Should some of our Eastern capitalists make Chauncey a center of operation in coal-mining and iron making, there would soon gather into its locality a large and thriving population. It being situated on the Ohio Central and at the terminus of Sunday Creek Valley, it would have the advantages of two valleys, Hocking and Sunday Creek.

Salina is located on Hocking River, about one mile above Chauncey. It has been noted for its salt manufactures under Gould & Green. It was a thriving village while those enterprising citizens had the management of the salt interests. Like Chauncey, it is now in a transition state. The time may soon come when Salina shall wake up and grow with the growth of the surrounding country, and be ranked among the noted towns of the Hocking Valley.

NORTH DOVER AND TRIMBLE, OR LOWER SUNDAY CREEK VALLEY.

Before entering upon a description of Lower Sunday Creek Valley, it will be in place to sketch some statistics of Dover and Trimble townships.

Dover was cut off from the western part of Ames and organized into a township April 4, 1811. The act that passed the Board of County Commissioners was the following: "Ordered that so much of the township of Ames as lies west of the thirteenth range be erected into a separate township by the name of Dover. Ordered, further, that the Clerk of the board notify the inhabitants of the township of Dover to meet at the house of Othniel Tuttle, in said township, on Saturday, the 20th of April instant, for the purpose of electing township officers." Dover then included the present townships of Ward, Green and Starr, of Hocking County, and Trimble, York and Dover, in Athens County. The principal settlements were, at that early date, on the waters of Sunday Creek.

The early settlers of Dover Township are mostly contained in the following list: Daniel Weethee, on sections 12 and 18, in Sunday Creek Valley; Josiah True, on sections 18 and 24; Abraham Pugsley, the father of a large family, settling in the same valley; Azel Johnson, joining farm of Daniel Weethee; Henry O'Neill, Samuel Tannehill, Barney J. Robinson, Cornelius Shoemaker, Nehemiah Davis (known as Elder Davis), James Pickett, Jeremiah Cass, Jonathan Watkins (father of a numerous family that settled on Sunday Creek), the Nye family, Reuben J. Davis, Resolved Fuller and brother, George Wilson, Benjamin Davis, Uriah Nash, Eliphalet Wheeler, Reuben Hurlbut, Samuel Stacey, Thomas Smith, Uriah Tippee, Abner Connett and others. The geological and geographical features will be noticed under the head of Lower Sunday Creek Valley.

These families were principally of the New England States; hardy pioneers who left comfortable homes in the East for the companionship of wild beasts and savages, in a distant wilderness. Such materials are required for successful frontier life.

Dover Township has three villages, two of which (Chauncey and Salina) have already been described. Millfield is located very pleasantly on the west bank of Sunday Creek, on sections 16 and 17. The town can number its half century of years, yet there being in it no distinguished manufactories its growth has not been very satisfactory. It has a flour-mill, two dry-goods stores, a blacksmith shop, an excellent school-house, two shoe shops, a postoffice, a wagonmaker's shop, and some other public buildings. The Ohio Central Railroad has a station in Millfield. Should capitalists open coal works in that village it might soon be a very thriving town.

After the division of what is called the "Coonskin library," which took place January, 1816, the Dover division was removed to the residence of Josiah True, near Millfield, where it continued to repose in comparative slumber till 1876, when it was waked up to become a unit of curiosity in the Centennial. The entire separation and removal did not take place, however, till Dec. 21, 1830, at which time "Dover Library Association" was incorporated with Daniel Weethee, Alanson Hibbard, Azariah Pratt, Sr., Josiah True, John B. Johnson, William Hyde and John Pugsley, the original proprietor of Millfield, as the original incorporators, and Daniel Weethee, Alanson Hibbard and Azariah Pratt as Directors for the first year.

TOWNSHIP TRUSTEES FROM 1825 TO 1883.

1825, Resolved Fuller, Daniel Weethee and Samuel B. Johnson; 1826, Jonathan Allen, Simon H. Mansfield and William Bagley; 1827, Jeremiah Morris, Simon H. Mansfield and Josiah True; 1828, Resolved Fuller, Simon H. Mansfield and Josiah True; 1829, Jeremiah Morris, Simon H. Mansfield and Horace Carter; 1830, Daniel Weethee, Simon H. Mansfield and Josiah True; 1831, Samuel Stephens, Jeremiah Morris and Josiah True; 1832–'33, Samuel Stephens, Robert Conn and Josiah True; 1834, John Armstrong, Robert Conn and Josiah True; 1835, Jeremiah Morris, Jonathan Connett and Josiah True; 1836–'37, John Armstrong, S. R. Fox and Josiah True; 1838, record lost; 1839, John Armstrong, Matthew McCune and David Tarrned; 1840, Mason B. Brown, Harry Clark and Josiah True; 1841, Jeremiah Morris, Matthew McCune and Josiah True; 1842, John Armstrong, Matthew McCune and Josiah True; 1843–'44, Albert Harper, Matthew McCune and Josiah True; 1845, William Hyde, Matthew McCune and Josiah True; 1846, Azariah Pratt, Matthew McCune and Josiah True; 1847, Henry Brown, Matthew McCune and Josiah True; 1848, Azariah Pratt, Matthew McCune and Josiah True; 1849, William Edwards, Austin Fuller, Josiah True; 1850–'51, Matthew McCune, Austin Fuller and W. S. Hyde; 1852, Matthew McCune, Austin Fuller and James Culver; 1853, Seth Fuller, Austin Fuller and John Spencer; 1854, Seth Fuller, W. S. Hyde and John Spencer; 1855, Samuel Augustine, W. S. Hyde and Woodruff Connett; 1856–'57, John Cradlebaugh, W. S. Hyde and Austin Fuller; 1858, John Cradlebaugh, W. S. Hyde and E. D. Harper; 1859–'60, John Cradlebaugh, Austin Fuller and O. G. Burge; 1861, Alexander Stephenson, Austin Fuller and O. G. Burge; 1862, Ebenezer Pratt, Joseph Tippy and W. S. Hyde; 1863, O. G. Burge, Joseph Tippy and W. S. Hyde; 1864, O. G. Burge, J. W. P. Cook and W. S. Hyde; 1865–'66, O. G. Burge, J. W. P. Cook and W. S. Hyde; 1867, O. G. Burge, R.

N. Fuller and W. S. Hyde; 1868, George Connett, Samuel Augustine and Ebenezer Pratt; 1869, Henry Brown, Woodruff Connett and F. L. Junod; 1870, Woodruff Connett, O. G. Burge and F. L. Junod; 1871, F. L. Junod, William Edwards and O. G. Burge; 1872, William M. Edwards, H. Connett and Ebenezer Pratt; 1873, William M. Edwards, William Cornell and Hiram Fuller; 1874, Hiram Fuller, William M. Edwards and William Connett; 1875, George Connett, A. B. White and L. A. Sprague; 1876, A. B. White, D. H. Cunningham and Henry Martin; 1877, Henry Martin, Ezra Cornell and J. W. P. Cook; 1878, Henry Martin, J. W. P. Cook and Hiram Fuller; 1879, Henry Martin, J. W. P. Cook and A. B. White; 1880, Austin True, F. L. Junod and Nathan Picket; 1881, Joel Sanders, Silas H. Stephenson and Samuel Augustine; 1882, Joel Sanders, Silas H. Stephenson and Samuel Augustine; 1883, Silas H. Stephenson, Daniel Fulton and John Brawley.

JUSTICES OF THE PEACE FROM 1825 TO 1883.

1826, D. Herrold; 1827–'31, Josiah True; 1832–'33, Simon H. Mansfield; 1834–'37, Josiah True; 1839, Frederick Cradlebaugh; 1841, John Armstrong; 1843, Josiah True; 1845, Charles R. Smith; 1846, Hiram Fuller; 1851, Charles R. Smith; 1852, J. W. P. Cook; 1853, Hiram Fuller; 1854, William Edwards; 1855, E. D. Varner; 1856, Hiram Fuller and C. R. Smith; 1858, Josephus Calvert; 1859, Hiram Fuller and John Smith; 1862, J. W. P. Cook, Hiram Fuller and John Smith; 1865, Job S. King; 1868, Hiram Fuller, Charles R. Smith and John Smith; 1871, Hiram Fuller, John Smith and Job S. King; 1874, Hiram Fuller, William M. Edwards and Job S. King; 1876, Hiram Fuller; 1877, Job S. King; 1878, John Cradlebaugh; 1879, Hiram Fuller and J. A. McKee; 1880, Andrew J. Learned; 1881, Silas H. Stephenson; 1882–'83, J. A. McKee.

A postoffice was established at Millfield in 1834, and at Chauncey in 1838.

TRIMBLE TOWNSHIP.

Trimble Township, so named from a former Governor of Ohio, was a part of Ames Township till 1811, and of Dover till 1827, at which time it was organized into a separate township. On its north, east and west are the counties of Perry, Morgan and Hocking; on the south is Dover Township. It is drained principally by the northern branches of Sunday Creek. Its original white settlers located their claims on the east and west branches, near the north and northwest limits of the township. Solomon Tuttle, Sr., with his son, Cyrus Tuttle, and his brother, Nial Tuttle, from Vermont, settled on the east branch of Sunday Creek in 1802. In their vicinity soon after, Joseph McDaniel and William Morrow located their families. William Bagley and his brother John Bagley, leaving Vermont in 1820, settled on the west branch of Sunday Creek, near the present Hartleyville.

John Bagley erected a factory and grist-mill. They were rude specimens, but they supplied the wants of the people. William Bagley settled on school section No. 16; farmed some and was associated with his brother John in the milling and factory business. Another brother, Samuel Bagley, being a tanner, erected the first tannery (the only one) in the township, 1822.

In 1822 a school was taught, near the forks of the creek (the present location of Sedalia) by Nancy Bagley, of Vermont, a sister of William, John and Samuel Bagley. This was the first school in the township. About 1824 John Morrow taught a school on the east branch, in the Tuttle, Morrow and Dew settlement. The school-house was a fair specimen of those pioneer buildings. It was a house 12 x 15 feet, composed of round logs, the ground for its floor; one log cut out on each side for light, oiled paper instead of glass. Door three feet by five, on wooden hinges, with a wooden latch, moved by a tow or leather string. In the end opposite to the door was the fireplace, occupying the principal part of the end, with a chimney composed of unhewn stone, or sticks and mud. In this rude specimen of the early seminaries, on one of its high wooden leg rough puncheon benches, sat our distinguished and honorable citizen, E. H. Moore, book in hand, legs dangling (being too short to reach the floor), eyes intent on spelling out the words of his lesson. In 1832 Mr. Moore taught school in the same place.

The Christian religion has always had a place on Sunday Creek, and Trimble Township has shared in its divine munificence. The Baptist, Methodist, and Christian denominations were the first to occupy the attention of the people. They are still the leading organizations. Other views have been proclaimed but have not been productive of any flattering results. The principal mill of Trimble Township was commenced at Oxford, now Trimble, by Jonathan Watkins in 1825. It was burned in 1865. After some years it was rebuilt, and continued as a water-mill till 1882. Since then it has been changed into a steam mill, and is furnished with all modern improvements in the flour-making line, and is doing an excellent business.

Agriculture is still, as it always has been, the chief occupation of its citizens. Mining of coal, however, has been such as to supply the home demand. In the future, mining will perhaps take the first rank. The minerals of the valley will be more fully noticed under the head of Sunday Creek Valley.

TOWNSHIP OFFICERS.

The first election for township officers was held at the residence of William Bagley, James Price, James Bosworth, and Jeremiah Cass being the Judges, and Samuel B. Johnson and Cyrus Tuttle, Clerks.

TOWNSHIP TRUSTEES.

1827, William Bagley, James Bosworth, Solomon Newton; 1828, Jeremiah Cass, Elijah Alderman, Solomon Newton; 1829, Joseph McDonald, James Price, Solomon Newton; 1830, David Eggleston, James Price, Solomon Newton; 1831, Jonathan Watkins, James Price, Solomon Newton; 1832, wanting; 1833, Elijah Alderman, Thomas Dew, John Ivers; 1834, Elijah Alderman, Luther Mingus, Enoch Rutter; 1835, wanting; 1836, Solomon Newton, Andrew McKee, William Shaner; 1837, Jonathan Watkins, Andrew McKee, William Shaner; 1838, Solomon Newton, Andrew McKee, Ebenezer Shaner; 1839, William McKee, Andrew McKee, John Ivers; 1840, Thomas L. Love, Andrew Rutter, wanting; 1841, James Hoge, W. J. Hartley, wanting; 1842, James Hoge, John B. Johnson, wanting; 1843, James Hoge, Isaac N. Joseph, William J. Hartley; 1844, William McClellan, Isaac N. Joseph, William J. Hartley; 1845, Andrew McKee, Caleb Carter, Isaac Blackwood; 1846, wanting; 1847, William McClellan, Andrew Dew, J. D. Davis; 1848, Andrew McKee, Andrew Dew, J. D. Davis; 1849-'50, William McClellan, Andrew Dew, J. D. Davis; 1851, William McClellan, William H. Peugh, S. T. Grow; 1852, wanting; 1853, James Hoge, John Ivers, wanting; 1854, Andrew Dew, John Ivers, William McClellan; 1855, wanting; 1856, Joseph Allen, B. Worrell, Andrew Dew; 1857, Benjamin Norris, John M. Johnson, Andrew Dew; 1858-'59, William H. Peugh, William McClellan, S. P. Grow; 1860-'61, William H. Peugh, William McClellan, L. H. Rhinehart; 1862, William H. Peugh, William McClellan,

Samuel Woodworth; 1863, Samuel Banks, John Shaner, Samuel Woodworth; 1864, Samuel Banks, John Gift, Dorsey McClellan; 1865-'66, Milton Monroe, John Gift, J. C. Lefever; 1867, William H. Peugh, Isaac Blackwood, Lemuel Bethel; 1868, Samuel Banks, J. M. Amos, Joseph Allen, 1869; Samuel Banks, E. H. Watkins, William Biddison; 1870, Samuel Banks, James S. Jennings, William Biddison; 1871, S. H. Johnson, J. W. Jones, Isaac Blackwood; 1872, David Glenn, William H. Peugh, Joshua Sands; 1873-'75, William H. Peugh, Joseph Allen, Jacob L. Wyatt; 1876, A. B. Johnson, William H. Peugh, Jacob L. Wyatt; 1877, William H. Peugh, A. B. Johnson, Jacob L. Wyatt; 1878, Jacob L. Wyatt, James H. Jones, James F. Kempton; 1879, James H. Jones, William H. Peugh, W. W. Anderson; 1880-'81, James H. Jones, William Biddison, William H. Peugh; 1882-'83, James H. Jones, Richard Daniels, William H. Peugh.

JUSTICES OF THE PEACE FROM 1827 TO 1883.

1827, William Bagley; 1830, James Price and Jeremiah Cass; 1833, Daniel Frazer and Samuel Mills; 1834, Emory Newton; 1836, Seth Pratt and Samuel Mills; 1838, Solomon Newton; 1839, Samuel Mills; 1840, David Allen; 1841, John Ivers; 1842, Morris Bryson; 1844, John Ivers; 1845, Morris Bryson; 1847, Isaac N. Joseph; 1848, George W. Roberts; 1850, Aquilla Norris and Benjamin Norris; 1851, Benjamin Norris and George W. Roberts; 1853, Alexander McClellan; 1854, William Biddison; 1856, Isaac N. Joseph; 1857, John M. Johnson (resigned Feb. 3, 1858); 1858, Morris Bryson; 1859, William H. Peugh; 1861, Morris Bryson; 1862, Lemuel Bethel; 1864, William Biddison; 1865, William Koons; 1867, J. S. Dew; 1868, Samuel Banks; 1869, James F. Kempton, resigned; 1870, James Rutter; 1871, J. L. Porter; 1874, E. N. Alderman; 1876, William H. Johnston; 1877, James Rutter; 1878, W. H. Johnston; 1880, W. W. Anderson; 1882, James N. Sands; 1883, Joseph W. Jones.

SUNDAY CREEK VALLEY.

Under this head will be included all that remains to be said of Trimble and North Dover, except such general remarks as will be appropriate to notice in the scientific chapter of the "History of Hocking Valley."

Under the above caption will be given a brief view of its topography, geological structure and its resources, together with its past history. Our space is too limited to enter into detail. We must leave the reader to amplify our thoughts and outline sketches as his knowledge and interest may dictate.

Sunday Creek Valley is fan-shaped, with its axis at Chauncey, near the mouth of the creek, and its radiating parts spreading out so as to include all the territory drained by Sunday Creek and its branches.

The springs which give rise to the extreme branches of Sunday Creek are wider apart than its head and mouth—wider than long.

Sunday Creek Valley has its bottom lands, yet they do not form one of its distinctive features. It is composed, principally, of ridges, spurs, inclined plains, ravines, gulches and valleys. It has a face for every point in the heavens. It has vastly more surface than sky. Its base is contracted, but the sum of its surfaces is very considerable. Though we thus truthfully describe its territory, we are happy to say that it has but a few rods of waste land. Sunday Creek Valley has every variety of soil and exposure. Its bottom lands are, in spots, composed of sand, produced by the disintegration of its sand rocks; in other localities they are alluvial; in other parts, clay, with a great variety of mixtures. Our northern surfaces are often steep, the strata not being dissolved by the extremes of heat and cold, or by storms. Our northern slopes are generally the most productive. Our southern hillsides are often rather poor, yet they have their special uses. Our east and west exposures are quite productive.

Sunday Creek Valley has its agricultural resources, still agriculture is not its specialty. Its soil produces fair crops of wheat, rye, Indian corn, potatoes, grass, turnips, and all kinds of vegetables suited to its latitude. Its hills are suited to the rearing of sheep, cattle, and all kinds of stock. It is a land adapted to vine and fruit culture. One advantage it has, worthy of special note; such is its variety of soil and exposures that there is scarcely ever a season without fruit, either on the ridges, on the slopes, in the ravines, or on the bottom lands. The soil, if scientifically cultivated, is quite productive, capable of sustaining a dense population.

MINERAL RESOURCES OF SUNDAY CREEK VALLEY.

Its mineral deposits are the most noted feature of Sunday Creek Valley. In its coal deposits it is, perhaps, superior to any other territory of equal size in the State. This will appear by an examination of its geological structure, which we proceed, briefly, to investigate.

Sunday Creek Valley is an erosion of the lower coal measures, there being no discoverable marks of volcanic action. In the gulches, ravines and valleys, the strata are in place on opposite sides—a proof that running water formed them. These depressions, therefore, are erosions, and the entire valley is a "wash-out" of past ages. The process is still in progress, every flood wafting tons of disintegrated rocks and minerals toward the Mexican Gulf. It will be readily seen that the main stream and its tributaries are increasing in length, are becoming wider from bank to bank, while their flow decreases in velocity. The waters are lowering the dividing ridges and spurs, while they are filling up deep cavities and evening the inclined planes at the bottoms of the principal streams. The washing-down process would, in time, make plain of the valley. In the gulches, ravines and valleys, the strata for 600 feet are vertically exposed. Shafts have been sunk to the fire-clay under the great seam of coal, and salt wells have penetrated 400 feet further. The strata are, therefore, known in a vertical section of 1,100 feet. We are more particularly concerned with the strata of the upper 700 feet. Beginning our examination of this vertical section twenty-six feet below the Nelsonville coal seam (great seam) we find our lowest coal vein two feet and six inches thick. This is a rich, gas-producing coal. Twenty-six feet above this vein is the great coal seam. In five wells its average thickness is nine feet three inches. In three shafts its average is about the same. This is for the entire surface of 35,000 acres. Seventy-five feet above the great vein is the Bailey's Run coal. In the lower Sunday Creek Valley this seam lies at the bases of our hills. Its average thickness is four feet six inches. Very excellent coke has been made from this seam of coal. It is an excellent gas-making and parlor coal. This coal is mined by drifting. The following analysis of a sample of this coal from section 34, Dover, was made by Prof. Wormley (State Chemist): "Specific gravity, 1.309; moisture 4.20; ash, 2.60; volatile combustible matter, 35.20; fire carbon, 58.00; total, 100.00 parts. Sulphur, 1.04; sulphur left in coke, 0.41; percentage of sulphur in coke, 0.67; gas per pound in cubic foot, 3.97; color of ash, gray; coke compact." The State Geologist makes the following remark: "This shows a very excellent coal. The ash is small and the fixed carbon is large, and the amount of gas is also large. The coal loses so much of its sulphur in coking that the coke is relatively free from it." Thirty-seven feet above the Bailey's Run coal seam, with a thick vein of iron ore between, is a vein of about two feet of coal. About seventy-five feet above this seam is another vein of coal two and one-half feet thick. About 200 feet above the last is the Pittsburg, or Pomeroy, coal vein, from four to eight feet thick. In this vertical section of 700 feet we can count thirteen horizons of iron ore and eleven horizons of limestone.

Sunday Creek Valley contains a vast amount of excellent sand rock for glass-making and building purposes. It has large quarries of flag-stone. Its deposits of fire-clay are immense. Our six coal seams will aggregate about twenty-seven feet. Our two workable seams average thirteen feet.

Such is a brief outline of the mineral resources of Sunday Creek Valley. This is claimed of the valley, that, for variety of minerals, amount and quality, as a whole, its peer cannot be found. Trimble Township and North Dover have more mineral wealth than can be found under an equal area (35,000 acres) anywhere else in Ohio, or perhaps in the world. We shall have occasion to strengthen these statements when the mineral resources of Hocking Valley are investigated. We shall now take up the history of this valley from the time that it began to be settled by the whites.

We have already given its civil history. Its schools, its social and religious history demand further attention. Society is the normal state of all living beings. Man is no exception to this general law. The world has been peopled by groups; groups have formed societies; societies have been gathered into villages, towns, cities, States, kingdoms and empires. Thus was America peopled; thus was Ohio settled; and by the same law Sunday Creek Valley received its first white inhabitants. The Ohio Company's purchase gave cast to the first settlers of the valley. Those that had a desire to go West from the New England States, hearing such flattering accounts of the district now forming Southeastern Ohio, purchased lands of that company, and moved West to occupy them. Sunday Creek Valley, therefore, received its first white population from New England. They brought with them, as a matter of necessity, their religion, manners, customs and educational spirit. But the valley to which they removed was truly a "howling wilderness." Savages occupied the lands that they had purchased, and, with various wild beasts, disputed with them the right of possession.

A change in their manner of living was a necessary consequence. New thoughts followed, and, consequently, a new course of action. In a few years they were comparatively a new people—Wilderness Yankees. They formed new ideas in every department of human thought. With minds as free as their breathing apparatus, they began to entertain new religious notions. They read their Bibles and did their own thinking. So soon as they were sufficiently numerous to have religious assemblies and form churches, the fruits of independent thinking were clearly seen. No New England churches were ever formed in Sunday Creek Valley. The inhabitants were principally what were called "New Lights," and afterward "Christians," more usually denominated "Disciples," and by their enemies, "Campbellites." Methodist and Baptist churches have often been formed, but their prosperity has not been very satisfactory.

Schools have always been sustained. Education belongs to New England life. A love for it is inherent in their very being. The branches taught were at first few, imperfectly understood, and unskillfully taught. In the early settlements, teachers knew nothing of geography, but little of English grammar, taught reading, writing and spelling. All higher branches of science were the great unknown.

SOCIAL PERIODS OF SUNDAY CREEK VALLEY.

These will be the better illustrated by examining their materials of dress. For the sake of convenience, we divide its past history into periods, named after the chief article of clothing.

1. *Buckskin Period.*—When the people had worn out their Eastern wardrobes, to replenish with like articles was impossible. They were, therefore, obliged to go like the savages, or clothe themselves with some domestic production. They tanned deer-skins, fashioned garments, and clothed their nakedness. Some tall courtships and interesting marriages belong to this primitive age.

2. *Linsey-Woolsey Period.*—The age of primitive simplicity soon began to yield to the march of Yankee progress. Flax and wool were combined and woven into cloth. Garments made of these materials became the fashionable wear of this advanced period; not, however, without the cry of "pride" and "extravagance."

3. *The Modern, or Silk Period.*—This period was never fully adopted, except by the "upper tens." The calico period is the

popular one of the valley. These four periods—the Buckskin, Linsey-Woolsey, Calico and Silk, mark the progress of society in Sunday Creek Valley.

BIOGRAPHICAL—DOVER.

William Bell, section 30, Dover Township, was born in Leicestershire, England, April 11, 1841, and came to America in 1864 and settled in this county, where he has since lived. Mr. Bell cleared thirty-three acres of land on middle branch of Bailey's Run. He moved to his present farm April 3, 1883. He was married May 2, 1869, to Jane R. Price, daughter of Abel C. Price, of Trimble Township. Mr. and Mrs. Bell have had five children, of whom two are living—William A. and Rebecca A. The deceased were—Sarah A., Frances E. and Lucy A. Mr. Bell owns 125 acres of land and is engaged in raising stock. Mrs. Bell was born in Dover Township near Kidwell's mill, Oct. 1, 1839, the same year Kidwell's mill was built.

Hiram Bingham, late of Salina, now of Athens Township, was born near Athens, July 22, 1826. He was brought up on a farm and educated in Athens. In 1851 he went to California and mined about three years; was then engaged in the dairy business, and afterward ran a meat market six years. He then went to Idaho where he lived two years, then resided one year in Wallawalla, Washington Territory. The steamer (Independence) that he and family took for the Golden State, wrecked off the coast of Jamaica Island, but they pulled in to Kingston and were all rescued. They were taken to Panama, where they remained a month, then went by steamer to San Francisco, arriving there March 6, 1852. They returned by the Nicaraugua route in 1866. Mr. Bingham has since resided in Athens County, except four years, when he was in Columbus, Ohio, in the grocery business. He engaged in the grocery business in Athens for two years. During the years of 1881 and 1882 he engaged in the manufacture of salt at Salina, Athens County, and in the spring of 1883 he bought a farm in Athens Township, where he removed about the first of April. He was first married to Lovina Lamb, daughter of Sylvanus Lamb. They had two children, one living—Surges. Mrs. Bingham died in 1848, and he married Miss Salama Weis, daughter of Jacob Weis, a native of Germany, who came to this county in 1819, and still resides here, at the age of eighty-five years. Mr. Bingham owns property in Athens.

Orrin R. Birge, Superintendent of the Agricultural Department at the Athens County Infirmary, and brother of O. G. Burge, of Chauncey, was born in Litchfield, Conn., Aug. 30, 1833. He was brought up and partially educated in his native town. The family removed to Cuyahoga County, Ohio, when Orrin was a boy. He has spent his life thus far on a farm. He came to Athens County about 1852. He was married Jan. 15, 1857, to Jane C., daughter of James Stephenson. They have but one child—James J. Mr. Birge has held his present position for the past ten years. He is a member of the Christian church.

Tobias Boudinot, section 17, Dover Township, was born in Meigs County, Ohio, March 27, 1822, and is a son of John Boudinot, of Knox County, Ohio, and a native of New Jersey. He was reared on the farm, and received a common-school education. He came to this township in 1839, where he has since lived. He was married Aug. 14, 1844, to Elizabeth, daughter of Charles Southerton, who came to this county in 1832. They had seven children, three living—Jennie E., Tobias T., and Cassius H. One son, Elmer H., died Jan. 29, 1882, in his twenty-first year. A daughter, Mrs. Lucy J. Peters, died at the age of twenty-two years and left two children. Mr. Boudinot owns 147 acres in this county and 320 acres in Carter County, Mo., and is engaged in farming and stock-raising. He was Infirmary Director for three years, and Township Trustee one term. He is a member of the Christian or Disciple church. His father is now ninety-three years old. He came to this county in 1839 and resided here until within the last few years. He was a soldier in the war of 1812. Our subject's grandfather's brother, Hon. Elias Boudinot, LL. D., was George Washington's private secretary; was President of the first Bible Society that ever assembled in the United States and was President of the first Continental Congress that ever assembled in America. He was also renowned for his generosity: he donated 339 acres of land adjoining Philadelphia to the American Bible Society, and gave $10,000 in cash to the same society, $13,000 to the poor, and $5,000 to purchase spectacles for the poor. He was of French descent.

John W. Brawley, section 13, was born in this township June 15, 1831, and is a son of James Brawley, who came to Athens County with his parents when a small boy and died here in April, 1873. Our subject was reared on a farm and received a common-school education. He was married July 4, 1859, to Susan, daughter

Charles Henry

of Hiram Fuller. They have four children—Nellie, Clarence, Ida and Mary. Nellie married George Merry. Mr. Brawley owns a farm of 118 acres and is engaged in farming and stock-raising.

Ormond G. Burge.—The Burge family differ in their spelling of the family name; our subject spells it with a "u," while his brother, Orrin R., and some others spell it with an "i." The subject of this sketch was born in Litchfield, Conn., July 7, 1820, and is a son of Orrin Burge, deceased, also a native of Litchfield, and of English descent. He brought his family to Cuyahoga County, Ohio, in 1830. Our subject came first to Athens County in 1838, and bought land in Waterloo Township. He remained in Nelsonville in the boot and shoe business from 1841 until 1846. He then came to Dover Township, where he has since resided and operated his farm at Chauncey. In 1856 he married Emily Coe, daughter of John Coe, a pioneer of Athens County. They have had six children—Lemuel, Caroline, Leanora, Wallace, Jane and Cora. Mrs. Burge died June 7, 1867. She was a member of the Free-Will Baptist church. Mr. Burge is a member of the Christian church. Mr. Burge held the office of Township Trustee of Dover Township for twelve years, and Assessor four or five years. He has recently sold his farm and resides with his son Lemuel in Chauncey.

William W. Burge, son of O. G. Burge, of Chauncey, was born in Dover Township, this county, June 5, 1855. He was reared on the farm and educated in Weethee's College at Mt. Auburn, this township. He married Ida M. Lapham Aug. 31, 1879. She is a daughter of Simon Lapham, of Cleveland. They have one child—Clara M., a bright-eyed little girl of two years. Mr. Burge is engaged in farming and stock-raising. He is a member of the Sons of Temperance and of the Christian church.

Simeon W. Cass was born in Dover Township, Oct. 11, 1821, and is a son of Jeremiah Cass, a native of Rhode Island, and an early settler at Amestown, this county. He was one of the party that cut the first road through the wilderness from Marietta to Amestown. He was a single man then and lived with a Mr. Wyatt. He married Sarah Wright, by whom he had eleven children. They reared three boys and seven girls. His father, Amos Cass, came to Marietta with his son and settled on Sunday Creek where he died many years ago. Jeremiah Cass removed with his family to Trimble Township, this county, when Simeon was an infant, and when he was about fifteen years old returned to Dover

Township. Mr. Cass was a soldier in the late war in Company H, One Hundred and Forty-first Ohio National Guards. He was married April 30, 1843, to Elsie J. Haning, daughter of Aaron Haning. They had five children, of whom three are living—Sarah, Emily and Adelaide C. One daughter, Mrs. Rhoda Davis, left nine children, and the other, Mrs. Mary J. Gibson, left two children. Mrs. Cass died Aug. 3, 1878. April 2, 1879, Mr. Cass married Sarah Simons, daughter of Admatha Simons, of England. They have had two children—Blanche G., deceased, and Susan F. Mr. Cass has been a member of the Christian church about twenty-five years, and has been Elder since the fall of 1863. His mother still lives in this township at the age of ninety-three years.

Charles P. Clester, section 7, was born in this township Oct. 2, 1848, and is a son of Samuel Clester, a native of Pennsylvania, who came to Athens County over forty years ago, where he died in 1869. Our subject was reared on the farm and educated at Weethee's College in this township. He was married in November, 1869, to Carrie McAfee, daughter of John McAfee, of this county. They have two children—Sadie and Carrie, aged twelve and nine years respectively. Mr. Clester owns 155 acres of land and is engaged in farming and stock-raising. He is a member of the Sugar Creek Methodist Episcopal church.

Hyrcanus Connett was born in this township Feb. 26, 1844. He was educated in the Ohio University at Athens. He worked for M. M. Green & Co. at Salina about eight years, then returned to the farm. He was married in March, 1871, to Elzina Bean, daughter of Isaiah Bean, of Pleasanton, Ohio. They have one child—Della May. Mr. Connett owns 160 acres of valuable land in Athens Township, but resides at present on the old home place in Dover Township. He is a member of the Methodist Episcopal church. Woodruff Connett, the father of the above, was born in Athens Township, this county, March 6, 1810, and is a son of Abner Connett, who came to this county in 1798 from Pennsylvania. He was reared on the farm and educated in a subscription school and has always been a farmer. He was married March 22, 1833, to Lucy P. Dorr, by whom he had two children—Lydia (now Mrs. Isaac Bassett) and Hyrcanus. Mrs. Connett died Jan. 22, 1881. Mr. Connett and his son own over 300 acres of valuable land.

Daniel Coots (originally spelled Kutz) was born in Somerset County, Pa., March 29, 1827, and is a son of David Coots, deceased, a native of Bedford County, Pa., who brought his family to Athens

County in 1837. They witnessed the building of the Hocking Canal, and saw some of the Irish rows among the hands employed on that work. Mr. Coots was reared on the farm, and for eighteen years was one of the most extensive farmers of the county. For the past four years he has had the mail route between Chauncey and Salina. He was married Feb. 14, 1855, to Frances R. Nye, daughter of Thedorus Nye, deceased. She was born in Chester, Meigs Co., Ohio. They have had eight children, four living— Ella M., Mary M., Frank T. and Emma B. The family are all members of the Methodist church.

John Coulson, section 8, Dover Township, was born in this township, Oct. 9, 1846. He was reared on the farm and educated at Weethee's College and at New Plymouth, Ohio. He learned the carpenter's trade when a boy, and still works some at building railroad bridges. He also learned surveying, and has followed that business more or less for the past fifteen years. He owns eighty-six acres of valuable land, and is engaged in farming and stock-raising. Mr. Coulson's father, James Coulson, was born in Washington County, Pa., Feb. 14, 1817, and came to this county in 1844. He was married in 1844, just before starting West, to Sarah A. Mountz, by whom he had seven children, four of whom are living —John, Samuel, Nancy and Daniel. There are 200 acres in the old home place, where his widow now lives. He died March 15, 1883. The deceased was twice elected and once appointed to the office of County Surveyor of Athens County. He was a Quaker in religious belief. He was an industrious and useful man, and a kind husband and father.

Ebenezer Dains, section 30, Dover Township, was born in Guernsey County, Ohio, May 10, 1820. He came to this county in 1831 with his parents, where he has since resided, with the exception of four years—one year in Perry County, Ohio, and three in Indiana. His father, Jacob B. Dains (deceased), was a native of New Jersey. Mr. Dains owns 133 acres of land, and is engaged in farming and stock-raising. He was married July 15, 1841, to Catherine Dewitt, daughter of James Dewitt. They have had thirteen children, of whom ten are living—George W., Jasper N., Mary, Elizabeth, James, Lydia, Sarah, William, Thomas and Eliza J. One son, John, died in his seventeenth year.

Joseph B. Doughty, druggist, of Chauncey, was born in Granville, Licking Co., Ohio, Jan. 19, 1846, and is a son of Rev. Richard Doughty, a Methodist Episcopal minister. Mr. Doughty began taking care of himself at the age of ten years; he worked on the farm, in coal mines, and clerked in stores several years. He was a soldier in the late war, in Company H, Eighty-fifth Ohio Infantry, and helped chase Morgan through Kentucky in 1863. He was discharged and then enlisted in Company F, One Hundred and Thirty-fifth Ohio Infantry, in the spring of 1864, and served for about ten months; eight months of the time he was in prison (having been captured at North Mountain) and was a part of the time in Andersonville. He went to Noblesville, Ind., in 1866, where he remained two years, and came to Hocking County in 1868. In 1871 he helped build the Straitsville branch of the Hocking Valley Railroad. Came to Chauncey in 1873, and in 1874 went to Perry County, Ohio. He returned to Chauncey in 1877, where he has since been engaged in the drug business. He was married in December, 1872, to Kate, daughter of Dr. A. J. Shrader, of Nelsonville. They have four children—Blanche M., Jessie S., Richard D. and Sarah I.

Thomas Ellis, a prominent farmer of Dover Township, is a native of Lincolnshire, England, and was born in the city of Grantham, May 21, 1817. His father, Richard Ellis, was a native of Doddington, England. Mr. Ellis emigrated from his native land to Dover Township in 1842, where he has since lived. He was married March 2, 1846, to Mary A. White, a daughter of John S. White. They had three children, two living—Mary and Sarah. For twenty-two years Mr. Ellis carried on a blacksmith shop in Millfield, when he sold out and bought his present farm on Sunday Creek, one mile north of Chauncey. It consisted of 510 acres, 160 of which he gave his daughter. He is now engaged in farming and stock-raising. Mr. Ellis still has in his possession a piece of the first carriage that was run in the Sunday Creek Valley. It was built by Mr. Reynolds, from Nova Scotia, in 1843.

Austin Fuller, deceased, late of Millfield, was born in Dover Township, this county, May 14, 1814, and was a son of Resolved Fuller. He was brought up on the farm, and educated in a subscription school. He was always a farmer. Oct. 19, 1835, he married Miss Mary Pratt, daughter of Azariah Pratt, and sister of Ebenezer Pratt, of this township. They had twelve children born to them, of whom eight are living—George, Resolved, Dudley, Carlin L., Abigail, Mary, Eva and Flavius. Abigail is the wife of Rev. Ephraim Wayman, of Chillicothe, Ill. Eva is the wife of Elder Samuel W. Brown, of Washington, Pa. One daughter, Mrs. Sarah Fuller Wyatt, died and left four children. A son, Melzer N., was also married, and left two children at his death. Mr. Fuller was a faithful member of the Methodist Episcopal church.

Dudley D. Fuller, of Millfield, was born March 4, 1847, son of Austin Fuller. He was reared on a farm, and educated in a common school and Weethee's College. He followed farming for some time. He enlisted in the late war in Company A, One Hundred and Twenty-ninth Ohio Infantry, and served nine months; was discharged and enlisted in the Navy Department, in which he served on the United States steamer Huntress until the close of the war. Mr. Fuller was married Oct. 8, 1876, to Mary J. Wyatt, daughter of George Wyatt. They have had four children, one living—Edith A. Mr. Fuller was appointed Postmaster at Millfield in March, 1879. He keeps a general store, doing an annual business of $8,000.

Russell N. Fuller, M. D., was born in this township Jan. 3, 1817. His father, Resolved Fuller, was a native of Connecticut, and came to this county in 1796. He walked the entire distance from Connecticut to this county with another boy. He was born in 1780, and was therefore but sixteen years old at that time. When he reached this then wilderness he had just three shillings, or $37\frac{1}{2}$ cents. He was industrious and economical, worked hard and grew wealthy. He bored the Chauncey salt well, and owned and operated the salt works there for some time. At one time he owned all the land where Chauncey now stands. He had a family of nine children, but two of whom are living—Russell N. and Hiram, of Marshfield, this county. The subject of this sketch was married in 1840 to Eliza B. Cooley, daughter of Caleb Cooley. They have eight children—Charles, Mary, Emma, Kate, Esther, John R., Milton and Henry H. The Doctor was Assessor of this township two terms, Township Trustee one term, and Township Treasurer one term. He commenced the practice of medicine in 1845, but has given up most of his practice of late. He owns a farm of 360 acres and is engaged in farming and stock-raising.

Daniel Fulton, section 29, Dover Township, was born in Alexander Township, this county, Aug. 21, 1822. His father, Loammia Fulton, was a native of Pennsylvania, and came with his parents to Athens County when about five years old, and settled in the woods among wolves, deer, panthers, wildcats and Indians. The subject of this sketch was reared on the farm and educated in a subscription school. He commenced to learn the carpenter's trade when seventeen years old. He worked on canal-locks on Hocking Canal about eight years, and built bridges several years. He has also carried on the farm until the present time. He was in the employ of the Hocking Valley Iron Company as their agent for three years. Mr. Fulton was married Dec. 24, 1846, to Lucy W., daughter of Josiah True. They have five children— Harmon, Mary and Emma (twins), Sarah Ida and John A. Mr. Fulton is a member of the Free-Will Baptist church. He owns 361 acres of valuable land, and is engaged in farming and stock-raising.

John Harvey, farmer, section 1, Dover Township, was born in Washington County, Ohio, Nov. 22, 1826. His father, James Harvey, a native of Ayrshire, Scotland, born in November, 1802, came to Barlow Township, Washington Co., Ohio, in 1818. Mr. Harvey spent his boyhood days on his father's farm and attended a subscription school. He learned the carpenter's trade with his father, and also learned the wagon-maker's trade. He followed the latter, of winters, for many years. He came to this county in 1853 and located in Dover Township, where he still lives. He enlisted in the late war in Company H, One Hundred and Forty first Ohio Infantry. He was married Feb. 5, 1854, to Sarah, daughter of Jonas Rice. They had six children—James R., John C., Mary, Nettie, J. Henry and Elinor H. Mr. Harvey owns 145 acres of land and is engaged in farming and stock-raising. He built several of the houses in this neighborhood, among them that of A. J. Willmarth, Alanson Courtney, Hugh Poston and Captain Phillips.

James C. Headley, section 12, Dover Township, was born in Monroe County, Ohio, April 3, 1840, son of Isaac Headley, of Morgan County, Ohio. He was reared on a farm and educated in a common school, and graduated from the Cincinnati Law School May 25, 1881. He was married April 20, 1865, to Rhoda Lewis, daughter of Jacob Lewis. Mr. and Mrs. Headley have had seven children, of whom five are living—Laired J. V., Sabra L. O., Irena L. S., Sitha A. F. and Lucretia J. Mr. Headley came to this county in 1869. For nine and a half years he ran a saw-mill, but at the present time is engaged in general farming.

William Henry was born in Wales, Oct. 2, 1836. He was educated in the public schools of Wales, and came to America in 1850, stopping in New York City; thence to Pittsburg and Pomeroy, Ohio, where he lived about a year. He then worked on railroads a while, and came to Chauncey in 1856, where he has since resided, with the exception of the time he was in the army, and has worked in the coal mines at the Chauncey Salt Works. He enlisted in May, 1862, in Company E, Seventy-fifth Ohio Infantry, and participated in the battles of Gettysburg, the Wilderness, and Fredericksburg, and was discharged in May, 1864, on account of disability, caused by a wound through the large part of the left leg, at the battle of Gettysburg. He was married May 26, 1858, to Lydia A. Birge, daughter of William A. Birge, of this county. They had six children, four of whom are living—Wilford, William, Winifred and John. Mr. Henry is a member of the Sons of Temperance.

William S. Hyde was born in Homer Township, Morgan Co., Ohio, Jan. 29, 1819, and is a son of William Hyde, a native of New York City, who came to Morgan County, Ohio, about 1817. In 1827 he removed to Millfield, this county, where he died Sept. 15, 1846. He owned large tracts of land around Millfield, and was extensively engaged in farming and in the mercantile business. Our subject was educated in a select school. He bought the farm where he now resides in 1860, and has recently sold it to the Buchtel Iron Company, but still resides here and is employed as the company's agent. He was married in the fall of 1843 to Hetta C. Andrews, daughter of Samuel Andrews. They have four children—Achsa, Emma, William and Maurice. Emma is married to Smith Jennings, of Nelsonville, and William to Adda Conant, and resides in Fairfield County, Ohio. Mr. Hyde was Infirmary Director of this county for nine years, and for many years was Trustee of Dover Township. He and his wife are members of the Methodist Episcopal church.

Norval W. James, shoemaker and farmer, was born in Coshocton County, Ohio, March 16, 1833, and is a son of William James, a native of Pennsylvania, who came to Ohio about 1832. The family removed to Muskingum County, Ohio, in 1844. Mr. James came to this county in 1847, where he still resides. He was a soldier in the late war, in Company I, Thirty-sixth Ohio Infantry, about five months. He participated in the battle of South Mountain, where he was wounded, on account of which he was discharged. He received a common-school education, and learned the shoemaker's trade in 1863, which he has since followed. He has worked at his trade in Millfield about fifteen years. He also carries on his farm of eighty-five acres on section 3. He was married Sept. 24, 1865, to Ruth, daughter of William S. Gardner. They have seven children—Jessie, Minnie, William S., Norval, Robert C., Ruth and an infant daughter. Mr. James was Postmaster at Millfield for three years.

William Johnson, section 30, Dover Township, was born in Ames Township, Athens Co., Ohio, April 13, 1828. His father, James Johnson, a native of Pennsylvania, settled at Somerset, Ohio, when only a few log cabins were there. The subject of this sketch was reared on a farm, and educated in a common school. He was married in March, 1853, to Elizabeth Gallington, daughter of Chester Gallington, of Helen Furnace, Ohio. They have had five children, of whom two are living—Lydia and Dow. Lydia is the wife of Noah Johnson. Mr. Johnson, subject of this sketch, owns 160 acres of land.

A. J. Learned, M. D., was born in Dover Township, Athens Co., Ohio, July 28, 1843. During his youth he worked on the farm in the summer and spent a part of the winter in attending the public schools. After he had attained some knowledge of the common branches, he entered the Weethee College, in Athens County. Aug. 19, 1861, he enlisted in the Eighteenth Ohio Infantry, and served until Nov. 9, 1864. He then came home, and June 15, 1867, was married to Mary Daines, by whom he has seven children. In 1873 Mr. Learned began the study of medicine, and soon afterward entered the Columbus Medical College, at Columbus, Ohio, where he graduated in 1877. He immediately began the practice of medicine, and has built up a fine practice, having an extended reputation as a physician.

Martin R. Learned was born in Washington County, Ohio, Jan. 17, 1820. His father, Daniel Learned, a native of Connecticut, born in 1767, moved to Washington County, Ohio, in 1814, and to Dover Township, Athens County, in 1821. His mother was Catherine (Gilliland) Learned, born in 1789, in New Jersey. He was reared on the old homestead and educated in a subscription school. Mr. Learned learned the trade of a millwright when young; followed that trade and the chair-making trade for about twenty years. He still has chairs in his possession that he made over forty years ago. He built several flat-boats some years ago, and during the high water he would run them down Sunday Creek to Hocking, thence to the Ohio River. For the past twenty years he has been engaged in farming. He was married Jan. 6, 1842, to Miss Ursula Wemer, a daughter of John Wemer.

They had four children, but one living—Eliza J., now the wife of James L. Howard. One daughter, Marietta, died at the age of thirty-four years. She was the wife of Sardine Cradlebaugh. Mr. Learned owns 162½ acres of valuable land. When the Learned family settled in the woods of Dover Township in 1821, there were numerous deer, wolves, bears, panthers, and a few elk. There are but two men in the township who were here when they came. Mr. Learned's father died March 28, 1862, at the age of ninety-five years. His mother is still living, and is ninety-four years old. She remains with her granddaughter, Mrs. Howard, on the old homestead, which our subject still owns. Daniel Learned was married twice, and was the father of twenty-four children.

Aaron Lewis, the oldest native of York Township now living in Athens County, was born Feb. 18, 1819, a son of Samuel Lewis, a native of Allegheny County, Pa., and an early settler of York Township, Athens County, having settled here prior to the war of 1812. Our subject was brought up mostly on the old homestead, and educated in a subscription school; often had to walk three miles through the deep snow in the woods to school. Mr. Lewis was married Dec. 25, 1844, to Sarah Fisk, daughter of Claudius L. Fisk. They had two children, both dead. One daughter, Emma J., left two children—Madge Dew and Mabel Russell, she having been married twice. Mrs. Lewis died Feb. 17, 1857, and Mr. Lewis again married, Sept. 14, 1859, Ruth C. Summers, daughter of Thomas Summers. They had seven children, six living—Douglas A., Francis M., Zua, Lee, Maggie and George W. Mr. Lewis went with his parents to the head of Raccoon, in York Township, when he was eleven years old, where he lived until the building of the Hocking Canal, when he returned to Hocking River, near Nelsonville, and has since resided in the valley. He removed to his present farm in Dover Township in 1875, where he owns 320 acres of valuable land, and is engaged in farming and stock-raising. He was Assessor of York Township for nineteen years, and was Trustee for that township many years. Mr. Lewis is in possession of an enormous elk horn, partially petrified, which was found in the Hocking River by a Mr. Schoonover in the winter of 1871-'2. It is supposed that it had lain beneath the sand and water for over 100 years.

Pulaski Lowry, an enterprising young business man, was born in Dover Township, this county, July 20, 1850. His father, William Lowry, was born in Athens Township in 1801, and was a son of Robert Lowry, a native of Ireland, and one of the first pioneers of Athens County. Our subject received a common-school education. He is now operating the Chauncey Salt Works, and makes twenty-five barrels of salt daily. This salt is of the purest and best quality. Mr. Lowry was married in June, 1872, to Sarah J. North, daughter of Henry North, of Chauncey. They have had six children, four of whom are living—Alvira, Almira, Alice and Mary.

Abram Martin, Superintendent of the Athens County Infirmary, was born in Lee Township, this county, Nov. 29, 1824. His father, Samuel Martin, was a native of Virginia, and an early settler of Athens County. His mother was Hepsibah Merritt Martin. Our subject was the fourth of nine children, five of them now living—David, of Vinton County, Ohio; Elijah, of Woodson County, Kansas; Abram; Josephus, of Vinton County, Ohio, and Nancy M., now Mrs. Cottrell, of Chariton County, Mo. Three of the deceased were grown—Harriet, Caleb and Thomas. Mr. Martin was reared on the farm and had very limited educational advantages, only having attended school for nine months in all. He was a soldier in the late war, in Company C, Thirty-sixth Ohio Infantry. for three years and one month, and participated in the battles of Louisburg, second Bull Run, South Mountain, Antietam, and many others. He was married Jan. 6, 1848, to Charlotte, daughter of George Robinette. They had eight children, seven of whom are living—Ettie R., Hattie B., Charles W., George W., David M., John M. and Ella. Mr. Martin has always lived in this county except about six years spent in Vinton County. He has held the present office since 1878. He owns a farm of 100 acres in Waterloo Township.

Henry F. McCoy, M. D., physician and surgeon, Millfield, was born in Waterloo Township, Athens Co., Ohio, May 12, 1849, and and is a son of Daniel McCoy (deceased), a native of East Scotland, who settled in Athens County about 1842. Our subject's mother died when he was sixteen years old, and this broke up the family and he was thrown entirely upon his own resources. He educated himself and taught school for seven years. During the last two years of his teaching he read medicine. During the winter of 1877-'78 he took a course of lectures at the Columbus (Ohio) Medical College, and practiced the following season in Nelsonville, Ohio.

He then returned to college, and graduated with high honors in the class of 1879. He at once removed to Chauncey, where he has built up a large and lucrative practice. He received two calls the day he located in Chauncey, and has practiced more or less every day since. He was married March 6, 1879, to Elizabeth, daughter of William Hawk, of Athens Township. They have one child— E. Maud. The Doctor is a Mason, and a member of the Methodist Episcopal church.

Joseph A. McKee, section 35, Dover Township, was born in Trimble Township, Dec. 26, 1835, and is a son of William McKee, now of Morgan County, Ohio, but a native of Greene County, Pa., who came to Athens County about 1820, and lived here till 1881. He is the father of seven children, four living—George W., Mary A., Sarah and Joseph A. One son, William W., was killed at the battle of Resaca in the late war. Mr. McKee was married Jan. 17, 1858, to Mahala Snyder, a daughter of George Snyder. They had nine children, seven of whom are living—Sarah E., Mary I., Clara, William A., George W., Joseph J. and John A. Mr. McKee was Clerk of Trimble Township for six years, and was elected Justice of the Peace for Dover Township in 1879, and re-elected in 1882. He has been Clerk of the Board of Education nearly ever since he became of age. He came to this township in February, 1868. He owns eighty acres of land, and is engaged in general farming.

James McKitrick, M. D., was born near Morristown, Belmont Co., Ohio, Oct. 1, 1815, and is a son of John McKitrick (deceased), a native of Washington County, Pa., and an early settler of Belmont County. James left home when quite small, and early learned the blacksmith's trade. At the age of twenty-one years he left the shop and engaged in the mercantile business in Morganville, Ohio, where he remained five years. He then read medicine under Dr. James Rusk, with whom he practiced six months. In 1844 he came to Millfield, where he built up a large practice and remained until 1865, and then came to Chauncey and practiced until 1881, when failing health compelled him to give up his practice, and he now resides on his farm adjoining Chauncey. His successor, Dr. H. F. McCoy, is a graduate from the Columbus Medical College, and a successful physician. Dr. McKitrick has always been an industrious and useful man. He has carried on his farm, and attended to his practice, enduring many privations and hardships. He was married March 29, 1845, to Miss Sarah W. Hyde, daughter of

William Hyde (deceased), an early settler of Athens County. They have one son—William S., who resides in Chauncey, and is a farmer and stock-raiser. The Doctor is a Presbyterian in religious faith, but is a member of the Methodist Episcopal church at Chauncey. He was always noted for his generosity and liberality, and always visited poor families when called, with or without pay.

Jeremiah Morris, deceased, late of Dover Township, was born in Washington County, Penn., April 7, 1797, and was a son of Joseph Morris, a native of New Jersey. He came to this county about 1825. He married Mary A. Southerton, by whom he had five children, two living—Joseph and Dianna; one son, Jeremiah, died at the age of twenty-one years. Mrs. Morris died Jan. 19, 1832. Mr. Morris married, July 14, 1833, Bethany L., daughter of Hamilton Lapham. She was born in New York State, Aug. 21, 1811. Mr. Morris died May 3, 1874. He was a member of the Christian church.

John Mourn, merchant, Chauncey, was born in York Township, Athens County, Oct. 14, 1831, and is a son of John Mourn, deceased, a native of Ireland, who came from Maryland to this county about 1818, and settled in the woods at Thompson's Ford, on Hocking River. He was the father of nine boys and one girl, of whom our subject was the third child. He was reared on the old homestead and received a common-school education. He started to California in the spring of 1852, overland route, arriving there the following October, and returned by the Nicaraugua steamship route in the fall of 1855, and settled in Dover Township, where he has since resided. He ran a saw-mill near Chauncey for three years, and was foreman of the Chauncey Salt Works for about eighteen years. In 1878 he became established in the mercantile business in Chauncey. He keeps a full line of everything usually kept in a first-class general store, and is doing a good business. He has held the office of Clerk of Dover Township for the past eight years, and for the past five years has held the office of Postmaster at Chauncey. In the fall of 1855 he married Sarah Six, a daughter of Leonard Six, deceased. They had six children, of whom three are living—Addie, John W. and James B. One daughter, Araminta, died at the age of sixteen years, and a son, Saudell S., died at the age of six years. Three of Mr. Mourn's brothers, Patrick, Robert and Thomas, were soldiers in the late war, in the Sixty-third Ohio Infantry. The two latter were sticken down with the measles while in the service and died soon after returning home. Mr. and Mr. Mourn are members of the Methodist Episcopal church.

William Ogg, section 7, Dover Township, farmer, stock-raiser and mechanic, was born in Hocking County, Ohio, May 14, 1833. His father, Andrew Ogg, came to Athens County when a young man and settled in Ames Township, and afterward removed to Hocking County. He returned with his family to Athens County in 1834, where he died in 1865. Our subject learned the carpenter's trade when a young man, and followed that avocation continually for twenty-eight years, when he began farming, though he occasionally works at his trade. He was married June 5, 1856, to Eliza Tippe. They have had seven children, three living—Wesley, Sarah and Joseph. Mr. Ogg owns 140 acres of valuable land. He and his wife are members of the Methodist Episcopal church.

Rev. J. Green Potter, section 30, was born in Jefferson County, N. Y., Oct. 27, 1828, and is a son of Jacob Potter, a native of Poultney, Vt., who removed to Jefferson County, N. Y., when a young man, and came with his family to this county in 1836, where the subject of this sketch has since resided. He was brought up on a farm and received a common-school education, but for the most part is a self-made man. He has been a local preacher in the United Brethren church for the past twelve years. Mr. Potter was married Oct. 15, 1855, to Sarah M. Thomas. They have had eight children, seven of whom are living—Henry G., Mary P., Hettie E., Lulu M., Frank, Minnie R. and A. Eugene. One daughter, Ella, died in her seventeenth year. Mr. Potter taught school a few years when a young man. His son, Henry G., is in the employ of the Chicago Stock Publishing Company. Miss Hettie is a prominent teacher of Athens County.

Ebenezer Pratt was born in Marietta, Ohio, June 19, 1813. His father, Azariah Pratt, was a native of Saybrook, Conn., and a descendant of Lieutenant William Pratt, who came from England to America in 1633, and was an early settler of Hartford. Azariah Pratt came to Marietta, Ohio, in the spring of 1788, but soon returned and remained until after the close of the Indian war. His wife, Sarah Nye, was in the fort at Marietta during that war, and saw the Indians attempt to kill George Meigs. Our subject came with some of the family to Dover Township in 1821 and did some work on their land, and one or two years later they moved here. He has since lived on the same farm. His educational advantages were very limited. He was married, Dec. 31, 1835, to Susan W. Wells, daughter of Varnam G. Wells. They had six children, four living—Mary, Minerva J., Panthea and Sarah; one daughter, Lucy, died at the age of forty-three years. Mr. Pratt was Trustee of Dover Township about twelve years. He owns 186 acres of valuable land, and is engaged in general farming.

William H. Price, son of John H. Price, was born in Licking County, Ohio, April 11, 1850. He was reared on a farm and received a common-school education. He came to Athens County in July, 1870; has worked at various avocations, but has followed mining coal the greater part of the time for the past five years. Mr. Price married Mary J. Larch, April 11, 1878. They have one child—William H. Mrs. Price's father, John Larch, is a resident of Athens County.

Peter Rush, section 30, Dover Township, was born in Bedford County, Penn., March 11, 1806. His father, John Rush, of Pennsylvania, brought his family to Perry County, Ohio, in 1812. The subject of this sketch came to this county about 1830, which was then inhabited by deer, wolves and other wild animals, and has lived here ever since. Mr. Rush was married Oct. 20, 1826, to Susannah Linscott, daughter of Israel Linscott. They have had eleven children, of whom four are living—Calvin, George, Almira and Minerva. Alva J. was married, and at his death left four children—Reburta, George, Barbara E. and Martha. George carries on the farm. Another son of our subject, Hiram, died at the age of eighteen years. Mr. Rush owns sixty-five acres of land.

Joel Sanders was born in Columbiana County, Ohio, March 16, 1814. His father, Benjamin Sanders, a native of Georgia, was a Quaker, but was excommunicated for marrying Sarah Wilkins. Joel was the third of their sixteen children, of whom seven are living—Milton, of Boston, Mass.; Joel; Jesse, in Iowa; Alusha N., of Chicago; Rebecca, of Wis.; Mrs. Margaret Ellis, of Iowa, and Mrs. Lizzie Donahue, of Davenport, Iowa. Mr. Sanders was married May 14, 1838, to Cynthia B., daughter of Ezra Johnson, an early settler of Athens County, who died here in 1873, in his eighty-fourth year. They have had five children, four living—Benjamin N., Charles D., Lewis W. and Chester L. One son, Joseph M., died in 1862 at the age of sixteen years. Mr. Sanders came to Athens County with his parents in 1830. He was Postmaster at Millfield for seven years; was Trustee of Dover Township three years, Superintendent of Infirmary eight years, Township Clerk seven years, and was elected Justice of the Peace in 1882. One son, Charles D., was a soldier in the late war.

Ebenezer Shaner was born in Muskingum County, Ohio, Jan. 7, 1812. His father, Adam Shaner, was born on Little Yah River, Pa., about 1784; and his grandfather, Matthias Shaner, was a German by birth and a Revolutionary soldier. Adam Shaner settled in Muskingum, Ohio, in 1805. The subject of this sketch was brought up on the farm and educated in a subscription school. He helped to operate the first saw-mill that was built in the vicinity of Zanesville. He came to this county in December, 1834, where he has since lived, except a short time spent in Morgan County. He was married March 18, 1834, to Mary A., daughter of Joseph Taylor. They have had eleven children, six living—Adam, Debora A., Lovina E., Samantha R., George and Hattie M. Mr. and Mrs. Shaner lost three sons in the late war while fighting for their country. Oliver P. was in Company A, Thirty-first Ohio Infantry. Davis was in Company A, Sixty-third Ohio Infantry, and Justice T. was in Company B, Seventy-fifth Ohio Infantry. The others, Elizabeth J. and Wm. H., were aged eighteen and two years respectively. Mr. Shaner was also a soldier in the late war, in Company A, Sixty-third Ohio Infantry. He was taken sick and was discharged after being in the hospital about eighteen months. He now draws a pension. Mr. Shaner has always been a farmer, and has seen many hardships and privations.

William O. Silvey, agent of the Hocking Valley Railroad Company, express agent and Postmaster at Salina, Athens County, was born in Marietta, Ohio, May 24, 1845, a son of John Silvey, a native of Pennsylvania, who resides in Middleport, Ohio. Our subject received his education in Wheelersburg, Ohio, working on a farm near by in summer, and attending school winters. He enlisted in the late war, in Company E, Thirty-third Ohio Infantry, for three years, and participated in the battles of Stone River, Chickamauga and Resaca. He was then taken sick and sent to Hospital No. 3, Nashville, but in a few days was detailed one of General Rosecrans's clerks, in which capacity he served until he was discharged in October, 1864. He worked at feeding horses for the Government a short time after returning from the war, then went to Racine, Ohio, where he engaged in the silversmith trade, but soon after abandoned it and engaged in the boot and shoe business. He went to Vincent Station on the M. & C. R. R. in 1868, where he learned telegraphy. He came to Salina in 1869, and clerked in the Salt Company's store, and had charge of the telegraph office here at the same time. As soon as the railroad was completed to Salina he entered into the employ of the company at Nelsonville, and about a month later took charge of the office at Salina, where he still remains. Mr. Silvey was married Oct. 26, 1871, to Aurelia Chamberlin, by whom he has one child—William H. Mrs. Silvey died Oct. 26, 1874, and he again married, May 1, 1877, Ruth Barker, daughter of Joseph Barker, an early settler of Athens County. This union has been blessed with two children—Effie May and Annie Aurelia, the former five years and the latter three years old. Mr. Silvey is a Mason and a member of the Methodist Episcopal church.

Charles R. Smith was born in Rhode Island, Dec. 12, 1817. His father, Stephen Smith, was a sea captain for many years, sometimes being absent from home two years at a time. Our subject received his early education at Providence and Newport, R. I., and in the Manual Labor School at Pawtucket. At the latter place he prepared for college and entered Brown University in 1835, but left at the close of the Sophomore year, on leave of absence, and finally drifted to Hocking Valley, Ohio, and never returned. When he came West he had no definite object in view, but came merely to see the world west of the mountains. His route here was via Long Island Sound, Hudson River, New York Central R. R. (then terminating at Utica), Erie Canal, Lake Erie, to Ashtabula; thence by stage to Steubenville; thence by Ohio River to Marietta; thence on horseback to Athens, arriving at the latter place in August, 1839. He clerked for ten months in Norman Root's store, when he was homesick and started home, but his finances gave out at Pittsburg, and he went to work to obtain money to complete his journey. While there he met Frederick Harbach, a young surveyor from Massachusetts, who was also homesick and without money. They talked matters over and concluded to go West, whereupon they put their scanty means together and bought a skiff and some provisions and floated down the Ohio River to the mouth of the Hocking, where our subject stopped off temporarily, while Harbach went to St. Louis, intending to send for Smith as soon as he should find a position for him; but he never sent for him. Mr. Smith then came to Chauncey, which was then just building up. After a short time as bookkeeper, he became clerk for Ewing, Vinton & Co., the original salt company, and afterward became superintendent of their business. The first coal that was shipped from Hocking Valley into the market was done under Mr. Smith's supervision. By his scientific system of bookkeeping and calculation, he showed to the Hocking Valley Coal and Salt Company that they were making no money on the salt produced, and they abandoned its manufacture in 1881. Our subject was appointed Postmaster of Chauncey in 1842, and the same year was elected to the office of Justice of the Peace. He filled both offices with credit to himself and satisfaction to the people for many years. For six years he was Infirmary Director, and for many years Treasurer of Dover Township. The Esquire was a prominent candidate before the Republican nominating convention in 1876, and in 1879 he left the party and now votes with the Democrats. He was married in December, 1842, to Eliza Everett, of Ames Township, a daughter of George Everett (deceased), an early settler of that township. They had four children, two of whom are living—Maria (now Mrs. Thomas Sheppard, of Nelsonville), and Charles R., Jr., of Chicago. One son, Frederick H., died in Missouri, May 15, 1873, at the age of twenty-six years. Mrs. Smith died July 17, 1849, and he again married, April 7, 1851, Rachel Haning, a daughter of Isaac Haning, by whom he has had four children, two living—George H., a merchant of Chauncey, and Mary A., now Mrs. Geo. H. Knight, of Providence, R. I. Mr. and Mrs. Smith are members of the Presbyterian church in Athens.

David Smith was born in Ward Township, Hocking Co., Ohio, June 19, 1849, a son of Robert H. Smith, of Missouri. Mr. Smith spent his boyhood days on the farm, and attended the common schools. At the age of twenty he came to Chauncey, and has since been engaged in mining coal. For the past two years he has worked in the mine at the Chauncey Salt Works. He was married March 19, 1872, to Anna, daughter of Nathan Pickett, an old settler of this county, but now a resident of Kansas. They had three children, two of whom are living—Nettie and Robert. He is a member of I. O. O. F.

William Smith was born in this township June 18, 1845, and is a son of John Smith, a native of Athens County. His grandfather, Samuel Smith, was a native of Virginia, and an early settler in Athens County. Mr. Smith was a soldier in the late war, in Company A, Sixty-third Regiment, Ohio Volunteer Infantry, and accompanied Sherman to the sea. He was married Jan. 1, 1866, to Dorcas, daughter of John Shannon. She was born in Waterloo Township, this county. Her father came with his parents to this county when a small boy. Mr. Smith's parents had fourteen children, nine of whom are now living—Isaac, Samuel, William, John, Elisha, Ezra, Mary, Elizabeth and Belle. The father died in 1873, at the age of sixty-nine. Mrs. Smith's parents had nine children, six of whom are living—Jackson, Sarah, Eleanor, Nancy, John and Dorcas.

Charles W. Southerton, Sunday Creek Valley, one and a half miles north of Chauncey, was born in Dover Township, where he now lives, May 22, 1831. His father, James Southerton, came to Athens County from England in 1820, and settled where our subject now resides. He married Harriet Renment, and they had eight children, four now living—James P., Harriet (Mansfield), Rhoda A. (White), and Charles W., who was brought up on the old homestead and received a common-school education. He owns 520 acres of valuable land, and is engaged in farming and stock-raising. He was married Dec. 9, 1857, to Lydia Deshler, daughter of Christopher Deshler. They had four children, but one of whom is living—Cora C. One son, Hiram W., died at the age of eight years. Mr. Southerton's father died in 1840.

James P. Southerton was born in the parish of Sussex, England, Dec. 17, 1811, and is a son of James Southerton, a native of the same place, who brought his family to this county in 1821, and settled in Dover Township. Our subject was educated in the select, or subscription, schools of the pioneer days. There was a log cabin where the family settled, and one acre slashed. Mr. Southerton has helped clear two farms. When he settled where he now lives it was in the woods. He was married in June, 1836, to Elizabeth H., daughter of James Musgrave, a native of Virginia. She was born in Tyler County, Va., and came to Muskingum County with her parents in 1833, and to this county in 1835. They have had thirteen children, of whom eight are living—Sarah A., William B., Clark N., L. Horton, Hiram, Maria, Edwin and Alice. Mr. Southerton has worked at the cooper's trade winters for the past thirty or more years. He owns 223 acres of valuable land, and is engaged in farming and stock-raising. Mrs. Southerton is a member of the Methodist church.

Jonathan Spaulding, section 1, Dover Township, was born in Hillsboro County, N. H., March 29, 1805, a son of A. Spaulding. He went with his parents to Windham County, Vt., in 1816, where the father died. Our subject went to Massachusetts in 1822, to Maryland in January, 1829, and Philadelphia in 1830.

He helped build the first railroad that was built in the United States, between Quincy and Milton, Mass., in about 1824. It was only four miles long. Mr. Spaulding worked at granite-stone cutting twelve years. From 1834 to 1836 he superintended the building of the first railroad that crossed the Allegheny Mountains. He helped build the first railroad out of Baltimore, and the first one out of Philadelphia. He also helped to run the first railroad engine ever run in the United States. In 1836 he helped build the limestone bridge on the turnpike across Will Creek, at Cumberland, Md., and in 1837 he came to Zanesville, Ohio, where he cut stone three years. He came to Athens County in 1840, where he has been farming and working at his trade until the last few years. He was married in March, 1836, to Melinda Parr, a native of Adams County, Pa. They had eight children, five living—Jonas R., William A., John M., Susan R. and Mary A. One son, Eli, died at the age of twenty-one years. Mrs. Spaulding died in January, 1870, and Mr. Spaulding was married in July, 1872, to Mrs. Sidney Bay, who died in January, 1873. His son, William A., lives on the old homestead with his father and runs the farm. He married Mary Hoisington, by whom he has two children—Lizzie and Bertie. The family are Methodists. John H. Spaulding married Charlotte Richmond and has two children—Harrie and Nellie. He lives adjoining the old homestead in Dover Township.

John A. Stephenson was born in Newark, Ohio, Feb. 21, 1835, and is a son of James A. Stephenson, who brought his family to Athens County in 1839. Our subject was reared on a farm and educated in Nelsonville. He farmed from 1857 to 1861, when he enlisted in the late war in Company H, Sixty-third Ohio Infantry, and served four years. He was in detached service all the time in the commissary department, under supervision of Colonel G. W. Baker. He was present at the battles of Corinth, Champion Hills, siege of Vicksburg, Brandon, Nashville, Iuka and others. He came to Chauncey in 1866. Oct. 29, 1857, he married Clara Birge, daughter of William A. Birge. They have four children—Ollie L. (now Mrs. J. K. Brown), James W., Gracie G. and Bertha B. Our subject's brother, James K. P. Stephenson, was killed at the battle of Bull Run, while in defense of his country. Mr. Stephenson has been a miner for the past seventeen years, and has worked all that time in the mine of the Chauncey Salt Works. He is a member of the Masonic fraternity.

Austin True, section 18, Dover Township, was born on the old homestead, where he now resides, March 6, 1818, and was a son of Josiah True (deceased). Mr. True was brought up on the old homestead, and received but limited educational advantages. He has always lived on the farm, and formerly was extensively engaged in dealing in stock, buying and shipping to Baltimore. He was married Feb. 11, 1844, to Jane, daughter of Resolved Fuller. They have had four children, three of whom are living—Hiram, Sarah and John. The first married Julia Weethee, and had one child—Marcus W. His wife died, and he then married Helen Moore. They have two children—Evelyn and Augusta. Sarah True married Levi Sprague, and has had five children—Florence L. (deceased), Wiley T., Warren V., Myra G. and Jennie E. John True married Mattie Maxwell, and has three children—Effie J., Laura E. and Lydia. Hiram was in the late war about nine months. He is now a physician in McConnelsville, Ohio. Mr. True owns about 1,000 acres of valuable land, and is engaged in farming and stock-raising. Mrs. True died in October, 1853. Mr. True never seeks for office or public favors.

J. P. Weethee is descended from New England parentage. His father, Daniel Weethee, and his mother, Lucy Wilkins, came from Southern New Hampshire to Ohio in 1798. Mr. Weethee settled in Dover Township, Athens County. Miss Wilkins being then single lived with her parents in the vicinity of Athens. After their marriage they began their log-cabin life on Sunday Creek, in North Dover. An unbroken wilderness covered that part of the county. The Indians were there, but were preparing to move toward the distant West. This couple had no company for some years but the red man and the wild beasts of the impenetrable forests—the bear, the panther and numerous packs of wolves, which congregated on hills and points in early eve to hold their night revels, and serenade the stars. Such a life was in gloomy contrast to the refined society of their New England homes. They were young, however, and a bright future was in anticipation.

Mrs. Weethee ended a long and quiet life on the same farm, while her husband, who survived her some years, died in Ames Township. They now sleep quietly together on a rise of ground, which commands a pleasing view of their early wilderness home.

J. P. Weethee, the subject of this memoir, was one of a numerous family born in a wilderness. His early thoughts were such as his surroundings would naturally suggest. His infancy, childhood and early youth were confined exclusively to Sunday Creek, and to what his Sunday Creek home was able to teach. His childhood was without any except parental instruction. His schooling in early youth was confined to two or three months in the year. His teachers knew nothing of the science of geography, had but limited knowledge of the higher rules of arithmetic, and very seldom taught even the first principles of English grammar. Under such imperfect tuition Mr. Weethee spent his first fifteen years. With a view to a more educational turn of life Mr. Weethee, in the fall of 1827, entered the Academical Department of the Ohio University. Being so imperfectly drilled in the primary branches, and knowing little else than the uncouth manners of backwoods boys, his progress in Latin and in other branches was by no means flattering to himself or to the expectations of his relatives. He has often remarked that his first year at the University was apparently thrown away, and yet it prepared his constitution for the severe drill which followed in after years. It was a preparatory year. In the fall of 1832, one-half year being occupied in teaching, Mr. Weethee took the degree of A. B., and that fall, about a month after his graduation, he commenced the study of medicine, under the private tuition of A. V. Medbery, M. D., a practicing physician of Athens. Under his instruction Mr. Weethee continued two years. The miscellaneous exercises of those two years opened up to Mr. Weethee a new field of future usefulness. During the vacation that followed his graduation, a camp-meeting was held by Rev. John Morgan and others, Cumberland Presbyterian ministers from the South (Alabama). In the great revival of that camp-meeting, Mr. Weethee made a profession of faith in Christ, and during the following winter joined the Athens church of that denomination.

During the two years of Mr. Weethee's medical studies he was occupied in Sabbath-schools, in various religious meetings and in Scripture investigations. Another field of future usefulness, one that seemed more vitally important, now called his attention—the ministry; for to do good, rather than to make money, appeared to Mr. Weethee the highest motive of existence. In the fall of 1834 Mr. Weethee went to Pittsburg, Penn., and placed himself under the care of the Pennsylvania Presbytery of the Cumberland Presbyterian church and commenced his studies for the ministry under Rev. J. Morgan, then Pastor of the Cumberland Presbyterian congregation at Uniontown, Pa. At that location was Madison College, whose first President was Rev. H. B. Bascom, the great orator of the time. Difficulties in the Methodist Episcopal church finally caused the college to suspend. By invitation of the trustees he opened a school in the college building. For the first three weeks he had but three pupils. He remained at the college eight years, graduated classes, and saw for years over 100 students during each session. Those were for Mr. Weethee (he being President) years of great mental exercise. He had at times to fill each professorship. He commenced teaching at sunrise, and usually heard from fifteen to twenty classes a day. On Saturdays he rode eighteen miles to a church, preached at night and on Sabbath at 11 A. M., and rode home in the afternoon ready to commence college exercises on Monday morning. He had no mental vacation. In 1842 Mr. Weethee was elected to the Presidency of Beverly College, Washington County, Ohio, and in the fall of that year he moved to Beverly and took charge of the institution. This college was placed under the care of the Pennsylvania Synod of the Cumberland Presbyterian church. It being in the vicinity of Marietta College, an old and well-established institution, its prospects were by no means flattering. During his first winter (1842-'3) Mr. Weethee took his first departure from what is generally regarded the "Orthodox faith."

On examining the prophecies relative to the future, more especially those of Daniel ii., vii., viii. and ix., and of the Apocalypse, Mr. Weethee concluded that those chains of prophecy were about to close, and as they brought the Son of Man again from heaven he believed that the advent was near. He considered it his duty to make public his convictions, being fully persuaded that the message would be glad tidings to all that loved his appearing. Opposition to those doctrines soon taught Mr. Weethee that Paul was mistaken when he said, "that a crown was laid up for all that loved his appearing," or that there were but few Christians. Opposition, however, did not deter him from proclaiming the truth. Wherever amongst all denominations a door was opened, Mr. Weethee was heard in heralding the coming Redeemer.

In the fall of 1844 Mr. Weethee, by invitation, visited Cincinnati, where he continued to preach during part of the winter. In the following spring (1845) he removed to Cincinnati and took charge of the Second Advent congregation, with which he continued till the spring of 1848. His ministerial labors while residing in the Queen City were constant and quite severe. In the spring of 1848 he removed to Boston, Mass., and took charge of the Chardon Street Church, where he remained till the fall of 1851. During his sojourn in Boston Mr. Weethee's labors in the great proclamation were more arduous than at Cincinnati. He was called to attend tent meetings in various parts of New England. He held protracted meetings in New York City, continuing six weeks, he speaking every night; also at Philadelphia, Lancaster, Baltimore, Brooklyn, Providence, Worcester, Bangor, Me., Woodstock on the St. John's, N. B., Halifax, Nova Scotia, and in various other locations in the East. While residing in Boston Mr. Weethee took his second departure from popular orthodoxy, the rejection of man's natural immortality, and the doctrine of endless torment. He holds Paul's declaration to be literally true, that "the wages of sin is death [not eternal conscious torments], but the gift of God is eternal life through Jesus Christ our Lord."

In the fall of 1851 Mr. Weethee returned again to Ohio, visiting Cleveland and Cincinnati. In a severe winter he returned from Cincinnati to Sunday Creek, the place of his nativity. In the fall of 1853 he took charge of the Amesville Academy, and continued in that institution two years teaching and preaching.

In the summer of 1855 he was elected President of Waynesburg College, located at Waynesburg, Greene Co., Pa. This college belonged, in its management, to the Pennsylvania Synod of the Cumberland Presbyterian Church. In the fall of 1855 Mr. Weethee removed to Waynesburg and entered upon his duties as President of the college. In that institution was a female department so constructed (not by the charter) as to give two heads to one institution. This arrangement did not suit his ideas of a college. Still he continued there till the fall of 1858, when he resigned and returned to Ohio. During Mr. Weethee's Presidency the number of students increased from 70 to 143. He was not forced to leave, but he deemed it best so to do. He graduated three classes. During his sojourn in Waynesburg he was called upon by the citizens to do much of the preaching. By request of the citizens he delivered a course of seven lectures, two hours each, to large audiences, on the nature and destiny of man.

In 1865 Mr. Weethee commenced teaching at his own residence which afterward grew into Weethee College, which was incorporated. Many students attended this institution. Its location is high and commanding and the site unusually healthy. Owing to its surroundings the institution has never commanded, at any one time, a large number of students; still it has had a reasonable patronage. Mr. Weethee put all his means into the buildings, apparatus and cabinet, and consequently cramped himself as to his pecuniary resources. From 1869 to 1875-'6 he was a worker in the Atlantic & Lake Erie Railway scheme, which afterward was changed to the Ohio Central. His labors of nearly seven years were lost in that enterprise. He was a Director and attended the last meeting of its board. That Ohio Central is the father of the present Ohio Central.

Mr. Weethee consumed time in geological researches to ascertain the mineral resources of Sunday Creek Valley. His reports are found in parts of the State geological reports of Dover and Trimble townships, Athens County. From 1876 to the present time (1883) he has resided at his own quiet home on Mount Auburn, North Dover, Sunday Creek Valley. He spends his time principally in writing on the prophetic Scriptures, which are published weekly in a religious periodical called *The Restitution*. His views on great moral and religious topics are unpopular, yet he is fearless in proclaiming his convictions. He thinks it safer to please God than to bow to the opinions of men. On all Scripture doctrines he consults the original Hebrew and Greek. What they teach he receives as the Divine voice.

Mr. Weethee's habits have always been strictly temperate, mostly teetotal. He has never made use of tobacco, regarding the practices of chewing and smoking filthy, intemperate and morally degrading. He never uses ardent spirits as a beverage. He pities the weakness of the drunkard, and utterly abhors the drunkard-makers. Had he the power dram-shops would immediately cease from the earth, and men from necessity would remain sober. He is therefore a high type of prohibitionism. He uses neither tea nor coffee. The proceeds of these habits he devotes to the proclamation of the glad tidings of Christ's coming and reign.

At the age of twenty-four years he married Miss Ann C. Krepps, of Philadelphia, with whom he is now living. She has always been to him, what every wife should be, a helpmate. A lady of deep religious convictions, she has always aided her husband, by her industry and strict economy, to carry the gospel to the poor. Depriving herself of all luxuries she saves means to send to the aid of missionary efforts in distant lands, especially to the Hebrews.

Ten miles due north of Athens in the valley of Sunday Creek, in a beautiful Gothic cottage on Mount Auburn, lives this couple in peace and in domestic quietude, Mrs. Weethee diligently occupied with her domestic affairs and with her garden of choice flowers, watching also the signs of the times, while her husband at his desk, pen in hand, choice books before and around him, sends forth weekly articles from the prophecies. Though living in retirement, yet by means of his pen he speaks weekly in various cities of the United States, Canada, England, Scotland, Holland, Switzerland, Jerusalem, India, New Zealand and to other parts of the world, looking for that blessed hope, the appearing of the Great God, even our Savior, Jesus, the Christ.

Laurentius Weethee, deceased, late of Dover Township, was born on the old homestead in North Dover, on Sunday Creek, March 10, 1810, and is a brother of Prof. Perkins Weethee, of this township. Our subject was educated in the common schools. The family removed out of the old house into the new one when he was four years old, and he lived there until his death, and ate within two feet of the same place for sixty-four years. He was married Feb. 25, 1826, to Lucy Nye. They had three children, but one now living—Lydia, now Mrs. Dr. Sprague, of Toronto, Canada, Mrs. Weethee died Feb. 23, 1864, and Oct. 1, 1865, he married Mrs. Nancy Johnson, daughter of John D. Johnson, of Pennsylvania. They had three children—Emma, Albert and Lucy. Mr. Weethee died March 28, 1879. He was a man of very marked character, honest, upright, benevolent, and the poor man's friend. He was a kind neighbor, and true Christian gentleman. He was a farmer and stock-raiser, and owned 540 acres of valuable land,

Andrew J. Willmarth was born in Fairfield, Franklin Co., Vt., June 17, 1811. His father, Rufus W. Willmarth, was also a native of Fairfield and a son of Ephraim Willmarth, a Revolutionary officer, who was wounded at the battle of Bennington. The Willmarths are descendants of John Willmarth, who came from England to America in a very early day. Our subject's Grandfather Willmarth and two brothers, John and Asa, were ship carpenters. Mr. Willmarth came to Muskingum County, Ohio, with his parents in 1818, and to this county in 1832, where he has since resided except three years spent in Clinton County, Ohio. He was married in the fall of 1833 to Sarah, daughter of Jacob Larue. They had one child—Sarah, now Mrs. Madison. Mrs. Willmarth died and he married, May 15, 1867, Mary, daughter of James Pugsley. Mr. Willmarth owns 137½ acres of valuable land.

BIOGRAPHICAL SKETCHES OF TRIMBLE TOWNSHIP.

Josiah Allen, dealer in hardware, furniture and lumber, senior member of the firm of Allen & Chadwell, is the oldest son of J. J. and Amanda R. (*nee* Fowler) Allen. He was born in Trimble Township, Athens Co., Ohio, Aug. 13, 1859, and lived with his parents until manhood. He attended the common schools and six terms at the Mt. Auburn College; during a part of that time was engaged as teacher of the grammar branches. He attended the National Normal University at Lebanon, Ohio, during the spring term of 1881. In the fall of 1878 he began teaching a Normal School at Trimble, and was thus engaged until 1882. He also attended the Ohio University at Athens during the spring term of 1879. June 1, 1882, he engaged in the lumber and hardware business near Trimble. Dec. 20, the same year, he established his present business in Trimble with Mr. Chadwell, and they now have a flourishing and increasing trade. Mr. Allen is a Master Mason, member of Bishopville Lodge, No. 470, A. F. & A. M. He is a member of the Disciple church and an ordained minister.

Thomas Biddison, farmer, the oldest son of William and Margaret (Forker) Biddison, was born in Perry County, Ohio, July 10, 1837. When fourteen years of age his parents removed to Athens County. At the age of twenty-one years he began farming for himself. Aug. 17, 1864, he enlisted in Company E, One Hundred and Seventy-fourth Ohio Infantry, as a private for one year, at Hartleyville, Ohio; was engaged with his regiment at Murfreesboro in 1864, and was wounded and sent to the hospital, and remained until February, 1865, when he received a furlough and was home one month. He then returned to Columbus and remained a short time; then to Camp Denison, where he was discharged, May 29, 1865. After his return home he purchased a farm, but sold it a year later and purchased a grist-mill in Morgan County. He ran his mill seven years and then sold out and rented land in Trimble Township, and farmed five years. He then purchased the farm on which he now resides. Jan. 8, 1860, he married Delilah, daughter of Morris and Emily (Edwards) Bryson, of Trimble Township. They have ten children—Henry, Maria, Elmer G., Luella, Sidney M., Silas, Ores A., Dilla M., Garfield, Clades L. and Rosie E.

William Biddison, Jr., farmer, is the second son of William and Margaret (Forker) Biddison. He was born in Perry County, Ohio, Dec. 10, 1847. When he was three years of age his parents removed to Athens County, where he was reared, and received a common-school education. March 5, 1865, he enlisted in Company A, One Hundred and Ninety-sixth Ohio Infantry, as a private for one year. He was with the command in the Shenandoah Valley; mustered out at Baltimore in September, 1865, and returned to Camp Chase, Ohio, where he was discharged Oct. 1, 1865. He then returned home and worked on a farm a year, and in the coal mines during the winter of 1866. In March, 1870, he rented land and farmed three years. He then removed to the home farm near Trimble and lived there four years. In April, 1877, he returned to the farm on school section, and has been farming to the present time. He has served as Township Trustee two years. Dec. 23, 1879, he married Loretta, daughter of S. T. and Mary (Swift) Kempton, of Trimble, Ohio. They have six children—Mary M., Laura A., William T., Dosie A., and Bertha M. and Bessie W. (twins), all at home. Raymond died in infancy. Mr. and Mrs. Biddison are members of the Disciple church.

Wm. H. Braddock, jeweler, is the oldest son of M. J. and Julia (Meloy) Braddock, of New Lexington, Ohio. He was born March 23, 1859, at New Lexington, Ohio, and lived there with his parents until nineteen years old, receiving a common-school education. March 3, 1879, he came to Trimble, Ohio, and worked at his trade as jeweler, in the store of G. A. Russell, until Oct. 23 of that same year, when his father-in-law gave him property in Trimble, where he located his present business and has continued to the present time with an increasing business. During the years 1880 and 1881 he had groceries in connection with his jewelry business. He is a Master Mason, member of Bishopville Lodge, No. 470, A. F. & A. M., Bishopville, Ohio. July 3, 1879, he married Clara, daughter of James and Mary A. (Vore) Duffee, of Trimble, Ohio. They had one child—William M. Mrs. Braddock is a member of the Disciple church.

Isaac E. Chappelear, proprietor of livery and feed stable at Corning, Perry County, and Trimble, Athens County, second son of James W. and Mary (Murphy) Chappelear, was born near Ringgold, Morgan Co., Ohio. At the age of twenty-one years he rented a farm in Morgan County, and farmed four years. From August, 1880, to August, 1881, he was engaged in the sale of patent medicines for M. C. Chappelear, of Zanesville, Ohio, traveling through the counties of Muskingum, Washington, Athens, Guernsey, Morgan, Noble and Harrison. In the fall of 1881 he was engaged in the hardware and grocery business at Byesville, Guernsey Co., Ohio, for three months, when he traded his stock of goods for lands in Missouri. In the spring of 1882 he established his livery and feed stables at Corning, Ohio, and in February, 1883, he opened his stables at Trimble. He is a Master Mason, member of Lodge No. 470, A. F. & A. M., Bishopville, Morgan Co., Ohio; was Senior Deacon of lodge from November, 1878, to November 1879, and Secretary from November, 1879, to November, 1880. He is a member of the Methodist Episcopal church.

Harvey D. Danford, M. D., physician, is the second son of John and Mary (Bradrick) Danford, and was born in Homer Township, Morgan Co., Ohio, Sept. 23, 1844. He lived with his parents on the farm until seventeen years of age, and received a common-school education. In October, 1861, he enlisted in Company F, Eighteenth Ohio Infantry, and was with that regiment some five months, when on account of his age he was sent home. Returning home he attended select school until June, 1863, when he enlisted in Company I, First Ohio Heavy Artillery, as a private for three years, or during the war. His command was first stationed at Covington, Ky.; from there to Lexington, Ky.; then at Fort Clay until February, 1864. They were then removed to Burside Point on the Cumberland River. In March they were removed to Knoxville, Tenn., and for several months were engaged in scouting the surrounding country; from there to Greenville, Tenn. In the spring of 1864 he was detailed by special order as an Orderly to Colonel C. G. Hawley, acting Brigadier-General, and served in that capacity until his term of service expired. July 25, 1865, he was discharged with his command at Knoxville, Tenn., and mustered out at Camp Denison, Ohio, Aug. 24 following, and returned home and attended school for a few months. Then engaged in the oil business for a short time. In the fall of 1866 he began the study of medicine with Dr. W. E. W. Shepard, of Nelsonville, Ohio; was with him three years, and during that time took two courses in the medical college of Cincinnati, Ohio, graduating March 1, 1870. May 1, 1870, he located at Trimble, Ohio, with Dr. John Dew. They practiced together three years. Dr. Danford is a member of Bishopville Lodge, No. 470, A. F. & A. M., Bishopville, Ohio; Athens Chapter, No. 39, R. A. M.; Athens Council, No. 15, R. & S. M., and Athens Commandery, No. 15, Knights Templar. April 10, 1872, he married Lydia, daughter of Morris and Emily (Edwards) Bryson, of Trimble. They have one child—Vernon G. Mr. Danford is a member of the Disciple church.

Silas J. Danford, dealer in general merchandise, is the senior member of the firm of Danford & Bradrick, Trimble, Ohio. He is the second son of John and Mary (Bradrick) Danford, and was born in Morgan County, Ohio, Feb. 7, 1848, and lived with his parents on the farm until manhood. He attended the common select schools and at the age of seventeen commenced teaching. In the spring of 1868 he attended the Iowa University at Mt. Pleasant, two terms. After leaving the University he taught school during the winter of 1868 and 1869. He returned to Morgan County, Ohio, in the spring of 1869, and resumed teaching, making his home at his father's. In the spring of 1871 he went to Iowa and Missouri in the interest of a patent hay-rake and fork, and was there three months. He returned home in the summer of 1871, and taught until the spring of 1873, when he went to Akron, Ohio, and attended the Akron Business College one term. He then taught until September, 1877, when he came to Trimble, Ohio, and purchased a grocery of E. N. Morehead. In the fall of 1880 he added dry goods, having at other times combined stationery and notions. In 1881 he added hardware in connection with his other business and continued the business alone until Dec. 1, 1881, when he formed a partnership with John F. Chadwell, and conducted the business under the firm name of Danford & Chadwell one year. In December, 1882, they dissolved partnership by mutual assent. He then rented his property to other parties and purchased the property and established the present firm where they now are doing an increasing business near the depot. Since the spring of 1878 he has been Township Treasurer. He is a member of the Disciple church.

M. P. Davis, M. D., physician, is the oldest son of Malon and Hylinda (Anderson) Davis. He was born near Long Island, N. J., May 13, 1813. His parents moved to Zanesville, Ohio, when he was a small boy, and from there to Wolf Creek, Morgan Co., Ohio, where he lived and worked on a farm and received a common-school education. He taught school during the winter months, and attended college for a time at Granville, Ohio. At the age of twenty-one years he began the study of medicine with Dr. E. W. Tinker, of Rosseau, Morgan Co., Ohio, and was with him about three years. In the spring of 1838, he located in Amesville, Athens County, and practiced there three years. He then removed to Perry County, Ohio, and practiced there two years; then lived in South Charleston, Ohio, one year, when he returned to Perry County and purchased a farm near Miller Town and carried on farming in connection with his practice until the spring of 1852. In April, 1852, he sold his property and purchased a farm near Trimble. In December, 1861, he enlisted in Company E, Sixty-third Ohio Volunteer Infantry, for three years as First Lieutenant. In May, 1862, he came home with the remains of his son who died at Corinth, and resigned his position and resumed the practice of his profession and farming until his death, Feb. 29, 1876. Dec. 13, 1838, he married Lydia A., daughter of Samuel and Mary H. (Tinker) Morrow, of Perry County, Ohio. Four children were born to them, only two now living—Amanda S. and Arius N. Lydia V. died at the age of two years. Malon Oscar died at Corinth, Miss., May 27, 1862. He was drummer of Company E, Sixty-third Ohio Volunteer Infantry. Mrs. Davis lives at the homestead with her son Arius.

Lewis W. Fulton, farmer, Trimble Township, Athens County, is the oldest son of Zephaniah and Laura (Fay) Fulton. He was born in Dover Township, Athens County, April 27, 1847, and lived with his parents until seventeen years of age, working on the farm and attending the common schools. Sept. 27, 1864, he enlisted in Company E, One Hundred and Seventy-fourth Regiment Ohio Volunteer Infantry, in Trimble, Ohio, as a private for one year, and was engaged in the battles of the Cedars near Stone River, Overhaul Creek, Decatur, Ala., near Kingston, N. C., joined Sherman near Goldsboro, N. C., and was present at Johnson's surrender, returning to Columbus, Ohio, where he was discharged July 6, 1865. He then returned home and purchased a farm in Trimble Township. In 1869 he sold his farm and removed to Doniphan County, Kas., and purchased lands and farmed one year. He then sold his lands and returned to Trimble Township and purchased the farm on which he at present resides, though he sold it in February, 1883, and is now employed by O. D. Jackson in managing his lumber interests. July 15, 1867, he married Miss Clarisa A., daughter of A. H. and Almira (Phillips) Chute, of Ward Township, Hocking County. They have three children—Laura L., Mary F. and Chester A., all at home. Two children, Augustus and Lucy, died in infancy. Himself and wife are members of the Disciple church.

Oliver D. Jackson, owner and proprietor of mines and store, and founder of the town of Jacksonville, is the only son of Joshua H. and Mary (Bean) Jackson. He was born in York Township,

Athens County, May 18, 1848, and lived there until 1854, when his parents removed to Ward Township, Hocking County. At the age of nineteen years he began teaching school, and taught during the winter season four years. Aug. 25, 1872, he and his father established a hardware store at New Straitsville, Perry Co., Ohio, under the firm name of J. H. Jackson & Son. In September, 1875, he purchased his father's interest and continued the business alone until May 1, 1877, when he sold a portion of his business there, and removed a portion of his stock to Bessemer and established a general mercantile store, and in November following removed his business to Buchtel, and April 1, 1878, he sold an interest in the business to the Akron Iron Company. He was then having full charge of the management of the store and live-stock business of the company until Sept. 10, 1882, when he sold his interest to the Akron Iron Company. In April, 1880, he purchased the first lands where he is now in business, and has added adjoining lands continually to the present time. He began business at this point Sept. 15, 1882, and is now shipping coal from his mines, and has a village laid out covering sixty acres. Sept. 7, 1875, he married Jane, daughter of David and Tryphena (Judd) Eggleston, of Ward Township, Hocking County. They have four children—Minnie E., William W., Frederick H. and Edward B.

J. W. Jenkins, miner, oldest son of William and Isabel (Roach) Jenkins, was born near Oakhill, Jackson Co., Ohio, Dec. 23, 1854, and lived there with his parents until sixteen years old, attending the common-schools. At the age of sixteen years he was employed as brakesman on the M. & C. R. R. After working there one year he returned home and attended school two years. He was then engaged mining ore near Ironton, Ohio, about six months; then was watchman on steamer Fleetwood, on the Ohio River, one year. In 1873 he went to the Ozark Iron Works, in Missouri, and was in charge of stone work for three months, when he went to Illinois and worked on a farm a short time, after which he returned home and attended school a year. He then taught and attended school alternately, two years. In 1877 he went to the Buchtel Furnace, Athens County, and worked there three years. In 1880 he was at Nelsonville a few months, and then went to Orbiston and worked until the fall of 1882, when he purchased property at Jacksonville, and is now engaged in sinking shafts at the mines. He is a member of Lodge No. 541, I. O. O. F., Haydenville, Ohio. May 7, 1878, he married Mary, daughter of P. D. and Nancy (Dennis)

Conner, of Orbiston, Hocking County. They have two children—Edward A. and Annie I.

Solomon H. Johnson, farmer and mill-owner, dealer in grain and stock at Trimble, Ohio, is the fifth son of John B. and Adaline S. (Tinker) Johnson. He was born Jan. 23, 1837, in Trimble Township, Athens County, and lived with his parents until manhood, receiving a common-school education. His father dying when he was eighteen years of age, he began managing the farm for his mother, and doing business for himself. In April, 1861, he enlisted in Company H, Twenty-second Ohio Volunteer Infantry, as a private, for three months, was appointed Corporal, and served as such during the term of his enlistment. He was in West Virginia and skirmished with the enemy there. He was discharged at Athens, Ohio, in August, 1861. He then re-enlisted in Company A, Sixty-third Ohio Volunteer Infantry, as a private, for three years. At the organization of his company he was commissioned Second Lieutenant and served as such until May 29, 1862, when he was promoted to First Lieutenant of same company, and served as such until the battle of Farmington, Tenn., where he received an injury from a shell which disabled him to such an extent that he resigned in October, 1862. He was at the battles of New Madrid, Mo., Island No. 10, Farmington, Iuka, Miss., second battle of Corinth, Miss. After he returned home in 1862, he resumed farming and stock-dealing for several years. During the years 1872 and 1873 he built a mill in partnership with his brother, S. M. Johnson, as half owner, and was thus engaged until February, 1878, when he sold his interest to his brother, continuing his farm and stock business, dealing in fine horses. In the spring of 1882 he formed a partnership for the construction of his present mill interest, the firm of Johnson, Wolf & Co., he being the senior member. He was elected Township Treasurer in the spring of 1876 and served two years. Jan. 22, 1865, he married Sarah E., daughter of David and Sarah (Dickson) Jones, of Hocking County. Mr. and Mrs. Johnson are members of the Disciple church.

J. H. Jones, farmer, second son of David and Sarah (Dickson) Jones, was born in Ward Township, Hocking Co., Ohio, April 1, 1840. In April, 1861, he enlisted in Company G, Twenty-second Ohio Volunteer Infantry, at Nelsonville, Ohio, as a private for three months, and was discharged at Athens, Ohio, in August, 1861. He then returned home and resumed farming until the spring of 1864, when he was called out 100 days in the Ohio

National Guards. Served four months and was discharged at Camp Chase in the fall of 1864. His regiment was on duty at Washington, D. C., when Early invaded Maryland. When discharged he returned home and resumed farming. In March, 1868, he purchased the farm where he now resides. He has served as Township Trustee for six years. Oct. 7, 1869, he married Nancy M., daughter of David and Mary (Morrow) Spencer, of Perry County, Ohio. They have five children—Edgar C., Carlos P., Oscar D., Orpha M. and Hannah E. Mr. and Mrs. Jones are members of the Disciple church.

J. W. Jones, farmer and dealer in real estate, oldest son of David and Sarah (Dixon) Jones, was born in York Township, Athens County, March 8, 1836, where he lived with his parents until ten years of age. Dec. 23, 1846, his father was drowned in Hocking River, near Nelsonville. His mother then removed to Homer Township, Morgan County, where he lived with her one year. He then lived with Jonathan Nesmith in Dover Township until fourteen years of age, when his mother removed to York Township and he lived with her and attended school during the winter. At the age of fifteen years he began hauling coal in Nelsonville, and worked during the summer and went to school during the winter for several years. In 1855 he was apprenticed to William Weller, of Nelsonville, to learn the boot and shoe trade and worked six months. The following year he worked at boot and shoe making for S. H. Tinker, of Nelsonville. He then had charge of a canal boat three months and dealt in stock. He then rented a farm until 1861. Sept. 1, 1861, he enlisted in Company A, Sixty-third Regiment Ohio Infantry, at Trimble, Ohio, as a private for three years; was in the battles of New Madrid, Island No. 10, Fort Pillow, Farmington, first and second battles at Corinth, and was one of a number who hauled two thirty-two pound Parrot guns by hand from New Madrid to Tiptonville, eighteen miles; also at Iuka and with his regiment to Eastport, Tenn., where he was detailed as Hospital Steward and served as such until discharged. He was discharged at Columbus, Ohio, Oct. 17, 1864. In February, 1865, he purchased a farm in Trimble Township and farmed and worked at the boot and shoe trade for two years. He then added more lands and farmed in partnership with his brother James until 1872 when he purchased his brother's interest. He sold his farm February, 1873. He was then employed by Thomas Ewing buying lands and prospecting until 1879. August, 1879, he purchased the Allen farm and has been engaged in farming and dealing in real estate and stock to the present time. He filled the office of Township Clerk, 1855 and 1856; Trustee, 1868, and Special Trustee nine years; was Land Appraiser in 1880, and is at present Justice of Peace. He is a Master Mason, member of Lodge No. 470, A. F. & A. M., Bishopville, Morgan County. Dec. 8, 1864, he married Martha E., daughter of George S. and Sarah (Smith) Anderson, of Hocking County. They had seven children—Sarah L., Ella L., James S., Joseph E., Elmer L., Alice B. and Silas H. His wife died Jan. 10, 1881, aged forty-two years. July 12, 1881, he married Laura, daughter of Jacob L. and Rebecca (Miller) Wyatt, of Trimble Township. They have one child—Frederick L. His wife is a member of the Disciple church.

James F. Kempton, fourth son of Stephen N. and Abigail (Tolbert) Kempton, was born in Trimble Township, Athens Co., Ohio, March 1, 1841, and lived with his parents on a farm until twenty years of age, attending the common school. April 27, 1861, he enlisted in Company H, Twenty-second Ohio Volunteer Infantry, as a private, for three months, and served his term of enlistment in West Virginia and Maryland; was discharged at Athens, Ohio, Aug. 31, 1861. In September, 1861, he re-enlisted in Company B, Seventy-fifth Ohio Volunteer Infantry, as a private, for three years, and was appointed Second Sergeant of his company. In 1862 he was promoted to First Sergeant of company, and served as such until November, 1863. He was taken prisoner at the battle of Gettysburg, Pa., July 22, 1863, and was confined in Libby and Belle Isle prisons, Va., for twenty days, when he was exchanged and returned to his command. In November, 1863, he was commissioned Second Lieutenant, and sent home on recruiting service, and was thus employed until April, 1864, when he returned to his regiment in Florida, and was promoted to First Lieutenant and assigned to the command of his company. At the battle of Gainsville, Florida, he and the majority of the regiment were taken prisoners; were in prison a short time in Macon, Ga., thence to Charleston, S. C., under fire of the Federal batteries two months. He was then removed to Columbia, S. C.; remained there until March 1, when he was removed to Wilmington, N. C., and then exchanged. Soon after he reported at Washington, D. C., and was discharged in March, 1865. He was engaged in the battles of McDowell, W. Va., Chancellorsville, John's Island, Gettysburg, Pa., White Point Landing, Camp Baldwin and Clay Ridge, Florida. Returning home he engaged in harness-making at Trimble, Ohio, until 1877. He then purchased a farm where he lived three years. He was then employed by the Akron Iron Company, in the huckstering business, two years and six months; then resumed farming. In January, 1883, he sold his farm to O. D. Jackson, and entered the store as clerk where he is employed at the present time. He has served six terms as Township Clerk, one term as Justice of the Peace and one term as Assessor. April 6, 1864, he married Emma, daughter of Samuel and Elizabeth (Edwards) Dupler, of Trimble Township. They have five children—Elfa E., Adda A., Sylvia E., Silas F. and Frank T. Mr. and Mrs. Kempton are members of the Disciple church.

Stephen T. Kempton, manufacturer and dealer in boots and shoes, is the oldest son of Stephen N. and Abigail (Tolbert) Kempton, and was born near North Killingly, Conn., Jan. 13, 1826. In his sixth year he came with his parents, to Amesville, Onio, where they lived one year, and then removed to Dover Township and lived one year. They then came to Trimble Township, where they lived two years. His father then purchased a farm near Trimble, known as the Tucker place, and farmed there two years. He then sold his farm and rented the Allen farm one year; then entered one quarter-section of land in section 13, Trimble Township. After coming of age Mr. Kempton went to learn the carpenter's trade of Daniel Fulton. After working a short time, business being dull, he abandoned the trade, and went to work for Bennett Woodworth to learn the boot and shoe trade, remaining with him two years. He then worked for himself near his father's one year, and then worked for G. W. Roberts, in Trimble, for several years on piece work. In December, 1852, he built a shop in Trimble, where he has carried on the boot and shoe business to the present time, farming some in connection with his business. During seven months in 1879 he was mining in Colorado. Sept. 6, 1849, he married Mary, daughter of James and Nancy (McClearie) Swift, of Pennsylvania. They had eight children—Amanda, wife of Warren Brison; Loretta, wife of W. Biddison; Charles F., John F., Angenetta, wife of J. P. McClearie, of North Carolina; Parker S., Minnie E. and U. S. Grant. Mr. and Mrs. Kempton are members of the Disciple church.

Peter Robins Kidwell, farmer and butcher, oldest son of William A. and Susan (Collins) Kidwell, was born in Guernsey County, Ohio, June 30, 1842. When a small boy his parents moved to Perry County and lived one year, then removed to Athens

County, and three years later removed to Hocking County and lived three years. They then returned to Athens County, Dover Township, where Peter R. lived with his parents, working on the farm, tending the grist-mill, and going to school till twenty-one years of age. He then worked in his father's mill for wages until 1865. During the year 1865 he was in the employ of the New York and Ohio Oil Company. He then rented and farmed until the spring of 1873, when he purchased the farm where he lives. Aug. 8, 1863, he married Miss Frances E., daughter of Zephaniah and Laura (Fay) Fulton. They have five children— Florence E., Chester A., William Z., Mary A. and Charles. Harvey R. died at the age of two years. Mr. Kidwell and wife are members of the Disciple church.

Samuel M. Lefever, carpenter, joiner, contractor and builder, undertaker and proprietor of the Central Hotel, Trimble, Ohio, is the fourth son of Isaac and Elizabeth (Step) Lefever. He was born in Trimble Township, July 6, 1840, and lived with his parents until nineteen years of age. At the age of nineteen he was apprenticed to C. C. Mingus to learn the carpenter's trade; was with him eighteen months. He then worked four months with D. Andrews and I. P. Lefever. Dec. 11, 1861, he enlisted in Company E, Seventy-fifth Ohio Volunteer Infantry, for three years as a private; was in the battles of Cedar Mountain, second Bull Run, Chancellorsville, Fredericksburg, Gettysburg, siege of forts Wagner and Gregg, before Charleston, and several minor engagements, during his term of service. Feb. 15, 1865, he was discharged at Jacksonville, Fla., and returned home. He worked with B. C. Lefever for two years, and then began contracting and building for himself, and has continued in the business to the present time, adding that of undertaking some nine years since. He is a Fellow Craft Mason, and member of Nelsonville Lodge. Jan. 14, 1871, he married Mary E., daughter of Isaac and Rachel (Burley) Hedley. They have two children—Webster E. E. and Isaac H. D.

John B. Love, farmer, is the oldest son of Thomas L. and Hannah (James) Love. He was born near Trimble, Ohio, Sept. 1, 1834, and lived with his parents until manhood, receiving a common-school education. At twenty-one years of age he leased land and farmed until 1861. Dec. 12, 1861, he enlisted in Company B, Seventy-fifth Ohio Volunteer Infantry, as a private, for three years, and was with his command in West Virginia. In September, 1862, he was discharged for disability, having received injuries from which he has never fully recovered. In 1863 he removed to Jefferson County, Iowa, and rented land eight years. He then returned to Trimble, Ohio, and purchased a portion of the home farm, where he still lives. He was Postmaster at Hartleyville one year. Dec. 27, 1853, he married Sarah A., daughter of Henry and Jane (Posey) May, of Morgan County, Ohio. They have three children —James L., of Hocking County; William C. and Sylva J. They have lost three children—Warwick A. in infancy, Riley M. in his second year, and Samuel F. at the age of seven years. Mr. and Mrs. Love are members of the Disciple church.

William Palmer, Superintendent of coal mines at Jacksonville, is the second son of William and Ann (Tickle) Palmer. He was born in Devonshire, England, Feb. 10, 1849, and lived there with his parents until fourteen years of age, attending the common schools. He then went to the lead mines at Cornwall, and worked there four years. When eighteen years of age he came to the United States with his older brother and began mining coal at Gilberton, Penn. They contracted to open a tunnel near Gilberton, and completed the work in six months. He then returned to England, and in December, 1868, came again to the United States, and was at Wheeling, W. Va., five months. Then he went to Benwood and mined two years and six months; from there to Sparta, Ill.; then returned to Jefferson County, Ohio, and mined at the Rush Run mines. February, 1871, he was engaged in opening new mines at Floodwood, Athens County. The company failing, he returned to Benwood; thence to Doanville, Athens County, opening new mines; thence to Straitsville, Perry County, then returned to Doanville; then engaged in opening the Hamley Run mines in Athens County; then to Shawnee, Perry County; then purchased land in Harden County, Ohio, with a view to farming, but a few months after changed his views and returned to Athens County, and leased the Desteiger coal mines and worked them one year. He then had charge of the Laurel Hill mines as superintendent two years; then removed to Columbus, Ohio, and contracted laying sewer-pipe six months; then returned to Laurel Hill; from there went to Buchtel, and mined three years; then to Orbiston, Hocking County, and was Superintendent of the mines twenty months. He then had charge of the Buchtel mines a few weeks, when he engaged to O. D. Jackson in 1882, to superintend opening his mines. He is a member of Buchtel Lodge, No. 712, I. O. O. F., and has filled the chair of Vice-Grand in his lodge. March 12, 1874, he married Martha E., daughter of Eli and Mary (Williams) Six, of Athens County. They had three children—Bessie A., John and Mary. They have lost two children—William E. died at the age of two years and six months, and Medoria died in infancy. Mrs. Palmer is a member of the Methodist Episcopal church.

C. H. Pettit, manufacturer of buggies and spring wagons, is the second son of John and Nancy (Deaver) Pettit. He was born in Deerfield Township, Morgan Co., Ohio, April 23, 1847, and lived there with his parents until seventeen years of age, receiving a common-school education. Sept. 4, 1864, he went to Afton, Union Co., Iowa, and worked in a saw-mill during the winter. In the spring of 1865 he went to work for Abraham Hunt, of Peoria, Mahaska Co., Iowa., to learn the carriage and wagon trade, and served as an apprentice until the spring of 1867, when he returned to Morgan County, Ohio, and worked at Deavertown, for Henry Deaver, on jour. work, near four years. Sept. 3, 1872, he came to Trimble and established his present business. He is agent for the Milburn wagon of Toledo, Ohio. April 10, 1872, he married Louisa, daughter of Morris and Emily (Edwards) Bryson, of Trimble. They have three children—Harley E., Barton H. and John Garfield. Mr. and Mrs. Pettit are members of the Disciple church.

J. W. Robinson, blacksmith and manufacturer of road and spring wagons, is the second son of Thomas W. and Magdaline (Haning) Robinson. He was born near Pomeroy, Meigs Co., Ohio, Sept. 16, 1857. When he was thirteen years of age his parents removed to Deavertown, Morgan County, where he lived until manhood. At the age of twenty-one years he went to work for Frank Deaver to learn the blacksmith's trade, and served an apprenticeship of three years. He then came to Trimble and established his present business. He is a Master Mason, member of Deavertown Lodge, No. 172, A. F. & A. M., Morgan County, Ohio. June 7, 1877, he married Lizzie, daughter of William and Mary (Particious) Tysinger, of Morgan County, Ohio. They have two children—Thomas W. and George W.

George A. Russell, dealer in general merchandise, oldest son of L. W. and Elizabeth A. (Morrow) Russell, was born near Chapel Hill, Perry Co., Ohio, July 10, 1841, and removed with his parents to Trimble, Athens County, in 1842, where he received a common-school education. In April, 1861, he enlisted in Company H, Twenty-second Ohio Volunteer Infantry, as a private for three months. He was appointed Second Sergeant of his company, and

Isaac Mathias

served as such during his term of enlistment. He was in the West Virginia campaign, and was discharged at Athens, Ohio, in August, 1861. Sept. 5, 1861, he re-enlisted in Company B, Seventy-fifth Ohio Volunteer Infantry, as a private, for three years. He was appointed First Sergeant of his company, and served as such until Oct. 31, 1862; was engaged in the battles of McDowell, Cross, Keys, South Mountain, second Bull Run, White Sulphur Springs Fredricksburg, Chancellorsville and Gettysburg. Oct. 31, 1862, he was promoted to Second Lieutenant and had command of his company from the battle of Chancellorsville to the battle of Gettysburg, where he was wounded and came home on furlough and remained two months. He returned to Annapolis, Md., and was discharged for disability Dec. 18, 1863. Returning home in 1863 he engaged in the mercantile business with his father at Trimble, Ohio, under the firm name of L. W. Russell & Son for one year, when he purchased his father's interest and conducted the business alone one year. He then sold an interest to John S. Dew, and conducted the business under the firm name of Russell & Dew for three years. He then purchased Dew's interest and continued the business alone until 1876, when he again became associated with his father under the firm name of L. W. Russell & Son, and was thus associated one year. He purchased his father's interest and has conducted the business alone to the present time. He has served as Township Treasurer a number of years, Treasurer of Special School Fund, and Postmaster from 1865 to the present time. He is a Master Mason, member of Lodge No. 470, A. F. & A. M., Bishopville, Ohio. May 8, 1864, he married Almira J., daughter of Dr. John S. and Angeline (Pugh) Dew, of Trimble, Ohio. They have four children—Clara B., Carlos A., John D. and Daisy. Mr. and Mrs. Russell are members of the Disciple church.

Hezekiah T. Sanders, owner and proprietor of saw and planing mill, Trimble, Ohio, is the oldest son of Levi and Henrietta (Martin) Sanders. He was born near Augusta, Carroll Co., Ohio, Nov. 5, 1826, and lived there with his parents, working on farm until fourteen years of age, and then learned the cooper's trade, working at it until twenty years of age. He then removed with his parents to Monroe Township, Perry County, where they lived two years, and he worked for his uncle in a saw-mill one year. He and his father then purchased a farm with a water-power saw-mill and carried on the mill and farm five years. They then traded their mill for some wild lands and cash and rented a farm near Nelsonville, where they lived two years. He then purchased lands in Ward Township, Hocking County, and improved it and lived there engaged in farming, cabinet-making and making chairs fourteen years. In 1864 he enlisted in Company G, One Hundred and Fifty-first Ohio National Guards, for 100 days; was stationed at Washington City and was engaged with Early's forces there in 1864; was discharged at Camp Chase, Ohio, and returned to his home and business in Hocking County. In 1869 he removed to Salt Lick Township, Perry County, and purchased property and carried on the cabinet and undertaking business until November, 1880, when he sold his property and purchased his present mill property. April 17, 1853, he married Sarah F., daughter of Mrs. Malinda Hines, of Perry County, Ohio. They have nine children—Byron H., Antoinette, Levi H., Horton L., Nora D., Rosa B., Riley S., Arvinie, Bertie R. Harvey B. died in infancy. Mr. and Mrs. Sanders are members of the Disciple church.

Seth Shaner, *M. D.*, farmer and physician near Hartleyville, Ohio, is the oldest son of Willian and Nancy (Tharp) Shaner. He was born in Trimble Township, Athens Co., Ohio, Feb. 15, 1838, where he has lived with his mother to the present time, his father dying when Seth was a small boy. He began teaching schoo in 1858 and taught during winter and farmed in summer for twelve years, excepting his military term. May 2, 1864, he enlisted in Company G, One Hundred and Forty-first Ohio National Guards, at Gallipolis, Ohio, for 100 days and served until September, 1864, when he was discharged at Gallipolis, Ohio, and returned home. In 1866 he began the study of medicine. In 1869 and 1870 he attended lectures at the Starling Medical College, Columbus, Ohio, and during the winter of 1873–'74 attended lectures at Jefferson Medical College, Philadelphia. He is now practicing medicine and farming in Trimble Township.

William Shaner, farmer near Hartleyville, Ohio, second son of William and Nancy (Tharp) Shaner, was born near Hartleyville, Athens County, May 5, 1840. Aug. 5, 1861, he enlisted in Company A, Thirty-first Ohio Volunteer Infantry, as a private for three years. After the battle of Corinth he was appointed Corporal and served as such until he re-enlisted as a veteran. He was in the battles of Stone River, Mill Springs, Chickamauga, Mission Ridge, Ringgold, Dallas, Resaca, Kennesaw Mountain and Marietta. In January, 1864, he re-enlisted as a veteran in the same company and regiment as a private;

was wounded at the siege of Atlanta, Aug. 7, 1864. He was then in field hospital for a time, thence to Chattanooga hospital, from there to Nashville, from there to Jeffersonville, Ind., from there to Camp Denison, where he was furloughed home, to the President's election. On his return to Denison, he was transferred to Columbus, Ohio, where he remained until March, 1865, when he was transferred to Company H, Sixth Regiment Veteran Reserve, and on duty on Johnson Island until June 1, 1865, when he was transferred to Cincinnati and remained one month; then returned to Johnson's Island, where he was discharged Aug. 5, 1865. He then returned home and purchased a farm, on which he now resides. He is a Master Mason, member of Lodge No. 470, A. F. & A. M., Bishopville, Ohio. Sept. 20, 1878, he married Nancy E., daughter of Elijah and Mary (Devore) Roberts, of Perry County, Ohio. They have one son—Dares A. Mr. Shaner is a member of the Methodist Episcopal church, and his wife of the Disciple church.

J. Taylor, farmer, third son of Charles and Mary A. (Seymour) Taylor, was born in Hampshire, England, Jan. 5, 1825. In 1837 he came with his parents to the United States, and settled in Muskingum County, Ohio, near Zanesville, where he lived until 1846, working on a farm and attending school. In 1846 he removed to Trimble Township, Athens County, and purchased wild lands and cleared a farm, where he has resided and farmed to the present time. April 7, 1852, he married Abigail, daughter of Stephen and Abigail (Talbert) Kempton, of Trimble Township. They have nine children, five sons and four daughters—Edward, of Trimble Township; Emily J., wife of Richard McKinley, of Trimble Township; Sarah E., James, Albert M., Alfred H., Joseph S., Mary and Flora F., all at home. Mary F. died at the age of two years. Mrs. Taylor is a member of the Disciple church.

Morgan W. Tharp, farmer, second son of James and Hannah (Withers) Tharp, was born in Muskingum County, Ohio, March 22, 1831. When he was six years old his parents moved to Trimble Township, Athens County. At the age of eighteen years he began working for wages on farms. When twenty-five years of age he rented and farmed four years. When twenty years of age he purchased a farm, on which his father lived until 1855, when he sold the farm, and, in 1860, purchased the one on which he now resides. Sept. 27, 1856, he married Mrs. Sarah Post, of Perry County. They have four children—James D., Amanda J., Rebecca E. and John W. Mrs. Tharp is a member of the Disciple church.

Thomas J. Tharp, farmer, fifth son of James and Hannah (Withers) Tharp, was born in Trimble Township, Athens County, Aug. 30, 1843, and lived with his parents until eighteen years of age, working on the farm and attending the common schools. Sept. 5, 1861, he enlisted in Company B, Seventy-fifth Ohio Volunteer Infantry, at Trimble, as a private, for three years; was in the battles of Monterey, Shaw's Ridge, McDowell, Franklin, Strasburg, Cross Keys, Cedar Mountain, Freeman Ford, Sulphur Springs, Waterloo Ridge, second battle Bull Run, Aldie, Chancellorsville, Gettysburg, Hagerstown, Fort Wagner, John's Island, Camp Baldwin, Gainesville, Pocataligo Bridge, and Charleston. His regiment was at Jacksonville, Fla., one year. He was home after the battle of Gettysburg two months on special recruiting service. Was discharged at Columbus, Ohio, Dec. 23, 1864, when he returned home. In March, 1865, he enlisted as a veteran in Company C, Fifth Regiment U. S. Troops, and was stationed at Washington, D. C., three months; Hartford, Conn., for a short time; Burlington, Vt.; Staten Island, New York, six months, where he was discharged, March 25, 1866. He then returned home and purchased a farm. In 1870 he sold his farm and rented two years. In 1872 he purchased where he now resides. May 5, 1866, he married Rebecca E., daughter of John B. and Adaline S. (Tinker) Johnson, of Trimble, Ohio. His wife died Sept. 24, 1866. Sept. 6, 1868, he married Clarissa, daughter of George W. and Harriet (Shaner) McDonald, of Trimble Township. They have four children—Lydia M., Georgia A. B., Hannah F. and Harriet E., all at home. Mrs. Tharp is a member of the Methodist Episcopal church.

Charles S. Tinker, farmer, the second son of Elisha and Lydia (Shepperd) Tinker, was born in Hampshire County, Mass., May 5, 1804. When a small boy his parents removed to Canada. At the beginning of the war of 1812 they returned to the United States and settled at Albany, N. Y., where they lived about five years. They then removed to Virginia, and lived one year; from there removed to Zanesville, Ohio, and lived until 1823. In 1823 his parents moved to Perry County, where they died. At the age of twenty-one years he began driving a dry-goods and notions wagon for his brother, S. H. Tinker, through the counties of Morgan, Perry, Washington, Athens, Meigs, Gallia and Lawrence; was employed thus two years. He then engaged in merchandising at Millfield for two years. He then removed to Athens and lived there four years, and then rented a farm near Millfield and farmed three years. In January, 1843, his father-in-law gave him the farm on which he now resides with his son, R. W. Dec. 12, 1827, he married Almira, daughter of Resolved and Elizabeth (Nash) Fuller, of Athens County. They have six children—Charles H., of Trimble Township; Eugene A., of Topeka, Kan.; Resolved W., on home farm; Austin H., in Ross County, Ohio; Roxana, widow of Henry Freeman, of Chauncey, Ohio.; Frances A., wife of H. Pierce, lawyer, of Alma, Kan. Three children are deceased—Elisha W., a physician, died May 12, 1879, at the age of thirty-six years; their second daughter, wife of Christopher Woodworth, of Dover Township; Lavina A., wife of John Boidenot, died Jan. 5, 1872, in Illinois. Mrs. Tinker died Feb. 16, 1875, in her sixty-eighth year. She was a member of the Methodist Episcopal church for a number of years before her death.

Josiah True, deceased, a companion and friend of Daniel Weethee, and one of the pioneers of the county, was born in New Hampshire, Oct. 25, 1776. He came to Marietta in 1793, and to Dover Township in 1800. He held the office of Justice of the Peace in Dover from 1815 till 1851, and was respected and popular. He died Sept. 16, 1855. Mr. True was one of the founders of the "Coonskin Library" of Ames Township, and always a leader in pioneer improvements. One of the first spinning wheels introduced into Dover was bought by him in 1803. Having accumulated a few bear and deer skins he carried them on his back to Zanesville, forty miles distant, purchased the wheel with the proceeds of the skins, and brought it home on his back. He walked all the way, and made the round trip of eighty miles in two days. Mr. True at a very early day bought some choice apples at Marietta and sowed the seeds from them, from which he established the first nursery attempted in the county. Most of the old orchards on Sunday and Monday Creeks were planted from this nursery, and some of the trees are still bearing.

Joshua Warehime, farmer, oldest son of John and Mariah (Niozum) Warehime, was born near Barnesville, Ohio, Aug. 8, 1830. When twelve years of age his parents removed to Noble County where he lived until manhood, working on a farm and attending the common schools. At the age of twenty-one years he rented lands and farmed two years. He then removed to Morgan County and purchased a farm, and lived there about twenty years. In 1869 he came to Athens County and purchased a farm where he lived nine years when he traded it for the one on which he now resides. Nov. 19, 1850, he married Nancy, daughter of Hugh and Jane (Moreland) McCathrin, of Noble County, Ohio. They have three children—Maria E., wife of Henry M. Copely, of Fairfield County; Margaret, wife of William H. Hilton, of Athens County, and Jacob, of Fairfield County. Mr. and Mrs. Warehime are members of the Protestant Methodist church.

William J. Wells, farmer, sixth son of William and Nancy (Stephens) Wells, was born in Monroe County, Ohio, Oct. 15, 1828, and lived there with his parents until manhood, working on a farm. He received a common-school education. At the age of twenty-one years he purchased a farm in Monroe County. In 1853 he removed to Morgan County, Ohio, and purchased a farm near Mountsville. In 1863 he removed to Saline County, Ill., and lived one year, when he returned to Morgan County, Ohio. In 1871 he came to Athens County and purchased the farm on which he now resides. Oct. 11, 1849, he married Hannah, daughter of Aaron and Elizabeth (Stephens) Morris, of Noble County, Ohio. They had four children—James, of Athens County; Aaron, of Morgan County; Nancy J., wife of Daniel Masters, of Hocking County; Mary E., wife of J. W. Howard, of Athens County. May 5, 1860, his wife died in her thirty-third year. May 10, 1861, he married Sarah, daughter of Simeon and Nancy (Timmons) Hale, of Morgan County. They have three children—Julia, wife of C. Edwards, of Athens County; Pearly and Bessie, at home.

Thomas R. White, dealer in drugs and medicines, son of G. K. and Hannah (Scott) White, was born in Morgan County, Ohio, April 7, 1851, and lived there with his parents until manhood. At the age of eighteen years he went to work on a farm for his uncle, F. D. Scott. When twenty years of age he engaged with Brown Manley Plow Company, of Malta, Ohio, as a carpenter, for three years, reading medicine during the time with a view of going into the drug business. In the spring of 1874 he purchased an interest in a portable saw-mill and ran the mill three years under the firm name of White & Hamilton. In September, 1877, he sold his mill interest, and in November of the same year purchased a drug store of Sanborn & Co., at Winsor, Morgan Co., Ohio, and was in the business there until May, 1880, when he sold his store to W. E. Gatewood and clerked for him three months. Oct. 19, 1881, he located in Trimble, where he is now engaged in the drug business, owning the property and doing a lively and increasing business. He was Township Clerk of Winsor

Township, Morgan Co., Ohio, one year. Dec. 14, 1879, he married Alice, daughter of Abel S. and Jane (Forsyth) Newton. They have two children, twin boys, Clifton S. and Clinton C.

Jacob L. Wyatt, farmer, the fifth son of John and Catherine (Michael) Wyatt, was born in Athens County, Ohio, Oct. 8, 1833. At twenty-one years of age he began farming on rented land. When twenty-seven years of age he purchased a farm in Trimble Township. In 1868 he sold his farm and rented until 1872, when he again purchased in Trimble Township. In 1874 he sold this farm and rented until 1876, when he purchased the farm on which he now resides. He has served as Township Trustee six years. Nov. 21, 1854, he married Rebecca, daughter of Samuel and Rachel (Cook) Miller, of Morgan County, Ohio. They had five children—Hester, wife of William Druggan, of Athens County; Alice, wife of Albert Johnson, of Morgan County; Laura, wife of Joseph Jones, of Athens County; Eva, at home; Mary, died in infancy. His wife was a member of the United Brethren church. She died Feb. 17, 1865. Aug. 8, 1866, he married Mrs. Maria, widow of Allen Miller, of Athens County. They have five children—George W., Charles G., Thomas L., Cora M. and Clara E., all at home. Allen G. died July 10, 1882, in his thirteenth year. Mr. and Mrs. Wyatt are members of the Disciple church.

Joseph Zimmerman, farmer, is the oldest son of Henry R. and Elizabeth (Brown) Zimmerman. He was born in Homer Township, Morgan Co., Ohio, Sept. 13, 1842. When ten years of age he came with his parents to Trimble Township, Athens County, where his father purchased a farm. April 1, 1861, he enlisted in Company H, Twenty-second Ohio Volunteer Infantry, at Trimble, as a private, for three months. When his term of service expired he was discharged at Athens, Ohio, Aug. 4, 1861. Oct. 20, 1861, he re-enlisted in Company A, Sixty-third Ohio Volunteer Infantry, as a private, at Chillicothe, Ohio, for three years. Before the second battle of Corinth he was appointed Third Sergeant of his company and served as such to the close of the war. Jan. 1, 1863, he entered the veteran service and was in the battle of Decatur, Ala.; from there he was with Sherman to the sea, participating in all the battles, and was discharged July 17, 1865. He returned home and purchased the farm on which he resides. Sept. 16, 1866, he married Lydia A., daughter of J. B. and Adaline S. (Tinker) Johnson, of Trimble Township. They have six children—Horace A., Mary E., Charles O., George A., Emet and Marcus D. Mrs. Zimmerman is a member of the Disciple church.

CHAPTER XXVIII.

LODI TOWNSHIP—AN AGRICULTURAL TOWNSHIP MIXE WITH PETRIFACTIONS AND INDIAN TRADITIONS.

ORGANIZATION AND BOUNDS—POPULATION—TOPOGRAPHY—PETRIFACTIONS—LEAD AND INDIAN TRADITIONS—FIRST ELECTION, FOURTEEN VOTES—THE PIONEERS—SCHOOLS AND SOME FEW REMARKS—CHURCHES, VILLAGES, BUSINESS — TOWNSHIP OFFICERS FROM 1827 TO 1883—BIOGRAPHICAL.

ORGANIZATION AND BOUNDS.

This township was organized in April, 1826, and its territory was originally a part of both Alexander and Carthage Townships. It is in township 4, range 13, and is bounded on the north by Canaan, and east by Carthage townships, south by Meigs County, and west by Alexander Township. It is a congressional township, six miles square, and has 23,040 acres of good, arable land. It is watered by Shade River, which enters the township at the northwest corner and, running diagonally, leaves the township at the extreme southeastern part. This divides the township almost equally in two parts, and the bottom lands along the stream are rich and fertile, yielding in corn and grasses abundant crops. The township is somewhat rough along the banks of the streams, and is a township of hills and valleys. The valleys are small, and the hills while not so fertile yield plentifully in grasses. Stock is an important element in the growing prosperity of the township.

POPULATION, ETC.

For the first thirty years of its settlement Lodi seemed to improve, and up to 1860 was well in the van of material progress, both in wealth and population. After the war she seemed to have first halted and then retrograded. The first census after becoming an independent organization was in 1830, when the population was 276. In 1840 it was. 754; 1850, 1,336, and in 1860 it reached 1,598. This was her largest population. Whether the war brought on the stagnation that followed, or it has arisen from other causes cannot be told; the fact only is of record that her population has slowly decreased, even its natural increase being lost. In 1870 the population was given at 1,551, and in 1880, 1,550. At this time the township has even signs of perfect repose.

PETRIFACTIONS.

There has not been much coal or iron development in this township, but quite a number of specimens of petrified pieces of wood, etc., have been found upon the banks and in the bed of Shade River, which has given that stream of water—the main watercourse between the Hocking and the Ohio rivers, into the latter of which it flows—considerable of a local reputation, and makes it a spot sought for by geologists and other men of science who delve in the hidden or wonderful works of nature. The principal petrifactions found have been in a gulch which leads into this river, on section 35, and it is in this ravine that signs of early days are found, showing that the Indians had found lead in its natural state, and had melted or separated it for their use from its impurities. Lead blossoms have been found at different times, and specimens of the ore showing from sixty to seventy per cent. of pure galena have been occasionally picked up. The trees along the banks of the river show that the Shawnee tribe was in some way connected with the Delawares, for on many trees will be found strange figures carved or cut in, such as turtles, etc. There is no doubt that a thorough exploration would develop much of interest to the scientific world, and also unfold much wealth which now lies hidden from the gaze of man.

ELECTION.

The first township election was held in the spring of 1827, and it is stated that but fourteen votes were polled. This is probably true, as three years later there were but 276 people in the township, which would give less than fifty votes, allowing a voting population of one to six of the inhabitants.

THE PIONEERS.

These men, like all the first settlers who became the advanced guard of civilization, had their troubles and trials, and also the pleasures, of pioneer life. Of the latter hunting was the main one, and of the former going to mill was one of their heaviest burdens; that is, it took much valuable time and fatiguing trips, for at first the burnt log as a mortar or a hand-mill did but little to supply a large family. There were not many settlers living in the surrounding townships when Joseph Thompson first settled in Lodi, and not many years after, or in 1815, before he began the erection of a mill. This was the first flouring or rather grist mill in all that section of country for many years. The farm property has since come into the possession of Henry Blazier. The mill has long since disappeared. The next mill mentioned was built in 1825 by Ezra Miller, of small size, and it, too, like the first one, has disappeared. A steam flouring mill now occupies the spot with a capacity equal to the demand. Near the center of the township another steam mill is in operation which fully supplies the wants of people in the surrounding country.

SCHOOLS.

Next to the milling interest, which was one of necessity, that which occupied to a large extent the adult population was the education of their children. In this regard the citizens of Lodi Township have exercised a wisdom which few have surpassed, and all could emulate with profit. The log cabin, with its rude and simple furniture, has given place to the well-built and well-finished and furnished school-houses of to-day. Pleasant Valley Seminary, located formerly at Jerseyville, was opened in December, 1867, and was under the superintendency of Prof. Daniel D. Clark, a graduate of the Ohio University. The public schools are all doing well and the attendance the past school session was fully up to the average.

The first religious society formed at Lodi was by the Methodists, in 1820, under the supervision of Rev. Goddard Curtis. They worshiped for many years in a small school-house on Shade River. At present the Methodists have two flourishing societies. About 1840 the Christians (or Campbellites) formed a society and built a church which, soon after its completion, was demolished by a large forest tree falling on it. They have since erected a good frame church at Jerseyville.

There are in Lodi Township three villages. Jerseyville is situated a mile and a half west of the center of the township, and contains two stores, one harness shop, one blacksmith shop, one hotel, a postoffice, one cabinet shop and two churches—Methodist Episcopal and Christian. Its population is about 175. Garden is situated two miles southeast of the center of the township, on the bank of Shade River. It contains a store, gunsmith shop, blacksmith shop, postoffice and one church—Methodist Episcopal.

Moretown is situated a mile and a half southwest of the center of the township. It has a population of about 150, and contains one store, two blacksmith shops and a postoffice. These are the only villages, the population being mostly agricultural. Yet while but little enterprise is being exhibited at this time, there is no township in the county where more true hospitality, intelligence and moral worth can be found than among the people of the beautiful hills and valleys of Lodi Township.

TOWNSHIP OFFICERS.

The following list contains the names of the principal township officers from 1827 to the present time:

1827-'28.—Trustees, Joseph Thompson, Elam Frost and John L. Kelly; Clerk, G. D. Drake; Justice of the Peace, Joseph Thompson.

1829.—Trustees, Joseph Thompson, Rufus P. Cooley and John L. Kelly; Clerk, G. D. Drake; Justice of the Peace, Rufus P. Cooley.

1830.-Trustees, Francis B. Drake, Thomas Miles and Abner Frost; Clerk, G. D. Drake; Justice of the Peace, Rufus P. Cooley.

1831.—Trustees, Joseph Thompson, Elam Frost and John L. Kelly; Clerk, G. D. Drake; Justice of the Peace, Rufus P. Cooley.

1832.—Trustees, Joseph Thompson, Thomas Miles and A. M. Williams; Clerk, Rufus P. Cooley; Justice of the Peace, Rufus P. Cooley.

1833.—Trustees, John Bodwell, Francis B. Drake and Abner Frost; Clerk, Joseph B. Force; Justice of the Peace, Joseph Thompson.

1834.—Trustees, Luther Dinsmore, John L. Kelly and J. B. Force; Clerk, Rufus P. Cooley; Justice of the Peace, Joseph Thompson.

1835.—Trustees, Luther Dinsmore, John L. Kelly and G. H. Cooley; Clerk, Rufus P. Cooley; Justices of the Peace, Rufus P. Cooley and Luther Dinsmore.

1836.—Trustees, Charles Brown, John L. Kelly and John Carlton; Clerk, Rufus P. Cooley; Justice of the Peace, Luther Dinsmore.

1837.—Trustees, Samuel Day, George Eaton and Cyrus O. McGrath; Clerk, John L. Kelly; Justice of the Peace, Smith C. Allen.

1838.—Trustees, Joseph Bobo, John Carlton and David Whaley; Clerk, John L. Kelly; Justice of the Peace, Churchill Creesy.

1839.—Trustees, Calvin P. Dains, Ezra H. Miller and Rufus P. Cooley; Clerk, John L. Kelly; Justice of the Peace, William Lee.

1840.—Trustees, Samuel Day, Wakeman Hull and Rufus P. Cooley; Clerk, John Cather; Justice of the Peace, Richard St. Clair.

1841.—Trustees, Samuel Day, Julius Stone and George Blazer; Clerk, John Cather; Justice of the Peace, Julius Stone.

1842.—Trustees, Samuel Day, Jehu Acley and Churchill Creesy; Clerk, Jonathan Witham; Justice of the Peace, David H. Miles.

1843.—Trustees, Wakeman Hull, Jehu Acley and Churchill Creesy; Clerk, John Cather; Justice of the Peace, Richard St. Clair.

1844.—Trustees, John Cather, Jehu Acley and Churchill Creesy.

1845.—Trustees, Joseph Cremer, John L. Kelly and John Whittington; Clerk, Stephen Gates; Justice of the Peace, David H. Miles.

1846.—Trustees, James G. Roberts, Wakeman Hull and John Whittington; Clerk, Joseph Cremer; Justice of the Peace, Isaac Woodyard.

1847.—Trustees, Julius Stone, Wakeman Hull and John L. Kelly; Clerk, Joseph Cremer; Justice of the Peace, Isaac Woodyard.

1848.—Trustees, William Jeffers, Wakeman Hull and John L. Kelly; Clerk, William H. Hull; Justice of the Peace, John Cather.

1849.—Trustees, William Jeffers, D. H. Miles and Amos Moore; Clerk, L. D. Evans; Justice of the Peace, Isaac Woodyard.

1850.—Trustees, William Jeffers, Joseph Cremer and William Bart; Clerk, Matthew Wilson; Justice of the Peace, Isaac Woodyard.

1851.—Trustees, Churchill Creesy, Ebenezer Williams and William Bart; Clerk, R. P. Cooley; Justice of the Peace, Lorenzo D. Evans.

1852.—Trustees, Churchill Creesy, Ebenezer Williams and D. H. Miles; Clerk, Isaac Bedell; Justice of the Peace, Isaac Woodyard.

1853.—Trustees, Joseph Cremer, Ebenezer Williams and D. H. Miles; Clerk, Isaac Bedell; Justice of the Peace, Isaac Woodyard.

1854.—Trustees, E. Williams, David Hart and William Jeffers; Clerk, Isaac Bedell; Justices of the Peace, Lorenzo D. Evans and David Hart.

1855.—Trustees, William Wilson, D. D. Miller and William Jeffers; Clerk, Isaac Bedell; Justices of the Peace, Lorenzo D. Evans and David Hart.

1856.—Trustees, John Kelly, D. D. Miller and William Jeffers; Clerk, Isaac Bedell; Justices of the Peace, Lorenzo D. Evans and David Hart.

1857.—Trustees, John Kelly, D. D. Miller and William Jeffers; Clerk, Isaac Bedell; Justices of the Peace, Lorenzo D. Evans and Elisha Langhead.

1858.—Trustees, John Kelly, David Hart and William Jeffers; Clerk, Isaac Bedell; Justices of the Peace, Lorenzo D. Evans and Elisha Langhead.

1859.—Trustees, John Kinney, David Hart and William Jeffers; Clerk, Isaac Bedell; Justices of the Peace, Lorenzo D. Evans and Elisha Langhead.

1860.—Trustees, John Cowan, Joseph Creesy and William Jeffers; Clerk, Isaac Bedell; Justices of the Peace, Lorenzo D. Evans and Elisha Langhead.

1861-'2.—Trustees, John Cowan, Joseph Creesy and Lewis Dains; Clerk, Isaac Bedell; Justice of the Peace, Benoni R. Pierce.

1863.—Trustees, John Cowan, Joseph Creesy and John Cather; Clerk, Isaac Bedell; Justice of the Peace, John Kelly.

1864.—Trustees, John Cowan, Joseph Creesy and James Wilson; Clerk, Isaac Bedell; Justice of the Peace, Nelson Lord.

1865.—Trustees, John Buck, A. J. Howard and Lewis Dains; Clerk, R. R. Cooley; Justice of the Peace, Nelson Lord.

1866.—Trustees, Moses Lawrence, A. J. Howard and F. J. Cremer; Clerk, R. R. Cooley; Justice of the Peace, Waldron S. Williams.

1867.—Trustees, William Jeffers, Joseph Creesy and F. J. Cremer; Clerk, John Cather; Justice of the Peace, Nelson Lord.

1868.—Trustees, William Jeffers, Joseph Creesy and F. J. Cremer; Clerk, John Cather; Justice of the Peace, William J. Shaffer.

1869.—Trustees, A. J. Howard, William Poston and John Cowan; Clerk, R. R. Cooley; Justice of the Peace, Lorenzo D. Evans.

1870.—Trustees, James Timoney, Hugh Meighen and E. M. Carsey; Clerk, Edgar Hermans; Justice of the Peace, John Cather.

1871.—Trustees, Asa Dains, John Kinney and James Timoney; Clerk, Edgar Hemans; Justice of the Peace, James Patterson.

1872.—Trustees, Moses Lawrence, W. S. Williams and Joseph Creesy; Clerk, Henry Butts; Justice of the Peace, L. D. Evans.

1873.—Trustees, Moses Lawrence, Joseph Creesy and Asa Dains; Clerk, G. W. Burson; Justice of the Peace, John Kinney.

1874.—Trustees, Joseph Creesy, Joseph Bishop and E. L. Sargent; Clerk, G. W. Burson; Justice of the Peace, John Kelly.

1875.—Trustees, O. Orr, Joseph Bishop and A. Dains; Clerk, G. W. Burson, Justice of the Peace, L. D. Evans.

1876.—Trustees, O. Orr, D. Ziggafoose and Joseph Bishop; Clerk, G. W. Burson; Justice of the Peace, W. S. Williams.

1877.—Trustees, D. Ziggafoose, Oscar Orr and M. Joston; Clerk, Edgar Hermans; Justice of the Peace, William Jeffers.

1878.—Trustees, Daniel Ziggafoose, M. Joston and W. L. Hawk. Clerk, E. L. Sargent; Justice of the Peace, L. D. Evans.

1879.—Trustees, James Bean, E. M. Carsey and John Kelly; Clerk, Jacob Wilson.

1880.—Trustees, Samuel Poston, E. M. Carsey and Oscar Orr; Clerk, Matthew Wilson; Justice of the Peace, William Jeffers.

1881.—Trustees, George German, S. T. Pierce and John Kelly; Clerk, Jacob Wilson; Justices of the Peace, W. S. Williams and S. T. Hull.

1882.—Trustees, W. M. Williams, E. M. Carsey and D. Ziggafoose; Clerk, L. Aton.

1883.—Trustees, E. M. Carsey, Daniel Ziggafoose and Dennis Timoney; Clerk, L. Aton; Justice of the Peace, William Jeffers.

BIOGRAPHICAL.

Richard Angell, deceased, son of John Angell, was born in England, April 6, 1790. When thirteen years of age his parents came to America, settling in New Jersey. He was married in August, 1811, to Mary Bougher, a native of Bucks County, Pa. In 1816 they removed to Allegheny County, Pa., where they resided till 1842. They then came to Lodi Township and settled on section 29. Mr. Angell bought two sections of land, of which but twenty-five acres was cleared. He was a member of the Presbyterian church. Though a man having large business interests he never had a lawsuit, and probably no man in the township had more friends or fewer enemies than he. Mr. Angell died Nov. 30, 1875, his wife having preceded him May 1, 1874. They had a family of ten children, eight now living—Jane, Richard, James, William, Hector, Mary, Thomas G. and Sarah Ann. John and David are deceased.

Thomas G. Angell, son of Richard and Mary Angell, was born in Allegheny County, Pa., Feb. 1, 1831. He came to Lodi Township, Athens Co., Ohio, when eleven years of age. He was reared on a farm receiving his education in the common schools. March 8, 1856, he married Mary, daughter of Richard Phillips. They have three children—Lydian M., Emma F. and Elmer G. May 2, 1864, Mr. Angell enlisted in the One Hundred and Forty-first Ohio Infantry. He was mustered out as First Lieutenant. He has a fine farm of 380 acres and one of the best residences in the township. He makes a specialty of Spanish merino sheep, having one of the best flocks in the county. Politically he is a Republican. He takes an active interest in politics, though no aspirant for office. He is a member of Athens Lodge, No. 25, A. F. & A. M.

Linza Aton, born Aug. 13, 1850, is a son of John and Margaret (Wheeler) Aton. He is the seventh of a family of eight children. His early life was spent on a farm and in attending the common schools. Jan. 9, 1869, he married Emma G. Snyder. They have three children, Lizzie C., John M., and Raymond L. Mr. Aton owns sixty acres of good, well-improved land, and is engaged in farming and stock raising. Politically he is a Republican. He has filled the offices of Assessor and Township Clerk with credit to himself and satisfaction to his friends.

S. C. Baker, son of James and Louisa (Worthen) Baker, was born in Meigs County, Ohio, Dec. 28, 1840. When quite young his parents moved to Coolville, Athens County, where his father was engaged in milling. When he was ten years of age they moved to Carthage Township. July 22, 1861, he enlisted in Company K, Thirty-ninth Ohio Infantry. He was in some of the hottest battles of the war, among them New Madrid, Corinth, Decatur, the Atlanta campaign and Bridges, S. C., where he was wounded and lay in the hospital three months. He was discharged July 24, 1865, having served four years. He was married Sept. 22, 1867, to Margery A. Nickerson. Mr. Baker owns an interest in a portable saw-mill. He has a good residence and twenty acres of land. Politically he is a Republican. He is a member of the Methodist Episcopal church.

James Beam, farmer, was born in Pennsylvania, March 28, 1841, a son of Jacob and Sarah Beam, natives of Pennsylvania. Coming to Ohio they located at Cincinnati, where they remained a short time, then moved to Meigs County, where our subject was reared. He enlisted at the age of twenty-one in Company I, Ninety-second Ohio Infantry, going into camp at Marietta, Ohio, where they remained two months; then went to Point Pleasant, Va.; then up the Kanawha to Jolly Bridge; from there to Nashville, Tenn.; then up the Cumberland to Carthage, where they had a skirmish with Morgan, just before his raid through Ohio. They then joined the Fourteenth Corps, commanded by General Thomas, at Murfreesboro; then moved on after Bragg, driving him beyond Chattanooga; then fought the battle of Chickamauga. He afterward participated in several battles, among them Mission Ridge and all the battles through Georgia, siege and flanking of Atlanta, then marched to the sea; then through the Carolinas and to Washington, D. C., where they were mustered out. He then returned home and located where he now resides. He was married Oct. 31, 1866, to Ann Eliza Fox, daughter of Rev. John O. Fox. By their union there are three children—John M., Althe L., Sarah F. Mrs. Beam died and he was again married, Sept. 22, 1878, to Alwillda C., daughter of Aaron C. Comstock. They have one child—Ann Eliza. Mr. Beam is politically a Republican.

Joseph Bishop is a native of Bethlehem, Pa., born Nov. 4, 1834. His father, Daniel Bishop, was also a native of Pennsylvania. He came to Athens County with his parents when ten years of age. He remained at home till the breaking out of the late civil war, when, Aug. 2, 1862, he enlisted in Company K, Seventy-third Ohio Infantry, and served three years. He was married Nov. 9, 1865, to Miss Coen, of Carthage Township. They have no children, but have an adopted son—Charles F. Flanders. Mr. Bishop owns a good farm of 174 acres all well improved and is engaged in farming and stock-raising. He is a member of Guysville Lodge, A. F. & A. M. Politically he is a Republican. He has served three years as Township Treasurer, and three years as School Trustee.

William Blackwood, one of the prominent farmers of Lodi Township, was born in Bedford County, Pa., Aug. 4, 1817, a son of James and Susan (McLean) Blackwood, the father of Irish and the mother of Scotch descent. When William was quite young his parents removed to Harrison County, Ohio, where he was reared and received a limited education in the subscription schools. He came to Lodi Township in 1851, and located on the farm where he now resides. He owns 340 acres of land, well improved, with good buildings, all gained by energy and good management, Mr. Blackwood commencing life by working for $10 per month; but by perseverance he has become one of the wealthiest men in the township. He was married Sept. 25, 1842, to Rachel Hill. They have seven children—Harvey L., Phœbe S., Amanda R., Melissa L., Lizzie R., Angie R. and Eva A.

John Burson is a native of Columbiana County, Ohio, born June 16, 1830. When eight years of age his parents came to Lodi Township, Athens County, where he was reared and educated. Feb. 25, 1855, he married Sarah C. Creamer, of Lodi Township. They are the parents of two children—Mary Dell and Herbert S. In 1859 Mr. Burson opened a general store on rather a limited scale, but by his fair and honorable dealing he has secured the confidence of his patrons and now has a large trade, keeping a complete line of the best goods, including dry goods, groceries, boots and shoes, and notions. He is a member of the Methodist Episcopal church, being at present Recording Steward, and is one of the substantial citizens of Lodi Township.

W. N. Burson, a native of Athens County, was born in February, 1852. He was reared a farmer and remained at home till of age. Jan. 16, 1872, he married H. C. Cather, a daughter of John Cather. In 1877 he opened a general merchandising store at Pratt's Fork, where he has since resided. He has a large stock of dry goods, groceries, boots and shoes, notions, etc., and commands a good country trade.

Quincy Cather, born in Lodi Township, Athens Co., Ohio, May 10, 1848, is a son of John Cather, an early settler of this township. He was reared on a farm, receiving his education in the common schools. In May, 1882, he opened a store of general merchandise, where he now has a large trade from the surrounding country. Nov. 10, 1870, he married Mary Peirce. They have three children—Edie, Emmett and Emily.

Lucius Coe, son of Chester and Roxy (Eggleston) Coe, was born in Onondaga County, N. Y., in December, 1811. His father was a native of Massachusetts, and his mother of Connecticut. When seventeen years of age he was employed as clerk in the grocery store of Nathaniel Eggleston; remained with him four years and then went to New York City, where he was a salesman in a variety store several years. In 1841 he came to Ohio and lived on a farm in Vinton County two years; then returned to New York City and remained till 1861, when he came to Lodi Township where he has since resided. He now has a large stock of dry goods, groceries, boots and shoes, etc. He was married Sept. 27, 1865, to Rebecca H. Sanders, a native of Carroll County, Ohio. They have two children—Harriet Jane and George A. Mr. Coe is a member of the Presbyterian church.

David Cowan, son of John and Mary (Means) Cowan, was born in Westmoreland County, Penn., Oct. 28, 1828. When he was eighteen months old his parents came to Ohio, locating in Guernsey County, where he was reared and educated. In 1856 he came to Athens County and located on the farm where he still resides. He has 200 acres of well-improved land on section 33, Lodi Township. He was married Jan. 16, 1859, to Mary E., daughter of Jacob Hank, of Lodi. Seven children have been born to them, five now living—Martha, Eva E., Sarah M., Cora E. and John. Mary and Fannie are deceased. Mr. Cowan is a member of the Methodist Episcopal church. Politically he is a Republican.

Joseph Creamer, deceased, was a native of Somerset County, Penn., born in May, 1805. When eighteen years of age he commenced to learn the tanner's trade, at which he worked the most of his life. When twenty-three years old he married Mary Morrison, also a native of Pennsylvania. They had a family of nine children—Asbury, Frank I., Norman (deceased), Belinda C., Sarah L., Mary A., S. M., Ella, Charles L. Mr. Creamer came to Athens County, locating in Lodi Township, in 1838. He held most of the township offices to the satisfaction of his constituents. He was a liberal supporter of the Methodist church, and it was mostly through his efforts that the church at Jerseyville was built. He was also largely instrumental in the building of the Jerseyville seminary. He died May 5, 1877, after a long and useful life.

S. M. Creamer is a native of Athens County, Ohio, born Aug. 9, 1843. He received a common-school education, being reared a farmer. In September, 1861, he enlisted in the Eighteenth Ohio Infantry, and served three years and three months. He was in the battles of Stone River, Mission Ridge, Lookout Mountain, Pulaski and Chattanooga. He married Hannah McClurg, a native of Westmoreland County, Penn. Six children have been born to them— Norman A., John L., Augustus B., V. May, Lulu B. and an infant. Mr. Creamer has a fine farm of 200 acres, and is extensively engaged in raising fine merino sheep. Politically he is a Republican. Mr. and Mrs. Creamer are members of the Methodist Episcopal church.

Joseph Creesy, son of Joseph and Elizabeth (Eastman) Creesy, was born in New Hampshire, Aug. 1, 1824, and came to Athens County, Ohio, in 1852. He is by trade a wheelwright, and for several years after coming here worked at his trade. He now owns a farm of 100 acres, all under a good state of cultivation, with a comfortable house and farm buildings. He has held the offices of Township Trustee and Land Appraiser, and by his fair-dealing has secured the confidence of all who know him. He was married Jan. 2, 1848, to Matilda Reynolds, a native of Athens County. They have two children—George and Anna.

E. E. Curtis, son of Joseph Curtis, was born in Meigs County, Ohio, April 1, 1840. When three years of age his parents removed to Tupper's Plains, where he was reared and educated. Aug. 5, 1861, he enlisted in the Second Virginia Cavalry, and served till June 3, 1865, taking an active part in several hard-fought battles, among them Cedar Creek, where he was wounded in the shoulder, and his horse shot from under him. Oct. 10, 1866, he married Susan Bean, of Lodi Township. They have three children—Mary E., Addie and James K. Mr. Curtis is by trade a wagon-maker. He is well-patronized, and has earned for himself and family a good home.

J. W. Dillenger, son of Charles and Amanda J. Dillenger, was born in Lodi Township, May 14, 1849. His early life was spent on the farm and in attending the schools of his township and Athens. In January, 1864, he enlisted in Company G, One Hundred and Eighty-fourth Ohio Infantry, and served till the fall of 1865. In September, 1874, he married Harriet, daughter of S. D. Miles, of Lodi. They have one child—Herbert F., born March 14, 1876. Mr. Dillenger has a good farm of 135 acres which he intends to have well improved. Politically he is a Republican. He is a member of the Grand Army of the Republic. His father, Charles Dillenger, was a native of New Jersey, and an early settler of Lodi Township. His mother, Amanda J. Simms, was a native of Virginia. They had a family of seven children—Sarah C., J. W., T. J., W. H., C. F., E. J. and Nancy E. Mr. Dillenger died in 1865.

Lorenzo Dow Evans, son of Dr. John and Eleanor (Day) Evans, was born in Sussex County, Del., Jan. 3, 1815. He was married Feb. 8, 1838, to Ann Wine, also a native of Delaware. Five children have been born to them, only three now living—William A., John L. and Elizabeth J. S. W. and Mary are deceased. S. W.

enlisted in the Eighteenth Ohio Infantry, and through the exposures of army life lost his health, though he lived till May 5, 1876. Mr. Evans enlisted in June, 1862, in the Ninety-second Ohio Infantry, Company I, and was discharged as First Lieutenant in August, 1863. He has been Justice of the Peace about thirty years, and has also served as Constable and Clerk. Politically he is a Republican. He has a farm of 250 acres, and makes a specialty of stock-raising. He is a member of the Methodist church, and has been a temperance man fifty years.

Abner Frost, son of Samuel and Esther Frost, was born in Meigs County, Ohio, Sept. 21, 1821. He received but a limited education, his early life being mostly spent in helping to clear a timbered farm. When he first moved on his present farm it was wild land, but he has brought it under a good state of cultivation and now has one of the finest farms in the township. He has 184 acres, all well improved, with a nice residence, and the largest barn in the township. In June, 1869, he went to Iowa and remained fourteen months, but returned again to his old home. He was married March 18, 1865, to Mary A., daughter of John and Ruth (Cass) Secoy. They have two children—Lucy, born March 30, 1867, and Minnie H., born Aug. 12, 1878.

Samuel Frost, deceased, son of Benjamin Frost, of English descent, was born Nov. 14, 1791. He was married Jan. 12, 1812, in Allegany County, N. Y., to Esther Miles, a native of Vermont. They came to Ohio in 1816, first settling in Meigs County. In 1825 they came to Athens County where he lived till his death. They had a family of eight children—Hiram, Miles, William, Abner, Luther, Rosannah, Elizabeth and Eunice. Mr. Frost was killed Dec. 14, 1855, by falling through the hatchway of a steamboat at Cincinnati. Esther Frost remained with her son Abner until her death, May 7, 1882, she being nearly eighty-six years old. She was born May 22, 1796.

Zimri Hoge, born Aug. 15, 1816, was the eldest of eleven children of John and Mary (Workman) Hoge, of Fayette County, Pa. His early life was spent on the farm and in attending school. When seventeen years of age he commenced to work at the carpenter's trade, following that occupation twenty years. In 1855 he moved on to the farm where he now lives, consisting of 150 acres under a good state of cultivation. He has a fine residence, furnished in accordance with the taste of a refined and cultured family. He was married March 24, 1842, to Margaret Brill, a native of Guernsey County, Ohio. They have five children—Melissa, Mary, Emeline, Eunice and Rosa.

William Howard, born in Holmes County, Ohio, Feb. 28, 1820, a son of Zadock Howard, a native of Greene County, Pa. When seventeen years of age he went to Morgan County and resided there about nine years. He was married April 14, 1840, to Sarah Ann Hutchinson, daughter of Richard Hutchinson. From this union there were six children—Nancy Jane, Fanny, McDonald, William Jasper, Mary Ellen and Sarah Elizabeth. They are all alive but Mary Ellen. He came to Athens County in 1846, and located on the farm where he still resides. He has 262 acres of well-improved land and a good residence. By industry and good management he has gained a comfortable home. His wife died June 30, 1859. He was married to Elizabeth Gaston, Oct. 17, 1861. From this union were two children—Elmer Elsworth and Annie May. Elmer is dead.

Hiram L. Hull, son of S. T. Hull, was born in Lodi Township, Athens County, Ohio, Dec. 17, 1848, and was reared and educated in his native township, residing at home until he arrived at manhood. March 24, 1866, he married Mary E. Smith. Seven children have been born to them, five living—Florence, Samuel, Charles, Lucy and Hattie. Allie and Absalom are deceased. Mr. Hull has a farm of 120 acres, under a good state of cultivation.

S. T. Hull, born in Delaware County, N. Y., July 16, 1819, was the youngest of ten children of Samuel and Rachel (Bostick) Hull. When he was four years of age, his parents moved to Ulster County, N. Y., where he was reared and educated, living there till he was twenty years of age. In 1839 he came to Athens County, locating in Lodi Township. He was married March 10, 1842, to Maria Witham. Five children were born to them, only four living—Augusta, Hiram S., Adaline and Jessie B. Samuel is deceased. S. T. Hull enlisted in November, 1861, in Company K, Seventy-third Ohio Infantry. He was in the battles of Cross Keys, Gettysburg, Lookout Valley, Mission Ridge, Chancellorsville, Resaca and Dallas. At the latter place he was wounded May 27, 1864, losing an arm. He was discharged Aug. 1, 1865, being mustered out as Sergeant. He lived eight years in Washington County, Ohio, and one year in Kansas, then returned to Lodi, where he still resides. He has held the office of Justice of the Peace five years.

Stephen W. Hull, son of Wakeman and Jane (Stewart) Hull, was born in Meredith, Delaware Co., N. Y., Jan. 13, 1818. May 29, 1836, he started for Athens County with a team, and arrived at Lodi Township, June 19. In 1836 he settled on the farm where he now resides. He has eighty-two acres of land, and a good residence. He has held several township offices, and was Postmaster one month under Buchanan and Lincoln's administrations. He has been married three times: the first time Oct. 19, 1839, to Mary P. Masters. They had two children—W. B. and N. N. Aug. 1, 1849, he married Nancy Wilmarth. One child was born to them—Edgar E. Aug. 20, 1874, he married Mary Elizabeth Jennings. They have two children—Nora Ann Elizabeth and Phœbe Lucinda Jane. Mr. Hull is an Elder in the Presbyterian church.

George Jeffers, son of 'Squire William Jeffers, was born in Lodi Township, Oct. 21, 1842. His early life was spent on the farm and in attending school. In August, 1860, he went to Mississippi and remained till the breaking out of the Rebellion. The day after the firing on Fort Sumter he took passage on the steamer West Moreland for the North, having agreed to volunteer in the Southern army in order to get away. In June, 1863, he enlisted in Company A, One Hundred and Twenty-ninth Ohio Infantry, for six months, but served nine months, being discharged in March, 1864. He returned home and remained on the farm with his father till Aug. 4, 1864, when he again enlisted in Company D, One Hundred and Seventy-fourth Ohio, and served eleven months. He was in the Nashville campaign under General Thomas, and participated in many hard-fought battles. He was discharged July 28, 1865, as Sergeant. Mr. Jeffers was married Jan. 18, 1868, to Elizabeth M. Burley, of this township. They have four children —Florence, Ida M., Mary M. and P. J. Mr. Jeffers owns a farm of 181 acres of well-improved land and is engaged in general farming and stock-raising. He is one of the most successful farmers of his age in the township. Politically he is a Republican.

George W. Jeffers was born in Carthage Township, Athens Co., Ohio, Jan. 19, 1825. When he was a child his parents moved to Lodi Township. His father died when he was small and he was obliged to rely on his own resources. He never had shoes to wear till he was eight years old. When nine years old he left home and lived with strangers three years. He then returned to live with his mother, and when only twelve years old commenced clearing heavily timbered land for the purpose of setting out an orchard and raising grain. In 1838 hard times came on, and the money could not be raised to pay the taxes, so the land was sold, but he afterward redeemed it. He chopped wood at 25 cents a cord and offered to make rails at 25 cents a hundred. He made hundreds of pounds of maple sugar, and sold it for 6 cents a pound, taking it in trade. When but fourteen years old he could do as much work in the harvest field as a man, and when fifteen could cut and split 200 rails a day. When twenty years old he was married to Mary Ann Kirgan. In 1849 he went to Henry County, Iowa, driving through with a team in nineteen days; had only 62½ cents left when he got there. He went to Marion and Clark counties and entered 160 acres in each county. He improved his land and afterward sold it for a good price. Feb. 23, 1857, he started for Cass County, Neb., and after a journey of fifteen days crossed the Missouri River on the ice, with three yokes of oxen and a heavily loaded wagon. He bought 320 acres of choice land for $1,700. He lived there fifteen years and had the privilege of helping to make Nebraska a State. In 1872 his family ties were broken, and he returned to Ohio. In 1876 he married Maggie Burson and settled in Pleasant Valley. He was a member of the Methodist church forty years, but in 1878 joined the Christian church, of which he is now an Elder. Mr. Jeffers has always assisted liberally in the building of churches and school-houses. In an early day he was called the strongest man at log-rollings and house-raisings, and was always ready to assist his neighbors in settling up the Hocking Valley. Mrs. Jeffers's father, James C. Burson, was born in Loudoun County, Va., in 1801, and died in 1870. He came to Athens County, Ohio, in 1839. March 10, 1822, he married Hannah Powell. They had eight children—Elizabeth, William, Catherine, John, Esther, James, Margaret and Hannah. Mr. Burson was an Elder in the Christian church the greater part of his Christian life, and strove to build up good society, and worked for the interest of his county. He cleared and got under cultivation seventy-five acres of land in the Hocking Valley, and saw very hard times as an early settler in raising his family. His widow still survives, and is in her eighty-fourth year.

Lewis H. Jeffers, born Dec. 4, 1838, in Athens County, is a son of William Jeffers. July 5, 1861, he enlisted in Company C, Thirtieth Ohio Infantry; was at the last battle of Bull Run, Champion Hill, siege of Vicksburg and Jackson, Miss., and was discharged Aug. 27, 1864. Sept. 30, 1864, he married Olive Brooks, of Alexander Township. They had nine children, seven of whom are living—Stella, Mary L., Wade E., George H., Emma M., Rodolph and Clyde Oottis. William and an infant son are deceased. Mr. Jeffers has 300 acres of land under a good state of cultivation, with a good residence and farm buildings.

William Jeffers, farmer and stock-raiser, was born in Athens County, Ohio, April 24, 1819. His father, George Jeffers, was a native of Pennsylvania, of English parentage. In 1826 he moved to the farm where the subject of our sketch still resides. William Jeffers was reared on a farm and educated in the common schools. In 1838 he married Mary Daily. Eight children were born to them, only six now living—L. H., George, William, S. C., C. F. and Elizabeth J. Winfield S. and Mary are deceased. Four sons were in the war of the Rebellion. Mr. Jeffers has been Justice of the Peace six years. He has a fine stock farm, making a specialty of Spanish merino sheep. He is a member of the Christian church. He is an enterprising man, and always takes an interest in anything that tends to the advancement of his county.

John Kelly, son of J. L. and Joanna Kelly, was born in Meigs County, Ohio, in November, 1824, and came to this township with his parents when an infant. He was married July 28, 1844, to Matilda Price. They have nine children—John L., Ivy, Adaline, Joseph, Joanna, Levi, Harriet, Charles and Effie. Mr. Kelly has served two terms as Justice of the Peace, and as Township Trustee. He is a member of the Christian church. Mrs. Kelly's grandmother, Margaret Snowdon, was the first white woman in Athens County.

J. L. Kelly, deceased, son of E. and Silence (Edmunds) Kelly, was born in Cayuga County, N. Y. His father came to Athens County, Ohio, with his family, and was one of the first settlers of Carthage Township. There was a family of four sons and two daughters. J. L. resided at home till nineteen years of age. When twenty-four he was married to Joanna Price, who was born in the block house at Marietta, Ohio. He lived in Meigs County two years, and in 1825 located in Lodi Township. He had a family of eleven children—John, Louisa, Perilla, L. E., Louis, Silence, Lucinda (deceased), Jane, Olive, William and Joanna.

John L. Kelly, son of John and Matilda (Price) Kelly, was born June 18, 1845, in Lodi Township, where he was reared and educated. June 20, 1862, he enlisted in the One Hundred and Twenty-ninth Ohio Infantry, and served a year. He was married Dec.

21, 1868, to Lydia Burley, who died leaving one child—Rosa. Dec. 25, 1876, he married Sarah Tower. They have three children—Maud, Lucas and Dessie. Mr. Kelly owns a farm of eighty acres, well improved.

John Kincade was born in 1815 in Clarksburg, Pa., a son of Joseph and Sarah Kincade. His parents came to Athens County when he was small, first settling in Guysville. He worked with his father in the mill and on the farm till manhood, then worked three years in the Coolville Mill. He then moved on the farm now called the Chalker farm; lived there a while and then went to Guysville and worked in the mills there three years; then moved one mile above Guysville and built the Kincade Mill, where he lived about thirty years. In 1881 he rented the Shade Valley Mills two years. He now is in Harmony. He was married April 1, 1840, to Harriet Hale. They had four children, only two now living—James Edwin and Justina. Mrs. Kincade died July 22, 1851. Jan. 1, 1852, he married S. E. Kelley. They have had eight children born to them—Mary Irena, John William, Laura A., Charles Ellsworth, Melville, Izetta May, Emma Dell and Edna Matilda. Politically Mr. Kincade is a Democrat. He has been a member of the Baptist church thirty-four years.

James Kyle, son of John Kyle, was born in Guernsey County, Ohio, Dec. 25, 1825. He was reared and educated in his native county, and when twenty-six years of age came to Lodi Township, locating at Garden, where he was engaged in the mercantile business eleven years. He is numbered among the best business men of Lodi Township and is always alive to the interests of the community. He was married when twenty years of age to Mary Jane Dean, a native of Marion County, Ohio. They have two children—Rachel Rebecca and Stephen W.

Samuel Poston, son of John and Isabel Poston, was born in Canaan Township, Athens Co., Ohio, June 7, 1837. He was married Nov. 15, 1857, to Elizabeth Ross, of Carthage Township. They have six children—Elsie D., Alice G., Effie J., Nettie F. Herbert and Elmer. The first four years after his marriage Mr. Poston resided in Canaan Township. He then moved to Lodi Township, living on the farm now owned by William Poston three years. He then returned to Canaan Township and resided two years, when he went to Bedford Township, Meigs County, and remained three years. In the spring of 1872 he came to Lodi Township and located on section 24, where he still resides. He has 287 acres, well improved, with a good residence and farm buildings. Politically Mr. Poston is a Prohibitionist. He has held the offices of Township Trustee and Assessor.

William Poston, born in Hampshire County, W. Va., Nov. 7, 1826, is a son of John and Isabella (McVicker) Poston, of English descent. In 1833 his parents came to Athens County, Ohio, and settled on Sugar Creek, where they lived two years and then moved to Canaan Township. William's early life was spent in assisting to clear wild timbered land. He attended the common schools, and by close study and observation has acquired a good practical education. When eighteen years of age he commenced life for himself by working by the month. Oct. 13, 1849, he married Miss T. Osborn, daughter of Ezra Osborn. In 1867 Mr. Poston came to Lodi Township and settled on the farm where he still resides. He has 175 acres mostly improved, with a good house well furnished. He has read law to some extent, and has been very successful in the profession. In politics he is an independent Democrat. He is no aspirant for office, but has served as Township Trustee. He is a firm believer in the Christian religion, and is always ready to do anything to advance its cause. Mr. and Mrs. Poston have six children—Mary Jane, Lydia Frances, John, Laura Elizabeth, Margaret Adaline and Cora Belle. He has given his children the advantage of a good education, so that they may be fitted for any position that they may be called upon to fill.

Isaac Sargent, a native of Washington County, Penn., was born June 1, 1817, and was a son of George and Sarah (Parkhurst) Sargent. He spent his youth on a farm, receiving but a limited education in the subscription schools. In 1836 he came to Athens County, settling in Lodi Township, where he has since resided with the exception of seven years spent in Meigs County. Mr. Sargent is by trade a shoemaker, but has worked at his trade only about twenty winters, the rest of his time being spent in farming. He now owns a farm of 200 acres, good, well-improved land, where he has all the comforts a good home can provide for his declining years. He was married Jan. 10, 1839, to Charlotte Davis, daughter of Calvin P. and Jane (Sloan) Davis. They have three children—Sarah Jane, Margaret Jane and E. L.

Windell Shott, son of John and Catharine (Learnes) Shott, was born in Prussia, Dec. 16, 1818, and was the fourth of a family of ten children. When he was eighteen years of age his parents came to America, landed at Baltimore after a voyage of seventy-three days. They went to Pittsburg, Penn., and remained three months; then came to Ohio, locating in Monroe County. Two months later Windell went to Belmont, where he lived about four years, when he went to Guernsey County and remained two years. He then returned to Monroe County, and in 1842 came to Athens County. He first lived on the old Beard farm a year, and then bought eighty acres where he now lives. He has by industry and frugality acquired a good property, owning at present 500 acres of well-improved land. In May, 1841, he married Catharine Timothy, a native of Guernsey County, Ohio, and a daughter of Peter and Elizabeth Timothy. They have ten children—Elizabeth, Mary, Catharine, John, Nicholas, William, Andrew, Sarah, Alice, Margaret. Mr. Shott was Postmaster a number of years, and it was through his influence that the mail-route from Guysville to Hull and Lottridge was established.

David G. Steuart, son of John Steuart, was born in Bath County, Va., Nov. 4, 1813. His grandfather, Wm. Steuart, was a native of Scotland, but educated at Belfast, Ireland. David G. was reared on a farm and received but a limited education. He came to Athens County, Ohio, in 1852, first settling in Athens Township. In 1876 he bought the farm where he now resides on section 17, Lodi Township, containing 120 acres of well-improved land, and makes a specialty of sheep-raising. He was married Nov. 18, 1844, to Rachel Calahan, of Virginia. They have two children—Charles H. and Elizabeth V. Politically Mr. Steuart is a Republican.

James K. Watkins, a native of Ohio, was born Sept. 26, 1833, a son of Andrew and Elizabeth Watkins, his father a native of Pennsylvania and his mother of Ohio. He was married Sept. 4, 1856, to Sarah A., daughter of Richard Angell, a prominent pioneer of Lodi Township. In 1864 Mr. Watkins bought the farm where he now resides. He has 100 acres of good land, well cultivated, and good farm buildings. Politically he is a Democrat.

Abraham M. Williams, deceased, was a native of New Jersey, born July 16, 1798, of German parentage. He was married to Margaret Force, a native of Rahway, N. J., born April 8, 1796, of French descent. In 1829 they came to Lodi Township, being among the first settlers, and located near Jerseyville, on what is known as the Burson farm. They reared a family of nine children —S. T., Henry C., Jeremiah M., Waldron S., Mary E., Margaret T., Harriet S, Wilbur M., William H. Margaret and Jeremiah are deceased, the latter dying a prisoner of war in 1862. Mr. Williams was a strong Union man; four of his sons were soldiers in the late war. He was a member of the Baptist church. He died in November, 1881. Mrs. Williams died May 29, 1869.

Wilbur M. Williams, son of Abraham M. Williams, was born in Lodi Township, March 6, 1837. He received a common-school education, residing on his father's farm till twenty-four years of age. Sept. 18, 1861, he enlisted in Company D, Eighteenth Ohio Infantry, and was in the service three years and two months, never being off duty during the time. He was in the battles of Stone River, Pulaski, and a number of others. He had his clothes torn by bullets, but was never wounded. He was discharged in November, 1864. Dec. 24, 1865, he married Belinda C. Cramer. Six children have been born to them—Stella M., Joseph E., Gladius, Mary M., Bertha B. and Anna. Mr. Williams has a fine farm of 340 acres, and is engaged in general farming, giving considerable attention to the raising of sheep. Politically he is a Republican. He is a member of the Methodist church.

Hiram G. Withers, M. D., a native of Ohio, was born Dec. 26, 1818, a son of Jonathan and Martha (Sarting) Withers, natives of Massachusetts. He was the second of a family of twelve children, eight sons and four daughters. His early life was spent in attending school and assisting on the farm, where he remained till twenty-two years of age. He then removed to Western Ohio. He commenced the study of medicine with Dr. Benj. Alworth, and finished with Dr. David McCune, receiving his certificate from the latter. He came to Athens County in 1860, and has built up a large practice. He has a good residence and is very pleasantly located in Jerseyville. Nov. 27, 1848, he married Ellen Stevenson. Six children have been born to them—William H., Mary E., Henry S., Agnes, Edward and Lucy N.

William Zinn, son of Moses and Theresa (Tharp) Zinn, was born in Franklin County, Ohio, Oct. 1, 1857. He was the fifth of six children. His early life was spent at Grove Point, where he received his education. When eighteen years of age he went to Columbus and engaged in the grocery business three years. He then went to Pottawattamie County, Iowa, and remained eighteen months. He then returned to Columbus and engaged in the wholesale flour business two years, when he came to Athens County and located at Canaanville, Ohio. February, 1883, he came to Hull's and bought out W. Shott. He keeps a large stock of dry goods, groceries, boots and shoes, notions, etc. and is laying the foundation of a good trade and successful business life.

William Blackstone, M. D., eldest son of John and Jemima Blackstone, came of English-Welsh ancestry. He was born in Botetourt County, Va., May 24, 1796. John Blackstone was a native of Kent County, Md., born March 9, 1772, and Jemima (King) Blackstone was a native of Virginia, born Sept. 19, 1773. When but a few years old William Blackstone was brought by his parents to Pickaway County, Ohio. Remaining there but a short time, the Blackstone's removed to Ross County, where they settled and made a farm near Bainbridge. On this farm the early years of William Blackstone were passed. Few indeed were the advantages offered the youth for obtaining an education, but young William's innate thirst for learning conquered adversity, and when he arrived at an age when he began teaching he was the most thorough scholar of any teacher in the pioneer schools of Southern Ohio. His first teacher was White Morgan, who taught in a log school-house in the Demitts Bottom, some two miles from the Blackstone cabin. When William had arrived at the age of about twenty-four his literary attainments and exemplary habits attracted the notice and admiration of Dr. Benjamin Doddridge, of Bainbridge, Ohio, himself a classical scholar, who taught him Greek and Latin and gave him a very fair education in the classics. During this time he also read medicine with Dr. Doddridge, from whom he obtained sufficient knowledge of the science of medicine to engage in the practice. Having received an offer from Dr. Luckey, of Circleville, Ohio, he went to that place and formed a partnership with him. He continued with Dr. Luckey about a year when he removed to Bloomingburg, Fayette County, and began the practice of medicine alone. About one year later he attended a course of lectures at Transylvania Medical College, at Louisville. On his return from Louisville he stopped at Bainbridge, Ohio, to participate in the most important and happy event in any man's life, his own marriage. On the 28th day of April, 1824, he was united in marriage with Julia M. Doddridge, eldest daughter of Benjamin and Sophia Doddridge, of Bainbridge, Ohio. She was born in Brook County, Va., Nov. 16, 1806. Her father, Dr. Doddridge, was a fine classical scholar, and graduate of Yale College. He came to Ohio as early as 1810, and was widely known and highly esteemed as an able physician and scholarly gentleman. Ohio at so early a period in its settlement as 1810 contained few such men of letters and polished physicians as Benjamin Doddridge. After their marriage Doctor and Mrs.

Blackstone went direct to Bloomingburg where the Doctor resumed the practice of medicine. About two years later they removed to Clarksville, Ohio; from there they removed to Piketon, Pike County, thence to Richmondale, Ross County; from there they went to the then new town of Waverly. In none of these places did they remain but two or three years at most, the Doctor all the time continuing the practice of medicine. During their stay at Waverly the Doctor attended the Ohio Medical College at Cincinnati, from which he graduated with honors in 1834. In 1839 Dr. Blackstone came to Athens, fresh from his graduation at Cincinnati, and being a fine literary scholar and learned in medicine he took rank at once among the very best physicians in all the Hocking Valley region. Of the eight children resulting from the union of William Blackstone and Julia Doddridge, but two survive—Doctor Benjamin Doddridge Blackstone, a practicing physician of Martinsville, Ind., and Doctor John King Blackstone, practicing at Hebron, Ind. The deceased were Julia M., wife of Dr. W. P. Johnson, of the Surgical Institute at Indianapolis, Ind.; Adaline O., died in infancy; William, Sophia Adela, Elizabeth Lillian and William Victor. In the pure moral life of Dr. Blackstone there is much to admire, much that is worthy of emulation. His professional life extended over about a half century, and during all these years of devotion to his profession he practiced medicine, not for the attainment of mercenary ends, but for the relief of suffering humanity. A member of the First Presbyterian Church of Athens, he was ever willing to lend his name or his influence to every moral enterprise. Doctor Blackstone died suddenly in his office at Athens, March 17, 1879. Mrs. Blackstone resides in her own quiet home in Athens, in the enjoyment of many devoted friends. She is a member of the Presbyterian church, in which she is an earnest, enthusiastic worker for the advancement of every worthy Christian enterprise.